GUYANA

FRENCH GUIANA

SURINAME

Essequibo River

RORAIMA

AMAPÁ

PARÁ

ATLANTIC OCEAN

Marajó Island

●Belém

Rio Amazonas

●Santarém

Rio Tocantins

PARÁ

MARANHÃO

CEARÁ

AMAZONAS

Rio Tapajós

Rio Xingu

RIO GRANDE DO NORTE

PARAIBA

PIAUÍ

PERNAMBUCO

Rio Araguaia

Rio Tocantins

ALAGOAS

Bananal Island

Rio São Francisco

SERGIPE

MATO GROSSO

BAHIA

BRAZIL

●Salvador

Rio Paraguay

●Cuiabá

GOIÁS

BRASÍLIA

●Corumbá

CHACO

MINAS GERAIS

NUEVA ASUNCIÓN

ALTO PARAGUAY

ESPÍRITO SANTO

CONCEPCIÓN

AMAMBAY

Rio Paraná

SÃO PAULO

OQUERÓN

RIO DE JANEIRO

PARAGUAY

SAN PEDRO

São Paulo ●

● Rio de Janeiro

PRESIDENTE HAYES

CANENDIYU

PARANÁ

MISIONES

ALTO PARANA

NEEMBUCU

ITAPUA

SANTA CATARINA

RIO GRANDE DO SUL

THE BIRDS OF SOUTH AMERICA

VOLUME II   THE SUBOSCINE PASSERINES

VOLUME II
THE SUBOSCINE PASSERINES

OVENBIRDS AND WOODCREEPERS
TYPICAL AND GROUND ANTBIRDS
GNATEATERS AND TAPACULOS
TYRANT FLYCATCHERS
COTINGAS AND MANAKINS

Project support has been provided by:
World Wildlife Fund (US),
World Wildlife Fund (Canada),
The MacArthur Foundation,
The McLean Contributionship,
RARE Center for Tropical Conservation,
Massachusetts Audubon Society,
and the Pan-American Section
of the International Council for Bird Preservation

THE BIRDS OF SOUTH AMERICA

by Robert S. Ridgely and Guy Tudor

In association with
The Academy of Natural Sciences of Philadelphia

UNIVERSITY OF TEXAS PRESS, AUSTIN

Printed in Singapore

First Edition, 1994

Requests for permission
to reproduce material from this work
should be sent to Permissions,
University of Texas Press,
Box 7819, Austin, TX 78713-7819.

⊗ The paper used in this publication
meets the minimum requirements of
American National Standard for
Information Sciences—Permanence of
Paper for Printed Library Materials,
ANSI Z39.48-1984.

LIBRARY OF CONGRESS CATALOGING-IN-PUBLICATION DATA
(Revised for vol. 2)

Ridgely, Robert S., 1946–
    The birds of South America.

    Ill on lining papers.
    Includes bibliographical references and indexes.
    Contents: v. 1. The oscine passerines   —   v. 2. The suboscine passerines.
    1. Birds—South America. I. Tudor, Guy, 1934–   . II. Brown, William L.
III. World Wildlife Fund (U.S.)
QL689.A 1R53   1989   598.298   88-20899
ISBN 0-292-70756-8 (V. 1)
ISBN 0-292-77063-4 (V. 2)

To the memory of
EUGENE EISENMANN,
one of the first ornithologists born in the neotropics,
who more than anyone else who ever lived
actively encouraged the serious study of its birds
by both visitors and residents alike.

And of
TED PARKER,
who loved the suboscines
more than any other group
of South American birds,
and who devoted the better part
of his all-too-short life
to their study.

And to the people of South America,
in whose hands the future of the world's finest avifauna lies.

CONTENTS

PREFACE

ALTHOUGH THE Preface to Volume I of *The Birds of South America* expressed our basic overall intentions, we feel that a new Preface for Volume II is in order.

The preparation of this volume, as might have been expected, has entailed far more time and effort than we had originally anticipated. However, we felt that the very complexities of the Suboscine Suborder necessitated a more comprehensive treatment than was presented for the Oscine Passerines of Volume I, and this has entailed more time. Furthermore, and for the same reason, we have felt compelled to somewhat expand the selection of species to be illustrated, even though their appearance tends to run "close" in many genera. Upon reflection, we consider that it is a testament to the designer skills at U.T. Press that they were able to fit all this information between the covers of one book!

A few words, if we may, concerning the reception granted our previous volume. We were very gratified by the many complimentary reviews published in various ornithological journals and birding magazines—satisfying enough, we might add, to revitalize our often flagging energies. We have, more than once, jokingly referred to this huge project as our "bête noire," "an albatross around our neck," and other appropriate similes from the Animal Kingdom. But, abetted by the encouragement of our friends and associates, we push on against the tide.

Unforeseen circumstances, it is true, could conceivably put a halt to the completion of this multivolumed project. When we started long ago, we discussed the possibility of our never finishing—a fate rendered unto more than a few overly ambitious projects in the past. We countered, though, what if we managed to get only the Passerines done? That's nearly 2,000 species dealt with . . . that's something, after all. This having been said, let us emphasize that as of now, we *do* look forward to our ultimately completing Volumes III and IV, as projected.

One minor aside. One of the thorniest issues, or so we felt at the time, was whether we really should start work at the end of the standard phylogenetic sequence, and what that first volume should be titled and how it should be numbered. We made the decision and waited for the brickbats—but our apprehension was misplaced. We have never heard anything but full agreement with our decision to bring out the whole work "backward."

As has been emphasized elsewhere, the legion of ornithologists and birders studying in and visiting all the countries of South America continues to grow rapidly. We delight in their interest and enthusiasm, and a concerted effort has been made to incorporate into our book the new and ever-expanding flow of information that results. We hope we have adequately acknowledged individuals where appropriate—certainly a major effort has been made to do so—and apologize (profusely!) if some snafu has resulted in someone's being forgotten or miscredited. Almost by definition, some information (particularly range statements) may be somewhat obsolete even before publication, but we have strived to bring together as much up-to-date and accurate information as was humanly possible.

A few weeks before writing this we learned of the death of our friend and colleague Ted Parker, in a plane crash on a mist-enshrouded ridge of coastal Ecuador. At the onset of this project Ted cooperated very closely with us, and indeed we were anxious to bring him aboard as a coauthor. The press of other commitments forced him ultimately to demur from so doing, much to our regret. Ted was at the vanguard of the modern, field-based era in Neotropical ornithology, and his loss represents a staggering blow. We miss him.

Lastly, let us express our deep-felt hope, one in which we know TAP would concur, that these volumes will continue to be useful, and that they will help inspire all manner of ornithological investigation in the great "Bird Continent."

ROBERT S. RIDGELY
GUY TUDOR

August 1993

ACKNOWLEDGMENTS

WORK ON THE more than 1000 species that comprise the South American suboscine groups in the Order Passeriformes has consumed more time and entailed far more effort than either of us could ever have imagined when we began this project some ten years ago. And not surprisingly, a growing number of individuals and institutions have been involved in its production, and these we would like to recognize and thank here.

Financial support for our work over the last five years has come from several sources, notably the MacArthur Foundation, the Massachusetts Audubon Society, and the McLean Contributionship. Many individuals, too many to acknowledge here, though we are grateful to each and every one, have provided support through the Academy of Natural Sciences of Philadelphia.

Virtually all of the people and institutions who assisted us during the preparation of Volume I of *The Birds of South America* have continued to do so with Volume II, and we cannot adequately express our gratitude to them all. A few individuals are, sadly, no longer with us, and the passing of several friends who were instrumental to our early progress should be noted here. They include the Peruvian conservationist Felipe Benavides, Tom Davis (fine tape recordist and expert on the birds of Surinam), indefatigable photographer John Dunning (who unquestionably photographed more species of neotropical birds than any other person ever has), Robin Hughes (expert birder of the southwestern Peru region), the well-known Venezuelan ornithologist William Phelps, Jr., and the renowned Brazilian ornithologist Helmut Sick. Finally, we especially mourn the recent death of our collaborator Bill Brown, a marvelous Canadian gentleman and coauthor of the acclaimed *Birds of Colombia*.

Individuals not mentioned in Volume I (a few of whom should have been, for which we apologize) who have assisted us in some way during the preparation of Volume II include David Agro, John Bates, Bob Behrstock, Rob Bierregaard, Paulo Boute, Jane Church, Jim Clements, Robert Clements, Mario Cohn-Haft, Nigel Collar, Paul Coopmans, Susan Davis, Dale Delaney, Davis Finch, John Fitzpatrick, Paulo Fonseca, Bruce Forrester, Kimball Garrett, Michael Gochfeld, Gary Graves, Jim Grootemat, Floyd Hayes, Steve Howell, Mort and Phyllis Isler (to whom we apologize for inadvertently neglecting to mention in Volume I their fine book on tanagers, published during the interval between Volume I's submission and publication, and which we saw in manuscript form), Lloyd Kiff, Al Maley, Manuel Marín, Burt Monroe, Jr., Storrs Olson, Larry O'Mealie, David Oren, Liz Pierson,

Gary Rosenberg, Rick Prum, Omar Rocha, Paul Scharf, Fred Sibley, Francisco Sornoza, Dante Teixera, Sophie Webb, Andrew Whittaker, David Wolf, and Kevin Zimmer.

We should particularly like to single out Paul Coopmans, Mark Robbins, Roberto Straneck, Bret Whitney, and Kevin Zimmer for having responded to so many requests for information, photographs, and tape recordings, Jane Church and Liz Pierson for their invaluable assistance in copy-editing the manuscript, Francisco Sornoza for having so ably helped to organize the Academy's ongoing research program in Ecuador, and Doug Stotz for his comprehensive review of virtually the entire manuscript. RSR would especially like to note his heavy use of the invaluable series of *Ornithological Gazetteers* published under the direction of Raymond Paynter and the Museum of Comparative Zoology, a series which now includes a volume on every South American country and which RSR consults daily. The recently published *Red Data Book* on neotropical birds (Collar et al. 1992) contains a wealth of new information on the scarcer birds of South America, and we would like to congratulate those authors on the successful completion of such a massive undertaking (now what we have to do is to save viable populations of all those rare, wonderful birds!).

The Academy of Natural Sciences of Philadelphia continues to be a stimulating and, dare one say, fun place for RSR to work, thanks in no small measure to the leadership of our systematics head, Frank Gill; both RSR and GT remain very grateful for the opportunities provided by our continuing association with that fine old institution. The American Museum of Natural History in New York continues to be strongly supportive of our work, and we deeply appreciate the total access we have to their incomparably rich collection.

Bill Brown, before his untimely death, having completed initial maps depicting the distribution of most South American bird species, RSR has now assumed responsibility for inputting new distributional and taxonomic data and thereby keeping these maps current; he has been ably assisted in this process by his wife, Peg, who has then kept each species' "camera-ready" map up to date. RSR has now become at least marginally computer-literate, thanks in no small part to his stepson Jackson Loomis and the continuing assistance of the Academy's Christine Bush; a quantum leap in RSR's productivity has been the result, for which he is most grateful. Michelle le Marchant continues in her intense commitment to the project and continues to be of administrative assistance to GT and to facilitate our communication. Finally, Peg Ridgely has been ever supportive and encouraging, even when the revision process seemed to be stretching on forever and when RSR continued to stay at the office too late; he considers himself a fortunate man indeed.

The cutoff date for new information to be added to this volume was March 1993.

THE BIRDS OF SOUTH AMERICA

VOLUME II   THE SUBOSCINE PASSERINES

ABBREVIATIONS

AMNH	American Museum of Natural History
ANSP	Academy of Natural Sciences of Philadelphia
C	*A Guide to the Birds of Colombia* (Hilty and Brown 1986)
CMNH	Carnegie Museum of Natural History
FMNH	Field Museum of Natural History
LSUMZ	Louisiana State University Museum of Zoology (now the Louisiana State University Museum of Science)
MCZ	Museum of Comparative Zoology
MECN	Museo Ecuatoriano de Ciencias Naturales
MZUSP	Museu de Zoologia do Universidade do São Paulo
P	*A Guide to the Birds of Panama* (Ridgely and Gwynne 1989)
UKMNS	University of Kansas Museum of Natural Science
UMMZ	University of Michigan Museum of Zoology
USNM	United States National Museum, Museum of Natural History at the Smithsonian Institution
V	*A Guide to the Birds of Venezuela* (Meyer de Schauensee and Phelps 1978)
VIREO	Visual Resources for Ornithology (at ANSP)
WFVZ	Western Foundation for Vertebrate Zoology
WWF	World Wildlife Fund, U.S.

PLAN OF THE BOOK

THE organization of Volume II of *The Birds of South America* follows very closely that used in Volume I, which should be referred to when necessary. A few changes that have been adopted, or issues that were not sufficiently addressed in Volume I, require a comment or explanation here.

THE MAIN TEXT

In order to more accurately summarize what that paragraph contains, we have changed the title of each species' first paragraph from *Identification* to *Description*.

Note that the numbering sequence for the plates in *A Guide to the Birds of Panama* was substantially changed in the revised edition of that book published in 1989; in this volume when we refer to a plate in that book (e.g., "P-27"), the *new* sequence is being used.

Astute readers will notice that in the present Volume more emphasis is placed on describing vocalizations than was our customary practice in Volume I. This increased emphasis is intentional, a result of our recognition that vocalizations play an especially important role in the discrimination of suboscine species, both amongst the birds themselves and for observers struggling to identify them.

NAMES

Several individuals have expressed to us their disappointment that we did not include Spanish and Portuguese bird names in Volume I (and will, we suppose, be disappointed that we continue not to do so in Volume II). Our explanation for not doing so should have been spelled out in Volume I, and it is as follows. There is still little international agreement among the various Spanish-speaking countries regarding Spanish names for birds: Argentines have their preferences, Venezuelans theirs, Ecuadorians still others, and so on. For us to have selected names would in many cases have required agonizing decisions, decisions that we strongly feel are best left to South American ornithologists whose first language is Spanish. Regarding Portuguese names for Brazilian birds, we should point out that a compendium of such vernacular names has recently been published (Willis and Oniki 1991), and if we had included Portuguese names, we would not in any case have diverged from their suggestions except where required by differing taxonomy. Our fervent hope is that, at some early juncture, a group of distinguished Spanish- and Portuguese-speaking ornithologists can be convened with the express goal of devising a list of Spanish and Portuguese names that we all can agree to use.

GEOGRAPHY

We should expressly note that our spelling of place names follows that used in the various *Ornithological Gazetteers* that have now been published, under the direction or authorship of Raymond Paynter, by the Museum of Comparative Zoology for every South American country. Van Remsen pointed out that the use in Volume I of the term *northwestern Bolivia* for the many Andean species whose ranges include La Paz, Cochabamba, and western Santa Cruz was technically not correct as these areas are not actually in the "north" of Bolivia; we have termed this area *western* in Volume II. Two states (provinces) have been formally subdivided since the preparation of Volume I: what was the state of Mato Grosso in Amazonian Brazil is now Mato Grosso and Mato Grosso do Sul, and the northern part of the east Ecuadorian province of Napo has now been split off as the province of Sucumbios.

HABITATS

We have employed a few ecological terms in Volume II that were not included in Volume I. These are the following:

Lomas. Low hills near the coast of western Peru and northern Chile whose sparse vegetation is supported by the *garúa* ("drizzle") which falls there, and by its relatively persistent cloud cover.

Monte. A term often used in eastern Argentina and adjacent areas to describe the small, isolated patches of woodland growing in mainly open terrain such as the pampas.

Restinga. Low and usually swampy woodland or scrub found near the coast in southeastern Brazil; *restinga scrub* also grows on coastal sand dunes. Although only recently recognized as ornithologically significant, both habitats are now known to support endemic bird species with extremely limited ranges and small populations and are thus of great international conservation interest.

MIGRATION

INCREASED attention has been given to the phenomenon of long-distance bird migration in South America in recent years, such that the summary presented here for the suboscine passerines is more comprehensive and accurate than what could be presented for the oscines in Volume I of *The Birds of South America*, though as always there are certain species whose status leaves room for doubt. As would be expected from the fact that only a few suboscines occur in North America (all of them tyrannids), virtually all of the suboscine long-distance migrants are austral migrants.

Table 1 lists the austral migrant suboscines, some of which may move only to a limited extent. Noteworthy is the fact that virtually all the austral migrants are tyrannids and that no woodcreeper, typical or ground antbird, tapaculo, or manakin (and only one cotinga, the White-tipped Plantcutter) is known to engage in such movements; the overwhelming majority of these latter groups occur only in the tropics. Table 2 lists the northern migrant suboscines (which we would actually prefer to call the boreal migrants); northern migrant species marked with an asterisk pass the northern winter mainly or entirely on the South American continent.

TABLE I.
Austral Migrants

Short-billed Miner	Black-fronted Ground-Tyrant
Bar-winged Cinclodes	Cinnamon-bellied Ground-Tyrant
Cordoba Cinclodes	Dark-faced Ground-Tyrant
Plain-mantled Tit-Spinetail	Chocolate-vented Tyrant
Wren-like Rushbird	Rusty-backed Monjita
Sharp-billed Canastero	Fire-eyed Diucon
Large Elaenia	Black-crowned Monjita
White-crested Elaenia	Yellow-browed Tyrant
Small-billed Elaenia	Blue-billed Black-Tyrant
Slaty Elaenia	White-winged Black-Tyrant
Southern Scrub-Flycatcher	Hudson's Black-Tyrant
White-crested Tyrannulet	Spectacled Tyrant
White-bellied Tyrannulet	Austral Negrito
Warbling Doradito	Black-backed Water-Tyrant
Subtropical Doradito	Rufous-tailed Attila
Dinelli's Doradito	Rufous Casiornis
Many-colored Rush-Tyrant	Swainson's Flycatcher
Yellow-billed Tit-Tyrant	Streaked Flycatcher
Vermilion Flycatcher	Piratic Flycatcher
Patagonian Tyrant	Variegated Flycatcher
Cliff Flycatcher	Crowned Slaty Flycatcher
Lesser Shrike-Tyrant	Tropical Kingbird
Gray-bellied Shrike-Tyrant	White-throated Kingbird
White-browed Ground-Tyrant	Fork-tailed Flycatcher
Ochre-naped Ground-Tyrant	White-tipped Plantcutter

TABLE 2.
Northern Migrants

Willow Flycatcher	Olive-sided Flycatcher*
Alder Flycatcher*	Great Crested Flycatcher
Acadian Flycatcher	Sulphur-bellied Flycatcher*
Eastern Wood-Pewee*	Gray Kingbird
Western Wood-Pewee*	Eastern Kingbird*

CONSERVATION

TREMENDOUS strides are now being made toward the conservation of South American birds, even as the primary and relatively little-altered habitats so many species depend on are still gradually being reduced in extent by human activities. We have learned so much in the last few years and decades—one can only hope that efforts to protect what is left can proceed apace. There are encouraging trends everywhere, ranging from a growing realization that ecotourism and other forms of "sustainable use" may play a positive role, to a reduction in international funding that is directed toward environmentally destructive projects. On the other hand, let's be realistic and recognize that human population levels continue to rise, rapidly in some countries, and that this—the ultimate cause of all environmental problems—stands to undermine any short-term progress we may be able to make.

One of the most encouraging and notable steps that has been taken recently is the publication of the exceedingly thorough and authoritative *Threatened Birds of the Americas* (Collar et al. 1992). No longer will conservation authorities in the various South American countries be able to claim that it was impossible to know what their bird conservation priorities should be: it is all spelled out in that extraordinary and exciting volume. Its appearance has virtually negated the need for the brief summary of endangered birds that we included in Volume I and which, for the sake of continuity, we will include here. One reason for so doing is that to a limited degree our criteria for including a species on such a list subtly differ. Collar et al. include several species that admittedly have very limited ranges (and thus are capable of supporting only small populations of the species in question) but whose habitats within that range are not known to be especially imperiled; an example is the Orinoco Softtail. We, however, tend to include certain more widely distributed species whose total numbers may not be quite so small but whose populations appear to be in steep decline because of human activities; an example is the Cock-tailed Tyrant. That having been said, we should emphasize that in the vast majority of cases we are in total agreement, and we can only encourage those interested in learning more about the topic to delve further by obtaining their own copy of *Threatened Birds of the Americas*.

ROYAL CINCLODES, *Cinclodes aricomae*
With a highly restricted range high in the Andes of southeastern Peru and adjacent Bolivia, the rare Royal Cinclodes, recently separated as a full species from the much more common Stout-billed Cinclodes found in Colombia and Ecuador, apparently ranges only in *Polylepis* groves. These are very limited in extent and are now being decimated by overgrazing and excessive wood-gathering.

MASAFUERA RAYADITO, *Aphrastura masafuerae*
Endemic to a single island (Masafuera) in the Juan Fernández Islands far off Chile, the population of this small furnariid has probably always been small and is currently estimated at fewer than 1000 individuals. Although it is not believed to be declining in numbers, the status of any species with a population this small needs to be continually monitored, especially as habitat changes on Masafuera have been extensive.

WHITE-BROWED TIT-SPINETAIL, *Leptasthenura xenothorax*
Endemic to the patches of *Polylepis*-dominated woodland in the high Andes of Apurímac and Cuzco, Peru, the White-browed Tit-Spinetail's population levels are declining as these woodlands, always limited in extent, continue to be cut by local people for firewood and to increase the extent of their pastures.

HOARY-THROATED SPINETAIL, *Poecilurus kollari*
The Hoary-throated Spinetail has been found only in the extreme north of Brazil, from whence it has been recorded from only a few sites in Roraima. Until more information is available, it seems reasonable to consider this spinetail as potentially threatened.

RUSSET-BELLIED SPINETAIL, *Synallaxis zimmeri*
Restricted to montane scrub in a limited region on the west slope of the Andes in Ancash, western Peru, the very distinct Russet-bellied Spinetail is threatened by the continued clearing of scrub and increasingly intensive cattle grazing. Some populations are theoretically protected by occurring within Huascarán National Park, but the park is itself evidently still under some threat from illegal activities.

APURIMAC SPINETAIL, *Synallaxis courseni*
The recently described Apurimac Spinetail is apparently confined to woodland undergrowth in one small mountainous area of the Andes in Apurímac, Peru. Given its extremely limited total range and the absence of protection for any of its habitat, we believe that its status requires continual monitoring (assuming political conditions permit). Whether the condition of its habitat is deteriorating seems to be unknown.

PINTO'S SPINETAIL, *Synallaxis infuscata*
Although little information is available, the forest-based Pinto's Spinetail, found only in a small area of northeastern Brazil and only recently split as a full species from the Rufous-capped Spinetail, seems certain to have declined because of massive deforestation in the region.

MARANON SPINETAIL, *Synallaxis maranonica*
This little-known and range-restricted spinetail, recently split as a full species from the much more widespread Plain-crowned Spinetail, is found only in woodland undergrowth in a limited part of the upper Río Marañón drainage in southern Ecuador and northwestern Peru. Because of deforestation and habitat degradation, little suitable habitat remains in its small range, and none of what still exists receives formal protection.

BLACKISH-HEADED SPINETAIL, *Synallaxis tithys*
Found in the undergrowth of deciduous forest and woodland in southwestern Ecuador and northwestern Peru, the Blackish-headed Spinetail has declined greatly because of the outright destruction of extensive areas of its habitat; much of the little that remains has been degraded by overgrazing, principally by goats. A major population is protected in Ecuador's Machalilla National Park.

PALE-TAILED CANASTERO, *Asthenes huancavelicae*
The several described races of this species (only recently recognized as deserving of full-species status) are each restricted to arid intermontane valleys of central Peru; several are known to be very rare, and all remain poorly known.

BERLEPSCH'S CANASTERO, *Asthenes berlepschi*
Restricted to a few valleys high in the Andes of western Bolivia; much of the very limited range of Berlepsch's Canastero has been significantly modified by agricultural activities. Recent information, however, does indicate that it may be capable of persisting even in such greatly modified habitats; more information is needed.

AUSTRAL CANASTERO, *Asthenes anthoides*
Found only on the steppes of southern Argentina and Chile, the Austral Canastero, though evidently formerly numerous, is now a very scarce and local resident of less disturbed areas, its numbers having declined because of the effects of severe overgrazing across almost its entire range. No substantial population receives formal protection.

STRIATED SOFTTAIL, *Thripophaga macroura*
With a limited range in the lowland forests of eastern Brazil, the always rare Striated Softtail is severely threatened by the near-total removal of forest within that area. Recent reports center on the region encompassing the Sooretama Reserve and the larger, privately held Rio Doce Reserve, both in northern Espírito Santo.

CANEBRAKE GROUNDCREEPER, *Clibanornis dendrocolaptoides*
A seemingly scarce inhabitant of streamside thickets in southeastern Brazil and adjacent Paraguay and Argentina, the little-known Canebrake Groundcreeper has likely been affected by the deforestation that has occurred across much of its range. More information is needed.

WHITE-THROATED BARBTAIL, *Premnoplex tatei*
Found only in the montane forests of northeastern Venezuela, populations of the White-throated Barbtail have declined as a result of extensive deforestation in that region. Small populations are protected, however, in several national parks.

GREAT XENOPS, *Megaxenops parnaguae*
A poorly known furnariid found very locally in the woodlands of northeastern Brazil, the distinctive Great Xenops is doubtless threatened by deforestation across much of its limited range.

RUFOUS-NECKED FOLIAGE-GLEANER, *Syndactyla ruficollis*
Endemic to the montane forests and woodlands of southern Ecuador and northwestern Peru, this foliage-gleaner (recently transferred from

the genus *Automolus*) has declined substantially because of forest destruction and deterioration in most of its always small range. Unlike some other species, however, it seems capable of persisting in quite degraded habitat. No population receives formal protection.

BOLIVIAN RECURVEBILL, *Simoxenops striatus*
Endemic to a restricted area of the yungas along the base of the Bolivian Andes from La Paz to western Santa Cruz, and seemingly very local, the Bolivian Recurvebill is threatened by continuing deforestation in much of that small range. One population is known to be protected within Amboró National Park.

ALAGOAS FOLIAGE-GLEANER, *Philydor novaesi*
Recently described from the remnant forests of highland Alagoas in northeastern Brazil, the Alagoas Foliage-gleaner is severely threatened by the near-total removal of forest and woodland habitat in its tiny range. None of its habitat presently receives protection.

HENNA-HOODED FOLIAGE-GLEANER, *Hylocryptus erythrocephalus*
Endemic to the deciduous woodlands and forests of southwestern Ecuador and northwestern Peru, this striking foliage-gleaner is, like the Rufous-necked, threatened by the near-total removal of wooded habitats over most of its range. Fortunately, however, the Henna-hooded persists quite well in degraded patches of woodland; a good population receives protection in Ecuador's Machalilla National Park.

MOUSTACHED WOODCREEPER, *Xiphocolaptes falcirostris*
Endemic to northeastern Brazil, where it appears always to have been local, the large Moustached Woodcreeper seems everywhere to occur at low densities in the increasingly fragmented woodlands of that region.

WHITE-BEARDED ANTSHRIKE, *Biatas nigropectus*
This very distinctive and secretive antshrike seems always to have been one of the scarcest bird species endemic to the forests of the southeastern Brazil region, and it now is certainly one of the rarest, with (so far as known) only a few small populations persisting in several areas, some of them (fortunately) well protected. Its status will need to be continually monitored.

PLUMBEOUS ANTVIREO, *Dysithamnus plumbeus*
Endemic to the lowland forests of southern Bahia and Espírito Santo, the Plumbeous Antvireo is now seriously threatened by the almost complete removal of primary forest within its original range. Populations receive protection within the Sooretama and (privately held) Rio Doce Reserves.

BICOLORED ANTVIREO, *Dysithamnus occidentalis*
This poorly known antbird is found only in two small disjunct areas on the slopes of the Andes in southwestern Colombia and northeastern Ecuador. The species has not been found in Colombia in recent years, and there are only a very few records of it from Ecuador; it apparently has specialized habitat requirements and has doubtless declined because of deforestation.

PECTORAL ANTWREN, *Herpsilochmus pectoralis*
A distinctive antwren found very locally in woodlands of northeastern Brazil, the Pectoral Antwren appears nowhere to be particularly numerous and everywhere to be declining as a result of continuing woodland destruction. As far as we are aware, no substantial population receives formal protection.

ASH-THROATED ANTWREN, *Herpsilochmus parkeri*
Known only from a single site in San Martín, northern Peru, the recently described Ash-throated Antwren seems almost certain to be threatened by the deforestation occurring in the region.

RIO DE JANEIRO ANTWREN, *Myrmotherula fluminensis*
This recently described species, still known from only one specimen and of uncertain taxonomic status, was found in lowland forest of Rio de Janeiro, Brazil. It must be presumed to be threatened by deforestation.

SALVADORI'S ANTWREN, *Myrmotherula minor*
Ranging only in the lowland forests of southeastern Brazil, numbers of the always uncommon Salvadori's Antwren have been substantially reduced by deforestation. If it can be confirmed to occur in western Amazonia as well (see main text for discussion of the problem), then the species as a whole can be considered not to be threatened.

BAND-TAILED ANTWREN, *Myrmotherula urosticta*
With a small range in the lowlands of southeastern Brazil, the Band-tailed Antwren is threatened by the near-total removal of forest within that area. Small populations exist in the Sooretama and (privately held) Rio Doce Reserves.

ALAGOAS ANTWREN, *Myrmotherula snowi*
Only recently described (and then subsequently raised to full species status), the Alagoas Antwren is, so far as known, restricted to one forest in Alagoas, Brazil, that found at Pedra Branca. That area is obviously greatly deserving of protection (it also supports several other acutely endangered bird species), but so far protected status has not been achieved.

YUNGAS ANTWREN, *Myrmotherula grisea*
Endemic to a limited area along the base of the Andes in Bolivia from La Paz to western Santa Cruz, populations of the apparently scarce and local Yungas Antwren have declined substantially because of deforestation. It occurs in Bolivia's Amboró National Park.

ORANGE-BELLIED ANTWREN, *Terenura sicki*
Recently described from the remnant forests of highland Alagoas in northeastern Brazil, the Orange-bellied Antwren is threatened by the near-total removal of forest within its minute range, virtually none of which presently receives any protection. Its numbers are, however, somewhat greater than those of the Alagoas Foliage-gleaner, whose range it shares.

YELLOW-RUMPED ANTWREN, *Terenura sharpei*
Endemic to a limited area along the base of the Andes in extreme southern Peru and Bolivia, the uncommon and local Yellow-rumped

Antwren has (like the Yungas Antwren) declined substantially as a result of widespread deforestation.

NARROW-BILLED ANTWREN, *Formicivora iheringi*
Restricted to remnant woodlands in a small area in interior southern Bahia, Brazil, the Narrow-billed Antwren's total population continues to decline as a result of deforestation. No habitat within its range receives formal protection.

BLACK-HOODED ANTWREN, *Formicivora erythronotos*
Dramatically rediscovered in the 1980s (after having gone unseen for over a century), the Black-hooded Antwren is confined to a distinctive coastal habitat (restinga) in southeastern Brazil. Much restinga has in recent decades been overwhelmed by urbanization; no area at present receives any formal protection.

RESTINGA ANTWREN, *Formicivora littoralis*
Recently described from the coastal scrub of Rio de Janeiro, Brazil, the Restinga Antwren is threatened by possible development within its minute range. As yet no population is receiving adequate protection.

SLENDER ANTBIRD, *Rhopornis ardesiaca*
With a range congruent with that of the Narrow-billed Antwren in interior southern Bahia, Brazil, the Slender Antbird's status gives equal cause for alarm. The two species often occur together in the same, mainly remnant, woodlands; protection of at least some portion of this diminishing habitat continues to be an urgent priority.

FRINGE-BACKED FIRE-EYE, *Pyriglena atra*
The acutely endangered Fringe-backed Fire-eye is now restricted to a few small plots of secondary woodland near Salvador in coastal Bahia, Brazil. None of these remnant areas receives formal protection, and doing so remains an urgent priority.

RECURVE-BILLED BUSHBIRD, *Clytoctantes alixii*
Restricted to forests in the lowlands of northern Colombia and adjacent northwestern Venezuela, populations of the Recurve-billed Bushbird have unquestionably undergone a severe decline as a result of the massive deforestation that has taken place across virtually all of its range. There is no recent information on its status; much of its range remains dangerous to enter, which fact may (if one chooses to be optimistic) actually be protecting some populations from further habitat deterioration.

BLACK-TAILED ANTBIRD, *Myrmoborus melanurus*
Restricted to a small area in the lowlands of northeastern Peru east of the lower Río Ucayali, and still known from only a small number of specimens, the Black-tailed Antbird seems to be very scarce and local even within its range, and its habitat requirements remain little understood.

GRAY-HEADED ANTBIRD, *Myrmeciza griseiceps*
Found only in the montane woodlands of southwestern Ecuador and northwestern Peru, the Gray-headed Antbird appears to be the rarest

and most local of the numerous bird species endemic to this region. Not only has deforestation tremendously fragmented its original range (never all that large), but this species seems less able than the others to persist in the degraded, often overgrazed woodlands found in many areas. It is not known to occur in any protected area.

SCALLOPED ANTBIRD, *Myrmeciza ruficauda*

Endemic to the lowlands of northeastern Brazil south to Espírito Santo, a region where deforestation has been severe, the Scalloped Antbird has declined substantially in overall numbers. The species does seem capable of persisting, at least locally, in patchy secondary habitat and is found in several protected areas.

GIANT ANTPITTA, *Grallaria gigantea*

This spectacular antpitta, known locally from the Andean slopes of southern Colombia and Ecuador, was rediscovered in 1992 in eastern Ecuador, but it has eluded researchers elsewhere in its range, where it may well have undergone a serious decline for as yet unascertained reasons (there still appears to be sufficient habitat for it in several regions).

TACHIRA ANTPITTA, *Grallaria chthonia*

Virtually nothing seems to be known about this antpitta, which has been found only at a single site in the subtropical forests of Táchira in western Venezuela. It is likely to be threatened by deforestation.

MOUSTACHED ANTPITTA, *Grallaria alleni*

As with its likely closest relative, the Tachira Antpitta, the Moustached Antpitta also remains virtually unknown in life. It has been found at only two sites, both in the subtropical zone above the Río Magdalena valley in the Colombian Andes. Although one of these sites is at least nominally protected as a national park (Cueva de los Guácharos), the species as a whole, still known from only two specimens, is almost certain to be threatened by deforestation.

BROWN-BANDED ANTPITTA, *Grallaria milleri*

This antpitta has not been found since 1942, when two specimens were obtained near the type locality in the northern part of Colombia's Central Andes. Apparently a forest inhabitant, it is certainly threatened by the deforestation that has removed so much of that range's original forest cover.

BICOLORED ANTPITTA, *Grallaria rufocinerea*

Apparently rare and local in temperate zone forests of the Colombian Andes, the little-known Bicolored Antpitta is almost certainly threatened by deforestation. One site from which it is known, Puracé National Park, is at least nominally protected.

BAHIA TAPACULO, *Scytalopus psychopompus*

This recently described tapaculo is known only from the type locality in the coastal lowlands of eastern Bahia, Brazil. Unknown in life, it is presumably a forest inhabitant; deforestation has been severe in much of the area near where it was found.

STRESEMANN'S BRISTLEFRONT, *Merulaxis stresemanni*
Still known from only two specimens taken in eastern Bahia, the Stresemann's Bristlefront remains unknown in life. As it occurs in a region where deforestation has been rampant, it must be presumed to be seriously at risk; as with the Bahia Tapaculo, more information is obviously needed.

BEARDED TACHURI, *Polystictus pectoralis*
Distributed very locally across South America in less disturbed grasslands, the Bearded Tachuri has for several decades been in steep decline virtually everywhere it occurs because of excessive burning and overgrazing of its habitat, as well as the outright conversion of that habitat to agricultural use. Nowhere does it appear to be numerous.

SHARP-TAILED GRASS-TYRANT, *Culicivora caudacuta*
Found only in the less-disturbed grasslands of interior Brazil, northern Bolivia, and Paraguay, the unique grass-tyrant has declined markedly because of excessive burning and grazing as well as the conversion of many areas to intensive agricultural use. In certain protected areas, such as Brazil's Emas National Park, the grass-tyrant can be quite numerous, but such areas are becoming fewer and fewer; there is some evidence it may be most widespread and numerous in northern Bolivia.

RUFOUS-SIDED PYGMY-TYRANT, *Euscarthmus rufomarginatus*
Found very locally in the savannas of eastern South America, this small tyrannid seems to be scarce throughout its range. Its numbers are dropping precipitously because of human alteration of much of its habitat, though populations presumably remain secure in some remote areas such as Bolivia's Serranía de Huanchaca and Surinam's Sipaliwini Savanna.

ASH-BREASTED TIT-TYRANT, *Anairetes alpinus*
Found extremely locally in patches of *Polylepis* woodland high in the Andes of Peru and Bolivia, the Ash-breasted Tit-Tyrant is known from but four localities. Woodlands at each site are being affected by local inhabitants' activities, principally overcutting for firewood.

ALAGOAS TYRANNULET, *Phylloscartes ceciliae*
Recently described from the remnant forests of highland Alagoas in northeastern Brazil, the Alagoas Tyrannulet remains tolerably numerous in the few areas of habitat left to it, but its overall numbers are doubtless but a small fraction of what they were a few decades ago, prior to the massive deforestation that has swept this region. As with the three other recently described endemic species of this area (Alagoas Antwren, Orange-bellied Antwren, and Alagoas Foliage-gleaner), none of the tyrannulet's habitat is protected.

RESTINGA TYRANNULET, *Phylloscartes kronei*
Recently described from the coastal restinga woodlands of southeastern Brazil, the Restinga Tyrannulet has a very restricted overall range, and its habitat is threatened by accelerating seashore development for second homes.

MINAS GERAIS TYRANNULET, *Phylloscartes roquettei*

Still known from only the type locality and its near vicinity in northern Minas Gerais in south-central Brazil, the sole specimen of the Minas Gerais Tyrannulet was obtained early in the 20th century, and the species has been observed on only one occasion since. The region is apparently severely impacted by deforestation; none of its habitat receives any protection.

SAO PAULO TYRANNULET, *Phylloscartes paulistus*

The Sao Paulo Tyrannulet seemed to be a scarce bird even before the ongoing wave of deforestation devastated so much of its originally forested habitat in southeastern Brazil, eastern Paraguay, and extreme northeastern Argentina—at least the total number of specimens taken is quite small. It is now extremely local; populations are found in several protected areas, notably Brazil's Iguaçú National Park and Cardoso State Park, and Paraguay's Mbaracayú Reserve.

ANTIOQUIA BRISTLE-TYRANT, *Phylloscartes lanyoni*

Only recently described from long-overlooked specimens taken in the foothill forests at the northern end of Colombia's Central Andes, the Antioquia Bristle-Tyrant remains virtually unknown in life. From what little information is available, it would appear likely to be at risk as a result of the extensive deforestation that has taken place in and near its known range.

PELZELN'S TODY-TYRANT, *Hemitriccus inornatus*

Known from only a single 19th-century specimen taken along the Rio Açana in northwestern Amazonian Brazil. Nothing is known about the Pelzeln's Tody-Tyrant in life. As the region is remote and presumably substantially undisturbed by human activities, it seems unlikely to be at risk, but given the absence of current information we include it here.

BUFF-BREASTED TODY-TYRANT, *Hemitriccus mirandae*

Endemic to the woodlands of northeastern Brazil, where it seems always to have been very locally distributed, the Buff-breasted Tody-Tyrant has been recorded at only a very few, scattered localities. A population is protected in the small Pedra Talhada Ecological Reserve in Alagoas.

KAEMPFER'S TODY-TYRANT, *Hemitriccus kaempferi*

Long known only from a single specimen taken in 1929 in Santa Catarina, Brazil, the Kaempfer's Tody-Tyrant was finally relocated in 1991, when a single bird was seen in secondary forest; a second specimen has also recently come to light. Although these records are gratifying, the species is definitely at risk from the deforestation that has overtaken most of the forests in the region to which it is confined; the site where it was recently found is only nominally protected.

FORK-TAILED PYGMY-TYRANT, *Hemitriccus furcatus*

This strikingly marked small tyrannid is endemic to the lowlands of Rio de Janeiro and São Paulo in southeastern Brazil, from which it has been recorded from only a small number of localities, in recent years apparently only at a few. Evidently never numerous, it is now gravely threatened by deforestation.

BUFF-CHEEKED TODY-FLYCATCHER, *Todirostrum senex*
In a situation comparable to that of the Pelzeln's Tody-Tyrant, the Buff-cheeked Tody-Flycatcher is known only from a single 19th-century specimen taken in western Amazonian Brazil, in this case at Borba on the lower Rio Madeira. The Borba region remains relatively remote and sparsely settled, so it would appear unlikely that the Buff-cheeked Tody-Flycatcher is at risk from human activities.

RUSSET-WINGED SPADEBILL, *Platyrinchus leucoryphus*
A rare tyrannid endemic to the humid forests of southeastern Brazil, eastern Paraguay, and northeastern Argentina, the Russet-winged Spadebill has seemingly always been a scarce species. In recent decades it has become decidedly rare and local as deforestation has eliminated many of its formerly occupied sites. A few populations are well protected, notably on the Brazilian side of Iguazú Falls and in Paraguay's Mbaracayú Reserve.

GRAY-BREASTED FLYCATCHER, *Lathrotriccus griseipectus*
Endemic to the woodlands of western Ecuador and northwestern Peru, the Gray-breasted Flycatcher has in recent years been found to be somewhat more numerous and widespread than had been thought; it was doubtless overlooked prior to its vocalizations becoming known. Nonetheless its overall population has been much reduced by the deforestation that has taken place across a major portion of its original range, and it amply deserves threatened status. Populations are protected in several national parks and reserves, with the largest population occurring in Ecuador's Machalilla National Park.

WHITE-TAILED SHRIKE-TYRANT, *Agriornis andicola*
The causes of the apparent rapid decline of the White-tailed Shrike-Tyrant from all or nearly all of its formerly wide Andean range (Ecuador to Chile and Argentina) remain enigmatic. In the case of this large tyrannid, habitat degradation and destruction seem *not* to have played a role; most of its high puna range remains little changed from a time when its numbers were evidently much greater than they are at present. A few still range in several nominally protected areas, notably Chile's Lauca National Park.

BLACK-AND-WHITE MONJITA, *Heteroxolmis dominicana*
Until recently the attractive Black-and-white Monjita occurred over a fairly wide area in southern Brazil, Paraguay, Uruguay, and northeastern Argentina where it favored open grassy, marshy country. For reasons that remain obscure (in the case of this species, habitat deterioration seems an inadequate explanation), the species has in recent years undergone a marked reduction in numbers and contraction in its range. There are no recent reports from Paraguay and only a few from Argentina; its stronghold appears to be the rolling hilly country of northeastern Rio Grande do Sul, Brazil.

COCK-TAILED TYRANT, *Alectrurus tricolor*

Restricted to less-disturbed grasslands from northern Bolivia and south-central Brazil south to northern Argentina, the charming Cock-tailed Tyrant is now extremely local as a result of overgrazing and excessive burning across the vast majority of its former range. Surviving numbers are doubtless greatest in Brazil, where some occur in well-protected areas such as Emas National Park, but overall the species has undergone a massive decline, and it is now totally absent from many areas where formerly present.

STRANGE-TAILED TYRANT, *Alectrurus risora*

Like its congener, the Strange-tailed Tyrant requires relatively undisturbed grasslands, in the Strange-tailed's case usually in marshier terrain. Although it was once found locally from southern Brazil to northern Argentina, the only recent reports of this spectacular and very aptly named tyrannid come from southern Paraguay and Corrientes, Argentina. None of its habitat is known to receive formal protection.

OCHRACEOUS ATTILA, *Attila torridus*

Endemic to the forests and woodlands of western Ecuador and adjacent Colombia, the Ochraceous Attila has declined drastically as a result of widespread deforestation. It does, however, seem tolerant of edge situations and appears capable of persisting in areas where forest has become quite fragmented. A population exists in Ecuador's Machalilla National Park.

SLATY BECARD, *Pachyramphus spodiurus*

Endemic to lighter woodland and plantations in western Ecuador and adjacent Peru, the Slaty Becard has, despite much field work in its range, been found at surprisingly few sites in recent years. Although it by no means requires undisturbed primary habitats, the relative paucity of recent reports is an indication that its overall numbers have declined substantially, for reasons that remain poorly understood (though woodland destruction has likely played a role). So far as known, no population occurs in a formally protected area.

YELLOW-HEADED MANAKIN, *Chloropipo flavicapilla*

This spectacular manakin is endemic to the subtropical zone forests of western Colombia, with a few records from the eastern Andes of Ecuador as well. Never numerous and apparently always local, there are relatively few recent reports of it; many areas where it was formerly found no longer provide suitable habitat because they have been converted to agricultural use. It surely deserves threatened status.

OPAL-CROWNED MANAKIN, *Pipra iris*

The exquisite little Opal-crowned Manakin is found only in the forests of lower Amazonian Brazil from the lower Rio Tapajós eastward, a region that has been heavily affected by development and population pressures in recent decades. Although it perhaps is not yet critically threatened, it is worth pointing out that this species is vulnerable to continuing forest destruction; no substantial portion of its range is protected.

GOLDEN-CROWNED MANAKIN, *Pipra vilasboasi*

This manakin is known from only one site in eastern Amazonian Brazil, the Rio Cururú in the Rio Tapajós drainage, from whence it was only recently described. Doubtless a forest inhabitant like all its close relatives, the stunning Golden-crowned Manakin is likely imperiled by the encroachment of cattle ranching, but no definite information on its status exists—indeed, no ornithologist other than its describer has ever seen it alive.

PERUVIAN PLANTCUTTER, *Phytotoma raimondii*

The Peruvian Plantcutter's range, along the Peruvian coast from Tumbes to Lima, has never been large, and the total extent of its specialized patchy low woodland habitat has always been extremely limited. In recent decades many such patches have been destroyed or altered, and as a result, the plantcutter's numbers have plummeted. The species deserves endangered status; so far as known, no population receives formal protection at present.

BUFF-THROATED PURPLETUFT, *Iodopleura pipra*

There are two forms of the very small Buff-throated Purpletuft, one (*leucopygia*) restricted to the remnant forests of northeastern Brazil, the other (nominate) found very locally in woodland and forest borders in the southeast. Both forms have declined drastically as a result of deforestation, and both should be recognized as endangered, *leucopygia* perhaps acutely so.

KINGLET CALYPTURA, *Calyptura cristata*

The tiny calyptura, known from a very limited area in southeastern Brazil centered on Rio de Janeiro, has not been seen since the 19th century when, judging from the number of specimens obtained, it cannot have been overly rare. Pessimists have already declared it extinct; despite the absence of any solid evidence to the contrary, we prefer to hold out the hope that it will yet be found. The species declined so long ago that no one really has any idea why, nor what its habitat was.

SWALLOW-TAILED COTINGA, *Phibalura flavirostris*

The attractive Swallow-tailed Cotinga enjoys a relatively wide range in southeastern Brazil, eastern Paraguay, and northeastern Argentina, with an apparently disjunct population in Bolivia. Nothing is known about its Bolivian status, but throughout the rest of its range the species seems to have undergone a steep decline, for reasons that remain obscure. There are only a very few recent reports of it from Paraguay and Argentina, and it is now very local in Brazil. Small numbers occur at least seasonally in Brazil's Itatiaia National Park.

BLACK-HEADED BERRYEATER, *Carpornis melanocephalus*

Endemic to the lowland forests of eastern Brazil, the Black-headed Berryeater has declined substantially as a result of the removal of forest from the vast majority of its range. Populations are protected in Espírito Santo at the Sooretama and (privately held) Rio Doce Reserves, and in the Lagamar area of São Paulo.

WHITE-CHEEKED COTINGA, *Zaratornis stresemanni*

Restricted to patches of *Polylepis*-dominated woodland high in the Andes of western Peru, the striking White-cheeked Cotinga is threatened by the continuing clearance of most of these woodlands for firewood. At least two sites where the cotinga is found, Huascarán National Park and Pampa Galeras Reserve, do receive formal protection.

BANDED COTINGA, *Cotinga maculata*

Endemic to the lowland forests of a limited area in eastern Brazil from Bahia to Rio de Janeiro, the beautiful Banded Cotinga is now severely threatened by the near-total loss of its habitat, so thorough has regional deforestation been. Recent reports come mainly from northern Espírito Santo, at the Sooretama and (privately held) Rio Doce Reserves.

WHITE-WINGED COTINGA, *Xipholena atropurpurea*

Restricted to the lowland forests of eastern Brazil, the stunning White-winged Cotinga has declined tremendously in recent decades because of deforestation. It remains, however, slightly more widespread and numerous than the sometimes-sympatric Banded Cotinga, being perhaps more resilient and apparently able to persist in patchy secondary habitat; it also had a larger original range. Populations are known from several protected areas.

LONG-WATTLED UMBRELLABIRD, *Cephalopterus penduliger*

Endemic to the montane forests on the west slope of the Western Andes in Colombia and Ecuador (wandering to the adjacent lowlands), this most spectacular of the umbrellabirds has declined markedly as a result of deforestation and, improbable though it may seem, shooting for food. Its capture for the export cage-bird market, formerly perhaps a factor (though numbers involved were certainly never large), is now illegal, and locally it is only very rarely kept in captivity. Populations are at least nominally protected in several national parks and reserves, though whether this altitudinal migrant's entire range of elevational requirements are incorporated in any is unknown.

THE PLATES

FACING PAGE TERMS

Note that, under more complex genera, major Groups (A, B, C, etc.) have been employed to associate visually similar species. Additional subsets within the Groups have been broken out where deemed useful; these are preceded by • (see "Plates and Facing Pages," vol. 1, p. 4).

Numbers represent a full species; modifying letters (e.g., 1a, 2b, etc.) refer to different subspecies, an age stage, or some other variation. If the gender symbol ($\male$, $\female$) is lacking, sexes are identical or nearly so in plumage. The subspecies illustrated here is specified; if none is, then the species is monotypic; i.e., it shows no racial variation.

Species *not illustrated* are listed in each Group under their most visually similar relatives; these are preceded by "*Also.*" The species sequence *within* each Group may not correspond exactly with that of the main text, although the Group sequences do.

Species-level *field marks* are not usually given; rather, we describe its genus or group and expect the reader to refer to the main text for most identification criteria.

Ranges are given (in very encapsulated form) for species which are not widespread; note that these refer to the entire species and are not merely the range of the listed subspecies. The following abbreviations are employed (apart from "standard" ones such as "se." for southeastern, "cen." for central, etc.):

se. S. Am. = southeastern South America (i.e., se. Brazil and adjacent e. Paraguay and ne. Argentina)	Par. = Paraguay
	Uru. = Uruguay
	Venez. = Venezuela
Amaz. = Amazonian or Amazonia	spp. = refers to several species
Arg. = Argentina	in a general way
Bol. = Bolivia	(e.g., *Geositta* spp.)
Col. = Colombia	ssp. = subspecies
Ecu. = Ecuador	$\male\male$, $\female\female$ = plural

Text page numbers are given for each genus and for major Groups within genera.

All birds on the same plate are drawn to *scale* unless divided by a solid line, which indicates that two different-size scales have been employed. Occasionally an inset is drawn to smaller scale; this is normally obvious but nonetheless is specified in a note at the bottom of that facing page.

PLATE 1: MINERS, EARTHCREEPERS, & ALLIES

Geobates Miners PAGE 24
A small and *very short-tailed* miner found only in open parts of *Brazilian cerrado.*
      1.   CAMPO MINER, *G. poecilopterus*

Geositta Miners   Plainly attired and short-tailed, the miners are found in open and usu- PAGE 24
ally arid terrain from the Ecuadorian Andes south to Patagonia and Tierra del Fuego; some species are
found at very high elevations, others along or near arid coasts. They are almost entirely terrestrial, though
all have conspicuous flight songs. Identification is often tricky and is based mainly on subtle differences in
bill shape, overall color tonality, patterning of *rufous on wing* (present in most species, but mostly evident
only in flight), and *extent and color of a pale area on rump* (likewise mainly visible in flight).
A. Typical miners; bills *short and slender;* uppertail-coverts *creamy* in many species. PAGE 25
• Occurring in open desert terrain of *w. Peru and n. Chile.*
      2.   COASTAL MINER, *G. p. peruviana* (Peru only)
    Also: Grayish Miner, *G. maritima*
• Occurring on *flatter terrain* mainly in altiplano and Patagonia.
      3.   COMMON MINER, *G. cunicularia titicacae*
      4.   SHORT-BILLED MINER, *G. antarctica* (Tierra del Fuego region)
    Also: Puna Miner, *G. punensis* (s. Peru to nw. Arg.)
• Occurring most often on *steep, rocky slopes* mainly at high elevations.
      5.   DARK-WINGED MINER, *G. saxicolina* (cen. Peru)
      6.   RUFOUS-BANDED MINER, *G. rufipennis fasciata*
    Also: Creamy-rumped Miner, *G. isabellina* (mostly cen. Chile; scarce)
B. Two miners with *distinctive bills* (but cf. *Upucerthia* earthcreepers). PAGE 29
      7.   THICK-BILLED MINER, *G. crassirostris* (w. Peru; scarce)
      8.   SLENDER-BILLED MINER, *G. t. tenuirostris*

Upucerthia Earthcreepers   Superficially much like *Geositta* miners, and with a similar overall dis- PAGE 31
tribution pattern in more open parts of Andes from Peru south to Patagonia, the earthcreepers differ in
their larger size, *longer and often more decurved bills* (in some species strikingly so), *longer tails* (often characteristically *cocked*), and *unbanded wings.* Identification to species is often difficult; pay particular attention to the *degree of bill curvature* and *extent of streaking below.*
A. *Bill strongly decurved;* either with *scaly throat* or *uniform below.* PAGE 31
      9.   SCALE-THROATED EARTHCREEPER, *U. dumetaria hypoleuca*
    10.   PLAIN-BREASTED EARTHCREEPER, *U. jelskii pallida*
    Also: Buff-breasted Earthcreeper, *U. validirostris* (mainly nw. Arg.; like 10)
              White-throated Earthcreeper, *U. albigula* (scarce in sw. Peru and
              n. Chile; like 10)
B. *Bill straighter;* underparts more or less *streaked.* PAGE 33
    11.   STRIATED EARTHCREEPER, *U. serrana* (Peru)
    12.   STRAIGHT-BILLED EARTHCREEPER, *U. ruficauda montana*
    Also: Rock Earthcreeper, *U. andaecola* (w. Bol. and nw. Arg.; nearest 12)

Ochetorhynchus Earthcreepers   A pair of rather small earthcreepers, often considered congeneric with PAGE 35
Upucerthia. One species ranges in *Bolivian foothills and lower slopes,* the other in *chaco of Par. and Arg.* Both
are found in *more wooded habitats* than *Upucerthia* earthcreepers, and Chaco (at least) is considerably more
arboreal and has *Phacellodomus-* (thornbird) like vocalizations.
    13.   CHACO EARTHCREEPER, *O. certhioides estebani*
    Also: Bolivian Earthcreeper, *O. harterti* (lacks rufous forehead)

Eremobius Earthcreepers PAGE 36
A distinctive earthcreeper of *Argentina's Patagonian steppes,* with *strikingly bicolored tail.*
    14.   BAND-TAILED EARTHCREEPER, *E. phoenicurus*

Chilia   Found only on *rocky mountainsides of cen. Chile,* the chilia is easily PAGE 37
identified by its *white bib,* and contrasting *rufous rump* and *blackish tail.*
    15.   CRAG CHILIA, *C. m. melanura*

PLATE 2: CINCLODES & HORNEROS

Cinclodes Cinclodes   A rather uniform group of about 13 fairly large furnariids which range PAGE 38 mainly in *Andes,* some at very high elevations, favoring open areas along *streams;* other species occur along *coastlines* from Peru to Arg. They are sturdily built birds, most with rather long tails, and almost all with a *white to rufous wing-band* (prominent in flight) and pale tail corners; a number have a striking white superciliary and contrasting white throat. Some resemble each other quite closely and can be confusing in the field; several have only recently been described or recognized as full species. Unlike earth-creepers, cinclodes have a bold demeanor and are frequently in the open; hence they are usually *easy to see.*

A. Distinctive *dark sooty brown* cinclodes; s. Tierra del Fuego and Falklands. PAGE 38

    1.   BLACKISH CINCLODES, *C. antarcticus maculirostris*

B. *"Standard"* cinclodes; size varies; some familiar, some very local. PAGE 39

    2.   CHILEAN SEASIDE-CINCLODES, *C. nigrofumosus*

    3.   GRAY-FLANKED CINCLODES, *C. o. oustaleti* (Chile and s. Arg.; smallish)

    4.   BAR-WINGED CINCLODES

        4a. *C. f. fuscus* (Chile and Arg.)

        4b. *C. f. albiventris* (Andes of n. Arg. to Peru)

        4c. *C. f. albidiventris* (Andes from Ecu. to Venez.)

    5.   STOUT-BILLED CINCLODES, *C. e. excelsior* (Andes of Col. and Ecu.)

    6.   LONG-TAILED CINCLODES, *C. pabsti* (extreme se. Brazil)

    7.   WHITE-WINGED CINCLODES, *C. a. atacamensis* (Andes of Peru to n. Chile and n. Arg.)

    Also: Peruvian Seaside-Cinclodes, *C. taczanowskii*

          Dark-bellied Cinclodes, *C. patagonicus* (nearest 2 and 3)

          Cordoba Cinclodes, *C. comechingonus* (Córdoba area, Arg.; most like 4c)

          Olrog's Cinclodes, *C. olrogi* (Córdoba area, Arg.)

          Royal Cinclodes, *C. aricomae* (rare in se. Peru and w. Bol.; resembles 5)

C. Unique *large* cinclodes of the *very high* Peruvian Andes; *immaculate white below.* PAGE 46

    8.   WHITE-BELLIED CINCLODES, *C. palliatus*

Furnarius Horneros   A small group of about 6 species (the exact number is still a matter of PAGE 46 debate), the horneros are chunky, rather *short-tailed* furnariids found in open areas through the lowlands of S. Am. *Rufous* predominates in most species, and many have a *bold white superciliary.* Horneros are perhaps best known for their distinctive *oven-shaped mud nests,* which in many parts of their range (especially in Arg.) are a conspicuous feature of the landscape. Their loud vocalizations also draw attention to these sometimes very familiar birds (especially Rufous).

A. *Bright rufous above;* contrasting crown (usually) and *prominent superciliary.* PAGE 47

    9.   PALE-LEGGED HORNERO, *F. leucopus tricolor*

    10.   BAND-TAILED HORNERO, *F. figulus pileatus* (e. Brazil)

    Also: Bay Hornero, *F. torridus* (river islands of w. Amazon; like 9 but darker)

          Lesser Hornero, *F. minor* (Amaz. river islands)

B. *"Plain"* horneros; Brazil and Bolivia southward. PAGE 50

    11.   CRESTED HORNERO, *F. cristatus* (chaco region)

    12.   RUFOUS HORNERO, *F. r. rufus*

Sylviorthorhynchus Wiretails The wiretail's *unique extremely long and filamentuous tail* renders it unmistakable. An inconspicuous inhabitant of undergrowth in *Nothofagus* forest and woodland in Chile and
Arg., most readily found by *voice*.

    1.   DES MURS' WIRETAIL, *S. desmursii*

Aphrastura Rayaditos A pair of delightful arboreal birds, numerous in wooded habitats in
s. S. Am., 1 only on the remote Juan Fernández Is. off Chile.

    2.   THORN-TAILED RAYADITO, *A. s. spinicauda*
   Also: Masafuera Rayadito, *A. masafuerae* (duller than 2; Juan Fernández Is.)

Leptasthenura Tit-Spinetails A distinctive group of small furnariids with *very long and strongly*
graduated ("spiky") tails found in open woodlands and scrub in Andes and across s. S. Am. to s. Brazil;
they favor more arid regions. All have small bills, and most have a "capped" look and several sport a *bushy*
crest. Some species resemble each other closely, especially those with streaked upperparts. All tit-spinetails
forage actively, moving restlessly from tree to tree, often hanging upside down as they glean branches
and twigs.

A. *Mantle streaked;* lower underparts well streaked to virtually plain.

    3.   ANDEAN TIT-SPINETAIL, *L. a. andicola*
    4.   RUSTY-CROWNED TIT-SPINETAIL (w. Peru)
        4a. *L. p. pileata*
        4b. *L. pileata cajabambae*
   Also: Streak-backed Tit-Spinetail, *L. striata* (w. Peru and n. Chile)
        White-browed Tit-Spinetail, *L. xenothorax* (resembles 4a; very local in
        se. Peru)
        Striolated Tit-Spinetail, *L. striolata* (se. Brazil)

B. *Mantle unstreaked;* tail solidly rufous in 2 species.
• With characteristic *capped or crested* appearance.

    5.   PLAIN-MANTLED TIT-SPINETAIL, *L. aegithaloides pallida*
    6.   TUFTED TIT-SPINETAIL, *L. platensis* (mostly Arg.)
    7.   BROWN-CAPPED TIT-SPINETAIL, *L. f. fuliginiceps* (w. Bol. and
        nw. Arg.)
    8.   ARAUCARIA TIT-SPINETAIL, *L. setaria* (se. Brazil area)
• *Lacks* capped effect; note *slender bill.*

    9.   TAWNY TIT-SPINETAIL, *L. yanacensis* (local in high Andes of Peru
        and Bol.)

Phleocryptes Rushbirds A small, chunky, short-tailed furnariid restricted to *marshes* from Peru
to Chile and Arg. *Common.*

    10.   WREN-LIKE RUSHBIRD, *P. m. melanops*

Limnornis and *Limnoctites* Reedhaunters
A pair of fairly large, hefty spinetails with simple patterns but *very distinctively shaped bills.* Found locally
in *marshes* from se. Brazil to e. Arg. and most easily located by *voice.*

    11.   CURVE-BILLED REEDHAUNTER, *Limnornis curvirostris*
    12.   STRAIGHT-BILLED REEDHAUNTER, *Limnoctites rectirostris*

Spartonoica Wren-Spinetails A single species of spinetail found locally in *marshes* from extreme s.
Brazil to Arg.; shy and hard to see well. The *spiky tail* and *streaked upperparts* with rufous cap are
distinctive.

    13.   BAY-CAPPED WREN-SPINETAIL, *S. maluroides*

Schoeniophylax Spinetails A rather large, distinctive spinetail with *relatively bold patterning* and
very long tail. Favors shrubby areas near water, ranging in s.-cen. S. Am.

    14.   CHOTOY SPINETAIL, *S. p. phryganophila*

Poecilurus Spinetails More "typical" spinetails found mainly in undergrowth of deciduous
woodland and scrub. They are similar in most respects to *Synallaxis* (Plate 4), and perhaps are congeneric,
but *Poecilurus* have more pronounced and solid black gular patches.

    15.   WHITE-WHISKERED SPINETAIL, *P. c. candei* (n. Col. and nw.
        Venez.)
    16.   OCHRE-CHEEKED SPINETAIL, *P. s. scutata* (ne. Brazil to
        nw. Arg.)
   Also: Hoary-throated Spinetail, *P. kollari* (near 15; extreme n. Brazil)

Synallaxis Spinetails   A large and difficult genus of obscure small furnariids with *usually long*   PAGE 65
and always strongly graduated tails ("double-pointed"); there are *Synallaxis* spinetails virtually throughout S. Am., the sole exception being the continent's far s. reaches. Several species have *very small ranges*
(but may there be quite numerous); some others are very locally distributed across broader areas. Many
Synallaxis have a *grizzled or plain black throat patch*, and also have *rufous crowns* and *rufous wing-coverts*. All
tend to skulk in dense lower growth, with most species in edge or secondary habitats, only a few actually occurring inside continuous forest. Attention is often drawn to them by their *frequently given*
vocalizations.

     Cranioleuca spinetails tend to be more arboreal, or to be more uniformly rufous above. Note that *Poeci-*
lurus spinetails are treated on Plate 3 (sometimes those species are placed in *Synallaxis*), and that the "*stic-*
tothorax pair" of *Synallaxis* spinetails are treated on Plate 5.

A. *Montane Synallaxis;* tail notably *long* in most.   PAGE 66
- Very *distinctive*, rare species of Ancash, Peru.
  - 1.   RUSSET-BELLIED SPINETAIL, *S. zimmeri*
- *All or mostly rufous;* the *S. unirufa* superspecies.
  - 2.   RUFOUS SPINETAIL, *S. u. unirufa* (w. Venez. to Peru)
  - 3.   BLACK-THROATED SPINETAIL, *S. castanea* (n. Venez.)
  - *Also:*   Rusty-headed Spinetail, *S. fuscorufa* (like 2 but back grayish; Santa
    Marta Mts.)
- "Typical" (with *rufous cap*, etc.); long tails either *rufous or brownish.*
  - 4.   AZARA'S SPINETAIL
    - 4a. *S. azarae urubambae*
    - 4b. *S. azarae superciliosa* (s. Bol. to nw. Arg.)
  - 5.   APURIMAC SPINETAIL, *S. courseni* (Apurímac, Peru)
  - *Also:*   Silvery-throated Spinetail, *S. subpudica* (tail brownish; E. Andes
    of Col.)

B. Standard *lowland Synallaxis* with rufous cap and wing-coverts.   PAGE 69
- *Edge and scrub habitats; tail grayish brown* in all but 6.
  - 6.   SOOTY-FRONTED SPINETAIL, *S. f. frontalis*
  - 7.   PALE-BREASTED SPINETAIL, *S. albescens inaequalis*
  - 8.   SPIX'S SPINETAIL, *S. spixi* (se. Brazil to ne. Arg.)
  - 9.   DARK-BREASTED SPINETAIL, *S. a. albigularis* (w. Amazonia)
  - *Also:*   Cinereous-breasted Spinetail, *S. hypospodia* (very local in s. Amazonia)
    Slaty Spinetail, *S. brachyura* (w. Col. and w. Ecu.)
- *Forest-based; dark* with *rufous/chestnut* tail.
  - 10.   RUFOUS-CAPPED SPINETAIL, *S. ruficapilla* (se. Brazil area)
  - 11.   CABANIS' SPINETAIL, *S. c. cabanisi* (e. Peru and n. Bol.)
  - *Also:*   Pinto's Spinetail, *S. infuscata* (near 10; local in ne. Brazil)
    Dusky Spinetail, *S. moesta* (like 11; local from e. Col. to n. Peru)
    Macconnell's Spinetail, *S. macconnelli* (like 11; local in ne. S. Am.)

C. *Synallaxis lacking* a rufous cap; a heterogeneous assembly.   PAGE 76
- Underparts *buff to mostly gray* (with or without a throat patch); tail *rufous/chestnut* in all but 15.
  - 12.   PLAIN-CROWNED SPINETAIL, *S. g. gujanensis*
  - 13.   WHITE-BELLIED SPINETAIL, *S. propinqua* (Amaz. river islands)
  - 14.   GRAY-BELLIED SPINETAIL, *S. cinerascens* (se. Brazil area)
  - 15.   BLACKISH-HEADED SPINETAIL, *S. tithys* (sw. Ecu. and
    nw. Peru)
  - *Also:*   White-lored Spinetail, *S. albilora* (nearest 12; pantanal woodland of
    sw. Brazil)
    Maranon Spinetail, *S. maranonica* (local in nw. Peru)
- *Foreparts chestnut/rufous* (except 16b); tail *black. Inside* Amaz. forests.
  - 16.   RUDDY SPINETAIL
    - 16a. *S. rutilans amazonica*
    - 16b. *S. rutilans omissa* (Belém region of Brazil)
  - *Also:*   Chestnut-throated Spinetail, *S. cherriei* (very local)
- *Streaky underparts;* n. Venez. region.
  - 17.   STRIPE-BREASTED SPINETAIL, *S. cinnamomea striatipectus*

Gyalophylax Spinetails   A *large* and *dark-looking* spinetail found locally in *arid interior ne.*   PAGE 81
Brazil. Tail more rounded and *bill more wedge-shaped* than in *Synallaxis.*
- 18.   RED-SHOULDERED SPINETAIL, *G. hellmayri*

"Synallaxis" Spinetails   This pair of spinetails of uncertain affinities has long been placed in   PAGE 82
Synallaxis, though we question whether that is where they actually belong; *Cranioleuca* or *Siptornopsis*
seem more likely. They are found in *sw. Ecu. and nw. Peru,* and both are marked by their *breast streaking.*

    1.   NECKLACED SPINETAIL, *S. s. stictothorax*

    Also: Chinchipe Spinetail, *S. chinchipensis* (upper Río Marañón valley)

Siptornopsis Spinetails   A *large* spinetail found locally in *mts. of nw. Peru.* Note the *conspicuous*   PAGE 83
dark breast streaking and *long grayish tail.*

    2.   GREAT SPINETAIL, *S. hypochondriacus*

Hellmayrea Spinetails   A *small, short-tailed,* almost wren-like spinetail found in undergrowth   PAGE 84
of temperate Andean forests from Venez. to Peru.

    3.   WHITE-BROWED SPINETAIL, *H. g. gularis*

Cranioleuca Spinetails   A large group of *mainly arboreal* spinetails found in forested and   PAGE 85
wooded habitats virtually throughout S. Am.; a minority range in shrubbery and marshes. Brown, rufous, and gray predominate, their rufous tails typically being *stiff* and having *"spiny tips,"* presumably to
better support them as they climb trunks and probe into airplants. *Facial patterns* are important for identification, with many species having either a *pale superciliary* or a *contrastingly colored crown* (most often
rufous). Bills, at least the lower mandibles, tend to be flesh-colored. Unlike *Synallaxis* spinetails, which
usually remain near the ground in dense growth and often are hard to see, *Cranioleuca* behave much more
like foliage-gleaners and are usually not too difficult to observe.

A. "Fancy," high Andean species of Peru and Bolivia; *pale crown in all but 1 form.*   PAGE 85

    4.   CREAMY-CRESTED SPINETAIL, *C. a. albicapilla*

    5.   LIGHT-CROWNED SPINETAIL, *C. a. albiceps* (crown buff in
        1 race)

    6.   MARCAPATA SPINETAIL, *C. m. marcapatae* (crown white in
        1 race)

B. "Standard" *Cranioleuca.*   PAGE 87

• With contrasting *rufous crown* (many very similar, resembling 8 or 9). Mainly *montane* in n. S. Am.
(except Pallid).

    7.   BARON'S SPINETAIL, *C. baroni capitalis* (large; n. and cen. Peru)

    8.   LINE-CHEEKED SPINETAIL, *C. a. antisiensis* (sw. Ecu. and
        nw. Peru)

    9.   ASH-BROWED SPINETAIL, *C. curtata cisandina* (mainly Andean
        e. slope, Col. to Bol.)

    Also: Streak-capped Spinetail, *C. hellmayri* (crown also streaked; Santa
        Marta Mts.)
        Tepui Spinetail, *C. demissa* (underparts gray)
        Pallid Spinetail, *C. pallida* (se. Brazil)
        Red-faced Spinetail, *C. erythrops* (entire face rufous; w. Col. and
        w. Ecu.)

• Crown *plain* to *notably streaked* (never rufous). Mainly *lowlands* (except Stripe-crowned).

    10.   GRAY-HEADED SPINETAIL, *C. s. semicinerea* (ne. and cen. Brazil)

    11.   OLIVE SPINETAIL, *C. obsoleta* (se. Brazil area)

    12.   STRIPE-CROWNED SPINETAIL, *C. p. pyrrhophia* (Bol. to Arg.)

    Also: Crested Spinetail, *C. subcristata* (Venez. and ne. Col.)

C. Miscellaneous *Cranioleuca,* mostly associated with marshes, river islands, or várzea forest.   PAGE 93

    13.   SULPHUR-BEARDED SPINETAIL, *C. sulphurifera* (marshes of
        extreme se. Brazil to e. Arg.)

    14.   RUSTY-BACKED SPINETAIL, *C. v. vulpina* (shrubbery near
        water)

    15.   SPECKLED SPINETAIL, *C. gutturata hyposticta*

    16.   SCALED SPINETAIL, *C. muelleri* (e. Amaz. Brazil; rare)

Certhiaxis Spinetails   PAGE 95
A pair of simply patterned, *rufous and white* spinetails found in and near lowland *marshes.*

    17.   YELLOW-CHINNED SPINETAIL, *C. c. cinnamomea*

    Also: Red-and-white Spinetail, *C. mustelina* (islands along Amazon and its
        tributaries)

5

TUDOR

PLATE 6: THISTLETAILS & CANASTEROS

Schizoeaca Thistletails   Small slender furnariids with *extremely long, "frayed" tails* found near   PAGE 96
treeline in Andes from Venez. to Bol. The species vary especially in dorsal color, face pattern, and chin-patch color; all have entirely *allopatric* distributions.

    1.   WHITE-CHINNED THISTLETAIL, *S. f. fuliginosa* (w. Venez. to n. Ecu., and in n. Peru)

    2.   MOUSE-COLORED THISTLETAIL, *S. griseomurina* (s. Ecu. and n. Peru)

    3.   EYE-RINGED THISTLETAIL, *S. palpebralis* (cen. Peru)

    4.   VILCABAMBA THISTLETAIL, *S. vilcabambae ayacuchensis* (s.-cen. Peru)

    5.   BLACK-THROATED THISTLETAIL, *S. h. harterti* (w. Bol.)

    Also: Ochre-browed Thistletail, *S. coryi* (w. Venez.)
        Perija Thistletail, *S. perijana* (Sierra de Perijá)
        Puna Thistletail, *S. helleri* (s. Peru)

Oreophylax Spinetails   Monotypic species restricted to *high mts. of se. Brazil.*   PAGE 100

    6.   ITATIAIA SPINETAIL, *O. moreirae*

Asthenes Canasteros   A large and confusing assemblage of small, rather dull-colored furna-   PAGE 100
riids found in Andes and Patagonia, with only 2 species north of Peru; outlying species are found in the chaco and in e. Brazil. *Many species resemble each other closely:* our Groups thus had to be narrowly defined, with only subtle differences between them. Tails are often *long*, in some species frequently held *cocked;* in virtually all of them the *outer rectrices are paler* (usually *rufous*). Most species show a chin patch, typically some shade of *rufous*. Canasteros inhabit open or semiopen terrain, often in *grassy* and especially *rocky* areas; here they are generally inconspicuous except when singing, scampering rapidly on the ground never far from cover. Note that the first 3 species listed were formerly united under the name of Creamy-breasted Canastero, *A. dorbignyi.*

A. *Upperparts unstreaked; uppertail mainly blackish* (rufous at most on outer 2 rectrices).   PAGE 101
• Mainly *black* uppertail *contrasting with rich rufous rump.*

    7.   RUSTY-VENTED CANASTERO, *A. d. dorbignyi* (w. Bol. to nw. Arg.)

    8.   DARK-WINGED CANASTERO, *A. a. arequipae* (w. Peru to n. Chile and nw. Bol.)

    Also: Pale-tailed Canastero, *A. huancavelicae* (local in valleys of cen. Peru)
        Berlepsch's Canastero, *A. berlepschi* (w. Bol.)
        Steinbach's Canastero, *A. steinbachi* (nw. Arg.)

• Mainly *dusky/blackish* uppertail, but rump *not* noticeably rufous.

    9.   SHARP-BILLED CANASTERO, *A. p. pyrrholeuca* (mainly Arg.)

    10.   SHORT-BILLED CANASTERO, *A. baeri* (mainly chaco)

    11.   DUSKY-TAILED CANASTERO, *A. h. humicola* (Chile)

    Also: Patagonian Canastero, *A. patagonica* (s. Arg.)

B. *Plain-backed,* but uppertail with *considerable rufous* (*more* than only on outer rectrices); throat often somewhat streaky.   PAGE 106

    12.   CANYON CANASTERO, *A. pudibunda grisior* (w. Peru)

    13.   RUSTY-FRONTED CANASTERO, *A. ottonis* (s.-cen. Peru)

    14.   CORDILLERAN CANASTERO, *A. m. modesta*

    Also: Maquis Canastero, *A. heterura* (w. Bol.; near 12 and 13)
        Cactus Canastero, *A. cactorum* (w. Peru; near 14)
        Cipo Canastero, *A. luiziae* (very local on serras of Minas Gerais, Brazil; grayish below)

C. Upperparts show *indistinct black streaking. Throat well streaked;* tail dull.   PAGE 110

    15.   STREAK-THROATED CANASTERO, *A. h. humilis* (Peru and w. Bol.)

D. Upperparts *decidedly to boldly black-streaked;* tail shapes and patterns *vary.*   PAGE 110

    16.   STREAK-BACKED CANASTERO, *A. wyatti graminicola* (Venez. to Peru; n. races grayer below)

    17.   AUSTRAL CANASTERO, *A. anthoides* (s. Arg. and s. Chile)

    18.   HUDSON'S CANASTERO, *A. hudsoni* (e. Arg. and Uru.)

    Also: Puna Canastero, *A. sclateri* (s. Peru to nw. Arg.; like 16)

E. Upperparts *crisply streaked with buff,* and/or *boldly streaked below;* tails tend to be spiky.   PAGE 113

    19.   SCRIBBLE-TAILED CANASTERO, *A. maculicauda* (local from s. Peru to nw. Arg.)

    20.   MANY-STRIPED CANASTERO, *A. f. flammulata* (Col. to w. Peru; Peru race less streaked below)

    21.   LINE-FRONTED CANASTERO, *A. u. urubambensis* (local in Peru and Bol.)

    Also: Junin Canastero, *A. virgata* (local in cen. and s. Peru)

Thripophaga Softtails　　　A diverse assemblage comprising 4 rare species, seemingly a "catch-all," none particularly resembling each other, and with very different, and seemingly unassociated, ranges. Their systematics likely will change in the future. Three species inhabit tropical lowland forests (2 of them with very limited ranges); the fourth (Russet-mantled) inhabits forest below treeline in a small area in the Peruvian Andes.　　　　　　　　　　　　　　　　　　　　　　　PAGE 115

　　　1.　ORINOCO SOFTTAIL, *T. cherriei* (1 site in s. Venez.)
　　　2.　STRIATED SOFTTAIL, *T. macroura* (e. Brazil)
　　　3.　PLAIN SOFTTAIL, *T. fusciceps dimorpha* (local in Amazonia)
　　Also:　Russet-mantled Softtail, *T. berlepschi* (russet with an ashy forecrown)

Phacellodomus Thornbirds　　　A comparatively homogeneous genus, thornbirds are *plainly attired* furnariids best known from their *conspicuous large stick nests,* around which they often linger, even when not breeding. Some species are marked by their *rufous forecrowns.* Thornbirds are most prevalent in semi-open areas of s. S. Am., with only a few (e.g., Red-eyed) ranging regularly into woodland and only the Common occurring in n. S. Am. All except Streak-fronted and Chestnut-backed range mainly or entirely in the lowlands.　　　　　　　　　　　　　　　　　　　　　　　　PAGE 118

A. *Smaller, with plain, drab whitish underparts.*　　　　　　　　　　　　PAGE 118
　　　4.　COMMON THORNBIRD, *P. r. rufifrons* (n. race lacks rufous forehead)
　　　5.　STREAK-FRONTED THORNBIRD, *P. s. striaticeps* (Andes from s. Peru to nw. Arg.)
　　Also:　Little Thornbird, *P. sibilatrix* (mainly n. Arg.)
B. Averaging *larger,* 2 species especially so; some with *light iris.*　　　　PAGE 120
　　　6.　GREATER THORNBIRD, *P. ruber* (e. Bol. and cen. Brazil to n. Arg.)
　　　7.　SPOT-BREASTED THORNBIRD, *P. maculipectus* (s. Bol. and nw. Arg.)
　　Also:　Freckle-breasted Thornbird, *P. striaticollis* (ne. Arg. to se. Brazil)
　　　　　Chestnut-backed Thornbird, *P. dorsalis* (large; nw. Peru)
C. Aberrant thornbird with throat (at least) *uniform bright rufous.*　　　PAGE 123
　　　8.　RED-EYED THORNBIRD, *P. erythrophthalmus ferrugineigula* (e. Brazil)

Clibanornis Groundcreepers　　　A *large* and *relatively boldly patterned* furnariid with distinctive *black scaling on sides of white throat,* the groundcreeper is found locally in lower growth of woodland near streams in se. S. Am.　　　　　　　　　　　　　　　　　　　　　　PAGE 123

　　　9.　CANEBRAKE GROUNDCREEPER, *C. dendrocolaptoides*

Anumbius Firewood-gatherers　　　Easily known by the combination of *white throat outlined with black spots* and *long graduated tail* with *white on outer rectrices,* the Firewood-gatherer ranges in open country from cen. Brazil to Arg. It builds a very conspicuous, large stick nest.　　　　　PAGE 124

　　　10.　FIREWOOD-GATHERER, *A. annumbi*

Coryphistera Brushrunners　　　Unique and unmistakable in appearance, the brushrunner is easily known by the combination of its *jaunty crest* and *profuse streaking* (especially below). Found in chaco woodland and scrub of s.-cen. S. Am., where mainly terrestrial.　　　　　　　PAGE 125

　　　11.　LARK-LIKE BRUSHRUNNER, *C. alaudina*

Pseudoseisura Cacholotes　　　A trio of *large* furnariids with *expressive, usually conspicuous bushy crests* (at least in 2 species), cacholotes are found in lighter woodland and scrub in e. and s. S. Am. Comportment and configuration bring to mind certain jays, though the cacholotes are often terrestrial; their *massive stick nests* are decidedly dissimilar. Notable for their *extraordinarily loud vocalizations.*　　PAGE 126

　　　12.　RUFOUS CACHOLOTE, *P. c. cristata* (ne. Brazil to n. Bol.)
　　　13.　BROWN CACHOLOTE, *P. lophotes argentina* (mainly w. Par. and n. and cen. Arg.)
　　　14.　WHITE-THROATED CACHOLOTE, *P. g. gutturalis* (Arg.)

PLATE 8: MISCELLANEOUS SMALL, MAINLY ARBOREAL FURNARIIDS

Metopothrix Plushcrowns PAGE 128
A *unique*-looking, small furnariid, mainly *olive and yellow* with *orange legs,* found in w. Amazonia.
1. ORANGE-FRONTED PLUSHCROWN, *M. aurantiacus*

Xenerpestes Graytails A pair of obscure, small, and seemingly rare arboreal furnariids with *grayish backs* and *contrasting colored foreheads* found in forests of nw. S. Am. Note *whitish superciliaries.* PAGE 129
2. EQUATORIAL GRAYTAIL, *X. singularis* (e. Ecu. and n. Peru)
3. DOUBLE-BANDED GRAYTAIL, *X. minlosi* (n. Col.)

Siptornis Prickletails PAGE 130
A small, vaguely *Xenops*-like furnariid found locally in Andean forests from Col. to n. Peru.
4. SPECTACLED PRICKLETAIL, *S. s. striaticollis*

Premnornis Barbtails A fairly small, *foliage-gleaner-like* furnariid found in understory of subtropical Andean forests. The tail is not "barbed." PAGE 131
5. RUSTY-WINGED BARBTAIL, *P. g. guttuligera*

Premnoplex Barbtails A pair of closely related, dark-plumaged, and inconspicuous small furnariids which range in understory of mossy, mainly Andean forests. PAGE 132
6. SPOTTED BARBTAIL, *P. b. brunnescens*
Also: White-throated Barbtail, *P. tatei* (ne. Venez.)

Roraimia Barbtails A *handsomely patterned* furnariid restricted to the *tepuis.* PAGE 133
7. RORAIMAN BARBTAIL, *R. a. adusta*

Margarornis Treerunners Two *distinctively patterned* furnariids which hitch up trunks and branches, woodcreeper-like, in Andean forests. PAGE 134
8. STAR-CHESTED TREERUNNER, *M. stellatus* (w. Col. and w. Ecu.)
9. PEARLED TREERUNNER, *M. squamiger peruvianus*

Pygarrhichas Treerunners PAGE 135
A unique, *white-bibbed,* strikingly nuthatch- (*Sitta*)like furnariid found in forests of *far-southern S. Am.*
10. WHITE-THROATED TREERUNNER, *P. albogularis*

Megaxenops Xenops Although with a *Xenops*-like (but much bigger) bill, the *mainly rufous* Great Xenops behaves more like a foliage-gleaner. PAGE 136
11. GREAT XENOPS, *M. parnaguae* (interior ne. Brazil)

Xenops Xenops A distinctive group of small, arboreal furnariids, most species with a *conspicuously upswept bill* and *silvery malar streak;* all show a rufous wing-band in flight. Found widely and often commonly in forest and woodland, creeping on slender branches. PAGE 137

A. Atypical; *lacks* upturned bill and malar streak. PAGE 137
12. RUFOUS-TAILED XENOPS, *X. milleri* (Amazonia)

B. Standard *Xenops; upturned bill* and *white malar streak.* PAGE 138
13. STREAKED XENOPS, *X. r. rutilans*
14. PLAIN XENOPS, *X. minutus genibarbis*
Also: Slender-billed Xenops, *X. tenuirostris* (nearest 13; Amazonia)

Heliobletus Treehunters Somewhat *Xenops*-like in overall appearance and behavior, but with a "normal" bill and plain wings. Found in forests of se. Brazil area. PAGE 140
15. SHARP-BILLED TREEHUNTER, *H. c. contaminatus*

Anabacerthia Foliage-gleaners A trio of comparatively small foliage-gleaners found in forests of Andes and se. Brazil area. Note that many other foliage-gleaner genera are depicted on succeeding plates. PAGE 141
16. WHITE-BROWED FOLIAGE-GLEANER, *A. amaurotis* (se. Brazil and ne. Arg.)
17. MONTANE FOLIAGE-GLEANER, *A. striaticollis montana*
Also: Scaly-throated Foliage-gleaner, *A. variegaticeps* (w. Col. and w. Ecu.; broad ochraceous brow)

PLATE 9: TUFTEDCHEEKS, TREEHUNTERS, *SYNDACTYLA* FOLIAGE-GLEANERS, ETC.

Pseudocolaptes Tuftedcheeks   A pair of large and attractively patterned furnariids with an *unmistakable and conspicuous white to pale buff tuft on sides of neck*. Both are found in montane forests. PAGE 143
  1. STREAKED TUFTEDCHEEK, *P. b. boissonneautii* (Venez. to Bol.)
  2. PACIFIC TUFTEDCHEEK, *P. johnsoni* (w. Col. and w. Ecu.)

Thripadectes Treehunters   *Large,* robust, stout-billed furnariids which skulk in undergrowth of PAGE 144 montane forests where they are only rarely observed. All are basically *Andean* in distribution and are similar in plumage, showing *at least some buff streaking or striping,* in some species *bold and extensive*.
A. Standard *large Thripadectes; streaked upperparts* (confined to *crown* in Streak-capped). PAGE 145
• *Underparts,* down over breast, *also streaked*.
  3. FLAMMULATED TREEHUNTER, *T. f. flammulatus* (w. Venez. to n. Peru)
  4. STRIPED TREEHUNTER, *T. h. holostictus* (w. Venez. to Bol.)
  Also: Peruvian Treehunter, *T. scrutator* (large like 3; Peru and Bol.)
• Ventral streaking/scaling *basically confined to throat*.
  5. BLACK-BILLED TREEHUNTER, *T. m. melanorhynchus* (Col. to Peru)
  Also: Streak-capped Treehunter, *T. virgaticeps* (n. Venez. to Ecu.)
B. *Smaller, dark Thripadectes* of Pac. slope. PAGE 148
  6. UNIFORM TREEHUNTER, *T. ignobilis*

Syndactyla Foliage-gleaners   Another essentially *Andean* genus, with 1 species (Buff-browed) also PAGE 148 found widely in se. S. Am. They range mainly inside montane forest. Bills are *short and straight,* and all species have *streaking on underparts,* against which the *pale and unstreaked throat* often stands out.
A. Mantle *pale-streaked* (but lightly so in Pac.-slope race of Lineated). Relatively hard to observe. PAGE 148
  7. LINEATED FOLIAGE-GLEANER, *S. subalaris mentalis* (Venez. to Peru)
  Also: Guttulated Foliage-gleaner, *S. guttulata* (n. Venez.)
B. Mantle *unstreaked*. Relatively easy to observe. PAGE 150
  8. BUFF-BROWED FOLIAGE-GLEANER, *S. r. rufosuperciliata*
  9. RUFOUS-NECKED FOLIAGE-GLEANER, *S. ruficollis* (sw. Ecu. and nw. Peru)

Cichlocolaptes Treehunters   A *large* arboreal furnariid endemic to forests of *e. Brazil*. Its *long bill* PAGE 151 and *prominent superciliary and streaking below* are distinctive. The s. race (São Paulo southward) is smaller with a darker, rufous tail.
  10. PALE-BROWED TREEHUNTER, *C. l. leucophrus*

Berlepschia Palmcreepers   An unmistakable, elegant, and rather slender furnariid *found almost exclusively in groves of Mauritia palms* in lowlands of Amazonia. PAGE 152
  11. POINT-TAILED PALMCREEPER, *B. rikeri*

9

PLATE 10: *PHILYDOR* FOLIAGE-GLEANERS & ALLIES

Simoxenops Recurvebills   A pair of foliage-gleaners found locally in forest undergrowth of PAGE 153
s. Amazonia. Both easily recognized by their *very heavy, upturned bills.*
       1.   PERUVIAN RECURVEBILL, *S. ucayalae* (se. Peru east very locally
          into Amaz. Brazil)
   Also: Bolivian Recurvebill, *S. striatus* (streaked above)

Hyloctistes Woodhaunters   A drab and easily confused foliage-gleaner found in undergrowth of PAGE 154
humid lowland forest west of Andes and in upper Amazonia. *Almost devoid of real field marks;* w. birds are
less streaked.
       2.   STRIPED WOODHAUNTER, *H. s. subulatus*

Ancistrops Hookbills   A *prominently streaked* foliage-gleaner with heavy, somewhat hooked PAGE 155
bill found in upper strata of humid Amaz. forests.
       3.   CHESTNUT-WINGED HOOKBILL, *A. strigilatus*

Philydor Foliage-gleaners   A rather uniform group of fairly slender foliage-gleaners found widely PAGE 156
in humid forests, mainly in Amazonia but others as far south as the s. Brazil region. Many are quite
boldly or even handsomely patterned; all show a *superciliary, often prominent.* None is streaked to any
great degree, usually not at all. Compared to *Automolus* foliage-gleaners, *Philydor* are more slenderly built,
and most are less skulking and therefore easier to see. They also seem to vocalize comparatively little.
A. More *arboreal* species; color of underparts *varies.* PAGE 156
       4.   CHESTNUT-WINGED FOLIAGE-GLEANER, *P. erythropterus*
          (Amazonia)
       5.   RUFOUS-RUMPED FOLIAGE-GLEANER, *P. erythrocercus lyra*
          (Amazonia)
       6.   BUFF-FRONTED FOLIAGE-GLEANER, *P. r. rufus* (foothills
          from Venez. to Bol., and in se. S. Am.)
       7.   OCHRE-BREASTED FOLIAGE-GLEANER, *P. lichtensteini* (se.
          Brazil region)
   Also: Rufous-tailed Foliage-gleaner, *P. ruficaudatus* (Amazonia; near 5)
B. More furtive species, mainly in *undergrowth; rich ochraceous* underparts. PAGE 160
       8.   PLANALTO FOLIAGE-GLEANER, *P. dimidiatus baeri* (interior
          s. Brazil)
       9.   CINNAMON-RUMPED FOLIAGE-GLEANER, *P. pyrrhodes*
          (Amazonia)
      10.   BLACK-CAPPED FOLIAGE-GLEANER, *P. atricapillus* (se. Brazil
          area)
   Also: Slaty-winged Foliage-gleaner, *P. fuscipennis* (nw. Col. and w. Ecu.;
          recalls 9)
          Alagoas Foliage-gleaner, *P. novaesi* (ne. Brazil; like 10)

Anabazenops Foliage-gleaners PAGE 163
Monotypic genus found in forests of *se. Brazil.* Virtually unmistakable *contrasting white collar.*
      11.   WHITE-COLLARED FOLIAGE-GLEANER, *A. fuscus*

10

PLATE 11: *AUTOMOLUS* FOLIAGE-GLEANERS, *SCLERURUS* LEAFTOSSERS, & ALLIES

Automolus Foliage-gleaners — A group of fairly large and *drab* foliage-gleaners found mainly in undergrowth of humid forest, especially in lowlands. They are confusing and often difficult to identify in the field, not only because most species are basically similar but also due to their furtive, reclusive behavior. Although generally similar to the more arboreal *Philydor* foliage-gleaners (cf. Plate 10), *Automolus* are *more robust in shape,* have heavier bills, and tend not to have a contrastingly colored superciliary; *eye-rings* and *contrastingly buff or white throats* are often present. Loud vocalizations, mainly given at dawn and dusk, often reveal their presence. PAGE 164

A. *Throat white to buffy-white.* PAGE 164

1. WHITE-EYED FOLIAGE-GLEANER, *A. leucophthalmus sulphurascens* (se. S. Am.)
2. WHITE-THROATED FOLIAGE-GLEANER, *A. r. roraimae* (tepuis)
3. DUSKY-CHEEKED FOLIAGE-GLEANER, *A. dorsalis* (local in w. Amazonia)

Also: Olive-backed Foliage-gleaner, *A. infuscatus*

B. *Throat buff to rich ochraceous.* PAGE 166

4. BUFF-THROATED FOLIAGE-GLEANER, *A. ochrolaemus turdinus* (throat *white* west of Andes)
5. BROWN-RUMPED FOLIAGE-GLEANER, *A. melanopezus* (local in w. Amazonia)
6. RUDDY FOLIAGE-GLEANER, *A. rubiginosus nigricauda* (some races paler; local in n. and w. S. Am.)

Also: Chestnut-crowned Foliage-gleaner, *A. rufipileatus*

Hylocryptus Foliage-gleaners — A pair of quite large foliage-gleaners, probably allied to *Automolus* but with distinctive *long bills* and *bright orange-rufous* on head. Both species have *restricted ranges* and *feed mainly in leaf litter* in deciduous woodland. PAGE 169

7. HENNA-HOODED FOLIAGE-GLEANER, *H. erythrocephalus* (sw. Ecu. and nw. Peru)
8. HENNA-CAPPED FOLIAGE-GLEANER, *H. rectirostris* (interior s. Brazil and n. Par.)

Sclerurus Leaftossers — Uniform genus of *obscure, dark brown* furnariids with *rather long slender bills* (less so in Short-billed), short legs, and *short black tails.* Identification to species is often difficult; watch especially for *pattern and color on throat.* Leaftossers are generally scarce, *inconspicuous, terrestrial* birds found in humid forests, both in lowlands and subtropical zone. PAGE 171

9. TAWNY-THROATED LEAFTOSSER, *S. mexicanus peruvianus*
10. GRAY-THROATED LEAFTOSSER, *S. a. albigularis* (local in foothills from Venez. to Bol.)
11. SHORT-BILLED LEAFTOSSER, *S. r. rufigularis* (Amazonia)
12. BLACK-TAILED LEAFTOSSER, *S. caudacutus brunneus* (Amazonia and e. Brazil)

Also: Rufous-breasted Leaftosser, *S. scansor* (e. Brazil to ne. Arg.; recalls 10)
Scaly-throated Leaftosser, *S. guatemalensis* (n. Col. and w. Ecu.; recalls 12)

Lochmias Streamcreepers — Leaftosser-like, but *distinctively spotted below,* the streamcreeper is found on or near the ground *near streams* locally through S. Am., mainly in *foothill* regions. PAGE 174

13. SHARP-TAILED STREAMCREEPER, *L. n. nematura* (Andean races lack superciliary)

11

GUDOR

PLATE 12: WOODCREEPERS I

Dendrocincla Woodcreepers   Midsized and *relatively plain* woodcreepers with *straight bills* found in PAGE 177 humid forests, all but 1 species in lowlands; Plain-brown is by far the most numerous and widespread. Most species, including Plain-brown, *habitually follow antswarms.*

A. *Large Dendrocincla of the Andes.* PAGE 177
      1.   TYRANNINE WOODCREEPER, *D. tyrannina*

B. *"Typical" Dendrocincla* of the *lowlands.* PAGE 178
      2.   PLAIN-BROWN WOODCREEPER
         2a. *D. fuliginosa meruloides*
         2b. *D. f. fuliginosa*
      3.   WHITE-CHINNED WOODCREEPER, *D. merula bartletti*
   Also: Plain-winged Woodcreeper, *D. turdina* (se. Brazil area)
         Ruddy Woodcreeper, *D. homochroa* (more rufescent; n. Col. and
         nw. Venez.)

Deconychura Woodcreepers   A pair of dull and obscure woodcreepers, both rather scarce, found PAGE 181 inside humid lowland and foothill forests. Both species have *relatively long tails* and narrow straight bills; ♂♂ are considerably larger than ♀♀.
      4.   LONG-TAILED WOODCREEPER, *D. longicauda pallida*
      5.   SPOT-THROATED WOODCREEPER, *D. s. stictolaema*

Glyphorynchus Woodcreepers   A *very small* woodcreeper found widely inside humid lowland forests, PAGE 183 and usually common. *Bill short, slightly upturned.*
      6.   WEDGE-BILLED WOODCREEPER, *G. spirurus castlenaudii*

Sittasomus Woodcreepers   A small, short-billed, *plain and unstreaked* woodcreeper which shows PAGE 184 *dramatic geographic variation* across its wide range; we depict 3 of the most divergent "types." Almost surely more than a single species is involved. Found in both deciduous and humid forests, though usually not in terra firme.
      7.   OLIVACEOUS WOODCREEPER
         7a. *S. griseicapillus amazonus* (Amazon basin)
         7b. *S. griseicapillus sylviellus* (se. Brazil region)
         7c. *S. griseicapillus reiseri* (ne. Brazil)

Nasica Woodcreepers PAGE 185
A *spectacular large* woodcreeper with *long pale bill* found in Amaz. forests, usually near water.
      8.   LONG-BILLED WOODCREEPER, *N. longirostris*

Drymornis Woodcreepers PAGE 185
A striking woodcreeper of *chaco woodlands* with *long, somewhat decurved bill.* Partially terrestrial.
      9.   SCIMITAR-BILLED WOODCREEPER, *D. bridgesii*

12

PLATE 13: WOODCREEPERS II

Dendrexetastes Woodcreepers   A fairly large woodcreeper of Amazonia marked by its *stout pale bill.*   PAGE 186
W. races have more inconspicuous streaking confined to breast.

    1.   CINNAMON-THROATED WOODCREEPER, *D. r. rufigula*

Hylexetastes Woodcreepers   A trio of *scarce and infrequently seen, large,* and relatively patternless   PAGE 187
woodcreepers with *very stout, dark red bills.* Allopatric Amaz. ranges.

    2.   UNIFORM WOODCREEPER, *H. uniformis* (cen. Amaz. Brazil)
    3.   BAR-BELLIED WOODCREEPER, *H. stresemanni undulatus*
        (w. Amaz. Brazil to n. Bol. and se. Peru)
    Also: Red-billed Woodcreeper, *H. perrotii* (Guianas to n. Brazil)

Dendrocolaptes Woodcreepers   Fairly large woodcreepers with *heavy straight bills, Dendrocolaptes* tend   PAGE 189
to have *complex patterns,* either *barred* or *barred and streaked,* but birds in lower Amaz. Brazil are plainer.
They range in humid forests, mainly in lowlands, and *often attend antswarms.* Complicated racial variation
in Barred and Black-banded Woodcreepers.

A. Northern South America through Amazonia.   PAGE 189

    4.   BARRED WOODCREEPER, *D. certhia medius*
    5.   BLACK-BANDED WOODCREEPER
        5a. *D. p. picumnus*
        5b. *D. picumnus pallescens* (se. Bol. to nw. Arg.)
    Also: Hoffmanns' Woodcreeper, *D. hoffmannsi* (cen. Amaz. Brazil)

B. *Eastern* South America.   PAGE 192

    6.   PLANALTO WOODCREEPER, *D. p. platyrostris*

Xiphocolaptes Woodcreepers   Very large and heavy woodcreepers with *impressively massive, somewhat*   PAGE 193
decurved bills, the *Xiphocolaptes* range widely in humid and deciduous forests and have entirely allopatric
ranges; the taxonomy of several species is still debated. Plumage patterns are usually complicated, with
most (all but Great Rufous) showing a *facial pattern.* Their far-carrying vocalizations often attract
attention.

A. Typical *Xiphocolaptes,* with streaking on foreparts.   PAGE 193

    7.   WHITE-THROATED WOODCREEPER, *X. a. albicollis* (se. Brazil
        area)
    8.   STRONG-BILLED WOODCREEPER, *X. promeropirhynchus*
        lineatocephalus
    Also: Moustached Woodcreeper, *X. falcirostris* (ne. Brazil)

B. Distinctive overall *bright rufous coloration.*   PAGE 196

    9.   GREAT RUFOUS WOODCREEPER, *D. m. major* (Bol. to n. Arg.)

13

Xiphorhynchus Woodcreepers   A confusing and widespread group of "typical" woodcreepers, all   PAGE 196
of them *streaked to some extent* (some very prominently). Bill shapes vary: in most it is fairly long and
somewhat decurved, but quite straight in some. In none is it as slender or as noticeably decurved as in
the generally similar but smaller *Lepidocolaptes* woodcreepers. *Xiphorhynchus* woodcreepers are found in
wooded and forested habitats almost throughout the lowlands of S. Am., the main exception being the
subtropical forests of the southeast; a few (Olive-backed, Spotted) range in montane forests of the Andes,
and only Straight-billed is regular in semiopen, scrubbier terrain. Included in the genus are several vexing
identification and taxonomic challenges, notably the Straight-billed/Zimmer's pair and the Spix's/"Elegant"/
Ocellated complex.

A. Bill rather *short, straight, and pale;* mainly várzea and scrub.   PAGE 197
      1.   STRAIGHT-BILLED WOODCREEPER, *X. p. picus* (n. races have
          whiter face)
      2.   STRIPED WOODCREEPER, *X. o. obsoletus*
    Also: Zimmer's Woodcreeper, *X. necopinus* (Amaz. Brazil; rare?)
B. Typical *Xiphorhynchus* with *long bills;* mainly *lowland* forest.   PAGE 199
• Pattern with ocellated or "tear-drop" effect.
      3.   OCELLATED WOODCREEPER, *X. ocellatus napensis*
      4.   SPIX'S WOODCREEPER, *X. spixii ornatus*
• Pattern of *linear streaking.*
      5.   CHESTNUT-RUMPED WOODCREEPER, *X. p. pardalotus*
          (ne. S. Am.)
      6.   BUFF-THROATED WOODCREEPER, *X. guttatus guttatoides*
          (Amazonia to Guianas and e. Brazil)
    Also: Cocoa Woodcreeper, *X. susurrans* (like 6 but smaller; n. Col. to
          Trinidad)
          Black-striped Woodcreeper, *X. lachrymosus* (*boldly* streaked; w. Col.
          and nw. Ecu.)
C. More *olive* coloration with *spotted pattern;* mainly foothills and montane forest.   PAGE 204
      7.   OLIVE-BACKED WOODCREEPER, *X. t. triangularis*
    Also: Spotted Woodcreeper, *X. erythropygius* (w. Col. and w. Ecu.)

Lepidocolaptes Woodcreepers   Fairly small and comparatively slender woodcreepers with *distinctive*   PAGE 205
pale, slender, and well-decurved bills; almost all show *neat, narrow streaking below,* though many are
*un*streaked above. Most species range in humid forest, either in lowlands or (especially Montane)
in montane areas; Streak-headed favors lighter woodland, whereas Narrow-billed is typical of cerrado
and scrub.

A. Standard *Lepidocolaptes;* note patterns, but *subspecific variation complex in some species.*   PAGE 206
      8.   LINEATED WOODCREEPER, *L. albolineatus duidae* (Amazonia to
          Guianas)
      9.   SCALED WOODCREEPER, *L. s. squamatus* (se. Brazil area)
    10.   LESSER WOODCREEPER, *L. f. fuscus* (e. Brazil, e. Par., ne. Arg.)
    Also: Montane Woodcreeper, *L. lacrymiger* (mostly Andes)
          Streak-headed Woodcreeper, *L. souleyetii* (n. S. Am.)
B. Distinctive, with *longer bill* and *broad white superciliary.*   PAGE 209
    11.   NARROW-BILLED WOODCREEPER, *L. a. angustirostris*

Campylorhamphus Scythebills   A distinct genus with *unmistakable, very long and strikingly decurved*   PAGE 210
bills, whose colors and shapes are (despite their English names) *not* particularly helpful for species recognition. Identifying to species can be difficult, though for the most part they *separate out by range.* The
various species are found mainly in humid or montane forest with only the Red-billed at all likely to
emerge into the semiopen. Despite their remarkable bills, behavior differs little from other woodcreepers'.

A. Rare, *large* scythebill with *Andean* distribution.   PAGE 211
    12.   GREATER SCYTHEBILL, *C. pucherani* (Col. to Peru)
B. *Standard* scythebills; all more or less *streaked.*   PAGE 211
    13.   RED-BILLED SCYTHEBILL
          13a. *C. trochilirostris napensis*
          13b. *C. trochilirostris lafresnayanus*
    14.   BLACK-BILLED SCYTHEBILL, *C. falcularius* (se. Brazil area)
    Also: Curve-billed Scythebill, *C. procurvoides* (Guianas to Amazonia)
          Brown-billed Scythebill, *C. pusillus* (Andes, Venez. to Peru)

PLATE 15: "FASCIATED" & "GREAT" ANTSHRIKES

Cymbilaimus Antshrikes — Both sexes of this pair of antshrikes are *narrowly barred nearly throughout* ("fasciated"); bills are proportionately massive. Found in humid lowland forests. PAGE 215

    1.   FASCIATED ANTSHRIKE, *C. lineatus intermedius*

    Also: Bamboo Antshrike, *C. sanctaemariae* (se. Peru and nearby)

Frederickena Antshrikes — Two very large (considerably larger than *Cymbilaimus*) but rather short-tailed antshrikes found at low densities in Amaz. and Guianan forests. Undulated is *wavily barred* ("undulated") in all plumages (including the *rufescent* ♀); ♀ Black-throated is *plain chestnut above*, coarsely barred *only below* (thus vaguely recalling some ♀ *Thamnophilus* antshrikes). PAGE 217

    2.   UNDULATED ANTSHRIKE, *F. unduligera fulva* (w. Amazonia; subadult)

    3.   BLACK-THROATED ANTSHRIKE, *F. viridis* (ne. S. Am.)

Mackenziaena Antshrikes — A pair of *large* and striking antshrikes which sneak in undergrowth of *forests and woodlands in se. S. Am.* Both species are notably long-tailed (especially Large-tailed); Tufted has a *prominent bushy crest*. PAGE 218

    4.   TUFTED ANTSHRIKE, *M. severa*

    5.   LARGE-TAILED ANTSHRIKE, *M. leachii* (♀ more heavily spotted, and with buff)

Hypoedaleus Antshrikes — A single species of relatively arboreal, large antshrike found in forests of se. S. Am., easily known by its *boldly white-spotted upperparts*. ♀ similar but buffier. PAGE 220

    6.   SPOT-BACKED ANTSHRIKE, *H. g. guttatus*

Batara Antshrikes — Absolutely unmistakable by virtue of its *very large size* and boldly banded upperparts, the Giant Antshrike is a shy and rarely seen inhabitant of forests from Bol. and n. Arg. to Brazil. PAGE 220

    7.   GIANT ANTSHRIKE

        7a. *B. cinerea argentina* (mainly Andean slopes, locally in chaco)

        7b. *B. c. cinerea* (larger; se. Brazil and ne. Arg.)

Taraba Antshrikes — A relatively numerous antshrike found widely in scrub and second-growth in tropical and subtropical lowlands. Both sexes are *bicolored*, ♀ being *rufous-chestnut* above. PAGE 221

    8.   GREAT ANTSHRIKE, *T. major semifasciatus*

15

1♀

1♂

2♂

3♂

4♂

4♀

5♂

6♂

7a♂

7b♀

8♂

TUDOR

Biatas Antshrikes   PAGE 222

Strikingly patterned, stout-billed antshrike of se. Brazil area. Rare and inconspicuous.

      1.   WHITE-BEARDED ANTSHRIKE, *B. nigropectus*

Sakesphorus Antshrikes   Midsized antbirds, rather variable in overall appearance: some are   PAGE 223
strongly crested whereas others show no crest at all (and still others are intermediate), and some are *boldly patterned* (whereas others are quite plain). Most occur in scrub or edge habitats in tropical lowlands, but Band-tailed is found inside humid forest.

A. *Black-hooded* effect in ♂♂; wings prominently *spotted and margined in both sexes.*   PAGE 223

      2.   COLLARED ANTSHRIKE, *S. b. bernardi* (sw. Ecu. and nw. Peru)

      3.   SILVERY-CHEEKED ANTSHRIKE, *S. cristatus* (ne. Brazil)

      4.   BLACK-BACKED ANTSHRIKE, *S. melanonotus* (n. Col. and n. Venez.)

      Also: Black-crested Antshrike, *S. canadensis* (closest to 2; ♀ streaked below)   PAGE 225

B. ♂♂ *mainly black* with white tail-tipping; ♀♀ distinctive.

      5.   BAND-TAILED ANTSHRIKE, *S. melanothorax* (ne. S. Am.)

      6.   GLOSSY ANTSHRIKE, *S. luctuosus* (Amaz. Brazil; ♂ with crest black)

Xenornis Antshrikes   PAGE 226

The only antshrike that is *streaked above;* ♂ has slaty gray face and underparts. Limited *nw. Col.* range.

      7.   SPECKLED ANTSHRIKE, *X. setifrons*

Thamnophilus Antshrikes   A large, complex genus found virtually throughout tropical and sub-   PAGE 227
tropical S. Am. A majority of the species are found in understory or (less often) borders of humid forest; these are treated on Plate 17 (Groups B–E). Those covered here, Group A (our "Barred" Group), are found *mainly in shrubby clearings and thickets.* ♂♂ are *barred at least ventrally;* ♀♀ show *barring only on underparts* (or, in some species, none at all). Despite their bold patterns, these antshrikes are *relatively unobtrusive,* tending to remain in heavy growth where they are heard much more often than seen.

A. ♂♂ more or less *barred below.*   PAGE 228

• ♂♂ *entirely barred;* ♀♀ *not* barred but show head streaking; iris yellow.

      8.   BARRED ANTSHRIKE, *T. doliatus radiatus*

      Also: Chapman's Antshrike, *T. zarumae* (sw. Ecu. and nw. Peru)

• ♂♂ either *entirely barred* or *more like* ♀♀; ♀♀ *barred below;* iris yellow.

      9.   LINED ANTSHRIKE, *T. tenuepunctatus berlepschi* (e. base of Andes from Col. to n. Peru)

      10.   CHESTNUT-BACKED ANTSHRIKE, *T. palliatus similis* (locally from e. Peru to e. Brazil)

      Also: Bar-crested Antshrike, *T. multistriatus* (Col.; nearest 9)

• ♂♂ *barred on breast only;* ♀♀ rather *dull* (cf. Group D, on Plate 17).

      11.   RUFOUS-CAPPED ANTSHRIKE (locally from Peru to Brazil)

      11a. *T. r. ruficapillus*

      11b. *T. ruficapillus marcapatae*

      11c. *T. ruficapillus jaczewskii*

      Also: Rufous-winged Antshrike, *T. torquatus* (♂ with black crown; interior e. Brazil)

16

TUDOR

The *Thamnophilus* antshrikes presented here (continued from Plate 16) are found *mainly in understory of forest and woodland,* to a lesser extent at borders. Diversity is greatest in the lowlands from Amazonia to the Guianas, with a few species in the Andes but only 1 west of them. ♂♂ are basically *gray to blackish,* often with *white wing markings;* ♀♀ tend to be brownish or rufescent and in many species also have wing markings (buffyish or white). As with the *Thamnophilus* in Group A, most of these antshrikes are comparatively inconspicuous birds, many of them ranging mainly as pairs independent of mixed flocks; *vocalizations* are important, both for locating them and for identification purposes.

These antshrikes are unusually confusing and difficult to analyze, for often ♂♂ and ♀♀ of the same species cannot be coherently "associated" visually, and furthermore intraspecific variation is in some cases more striking than the differences between species. In the following categories it has been found more useful to emphasize the ♂ *plumages for our main Groups,* but usually to break out ♀ *plumages for our subsets.*

B. Rather large and dark. ♂♂ with *wings obviously white-fringed;* ♀♀ variable. PAGE 232

    1.   BLACKISH-GRAY ANTSHRIKE
        1a. *T. n. nigrocinereus*
        1b. *T. nigrocinereus tschudii*
    Also: Castlenau's Antshrike, *T. cryptoleucus* (along Amazon; ♀ all black)

C. ♂♂ gray to black, *with or without wing-spots;* ♀♀ *all distinctive.* PAGE 234
• ♀♀ *rufous* with *blackish hood.*

    2.   BLACK ANTSHRIKE, *T. n. nigriceps* (n. Col.)
    Also: Cocha Antshrike, *T. praecox* (local in ne. Ecu.)

• ♀♀ *entirely rufous to chestnut.*

    3.   WHITE-SHOULDERED ANTSHRIKE
        3a. *T. aethiops injunctus*
        3b. *T. a. aethiops*

D. ♂♂ *like Group C* (but never black); ♀♀ rather *dull* (see also Plate 16). PAGE 236
• ♀♀ warm brown with *gray face; Andes.*

    4.   UNIFORM ANTSHRIKE, *T. unicolor grandior* (Col. to cen. Peru)
    Also: Upland Antshrike, *T. aroyae* (s. Peru and Bol.)

• ♀♀ recall ♀ Eastern Slaty-, but *without* wing markings.

    5.   PLAIN-WINGED ANTSHRIKE, *T. s. schistaceus* (nw. race cap black)
    Also: Mouse-colored Antshrike, *T. murinus*

E. *Both sexes with pronounced white wing markings* (except ♀ Variables in Peru). PAGE 239
• ♂♂ rather "standard" gray *Thamnophilus;* ♀♀ all differ.

    6.   EASTERN SLATY-ANTSHRIKE, *T. p. punctatus* (e. of Andes)
    7.   AMAZONIAN ANTSHRIKE, *T. a. amazonicus*
    8.   STREAK-BACKED ANTSHRIKE, *T. i. insignis* (tepuis)
    Also: Western Slaty-Antshrike, *T. atrinucha* (nw. Venez. to w. Ecu.).

• E. races (e.g., 9a) recall Eastern Slaty- (some with tawny on belly); Andean races (e.g., 9b, 9c) *very different.*

    9.   VARIABLE ANTSHRIKE
        9a. *T. caerulescens gilvigaster*
        9b. *T. caerulescens aspersiventer*
        9c. *T. caerulescens melanochrous*

Megastictus Antshrikes   An uncommon species of *Thamnophilus*-like antshrike found in Amazonia. Unmistakable *large round white spots on wing* (buff in ♀). PAGE 244
    10.   PEARLY ANTSHRIKE, *M. margaritatus*

Pygiptila Antshrikes   A rather common *Thamnophilus*-like antshrike with *disproportionately short tail and large bill.* Amazonia and Guianas. PAGE 245
    11.   SPOT-WINGED ANTSHRIKE, *P. stellaris occipitalis*

NOTE: *Tschudii* race of Blackish-gray Antshrike (1b), nominate race of White-shouldered Antshrike (3b), and *melanochrous* race of Variable Antshrike (9c) are all drawn at a smaller scale.

17

Thamnistes Antshrikes A single fairly common species of antshrike found in *forest canopy* on PAGE 245
Andean slopes south to Bol. Note brownish plumage, *fairly stout bill*. Sexes alike.

    1.   RUSSET ANTSHRIKE, *T. anabatinus rufescens*

Thamnomanes Antshrikes Four rather similar and easily confused antshrikes of humid forest PAGE 247
lower growth in Amazonia, where they are regularly found as leaders of mixed understory flocks. ♂♂ are
uniform and essentially *some shade of gray;* ♀♀ are more olive brown, *more rufescent on belly.*

    2.   SATURNINE ANTSHRIKE, *T. s. saturninus* (south of Amazon)
    3.   CINEREOUS ANTSHRIKE, *T. caesius hoffmannsi*
    Also: Dusky-throated Antshrike, *T. ardesiacus* (nearest 2)
           Bluish-slate Antshrike, *T. schistogynus* (nearest 3; sw. Amazonia)

Dysithamnus Antvireos A group of rather small, *chunky* antbirds with short tails, larger and PAGE 250
heavier-billed than the *Myrmotherula* antwrens so often found with them, less slender and shorter-tailed
than *Thamnomanes* antshrikes. Behavior rather sluggish, hopping in lower growth of humid forest,
gleaning in foliage. Most are found in *foothill or subtropical forests;* none occurs in Amaz. lowlands.

A. "Plain" and "fancy" antvireos; ♀♀ with *rufescent crowns.* PAGE 250

    4.   PLAIN ANTVIREO, *D. mentalis olivaceus*
    5.   SPOT-BREASTED ANTVIREO, *D. stictothorax* (se. Brazil area)
    6.   RUFOUS-BACKED ANTVIREO, *D. xanthopterus* (se. Brazil)
    Also: Spot-crowned Antvireo, *D. puncticeps* (w. Col. and nw. Ecu.)

B. "Plumbeous" antvireos (♂♂ *slaty*); ♀♀ dissimilar. PAGE 253

    7.   PLUMBEOUS ANTVIREO, *D. plumbeus* (se. Brazil)
    8.   WHITE-STREAKED ANTVIREO, *D. l. leucostictus* (locally in mts.
           from Venez. to Ecu.)
    Also: Bicolored Antvireo, *D. occidentalis* (Andean slopes of sw. Col. and ne. Ecu.)

Herpsilochmus Antwrens A complex and difficult genus of rather long-tailed antwrens found in PAGE 255
canopy and borders of humid forest (usually), a few species in more deciduous woodland or even scrub.
Problems are greatest among the species we place in our Group B, all of which resemble each other very
closely indeed. Points to watch for especially are:

  1. *tail pattern* (whether spotted above, or merely with outer feathers edged white);
  2. *back* (whether plain, or mottled/streaked with black and white);
  3. *crown pattern of* ♀ (whether spotted or not, and with what color, rufescent or white);
  4. *face and breast color of* ♀ (in some species at least tinged buff).

A. ♂♂ with *patterned breast;* ♀♀ have *crowns and underparts ochraceous to buff.* Brazil. PAGE 255

    9.   LARGE-BILLED ANTWREN, *H. longirostris* (mainly int. Brazil)
    10. PECTORAL ANTWREN, *H. pectoralis* (local in ne. Brazil)

B. ♂♂ *plain grayish white* below; ♀♀ with *spotted or streaked crown* and buff-tinged *breast.* PAGE 257
• *Tail with dorsal white spots; north* of Amazon.

    11. SPOT-TAILED ANTWREN, *H. sticturus* (ne. S. Am.)
    12. SPOT-BACKED ANTWREN, *H. dorsimaculatus* (upper Orinoco and
          Rio Negro drainages)
    Also: Dugand's Antwren, *H. dugandi* (local in w. Amazonia)
           Todd's Antwren, *H. stictocephalus* (mainly Guianas)
           Roraiman Antwren, *H. roraimae* (tepuis)
• *Tail dorsally edged white; south* of Amazon.

    13. BLACK-CAPPED ANTWREN, *H. atricapillus*
    Also: Pileated Antwren, *H. pileatus* (ne. Brazil)
           Creamy-bellied Antwren, *H. motacilloides* (cen. and s. Peru)
           Ash-throated Antwren, *H. parkeri* (San Martín, Peru)

C. Both sexes *mainly yellowish below;* ♀♀ with rufous crown. PAGE 262

    14. RUFOUS-WINGED ANTWREN, *H. rufimarginatus scapularis*
    15. YELLOW-BREASTED ANTWREN, *H. axillaris aequatorialis* (locally
          on Andean slopes from Col. to Peru)

Microrhopias Antwrens An attractive antwren found widely in lower growth of humid low- PAGE 264
land forests, readily known by its *fairly long tail*, often fanned and partially cocked, *showing much white.*
♀♀ show striking geographic variation in plumage.

    16. DOT-WINGED ANTWREN
        16a. *M. quixensis bicolor*
        16b. *M. quixensis emiliae*

18

Myrmotherula Antwrens   A large and complex genus of *small, short-tailed* antbirds found mainly   PAGE 265
in *humid lowland forest* (only a few species out into secondary growth or in borders, or in subtropical
zone). Many species are *hard to identify* (see text for details), in part because interspecific distinctions are
often minor, in part because these antwrens are often hard to see well for very long. Many species *regularly forage with understory flocks,* but most members of Group A favor forest *canopy and borders.*

A. *"Pygmy"/"Streaked"* assemblage. Both sexes *prominently streaked above.*   PAGE 266
- "Pygmy" group: both sexes *pale yellow below* (streaking typically *sparse*).
  1. PYGMY ANTWREN, *M. b. brachyura*
  2. SHORT-BILLED ANTWREN, *M. obscura* (w. Amazonia)
  3. SCLATER'S ANTWREN, *M. sclateri* (sw. Amazonia)
  Also: Yellow-throated Antwren, *M. ambigua* (sw. Venez. area)
- "Streaked" group: ♂♂ *streaked black and white,* ♀♀ *ochraceous buff below* with *variable* dark streaking.
  4. STREAKED ANTWREN, *M. surinamensis multostriata*
  5. STRIPE-CHESTED ANTWREN, *M. longicauda australis* (e. base of
  Andes)
  Also: Cherrie's Antwren, *M. cherriei* (mainly upper Orinoco drainage)
  Klages' Antwren, *M. klagesi* (lower Amazon; very local)

B. *Large spots on tertials* (both sexes), throat concolor. On or near ground, usually not in mixed flocks.   PAGE 271
  6. PLAIN-THROATED ANTWREN, *M. h. hauxwelli*
  7. RUFOUS-BELLIED ANTWREN, *M. guttata* (ne. S. Am.)

C. *"Stipple-throated"* assemblage. ♂♂ generally *browner-backed,* though *may or may not have a chestnut*   PAGE 272
saddle; both sexes show wing-spotting.
- Sexes *similar,* both with stippled throat; tail rather short.
  8. STAR-THROATED ANTWREN, *M. gularis* (se. Brazil)
- Typical "stipple-throats" (vestigial in ♂ 11); tails comparatively long.
  9. STIPPLE-THROATED ANTWREN, *M. h. haematonata*
  10. WHITE-EYED ANTWREN, *M. leucophthalma sordida* (s. Amazonia)
  11. RUFOUS-TAILED ANTWREN, *M. e. erythrura* (w. Amazonia)
  Also: Foothill Antwren, *M. spodionota* (e. Ecu. and e. Peru)
  Brown-bellied Antwren, *M. gutturalis* (ne. S. Am.)
  Checker-throated Antwren, *M. fulviventris* (w. Col. and w. Ecu.)
- ♀'s throat stippled (except in 1 race), but ♂'s throat *black;* variable.
  12. ORNATE ANTWREN
  12a. *M. ornata saturata*
  12b. *M. ornata atrogularis*

D. *Silky white flank feathers* (but grayer in e. Brazil race of White-flanked). Recent evidence shows that   PAGE 278
Black-hooded Antwren belongs in genus *Formicivora.*
  13. WHITE-FLANKED ANTWREN, *Myrmotherula axillaris melaena*
  14. BLACK-HOODED ANTWREN, *Formicivora erythronotos* (se. Brazil;
  very rare)

E. *"Slaty"/"Gray"* assemblage. Most ♂♂ have *throat black,* concolor in some. ♀♀ often difficult.   PAGE 280
- Typical "gray" *Myrmotherula.* ♂♂ (and some ♀♀) have *wing-coverts spotted or fringed white;* ♀♀ gray
to brown above.
  15. LONG-WINGED ANTWREN, *M. longipennis garbei*
  16. IHERING'S ANTWREN, *M. iheringi* (sw. Amazonia)
  17. BAND-TAILED ANTWREN, *M. urosticta* (se. Brazil)
  18. GRAY ANTWREN, *M. m. menetriesii* (♂♂ of some races have throat
  concolor)
  19. LEADEN ANTWREN, *M. assimilis* (islands along Amazon)
  Also: Slaty Antwren, *M. schisticolor* (foothills and lower Andean slopes)
  Rio Suno Antwren, *M. sunensis* (w. Amazonia)
  Rio de Janeiro Antwren, *M. fluminensis* (se. Brazil; very rare)
  Salvadori's Antwren, *M. minor* (se. Brazil; Amazonia?)
- ♂♂ with *wing-coverts unmarked.*
  20. UNICOLORED ANTWREN, *M. u. unicolor* (e. Brazil)
  Also: Alagoas Antwren, *M. snowi* (ne. Brazil; like 20)
  Plain-winged Antwren, *M. behni* (local in foothills, Guianas to Ecu.)
  Yungas Antwren, *M. grisea* (w. Bol. foothills; ♂ throat concolor)

19

PLATE 20: *TERENURA & FORMICIVORA* ANTWRENS, *DRYMOPHILA* ANTBIRDS, ETC.

Terenura Antwrens Small and inconspicuous antwrens which range mostly high in canopy of humid forest, most species in lowlands, a few in foothills and lower subtropical zone. Relatively *slender* and *long-tailed* (compared to other antwrens), in shape they rather more resemble certain tyrannulets (e.g., *Mecocerculus* and *Phyllomyias*). Distinctive is the *patch of rufous on lower back and rump* (yellow in 1 species) shown by both sexes of all species except ♂ Orange-bellied Antwren.

A. *Streaked head* (both sexes); most also with *rufous back*. E. Brazil region.
- 1. STREAK-CAPPED ANTWREN, *T. maculata* (se. Brazil area)
- *Also:* Orange-bellied Antwren, *T. sicki* (♂ with black back; ♀ orange below; very local in ne. Brazil)

B. Standard *Terenura*; ♀ ♀ lack ♂ ♂' *black crown*.
- 2. ASH-WINGED ANTWREN, *T. s. spodioptila* (ne. S. Am.)
- 3. RUFOUS-RUMPED ANTWREN, *T. c. callinota* (foothills and subtropics, mainly Andes)
- 4. YELLOW-RUMPED ANTWREN, *T. sharpei* (local in foothills of s. Peru and w. Bol.)
- *Also:* Chestnut-shouldered Antwren, *T. humeralis* (much like 3; w. Amazonia)

Drymophila Antbirds Small but *strikingly long-tailed* antbirds found in lower growth of forest and woodland, especially favoring areas with *dense stands of bamboo*. Most species range in se. S. Am., with 1 in Andes and another in w. Amazonia. Most are *prominently streaked or spotted*, and many show an obvious eyebrow.

A. *Se. Brazil and adjacent areas.*
- Tail *shorter and banded above;* note *ocellated back pattern.*
  - 5. SCALED ANTBIRD, *D. squamata stictocorypha*
- Tail *long and uniformly colored above.*
  - 6. FERRUGINOUS ANTBIRD, *D. ferruginea*
  - 7. RUFOUS-TAILED ANTBIRD, *D. genei*
  - 8. DUSKY-TAILED ANTBIRD, *D. malura*
  - *Also:* Bertoni's Antbird, *D. rubricollis* (much like 6)
  - Ochre-rumped Antbird, *D. ochropyga* (nearest 7)

B. Mostly *Andes* and *Amazonia.*
- 9. LONG-TAILED ANTBIRD, *D. c. caudata* (Andes and n. Venez.)
- *Also:* Striated Antbird, *D. devillei* (sw. Amazonia)

Formicivora Antwrens Small, *fairly long-tailed* antwrens found in *scrub and light woodland*, mainly in e. and s.-cen. S. Am. ♂ ♂ of most species have a *striking white "fringe" bordering black underparts*; ♀ ♀ vary below (some uniform, others streaked). Although long considered to be a *Myrmotherula* antwren (and shown by us on Plate 19), the Black-hooded Antwren has recently been shown to almost certainly be a *Formicivora*.

A. *Aberrant; slaty* with "white fringe" *restricted to flanks*.
- 10. NARROW-BILLED ANTWREN, *F. iheringi* (local in cen. Bahia and cen. Minas Gerais, Brazil)

B. Typical *Formicivora.*
- 11. WHITE-FRINGED ANTWREN, *F. g. grisea* (♀ ♀ of some races streaked below)
- 12. RUSTY-BACKED ANTWREN, *F. r. rufa*
- 13. BLACK-BELLIED ANTWREN, *F. m. melanogaster* (mainly e. and s. Brazil)
- *Also:* Serra Antwren, *F. serrana* (se. Brazil)
- Restinga Antwren, *F. littoralis* (very local in se. Brazil)

Myrmorchilus Antbirds A fairly large antbird found in arid woodland and scrub in *chaco* and *caatinga* regions. Note *boldly streaked upperparts in both sexes*.
- 14. STRIPE-BACKED ANTBIRD, *M. strigilatus suspicax*

20

PLATE 21: *CERCOMACRA* ANTBIRDS, *PYRIGLENA* FIRE-EYES, BUSHBIRDS, ETC.

Cercomacra Antbirds   Midsized antbirds with *rather long tails* (with or without white tip- PAGE 303
ping) and slender bills found in lower growth of forest and woodland, especially at borders and in thickets, where generally inconspicuous. Both sexes are simply patterned, ♂ ♂ basically black to gray with (except in n. races of Gray) *white spotting or fringing on wing-coverts;* color of underparts and extent of
markings on wing-coverts in ♀ ♀ *varies.*

A. *Canopy vine tangle habitat* unique in genus; note *bold white tail-tips.* PAGE 304

    1.   GRAY ANTBIRD
         1a. *C. c. cinerascens* (north of Amazon)
         1b. *C. cinerascens sclateri* (south of Amazon)

B. ♂ ♂ *gray to dark slaty,* ♀ ♀ *bright ochraceous to rufous below; no* tail-tipping (or at most faintly fringed). PAGE 304

    2.   RIO DE JANEIRO ANTBIRD, *C. brasiliana* (se. Brazil; rare)
    3.   BLACKISH ANTBIRD, *C. nigrescens approximans* (Amazonia)
    Also: Dusky Antbird, *C. tyrannina* (n. S. Am.; like 2)
           Black Antbird, *C. serva* (w. Amazonia; nearest 3)

C. *Black* ♂ ♂ much alike; ♀ ♀ *blackish to ashy gray below,* most with *whitish streaking/mottling* on throat. PAGE 307
Tail *boldly white-tipped.* Most species *range-restricted; all allopatric.*

    4.   JET ANTBIRD, *C. nigricans* (locally from Venez. to w. Ecu.)
    5.   MATO GROSSO ANTBIRD, *C. melanaria* (n. Bol. and sw. Brazil)
    Also: Bananal Antbird, *C. ferdinandi* (local in cen. Brazil; ♀ like 4)
           Rio Branco Antbird, *C. carbonaria* (local in n. Brazil; ♀ with
           ochraceous belly)
           Manu Antbird, *C. manu* (local in bamboo thickets of sw. Amazonia)

Rhopornis Antbirds   Large but *slender* and *quite long-tailed* antbird found only in remaining PAGE 310
woodlands of small area in *s. Bahia, Brazil.*

    6.   SLENDER ANTBIRD, *R. ardesiaca*

Pyriglena Fire-eyes   *Large* and *quite long-tailed* antbirds with comparatively short bills. PAGE 310
Both sexes have *distinctive bright red eyes.* ♂ ♂ are *jet black* with a semiconcealed white dorsal patch or
(additionally) with white markings on wings. Note extreme racial variation in ♀ White-backed; ♀ ♀ of
other species resemble *maura* or *pacifica* races of White-backed (but lack the supraloral). Fire-eyes are
found in forest and woodland undergrowth, where regularly encountered at army antswarms.

    7.   WHITE-SHOULDERED FIRE-EYE, *P. leucoptera* (se. Brazil area)
    8.   WHITE-BACKED FIRE-EYE
         8a. *P. leuconota maura*
         8b. *P. leuconota picea*
         8c. *P. leuconota pacifica*
    Also: Fringe-backed Fire-eye, *P. atra* (very rare and local in e. Bahia, Brazil)

Neoctantes Bushbirds PAGE 313
Monotypic genus found in forests of Amazonia, marked by *distinctive bill with upturned lower mandible.*

    9.   BLACK BUSHBIRD, *N. niger* (♂ all black)

Clytoctantes Bushbirds   With an *even more extremely modified bill* (larger, and also laterally com- PAGE 314
pressed) than the previous genus, striking and rarely seen *Clytoctantes* bushbirds are found locally in lowland forests.

    10.   RECURVE-BILLED BUSHBIRD, *C. alixii* (n. Col.; ♀ chestnut
           brown)
    Also: Rondonia Bushbird, *C. atrogularis* (s. Amaz. Brazil; ♂ blacker, ♀
           chestnut with black throat patch)

21

Myrmoborus Antbirds — Small group of rather chunky and short-tailed antbirds found in undergrowth of forests and woodlands of Amazonia, where most species are numerous though never conspicuous. Most show a distinctive *black face or mask*. ♂ ♂ are *predominantly gray*; ♀ ♀ *vary* (even within the same species; see text). — PAGE 315

A. Wings *plain* (♂ ♂), or only lightly dotted (♀ ♀). — PAGE 315

    1.   WHITE-BROWED ANTBIRD, *M. l. leucophrys*

    2.   ASH-BREASTED ANTBIRD, *M. l. lugubris* (locally along Amaz. rivers; ♀ ♀ westward show mask)

B. Wings *boldly fringed white* (*or buff*) in *both* sexes. — PAGE 317

    3.   BLACK-FACED ANTBIRD, *M. myotherinus elegans* (some ♀ ♀ all buff below)

    4.   BLACK-TAILED ANTBIRD, *M. melanurus* (local and rare in ne. Peru; ♀ lacks mask)

Dichrozona Antbirds — Monotypic genus of *very small*, short-tailed antbird found at low densities in undergrowth of terra firme forest in Amazonia. Note the *bold rump band* and *wing-banding*; ♀ quite similar. — PAGE 318

    5.   BANDED ANTBIRD, *D. cincta stellata*

Hylophylax Antbirds — Group of small antbirds found widely in undergrowth of humid lowland forests, where they are usually numerous but inconspicuous. *Complex and attractive plumage patterns* in most species, with back and breast *usually spotted* (back *scaled* in most races of Scale-backed). — PAGE 319

A. "Spot-backed" Group; both sexes with *breast boldly spotted*. — PAGE 319

    6.   SPOT-BACKED ANTBIRD, *H. n. naevia*

    7.   DOT-BACKED ANTBIRD, *H. p. punctulata* (markedly rarer than 6)

    Also: Spotted Antbird, *H. naevioides* (back solid rufous; w. Col. and w. Ecu.)

B. "Scale-backed": ♀ ♀ highly *variable*, some races *lack* fringing. — PAGE 321

    8.   SCALE-BACKED ANTBIRD

    8a. *H. poecilinota lepidonota*

    8b. *H. poecilinota nigrigula*

Hypocnemis Antbirds — Small antbirds found in lower growth of forest borders and woodland in Amaz. lowlands. Although *short-tailed*, their *streaky* or *spotted* overall patterns recall those of *Drymophila* antbirds. Most forms have *yellowish underparts* and/or *rusty flanks*. — PAGE 322

    9.   WARBLING ANTBIRD

    9a. *H. cantator peruviana* (widespread)

    9b. *H. c. subflava* (localized in se. Peru and nw. Bol.)

    Also: Yellow-browed Antbird, *H. hypoxantha* (nearest 9b; w. Amazonia)

Myrmochanes Antbirds — Very distinctive *small* antbird found *exclusively on river islands in w. Amazonia*. Both sexes (note virtual *lack* of dimorphism) are *bicolored*. — PAGE 324

    10.   BLACK-AND-WHITE ANTBIRD, *M. hemileucus*

Hypocnemoides Antbirds — A pair of very similar small antbirds found *near water* in Amazonia, where mainly allopatric (though with some overlap). Note the *white tail-tipping*, and, in ♀ ♀, the *gray and white mottled underparts*. — PAGE 325

    11.   BAND-TAILED ANTBIRD, *H. maculicauda* (south of Amazon)

    Also: Black-chinned Antbird, *H. melanopogon* (mainly north of Amazon)

Sclateria Antbirds — Monotypic genus of *long-billed* and rather long-legged antbird found *near water* in Amaz. lowlands. Note striking geographical variation in underparts. — PAGE 326

    12.   SILVERED ANTBIRD

    12a. *S. n. naevia* (more eastern)

    12b. *S. naevia argentata* (more western)

22

Percnostola Antbirds   A pair of antbirds found in different parts of Amazonia, both mainly   PAGE 327
at forest edges. Although rather dissimilar as antbirds go, ♂ ♂ of both species (and ♀ ♀ of Black-headed)
do show *pronounced fringing on wing-coverts.* Note that 3 species recently usually placed in *Percnostola* are
here returned to the genus *Schistocichla* (which follows).

    1.   WHITE-LINED ANTBIRD, *P. lophotes* (se. Peru)
    2.   BLACK-HEADED ANTBIRD (locally from Guianas to Peru)
        2a. *P. rufifrons minor* (more western)
        2b. *P. r. rufifrons* (more eastern)

Schistocichla Antbirds   A uniform group of 3 species found in Amaz. forest undergrowth,   PAGE 329
where they are inconspicuous and infrequently seen. All are round-headed (none showing any crest, unlike the true *Percnostola* antbirds). ♂ ♂ are *basically gray,* ♀ ♀ *rufous at least below;* both sexes show *spotting
on wing-coverts* (white in ♂ ♂, rufous-buff in ♀ ♀).

    3.   SPOT-WINGED ANTBIRD, *S. leucostigma subplumbea*
    4.   SLATE-COLORED ANTBIRD, *S. schistacea* (w. Amazonia)
    5.   CAURA ANTBIRD, *S. c. caurensis* (s. Venez.)

Myrmeciza Antbirds   A complex group of forest-inhabiting antbirds found widely in tropi-   PAGE 331
cal lowlands, where many species are mostly terrestrial, others foraging through lower growth. As with
the previous 2 genera, *Myrmeciza* tend to be shy and infrequently seen birds. Although for the most part
we follow traditional taxonomy, preliminary evidence indicates that the numerous species currently placed
in the genus are likely not a monophyletic unit, but exactly how the genus should be subdivided and/or
combined with related genera remains uncertain. We here present mainly the species comprising what was
formerly considered the genus *Myrmoderus,* with the rest of the *Myrmeciza* following on Plate 24. "*Myrmoderus*" antbirds are relatively (compared to true *Myrmeciza*) small and slim and tend to be *colorfully and
intricately patterned;* only 1 species shows a bare orbital patch.

A. Two aberrant, dissimilar *Myrmeciza.*   PAGE 331

    6.   GRAY-HEADED ANTBIRD, *M. griseiceps* (sw. Ecu. and nw. Peru;
        scarce and local)
    7.   YAPACANA ANTBIRD, *M. disjuncta* (sw. Venez. area; ♀ buffy
        below)

B. Typical "*Myrmoderus*": ♂ ♂ *brown-backed* with black bib, ♀ ♀ usually *rufous below;* both sexes with   PAGE 333
    wing-spotting.

    8.   CHESTNUT-TAILED ANTBIRD, *M. h. hemimelaena*
    9.   BLACK-THROATED ANTBIRD, *M. a. atrothorax*
   Also: Gray-bellied Antbird, *M. pelzelni* (sw. Venez. area; ♀ mostly whitish
        below)

C. *Ornately* patterned "*Myrmoderus*"; mainly terrestrial.   PAGE 335
• Larger, with *bare blue orbital patch;* ♂ has *full* black bib.

    10.   FERRUGINOUS-BACKED ANTBIRD, *M. ferruginea* (ne. S. Am.)
• *Scaly breast* in ♂ ♂, *masked effect* in ♀ ♀; *e. Brazil.*

    11.   SCALLOPED ANTBIRD, *M. ruficauda*
    12.   SQUAMATE ANTBIRD, *M. squamosa*
    13.   WHITE-BIBBED ANTBIRD, *M. loricata*

23

Myrmeciza Antbirds Coverage of the members of the rather heterogeneous genus *Myrme-* PAGE 337
ciza here continues from Plate 23. Presented here are several species long considered members of *Myrme-*
ciza, together with 2 species for many decades separated in the genus *Sipia.* The genus *Gymnocichla* seems
closely allied, but for now follows as a separate, monotypic genus. These *Myrmeciza* are almost all found
in lower growth of humid lowland forests, with a few mostly or entirely in foothills and only White-
bellied in more deciduous habitats. Most are *dark* (some black) and *simply patterned,* with many showing
either a *bare blue orbital patch* or *spotting on wing-coverts* (sometimes both). All these species tend to be shy
and unobtrusive, though most have characteristic and frequently heard songs which at least make their
presence known. Several (especially Sooty and Immaculate) are confirmed army ant followers, and almost
all will appear at swarms at least adventitiously.

D. *Large and robust,* with *heavy bill;* most show a *bare blue orbital patch.* ♂ ♂ *slaty to black* (only Plum- PAGE 337
beous with wing-spots); all ♀ ♀ *dissimilar.*

1. PLUMBEOUS ANTBIRD, *M. hyperythra* (w. Amazonia)
2. SOOTY ANTBIRD, *M. f. fortis* (w. Amazonia)
3. WHITE-SHOULDERED ANTBIRD, *M. melanoceps* (w. Amazonia)
4. GOELDI'S ANTBIRD, *M. goeldii* (se. Peru and adjacent Bol. and Brazil)
Also: Immaculate Antbird, *M. immaculata* (w. Venez. to w. Ecu.; ♀ dark brown)

E. Smaller *Myrmeciza;* most *lack* prominent orbital patch. PAGE 340
• *Bright rufous back* and white midbelly; ♀ *lacks* black bib.

5. WHITE-BELLIED ANTBIRD, *M. longipes griseipectus* (deciduous woodlands in n. S. Am.)

• Quite dark with *wings typically spotted;* ♀ ♀ usually browner. Includes "*Sipia*" (7 and 8).

6. CHESTNUT-BACKED ANTBIRD, *M. exsul maculifer* (w. Col. and w. Ecu.)
7. ESMERALDAS ANTBIRD, *M. nigricauda* (sw. Col. and w. Ecu.)
8. STUB-TAILED ANTBIRD, *M. berlepschi* (w. Col. and nw. Ecu.)
Also: Dull-mantled Antbird, *M. laemosticta* (n. Col. and nw. Venez.; nearest 7)

Gymnocichla Antbirds A fairly large antbird found in humid woodlands of *n. Col.;* closely PAGE 343
related to *Myrmeciza.* ♂ ♂ have *unique bare blue crown;* ♀ ♀ are *quite bright rufous brown* with a *blue orbital
area.*

9. BARE-CROWNED ANTBIRD, *G. nudiceps sanctamartae*

Myrmornis Antbirds An *oddly proportioned, chunky* antbird with *short legs, stubby tail,* and PAGE 344
long bill. Mainly *terrestrial,* shuffling about inside humid lowland forests.

10. WING-BANDED ANTBIRD, *M. t. torquata* (locally from n. Col. to Amaz. Brazil)

All of the antbirds on this plate forage almost exclusively at army antswarms—these are the original "ant-birds." In fact, however, the ants themselves are eaten only by accident; rather, what is occurring is that these antbirds (and some other birds, notably a variety of woodcreepers) are pursuing arthropods attempting to flee the onrushing swarm of ants.

An army antswarm presents one of the most fascinating spectacles to be seen in the neotropics, and a good one is always the center of much bird activity. According to E. O. Willis, whose studies of ant-following antbirds are models of depth and comprehensiveness, the primary ants whose swarms are followed by birds are in the genus *Eciton*, which has a wide range in the lowlands from Mexico to Arg.; the smaller swarms of *Labidus praedator* are also followed to some extent. A swarm is active mainly from mid-morning to midafternoon, before and after which the ants conglomerate into what is termed a bivouac; rain reduces or ends activity. Swarms are best located by listening for the antbirds' characteristic chirring call notes and songs; the ants cannot travel very rapidly or very far, and therefore the same swarm can often be relocated on successive days.

Pithys Antbirds   A pair of striking antbirds, the unique White-plumed being wide-spread in Amaz. forests, the White-masked being known from only a single (hybrid?) specimen. Sexes alike.   PAGE 345

    1.   WHITE-PLUMED ANTBIRD, *P. a. albifrons*
    Also: White-masked Antbird, *P. castanea* (extreme n. Peru)

Gymnopithys Antbirds   Fairly small, chunky, and short-tailed antbirds found in humid lowland forests. Bicolored and Rufous-throated are quite similar aside from their coloration below, whereas White-throated and Lunulated form a rather different pair of species (being sexually dimorphic, etc.). Note that Bicolored may be composed of cis- and trans-Andean semispecies.   PAGE 346

    2.   BICOLORED ANTBIRD, *G. leucaspis castanea*
    3.   RUFOUS-THROATED ANTBIRD, *G. r. rufigula* (ne. S. Am.)
    4.   WHITE-THROATED ANTBIRD, *G. salvini maculata* (sw. Amazonia)
    Also: Lunulated Antbird, *G. lunulata* (e. Ecu. and ne. Peru)

Rhegmatorhina Antbirds   A very attractive group of 5 or 6 species of ant-following antbirds found in Amazonia, mainly in *Brazil*; their often small ranges are *entirely allopatric*. All have *very prominent bare ocular areas* (pale blue to yellowish green) and *fairly long crest feathers* (though these are often held down against the crown). Most ♀ ♀ (except 5) show an "ocellated" *barred pattern on mantle*, extending to the underparts in 6 and 7.   PAGE 349

A. Elongated crest feathers *"normal."*   PAGE 349

    5.   BARE-EYED ANTBIRD, *R. gymnops* (east of lower Rio Tapajós)
    6.   WHITE-BREASTED ANTBIRD, *R. hoffmannsi* (east of Rio Madeira)
    7.   HARLEQUIN ANTBIRD, *R. berlepschi* (west of lower Rio Tapajós)
    Also: Chestnut-crested Antbird, *R. cristata* (all rufous below; extreme se. Col. and nw. Brazil)

B. Elongated crest feathers *decomposed* (pale ashy or golden in color).   PAGE 351

    8.   HAIRY-CRESTED ANTBIRD, *R. melanosticta purusiana* (w. Amazonia)

Skutchia Antbirds   A fairly large antbird found in a limited area in Amaz. Brazil, between lower Rio Tapajós and lower Rio Madeira. Its bare skin around the eye is inconspicuous, but the *white loral plumes* and *barred band on breast* are not. Sexes similar.   PAGE 352

    9.   PALE-FACED ANTBIRD, *S. borbae*

Phlegopsis Bare-eyes   Quite large and *boldly patterned* antbirds found in Amazonia, marked especially by their *striking bare red ocular areas* (less so in ♀ of 10).   PAGE 353

    10.   REDDISH-WINGED BARE-EYE, *P. erythroptera* (w. Amazonia)
    11.   BLACK-SPOTTED BARE-EYE, *P. n. nigromaculata*

Phaenostictus Antbirds   A spectacular, rather long-tailed antbird of w. Col. and nw. Ecu., easily known by its *overall spotted appearance* and *very large bare blue ocular region*. Sexes similar.   PAGE 354

    12.   OCELLATED ANTBIRD, *P. mcleannani pacificus*

25

1

2

3

4♀

4♂

5♂

6♀

7♂

8♀

9

10♂

10♀

11

12

GTUDOR

Formicarius Antthrushes   *Dark and plain* antbirds of the forest floor, mostly in lowlands and   PAGE 356
foothills. Here they walk about with jaunty manner and *short tail cocked high*, looking like nothing so
much as small rails; like rails, they are shy and heard more often than seen, with *distinctive vocalizations.*
They show *no streaked or barred pattern below;* most have a bit of bare skin in front of and behind the eye.

    1.   BLACK-FACED ANTTHRUSH, *F. a. analis*
    2.   RUFOUS-CAPPED ANTTHRUSH, *F. colma ruficeps*
    3.   RUFOUS-BREASTED ANTTHRUSH, *F. rufipectus thoracicus*
       (mainly Andean slopes)
Also: Black-headed Antthrush, *F. nigricapillus* (w. Col. and w. Ecu.)
       Rufous-fronted Antthrush, *F. rufifrons* (very local in se. Peru)

Chamaeza Antthrushes   Generally larger and *plumper* than the previous genus (but otherwise   PAGE 359
not dissimilar in shape), *Chamaeza* antthrushes all show a *bold streaked, scalloped, or barred pattern below.*
The various species look quite alike and are often not easy to identify. All are unobtrusive, terrestrial birds
of humid forest (especially in *montane* areas), heard far more often than seen; *voice* is often a good distinguishing character.

A. Typical *Chamaeza*, *streaked to scalloped below.* All very much *alike.*   PAGE 360

    4.   RUFOUS-TAILED ANTTHRUSH, *C. ruficauda* (se. Brazil)
    5.   NOBLE ANTTHRUSH, *C. n. nobilis* (Amaz. lowlands; large)
Also: Scalloped Antthrush, *C. turdina* (locally in n. Venez. and w. Col.)
       Cryptic Antthrush, *C. meruloides* (se. Brazil)
       Short-tailed Antthrush, *C. campanisona*

B. Dense *barring below.*   PAGE 364

    6.   BARRED ANTTHRUSH, *C. m. mollissima* (local in Andes from Col.
       to Bol.)

Pittasoma Antpittas   A pair of quite large and *very handsomely and boldly patterned* antpittas   PAGE 364
found in wet forests of *w. Col. and w. Ecu.* Both species are shy, terrestrial, and all too infrequently seen
(perhaps most often at antswarms). Longer-billed than *Grallaria* antpittas. Somewhat sexually dimorphic.

    7.   RUFOUS-CROWNED ANTPITTA
       7a. *P. r. rufipileatum* (nw. Ecu.)
       7b. *P. rufipileatum rosenbergi* (Chocó, Col.)
Also: Black-crowned Antpitta, *P. michleri* (nw. Col.)

Grallaria Antpittas   The genus *Grallaria* contains some of South America's most fabled   PAGE 366
birds. Almost all are secretive and infrequently seen, and many are rare and highly range-restricted, several
species having only recently been discovered, others being known only from a few old specimens. As a
group, *Grallaria* antpittas are easily known by their characteristic shape: *very long legs* (almost always blu-
ish gray), *very short tail* (essentially invisible in the field), and *chunky round shape.* Although not colorful,
most species are attractively patterned in shades of brown, rufous, and gray; some are boldly *barred,
scaled,* or *streaked.* Antpittas are primarily *terrestrial*, hopping or running, often rapidly, in dense undergrowth; most occur in forest, with a few found in secondary scrub or páramo. All are heard more often
than seen, and their *simple but often beautiful songs* are usually distinctive; some habitually sing from
slightly elevated perches. Although 1 species or another is found through much of forested S. Am. (except
in the far south), *Grallaria* reaches by far its highest diversity in the *Andes.*

   We divide this large genus into several Groups, with coverage continuing on Plate 27. Our first Group
comprises the classic, "typical" *Grallaria* antpittas (the *Grallaria* subgenus) and includes the largest members of the genus and some of South America's more spectacular birds.

A. "*Barred*" and "*scaled*" antpittas; *malar streaks* often evident.   PAGE 366
• *Very large* with *boldly barred underparts.*

    8.   GIANT ANTPITTA, *G. gigantea hylodroma* (rare in s. Col. and Ecu.)
    9.   UNDULATED ANTPITTA, *G. squamigera canicauda* (w. Venez. to Bol.)
Also: Great Antpitta, *G. excelsa* (rare in Venez.)

• Mainly medium-sized (except e. Brazil races of Variegated), with more or less obvious *pale malar
stripe;* most *scaled above.*

   10.   VARIEGATED ANTPITTA, *G. varia imperator* (disjunct in e. Brazil
       area, ne. S. Am., and upper Amazonia)
   11.   SCALED ANTPITTA, *G. guatimalensis regulus* (mainly Andean slopes
       and tepuis)
Also: Tachira Antpitta, *G. chthonia* (very local in w. Venez.; like 11)
       Moustached Antpitta, *G. alleni* (very local in w. Col.; like 11)
       Plain-backed Antpitta, *G. haplonota* (n. Venez. and Ecu.; midthroat pale)

26

1

2

3

4

5

6

7a♂

7b♀

8

9

10

11

GTUDOR

Grallaria Antpittas We here continue coverage of the *Grallaria* antpittas from Plate 26. PAGE 372
Groups B and C comprise the *Oropezus* subgenus: a large set of antpittas with *plain patterns* (*no apparent barring, scaling, or streaking*), found almost exclusively in the *Andes*. Group D comprises the *Hypsibemon* subgenus, also almost entirely *Andean* in distribution; these show *prominent streaking,* usually just on underparts but in 1 species (Stripe-headed) also on the crown and mantle. Group E comprises a pair of species in the *Thamnocharis* subgenus; these inhabit *Amaz. lowland forests* and resemble *Hypsibemon* in their *streaking below,* but have even longer flank feathers and shorter tails.

B. *Simply patterned Grallaria* found mainly in *temperate* zone of *Andes*. PAGE 372
- Medium sized with *olive brown upperparts.*
  - 1. TAWNY ANTPITTA, *G. q. quitensis* (Col. to n. Peru)
  - 2. RUFOUS-FACED ANTPITTA, *G. erythrotis* (Bol.)
- Smallish and *mainly dull brown.*
  - *Not illustrated:* Brown-banded Antpitta, *G. milleri* (Cen. Andes of Col.; rare)
- *Rather small; pale rufous to chestnut predominating.*
  - 3. RUFOUS ANTPITTA (sw. Venez. to Bol.)
    - 3a. *G. r. rufula*
    - 3b. *G. r. cajamarcae* (n. Peru)
  - 4. GRAY-NAPED ANTPITTA, *G. g. griseonucha* (w. Venez.)
  - 5. BICOLORED ANTPITTA, *G. rufocinerea* (Col.; rare)
  - *Also:* Chestnut Antpitta, *G. blakei* (local in cen. Peru; like 3a)
- *Large; dark gray underparts.*
  - 6. CHESTNUT-NAPED ANTPITTA, *G. n. nuchalis* (Col. to n. Peru)
  - *Also:* Pale-billed Antpitta, *G. carrikeri* (local in n. Peru)

C. *Simply patterned Grallaria* found mainly in *subtropical* zone of *Andes*. All allopatric; the *G. hypoleuca* PAGE 376
superspecies.
- *Back rufous brown.*
  - 7. YELLOW-BREASTED ANTPITTA, *G. flavotincta* (w. Col. and w. Ecu.)
  - 8. RUSTY-TINGED ANTPITTA, *G. przewalskii* (n. Peru)
  - *Also:* White-bellied Antpitta, *G. hypoleuca* (Col. and e. Ecu.; nearest 7)
    - Bay Antpitta, *G. capitalis* (cen. Peru; all rusty below)
- *Back bright rufous* or with *rufous cap.*
  - 9. RED-AND-WHITE ANTPITTA, *G. erythroleuca* (s. Peru)
  - 10. WHITE-THROATED ANTPITTA, *G. albigula* (extreme s. Peru to nw. Arg.)

D. Montane *Grallaria* with *conspicuous streaking.* PAGE 379
- Obvious streaking *only on underparts.*
  - 11. SANTA MARTA ANTPITTA, *G. bangsi*
  - 12. CHESTNUT-CROWNED ANTPITTA, *G. ruficapilla albiloris* (Venez. to n. Peru)
  - *Also:* Cundinamarca Antpitta, *G. kaestneri* (local in E. Andes of Col.)
    - Watkins' Antpitta, *G. watkinsi* (sw. Ecu. and nw. Peru; like 12 but paler and pink-legged)
- Distinctive; *heavily scalloped below* and *streaked at least on head.*
  - 13. STRIPE-HEADED ANTPITTA, *G. a. andicola* (Peru and w. Bol.)

E. *Large;* restricted to *w. Amaz. lowlands*. Note white streaks on rump and very short tail. The *Thamno-* PAGE 382
charis subgenus.
- 14. OCHRE-STRIPED ANTPITTA, *G. dignissima* (e. Ecu. and ne. Peru)
- *Also:* Elusive Antpitta, *G. eludens* (se. Peru; like 14 but throat white)

27

Myrmothera Antpittas A pair of *dull brownish* antpittas, 1 in Amaz. lowland forests, the other PAGE 383
on the tepuis. Resemble *Grallaria,* but have more slender bills. Both shy and difficult to see, though vocal.

    1.   THRUSH-LIKE ANTPITTA, *M. c. campanisona*
    Also: Tepui Antpitta, *M. simplex* (dingy breast *un*streaked)

Hylopezus Antpittas Similar to *Myrmothera,* and equally vocal but hard to see; likewise PAGE 384
found principally in humid lowland forests, Speckle-breasted also being montane in se. Brazil. All have
streaking or spotting on breast.

A. *Wide ochraceous eye-ring; very bold* spotting/streaking on breast. PAGE 384
    2.   SPOTTED ANTPITTA, *H. macularius diversus*
    Also: Streak-chested Antpitta, *H. perspicillatus* (w. Col. and w. Ecu.)

B. More *"plain-faced"*; streaking/spotting on breast typically *finer.* PAGE 386
    3.   WHITE-LORED ANTPITTA, *H. f. fulviventris* (e. Ecu. and se. Col.)
    4.   WHITE-BROWED ANTPITTA, *H. ochroleucus* (ne. Brazil)
    5.   SPECKLE-BREASTED ANTPITTA, *H. nattereri* (se. Brazil area)
    Also: Fulvous-bellied Antpitta, *H. dives* (w. Col.; nearest 3)
          Amazonian Antpitta, *H. berlepschi* (s. Amazonia; nearest 3)

Grallaricula Antpittas Short-billed and *very small* antpittas, smaller than any *Grallaria,* the PAGE 389
members of this genus are *skulking* inhabitants of humid forest lower growth. Although generally found
close to the ground, they only briefly drop to the ground itself. *Grallaricula* antpittas are found mainly in
the subtropical zone of the *Andes,* where some species are believed to have very small ranges and are
scarce (though to some extent they may just be overlooked). Some species have musical vocalizations, but
on the whole *less vocal* than other antpittas.

A. Typical small *Grallaricula;* note the wide variation in the commonest species (even to bill color). PAGE 389
• Distinctive *rufous head* and *gray underparts.*
    6.   HOODED ANTPITTA, *G. cucullata* (mainly Col.)
• Variably patterned below, from *plain rufous* to *boldly streaked or scalloped.*
    7.   OCHRE-BREASTED ANTPITTA, (relatively numerous)
          7a. *G. flavirostris zarumae*   7b. *G. flavirostris boliviana*
    8.   PERUVIAN ANTPITTA, *G. peruviana* (s. Ecu. and n. Peru; rare)
    Also: Scallop-breasted Antpitta, *G. loricata* (n. Venez.; like 8)
          Ochre-fronted Antpitta, *G. ochraceifrons* (rare in n. Peru; closest to 8)
          Rusty-breasted Antpitta, *G. ferrugineipectus* (Venez. to n. Col., and
          Peru and Bol.; *plain* below)

B. Somewhat larger than Group A; share *slaty gray crown.* PAGE 392
    9.   SLATE-CROWNED ANTPITTA, *G. nana occidentalis*
    10.   CRESCENT-FACED ANTPITTA, *G. lineifrons* (e. Ecu. and s. Col.;
          scarce)

Conopophaga Gnateaters *Plump, short-tailed,* and *long-legged* like antpittas, the gnateaters differ PAGE 395
in their *unmistakable postocular tufts* present in all but 1 species. They also differ in not being as vocal.
They are sexually dimorphic (unlike the vast majority of antpittas), ♀♀ usually having a grayer and less
prominent postocular, and with *rufous breast* in many species. Gnateaters are inconspicuous inhabitants of
humid forest undergrowth, favoring treefalls and borders; some are montane (in Andes and e. Brazil region), but most range in Amazonia. We employ geographical groupings below.

A. *Andes;* mainly subtropical zone. ♂♂ gray below. PAGE 395
    11.   CHESTNUT-CROWNED GNATEATER, *C. castaneiceps brunneinu-
          cha* (Col. to Peru)
    Also: Slaty Gnateater, *C. ardesiaca* (s. Peru and Bol.; ♀ gray below)

B. *E. Brazil* area; ♀♀ much more alike than ♂♂. PAGE 397
    12.   RUFOUS GNATEATER (postocular tuft white in ♂)
          12a. *C. lineata vulgaris* (se. Brazil)
          12b. *C. lineata cearae* (ne. Brazil)
    13.   BLACK-CHEEKED GNATEATER, *C. m. melanops*

C. *Amazonian lowlands* east to ne. Brazil. PAGE 398
• ♀♀ *rufous*-breasted.
    14.   ASH-THROATED GNATEATER, *C. peruviana* (w. Amazonia)
    15.   CHESTNUT-BELTED GNATEATER, *C. aurita occidentalis*
• ♀♀ *gray*-breasted; ♂♂ with full black hood at least.
    16.   BLACK-BELLIED GNATEATER, *C. melanogaster* (s. Amaz. Brazil)
    Also: Hooded Gnateater, *C. roberti* (e. Amaz. Brazil)

28

G TUDOR

PLATE 29: LARGER TAPACULOS

Pteroptochos Huet-huets and Turcas
Very large tapaculos found principally in Chile, the Black-throated also into adjacent Arg. Their *very long legs and strong feet* are characteristic. All species are primarily terrestrial, the 2 huet-huets (possibly conspecific) in austral forest, the turca in matorral and scrub in cen. Chile.

        1.   BLACK-THROATED HUET-HUET, *P. tarnii*
        2.   MOUSTACHED TURCA, *P. m. megapodius*
    Also: Chestnut-throated Huet-huet, *P. castaneus* (s.-cen. Chile; like 1)

Scelorchilus Tapaculos   Another pair of *distinctively patterned* tapaculos, generally similar to
the huet-huets but considerably smaller and with less strong feet, and likewise found primarily in *Chile*.

        3.   CHUCAO TAPACULO, *S. r. rubecula* (s. forests)
        4.   WHITE-THROATED TAPACULO, *S. a. albicollis* (matorral scrub of cen. Chile)

Rhinocrypta Gallitos   A distinctive *large* and *bushy-crested* tapaculo found in the chaco and n.
Patagonian scrub of s.-cen. S. Am.

        5.   CRESTED GALLITO, *R. lanceolata*

Teledromas Gallitos   A *plain* and *pale* tapaculo which runs on the ground (sometimes incredibly rapidly) in arid scrub of *w. Arg.*

        6.   SANDY GALLITO, *T. fuscus*

Merulaxis Bristlefronts   A pair of quite long-tailed tapaculos with *unique bristles springing from*
above the lores; both species range in forest undergrowth of *se. Brazil.* Sexes dimorphic.

        7.   SLATY BRISTLEFRONT, *M. ater*
    Also: Stresemann's Bristlefront, *M. stresemanni* (very rare in s. Bahia)

Liosceles Tapaculos
The only tapaculo in Amazonia, where it inhabits the ground inside terra firme forest.

        8.   RUSTY-BELTED TAPACULO, *L. t. thoracicus*

Acropternis Tapaculos   A splendid large tapaculo with a *unique, boldly spotted appearance*
found in dense undergrowth of montane forest in the n. Andes. Vocal, but furtive.

        9.   OCELLATED TAPACULO, *A. orthonyx infuscata*

29

GUDOR

PLATE 30: SMALLER TAPACULOS

Eugralla Tapaculos
A mainly gray tapaculo with *quite conspicuous contrasting rufous flanks*
PAGE 409
and *yellow legs* found in austral forests of *s. Chile and adjacent Arg.*
      1.   OCHRE-FLANKED TAPACULO, *E. paradoxa*

Myornis Tapaculos
PAGE 410
A *rather long-tailed*, essentially gray tapaculo found in undergrowth of montane forest in n. Andes.
      2.   ASH-COLORED TAPACULO, *M. senilis*

Scytalopus Tapaculos
An exceptionally complex genus of small, short-tailed birds which
PAGE 411
creep about on or near the ground, where they are hard to see and fly very little. Most species occur in forest or woodland undergrowth, and few in more open terrain (there usually hopping on and among rocks instead of moving through dense tangles). Maximum diversity is reached in the Andes, but several species range far into s. S. Am. (the Magellanic even reaching Cape Horn); others are endemic to the e. Brazil region, and a few occur extralimitally in s. Middle America. All *Scytalopus* are essentially some shade of gray or blackish, some with contrasting white or gray on the head and many showing rufous with dark barring on the flanks and rump. *Many species cannot be identified on plumage characters alone* and must be distinguished on the basis of *vocalizations;* these are given relatively frequently and with practice can be quite distinctive. Bear in mind that *their taxonomy is still actively developing* and that several species may be split further than in the arrangement presented here. In addition, several forms now known to represent separate species have yet to be actually described. Immatures of *all* species are *brownish*, with coarse barring (see 10b).

A. Mainly in *Andes.*
PAGE 412
      3.   UNICOLORED TAPACULO (w. Venez. to Bol.)
            3a. *S. unicolor latrans* (w. Venez. to n. Peru)
            3b. *S. u. unicolor*
      4.   LARGE-FOOTED TAPACULO, *S. macropus* (Peru)
      5.   RUFOUS-VENTED TAPACULO, *S. femoralis micropterus* (Col. to Peru)
      6.   WHITE-CROWNED TAPACULO, *S. b. bolivianus* (w. Venez. to Bol.)
      7.   BROWN-RUMPED TAPACULO, *S. latebricola meridanus* (w. Venez. to Ecu.)
      8.   MAGELLANIC TAPACULO, *S. magellanicus* (s. Chile and s. Arg.)
      9.   ANDEAN TAPACULO (w. Venez. to nw. Arg.; variable)
            9a. *S. griseicollis simonsi*
            9b. *S. griseicollis superciliaris* (nw. Arg.)
   Also: Santa Marta Tapaculo, *S. sanctaemartae*
            Narino Tapaculo, *S. vicinior* (sw. Col. and nw. Ecu.; like 5)
            Tacarcuna Tapaculo, *S. panamensis* (extreme nw. Col.)
            Caracas Tapaculo, *S. caracae* (n. Venez.; like 7)
            Dusky Tapaculo, *S. fuscus* (cen. Chile; darker than 8)

B. *E. Brazil* region.
PAGE 420
     10.   MOUSE-COLORED TAPACULO, *S. speluncae*
            10a. adult   10b. immature
     11.   WHITE-BREASTED TAPACULO, *S. indigoticus*
   Also: Bahia Tapaculo, *S. psychopompus* (like 11)
            Brasilia Tapaculo, *S. novacapitalis*

Psilorhamphus Bamboowrens
A unique small "tapaculo" (it doesn't look or act like one) with *finely*
PAGE 421
dotted plumage found in *bamboo stands* of *se. Brazil area.* ♀ somewhat browner.
     12.   SPOTTED BAMBOOWREN, *P. guttatus*

Melanopareia Crescent-chests
A distinctive quartet of *attractively patterned* tapaculos found locally in
PAGE 422
scrub and semiopen terrain. Appearance, behavior, and vocalizations are decidedly *un*tapaculo-like (more resembling antbirds). ♀ ♀ generally similar.
     13.   COLLARED CRESCENT-CHEST, *M. torquata rufescens* (mainly interior Brazil)
     14.   OLIVE-CROWNED CRESCENT-CHEST, *M. maximiliani argentina* (Bol. to n. Arg.)
     15.   ELEGANT CRESCENT-CHEST, *M. e. elegans* (w. Ecu. and nw. Peru)
   Also: Maranon Crescent-chest, *M. maranonica* (upper Río Marañón valley of nw. Peru and s. Ecu.; like 15)

30

Suiriri Flycatchers   Now considered a single species, though there are 2 distinctly different   PAGE 427
"types," as illustrated. Found in scrubby woodland, cerrado, and campos in interior s.-cen. S. Am.

    1.   **SUIRIRI FLYCATCHER**
        1a. *S. suiriri affinis* (mainly Brazil)   1b. *S. s. suiriri* (chaco region)

Elaenia Elaenias   A well known, generally numerous group of flycatchers; 1 species or   PAGE 428
another is found throughout S. Am. (in some areas 6 or more species occur). Most are predominantly
olive with 2 or 3 usually well marked wing-bars; many have yellower bellies, and others show a prominent
crest or eye-ring. Bills are small (though not as stubby as in *Sublegatus*), with pale lower mandibles.

    Elaenias are perhaps best known for the difficulty one often has in trying to identify them. Our Groups
and subgroups have been drawn to reflect the reality that *the differences between many species are extremely
subtle:* many species within the following Groups look virtually identical to each other, and even the differences between Groups are relatively minor. In particular, the points you need to look for are:

    1. relative size;
    2. presence or absence of a crest (and if present, its shape);
    3. presence or absence of white in crown (sometimes hard to see);
    4. number of wing-bars (2 or 3—beware molt stage, which sometimes obscures the upper one);
    5. color of belly.

    Habitat and *range* are also important; but remember that many species are migratory and others are
prone to wandering. *And if your bird is vocalizing, pay special attention to that.*

A. "Typical," confusing elaenias.   PAGE 429
• With *obvious shaggy or bushy crests* (when alert); all rather large, and *belly clear yellowish.*
        2.   **YELLOW-BELLIED ELAENIA**, *E. f. flavogaster*
        3.   **MOTTLE-BACKED ELAENIA**, *E. gigas* (e. base of Andes)
      Also: Large Elaenia, *E. spectabilis* (less crested)
             Noronha Elaenia, *E. ridleyana* (off ne. Brazil)
• With decidedly *olivaceous tone* (especially above) and *yellowish belly.*
        4.   **HIGHLAND ELAENIA**, *E. obscura sordida* (Andes from Peru to
             Arg., and in se. S. Am.)
        5.   **SIERRAN ELAENIA**, *E. p. pallatangae* (Andes, Col. to Bol.; tepuis)
      Also: Mountain Elaenia, *E. frantzii* (Col. and Venez.)
• Medium-sized; *very* similar, with belly pale yellowish to white.
        6.   **PLAIN-CRESTED ELAENIA**, *E. cristata* (savannas of e. S. Am.)
        7.   **WHITE-CRESTED ELAENIA**, *E. albiceps chilensis*
      Also: Lesser Elaenia, *E. chiriquensis* (widespread in drier areas)
             Caribbean Elaenia, *E. martinica* (Netherlands Antilles)
             Small-billed Elaenia, *E. parvirostris* (breeds s. S. Am., migrating north)
             Olivaceous Elaenia, *E. mesoleuca* (se. S. Am.)

B. Relatively distinctive elaenias. Coloration decidedly brownish or gray.   PAGE 438
        8.   **SLATY ELAENIA**, *E. strepera* (breeds Bol. and n. Arg., migrating n.)
        9.   **BROWNISH ELAENIA**, *E. pelzelni* (islands in Amazon River)
      10.   **RUFOUS-CROWNED ELAENIA**, *E. ruficeps* (savannas of ne. S. Am.)
      Also: Great Elaenia, *E. dayi* (tepuis)

Sublegatus Scrub-Flycatchers   A difficult, small genus of midsized flycatchers, close to *Elaenia* but   PAGE 440
differing in shorter, all-black bills and less conspicuous and noisy behavior.

      11.   **NORTHERN SCRUB-FLYCATCHER**, *S. arenarum glaber*
      Also: Amazonian Scrub-Flycatcher, *S. obscurior*
             Southern Scrub-Flycatcher, *S. modestus* (s.-cen. S. Am.)

Myiopagis Elaenias   Another difficult, obscure genus. Thought closely related to true   PAGE 442
Elaenia but really does not much resemble them, being smaller and more slender with a darker-crowned
look and different wing markings. All have a *coronal stripe* (either white or yellow). More birds of forest
and woodland canopy and interior than *Elaenia*, and generally less conspicuous and noisy.

A. *Prominent yellowish to white wing-bars;* usually in forest.   PAGE 443
      12.   **FOREST ELAENIA**, *M. gaimardii guianensis*
      13.   **GRAY ELAENIA** (disjunctly in humid forest)
             13a. *M. c. caniceps*   13b. *M. caniceps cinerea*
      Also: Yellow-crowned Elaenia, *M. flavivertex* (locally in Amazonia)
B. *Wing-bars obscure* or lacking, pale brownish to whitish; typically in drier habitats than Group A.   PAGE 445
      14.   **PACIFIC ELAENIA**, *M. subplacens* (w. Ecu. and nw. Peru)
      Also: Greenish Elaenia, *M. viridicata* (locally in woodland south to s. Brazil)

31

Phaeomyias and *Pseudelaenia* Tyrannulets   Mouse-colored widespread in semiopen areas; Gray-
and-white restricted to desert scrub in sw. Ecu. and nw. Peru. Both dull, though white evident in crest of
Gray-and-white.

    1. MOUSE-COLORED TYRANNULET, *Phaeomyias murina ignobilis*
   Also: Gray-and-white Tyrannulet, *Pseudelaenia leucospodia*

Camptostoma Beardless-Tyrannulets
Notably dull, this bushy-crested tyrannulet is widespread in semiopen areas.

    2. SOUTHERN BEARDLESS-TYRANNULET, *C. o. obsoletum*

Tyrannulus Tyrannulets   Stubby bill; characteristic voice. Widespread in tropical lowlands.
    3. YELLOW-CROWNED TYRANNULET, *T. elatus*

Ornithion Tyrannulets   Two very small, quite dissimilar tyrannulets of humid tropical lowlands. Tail short (especially in Brown-capped), both with a rather prominent white superciliary.

    4. BROWN-CAPPED TYRANNULET, *O. b. brunneicapillum* (nw. S. Am.)
    5. WHITE-LORED TYRANNULET, *O. inerme* (Amazonia; e. Brazil)

Zimmerius Tyrannulets   Rather "typical" (and often confusing) small tyrannulets, found
mainly in montane areas (especially on lower Andean slopes), with only the Slender-footed found in lowlands. All have stubby bills and can be known by wing pattern, in which *yellow edging is very evident* but
actual wing-bars are obscure or lacking. Tend to perch horizontally with *tail often partially cocked.*
A. *Contrasting* supraloral and *dark* iris; subtropical.

    6. GOLDEN-FACED TYRANNULET, *Z. c. chrysops* (Venez. to n. Peru)
   Also: Peruvian Tyrannulet, *Z. viridiflavus* (yellower below; cen. Peru)
     Venezuelan Tyrannulet, *Z. improbus* (Venez. and n. Col.)
B. *Weak* facial pattern with *pale* iris; most in tropical zone.

    7. BOLIVIAN TYRANNULET, *Z. b. bolivianus* (Andes, s. Peru to Bol.)
    8. SLENDER-FOOTED TYRANNULET, *Z. g. gracilipes*
   Also: Paltry Tyrannulet, *Z. villissimus* (nw. Col.)
     Red-billed Tyrannulet, *Z. cinereicapillus* (e. Ecu. and e. Peru; scarce)

Phyllomyias Tyrannulets   Confusing small tyrannulets found mainly on slopes of Andes and in
other highland areas, mostly in canopy and borders of forest and woodland. Resemble *Zimmerius* except
that *most show wing-bars* (obscure in some). Most perch quite horizontally, but tails are usually *not* cocked.
Phylloscartes have longer bills and a different posture. See also Plates 33 and 34.
A. Wing-bars *obscure.*

    9. SOOTY-HEADED TYRANNULET, *P. g. griseiceps* (n. S. Am.)
B. Mainly *se. South America*, with all but Gray-capped having basically *concolor crowns.*

    10. GRAY-CAPPED TYRANNULET, *P. griseocapilla*
    11. PLANALTO TYRANNULET, *P. fasciatus brevirostris*
   Also: Greenish Tyrannulet, *P. virescens*
     Reiser's Tyrannulet, *P. reiseri* (disjunct, cen. Brazil and ne. Venez.)
     Rough-legged Tyrannulet, *P. burmeisteri* (also Andes of Bol. and n. Arg.)
C. Mainly in *northern Andes* with more or less *contrasting gray to dusky crowns.* A few have a dark auricular
 patch like *Phylloscartes.*

    12. SCLATER'S TYRANNULET, *P. s. plumbeiceps* (s. Peru to nw. Arg.)
    13. PLUMBEOUS-CROWNED TYRANNULET, *P. plumbeiceps*
    14. ASHY-HEADED TYRANNULET, *P. cinereiceps*
    15. TAWNY-RUMPED TYRANNULET, *P. uropygialis*
   Also: White-fronted Tyrannulet, *P. zeledoni*
     Black-capped Tyrannulet, *P. nigrocapillus*

Mecocerculus Tyrannulets   Found mainly in Andean forests, with White-throated also on outlying highlands. Typical tyrannulets with a *bold superciliary* (usually) and *wing-bars;* bill relatively slender.
A. Typical *horizontal* posture; usually grayish below, 2 species with white underside of tail.

    16. RUFOUS-WINGED TYRANNULET, *M. calopterus* (w. Ecu, n. Peru)
    17. WHITE-BANDED TYRANNULET, *M. stictopterus taeniopterus*
    18. SULPHUR-BELLIED TYRANNULET, *M. minor*
   Also: White-tailed Tyrannulet, *M. poecilocercus*
     Buff-banded Tyrannulet, *M. hellmayri* (s. Peru to n. Arg.)
B. *Upright* posture; contrasting *white throat.*

    19. WHITE-THROATED TYRANNULET, *M. leucophrys notatus*

32

Stigmatura Wagtail-Tyrants   Distinctive and attractive small flycatchers with *long, graduated, white-*   PAGE 468
tipped tails; the tail is rarely or never actually wagged, but is often *fanned* and held *cocked.* Both species
also have populations in *ne. Brazil.*

     1.   GREATER WAGTAIL-TYRANT, *S. b. budytoides* (mainly chaco)
     Also: Lesser Wagtail-Tyrant, *S. napensis* (mainly Amazon islands)

Inezia Tyrannulets   A small genus of 3 at least superficially diverse tyrannulets, all found in   PAGE 470
semiopen shrubby (*nonforest*) terrain.

     2.   PALE-TIPPED TYRANNULET, *I. subflava caudata* (n. Col. to ne. Brazil)
     Also: Slender-billed Tyrannulet, *I. tenuirostris* (resembles S. Beardless-
         Tyrannulet; ne. Col. and nw. Venez.)
         Plain Tyrannulet, *I. inornata* (resembles 4; n. Bol. to nw. Arg.)

Serpophaga Tyrannulets   Another rather diverse group of tyrannulets, though all are more or   PAGE 472
less *grayish* (not olive) with a *semiconcealed white coronal patch.*
A. More slender species; elongated but flat, blackish crest feathers.   PAGE 472

     3.   WHITE-CRESTED TYRANNULET, *S. s. subcristata* (s. S. Am.)
     4.   WHITE-BELLIED TYRANNULET, *S. munda* (Bol. to w. Arg.)
     5.   RIVER TYRANNULET, *S. h. hypoleuca* (Amaz. river islands)
B. Plumper species with *contrasting black tail.* Both *closely associated with water.*   PAGE 474

     6.   SOOTY TYRANNULET, *S. nigricans* (s. Brazil to n. Arg.)
     Also: Torrent Tyrannulet, *S. cinerea* (paler body; Andean streams)

Polystictus Tachuris   Two very different looking (congeneric?) small tyrannids, Bearded   PAGE 475
occurring locally in less disturbed grasslands, Gray-backed being a rare and local e. Brazil endemic.

     7.   BEARDED TACHURI, *P. p. pectoralis*
     8.   GRAY-BACKED TACHURI, *P. superciliaris*

Culicivora Grass-Tyrants   A very small and distinctive tyrannid; note its *long frayed tail* and   PAGE 477
streaky upperparts. Local in less disturbed tall grass savannas of interior s.-cen. S. Am.

     9.   SHARP-TAILED GRASS-TYRANT, *C. caudacuta*

Euscarthmus Pygmy-Tyrants   PAGE 478
A pair of small, *predominantly brown* flycatchers found in brushy areas and savannas.

     10.   TAWNY-CROWNED PYGMY-TYRANT, *E. m. meloryphus*
     Also: Rufous-sided Pygmy-Tyrant, *E. rufomarginatus* (mainly e. Brazil; rare)

Pseudocolopteryx Doraditos   Four slender, rather plain flycatchers of *marshes* (and sometimes adja-   PAGE 479
cent shrubbery). All are *uniform and often quite bright yellow below,* the head with some brown or blackish.

     11.   WARBLING DORADITO, *P. flaviventris* (s. S. Am.)
     12.   CRESTED DORADITO, *P. sclateri* (also locally north to Trinidad)
     Also: Subtropical Doradito, *P. acutipennis* (also locally north to Col. Andes)
         Dinelli's Doradito, *P. dinellianus* (local, mainly in Arg.)

Tachuris Rush-Tyrants   PAGE 482
Unmistakable with gaudy, *multicolored* plumage, found in *marshes* from Peru to Chile and Arg.

     13.   MANY-COLORED RUSH-TYRANT, *T. r. rubrigastra*

Anairetes Tit-Tyrants   Small flycatchers of scrub and low woodland in the Andes, Patagonia,   PAGE 483
and Chile, most of them easily recognized by their *crests* and/or *streaky* plumage.

     14.   TUFTED TIT-TYRANT, *A. parulus aequatorialis*
     15.   PIED-CRESTED TIT-TYRANT, *A. reguloides albiventris* (w. Peru)
     Also: Yellow-billed Tit-Tyrant, *A. flavirostris* (nearest 14; Peru to Arg.)
         Juan Fernandez Tit-Tyrant, *A. fernandezianus*
         Black-crested Tit-Tyrant, *A. nigrocristatus* (much like 15; n. Peru and
         extreme s. Ecu.)
         Ash-breasted Tit-Tyrant, *A. alpinus* (unstreaked and gray; rare at high
         elevations in Peru and Bol.)

Uromyias Tit-Tyrants   Found locally in high montane forests of Andes from Col. to Peru.   PAGE 487
They differ from *Anairetes* tit-tyrants in their flat crests and longer tails, also in behavior.

     16.   AGILE TIT-TYRANT, *U. agilis* (Col. and Ecu.)
     17.   UNSTREAKED TIT-TYRANT, *U. agraphia* (Peru)

33

PLATE 34: *PHYLLOSCARTES* TYRANNULETS & BRISTLE-TYRANTS, *MIONECTES* FLYCATCHERS, & ALLIES

Capsiempis Tyrannulets   A small, *very yellow* tyrannulet found locally in woodland and edge
(*especially in bamboo*) in tropical lowlands.

        1.   YELLOW TYRANNULET, *C. flaveola amazona*

Phylloscartes Tyrannulets and Bristle-Tyrants
A diverse group of small tyrannulets, united by their *rather long and slender bills* and *fairly long tails*. Many have complex facial patterns which typically include a *grizzled facial area* and a *dark patch on ear-coverts*; none shows a really prominent superciliary (most none at all). They divide into 2 groups:

   1. typical "true" *Phylloscartes* which glean actively in foliage, perch horizontally, and cock their tails;

   2. bristle-tyrants (formerly separated in *Pogonotriccus*), less active and tend to perch vertically.

   All are found exclusively or primarily in humid forest, with most species in foothill, montane, or subtropical areas. They are mostly absent from Amazonia.

A. "True" *Phylloscartes* with *rather weak facial pattern*, but wing-bars *prominent*.

        2.   MOTTLE-CHEEKED TYRANNULET, *P. v. ventralis* (Andes of Peru to n. Arg., and in se. Brazil area)

      Also: Alagoas Tyrannulet, *P. ceciliae* (very local in ne. Brazil)

                Restinga Tyrannulet, *P. kronei* (very local in se. Brazil)

                Olive-green Tyrannulet, *P. virescens* (mainly in Guianas)

                Ecuadorian Tyrannulet, *P. gualaquizae* (Ecu. and n. Peru)

B. "True" *Phylloscartes* with *obvious black or rufous on brow or lores*; all scarce or "range-restricted."

        3.   BLACK-FRONTED TYRANNULET, *P. nigrifrons* (tepuis)

        4.   RUFOUS-LORED TYRANNULET, *P. flaviventris* (n. Venez.; local in Andean foothills of s. Peru and Bol.)

      Also: Rufous-browed Tyrannulet, *P. superciliaris* (local in nw. S. Am.)

                Minas Gerais Tyrannulet, *P. roquettei* (very local in se. Brazil)

C. "True" *Phylloscartes* endemic to se. Brazil region; all with *distinctive facial patterns*, but *no wing-bars*.

        5.   BAY-RINGED TYRANNULET, *P. sylviolus*

        6.   OUSTALET'S TYRANNULET, *P. oustaleti*

        7.   SERRA DO MAR TYRANNULET, *P. difficilis*

      Also: Sao Paulo Tyrannulet, *P. paulistus*

D. Subgenus "*Pogonotriccus*," the bristle-tyrants. All with more upright posture than previous Groups;
   most show *auricular patch* and *gray crown*.

        8.   VARIEGATED BRISTLE-TYRANT, *P. p. poecilotis* (Venez. to Peru)

        9.   MARBLE-FACED BRISTLE-TYRANT, *P. o. ophthalmicus* (n. Venez. to Bol.)

      10.   SPECTACLED BRISTLE-TYRANT, *P. orbitalis* (s. Col. to Bol.)

      11.   SOUTHERN BRISTLE-TYRANT, *P. eximius* (se. Brazil area)

      Also: Chapman's Bristle-Tyrant, *P. chapmani* (tepuis)

                Venezuelan Bristle-Tyrant, *P. venezuelanus* (n. Venez.)

                Antioquia Bristle-Tyrant, *P. lanyoni* (very local in n. Col.)

Leptopogon Flycatchers   Slender and rather long-tailed flycatchers which look much like large
Phylloscartes bristle-tyrants, but with proportionately *even longer bills*. Most have *gray crowns* and (except some races of Slaty-capped) *ochraceous wing-bars*. All perch vertically and frequently wing-lift. All but Sepia-capped range in the *Andes*.

      12.   SEPIA-CAPPED FLYCATCHER, *L. amaurocephalus peruvianus*

      13.   RUFOUS-BREASTED FLYCATCHER, *L. r. rufipectus* (w. Venez. to n. Peru)

      Also: Slaty-capped Flycatcher, *L. superciliaris* (Venez. to Bol.)

                Inca Flycatcher, *L. taczanowskii* (e. Peru)

Mionectes Flycatchers   *Plain*, usually mostly olive flycatchers with slim build and slender bills.
"True" *Mionectes* are quite *streaked* and have a *prominent white postocular spot*; members of the subgenus "*Pipromorpha*" have *lower underparts ochraceous-rufous*. All wing-lift frequently and are found in lower growth of forest and borders, "true" *Mionectes* on or near the Andes from Venez. to Bol., "*Pipromorpha*" in more humid lowlands.

A. "True" *Mionectes*; mainly *dark olive* with *streaking below, white postocular spot*.

      14.   STREAK-NECKED FLYCATCHER, *M. striaticollis poliocephalus*

      Also: Olive-striped Flycatcher, *M. olivaceus*

B. Subgenus "*Pipromorpha*"; *lower underparts ochraceous or rufous*.

      15.   OCHRE-BELLIED FLYCATCHER, *M. oleagineus chloronotus*

      16.   GRAY-HOODED FLYCATCHER, *M. rufiventris* (se. Brazil area)

      Also: McConnell's Flycatcher, *M. macconnelli* (Guianas to Amazonia; like 15)

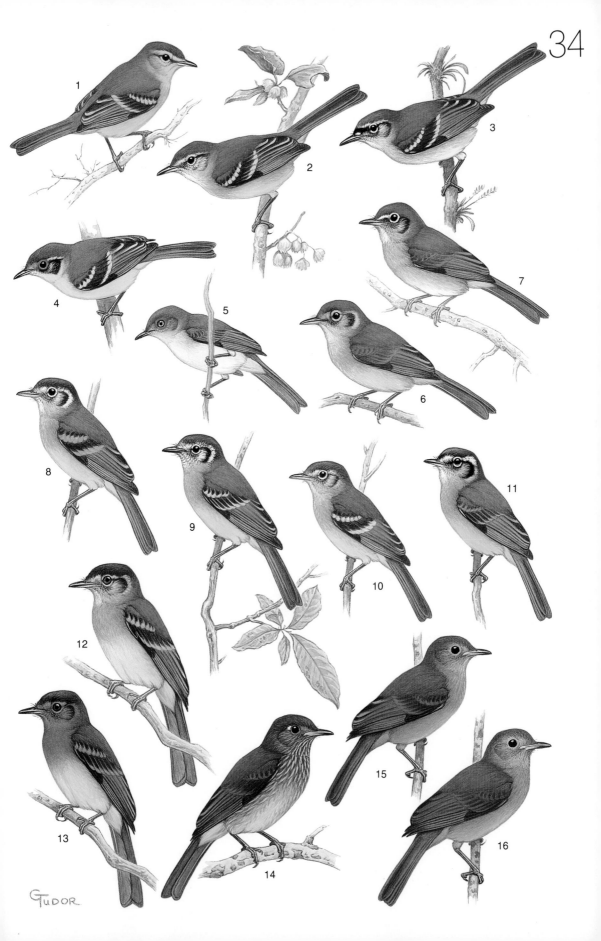

34

Myiornis Pygmy-Tyrants *Tiny* flycatchers found along borders of humid forest, both in tropics and subtropics. *Chunky* and round, with *very short tails* (especially in Short-tailed and Black-capped). PAGE 507

    1.   SHORT-TAILED PYGMY-TYRANT, *M. ecaudatus*
    2.   EARED PYGMY-TYRANT, *M. auricularis* (se. Brazil area)
    Also: Black-capped Pygmy-Tyrant, *M. atricapillus* (w. Col. and nw. Ecu.)
          White-bellied Pygmy-Tyrant, *M. albiventris* (se. Peru and w. Bol.)

Oncostoma Bentbills *Bent-downward bill;* otherwise reminiscent of lowland *Hemitriccus*. PAGE 509

    3.   SOUTHERN BENTBILL, *O. olivaceum* (n. Col.)

Lophotriccus Pygmy-Tyrants Small, predominantly olive flycatchers found in undergrowth of humid forest and woodland. *Broad, flat, transverse crests* with *feathers edged rufous, gray, or olive.* PAGE 510

    4.   SCALE-CRESTED PYGMY-TYRANT, *L. pileatus squamaecristae*
        (mts. from Venez. to Peru)
    5.   DOUBLE-BANDED PYGMY-TYRANT, *L. v. vitiosus*
    Also: Long-crested Pygmy-Tyrant, *L. eulophotes* (locally in sw. Amazonia)
          Helmeted Pygmy-Tyrant, *L. galeatus* (ne. S. Am.)

Atalotriccus Pygmy-Tyrants PAGE 512
Resembles *Lophotriccus,* but *lacking their crests,* and found in dry scrub and low woodland in n. S. Am.

    6.   PALE-EYED PYGMY-TYRANT, *A. pilaris venezuelensis*

Hemitriccus Tody-Tyrants A difficult, obscure group found through much of S. Am., though PAGE 513
many are rare or range-restricted. Compared to *Todirostrum, Hemitriccus* larger, have narrower and less flattened bills, and perch more erectly. Identification difficult, especially in our lowland Group. Watch for *wing pattern* (presence or absence of wing-bars and pale tertial edging), *color and pattern of underparts* (especially the degree of flammulation), *facial pattern* (often buff or rufous is present), and *iris color.* Typically found in lower growth of humid forest and woodland, with only Pearly-vented in drier scrub.

A. *Lowland Group.* Most *flammulated below* to some extent; most with pale iris. PAGE 514
• *Belly whitish;* widespread in drier areas.
    7.   PEARLY-VENTED TODY-TYRANT, *H. margaritaceiventer wucheri*
    Also: Pelzeln's Tody-Tyrant, *H. inornatus* (1 specimen from nw. Brazil)
• *Belly more or less yellowish; Amaz./Guianan lowlands.* Most similar to 9.
    8.   STRIPE-NECKED TODY-TYRANT, *H. s. striaticollis*
    9.   WHITE-EYED TODY-TYRANT, *H. z. zosterops*
    Also: Johannes' Tody-Tyrant, *H. iohannis* (like 8; w. Amazonia)
          Snethlage's Tody-Tyrant, *H. minor* (e. and cen. Amazonia)
          Zimmer's Tody-Tyrant, *H. minimus* (e. Amaz. Brazil and ne. Bol.; rare)
• *Uniform* (not flammulated), with *dark iris.*
    10. BOAT-BILLED TODY-TYRANT, *H. josephinae* (ne. S. Am.; rare)

B. *Montane and e. Brazil groups.* More distinctive than Group A, many showing *buff to ochraceous on face.* PAGE 519
• *Essentially Andean.* Rather divergent in appearance; all but 11 quite *rare.*
    11. BLACK-THROATED TODY-TYRANT, *H. granadensis lehmanni*
    12. BUFF-THROATED TODY-TYRANT, *H. rufigularis* (Ecu. to Bol.)
    Also: Yungas Tody-Tyrant, *H. spodiops* (resembles Group A; only Bol.)
          Cinnamon-breasted Tody-Tyrant, *H. cinnamomeipectus* (recalls 13)
• Confined to *e. Brazil.*
    13. BUFF-BREASTED TODY-TYRANT, *H. mirandae* (rare)
    14. FORK-TAILED TODY-TYRANT, *H. furcatus* (rare)
    15. EYE-RINGED TODY-TYRANT, *H. orbitatus*
    16. HANGNEST TODY-TYRANT, *H. n. nidipendulus*
    Also: Kaempfer's Tody-Tyrant, *H. kaempferi* (very local; much like 13)

C. "True" *Hemitriccus* bamboo-tyrants. Confined to *bamboo thickets;* iris dark. PAGE 524
    17. DRAB-BREASTED BAMBOO-TYRANT, *H. diops* (se. Brazil area)
    18. FLAMMULATED BAMBOO-TYRANT, *H. flammulatus* (sw. Amaz.)
    Also: Brown-breasted Bamboo-Tyrant, *H. obsoletus* (se. Brazil)

Pseudotriccus Pygmy-Tyrants Inconspicuous flycatchers found in undergrowth of Andean forests. PAGE 526
Frequent bill snapping and wing-whirring often draw attention.

    19. BRONZE-OLIVE PYGMY-TYRANT, *P. p. pelzelni* (Col. to Peru)
    20. RUFOUS-HEADED PYGMY-TYRANT, *P. ruficeps* (Col. to Bol.)
    Also: Hazel-fronted Pygmy-Tyrant, *P. simplex* (se. Peru and Bol.; like 19)

35

Todirostrum Tody-Flycatchers   Small flycatchers characterized by their *extremely spatulate bills,* found   PAGE 528
widely through the neotropics. Most range in *lowlands* (only a few exclusively in the subtropics, and none
higher), and most occur basically in *nonforest habitats.* Thus both in overall range and habitats they differ
from the similar *Hemitriccus* tody-tyrants, from which they further can be distinguished by their usually
somewhat *horizontal posture* with *tail held partially cocked.*

A. *T. sylvia* Group. Lacking bright yellow below, but *usually with rusty on face.* Found in *undergrowth,*
   difficult to see. Iris usually dark.   PAGE 529

- *Rusty-cinnamon on face* (extensive to only a trace on loral area).
  1. OCHRE-FACED TODY-FLYCATCHER, *T. p. plumbeiceps*
     (s. S. Am.)
  2. SMOKY-FRONTED TODY-FLYCATCHER, *T. fumifrons* (ne. S. Am.)
  Also: Ruddy-Tody-Flycatcher, *T. russatum* (tepuis)
     Rusty-fronted Tody-Flycatcher, *T. latirostre* (Amazonia to s. Brazil)
     Buff-cheeked Tody-Flycatcher, *T. senex* (1 specimen from w. Amaz. Brazil)

- *Head dark gray without rusty.*
  3. SLATE-HEADED TODY-FLYCATCHER, *T. sylvia griseolum*
     (n. S. Am.)

B. *T. cinereum* Group. *More or less bright yellow below.* More arboreal than Group A.   PAGE 532
- "Typical" of Group, and *common;* usually *pale iris.*
  4. SPOTTED TODY-FLYCATCHER, *T. m. maculatum* (Amazonia)
  5. COMMON TODY-FLYCATCHER, *T. c. cinereum*
  Also: Yellow-lored Tody-Flycatcher, *T. poliocephalum* (se. Brazil)
     Maracaibo Tody-Flycatcher, *T. viridanum* (nw. Venez.)

- *Broad yellow wing-band;* usually *dark iris.* Much *scarcer* than above subgroup.
  6. BLACK-BACKED TODY-FLYCATCHER, *T. pulchellum* (se. Peru)
  Also: Golden-winged Tody-Flycatcher, *T. calopterum* (w. Amazonia; back *olive*)

C. *T. pictum* Group. *Smaller and shorter-tailed* than Group B, all with olive back contrasting with *black*   PAGE 535
   crown.
  7. YELLOW-BROWED TODY-FLYCATCHER, *T. chrysocrotaphum
     neglectum* (Amazonia)
  8. PAINTED TODY-FLYCATCHER, *T. pictum* (ne. S. Am.)
  Also: Black-headed Tody-Flycatcher, *T. nigriceps* (nw. S. Am.)

Poecilotriccus Tody-Tyrants   Plump, *boldly patterned* small flycatchers found in *dense low forest tan-*   PAGE 537
gles (especially *bamboo*) or shrubby clearings (Rufous-crowned). All but Rufous-crowned are *scarce or lo-*
cal. Black-and-white is sexually dimorphic (♀ more like others).
  9. BLACK-AND-WHITE TODY-TYRANT, *P. c. capitalis* (w. Amaz.)
  10. WHITE-CHEEKED TODY-TYRANT, *P. albifacies* (se. Peru)
  11. RUFOUS-CROWNED TODY-TYRANT (Andes, Venez. to Ecu.)
     11a. *P. r. ruficeps*
     11b. *P. ruficeps melanomystax*

Taeniotriccus Tyrants   A *boldly patterned* flycatcher found locally in ne. S. Am. Poorly known,   PAGE 539
probably in forest undergrowth. Note *crest* and *unique wing pattern.*
  12. BLACK-CHESTED TYRANT, *T. andrei*

Corythopis Antpipits   A pair of very distinctive, basically *terrestrial* flycatchers of humid   PAGE 540
forest, where they walk about *pumping their tails.*
  13. RINGED ANTPIPIT, *C. torquata anthoides* (Amazonia)
  Also: Southern Antpipit, *C. delalandi* (se. Brazil area)

Platyrinchus Spadebills   Small, round, short-tailed flycatchers with *extremely wide flat bills,* all   PAGE 542
found *inside humid forest.* All are more or less solitary, and usually hard to see. Mainly in Amazonia.
A. *Relatively simple facial patterns.* Bills average *broader* than next Group.   PAGE 542
  14. WHITE-CRESTED SPADEBILL, *P. platyrhynchos senex*
  15. YELLOW-THROATED SPADEBILL, *P. f. flavigularis* (local in Andes)
  Also: Cinnamon-crested Spadebill, *P. saturatus* (mainly ne. S. Am.)
B. *Bolder, more complex facial patterns.*   PAGE 544
  16. WHITE-THROATED SPADEBILL, *P. mystaceus zamorae* (mostly in
     montane areas)
  17. RUSSET-WINGED SPADEBILL, *P. leucoryphus* (se. Brazil area; rare)
  Also: Golden-crowned Spadebill, *P. coronatus* (mainly Amazonia)

36

Tolmomyias Flycatchers   A group of *wide-billed* flycatchers found in forests and woodland in   PAGE 546
tropical lowlands, mostly remaining rather high in trees. Dull-plumaged and *hard to identify;* pay particular attention to voices and wing pattern. Cf. especially the narrower-billed *Myiopagis* elaenias (Plate 31).

    1.   YELLOW-OLIVE FLYCATCHER, *T. s. sulphurescens*
    2.   GRAY-CROWNED FLYCATCHER, *T. p. poliocephalus* (Amazonia
        to e. Brazil)
    3.   YELLOW-BREASTED FLYCATCHER, *T. f. flaviventris*
  Also: Yellow-margined Flycatcher, *T. assimilis*

Rhynchocyclus Flatbills   These are the *widest-billed* flycatchers. Sombre and basically olive, they   PAGE 550
range *inside humid forest* at lower levels, often accompanying mixed flocks, but with rather stolid behavior.

    4.   OLIVACEOUS FLATBILL, *R. olivaceus aequinoctialis* (lowlands,
        mainly Amazonia to e. Brazil)
    5.   FULVOUS-BREASTED FLATBILL, *R. fulvipectus* (Andes, Venez.
        to Bol.)
  Also: Pacific Flatbill, *R. pacificus* (w. Col. and nw. Ecu.)
        Eye-ringed Flatbill, *R. brevirostris* (nw. Col.)

Ramphotrigon Flatbills   Similar in general aspect to the previous genus (and also with fairly   PAGE 552
wide bills) but with more prominent wing-bars and different facial patterns. Nonetheless, recent evidence
indicates that the 2 genera are not all that closely related. Found in understory of humid lowland forest.

    6.   LARGE-HEADED FLATBILL, *R. m. megacephala* (local from Ama-
        zonia to se. Brazil)
    7.   RUFOUS-TAILED FLATBILL, *R. ruficauda* (Amazonia to
        Guianas)
  Also: Dusky-tailed Flatbill, *R. fuscicauda* (local in w. Amazonia)

Cnipodectes Twistwings   An *essentially dull brown* flycatcher found in lower growth of humid   PAGE 554
forest, the adult ♂ twistwing has unusually twisted outer primaries (hard to see in the field). ♀♀ are
considerably smaller than ♂♂.

    8.   BROWNISH TWISTWING, *C. s. subbrunneus*

Onychorhynchus Flycatchers   *Uniform and brown* the vast majority of the time, the Royal Flycatch-   PAGE 555
er's glory is its *spectacular, highly colored transverse crest.* Unfortunately this is only rarely seen under normal
field conditions, usually being laid flat over the nape, *imparting a distinctive "hammerhead" effect.* Found
in forest and woodland undergrowth in tropical lowlands.

    9.   ROYAL FLYCATCHER
        9a. *O. c. coronatus*
        9b. *O. c. occidentalis* (w. Ecu.; drawn at smaller scale)

Myiotriccus Flycatchers   An exceptionally attractive ("cute") flycatcher found at *edge of Andean*   PAGE 557
forests. Unmistakable on account of *white on face* and *bright yellow rump.* Upright posture.

    10.   ORNATE FLYCATCHER, *M. ornatus phoenicurus*

Myiobius Flycatchers   Easily known by their *lively behavior* in which their *yellow rumps and*   PAGE 558
black tails are conspicuously displayed. *Species-level identification, however, is often difficult* (see text). Found
inside lower growth of humid forest and woodland, often with mixed flocks.

    11.   SULPHUR-RUMPED FLYCATCHER
        11a. *M. b. barbatus*
        11b. *M. barbatus mastacalis* (se. Brazil)
    12.   TAWNY-BREASTED FLYCATCHER, *M. villosus* (Andes, Venez.
        to Bol.)
  Also: Black-tailed Flycatcher, *M. atricaudus*

Terenotriccus Flycatchers   A *small rufescent and gray* flycatcher found inside humid lowland forest   PAGE 561
and woodland; usually common. *Upright posture.*

    13.   RUDDY-TAILED FLYCATCHER, *T. erythrurus signatus*

37

PLATE 38: *MYIOPHOBUS* FLYCATCHERS, PEWEES, ETC.

Pyrrhomyias Flycatchers | *Mainly cinnamon-rufous; forest borders and clearings in Andes.* |
1.   CINNAMON FLYCATCHER, *P. c. cinnamomea*

Myiophobus Flycatchers   A fairly large group of mainly forest-inhabiting flycatchers which superficially resemble *Empidonax*, though all species (at least ♂ ♂) have a brightly colored semiconcealed
coronal patch. Most are dull-colored, more or less olive or brown, usually with *buff to ochraceous wing-bars.*
A.   Solitary, *forest understory* species, all found in the *Andes*. Underparts *yellowish to grayish olive.*
2.   FLAVESCENT FLYCATCHER, *M. flavicans superciliosus*
3.   RORAIMAN FLYCATCHER, *M. r. roraimae* (mainly tepuis)
Also: Orange-crested Flycatcher, *M. phoenicomitra* (local, s. Col. to n. Peru)
Unadorned Flycatcher, *M. inornatus* (s. Peru and Bol.)
B.   Flock-associated, *forest canopy and edge* species in *Andes*. Underparts *clear yellow to ochraceous.*
4.   HANDSOME FLYCATCHER, *M. p. pulcher* (Col. and n. Ecu.)
5.   OCHRACEOUS-BREASTED FLYCATCHER, *M. ochraceiventris*
(Peru and w. Bol.)
Also: Orange-banded Flycatcher, *M. lintoni* (s. Ecu. and n. Peru; local)
C.   In *more open, shrubby habitats* than previous Groups, found in *lowlands*. Underparts *usually streaked.*
6.   BRAN-COLORED FLYCATCHER (comparatively common)
6a. *M. fasciatus auriceps*   6b. *M. fasciatus rufescens* (w. Peru)
Also: Olive-chested Flycatcher, *M. cryptoxanthus* (locally in e. Ecu. and ne. Peru)

Mitrephanes Tufted-Flycatchers   Small pewee-like flycatchers with *short, somewhat bushy crests.*
7.   COMMON TUFTED-FLYCATCHER, *M. phaeocercus berlepschi*
(w. Col. and nw. Ecu.)
Also: Olive Tufted-Flycatcher, *M. olivaceus* (e. Peru and w. Bol.)

Lathrotriccus, Empidonax, and Aphanotriccus Flycatchers
Drab flycatchers with bold wing-bars and (usually) an eye-ring or supraloral, found in forest and woodland lower growth and shrubby areas. Often hard to identify, and the 3 N. Am. migrants can be impossible unless they are vocalizing. Confusion is also possible with other genera, e.g., *Contopus*.
8.   EULER'S FLYCATCHER, *L. euleri bolivianus*
9.   GRAY-BREASTED FLYCATCHER, *L. griseipectus* (w. Ecu. and nw. Peru)
Also: Black-billed Flycatcher, *A. audax* (n. Col.)
"Traill's" (Willow and Alder) Flycatcher, *E. traillii* and *E. alnorum*
Acadian Flycatcher, *E. virescens* (w. Col. and w. Ecu.)

Contopus Pewees and Flycatchers
Drab flycatchers *usually found perched erectly at edge of forest*, hawking insects. They resemble the previous
Group but *never show a complete eye-ring* and have *less well marked wing-bars; tails are proportionately longer.*
Several resident species are *quite uniform*, blackish to olive grayish.
A.   *Smaller* pewees. The wood-pewees are N. Am. migrants resembling Tropical.
10.   BLACKISH PEWEE, *C. nigrescens* (very local in foothills)
11.   TROPICAL PEWEE, *C. cinereus pallescens*
Also: White-throated Pewee, *C. albogularis* (resembles 10; very local in
Guianas and ne. Brazil)
Eastern Wood-Pewee, *C. virens*   Western Wood-Pewee, *C. sordidulus*
B.   *Larger* pewees. May show *conspicuous crest.*
12.   SMOKE-COLORED PEWEE
12a. *C. fumigatus brachyrhynchus* (Bol. and nw. Arg.)
12b. *C. fumigatus ardosiacus* (Venez. to Peru)
Also: Olive-sided Flycatcher, *C. borealis* (N. Am. migrant)

Cnemotriccus Flycatchers   Found in undergrowth in tropical lowlands. *Pale superciliary.*
13.   FUSCOUS FLYCATCHER, *C. f. fuscatus*

Sayornis Phoebes
A distinctive *black and white* flycatcher strongly tied to *Andean streams and rivers.* Often pumps tail.
14.   BLACK PHOEBE, *S. nigricans angustirostris*

Pyrocephalus Flycatchers   Found widely in open areas, ♂ instantly known by *flaming red and*
blackish plumage; ♀ shows some streaking and *usually some red on underparts.*
15.   VERMILION FLYCATCHER
15a. *P. rubinus obscurus*   15b. *P. rubinus obscurus* (dark morph, found in
w. Peru and n. Chile)   15c. *P. rubinus piurae*

NOTE: Figures 12b, 14, 15a, and 15b are drawn to a smaller scale.

38

Colorhamphus Tyrants
A small, *rather gray* flycatcher with *rufous wing-bars* found in *forests of Chile and s. Arg.*
        1.   PATAGONIAN TYRANT, *C. parvirostris*

Ochthoeca and *Silvicultrix* Chat-Tyrants
Attractive midsized flycatchers found *mostly at higher elevations in the Andes.* They occur either in forest
understory or at edge, with some species out into more open, shrubbier terrain. Most show a *long, bold
superciliary* (usually white, in a few species yellow or buff), and many have *prominent rufous wing-bars*
(their extent varying racially in some species). The genus *Silvicultrix* was recently erected for 4 species of
forest understory chat-tyrants.
A. *Smaller* species, favoring *forest undergrowth and edge.*
• *Dark slaty* with short eyebrow; most races with *some chestnut below.*
        2.   SLATY-BACKED CHAT-TYRANT, *O. cinnamomeiventris thoracica*
• *Yellow-olive to ashy gray below;* eyebrow variably yellow to white. *Silvicultrix.*
        3.   YELLOW-BELLIED CHAT-TYRANT, *S. diadema gratiosa*
        4.   CROWNED CHAT-TYRANT, *S. f. frontalis*
      Also: Golden-browed Chat-Tyrant, *S. pulchella* (e. Peru and w. Bol.)
              Jelski's Chat-Tyrant, *S. jelskii* (s. Ecu. and nw. Peru)
• Distinctive *rufous chest* contrasting with pale belly.
        5.   RUFOUS-BREASTED CHAT-TYRANT, *O. rufipectoralis obfuscatus*
B. *Larger* and rangier species (except *O. piurae*), more conspicuous in *semiopen scrub.*
• *Gray underparts;* eyebrow white
        6.   WHITE-BROWED CHAT-TYRANT, *O. leucophrys leucometopa*
      Also: Piura Chat-Tyrant, *O. piurae* (nw. Peru)
• *Rufescent underparts;* eyebrow white to rufous.
        7.   BROWN-BACKED CHAT-TYRANT, *O. fumicolor brunneifrons*
      Also: D'Orbigny's Chat-Tyrant, *O. oenanthoides* (white eyebrow)

Myiotheretes Bush-Tyrants   A group of 4 large flycatchers found in the *Andes,* principally at high
elevations; note that 2 species (Red-rumped and Rufous-webbed) formerly placed in this genus have recently been separated out (see below). Most are fairly conspicuous birds found in forest edge or shrubby
terrain (Smoky found more inside forest). All show *rufous in wing* (prominent in flight). *Throat streaking*
is prominent in most, and all but Smoky have rufous on belly.
A. *Smaller, forest-based* bush-tyrants.
        8.   SMOKY BUSH-TYRANT, *M. f. fumigatus*
      Also: Santa Marta Bush-Tyrant, *M. pernix*
              Rufous-bellied Bush-Tyrant, *M. fuscorufus* (e. Peru and w. Bol.)
B. *Large* bush-tyrant of semiopen areas.
        9.   STREAK-THROATED BUSH-TYRANT, *M. s. striaticollis*

Polioxolmis Bush-Tyrants   Single species of *mainly gray* tyrant with rufous in wings and tail
found high in Andes of (mostly) Peru and Bol., mainly in *Polylepis* woodlands. The genus was recently
separated from *Myiotheretes,* and earlier the species was often placed in *Xolmis.*
        10.   RUFOUS-WEBBED BUSH-TYRANT, *P. r. rufipennis*

Cnemarchus Bush-Tyrants   An attractive and boldly patterned large tyrannid found locally in the
high Andes from Col. to Bol. The genus was recently resplit from *Myiotheretes.*
        11.   RED-RUMPED BUSH-TYRANT, *C. e. erythropygius*

Hirundinea Flycatchers   Easily known by its *long pointed wings* (showing *much rufous in flight*)
and its unusual *cliff habitat* (sometimes using buildings as a replacement). Local across much of S. Am.,
wherever there is appropriate habitat.
        12.   CLIFF FLYCATCHER
              12a. *H. ferruginea bellicosa* (s. S. Am.)
              12b. *H. ferruginea sclateri* (Andes; tepui birds similar)

NOTE: Rufous-webbed Bush-Tyrant (10) and the *sclateri* race of Cliff Flycatcher (12b) are depicted at a
smaller scale.

39

G TUDOR

PLATE 40: SHRIKE-TYRANTS, GROUND-TYRANTS, & ALLIES

Agriornis Shrike-Tyrants   *Large and stout* flycatchers with *heavy and strongly hooked bills,* found in
open areas high in the Andes and in lowlands of Chile and Arg. Relatively drab-colored, with all species
showing some *throat streaking* (usually prominent) and some *white in tail.*

A. *Small* shrike-tyrant. Mainly Argentina.
    1.   LESSER SHRIKE-TYRANT, *A. murina*

B. Typical, *large* shrike-tyrants with *strongly hooked bills.*
• Outer tail feathers *mostly or entirely white.*
    2.   BLACK-BILLED SHRIKE-TYRANT, *A. montana insolens*
    Also: White-tailed Shrike-Tyrant, *A. andicola* (rare)
• Tail mainly dark (*only outer web white*).
    3.   GREAT SHRIKE-TYRANT, *A. livida fortis* (Chile and adjacent Arg.)
    Also: Gray-bellied Shrike-Tyrant, *A. microptera* (mainly Arg. and Bol.)

Ochthornis Water-Tyrants   A small, dull-colored flycatcher found *along rivers in Amazonia.*
Placed here because of superficial similarity to Little Ground-Tyrant, alongside which it is often found.
    4.   DRAB WATER-TYRANT, *O. littoralis*

Muscisaxicola Ground-Tyrants   *Mainly terrestrial* flycatchers found (except for Little) in *open grassy or*
rocky areas of Andes, especially at *high elevations,* south to Tierra del Fuego. Many species are migratory,
some highly so. Plainly colored (predominantly gray to brownish gray), the various species can be difficult to tell apart, particularly as they are often wary and hard to approach. The key features to check are
the *pattern and coloration on the head,* especially the presence or extent of a *white superciliary or supraloral,*
or the presence of *patches or areas of black or some shade of rufous* (varying to yellowish). All have rather
slender black bills, long pointed wings, *contrasting blackish tails with white outer webs,* and long legs. Flight
is markedly swift, graceful, and controlled; upon landing, ground-tyrants habitually flick their wings
and tail.

A. Distinctly *small* ground-tyrants with *rufescent wing-edging* (sometimes shown by immatures of other
   species).
    5.   SPOT-BILLED GROUND-TYRANT, *M. m. maculirostris*
    Also: Little Ground-Tyrant, *M. fluviatilis* (along rivers in Amazonia)

B. Typical ground-tyrants; note *forehead and crown patterns.*
• Crown *uniform,* or progressively *more rufous to rear;* some species with *white superciliary.*
    6.   PLAIN-CAPPED GROUND-TYRANT, *M. alpina grisea* (Col. to
       w. Bol.)
    7.   PUNA GROUND-TYRANT, *M. juninensis* (mainly Peru and Bol.)
    8.   RUFOUS-NAPED GROUND-TYRANT, *M. r. rufivertex*
    Also: Cinereous Ground-Tyrant, *M. cinerea* (mainly Bol. to Arg. and Chile;
       most like 6)
       White-browed Ground-Tyrant, *M. albilora* (s. breeder, migrating to
       Ecu.; most like 7)
• *Large* ground-tyrants, with *forehead broadly white.*
    9.   OCHRE-NAPED GROUND-TYRANT, *M. f. flavinucha* (s. breeder,
       migrating to Peru)
    Also: White-fronted Ground-Tyrant, *M. albifrons* (mainly Peru and Bol.)
• *Forehead or foreface black;* s. breeders, migrating north as far as Peru.
    10.   BLACK-FRONTED GROUND-TYRANT, *M. frontalis*
    11.   CINNAMON-BELLIED GROUND-TYRANT, *M. capistrata*
    12.   DARK-FACED GROUND-TYRANT, *M. m. macloviana*

Muscigralla Field-Tyrants   An odd little flycatcher of *arid sw. Ecu. and w. Peru. Plump* and *very*
short-tailed, with *extremely long legs.*
    13.   SHORT-TAILED FIELD-TYRANT, *M. brevicauda*

Neoxolmis Tyrants   A *large* terrestrial flycatcher of *Patagonian steppes,* migrating north
into the pampas. More *boldly patterned and colored* than any ground-tyrant.
    14.   CHOCOLATE-VENTED TYRANT, *N. rufiventris*

40

GTUDOR

PLATE 41: MONJITAS & SOME OTHER OPEN-COUNTRY TYRANTS

Xolmis and *Heteroxolmis* Monjitas PAGE 609

Striking and fairly large flycatchers found widely in semiopen terrain in s.-cen. and s. S. Am., reaching their highest diversity in Arg. Most are *simply but boldly patterned in white, black, and gray,* the Rusty-backed pair being quite different (rusty dorsally). One species, the Fire-eyed Diucon, was formerly separated in the genus *Pyrope;* another, the Black-and-white, recently had a new genus, *Heteroxolmis,* raised for it. All the monjitas tend to take conspicuous perches, from there dropping to the ground to pursue prey.

A. Pair of monjitas found in *Argentina;* both species with *rusty brown back.* PAGE 609

1. RUSTY-BACKED MONJITA, *X. rubetra*

Also: Salinas Monjita, *X. salinarum* (very local in nw. Arg.; paler)

B. *Typical* monjitas. PAGE 610

2. FIRE-EYED DIUCON, *X. p. pyrope* (Chile and s. Arg.)
3. GRAY MONJITA, *X. c. cinerea* (Brazil to n. Arg.)
4. BLACK-CROWNED MONJITA, *X. coronata* (Arg., migrating a bit northward)
5. WHITE MONJITA, *X. i. irupero* (mainly e. Bol. to cen. Arg.)
6. BLACK-AND-WHITE MONJITA, *H. dominicana* (very local in se. S. Am.)

Also: White-rumped Monjita, *Xolmis velata* (mainly Brazil)

Satrapa Tyrants PAGE 614

A distinctive *dark olive and yellow* tyrannid, widespread but never really common in groves of trees and clearings in s.-cen. S. Am. and Venez.

7. YELLOW-BROWED TYRANT, *S. icterophrys*

Machetornis Tyrants PAGE 615

A *superficially kingbird-like flycatcher, partially terrestrial* in open parts of S. Am. (not in Amazonia). Often associates with grazing animals.

8. CATTLE TYRANT, *M. r. rixosus*

Tumbezia Tyrants PAGE 616

A small, brightly colored flycatcher found only in *lowlands of nw. Peru.* Perhaps most closely related to *Ochthoeca* chat-tyrants (see Plate 39).

9. TUMBES TYRANT, *T. salvini*

Muscipipra Gray Tyrants PAGE 617

An unmistakable sleek, gray and black tyrannid with *a long divided tail. Se. Brazil region.*

10. SHEAR-TAILED GRAY TYRANT, *M. vetula*

Gubernetes Tyrants PAGE 618

An unmistakable and spectacular, *very large* tyrannid with *very long forked tail, bold pectoral collar,* etc. Local in open country, usually near water, in s.-cen. S. Am.

11. STREAMER-TAILED TYRANT, *G. yetapa*

41

GTUDOR

Colonia Tyrants A distinctive, mainly black flycatcher with *contrasting pale crown* and PAGE 619
elongated central tail feathers. Found at edge of humid tropical forest and in clearings, perched high.
      1.   LONG-TAILED TYRANT, *C. c. colonus*

Knipolegus Tyrants and Black-Tyrants PAGE 619
Midsized, often sexually dimorphic flycatchers found mainly in s. S. Am., with outlying species in the
Andes and the Amazon and Orinoco basins. Typical ♂♂ are *basically black or gray,* often with a *pale blue*
bill and sometimes a crest, red iris, or *white wing-stripe* (usually visible only in flight, but then very conspicuous). ♀♀ may simply be duller versions of ♂♂, or (more often) are *browner above* and *streaked below.*
Most *Knipolegus* are found at forest edge or in lighter woodland, but some range out into more open
cerrado habitat (e.g., Crested) or are more restricted to forest understory (e.g., Andean). As a group, they
are strikingly quiet birds; several species do have aerial displays.
A. Sexes similar (*hen-plumaged*). Andes and tepuis. PAGE 620
      2.   RUFOUS-TAILED TYRANT, *K. poecilurus peruanus*
B. "Standard" *Knipolegus:* ♂♂ *ashy gray to shiny black;* ♀♀ either *duller* (1 species) or (more frequently) PAGE 621
    very different, *mottled or streaked below* with variable amount of *rufous at base of tail.*
•   ♂♂ *ashy gray to shiny black.*
      3.   CINEREOUS TYRANT, *K. striaticeps* (chaco region)
      4.   ANDEAN TYRANT, *K. signatus cabanisi* (Andes of Peru to Arg.;
          in n. Peru ♂♂ are black)
      5.   BLUE-BILLED BLACK-TYRANT, *K. cyanirostris* (se. S. Am.)
    Also: Riverside Tyrant, *K. orenocensis* (locally in Amazon and Orinoco
          systems; races either gray or black)
          Amazonian Black-Tyrant, *K. poecilocercus* (locally in Amazon and
          Orinoco systems)
•   ♂♂ *shiny black* with *white wing-stripe.*
      6.   WHITE-WINGED BLACK-TYRANT, *K. a. aterrimus* (♀♀ vary)
    Also: Hudson's Black-Tyrant, *K. hudsoni* (Patagonia to chaco area; scarce)
C. Sexes similar (*cock-plumaged*): *glossy black* with *white in wing;* mainly in s. Brazil. PAGE 627
      7.   VELVETY BLACK-TYRANT, *K. nigerrimus*
      8.   CRESTED BLACK-TYRANT, *K. lophotes*

Hymenops Tyrants Related to *Knipolegus*, also sexually dimorphic, but with *much more* PAGE 628
white in wing (rufous in ♀) and unusual *fleshy yellow wattle around eye.* Marshy areas in s. S. Am.
      9.   SPECTACLED TYRANT, *H. p. perspicillatus*

Lessonia Negritos A pair of small, basically terrestrial flycatchers found in *open areas near* PAGE 629
water. Genus distinctive (♂♂ unique), but distinguishing the 2 species is often not easy.
      10.   AUSTRAL NEGRITO, *L. rufa* (s. S. Am.)
    Also: Andean Negrito, *L. oreas* (Andes of Peru to n. Chile and n. Arg.)

Fluvicola Water-Tyrants A pert, attractive trio of *boldly patterned* tyrannids, found *near water* PAGE 631
across much of tropical S. Am. Unlike the next genus, *these forage mostly on ground.*
      11.   BLACK-BACKED WATER-TYRANT, *F. albiventer* (Arg. to Amaz.)
      12.   MASKED WATER-TYRANT, *F. n. nengeta* (w. Ecu. and nw. Peru,
          and e. Brazil)
    Also: Pied Water-Tyrant, *F. pica* (n. S. Am.; like 11)

Arundinicola Marsh-Tyrants Single species favoring *shrubbery near water* in tropical lowlands, with PAGE 633
white-headed ♂ unmistakable and conspicuous. Plumper than previous genus, perching more upright.
      13.   WHITE-HEADED MARSH-TYRANT, *A. leucocephala*

Alectrurus Tryants A splendid pair of bizarre and boldly patterned flycatchers found very PAGE 633
locally in *s. grasslands.* Males have *spectacularly modified tails* (among the oddest of all S. Am. birds): in
Cock-tailed *compressed into a vertically oriented fan shape,* and in Strange-tailed there are *2 broad pennants*
which protrude far beyond the rest of tail. ♀♀ are mottled brown and buffy, Strange-tailed with rudimentary pennants.
      14.   COCK-TAILED TYRANT, *A. tricolor*
      15.   STRANGE-TAILED TYRANT, *A. risora* (breeding)

42

1♂ 2 3♂ 4♂ 5♀ 5♂ 6♂ 6♀ 7♀ 8 9♂ 9♀ 10♂ 10♀ 11 12 13♂ 14♂ 14♀ 15♂

TUDOR

Attila Attilas — Fairly large, bulky tyrannids (formerly classified as cotingas) marked   PAGE 636
by their *heavy, straight, prominently hooked bills*. Most are *more or less rufescent* (the major exception being
the widespread but variable Bright-rumped, which is usually olive but can be more gray or rufous), and
all show at least a somewhat paler rump. Found widely in lowland or foothill forests and woodlands, but
generally inconspicuous aside from their far-carrying calls.

A. *Head more or less contrastingly gray.*   PAGE 636

    1.   RUFOUS-TAILED ATTILA, *A. phoenicurus* (se. Brazil to Amazonia)

    2.   GRAY-HOODED ATTILA, *A. r. rufus* (se. Brazil)

    Also: Citron-bellied Attila, *A. citriniventris* (upper Amazonia; scarce)

B. Head and back rather *uniform.*   PAGE 638

    3.   CINNAMON ATTILA, *A. cinnamomeus* (Amazonia to Guianas)

    4.   WHITE-EYED ATTILA, *A. bolivianus nattereri* (Amazonia)

    5.   BRIGHT-RUMPED ATTILA, *A. s. spadiceus*

    Also: Ochraceous Attila, *A. torridus* (w. Ecu.; recalls 3)

Casiornis — More delicately built than other flycatchers on this plate, the 2 *Casior-*   PAGE 641
nis also have relatively slight bills. In other respects, however, they resemble *Myiarchus*, though less vocal
and *more predominantly rufous*. Crown feathers are often raised.

    6.   RUFOUS CASIORNIS, *C. rufa* (s.-cen. S. Am.)

    7.   ASH-THROATED CASIORNIS, *C. fusca* (ne. Brazil)

Rhytipterna Mourners — A confusing genus: note that Grayish and Rufous Mourners look   PAGE 642
remarkably like 2 pihas (Screaming and Rufous), whereas Pale-bellied closely resembles a *Myiarchus*
flycatcher—actually, none of the 3 *Rhytipterna* species look much like each other!

    8.   GRAYISH MOURNER, *R. simplex frederici* (Amaz. forests)

    9.   PALE-BELLIED MOURNER, *R. immunda* (local in Amaz.
savannas)

    Also: Rufous Mourner, *R. holerythra* (w. Col. and nw. Ecu.)

Myiarchus Flycatchers — A widespread and *exceptionally confusing* group of flycatchers. The ge-   PAGE 645
nus itself is quite recognizable: all are midsized to fairly large flycatchers, some shade of olivaceous above,
often with *darker crown* (and crown feathers are often raised into a *bushy crest*), some species with *rufous
or pale edging or tipping on tail feathers*; throat and breast are pale gray, contrasting with pale yellow underparts. Identifying to species level is usually hard, sometimes impossible. *Voice, habitat*, and *range* are often
more helpful than appearance; see text for details. As a group they are widespread in semiopen wooded
areas (a few in canopy of more or less continuous forest, others in more open arid regions), primarily in
the lowlands, a few up into the Andes. Although typically not very conspicuous, *Myiarchus* flycatchers do
vocalize quite a bit, and attention is thus often drawn to them.

A. The only mostly *rufous Myiarchus.*   PAGE 645

    10.   RUFOUS FLYCATCHER, *M. semirufus* (nw. Peru)

B. Conspicuous *rufous in tail*; somewhat larger.   PAGE 646

    11.   BROWN-CRESTED FLYCATCHER, *M. t. tyrannulus*

    Also: Great Crested Flycatcher, *M. crinitus* (N. Am. migrant to nw. S. Am.)

C. "Typical" *Myiarchus*; many species *extremely similar.*   PAGE 647

    12.   SWAINSON'S FLYCATCHER, *M. swainsoni pelzelni*

    13.   SHORT-CRESTED FLYCATCHER, *M. f. ferox*

    14.   SOOTY-CROWNED FLYCATCHER, *M. phaeocephalus* (w. Ecu.
and nw. Peru)

    Also: Venezuelan Flycatcher, *M. venezuelensis* (n. Venez. and ne. Col.)

        Panama Flycatcher, *M. panamensis* (w. Col. and nw. Venez.)

        Pale-edged Flycatcher, *M. cephalotes* (Andes south to Bol.)

        Apical Flycatcher, *M. apicalis* (w. Col.)

        Dusky-capped Flycatcher, *M. tuberculifer* (widespread; most races
smaller than usual *Myiarchus*)

Sirystes — Patterned rather like a *Myiarchus* but in *shades of white and gray* (no   PAGE 653
yellow), with black crown, wings, and tail (wings and tail with some white). Behavior and voice also
recall *Myiarchus*. Canopy of humid lowland forest.

    15.   SIRYSTES, *S. sibilator subcanescens*

43

Megarynchus Flycatchers   Large flycatcher with *massive bill*. Widespread in lowlands.   PAGE 654

    1.   BOAT-BILLED FLYCATCHER, *M. p. pitangua*

Pitangus and *Philohydor* Kiskadees   *Boldly black-and-white-striped heads,* mostly bright yellow under-   PAGE 655
parts. Great conspicuous and vociferous, whereas Lesser more retiring and *found only near water.* Widespread in lowlands.

    2.   GREAT KISKADEE, *Pitangus s. sulphuratus*

    3.   LESSER KISKADEE, *Philohydor l. lictor*

Phelpsia and *Myiozetetes* Flycatchers   Midsized flycatchers, all with *rather short bills;* plumage pat-   PAGE 656
terns differ, varying from the classic "kiskadee pattern" to duller birds lacking head striping. Noisy, conspicuous birds found mainly in clearings and edge situations, some often near water.

A. Larger, with *clear yellow underparts.*   PAGE 657

• Crown and cheeks *black,* back *browner.*

    4.   WHITE-BEARDED FLYCATCHER, *P. inornata* (Venez.)

    Also: Rusty-margined Flycatcher, *M. cayanensis*

• Crown and cheeks *dark gray,* back *more olive.*

    5.   SOCIAL FLYCATCHER, *M. s. similis*

    Also: Gray-capped Flycatcher, *M. granadensis;* (head pattern reduced)

B. *Small; no* head pattern, chest streaky.   PAGE 660

    6.   DUSKY-CHESTED FLYCATCHER, *M. l. luteiventris*

Conopias Flycatchers   Resemble typical *Myiozetetes* but with *proportionately longer bills.* They   PAGE 660
also have different nesting behavior and are *much more forest-based birds.* None are common.

    7.   THREE-STRIPED FLYCATCHER, *C. t. trivirgata* (locally in Ama-
          zonia, se. Brazil region)

    8.   LEMON-BROWED FLYCATCHER, *C. c. cinchoneti* (locally in Andes)

    Also: White-ringed Flycatcher, *C. albovittata* (w. Col. and nw. Ecu.)

            Yellow-throated Flycatcher, *C. parva* (local, mainly ne. S. Am.)

Myiodynastes Flycatchers   Fairly large flycatchers with stout bills; all but Baird's show a *bold dark*   PAGE 663
malar streak, and all but 1 subspecies of Streaked have *tails mainly rufous.* Conspicuous and noisy birds,
found mainly in lightly wooded or edge situations; second pair migratory.

A. *Indistinct* chest streaking, *some buff on throat or chest.*   PAGE 663

    9.   BAIRD'S FLYCATCHER, *M. bairdii* (sw. Ecu. and nw. Peru)

    Also: Golden-crowned Flycatcher, *M. chrysocephalus* (Andes)

B. *Heavily streaked throughout.*   PAGE 665

    10.   STREAKED FLYCATCHER, *M. m. maculatus*

    Also: Sulphur-bellied Flycatcher, *M. luteiventris* (N. Am. migrant to Amaz.)

Legatus Flycatchers   Rather small flycatcher with streaky underparts, *stubby bill,* and dusky   PAGE 666
(*not rufous*) tail. Wide-ranging in tropical lowlands, often near oropendola or cacique colonies.

    11.   PIRATIC FLYCATCHER, *L. l. leucophaius*

Empidonomus and *Griseotyrannus* Flycatchers   PAGE 667
A pair of flycatchers (genera recently split), dissimilar in appearance though much alike in behavior and
voice. Both are found in lightly wooded or edge situations and are highly migratory.

    12.   CROWNED SLATY FLYCATCHER, *G. a. aurantioatrocristatus*

    Also: Variegated Flycatcher, *E. varius* (plumage much like Piratic)

Tyrannopsis Flycatchers   *Dull-looking,* with *short bill and tail.* Favors *Mauritia* palms.   PAGE 669

    13.   SULPHURY FLYCATCHER, *T. sulphurea* (local in Amazonia)

Tyrannus Kingbirds and Flycatchers   Fairly large flycatchers, the kingbirds are *familiar and*   PAGE 670
conspicuous birds of semiopen and open terrain. All are to some extent migratory.

A. "Typical" neotropical kingbirds; note *largish bills, dark ear-coverts.*   PAGE 670

• Back *olivaceous.*

    14.   TROPICAL KINGBIRD, *T. m. melancholicus*

    Also: White-throated Kingbird, *T. albogularis* (Brazil to Amazonia)

• Back *grayer,* like crown.

    15.   SNOWY-THROATED KINGBIRD, *T. niveigularis* (mainly w. Ecu.)

    Also: Gray Kingbird, *T. dominicensis* (n. S. Am.; belly white)

B. Smaller bill and "*black-capped;*" Fork-tailed with *tail streamers.*   PAGE 673

    16.   FORK-TAILED FLYCATCHER, *T. s. savana* (much smaller scale)

    Also: Eastern Kingbird, *T. tyrannus* (N. Am. migrant mainly to Amazonia)

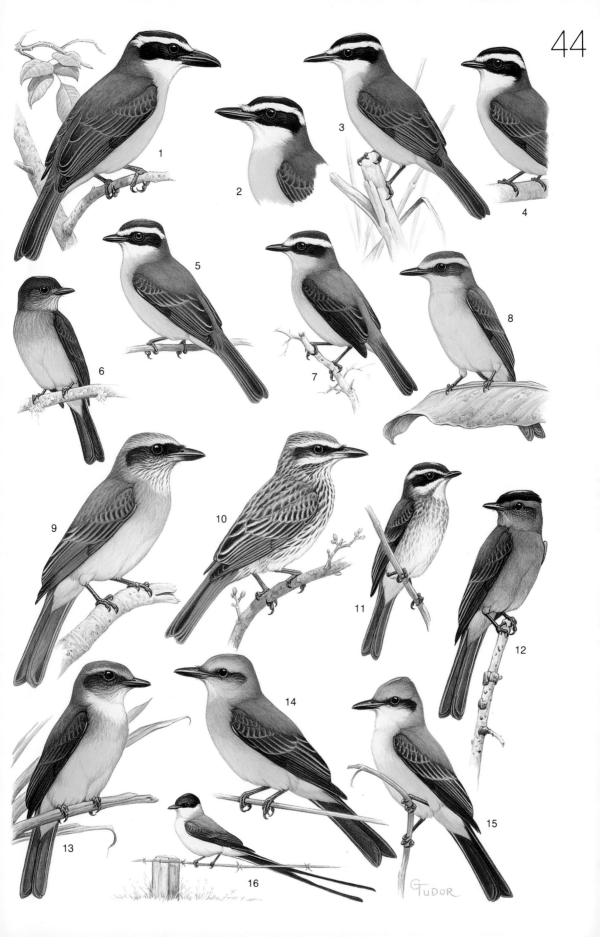

44

TUDOR

Xenopsaris Resembles a slender small becard (especially ♂ Cinereous) but with PAGE 675
sexes alike; immature has crown brown. Very local in riparian areas and lighter woodland.
> 1. XENOPSARIS, *X. a. albinucha*

Pachyramphus Becards Arboreal birds found widely through the neotropics, becards have PAGE 676
broad and somewhat hooked bills (stouter in the *Platypsaris* subgenus) and rather subdued coloration and
simple patterns. They look *large-headed,* and some species often raise their crown feathers into a *rounded
bushy crest.* They tend to forage quietly in foliage and are not overly conspicuous birds, though their oft-
repeated, usually melodic songs do often attract attention.

A. *Distinctive* becards (not necessarily closely related). PAGE 676
- *Bright olive back* and/or *yellowish face;* ♀ ♀ lack black crown but have chestnut shoulders.
> 2. GREEN-BACKED BECARD, *P. v. viridis* (s. and e. S. Am.)
> 3. YELLOW-CHEEKED BECARD, *P. xanthogenys* (e. slope of Andes
>   in Ecu. and Peru)
> 4. BARRED BECARD, *P. v. versicolor* (Andes)
- *Both* sexes unique; rare and local in ne. S. Am.
> 5. GLOSSY-BACKED BECARD, *P. surinamus*

B. *"Typical"* becards; most ♂ ♂ gray, black, and white; ♀ ♀ usually very different. PAGE 679
- Wing and tail-tips *boldly marked with white* (♂ ♂) or ochraceous (♀ ♀).
> 6. WHITE-WINGED BECARD, *P. polychopterus nigriventris* (a dark
>   race; other ssp. paler)
> 7. BLACK-CAPPED BECARD, *P. m. marginatus* (mainly Amazonia)
> *Also:* Black-and-white Becard, *P. albogriseus* (nw. S. Am.)
- Wings and tail *only edged* white; ♀ ♀ *cinnamon-rufous.*
> 8. SLATY BECARD, *P. spodiurus* (mainly w. Ecu.)
> *Also:* Cinereous Becard, *P. rufus* (Amazonia northward)
- *Both* sexes *cinnamon-rufous.*
> 9. CHESTNUT-CROWNED BECARD, *P. c. castaneus*
> *Also:* Cinnamon Becard, *P. cinnamomeus* (nw. S. Am.)

C. *Platypsaris* subgenus; larger, more *bull-headed* and *stout-billed.* ♂ ♂ gray to slaty; ♀ ♀ vary from *all* PAGE 683
rufous to having *crown and back gray.*
> 10. CRESTED BECARD, *P. v. validus* (s. S. Am.)
> 11. PINK-THROATED BECARD, *P. minor* (Amazonia)
> *Also:* One-colored Becard, *P. homochrous* (nw. S. Am.)

Tityra Tityras A trio of wide-ranging and quite conspicuous arboreal birds, nesting PAGE 686
in holes in snags; all are bull-headed, thick-billed, and short-tailed. Crisp-looking ♂ ♂ are *pearly gray and
black;* ♀ ♀ are *dingier and often browner* (well-streaked in Black-tailed). The 2 larger species have *pinkish
red orbital areas and basal bills.*
> 12. BLACK-CROWNED TITYRA, *T. inquisitor pelzelni*
> 13. BLACK-TAILED TITYRA, *T. c. cayana*
> *Also:* Masked Tityra, *T. semifasciata* (most like 13)

45

Sapayoa   PAGE 689
An obscure *olive* bird of humid forests in *w. Col. and nw. Ecu.* Not a true manakin.
              1.   BROAD-BILLED SAPAYOA, *Sapayoa aenigma*

Schiffornis Mourners   Three obscure birds which inhabit humid forest undergrowth in low-   PAGE 690
lands and foothills, best known from their *loud whistled songs.* Sexes are alike. Not true manakins.
              2.   THRUSH-LIKE MOURNER, *S. turdinus amazonus*
              3.   VARZEA MOURNER, *S. major* (várzea forests in Amazonia)
        Also: Greenish Mourner, *S. virescens* (se. Brazil area)

Tyranneutes Tyrant-Manakins   A pair of plain and *very small* birds found inside Amaz. and Guianan   PAGE 693
forests; not true manakins. Sexes alike. Best known from ♂ ♂' *interminably repeated songs.*
              4.   DWARF TYRANT-MANAKIN, *T. stolzmanni*
        Also: Tiny Tyrant-Manakin, *T. virescens* (ne. S. Am.)

Neopelma Tyrant-Manakins   *Plain* forest or woodland-inhabiting birds, with allopatric ranges.   PAGE 694
Larger than preceding, they resemble certain elaenias (especially *Myiopagis*), and like them have yellow
coronal patches, but note *plain wings.* Sexes alike. Inconspicuous, best known from ♂ ♂' vocalizations.
              5.   PALE-BELLIED TYRANT-MANAKIN, *N. pallescens* (e. Brazil)
              6.   SULPHUR-BELLIED TYRANT-MANAKIN, *N. sulphureiventer*
                  (sw. Amazonia)
        Also: Wied's Tyrant-Manakin, *N. aurifrons* (se. Brazil)
                  Saffron-crested Tyrant-Manakin, *N. chrysocephalum* (ne. S. Am.)

Neopipo Tyrant-Manakins   Found locally in Amazonia, little known and apparently rare. Not a   PAGE 697
true manakin. Sexes alike. *Looks incredibly like the more common Ruddy-tailed Flycatcher* (Plate 37).
              7.   CINNAMON TYRANT-MANAKIN, *N. cinnamomea*

Piprites   A pair of distinctive but dissimilar birds of uncertain affinities, long   PAGE 698
thought to be (and called) manakins. Found in *canopy of humid forest,* often with mixed flocks.
              8.   WING-BARRED PIPRITES, *P. chloris tschudii*
              9.   BLACK-CAPPED PIPRITES, *P. pileatus* (se. Brazil area)

Heterocercus Manakins   Three closely related, *large,* and *chunky* manakins with characteristic   PAGE 700
silvery white gorgets (*gray* in ♀ ♀). All favor *woodland near water,* with allopatric ranges in Amazonia.
             10.   FLAME-CRESTED MANAKIN, *H. linteatus* (Amaz. Brazil)
             11.   YELLOW-CRESTED MANAKIN, *H. flavivertex* (ne. S. Am.)
        Also: Orange-crested Manakin, *H. aurantiivertex* (e. Ecu. and ne. Peru)

Chloropipo Manakins   Rather long-tailed manakins found in understory of humid forests,   PAGE 702
mainly in *montane or foothill areas.* All are inconspicuous and quiet birds, not often encountered.
A. Sexes *similar;* dull green to olive.   PAGE 702
             12.   GREEN MANAKIN, *C. h. holochlora* (Col. to e. Peru)
        Also: Olive Manakin, *C. uniformis* (tepuis)
B. Sexes *differ;* both species with white underwing.   PAGE 703
             13.   YELLOW-HEADED MANAKIN, *C. flavicapilla* (Andes of Col.)
             14.   JET MANAKIN, *C. unicolor* (Ecu. and Peru; ♂ like 15)

Xenopipo Manakins   *All black* manakin found in *woodlands of savanna regions of ne. S. Am.*   PAGE 705
             15.   BLACK MANAKIN, *X. atronitens* (♀ much like 14)

·*Chiroxiphia* Manakins   Fairly large manakins, ♂ ♂ of all species with *contrasting blue backs.*   PAGE 705
Orange to flesh-colored legs in both sexes. Allopatric inside forest and woodland, mainly in lowlands.
A. "Typical" *Chiroxiphia* (underparts black).   PAGE 706
             16.   BLUE-BACKED MANAKIN, *C. p. pareola* (1 race has yellow crown)
        Also: Yungas Manakin, *C. boliviana* (e. slope of Andes in s. Peru and Bol.)
                  Lance-tailed Manakin, *C. lanceolata* (n. Col. and n. Venez.)
B. *Larger and much bluer;* se. South America.   PAGE 708
             17.   BLUE MANAKIN, *C. caudata*

Antilophia Manakins   *Frontal crest* of both sexes unique. *Gallery forests of interior Brazil.*   PAGE 709
             18.   HELMETED MANAKIN, *A. galeata*

46

1♂ 2 3 4 5 6 7♂ 8 9♂ 10♀ 10♂ 11♂ 12 13♂ 14♀ 15♂ 16♂ 16♀ 17♂ 18♂ 18♀

TUDOR

Manacus Manakins   ♂♂ *boldly patterned with white or yellow collar and throat;* ♀♀ much
duller, olive like so many other ♀ manakins but with *bright orange legs.*
         1.   WHITE-BEARDED MANAKIN, *M. m. manacus*
       Also: Golden-collared Manakin, *M. vitellinus* (w. Col.)

Ilicura Manakins   A distinctive genus endemic to montane forests of se. Brazil. *Colorful*
and ornately patterned ♂ unmistakable; ♀ has *gray face, orange eye,* and *pointed tail.*
         2.   PIN-TAILED MANAKIN, *I. militaris*

Corapipo Manakins   Pair of manakins occurring locally in humid forests of n. S. Am. ♂♂
have contrasting *white throats;* ♀♀ more *grayish or whitish below* than ♀ *Pipra* manakins.
         3.   WHITE-THROATED MANAKIN, *C. gutturalis* (ne. S. Am.)
       Also: White-ruffed Manakin, *C. leucorrhoa* (nw. S. Am.; local)

Masius Manakins   Monotypic genus found in *Andean forests* (at *higher elevations* than
most other manakins). ♂ with *yellow on crown, throat,* and *wing,* ♀ with *yellow chin patch.*
         4.   GOLDEN-WINGED MANAKIN, *M. c. chrysopterus*

Machaeropterus Manakins   Trio of small manakins found mainly in lowland forests, to a lesser ex-
tent (especially Club-winged) in foothills. Coloration and pattern diverse, 2 species showing *streaked effect*
below, blurry in ♀♀.
         5.   STRIPED MANAKIN, *M. regulus striolatus*
         6.   FIERY-CAPPED MANAKIN, *M. p. pyrocephalus*
         7.   CLUB-WINGED MANAKIN, *M. deliciosus* (w. Col. and w. Ecu.)

Pipra Manakins   Small manakins found mainly in humid lowland forests, a few species
on e. slope of Andes in foothills and subtropical zone (these mainly in first subset of Group A). ♂♂ are
boldly patterned, brightly colored, and easily recognizable, especially because *for the most part all species within*
each of our Groups have allopatric ranges. ♀♀ are much duller and more difficult, but *differences between*
Groups are basically consistent, and thus ♀♀ can usually be identified by *range.*
A. *"Crowned"* Group: *small.* ♂♂ typically have *blue or white crown patches,* and often *rumps* as well; ♀♀
     united by *viridian green upperparts.*
-   ♂♂ usually *black;* iris *dark.*
         8.   BLUE-CROWNED MANAKIN
           8a. *P. c. coronata*
           8b. *P. coronata exquisita*
         9.   BLUE-RUMPED MANAKIN, *P. i. isidorei* (e. slope of Andes, Col.
            to n. Peru)
       10.   WHITE-FRONTED MANAKIN, *P. s. serena* (ne. S. Am.)
       Also: Cerulean-capped Manakin, *P. coeruleocapilla* (e. slope of Andes, cen.
            and s. Peru)
            Orange-bellied Manakin, *P. suavissima* (tepuis; like 10)
-   ♂♂ mainly *green;* iris *light.* All in *Amaz. Brazil.*
       11.   SNOW-CAPPED MANAKIN, *P. n. nattereri*
       12.   OPAL-CROWNED MANAKIN
           12a. *P. i. iris*   12b. *P. iris eucephala*
       Also: Golden-crowned Manakin, *P. vilasboasi* in (s. Pará, Brazil)
B. ♂ *all black with extensive white crown;* ♀ with *gray crown* (especially westward). *Iris red.*
       13.   WHITE-CROWNED MANAKIN, *P. pipra comata*
C. ♂♂ with *golden to scarlet heads,* and usually a white iris; ♀♀ *dull olive above.*
       14.   GOLDEN-HEADED MANAKIN, *P. e. erythrocephala* (north of
            Amazon)
       15.   ROUND-TAILED MANAKIN, *P. chloromeros* (e. Peru and n. Bol.)
       16.   SCARLET-HORNED MANAKIN, *P. cornuta* (tepuis)
       Also: Red-headed Manakin, *P. rubrocapilla* (south of Amazon)
            Red-capped Manakin, *P. mentalis* (w. Col. and w. Ecu.)
D. ♂♂ differ from Group C in their *"hooded"* effect, with *yellow and/or red extending from face to belly;*
     ♀♀ *brighter yellow below.* The *P. aureola* superspecies.
       17.   WIRE-TAILED MANAKIN, *P. filicauda* (nw. Amazonia and Venez.)
       18.   BAND-TAILED MANAKIN, *P. fasciicauda scarlatina* (south of
            Amazon)
       Also: Crimson-hooded Manakin, *P. aureola* (locally in ne. S. Am.)

47

Oxyruncus Sharpbills   A single species of uncertain affinities, often considered a monotypic family but here considered a cotinga, the Sharpbill ranges *very locally* in humid forests, especially in lower montane areas. Distinctive are its *sharply pointed bill* and *conspicuously scaled and spotted face and underparts*. Races vary in amount of yellow below.   PAGE 731

1.   SHARPBILL, *O. c. cristatus* (tepuis; lower Amaz. Brazil; se. Brazil to Par.; e. Peru and w. Bol.)

Phytotoma Plantcutters   A group of 3 closely related *stubby-billed* species, the plantcutters are found in s. S. Am., favoring low woodland and semiopen areas; their ranges are nonoverlapping. They once comprised their own family but are now considered cotingas. ♂♂ are *attractively patterned in gray, black, and rufous*; ♀♀ are *conspicuously streaked* but retain the *distinctive tail patterns* of their respective mates.   PAGE 732

A. Undertail dark gray *tipped white*.   PAGE 733

2.   WHITE-TIPPED PLANTCUTTER, *P. r. rutila* (Bol. to cen. Arg.)
Also: Peruvian Plantcutter, *P. raimondii* (local in nw. Peru)

B. Undertail *rufous tipped blackish*.   PAGE 734

3.   RUFOUS-TAILED PLANTCUTTER, *P. rara* (Chile and s. Arg.)

Iodopleura Purpletufts   Rather scarce *little* cotingas ranging in canopy and borders of humid lowland forest, the purpletufts can be known by their characteristic silhouette (*stubby bill, short tail, long wings*) as they perch on prominent high branches, looking vaguely swallow-like. The *pectoral tuft* for which the genus is named is usually inconspicuous and in ♀♀ is white or vestigial.   PAGE 735

A. Larger; *sooty and white pattern*.   PAGE 735

4.   WHITE-BROWED PURPLETUFT, *I. isabellae* (Amazonia).
Also: Dusky Purpletuft, *I. fusca* (ne. S. Am.; *no* white on face)

B. *Smaller* and grayer; rare in e. Brazil.   PAGE 736

5.   BUFF-THROATED PURPLETUFT, *I. p. pipra*

Calyptura Calypturas   The *smallest* cotinga. A bizarre little bird, endemic to *se.* Brazil, bearing a remarkable resemblance to holarctic kinglets (*Regulus* spp.). Should be easily recognized if it is ever seen again—the species has not been found since the 19th century and could be *extinct*.   PAGE 737

6.   KINGLET CALYPTURA, *C. cristata*

Laniisoma Mourners   A monotypic genus apparently most closely related to the *Laniocera* mourners (see Plate 51). Elegant Mourner (formerly the Shrike-like Cotinga, though hardly "shrike-like") is a rarely encountered bird of humid forest found locally on e. slope of Andes and in se. Brazil. Races vary in amount of *ventral barring* and in color of ♀'s crown; immatures show *rufous tipping on wing-coverts*.   PAGE 738

7.   ELEGANT MOURNER
7a. *L. e. elegans* (se. Brazil)
7b. *L. e. buckleyi* (Andes; immature)

Phibalura Cotingas   The *boldly patterned* Swallow-tailed Cotinga differs from all other cotingas in the shape of its *deeply forked tail*. ♀ has grayer head and is more scaled below. It is not a true forest bird (unlike so many other cotingas), being found locally in clearings and forest borders mainly in *se. Brazil* region.   PAGE 739

8.   SWALLOW-TAILED COTINGA, *P. f. flavirostris*

Carpornis Berryeaters   The 2 berryeaters are restricted to the interior of humid forest in *e. Brazil*, where they are inconspicuous aside from their *distinctive loud calls*. ♀♀ have olive heads, but their overall patterns resemble ♂♂'.   PAGE 740

9.   HOODED BERRYEATER, *C. cucullatus*
10.   BLACK-HEADED BERRYEATER, *C. melanocephalus*

Ampelion Cotingas   A distinctive pair of easily recognized, midsized cotingas found in the   PAGE 741
Andes. Sexes are alike, and both species have *reddish nuchal crests* which are expandable laterally and can
be spectacular. They are conspicuous birds which often perch in the open, but Chestnut-crested is scarce.
> 1.   RED-CRESTED COTINGA, *A. rubrocristatus*
> 2.   CHESTNUT-CRESTED COTINGA, *A. r. rufaxilla*

Zaratornis and *Doliornis* Cotingas   PAGE 742
A pair of cotingas, both found at high elevations in the Andes of *Peru*. They resemble the more numerous
and widespread *Ampelion* cotingas.
> 3.   WHITE-CHEEKED COTINGA, *Z. stresemanni* (local in w. Peru)
> *Also:*   Bay-vented Cotinga, *D. sclateri* (very local in e. Peru)

Ampelioides Fruiteaters   A monotypic genus, somewhat like *Pipreola*, but even stouter, with   PAGE 744
heavy bill and short tail. Its *bold scalloped pattern* is unique; ♀ has blacker scalloping below, olive crown.
Found locally in humid Andean forests, principally in lower subtropics.
> 4.   SCALED FRUITEATER, *A. tschudii*

Pipreola Fruiteaters   A fine group of *brightly colored* and *boldly patterned* cotingas found   PAGE 744
mainly in the Andes (a single divergent species on the tepuis). Distinctive is their *plump shape,* with short-
ish tail and vertical posture (reminiscent of a trogon). So, too, are their colored soft parts: *the bill is always
some shade of red in* ♂♂ (and some ♀♀), iris is often pale, and legs are often red or orange. All but the
tepui endemic are *predominantly some shade of green (often bright)*, ♂♂ with either *black on head* or with
golden to red on chest; ♀♀ are more *barred or streaked below*. Note that similar ♂ patterns can crop up in
unrelated species Groups. Although colorful, fruiteaters are usually inconspicuous birds, with quiet demeanor and slow movements; further, they tend to remain inside forest and rarely or never perch in exposed sunny positions. Vocalizations are thin and exceptionally high-pitched.
A. *Large and boldly barred below;* ♂ has *black hood.* Iris color varies.   PAGE 745
> 5.   BARRED FRUITEATER, *P. a. arcuata*
B. Both sexes moss green with "hooded" effect, *dark iris,* and *coral red legs.*   PAGE 745
> 6.   GREEN-AND-BLACK FRUITEATER, *P. riefferii chachapoyas*
> *Also:*   Band-tailed Fruiteater, *P. intermedia* (Peru and Bol.)
C. Both sexes emerald green with *yellow iris,* coral red bill, and *olive-gray legs.* ♂♂ superficially appear   PAGE 747
   diverse; ♀♀ (except Black-chested) yellow-streaked to throat. The *P. aureopectus* superspecies.
> 7.   BLACK-CHESTED FRUITEATER, *P. lubomirskii* (s. Col. to
>   n. Peru)
> 8.   MASKED FRUITEATER, *P. pulchra* (Peru)
> *Also:*   Orange-breasted Fruiteater, *P. jucunda* (♂ has *black head;* w. Col. and
>   w. Ecu.)
>   Golden-breasted Fruiteater, *P. aureopectus* (♂ has *green head;* Venez.
>   and Col.)
D. ♂♂ diverse, though all share a *fiery red chest patch;* ♀♀ all have green *barring* on lower underparts.   PAGE 749
•   ♂♂ with lower underparts mainly *yellow.*
> 9.   SCARLET-BREASTED FRUITEATER, *P. f. frontalis* (Ecu. to Bol.)
> *Also:*   Handsome Fruiteater, *P. formosa* (♂ has *black head;* Venez.)
•   ♂♂ with lower underparts mainly *green; very small.*
> 10.   FIERY-THROATED FRUITEATER, *P. chlorolepidota* (s. Col. to
>   n. Peru)
E. Both sexes unique; confined to *tepuis.*   PAGE 751
> 11.   RED-BANDED FRUITEATER, *P. w. whitelyi*

49

GTUDOR

PLATE 50: "TRUE" COTINGAS

Porphyrolaema Cotingas   A single species of cotinga found in w. Amazonia, where at best un-   PAGE 752
common in forest canopy. Both sexes have *distinctive pale fringing* on back feathers, and ♀ is *profusely barred below.*

      1.   PURPLE-THROATED COTINGA, *P. porphyrolaema*

Cotinga Cotingas   A distinctive group of beautiful arboreal cotingas found in canopy of   PAGE 752
humid lowland tropical forest, most species with allopatric ranges, 2 of them (Purple-breasted and Plum-throated) occurring with the more widespread Spangled. ♂ ♂ are all *some shade of intense blue,* always with purple at least on throat (in some species on lower underparts as well); ♀ ♀ are brown, often *quite scaled or spotted, especially below.* A characteristic dove-like expression is imparted by their *small dark heads* and *large dark eyes.*

A. ♂ ♂ *deeper,* more *cobalt* blue; *more extensive purple below.* ♀ ♀ *conspicuously scaled and spotted.*   PAGE 753
      2.   BANDED COTINGA, *C. maculata* (se. Brazil)
    Also: Purple-breasted Cotinga, *C. cotinga* (no blue chest band; ne. S. Am.)
             Blue Cotinga, *C. nattererii* (less purple below; nw. Venez. to nw. Ecu.)
B. ♂ ♂ *paler,* more *turquoise* blue; *only throat purple.* ♀ ♀ more uniform, *scaling and spotting reduced.*   PAGE 754
      3.   PLUM-THROATED COTINGA, *C. maynana* (w. Amazonia)
      4.   SPANGLED COTINGA, *C. cayana* (Amazonia to Guianas)

Xipholena Cotingas   A trio of cotingas similar in some respects to *Cotinga,* but looking   PAGE 755
quite different. Both sexes have *whitish eyes.* ♂ ♂ are basically bichromatic, *purple to blackish with startling white wings,* also a white tail in 1 species; ♀ ♀ look much alike, *gray with white wing-edging.* All are arboreal in humid tropical lowland forest, with essentially allopatric ranges.

      5.   POMPADOUR COTINGA, *X. punicea* (Guianas to cen. Amazonia)
      6.   WHITE-TAILED COTINGA, *X. lamellipennis* (lower Amaz. Brazil)
    Also: White-winged Cotinga, *X. atropurpurea* (e. Brazil)

Carpodectes Cotingas   A single species of large cotinga found in wet forests of *w. Colombia*   PAGE 758
and nw. Ecuador. ♂ is *pure white,* ♀ much like a large ♀ *Xipholena* cotinga.
      7.   BLACK-TIPPED COTINGA, *C. hopkei*

Conioptilon Cotingas   Recently described monotypic genus *found very locally in se. Peru low-*   PAGE 759
lands. Distinctive *gray and black plumage.* Sexes alike.
      8.   BLACK-FACED COTINGA, *C. mcilhennyi*

50

Laniocera Mourners   A pair of inconspicuous mourners found in understory of humid for-   PAGE 759
est, 1 (which is rufous) found west of the Andes, the other (which is gray) east of them. *Wing-spotting*
distinguishes them from the pihas and *Rhytipterna* mourners (Plate 43). Immatures are more scaled or
spotted below.

1.   CINEREOUS MOURNER, *L. hypopyrrha* (immature)
Also: Speckled Mourner, *L. rufescens* (mostly rufous; w. Col. and nw. Ecu.)

Lipaugus Pihas   A rather uniform group of plain and somewhat thrush-like cotingas   PAGE 761
found inside or in subcanopy of humid forest, some in lowlands and others in montane areas. A majority
are *wholly or predominantly gray* (1 of these also with a rose collar), and 2 others are mainly olive and 1 is
rufous. Most species are either scarce or have small ranges; only the Screaming and Rufous are really
numerous in their ranges. At least some species are *very vocal*, with loud and arresting calls drawing immediate attention.

A. *"Olive green"* pihas; local in Andes.   PAGE 761
2.   GRAY-TAILED PIHA, *L. subalaris* (foothills on e. slope of Andes,
s. Col. to ne. Peru)
Also: Olivaceous Piha, *L. cryptolophus* (Col. to e. Peru)

B. *Non-Andean* pihas; color variable.   PAGE 762
3.   SCREAMING PIHA, *L. vociferans* (east of Andes)
4.   RUFOUS PIHA, *L. unirufus castaneotinctus* (west of Andes)
5.   ROSE-COLLARED PIHA, *L. streptophorus* (tepuis; ♀ lacks collar)
Also: Cinnamon-vented Piha, *L. lanioides* (brownish gray and larger;
se. Brazil)

C. *Largest* and *longest-tailed* pihas; mainly or all *gray*. Andes.   PAGE 765
6.   SCIMITAR-WINGED PIHA, *L. uropygialis* (Bol.)
Also: Dusky Piha, *L. fuscocinereus* (mainly Col. and Ecu.)

Tijuca Cotingas   PAGE 766
A pair of large, piha-like cotingas found only in forests on *high mts. of se. Brazil.*
7.   BLACK-AND-GOLD COTINGA, *T. atra*
Also: Gray-winged Cotinga, *T. condita* (recalls ♀ of larger 7)

Procnias Bellbirds   A trio of splendid large cotingas, well known for ♂ ♂' *bizarre orna-*   PAGE 767
mentation and *resoundingly loud calls.* They range locally in n. and e. S. Am., mainly in canopy of humid
forest, where they are inconspicuous except when vocalizing.
8.   BARE-THROATED BELLBIRD, *P. nudicollis* (se. S. Am.)
9.   BEARDED BELLBIRD, *P. averano carnobarba* (Venez. to ne. Brazil)
Also: White Bellbird, *P. alba* (♂ with single long wattle, ♀ with olive head;
ne. S. Am.)

NOTE: Bare-throated Bellbird (8) is drawn to a smaller scale.

51

PLATE 52: FRUITCROWS, UMBRELLABIRDS, RED-COTINGAS, COCKS-OF-THE-ROCK, ETC.

Gymnoderus Fruitcrows   A rather *ungainly* large cotinga found *along rivers and lakes in Ama-*
zonia. Bare bluish skin and wattles on sides of neck (less in ♀) is unique; also note ♂'s *silvery wings.*
>   1.   BARE-NECKED FRUITCROW, *G. foetidus*

Querula Fruitcrows   A stocky, short-tailed, *mostly black* cotinga found in small flocks in hu-
mid tropical forests. Only ♂♂ have *purple throat.*
>   2.   PURPLE-THROATED FRUITCROW, *Q. purpurata*

Haematoderus Fruitcrows   Spectacular and unmistakable, the *large, mainly red* Crimson Fruit-
crow is a rare inhabitant of forest canopy, mainly in ne. S. Am.
>   3.   CRIMSON FRUITCROW, *H. militaris* (♀♀ and immature ♂♂
>   have entire mantle dark brown)

Pyroderus Fruitcrows
Easily known by the *fiery red ruff,* present in both sexes. Found locally, mainly in *subtropical* forests.
>   4.   RED-RUFFED FRUITCROW, *P. s. scutatus* (some races have lower
>   underparts rufous-chestnut)

Cephalopterus Umbrellabirds   *Huge, black* cotingas with a *unique "umbrella" crest* (expandable) and
long chest wattle (extensible), both crest and wattle smaller in ♀♀. Canopy and borders of humid forest, in
Amazonia mainly along rivers.
>   5.   AMAZONIAN UMBRELLABIRD, *C. ornatus* (locally in Amazonia
>   and on e. slope of Andes)
>   *Also:*   Long-wattled Umbrellabird, *C. penduliger* (locally in sw. Colombia
>   and w. Ecuador; iris dark)

Perissocephalus Capuchinbirds
A strange, *bald-headed,* and "cowled" large cotinga found inside humid forests of ne. S. Am. Weird voice.
>   6.   CAPUCHINBIRD, *P. tricolor*

Phoenicircus Red-Cotingas   Pair of beautiful, *mainly red and black/brown* cotingas found locally in-
side Amaz. and Guianan forests. Usually scarce. They look vaguely like gigantic manakins.
>   7.   GUIANAN RED-COTINGA, *P. carnifex* (ne. S. Am.)
>   *Also:*   Black-necked Red-Cotinga, *P. nigricollis* (w. and cen. Amazonia)

Rupicola Cocks-of-the-rock   Unmistakable pair of large cotingas (formerly placed in their own
family), ♂♂ *brilliantly colored and ornamented,* both sexes with *laterally compressed frontal crests* (smaller in
the browner ♀♀). Found locally in forested areas, the Andean near streams and gorges, the Guianan near
rocky outcrops.
>   8.   ANDEAN COCK-OF-THE-ROCK, *R. p. peruviana* (Andes from
>   Venez. to Bol.; ♂ of w. race scarlet)
>   *Also:*   Guianan Cock-of-the-rock, *R. rupicola* (ne. S. Am.; ♂'s wings quite
>   different)

52

1♂

2♂

4

3♂

5♂

6

7♀

7♂

8♀

8♂

GTUDOR

ORDER PASSERIFORMES

The Suboscines

WITH this second volume of *The Birds of South America,* we complete coverage of the species that as a group are usually called the passerines.

The Order Passeriformes comprises well over half the species of birds in the world. They are essentially cosmopolitan, occurring everywhere except on Antarctica and some very remote oceanic islands. In South America, as elsewhere, passerine birds can be found in virtually every conceivable terrestrial habitat. None, however, is truly aquatic; a very few (such as *Cinclus* dippers) feed in or at the edge of fresh water, and a very few others (such as *Cinclodes* cinclodes) feed at the edge of salt water. They are usually small in size, with the largest species in South America being certain crow- (*Corvus-*)sized cotingas and oropendolas. Often also termed "the perching birds," passerines have feet that are adapted for perching, with four toes on the same level and a large and nonreversible hallux directed to the rear. The young are nidicolous, hatching blind and helpless with only sparse down.

Passerine birds are characterized by having a syrinx that is adapted for singing. The two suborders, Tyranni (the suboscines) and Passeri (the oscines), differ in their syringeal morphology, which is simpler in the suboscines than it is in the oscines. Many suboscine birds are nonetheless capable of producing varied and often beautiful songs (though they are rarely the equal of certain oscines), and many are notably vocal. The vast majority of suboscine birds occur in the neotropics; only a few small families, such as the pittas (Pittidae) and broadbills (Eurylamidae), occur in the Old World.

Although the Order Passeriformes, Suborder Tyranni, and Suborder Passeri form well-defined taxonomic units, relationships at the family and subfamily levels remain controversial. As in Volume I, we have in the main adhered to the family sequence and classification found in the 1983 AOU Check-list. This differs quite significantly from that employed by Meyer de Schauensee (1966, 1970); in addition, several departures suggested by Sibley and Monroe (1990) have been incorporated. The more important "higher order" changes that result are summarized here (details and references are given in lower-order introductions).

1. The woodcreepers, formerly given full family rank (Dendrocolaptidae), are now considered to comprise a subfamily (Dendrocolaptinae) within the ovenbirds (Furnariidae) and are placed at the end of the sequence.

2. What was formerly considered to be the antbird family (Formicariidae) has been split into two families: the typical antbirds (Thamnophilidae) and the ground antbirds (Formicariidae, including the genera *Formicarius, Chamaeza, Grallaria, Pittasoma, Myrmothera, Hylopezus,* and *Grallaricula*).

3. The gnateaters are once again given full family rank (Conopophagidae). *Corythopis* is, however, a tyrannid genus.

4. Tyrant flycatcher (Tyrannidae) taxonomy remains exceptionally complex and difficult. The existence of several subfamilies (e.g., Elaeniinae, Pipromorphinae, Fluvicolinae, Tyranninae, and Tityrinae) has been suggested by various authors, but their limits remain uncertain, with the allocation of certain genera being problematic. We thus have not broken out any such units within what used to be considered "typical" tyrant flycatchers. The sequence of genera we

employ is essentially "reversed" from what is found in Meyer de Schauensee (1966, 1970), follow-ing the sequence suggested by M. A. Traylor, Jr., in *Birds of the World,* vol. 8.

5. There seems to be universal agreement that the manakins and the cotingas, both formerly given full family status (Pipridae and Cotingidae, respectively), should be considered as only subfamilies (Piprinae and Cotinginae) within the Tyrannidae. Note that there is ongoing debate concerning the allocation of certain genera to the three subfamilies (Tyranninae, Piprinae, Co-tinginae), with some genera seeming intermediate or still considered *incertae sedis* (notably *Sa-payoa*). Some details and references for these "problem" genera are provided in the appropriate generic introductions.

6. What were formerly considered to be three separate small families, the cocks-of-the-rock (Rupicolidae), the plantcutters (Phytotomidae), and the Sharpbill (Oxyruncidae), are no longer believed to deserve recognition as full families and are now considered to belong within the cotinga (Cotinginae) subfamily in the Tyrannidae.

As in Volume I, we should emphasize that the sequence employed *is not necessarily an indica-tion of relationship.* Our desire to associate various "similar-appearing" genera and species to-gether has taken precedence.

Furnariidae

OVENBIRDS AND WOODCREEPERS

THE ovenbirds and the woodcreepers are now usually considered to belong to the same family (1983 AOU Check-list; Sibley and Ahlquist 1990) and are so treated here.

Furnariinae

OVENBIRDS

A LARGE and exceptionally diverse subfamily which, despite their rather dull plumage, includes some of the most interesting of all South American birds. They are exclusively neotropical in distribution, with diversity being greatest in the Andes and in south-central South America. Species have radiated into nearly every conceivable niche and habitat, from lowland and montane forests (at varying heights from the ground to the canopy) to grasslands, marshes, and even rocky areas and meadows near the level of permanent snow in the Andes; several *Cinclodes* are among the most marine of all passerine birds, occurring strictly along the immediate shoreline. Some, such as several of the *Furnarius* horneros, are among the most familiar of all South American birds, but many others are much more obscure in both appearance and behavior, and many have very restricted ranges and habitat requirements. None is brightly colored (though a few are quite strikingly patterned), and virtually all are predominantly some shade of brown, rufous, or gray; the sexes are alike. Many genera have somewhat decomposed tail feathers (reaching an extreme in the *Sylviorthorhynchus* wiretail), in some ending in bare and somewhat stiffened shafts; unlike the woodcreepers, however, none routinely uses its tail for support. All species are essentially insectivorous. Most species are very vocal, though their songs usually consist only of simple trills or chatters and rarely have any musical quality. There is stunning variation in nest structure and placement, though all species build an essentially closed nest with a side entrance. The conspicuous mud nests of *Furnarius* horneros are well known, and because of their fancied resemblance to a Dutch oven, gave rise to the often-used English name of *ovenbird* for the genus and family. Many other species build stick nests (enormous in some); and others place their nest at the end of a burrow or in holes in trees or walls.

Vaurie (1980) proposed major changes in the taxonomy of the furnariids, especially at the generic level. For the most part, however, his revisions have not been well received by ornithologists familiar with the birds in life, and the vast majority of his suggested generic changes to the taxonomy employed by Meyer de Schauensee (1966, 1970) have not, therefore, been followed here.

Geobates Miners

A monotypic genus typical of the Brazilian cerrado. It is closely related to *Geositta* of the Andes and austral South America but differs in its small size, very short tail, and wing pattern; its distribution is also completely different. Vaurie (1971, 1980) suggested merging *Geobates* into *Geositta*.

Geobates poecilopterus

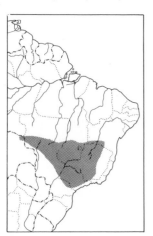

CAMPO MINER   PLATE: 1

DESCRIPTION: 12.5 cm (5"). *A short-tailed miner of the cerrado and campos of interior s. Brazil.* Fawn brown above with narrow buff superciliary; wings dusky with *mainly rufous secondaries, a rufous band across primaries* (the rufous especially visible in flight), and pinkish chestnut underwing-coverts; *tail rufous with a broad black subterminal band,* central pair of feathers mainly dusky. Throat white; remaining underparts dull buff flammulated with brown on breast.
SIMILAR SPECIES: No other miner occurs with this species, which otherwise is likely to be confused only with much larger Rufous Hornero.
HABITAT AND BEHAVIOR: Rare to locally (or temporarily) fairly common in open grassy cerrado and campos, occurring only where there are at most a few scattered small trees. Often most numerous on terrain that has recently been burned, appearing as if by magic when the ground is still charred, sometimes when it is still smoking! Terrestrial and usually inconspicuous, though often quite tame once located; may crouch when approached, trying to avoid detection, but then flushes abruptly. Only rarely perches on a shrub; occasionally a bird is seen flying high overhead (dispersing?). Usually found singly or in pairs, rarely or never in flocks, though sometimes congregating in loose "colonies" in particularly suitable habitat. The male's song, usually given in a display flight in which the bird hovers up to 50 m above the ground, is a simple, repeated, semimusical "zhliip" or "zh-zh-zh-leeép."
RANGE: Interior s.-cen. Brazil (Minas Gerais and São Paulo west locally to s. Mato Grosso) and adjacent ne. Bolivia (ne. Santa Cruz on Serranía de Huanchaca). Mostly 500–1200 m.

Geositta Miners

Rather similar plain, short-tailed, mainly terrestrial furnariids found in open, usually arid country, the miners in many respects resemble the larks, Alaudidae (found principally in the Old World). Most miners range at high elevations in the Andes, with a few occurring on the Peruvian and Chilean coasts, others as far south as Patagonia and Tierra del Fuego; only one, the Short-billed, is believed to be migratory. In flight many species show rufous on the wing and/or a pale area on the rump and base of the tail; the details of these patterns, together with bill shape and overall coloration, are important characters for species identification. Miners nest in burrows dug into level ground or banks; most species excavate their own (presumably the derivation of the name *miner*), but some use burrows dug by other birds (notably *Upucerthia* earthcreepers) or by rodents (especially *Ctenomys* spp.).

GROUP A

Typical miners; bills *short and slender;* uppertail-coverts *creamy* in many species.

Geositta peruviana

COASTAL MINER

PLATE: I

DESCRIPTION: 14 cm (5½″). *Barren or desert-like areas along coast of Peru.* Pale sandy brownish above with narrow whitish superciliary and indistinct eye-ring; sandy edging on wing-coverts and tertials, and flight feathers mainly tawny-buff (showing at rest but more conspicuous as a *wide band* in flight); tail dusky and buff, paler at base and with outer web of outermost rectrix whitish. *Uniform whitish below.*

SIMILAR SPECIES: This miner occurs at *lower elevations* than any other miner in its range, though it does overlap to some extent with Grayish Miner. Grayish is somewhat darker and grayer above, its entire wing is dark, and it has a pinkish area on flanks. Cf. also Short-tailed Field-Tyrant (similar in overall coloration and habits).

HABITAT AND BEHAVIOR: Uncommon to locally common in arid, often sandy, terrain, sometimes around buildings but always where vegetation is sparse (at most scattered low shrubs) or nonexistent. Mostly terrestrial and quite active, running rapidly in short bursts, then pausing and remaining motionless; sometimes perches on low branches or walls. Usually occurs singly or in pairs, seldom in flocks. Its call is a simple "tswit" or "tsweet," often uttered as it flushes; displaying males hover into the wind and give a lengthy musical twittering. Numerous at various sites on and near Paracas Peninsula.

RANGE: Coastal w. Peru (Tumbes south to Ica). To 400 m.

Geositta maritima

GRAYISH MINER

DESCRIPTION: 14 cm (5½″). *Barren Pacific slope deserts from cen. Peru to n. Chile.* Resembles Coastal Miner but is somewhat darker and *more grayish above* and has a *more blackish tail* with no paler area at base (but retains pale outermost rectrices), *completely dark wings* (no pale band shows even in flight), and *contrastingly pinkish buff flanks* (often conspicuous in the field; Coastal's underparts are uniform whitish).

HABITAT AND BEHAVIOR: Uncommon to locally common in open barren terrain, usually in rocky places but also in areas where sand is

more prevalent. Unlike Coastal Miner, Grayish does not occur along the immediate coast but favors hilly areas a short distance inland and on up the dry w. slope of Andes. Small numbers are found locally in "absolute" desert with little or no vegetation. Behavior similar to Coastal Miner's, though Grayish seems more apt to occur in small, loose flocks in the nonbreeding season. When flushed it often flies off for long distances. Can be found along the road between Arica and Putre in Tarapacá, northernmost Chile; here it is usually the first bird one encounters, at about 2500 m, after ascending through the zone of lifeless desert. Also numerous at the Lomas de Lachay north of Lima, Peru.

RANGE: W. Peru (north to Ancash) and n. Chile (south to Atacama). To about 2900 m (in Chile).

Geositta cunicularia

COMMON MINER   PLATE: I

DESCRIPTION: 14–15 cm (5½–6"). *Level open areas from Peruvian altiplano and s. Brazil south to Tierra del Fuego. Bill rather slender and slightly decurved,* pale at base of lower mandible. Pale grayish brown above with narrow buffy whitish superciliary; *flight feathers mainly pale rufous* (showing at rest but much more conspicuous in flight); tail dusky, *creamy buff at base and on outer rectrices* (most prominent in flight). Below buffy whitish, with *indistinct brownish streaking on breast.* Foregoing applies to *froberni* group (with *titicacae* and *juninensis*) of altiplano of Peru, Bolivia, and n. Chile; *titicacae* has the most extensive pale area at base of tail and the least breast streaking. Nominate group (with *hellmayri* and *fissirostris*) of s. part of range similar but duller generally (less rufescent on wings and with less contrasty creamy basal tail), with heavier breast streaking. *Deserticolor* of coastal s. Peru and n. Chile (south to Atacama) is markedly smaller, somewhat paler ("sandier") above and whiter (less buffyish) below, with a whiter superciliary.

SIMILAR SPECIES: Short-billed Miner (overlapping with Common in Patagonia) has shorter and straighter bill, more mottled breast lacking discrete streaks, and no rufous in wings (this absence most evident in flight). Puna Miner (overlapping with Common in altiplano) has uniform whitish underparts without any breast streaking.

HABITAT AND BEHAVIOR: Fairly common to common on open, more or less level plains, gently rolling hillsides, and sandy areas. In Chile, Argentina, and Brazil occurs even on coastal sand dunes; *deserticolor* favors the sparse, low loma vegetation found on coastal hills. Short grass cover, sometimes with a scattering of low shrubs, is preferred; long grass and truly barren areas are avoided. Common Miners are usually inconspicuous, found singly or in pairs feeding on the ground, occasionally pausing erectly to look up; though mainly terrestrial, they sometimes perch on fence posts, low shrubs, and the like. They are always most evident in flight, when the pale basal tail and rufous in the wing flash conspicuously. When alarmed they often crouch in an attempt to escape detection, or they may run off rapidly; when flushed they are apt to fly for long distances. Nonbreeding birds may gather in flocks but do not usually associate with other birds. Nesting males have an undulating flight display in which they fly fairly low over the ground and occasionally mount higher, descending with fluttering wings, all the while giving a repeated series of rather loud, semimusical notes (somewhat sharper in nominate *cunicularia*).

RANGE: Peru (north in Andes to Junín, along coast from s. Ica southward), w. Bolivia, Chile (in Andes of Tarapacá, along coast south to Antofogasta, in lowlands and foothills from Atacama southward, and on Patagonian plains of Aysén and Magallanes south to n. Isla Grande), Argentina (in Andes north locally to Jujuy, in mountains of w. Córdoba, and in Patagonia and lowlands north at least locally to s. Córdoba and s. Corrientes; ranges south in small numbers to n. Isla Grande), Uruguay, and extreme s. Brazil (resident in s. and coastal Rio Grande do Sul); 1 record (an austral migrant?) from se. Paraguay (specimen from Villarica in Guairá; Vaurie 1980). Southernmost breeders are migratory, but *contra* Fjeldså and Krabbe (1990), the species is a breeding resident north to s. Brazil. To 4800 m (in Peruvian altiplano; *deserticolor* to at least 2400 m in the Arequipa area).

NOTE: Its distribution, small size, and other factors make us suspect that *deserticolor* (with *georgei;* Loma Miner) of coastal s. Peru and n. Chile could deserve full species status, but the possibility of intergradation with *G. c. fissirostris* in Atacama, Chile, still needs to be investigated. Fjeldså and Krabbe (1990) suggest that because of certain vocal differences, nominate *cunicularia* (Brazil to Patagonia) may deserve specific separation from other forms.

Geositta punensis

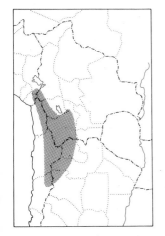

PUNA MINER

DESCRIPTION: 14.5 cm (5¾″). *Altiplano of extreme s. Peru south to n. Chile and nw. Argentina.* Resembles Common Miner, with which locally sympatric, but slightly smaller and with bill a bit *shorter.* Puna is also paler and sandier above and *uniform whitish below* with *none of Common's breast streaking.*

SIMILAR SPECIES: Grayish Miner occurs mainly or entirely at lower elevations, is grayer above, lacks rufous in wings, and has a distinctive pinkish area on flanks.

HABITAT AND BEHAVIOR: Fairly common on level and open, often barren, plains. Behavior similar to Common Miner's. Likewise has a rather lengthy song given mainly in a flight display.

RANGE: Andes of s. Peru (north to Moquegua and s. Puno), w. Bolivia, n. Chile (south to Atacama), and nw. Argentina (south to Catamarca). 3000–5000 m.

Geositta antarctica

SHORT-BILLED MINER   PLATE: 1

DESCRIPTION: 15.5 cm (6″). *Breeds on steppes in Fuegian region,* migrating north into w. Argentina. *Bill quite short and straight.* Above grayish brown with narrow whitish superciliary and whitish uppertail-coverts; wings quite long, brownish (*showing no rufous, even in flight*). Below dull whitish, *mottled* lightly with dusky on breast.

SIMILAR SPECIES: Very similar Common Miner has a longer and more decurved bill; in flight shows obvious rufous on flight feathers (Short-billed's wings in flight look *relatively uniform*); and has definite, though fine, *streaks* on breast. A good look is required to be certain!

HABITAT AND BEHAVIOR: Uncommon to locally common on open, barren, windswept steppes with sparse, short grass and a scattering of small shrubs, and in sandy open places near coast. Behavior similar to Common Miner's, though Short-billed's song, most often given from the ground, is a rather different, simpler "weetuk-weetuk-weetuk-weetuk-weetuk." These 2 miners occur together locally, and Vuilleumier (1991) has even found them nesting in mixed "colonies." Short-billed is numerous on the heavily sheep-grazed grasslands of n. part of Isla Grande (e.g., around Porvenir in Chile, and Río Grande in Argentina) but is less common as a breeder north of the Straits of Magellan.

RANGE: Breeds in s. Chile and s. Argentina (on northern, nonforested parts of Isla Grande and north to w. Santa Cruz, Argentina); during austral winter migrates north along e. base of Andes as far as Mendoza, Argentina. Below 1000 m.

Geositta saxicolina

DARK-WINGED MINER   PLATE: I

DESCRIPTION: 16.5 cm (6½″). *High Andes of w.-cen. Peru.* Grayish brown above with *cinnamon-buff superciliary and sides of neck* and tinge on forehead; wings uniform dusky brown (showing less pale edging on wing-coverts and tertials than other miners and *showing no rufous in flight*); *rump and basal half of tail creamy buff*, as are outermost rectrices. *Pale buff below* with *no breast streaking or flammulation*.

SIMILAR SPECIES: Common Miner lacks obvious buff on face and underparts, has breast streaking, and shows prominent rufous on wings in flight (Dark-winged's wings in flight look *uniform* and *dark*).

HABITAT AND BEHAVIOR: Fairly common on sparsely vegetated rocky slopes at high elevations. Usually quite conspicuous, seen singly or in pairs, perching on boulders or running on grassy areas or patches of dirt. Rather easily found in the Marcapomacocha area in Andes high above Lima.

RANGE: Andes of cen. Peru (w. Junín, Huancavelica, and adjacent Lima and Pasco). Mostly 4000–4900 m.

Geositta rufipennis

RUFOUS-BANDED MINER   PLATE: I

DESCRIPTION: 17–18 cm (6¾–7″). *High Andes of w. Bolivia, w. Argentina, and Chile.* Above buffy brown to grayish brown with narrow buffy whitish superciliary or postocular (variable in extent); wings with *contrastingly rufous flight feathers with a black subterminal band* (conspicuous in flight, though mostly hidden at rest); *tail mainly rufous* with a dusky terminal band. Below dingy buffy whitish, *often showing some pinkish cinnamon on flanks* (distinctive when present, though sometimes absent or hidden by wings).

SIMILAR SPECIES: This rather large but short-billed miner lacks the pale rump and uppertail-coverts of most other miners (e.g., smaller

Common) but *shows much more rufous on tail;* its wing pattern in flight is very striking, with the blackish subterminal edge contrasting more with the rufous. Cf. especially Creamy-rumped Miner.

HABITAT AND BEHAVIOR: Uncommon to locally common on rocky slopes with scattered bushes and grassy areas; sometimes feeds on fields or near water (seepage zones, along streams). Behavior much like other miners', though Rufous-banded seems more confiding and gregarious, even in breeding season often occurring in small groups and regularly in flocks during austral winter. Its song, recalling a shorebird's or even a canary's, is a lengthy and quite musical trilling interspersed with somewhat sharper notes, e.g., "treetreetreetree-trrrrr-treetreetreetree . . . " or "dree-dree-dreedreédreé!" It sings either during a hovering flight display or while perched atop a boulder or other spot with a commanding view. Particularly numerous in Andes of Santiago, Chile, where by far the most common miner.

RANGE: Andes of w. Bolivia (north to La Paz), w. Argentina (south to w. Santa Cruz; also in mts. of w. Córdoba), and Chile (s. Antofogasta south to Aysén). To 4400 m (in Bolivia); down to 650 m (even lower?) in Chile.

Geositta isabellina

CREAMY-RUMPED MINER

DESCRIPTION: 18 cm (7"). A *large* miner found locally at *high elevations* in Andes of *cen. Chile and Argentina*. Resembles Rufous-banded Miner but has longer and more decurved bill, paler (more isabelline) upperparts, *more uniform wings in flight* (flight feathers dull rufous, with less contrasting dusky subterminal band), and *creamy whitish rump and uppertail-coverts* (contrasting with tail).

SIMILAR SPECIES: Cf. also the smaller Common Miner, likewise with a creamy basal tail but showing breast streaking, etc.

HABITAT AND BEHAVIOR: Rare to locally uncommon on barren rocky slopes at high elevations, feeding mainly on small patches of short grass. Behavior much like Rufous-banded Miner's, though Creamy-rumped always seems much less numerous and is never as gregarious (usually found singly or in pairs). Creamy-rumped's song is also similar, and likewise is given both in flight and from a perch, often atop a boulder with a commanding view (S. Howell). Can be found near Laguna Horcones in Mendoza, Argentina, and above the Portillo ski resort in Santiago, Chile.

RANGE: Andes of cen. Chile (Atacama south to Talca) and w. Argentina (San Juan and Mendoza; records from farther north are regarded as uncertain, though they could pertain to austral migrants). 3000–4500 m, lower (to 2000 m) during austral winter.

GROUP B

Two miners with *distinctive bills* (but cf. *Upucerthia* earthcreepers).

Geositta crassirostris

THICK-BILLED MINER   PLATE: I

DESCRIPTION: 17–17.5 cm (6¾–7"). *Local on w. slope of Andes in Peru. Bill thick and rather decurved; legs whitish.* Above dark brown to grayish

brown, feathers of mantle edged paler with a *mottled or scaled effect* (less so when in worn plumage), and with narrow whitish superciliary; wings with rufous band (conspicuous in flight) on otherwise blackish flight feathers; *tail mostly rufous basally,* with blackish subterminal band and narrow pale tip. Below grayish white, mottled or streaked with dusky on breast.

SIMILAR SPECIES: This miner is readily recognized in its restricted range and habitat by its large size, heavy bill (especially thick at base), whitish legs, and overall dark upperparts which lack a pale rump. All the earthcreepers have longer tails.

HABITAT AND BEHAVIOR: Uncommon on steep rocky slopes with scattered bushes and cacti; also occurs on the coastal hills locally known as lomas which support a characteristic low "fog vegetation." Found singly or in pairs, walking on level patches of grass or dirt or perching atop boulders. Its calls are described (Koepcke 1970) as loud, a "keen keen" and "reetreetreetreet. . . ." Small numbers can be found along the road to Juliaca above Arequipa, and above Nazca along the road to Pampa Galeras in s. Ayacucho.

RANGE: Locally on w. slope of Andes in Peru (Lima south to Arequipa). 600–3000 m.

NOTE: See T. S. Schulenberg (*Bull. B. O. C.* 107[4]: 185–186, 1987) for more information on the distribution of this species.

Geositta tenuirostris

SLENDER-BILLED MINER   PLATE: I

DESCRIPTION: 18.5–19 cm (7¼–7½"). A large miner with a *very long, thin, somewhat decurved bill reminiscent of an earthcreeper's.* Above pale sandy to grayish brown with a narrow pale buff superciliary; in flight shows *mainly rufous flight feathers* (only the tips of outer remiges are dusky) and *mostly rufous tail* (without a darker subterminal band and with only central rectrices dusky). Below pale buffyish with *pronounced brownish flammulation or streaking on breast.* Birds from Ecuador (*kalimayae;* N. Krabbe, *Bull. B.O.C.* 112[3]: 166–169, 1992) are slightly smaller, grayer overall, with slightly more profuse streaking on breast and more extensive dusky on wings and tail.

SIMILAR SPECIES: No other miner has such a long, slender bill, but aside from this and its concolor (not pale) rump and basal tail, Slender-billed resembles the smaller Common Miner. Cf. *Upucerthia* earthcreepers, all of which have notably longer tails.

HABITAT AND BEHAVIOR: Uncommon to fairly common on puna and drier páramo grasslands and meadows and adjacent ploughed fields, sometimes also on terraced fields of alfalfa; unlike other miners, this species is often associated with water. Found singly or in pairs, walking about on the ground with a waddling gait similar to a hornero's. Often rather tame. Like other miners, it has a flight display during which male circles and hovers above its territory while pouring forth a simple repetitive song; it sometimes also sings while perched.

RANGE: Andes of n. Ecuador (locally in w. Cotopaxi), and in Peru (north to Cajamarca), w. Bolivia, nw. Argentina (south to w. La

Rioja), and extreme n. Chile (seen in Feb. 1990 near Parinacota in Lauca Nat. Park, Arica; M. Sallaberry et al.). 2500–4600 m.

Upucerthia Earthcreepers

Earthcreepers are fairly large, plainly attired, mostly terrestrial furnariids found mainly high in the Andes, though a few species range lower and one occurs down across the Patagonian plains to sea level. Only the Scale-throated is migratory. Their bills are long, strikingly decurved in some species, and their long tails are characteristically held cocked. Much like miners, earthcreepers nest in burrows dug into banks. In many respects (but not in nesting) they are convergent with several thrashers (*Toxostoma* spp.) found in the deserts of sw. United States and n. Mexico.

GROUP A   *Bill strongly decurved;* either with *scaly throat* or *uniform below.*

Upucerthia dumetaria

SCALE-THROATED EARTHCREEPER   PLATE: 1

DESCRIPTION: 21.5 cm (8½″). *Bill long, slender, strikingly decurved.* Uniform dull grayish brown above with long, narrow, whitish superciliary; flight feathers show a wash of dull rufous in flight; *outer rectrices rather prominently tipped pale buff or whitish* (visible mainly in flight). Dull buffy whitish below, whitest on throat, *feathers of lower throat and chest tipped dusky giving pronounced scaly effect.* Extent of scaling below seems to vary individually, juveniles having the most. *Saturatior* (lowland Chile from Aconcagua to Valdivia, and in adjacent Argentina in w. Neuquén and Chubut) has a shorter bill and is darker above.
SIMILAR SPECIES: This is the only earthcreeper with pale tail-tipping, often easily seen as the bird flushes; also the only earthcreeper with obvious scaling on foreneck.
HABITAT AND BEHAVIOR: Fairly common to common (but much less numerous northward) on shrubby and brush-covered slopes and plains, seemingly not as tied to quebradas or steep slopes as are many other earthcreepers, and numerous in Patagonian steppe country. Found singly or in pairs, and generally reclusive, usually skulking on or near the ground in or near heavy cover, retreating inside when disturbed. At other times, however, it may be bolder, hopping about in the open with tail cocked at a shallow angle or perching atop a bush. The song in cen. Chile is a spritely, rather musical "tr, tr, trreetrree-trreetrritrritrri" with a slight ascending effect.
RANGE: Andes of extreme s. Peru (s. Puno), w. Bolivia, Chile (where also in lowlands and foothills, especially in cen. and far s. sectors; recorded north locally to s. Tarapacá), and w. and s. Argentina, southward spreading out across Patagonia and south to Tierra del Fuego; in austral winter migrates north into ne. Argentina as far as Santiago del Estero, Entre Ríos, and n. Buenos Aires, rarely reaching s. Uruguay (May–Aug. sightings from se. San José). To 3900 m (in Bolivia).

Upucerthia jelskii

PLAIN-BREASTED EARTHCREEPER   PLATE: I

DESCRIPTION: 19–19.5 cm (7½–7¾"). A *uniform-looking* earthcreeper of *Andes of Peru, w. Bolivia, and extreme n. Chile and nw. Argentina. Long, slender, strikingly decurved bill.* Above uniform light brown with long, narrow, buff superciliary; a small area of rufous (visible mainly in flight) shows on inner primaries; tail mostly rufous-chestnut. *Below uniform dull buff,* feathers of lower throat sometimes faintly scaled dusky (younger birds?). Foregoing applies to *pallida* of most of range; *saturata* (Ancash and w. Pasco in cen. Peru) is more grayish buff below and has virtually no rufous on wings; nominate race (Lima to Huancavelica in Peru) also shows little rufous on wings.

SIMILAR SPECIES: Cf. very similar White-throated Earthcreeper, which overlaps with Plain-breasted in sw. Peru and n. Chile.

HABITAT AND BEHAVIOR: Fairly common on shrubby hillsides with scattered grassy or bare areas and along dry washes and ravines. Behavior similar to Scale-throated Earthcreeper's and usually equally sneaky, often hiding beneath bushes or rocks, rapidly running or half-flying while crossing open areas, rarely lingering in exposed positions. Often carries its tail at a more acute angle than Scale-throated. Feeding birds use their sickle-shaped bills to probe into loose, often sandy, soil. Plain-breasted Earthcreepers are usually quiet, though in breeding season males will sing a long, simple series of rather dry trilled notes from atop a bush or rock.

RANGE: Andes of cen. and s. Peru (north to Ancash), w. Bolivia, extreme n. Chile (Arica), and nw. Argentina (San Antonio de los Cobres in w. Salta). Mostly 3500–4500 m.

NOTE: Considered conspecific with *U. validirostris* by Vaurie (1980), though not in his earlier work (Vaurie 1971). As Vaurie (1980) points out, there does appear to be a cline in increased rufous in the wing southward (with the most in *U. validirostris*), but the break in size (*validirostris* is considerably larger) seems quite marked. *U. validirostris* has recently been taken in extreme s. Bolivia (J. Cabot, *Bull. B. O. C.* 110[2]: 195, 1990), and *U. jelskii pallida* is known from one locality in nw. Argentina; thus apparently these two forms overlap locally, though whether they ever occur syntopically remains uncertain. Intergradation may occur, but if so it is as yet unreported. If they are ultimately considered conspecific, we suggest the English name "Plain Earthcreeper."

Upucerthia validirostris

BUFF-BREASTED EARTHCREEPER

DESCRIPTION: 20–21 cm (8–8¼"). A *large* earthcreeper of *Andes of nw. Argentina and adjacent Bolivia.* Very similar to Plain-breasted Earthcreeper (with which perhaps conspecific) but somewhat larger with an *even longer bill.* Differs further in having more rufous on flight feathers. Despite the difference implied by the 2 species' English names, the color of their underparts is virtually identical.

HABITAT AND BEHAVIOR: Uncommon to fairly common on shrubby slopes with scattered grassy or bare areas and along dry washes or ravines. Behavior similar to Plain-breasted Earthcreeper's, as is its shrill, trilled song. Quite numerous near Abra del Infiernillo west of Tafí del Valle in Tucumán.

RANGE: Andes of extreme s. Bolivia (Potosí at Quetena Chica) and nw. Argentina (south to Mendoza, and in w. Córdoba). 2000–4000 m.

NOTE: See comments under Plain-breasted Earthcreeper.

Upucerthia albigula

WHITE-THROATED EARTHCREEPER

DESCRIPTION: 19.5 cm (7¾"). *W. slope of Andes in sw. Peru and extreme n. Chile.* Closely resembles Plain-breasted Earthcreeper (*pallida*), with which locally sympatric though usually occurring at somewhat *lower elevations.* Differs in its more extensively rufous-chestnut primaries (most evident in flight) and usually in its whiter, more contrasting throat, broader and whiter superciliary, and more rufous-chestnut tail (contrasting more with upperparts; most evident in flight).

HABITAT AND BEHAVIOR: Rare to uncommon on sparsely vegetated hillsides and along arid quebradas, locally also in heavily grazed pastures and fields with intervening hedgerows. Behavior similar to Plain-breasted Earthcreeper's, as is its song, though White-throated's tends to be more musical (not as dry) and slower, "cht, cht, ch-ch-chchchchi-chichi." A few pairs of this rare earthcreeper reside along the side road into Putre, in Arica, Chile; Plain-breasted Earthcreepers are also found here but are more numerous at slightly higher elevations.

RANGE: W. slope of Andes in sw. Peru (north to the Nazca-Puquio road in Ayacucho) and extreme n. Chile (Arica). 2500–4000 m.

NOTE: For more information on this until recently poorly known species, see T. S. Schulenberg (*Condor* 89[3]: 654–658, 1987).

GROUP B

Bill straighter; underparts more or less *streaked.*

Upucerthia serrana

STRIATED EARTHCREEPER   PLATE: I

DESCRIPTION: 20.5 cm (8"). *Andes of Peru.* Rather long and decurved bill (but curvature much less extreme than in previous 4 species). Above grayish brown, somewhat duskier on crown, and with long, narrow, whitish superciliary and pale shaft streaking on crown and back; *wings and tail contrastingly rufous* (easily seen on perched birds). Throat white, remaining underparts pale dingy grayish brown *prominently streaked with whitish.*

SIMILAR SPECIES: Plain-breasted Earthcreeper is somewhat paler generally, lacks streaking below, and its rufous wings and tail contrast much less.

HABITAT AND BEHAVIOR: Uncommon to locally fairly common on or near ground on rocky shrubby slopes and in patches of *Polylepis* woodland; favors somewhat more vegetated terrain than Plain-breasted Earthcreeper. Found singly or in pairs, usually inconspicuous, hopping on ground with tail half-cocked, probing with its bill into loose soil or rock crevices like other earthcreepers. Its song is described as a harsh trill introduced by 3 separated notes, "keep kip kip trrrrrrrrr-r-r-r" (Fjeldså and Krabbe 1990).

RANGE: Andes of Peru (Cajamarca south to Huancavelica). Mostly 2800–4200 m.

Upucerthia ruficauda

STRAIGHT-BILLED EARTHCREEPER   PLATE: 1

DESCRIPTION: 18.5 cm (7¼″). *Andes of s. Peru to s. Argentina.* Bill so slightly decurved that it looks *virtually straight*. Above pale brown with *narrow whitish superciliary*, becoming more rufescent on rump; an indistinct rufous area shows on inner part of primaries in flight; tail looks mostly rufous, central pair of rectrices duskier, and inner webs of all but outermost pair blackish. *Throat and breast white*, lower underparts pale brownish *with blurry whitish streaking*. Foregoing applies to *montana* of n. part of range south at least to n. Chile and w. Bolivia; nominate race of remainder of range has duller whitish throat and breast.

SIMILAR SPECIES: Rock Earthcreeper has slightly more decurved bill, more ochraceous superciliary, darker upperparts, more uniform and buffier underparts (lacking the contrasting white-bibbed effect) with streaking more confined to sides, and completely rufous tail. Rock carries its tail at a much less acute angle than Straight-billed typically does. Cf. also certain canasteros (all with shorter bills; Rusty-vented is most similar) and Band-tailed Earthcreeper.

HABITAT AND BEHAVIOR: Uncommon to locally fairly common in ravines with low shrubs (sometimes *Polylepis* scrub) and on slopes with bunchgrass and scattered shrubs; seems quite tied to the presence of boulders or piles of jumbled rocks. Found singly or in pairs and usually quite secretive and shy, hopping or running rapidly on ground or perching on rocks, *almost always with its tail cocked very high* (sometimes held so far forward it almost touches the head!). Foraging birds can sometimes be located through their sharp, single "kweep" contact note. The song, given from a rock, is a fast series of "pu" notes quickly rising into 2 or 3 loud, penetrating, more spaced "pee" or "wheet" notes (Fjeldså and Krabbe 1990). Readily found in the shrubby quebradas below Putre, along the road down to Arica, Chile.

RANGE: Andes of s. Peru (north to Arequipa), w. Bolivia, Chile (Tarapacá south locally to Santiago, rarer southward), and w. Argentina (south to s. Chubut). Mostly 2300–4300 m, but much lower (reportedly to 300 m) in s. Argentina.

Upucerthia andaecola

ROCK EARTHCREEPER

DESCRIPTION: 18.5 cm (7¼″). *Andes of w. Bolivia to nw. Argentina.* Resembles Straight-billed Earthcreeper but bill somewhat more decurved. Further differs in having a *buff superciliary*, generally darker upperparts, *entirely rufous tail*, and more uniform buffyish underparts (foreneck not whiter) with *streaking darker and more confined to flanks*.

SIMILAR SPECIES: Birds running on the ground with cocked tail might be confused with certain canasteros, though these are always smaller with dissimilar (shorter and less decurved) bills.

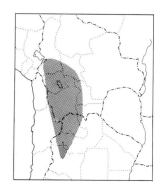

HABITAT AND BEHAVIOR: Uncommon to fairly common in quebradas and on steep rocky hillsides with bunchgrass and scattered bushes. Behavior similar to Straight-billed Earthcreeper's, though Rock never seems to cock its tail at as acute an angle and on the whole is more confiding and easier to see. The song, usually given from atop a shrub, is a piercing "veetveet-veeveeveeveeveeeee-veet-viree-veetvee-vee" (B. Whitney, *in* Fjeldså and Krabbe 1990). Quite numerous along the Cachi road in Salta, Argentina.

RANGE: Andes of w. Bolivia (north to La Paz), nw. Argentina (south to Catamarca), and adjacent n. Chile (e. Antofogasta). Mostly 2600–4200 m.

Ochetorhynchus Earthcreepers

A pair of furnariids found in arid woodlands of interior s.-cen. South America. Their generic placement has been debated, but we feel that the evidence now available indicates that they should be separated from *Upucerthia*. In *Birds of the World*, vol. 7, they and *U. ruficauda* (Straight-billed Earthcreeper) were separated in the genus *Ochetorhynchus*. Meyer de Schauensee (1966, 1970) reunited them in *Upucerthia*, where they had been placed in *Birds of the Americas*, vol. 13, part 4. Vaurie (1980) also placed them in *Upucerthia*, partly because he did not want generically to separate *ruficauda* and *andaecola* (Rock Earthcreeper), which he considered to be closely related. We agree with this latter contention but suggest that *certhioides* and *harterti* differ markedly from other *Upucerthia* species. Not only is *certhioides*'s voice very unlike that of any *Upucerthia* (more resembling a *Phacellodomus* thornbird), so too is its more arboreal behavior. Further, sometimes its nests are constructed of twigs (made either by itself or by other furnariids), and sometimes they are placed in tree or rock hollows or even hornero nests. The nest of the closely related *O. harterti* remains undescribed.

Ochetorhynchus certhioides

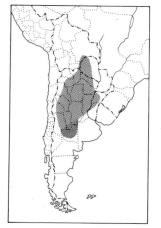

CHACO EARTHCREEPER   PLATE: 1

DESCRIPTION: 17 cm (6¾"). *Dry chaco woodland.* Bill almost straight. Above mostly brown with *rufous forehead* and buff superciliary; flight feathers basally rufous (visible mainly in flight); tail mostly rufous brown, brownest on central rectrices. *Throat white, contrasting* with pale grayish brown remaining underparts. Foregoing applies to *estebani* (n. part of range); nominate and *luscinia* (remainder of range) are somewhat darker generally, especially below, and have a *rufous superciliary* in addition to the rufous forehead.

SIMILAR SPECIES: Almost all other earthcreepers occur at higher elevations, and none (except Bolivian, which see) is as arboreal. Band-tailed Earthcreeper occurs farther south in Argentina, is streaked below, and lacks rufous forehead. Cf. also Common Thornbird.

HABITAT AND BEHAVIOR: Uncommon to fairly common but inconspicuous (most easily found when singing) in lower growth of dry woodland and chaco scrub, especially where undergrowth (e.g., terrestrial bromeliads) is dense. Usually found singly or in pairs, most often foraging in low trees and shrubs but sometimes dropping to ground. Seems not to cock its tail. The song is a series of 6–10 loud, penetrating notes which are either steady in pitch or descend slightly, e.g., "cheeé-cheeé-cheeé-cheeé-cheeé-cheéw," quite reminiscent of a *Phacellodomus* thornbird and unlike any *Upucerthia* earthcreeper.

RANGE: Se. Bolivia (Estancia Perforación in s. Santa Cruz, and probably also in Tarija), w. Paraguay, and n. and cen. Argentina (south to Mendoza, La Pampa, and Santa Fe, and east to w. Corrientes and nw. Entre Ríos). To about 1700 m.

NOTE: See comments under Bolivian Earthcreeper.

Ochetorhynchus harterti

BOLIVIAN EARTHCREEPER

DESCRIPTION: 17 cm (6¾"). Andean valleys of *s. Bolivia*. Resembles Chaco Earthcreeper (no overlap). Differs most strikingly in *lacking Chaco's rufous forehead*. In addition, Bolivian's entire underparts are paler, so its whitish throat contrasts *less*, and its uppertail-coverts are more rufescent. Bolivian has a buff superciliary (much as in the *estebani* race of Chaco).

SIMILAR SPECIES: Occurs at lower elevations than Rock and Straight-billed Earthcreepers. Common Thornbird in area of overlap has rufous forehead.

HABITAT AND BEHAVIOR: Uncommon in lower growth and borders of deciduous woodland and arid scrub with a special predilection for patches of terrestrial bromeliads. Its behavior seems to differ little from Chaco Earthcreeper's, though Bolivian seems to forage more often on or near ground. One call that has been heard is a sharp "peeyp!" repeated at about 2-second intervals (R. A. Rowlett and RSR). We are not familiar with Bolivian's song; A. W. Kratter et al. (1993) describe it as being similar but with "on average more notes." Can be found east of Comarapa in w. Santa Cruz.

RANGE: Andean valleys of s. Bolivia (Cochabamba, w. Santa Cruz, and Chuquisaca). 1430–2960 m.

NOTE: Considered by Vaurie (1980) as a subspecies of *O. certhioides*. While we agree that *estebani*, the race of *O. certhioides* that comes closest to the range of *O. harterti*, is also the closest in generally paler plumage to that seen in *O. harterti*, *estebani* has no less rufous on its forehead than the other races of *O. certhioides*. Further, in Bolivia (where the species' ranges come closest), the elevations at which *O. harterti* occurs lie considerably above those recorded for *O. certhioides* (which occurs higher in Argentina). For more natural history and distribution information on this species, see Remsen et al. (1988).

Eremobius Earthcreepers

A monotypic genus closely related to *Upucerthia* and found in s. Argentina and immediately adjacent s. Chile. In comportment *Eremobius* seems intermediate between *Upucerthia* and certain *Asthenes* canasteros. It places its large twig nest in a low shrub; thus its nesting behavior is similar to some *Asthenes'* but differs strikingly from *Upucerthia*'s.

Eremobius phoenicurus

BAND-TAILED EARTHCREEPER   PLATE: I

DESCRIPTION: 18 cm (7″). *Patagonian steppes of s. Argentina and adjacent Chile.* Bill almost straight. Above mostly pale grayish brown with *long, narrow, white superciliary* and somewhat more rufescent ear-coverts; *tail mostly black with basal half of all but central rectrices contrastingly rufous-chestnut.* Throat white; remaining underparts dull grayish, *distinctly streaked with white on breast and down flanks,* and tinged buffy on belly.

SIMILAR SPECIES: Larger Scale-throated Earthcreeper has a longer and much more decurved bill, shows scaling (not streaking) on foreneck, and its tail (showing virtually no rufous) is not bicolored. Straight-billed Earthcreeper occurs mainly at higher elevations (though with some overlap in s. Argentina); it has a mainly rufous tail.

HABITAT AND BEHAVIOR: Uncommon on sparsely vegetated shrubby plains, mostly on level ground (showing no special predilection for ravines). Mainly terrestrial, running rapidly on ground, usually with its tail cocked high; though rarely remaining long in the open, it is often quite confiding, more so than Scale-throated. Feeds by probing into sandy ground or around stones, also while hopping about inside the cover of a shrub. Singing birds sometimes perch conspicuously atop bushes but more often remain hidden; the song is a short, fast, dry trill which sometimes ends with a distinctive, sharply emphasized "wheeék" note or series of notes (R. Straneck; RSR); an alarm call is a repeated husky "suwee" (B. Whitney; RSR). Small numbers occur on Valdés Peninsula in Chubut.

RANGE: S. Argentina (Neuquén and Río Negro south to s. Santa Cruz) and extreme s. Chile (Nov. 1989 specimen from near Punta Delgada in ne. Magallanes; F. Vuilleumier and A. Capparella). Records from farther north in Argentina are considered doubtful (J. R. Navas, *Rev. Museo Arg. Cienc. Nat. "Bernardino Rivadavia"* 7[3]: 294–301, 1971). To 1200 m.

Chilia

A monotypic and distinct genus almost certainly most closely related to the earthcreepers (though considered by Vaurie [1980] to be closest to *Cinclodes*). A Chilean endemic, with restricted rocky habitat. Its nest is made of twigs and set in a fissure of a rock (Johnson 1967).

Chilia melanura

CRAG CHILIA   PLATE: I

DESCRIPTION: 18.5 cm (7¼″). *Steep rocky slopes and cliffs in mountains of cen. Chile.* Bill *very straight* (sometimes almost looking upturned). Above mostly brown with narrow white superciliary and *contrasting*

rufous rump, uppertail-coverts, and crissum; tail mainly blackish. Lower face, throat, and breast sharply white, belly dull brown. Atacamae (of n. end of range in Atacama and Coquimbo) is paler generally.

SIMILAR SPECIES: Earthcreeper-like but *boldly patterned*, the Crag Chilia is not likely to be confused in its limited range and habitat. N. Am. observers will be struck by its superficial similarity to the Canyon Wren (*Catherpes mexicanus*).

HABITAT AND BEHAVIOR: Uncommon to fairly common on arid rocky slopes with at most sparse shrubby vegetation, and on cliffs. Usually in pairs, hopping and running about on ground with tail partially cocked, often perching or climbing around on boulders, but flying relatively little. For most of the year it is easiest to see in the relative cool of early morning, for it becomes very elusive during the sun-baked midday. The chilia forages mainly by probing into crevices of rocks (it has also been seen feeding at cactus flowers) and often keeps up a steady "cht, ch-ch, cht, ch-ch . . ." fussing. Its song is a short staccato chatter, jumbled at the beginning and end and with 4–7 loud, piercing "teet" notes in the middle (B. Whitney, *in* Fjeldså and Krabbe 1990). Small numbers can be seen along lower part of the road to the Yeso Reservoir and on upper part of the Farallones road, both in the Santiago Andes.

RANGE: Cen. Chile (Atacama south to Colchagua). Mostly 1400–2400 m, perhaps somewhat lower in winter.

Cinclodes Cinclodes

A fairly uniform group of sturdily built and rather plainly attired furnariids found mainly in the Andes, with some species along coastlines from Peru southward and others on isolated highlands in Argentina and southern Brazil. Only one, the widespread Bar-winged, is migratory. Cinclodes are particularly fond of the vicinity of water, especially rushing mountain streams. Unlike the superficially similar earthcreepers, they have at most only slightly decurved bills and also differ in their usually much bolder, more confiding behavior. Most species show a white to rufous wing-band, prominent in flight, and pale tail-corners; the wing-band is shown off to good effect during the exuberant wing-flapping displays given by all species. The nest, in a hole or burrow, sometimes natural but often excavated by the birds themselves, is usually placed in a bank, less often in a wall or even an old building.

GROUP A

Distinctive *dark sooty brown* cinclodes; s. Tierra del Fuego and Falklands.

Cinclodes antarcticus

BLACKISH CINCLODES   PLATE: 2
Other: Tussock-bird (Falklands)

DESCRIPTION: 19–20 cm (7½–8"). *Coastlines of s. Tierra del Fuego and Falklands*. Bill blackish, usually with a yellowish base. *Maculirostris* (of

Fuegian area) is *uniform dark sooty,* slightly paler on throat. Nominate race (of Falklands) is somewhat smaller, more sooty brown, and shows a faint rufescent wing-band in flight.

SIMILAR SPECIES: Not likely to be confused, though it has the configuration and size of a *Turdus* thrush (cf. Austral Thrush, the only thrush that occurs with it but which differs in coloration).

HABITAT AND BEHAVIOR: Uncommon to locally very common along coasts, both in rocky areas and on gravelly beaches; regularly found where seals and sea lions haul out of the water and at colonies of nesting seabirds. Now essentially confined to islands where introduced predators are scarce or absent. On Falklands found primarily on the smaller "out" islands such as Carcass Is., whereas in Tierra del Fuego it occurs only in the far south (e.g., areas around Navarino Is. and on Cape Horn). Likely was formerly more numerous and widespread. Blackish Cinclodes is sometimes astonishingly tame, doubtless accounting for its decline where cats and rats are numerous; some individuals almost seem inquisitive, at times hopping about unconcernedly at your feet, even inspecting your shoes! Forages mainly by searching for insects and marine invertebrates in the kelp mats which are so prevalent on the coastlines it inhabits, but also perches freely in trees planted around sheep stations. The song is a loud series of sharp staccato notes interspersed with more musical trills, often continued for several minutes; this is sometimes given as part of a flight display, or the bird may remain perched, repeatedly raising and flapping both wings simultaneously like other cinclodes.

RANGE: Extreme s. Chile and Argentina (from Beagle Channel southward, and on Mitre Peninsula and Diego Ramirez Is.); Falkland Is. Below 100 m.

GROUP B

"Standard" cinclodes; size varies; some familiar, some very local.

Cinclodes nigrofumosus

CHILEAN SEASIDE-CINCLODES

PLATE: 2

Other: Seaside Cinclodes

DESCRIPTION: 21.5 cm (8½"). *Rocky coastlines of n. and cen. Chile;* a Peruvian form, *C. taczanowskii,* sometimes considered conspecific with this species, is here considered a distinct species. *Mostly dark sooty brown above* with a *very narrow* whitish superciliary; a rufous-buff wing-band shows mainly in flight; outer rectrices tipped buff. *Throat white* extending to sides of neck; remaining underparts brown with white shaft streaking on breast.

SIMILAR SPECIES: Dark-bellied Cinclodes is smaller with a less heavy bill and is much grayer generally (not so brown) with a more prominent white superciliary. Cf. also Peruvian Seaside-Cinclodes.

HABITAT AND BEHAVIOR: Rare to fairly common (scarcer northward) along rocky coastlines. Never occurs away from immediate coast; indeed it and closely related Peruvian Seaside-Cinclodes have been called "the most maritime of all passerine birds" (R. A. Paynter, Jr., *Bull. B. O. C.* 91[4]: 11–12, 1971), but despite this Paynter could find no evidence that they had a functional salt gland. Forages singly or as separated pairs on rocks, often in areas exposed to heavy surf, where it feeds much like certain rock-favoring shorebirds (e.g., Ruddy Turnstone and Surfbird), though it sometimes holds its tail partially cocked. The song, a long and loud trilling often accompanied by repeatedly flaring the wings open and shut, exposing the wing-band, is usually delivered as the bird perches atop a boulder. Quite readily found around Valparaiso, especially along the coast road just to the north. RANGE: Coast of n. and cen. Chile (Arica south to Valdivia).

NOTE: See comments under Peruvian Seaside-Cinclodes.

Cinclodes taczanowskii

PERUVIAN SEASIDE-CINCLODES
Other: Seaside Cinclodes, Surf Cinclodes

DESCRIPTION: 21.5 cm (8½"). *Rocky coastlines of cen. and s. Peru.* Sometimes considered conspecific with preceding species but is somewhat paler and less sooty (especially on back, rump, and underparts) and has *white throat markedly less contrasting and extensive* (the throat is only faintly white-streaked), *virtually no white superciliary, wing-coverts tipped pale buff* (in Chilean very faint), and slightly whiter tail-tips.
HABITAT AND BEHAVIOR: Uncommon to fairly common along rocky coastlines. Behavior, including voice, similar to Chilean Seaside-Cinclodes's. Readily seen at Paracas Peninsula.
RANGE: Coast of cen. and s. Peru (Ancash south to Tacna).

NOTE: We follow Vaurie (1980) and *Birds of the World*, vol. 7, in considering *C. taczanowskii* as a species separate from *C. nigrofumosus* of Chile (which then becomes monotypic); Meyer de Schauensee (1966, 1970) considered them conspecific. The gap between the two forms has been considerably narrowed by the late R. A. Hughes's recent sightings (pers. comm.) of birds that appeared to be typical *taczanowskii* at Ite in Tacna, Peru; this is only some 70 km north of the northernmost locality for true *nigrofumosus*, at Arica in Chile. Despite their close approach, there is no evidence of intergradation between the two. It seems confusing to call *nigrofumosus* the Seaside Cinclodes and *taczanowskii* the Surf Cinclodes, as has been suggested (Meyer de Schauensee 1966)—at least we can never remember which is which! We prefer to use geographical epithets.

Cinclodes oustaleti

GRAY-FLANKED CINCLODES   PLATE: 2

DESCRIPTION: 16.5—17 cm (6½—6¾"). *Mainly in Chile* (including Juan Fernández Is.). *Mostly sooty gray above* with narrow white superciliary; underwing-coverts and axillars white, with a buff wing-band showing mainly in flight; outer tail feathers tipped rufous-buff. Throat white indistinctly flecked with dusky; *breast and flanks grayish*, lightly spotted and streaked with white, *the flanks more or less contrasting with whitish median belly.* *Hornensis* of extreme south is slightly larger and grayer than nominate subspecies.
SIMILAR SPECIES: Dark-bellied Cinclodes is appreciably larger with somewhat longer and heavier bill, a more conspicuous superciliary, more discrete white streaks on breast, and less contrasting flanks; its underwing-coverts are gray (Gray-flanked's are white, but this is hard to see in the field). Sympatric race of Bar-winged Cinclodes (nomi-

nate) is more similar and is about the same size but is paler grayish brown above, has a buffier superciliary, lacks the contrasting grayish flanks, and never looks streaked below; its tail-corners are paler (not as buffy; this is often helpful as a bird flushes).

HABITAT AND BEHAVIOR: Uncommon in open grassy and rocky areas, usually (*contra* Fjeldså and Krabbe 1990) near streams in mountainous regions; during austral winter descends to lowlands, some birds regularly reaching coast; perhaps only a summer visitor to s. end of its range. Generally found singly or in pairs and, though fairly bold and conspicuous, usually the least numerous cinclodes in its range. Its behavior, including voice, is similar to that of the better-known cinclodes (see under Bar-winged). Small numbers nest in Andes of Santiago, Chile, mostly at quite high elevations (Dark-bellied lower).

RANGE: Chile (Antofogasta south to Aysén, and in s. Magallanes) and adjacent Argentina (locally from Mendoza to w. Chubut, and in Tierra del Fuego); Juan Fernández Is. off Chile. Mostly below 3000 m (occasionally nesting higher).

NOTE: See comments under Olrog's Cinclodes.

Cinclodes olrogi

OLROG'S CINCLODES

DESCRIPTION: 17 cm (6¾"). *Recently described from the Córdoba, Argentina, area.* Superficially resembles sympatric Cordoba Cinclodes but differs in its *striking white wing-band* (not rufous) and somewhat more mottled breast; tail-corners are dull rufous.

SIMILAR SPECIES: White-winged Cinclodes, which also breeds in w. Córdoba and also favors vicinity of streams, is larger with a longer bill and white tail-corners; underparts of White-winged's sympatric race (*schocolatinus*) are quite dark and uniform, without the mottled effect on breast of Olrog's. Cf. also Gray-flanked Cinclodes (no overlap).

HABITAT AND BEHAVIOR: Uncommon in open grassy and rocky areas, where it almost always feeds along or near streams. Behavior similar to that of syntopic Cordoba Cinclodes, though Olrog's seems less numerous and much more restricted to vicinity of water. Small numbers can be found on the Pampa de Achala.

RANGE: N.-cen. Argentina (mts. of w. Córdoba and ne. San Luis). Breeds 1600–2800 m, in winter descending to about 900 m.

NOTE: A recently described species: M. Nores and D. Yzurieta, *Acad. Nac. Córdoba Misc.* 61: 4–8, 1979. Olrog (1979) considered *olrogi* a race of *C. oustaleti,* whereas Nores later (*Hornero* 12: 262–273, 1986) treated it as a race of *C. fuscus* because of its similarity to a recently described race, *riojanus,* of *C. fuscus* from nearby La Rioja. We believe it more likely that Olrog was correct and that *C. olrogi* is more closely allied to *C. oustaleti,* but treat it as a full species.

Cinclodes patagonicus

DARK-BELLIED CINCLODES

DESCRIPTION: 20.5 cm (8"). *Cen. and s. Chile and adjacent Argentina south to Tierra del Fuego.* Resembles Gray-flanked Cinclodes but is *substantially larger* and has a longer and heavier bill (more like the 2 spe-

cies of seaside-cinclodes). Other differences include a *bolder and wider white superciliary,* being darker generally, and having *more distinct white streaking on breast* and less contrast between flanks and median belly.

SIMILAR SPECIES: Cf. also Chilean Seaside-Cinclodes and nominate race of Bar-winged Cinclodes.

HABITAT AND BEHAVIOR: Fairly common to common in a variety of habitats but *invariably near water* (protected saltwater shorelines, lakeshores, and along rivers and rocky streams). Especially numerous in Tierra del Fuego, where apparently resident, occurring near open water at sea level during winter. Behavior similar to that of other cinclodes, but Dark-bellied often seems more animated and "cocky" in its mannerisms and is often very bold. Along rocky rivers and streams it may recall a *Cinclus* dipper (perhaps even acting as its ecological replacement?). Has a variety of sharp call notes, e.g., "tjit," sometimes repeated; its song is rather different, starting with several more musical phrases then ending with a descending chatter, "pur-r-r-ree-pree-pree-pree-tr-r-r-r-r-r-r-r-r-r."

RANGE: Chile (north to Antofogasta) and w. Argentina (north to sw. Mendoza) south to Tierra del Fuego (even at Cape Horn). Mostly below 1200 m (but recorded to 2300 m in cen. Chile).

Cinclodes fuscus

BAR-WINGED CINCLODES   PLATE: 2

DESCRIPTION: 17–17.5 cm (6¾–7"). *A small, widespread, and generally numerous cinclodes. Bill comparatively short and slender.* Nominate *fuscus* (nesting in Chile from Atacama southward, and in Argentina from Mendoza, La Pampa, and s. Buenos Aires southward, migrating northward) is dingy grayish brown above with buff to buffy whitish superciliary; a *cinnamon-buff wing-band* is visible mainly in flight, as are its buffy whitish tail-corners and entire outer web of outermost pair of rectrices. Throat whitish, feathers scaled with dusky brown; remaining underparts pale dingy grayish brown. All other races are browner and paler (less dingy and gray); *albiventris* group (of nw. Argentina and n. Chile north through Peruvian Andes) is paler buffy whitish below and has a buffy whitish wing-band, whereas *albidiventris* group (Andes of Ecuador north to Venezuela) has a truly *rufous wing-band,* more rufous tail-corners, and is more brownish below.

SIMILAR SPECIES: Usually the most common and most familiar cinclodes; learn it well, as in most areas there is at least 1 other cinclodes with which it can be confused. In Ecuador and Colombia, cf. larger, heavier-billed Stout-billed Cinclodes. White-winged Cinclodes is larger, has a longer tail and markedly longer bill, more rufous back, and striking pure white wing-band and tail-corners. In and near Córdoba, Argentina, cf. localized Cordoba and Olrog's Cinclodes; in extreme se. Brazil, cf. Long-tailed Cinclodes. Gray-flanked Cinclodes, darker and sootier above with a whiter superciliary, shows more contrast between its dark flanks and whitish median belly.

HABITAT AND BEHAVIOR: Common in a variety of open grassy habitats (including páramo and puna grasslands, and the steppes of Patagonia), usually along streams, lakeshores, or rivers. Mainly terrestrial and often confiding, foraging while walking on ground, picking at grass or rocks, sometimes probing into damp soil or animal droppings. Frequently in pairs, flying swiftly across open ground or up and down watercourses; the tail is often cocked upon alighting but generally not while feeding. The song is a short, fast, high trill, sometimes given in flight but more often from an exposed perch while simultaneously wing-flapping in the typical *Cinclodes* display.

RANGE: Andes of w. Venezuela (north to s. Lara), Colombia (in E. Andes from Boyacá south to Cundinamarca and in Cen. Andes from Cauca southward; also Santa Marta Mts.), Ecuador, Peru, w. Bolivia, Chile, and Argentina; in s. part of the last two also breeds in lowlands, in Argentina north to La Pampa and s. Buenos Aires, and in austral summer south to Tierra del Fuego. In austral winter nominate *fuscus* migrates north to extreme s. Paraguay (2 seen in Neembucú in June 1991; RSR and P. Scharf et al., photos VIREO), ne. Argentina (Corrientes), Uruguay, and extreme s. Brazil (Rio Grande do Sul). To 5000 m.

Cinclodes comechingonus

CORDOBA CINCLODES

Other: Chestnut-winged, Comechingones, or Sierran Cinclodes

DESCRIPTION: 17 cm (6¾″). *Córdoba, Argentina.* Resembles Bar-winged Cinclodes and has sometimes been considered a race of that species. Differs in its *deep rufous wing-band and tail-corners* (not just cinnamon-buff) and *mostly yellowish lower mandible* (Bar-winged's bill usually all dark, with at most the base of lower mandible pale).

SIMILAR SPECIES: The other 2 cinclodes breeding in Córdoba mts., White-winged and Olrog's, both have *white* wing-bands. Note that nominate race of Bar-winged can occur with Cordoba Cinclodes during austral winter.

HABITAT AND BEHAVIOR: Common in open grassy and rocky areas, most numerous near water but also regularly occurring (more often than most cinclodes) at some distance from it. Behaves much like Bar-winged Cinclodes; in our experience (*contra* Fjeldså and Krabbe 1990), Cordoba does not cock or wag its tail any more than Bar-winged, nor is it especially shy. Breeding birds give a variety of exuberant chips and trills, many with a descending effect; the song is rather more complex than most songs of Bar-winged. Numerous on the Pampa de Achala.

RANGE: N.-cen. Argentina (breeding in mts. of w. Córdoba and ne. San Luis, in austral winter occurring north to e. Tucumán and w. Santiago del Estero). Breeds 1600–2400 m, in winter descending to 1000 m.

NOTE: This taxon has sometimes been considered only a race of *C. fuscus* (e.g., Meyer de Schauensee 1966), though in our view it deserves full species status. In the area where *C. comechingonus* breeds, *C. fuscus* is found *only* as a winter visitor; sympatric breeding does *not* occur (*contra* Vaurie 1980, p. 38). Several English names have been suggested. Because by far the major portion of its breeding range lies within Córdoba, we favor Cordoba Cinclodes. The wing-band is not really "chestnut" (being rufous), and the name "Comechingones," derived from one of the mt. ranges on which it breeds, seems overly obscure.

Cinclodes excelsior

STOUT-BILLED CINCLODES

PLATE: 2

DESCRIPTION: 20.5 cm (8″). *Páramos of Cen. Andes of Colombia and Ecuador; C. aricomae of s. Peru and w. Bolivia is considered a separate species* (see below). Bill *rather long, heavy, and markedly decurved.* Above dark brown with whitish superciliary; a rufous-buff wing-band and dull buff tail-corners show mainly in flight. Throat whitish scaled with dusky; remaining underparts dull buffy whitish, brownest on sides and flanks, with *usually prominent brownish scaling on breast.*

SIMILAR SPECIES: Often confused with Bar-winged Cinclodes and regularly occurs with it. Bar-winged is considerably smaller, has a finer and shorter bill with no curvature, and its breast is usually only lightly scaled.

HABITAT AND BEHAVIOR: Uncommon to fairly common in páramo and grassy areas, usually near water and at least some woody vegetation (low bushes or *Polylepis* woodland); at least in Ecuador also occurs at elevations well above where even small shrubs can grow (e.g., on slopes of Volcán Cotopaxi). Forages while walking on ground, probing into grass or among rocks; perches freely in trees, especially when alarmed. Nests in holes that it digs in roadcuts and other banks; G. R. Graves and G. Arango (*Condor* 90[1]: 251–253, 1988) present more information on nesting in Colombia, and nesting behavior in Ecuador appears not to differ (RSR). Singing birds give a trilled "tr-r-r-r-r-r-r-reeet," usually accompanied by a wing-flapping display, and also have a sharp call note.

RANGE: Andes of Colombia (Nevado del Ruiz/Nevado del Tolima complex in Cen. Andes of Tolima, and in s. Nariño) and Ecuador (south to Azuay at El Cajas). 3300–5000 m.

NOTE: See comments under Royal Cinclodes. Vaurie (1980) considered *excelsior* to belong in the genus *Geositta.* Subsequent opinion, however, based on the species' behavior and morphology, has been unanimous in suggesting that this treatment was incorrect and that *excelsior* belongs in the genus in which it has traditionally been placed, *Cinclodes.*

Cinclodes aricomae

ROYAL CINCLODES

DESCRIPTION: 20.5 cm (8″). *Very local in high Andes of s. Peru and adjacent Bolivia.* Resembles geographically distant Stout-billed Cinclodes, and is sometimes considered conspecific; bill shape similar. Royal has *considerably darker and browner lower underparts,* buffier (less white) superciliary, and in flight shows *more prominent rufous wing-band* which contrasts more because of its darker flight feathers.

SIMILAR SPECIES: Cf. smaller and slimmer-billed Bar-winged Cinclodes.

HABITAT AND BEHAVIOR: Rare in patches of *Polylepis* woodland on steep rocky slopes; perhaps occurs away from such patches, but if so this has not yet been noted. Feeds by hopping on rocks in and near woodland, flicking off pieces of moss and earth to expose hidden prey items. Only recently rediscovered (see J. Fjeldså, N. Krabbe, and T. A. Parker III, *Bull. B. O. C.* 107[3]: 112–114, 1987), and considered by these authors to be threatened by local inhabitants' ongoing destruction of *Polylepis* woodlands for firewood.

RANGE: Locally in Andes of s. Peru (southeast of Abancay in Apurímac; Abra Málaga area above Ollantaytambo in Cuzco; Aricoma pass in Puno) and extreme w. Bolivia (a single specimen taken at Tilotilo in La Paz). 3600–4700 m.

NOTE: Often regarded as a subspecies of *C. excelsior,* but J. Fjeldså and N. Krabbe (pers. comm.) now feel that *C. aricomae* deserves full species rank based on its somewhat different plumage pattern, different habitat, and highly disjunct range. We employ the English name suggested by Fjeldså and Krabbe (1990), though we do not see anything particularly "royal" about the species (perhaps Polylepis Cinclodes would have been a better choice).

Cinclodes pabsti

LONG-TAILED CINCLODES   PLATE: 2

DESCRIPTION: 21.5 cm (8½"). *A large cinclodes found locally in extreme se. Brazil.* Grayish brown above with whitish superciliary; wings duskier, *coverts and remiges prominently tipped and edged cinnamon-buff* and with wing-band of same color visible mainly in flight; *tail-corners broadly tipped cinnamon-buff.* Throat white; remaining underparts pale brownish.

SIMILAR SPECIES: Likely to be confused only with Bar-winged Cinclodes (though the two have never been found together). Bar-winged is a substantially smaller, shorter-tailed bird whose closed wing is much plainer and whose throat is obviously speckled with dusky. Cf. also Chalk-browed Mockingbird.

HABITAT AND BEHAVIOR: Uncommon to fairly common in open grasslands, almost always near water (streams, ponds, etc.), sometimes around farmhouses. Behavior much like other *Cinclodes',* with similar trilled song and wing-flapping display. Can be found on the plateau around São Francisco de Paula and along the road from there north toward Aparados da Serra Nat. Park, where it also occurs.

RANGE: Extreme se. Brazil (se. Santa Catarina and ne. Rio Grande do Sul). 750–1700 m.

Cinclodes atacamensis

WHITE-WINGED CINCLODES   PLATE: 2

DESCRIPTION: 21 cm (8¼"). *A striking and fairly large cinclodes found along streams in high Andes from Peru to Argentina. Bill quite long. Above rufous brown with bold white superciliary; wings duskier with broad white wing-band and patch on primary-coverts* (especially prominent in flight but also visible on closed wing); tail blackish with white corners. Throat white, lower throat faintly mottled darker; remaining underparts pale buffy grayish, browner on flanks and crissum. *Schocolatinus* (Córdoba and San Luis, Argentina) is darker brown (not so rufous) above and darker below (with contrastingly white throat).

SIMILAR SPECIES: This species is widely sympatric with, but almost always outnumbered by, the *albiventris* type of Bar-winged Cinclodes. Bar-winged is smaller and proportionately shorter-tailed and shorter-

billed, is less rufescent above with a buffier superciliary, and has a less flashy, not so pure white wing-band with much less white showing on closed wing. In Córdoba area, Olrog's Cinclodes is smaller and has rufous-buff (not white) tail-corners.

HABITAT AND BEHAVIOR: Uncommon to fairly common along rocky streams in puna grassland or shrubby terrain, sometimes also where there are small patches of low *Polylepis* woodland. In behavior and voice is much like other *Cinclodes* but is much more restricted to clear running water, being rarely or never found away from it.

RANGE: Andes of Peru (north to Ancash and Pasco), w. Bolivia, n. and cen. Chile (mainly in Tarapacá and Antofogasta, more rarely south to Santiago), and w. Argentina (south rarely to Mendoza; also in mts. of w. Córdoba and ne. San Luis). Mostly 2200–4500 m (sometimes to 5000 m), but lower in Córdoba area of Argentina (down to 900 m in winter), and twice seen near sea level in Arequipa, Peru, by R. A. Hughes (pers. comm.).

GROUP C

Unique *large* cinclodes of the *very high* Peruvian Andes; *immaculate white below.*

Cinclodes palliatus

WHITE-BELLIED CINCLODES   PLATE: 2

DESCRIPTION: 24 cm (9½"). *An unmistakable, very large cinclodes found very high in Peruvian Andes. Crown pale brownish gray* with a black loral spot; otherwise rich rufous brown above with *broad white wing-band* very conspicuous in flight and visible even on closed wing; tail duskier with small white tail-corners. *Pure snowy white below.*

HABITAT AND BEHAVIOR: Rare and local in boggy areas with short grass and *Distichia* cushion plants, occasionally moving up onto adjacent rocky slopes. This species, by far the most spectacular and elegant *Cinclodes,* behaves rather differently from the others and in some ways more resembles a *Mimus* mockingbird, though the cinclodes is usually wary. It generally occurs in pairs which are usually conspicuous as they run rapidly out on open, damp ground, pausing abruptly to feed. The tail is usually held high and is sometimes also angled sideways. A loud "chec" has been heard (M. Robbins), as has a long, trilled chattering (Fjeldså and Krabbe 1990). A few pairs can be found high above Lima along the road to Marcapomacocha.

RANGE: Andes of cen. Peru (locally in Junín, Lima, and Huancavelica; the old record supposedly from Moyobamba in San Martín is unquestionably erroneous). 4400–5000 m.

Furnarius Horneros

The horneros form a small and distinct genus of chunky, somewhat thrush-like furnariids found in open or semiopen areas through the lowlands of South America, especially near water. Their tails are short (markedly shorter than in cinclodes and earthcreepers), and most have a rather long, slender bill. Rufous and brown predominate, accentuated in many species by a bold white eyebrow. Horneros forage mostly on the ground, where they probe with their bills or flick aside leaves; they have a distinctive strutting gait, lifting each foot high as they move along, often holding the head back and thrusting the breast forward. Many are bold in demeanor, and all are very vocal. Some horneros are conspicuous and numerous, notably the Rufous, which over wide parts of its range ranks as one of the best-known birds. Others, such as two found on Amazonian river islands, the Bay and Lesser, are much scarcer and more unobtrusive.

The remarkable mud nests of almost all species are shaped much like an old-fashioned oven, hence their English name *ovenbird; horno* is Spanish for oven, and *hornero* means baker. The nests of the most familiar species, Rufous, are very conspicuous, but those of the others are usually placed in much less obvious situations, typically on a shaded large horizontal limb. Nests of the Band-tailed Hornero, however, have recently been described as strikingly different: a shallow open cup constructed of grasses and other plant material placed in an arboreal bromeliad or under the eaves of a house (A. Studer and J. Veilliard, *Ararajuba* 1:39–41, 1990).

GROUP A

Bright rufous above; contrasting crown (usually) and *prominent superciliary*.

Furnarius leucopus

PALE-LEGGED HORNERO

PLATE: 2

DESCRIPTION: 16.5–19 cm (6½–7½"). *Legs typically pale yellowish to flesh* but varying to grayish in *assimilis* (mainly of Brazil) or brownish gray in *cinnamomeus* (w. Ecuador and Peru); iris usually brown, but pale hazel to creamy yellow in *cinnamomeus;* bill usually pale with at least base of maxilla blackish. Nominate group (with *tricolor*) of Amaz. to e. Brazil is *mostly bright orange-rufous above* with contrasting brownish gray crown and cheeks and long, broad, white superciliary; primaries blackish with rufous band showing in flight. Throat white; *remaining underparts pale rich cinnamon-buff,* whitest on midthroat and belly. Birds from Caribbean Colombia and nw. Venezuela (*longirostris* and *endoecus*) similar but with grayer crown; see V-20, C-24. *Cinnamomeus* of Pacific slope of Ecuador and nw. Peru is considerably larger with a longer and heavier bill, grayer crown, and whiter underparts. SIMILAR SPECIES: Generally the most numerous and widespread hornero across tropical South America. Bay Hornero is much more rufescent below; Lesser is considerably smaller and duller; and Band-tailed, compared to sympatric *tricolor* Pale-legged, is duller below and almost always shows a blackish terminal tail-band. HABITAT AND BEHAVIOR: Fairly common to very common in a variety of open to semiopen habitats in both humid and arid regions, in the latter mainly near water and in agricultural areas. Usually seen singly or in separated pairs which walk on ground, often nodding head back and forth. In some areas (e.g., w. Ecuador and nw. Peru), Pale-legged

Horneros often strut around boldly in the open, whereas in other areas (e.g., much of Amazonia) they tend to be more unobtrusive, more often remaining in or near cover, sometimes even walking about inside forest or woodland. Feeds by picking or probing into ground or grass or by flipping aside leaves with the bill. Although mainly terrestrial, also perches freely on large horizontal tree limbs, fence posts, etc. The frequently heard song is an arresting series of loud notes that gradually slow and descend in pitch, sometimes given more or less in unison by both members of a pair.

RANGE: Caribbean n. Colombia (Córdoba eastward, and south in middle Río Magdalena valley to e. Antioquia; 1 sighting from east of Andes in Norte de Santander) and nw. Venezuela (east to Falcón and Lara); w. Ecuador (north to w. Esmeraldas and Pichincha) and nw. Peru (south to Ancash); Guyana, Amaz. and e. Brazil (in Amazonia east only to around Santarém; south to Mato Grosso, s. Goiás, Bahia, and e. Minas Gerais), n. Bolivia (south to La Paz, Cochabamba, and Santa Cruz), and e. Peru (Loreto to Puno and Madre de Dios). To 2300 m (in s. Ecuador); nominate group to at least 1100 m.

NOTE: See comments under Bay Hornero. The two disjunct populations found in nw. South America, though currently classified as races of *F. leucopus,* may represent separate species. *Cinnamomeus* of w. Ecuador and nw. Peru is particularly divergent, especially in its notably larger size and pale iris; if split, it could be called Pacific Hornero. Birds of Caribbean Colombia and nw. Venezuela (*longirostris* group) are more similar to the cis-Andean nominate group, but if split they could be called Caribbean Hornero.

Furnarius torridus

BAY HORNERO

Other: Pale-billed Hornero

DESCRIPTION: 18.5 cm (7¼"). Mainly or entirely on *river islands in w. Amazonia.* Sometimes regarded as a dark morph of Pale-legged Hornero (*F. leucopus tricolor*), with which it may be sympatric; as yet they seem not to have been found at precisely the same locality. Resembles nominate group of that species, with similar soft-part colors: pinkish legs, mostly pale (whitish to horn or grayish) bill with dark restricted to base of maxilla. Differs in being somewhat larger, with generally more "saturated" plumage: *upperparts uniform rufous-chestnut* with *crown virtually concolor* (not grayer); less prominent buffy grayish superciliary; *underparts darker,* mainly *rufous* except for white throat. SIMILAR SPECIES: Cf. also the considerably smaller Lesser Hornero, with which Bay is locally sympatric.

HABITAT AND BEHAVIOR: Uncommon on or near ground in riparian woodland and forest and at borders on river islands in upper Amazon basin; found both in *Cecropia*-dominated woodland and in older forest (Rosenberg 1990). Behavior similar, so far as known, to Pale-legged Hornero's; the 2 species have been collected at several of the same localities in w. Brazil and ne. Peru, but how and if their ecological relationships differ remains unknown. We do not know its voice.

RANGE: Along Amazon River in extreme w. Brazil (at São Paulo de Olivença and Panelas Is.), s. Colombia (sightings from Leticia area), ne. Peru (up Río Ucayali almost to Pucallpa, on lower Río Huallaga at Santa Cruz, and along Río Napo), and extreme ne. Ecuador (1991 sightings near Lagartococha; RSR). Below 200 m.

NOTE: *F. torridus* has sometimes been considered a dark morph of *F. leucopus tricolor*, e.g., in *Birds of the Americas* (vol. 13, part 4) and by C. Vaurie (*Am. Mus. Novitates* 2515, 1973). J. T. Zimmer (*Am. Mus. Novitates* 860, 1936), who was followed by Meyer de Schauensee (1966, 1970), came to the opposite conclusion. Although there is some individual variation in color tonality and other characters, all the specimens we examined seem to be readily assignable to one group or the other, with no evident intermediates; hence we tentatively continue to regard *F. torridus* as a full species. As the bill color of *F. torridus* seems similar to that of *F. leucopus*, the previously suggested English name, Pale-billed Hornero, is misleading as it suggests a nonexistent difference. We feel "Bay" accurately conveys the saturated color tone of *F. torridus* as compared with *F. leucopus*, much as, for instance, Bay Antpitta (*Grallaria capitalis*) is more saturated than Rusty-tinged Antpitta (*G. przewalskii*).

Furnarius figulus

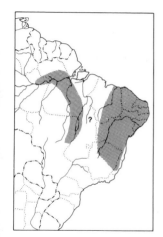

BAND-TAILED HORNERO

PLATE: 2

Other: Wing-banded Hornero

DESCRIPTION: 16.5 cm (6½"). *Lower Amaz. and e. Brazil*. Iris dark; *legs dull grayish. Pileatus* (lower Amaz. Brazil south to upper Rio Araguaia) cinnamon-rufous above with *contrasting dark brown crown and cheeks* and whitish superciliary; primaries blackish with 2 rufous bands visible on outer feathers (they are hard to discern in the field and seem to merge into a single band on inner flight feathers); *tail feathers tipped with black mostly on their inner webs* (extent of tipping is variable; a few birds show none). *Uniform drab buffyish below* with somewhat whiter throat and midbelly. Nominate race (e. Brazil) similar but crown essentially *concolor* with remaining upperparts.

SIMILAR SPECIES: Pale-legged Horneros of nominate group (widely sympatric with Band-tailed) are brighter generally, with more orangey upperparts and buffier underparts (contrasting more with the purer white throat); have pinkish legs; never show black tail-tipping; and have only 1 wing-band. Cf. also Lesser Hornero.

HABITAT AND BEHAVIOR: Uncommon to fairly common in semiopen areas, parks and gardens, and woodland borders, the main requirement seeming to be the proximity of water (whether still or flowing seems unimportant). Behaves much like Pale-legged Hornero, with which sometimes syntopic; Band-tailed may favor somewhat less wooded habitats. Band-tailed's primary song resembles Pale-legged's explosive series of notes which gradually slow and descend, though Band-tailed also has a quite different call (given mainly in alarm?), a comparatively subdued series of 6–10 sharp staccato notes, e.g., "chu, chu, che-che-ch-ch-ch-cheh," sometimes slower and then sounding almost like a *Formicivora* antwren.

RANGE: Lower Amaz. Brazil (from just below Manaus downriver to mouth of Rio Xingu, and south to upper Rio Araguaia drainage in Goiás) and e. Brazil (south to Minas Gerais and Espírito Santo, spreading southward in recent decades and reported uncertainly even from Rio de Janeiro). To 600 m.

NOTE: All the horneros to some degree show a wing-band. Calling *F. figulus* the Wing-banded Hornero (Meyer de Schauensee 1966, 1970) implies that it alone has such a band. However, this is the only hornero that ever shows a tail-band.

Furnarius minor

LESSER HORNERO

DESCRIPTION: 15 cm (6"). A *small, dull* hornero found locally on *river islands along the Amazon and its major tributaries*. Resembles locally sympatric *pileatus* race of Band-tailed Hornero but is *smaller* and has crown and cheeks slightly paler and grayer, a less contrasting superciliary, and somewhat more richly colored and buffier underparts with *more contrasting white throat*.

SIMILAR SPECIES: Pale-legged and Bay Horneros are both larger and have pale flesh-colored (not dark grayish) legs; both are much more richly colored, etc.

HABITAT AND BEHAVIOR: Uncommon to fairly common on or near ground in younger successional habitats on river islands, both in early-succession *Tessaria*-dominated scrub and in older *Cecropia*-dominated woodland; sometimes forages out onto more open, sandy or muddy habitats. Behavior much like Pale-legged Hornero's, though Lesser is usually not particularly conspicuous. Lesser's song is much harsher and more run together, "chk, chk, ch-ch-ch-ch-ch-ch-ch-ch-ch."

RANGE: Amaz. Brazil (along the Amazon and its major tributaries downriver to the lower Rio Tapajós and Santarém area), s. Colombia (Leticia area), ne. Peru (south to the lower Río Huallaga at Santa Cruz), and e. Ecuador (along the Río Napo upriver to near Limoncocha). To 300 m.

GROUP B

"*Plain*" horneros; Brazil and Bolivia southward.

Furnarius cristatus

CRESTED HORNERO   PLATE: 2

DESCRIPTION: 15.5 cm (6"). *Chaco of n. Argentina, w. Paraguay, and adjacent Bolivia. Prominently crested*. Above buffy brown with whitish lores and slightly rufescent forehead; primaries somewhat duskier but rufous wing-band obscure or absent; tail rufous. Below mostly pale pinkish buff; throat contrastingly white, also whiter on midbelly.

SIMILAR SPECIES: Rufous Hornero is similarly colored but markedly larger and lacks the crest.

HABITAT AND BEHAVIOR: Fairly common in chaco scrub and woodland, clearings, and around houses. Behavior similar to Rufous Hornero's, as are its vocalizations, though Crested's average shriller and higher-pitched. Except in heart of its range, Crested is usually not as conspicuous or confiding. Particularly numerous around and west of Filadelfia in Paraguay.

RANGE: Se. Bolivia (Chuquisaca and Tarija), w. Paraguay (only well west of the Río Paraguay), and n. Argentina (south to n. San Luis, n. Córdoba, Santa Fe, and nw. Entre Ríos). To 1000 m (in Córdoba, Argentina).

Furnarius rufus

RUFOUS HORNERO

PLATE: 2

DESCRIPTION: 18–20 cm (7–8″). *The* widespread and numerous hornero of s. half of South America; looks *very plain*. Above rufous brown with slightly grayer crown and rufescent forehead, pale lores, and faint buffyish superciliary; flight feathers duskier with indistinct cinnamon wing-band showing in flight; tail rufous. Below slightly paler buffy brown, paler on midbelly and whitest on throat and crissum. Nominate race of most of Argentina, Uruguay, and s. Brazil is considerably larger than other races. *Albogularis* (e. Brazil south to São Paulo) is brighter and more uniformly buff below (except for its white throat).

SIMILAR SPECIES: One of the most familiar birds in many parts of its range, the inaccurately named Rufous Hornero (it is almost the *least* rufous of the horneros and would better be called the Brown, Plain, or even Common Hornero!) quickly becomes an easily recognized fixture, though at a glance it could be confused with a thrush. Cf. smaller and obviously crested Crested Hornero.

HABITAT AND BEHAVIOR: Common to very common and widespread in most open or semiopen habitats throughout much of its range, though at n. end of its range in Brazil *albogularis* seems considerably less numerous. Very familiar, the Rufous Hornero is Argentina's national bird. It is frequently seen around houses and along roads, boldly strutting around on the ground or perching on exposed branches or any other commanding vantage point; though it is plainly attired, its jaunty demeanor quickly gains it admirers. In some areas its mud nests, which are used only once but take several years to disintegrate, seem to be on almost every telephone pole or fence post; sometimes a new nest is constructed on top of an old one. After having been used by horneros, these "mud ovens" are frequently taken over by other species such as White-rumped Swallows, Brown-chested Martins, or Saffron Finches. The Rufous Hornero's song, a sudden and loud series of notes, almost raucous at close range, at first rises and then slowly drops off, like other horneros'; it is often given as a duet by a pair. Also given are a variety of sharp "chak!" notes.

RANGE: N. and e. Bolivia (La Paz and Beni east and south through Santa Cruz and Tarija), s. Brazil (north to Goiás, s. Piauí, and Alagoas; spreading into formerly forested areas in lowlands near Atlantic coast), Paraguay, Uruguay, and n. and cen. Argentina (south in small numbers to Río Negro and ne. Chubut). Mostly below 2500 m (recorded to 3500 m in Bolivia).

Sylviorthorhynchus Wiretails

A small furnariid found in the undergrowth of temperate forest in s. South America. The wiretail's tail, unique among neotropical passerines, has only six rectrices, the central pair extremely elongated, the next pair only about half as long, and the outermost vestigial. The bill is narrow and straight, somewhat like a gnatwren's (*Ramphocaenus*).

The enclosed nest, made of grass and placed near the ground, is ball-shaped with a side entrance (Johnson 1967).

Sylviorthorhynchus desmursii

DES MURS' WIRETAIL

PLATE: 3

DESCRIPTION: 19–23 cm (7½–9″). *Forests of cen. and s. Chile and adjacent Argentina. Extraordinarily long, narrow, and filamentous central pair of tail feathers.* Rufous brown above, most rufescent on forecrown and wings, with narrow whitish superciliary and mottled cheeks. Below buffy whitish, buffiest on breast.

SIMILAR SPECIES: So thin are the wiretail's central rectrices that at times they are almost invisible in the field; thus it may resemble a tailless spinetail or even a gnatwren. However, nothing really similar occurs with it.

HABITAT AND BEHAVIOR: Uncommon to fairly common in undergrowth of *Nothofagus*-dominated forest and secondary woodland, especially where there are dense and extensive stands of *Chusquea* bamboo; seems less numerous in Argentina than in Chile. Forages mainly in pairs, is skulking and reclusive, and is difficult to find when silent; fortunately it vocalizes often. The "purpose" of the unique tail is unknown; it almost seems maladaptive in the heavy cover the bird favors. The fairly loud song, frequently given at least in breeding season, consists of a repeated rollicking phrase preceded by several faint husky notes, "zhree-zhree-chdreuw-chdreuw-chdreuw-chdreuw-chdreuw-chdreuw."

RANGE: Cen. and s. Chile (Aconcagua south to n. Magallanes) and adjacent Argentina (Neuquén south to w. Santa Cruz). To about 1000 m.

Aphrastura Rayaditos

A pair of small and easily recognized furnariids with conspicuous protruding shafts on their stiffened tail feathers. They are found in far s. South America, one species only on the Juan Fernández Is. On the mainland the charming and energetic Thorn-tailed Rayadito is among the most frequently seen birds in wooded habitats. Its nest is placed behind a piece of bark or in a hole.

Aphrastura spinicauda

THORN-TAILED RAYADITO

PLATE: 3

DESCRIPTION: 14–14.5 cm (5½–5¾″). *Cen. and s. Chile and adjacent Argentina.* Unmistakable. *Crown and auriculars black with long and broad buff superciliary;* above brown, becoming rufous on rump; wings blackish, coverts tipped buff and whitish, flight feathers with *2 broad buff bands* (visible even on closed wing); *tail mainly rufous,* the feathers *terminating in stiff, narrow, protruding shafts.* Below whitish, whitest on throat. *Fulva* (Chiloé Is. off s. Chile) differs strikingly from nominate race (remainder of range) in being *bright pale ochraceous below.*

SIMILAR SPECIES: Cf. only Masafuera Rayadito, confined to Juan Fernández Is. off Chile.

HABITAT AND BEHAVIOR: Common to very common in a variety of

forested and wooded habitats ranging from tall undisturbed *Nothofagus* (Southern Beech) forest (where perhaps most common) through young second-growth to low scrub and tussock grass, *Poa flabellata* (the last on the windswept islands of Fuegian region). One of the most numerous birds in its habitat and range, especially in the lake district of Chile; also the most numerous landbird on Diego Ramirez Is. (Vuilleumier 1991). Thorn-tailed Rayaditos are almost always found in groups, sometimes quite large (up to 15 or more birds, perhaps especially in winter); often a few other species, e.g., White-throated Treerunner, join them to form a mixed flock. They forage at all levels, energetically and nervously inspecting both foliage and branches and trunks, sometimes cocking the tail; when on trunks, they seldom use their tail for support (which seems puzzling, given their stiff protruding "spines"). They behave much like holarctic tits (*Parus* spp.) and are equally bold in demeanor, often approaching the observer very closely. They utter a variety of calls, the most frequent a short, dry trill, "trrrrrrrreet," sometimes continued for 5 or more seconds or interrupted by various "tic" notes; agitated birds often give a long-continued scolding "tsii-tsii-tsii-tsii-tsii. . . ."
RANGE: Cen. and s. Chile (north to Coquimbo) and adjacent Argentina (north to Neuquén) south to Tierra del Fuego (where present even on Cape Horn and Staten Is.), and on Diego Ramirez Is. off extreme s. Chile; accidental on Falkland Is. Mainly below 1200 m, in small numbers up to 2000 m.

Aphrastura masafuerae

MASAFUERA RAYADITO

DESCRIPTION: 16.5 cm (6½"). *Juan Fernández Is. off Chile.* Larger, with a longer bill and tail than the mainland species, and duller plumage. Differs in having *crown and auriculars dusky brown* with *dull buffy grayish superciliary,* and underparts drab buffy grayish.
HABITAT AND BEHAVIOR: Uncommon in areas dominated by *Dicksonia* ferns, perhaps especially along stream courses. Although believed by Vaurie (1980, p. 60) to be "probably very rare, perhaps vanishing or extinct," more recent observations indicate that numbers, though not large, have probably not declined in the 20th century, with a total population of 500–1000 birds. Masafuera Rayadito differs strikingly from its mainland counterpart in occurring singly or in pairs, never in flocks. An often-given churring call frequently reveals its presence in the dense low vegetation it favors. All the information above is derived from M. de L. Brooke ("The Birds of the Juan Fernández Islands, Chile," ICBP Study Report No. 16, 1987 and *Bull. B. O. C.* 108[1]: 4–9, 1988).
RANGE: Juan Fernández Is. on Isla Alejandro Selkirk (formerly Isla Masafuera) off Chile. 600–1300 m.

Leptasthenura Tit-Spinetails

The tit-spinetails, a distinctive group of small, slender, long-tailed furnariids, are found mostly in scrub and woodland patches at higher

elevations in the Andes, but several species occur in the lowlands of
e. South America. Their tails are especially striking, the feathers very
graduated and pointed, the tips of the central pair projecting as a
"double point" (more extreme in some species). Shades of brown, rufous, and grayish predominate; some species show quite prominent
bushy crests. They forage actively and acrobatically in foliage, often
hanging upside down, and are certain to remind observers of tits
(*Parus* spp.). Nests are placed in holes, both in the abandoned nests
of other furnariids (including larger species such as the Firewood-
gatherer, *Anumbius*) or in banks, trees, walls, or houses.

GROUP A   *Mantle streaked;* lower underparts well streaked to virtually plain.

Leptasthenura andicola

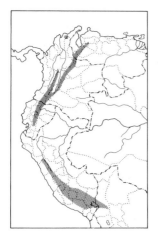

ANDEAN TIT-SPINETAIL   PLATE: 3

DESCRIPTION: 16.5–17 cm (6½–6¾"). Andes of w. Venezuela to
w. Bolivia; *the only tit-spinetail north of Peru*. Nominate race and *certhia*
(Venezuela to Ecuador) have *crown streaked black and rufous* with conspicuous white superciliary and narrow frontlet; back dark brown
streaked white; wings and tail brown, rectrices edged paler. Below
brown *extensively streaked white* (boldest on breast) with chin white.
Birds from Peru and Bolivia (*peruviana*) are more boldly streaked below (streaks outlined with blackish), whereas birds from Colombia's
E. Andes (*exterior*) and Santa Marta Mts. (*extima*) have a rufous patch
at base of primaries and belly essentially *unstreaked*.
SIMILAR SPECIES: *The most streaked tit-spinetail.* Streak-backed, Rusty-
crowned, and White-browed Tit-Spinetails all show prominent streaking on back, but streaking or spotting below is confined to throat
and chest. Many-striped Canastero has similar streaked plumage but
differs markedly in tail shape and color, shows rufous in wing, and has
an orange-rufous chin spot. Tit-tyrants (*Anairetes* spp.) are, despite
their similar-sounding English name, quite different: smaller, much
shorter-tailed, etc.
HABITAT AND BEHAVIOR: Fairly common to rather rare and local
(much less numerous in Peru and Bolivia) in low woodland near treeline, páramo with scattered bushes, and patches of *Polylepis* woodland.
The ecological relationships with other tit-spinetails in Peru and Bolivia are complex and still not well understood. Usually found in pairs
or small groups, Andean Tit-Spinetails forage restlessly, moving rapidly from bush to bush, often hanging upside down as they inspect
leaves, branches, or flowers, mainly in outer foliage; they sometimes
accompany loose mixed flocks. Although often inconspicuous because
of the dense nature of their favored habitats, they are not shy and
sometimes allow a close approach. They give a hesitating, descending
series of high-pitched notes and trills and various other "tik" calls.
RANGE: Andes of w. Venezuela (north to Trujillo), Colombia
(E. Andes, and north in Cen. Andes to Tolima), Ecuador (south on
w. slope to Azuay, on e. slope only to Cotopaxi and sw. Napo), Peru

(Ancash south locally to Arequipa and Puno), and w. Bolivia (La Paz). 3000–4500 m.

Leptasthenura striata

STREAK-BACKED TIT-SPINETAIL

Also: Streaked Tit-Spinetail

DESCRIPTION: 16.5–17 cm (6½–6¾"). *Andes of w. Peru and n. Chile.* Resembles Andean Tit-Spinetail but in area of overlap (Peru) occurs at somewhat *lower* elevations. *Generally much less streaked,* the streaking confined to crown and back (on back narrower and less contrasting), and with a narrower superciliary; has a *rather prominent rufous patch at base of primaries. Below mottled pale grayish,* the throat whiter with black speckling; *albigularis* of Huancavelica, Peru, lacks throat speckling and shows almost no superciliary.

SIMILAR SPECIES: Plain-mantled Tit-Spinetail has back uniform grayish, *not* streaked. In Peru cf. also Rusty-crowned Tit-Spinetail.

HABITAT AND BEHAVIOR: Fairly common to locally common in montane scrub, sometimes quite sparse, and (southward) in patches of *Polylepis* woodland. Behavior, including vocalizations, similar to Andean Tit-Spinetail's. Numerous in the shrub zone below Putre in n. Chile.

RANGE: Andes of w. Peru (north to Ancash) and n. Chile (Tarapacá). Mostly 2000–4000 m but occurs lower (mainly 1500–2500 m) in Lima and Ancash, Peru.

NOTE: Although this species has traditionally been called the Streaked Tit-Spinetail (Meyer de Schauensee 1966, 1970), this name makes little sense, for it is much *less* streaked than the otherwise rather similar Andean Tit-Spinetail.

Leptasthenura pileata

RUSTY-CROWNED TIT-SPINETAIL   PLATE: 3

DESCRIPTION: 17 cm (6¾"). *Andes of w. Peru.* Nominate race of Lima has *crown uniform rufous* with narrow white superciliary; above otherwise grayish brown streaked with whitish; wings and tail brownish dusky, rectrices edged paler and with ashy patch on primaries. *Throat and upper chest white boldly checkered with black;* remaining underparts mottled dull pale brownish. *Cajabambae* (north of Lima) has *black streaking on crown,* whereas *latistriata* (Huancavelica and Ayacucho) resembles nominate but is more broadly streaked above, more streaked on breast, and darker on belly.

SIMILAR SPECIES: Nominate race and *latistriata,* with their *unstreaked* rufous crowns, are distinctive among the tit-spinetails with streaked mantles except for the range-restricted White-browed (which see). *Cajabambae* is more confusing. The similar Streak-backed Tit-Spinetail (which in area of sympatry usually occurs at lower elevations) differs most markedly in having a quite prominent rufous patch on wing and also has less distinct speckling on throat. Andean Tit-Spinetail is much more obviously streaked below.

HABITAT AND BEHAVIOR: Fairly common in montane scrub and patches of low woodland (including *Polylepis*). Behavior, including vocalizations, much like Andean Tit-Spinetail's. Readily seen in shrubbery of Santa Eulalia valley above Lima (the "fancy," rufous-crowned race). RANGE: Andes of w. Peru (Cajamarca south to Huancavelica and Ayacucho). Mostly 2500–3500 m, locally down to 2000 m and up to 4000 m.

NOTE: More than one species may be involved. See comments under White-browed Tit-Spinetail.

Leptasthenura xenothorax

WHITE-BROWED TIT-SPINETAIL

DESCRIPTION: 17 cm (6¾"). *Very local in high Andes of se. Peru*. Closely resembles nominate Rusty-crowned (with which perhaps conspecific), thus with *solid rufous crown*. Differs mainly in its *plain smoky grayish underparts* showing no mottling; the throat and chest checkering may be even bolder and is sharply demarcated from underparts.
SIMILAR SPECIES: The only other tit-spinetail occurring with this species is the very different Tawny.
HABITAT AND BEHAVIOR: Uncommon and local in patches of *Polylepis* woodland. Behavior and voice much like Andean Tit-Spinetail's. Small numbers can be seen along the Abra Málaga road above Ollantaytambo where, as apparently elsewhere in its very limited range, this species is threatened by continued cutting of trees for firewood and pasturage.
RANGE: Andes of se. Peru (southeast of Abancay in Apurímac, and a few sites in Cuzco). 3700–4500 m.

NOTE: Vaurie (1980) considered *L. xenothorax* conspecific with *L. pileata*; indeed Vaurie seems implicitly to have favored not recognizing *xenothorax* even at the subspecific level. However, recently obtained specimens and observations appear to support the continued recognition of *L. xenothorax* as a full species (e.g., Fjeldså and Krabbe 1990). We note that the plumage of *L. p. cajabambae* differs more strikingly from *L. p. pileata* than does *L. xenothorax*; possibly *L. cajabambae* (Cajamarca Tit-Spinetail) deserves species status. We also believe that *L. xenothorax*'s English name of White-browed is rather misleading as it is the Andean Tit-Spinetail that has the most prominent white brow in the genus. *L. xenothorax* perhaps should have been called "Cuzco Tit-Spinetail."

Leptasthenura striolata

STRIOLATED TIT-SPINETAIL

DESCRIPTION: 16–16.5 cm (6¼–6½"). Recalls several tit-spinetails with streaked backs found in Andes, but note its *separate range* in *se. Brazil*. Crown black streaked with rufous and with buffy whitish superciliary; *mantle brown boldly streaked with buffyish*, rump plain brown; tail dark brown, outer feathers rufous. Dull ochraceous below, speckled with brown on throat and upper chest.
SIMILAR SPECIES: Araucaria Tit-Spinetail has a chestnut mantle with *no* streaking and generally shows an obvious crest; it is virtually confined to *Araucaria* trees (for which Striolated, though sometimes foraging in them, shows no special affinity).
HABITAT AND BEHAVIOR: Fairly common to common in a variety of wooded and shrubby habitats and in gardens. Behavior, including its high-pitched and slightly descending song, similar to Andean Tit-Spinetail's.

RANGE: Se. Brazil (Paraná south to n. Rio Grande do Sul). Mostly 500–1100 m.

GROUP B *Mantle unstreaked;* tail solidly rufous in 2 species.

Leptasthenura aegithaloides

PLAIN-MANTLED TIT-SPINETAIL PLATE: 3

DESCRIPTION: 16–16.5 cm (6¼–6½"). Crown dusky streaked cinnamon-buff, and narrow whitish superciliary; *above otherwise pale brownish gray,* with whitish streaking on nape; wings dusky with cinnamon-rufous patch at base of flight feathers; tail dusky, outer feathers edged whitish. *Throat white,* with its sides and upper chest faintly streaked whitish and dull brown; lower underparts pale buffy grayish. Foregoing applies to *pallida* of most of Argentinian range and to *grisescens* of coastal s. Peru and n. Chile; nominate race of most of Chilean range is similar but darker generally. *Berlepschi* of the altiplano of s. Peru, w. Bolivia, n. Chile, and nw. Argentina is larger and decidedly buffier on lower underparts.

SIMILAR SPECIES: Tufted Tit-Spinetail always shows a conspicuous crest (rearcrown feathers of Plain-mantled are at most ruffled), and its entire throat is lightly speckled (not pure white in middle). Brown-capped Tit-Spinetail shows *no* streaking.

HABITAT AND BEHAVIOR: Fairly common in low open scrub, rocky ravines with scattered shrubbery, loma vegetation (in coastal s. Peru and n. Chile), matorral (in Chile), and gardens. Usually in pairs or small groups, clambering about acrobatically in shrubs and low trees, sometimes dropping down into clumps of tall grass or even to ground. Its song in Argentina is an irregular, high, descending trilled series of notes, e.g., "tsit, tsit, tsit, tseedeleetseedeleetseedeleetseedelee"; foraging birds give a variety of chipping contact calls.

RANGE: Coastal s. Peru (north to Arequipa) and n. Chile (south to Atacama); altiplano of extreme s. Peru (Puno), w. Bolivia, n. Chile (south to Antofogasta), and nw. Argentina (south to Catamarca and Tucumán); lowlands of cen. and s. Chile (north to s. Coquimbo); lowlands of cen. and s. Argentina (north to La Rioja, San Luis, La Pampa, and s. Buenos Aires) south locally to n. Tierra del Fuego in Magallanes, Chile; in austral winter *pallida* is recorded north to Tucumán and Santiago del Estero, Argentina, where it overlaps locally with resident *berlepschi.* To 4300 m.

NOTE: More than one species may be involved.

Leptasthenura platensis

TUFTED TIT-SPINETAIL PLATE: 3

DESCRIPTION: 16–16.5 cm (6¼–6½"). *Mainly Argentina.* Resembles sympatric race (*pallida*) of Plain-mantled Tit-Spinetail. Differs in showing a *distinct bushy crest* with streaking finer on crown and more diffused on nape, *completely speckled throat* (not pure white in middle), and pale cinnamon (not whitish) edges to outer rectrices.

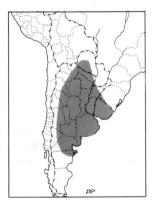

HABITAT AND BEHAVIOR: Fairly common to common in light woodland (including monte) and adjacent shrubbery. More a bird of wooded areas than Plain-mantled Tit-Spinetail (which favors scrubby, more open situations), though there is some overlap, especially in austral winter. General behavior is similar to Plain-mantled's, as are vocalizations, though Tufted's are even weaker and higher-pitched.

RANGE: S. Paraguay (only 2 records: a specimen from Lichtenau in the chaco of Presidente Hayes, and a pair seen north of Pilar in Neembucú in June 1991 by RSR and P. Scharf et al.), extreme s. Brazil (w. Rio Grande do Sul), Uruguay, and Argentina (south to n. Chubut; 1 record of a likely vagrant from Paso Ibáñez in Santa Cruz; not recorded from Misiones). To about 1000 m.

Leptasthenura fuliginiceps

BROWN-CAPPED TIT-SPINETAIL   PLATE: 3

DESCRIPTION: 16.5 cm (6½"). A *plain, brownish, and unstreaked tit-spinetail of Bolivian and Argentinian Andes.* Above mostly pale sandy brown with *contrasting brown crown* (usually raised into a *short bushy crest*) and buffyish superciliary; *wings and tail contrastingly rufous.* Below dingy pale buff, buffiest on lower belly.

SIMILAR SPECIES: Tawny Tit-Spinetail has a longer bill and lacks the crest and "capped" effect; it also is much brighter ochraceous below. Plain-mantled Tit-Spinetail is streaked on crown, neck, and throat and has mainly dusky tail.

HABITAT AND BEHAVIOR: Fairly common in patches of low woodland (including scraggly *Polylepis*), adjacent scrubby growth, and hedgerows; favors drier regions. Behavior and vocalizations similar to Plain-mantled Tit-Spinetail's, with which it sometimes occurs, though generally Brown-capped prefers ravines and steeper slopes, Plain-mantled more level plains. Numerous in various areas above Cochabamba.

RANGE: Andes of w. Bolivia (north to La Paz) and w. Argentina (south to n. Mendoza; also in mts. of w. Córdoba and ne. San Luis). Mostly 2000–3300 m, occasionally lower (especially in winter?), and recorded to 3900 m in Cochabamba.

Leptasthenura setaria

ARAUCARIA TIT-SPINETAIL   PLATE: 3

DESCRIPTION: 17 cm (6¾"). A *boldly patterned* tit-spinetail of *Araucaria groves in se. Brazil region;* bill relatively long and slender. *Prominently crested.* Crown black with fine white streaks and a narrow white superciliary; *upperparts contrastingly chestnut,* more blackish on wings; tail very long, mostly rufous-chestnut with black central rectrices. Throat white flecked with dusky; remaining underparts dull pale ochraceous, tawny on crissum.

SIMILAR SPECIES: The only other tit-spinetail in its range is the very different Striolated, which is not crested, has streaked mantle, etc.

HABITAT AND BEHAVIOR: Fairly common in *Araucaria* groves. Almost entirely confined to these trees, doing most if not all of its acrobatic feeding in them, and rarely seen anywhere else, even occurring in planted groves around buildings and in gardens. This small slender bird often forages high above ground and is sometimes hard to see as it is so easily concealed amongst the *Araucaria's* large and dense needles. The high-pitched, descending trilled song and various other calls are typical of the genus and often draw attention. Readily found wherever *Araucaria* occurs in highlands of ne. Rio Grande do Sul.

RANGE: Se. Brazil (s. Rio de Janeiro, where found recently at Itatiaia Nat. Park, south to n. Rio Grande do Sul) and ne. Argentina (Misiones). To at least 1100 m.

Leptasthenura yanacensis

TAWNY TIT-SPINETAIL

PLATE: 3

DESCRIPTION: 16.5 cm (6½"). *Locally high in Andes of Peru and w. Bolivia.* Bill relatively long and slender. *Above uniform tawny brown,* becoming rufous on forecrown, and with dull buff superciliary; wings duskier, feathers broadly edged with rufous; rather long tail rufous. *Below uniform bright ochraceous.*

SIMILAR SPECIES: Brown-capped Tit-Spinetail is crested and has a stubbier bill; it looks distinctly "dark-capped" and is sandier brown above and duller below.

HABITAT AND BEHAVIOR: Rare to locally fairly common in groves of *Polylepis* woodland (sometimes even where low and sparse) and on steep slopes with rocks, bunchgrass, and low shrubs. General behavior similar to other tit-spinetails' but reported (Fjeldså and Krabbe 1990) to be more vocal, with a long trilled song and various chattering calls.

RANGE: Andes of Peru (recorded from various localities on slopes of Cordillera Blanca in Ancash, in n. Lima, and locally above treeline along e. slope of Andes in Cuzco and Puno) and w. Bolivia (locally from La Paz south to Tarija). 3200–4600 m.

Phleocryptes Rushbirds

A monotypic genus of small furnariid found widely in reedbeds of s. South America. Its globular nest has a protected side entrance near the top and is attached to reed stems out over the water.

Phleocryptes melanops

WREN-LIKE RUSHBIRD

PLATE: 3

DESCRIPTION: 13.5–14.5 cm (5¼–5¾"). A chunky small furnariid of *southern reedbeds. Crown dark brown contrasting with broad buffy whitish superciliary;* back streaked black, brown, and whitish, becoming uniform brown on rump; wings dusky with *conspicuous rufous band on coverts and across base of remiges; fairly short tail* mostly brown and black, feathers tipped buff. Below buffy whitish (buffier in fresh plumage, whiter when worn). *Schoenobaenus* of altiplano in Peru, Bolivia, and extreme nw. Argentina is *markedly larger* and longer-billed than races found in lowlands (nominate group, including *brunnescens* and *loaensis* of Pacific coast).

SIMILAR SPECIES: Bay-capped Wren-Spinetail has a rufous crown, much less obvious superciliary, and longer, more pointed tail; it occurs only in Argentina, Uruguay, and s. Brazil. Cf. also Grass Wren (*Cistothorus*).

HABITAT AND BEHAVIOR: Locally common in reedbeds growing in both fresh and brackish water, rarely leaving their confines. Rushbirds are usually inconspicuous, though this is mostly due to the inaccessible nature of most of their habitat; they are not especially shy and often are quite curious, approaching to investigate squeaking noises. Observers will be struck by their similarity to the Marsh Wren (*Cistothorus palustris*) of North America and to certain *Acrocephalus* warblers of the Old World; while feeding they often drop down to mud or floating vegetation and sometimes even hop in shallow water. The most frequent vocalization is very unbird-like, consisting only of a repeated but somewhat syncopated ticking, often several ticks per second and sometimes continued for several minutes. This sounds mechanical (almost like 2 pebbles being tapped together) but is vocal, as the bill does not necessarily close with each tick (Belton 1985).

RANGE: W. Peru (north along coast to Trujillo, in highlands to Junín), w. Bolivia (La Paz southeast to w. Santa Cruz and in Oruro, mainly in highlands but in Santa Cruz also in lowlands), Chile (south locally to Aysén; very local in north), Paraguay (few records), s. Brazil (common resident in Rio Grande do Sul and coastal Santa Catarina; single records from São Paulo and Rio de Janeiro), Uruguay, and Argentina (south to Chubut); 1 record from Tierra del Fuego (a specimen from near Ushuaia). No definite evidence of austral migration, though the scatter of records from Paraguay and se. Brazil is suggestive. To 4300 m.

Limnornis and *Limnoctites* Reedhaunters

A pair of comparatively large, marsh-inhabiting spinetails found locally in se. South America. Despite the comments of Vaurie (1980), who considered them congeneric, we continue to favor separating them as monotypic genera, though we treat them together here because of their overall similarity. *Limnoctites* is considerably slighter and has a strikingly different bill; its tail is longer and its feathers are stiffer and much more pointed. Their vocalizations are dissimilar. *Limnornis* builds a round nest with a side entrance which is attached to reeds (Belton 1985), whereas the nest of *Limnoctites* seems undescribed.

Limnornis curvirostris

CURVE-BILLED REEDHAUNTER   PLATE: 3

DESCRIPTION: 16–16.5 cm (6¼–6½″). *Reedbeds of e. Argentina, Uruguay, and s. Brazil. Rather long, decurved bill.* Above brown, more rufescent on wings, rump, and especially on its fairly short and rounded tail; superciliary white. Whitish below, whitest on throat and tinged buff on flanks.

SIMILAR SPECIES: Straight-billed Reedhaunter has a straighter bill, is grayer above, and has a longer, narrower, and "spikier" tail. Rufous Hornero is superficially similar but occupies an entirely different habitat.

HABITAT AND BEHAVIOR: Uncommon to fairly common in reedbeds growing in water, especially where these are extensive and fringe large coastal lagoons. Found singly or in pairs, this well-named species seems never to leave reedbeds. Unless singing, it is usually difficult to see, creeping about within cover and rarely flying any distance. Especially in early morning its distinctive loud song is often delivered from a more or less exposed vantage point; it consists of a fast series of harsh, strident notes, at first rapidly rising, then sliding down and weakening, e.g., "dr-rrrrrrri-di-di-di-dr-rrrrreuw." Readily seen at Taim Ecological Station in Rio Grande do Sul, Brazil.

RANGE: Extreme s. Brazil (coastal Rio Grande do Sul), s. Uruguay, and e. Argentina (mainly Entre Ríos and e. Buenos Aires; also a recent sight report from s. Misiones). Below 100 m.

Limnoctites rectirostris

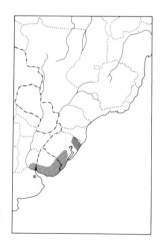

STRAIGHT-BILLED REEDHAUNTER   PLATE: 3

DESCRIPTION: 16 cm (6¼"). *Local in sedgy marshes of se. Brazil, Uruguay, and e. Argentina. Very long, virtually straight bill.* Grayish brown above, *grayest on crown,* with indistinct whitish superciliary; wings contrastingly rufous; *rather long, graduated, and pointed tail* also rufous, the spines protruding. Whitish below, whitest on throat and tinged buff on sides. Immature more cinnamon above and much more ochraceous below.

SIMILAR SPECIES: Curve-billed Reedhaunter is considerably heavier-bodied (though shorter-tailed) with an obviously decurved bill; it is browner above (showing no grayish), and its tail is broader with the feathers rounder and lacking the protruding "spines." The 2 reedhaunters appear never to occur together in the same marsh. Cf. also Sulphur-bearded Spinetail.

HABITAT AND BEHAVIOR: Uncommon to fairly common but very local in small marshes and swales that support beds of the spiny sedge *Eryngium.* Usually in pairs and reclusive, creeping about in dense low vegetation much of the time. Easiest to see when vocalizing, as it may then mount to a more exposed perch; the song is a series of high-pitched notes, all on essentially the same pitch, ending in a trill, e.g., "tsi-tsi-tsi-tsi-tsi-titititititi." The effect is like that of songs of many other small furnariids, e.g., various tit-spinetails and canasteros. Found in fair numbers in highlands of ne. Rio Grande do Sul, Brazil, along the road between São Francisco de Paula and Aparados da Serra Nat. Park.

RANGE: Extreme s. Brazil (Rio Grande do Sul; seems likely in adjacent Santa Catarina), s. Uruguay, and e. Argentina (Entre Ríos; recently reported from near Villa Ballestar in n. Buenos Aires). To 1100 m.

Spartonoica Wren-Spinetails

A monotypic genus of small furnariid found locally in marshes of the pampas region. Although Vaurie (1980) was convinced that its closest relative was *Synallaxis* (almost considering it a subgenus), we are not so confident, partly because of its streaked upperparts (not shown by any *Synallaxis*) and also because its behavior and habitat differ so radically. We suspect its closest relative may be *Asthenes*, in which genus it was for a time placed (e.g., *Birds of the Americas*, vol. 13, part 4). Nest form varies, but evidently it is placed near the ground and usually is open at the top, the latter unique among the Furnariidae (Vaurie 1980). Note that Meyer de Schauensee (1966, 1970) erred in spelling the generic name, which is *Spartonoica* (not *Spartanoica*).

Spartonoica maluroides

BAY-CAPPED WREN-SPINETAIL   PLATE: 3

DESCRIPTION: 14–14.5 cm (5½–5¾"). *Marshes of Argentina, Uruguay, and s. Brazil.* Iris pale bluish gray to white. Above mostly sandy brown *boldly streaked with black on nape and mantle; crown contrastingly rufous;* indistinct whitish superciliary; wings with cinnamon area at base of flight feathers; tail long and strongly graduated with feathers very pointed, mostly brown. Below whitish, tinged dull buff on sides and flanks.

SIMILAR SPECIES: Resembles Hudson's Canastero, and the two can occur together; though the canastero is not a confirmed marsh bird, it often occurs in damp grassy places. The canastero lacks the rusty crown and shows sparse but relatively prominent black streaking on flanks. Cf. also Sulphur-bearded Spinetail (which is unstreaked above, lacks rusty crown, etc.), and much shorter-tailed Grass Wren (which regularly occurs with Bay-capped).

HABITAT AND BEHAVIOR: Uncommon to locally fairly common (perhaps mostly overlooked) in marshes with extensive growths of sedges (e.g., *Eryngium*) and reedbeds, in both fresh and brackish water; also sometimes occurs in tall grass and forbs on drier ground. This slender spinetail is usually very reclusive and shy, even when nesting rarely perching in the open for long. A flushed bird usually flies a short distance low over the vegetation before pitching back in and, more often than not, disappearing. The distinctive song is a very dry, mechanical-sounding, reeling trill lasting 2–3 seconds.

RANGE: Extreme s. Brazil (s. Rio Grande do Sul), Uruguay, and cen. Argentina (Corrientes, Entre Ríos, and Buenos Aires west locally to Córdoba and Mendoza, and south to Río Negro). To about 900 m.

Schoeniophylax Spinetails

With striking plumage and an exceptionally long tail, the distinctive Chotoy Spinetail of s.-cen. South America is not likely to be confused. Vaurie (1980) considered it a subgenus of *Synallaxis;* we prefer, however, to maintain it as distinct because of its different morphological features and very distinctive voice.

Schoeniophylax phryganophila

CHOTOY SPINETAIL   PLATE: 3

DESCRIPTION: 19–22 cm (7½–8¾"). *Boldly patterned* with *extremely long tail.* Crown mostly chestnut, duskier on forecrown, and with narrow whitish superciliary; above otherwise sandy brown *boldly streaked with blackish;* lesser wing-coverts contrastingly rufous-chestnut; *very strongly graduated tail grayish brown.* Chin yellow; *patch on middle of lower throat black,* sides of throat white; *band across chest cinnamon;* remaining underparts whitish, tinged dull buff on flanks. Immatures are duller generally and lack the rufous crown and complex throat pattern. *Petersi* of interior e. Brazil is smaller.

SIMILAR SPECIES: Virtually unmistakable, the Chotoy has a much longer tail than any *Synallaxis* spinetail, none of which is streaked above. *Leptasthenura* tit-spinetails are somewhat alike in overall shape but differ in color pattern and behavior.

HABITAT AND BEHAVIOR: Fairly common to common in semiopen areas with scattered trees and bushes, gallery and monte woodland, and gardens; most numerous near water. Usually in pairs or small (family?) groups which remain inside cover much of the time, rarely flying any great distance. The presence of this striking spinetail is, however, often revealed by its quite conspicuous large stick nest with a tubular entrance on the side and by its distinctive low chuckling or gurgling call, "cho-cho-cho-cho-chchchchchchchuh." Presumably the English name is onomatopoeic.

RANGE: N. and e. Bolivia (Santa Cruz west locally to Beni, and south to Tarija), extreme sw. and s. Brazil (s. Mato Grosso and Mato Grosso do Sul, and s. Rio Grande do Sul), Paraguay (all but the extreme east), Uruguay, and n. Argentina (south to n. Buenos Aires); interior e. Brazil (n. Minas Gerais and w. Bahia). To about 500 m.

Poecilurus Spinetails

This trio of spinetails, united by their pronounced black gular patch and found in three disjunct areas of mainly deciduous woodland, is perhaps best classified as only a subgenus of *Synallaxis* (as urged by Vaurie 1980). M. Braun and T. A. Parker III (*Neotropical Ornithology,* AOU Monograph no. 36, p. 339, 1985) considered their relationship to *Synallaxis* "uncertain." C. J. Marinkelle (*in* Vaurie 1980) described the seemingly different nest as being of similar construction but placed in a tree cavity; Vaurie (op. cit., p. 87) "hesitated to accept" this.

Poecilurus candei

WHITE-WHISKERED SPINETAIL   PLATE: 3

DESCRIPTION: 16 cm (6¼"). A *handsome* spinetail of *Caribbean lowlands of n. Colombia and nw. Venezuela. Above mostly bright rufous to*

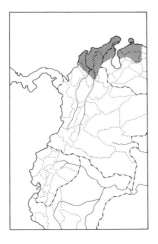

cinnamon-rufous with dark gray crown, *rufous postocular stripe,* and *black cheeks;* terminal half of tail black. *Chin and malar streak white,* contrasting with *black median throat;* below mostly cinnamon-rufous, white on median belly. *Atrigularis* (mainly in Río Magdalena valley of s. Bolívar) is rather different: postocular lacking, malar smaller and flecked with gray, back brown, base of tail darker and more chestnut (so less contrast with black distal half of tail), and flanks more olivaceous; see C-24.

HABITAT AND BEHAVIOR: Fairly common to common in arid scrub and deciduous woodland. Usually in pairs which forage mainly by hopping on ground, often with tails partially cocked. Although not particularly shy, they can be hard to see because their favored habitat is so dense. The frequently given call is a repeated nasal "a-dít-dít-du" (Hilty and Brown 1986). Readily found in w. Falcón, Venezuela.

RANGE: Caribbean n. Colombia (west to Sucre and n. Bolívar) and nw. Venezuela (east to Falcón and Lara). To at least 300 m.

NOTE: *Atrigularis* is morphologically quite distinct and might almost be regarded as a separate species (Magdalena Spinetail) but for the reported occurrence of specimens with apparent intermediate characters (*Birds of the Americas,* vol. 13, part 4).

Poecilurus kollari

HOARY-THROATED SPINETAIL

DESCRIPTION: 15.5 cm (6"). Very limited area in *extreme n. Brazil.* Resembles nominate White-whiskered Spinetail (no overlap), differing in its brown-tinged crown, grayish (not black) cheeks, entirely rufous tail, and black throat flecked with white (especially in malar area).

SIMILAR SPECIES: Nothing really similar in its small range.

HABITAT AND BEHAVIOR: Virtually unknown in life. In Aug. 1992, B. Forrester et al. (pers. comm.) found a pair in seasonally flooded forest along the Rio Tacutu near Conçeicão do Maú. We do not know its voice.

RANGE: Extreme n. Brazil (n. Roraima); likely occurs in adjacent s. Guyana.

Poecilurus scutatus

OCHRE-CHEEKED SPINETAIL   PLATE: 3

DESCRIPTION: 15.5 cm (6"). *Ne. Brazil to nw. Argentina.* Nominate race (all of Brazilian part of range except Mato Grosso) has crown and upper back olive brown with remainder of upperparts rufous; *white superciliary* tinged buff behind eye. Chin white, with *prominent and fairly large patch of black on center of throat;* sides of head and neck, breast, and flanks ochraceous buff, whiter on median belly. *Whitii* (Mato Grosso westward) similar but with olive brown back and rump (only wings and tail are rufous).

SIMILAR SPECIES: Slightly larger White-lored Spinetail lacks distinct superciliary and black throat patch and has underparts all cinnamon except for white throat.

HABITAT AND BEHAVIOR: Uncommon in tangled undergrowth and

thickets of deciduous woodland and borders of humid forest; in nw. Argentina also found in undergrowth of humid foothill forest. Behavior much like White-whiskered Spinetail's, likewise usually found in pairs which seem notably sedentary; Ochre-cheeked seems not to feed so persistently on the ground. Its frequently given call, a shrill "tweeeyt, to-weét?" with a distinctive leisurely cadence, is often repeated endlessly; it resembles the song of Gray-bellied Spinetail (*Synallaxis cinerascens*). Several pairs range in the woods near the swimming pool at Brasília Nat. Park; also frequent in Calilegua Nat. Park in Salta, Argentina.

RANGE: E. and s.-cen. Brazil (Pernambuco and Ceará west to s. Pará on the Serra dos Carajás, Goiás, and s. Mato Grosso, and south to São Paulo and s. Minas Gerais), e. Bolivia (Santa Cruz, Chuquisaca, and Tarija), and nw. Argentina (Jujuy and Salta). To 1700 m (in Bolivia).

Synallaxis Spinetails

One of the larger and more confusing genera of neotropical birds. We recognize no fewer than 27 species of *Synallaxis* spinetails in South America (there is another one in Middle America). We have excluded from *Synallaxis* the genus *Gyalophylax* and the 3 species comprising the genus *Poecilurus;* both have sometimes been considered subgenera within *Synallaxis*.

At least 1 *Synallaxis* is found virtually everywhere on the continent except in far austral regions, and up to 3 or 4 species may be locally sympatric. However, numerous *Synallaxis* have very restricted ranges, whereas others may have broader distributions in which they are found only locally. These small furnariids are characterized by their usually long, always strongly graduated and "double-pointed" tails. Although Vaurie (1980) gave it great significance in forming his groupings, we have ignored the number of rectrices (either 8 or 10) in forming our Groups, concluding that the number appears to represent only a species-level character.

Many *Synallaxis* have a rufous crown, and all show rufous on the wing (at least on the coverts); many also have a "gular" or throat patch, usually grizzled black and white, sometimes solid black. Plumage patterns vary, but many species closely resemble one another, often making identification to species level tricky; pay particular attention to facial pattern, tail color, and (perhaps most important) the often endlessly reiterated and usually distinctive vocalizations. Juveniles of most or all species are duller and less patterned.

Synallaxis spinetails skulk in thick vegetation near the ground; some are found in humid forest undergrowth, but most range primarily in thickets and shrubbery in more open areas or at forest and woodland borders. Nests, often bulky globular or ball-shaped structures made of sticks and stiff grass with a side entrance, are usually attached to a low branch (less often on or near the ground) and are less conspicuous than the stick nests of certain other furnariids (e.g., *Phacellodomus* thornbirds).

GROUP A

Montane Synallaxis; tail notably *long* in most.

Synallaxis zimmeri

RUSSET-BELLIED SPINETAIL   PLATE: 4

DESCRIPTION: 16.5 cm (6½"). *W. slope of Andes in cen. Peru. Crown gray,* becoming olivaceous gray on back, and with narrow, interrupted whitish eye-ring; rump and extensive area on wing-coverts and inner flight feathers rufous; tail dusky, outer feathers increasingly rufous. *Throat pale ashy gray; remaining underparts pinkish rufous.*

SIMILAR SPECIES: The only *Synallaxis* so far south on w. slope of Andes.

HABITAT AND BEHAVIOR: Locally fairly common in dense montane scrub, which in many areas is being degraded by livestock. Forages in pairs, gleaning inside bushes and low trees, probing into clumps of moss. The song consists of a fast, snarling "quik-quik" repeated every few seconds. All information from Fjeldså and Krabbe (1990). Seems likely to deserve threatened status.

RANGE: W. slope of Andes in cen. Peru (cen. and s. Ancash on w. slope of Cordillera Negra, in drainages of Ríos Casma and Huarmey). 1800–2900 m.

NOTE: A very distinct species of *Synallaxis,* possibly even deserving generic separation.

Synallaxis unirufa

RUFOUS SPINETAIL   PLATE: 4

DESCRIPTION: 17–18 cm (6¾–7"). Andes of w. Venezuela to s. Peru. *Essentially uniform bright rufous* (somewhat darker, more chestnut above) with contrasting black lores. *Munotzebari* (Sierra de Perijá) is slightly paler, more cinnamon below, and has a suggestion of a cinnamon superciliary. *Meridana* (Andes of w. Venezuela) is also slightly paler and sometimes shows a tiny black chin spot.

SIMILAR SPECIES: Quite easily confused with Rufous Wren (the 2 species are locally syntopic), though the wren shows faint dark barring on wings and tail (never present on the spinetail) and its tail is more rounded, whereas the spinetail's is frayed and double-pointed. The spinetail usually travels in pairs, the wren in groups. Cf. also Black-throated Spinetail (no overlap).

HABITAT AND BEHAVIOR: Uncommon to fairly common but somewhat local in undergrowth of montane forest and forest borders, frequently in thickets of *Chusquea* bamboo. A skulking bird which usually keeps to dense cover, thus most often recorded only by voice. Generally forages in pairs, less often in family groups, sometimes accompanying mixed flocks but at least as often found independently. Its most frequent song is a simple, upslurred, rather shrill "kweeík" or "kuh-kweeík," often repeated steadily every 1–2 seconds for protracted periods.

RANGE: Andes of w. Venezuela (north to Trujillo), Colombia, Ecuador (south on w. slope to Cotopaxi), and Peru (south to n. Cuzco on Cordillera de Vilcabamba); Sierra de Perijá on Venezuela-Colombia border. Mostly 1700–3200 m.

NOTE: See comments under Black-throated Spinetail.

Synallaxis castanea

BLACK-THROATED SPINETAIL PLATE: 4

DESCRIPTION: 18.5 cm (7¼"). *Mts. of n. Venezuela;* formerly considered conspecific with Rufous Spinetail. Resembles paler races of Rufous Spinetail (no overlap) but with longer tail (tips more rounded) and *contrasting black throat patch.* Voice also differs (see below).

HABITAT AND BEHAVIOR: Fairly common in undergrowth of montane forest and forest borders. Behavior similar to Rufous Spinetail's, but Black-throated's voice differs characteristically, often being given by both members of a pair, first a fast, staccato "ke-che-che-che-che," quickly followed by a louder "ker-cheé-cheé." Readily found around Colonia Tovar, e.g., along first part of the road down to Limón.

RANGE: Coastal mts. of n. Venezuela (Aragua east to Miranda and Distrito Federal). 1300–2200 m.

NOTE: Long considered a race of *S. unirufa*, but C. Vaurie and P. Schwartz (*Am. Mus. Novitates* 2483, 1972) demonstrated that *S. castanea* is best considered a separate species, especially on the basis of its rather different voice.

Synallaxis fuscorufa

RUSTY-HEADED SPINETAIL

DESCRIPTION: 17 cm (6¾"). *Santa Marta Mts. of n. Colombia.* Resembles paler races of Rufous Spinetail (no overlap) but foreparts more orange-rufous, *back contrastingly grayish olive,* and flanks somewhat more extensively grayish olive. See C-24.

SIMILAR SPECIES: The only *Synallaxis* spinetail occurring at high elevations on Santa Marta Mts.

HABITAT AND BEHAVIOR: Fairly common to common in undergrowth of montane forest and forest borders. Behavior similar to Rufous Spinetail's, though Rusty-headed tends to forage more often at greater heights above ground; perhaps for this reason it is much easier to see. Its song, often repeated for long periods, is a short nasal "dit-dit-du" (Hilty and Brown 1986). Easily found along upper part of the San Lorenzo ridge road.

RANGE: Santa Marta Mts. of n. Colombia. Mostly 2000–3000 m, in smaller numbers down to about 1000 m.

Synallaxis azarae

AZARA'S SPINETAIL PLATE: 4

Includes: Elegant Spinetail, Buff-browed Spinetail

DESCRIPTION: 17–17.5 cm (6¾–7"). *Widespread and generally numerous in Andes from Venezuela to Argentina;* includes Elegant and Buff-browed Spinetails, both of which have been considered sepa-

rate species. Above olive brown with *contrasting rufous crown* (except for brown frontlet), *most of wing and long pointed tail rufous*. Throat mixed black and white; remaining underparts vary from almost uniformly gray to whitish, with olivaceous or buff flanks. Geographic variation in this species is complex. More northerly races (south to n. Peru) are relatively pale below (see C-25), reaching an extreme in *ochracea* (s. Ecuador and nw. Peru), in which most of underparts look whitish (some birds even have a pale superciliary). Birds (including "*urubambae*") from cen. Peru south to Cochabamba, Bolivia, are notably dark and gray below; Remsen et al. (1988) suggest that all the described races from cen. Peru to w. Bolivia should be subsumed into nominate *azarae*. Birds from Santa Cruz, Bolivia, south into Argentina (including *superciliosa*) show a *usually prominent buff superciliary* and revert to being relatively pale below. Birds from the intervening area in Bolivia are variable and intermediate.

SIMILAR SPECIES: This basically montane *Synallaxis* is the most frequently encountered spinetail in the Andes. In ne. Colombia cf. the Silvery-throated Spinetail, and in s. Peru the Apurimac Spinetail. Sooty-fronted Spinetail, though basically found in lowlands, occurs sympatrically with slightly larger and longer-tailed Azara's in Andean valleys of s. Bolivia (though unlike Azara's, Sooty-fronted is *not* a forest-based bird); the race of Azara's in area of overlap shows a buff brow which Sooty-fronted lacks.

HABITAT AND BEHAVIOR: Fairly common to common in shrubby forest borders, undergrowth of secondary woodland, and overgrown clearings; in s. part of range occurs also in lower growth of montane forest. Furtive and difficult to see, creeping about in dense shrubbery, grass, or ferns, almost always close to ground; heard far more often than seen, but even after tape playback will usually skulk and rarely perch in the open for more than an instant. Generally occurs in pairs, remaining independent of mixed flocks. Its voice, which seems not to vary over its extensive range, is a repeated, sharp "ka-kweeék."

RANGE: Andes of w. Venezuela (north to Trujillo), Colombia, Ecuador, Peru (south on w. slope to Cajamarca), Bolivia, and n. Argentina (south to Tucumán and Catamarca). In most of range mainly 1500–3200 m, but regularly occurs lower in sw. Ecuador (down to 900 m), and in s. Bolivia and Argentina ranges mainly 500–1500 m.

NOTE: We include both the Elegant Spinetail (*S. elegantior*, with *media*, *ochracea*, and *fruticicola*) of Venezuela to n. Peru and the Buff-browed Spinetail (*S. superciliosa*, with *samaipatae*) of s. Bolivia and Argentina as races of *S. azarae*. *S. elegantior*, after having long been considered part of *S. azarae* (e.g., *Birds of the World*, vol. 7, and Meyer de Schauensee 1966, 1970), was separated as a full species by C. Vaurie and P. Schwartz (*Am. Mus. Novitates* 2483, 1972) and Vaurie (1980), based on supposed differences in their primary songs. However, recent field work has not confirmed this; see, for example, the comments of Fjeldså and Krabbe (1990), who nonetheless continue to regard *S. elegantior* as distinct, and those of Remsen et al. (1988). The latter also present evidence, with which we concur, for regarding *superciliosa* as conspecific with *S. azarae*; this is based on the frequency of birds in Bolivia with variable and intermediate plumages and on the similarity of their voices. As the plumages of the expanded species are so geographically variable, the use of a descriptive specific epithet seems precluded; we hence retain Azara's Spinetail as the English name for the enlarged species.

Synallaxis courseni

APURIMAC SPINETAIL

PLATE: 4

Other: Coursen's Spinetail

DESCRIPTION: 19 cm (7½"). Recently described from *Apurímac, s. Peru*. Resembles nominate race of Azara's Spinetail but even grayer overall and with *tail notably longer and brownish dusky* (not rufous). Azara's apparently does not occur sympatrically with this species.

HABITAT AND BEHAVIOR: Locally common in undergrowth and borders of montane forest, favoring areas of bamboo under small, gnarled, moss-covered trees. Behavior, including vocalizations, much like that of Azara's Spinetail (Fjeldså and Krabbe 1990).

RANGE: Andes of s. Peru (northwest of Abancay in Apurímac). 2450–3500 m.

NOTE: A recently described species: E. R. Blake, *Auk* 88(1): 179, 1971. Fjeldså and Krabbe (1990) suggest that *courseni* could prove to be only a subspecies of *S. azarae*, and we fully agree. It seems best to highlight *S. courseni*'s extremely limited range in its English name.

Synallaxis subpudica

SILVERY-THROATED SPINETAIL

DESCRIPTION: 19 cm (7½"). *E. Andes of Colombia*. Resembles geographically distant Apurimac Spinetail but more olivaceous brown generally (not so gray); likewise has a *very long grayish brown tail*. From most angles throat is not really very "silvery." See C-25.

SIMILAR SPECIES: Azara's Spinetail is similar but has rufous tail; calls of the two differ markedly.

HABITAT AND BEHAVIOR: Fairly common to common in shrubby forest and woodland borders, overgrown clearings, and bushy hedgerows. Behavior similar to Azara's Spinetail's, likewise usually in pairs, but Silvery-throated is generally easier to see—in part because of the somewhat more open nature of its habitat. Its song is a fast, coalescing series of chattered notes which gradually drop in pitch and become less loud, "chí-chi-chi-che-che-che-chu-chu-chu," much like a *Cranioleuca* spinetail's.

RANGE: E. Andes of n. Colombia (Boyacá and Cundinamarca). Mostly 2000–3200 m.

GROUP B

Standard *lowland Synallaxis* with rufous cap and wing-coverts.

Synallaxis frontalis

SOOTY-FRONTED SPINETAIL

PLATE: 4

Includes: Gray-browed Spinetail

DESCRIPTION: 16 cm (6¼"). Wide range from e. Brazil to Bolivia and n. Argentina. Above olive brown with *rufous crown* (except for dark frontlet); *most of wings and tail also rufous;* some birds have a faint short whitish streak behind or above eye. Upper throat whitish, lower throat

flecked with black; sides of throat and breast grayish, becoming whitish on midbelly and olivaceous brown on flanks.

SIMILAR SPECIES: Pale-breasted and Cinereous-breasted Spinetails are similar, but both have dull dark brown tails; Pale-breasted is white below and shows less rufous on wing. The songs of all three differ strikingly. In s. Bolivia confusion is also likely with Azara's Spinetail (also with rufous tail), though the race of Azara's found there has a distinctive buff superciliary never found in Sooty-fronted. *All* of these spinetails have similar dark "sooty" frontlets.

HABITAT AND BEHAVIOR: Uncommon to locally common in undergrowth and borders of low woodland, gallery woodland, chaco scrub, monte, and fields and savannas with scattered bushes. Favors more wooded or shrubby (less grassy) areas than Pale-breasted Spinetail and seems most numerous in Bolivia and Argentina. Usually inconspicuous, foraging in pairs within cover and close to ground. The song is a sharp "ka-kwee-eék" or simply "ka-kweek," similar to that of Azara's Spinetail.

RANGE: E. and interior Brazil (Maranhão, Ceará, and Paraíba south and west to s. Mato Grosso, Mato Grosso do Sul, and São Paulo; also in s. Rio Grande do Sul, but not found in coastal se. Brazil), n. and e. Bolivia (west to Beni), Paraguay, Uruguay, and n. Argentina (south to Mendoza, La Pampa, and n. Buenos Aires). Perhaps partially migratory in extreme south of range. To 2500 m (in Cochabamba and Santa Cruz, Bolivia).

NOTE: C. Vaurie (*Ibis* 113[4]: 520, 1971) showed that what was described as *S. poliophrys* (Gray-browed Spinetail) was a misidentified specimen of *S. frontalis*. Although it was labeled as having been taken in French Guiana, Vaurie hypothesized that it likely had been obtained in e. Brazil.

Synallaxis hypospodia

CINEREOUS-BREASTED SPINETAIL

DESCRIPTION: 15.5 cm (6"). *Local from s. Peru to ne. Brazil.* Resembles Sooty-fronted Spinetail but smaller and with *shorter, dull dark brown tail* (not rufous).

SIMILAR SPECIES: Pale-breasted Spinetail shares the dull brownish tail but differs in being much more whitish (less gray) below; their voices differ markedly. Spix's Spinetail (limited overlap) has longer and spikier tail, and its solidly rufous crown lacks Cinereous-breasted's dusky frontlet. Dark-breasted Spinetail is especially similar, differing only in its slightly brighter rufous crown, slightly purer gray sides of head and chest, and somewhat shorter, not so dark, and "spikier" tail (Cinereous-breasted's tail tips are more rounded).

HABITAT AND BEHAVIOR: Fairly common but *very* local (inexplicably so) in low shrubby areas with intermixed tall grass, often but not always near water. Skulking behavior is similar to much more numerous and widespread Sooty-fronted Spinetail's; the two may occur in close proximity. Cinereous-breasted's song is a fast and fairly loud series of chippered notes, coalescing at the end, "chew, chew-chee-chee-chee-ee-ee-ee-ee-ee-eu," somewhat similar to the song of Dark-breasted Spinetail.

RANGE: Very locally in se. Peru (Santa Ana in Cuzco and unpublished LSUMZ specimens from Pampas de Heath in Madre de Dios), n. Bolivia (a few localities in s. Beni and Santa Cruz), and s. Amaz. and ne. Brazil (Rio Juruá, Rio Madeira, and Itacoatiara east to w. Minas Gerais, Bahia, Alagoas, and Ceará). Records from farther north in Peru (San Martín and Junín) seem uncertain and are likely based on misidentified specimens; 6 specimens of Dark-breasted Spinetail in ANSP from San Martín and Junín were originally misidentified as Cinereous-breasted and may be the source of the confusion. Some of the published Amaz. Brazil records of Cinereous-breasted may also be the result of confusion with Dark-breasted Spinetail. To 700 m.

Synallaxis albescens

PALE-BREASTED SPINETAIL

PLATE: 4

DESCRIPTION: 16–16.5 cm (6¼–6½"). *Widespread* and usually numerous in open grassy areas. Above pale olive to grayish brown with rufous to cinnamon-rufous crown (except for dusky frontlet) and wing-coverts, and *dull brownish tail. Below mostly whitish,* with some black flecking on lower throat and a grayish tinge on breast.
SIMILAR SPECIES: Cinereous-breasted Spinetail is a bit smaller and is darker and more grayish generally; its voice differs. Dark-breasted Spinetail has a shorter and spikier tail, is darker and grayer generally than Pale-breasted, especially on breast, and shows more black on lower throat; the two occur together only very locally.
HABITAT AND BEHAVIOR: Fairly common to common in open grassy areas with scattered bushes or hedgerows, savannas, shrubby areas, and damp sedgy meadows. Behavior similar to that of other open-country *Synallaxis,* usually in pairs and inconspicuous unless vocalizing, which it frequently does. Although it sometimes sings from a concealed position, more often a singing bird mounts into a bush or low tree to tirelessly give its nasal "weé-bzü" (which to N. Am. observers will recall Willow Flycatcher's "fítz-bew"). The song of Argentinian birds is strikingly shriller and higher-pitched, "whzií-whzeeu."
RANGE: N. Colombia (Caribbean lowlands, Ríos Cauca and Magdalena valleys, and east of the Andes south to Meta and Vichada, with a few records from the Leticia area), Venezuela (including Margarita Is.), Guianas, most of Brazil (locally in Amazonia, especially westward; more widespread elsewhere, except absent from the coastal southeast and from all but w. tips of Santa Catarina and Rio Grande do Sul), Paraguay, n. and e. Bolivia, se. Peru (a few records from Tambopata Reserve in Madre de Dios, perhaps pertaining to austral migrants), and n. and cen. Argentina (south to Mendoza, La Pampa, and Buenos Aires; also a 1992 record of a presumed vagrant on Valdés Peninsula in ne. Chubut); Trinidad; seems likely in n. Uruguay. Also Costa Rica and Panama. Mostly below 1500 m.

NOTE: In *Birds of the Americas,* vol. 13, part 4, what is now considered *S. albigularis* was treated as a race of *S. albescens;* shortly thereafter they were demonstrated to be separate species, which they certainly are. It was presumably the former inclusion of *albigularis* in *S. albescens* that caused Meyer de Schauensee (1966, 1970) incorrectly to incorporate w. Amazonia (e.g., e. Ecuador) into the range of *S. albescens.*

Synallaxis spixi

SPIX'S SPINETAIL   PLATE: 4

Other: Chicli Spinetail

DESCRIPTION: 16 cm (6¼"). *Se. Brazil area.* Grayish to olive brown above with *entirely rufous crown* (*no* dusky frontlet) and rufous wing-coverts; long, pointed, grayish brown tail. *Mostly gray below,* paler on midbelly and browner on flanks, flecked with white on upper throat and more or less solid black on lower throat.

SIMILAR SPECIES: Cinereous-breasted Spinetail has shorter, sootier, and less pointed tail; though most of its crown is rufous, it does have a dusky frontlet lacking in Spix's. Their ranges only barely overlap. Pale-breasted Spinetail shows a dark frontlet and is much paler below; its song differs markedly. Cf. also Rufous-capped Spinetail (more of a forest bird, etc.).

HABITAT AND BEHAVIOR: Fairly common to common in shrubby and grassy areas and woodland borders, often but not always near water. Behavior similar to that of other *Synallaxis* spinetails favoring more or less open terrain, usually hopping or creeping about in dense cover, perching in the open mainly when singing. Song is a constantly reiterated, fast "whít, di-di-di" (closely recalling song of geographically distant Dark-breasted Spinetail).

RANGE: Se. Brazil (north to Minas Gerais and Espírito Santo), e. Paraguay, Uruguay, and ne. Argentina (south to n. Buenos Aires). To about 2050 m.

NOTE: *S. spixi* has gone by the onomatopoeic name of Chicli Spinetail in recent literature, an unfortunate choice for, *unlike* several of its congeners, its more complex song bears no resemblance whatsoever to "chicli." We suspect that the name "chicli" was originally attached to the more wide-ranging and numerous *S. frontalis,* for which it *would* be a good English name, but that it subsequently was inadvertently (or at least incorrectly) transferred to *S. spixi.* We prefer to reduce the confusion by employing the simple patronym (also employed in *Birds of the Americas,* vol. 13, part 4).

Synallaxis albigularis

DARK-BREASTED SPINETAIL   PLATE: 4

DESCRIPTION: 15.5 cm (6"). *W. Amazonia.* Above olive to grayish brown with fairly bright rufous crown (except for dark frontlet) and wing-coverts; *rather short, spiky, grayish brown tail. Upper throat white* (often quite conspicuous), lower throat flecked with black; *remaining underparts gray,* becoming whitish on midbelly and browner on flanks. *Rodolphei* (se. Colombia and e. Ecuador) is darker generally, especially below.

SIMILAR SPECIES: Pale-breasted Spinetail (limited overlap) has longer tail and is paler below; its voice differs characteristically. Dusky Spinetail is darker and more uniform below, has a chestnut tail, and is much more of a forest bird. Cf. also Cinereous-breasted Spinetail (no known overlap, though ranges come close).

HABITAT AND BEHAVIOR: Common in overgrown and (especially)

grassy clearings, shrubby woodland borders, and low riparian growth (particularly on river islands and banks, where favoring areas dominated by dense stands of *Gynerium* cane). Behavior similar to numerous other spinetails', and likewise hard to see well, even when birds are singing from all around, as they often are. Song is an oft-repeated, fast "whít, di-di-di," sometimes with an extra "di." Seems particularly numerous near e. base of Andes in Ecuador, where it is spreading and increasing in numbers as a result of accelerating deforestation.

RANGE: Se. Colombia (north to s. Meta), e. Ecuador, e. Peru (south to Madre de Dios), and w. Amaz. Brazil (east locally along the Amazon to near the mouth of the Rio Negro); seems likely in extreme nw. Bolivia. Up to at least 1200 m.

Synallaxis brachyura

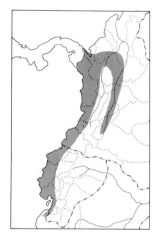

SLATY SPINETAIL

DESCRIPTION: 15.5–16 cm (6–6¼"). *W. Colombia to extreme nw. Peru.* Resembles Dark-breasted Spinetail (found only east of Andes) but with somewhat longer tail and darker generally (grayer on back and more uniformly gray below). See C-25.

SIMILAR SPECIES: In much of its range the only *Synallaxis* spinetail present. In sw. Ecuador and nw. Peru, cf. rather different Blackish-headed and Necklaced Spinetails which mainly inhabit more arid regions; there is some overlap, particularly with Blackish-headed. In w. Colombia Pale-breasted Spinetail also occurs, but it is much whiter below, etc. Higher in Andes cf. Azara's Spinetail, differing in its notably longer rufous tail, vocalizations, and other characters.

HABITAT AND BEHAVIOR: Fairly common to common in shrubby forest and woodland borders, densely overgrown clearings, and gardens in more humid regions. Behavior similar to many other *Synallaxis*', but more likely to forage higher above ground and to leave dense cover, so generally easier to see. Its song is a low, throaty churring often introduced by a few notes, e.g., "ch-ch-chirrrrr" or just the "chirrrrr" given alone.

RANGE: W. Colombia (Pacific lowlands, more humid Caribbean lowlands, and Río Magdalena valley south to Huila), w. Ecuador, and extreme nw. Peru (Tumbes). Also Honduras to Panama. The published records from Goiás, Brazil ("*jaraguana*"), were based on misidentified specimens of Cinereous-breasted Spinetail (Vaurie 1980). To 2000 m.

Synallaxis ruficapilla

RUFOUS-CAPPED SPINETAIL   PLATE: 4

DESCRIPTION: 16 cm (6¼"). *A boldly marked spinetail of forest undergrowth from e. Brazil to e. Paraguay and ne. Argentina. Entire crown bright rufous bordered below by a buff streak* and dusky cheeks; above otherwise mostly brown, wing-coverts and relatively short *tail rufous-chestnut*. Throat silvery grayish, becoming gray on breast and pale dull ochraceous on belly.

SIMILAR SPECIES: Not likely confused in range, where no other *Synallaxis* shares the buff below the rufous crown. Cf. Spix's Spinetail (in more open terrain) and Pinto's Spinetail (no overlap).

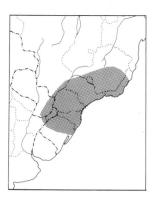

HABITAT AND BEHAVIOR: Fairly common to common in undergrowth and borders of forest and second-growth woodland, particularly favoring thickets of *Chusquea* bamboo; perhaps less numerous in Paraguay and Argentina. Usually in pairs, hopping about in lower growth, often quite bold and relatively easy to see; sometimes accompanies flocks of understory birds. Song is a somewhat nasal, fast "di-di-di-reét" often repeated for sustained periods, more rapidly when excited.

RANGE: Se. Brazil (Minas Gerais and Espírito Santo south to n. Rio Grande do Sul), e. Paraguay (Canendiyu, Alto Paraná, and Itapúa), and ne. Argentina (Misiones). Up to at least 1400 m.

NOTE: See comments under Pinto's Spinetail.

Synallaxis infuscata

PINTO'S SPINETAIL

Other: Plain Spinetail

DESCRIPTION: 16 cm (6¼"). *Very local in ne. Brazil.* Resembles Rufous-capped Spinetail (with which formerly considered conspecific), differing in having only a slight suggestion of the buff stripe below rufous crown, grayer back (hence the rufous crown contrasts more), and *more uniform dark gray underparts* (not paler ochraceous on belly).

HABITAT AND BEHAVIOR: Uncommon to fairly common but local in densely overgrown clearings and shrubby forest and woodland borders. Usually forages in pairs, remaining in dense cover and close to ground much of the time; seems not to follow mixed flocks. Foraging birds frequently give a sharp, nasal "enk-enk" (sometimes 3 or 4 "enk"s in series); whether this is the full song is unknown. Although fairly numerous at Pedra Branca near Murici in Alagoas (seen by RSR and T. Schulenberg in Oct. 1987), overall numbers of this species must have declined substantially in recent decades because of deforestation.

RANGE: Ne. Brazil (recorded from a few localities in Alagoas and Pernambuco, and from a series of 5 unpublished specimens in LSUMZ taken by E. Dente in the 1970s at Coroatá in ne. Maranhão). To 500 m.

NOTE: Described as a subspecies of *S. ruficapilla* by O. Pinto in 1950, *infuscata* was raised to full species rank by Vaurie (1980), and this treatment appears to be correct. We suggest that naming *S. infuscata* after its describer, the great Brazilian ornithologist Oliveiro Pinto, would be appropriate; it is no "plainer" than several other *Synallaxis*.

Synallaxis cabanisi

CABANIS' SPINETAIL   PLATE: 4

DESCRIPTION: 15.5 cm (6"). *Near e. base of Andes in Peru and Bolivia.* Above brown with *entirely rufous crown* (*no* dusky frontlet), mainly rufous wings, *and short, often very frayed-looking rufous-chestnut tail.* Throat mixed silvery gray and black (whiter on submalar area); remaining underparts dull grayish olive brown. Foregoing applies to nominate *cabanisi* of Peru; *fulviventris* of Bolivia is markedly paler generally and plainer dingy buff below (lacking grayish tone).

SIMILAR SPECIES: Cf. Dusky and Macconnell's Spinetails (both have a dusky frontlet which Cabanis' lacks; all have allopatric ranges). Dark-breasted Spinetail has a brown tail, shows a dusky frontlet, and is

mainly found in grassy clearings (not the woodland undergrowth of Cabanis').

HABITAT AND BEHAVIOR: Uncommon to fairly common but somewhat local in rank undergrowth of secondary woodland and forest borders, also in areas dominated by dense stands of *Gynerium* cane along rivers. Usually in pairs, creeping and hopping about on or near ground. Very furtive, it most often reveals its presence by its frequently given abrupt and nasal "nyap" or "nyap-nyap" calls; we do not know if it also has a territorial song. Numerous near Hacienda Amazonia in n. Cuzco, Peru.

RANGE: E. Peru (north to Huánuco) and n. Bolivia (south to s. Beni and Cochabamba). 200–1350 m.

NOTE: Sometimes considered conspecific with *S. moesta* (Dusky Spinetail), as has been *S. macconnelli* (Macconnell's Spinetail); Meyer de Schauensee (1966, 1970) treated *macconnelli* and its associated subspecies as conspecific with *S. cabanisi*, leaving *S. moesta* as a separate species. Vaurie (1980), however, considered the three as distinct species. We believe the latter's treatment is preferable, as they appear to comprise a superspecies with, for *Synallaxis*, a relatively heavy bill and short tail. The species exhibit minor morphological and vocal differences; *brunneicaudalis*, the very dark southernmost race of *S. moesta*, differs strikingly from the northernmost race (nominate) of *S. cabanisi*.

Synallaxis moesta

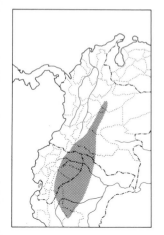

DUSKY SPINETAIL

DESCRIPTION: 15.5 cm (6"). *Near e. base of Andes from Colombia to n. Peru.* Nominate race (the northernmost, ranging from w. Casanare to w. Meta) resembles Cabanis' Spinetail but shows a *dusky frontlet;* see C-25. The 2 more southerly races of Dusky Spinetail (*obscura* and *brunneicaudalis*) are markedly darker and grayer on back and *especially on underparts.*

SIMILAR SPECIES: Cf. Cabanis' Spinetail (no overlap). Dark-breasted Spinetail has a brown (not rufous-chestnut) tail and mainly inhabits grassy clearings (not the woodland and forest undergrowth of Dusky).

HABITAT AND BEHAVIOR: Uncommon and seemingly local (overlooked?) in dense undergrowth and thickets of humid forest borders and secondary woodland; sometimes in bamboo thickets. Behavior much like Cabanis' Spinetail's. One call is a low nasal chattering, "rha-a-a-a-a-a-a" (P. Coopmans, RSR); we do not know if it also has a territorial "song." Can be found north of Archidona along the road to Loreto in w. Napo, Ecuador.

RANGE: Along e. base of Andes in Colombia (north to Casanare) and in e. Ecuador (Napo to Zamora-Chinchipe) and n. Peru (recorded from mouth of Río Curaray into the Río Napo in Loreto [questionably?], and at Moyobamba in San Martín). 200–1200 m.

NOTE: See comments under Cabanis' Spinetail.

Synallaxis macconnelli

MACCONNELL'S SPINETAIL

DESCRIPTION: 15.5 cm (6"). *Local in ne. South America.* Closely resembles geographically distant Cabanis' Spinetail, especially Cabanis' nominate race, but with *dusky frontlet* and throat more blackish with

less silvery gray edging; see V-19 (there called Dusky Spinetail). *Obscurior* (Surinam to Amapá) is reportedly slightly darker, whereas *yavii* (Cerro Yaví in n. Amazonas, Venezuela) is reportedly slightly paler.

SIMILAR SPECIES: This dark spinetail with its rather short rufous-chestnut tail is unlikely to be confused in its range. Plain-crowned Spinetail lacks rufous crown; Pale-breasted Spinetail is much paler generally and has a brown tail.

HABITAT AND BEHAVIOR: Fairly common but local in dense shrubbery at borders of forest and in woodland undergrowth. Like Cabanis' and Dusky Spinetails, Macconnell's is a skulking bird, difficult to observe without tape playback. Its call in Surinam is a repeated, low, gravelly "kir-r-r-r-r-r, kik," the "kik" much softer and inaudible except at close range (T. Davis). Reasonably numerous around the Voltzberg dome and at Foengoe Is. in Surinam.

RANGE: Tepui slopes of s. Venezuela (Bolívar and n. Amazonas, and on Cerro de la Neblina in s. Amazonas); Surinam, French Guiana, and Amapá, Brazil; seems likely in Guyana. To 1900 m in Venezuela.

NOTE: See comments under Cabanis' Spinetail.

GROUP C

Synallaxis lacking a rufous cap; a heterogeneous assembly.

Synallaxis gujanensis

PLAIN-CROWNED SPINETAIL   PLATE: 4

DESCRIPTION: 16–16.5 cm (6¼–6½"). A *very plain* spinetail found locally from Guianas into Amazonia. *Head grayish brown* with slightly darker crown and dingy whitish lores, becoming dull olive brown on back; *wings and tail contrastingly rufous,* rectrices quite pointed. *Below dingy buff to dingy grayish buff,* whitest on throat, paler on midbelly.

SIMILAR SPECIES: *Lacks* the rufous on crown and black on lower throat shown by several other otherwise similar *Synallaxis* spinetails. Plain-crowned most resembles White-bellied Spinetail, which occurs with it on some river islands, but White-bellied has a black throat patch and otherwise essentially gray and white underparts (not buffyish). Rusty-backed Spinetail (a *Cranioleuca*), which also often occurs with Plain-crowned, has entire upperparts rufous. Cf. also Maranon and White-lored Spinetails.

HABITAT AND BEHAVIOR: Fairly common to common in undergrowth of várzea forest and woodland and in younger riparian growth (especially on river islands where it seems particularly numerous, e.g., in dense stands of *Gynerium* cane). Very skulking, usually foraging on or near the ground, generally moving about as pairs which keep in contact through their distinctive "keék, uh" call; it is given by both sexes, usually at intervals of at least a few seconds.

RANGE: E. and s. Venezuela (e. Monagas south to Bolívar and in n. Amazonas), Guianas, Amaz. Brazil (north of the Amazon in n. Roraima, Amapá, and along the Amazon itself, south of it from n. Maranhão westward), n. Bolivia (south to La Paz, Cochabamba, and Beni), e. Peru, e. Ecuador (islands in the Río Napo and lower Río Aguarico), and se. Colombia (north to w. Meta). To 1200 m (in Colombia).

NOTE: We follow Vaurie (1980) in considering *S. albilora* (with *simoni*; White-lored Spinetail) and *S. maranonica* (Maranon Spinetail) as species separate from *S. gujanensis*; Meyer de Schauensee (1966, 1970) treated them as conspecific. The three differ quite strikingly in plumage, and their voices, though similar in quality, differ markedly in phraseology.

Synallaxis albilora

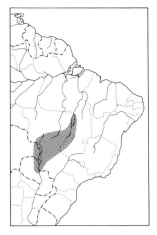

WHITE-LORED SPINETAIL

Other: Ochre-breasted Spinetail

DESCRIPTION: 16 cm (6¼"). *Mainly interior sw. Brazil;* sometimes considered conspecific with Plain-crowned Spinetail. Resembles that species (no overlap) but with browner back (thus the grayish head contrasts more), *white lores* (often quite prominent), and *mostly bright ochraceous underparts* (only the throat is white); the rectrices are rounder.

SIMILAR SPECIES: Not likely confused in its restricted range. Ochre-cheeked Spinetail has a black patch on lower throat and a fairly obvious white superciliary.

HABITAT AND BEHAVIOR: Common in undergrowth of deciduous and gallery woodland and in riparian shrubbery. Behavior similar to Plain-crowned Spinetail's; likewise partially terrestrial, but because of the more open nature of its habitat, White-lored is generally much easier to observe. Its song is a sharp and piercing "keeeu, kit-kweeit," usually delivered at a rather leisurely pace, once every 3–5 seconds. Numerous in woodlands of pantanal in w. Mato Grosso.

RANGE: Interior sw. Brazil (Goiás north to Bananal Is., s. Mato Grosso, and w. Mato Grosso do Sul) and adjacent Bolivia (extreme e. Santa Cruz) and n. Paraguay (e. Alto Paraguay, ne. Presidente Hayes, and n. Concepción). To 1000 m.

NOTE: See comments under Plain-crowned Spinetail. Meyer de Schauensee (1966) named this species the "Ochre-breasted Spinetail," although Hellmayr had already suggested White-lored Spinetail (*Birds of the Americas,* vol. 13, part 4). We believe the advantage of retaining a name that "agrees with" its Latin species name is compelling, especially given the number of other spinetails with ochre on the breast.

Synallaxis maranonica

MARANON SPINETAIL

DESCRIPTION: 15.5 cm (6"). *Río Marañón valley of nw. Peru and adjacent Ecuador;* sometimes considered conspecific with Plain-crowned Spinetail. Resembles that species (no overlap) but *markedly grayer and more uniform below* (throat with only slight whitish mottling and only a faint olivaceous brown tinge on lower flanks); back is somewhat browner and tail is shorter with considerably rounder rectrices.

SIMILAR SPECIES: Readily recognized in its restricted range by the lack of rufous on crown and black on lower throat, both shown by all other *Synallaxis* occurring with or near it.

HABITAT AND BEHAVIOR: Uncommon to locally fairly common in undergrowth of deciduous woodland and forest, to a lesser extent also in humid forest and regenerating secondary scrub. Usually in pairs, foraging independently of mixed flocks; hops on or near ground and is generally difficult to see. The song, given by both sexes, is a very slowly paced, nasal "kiweeu . . . keeeu," often with an interval of 5–10 or more seconds between paired phrases.

RANGE: Nw. Peru (n. Cajamarca) and extreme s. Ecuador (s. Zamora-Chinchipe in the Zumba area; ANSP). 500–1100 m.

NOTE: See comments under Plain-crowned Spinetail.

Synallaxis propinqua

WHITE-BELLIED SPINETAIL   PLATE: 4

DESCRIPTION: 16 cm (6¼"). *Local on river islands in Amazon system.* Proportionately long bill. Above mainly brownish gray contrasting with mainly rufous wings and tail; rectrices very pointed. Chin silvery gray with *black patch on lower throat* (depending on angle, can be quite conspicuous); breast gray, becoming *distinctly white on median belly,* brownish on flanks.

SIMILAR SPECIES: Plain-crowned Spinetail shows no black on throat and has remaining underparts uniform dingy buffyish.

HABITAT AND BEHAVIOR: Fairly common to common but very local in early succession growth on river islands, most often in young *Gynerium* cane interspersed with low bushes and tangles. Considered an "obligate island species" (Rosenberg 1990). *Synallaxis* spinetails are not a conspicuous lot, but White-bellied is perhaps the hardest of all to observe; pairs or single birds creep about on or near ground, almost never in the open. Fortunately they have an unmistakable, strange song with an unusual nasal mechanical quality, typically a repeated "eh-ehhhhhhhh," with excited birds sometimes lengthening this into a series of descending chirring notes that recall a *Laterallus* crake's.

RANGE: Locally along rivers in e. Ecuador (islands in the Río Napo and lower Río Aguarico, and at Sarayacu in the Río Pastaza drainage), extreme s. Colombia (sightings along the Amazon near Puerto Nariño), ne. Peru (along the Amazon, Río Napo, and Río Ucayali as far south as Lagarto; reports from Madre de Dios require confirmation), n. Bolivia (along Río Beni in n. Beni), Amaz. Brazil (east to the lower Rio Tocantins), and French Guiana (Oyapock River). To 300 m.

Synallaxis cinerascens

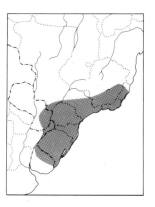

GRAY-BELLIED SPINETAIL   PLATE: 4

DESCRIPTION: 14 cm (5½"). A *small* and short-billed spinetail of *se. Brazil to e. Paraguay and n. Uruguay.* Above mostly olive brown, grayer on face, with rufous wing-coverts and rufous-chestnut tail. Upper throat white, patch on lower throat black; *remaining underparts nearly uniform gray.*

SIMILAR SPECIES: Spix's Spinetail, also mainly gray below (though its midbelly is whiter), has a rufous crown and longer brown tail; it inhabits much more open terrain.

HABITAT AND BEHAVIOR: Uncommon to locally fairly common in lower growth of humid forest and more mature secondary woodland. Although sometimes found around forest openings, the Gray-bellied, unlike so many *Synallaxis,* seems not to favor forest borders. Usually found singly or in pairs, inconspicuous, and not apt to be found unless vocalizing. Its song is a distinctive, thin, piercing "wheeeyt? beeeyt," sometimes varied to "wheeeyt bu-beeeyt."

RANGE: Se. Brazil (north to s. Minas Gerais and Rio de Janeiro; reports from s. Goiás require confirmation), e. Paraguay (west to Paraguarí), ne. Argentina (Misiones and e. Corrientes), and n. Uruguay (locally in Artigas, Cerro Largo, and Rocha). To about 1100 m.

Synallaxis tithys

BLACKISH-HEADED SPINETAIL

PLATE: 4

DESCRIPTION: 14.5 cm (5¾"). *Sw. Ecuador and adjacent Peru. Head and neck dark gray becoming black on foreface* and olivaceous gray on back and rump; wing-coverts contrastingly bright cinnamon-rufous (the *brightest* in genus), *tail sooty*. Throat black, somewhat grizzled with white along malar; remaining underparts gray, palest on midbelly.

SIMILAR SPECIES: The conspicuous black on the face of this attractive *Synallaxis* is unique.

HABITAT AND BEHAVIOR: Uncommon in thick undergrowth of deciduous forest and woodland and in adjacent scrub. Behavior similar to many other *Synallaxis*', usually in pairs and tending to be inconspicuous and remaining close to ground, often feeding on the ground itself. The song is a short, dry, slightly ascending trill, "t-t-t-t-t-tit," repeated every few seconds. Overall numbers have declined because of deforestation, and grazing in much of what forest remains, and the species likely deserves threatened status. It occurs in Chongon Hills, and a substantial population is found in Ecuador's Machalilla Nat. Park.

RANGE: Sw. Ecuador (north to cen. Manabí, and inland to w. Loja) and extreme nw. Peru (Tumbes). To 1100 m.

Synallaxis rutilans

RUDDY SPINETAIL

PLATE: 4

DESCRIPTION: 14–15 cm (5½–6"). Forest undergrowth from Guianas to Amazonia. W. birds (including *caquetensis;* Colombia and Ecuador eastward north of Amazon to lower Rio Negro in Brazil) are *mainly rich chestnut* with *contrasting black lores and a black throat patch;* wings and belly duskier; rather short and often frayed tail black. E. birds (including nominate and *dissors;* s. Venezuela, Guianas, Amaz. Brazil from Rio Negro eastward and between Rios Tapajós and Tocantins) similar but more olivaceous brown on hindcrown, back, and rump; see V-19, C-25. Birds from most of the rest of range (including *amazonica*) are more or less intermediate. Very different, however, is the variable *omissa* of e. Amaz. Brazil from Rio Tocantins eastward. *Omissa* is normally more or less uniform dark brownish gray with a black throat and tail and extensive rufous-chestnut on wing-coverts. Some individuals show a rufescent tinge on the breast and even the back; reportedly a few are colored "exactly like *S. r. rutilans*" (*Birds of the World,* vol. 7, p. 91).

SIMILAR SPECIES: In most of its range, the richly colored Ruddy Spinetail is likely confused only with the usually rarer Chestnut-throated Spinetail. Ruddy always has a black throat patch (lacking in Chestnut-throated), though the black can be hard to see. Although the dull and dark *omissa* form can be confusing, no other *Synallaxis* shares its rufous-chestnut wing-coverts *and* black tail.

HABITAT AND BEHAVIOR: Uncommon to locally fairly common in undergrowth of terra firme forest, sometimes around small open areas such as treefalls but not usually at forest borders. Usually forages in pairs which remain on or close to ground, searching leaf litter, tangles, and dead leaf clusters. Its song is a repetition of the phrase "keé-kawow, keé-kawow . . . " or "keé-kow, keé-kow . . . ," sometimes rapidly given in succession for long periods; both members of the pair give it. Numerous in forest at Junglaven, in Amazonas, Venezuela.

RANGE: Guianas, s. Venezuela (Bolívar and Amazonas), se. Colombia (north to Meta and Vaupés), e. Ecuador (few records), e. Peru, n. Bolivia (south to La Paz and n. Santa Cruz), and Amaz. Brazil (south to sw. Mato Grosso and sw. Pará; east to n. Maranhão; the São Paulo record seems doubtful). To 900 m.

NOTE: *S. omissa* (Para Spinetail) may prove to be a full species; the nature of the intergradation between it and nominate *rutilans* seems little studied, and we do not know its voice.

Synallaxis cherriei

CHESTNUT-THROATED SPINETAIL

DESCRIPTION: 14 cm (5½"). *Very* local in Amazonia. Resembles nominate/*dissors* type of Ruddy Spinetail (with olivaceous brown upperparts) but *throat orange-rufous* (with *no* black, but decidedly not "chestnut").

SIMILAR SPECIES: In addition to lacking Ruddy Spinetail's black throat (which can be hard to see clearly), Chestnut-throated has a *paler* throat and breast, which thus *contrast* more with its grayish belly (Ruddy's rufous-chestnut throat and breast blend more into its dull brownish belly).

HABITAT AND BEHAVIOR: Rare to occasionally fairly common but very local (inexplicably so) in undergrowth of secondary woodland and the borders of humid forest; at least at Alta Floresta in Mato Grosso, its distribution seems quite closely tied to stands of *Guadua* bamboo. Behavior much like Ruddy Spinetail's, and the two are found syntopically at a few sites. In general Ruddy takes over in understory of terra firme, leaving Chestnut-throated to occupy forest borders and other "disturbed" habitats. Its call, a repeated "prrrrr-preéyt, prrrrr-preéyt, prrrrr-preéyt . . . ," is very different from Ruddy's but seems to be given just as persistently.

RANGE: Very locally in extreme se. Colombia (Putumayo at "Guascayaco"; FMNH), e. Ecuador (a few sites in w. Napo), and e. Peru (known only from the Moyobamba area of San Martín and the Hacienda Luisiana area in Ayacucho); s. Amaz. Brazil (a few localities in Rondônia, Alta Floresta and Rio do Cágado in Mato Grosso, and

s. Pará from the lower Rio Xingu south to the Serra dos Carajás and Gorotire). To 1100 m.

NOTE: For notes on this species in Brazil, see D. C. Oren and J. M. C. da Silva (*Bol. Mus. Par. Emílio Goeldi*, sér. Zool. 3[1]: 1–9, 1987).

Synallaxis cinnamomea

STRIPE-BREASTED SPINETAIL   PLATE: 4

DESCRIPTION: 14–15 cm (5½–6″). *Ne. Colombia to Trinidad and Tobago.* Quite variable. *Striatipectus* group of Venezuela is mostly dull brown above with *buff to fulvous superciliary;* wings mostly rufous, tail dull chestnut. Chin white, lower throat narrowly streaked black and white; *remaining underparts mostly buff with crisp dusky streaking.* Nominate race (ne. Colombia) is more rufescent above (especially on face) with rufous superciliary, and (aside from its black-and-white-streaked throat) its underparts are *mostly rufous with blurry fulvous streaking;* see C-25. Trinidad and Tobago birds differ more. On Trinidad, *carri* is dark brown above with no superciliary, its throat is blacker with narrower white streaking, and its underparts are dull olive brown with *little streaking;* on Tobago, *terrestris* is paler and more olivaceous brown generally and has *some blurry buff streaking on breast* (only).

SIMILAR SPECIES: No other *Synallaxis* has streaked underparts; as the species' behavior is typical of the genus, Stripe-breasted seems unlikely to be confused with other furnariids.

HABITAT AND BEHAVIOR: Uncommon to fairly common in undergrowth of humid forest borders, secondary woodland, and deciduous woodland; on Trinidad and Tobago also in forest undergrowth, and seems especially numerous on Tobago. Skulking behavior much like that of other *Synallaxis'*. The song is a repeated "chík-kweeik? chík-kweeik? . . . ," the second note with a querulous quality, often continued rapidly for some time, occasionally for protracted periods. The overall effect, which seems not to vary geographically, is reminiscent of Azara's Spinetail's song.

RANGE: Lower slopes of coastal mts. of n. Venezuela (east to Paria Peninsula), and lower slopes of Andes of w. Venezuela and ne. Colombia (south to Cundinamarca); Sierra de Perijá on Venezuela-Colombia border; Trinidad and Tobago. Mostly below 1500 m, rarely up to 2100 m.

NOTE: The distinctive birds of Trinidad (*carri;* Trinidad Spinetail) and of Tobago (*terrestris;* Tobago Spinetail) may prove to be full species.

Gyalophylax Spinetails

A monotypic genus endemic to ne. Brazil, the little-known *Gyalophylax* has sometimes been subsumed into *Synallaxis* (e.g., by Vaurie 1980). Although it is obviously closely related, we feel it deserves recognition on the basis of its almost wedge-shaped bill (with lower mandible slightly upturned) and rather rounded (though still graduated) tail; additionally, it has 12 rectrices (vs. only 8 or 10 in all *Synallaxis*).

Gyalophylax hellmayri

RED-SHOULDERED SPINETAIL   PLATE: 4

DESCRIPTION: 18 cm (7"). A *large*, dark-looking spinetail of *arid interior ne. Brazil*. Iris yellow-orange. *Mostly uniform dingy brownish gray* (almost mauve), slightly buffier on midbelly and with *large, solid black triangular throat patch; wing-coverts contrastingly bright rufous-chestnut; tail rather long and blackish*.

SIMILAR SPECIES: Larger than any potentially sympatric *Synallaxis* spinetail, none of which shares its combination of uniform dark plumage with contrasting rufous wing-coverts and black throat patch. Cf. Pale-breasted Spinetail.

HABITAT AND BEHAVIOR: Rare to uncommon in low scrub and undergrowth of sparse deciduous woodland. Behavior similar to that of *Synallaxis* spinetails, tending to skulk in dense growth near the ground and showing itself most advantageously soon after dawn. Its song is an abrupt chirring which gradually becomes more stuttering and fades in volume (somewhat recalling a *Laterallus* crake); a more frequent call is a fast, endlessly repeated "ka-chew, ka-chew, ka-chew . . ." (D. Finch).

RANGE: Ne. Brazil (n. Bahia, w. Pernambuco, and Piauí). To about 500 m.

GROUP D

Small "*Synallaxis*" Spinetails (perhaps better placed in *Cranioleuca* or *Siptornopsis*). A pair of spinetails found in arid scrub of sw. Ecuador and nw. Peru. Their generic affinities are uncertain (see below). We retain them in their traditional genus, *Synallaxis;* they may deserve to be placed in their own genus (though no name is available).

Synallaxis stictothorax

NECKLACED SPINETAIL   PLATE: 5

DESCRIPTION: 12.5 cm (5"). *Lowlands of sw. Ecuador and nw. Peru*. Forehead streaked black and white becoming grayish brown on crown and upper back, brown on back, and cinnamon-rufous on rump; *long narrow superciliary white;* wings mainly rufous with outer remiges dusky; tail mostly rufous with inner web of central pair of rectrices blackish, producing a quite marked *bicolored effect*. Below white, *purest on throat,* with *fine dusky streaking across breast* (sometimes inconspicuous) and pale buff flanks. Foregoing applies to nominate race of sw. Ecuador; *maculata* of nw. Peru differs in having tail almost entirely rufous (dusky only on tips of central rectrices).

SIMILAR SPECIES: Cf. Chinchipe Spinetail (no overlap). Otherwise this distinctive, scrub-inhabiting spinetail is not likely to be confused in its limited range; it can look vaguely wren-like.

HABITAT AND BEHAVIOR: Fairly common in arid scrub and borders of light deciduous woodland. Usually in pairs, gleaning in foliage, generally easy to observe as not particularly shy and often in the semiopen. Its most common song is an often explosive series of sputtering notes which start loudly and then gradually slow and trail off, e.g., "ch-ch-

chéh-chéh-chéh-chéh-cheh-cheh-ch-ch-ch, ch, ch, ch"; sometimes only the "ch" notes are given in series. It often calls while perched on or close to its conspicuous ball-shaped nest made of sticks.

RANGE: Sw. Ecuador (north to cen. Manabí) and nw. Peru (south to La Libertad). Below 200 m.

NOTE: Does not include *S. chinchipensis* (Chinchipe Spinetail) of Peru's upper Río Marañón valley. Whether *S. stictothorax* (and *S. chinchipensis*) belongs in the genus *Synallaxis* seems doubtful. In plumage both are atypical for that genus, as pointed out decades ago in *Birds of the World*, vol. 7. Vocally *stictothorax* reminds us strongly of certain *Cranioleuca*, and in its more or less arboreal behavior it resembles that genus as well. The plumage similarity to the much larger *Siptornopsis*, whose voice and behavior we do not know, is also striking. Given the uncertainty, we retain both in *Synallaxis*.

Synallaxis chinchipensis

CHINCHIPE SPINETAIL

DESCRIPTION: 13.5 cm (5¼"). *Upper Río Marañón valley of nw. Peru;* formerly regarded as conspecific with Necklaced Spinetail. Resembles that species but slightly larger and with longer bill; in addition, its superciliary is much less strongly marked and buffyish (not bold and pure white), its breast is spotted (not streaked) dusky, and its flanks are grayish (not buff); its tail, with extensive dusky, has pattern of nominate Necklaced.

SIMILAR SPECIES: Great Spinetail (*Siptornopsis*) has a similar pattern but is *much* larger, etc.; it occurs at much higher elevations in nw. Peru.

HABITAT AND BEHAVIOR: Unknown to us in life.

RANGE: Nw. Peru (upper Río Marañón valley in Cajamarca, mainly in the drainage of one of its affluents, the Río Chinchipe). To at least 400 m.

NOTE: This form seems always to have been regarded as a race of *S. stictothorax* of the Pacific lowlands, but we feel that its plumage and morphological differences warrant considering it a separate species. As both species are found only at low elevations, they are presently not in contact, being separated by the Andes.

Siptornopsis Spinetails

A large and long-tailed spinetail of uncertain affinities found in the upper Río Marañón valley of n. Peru. Its similarity in color and pattern to the Necklaced and Chinchipe Spinetails was first remarked upon in *Birds of the World*, vol. 7.

Siptornopsis hypochondriacus

GREAT SPINETAIL   PLATE: 5

DESCRIPTION: 18.5 cm (7¼"). *A large and long-tailed spinetail of slopes above upper Río Marañón valley in n. Peru. Brown above,* palest on rump and darkest on crown, with *long white superciliary* and dusky lores and auriculars; lesser wing-coverts rufous (but otherwise *no rufous on wings*). Below white, dingier on belly, with *bold brown streaking narrow*

across breast and broad down sides and flanks. Immature similar but less extensively streaked below.

SIMILAR SPECIES: Much larger, though similarly patterned, than Necklaced and Chinchipe Spinetails; both these species are found at lower elevations. Baron's Spinetail is almost as large and is superficially similar but has rufous crown, wings, and tail and lacks streaking below. Cf. Common and Chestnut-backed Thornbirds, both of which have much more rufous above and no breast streaking.

HABITAT AND BEHAVIOR: Not well known. Fjeldså and Krabbe (1990) say it occurs in pairs in dense humid montane shrubbery, sometimes with alders (*Alnus*) intermixed, and that it has "a loud chatter"; yet M. J. Braun and T. A. Parker III (*Neotropical Ornithology*, AOU Monograph no. 36, pp. 333–346, 1985) write that it inhabits "desert scrub." It is said to build a "huge, roofed stick nest like those of *Phacellodomus* [thornbirds]" (T. A. Parker III).

RANGE: N. Peru (slopes above upper Río Marañón valley in Cajamarca, La Libertad, and n. Ancash). 2000–3000 m.

Hellmayrea Spinetails

Found in forests of the n. Andes, the monotypic genus *Hellmayrea* differs from *Synallaxis* in its markedly short tail and lack of rufous in the wing. The species was formerly often placed in *Synallaxis*, e.g., by Meyer de Schauensee (1966, 1970). M. J. Braun and T. A. Parker III (*Neotropical Ornithology*, AOU Monograph no. 36, pp. 333–346, 1985) discussed its relationships and suggested resurrecting the genus *Hellmayrea* for *gularis*, indicating that it is probably more closely related to *Cranioleuca* than to *Synallaxis*.

Hellmayrea gularis

WHITE-BROWED SPINETAIL   PLATE: 5

DESCRIPTION: 13–13.5 cm (5–5¼"). *A small, short-tailed spinetail of temperate forest from Venezuela to Peru*. Above mostly rufous brown, most rufous on tail, and with *white lores and narrow superciliary. Throat white* margined with dusky; remaining underparts uniform buffy brown. Foregoing applies to nominate race of Colombia and Ecuador. *Cinereiventris* of Venezuelan Andes and *brunneidorsalis* of Sierra de Perijá similar but more grayish below, with brown restricted to sides and flanks; see V-19. *Rufiventris* of Peru also resembles nominate but is more rufescent above and brighter, more cinnamon below.

SIMILAR SPECIES: Because of its notably short tail, this species can be confused with the similarly colored (and also short-tailed) Mountain Wren. Rufous Spinetail has a much longer tail and lacks the white superciliary and throat. *Schizoeaca* thistletails also have much longer tails and differ in varying plumage details.

HABITAT AND BEHAVIOR: Uncommon in dense tangled undergrowth and borders of montane forest, often in thickets of *Chusquea* bamboo. Usually found singly or in pairs, generally not accompanying mixed flocks; forages, sometimes quite acrobatically, mainly by probing into clumps of moss and curled-up dead leaves. Although generally quiet and unobtrusive, the White-browed Spinetail is not too difficult to observe and for an Andean forest bird is surprisingly unwary. The infrequently heard song, reminiscent of the songs of several *Cranioleuca*, is a series of high-pitched notes that end in a trill, e.g., "chit-chit-chit-chit-chi-chi-chichichichichichi."

RANGE: Andes of w. Venezuela (north to Trujillo), Colombia (north in W. Andes to Antioquia), Ecuador (south on w. slope to Azuay), and n. and cen. Peru (south to Junín); Sierra de Perijá on Venezuela-Colombia border. Mostly 2500–3500 m.

Cranioleuca Spinetails

A large but quite homogeneous group of small furnariids found in a variety of wooded and forested habitats from the lowlands up to tree-line in the Andes; only one species, the atypical Sulphur-bearded, inhabits really open terrain (marshes). Most are rather plain birds with shades of brown and gray predominating; all but the Sulphur-bearded have the wings (in some species just the wing-coverts) and tail rufous, and many species also show a rufous crown and pale superciliary. Immatures are often much buffier or browner, and more uniform.

Cranioleuca differ from *Synallaxis* spinetails in their arboreal behavior and their shorter and differently shaped, graduated, and "double-pointed" tails. The tail-tips of all species except the Rusty-backed, Speckled, and Scaled are stiffened, presumably to support them as they creep up trunks and along branches. Their active and acrobatic foraging is similar to that of many foliage-gleaners, though *Cranioleuca* spinetails tend to be more conspicuous. Nests, composed primarily of moss and usually attached to the tip of a drooping limb, are often obvious, being fairly large oval or ball-shaped structures with a side entrance. Vaurie (1971, 1980) proposed merging the genus *Cranioleuca* into *Certhiaxis,* a move that subsequent authors have usually not followed as it created a genus that is "suspiciously heterogeneous" (J. W. Fitzpatrick, *Auk* 99[4]: 812, 1982).

GROUP A

"Fancy," high Andean species of Peru and Bol.; *pale crown* in all but 1 form.

Cranioleuca albicapilla

CREAMY-CRESTED SPINETAIL   PLATE: 5

DESCRIPTION: 17 cm (6¾"). *Semiarid interior Andean valleys of s.-cen. Peru. Bill pale,* grayish to flesh. *Crown creamy white, becoming buffier to rear* (feathers often raised expressively into a *bushy crest*), and narrow whitish postocular stripe; otherwise brownish olive above with contrasting rufous wing-coverts and tail. Throat white; remaining underparts drab pale buffy grayish. *Albigula* (Cuzco and adjacent Apurímac)

similar to nominate of remainder of range but crown deeper buff and underparts tinged more ochraceous.

SIMILAR SPECIES: Marcapata Spinetail is smaller with a black bill, has crown either rufous or white (depending on race) margined with black, and inhabits montane forest, not the semiarid scrub favored by Creamy-crested. Cf. also Baron's Spinetail.

HABITAT AND BEHAVIOR: Fairly common to common in dense semi-arid woodland, frequently near streams, and often in areas where the habitat is quite patchy and disturbed; also ranges locally up into *Polylepis*-dominated woodland. Usually found singly or in pairs, hitching along branches and probing into clumps of moss, bark crevices, and epiphytes. Inconspicuous unless vocalizing, but its song is loud and quite frequently given, a descending series of semimusical notes, "tch, tch, chee-chee-cheechee-ee-ee-ee-ee-ew." This strikingly attractive *Cranioleuca* is readily found around the Peñas ruins above Ollantaytambo in Cuzco.

RANGE: Semiarid Andean valleys and slopes in cen. and s. Peru (Junín south to Cuzco). Mostly 2500–3600 m.

Cranioleuca albiceps

LIGHT-CROWNED SPINETAIL   PLATE: 5

DESCRIPTION: 15.5 cm (6"). *Andes of w. Bolivia and extreme s. Peru.* Nominate race (La Paz, Bolivia, and Puno, Peru) has *crown white or white tinged buff outlined laterally by black*; superciliary and sides of head dark grayish; nape and rump olive brownish; entire mantle and tail rufous. Chin white; remaining underparts and sides of head dull olive brownish. *Discolor* (Cochabamba and Santa Cruz, Bolivia) very similar aside from its *rich buff crown*.

SIMILAR SPECIES: Slightly larger Marcapata Spinetail of s. Peru also has 2 races with strikingly different crown colors, white and rufous. Both races have distinctly whiter superciliaries and more extensively white throats than Light-crowned. Where Marcapata comes closest to range of Light-crowned, Marcapata's crown is rufous whereas Light-crowned's is white.

HABITAT AND BEHAVIOR: Fairly common in lower and middle growth and borders of montane forest, often associated with stands of *Chusquea* bamboo. Usually found singly or in pairs (less often in larger, presumably family, groups), hitching along limbs and smaller branches, probing and rummaging in moss, epiphytes, and suspended dead leaves; less often and more briefly may creep up trunks like a woodcreeper. Its most common song is a rather long series of shrill notes which gradually descend and fade away (thus more or less like numerous other *Cranioleuca*). Readily seen at "Siberia" above Comarapa in Santa Cruz (buff-crowned birds) and near Chuspipata in the La Paz yungas (white-crowned birds).

RANGE: Andes of extreme s. Peru (s. Puno) and w. Bolivia (La Paz, Cochabamba, and w. Santa Cruz). Mostly 2400–3300 m.

NOTE: See comments under Marcapata Spinetail.

Cranioleuca marcapatae

MARCAPATA SPINETAIL

PLATE: 5

DESCRIPTION: 16 cm (6¼"). *Andes of Cuzco, Peru.* Nominate race (Cuzco, Peru) has *crown rufous outlined laterally by black; narrow superciliary whitish,* sides of head and nape grayish; entire mantle and tail rufous, rump grayish olive. *Throat white,* becoming dull buffy grayish on remaining underparts. *Weskei* (n. Cuzco on Cordillera Vilcabamba) very similar aside from its *white crown.*

SIMILAR SPECIES: Cf. similar Light-crowned Spinetail, found farther south on e. slope of Andes. Ash-browed Spinetail also has a rufous crown and somewhat resembles nominate Marcapata but is somewhat smaller and lacks Marcapata's rufous back; Ash-browed ranges at lower elevations and is more arboreal.

HABITAT AND BEHAVIOR: Uncommon in lower growth and borders of montane forest, frequently associated with patches of *Chusquea* bamboo. Behavior similar to Light-crowned Spinetail's. One vocalization is a fast, descending "skwa, ski-ski-ski-skee-skee, tuhtuhtuh," another (Parker and O'Neill 1980) a descending series of staccato notes, "tu-tu-tu-tu-tu"; both are similar to the calls of many other *Cranioleuca* spinetails (including Light-crowned). Small numbers can be seen along n. side of the Abra Málaga road above Ollantaytambo (rufous-crowned birds).

RANGE: Andes of s. Peru (Cuzco). 2700–3400 m.

NOTE: For the description of *weskei,* a discussion of the variation in this species and the closely related *C. albiceps,* and a fine painting by L. McQueen depicting all four forms involved, see J. V. Remsen, Jr. (*Wilson Bull.* 96[4]: 515–523, 1984). As Remsen points out, maintaining the traditional two-species concept seems appropriate until more information is available concerning the contact zones among the four forms; possibly all will ultimately best be united in a single species or (less likely) split into four.

GROUP B

"Standard" Cranioleuca.

Cranioleuca baroni

BARON'S SPINETAIL

PLATE: 5

Other: Southern Line-cheeked Spinetail

DESCRIPTION: 16.5–17.5 cm (6½–7"). A *large* spinetail of *high Andes of n. and cen. Peru;* sometimes considered conspecific with Line-cheeked Spinetail. *Crown rufous* bordered below by a *narrow white superciliary;* cheeks streaked blackish and white; *upperparts otherwise brownish gray,* with contrasting mainly rufous wings and tail. *Throat pure white* becoming more grayish white with somewhat mottled effect on remaining underparts. Foregoing applies to *capitalis* and *zaratensis* of s. end of range (in Huánuco, Pasco, and Lima); nominate race is more olivaceous gray and less mottled on lower underparts but retains the striking white throat. Although not geographically correlated, there seems to be substantial variation in size, with *zaratensis* averaging the smallest and *capitalis* the largest.

SIMILAR SPECIES: Line-cheeked Spinetail (no overlap) is usually much smaller, browner above, and drabber and buffier below. Great Spinetail

(*Siptornopsis*) has a longer, brown tail and lacks the rufous crown and extensively rufous wings. Creamy-crested Spinetail has a pale bill and buffy whitish (not rufous) crown.

HABITAT AND BEHAVIOR: Uncommon to locally fairly common in montane forest and woodland, especially in areas that are not very humid; also occurs locally in patches of *Polylepis* woodland. Usually found singly or in pairs, sometimes loosely associated with small mixed flocks; forages mainly by creeping on larger branches and trunks, inspecting epiphytes, clumps of moss, and bark. Its loud, shrill, descending song is similar to that of many other *Cranioleuca;* also gives several sharp, single-noted calls. Can be seen near Lago Llanganuco in Huascarán Nat. Park in Ancash, Peru.

RANGE: Andes of n. and cen. Peru (Amazonas and cen. Cajamarca south to Pasco and Lima). Mostly 2300–3700 m.

NOTE: *C. baroni* (with *capitalis* and *zaratensis*) has often been regarded as conspecific with *C. antisiensis* (e.g., Meyer de Schauensee 1966, 1970), though not in *Birds of the World,* vol. 7. The two differ strikingly in size and several plumage characters. Contrary to the comments in Vaurie (1980), we find no significant approach to *C. baroni* in specimens of *C. antisiensis palamblae* at AMNH or ANSP; the most southerly form, *zaratensis,* does seem to average smaller. We believe the better course is to regard the two as separate species.

Cranioleuca antisiensis

LINE-CHEEKED SPINETAIL   PLATE: 5

Other: Northern Line-cheeked Spinetail

DESCRIPTION: 14.5 cm (5¾"). *Andes of sw. Ecuador and nw. Peru. Crown rufous* bordered below by *narrow whitish superciliary;* lores buff, and cheeks indistinctly streaked pale buff; upperparts otherwise olivaceous brown with contrasting rufous wings and tail. Throat whitish, becoming dull buffy brownish on remaining underparts.

SIMILAR SPECIES: Ash-browed Spinetail is generally darker with a less prominent superciliary; the two are not known to occur together, Ash-browed being found basically on e. slope of Andes and at lower elevations. Red-faced Spinetail overlaps with Line-cheeked only marginally if at all (occurring farther north on w. slope of Andes) and has *entire* head (not just crown) rufous. However, beware immature Red-faceds, which may have rufous more or less restricted to crown and show a buff superciliary. Cf. also Baron's Spinetail (no overlap).

HABITAT AND BEHAVIOR: Fairly common to common in canopy and borders of montane forest, woodland, and even quite degraded secondary scrub. Behavior similar to that of Baron's Spinetail, foraging at all levels, frequently with mixed flocks. Has a variety of chippering and scolding calls; the song is a series of loud and well-enunciated shrill notes which (typical for the genus) gradually fade, weaken, and drop in pitch. Easily seen in woodland patches around Celica in Loja, Ecuador.

RANGE: Andes of sw. Ecuador (Azuay, El Oro, and Loja; sightings from farther north are regarded as uncertain, as they may pertain to immature Red-faced Spinetails) and nw. Peru (south to n. Cajamarca and Lambayeque). Mostly 1100–2900 m.

NOTE: See comments under Baron's Spinetail.

Cranioleuca curtata

ASH-BROWED SPINETAIL

PLATE: 5

DESCRIPTION: 14.5 cm (5¾"). Mainly on *e. slope of Andes* from Colombia to Bolivia. *Crown rufous-chestnut* with variable amount of dusky on forecrown and *indistinct grayish superciliary;* above otherwise olive brown with contrasting rufous-chestnut wings and tail. Throat whitish; remaining underparts dull brownish olive. Immature rather strikingly different, with upperparts much like adult but with superciliary, sides of head, and most of underparts orange-ochraceous. Iris hazel to reddish brown; neither specimen labels nor our extensive experience with living birds over much of the species' range have uncovered any evidence to indicate that it is white, as claimed by Hilty and Brown (1986) for the E. Andes of Colombia (where possibly different?).

SIMILAR SPECIES: Crested Spinetail replaces Ash-browed northward on e. slope of Andes in Colombia; it differs most notably in having a pale bill and in lacking the rufous crown. Line-cheeked Spinetail, mainly of w. slope of Andes (no known overlap with Ash-browed), is quite similar but paler generally with a bolder, whiter superciliary.

HABITAT AND BEHAVIOR: Uncommon to fairly common in montane forest, sometimes coming out into trees in adjacent clearings, foraging especially at middle levels and borders though also sometimes well up into canopy. Behavior similar to that of many other *Cranioleuca* spinetails, feeding primarily by hitching along branches, often quite acrobatically (sometimes even upside down), and rummaging in epiphytes and tangles; frequently with mixed flocks. Its call, a series of shrill notes which gradually drop in pitch and fade in intensity, resembles that of several other *Cranioleuca*.

RANGE: Andes of Colombia (w. slope of E. Andes from Santander south to head of Río Magdalena valley in Huila; e. slope of E. Andes from w. Caquetá southward [also farther north?]) and e. slope of Andes in Ecuador, Peru, and w. Bolivia. Mostly 900–2000 m, in small numbers up to 2500 m at least in Colombia.

NOTE: G. R. Graves (*Condor* 88[1]: 120–122, 1986) has shown that what was long called *Cranioleuca furcata* (Fork-tailed Spinetail) was only the immature plumage of *C. curtata*. C. Vaurie (*Ibis* 113: 517–519, 1971) had incorrectly concluded that it was a valid species.

Cranioleuca hellmayri

STREAK-CAPPED SPINETAIL

DESCRIPTION: 14 cm (5½"). *Colombia's Santa Marta Mts.* Resembles Ash-browed Spinetail (no overlap) but with *pale iris* (pale straw to white). Further, its rufous crown is *streaked with black,* superciliary more whitish, and sides of head more streaked. See C-24 (where iris is incorrectly colored).

SIMILAR SPECIES: The only other spinetail in montane forests of Santa Marta Mts. is the very different Rusty-headed, a *Synallaxis* with allrufous head, neck, and breast.

HABITAT AND BEHAVIOR: Common in montane forest, secondgrowth woodland, and borders. Behavior, including voice, similar to Ash-browed Spinetail's. Easily seen along the San Lorenzo ridge road.

RANGE: Santa Marta Mts. of n. Colombia. 1600–3000 m.

Cranioleuca demissa

TEPUI SPINETAIL

DESCRIPTION: 14.5 cm (5¾"). *Tepuis of s. Venezuela area.* Resembles Ash-browed Spinetail (no overlap) but *distinctly grayer below.* Immatures are more brownish below. See V-19 (but note that it should be grayer below).
SIMILAR SPECIES: The only *Cranioleuca* in its range.
HABITAT AND BEHAVIOR: Fairly common in canopy and borders of montane forest and woodland. Behavior, including vocalizations, much like Ash-browed Spinetail's. Readily found along upper part of the Escalera road in e. Bolívar.
RANGE: Tepuis of s. Venezuela (Bolívar and Amazonas south to Cerro de la Neblina) and adjacent Guyana (Mt. Ayanganna) and Brazil (n. Roraima). 1100–2450 m.

Cranioleuca pallida

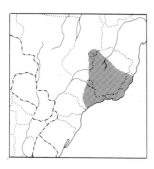

PALLID SPINETAIL

DESCRIPTION: 14 cm (5½"). *Se. Brazil.* Resembles geographically distant Ash-browed Spinetail but with somewhat more prominent and whiter superciliary, and a little paler below. Note that the species is not especially "pallid" (e.g., far less so than Gray-headed).
SIMILAR SPECIES: Olive Spinetail lacks the rufous crown and is probably never sympatric with Pallid.
HABITAT AND BEHAVIOR: Fairly common in canopy and borders of montane forest and woodland, sometimes coming out into tall trees in adjacent clearings. Behavior, including vocalizations, similar to Ash-browed Spinetail's. Numerous at Itatiaia Nat. Park.
RANGE: Se. Brazil (Brasília, cen. Minas Gerais, and Espírito Santo south to se. São Paulo). 700–2150 m.

Cranioleuca erythrops

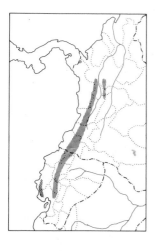

RED-FACED SPINETAIL

DESCRIPTION: 14 cm (5½"). *W. Colombia and w. Ecuador.* Resembles Ash-browed Spinetail but *entire face rufous* and lacks mottling on breast. See C-25, P-14. Immature has rufous on head reduced to the crown and may show a buff superciliary.
SIMILAR SPECIES: Line-cheeked Spinetail (limited or no range overlap) has rufous on head confined to crown.
HABITAT AND BEHAVIOR: Fairly common in canopy and borders of montane forest and taller woodland. Behavior, including vocalizations, much like Ash-browed Spinetail's.
RANGE: W. Colombia (w. slope of W. Andes and w. slope of Cen. Andes from Antioquia to Quindío) and w. Ecuador (mainly on w. slope of Andes south to e. Guayas; an isolated population on the coastal cordillera in sw. Manabí and w. Guayas). Also Costa Rica and Panama. Mostly 600–1600 m, in smaller numbers up to 2100 m in Colombia, locally down to near sea level in sw. Ecuador.

Cranioleuca semicinerea

GRAY-HEADED SPINETAIL   PLATE: 5

DESCRIPTION: 14 cm (5½"). *Local in ne. and s.-cen. Brazil. Bill pinkish. Head and neck pale ashy gray,* slightly paler on forehead and with faint

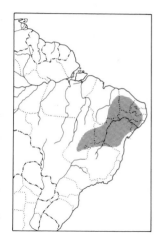

whitish superciliary, becoming *dingy pale grayish below;* remaining upperparts entirely rufous. *Goyana* (s. Goiás) is similar but has darker crown and auriculars and somewhat more prominent superciliary.

SIMILAR SPECIES: Nothing similar in range, where no other *Cranioleuca* is present.

HABITAT AND BEHAVIOR: Rare to uncommon in canopy and borders of forest and taller woodland, both in rather arid areas and in more humid regions. Usually in pairs, with active arboreal behavior typical of many other members of the genus. Its song is a thin and very high-pitched "tseet-tseet-tseet-tseet-tititititi" fading away toward the end, in quality and pattern much like that of many other *Cranioleuca.* Small numbers can be found in woodland south of Jequié in s. Bahia.

RANGE: Locally in ne. and s.-cen. Brazil (Ceará and Alagoas south to s. Bahia and extreme n. Minas Gerais, and west to s. Goiás). To 800 m.

NOTE: For more information on this species, see D. M. Teixera and G. Luigi (*Rev. Brasil. Biol.* 49[2]: 605–613, 1989).

Cranioleuca subcristata

CRESTED SPINETAIL

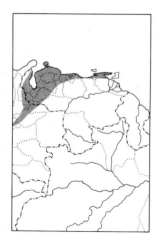

DESCRIPTION: 14 cm (5½"). *N. and w. Venezuela and ne. Colombia. Bill flesh-colored.* Olive brown above with *faint blackish streaks on crown* and indistinct pale superciliary; wings and tail contrastingly rufous. Uniform dingy pale olivaceous brown below. See V-19, C-25.

SIMILAR SPECIES: Although notably dull colored (and despite its English name, it shows no crest), this typical *Cranioleuca* is unlikely to be confused in range, where it is the only member of its genus present. Plain-crowned Spinetail (a *Synallaxis*) is similar in plumage but differs greatly in behavior and has a dark bill; their ranges do not overlap.

HABITAT AND BEHAVIOR: Fairly common to common in a variety of forested and wooded habitats, sometimes ranging out into secondary scrub as well; occurs both in humid and fairly dry regions. Behavior similar to numerous other arboreal *Cranioleuca* spinetails'; its most common song, a series of high, shrill notes followed by a descending trill, is also strongly reminiscent. Readily found in woodland around Caracas.

RANGE: N. and w. Venezuela (east to Paria Peninsula) and ne. Colombia (lower slopes of E. Andes south to s. Boyacá). Mostly below 1500 m.

Cranioleuca obsoleta

OLIVE SPINETAIL   PLATE: 5

DESCRIPTION: 14 cm (5½"). A *drab and uniform,* short-billed *Cranioleuca* of se. Brazil area. *Uniform brownish olive above* with whitish superciliary and contrasting rufous wing-coverts (*only*) and tail. Pale drab buffy olivaceous below, palest on throat.

SIMILAR SPECIES: Pallid Spinetail has rufous on crown and entire wing. Cf. also Stripe-crowned Spinetail, which replaces Olive southward and westward.

HABITAT AND BEHAVIOR: Fairly common to common in canopy and borders of humid forest and secondary woodland, including *Araucaria*

woodland. Usually in pairs, foraging actively and acrobatically, mainly by creeping on trunks and larger branches, often inspecting moss clumps and epiphytes; frequently with mixed flocks. Its song, similar to that of many other *Cranioleuca,* is an accelerating series of high-pitched but gradually descending notes that end in a trill. Numerous at various localities in highlands of ne. Rio Grande do Sul.

RANGE: Se. Brazil (s. São Paulo south to Rio Grande do Sul; old published records from farther north are regarded as unverified), e. Paraguay (a few reports from Canendiyu, Alto Paraná, Caazapá, and Misiones), and ne. Argentina (Misiones and e. Corrientes). To about 1000 m.

NOTE: Belton (1985) suggests that *obsoleta* may be only a subspecies of *C. pyrrhophia,* based on birds with apparently intermediate plumage and size that he obtained in Rio Grande do Sul. Some specimens of *C. pyrrhophia* in AMNH do indeed show very reduced crown streaking, indicating a possible approach to *C. obsoleta.* Belton also comments that they seem to respond to each others' songs, but as so many *Cranioleuca* have such similar voices, we would expect many species to respond to another's voice.

Cranioleuca pyrrhophia

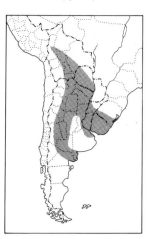

STRIPE-CROWNED SPINETAIL   PLATE: 5

DESCRIPTION: 14.5 cm (5¾"). Bolivia to Argentina. *Crown conspicuously streaked buff and blackish,* bordered below by a *broad white superciliary* and blackish postocular line; otherwise mostly brownish gray above with contrasting rufous wing-coverts and tail. *Mostly whitish below,* whitest on throat and lower face, tinged buff on flanks. Birds from Bolivian highlands (*striaticeps* and *rufipennis*) are browner above with more extensive crown streaking; many birds from Rio Grande do Sul, Brazil, show *reduced* crown streaking.

SIMILAR SPECIES: Smaller Olive Spinetail lacks the streaked crown, has a less conspicuous superciliary, and is much drabber (not so white) below. Little Thornbird is duller generally with inconspicuous streaking on crown restricted to forehead, less conspicuous superciliary, and mainly brown wings and tail. Streak-fronted Thornbird is larger and has less conspicuous crown streaking and rounded (not "spiky") tail-tips.

HABITAT AND BEHAVIOR: Fairly common to common in various types of low woodland and scrub, including chaco; widespread, persisting in thickets and hedgerows in many agricultural regions. Behavior much like Olive Spinetail's, though Stripe-crowned often seems tamer and is even more active and acrobatic. Its vocalizations also seem very similar. Because of the low and relatively open nature of its habitat, this attractive *Cranioleuca* is generally easy to see.

RANGE: S. Bolivia (north in semiarid Andean valleys to La Paz, and generally in lowlands from s. Santa Cruz southward), n. and cen. Argentina (south to Neuquén and Río Negro; absent from pampas of much of Buenos Aires, etc.), w. Paraguay, Uruguay, and extreme s. Brazil (s. Rio Grande do Sul). To 3100 m (in Bolivia); up to only about 1800 m in Argentina.

NOTE: See comments under Olive Spinetail.

GROUP C

Miscellaneous *Cranioleuca,* mostly associated with marshes, river islands, or várzea forest.

Cranioleuca sulphurifera

SULPHUR-BEARDED SPINETAIL

PLATE: 5

DESCRIPTION: 15 cm (6"). *Marshes of e. Argentina to extreme s. Brazil.* Iris orange-hazel. Above olive brown with indistinct buffy whitish superciliary; wing-coverts contrastingly rufous and with *buff patch in flight feathers* (showing as a stripe in flight); tail brown, outer feathers more rufescent. *Lower face, throat, and breast lightly streaked whitish and gray* with *small patch of lemon yellow on throat,* becoming whitish on belly and buff on flanks.

SIMILAR SPECIES: No other *Cranioleuca* inhabits marshes to such an extent. Most resembles Stripe-crowned Spinetail, but that species has crown streaking, more prominent superciliary, pure white throat, etc. Yellow-chinned Spinetail looks more strikingly bicolored, with rufous upperparts and white underparts. Cf. also Bay-capped Wren-Spinetail and Hudson's Canastero.

HABITAT AND BEHAVIOR: Uncommon to locally fairly common in reedbeds of marshes, sometimes venturing into adjacent shrubbery. Often occurs with Curve-billed Reedhaunter. Although not particularly shy, Sulphur-bearded is often difficult to see, mainly because of the mostly inaccessible nature of its habitat. Early in the morning on calm days it may perch in the open atop grass clumps or low bushes. The song consists of an upslurred trill followed by a fast series of harsh notes which gradually drop off, e.g., "d-d-d-r-r-i-i, dirip, dirip, dirip, drip-drip-dreeuw-dreew"; sometimes the upslurred trill follows the other notes. Numerous in marshes near Belén de Escobar north of Buenos Aires.

RANGE: Extreme s. Brazil (s. Rio Grande do Sul), Uruguay, and e. Argentina (s. Corrientes, s. Santa Fe, and s. Córdoba south to e. Río Negro). Below 300 m.

Cranioleuca vulpina

RUSTY-BACKED SPINETAIL

PLATE: 5

DESCRIPTION: 14–14.5 cm (5½–5¾"). *Uniform rufous above* with *narrow whitish superciliary* and grayish cheeks with faint paler streaking. *Below uniform drab buffy grayish,* palest on throat and with somewhat streaked effect on chest. *Reiseri* (ne. Brazil in Piauí, Pernambuco, and w. Bahia) has brighter cinnamon-rufous upperparts and is paler and a little buffier below with no streaked effect on chest.

SIMILAR SPECIES: The most uniformly rufous above of any *Cranioleuca.* Yellow-chinned and Red-and-white Spinetails are much whiter below and have longer bills and a less evident superciliary.

HABITAT AND BEHAVIOR: Fairly common to common near water in shrubby thickets and woodland undergrowth; in many parts of Amazonia most numerous on river islands. Usually in pairs which forage actively in dense tangled growth and are often hard to see well. The song is a fairly long (lasting about 3 seconds) and rapid series of chortling notes, somewhat more enunciated at the beginning, which gradually weaken and accelerate, "ch-ch-ch-chchchchchewewewewewew"; it is usually given at fairly long intervals.

RANGE: Cen. Venezuela (Delta Amacuro west through the llanos and n. Bolívar and n. Amazonas to Barinas and Apure) and ne. Colombia (south to Vichada and Meta); much of Brazil south to n. São Paulo, n. Paraná, and Mato Grosso do Sul (but absent from the coastal east and mostly from north of n. bank of the Amazon), n. Bolivia (Pando, Beni, and Cochabamba), e. Peru (south along the Río Ucayali to Lagarto), extreme s. Colombia (along the Amazon near Leticia), and e. Ecuador (mouth of the Río Lagarto into the Río Aguarico, and numerous recent records from islands in the Río Napo up to near Limoncocha). To 1000 m.

NOTE: Does not include *C. dissita* (Coiba Spinetail) from Coiba Is. in Pacific Ocean off w. Panama; despite the tremendous range disjunction, this form was formerly considered only a subspecies of *C. vulpina* (see Ridgely and Gwynne 1989).

Cranioleuca gutturata

SPECKLED SPINETAIL

PLATE: 5

DESCRIPTION: 14.5 cm (5¾"). Amazonia to s. Venezuela and the Guianas; iris often whitish or yellow. Dark olive brown above with rufous-chestnut crown and narrow buff superciliary; most of wings and tail also rufous-chestnut. Chin yellowish ochre; remaining underparts dull buff *thickly speckled with blackish on breast,* speckles becoming more obscure on belly and washed with dull olivaceous brown on flanks.

SIMILAR SPECIES: Over most of its range this well-named spinetail is readily known on the basis of its speckled or spotted underparts. Cf. Scaled Spinetail and Orinoco Softtail, both very range-restricted.

HABITAT AND BEHAVIOR: Uncommon to locally fairly common in lower growth and borders of humid forest, principally in várzea but also ranging locally in terra firme. Usually found singly or in pairs, frequently accompanying mixed flocks; forages mainly by hopping along branches and trunks, probing into epiphytes and rummaging in dead leaf clusters. Although this species has been quiet in our experience, a sharp squeaky call and a rolling chatter have been heard in Surinam (T. Davis).

RANGE: S. Venezuela (s. Bolívar and Amazonas), se. Colombia (recorded only from w. Caquetá, Putumayo, and s. Amazonas, but probably ranges northward as well), e. Ecuador, e. Peru, n. Bolivia (south to La Paz and Cochabamba), Amaz. Brazil (south to Rondônia, and east to the lower Rio Tocantins; absent from upper Rio Negro drainage), and French Guiana and Surinam. To 1100 m.

Cranioleuca muelleri

SCALED SPINETAIL

PLATE: 5

DESCRIPTION: 16 cm (6¼"). *Local along lower Amazon in Brazil.* Above much like the much better known Speckled Spinetail. Below dull buffy whitish, *feathers edged dark olive giving a coarse, scaly appearance,* becoming uniform olivaceous on flanks.

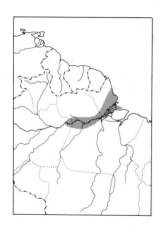

SIMILAR SPECIES: Speckled Spinetail is smaller and obviously speckled (not scaled) on breast.

HABITAT AND BEHAVIOR: Unknown in life.

RANGE: Lower Amaz. Brazil (from near mouths of Rios Tapajós and Jamundá east to Amapá and Mexiana Is.). Below 200 m.

Certhiaxis Spinetails

A pair of bicolored, basically rufous and white spinetails found near water in the lowlands. The bill is longer and more slender than in *Cranioleuca*.

Certhiaxis cinnamomea

YELLOW-CHINNED SPINETAIL   PLATE: 5

Other: Yellow-throated Spinetail

DESCRIPTION: 14–14.5 cm (5½–5¾"). *Widespread near water in n. and s. South America. Mostly cinnamon-rufous* to rufous brown above with indistinct pale grayish superciliary, the lores and small area behind eye dusky; flight feathers tipped dusky. *Below uniform white* faintly tinged buff, especially on flanks; *chin spot pale yellow.* Races of n. Colombia and n. Venezuela (*fuscifrons, marabina,* and *valenciana*) have a dusky frontlet; see C-25.

SIMILAR SPECIES: Although the yellow chin can be hard to see in the field, this clean-cut, marsh-loving spinetail is easily known from its basically bicolored appearance: rufous above, white below. Rusty-backed Spinetail, sometimes with it, is considerably dingier below. Cf. Red-and-white Spinetail.

HABITAT AND BEHAVIOR: Fairly common to common in marshes (especially reedbeds), water ditches, wet grassy areas, mangroves, and bordering shrubbery. Active and conspicuous for a marsh bird, often feeding in bushes or hopping in the open on floating vegetation, e.g., the mats of water hyacinth so prevalent in many areas. Sings loudly and frequently, a repeated churring rattle, "chu-chu-chchchchcchchchchchchcu," with quality reminiscent of certain *Laterallus* crakes; also has various other shorter calls.

RANGE: N. and extreme ne. Colombia (Caribbean lowlands and Río Magdalena valley south to Huila; east of Andes in n. Arauca), most of Venezuela (not in most of Amazonas), Guianas, most of Brazil (except extreme west and apparently parts of s. Amazonia), extreme s. Colombia (along Amazon near Leticia), n. and e. Bolivia (Beni south to Tarija), Paraguay, Uruguay (locally in Durazno, Soriano, and Rocha), and n. Argentina (south to Salta, ne. Córdoba, and n. Buenos Aires); Trinidad. To 500 m.

NOTE: We agree with Hilty and Brown (1986) who slightly altered this species' English name from "Yellow-throated" to better reflect that the yellow is so inconspicuous.

Certhiaxis mustelina

RED-AND-WHITE SPINETAIL

DESCRIPTION: 14 cm (5½"). *Local along rivers in Amazonia.* Resembles Yellow-chinned Spinetail but is brighter rufous above with completely bright rufous crown, *sharply contrasting black lores,* and *no* pale grayish superciliary; also *lacks* yellow on chin. The sympatric race of Yellow-chinned in Amazonia, *pallida,* is comparatively dull. See C-25.

HABITAT AND BEHAVIOR: Uncommon to fairly common in grassy areas and shrubbery near water, especially on river islands. Behavior similar to Yellow-chinned Spinetail's; the two are locally syntopic, e.g., on certain islands in the Amazon near Leticia, Colombia. Vocalizations are also similar, though a commonly given call is an emphasized "chuk-cheh" or "chuk-cheh-cheh."

RANGE: Amaz. Brazil (mostly near Amazon River from near Belém westward, occurring upriver along the Rio Madeira to the Bolivian border), extreme s. Colombia (along the Amazon near Leticia), and e. Peru (along the Amazon and upriver along the Río Ucayali to Lagarto). Below 150 m.

Schizoeaca Thistletails

Small furnariids found in woodland undergrowth near treeline in the Andes from Venezuela to Bolivia, with an outlying form on the Sierra de Perijá, the thistletails are characterized by their very long and strongly graduated tails whose feathers are frayed and decomposed-looking. The various taxa exhibit a "chaotic" pattern of geographic variation which principally involves dorsal color (rufous to olive brown), the presence or absence of an eye-ring and superciliary whose color ranges from white to pale grayish or ochraceous, and the color of the chin patch (white or rufous). Meyer de Schauensee (1966, 1970) recognized six species in the genus; two species have been described subsequently. Vaurie (1980) suggested considering all forms as subspecies of a highly polytypic *S. fuliginosa.* However, J. V. Remsen, Jr. (*Proc. Biol. Soc. Wash.* 94 [4]: 1068–1075, 1981), with whom we concur, felt that continuing to separate the genus into distinct species was the most appropriate course.

All taxa have allopatric distributions. For ease of comparison, we have treated them by *proceeding from north to south in the Andes.* Further, comparisons are made *only* to species that occur in areas immediately to the north or south of the species in question.

Schizoeaca coryi

OCHRE-BROWED THISTLETAIL

DESCRIPTION: 18 cm (7"). *W. Venezuela.* Olive brown above, crown slightly grayer, with *contrasting ochre superciliary, face, and chin patch.* Remaining underparts drab brownish gray. See V-19.

SIMILAR SPECIES: White-chinned Thistletail, occurring to the south, has a whitish eye-ring, superciliary, and chin patch and is much more rufescent above. Cf. also Perija Thistletail.

HABITAT AND BEHAVIOR: Uncommon to fairly common in dense undergrowth of low montane woodland and forest borders. Behavior, including vocalizations, much like White-chinned Thistletail's.

RANGE: Andes of w. Venezuela (Trujillo, Mérida, and n. Táchira). Mostly 3000–4100 m.

Schizoeaca perijana

PERIJA THISTLETAIL

DESCRIPTION: 19 cm (7½″). *Sierra de Perijá on Venezuela-Colombia border.* Olive brown above, slightly grayer on crown, with *indistinct grayish superciliary. Chin patch ochre;* remaining underparts drab brownish gray.

SIMILAR SPECIES: Ochre-browed Thistletail (no overlap) has ochre on sides of head as well as on chin.

HABITAT AND BEHAVIOR: Nothing seems to be on record, though presumably much like its congeners'.

RANGE: Sierra de Perijá on Venezuela-Colombia border. 3000–3400 m.

NOTE: A newly described species: W. H. Phelps, Jr., *Bol. Soc. Venez. Cienc. Nat.* 33: 43–53, 1977.

Schizoeaca fuliginosa

WHITE-CHINNED THISTLETAIL   PLATE: 6

DESCRIPTION: 18.5–19 cm (7¼–7½″). *Disjunct distribution from w. Venezuela to cen. Peru;* absent from s. Ecuador and extreme n. Peru. N. birds have gray irides. *Chestnut brown above* with *narrow white eye-ring* and indistinct short pale grayish superciliary. *Uniform gray below* with *whitish chin patch.* Foregoing applies to nominate race (w. Venezuela to e. Ecuador) and *peruviana* (Amazonas and San Martín, Peru); *peruviana* slightly more mottled on belly and with less prominent eye-ring. *Fumigata* (w. Nariño, Colombia, and nw. Ecuador) similar but with underparts browner and drabber (less pure gray). *Plengei* (Huánuco, Peru; J. P. O'Neill and T. A. Parker III, *Bull B.O.C.* 96[4]:136–141, 1976) has whiter superciliary and some whitish streaking on lower throat and breast.

SIMILAR SPECIES: Mouse-colored Thistletail, occurring between ranges of nominate and *peruviana* White-chinneds, is duller and more olive brown above (showing no rufous) and has a barely discernible superciliary. Ochre-browed Thistletail, occurring north of White-chinned, differs strikingly in its ochraceous face and chin patch. Eye-ringed Thistletail, occurring just south of *plengei* White-chinned, has an orange-rufous chin patch and no discernible superciliary.

HABITAT AND BEHAVIOR: Uncommon to locally fairly common in dense undergrowth and borders of low montane woodland and forest borders near and just below treeline (in Peru called *pajonal*) and in patches of woodland above treeline (including groves of *Polylepis*). Found singly or in pairs, most often independently of mixed flocks, hopping and fluttering through dense vegetation with tail partially cocked; flights are short and weak. Although not particularly shy, this species is often hard to see well because of its very dense habitat. Forages by gleaning, often quite acrobatically, for insects from leaves and slender branches. The song, given by both sexes, is a high-pitched, thin trill which descends slightly; also a sharp "pyeek" call note in alarm or as a contact note.

RANGE: Andes of extreme w. Venezuela (sw. Táchira on the Páramo de Tamá), Colombia (E. Andes south to Nariño, Cen. Andes in Caldas and Tolima, W. Andes in Nariño), and Ecuador (on w. slope south to Pichincha, on e. slope south to nw. Morona-Santiago on the Sangay massif); Andes of n. and cen. Peru (Amazonas and San Martín; Huánuco on Cordillera Carpish). Mostly 2800–3500 m, but recorded lower (to 2400 m) in Peru.

Schizoeaca griseomurina

MOUSE-COLORED THISTLETAIL   PLATE: 6

DESCRIPTION: 18.5–19 cm (7¼–7½"). *S. Ecuador and extreme n. Peru. Olive brown above* with *narrow but very bold white eye-ring* and faint grayish postocular stripe. Uniform grayish below with whitish chin patch.

SIMILAR SPECIES: White-chinned Thistletail (races of which occur both north and south of this species) is much more rufescent above and has a more prominent pale superciliary and a less conspicuous and contrasting eye-ring.

HABITAT AND BEHAVIOR: Uncommon to locally fairly common in dense undergrowth of low humid woodland and forest borders near and just below treeline, locally (e.g., at El Cajas in Azuay, Ecuador) also in patches of *Polylepis*-dominated woodland above treeline. Behavior, including vocalizations, much like White-chinned Thistletail's. Readily found at the Cajanuma station of Podocarpus Nat. Park.

RANGE: Andes of s. Ecuador (north to Palmas and El Cajas in Azuay and the Gualaceo-Limon road in Morona-Santiago) and extreme n. Peru (n. Piura and nw. Cajamarca). 2800–4000 m.

Schizoeaca palpebralis

EYE-RINGED THISTLETAIL   PLATE: 6

DESCRIPTION: 18.5–19 cm (7¼–7½"). *Cen. Peru in Junín. Chestnut brown above* with *narrow but bold white eye-ring*. Uniform gray below, some birds with a little whitish mottling, with *orange-rufous chin patch*.

SIMILAR SPECIES: White-chinned Thistletail (*plengei*, occurring just to the north) has a whitish chin patch and fairly prominent white superciliary. Vilcabamba Thistletail, occurring just to the south, has olive brown upperparts with no rufescent tone and no eye-ring.

HABITAT AND BEHAVIOR: Nothing seems to be on record, though presumably much like its congeners'.

RANGE: Andes of cen. Peru in Junín. About 3300 m.

Schizoeaca vilcabambae

VILCABAMBA THISTLETAIL   PLATE: 6

DESCRIPTION: 18.5–19 cm (7¼–7½"). *S. Peru in Ayacucho and n. Cuzco.* Olive brown above (with eye-ring and superciliary *absent or*

barely apparent). *Chin patch rich rufous;* remaining underparts grayish, some birds slightly mottled paler. Foregoing applies to *ayacuchensis* of Ayacucho; nominate race of Cuzco has paler and less extensive rufous chin patch and *decidedly scaly effect on underparts.*

SIMILAR SPECIES: Eye-ringed Thistletail, found to the north, is rufescent above with prominent eye-ring. Puna Thistletail, found to the south, is more rufescent above with at least an indistinct pale superciliary and shows some blackish on lower throat.

HABITAT AND BEHAVIOR: Nothing seems to be on record, though presumably much like its congeners'. Judging from the number of specimens that were obtained in a relatively short time, the species must at least locally be not uncommon.

RANGE: Andes of s. Peru (n. Ayacucho at and near Puncu, and n. Cuzco on n. end of Cordillera de Vilcabamba). 2800–3500 m.

NOTE: A newly described species: C. Vaurie, J. S. Weske, and J. W. Terborgh, *Bull. B. O. C.* 92(5): 142–144, 1972. In that paper, both *vilcabambae* and *ayacuchensis* were described as races of *S. fuliginosa.*

Schizoeaca helleri

PUNA THISTLETAIL

DESCRIPTION: 18 cm (7″). *S. Peru in s. Cuzco and Puno.* Resembles Vilcabamba Thistletail. Differs in its more rufescent upperparts (especially tail) with indistinct pale superciliary and at most a faint eye-ring; very small area of rufous on upper chin, *lower throat blackish flecked with pale gray;* and more uniform grayish underparts with *no* mottled or scaly effect.

SIMILAR SPECIES: Black-throated Thistletail, found to the south, has much more ochraceous sides of head and a more extensively and solidly blackish throat.

HABITAT AND BEHAVIOR: Uncommon in undergrowth of low montane woodland and forest borders near treeline. Behavior, including vocalizations, similar to White-chinned Thistletail's. Can be found along the upper Paucartambo-Shintuya road.

RANGE: Andes of s. Peru in s. Cuzco and Puno. 2800–3600 m.

Schizoeaca harterti

BLACK-THROATED THISTLETAIL   PLATE: 6

DESCRIPTION: 18 cm (7″). *W. Bolivia.* Above brown, more rufescent on crown and tail, with narrow whitish eye-ring and *pale buffyish superciliary.* Cheeks and sides of neck washed with ochraceous, brightest on malar region; chin patch whitish, *lower throat blackish;* remaining underparts uniform dull grayish. Birds from Cochabamba and w. Santa Cruz (*bejaranoi;* J. V. Remsen, Jr., *Proc. Biol. Soc. Wash.* 94[4]: 1068–1075, 1981) are somewhat more extensively and intensely ochraceous on cheeks and sides of neck.

SIMILAR SPECIES: Puna Thistletail, found to the north, is duller overall with grayish sides of head, less marked facial pattern, and duller brown crown.

HABITAT AND BEHAVIOR: Fairly common to common in dense under-

growth of low montane woodland and forest borders. Behavior, including vocalizations, similar to White-chinned Thistletail's.

RANGE: W. Bolivia (La Paz, Cochabamba, and w. Santa Cruz). Mostly 2900–3400 m.

Oreophylax Spinetails

A single species found in the mountains of se. Brazil where it is restricted to a higher elevation zone than any other Brazilian endemic. Since the early 20th century treated as a monotypic genus, *Oreophylax*, but Vaurie (1980) suggested considering it congeneric with the Andean genus *Schizoeaca*. Based especially on its voice, we feel it could be at least as close to *Asthenes* and thus tentatively leave it in *Oreophylax*. The recent discovery farther north in e. Brazil of an outlying species of *Asthenes* also suggests that *Asthenes* may be *Oreophylax*'s closest relative.

Oreophylax moreirae

ITATIAIA SPINETAIL   PLATE: 6
Other: Italiata Thistletail

DESCRIPTION: 19 cm (7½"). *High mts. of se. Brazil*. Above dull olivaceous brown with faint buffyish superciliary; wings and tail somewhat more rufescent; *tail very long and strongly graduated, with feathers pointed and somewhat frayed*. Chin patch pale orange-rufous; remaining underparts dingy pale buffyish.

SIMILAR SPECIES: Confusion in its limited range unlikely. Rufous-capped and Spix's Spinetails (*Synallaxis*) are quite different, have rufous on crown, etc. Cf. also Cipo Canastero (no overlap).

HABITAT AND BEHAVIOR: Uncommon to locally fairly common onto low shrubby clearings and coarse grassy areas in highlands of se. Brazil. Usually in pairs, hopping close to or even on ground, and inconspicuous except when singing, when it may mount to the top of a bush or rock. The song, a jumbled series of fairly fast and musical notes, ends in a chippered trill, "whyee-whee-whee-dwee-dwee-dwee-didididididideu." Readily found along the upper Agulhas Negras road in Itatiaia Nat. Park.

RANGE: High mts. of se. Brazil (s. Espírito Santo south to ne. São Paulo). 2000–2800 m.

Asthenes Canasteros

The canasteros are a rather heterogeneous group of small and usually long-tailed furnariids found in open or semiopen terrain primarily in the Andes and Patagonia, with only two species north of Peru; outlying species occur in e. Brazil and the chaco. Many favor rocky and/or grassy terrain. Because so many species resemble each other very closely, we have had to define our Groups and subsets narrowly, with in some cases only subtle differences from one another. Most observers would include canasteros among the most difficult neotropical genera to identify, in part because many species are so often shy and hard to see well. Although primarily terrestrial, all canasteros do mount onto rocks and into bushes or low trees, especially to sing. Many habitually cock their tails.

Tail shapes vary; feathers are broad and rounded in some species, including our first two Groups, but in others, including our second two Groups, they are narrower, more pointed, and frayed. Virtually all species' outer rectrices or outer webs are paler, usually rufous but grayish in a few. Many show a narrow rufous wing-stripe, visible especially in flight. Most show a small chin patch, most often orange-rufous but in some species buff or whitish; certain individuals (younger birds?) of some species lack the patches.

From an identification perspective, the key general characters to watch for are the presence or absence of the following.

1. Streaking above.
2. Streaking below (especially on foreneck).
3. A chin patch (and its color).
4. Rufous on the tail (and its pattern).

Nests are usually large, interwoven stick structures placed in a bush, low tree, or among rocks; the vernacular name *canastero* means "basket-maker." Some species' nests are enormous and very conspicuous, whereas others' are smaller and partially composed of grass.

Although Vaurie (1980) subsumed the genus *Asthenes* in *Thripophaga*, this merger, which we believe incorrect, has not been followed by most subsequent authors.

GROUP A

Upperparts unstreaked; uppertail mainly blackish (rufous at most on outer 2 rectrices).

Asthenes dorbignyi

RUSTY-VENTED CANASTERO   PLATE: 6
Other: Creamy-breasted Canastero

DESCRIPTION: 15.5–16.5 cm (6–6½″). Bolivia and nw. Argentina; what was formerly known as the Creamy-breasted Canastero has been split into 3 allospecies; Dark-winged (*A. arequipae*) and Pale-tailed (*A. huancavelicae*) Canasteros follow. Rather pale sandy brown above with an indistinct pale grayish superciliary, *mainly rufous wings,* and a *rich rufous rump which contrasts with mostly black tail* (outer feathers rufous). Creamy whitish below with chestnut chin patch, pale rufous on flanks and crissum.

SIMILAR SPECIES: A relatively highly colored and often numerous canastero usually found in gorges and on slopes with shrubby vegetation or cacti (*not just grass*). It usually can be known by its rump-tail contrast, very evident in flight. Cf. very similar Berlepsch's and Steinbach's Canasteros. Also easily confused with Streak-fronted Thornbird, and the two regularly occur together; the thornbird is somewhat larger, never shows a chin patch (sometimes the canastero's is not very obvious), and its uppertail is duskier (not so black) and contrasts less with the rump.

HABITAT AND BEHAVIOR: Fairly common in a variety of habitats with scrubby, sparse, low shrubby vegetation (often where there are some columnar cacti), locally even in hedgerows in agricultural areas and around houses; especially favors gorges and steep slopes. Usually in pairs; feeds mainly while hopping on the ground, scampering from underneath one bush to another, rarely in the open for long. When on the ground the tail is usually held cocked. The song, not especially different from those of many other canasteros', is a series of accelerating high-pitched notes which end in a trill. The very large (up to 3–4 m across) and conspicuous stick nest is placed in small trees, shrubs, or among the arms of columnar cacti.

RANGE: Andes of w. Bolivia (north to La Paz) and nw. Argentina (mainly south to Tucumán, also in Mendoza). Mostly 2500–4000 m.

NOTE: We follow J. Fjeldså and T. S. Schulenberg (ms., *in* Collar et al. 1992) in regarding *A. huancavelicae* (Pale-tailed Canastero) and *A. arequipae* (Dark-winged Canastero) as full species, reserving the well-known English name of Creamy-breasted Canastero for the expanded species concept. *A. huancavelicae* appears to be a very distinct species (despite not being recognized even at the subspecific level by Vaurie 1980), *A. arequipae* perhaps somewhat less so (we thought some specimens of *A. dorbignyi consobrina* in AMNH appeared to show evidence of intergradation with *A. arequipae*).

Asthenes arequipae

DARK-WINGED CANASTERO   PLATE: 6

Other: Creamy-breasted Canastero

DESCRIPTION: 15.5–16.5 cm (6–6½"). Andes from w. Peru to n. Chile and adjacent Bolivia. Here considered a separate species from *A. dorbignyi*, Rusty-vented (formerly Creamy-breasted) Canastero. Iris usually pale grayish. Dark grayish brown above with indistinct pale grayish superciliary, *blackish ear-coverts, mainly blackish wings,* and *rich rufous rump which contrasts with mostly black tail* (outer feathers rufous). Creamy whitish below with chestnut chin patch and contrasting rufous on flanks and crissum. An undescribed race from Lima and Ayacucho is markedly darker, with almost solidly black wings and less rufous on flanks, crissum, and rump.

SIMILAR SPECIES: This strikingly patterned and colored canastero is readily known in its limited range and habitat. Cf. Rusty-vented Canastero (no overlap).

HABITAT AND BEHAVIOR: Fairly common in and near groves of *Polylepis* trees, also in adjacent montane scrub; locally (at least in Arequipa, Peru) also in arid scrub with scattered cacti. Behavior much like Rusty-vented Canastero's, but often more arboreal when in *Polylepis*, sometimes hopping on branches up to 5–6 m above ground. The tail is usually held cocked when hopping on the ground but is held at a more normal angle when in trees. Song is similar to Rusty-vented's but shorter and lacking Rusty-vented's sharp introductory notes. Builds a conspicuous stick nest much like Rusty-vented's. Readily found around Putre in n. Chile.

RANGE: Andes of w. Peru (s. Lima and adjacent Ayacucho south locally through Arequipa, Mocquegua, Tacna, and s. Puno), w. Bolivia (locally in extreme sw. La Paz and nw. Oruro), and n. Chile (Tarapacá). Mostly 3500–4800 m, locally (in Arequipa, Peru) down to 2500 m.

NOTE: See comments under Rusty-vented Canastero.

Asthenes huancavelicae

Asthenes berlepschi

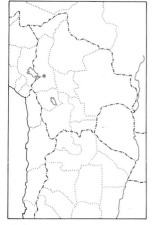

Asthenes steinbachi

PALE-TAILED CANASTERO
Other: Creamy-breasted Canastero

DESCRIPTION: 15.5–16.5 cm (6–6½″). Local in arid intermontane valleys of Andes in *cen. Peru*. Here considered a separate species from *A. dorbignyi*, Rusty-vented (formerly Creamy-breasted) Canastero. Grayish brown above with rather prominent whitish superciliary, mainly rufous wings, and *strikingly pale tail* (*whitish* in *usheri* of Apurímac and Ayacucho; *pale cinnamon* in nominate *huancavelicae* of Huancavelica and Ayacucho; *mainly cinnamon* in an undescribed race from Ancash). Mainly grayish to creamy white below with at most a faint pale rufous chin patch, some pinkish buff on flanks and crissum. SIMILAR SPECIES: The pale tail should be distinctive, regardless of race. HABITAT AND BEHAVIOR: Locally fairly common in sparse arid scrub with scattered small trees and columnar cacti; however, more n. forms (including *usheri*) are described as being rare. Usually in pairs, running rapidly on ground with tail cocked; sings from low trees and bushes. The song of *usheri* is a fairly high-pitched, intense trill which lasts about 2 seconds, quite different from Rusty-vented and Dark-winged Canasteros' (Fjeldså and Krabbe 1990). Bulky stick nests are apparently invariably placed in cacti. The n. forms are believed to be threatened by habitat disturbance (Collar et al. 1992). RANGE: Locally in intermontane valleys of cen. and s.-cen. Peru (very locally in Ancash; apparently also in Huánuco above Santa María del Valle; locally in Huancavelica, Ayacucho, and Apurímac). Mostly 1800–3700 m.

NOTE: See comments under Rusty-vented Canastero.

BERLEPSCH'S CANASTERO

DESCRIPTION: 16.5 cm (6½″). *W. Bolivia*. Closely resembles Rusty-vented Canastero. Slightly larger with a somewhat longer and stouter bill; chin patch either absent or tiny; outer 2 pairs of rectrices entirely rufous (not just their outer webs), and the third rufous basally. HABITAT AND BEHAVIOR: Uncommon in low semiarid montane scrub and hedgerows in mainly agricultural terrain. Seen singly or in pairs, usually skulking within hedgerows, occasionally somewhat more in the open. In 1991 J. Fjeldså (*in* Collar et al. 1992) found this canastero around the village of Sorata, where a small population persists despite the near-total removal of natural habitat in the vicinity. RANGE: Andes of w. Bolivia (La Paz near the Nevado Illampu in the Cordillera Real). 2700–3700 m.

NOTE: This little-known form is perhaps only a race of *A. dorbignyi*.

STEINBACH'S CANASTERO
Also: Chestnut Canastero

DESCRIPTION: 16 cm (6¼″). *W. Argentina*. Closely resembles Rusty-vented Canastero. Differs in *lacking* a chin patch (lower throat only flecked black) and *shows more rufous on sides of tail* (outer 2 pairs of rectrices entirely rufous, not just the outer web of outermost pair).

SIMILAR SPECIES: Can be distinguished from more common Rusty-vented Canastero only with great care. Both characters useful in the field are difficult to confirm: chin patches of *all* canasteros are sometimes hard to see, and their tail patterns are usually visible only briefly, most often when the birds are in flight. Steinbach's usually occurs at lower elevations than Rusty-vented; whether the two ever occur syntopically is unknown.

HABITAT AND BEHAVIOR: Rare to uncommon in sparse scrub, often in ravines or washes, and usually in arid regions. Behavior similar to Rusty-vented Canastero's. We do not know the voice of Steinbach's. Small numbers can be found in valleys south of Cachi in w. Salta, along the road toward Cafayete.

RANGE: Andes of w. Argentina (w. Salta south locally to Mendoza). Mainly 1500–2500 m, but recorded down to 800 m during austral winter.

NOTE: The English name of "Chestnut" Canastero was invented by Meyer de Schauensee (1966, 1970) and has been used in subsequent literature. It seems an unfortunate and misleading choice, as the species is no more chestnut than its congeners. We prefer to revert to the patronym used in *Birds of the Americas*, vol 13, part 4.

Asthenes pyrrholeuca

SHARP-BILLED CANASTERO　　　　PLATE: 6

Other: Lesser Canastero

DESCRIPTION: 16.5 cm (6½″). Breeds mainly in *s. Argentina*, migrating northward. A *plain* canastero with *comparatively long tail. Bill straight and thin*. Above uniform pale grayish brown, some individuals with an indistinct narrow buffy grayish superciliary; wings slightly more rufescent and tail mainly dusky, basally more brownish, with outer feathers dull rufous. Chin patch pale orange-rufous; remaining underparts pale grayish, tinged buffyish on flanks and crissum. An apparently unnamed form resident near salt lagoons of Santiago del Estero is very dark overall (especially dorsally); it may represent a distinct species.

SIMILAR SPECIES: The often sympatric Short-billed Canastero has a markedly heavier bill (quite evident in the field), proportionately shorter tail, and shows a larger rufous chin patch. Cordilleran Canastero gives a more streaked effect on the sides of head and neck and on lower throat, and is buffier (not so grayish) below; it, too, has a proportionately shorter tail. Cordilleran favors grassy areas (not the scrub of Sharp-billed) and is more terrestrial.

HABITAT AND BEHAVIOR: Fairly common to common in low shrubby areas on plains and hillsides of Patagonia, and in sparse scrub on lower mountain slopes of Chile; during the austral winter also occurs in chaco scrub and low woodland. A form is also apparently a very local resident in halophytic scrub near saline lagoons in nw. Argentina. Mainly arboreal while foraging, the Sharp-billed feeds amongst shrubby growth and is often very hard to see well; less often it drops to ground where it runs rapidly between places of concealment. It seldom flies very far. The tail is sometimes held partially cocked. The song is a fast, fairly musical and rollicking "whi-di-di-di-wheediyiu-wheedi-yiu-wheediyiu," usually given from within cover, less often (generally in early morning) from an exposed perch atop a bush. Both sexes sing (Wetmore 1926).

RANGE: Breeds in cen. Argentina (Mendoza, La Pampa, and s. Buenos Aires south to Santa Cruz; n. limit of breeding uncertain, with apparently outlying resident populations [this or an undescribed species?] in n. Córdoba and sw. Santiago del Estero) and cen. Chile (Aconcagua south locally to Aysén); in austral winter migrates north as far as s. Bolivia (Tarija), w. and s. Paraguay (few records), and s. Uruguay (records from Colonia and Salto). Seems possible in extreme s. Brazil. Mostly below 2000 m, small numbers to 3000 m.

NOTE: *A. pyrrholeuca* is not a particularly small canastero, and we are uncertain as to the derivation of its usual English name, Lesser Canastero; at a minimum, it is rather misleading and unhelpful. However, its sharply pointed bill shape is unique among *Asthenes* and highlights one of the main differences from the Short-billed Canastero, the species with which it is most often confused.

Asthenes baeri

SHORT-BILLED CANASTERO PLATE: 6

DESCRIPTION: 15.5 cm (6"). *N. Argentina and adjacent Bolivia, Paraguay, extreme s. Brazil, and Uruguay. Bill rather short and stout,* often imparting a "snub-nosed" effect. In coloration much like Sharp-billed Canastero, but with *broader and gray superciliary, more pronounced orange-rufous chin patch,* and blacker central rectrices. Also has a *distinctly shorter tail than Sharp-billed.*

SIMILAR SPECIES: Cf. Sharp-billed Canastero. Also resembles Little Thornbird (with which frequently sympatric), which lacks the chin patch but has a rufous shoulder patch. Even nest placement sometimes helps: the thornbird's is typically near the tip of a branch, the canastero's supported by 2 forking branches.

HABITAT AND BEHAVIOR: Uncommon to fairly common in chaco scrub and low woodland, and in thickets and monte woodland. Behavior similar to Sharp-billed Canastero's, though Short-billed seems to drop to the ground less often. Its song, distinctly different, is a series of fast, descending notes that end in a wiry and more mechanical-sounding trill (somewhat recalling song of a *Cranioleuca* spinetail); often the even, wiry trill is given alone with no introductory notes.

RANGE: Se. Bolivia (north to s. Santa Cruz at Estancia Perforación), w. Paraguay, Uruguay, extreme sw. Brazil (w. Rio Grande do sul) and n. and cen. Argentina (south to Mendoza, La Pampa, and s. Buenos Aires). No evidence of migration. Below 800 m.

Asthenes patagonica

PATAGONIAN CANASTERO

DESCRIPTION: 15.5 cm (6"). *Patagonian steppes.* Resembles Sharp-billed and Short-billed Canasteros; bill shape intermediate. Differs from both in having *no* orange-rufous chin patch (*throat white finely speckled with black*) and *more extensively blackish tail* (with rufous restricted to outer web of outermost rectrix).

SIMILAR SPECIES: The chin color and tail pattern of canasteros are often hard to see well; thus distinguishing Sharp-billed, Short-billed, and Patagonian is often not easy, especially given the brief views they all too often afford. Note that Patagonian mainly overlaps with Sharp-billed (Short-billed ranges mostly northward); Patagonian and Sharp-billed have strikingly different songs.

HABITAT AND BEHAVIOR: Uncommon to fairly common in low shrubby growth on plains of Patagonia. Behavior similar to Sharp-billed Canastero's, and often found with it but usually in smaller numbers. Patagonian's song is a loud, rather strident and penetrating trill on a single pitch. Can be seen on Valdés Peninsula.

RANGE: S. Argentina (s. Mendoza, La Pampa, and s. Buenos Aires south at least locally to n. Santa Cruz at Bosque Petrificado Nat. Monument). No evidence of migration. To at least 700 m.

Asthenes humicola

DUSKY-TAILED CANASTERO   PLATE: 6

DESCRIPTION: 15.5 cm (6"). *Chile.* Brown above with short whitish superciliary; *lesser wing-coverts contrastingly rufous; tail essentially blackish* (even the dingy grayish lateral rectrices showing virtually no rufous). *Throat white with fine black speckling; breast dingy grayish with fine white streaking;* lower underparts dull brownish gray with flanks and crissum tawny. Foregoing applies to nominate race of cen. Chile; *goodalli* (sw. Antofagasta; Marin et al. 1991) has brighter cinnamon flanks and crissum, whereas *polysticta* (s. Concepción to Malleco) has blacker streaking below and duller flanks and crissum.

SIMILAR SPECIES: Not known to overlap with Patagonian Canastero, which in any case has streaking restricted to throat, lacks rufous shoulders, and has rufous on outer web of outermost rectrix. Cordilleran Canastero has much more rufous in tail and an orange-rufous chin spot surrounded by streaking (effect very different).

HABITAT AND BEHAVIOR: Uncommon to fairly common in dense thickets in matorral. Behavior similar to Sharp-billed Canastero's, but usually even more difficult to observe. The song has been described (Fjeldså and Krabbe 1990) as a loud, clear trill, but all we have heard is a sharply enunciated ticking, "ts-ts-ts-ts-ts-ts-ts."

RANGE: Chile (sw. Antofagasta south to Malleco). The old record from Mendoza, Argentina, "requires confirmation" (Narosky and Yzurieta 1987). To about 1200 m.

GROUP B

Plain-backed, but uppertail with *considerable rufous (more* than only on outer rectrices); throat often somewhat streaky.

Asthenes pudibunda

CANYON CANASTERO   PLATE: 6

DESCRIPTION: 16.5 cm (6½"). *W. Peru.* Brown above with indistinct narrow buffy grayish superciliary; *wings and tail mainly rufous-chestnut.*

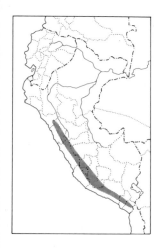

Mostly grayish below with pale cinnamon chin patch in *grisior* (M. Koepcke, *Am. Mus. Novitates* 2028, 1961) of Huancavelica southward (orange-rufous in nominate race of Lima; chestnut in *neglecta* of La Libertad and Ancash); some indistinct pale streaking on sides of head and lower throat (especially in *grisior*).

SIMILAR SPECIES: Best known by its mainly rufous-chestnut tail (even from above showing virtually no dusky). Does not occur with either Maquis or Rusty-fronted Canasteros (both similar) but sometimes found with differently marked Dark-winged Canastero.

HABITAT AND BEHAVIOR: Uncommon to fairly common on rocky slopes with bushes and low trees (often *Polylepis*), also often in gorges. Usually in pairs which hop on ground or in foliage or along branches in shrubs and trees; the tail is usually held cocked at an acute angle. Not as hard to see as some other congeners. Its song, an accelerating loud trill with a few introductory notes, falls toward the end (Fjeldså and Krabbe 1990). Can be seen along the Santa Eulalia road well above Huinco, in Lima.

RANGE: Andes of w. Peru (La Libertad and Ancash south locally to Tacna). 2400–3500 m.

Asthenes ottonis

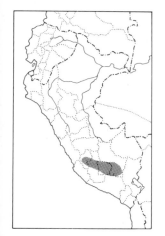

RUSTY-FRONTED CANASTERO   PLATE: 6

DESCRIPTION: 18 cm (7"). *S.-cen. Peru*. Above brown with *rufous fore-head* and narrow buffy grayish superciliary; *wings and long, gradu-ated, and rather pointed tail mainly rufous-chestnut*. Chin patch orange-rufous; remaining underparts grayish with fine white streaking on lower throat and breast.

SIMILAR SPECIES: The only canastero in its limited range with a mostly rufous tail. Streak-fronted Thornbird, which regularly occurs with this species, is larger with a shorter tail, whiter below with no chin spot, and has more dusky on wings and rufous only on lateral tail feathers.

HABITAT AND BEHAVIOR: Fairly common in arid montane scrub and woodland, patches of low *Polylepis* woodland, and sparsely vegetated (often overgrazed) arid scrub. Found singly or in pairs, and hard to see well as it seldom remains in the open for more than a few seconds. It often scampers rapidly on the ground between places of concealment, usually with the tail held high; flights are brief and weak. The song is a rapidly descending series of short, high-pitched notes, "bzee-bzée-bzee-di-di-di-di-d-d-d" (Parker and O'Neill 1980). Quite readily found above the Peñas ruins and up w. side of the Abra Málaga road in Cuzco; also occurs around the Urpicancha lakes.

RANGE: Andes of s.-cen. Peru (Huancavelica east to Cuzco). 2750–4000 m.

Asthenes heterura

MAQUIS CANASTERO
Also: Iquico Canastero

DESCRIPTION: 16.5 cm (6½"). *W. Bolivia*. Similar to Rusty-fronted Canastero (no overlap) but *lacks* its rufous forehead and shows virtu-ally *no* streaking on foreneck.

SIMILAR SPECIES: Cf. also the similar Canyon Canastero (no overlap) which has a slightly longer bill and proportionately shorter tail with markedly less pointed feathers.

HABITAT AND BEHAVIOR: Uncommon in arid montane scrub and low woodland, and in thick hedgerows in mainly agricultural terrain. Behavior much like Rusty-fronted Canastero's; we do not know the voice of Maquis. Can be found at several sites above Cochabamba (City).

RANGE: Andes of w. Bolivia (La Paz and Cochabamba). 3000–4200 m.

NOTE: *Heterura* has been considered only a subspecies of *A. pudibunda* (Meyer de Schauensee 1966, 1970), but we concur with Vaurie (1980) that it likely is closer to *A. ottonis,* agreeing in its finer bill and longer tail. Treating them as allospecies seems the most reasonable course. The English name of Iquico Canastero, derived from the name of the species' type locality, has been used in some references (e.g., *Birds of the Americas*, vol. 13, part 4; Meyer de Schauensee 1966). More recently, the name Maquis Canastero, derived from a name applied to scrub habitat (originally in a Mediterranean context), has been suggested (Fjeldså and Krabbe 1990; Sibley and Monroe 1990). Not having a strong preference, we employ the latter.

Asthenes modesta

CORDILLERAN CANASTERO   PLATE: 6

DESCRIPTION: 14.5–15 cm (5¾–6″). *Widespread and often numerous in grasslands from Peru to s. Argentina.* Above sandy grayish brown with narrow buffy whitish superciliary; wings more rufescent (*sometimes showing as a patch at base of secondaries*); *tail rufous and dusky* (outer webs mostly rufous, inner webs mostly dusky, but in the field tail *looks mainly rufous* with dusky only on middle of central rectrices). Chin patch orange-rufous (lacking in some individuals), *surrounded by fine dusky and whitish streaking on sides of head and lower throat;* remaining underparts buffy whitish. Southernmost birds (cen. Argentina and Chile southward; various marginal races recently named) slightly smaller, darker and less sandy above, and more whitish with less of a buff tinge below.

SIMILAR SPECIES: Various somewhat similar canasteros can be confused with this species, but most, if seen well, show dark streaking on back (*Cordilleran is always plain-backed*). Streak-throated is the most similar, but its streaky effect on *foreneck* is more pronounced and it has a mainly dusky tail and back streaking. Sharp-billed Canastero is also plain-backed, but it lacks any foreneck streaking and has a broader and more diffused superciliary, different bill, and different tail pattern with only lateral feathers contrastingly rufous.

HABITAT AND BEHAVIOR: Fairly common to locally common in open grassy areas, often where there are boulders, and usually in arid regions. Mainly terrestrial, hopping and running rapidly on ground, often holding the tail cocked at an acute angle; frequently seen perched along or scampering across tracks or little-used roads. Usually easy to see, at times even rather tame, perching unsuspiciously on a boulder or atop a grass clump. The song is a short series of semimusical notes that slightly but distinctively *ascend in pitch*.

RANGE: Andes of cen. and s. Peru (north to Junín), w. Bolivia, Chile (south locally to steppes of Aysén and n. Magallanes), and Argentina (south to Santa Cruz, and extending east across Patagonian lowlands as far north as s. Buenos Aires; also in mts. of w. Córdoba and ne. San Luis). To about 4500 m.

Asthenes cactorum

CACTUS CANASTERO

DESCRIPTION: 14.5 cm (5¾"). *Local in w. Peru.* Resembles nominate Cordilleran Canastero but occurs at much lower elevations and in a different habitat. *Bill strikingly longer;* chin patch larger, paler, and more diffused; seems to show much less streaky effect on sides of head and foreneck; breast whiter; central tail feathers mainly dusky.

SIMILAR SPECIES: The only canasteros at all likely to occur with this range- and habitat-restricted species are the dissimilar Canyon and Dark-winged.

HABITAT AND BEHAVIOR: Uncommon on open, very arid slopes with scattered columnar cacti and boulders. Behavior much like Cordilleran Canastero's, also mainly terrestrial and often cocking its tail at an acute angle, but Cactus also frequently forages by hopping high on the arms of cacti. The song is described (Fjeldså and Krabbe 1990) as a long, fast, weak trill, seemingly differing from Cordilleran's. Can be found in small numbers near the Lomas de Lachay north of Lima [city], e.g., along the side road toward Samán.

RANGE: W. slope of Andes in w. Peru (Lima south locally to Arequipa). To 2500 m.

NOTE: *Cactorum* has been considered conspecific with *A. modesta* (e.g., by Vaurie 1980) but seems likely to be a distinct species, based especially on its different habitat and elevational preferences, morphology, and song.

Asthenes luizae

CIPO CANASTERO

DESCRIPTION: 17 cm (6¾"). *Serras of e. Minas Gerais, Brazil.* Above uniform brown to grayish brown with narrow whitish superciliary; central tail feathers dusky brown, outer tail feathers rufous-chestnut. *Chin patch white with fine black streaks; remaining underparts uniform grayish.*

SIMILAR SPECIES: No other canastero occurs anywhere near its range.

HABITAT AND BEHAVIOR: Fairly common but very local on steep slopes with scattered bushes and ground bromeliads, favoring areas with numerous tumbled rocks and boulders (many of them loose). Behavior similar to many other canasteros', mainly terrestrial, running rapidly on rocky slopes, often disappearing into the numerous crevices. The tail is usually held partially cocked. The song is described as a series of loud, sharp notes descending in pitch, ending with a series of softer lower notes; it is usually delivered from an exposed perch (M. Pearman). We have also heard it give a very brief series of rising high-pitched notes. The Cipo Canastero can be seen quite readily at the type locality, most easily in the early morning when it is more likely to be calm. Its habitat appears not to be under any threat and in fact lies adjacent to, but unfortunately not in, the newly established Serra do Cipó Nat. Park.

RANGE: Interior se. Brazil (Serra do Cipó in e. Minas Gerais); perhaps will be found on Serra do Espinaço. 1000–1200 m.

NOTE: A newly described species: J. Vielliard, *Ararajuba* 1: 121–122, 1990. Much valuable information on this remarkable discovery is also presented by M. Pearman (*Bull. B. O. C.* 110[3]: 145–153, 1990).

GROUP C

Upperparts show *indistinct black streaking. Throat well streaked;* tail dull.

Asthenes humilis

STREAK-THROATED CANASTERO   PLATE: 6

DESCRIPTION: 15.5–16 cm (6–6¼″). *Peru and Bolivia.* Above grayish brown, *back indistinctly streaked darker,* and with narrow whitish superciliary; *rather short tail mostly dusky,* outer feathers edged paler grayish. Chin patch rufous, *surrounded by quite prominent dusky and whitish streaking on sides of head, throat, and chest;* remaining underparts buffy whitish. *Robusta* (Cuzco, Peru, southward) slightly larger and darker.
SIMILAR SPECIES: Cordilleran Canastero has *plain* back (but back streaking of Streak-throated is usually not prominent in the field), less streaking on sides of head and foreneck (but shows some), and much more rufous in tail; this last is usually the best distinguishing feature.
HABITAT AND BEHAVIOR: Fairly common to common in puna grassland, mainly in arid regions, usually where the grass is rather short (especially compared to the tall grass favored by many other canasteros), and often most numerous where there are rocks or boulders at least nearby. Found singly or in pairs, feeding mostly while hopping about on the ground, usually with tail held partially cocked. Not very shy, sometimes perching for protracted periods atop a rock or clump of grass, often while vocalizing. The song is a trill of varying lengths.
RANGE: Andes of Peru (s. Cajamarca south to Ayacucho, and in Cuzco and Puno) and w. Bolivia (La Paz). 2700–4800 m.

GROUP D

Upperparts *decidedly to boldly black-streaked;* tail shapes and patterns *vary.*

Asthenes wyatti

STREAK-BACKED CANASTERO   PLATE: 6

DESCRIPTION: 15.5–18 cm (6–7″). Local from *Venezuela and Colombia to s. Peru. Graminicola* (cen. and s. Peru) is brown above *rather prominently streaked with black* and with narrow buffy superciliary; wings more rufescent (brightest at base of flight feathers); *rather long tail dusky with outer 3 pairs of rectrices rufous.* Chin patch orange-rufous; *remaining underparts dull tawny-buff. Aequatorialis* group of subspecies (cen. Ecuador northward) smaller, *sanctaemartae* of Colombia's Santa Marta Mts. markedly so, but with longer bill and *dingy buffy grayish underparts;* see V-19, C-24. *Azuay* from s. Ecuador is also quite distinct, with largely rufous wing, dull tawny-buff underparts like *gra-*

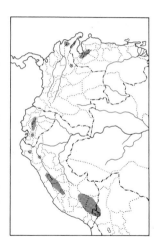

minicola, and more rufous on tail (even on central rectrices); it is quite large.

SIMILAR SPECIES: Puna Canastero overlaps with very similar *graminicola* form of Streak-backed in extreme s. Peru. Only their tail pattern differs: Puna has black at base of outer 3 tail feathers, whereas Streak-backed's are all rufous. Streak-throated Canastero lacks rufous on tail, has more streaking on foreneck and sides of neck, and is dingier and grayer below (not so buffy).

HABITAT AND BEHAVIOR: Uncommon to locally fairly common in páramo and puna grasslands, often (especially northward?) where there are rocks and some low shrubs. In Colombia and Ecuador tends to occur in drier areas than Many-striped Canastero, though locally they are sympatric (e.g., on Cotopaxi and Chimborazo volcanos in Ecuador). Mostly terrestrial, scampering rapidly between tussocks of grass or surveying its domain from atop a bush or rock. The song of *aequatorialis* is a very fast trill lasting about 2 seconds and accelerating and rising slightly in pitch; we are not familiar with the songs of other races, but that of *graminicola* is described (Fjeldså and Krabbe 1990) as similar.

RANGE: Andes of w. Venezuela (Trujillo and Mérida) and extreme ne. Colombia (E. Andes in n. Santander); n. and cen. Ecuador (Cotopaxi south to Chimborazo, and very locally from Azuay south to its border with Zamora-Chinchipe); locally in Peru (seen by T. A. Parker III north of Cruz Blanca in Piura; seen by F. Vuilleumier at Las Lagunas in Cajamarca; and from Ancash and Junín south locally into Puno); Sierra de Perijá on Venezuela-Colombia border, and Santa Marta Mts. of n. Colombia. Mostly 3000–4500 m, but occasionally found higher (to 5000 m) and recorded down to 2400 m on Santa Marta Mts.

NOTE: This species is closely related to *A. sclateri. A. wyatti* and *A. sclateri punensis* appear to overlap in Puno, Peru, but there may be some intergradation; more study is needed. Plumages of the more northerly group of races of *A. wyatti* differ strikingly from *graminicola* of Peru and the little-known *azuay* of s. Ecuador. The latter two perhaps should be specifically separated from *A. wyatti,* as indeed they were by Chapman (1926). Vocally all the "streak-backed" canasteros (*A. wyatti, A. sclateri,* and *A. anthoides*) appear similar.

Asthenes sclateri

PUNA CANASTERO

Other: Puno Canastero
Includes: Cordoba Canastero

DESCRIPTION: 18 cm (7″). *S. Peru to nw. Argentina;* includes what was formerly called Cordoba Canastero. Closely resembles *graminicola* race of Streak-backed Canastero, perhaps distinguishable only in the hand. Puna Canastero differs in having *only terminal third of outer 3 pairs of rectrices rufous* (Streak-backed's are *entirely* rufous).

SIMILAR SPECIES: Cordilleran Canastero has much more rufous on tail and an unstreaked back.

HABITAT AND BEHAVIOR: Uncommon in puna grassland, especially where the grass is fairly long and most often where there are some

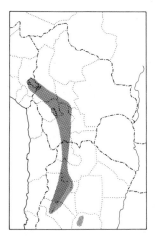

rocks or in ravines. Behavior much like Streak-backed Canastero's, as apparently is its voice. Small numbers can be seen on the Pampa de Achala in Córdoba, Argentina (where outnumbered by Cordilleran Canastero), and at the Abra del Infiernillo in Tucumán.

RANGE: Andes of extreme s. Peru (locally near Lake Titicaca in Puno), w. Bolivia (locally in La Paz, Cochabamba, and Potosí), and nw. Argentina (locally from Salta south to La Rioja, and in mts. of w. Córdoba). 1800–4000 m.

NOTE: We follow J. R. Navas and N. A. Bo (*Com. Museo. Arg. Cienc. Nat. "Bernardino Rivadavia"* 4[11]: 85–93, 1982) in considering *A. punensis* (with *cuchacanchae* and *lilloi*) conspecific with *A. sclateri*. *A. sclateri* (Cordoba Canastero) was formerly usually considered a monotypic species endemic to the Córdoba hills; that name has priority over *punensis*. The *punensis* group has also been considered (Meyer de Schauensee 1966) conspecific with *A. anthoides* (Austral Canastero), but this seems surely wrong. We consider the best English name for the expanded species to be Puna Canastero. *A. sclateri* used to be called Cordoba Canastero, but that seems inappropriate given its now greatly enlarged range; *A. punensis* used to be called Puno Canastero (from its type locality in Puno, Peru), but that too seems misleading given its extensive range. However, all forms are found in puna grasslands.

Asthenes anthoides

AUSTRAL CANASTERO   PLATE: 6

DESCRIPTION: 16.5 cm (6½"). *S. Argentina and s. Chile,* occurring farther south than any other canastero and only marginally overlapping with any of them. *Above sandy brown conspicuously streaked with blackish* and with narrow whitish superciliary; cinnamon patch on flight feathers (visible as a wing-band in flight, becoming whitish on outer primaries); *tail rather short, feathers very pointed,* mainly dusky *prominently edged with buffy whitish.* Chin patch orange-rufous; lower throat finely streaked with black and with black dots on sides of neck; remaining underparts drab grayish buff with some fine blackish streaking on flanks.

SIMILAR SPECIES: No other canastero in its range is *streaked above.*

HABITAT AND BEHAVIOR: Rare to uncommon but now very local in less intensively grazed Patagonian steppes, usually where there is a fairly dense growth of low shrubs interspersed with patches of tall grass. Found singly or in pairs, feeding mostly while hopping on the ground, often with tail cocked. Easiest to see when perched atop a bush or fence; this happens most often when the nearly endless Patagonian winds finally abate. The song is reported to be a short trill reminiscent of Streak-backed Canastero's (B. Whitney *in* Fjeldså and Krabbe 1990). Numbers, formerly apparently large, have declined greatly in recent decades, almost certainly as a result of widespread overgrazing by sheep. Certainly deserves formal threatened status. Small numbers persist in a few areas northeast of Punta Arenas in Chile and at Punta Dungeness in Santa Cruz, Argentina.

RANGE: S. Argentina (s. Neuquén southward) and extreme s. Chile (locally in Aysén and in Magallanes) south to Tierra del Fuego (including Staten Is.). In the past recorded north in Chile to Concepción and (as a presumed austral migrant) to Aconcagua, but not recorded from so far north for many decades. We regard the two published specimens from Buenos Aires as unverified. One very early specimen from Falkland Is., taken by Darwin in the 1830s, is now usually regarded as having been mislabeled. To 1500 m.

Asthenes hudsoni

HUDSON'S CANASTERO   PLATE: 6

DESCRIPTION: 18 cm (7"). *E. Argentina and Uruguay.* Sandy brown above *conspicuously streaked with blackish and silvery grayish* and with narrow whitish superciliary; cinnamon patch on flight feathers (visible as a wing-band in flight, becoming whitish on outer primaries); *tail long, feathers very pointed,* mainly dusky *prominently edged with silvery gray.* Chin patch usually white (often quite prominent), less often orange-rufous; remaining underparts rich to drab buff, *flanks with sparse but quite noticeable black streaking.* Juvenile quite prominently streaked with dusky on foreneck.

SIMILAR SPECIES: The only canastero found primarily in the pampas region. Short-billed Canastero, the only other *Asthenes* found widely in the pampas (in scrub and monte), is unstreaked above, etc. Hudson's most resembles Austral Canastero (found in Patagonian steppes well to the south) but has a longer tail with more prominent silvery edging and also is streaked with silvery on mantle. Bay-capped Wren-Spinetail (sometimes syntopic) is smaller, has rufous on crown, and lacks flank streaking. Cf. also Firewood-gatherer.

HABITAT AND BEHAVIOR: Uncommon to locally fairly common in tall grass and sedges in and near marshes or seasonally flooded areas. Usually in pairs, secretive and hard to see unless singing, hopping and running on the ground and hiding among tussocks of grass. The song, usually delivered from a somewhat exposed position, is a short trill of semimusical notes that rise in pitch; it is similar to songs of other members of our "streak-backed" Group. Can be found around marshes near General Lavalle in Buenos Aires, particularly toward Punta Norte.

RANGE: Extreme s. Brazil (one record from s. Rio Grande do Sul), Uruguay, and e. Argentina (Entre Ríos, Santa Fe, and se. Córdoba south locally to Río Negro). Records (Vaurie 1980) for se. Paraguay, and for sw. Chubut in s. Argentina, are regarded as unverified. To 950 m.

GROUP E

Upperparts *crisply streaked with buff,* and/or *boldly streaked below;* tails tend to be spiky.

Asthenes maculicauda

SCRIBBLE-TAILED CANASTERO   PLATE: 6

DESCRIPTION: 17 cm (6¾"). Local from *extreme s. Peru to nw. Argentina. Above blackish brown narrowly streaked with buff,* with *almost solidly rufous forecrown* and narrow buff superciliary; tail long and pointed, *rufous with irregular linear black markings* (the unique "scribbles" are hard to discern in the field). Pale dull buffyish below with *no chin patch;* some dusky streaking (less southward?) across breast and down flanks.

SIMILAR SPECIES: Junin Canastero (sympatric or nearly so in extreme s. Peru) has no rufous on crown, a uniform brown tail (less rufescent than Scribble-tailed's and with no "scribbles"), and a pale rufous chin patch. Cf. also Puna Canastero.

HABITAT AND BEHAVIOR: Rare to uncommon and apparently local in puna grassland, mostly (entirely?) where the bunchgrass is especially tall and luxuriant or where there is a lusher admixture of low shrubs. Creeps and hops about on ground, usually within or very near cover; does not cock its tail. The song is a fast series of rolled "trree" notes which culminate in a trilled chipper, e.g., "trree-trree-trree-trreetrree-trreetritritritititi"; usually sings from the upper part of a clump of bunchgrass. Small numbers of this canastero, arguably the most handsome member of the genus, can be found near the Abra del Infiernillo west of Tafi del Valle in Tucumán, Argentina.

RANGE: Locally in Andes of extreme s. Peru (south of Limbani in Puno) and w. Bolivia (La Paz and Cochabamba); nw. Argentina (Tucumán and adjacent Catamarca, perhaps also in Salta). Mostly 3000–4300 m.

Asthenes virgata

JUNIN CANASTERO

DESCRIPTION: 17 cm (6¾"). Local in *cen. and s. Peru*. Resembles Scribble-tailed Canastero (limited overlap in extreme s. Peru) but has *no rufous on forecrown* (entire crown blackish with narrow buff streaking); *shorter, solidly brown tail; pale rufous chin patch* (at least in most individuals); and more whitish or grayish (not so buffy) on lower underparts.

SIMILAR SPECIES: Also closely resembles Peruvian race (*taczanowskii*) of Many-striped Canastero; Many-striped differs in its basically whitish throat, more extensive rufous on wing, and blacker (not so brown) mottling on underparts.

HABITAT AND BEHAVIOR: Rare to uncommon and local in puna grassland, apparently mostly (entirely?) in areas where the bunchgrass is relatively lush (and less intensively grazed) and mostly near patches of *Polylepis* woodland. Behavior (including vocalizations) similar to Scribble-tailed Canastero's. Small numbers can be found along w. side of the Abra Málaga road above Ollantaytambo in Cuzco, Peru.

RANGE: Locally in Andes of cen. and s. Peru (Lima, Junín, Ayacucho, Cuzco, and Puno). 3300–4300 m.

NOTE: *Virgata* could prove to be a subspecies of *A. flammulata,* the s. race of which (*taczanowskii*) approaches *A. virgata* in several plumage characters.

Asthenes flammulata

MANY-STRIPED CANASTERO   PLATE: 6

DESCRIPTION: 16 cm (6¼"). *Colombia to cen. Peru.* Nominate race of Ecuador and Nariño, Colombia, is blackish brown above prominently streaked with tawny on crown and buffy whitish on mantle and with narrow pale buff whitish superciliary; *wings mainly chestnut;* rather short tail mostly dark brown, feathers pointed and margined with ru-

fous. Chin patch orange-buff; *remaining underparts whitish prominently streaked with dusky-brown.* Colombian birds (*multostriata* and *quindiana*) are more solidly streaked rufous on forecrown; *multostriata* (E. Andes) has darker, rufous-chestnut chin patch. Peruvian birds (*taczanowskii* and *pallida*) differ more markedly, with *whitish throat* and *reduced* dark streaking below (almost none on belly).

SIMILAR SPECIES: The not-so-handsome Streak-backed Canastero is much less streaked generally, especially below. In cen. Peru, cf. very similar Junin Canastero. Andean Tit-Spinetail lacks the rufous wings.

HABITAT AND BEHAVIOR: Uncommon and local to (northward) fairly common in páramo and puna grasslands, especially where there are a few scattered bushes or *Espeletia* and at edge of woodland patches. Behavior (including vocalizations) similar to Scribble-tailed Canastero's.

RANGE: Andes of Colombia (E. Andes from Norte de Santander southward, Cen. Andes from Caldas southward, W. Andes only in Nariño), Ecuador (on w. slope south locally to El Oro), and Peru (south locally to Ancash and Junín). Mostly 3000–4500 m.

Asthenes urubambensis

LINE-FRONTED CANASTERO   PLATE: 6

DESCRIPTION: 16 cm (6¼"). *Very local in Peru and Bolivia. Above uniform umber brown,* with pale streaking confined to forecrown and sides of neck; fairly long and conspicuous whitish superciliary. Chin patch orange-buff; *remaining underparts streaked whitish and dusky-brown.* *Huallagae* (south to Pasco, Peru) has streaking below more extensive and contrasting.

SIMILAR SPECIES: Distinctive; the only canastero that is uniform above and streaked below.

HABITAT AND BEHAVIOR: Rare to uncommon and local in low woodland near treeline and in *Polylepis* groves. Mainly arboreal, hopping and sidling along branches; does not cock tail. Its song is an ascending trill (Fjeldså and Krabbe 1990). Small numbers can be found on e. slope of the Abra Málaga road above Ollantaytambo in Cuzco, Peru.

RANGE: Locally on e. slope of Andes in Peru (San Martín, La Libertad, Huánuco, Pasco, Cuzco, and Puno) and w. Bolivia (La Paz and Cochabamba). Mostly 3200–4300 m.

Thripophaga Softtails

The genus *Thripophaga* may not be a monophyletic assemblage, but it is maintained here, following Meyer de Schauensee (1966, 1970), because we remain uncertain how else to allocate several species. Vaurie (1980) tremendously expanded the genus *Thripophaga* by including in it the seemingly rather distantly related genus *Asthenes*. He also transferred *fusciceps* and *berlepschi,* species placed in *Thripophaga* by Meyer de Schauensee (and by us), to the genus *Phacellodomus.* The four species comprising *Thripophaga* are admittedly a rather heterogeneous lot, though all have broadly rounded, unpointed rectrices, and all are rare and local. The "true" *Thripophaga* is *macroura,* a scarce forest-inhabiting endemic of se. Brazil. The latter's nest is a ball-shaped structure of twigs placed on a horizontal branch (Collar et al. 1992).

Thripophaga cherriei

ORINOCO SOFTTAIL   PLATE: 7

DESCRIPTION: 14.5 cm (5¾"). *Known from only a single site in s. Venezuela.* Iris yellow. Olive brown above with indistinct whitish superciliary; more chestnut on wings, and tail rufous-chestnut. *Distinct chin patch orange-rufous;* remaining underparts somewhat paler olive brown, *breast and sides of neck with narrow but distinct buffy whitish streaking.*
SIMILAR SPECIES: Similar Speckled Spinetail (*Cranioleuca*), which likely occurs sympatrically, has a pale breast spotted with dusky, rufous-chestnut crown, and no orange-rufous gular patch.
HABITAT AND BEHAVIOR: Virtually unknown in life. Recorded from "rain forests and small clearings along river banks and small caños" (Meyer de Schauensee and Phelps 1978, p. 193).
RANGE: S. Venezuela (Capuana, near the Orinoco River in nw. Amazonas). 150 m.

Thripophaga macroura

STRIATED SOFTTAIL   PLATE: 7

DESCRIPTION: 18 cm (7"). *Lowlands of e. Brazil.* Above rufous brown, streaked with buff on crown and back, and with indistinct buffy whitish superciliary; wings rufous-chestnut, *tail contrastingly bright cinnamon. Distinct chin patch orange-rufous;* remaining underparts dull brown *narrowly streaked whitish.*
SIMILAR SPECIES: Pale-browed Treehunter is notably larger with substantially heavier bill, more conspicuous superciliary, and broader streaking below; in area of overlap with Striated Softtail, *both* species have contrasting cinnamon-colored tail.
HABITAT AND BEHAVIOR: Rare in lower growth and middle levels of humid forest and forest borders. Usually skulking, but single individuals or pairs sometimes accompany mixed flocks; forages mainly while hopping around inside vine tangles, less often in terminal foliage and along branches. Its most common vocalization is a simple repetition of a single strident note, "tch-tch-tch-tch-tch-tch-tch-tch . . . ," sometimes with chatters interspersed. Although small numbers occur at the Sooretama Reserve in Espírito Santo, on the whole this is a scarce and infrequently encountered Brazilian endemic which, though perhaps often overlooked, certainly deserves threatened or endangered status.
RANGE: Locally in se. Brazil (s. Bahia south through e. Minas Gerais and Espírito Santo to n. Rio de Janeiro). To 1000 m.

Thripophaga fusciceps

PLAIN SOFTTAIL   PLATE: 7

DESCRIPTION: 16.5–19 cm (6½–7½"). A *drab* and *uniform*-looking furnariid found *locally* in Amazonia. Bill bluish horn; iris hazel. *Mostly*

drab olivaceous brown, slightly darker above, with indistinct but rather wide pale buffyish superciliary and frontlet; wings and tail rufous. Females average paler than males, especially on brow and foreneck. Nominate race (Bolivia) is considerably larger than the similarly plumaged *dimorpha* (found disjunctly in se. Peru and in e. Ecuador and adjacent Peru). *Obidensis* (widely disjunct in lower Amaz. Brazil) is intermediate in size and is darker and browner generally.

SIMILAR SPECIES: Vaguely recalls certain foliage-gleaners, but note the softtail's arboreal habits and *unstreaked* appearance. Common Thornbird is similar though browner and more uniformly colored; they are not known to overlap, and the thornbird inhabits more open terrain.

HABITAT AND BEHAVIOR: Generally rare and local in vine tangles and thick vegetation at borders of humid forest, mainly in várzea and transitional forest; judging from the number of specimens, *obidensis* may be locally more numerous in e. Amaz. Brazil. Usually in pairs or small (presumed family) groups, clambering about at mid-levels, usually not with mixed flocks. The call in se. Peru is a sharp, loud, descending churring, often given excitedly in rapid series as a duet by members of a pair.

RANGE: Locally in ne. Ecuador (a few Napo records) and adjacent ne. Peru (specimen from mouth of the Río Curaray into the Napo); se. Peru (Pasco to Madre de Dios and Puno) and n. Bolivia (Beni, La Paz, and Cochabamba); e. Amaz. Brazil (from near mouth of Rio Madeira into the Amazon east to near mouth of the Rio Tapajós). To about 500 m.

Thripophaga berlepschi

RUSSET-MANTLED SOFTTAIL

DESCRIPTION: 18 cm (7"). *Local in Andes of n. Peru.* Bill bluish horn; iris hazel to orange. *Rufous above* with *crown and chin pale grayish buff,* fading to buffy olive on hindcrown; rump olivaceous brown. *Breast also rufous,* becoming olivaceous brown on belly. Juvenal has head, neck, and most of underparts scaled with dusky.

SIMILAR SPECIES: Basically a rufous furnariid with contrastingly paler, ashy crown; it somewhat recalls certain *Cranioleuca* spinetails, especially Marcapata and Light-crowned, but overlaps with neither.

HABITAT AND BEHAVIOR: Little known. Rare in undergrowth of montane forest and stunted woodland. Found in forest just below treeline in La Libertad, where a few were captured in mist-nets and the species was seen infrequently, once in an area with a heavy *Chusquea* bamboo understory (M. Robbins). Pairs and small groups have been seen accompanying small understory flocks (T. A. Parker III, *in* Collar et al. 1992). Its voice seems to be unknown.

RANGE: Locally in Andes of n. Peru (Amazonas on Cordillera de Colán south to e. La Libertad). 2450–3350 m.

NOTE: Vaurie (1980) placed this species in the genus *Phacellodomus.* Behaviorally it seems closer to *Cranioleuca* (M. Robbins).

Phacellodomus Thornbirds

A fairly uniform genus of plain, unstreaked furnariids found in a variety of habitats and regions in South America, though most range in semiopen, often arid terrain, and none is found in humid lowland forests. Vaurie (1980) placed three additional species in the genus: *dendrocolaptoides* (which we accept as being closely related to *Phacellodomus* but maintain in its own monotypic genus, *Clibanornis*) and *fusciceps* and *berlepschi* (both of which we retain in the genus *Thripophaga*). Many thornbirds have contrasting rufous crowns or forecrowns, often with the feathers stiffened and somewhat streaky. Their bills are rather stout and slightly decurved, their tails well rounded and unstiffened. Except when giving voice to their often loud songs, thornbirds are normally inconspicuous. Nests, however, are very conspicuous: they are large cylindrical structures made of sticks, often with several chambers, and are usually attached to near the tip of a drooping branch.

GROUP A   *Smaller,* with *plain, drab whitish underparts.*

Phacellodomus rufifrons

COMMON THORNBIRD   PLATE: 7

Other: Rufous-fronted Thornbird, Plain (-fronted) Thornbird

DESCRIPTION: 15.5–16.5 cm (6–6½"). *Highly disjunct distribution* in semiarid parts of tropical South America. Nominate race and *sincipitalis* (s.-cen. South America), as well as *peruvianus* (Río Marañón valley of nw. Peru and adjacent Ecuador), are *drab brown above* with *rufous forecrown,* somewhat streaked effect on entire crown, and pale superciliary and lores. Below dull buffy whitish, brownest on flanks. *Specularis* (ne. Brazil from Maranhão to Pernambuco) similar but with rufous patch on primaries and some rufous on shoulders and even a little on tail. *Plainest* race is the rather small *inornatus* of Venezuela and ne. Colombia: it *lacks* rufous forecrown (see V-19, C-25).

SIMILAR SPECIES: Very dull and nondescript, particularly in n. part of its range, where best known from its *lack* of obvious field marks. Elsewhere the rufous forecrown, usually quite evident, is the best character. Cf. similar Little (in chaco region) and Streak-fronted (in Andes) Thornbirds, with which Common may overlap marginally.

HABITAT AND BEHAVIOR: Fairly common to common in a variety of semiopen and more lightly wooded habitats, ranging from trees around ranch houses and in pastures to fairly humid woodland (especially at borders) along the base of the Andes in s. Bolivia and nw. Argentina. Usually in pairs or small groups; mainly arboreal (though feeding birds sometimes drop to the ground) and generally quite conspicuous, especially when around its obvious, large (often 2 m or more long) stick nests; the latter are attached to forks near tips of large, often drooping branches. These nests are sometimes multichambered, and all or a portion may be usurped by other birds. Common Thornbirds sing frequently, most often a loud, abrupt series of forceful "cheh" or "chit" notes which start slowly, then accelerate and descend. Often both members of a pair call in sequence.

RANGE: Venezuela (Sucre and Monagas west to Lara, Barinas, and Apure, and south to n. Bolívar) and ne. Colombia (llanos south to ne. Meta); nw. Peru (Amazonas, Cajamarca, and San Martín, in upper Río Marañón valley) and extreme s. Ecuador (Zumba region of s. Zamora-Chinchipe; ANSP); e. and s.-cen. Brazil (Maranhão and Pernambuco south through most of Bahia to n. Minas Gerais; s. Mato Grosso, Mato Grosso do Sul, and nw. Paraná), n. Paraguay, e. and s. Bolivia (west to Beni), and nw. Argentina (south to Tucumán). Mostly below 1300 m, but reportedly (Vaurie 1980) to 2000 m in Argentina.

NOTE: Several English names for this species have been proposed recently, none of them appropriate for the species as a whole. We propose the name Common Thornbird for this geographically variable species so long as all forms are considered conspecific. If the three disjunct populations presently considered to comprise *P. rufifrons* are split as full species, northerly birds (without rufous forecrowns) could be called the Plain Thornbird (*P. inornatus*), Marañón birds the Maranon Thornbird (*P. peruvianus*), and southerly birds the Rufous-fronted Thornbird (*P. rufifrons*).

Phacellodomus sibilatrix

LITTLE THORNBIRD

DESCRIPTION: 14 cm (5½"). *N. Argentina and adjacent areas.* Resembles geographically closest race of Common Thornbird (*sincipitalis*; these 2 species are seemingly not sympatric anywhere) but *substantially smaller*. Little differs further in showing *virtually no rufous on forecrown* (though its forecrown does show the same vaguely streaky effect) and in having a *small rufous patch on shoulders* and more rufous on its outer rectrices.

SIMILAR SPECIES: The somewhat larger Short-billed Canastero has a smaller bill and is more grayish (not so brownish) overall; it shows a distinct orange-rufous chin patch but lacks the thornbird's rufous shoulders.

HABITAT AND BEHAVIOR: Uncommon to fairly common in chaco woodland and scrub. Usually in pairs or small groups, sometimes (perhaps especially when not breeding) with loose mixed flocks, and often very confiding; primarily arboreal, though feeding birds sometimes drop to the ground where they hop about with partially cocked tails. The song is a series of shrill, well-enunciated "cheep" notes with slightly descending effect, similar to Common Thornbird's but somewhat higher-pitched; also gives various sharp "chip" notes while foraging. Quite numerous in woodland around Filadelfia in w. Paraguay.

RANGE: S. Bolivia (s. Santa Cruz at Estancia Perforación), w. Paraguay, w. Uruguay, and n. Argentina (south to La Rioja, Córdoba, and n. Buenos Aires). To 2000 m (in Jujuy, Argentina).

Phacellodomus striaticeps

STREAK-FRONTED THORNBIRD   PLATE: 7

DESCRIPTION: 17 cm (6½"). *Andes from s. Peru to nw. Argentina.* Drab brown above with *rufous forecrown*, finely streaked with grayish on

crown, and pale superciliary; shoulders rufous and *flight feathers cinnamon-rufous basally* (showing as a *patch* even on closed wing); *outer rectrices rufous,* their tips and central pair dusky. Below whitish with pale buff wash on flanks. *Griseipectus* (s. Peru) has breast washed more grayish.

SIMILAR SPECIES: Resembles Common Thornbird of lowlands; despite its English name, in the field the Streak-fronted shows no more streaking on its crown than the Common. In area of possible overlap (none is known), look for Common's *lack* of rufous in wings or tail. Streak-fronted also resembles various *Asthenes* canasteros, especially Rusty-vented; the somewhat smaller canastero has a chestnut chin patch (admittedly sometimes obscure), shows more rufous on wing, and has rich rufous rump contrasting with blacker tail. Cf. also the scarce Steinbach's Canastero.

HABITAT AND BEHAVIOR: Uncommon to common in montane scrub and adjacent agricultural fields, generally in semiarid regions and often where there are cacti; also quite regular around houses. Seems less numerous in Peru than elsewhere. Forages both in shrubbery and while hopping, with tail partially cocked, on the ground; usually in pairs or small groups. Generally reasonably confiding. Perhaps easiest to see when building or repairing its conspicuous nests, which birds seem to build or at least repair throughout the year; these nests are routinely placed in a very obvious situation, with the crossbar of a telephone pole often being used as a support. The song resembles Common Thornbird's.

RANGE: Andes of s. Peru (intermontane valleys north to Apurímac and Cuzco), w. Bolivia, and nw. Argentina (south to Tucumán and Catamarca). Mostly 2800–4200 m, moving lower during austral winter.

GROUP B   Averaging *larger,* 2 species especially so; some with *pale iris.*

Phacellodomus ruber

GREATER THORNBIRD   PLATE: 7

DESCRIPTION: 20.5 cm (8″). A *large* thornbird of interior s.-cen. South America. *Iris bright yellow.* Brown above, *more rufous on crown, wings, and tail* (especially outer rectrices); more grayish on face and dusky on auriculars and with *pale lores* (but generally *no* superciliary shows). *Below pure whitish;* some birds in fresh plumage have dark scaling on foreneck.

SIMILAR SPECIES: Freckle-breasted Thornbird is quite similar, and in areas of actual or potential overlap the two are *easily* confused. Freckle-breasted is smaller, its wings are more or less concolor olive brown with dull rufous showing only on flight feathers (Greater's entire wing is contrastingly rufous), and its tail shows less rufous. Freckle-breasted is also more apt to show a faint superciliary and has less whitish on lores. Apparently depending on molt stage, breast patterns of the 2 species can be surprisingly alike.

HABITAT AND BEHAVIOR: Uncommon to fairly common in undergrowth of gallery woodland and in shrubby areas, almost invariably *near water,* sometimes foraging out into adjacent reedbeds or other emergent vegetation. Usually in pairs and generally quite skulking, hopping on or near the ground. More conspicuous when singing, then often mounting to near the top of a bush or low tree, though never far from cover. The song, heard rather frequently throughout the year, is a series of loud, arresting notes which start almost explosively, then gradually accelerate and become somewhat less loud and emphatic, "kur-cheé-chee-chee-chee-che-che-che-chew-chew-chew-chew-chu-chu-chu-chuchuchu." Particularly numerous in pantanal of Mato Grosso, Brazil, and Paraguay.

RANGE: N. and e. Bolivia (west to La Paz and Beni), interior cen. Brazil (s. Mato Grosso and Mato Grosso do Sul east to nw. São Paulo, nw. Minas Gerais, w. Bahia, and n. Goiás), Paraguay (but absent in extreme west and east), n. Argentina (south in northwest to Tucumán, and near the Río Paraguay south to Santa Fe and Entre Ríos; an old record from Buenos Aires is regarded as uncertain), and extreme s. Brazil (w. Rio Grande do Sul). Likely occurs in n. Uruguay. Mostly below 1100 m, locally to 1400 m in Bolivia.

Phacellodomus striaticollis

FRECKLE-BREASTED THORNBIRD

DESCRIPTION: 18 cm (7″). *Ne. Argentina to se. Brazil.* Resembles Spot-breasted Thornbird (no overlap; the two were formerly considered conspecific) but has *iris yellow* (not gray), browner (less rufous) crown which lacks white shaft streaking, less prominent pale superciliary, and is *considerably paler below* (especially on ground color of breast, which shows only *minute white freckling*).

SIMILAR SPECIES: Quite easily confused with Greater Thornbird, which also has yellow eye. Greater, as its name implies, is larger, though this is difficult to ascertain in the field where its more extensive and contrasting rufous in wing and tail is a better field mark. Greater also usually shows more prominent pale lores, almost no superciliary, is whiter below, and may show some dusky scaling on foreneck (especially on sides); a few may even have some white spotting on breast (again restricted to *sides*).

HABITAT AND BEHAVIOR: Uncommon to fairly common in borders of gallery woodland and monte and in thickets in more open grassy or marshy terrain; almost always *near water.* Usually in pairs which skulk near the ground and, like Greater Thornbird, sometimes forages out into emergent marsh vegetation. Freckle-breasted's song is similar to Greater's, though more often with an extended series of comparatively soft preliminary notes before the much louder main song.

RANGE: Ne. Argentina (e. Formosa south to e. Córdoba and n. Buenos Aires; only uncertainly recorded from Misiones), Uruguay, and se. Brazil (north locally to e. Paraná). To about 700 m.

NOTE: See comments under Spot-breasted Thornbird.

Phacellodomus maculipectus

SPOT-BREASTED THORNBIRD

PLATE: 7

Other: Freckle-breasted Thornbird (in part)

DESCRIPTION: 18 cm (7″). *S. Bolivia and nw. Argentina;* formerly considered conspecific with Freckle-breasted Thornbird. Iris gray (*not yellow*). Dull brown above with rufous crown showing sometimes quite prominent white shaft streaks, and short but rather contrasting whitish superciliary; *flight feathers edged dull rufous;* tail mostly brown, outer feathers rufous. Throat buffy whitish, *sides of throat and breast becoming orange-rufous with small white chevron-shaped markings;* belly pale ochraceous, deepest on flanks.

SIMILAR SPECIES: Cf. Freckle-breasted Thornbird (no overlap).

HABITAT AND BEHAVIOR: Uncommon in undergrowth and borders of deciduous and semihumid woodland. Unlike Freckle-breasted Thornbird, this species shows no particular predilection for vicinity of water. Usually in pairs, skulking in dense growth near ground. Its song, more or less typical of genus, is a series of loud, emphasized notes, "kew, keeé-keee-keee-keee-keee-keeh," perhaps averaging slightly higher pitched and faster than songs of Freckle-breasted. Can be found north of Salta (city) along the road to Jujuy (city).

RANGE: Andean slopes and intermontane valleys of s. Bolivia (north to w. Santa Cruz) and nw. Argentina (south to La Rioja). About 1000–2500 m.

NOTE: *P. maculipectus* is here treated as a species distinct from *P. striaticollis,* following the evidence presented by Nores and Yzurieta (1981). These authors indicate that the two taxa, in addition to their plumage differences, also differ in nest shape and placement: the nest of *P. maculipectus,* typical of the genus, is large, cylindrical, and placed near the tip of a drooping branch, whereas the nest of *P. striaticollis* is smaller, more spherical, and more apt to be placed in the fork of a branch. However, our field experience does not support their contention that the two taxa show marked vocal differences.

Phacellodomus dorsalis

CHESTNUT-BACKED THORNBIRD

DESCRIPTION: 19.5 cm (7¾″). A *large* thornbird of *upper Río Marañón valley of nw. Peru.* Iris bluish gray or bluish white; bill long and straight, lacking decurved effect of other thornbirds'. Grayish brown above, crown somewhat rufescent and with streaked effect, and lores pale; *smudgy rufous-chestnut "saddle" across back;* wings and tail mostly rufous. Whitish below with *band of rufous speckling across breast* and rufous-tinged flanks.

SIMILAR SPECIES: Not likely confused in its *limited range.* Cf. Common Thornbird (occurring farther down Río Marañón valley, with no recorded overlap); it lacks rufous on back and across breast, etc.

HABITAT AND BEHAVIOR: Uncommon in dense low scrub growing in arid regions. The large cylindrical nests, typical of the genus and usually placed near the tip of a tree branch, are conspicuous, but usually the birds themselves are not (M. Robbins). Voice seems to be undescribed.

RANGE: Nw. Peru (upper Río Marañón valley in s. Cajamarca and La Libertad; a sighting from Ancash on e. slope of Cordillera Blanca, *fide* Fjeldså and Krabbe 1990). Mostly 2000–2700 m.

GROUP C

Aberrant thornbird with throat (at least) *uniform bright rufous.*

Phacellodomus
erythrophthalmus

RED-EYED THORNBIRD

PLATE: 7

DESCRIPTION: 17 cm (6¾"). *E. Brazil. Ferrugineigula* (north to s. São Paulo) has *red iris;* it is brown above and on sides of head with *deep rufous crown;* outer rectrices rufous. *Throat and breast orange-rufous,* fading to buffy whitish on belly and brownish on flanks. Nominate race (south to ne. São Paulo) has *orange iris,* rufous on crown restricted to forecrown, tail entirely rufous, and *throat (only) deeper rufous* with remaining underparts entirely olivaceous brown.

SIMILAR SPECIES: Completely unlike any other thornbird: much more rufous below, lacking "streaky" effect on crown, etc. Superficially looks more like a *Philydor* foliage-gleaner, though lacking the bold superciliary shown by members of that genus.

HABITAT AND BEHAVIOR: Uncommon and inconspicuous in lower growth and borders of swampy woodland and in second-growth areas with dense thickets and tall grass; more a bird of wooded habitats than Freckle-breasted Thornbird, though both regularly occur in close proximity. Red-eyed is an inveterate skulker, hopping about in thick, low, damp vegetation and rarely emerging even when singing. The song of *ferrugineigula* is a short series of loud, ringing notes preceded by a single softer one, "ku, keeé-keeé-keeé-keeé-keeé-kuh," quite distinct from songs of other thornbirds.

RANGE: E. Brazil (s. Bahia south to s. Rio Grande do Sul). To at least 750 m.

NOTE: *Ferrugineigula* may prove to be a separate species, and if so treated it would retain the name of Red-eyed Thornbird, with *P. ferrugineigula* being best called the Orange-eyed Thornbird. Willis and Oniki (1991) mention that *ferrugineigula* and nominate *erythrophthalmus* "occur together" (but give no details). *P. erythrophthalmus* differs markedly from the other species currently classified in the genus *Phacellodomus;* these differences include its plumage, voice, and (*fide* Vaurie 1980) nest (suspended from the top, not supported from below). It was separated in the genus *Drioctistes* in *Birds of the Americas,* vol. 13, part 4. Despite its having been merged into *Phacellodomus* in *Birds of the World,* vol. 7, and in all subsequent references, maintaining *Drioctistes* may prove to be a better course.

Clibanornis Groundcreepers

A rare and local inhabitant of woodland near streams in se. South America, the monotypic genus *Clibanornis* seems allied to *Phacellodomus,* so much so that Vaurie (1980) transferred it to that genus. Vocally, however, it is not especially similar to *Phacellodomus;* this, combined with its marked plumage and morphological differences, convinces us that the genus is best maintained. Formerly the genus had been associated with *Cinclodes* (e.g., *Birds of the Americas,* vol. 13, part 4; followed by Meyer de Schauensee 1966, 1970), but given its forest-based habitat, a close relationship to that genus seems unlikely. The nest remains undescribed.

*Clibanornis
dendrocolaptoides*

CANEBRAKE GROUNDCREEPER

DESCRIPTION: 21.5 cm (8½"). *Limited area in se. Brazil region*. Rufous brown above, darker and more chestnut on crown and tail, and with *bold pale grayish postocular stripe*, pale lores, and dusky auriculars. *Throat white, spotted and scaled with black on its sides;* below dull gray, with sides, flanks, and crissum washed with brown.

SIMILAR SPECIES: Superficially thornbird-like, though larger than any (even the Greater) and more boldly marked on the head.

HABITAT AND BEHAVIOR: Rare in lower growth of gallery forest and bamboo thickets, usually near streams. Not well known in life; usually in pairs, reclusive and difficult to see in its dense habitat (Belton 1984). Its song is a series of loud, strident, staccato notes, e.g., "chet, chet, chet-chit-chit" (W. Belton recording); the effect is not particularly like a *Phacellodomus*. The Canebrake Groundcreeper is likely threatened by deterioration or elimination of much of its streamside habitat, though the degree to which it is capable of persisting in degraded, patchy remnants is unknown.

RANGE: Se. Brazil (s. São Paulo south to n. Rio Grande do Sul), ne. Argentina (Misiones), and e. Paraguay (recorded from Alto Paraná by Bertoni in the early 20th century; recently only by Brooks et al. [1992] at Estancia La Golondrina in s. Caaguazú). To about 800 m.

Anumbius Firewood-gatherers

Although comparatively obscure in appearance, the Firewood-gatherer's conspicuous large stick nests attract attention. The species inhabits open terrain from s. Brazil to cen. Argentina. Despite its notably different tail, it likely is most closely related to the *Phacellodomus* thornbirds.

Anumbius annumbi

FIREWOOD-GATHERER

DESCRIPTION: 19.5 cm (7¾"). *Open country of s.-cen. South America*. Above pale sandy brown, back sparsely but boldly streaked with blackish, and with rufous forecrown and whitish superciliary; flight feathers edged rufescent; *tail long and graduated,* feathers strongly pointed and *outer feathers dusky broadly tipped white (conspicuous in flight)*. *Throat white outlined with black spotting* and contrasting with pale dull buffyish remaining underparts; some indistinct streaking on breast. The species is monotypic; specimens of "*machrisi*" from Goiás can be matched by birds from Rio Grande do Sul (D. Stotz, pers. comm.).

SIMILAR SPECIES: Vaguely recalls a canastero, thornbird, or Chotoy Spinetail, though none of these shows such obvious white in tail. Long-tailed silhouette somewhat recalls shape of Wedge-tailed Grass-Finch (*Emberizoides*) or Great Pampa-Finch (*Embernagra*).

HABITAT AND BEHAVIOR: Uncommon to locally common in savannas, grasslands, and pastures with scattered small trees and at edge of relatively sparse open woodland; avoids more continuously wooded areas and may spread into regions opened up for agriculture, there using hedgerows, windbreaks, and trees around houses; less numerous in most of Brazilian portion of range. Except around their nests, Firewood-gatherers are relatively inconspicuous, usually feeding on the ground in or near cover. Their large nests are constructed mainly of long and frequently thorny twigs (also assorted debris, most frequently placed on or near the entrance). Nests are usually placed in the open, most frequently in a low tree but sometimes on phone poles or other structures. Each year a new chamber is constructed, often with the old nest used as a base; after several years the resulting structure can be astonishingly large. Pairs, which tend to be very sedentary, frequently perch near their nests and often vocalize while perching nearby. Their most common song is a repeated, gravelly, fast "chit, chit, chit, che-che-che-che-ee-ee-ee-ee-eu" with a descending effect.

RANGE: S. Brazil (Goiás south through Minas Gerais to Rio Grande do Sul), Paraguay (except in northwest), Uruguay, and n. and cen. Argentina (south to ne. Chubut). To 1000 m.

Coryphistera Brushrunners

This unique and boldly patterned furnariid, found in woodlands of s.-cen. South America, is especially typical of the chaco.

Coryphistera alaudina

LARK-LIKE BRUSHRUNNER   PLATE: 7

DESCRIPTION: 16.5 cm (6½"). Unmistakable, *conspicuously streaked* and *strongly crested* furnariid found in *chaco woodland*. Bill and legs mainly orange to reddish pink. Above streaked grayish brown, blackish, and white, with mainly *blackish crest* (usually held erect), *white oval patches above and below eye* (the lower one larger), and cinnamon-rufous earcoverts; tail blackish with outer feathers basally rufous (visible especially in flight). *Below white profusely streaked with rufous to cinnamon-buff*, more spotted on throat. There is some variation (individual? geographical?) in heaviness of streaking and overall saturation.

SIMILAR SPECIES: No other furnariid matches this species' ornate and attractive pattern.

HABITAT AND BEHAVIOR: Fairly common to common in chaco woodland and scrub, adjacent agricultural fields, and (east of the Río Paraguay) monte and espinilho woodland. Brushrunners are very social birds and almost always occur in small groups (during the austral winter of up to 12–15 birds); these sometimes associate with mixed flocks, Picui Ground-Doves (*Columbina picui*) and Bay-winged Cowbirds (*Molothrus badius*) being especially frequent companions. Brushrunners forage almost entirely on the ground, most often in the open but near cover, scurrying about with head and neck held high, looking much like small quail. When alarmed they flush and perch in bushes and low trees. A variety of semimusical chatters and trills are given, often by several birds more or less at once. The nest, like a large thornbird's with a small side entrance, is generally placed in a fork or with support from below (not, unlike the thornbirds', near the tip of a branch). Groups of brushrunners apparently roost in their nests even when not breeding, and we suspect that "helpers" may assist breeding pairs.

RANGE: Se. Bolivia (north to s. Santa Cruz), w. Paraguay (mainly well west of the Río Paraguay, also in small numbers north of Pilar in Neembucú), extreme s. Brazil (sw. Rio Grande do Sul), and n. and cen. Argentina (south to Mendoza, La Pampa, extreme s. Buenos Aires, and Entre Ríos); likely occurs in w. Uruguay. *Contra* some sources (e.g., Olrog [1979]), there is no recent evidence of migration, and it definitely breeds in Paraguay. Mostly below 500 m.

Pseudoseisura Cacholotes

A distinct genus with no evident close relatives (Vaurie 1980), the cacholotes are among the largest furnariids; two species (Rufous and Brown) have distinctive bushy crests and piercing yellow irides, whereas the third (White-throated) is less conspicuously crested and usually dark eyed. Cacholotes range in lighter woodland and scrub in e. and s. South America; the three species are nearly allopatric. In nesting and other behavior they seem to be "exaggerated" thornbirds. Their stick nests can, however, be much larger, especially the Brown Cacholote's whose nests can be up to 2–3 m across; ½-m-long sticks are sometimes incorporated. Nests of the White-throated Cacholote are smaller. Cacholotes are also well known for their amazingly loud and raucous voices.

Pseudoseisura cristata

RUFOUS CACHOLOTE   PLATE: 7

DESCRIPTION: 23 cm (9"). Ne. Brazil west disjunctly to n. Bolivia. Iris golden yellow. *Expressive bushy crest. Uniform cinnamon-rufous,* very slightly paler below; crest feathers ashy gray. Birds from Beni, Bolivia (perhaps under the name *unirufa,* despite the comments in *Birds of the Americas,* vol. 13, part 4, p. 182) appear paler and more cinnamon and lack gray in crest.

SIMILAR SPECIES: Brown Cacholote (no known overlap) is larger, darker on crest, and grayer on back and underparts (such that its more rufous throat and face contrast more).

HABITAT AND BEHAVIOR: Uncommon to locally fairly common in dry caatinga woodland (ne. Brazil), often even in areas that have been severely overgrazed, and in gallery woodland in more humid, often somewhat marshy situations (Mato Grosso to n. Bolivia). Rufous Cacholotes are mainly arboreal but regularly drop to the ground to feed, walking about with an almost comical, lurching gait. In general comportment and especially in their slow, undulating flight cacholotes bear an uncanny resemblance to certain jays (Corvidae). Their voice is extraordinary, a loud and very far-carrying series of notes of very different but always nonmusical qualities, some gurgling, others cackling or churring, the whole gradually winding down to a stuttering stop; this is often given by both members of a pair in unison or as a duet. Seems especially numerous in arid parts of the caatinga.

RANGE: Ne. Brazil (extreme e. Maranhao, Paraíba, and Pernambuco south to cen. Minas Gerais); sw. Brazil (s. Mato Grosso and Mato Grosso do Sul) and adjacent Bolivia (extreme e. Santa Cruz) and n. Paraguay (Alto Paraguay); n. Bolivia (Beni). To at least 500 m.

Pseudoseisura lophotes

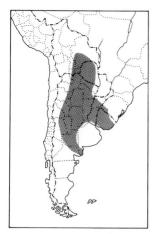

BROWN CACHOLOTE
PLATE: 7

DESCRIPTION: 26 cm (10¼"). Iris straw yellow. *Expressive bushy crest.* Above brown, *crest feathers darker* (more blackish or grayish); rump and tail rufous. Throat, face, and crissum rufous; remaining underparts brown, feathers edged whitish giving vaguely barred or scaled effect (especially in birds in fresh plumage). Birds from n. Argentina southward (*argentina*; K. C. Parker, *Auk* 77[2]: 226–227, 1960) are darker generally with more prominent pale edging below; birds from Santa Cruz, Bolivia, are paler and more uniform; birds from w. Paraguay intermediate.

SIMILAR SPECIES: Rufous Cacholote is smaller and more smoothly rufous or cinnamon-rufous below with no contrasting feather edging; the 2 species do not occur together.

HABITAT AND BEHAVIOR: Uncommon to fairly common in chaco woodland and scrub and (east of Río Paraguay) in monte and espinilho woodland. Behavior and vocalizations similar to Rufous Cacholote's.

RANGE: S. Bolivia (Santa Cruz at Guanacos and Estancia Perforación), w. Paraguay, extreme s. Brazil (sw. Rio Grande do Sul), Uruguay, and n. and cen. Argentina (south to Mendoza, La Pampa, extreme s. Buenos Aires, Santa Fe, and Entre Ríos; not in Misiones). To 900 m.

Pseudoseisura gutturalis

WHITE-THROATED CACHOLOTE
PLATE: 7

DESCRIPTION: 24 cm (9½"). *W. and cen. Argentina.* Iris (usually?) dark; *crest short* (often not evident). Dull grayish to grayish brown above, with lores and narrow partial eye-ring whitish. *Small patch on throat white*, with small black patch below; remaining underparts dull grayish to sandy brown, *ochroleuca* (C. Olrog, *Neotropica* 5: 42, 1959) of Andes south to Mendoza sandier.

SIMILAR SPECIES: Brown Cacholote is somewhat larger and is decidedly less grayish overall, with throat rufous instead of white; Brown's crest is usually very conspicuous, whereas White-throated's is usually held depressed. The 2 species overlap only marginally.

HABITAT AND BEHAVIOR: Uncommon to locally fairly common in Patagonian scrub and in sparse shrubbery growing in open, barren, sandy or stony Andean valleys. Behavior and cacaphonous voice similar to other cacholotes', though more terrestrial; White-throated Cacholote

seems to run more rapidly and easily than its congeners, with less waddling or lurching.

RANGE: W. and cen. Argentina (w. Salta south to n. Santa Cruz, and east across the plains of La Pampa and Río Negro to extreme s. Buenos Aires). To 2900 m.

Metopothrix Plushcrowns

A monotypic genus, so unusual in overall appearance and color pattern among the Furnariidae that its familial affinity was questioned until J. A. Feduccia (1970, *in* Vaurie 1980) showed that its cranial structure was typical of the furnariids. Unpublished information (RSR) on its nesting in Ecuador is also consistent with placement in the Furnariidae: on three occasions birds have been seen either entering or constructing stick nests almost ½ m across and with a side entrance, not dissimilar in overall form from those of *Phacellodomus* thornbirds. We have seen these usually conspicuous nests placed on lateral branches of trees 4 to as much as 20 m above the ground (R. M. Fraga [*Hornero* 13(3): 236, 1992] has also very recently described just such a nest); we once observed two nests in very close proximity attended by four plushcrowns.

Metopothrix aurantiacus

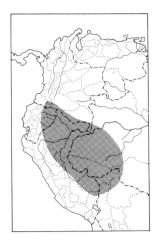

ORANGE-FRONTED PLUSHCROWN PLATE: 8

DESCRIPTION: 11.5 cm (4½″). A small, warbler-like bird with *rather bright orange legs* found in w. Amazonia. Grayish olive above with *bright orange forehead* (feathers stiffened and plush-like, but this is usually not evident in the field), becoming *bright yellow on foreface and throat;* wings dusky, coverts narrowly edged yellowish. Lower underparts pale yellowish. Immature lacks orange and yellow on head.

SIMILAR SPECIES: Virtually unmistakable, utterly unlike any other furnariid. More resembles a small tanager, perhaps most like Orange-headed, though none of these has orange legs.

HABITAT AND BEHAVIOR: Uncommon and local in canopy and borders of second-growth and riparian woodland, also sometimes out into trees and shrubs in clearings. Usually in pairs or small groups which generally feed independently of mixed flocks but sometimes accompany them. Forages mainly by gleaning, sometimes actively and even acrobatically (often briefly hanging upside down), for insects in foliage and among twigs. Has also occasionally been seen feeding on fruit, and we have once seen plushcrowns at flowers (nectar? insects?). The only call seems to be a short series of high, thin, sibilant notes, e.g., "tsweet-tsweet," sometimes given singly or varied to a "tswit-tsweét, tswi-tsweét." Readily seen in second-growth around Tena in eastern Ecuador.

RANGE: Se. Colombia (north to Putumayo), e. Ecuador (mainly in Napo), e. Peru (south to Madre de Dios), n. Bolivia (Beni), and

w. Amaz. Brazil (east to middle Rio Purus). Mostly below 700 m, but to 1000 m in s. Peru (*fide* D. Stotz).

Xenerpestes Graytails

A pair of obscure grayish furnariids with rounded tails which are found locally in forests of nw. South America. The graytails remain little known and seem rare, although the scarcity of records may only reflect the relative difficulty in seeing, identifying, and collecting them. Their inclusion in the Furnariidae has been questioned, but a large stick nest seen in Panama and believed to have been built by the Double-banded Graytail (Ridgely and Gwynne 1989) suggests that this arrangement is probably correct.

Xenerpestes singularis

EQUATORIAL GRAYTAIL · PLATE: 8

DESCRIPTION: 11.5 cm (4½"). *Rare in foothills along e. base of Andes in Ecuador and n. Peru.* Iris hazel. *Olive gray above* with *rufous forehead* and narrow white superciliary; wings and tail duskier. Below creamy whitish with *conspicuous blurry gray streaking,* crissum buffier.

SIMILAR SPECIES: Recalls certain small sympatric furnariids in shape (e.g., Ash-browed Spinetail) but smaller and grayer above than any and with more warbler-like foraging behavior. As the graytail often forages high in very tall trees where color and pattern are often difficult to discern, sometimes its distinctive behavior (see below) is the best clue. Streaking below and lack of wing-bars immediately distinguish it from Double-banded Graytail (no overlap). Cf. also *Herpsilochmus* antwrens (though they all show wing-bars) and Gray-mantled Wren (*Odontorchilus*), though it lacks streaking below.

HABITAT AND BEHAVIOR: Rare and seemingly local in canopy and borders of montane forest. Usually seen singly or in pairs foraging well above ground with mixed flocks of insectivorous birds, sometimes coming lower at forest edge. Feeds by gleaning actively from leaves, twigs, and small branches, generally near their outer part, characteristically clinging to their undersides; occasionally one briefly creeps along a branch. We have not heard its voice. Small numbers are seen fairly regularly in the vicinity of Zamora, Ecuador.

RANGE: Locally along e. base of Andes in Ecuador (north to Napo near Archidona) and n. Peru (near Carmen in n. Cajamarca and northwest of Rioja in n. San Martín). 1000–1700 m.

NOTE: For additional notes on this species, see T. A. Parker III and S. A. Parker, *Auk* 97(1): 203–205, 1980.

Xenerpestes minlosi

DOUBLE-BANDED GRAYTAIL · PLATE: 8

DESCRIPTION: 11 cm (4¼"). *N. Colombia.* Iris hazel. Olive gray above with *blackish forehead* and *narrow white superciliary;* wings duskier with

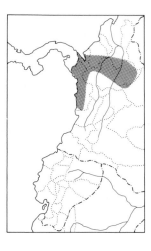

2 bold white wing-bars. Below uniform creamy whitish, sometimes with slight dark mottling on sides of chest.

SIMILAR SPECIES: Overall pattern vaguely recalls certain nonbreeding wood warblers (e.g., Cerulean and Bay-breasted). Cf. Equatorial Graytail (no overlap).

HABITAT AND BEHAVIOR: Rare to locally uncommon in canopy and borders of humid and deciduous forest and borders. Behavior (in Panama) seems not to differ appreciably from Equatorial Graytail's, though Double-banded apparently associates less frequently with mixed flocks and seems particularly to favor viny tangles at mid-levels where it is often hard to see well. Its voice is unknown to us.

RANGE: Locally in lowlands of nw. Colombia (Pacific lowlands south to lower Río San Juan, and east across humid Caribbean lowlands to middle Río Magdalena valley in nw. Santander and w. Boyacá). Also e. Panama. To 900 m.

Siptornis Prickletails

A small, *Xenops*-like furnariid found in the Andes of nw. South America. Vaurie (1980) suggested *Siptornis* might be most closely related to the *Cranioleuca* group of spinetails, and this seems borne out by the recent discovery (*fide* P. Greenfield) of its *Cranioleuca*-like nest in Ecuador. This was a spherical mass of moss and other plant material with an entrance from below, placed near the tip of a lateral branch. The name "prickletail," though distinctive sounding, is actually quite misleading; the tail is indeed double pointed but is not in the least prickly, its spines not even protruding.

Siptornis striaticollis

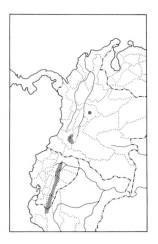

SPECTACLED PRICKLETAIL

PLATE: 8

DESCRIPTION: 12 cm (4¾"). *Local in Andes from s. Colombia to n. Peru.* Bill *thin* and somewhat warbler-like. Rufous brown above with *chestnut crown,* dark lores, and *bold, short white postocular stripe and incomplete eye-ring;* wing-coverts and tail rufous-chestnut. Below brownish gray with very fine whitish streaking on throat and chest. Foregoing applies to nominate race of Colombia. *Nortoni* (G. R. Graves and M. B. Robbins, *Proc. Biol. Soc. Wash.* 100[1]: 121–124, 1987) of Ecuador and n. Peru has less prominent eye-ring and is *much more prominently streaked with whitish on throat and chest.*

SIMILAR SPECIES: Most resembles Streaked Xenops, sometimes foraging in the same flock; the xenops has an upturned bill and white malar streak and lacks the contrasting white around eye.

HABITAT AND BEHAVIOR: Rare to locally uncommon in montane forest and forest borders. Forages rather actively, usually accompanying mixed flocks and remaining at mid-levels. Hitches along moss-covered limbs, pausing to probe in moss, leaves, or crevices in bark; occasionally one briefly hangs upside down to inspect a leaf, or more often taps softly on wood, sometimes using its (soft) tail as a brace. A peculiar high-pitched trill has been heard (J. W. Eley). Small numbers can be found in forest patches above Zamora along the road to Loja.

RANGE: Locally in Andes of Colombia (w. slope of E. Andes in Cundinamarca, and around head of Río Magdalena valley), e. Ecuador, and extreme n. Peru (n. Cajamarca). 1300–2300 m.

Premnornis Barbtails

A small, forest understory furnariid found in the Andes. Vaurie (1980) suggested that *Premnornis* (as well as *Premnoplex*) be merged into *Margarornis*. However, we are reluctant to do so, mainly because behaviorally *Premnornis* is much more like various foliage-gleaners than like other "treerunners" and "barbtails." Further, the tail of *Premnornis*, though somewhat stiffened, is not barbed at all; thus its English name is a misnomer. D. W. Rudge and R. J. Raikow (*Condor* 94[3]: 760–766, 1992) present anatomical evidence suggesting that *Premnornis*, *Premnoplex*, *Margarornis*, and *Roraimia* comprise a monophyletic unit.

Premnornis guttuligera

RUSTY-WINGED BARBTAIL   PLATE: 8

DESCRIPTION: 14.5 cm (5¾"). A nondescript *small* foliage-gleaner found from Venezuela to Peru. Brown above with buff superciliary and streaks on sides of neck and (sparsely) on back; wings and tail rufous, coverts tipped buff. Throat dull buffy whitish; remaining underparts brown with *conspicuous broad buff scalloped streaking*.

SIMILAR SPECIES: Lineated and Buff-browed Foliage-gleaners are similarly plumaged but considerably larger. Lineated varies racially, but the subspecies that are more broadly streaked below also show much more streaking above than Rusty-winged. Buff-browed is more olive brown (not so dark) generally and shows no streaking on upperparts. Smaller Spotted Barbtail is much deeper buff on throat, is unstreaked above, and has more of a spotted (not streaked) effect below; it behaves differently, unobtrusively creeping up branches (not actively gleaning).

HABITAT AND BEHAVIOR: Uncommon to locally fairly common in lower and middle growth of montane forest. Usually found singly, most often when accompanying mixed flocks of understory birds. Rusty-winged Barbtail behaves much like numerous other foliage-gleaners and certain *Cranioleuca* spinetails as it clambers about actively in dense, often viny or tangled, foliage, frequently inspecting clusters of dead leaves; unlike Spotted Barbtail, Rusty-winged almost never hitches up or along limbs and only rarely and briefly uses its tail for support. Unlike most foliage-gleaners, Rusty-winged Barbtail seems strikingly unvocal; we have never knowingly heard its song.

RANGE: Andes of extreme w. Venezuela (sw. Táchira), Colombia, nw. and e. Ecuador (on w. slope known only from Pichincha), and e. Peru (south to Puno); Sierra de Perijá on Venezuela-Colombia border. Published sightings from Cochabamba, Bolivia (Remsen and Ridgely 1980), are regarded as uncertain. Mostly 1600–2500 m, but recorded lower (down to at least 1300 m) in Peru.

Premnoplex Barbtails

A pair of small, dark furnariids found inside montane forests, mainly in the Andes. Both species are inconspicuous and quiet. The nest of the Spotted Barbtail is a rather large, globular structure made of moss and other plant material, with an entrance from below.

Premnoplex brunnescens

SPOTTED BARBTAIL   PLATE: 8

DESCRIPTION: 13.5–14 cm (5¼–5½"). A small, *dark* furnariid of Andean forest understory. Dark brown above with indistinct broken buff superciliary; *tail brownish black* with stiff protruding spines. *Throat buff to tawny-buff;* remaining underparts dark brown *profusely marked with large oval buff spots outlined by black.*
SIMILAR SPECIES: Rusty-winged Barbtail has rufous wings and tail and looks more streaked (less spotted) below. Wedge-billed Woodcreeper's overall pattern resembles barbtail's, but the woodcreeper's slender, long-tailed shape is quite different and its tail is rufous. Pearled Treerunner is much more arboreal and much brighter rufous above with a bold white superciliary.
HABITAT AND BEHAVIOR: Fairly common in undergrowth of montane forest, to a lesser extent at forest borders. A quiet and unobtrusive bird, usually found singly creeping on a mossy branch or trunk; the tail (despite its protruding barbs) generally is not used for support. Less often this species moves about in pairs, and occasionally one accompanies a mixed flock. Its true numbers are usually better revealed by mist-netting. Although not very vocal, it occasionally gives a song consisting of a series of high thin notes followed by a trill, the overall effect reminiscent of a *Cranioleuca* spinetail. Its distinctive high sharp "teep!" or "teeyk!" call note is more often heard (B. Whitney; RSR).
RANGE: Mts. of n. Venezuela (east to Miranda), and Andes of w. Venezuela, Colombia, Ecuador (south on w. slope to El Oro), e. Peru, and w. Bolivia (La Paz and Cochabamba); Sierra de Perijá on Venezuela-Colombia border, Santa Marta Mts. of n. Colombia, and Cerro Tacarcuna in nw. Chocó, Colombia. Also Costa Rica and Panama. Mostly 900–2500 m, in small numbers locally down to 650–700 m in w. Colombia and w. Ecuador.

Premnoplex tatei

WHITE-THROATED BARBTAIL

DESCRIPTION: 14 cm (5½"). *Mts. of ne. Venezuela.* Resembles Spotted Barbtail (no overlap), differing as follows: *white or whitish superciliary, throat, and spotting on underparts;* spotting on breast denser with indi-

vidual spots larger; and more white streaking on sides of neck and nape.

SIMILAR SPECIES: Nothing similar in its limited range.

HABITAT AND BEHAVIOR: Uncommon in lower growth of montane forest. Behavior much like Spotted Barbtail's, likewise favoring understory of wet mossy forest. Vocally it appears to be similar (T. Meyer). Can be found on slopes of Cerro Humo in Sucre, but overall numbers have doubtless declined greatly because of deforestation across much of its small range.

RANGE: Mts. of ne. Venezuela (ne. Anzoategui, n. Monagas, and Sucre). 800–2400 m.

NOTE: It has been suggested that *tatei* (and *pariae*) are only subspecies of *P. brunnescens* (e.g., *Birds of the World*, vol. 7, and Vaurie 1980). However, the throat color of *rostratus*, the race of *P. brunnescens* found in n. Venezuela, shows no approach to the white of *tatei* and *pariae*, and in fact is a deeper buff than that found in many other races of *P. brunnescens*.

Roraimia Barbtails

A striking furnariid endemic to the tepuis, the Roraiman Barbtail, named for the large mountain (Cerro Roraima) that straddles the Venezuela-Guyana frontier, has usually been classified in its own genus. Meyer de Schauensee and Phelps (1978) and Vaurie (1980), however, placed it in *Margarornis*, which *adusta* resembles in its general color pattern, protruding tail spines, and overall behavior (though it tends to stay lower in trees). We thus suspect that subsuming *Roraimia* may prove to be the correct course, but D. W. Rudge and R. J. Raikow (*Condor* 94[3]: 760–766, 1992) maintained the genus as distinct.

Roraimia adusta

RORAIMAN BARBTAIL   PLATE: 8

DESCRIPTION: 14.5 cm (5¾"). *Tepuis of s. Venezuela and adjacent areas. Chestnut above, brightest on sides of neck and nape and extending forward as a superciliary;* crown and auriculars blackish brown. Throat white, *remaining underparts coarsely streaked dingy buff and dark brown,* crissum more uniform brown.

SIMILAR SPECIES: This boldly patterned and relatively colorful furnariid resembles nothing else in its limited range.

HABITAT AND BEHAVIOR: Uncommon in lower growth of montane forest, less often at borders; perhaps especially in rather stunted, very mossy forest. Usually found singly or in pairs, foraging almost entirely by hitching or sidling up vertical trunks, usually within 5 m of the ground. Sometimes uses its tail for support. In overall comportment reminiscent of a Wedge-billed Woodcreeper and like that species often moves independently of mixed flocks. Seems very quiet; we have not heard vocalizations. Small numbers occur near the top of the Escalera in e. Bolívar, Venezuela.

RANGE: Tepuis of s. Venezuela (Bolívar and n. Amazonas) and adjacent Guyana and extreme n. Brazil (Roraima). 1000–2500 m.

Margarornis Treerunners

A pair of attractively patterned furnariids found in Andean forests; two additional species occur in s. Middle America. Their tail feathers end in bare shafts, and both species habitually creep up trunks and branches much like woodcreepers. The nest is a small ball-shaped structure, made primarily of moss, with a side entrance.

Margarornis stellatus

STAR-CHESTED TREERUNNER   PLATE: 8

Other: Fulvous-dotted Treerunner

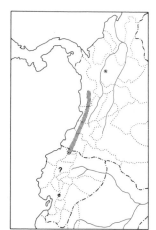

DESCRIPTION: 15 cm (6″). *Local in mossy forests of w. Colombia and w. Ecuador.* Uniform bright chestnut above with indistinct paler superciliary. *Throat contrastingly white,* feathers of lower throat black-edged; remaining underparts rufous-chestnut with a slight mottled effect, *chest with small but conspicuous white "stars" edged with black.*

SIMILAR SPECIES: The striking white throat on this otherwise essentially rufous bird is the key; the neat white stars on chest are also quite evident at close range. Pearled Treerunner is much more profusely spotted below and shows an obvious superciliary; it occurs at higher elevations. Cf. also Wedge-billed Woodcreeper.

HABITAT AND BEHAVIOR: Rare to locally uncommon in very humid montane forest, especially mossy cloud forest. Occurs singly and in pairs, foraging from middle levels up into canopy, mainly by methodically hitching up trunks, sometimes using its tail for support, probing and pecking into moss and bromeliads. Frequently seen with mixed flocks. Very quiet; we have never heard it vocalize.

RANGE: W. Colombia (n. end of Cen. Andes at Valdivia in Antioquia, and locally on w. slope of W. Andes from s. Chocó southward) and w. Ecuador (Carchi south locally to Chimborazo at Pagma). 1200–2200 m.

NOTE: Although it or a variant has long been in use, the English name Fulvous-dotted Treerunner is very misleading; the bird's basic color is only vaguely fulvous, actually more a rich rufous, but the dots themselves are startlingly white. We prefer our newly coined but far more evocative name of Star-chested Treerunner.

Margarornis squamiger

PEARLED TREERUNNER   PLATE: 8

DESCRIPTION: 15 cm (6″). An *attractive* and *boldly patterned* furnariid of Andean forests from Venezuela to Bolivia. Bright rufous-chestnut above, somewhat duller and browner on crown, with *bold creamy white superciliary.* Throat creamy white; remaining underparts brown *profusely marked with large tear-shaped creamy white and black-edged spots,* extending up onto sides of neck. Foregoing applies to *peruvianus* (e. slope of Peruvian Andes from Amazonas to Cuzco). Nominate race (Puno, Peru, south into Bolivia) similar but superciliary, throat, and spotting below more yellow-tinged, and crown rufous (uniform with upperparts). *Perlatus* (northward from nw. Peru) like *peruvianus* but with pure white superciliary and throat, and white spotting below.

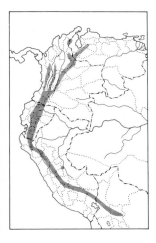

SIMILAR SPECIES: So strikingly patterned that confusion is unlikely with other furnariids. Cf. very similar Beautiful Treerunner (see below). Montane Woodcreeper has similar overall pattern but differently shaped bill, lacks eyebrow, and is streaked (not spotted) below.

HABITAT AND BEHAVIOR: Fairly common to locally common in montane forest, forest borders, and woodland (including patches of *Polylepis*-dominated woodland above true treeline). Usually found singly or in pairs, hitching along mossy branches and trunks from mid-levels up into canopy, often using its tail for support, sometimes moving out onto slender terminal twigs. Easy to see and usually a prominent member of mixed foraging flocks in Andean forests. Pearled Treerunners are not very vocal, though they occasionally give a few weak, high thin trills or single notes.

RANGE: Andes of w. Venezuela (north to Trujillo), Colombia, Ecuador, nw. and e. Peru (south on w. slope to Piura and Cajamarca), and w. Bolivia (south to w. Santa Cruz); Sierra de Perijá on Venezuela-Colombia border. Mostly 1800–3800 m.

NOTE: Beautiful Treerunner (*M. bellulus*) of Darién, Panama, mts., has been recorded virtually on the Colombian border on both Cerro Quía and Cerro Tacarcuna and surely occurs on their Colombian slopes as well. It differs from Pearled Treerunner (*M. squamiger*) in being duller and browner above (less rufous) and in having a less prominent and buffier superciliary and smaller and sparser spots on underparts. Vaurie (1980) treated *bellulus* as a subspecies of *M. squamiger,* and others have also questioned its specific status; we do as well.

Pygarrhichas Treerunners

A monotypic, very distinctive genus of arboreal furnariid endemic to the far southerly forests of South America; it seems to have no close relative. The nest is placed in a hole dug, apparently by the treerunners themselves, into a branch of dead wood (Johnson 1967).

Pygarrhichas albogularis

WHITE-THROATED TREERUNNER   PLATE: 8

DESCRIPTION: 14.5–15 cm (5¾–6"). *A very distinctive, nuthatch-(Sitta)-like bird of Fuegian forests of Chile and adjacent Argentina.* Bill long, slender, and *strongly upswept,* with *most of lower mandible ivory white to pinkish white.* Above brown with blackish auriculars, some birds variably mixed with chestnut on scapulars and back; lower back, most of wings, and tail rufous; *rather short tail* ends in long protruding spines. *Below mostly white, pure white on throat and breast,* variably (especially immatures?) scaled with dark brown (sometimes quite broadly) on belly, brownest on flanks.

SIMILAR SPECIES: Virtually unmistakable; does occur with similarly colored Thorn-tailed Rayadito.

HABITAT AND BEHAVIOR: Uncommon to locally fairly common in *Nothofagus* (Southern Beech)-dominated forest, also regularly at borders and sometimes into trees in clearings, but generally where there are at least some tall trees. Usually found singly or in pairs, foraging actively at all levels, creeping about energetically on trunks (sometimes even moving downward head first) and branches. Generally moves like a nuthatch (*Sitta* spp.), holding the tail away from the substrate, but regularly uses its tail to brace itself when prying at a piece of bark. Often with flocks of Thorn-tailed Rayaditos and other birds; like the rayadito, sometimes so tame as to be almost oblivious of an observer. The most common call is a loud, often rapidly repeated, rather metallic "tsi-dik" or simply "tsik."

RANGE: Cen. and s. Chile (north to Santiago) and adjacent w. Argentina (north to s. Mendoza) south to Tierra del Fuego. To at least 1200 m.

Megaxenops Xenops

Confined to woodland in ne. Brazil, the Great Xenops is, despite its rather *Xenops*-like bill, probably more closely allied to certain foliage-gleaners (*Philydor?*). The bill shape of another furnariid genus, *Simoxenops* (recurvebills) of Amazonia, is fairly similar.

Megaxenops parnaguae

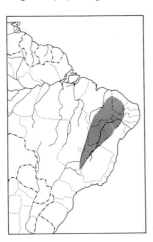

GREAT XENOPS   PLATE: 8

DESCRIPTION: 16 cm (6¼"). *Caatinga woodland of ne. Brazil. Bill heavy, with lower mandible sharply upturned* and pale at base. *Mostly bright cinnamon-rufous,* somewhat paler below and deeper rufous on wings and tail; apparently shows some dark gray skin around eye; *throat contrastingly white.*

SIMILAR SPECIES: Combination of striking bill and basically bright rufous plumage renders this splendid bird virtually unmistakable.

HABITAT AND BEHAVIOR: Rare to uncommon in caatinga and semi-humid woodland and forest; perhaps locally more numerous, but still little known and found in a region that remains relatively unfrequented by ornithologists. As Teixera et al. (1989) recently confirmed from field observations, the Great Xenops is not a true xenops at all: apart from not having a stiffened tail, it forages in a totally different manner, gleaning more like a foliage-gleaner, never hitching on trunks or branches for any extended period, or pecking at wood. Accompanies mixed flocks of understory birds and has been seen prying off pieces of bark with the bill, evidently to expose insects hiding beneath (E. O. Willis, *in* Vaurie 1980). The song is a distinctive, bubbly series of closely spaced notes which last about 3 seconds and start quietly, then rapidly become louder and higher in pitch before accelerating as they trail off at the end. Also gives single, loud, sharp call notes, these sometimes delivered in a short series (B. Whitney and J. F. Pacheco, in prep.). The Great Xenops has been found recently on the Chapada do Araripe in s. Ceará and in Serra da Capivara Nat. Park in s. Piauí, but the species as a whole is likely threatened by deforestation across most of its range.

RANGE: Interior ne. and e.-cen. Brazil (Piauí, Ceará, and w. Pernambuco south locally through w. Bahia to w. Minas Gerais). To 1100 m.

Xenops Xenops

A distinctive group of small arboreal furnariids, most xenops are marked by their laterally compressed bill with the lower mandible strongly upturned, rufous or buff wing-band, and unique silvery malar streak. The Rufous-tailed Xenops lacks the upturned bill and silvery malar streak and for these reasons was described in a separate genus, *Microxenops*. Vaurie (1980) advocated the merger of *Heliobletus* (Sharp-billed Treehunter) into *Xenops*, but recent information does not support this.

All the xenops behave much like *Picumnus* piculets; one or another species occurs in almost all lowland and subtropical forests, and up to three may be sympatric. Xenops nest in a small hole dug into soft wood; though they often dig their own, they sometimes use natural cavities or holes dug by other birds (e.g., piculets).

GROUP A

Atypical; *lacks* upturned bill and malar streak.

Xenops milleri

RUFOUS-TAILED XENOPS   PLATE: 8

DESCRIPTION: 11 cm (4¼"). *Bill essentially straight* (lower mandible *not* upturned); *no white malar streak*. Crown dusky, narrowly but sharply streaked with buff; above otherwise brown streaked with pale buff and with pale buff superciliary; rump and *entire tail rufous;* wings blackish with cinnamon band across base of flight feathers. Below rather uniformly and blurrily streaked brownish olive and buffy whitish.
SIMILAR SPECIES: Best distinguished from other xenops by its *plain face* (with no malar streak); rufous tail and straight bill are also distinctive but are more difficult to see unequivocably under normal field conditions. Of all the xenops, Rufous-tailed is the most streaked above and the palest below.
HABITAT AND BEHAVIOR: Rare to locally fairly common in canopy and borders of humid forest, in Brazil primarily in terra firme (D. Stotz), but at least in Ecuador also in várzea. Behaves much like other, more familiar xenops, working along or beneath slender branches and in vine tangles, swiveling from side to side and pausing from time to time to peck at dead wood or flake off small pieces of bark. Tail is rarely or never used for support. Usually found singly, almost always accompanying a mixed flock of canopy or subcanopy birds. We do not know its voice.
RANGE: S. Venezuela (s. Bolívar and Amazonas), se. Colombia (north to Meta and Vaupés), e. Ecuador, e. Peru (south to Madre de Dios), Amaz. Brazil (south to Rondônia at Cachoeira Nazaré and sw. Pará on the Rio Cururu; east to around the mouth of the Rio Tapajós), French Guiana, and Surinam. Probably occurs in n. Bolivia. There are only a

few records of this probably under-recorded species from most parts of its rather broad range. To 600 m.

GROUP B

Standard *Xenops; upturned bill* and *white malar streak.*

Xenops rutilans

STREAKED XENOPS

PLATE: 8

DESCRIPTION: 12–12.5 cm (4¾–5″). Wide-ranging, but local in Amazonia (only in south; absent from north). Above rufous brown, *duskier on crown, lightly streaked on crown, neck, and upper back with buff;* superciliary pale buff and with *prominent silvery white malar streak;* rump and tail rufous, tail with black on inner webs of some inner rectrices (but hard to see in the field); wings mostly rufous, with some black in flight feathers (a rufous wing-band showing in flight). Throat whitish; remaining underparts olive brown *narrowly but extensively streaked with whitish.*

SIMILAR SPECIES: *Very* similar to Slender-billed Xenops, which see; Slender-billed is found only in *humid lowland forests* where Streaked normally does not occur. Plain Xenops is much less generally streaked, showing no streaks above and at most only a few on chest. Cf. also Spectacled Prickletail, especially in e. Ecuador and n. Peru, and (in se. Brazil region) Sharp-billed Treehunter.

HABITAT AND BEHAVIOR: Uncommon to fairly common in montane forest, second-growth woodland, and borders; mainly in Venezuela, w. Ecuador and adjacent Peru, and more widely from Bolivia and n. Argentina eastward, also in deciduous forest and woodland. Behavior similar to other xenops' (see under Rufous-tailed), though like Plain Xenops, Streaked more often forages lower. The call, seldom heard, is a short descending series of 3–5 well-separated, shrill notes.

RANGE: N. Venezuela (east to Paria Peninsula, and south onto the n. fringe of the llanos), w. Colombia (Andean slopes), Ecuador (in w. lowlands north to w. Esmeraldas; also on both e. and w. slopes of Andes), Peru (mostly on e. slope of Andes; also in lowlands of extreme northwest), Bolivia (Andean slopes and lowlands), cen. and s. Brazil (north very locally in Amazonia to the Amazon; south to Rio Grande do Sul), e. Paraguay, and n. Argentina (in the northwest south to Tucumán, in the northeast only in ne. Corrientes and Misiones); Sierra de Perijá on Venezuela-Colombia border and Santa Marta Mts. in n. Colombia; Trinidad. Also Costa Rica and Panama. Sight reports from French Guiana (Tostain 1992) require corroboration. To about 2400 m, occasionally higher.

Xenops tenuirostris

SLENDER-BILLED XENOPS

DESCRIPTION: 11.5 cm (4½″). Local in *Amazonia.* Very similar to Streaked Xenops but slightly smaller (shorter tailed). Its bill is slightly more slender, but this is of marginal or no value in the field. Of greater use are its *sparser pale streaking on underparts* and *more extensive black in tail:* usually *both* webs of 3d and 4th rectrices are black, this sometimes

extending to 2d and 5th. Slender-billed's black in tail can be seen in the field, whereas in Streaked it is usually invisible, the entire uppertail looking rufous. See V-19, C-25. Streaked does not occur in much of Amazonia.

SIMILAR SPECIES: Rufous-tailed Xenops lacks silvery malar stripe, is more streaked above and paler below, and has *no* black in tail.

HABITAT AND BEHAVIOR: Rare to locally uncommon in canopy and borders of humid forest, in both terra firme and várzea, at least in Brazil with perhaps a predilection for riverine forest (D. Stotz). Behavior much like that of other xenops' (see under Rufous-tailed). A thin trill has been heard (D. Stotz).

RANGE: S. Venezuela (locally in Bolívar and Amazonas), extreme n. Brazil (Roraima on Rio Quitauaú, *fide* D. Stotz), se. Colombia (north at least to Caquetá and Vaupés), e. Ecuador, e. Peru, n. Bolivia (Pando and Beni), and s. Amaz. Brazil (south to s. Mato Grosso at Rio do Cágado, and east to the lower Rio Tapajós area and sw. Pará at Rio Cururu); Surinam and French Guiana. To 1000 m.

Xenops minutus

PLAIN XENOPS

PLATE: 8

DESCRIPTION: 11.5–12.5 cm (4½–5″). *Lower mandible sharply upturned. The least streaked xenops.* Above olive brown with pale buff superciliary and *prominent silvery white malar streak;* rump and tail rufous, tail with mainly black 3d and 4th rectrices; wings mainly rufous, with considerable black on flight feathers (a cinnamon-rufous wing-band shows in flight). Throat whitish; remaining underparts pale dull brown with some whitish streaking or mottling on chest. Nominate *minutus* of e. Brazil and adjacent Paraguay and Argentina is markedly smaller than all other races, has a proportionately smaller bill, a whiter throat, and less mottling on chest.

SIMILAR SPECIES: [All other xenops are more streaked, particularly on underparts.] In a quick view, a Plain Xenops could be mistaken for a Wedge-billed Woodcreeper.

HABITAT AND BEHAVIOR: Uncommon to fairly common in a variety of forested and wooded habitats, also sometimes out into trees in adjacent clearings. The most widespread and generally numerous xenops in lowlands, though tending to be scarcer in Amazonia. Behavior similar to other xenops' (see under Rufous-tailed), though more than any of the others, Plain forages in lower strata (and as a result is much more often captured in mist-nets). Only occasionally is a Plain seen in the same flock as one of its congeners; more often Plain remains in understory, the others in canopy or subcanopy. Although usually not very vocal, Plain occasionally gives a sharp "peek" call note; the song is a high-pitched but descending series of fast notes which accelerate into a trill. Like *Picumnus* piculets, this species and the other xenops are often first located by their soft tapping.

RANGE: Guianas, Venezuela, Colombia, Ecuador (south in the west to El Oro), e. Peru, n. Bolivia (south to La Paz, Cochabamba, and Santa Cruz), and Amaz. Brazil (south to s. Mato Grosso and n. Goiás, and east to Maranhão); e. Brazil (Pernambuco south to Santa Catarina), e. Paraguay (west to Canendiyu and Caaguazú), and ne. Argentina (Misiones). Also Mexico to Panama. Mostly below 1000 m, in small numbers to 1500 m or even higher.

NOTE: The disjunct nominate form of e. Brazil region is strikingly different from all other races of this species and may deserve full species status (though it does not seem to differ vocally). It would become *X. minutus* (Minute Xenops), the species elsewhere being called *X. genibarbis* (Plain Xenops).

Heliobletus Treehunters

Heliobletus seems closely related to *Xenops* but has a "normal" bill (not laterally compressed as in *Xenops*) and lacks the classic xenops wing pattern (i.e., with a rufous wing-band, etc.). Vaurie (1980) considered it congeneric with *Xenops,* and he may be correct, but because of their differences we prefer to maintain *Heliobletus* as distinct. Although its usual group name of "treehunter" is somewhat misleading (all the other "treehunters," including the sympatric *Cichlocolaptes,* are larger birds), it seems equally misleading to call it a "xenops," as Vaurie (op. cit.) suggested, if indeed there is a good chance that it isn't one.

Heliobletus contaminatus

SHARP-BILLED TREEHUNTER
Other: Sharp-billed Xenops

PLATE: 8

DESCRIPTION: 13.5 cm (5¼"). *Se. Brazil area.* Above olive brown, crown streaked with blackish and *back more broadly streaked with buffy whitish,* and with *long yellowish buff superciliary;* tail rufous. *Throat yellowish buff extending onto sides of neck as partial collar;* remaining underparts broadly and blurrily streaked olive brown and buffy whitish, brownest on flanks. Foregoing applies to *camargoi* of most of range; nominate race of Rio de Janeiro northward has *back more narrowly streaked or plain* and less extensive streaking on belly.
SIMILAR SPECIES: Streaked Xenops has sharply upturned bill, silvery malar streak, and much rufous in wing. White-browed Foliage-gleaner has whiter superciliary and throat, lacks pale streaking on back, and is less streaked below; the foliage-gleaner remains in forest lower growth.
HABITAT AND BEHAVIOR: Uncommon to locally fairly common in canopy, middle levels, and borders of humid and montane forest. Usually found singly or in pairs, habitually accompanying mixed flocks of canopy and subcanopy birds. Climbs about on slender branches and amongst viny tangles, gleaning insects from branches, leaves, and epiphytes; does not use tail for support, though it often hangs upside down. We have not noted it pecking or tapping into soft wood as xenops so often do. Usually quiet but occasionally gives a harsh rattled trill and a soft "tick" note. Numerous at Boracéia in São Paulo (D. Stotz) and in Rio Grande do Sul, Brazil.
RANGE: Se. Brazil (north to São Paulo, s. Minas Gerais, and Espírito

Santo), e. Paraguay (Canendiyu and Alto Paraná), and ne. Argentina (Misiones). To 1800 m.

Anabacerthia Foliage-gleaners

Three species of relatively small, arboreal foliage-gleaners, found mainly in the Andes and the highlands of Middle America, with an outlying species in the se. Brazil region. Vaurie (1980) merged the genus into his greatly expanded *Philydor*. We are not convinced that the species placed in *Anabacerthia* in *Birds of the World*, vol. 7, and Meyer de Schauensee (1966, 1970) form a monophyletic unit; in particular, the Brazilian *A. amaurotis* appears to stand apart.

Anabacerthia amaurotis

WHITE-BROWED FOLIAGE-GLEANER PLATE: 8

DESCRIPTION: 15.5 cm (6"). *Se. Brazil area.* Rufous brown above, darker on ear-coverts and crown, where feathers are basally whitish (usually hidden) and tipped blackish; *broad creamy white superciliary;* contrasting bright rufous tail. *Throat whitish;* remaining underparts brownish olive with blurry whitish streaking extending up onto sides of neck from breast.

SIMILAR SPECIES: More common Buff-browed Foliage-gleaner frequently occurs with this species, and the two can be confused; Buff-browed's superciliary is narrower and distinctly buff (not wide and creamy), its ear-coverts are not as dark or contrasting, and it is more uniformly olive brown above. Sharp-billed Treehunter is smaller, has a buffier superciliary and throat, and is streaked on back. Pale-browed Treehunter is considerably larger, streaked on crown and back, and more sharply streaked below.

HABITAT AND BEHAVIOR: Rare to locally fairly common in lower growth of humid and montane forest. Inconspicuous and seldom seen; forages singly, usually close to the ground, and most often in the company of understory flocks (regularly with other foliage-gleaners and Red-crowned Ant-Tanagers). In our limited experience, it shows no special predilection for bamboo; D. Stotz (pers. comm.) has noted it frequently feeding in dead leaves. Its song consists of a stuttering chatter lasting several seconds, followed by 3–4 loud shrieking notes, e.g., "t-t-t-t-t-t-t-t, jreék-jreék-jreék." Apparently relatively numerous in Serra dos Órgãos Nat. Park in Rio de Janeiro (Scott and Brooke 1985) and at Boracéia in São Paulo (D. Stotz).

RANGE: Se. Brazil (s. Espírito Santo on the Serra do Caparão south locally to n. Rio Grande do Sul), se. Paraguay (1992 sightings from s. Alto Paraná and n. Caazapá; Brooks et al. [1992]), and ne. Argentina (Misiones). To 1500 m.

Anabacerthia striaticollis

MONTANE FOLIAGE-GLEANER PLATE: 8

DESCRIPTION: 16–16.5 cm (6¼–6½"). Mts. from Venezuela to Bolivia. Uniform brown above with *conspicuous buffy whitish eye-ring and*

narrow postocular streak; tail contrastingly rufous. Throat buffy whitish faintly scaled darker; *remaining underparts uniform dull olivaceous buff* with narrow pale streaking on breast. Foregoing applies to *montana* (with *yungae*) of extreme s. Colombia southward; birds from farther north show little or no breast streaking (see C-26), whereas *anxia* (Santa Marta Mts.) has throat and postocular more yellowish buff.

SIMILAR SPECIES: A drab foliage-gleaner; note its montane distribution, arboreal behavior, and spectacled look. Resembles several *Philydor* foliage-gleaners, in particular Rufous-rumped, which regularly occurs with it on lower Andean slopes. The race of Rufous-rumped most similar to Montane (*subfulvus* of s. Colombia to n. Peru) is more rufescent (less olive) above and has a bolder superciliary and more contrasting, ochraceous throat. Cf. also Scaly-throated Foliage-gleaner of w. slope (no known overlap, though the two replace each other altitudinally on w. slope of W. Andes in Colombia).

HABITAT AND BEHAVIOR: Fairly common and generally widespread in canopy and borders of montane forest; the most frequently seen foliage-gleaner in many subtropical Andean forests. Relatively easy to watch, the Montane Foliage-gleaner forages actively, sometimes even acrobatically, at middle and upper tree levels, clambering along branches, often hanging upside down or moving out onto terminal twigs, pausing to inspect epiphytes and dead leaves. One or 2 regularly accompany many mixed flocks. Not very vocal, but foraging birds give an occasional sharp "peck" call; dawn song is a series of tyrannid-like, irregularly paced "pik" or "peck" notes.

RANGE: Mts. of n. Venezuela (east to Miranda), and Andes of w. Venezuela, Colombia (south on w. slope of W. Andes to Cauca), e. Ecuador, e. Peru, and w. Bolivia (La Paz and Cochabamba); Sierra de Perijá on Venezuela-Colombia border and Santa Marta Mts. of n. Colombia. Mostly 900–2300 m.

Anabacerthia variegaticeps

SCALY-THROATED FOLIAGE-GLEANER
Other: Spectacled Foliage-gleaner

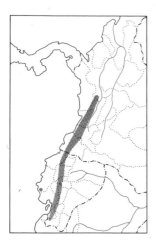

DESCRIPTION: 16.5 cm (6½"). *W. Colombia and w. Ecuador. Crown dusky* with some olivaceous streaking, contrasting with *wide, bright ochraceous postocular stripe and ochraceous eye-ring,* and dusky ear-coverts; otherwise *rufous brown above* with rufous-chestnut tail. Throat yellowish buff, feathers obscurely edged dusky resulting in a scaly look; *breast blurrily streaked ochraceous and brownish olive,* becoming olive brown on flanks. See C-26.

SIMILAR SPECIES: This handsome foliage-gleaner is unlikely to be confused in its relatively limited range. Montane Foliage-gleaner is duller and more uniform, with much less contrasting facial pattern, no ochraceous streaking on breast, etc.

HABITAT AND BEHAVIOR: Uncommon to fairly common in canopy and borders of montane forest and forest borders. Behavior much like Montane Foliage-gleaner's. Like that species, the much prettier Scaly-throated tends to feed toward the outer part of trees and regularly to come quite low; hence it is likewise easy to observe. Numerous at Tinalandia in Ecuador.

RANGE: W. slope of W. Andes in Colombia (north to s. Chocó) and w. Ecuador (south to w. Loja; an isolated population on the coastal cordillera in sw. Manabí). Also Mexico to Panama. Mostly 700–1700 m.

NOTE: The systematic position of the South American taxon *temporalis* remains uncertain. *Birds of the World*, vol. 7, treated *temporalis* as a separate monotypic species, with Middle American *variegaticeps* a subspecies of *A. striaticollis*. We do not know the rationale for Meyer de Schauensee's (1966, 1970) shift in which he placed *temporalis* as a subspecies of *A. variegaticeps;* this was followed by Vaurie (1980). On virtually all plumage characters, the arrangement in *Birds of the World* seems more reasonable, but in the absence of significant new information, we are loathe to alter the now generally accepted arrangement. The two English names for *A. variegaticeps* (with *temporalis*), "Scaly-throated" and "Spectacled" Foliage-gleaner, have been used almost interchangeably in recent literature. Because so many South American foliage-gleaners are equally "spectacled" (even if few in Middle America are—this is why E. Eisenmann suggested changing *A. variegaticeps*'s name in the first place), we favor the name Scaly-throated.

Pseudocolaptes Tuftedcheeks

A pair of large and handsomely patterned furnariids found in montane forests; another species is found in s. Central America. Their conspicuous "tufts" on the sides of the neck are unique. An unusual feature is that females' bills are consistently longer and slightly more decurved than males'. The nest, a ball-shaped structure with a tubular entrance from below, is placed in a hole or wedged into a crevice, usually not very high above the ground.

Pseudocolaptes boissonneautii

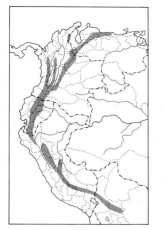

STREAKED TUFTEDCHEEK   PLATE: 9

DESCRIPTION: 20.5–21.5 cm (8–8½"). A striking, large, arboreal furnariid found in mts. from Venezuela to Bolivia. Mostly brown above, crown duskier and with narrow buff superciliary and *streaked with buff on both crown and back* (finer on crown, *broader on back*); wing-coverts variably edged with rufescent; rump and tail bright rufous. Throat whitish, *feathers on sides of neck lengthened and flaring back to form a prominent snowy white tuft;* breast buffy whitish with variable amount of brown scaling, gradually deepening to fulvous on belly. The even more striking immatures have blacker crown (contrasting with brown back) with little or no streaking, are more boldly scaled with blackish on breast, and are more rufous on belly.

SIMILAR SPECIES: Cf. Pacific Tuftedcheek, found only in W. Andes of Colombia and Ecuador; otherwise unmistakable.

HABITAT AND BEHAVIOR: Uncommon to fairly common in canopy and borders of montane forest and woodland, also sometimes out into tall trees in clearings. Found singly or in pairs, often with mixed flocks and usually remaining well above ground. Tuftedcheeks forage primarily by probing into bromeliads and other epiphytic plants, often propping themselves with their tails and hammering or rummaging about noisily; they often work methodically along major horizontal limbs, less often on vertical trunks. They are not particularly vocal, though feeding birds periodically give a loud "chut!"; the infrequently heard song is a combination of "chut" notes and trills, e.g., "chut-chut-cheeee-e-e-e-e."

RANGE: Mts. of n. Venezuela (east to Miranda), and Andes of Venezuela, Colombia, Ecuador, Peru (south on w. slope to Cajamarca), and w. Bolivia (La Paz, Cochabamba, and w. Santa Cruz); Sierra de Perijá on Venezuela-Colombia border. Mostly 1700–3100 m.

NOTE: See comments under Pacific Tuftedcheek.

Pseudocolaptes johnsoni

PACIFIC TUFTEDCHEEK PLATE: 9
Other: Buffy Tuftedcheek

DESCRIPTION: 20.5 cm (8"). *Local on Pacific slope of Andes in Colombia and Ecuador.* Here regarded as a separate species from Buffy Tuftedcheek of Costa Rica and Panama. Differs from Streaked Tuftedcheek (which replaces Pacific at higher elevations) in having *tuft on sides of neck tinged buff, unstreaked rufous-chestnut back* (not brown broadly streaked buff), *breast darker with only sparse white chevrons* (lacking scaled effect and not as conspicuous as in Streaked), and belly richer and deeper rufous.

HABITAT AND BEHAVIOR: Rare to uncommon and seemingly very local in canopy and borders of montane forest, primarily in very wet cloud forest zone of foothills. Behavior similar to Streaked Tuftedcheek's, as are many of its vocalizations; the 2 species are not known to be anywhere sympatric. Can be found in the patchy forest west of Piñas in El Oro, Ecuador.

RANGE: Locally on w. slope of W. Andes in sw. Colombia (north to Valle; apparently not recorded from Nariño but must occur) and Ecuador (recorded from Pichincha, Chimborazo, Azuay, and El Oro). Mostly 900–1500 m.

NOTE: This species has a complex taxonomic history. It was long confused with *P. boissonneautii* and not accurately diagnosed until 1936 when J. T. Zimmer (*Am. Mus. Novitates* 862) concluded that *johnsoni* was restricted to the Andes' west slope; he felt it had affinities with *P. lawrencii* of s. Central America. Vaurie (1980) attempted to demonstrate that birds that were named *johnsoni* were merely immatures of *P. boissonneautii;* this clearly has proven to be incorrect as the plumage characters defining *johnsoni* cluster in its limited range and differ from those of young *P. boissonneautii.* Robbins and Ridgely (1990) emphasized that the plumage differences between *johnsoni* and nominate *lawrencii* were as great as those between the altitudinally segregated *johnsoni* and *boissonneautii,* and that nominate *lawrencii* was (like *boissonneautii*) also found exclusively at higher elevations. We believe the best way to show their biological and systematic relationships is to treat the three taxa as separate species. No one seems to have given *johnsoni* an English name; we suggest emphasizing its limited range entirely on the Andes' Pacific slope.

Thripadectes Treehunters

A mainly Andean group of large, robust furnariids with heavy black bills; another species is found in the mts. of Costa Rica and w. Panama.

All range in the undergrowth of montane forest and are furtive, shy, and difficult to identify, in part because they are so hard to see well. They are very similar, all showing buff striping or streaking to varying extents. Nests are placed at the end of burrows which the birds dig into banks, often along forest trails.

GROUP A

Standard *large Thripadectes; streaked upperparts* (confined to *crown* in Streak-capped).

Thripadectes flammulatus

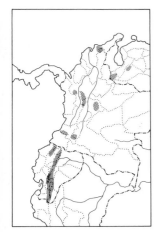

FLAMMULATED TREEHUNTER   PLATE: 9

DESCRIPTION: 24 cm (9½"). Mainly Andes from Venezuela to n. Peru. *The most boldly patterned treehunter. Above and below mostly blackish with conspicuous buff striping,* becoming browner on belly; wings, rump, and tail rufous-chestnut. *Bricenoi* (Mérida, Venezuela) is somewhat paler overall with less crisp striping.

SIMILAR SPECIES: Cf. Peruvian Treehunter, which replaces this species southward (no overlap). Striped Treehunter has a similar plumage pattern, though its ground color is duskier (not so blackish) and its buff streaking is not so wide, resulting in a much less contrasty effect; it tends to show virtually no streaking on belly and is also notably smaller.

HABITAT AND BEHAVIOR: Uncommon in undergrowth of montane forest and dense growth at forest and woodland borders, sometimes in areas dominated by *Chusquea* bamboo but also (in smaller numbers?) in places lacking it. All treehunters are furtive and rarely seen, this species and perhaps the Peruvian notably so; mist-netting sometimes reveals that they are more numerous than expected. On the rare occasions when a Flammulated Treehunter is encountered, usually it is a single individual foraging low, most often apart from a mixed flock. Its infrequently heard song is a series of harsh, grating notes which stutter at first and then slightly accelerate; foraging birds give single sharp "chek" notes of similar quality.

RANGE: Andes of w. Venezuela (Mérida), Colombia (seemingly local, but likely under-recorded), Ecuador (south on w. slope to Pichincha), and extreme n. Peru (Cerro Chinguela in Piura, and Cordillera del Condor in Cajamarca); Santa Marta Mts. of n. Colombia. Mostly 2000–3500 m, but has been recorded (ANSP) down to 800 m on w. slope of Andes in Cauca, Colombia.

Thripadectes scrutator

PERUVIAN TREEHUNTER
Other: Buff-throated Treehunter

DESCRIPTION: 24 cm (9½"). *E. slope of Andes in Peru and w. Bolivia.* Resembles Flammulated Treehunter (no overlap) but *brown above* (not blackish) with *more diffused buff streaking* which does not extend down over lower back; also brownish below (not so blackish) with buff streaking less prominent and not extending over lower belly.

SIMILAR SPECIES: Striped Treehunter is notably smaller and more narrowly buff-streaked, both above and below; streaking on upperparts

extends farther down back than Peruvian's, whereas streaking on underparts stops higher on breast.

HABITAT AND BEHAVIOR: Uncommon in undergrowth of montane forest and dense growth at forest and woodland borders. Behavior much like Flammulated Treehunter's; its voice is also reportedly (Parker et al. 1985) similar.

RANGE: E. slope of Andes in Peru (Amazonas south locally to Cuzco, presumably also in Puno) and w. Bolivia (recorded only from Cochabamba, in the Chapare at km 104 on the Villa Tunari road). About 2450–3200 m.

NOTE: Fjeldså and Krabbe (1990) suggest that *scrutator* might better be regarded as a subspecies of *T. flammulatus*. The similarity of their voices indeed indicates a close relationship, but we believe a more appropriate treatment is to regard them as closely related allospecies, as proposed by F. Vuilleumier (*in* Vaurie 1980). The species' usual English name has been Buff-throated Treehunter (Meyer de Schauensee 1966, 1970). However, its throat is not actually buff but rather has a pattern exactly like that found in *T. flammulatus* (i.e., boldly streaked dusky and buff), and we cannot explain how the name "Buff-throated" could have been selected. It is misleading as it suggests a nonexistent distinguishing character. As *T. scrutator*'s range lies almost entirely within Peru, we feel "Peruvian" is a much more appropriate modifying name.

Thripadectes holostictus

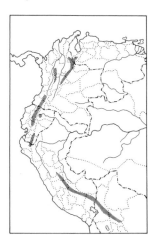

STRIPED TREEHUNTER   PLATE: 9

DESCRIPTION: 20.5–21.5 cm (8–8½"). Andes from Venezuela to Bolivia. *Above dusky brown prominently streaked with buff;* wings more rufescent, rump and tail rufous-chestnut. Below brown, throat and breast with blurry buff streaking (its extent and pattern varying individually, with some birds, especially southward, showing little or none).

SIMILAR SPECIES: A confusing bird, essentially "intermediate" in appearance between the more boldly striped Flammulated and Peruvian Treehunters and the more uniform Streak-capped and Black-billed Treehunters. Cf. those species. Lineated Foliage-gleaner is also quite similar, especially on e. slope of Andes (where Lineated is more streaked), but it is smaller, shows a narrow buff postocular stripe, and has an essentially unmarked buff throat.

HABITAT AND BEHAVIOR: Uncommon in undergrowth of montane forest and dense growth at forest and woodland borders, sometimes in *Chusquea* bamboo. Behavior similar to Flammulated Treehunter's, and likewise seldom encountered; Striped usually occurs at lower elevations, though there seems to be considerable overlap, perhaps especially on w. slope of Andes. Its song is rather different, a fast chipper with a slight descending effect (P. Coopmans recording).

RANGE: Locally in Andes of extreme w. Venezuela (sw. Táchira), Colombia (not in W. Andes north of Cauca, nor around head of Río Magdalena valley; probably under-recorded), Ecuador (south on w. slope to Chimborazo), Peru (seemingly not recorded north of Pasco, but probably occurs), and w. Bolivia (La Paz and Cochabamba). Mostly 1500–2500 m but has been recorded (ANSP) down to 900 m on w. slope of Andes in Cauca, Colombia.

Thripadectes
melanorhynchus

BLACK-BILLED TREEHUNTER   PLATE: 9

DESCRIPTION: 21 cm (8¼"). Local on *e. slope of Andes from Colombia to Peru.* Above mainly dark brown, duskier on crown, *crown and back narrowly streaked with buff;* wings rufescent, rump and tail rufous-chestnut. *Throat quite bright ochraceous, feathers edged with black giving a scaly appearance;* remaining underparts uniform brown to ochraceous brown *with virtually no streaking.* Note that *all* the larger treehunters have black bills.

SIMILAR SPECIES: Most resembles Streak-capped Treehunter with which apparently locally sympatric, at least in ne. Ecuador; Streak-capped shows less streaking on upperparts (essentially confined to crown) and has more streaked pattern on throat (not so "scaly"). Striped Treehunter is more streaked overall, especially on underparts.

HABITAT AND BEHAVIOR: Uncommon to locally fairly common in undergrowth and dense borders of montane forest and secondary woodland. Its reclusive behavior is similar to other treehunters' (see under Flammulated), though at least in its Ecuadorian range, Black-billed seems more numerous and widespread. A sharp, loud "kyip" note is commonly given, often in fairly rapid series; we do not know if it also has a chattered true song. Quite numerous north of Archidona along the road to Loreto in Napo, Ecuador.

RANGE: E. slope of Andes in Ecuador (north to Sucumbios) and Peru (south to Puno); 1 record from Colombia (an AMNH specimen taken in 1913 above Villavicencio in w. Meta; almost surely also occurs southward). 1000–1700 m.

Thripadectes virgaticeps

STREAK-CAPPED TREEHUNTER

DESCRIPTION: 21.5 cm (8½"). Mts. from Venezuela to Ecuador. Resembles slightly smaller Black-billed Treehunter, differing principally in having a grayer crown and nape, *almost unstreaked back,* and *more streaked* (less "scaly") *throat,* the streaks extending down over upper chest as well. See V-20, C-26. Birds from Pacific slope and n. end of Colombia's Cen. Andes (nominate and *sclateri*) have longer bills than those from elsewhere.

SIMILAR SPECIES: Striped Treehunter is considerably more prominently streaked, both above and below. Smaller Uniform Treehunter is much plainer overall, unstreaked above, and browner below (not ochraceous on belly) with less prominent streaking on throat.

HABITAT AND BEHAVIOR: Uncommon in undergrowth of montane forest and at thickly vegetated forest borders. Furtive behavior similar to other treehunters' (see under Flammulated); like them, seldom seen and usually encountered apart from mixed flocks. In n. Venezuela a commonly given call is a fast, sharp "ch-di-dit!" repeated at several-second intervals.

RANGE: Mts. of n. Venezuela (Carabobo east to Distrito Federal), and Andes of w. Venezuela (sw. Lara at Anzoátegui, and in sw. Táchira),

Colombia (local: mainly in W. Andes from s. Chocó southward, also at n. end of Cen. Andes and from head of Río Magdalena valley southward on e. slope), and n. Ecuador (on e. slope only in w. Napo, on w. slope south to Pichincha). Mostly 1300–2100 m, locally down to 900 m on Pacific slope in Nariño, Colombia.

GROUP B

Smaller, dark Thripadectes of Pac. slope.

Thripadectes ignobilis

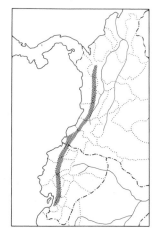

UNIFORM TREEHUNTER

PLATE: 9

DESCRIPTION: 19 cm (7½"). *W. Colombia and w. Ecuador. Short, stout bill,* base of lower mandible somewhat reddish. Above dark rufescent brown *with no streaking* except for a *short, thin, buff postocular streak,* somewhat duskier on crown; tail rufous-chestnut. *Below dull brown,* throat with buff streaking, extending more sparsely down over chest. SIMILAR SPECIES: Streak-capped Treehunter is larger with markedly longer bill, shows some streaking on crown, and is much more ochraceous on belly (not basically dull uniform brown); it usually occurs at higher elevations, though there is some overlap. HABITAT AND BEHAVIOR: Uncommon in lower growth of montane forest, forest borders, and mature second-growth woodland. Although furtive, Uniform seems easier to see than other *Thripadectes,* foraging more often well above ground (occasionally as high as subcanopy); it also accompanies mixed flocks more frequently. Its song is a series of 6–8 rapidly delivered "kyip" notes, usually delivered soon after dawn. Seen regularly in cloud forest west of Piñas in El Oro, Ecuador. RANGE: Pacific slope of W. Andes in w. Colombia (north to Chocó) and w. Ecuador (south to El Oro). Mostly 700–1700 m.

NOTE: This distinctive treehunter perhaps deserves to be generically separated from the other *Thripadectes,* as suggested in *Birds of the Americas,* vol. 13, part 4. No name seems to be available, however.

Syndactyla Foliage-gleaners

A mainly Andean genus of fairly typical, midsized foliage-gleaners; one species (Buff-browed) is also found in se. South America. They are united by their relatively short, straight bills and rather prominent streaking on underparts; their unstreaked pale throats often stand out. Vaurie (1980) merged the genus into his expanded *Philydor.* The Rufous-necked Foliage-gleaner, usually placed in *Automolus,* is here placed in *Syndactyla* because of vocal similarities and other factors.

GROUP A

Mantle *pale-streaked* (but lightly so in Pac.-slope race of Lineated). Relatively hard to observe.

Syndactyla subalaris

LINEATED FOLIAGE-GLEANER

PLATE: 9

DESCRIPTION: 18–18.5 cm (7–7¼"). Andes from Venezuela to Peru. Mostly brown above, more blackish on crown and nape, with indistinct narrow buff postocular streak and *buff streaking from crown to*

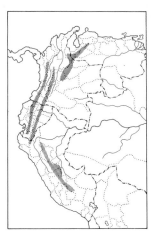

back; wings more rufescent, tail rufous. *Throat plain yellowish buff;* remaining underparts brown streaked with yellowish buff, belly browner. Foregoing applies to *mentalis* group of most of range. Nominate race (with *tacarcunae*) of Pacific slope has brown crown (though nape is still blackish, with an almost contrasting effect) and is *more narrowly streaked with buff above* (*often showing mainly as a band on nape*); also usually less streaked on underparts. Juvenile much more rufescent generally, with an orange-ochraceous postocular streak, and streaking on back and breast see P-14.

SIMILAR SPECIES: Easily confused with several sympatric furnariids. Of the *Thripadectes* treehunters, Striped and Uniform are the most similar. Striped especially resembles east-slope Lineateds, but the treehunter is larger and stouter with a heavier bill and shows more streaking on its buff throat. Uniform differs from west-slope Lineateds in being slightly larger and stouter-billed and more uniform generally (showing *no* streaking above, below only on throat). Striped Woodhaunter is always duller and longer-billed. West of Andes, where sympatric Lineateds have streaking mainly on nape, the woodhaunter is almost unstreaked above; on e. slope of Andes, where woodhaunter is somewhat more streaked, Lineated's streaking is always more extensive and crisper (both above and below). Does not overlap with Guttulated Foliage-gleaner; cf. also Buff-browed Foliage-gleaner and smaller and less-streaked Montane Foliage-gleaner.

HABITAT AND BEHAVIOR: Uncommon to fairly common in lower and middle growth of montane forest and, to a lesser extent, forest borders. Seen singly or in pairs, most often accompanying a mixed flock, hopping and clambering along limbs and trunks, inspecting foliage, epiphytes, and dead leaves. Its frequent song is a distinctive accelerating series of harsh nasal notes, stuttering at first, "anh, anh, anh-anh-anh-anhanhanhanh."

RANGE: Andes of w. Venezuela (north to s. Lara), Colombia, Ecuador (on w. slope south to El Oro), and Peru (south to Cuzco on the Cordillera de Vilcabamba; citations for Puno [Meyer de Schauensee 1966] are apparently unfounded); slopes of Cerro Tacarcuna in nw. Chocó, nw. Colombia. Also Costa Rica and Panama. Mostly 1000–2000 m.

Syndactyla guttulata

GUTTULATED FOLIAGE-GLEANER

DESCRIPTION: 18.5 cm (7¼"). *Mts. of n. Venezuela.* Resembles Lineated Foliage-gleaner (no overlap), differing in its *essentially unstreaked crown, more prominent buff superciliary,* and *wider and more extensive buff streaking below* (extending down over belly); sides of throat have a more scaled (less streaked) pattern.

SIMILAR SPECIES: In its limited range not likely confused. Cf. Streak-capped Treehunter.

HABITAT AND BEHAVIOR: Uncommon in lower and middle growth of montane forest and forest borders. Behavior much like Lineated Foliage-gleaner's, as is its equally frequently given call. Regularly found in Henri Pittier Nat. Park in Aragua, both at Rancho Grande and along the Choroni road.

RANGE: Mts. of n. Venezuela (Sucre, n. Monagas, and ne. Anzoátegui; Yaracuy east to Distrito Federal). 800–2100 m.

GROUP B

Mantle *unstreaked*. Relatively easy to observe.

Syndactyla rufosuperciliata

BUFF-BROWED FOLIAGE-GLEANER   PLATE: 9

DESCRIPTION: 17.5–18 cm (6¾–7″). Above uniform brownish olive with *prominent buff superciliary* but no streaking except on sides of neck; tail rufous. *Throat whitish;* remaining underparts brownish olive *with broad blurry whitish to pale buff streaking.* Nominate race of se. Brazil slightly smaller, whereas Andean birds south to w. Bolivia (*cabanisi* and *similis*) are somewhat richer brown above and have streaking below slightly yellower.
SIMILAR SPECIES: Lineated Foliage-gleaners in Peru are buff-streaked on crown and back and show a less obvious superciliary. In se. Brazil, the less numerous White-browed Foliage-gleaner can be confused with Buff-browed, but White-browed has more rufescent upperparts, creamy whitish superciliary, and contrastingly dark ear-coverts. Cf. also the smaller Sharp-billed Treehunter.
HABITAT AND BEHAVIOR: Fairly common to common in a variety of forested and wooded habitats, also regularly at borders; Buff-browed is a less strictly forest bird than Lineated Foliage-gleaner. Usually easier to see than other foliage-gleaners, not so tied to thick tangled habitat and sometimes foraging among terminal branches more or less in the open; also often relatively unsuspicious, sometimes even perching "normally" on a branch for protracted periods. Pairs frequently accompany mixed flocks, foraging at all levels though most often at low and middle heights. Its frequently heard song is a fast series of loud but less nasal notes than Lineated's, "kuh-kuh-kuh-kihkihkihkikikikiku"; it seems not to vary across the species' broad range. Various other contact calls are also given.
RANGE: E. slope of Andes in extreme s. Ecuador (Cordillera del Condor in se. Zamora-Chinchipe), Peru, Bolivia, and nw. Argentina (south to La Rioja); se. Brazil (north to s. Minas Gerais at Caraça), Uruguay, se. Paraguay (west to Paraguarí), and ne. Argentina (west to e. Chaco and ne. Santa Fe near the Río Paraguay, and south to n. Buenos Aires). Mostly 1300–2500 m in Andes; mostly below 1600 m in se. South America.

Syndactyla ruficollis

RUFOUS-NECKED FOLIAGE-GLEANER   PLATE: 9

DESCRIPTION: 18–18.5 cm (7–7¼″). *Mts. of sw. Ecuador and nw. Peru.* Above rufescent brown with *superciliary and sides of neck contrastingly orange-rufous;* wings rufescent, tail rufous. *Throat cinnamon-buff* (brightest at its sides) with remaining underparts olive brown, broadly streaked buffyish on breast.
SIMILAR SPECIES: Not likely confused in its limited range.
HABITAT AND BEHAVIOR: Uncommon to fairly common in lower and

middle growth of montane forest, second-growth woodland, and borders; favors moderately humid areas, though smaller numbers also occur in more deciduous woodland. Usually found singly or in pairs (occasionally more), most often while accompanying mixed flocks; forages in typical foliage-gleaner fashion mainly by hitching along major horizontal limbs and on trunks, inspecting bromeliads and other epiphytic plant growth. Its frequently heard song is a series of harsh, nasal, ratchetty notes which start slowly and then speed up, "anh, anh-anh-anhanhanhanhanhanh," sometimes almost ending in a roll; it strongly resembles Lineated and Guttulated Foliage-gleaners' songs. Feeding birds also give single sharp "ank" notes of similar quality. Although it remains numerous in woodland patches west of Celica, Ecuador, overall numbers have doubtless declined substantially in recent decades because of forest destruction over significant portions of its always limited range. Although capable of persisting in relatively small and degraded forest fragments, it deserves threatened status.

RANGE: Andes of extreme sw. Ecuador (w. and s. Loja) and nw. Peru (south to Lambayeque and Cajamarca; the citation for the Río Marañón valley at La Lejía in Amazonas [Meyer de Schauensee 1966] is apparently without foundation). Mostly 1300–2700 m, locally down (in less disturbed forest) to 600 m.

NOTE: Usually placed in the genus *Automolus* (e.g., Meyer de Schauensee 1966, 1970; Vaurie 1980). Several recent authors (e.g., Parker et al. 1985; Fjeldså and Krabbe 1990) have, however, commented on the striking similarity of this species' vocalizations to those of several *Syndactyla* and their dissimilarity to those of *Automolus* and have suggested that its affinities lie with the former. We agree entirely, adding that both its subtropical-zone distribution and overall plumage pattern also lie more with *Syndactyla*.

Cichlocolaptes Treehunters

A monotypic genus endemic to the forests of e. Brazil. Vaurie (1980) merged it into his expanded *Philydor*.

Cichlocolaptes leucophrus   **PALE-BROWED TREEHUNTER**   PLATE: 9

DESCRIPTION: 20.5–22.5 cm (8–8¾"). *E. Brazil.* Long, straight bill. Above rufous brown with whitish to pale buff superciliary and narrow streaking on crown and back, somewhat wider on back; *tail contrastingly bright pale cinnamon*. Throat whitish, feathers at sides narrowly scaled with brown; *remaining underparts conspicuously streaked buffy white and brown*. Foregoing applies to nominate race (south to Rio de Janeiro); *holti* (São Paulo southward; O. Pinto, *Rev. Arg. Zoog.* 1[3]: 166, 1941) is *substantially smaller* and has a *rufous tail*, browner back, and wider, more prominent, superciliary.

SIMILAR SPECIES: Striated Softtail, locally sympatric with the large nominate form of the treehunter, is markedly smaller and has a more slender bill, narrower pale superciliary, finer streaking below, and a small orange-rufous chin patch. Pale-browed Treehunter's southern

holti form resembles sympatric White-browed Foliage-gleaner, but latter differs in its lack of back streaking, blurrier and less extensive streaking on underparts, and more slender bill. Cf. also Buff-browed Foliage-gleaner.

HABITAT AND BEHAVIOR: Rare to locally fairly common in humid and montane forest and forest borders; D. Stotz (pers. comm.) believes it is most numerous where very humid conditions permit abundant epiphytic growth, such as on Serra do Mar in São Paulo (e.g., at Boracéia). Usually seen singly, less often in pairs, Pale-browed Treehunter forages at all levels from lower growth inside forest to subcanopy, clambering about on larger limbs and often feeding in bromeliads (into which it occasionally disappears!) and other epiphytic plants; at times its foraging is reminiscent of *Pseudocolaptes* tuftedcheeks'. The most common song, a loud ringing "wreeyp! wreeyp! wreeyp-wreeyp-wreeyp" (with a varying number of "wreeyp" notes), is sometimes interspersed with a loud, fast chattering. The species, though doubtless much reduced in overall numbers, does have populations in several well-protected areas (e.g., Itatiaia Nat. Park and the Sooretama and Nova Lombardia reserves).

RANGE: E. Brazil (s. Bahia south to ne. Santa Catarina); the published record from Rio Grande do Sul is regarded as uncertain (Belton 1984). To 1400 m.

NOTE: Two species could be involved, though specimens from Serra do Bocaina in ne. São Paulo are intermediate (Pinto 1978; D. Stotz, pers. comm.), and their voices appear to be similar. If split, *C. leucophrus* could be called Pale-tailed Treehunter, leaving Pale-browed Treehunter for *C. holti*. The correct spelling of the specific name is *leucophrus* (Sibley and Monroe 1990) and not *leucophrys, contra* Meyer de Schauensee (1966, 1970).

Berlepschia Palmcreepers

A splendid, boldly patterned furnariid of Amazonia whose distribution is strictly tied to the presence of *Mauritia* palms.

Berlepschia rikeri

POINT-TAILED PALMCREEPER   PLATE: 9

DESCRIPTION: 21.5 cm (8½"). A striking large furnariid *confined to Mauritia palm groves in Amazonia.* Unmistakable, by many considered the most attractive furnariid. Long, straight bill. *Head, neck, and underparts black conspicuously streaked with white; mantle, wings, and tail contrastingly bright rufous-chestnut;* rectrices quite pointed.

HABITAT AND BEHAVIOR: Rare to locally uncommon in *Mauritia* palmgroves, and therefore local in many regions; these groves occur in both essentially open, savannalike areas and mainly forested regions. Usually occurs as widely dispersed pairs. The palmcreeper is strictly arboreal and, unless vocalizing, surprisingly inconspicuous as it rummages about much of the time toward the base of large fan-shaped palm fronds. The song is an unmistakable and very loud, far-carrying

series of ringing notes which last for 3–5 seconds, "dedede-kree! kree! kree! kree! kree! kree! kree! kree! kree! kree!" Birds seem to vocalize infrequently, mainly in early morning; in response to tape playback, a bird may fly in from a long distance but even then will often remain difficult to see well. Recognition of this song has led to several major range extensions in recent years, but nonetheless *Berlepschia* seems nowhere really numerous; it can be found in the outskirts of Manaus, Brazil, and (*fide* D. Delaney) Puerto Ayacucho in Amazonas, Venezuela. RANGE: Locally in the Guianas, s. Venezuela (Canaima, Bolívar; Puerto Ayacucho and near Cerro Duida in Amazonas), extreme se. Colombia (1989 sightings [M. Pearman; P. Coopmans] north of Leticia in Amazonas), Amaz. Brazil (south to s. Mato Grosso, s. Goiás, w. Bahia, and s. Piauí), nw. Bolivia (Pando, n. La Paz, and w. Beni), and extreme se. Peru (Tambopata Reserve in Madre de Dios); ne. Ecuador (numerous records [including VIREO photos] since 1988 from La Selva and near Tena). To at least 600 m.

Simoxenops Recurvebills

A pair of scarce, foliage-gleaner-like furnariids found primarily in sw. Amazonia. Both have strikingly heavy, upturned bills. Vaurie (1980) merged the genus into his expanded *Philydor*. Vocal similarities suggest that *Simoxenops* may actually be more closely related to the montane *Syndactyla* foliage-gleaners (which genus was also included in *Philydor* by Vaurie [1980]).

Simoxenops ucayalae

PERUVIAN RECURVEBILL   PLATE: 10

DESCRIPTION: 19 cm (7½″). Very local in s. Amazonia. *Massive bill with lower mandible strongly upturned,* mostly bluish horn with blackish along ridge. Above rufescent brown, somewhat duller on crown and wings, and with indistinct narrow ochraceous superciliary; rump and tail rufous-chestnut. *Below orange-rufous,* slightly flammulated on sides of throat and chest. Immature has more prominent superciliary and conspicuous black scalloping on underparts.
SIMILAR SPECIES: Cf. Bolivian Recurvebill. *Automolus* foliage-gleaners have much more slender bills and are less ochraceous generally than this species; Chestnut-crowned and Brown-rumped are the most similar and regularly occur with the recurvebill.
HABITAT AND BEHAVIOR: Rare to locally uncommon in undergrowth of humid forest, primarily in or near thickets of *Guadua* bamboo. Found singly or in pairs, usually independently of mixed flocks, and difficult to see, in part because of its dense habitat. Has been seen hammering on stalks of dead bamboo, presumably trying to find food (M. Robbins). Foraging birds sometimes give a repeated, quite loud "chak" or "chek" call by which they may sometimes be located. More distinctive is the territorial song, a faster and sharply ascending series of notes of similar harsh nasal quality, lasting about 5 seconds; this is

somewhat reminiscent of a *Syndactyla* foliage-gleaner. Small numbers occur at Tambopata Reserve in Madre de Dios, Peru.

RANGE: Se. Peru (s. Ucayali and Madre de Dios) and extreme nw. Bolivia (Pando at Camino Mucden); recorded also from much farther east in Amaz. Brazil (Alta Floresta in n. Mato Grosso, and near e. bank of the lower Rio Xingu south of Altamira). Novaes (1978) discussed an additional specimen in the Goeldi Museum taken at an uncertain locality, probably either at Sena Madureira in Acre or at Humaitá on the middle Rio Madeira. To 1300 m.

NOTE: Natural history information on this species was published by Parker (1980).

Simoxenops striatus

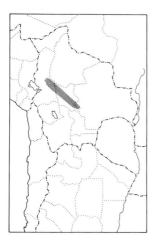

BOLIVIAN RECURVEBILL

DESCRIPTION: 19 cm (7½"). *Foothills of w. Bolivia*. Similar to Peruvian Recurvebill (no overlap) but bill slightly less massive; differs further in being darker and browner above with *prominent buff streaking on head, neck, and back* and with somewhat more prominent ochre superciliary.
SIMILAR SPECIES: Other vaguely similar foliage-gleaners have differently shaped bills, as do *Thripadectes* treehunters.
HABITAT AND BEHAVIOR: Rare to uncommon in montane forest, favoring dense tangled undergrowth and vine tangles at middle levels; unlike Peruvian Recurvebill, the Bolivian apparently shows no preference for bamboo. Not well known. Behavior seems similar to Peruvian Recurvebill's, though Bolivian sometimes forages higher while accompanying mixed flocks of middle level and subcanopy birds. Vocalizations are much like Peruvian Recurvebill's. Much behavioral information derived from Parker et al. (1992).
RANGE: Locally in foothills along base of Andes in w. Bolivia (La Paz, Cochabamba, and w. Santa Cruz). 670–900 m.

Hyloctistes Woodhaunters

A drab foliage-gleaner with a fairly long bill, found in humid lowland forests west of the Andes and in w. Amazonia. Vaurie (1980) merged the genus into his expanded *Philydor*.

Hyloctistes subulatus

STRIPED WOODHAUNTER   PLATE: 10
Other: Striped Foliage-gleaner

DESCRIPTION: 17–17.5 cm (6¾–7"). Dull and confusing. Nominate race (east of Andes) olive brown above, somewhat duskier on crown, with *buff streaking on crown, neck, and mantle;* wings somewhat more rufescent; rump and tail rufous-chestnut. *Throat pale buffyish;* remaining underparts dull olivaceous brown, *breast somewhat flammulated with buff. Assimilis* (west of Andes; we consider *cordobae* synonymous) similar but slightly darker above with buff streaking restricted to a little on crown; also somewhat less flammulated below.
SIMILAR SPECIES: Lineated Foliage-gleaner is more sharply and exten-

sively streaked with buff on hindneck, mantle, and breast but otherwise is quite similar and easily confused; note their different vocalizations, and that Lineated is more montane (though with some overlap). Uniform Treehunter overlaps with the woodhaunter on w. slope of Andes; treehunter is darker generally with a shorter but stouter bill and has throat nearly uniform with rest of underparts (not contrastingly paler). Other treehunters are larger, etc. Buff-throated Foliage-gleaners found east of Andes are unstreaked above, have less breast flammulation, and also have a more or less prominent eye-ring; those found west of Andes differ in their contrastingly whitish throat. Rusty-winged Barbtail is markedly smaller and smaller-billed and much more prominently marked below; it is more montane.

HABITAT AND BEHAVIOR: Uncommon to locally fairly common in lower and middle growth of humid forest and mature secondary woodland. Woodhaunters are usually found singly, often accompanying mixed understory flocks; they forage much like *Automolus* foliage-gleaners, hopping, rummaging, and probing in tangled vegetation and among epiphytes. Songs vary geographically, with birds east of Andes giving 2 (occasionally up to 4) loud ringing "teeuw" notes often followed by a softer and lower-pitched rattling, "tr-r-r-r-r-r," the effect similar to Chestnut-winged Hookbill's song. Birds west of Andes seem only to give a series of 5–8 sharp fast notes, "kyip-kyip-kyip-kyip-kyip," sometimes repeated tirelessly. A "squirp!" call note is given throughout range.

RANGE: W. Colombia and w. Ecuador (south to e. Guayas and nw. Azuay); s. Venezuela (Amazonas and Bolívar), e. Colombia (north to Meta and Vaupés), e. Ecuador, e. Peru, n. Bolivia (Pando, Beni, and La Paz), and w. and cen. Amaz. Brazil (mainly south of the Amazon, ranging east to n. Mato Grosso at Alta Floresta and the lower Rio Tapajós; north of the Amazon only in the upper Rio Negro drainage). Also Nicaragua to Panama. Mostly below 1100 m, in small numbers to 1700 m.

NOTE: Based primarily on their strikingly different primary vocalizations, more than one species may be involved, ranging on either side of the Andes. If split, the cis-Andean *H. subulatus* could be called the Eastern Woodhaunter, the trans-Andean *H. virgatus* (with *assimilis*) the Western Woodhaunter. Given the number of foliage-gleaners in various genera, we feel it is more helpful to separate *Hyloctistes* as a "woodhaunter" and not call it a "foliage-gleaner."

Ancistrops Hookbills

A monotypic genus of heavy-bodied foliage-gleaner found in forests of Amazonia. It is characterized by its stout and somewhat hooked bill with a somewhat upturned lower mandible. Vaurie (1980) merged the genus into his expanded *Philydor*.

Ancistrops strigilatus

CHESTNUT-WINGED HOOKBILL   PLATE: 10

DESCRIPTION: 19 cm (7½"). W. and cen. Amazonia. *Bill heavy and hooked* (hook hard to see in the field). Above dark olive brown *rather*

prominently streaked with yellowish buff and with narrow pale buff superciliary; *wings and tail contrastingly rufous. Below yellowish buff narrowly but conspicuously streaked with dusky-olive* except on throat.

SIMILAR SPECIES: Overall pattern is quite like Chestnut-winged Foliage-gleaner's, and the two sometimes forage in the same flock, but the more slender foliage-gleaner is unstreaked and has a fairly contrasting orangey throat.

HABITAT AND BEHAVIOR: Uncommon to locally fairly common in middle levels and canopy of humid forest, mainly in terra firme but sometimes in várzea as well. Usually seen singly or in pairs, most often accompanying a mixed flock in subcanopy. Forages, often quite sluggishly, mainly along larger limbs and in vine tangles and generally is not difficult to see. The song is a nasal and somewhat querulous "tyeeuw-tyeeuw," often followed by or interspersed with a chattering which may continue at varying intensities for 5–10 or even more seconds; it resembles the song of the cis-Andean Striped Woodhaunter.

RANGE: Se. Colombia (north to Meta and Vaupés), e. Ecuador, e. Peru, nw. Bolivia (La Paz and Pando), and w. and cen. Amaz. Brazil (east to the lower Rio Tapajós area, and south to Rondônia and n. Mato Grosso at Alta Floresta). Mostly below 500 m (recorded to 900 m in s. Peru).

Philydor Foliage-gleaners

A rather uniform genus of about 10 species of fairly large furnariids found widely in humid forests, both in Amaz. lowlands and in montane areas (though none occurs above 2000 m). About half are arboreal and reasonably conspicuous, whereas the others are more furtive, foraging in lower growth where they are less often seen. Unlike many of their closer relatives, *Philydor* foliage-gleaners show little or no streaking, but all species have a superciliary, often bold. Compared to *Automolus* foliage-gleaners (Plate 11), *Philydor* are more slender and more strongly patterned; they also vocalize less often and less loudly. *Philydor* nests are placed in holes in trees or (perhaps most often) in dead snags; sometimes (or in some species?) they are dug into banks. Vaurie (1980) placed 7 other genera (*Simoxenops, Hyloctistes, Ancistrops, Anabazenops, Anabacerthia, Cichlocolaptes,* and *Syndactyla*) in *Philydor*. Although some of these mergers may prove to be correct, we prefer to await a more complete behavioral (and, ideally, also biochemical) analysis before creating such a variable grouping, and thus retain the generic arrangement of Meyer de Schauensee (1966, 1970).

GROUP A   More *arboreal* species; color of underparts *varies.*

Philydor erythropterus   **CHESTNUT-WINGED FOLIAGE-GLEANER**   PLATE: 10

DESCRIPTION: 18.5 cm (7¼"). Amazonia. *Above olive grayish with lores and (especially) throat pale ochraceous orange,* narrow buff superciliary,

and fine streaking on auriculars; *wings and tail contrastingly rufous-chestnut.* Remaining underparts pale dingy buffyish with some vague pale shaft streaking.

SIMILAR SPECIES: Chestnut-winged Hookbill has stouter bill and heavier body but is best distinguished by its streaking (both above and below) and lack of rather contrasting orangey throat. Other arboreal *Philydor* foliage-gleaners have wings concolor with back.

HABITAT AND BEHAVIOR: Uncommon to locally fairly common in middle levels and canopy of terra firme forest. Seen singly or in pairs, usually accompanying mixed flocks of canopy birds. Often forages more or less in the open, actively sidling along limbs or clambering about in terminal foliage, regularly inspecting tangles and curled dead leaves. The song, rather infrequently heard, is a fast, semimusical, descending trill.

RANGE: S. Venezuela (locally in s. Bolívar and adjacent ne. Amazonas); se. Colombia (north to w. Meta), e. Ecuador, e. Peru, n. Bolivia (Pando, Beni, and La Paz), and Amaz. Brazil (south to s. Mato Grosso on the Serra dos Parecis, and east to e. Pará in the Belém area). To 1200 m.

Philydor erythrocercus

RUFOUS-RUMPED FOLIAGE-GLEANER   PLATE: 10

DESCRIPTION: 16.5–17 cm (6½–6¾″). Guianas to Amazonia, extending up onto e. slope of Andes. Does not include Slaty-winged Foliage-gleaner, found west of the Andes and sometimes considered conspecific. Olive brown above with buff lores and superciliary; *rump and tail contrastingly rufous.* Below dingy pale buffy olivaceous, tinged olive on flanks. Foregoing applies to nominate/*lyra* of Guianas and s. Amazonia west to Peru. *Subfulvus* of se. Colombia to ne. Peru similar but rump with less rufous (essentially restricted to uppertail-coverts), and often more ochraceous below. *Ochrogaster* of foothills and lower subtropical zone on e. slope of Andes from cen. Peru to Bolivia is even more strongly ochraceous-tinged below (*especially on throat*) and shows considerable rufous on rump.

SIMILAR SPECIES: *Subfulvus* race of Rufous-rumped, which shows less rufous on rump, is especially easily confused with Rufous-tailed Foliage-gleaner. Best distinguishing points (not easy to confirm in the field) are Rufous-tailed's faint olivaceous mottling on breast and its completely olive rump contrasting with rufous tail. Rufous-tailed is never as ochraceous below as *ochrogaster* or (sometimes) *subfulvus* Rufous-rumped, but Rufous-tailed can look quite yellowish throated. Buff-fronted Foliage-gleaner also somewhat resembles *ochrogaster* Rufous-rumped (they overlap on e. slope of Andes), but Buff-fronted is larger, contrastingly rufous on wings, and shows some buff on forehead.

HABITAT AND BEHAVIOR: Uncommon in lower growth and (especially) middle levels of humid forest (occasionally at borders), in lowlands mainly in terra firme, on e. slope of Andes ranging up into montane forest. Behavior much like Chestnut-winged Foliage-gleaner's, but Rufous-rumped is more apt to occur lower (and therefore is much more likely to be captured in mist-nets). Its rather infrequently heard song (at least in Ecuador) is an undistinctive, slightly descending series of high-pitched notes.

RANGE: Guianas, Amaz. Brazil (south to n. Goiás on Bananal Is. and s. Mato Grosso on the Serra dos Parecis, and east to n. Maranhão), n. Bolivia (south to La Paz, Cochabamba, and n. Santa Cruz), e. Peru, e. Ecuador (most numerous in foothills), and se. Colombia (north to w. Meta). To about 1600 m.

NOTE: Does not include *P. fuscipennis* (Slaty-winged Foliage-gleaner) of nw. Colombia and w. Ecuador, which differs markedly in several plumage characters. Sibley and Monroe (1990) suggest that *P. ochrogaster* (Ochre-bellied Foliage-gleaner) of Peru and Bolivia be treated as a separate species, and its foothill distribution, above the lowland range of the different-appearing race *lyra*, would seem to suggest that this might be correct. No intermediate specimens are known (*fide* J. V. Remsen, Jr.), but some specimens of *subfulvus* from s. Ecuador do seem to show intermediacy toward *ochrogaster*. Pending a more thorough examination of their contact zone, and given the apparent similarity of their primary vocalizations (Parker et al. 1992), we retain *ochrogaster* as a subspecies of *P. erythrocercus*.

Philydor ruficaudatus

RUFOUS-TAILED FOLIAGE-GLEANER

DESCRIPTION: 17 cm (6¾"). S. Venezuela and the Guianas to Amazonia. Olive brown above (*including rump*) with buff lores and superciliary; *tail contrastingly rufous*. Below dingy pale buffy olivaceous, the throat tinged yellowish and with *some olivaceous mottling on breast*, flanks tinged olive. See V-20, C-26. *Flavipectus* (tepui region) has more ochraceous superciliary and auriculars.

SIMILAR SPECIES: *Often* confused with the frequently sympatric Rufous-rumped foliage-gleaner. Nominate/*lyra* group of that species (e. and s. Amazonia) differs in having rufous extending to rump and no breast mottling; as it has less rufous on rump, *subfulvus* (nw. Amazonia) is even more similar, differing mainly in lacking breast mottling. HABITAT AND BEHAVIOR: Uncommon in middle levels and subcanopy of terra firme forest. General behavior similar to Rufous-rumped's, though Rufous-tailed almost always is seen accompanying canopy flocks (sometimes with Chestnut-winged Foliage-gleaner), whereas Rufous-rumped seems to accompany understory flocks. We do not know Rufous-tailed's voice. RANGE: Guianas, s. Venezuela (Bolívar and Amazonas), se. Colombia (north to Meta and Vaupés), e. Ecuador (few records), e. Peru, n. Bolivia (south to La Paz and Cochabamba), and Amaz. Brazil (mainly south of the Amazon, where ranging south to n. Mato Grosso, and east to n. Maranhão; north of the Amazon only in Amapá and adjacent Pará, and close to the Venezuelan border). Mostly below 800 m, but recorded to 1300 m in Venezuela.

Philydor rufus

BUFF-FRONTED FOLIAGE-GLEANER   PLATE: 10

DESCRIPTION: 18.5–19 cm (7¼–7½"). Mainly montane from Venezuela to s. Brazil and ne. Argentina. Bill mostly or entirely black, but trans-Andean *riveti*'s bill is pale. *Forehead and broad superciliary ochra-*

ceous buff contrasting with gray crown and stripe behind eye; otherwise olive brown above with somewhat contrasting rufous wings and rufous-brown tail. Below uniform ochraceous buff. Foregoing applies to nominate group of se. South America. Birds from most of Andean range and Venezuela (*columbianus* group) are similar but duller, with less contrasting head pattern (less gray on crown, less buff on forehead); see V-20. Birds from w. slope of Andes (*riveti*) are somewhat smaller, shorter tailed, darker overall with olivaceous wash on underparts aside from throat, and likewise have dull head pattern; see C-26.

SIMILAR SPECIES: In se. South America confusion is most likely with smaller Ochre-breasted Foliage-gleaner which, however, has *entirely grayish crown* (locally sympatric nominate Buff-fronted has a *conspicuous* buff forehead). In higher mts. of se. Brazil, cf. also Brown Tanager (*Orchesticus*), which has an astonishingly similar coloration and plumage pattern but can be known by its considerably heavier bill. In Peru and Bolivia, Buff-fronted Foliage-gleaner can be confused with *ochrogaster* race of Rufous-rumped, which is smaller and has no rufous on wings and no buff on forehead. Russet Antshrike has somewhat similar overall pattern and often occurs with Buff-fronted on lower Andean slopes, sometimes in the same flock, but differs substantially in its bull-headed, short-tailed shape and very heavy bill.

HABITAT AND BEHAVIOR: Uncommon to locally fairly common in subcanopy and canopy of humid and montane forest, sometimes coming lower at borders; perhaps most numerous in se. South America. In se. Peru lowlands this mainly montane foliage-gleaner occurs primarily in riparian forest (D. Stotz). Usually seen singly and in pairs, most often with mixed flocks, and generally quite conspicuous. Forages by hopping and twisting along branches and in terminal foliage, often quite acrobatically hanging upside down as it searches for prey. The most frequently heard vocalization, apparently much alike throughout its range, is a slightly descending, fast series of rather sharp, metallic, woodpecker-like notes, "whi-ki-ki-ki-ke-ke-ke-kuh-kuh."

RANGE: Coastal mts. of n. Venezuela (Carabobo east to Miranda); locally in mts. of s. Venezuela (n. Amazonas and nw. Bolívar); Andes of Colombia (E. Andes from Santander to Cundinamarca; Cen. Andes in Antioquia and Caldas; W. Andes from s. Chocó southward), Ecuador (on w. slope south to Pichincha and in El Oro, on e. slope south locally from w. Napo), e. Peru (where also ranging down into adjacent lowlands in Madre de Dios), and w. Bolivia (south to Chuquisaca); s. Brazil (Espírito Santo south to n. Rio Grande do Sul, and inland locally to s. Mato Grosso), e. Paraguay, and ne. Argentina (Misiones and ne. Corrientes). Also Costa Rica and w. Panama. To 1800 m.

NOTE: More than one species is perhaps involved.

Philydor lichtensteini **OCHRE-BREASTED FOLIAGE-GLEANER** PLATE: 10

DESCRIPTION: 18 cm (7″). *Se. Brazil area.* Rather short bill. *Crown and nape grayish* with slight scaly effect, merging into brown back; *long*

ochraceous buff superciliary and gray stripe behind eye; wings rufous and tail rufous-brown. Ochraceous below, tinged olivaceous on sides and flanks.

SIMILAR SPECIES: Frequently sympatric Buff-fronted Foliage-gleaner is larger and shows a buff forehead, prominent in the field. Cf. also Planalto Foliage-gleaner.

HABITAT AND BEHAVIOR: Fairly common to common in middle levels and canopy of humid forest and mature secondary woodland. Behavior much like Buff-fronted Foliage-gleaner's, though tending to be less conspicuous, foraging more by inspecting dead leaves and tangles in less exposed situations (not as often out among terminal branches). Its descending primary vocalization also is similar to Buff-fronted's. Seems capable of persisting in degraded and patchy woodland. Numerous around Iguazú Falls.

RANGE: Se. Brazil (s. Bahia south to n. Rio Grande do Sul, and inland to s. Goiás and s. Mato Grosso do Sul), e. Paraguay (Amambay southward), and ne. Argentina (Misiones). To 800 m.

GROUP B

More furtive species, mainly in *undergrowth; rich ochraceous* underparts.

Philydor dimidiatus

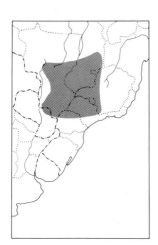

PLANALTO FOLIAGE-GLEANER   PLATE: 10
Other: Russet-mantled Foliage-gleaner

DESCRIPTION: 17–17.5 cm (6¾–7″). A *uniform*-looking foliage-gleaner found primarily on *Brazil's central plateau. Above bright olive brown* with *long superciliary and sides of neck rich ochraceous;* wings slightly more rufescent than back; tail rufous-chestnut. *Below uniform rich ochraceous,* washed with olivaceous on flanks. Foregoing applies to *baeri* of Goiás and Minas Gerais. Nominate race of Mato Grosso and Paraguay similar but apparently with more uniform and brighter *cinnamon brown back.*

SIMILAR SPECIES: Buff-fronted and Ochre-breasted Foliage-gleaners both show gray on crown and are much less richly colored below. Henna-crowned Foliage-gleaner is larger, lacks any superciliary, and its crown and nape contrast with back.

HABITAT AND BEHAVIOR: Rare to locally uncommon in lower and middle growth of humid and gallery forest and woodland. Usually found singly or in pairs, most often not with mixed flocks, foraging along limbs and among epiphytic vegetation. Its loud song is a distinctive series of strongly emphasized, harsh metallic "chek" notes preceded by a softer accelerating chatter and ending with a slowing chatter, thus "chededede-chéh-chéh-chéh-chéh-chéh-chéh-chéh-chéh-chéh-cheh-che-che-ch-ch-ch." Foraging birds give a loud, nasal, single or doubled "chéh" note. Can be found near the public pool at Brasília Nat. Park.

RANGE: Locally in interior s. Brazil (s. Mato Grosso and Goiás south to w. Paraná and sw. Minas Gerais) and extreme ne. Paraguay (Concepción). To 1200 m.

NOTE: The English name of this scarce and obscure species (we still have not seen a specimen of the nominate race) has generally been given as the Russet-mantled

Foliage-gleaner. Although its mantle is somewhat rufescent, it is not markedly more so than the rest of its upperparts; in fact, the species gives a rather uniform impression. We prefer to change the species' name to highlight its limited range, essentially restricted to the central plateau of Brazil, the planalto.

Philydor pyrrhodes

CINNAMON-RUMPED FOLIAGE-GLEANER PLATE: 10

DESCRIPTION: 16.5–17 cm (6½–6¾"). Guianas and s. Venezuela to Amazonia. Brown above with *bright cinnamon lores and superciliary* and *contrasting slaty wings; rump and tail bright pale cinnamon*. Entire underparts rich bright ochraceous.

SIMILAR SPECIES: One of the handsomest foliage-gleaners and essentially unmistakable in its *Amazonian* range.

HABITAT AND BEHAVIOR: Rare to uncommon in lower and (less often) middle growth of humid forest, ranging both in terra firme (where most often near streams) and várzea; shows a predilection for areas where understory palms are numerous. Usually found singly or in pairs, most often independent of mixed understory flocks but occasionally with them. Rather shy and often difficult to see well, tending to remain in thick cover, clambering about in foliage and rummaging in hanging dead leaves and other suspended debris. Foraging birds sometimes give a loud "chak!" call; we do not know any primary vocalization.

RANGE: Guianas, s. Venezuela (Bolívar and Amazonas), se. Colombia (north to Meta and Vaupés), e. Ecuador, ne. and se. Peru, n. Bolivia (Pando, Beni, and ne. Santa Cruz), and Amaz. Brazil (east to n. Maranhão, and south to Rondônia and w. Mato Grosso). To 700 m.

Philydor fuscipennis

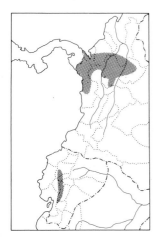

SLATY-WINGED FOLIAGE-GLEANER

Other: Rufous-rumped Foliage-gleaner (in part)

DESCRIPTION: 17 cm (6¾"). *Nw. Colombia and w. Ecuador;* sometimes considered conspecific with Rufous-rumped Foliage-gleaner, found east of Andes. Resembles Cinnamon-rumped Foliage-gleaner (also found only east of Andes) but has dusky wings, rufous rump and tail (not nearly so bright or pale), and (except on throat) considerably duller and more olivaceous underparts. See P-20.

SIMILAR SPECIES: In its range west of Andes, this relatively boldly patterned foliage-gleaner is easily recognized; note especially its bold buff superciliary and contrasting dusky wings.

HABITAT AND BEHAVIOR: Uncommon and somewhat local in lower and middle growth of humid forest and mature second-growth woodland, occasionally at borders. Behavior much like Cinnamon-rumped Foliage-gleaner's, though usually more conspicuous and regularly with flocks. Foraging birds give a sharp "chef!" call; we do not know any primary vocalization. Small numbers occur at the Río Palenque Field Station in Pichincha, Ecuador.

RANGE: Nw. Colombia (humid Caribbean lowlands east to n. Santander and n. Caldas, and Pacific lowlands of Chocó); w. Ecuador (locally from s. Pichincha to nw. Azuay). Also Panama. To 1200 m.

NOTE: Until recently (Hilty and Brown 1986, Ridgely and Gwynne 1989) considered conspecific with *P. erythrocercus* (Rufous-rumped Foliage-gleaner). We remain uncertain what its closest relative in *Philydor* is; it and *P. erythrocercus* may form a superspecies pair, or *P. fuscipennis* may be more closely related to the at least superficially similar *P. pyrrhodes*.

Philydor atricapillus

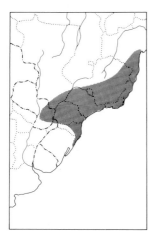

BLACK-CAPPED FOLIAGE-GLEANER   PLATE: 10

DESCRIPTION: 16.5–17 cm (6½–6¾"). *Se. Brazil area. Crown, stripe behind eye, and stripe outlining lower edge of ear-coverts black* contrasting sharply with bright buff postocular stripe, whitish ocular area, and *orange-rufous nape and sides of neck;* back rufescent brown becoming *bright cinnamon-rufous on rump and tail;* wings dusky brown. *Below uniform bright ochraceous.* The reported north-south cline in overall tonality, from bright and rufescent to dull and olivaceous (Vaurie 1980), is *not* evident in MZUSP or AMNH specimens (D. Stotz; RSR).

SIMILAR SPECIES: Exceptionally handsome, this foliage-gleaner is readily recognized. In Alagoas, ne. Brazil, cf. the closely related and newly described Alagoas Foliage-gleaner (but no overlap).

HABITAT AND BEHAVIOR: Uncommon to locally fairly common but usually inconspicuous in lower growth of humid forest and mature secondary woodland, sometimes where there are extensive bamboo thickets. Generally seen singly or in pairs accompanying mixed understory flocks; forages actively and often even acrobatically, sometimes even clinging onto trunks, probing into crevices and dead leaves from a variety of occasionally contorted positions. The song is a rather musical, fast trill which descends in pitch (somewhat reminiscent of Long-billed Gnatwren's song except for the drop in pitch). It also gives an irregular series of 3–7 squeaky notes (D. Stotz). Overall numbers have declined because of widespread deforestation across much of its range, but the species seems capable of persisting in somewhat degraded and patchy woodland.

RANGE: Se. Brazil (s. Bahia south to ne. Rio Grande do Sul, and inland to s. Mato Grosso do Sul), e. Paraguay (west to Paraguarí), and ne. Argentina (Misiones). To 1050 m.

NOTE: *Philydor hylobius* (Neblina Foliage-gleaner) was described in 1956 on the basis of two specimens from Cerro de la Neblina in Amazonas, Venezuela. Vaurie (1980) considered *hylobius* an "isolated population" of *P. atricapillus,* seemingly not even giving it subspecific rank. R. W. Dickerman et al. (*Auk* 103[2]: 431–432, 1986), however, demonstrated conclusively that *hylobius* was only the juvenal plumage of the White-throated Foliage-gleaner (*Automolus roraimae*).

Philydor novaesi

ALAGOAS FOLIAGE-GLEANER

DESCRIPTION: 18 cm (7"). *Ne. Brazil in Alagoas.* Resembles Black-capped Foliage-gleaner (clearly its northerly replacement), but differs in somewhat larger size and *less striking and contrasting head pattern,* with browner (not so pure black) crown, narrower buff superciliary, and *much browner (not orange-rufous) nape and sides of neck.*

SIMILAR SPECIES: The only *Philydor* foliage-gleaner in its limited range.

HABITAT AND BEHAVIOR: Apparently rare in undergrowth of second-growth woodland and woodland borders. Recently discovered on the slopes of Pedra Branca (= "Serra" Branca; Collar et al. 1992), a range of low coastal mts. north of Murici in Alagoas. The *least* numerous of the 4 bird species recently described from there (the others being Alagoas Tyrannulet and Alagoas and Orange-bellied Antwrens), and as the area is one of the very few in ne. Brazil with any forest extant, the foliage-gleaner deserves formal endangered status; an effort is currently underway to protect at least some of the forest that remains (Collar et al. 1992). Behavior similar to Black-capped Foliage-gleaner's, likewise usually seen singly or in pairs while accompanying small mixed flocks of understory birds. In Oct. 1987, RSR and T. Schulenberg heard no vocalizations; D. M. Teixera and L. P. Gonzaga (*Bol. Mus. Par. Emílio Goeldi,* Zool., nov. sér., no. 124, 1983) describe a descending series of whistles, "uü-uü-uü-uü-uü," and a "thürr" alarm call.

RANGE: Ne. Brazil (Alagoas). 400–550 m.

NOTE: A newly described species: D. M. Teixera and L. P. Gonzaga (op. cit.).

Anabazenops Foliage-gleaners

A monotypic genus of strikingly patterned foliage-gleaner found in se. Brazil. Its rather heavy bill has a relatively straight culmen and upturned gonys. Vaurie (1980) merged the genus into his expanded *Philydor.*

Anabazenops fuscus

WHITE-COLLARED FOLIAGE-GLEANER   PLATE: 10

DESCRIPTION: 19–19.5 cm (7½–7¾"). A *strikingly patterned* foliage-gleaner found only in *se. Brazil.* Rather heavy straight bill mostly bluish horn with blackish on ridge. Above brown with *very contrasting white superciliary, throat, and sides of neck, the last extending around nape as a nuchal collar;* tail rufous. Remaining underparts buffy whitish, brownest on crissum.

SIMILAR SPECIES: No other foliage-gleaner shows such a contrast; cf. White-eyed Foliage-gleaner (lacks collar, etc.). Female of sympatric White-bearded Antshrike has a similar pattern, but its bill is stouter and less pointed and its crown and wings are rufous.

HABITAT AND BEHAVIOR: Fairly common in lower growth of humid forest, mature secondary woodland, and borders; particularly favors areas with extensive stands of bamboo. Found singly or in pairs, regularly with mixed flocks, and generally bold and not difficult to observe, sometimes foraging for extended periods at quite close range. Its call is a burry "wrr-jek, wrrjejek, wrrjejek, wrrjejek" with a distinctive cadence. Readily seen at lower elevations of Itatiaia Nat. Park.

RANGE: Se. Brazil (Espírito Santo and cen. Minas Gerais south to e. Santa Catarina). 500–1200 m (lower?).

Automolus Foliage-gleaners

Drab, fairly large foliage-gleaners with generally rather heavy bills (varying somewhat in length). More robust than the generally similar *Philydor* foliage-gleaners, *Automolus* usually lack a superciliary; some species have indistinct eye-rings and many have contrastingly colored, white or buff, throats. Juvenal plumages are more ochraceous generally, often especially on the underparts, this most marked in White-throated and Dusky-cheeked. These birds of the understory of humid lowland forest (none is as arboreal as most *Philydor*) tend to be shy and inconspicuous, lurking in heavy cover. They advertise their presence through their far-carrying vocalizations, given especially at dawn and dusk. Nests are placed at the end of burrows dug into earthen banks. Note that three species often placed in *Automolus* are here separated generically: *erythrocephalus* and *rectirostris* are placed in *Hylocryptus,* and *ruficollis* has been transferred to *Syndactyla.*

GROUP A

Throat white to buffy-white.

Automolus leucophthalmus

WHITE-EYED FOLIAGE-GLEANER   PLATE: II

DESCRIPTION: 19–19.5 cm (7½–7¾"). *E. Brazil and adjacent Paraguay and Argentina. Iris white.* Above rufescent brown with rump and tail bright cinnamon-rufous. *Throat white* (often puffed out), becoming pale ochraceous on sides of breast and darkening to dull brownish on belly.

SIMILAR SPECIES: The only *Automolus* foliage-gleaner in its range. Greater Thornbird, also pale eyed (though iris *yellow,* not white), is superficially similar but occupies an entirely different habitat (shrubbery and damp thickets, not forest and woodland undergrowth).

HABITAT AND BEHAVIOR: Uncommon to fairly common in undergrowth of humid forest and secondary woodland, often where there is a dense understory of bamboo, sometimes in tangles at borders. Usually seen singly or in pairs and, for an *Automolus* foliage-gleaner, not too shy or difficult to see; regularly accompanies mixed flocks. Forages by rummaging through viny thickets and among dead leaves. All of its calls are loud and attract attention, the most characteristic being a fast rhythmic "ki-deee, ki-dee, ki-dee, ki-dee, ki-dee, ki-dee," sometimes varied to a "ki-trrr, ki-trrr, ki-trrr, ki-trrr." This species continues to be relatively widespread despite much forest destruction across its range; it persists well in degraded and fragmented woodland patches.

RANGE: E. Brazil (Paraíba south to Rio Grande do Sul, and inland into s. Goiás and se. Mato Grosso), e. Paraguay (west to Paraguarí), and ne. Argentina (Misiones and probably ne. Corrientes). To about 1000 m.

Automolus roraimae

WHITE-THROATED FOLIAGE-GLEANER   PLATE: II
Includes: Neblina Foliage-gleaner

DESCRIPTION: 18 cm (7"). *Tepuis of s. Venezuela.* Above dark rufescent brown, somewhat sootier on crown, with *white superciliary* and *blackish*

cheeks; rump and tail rufous-chestnut. *Throat white to buffy whitish, contrasting* with brown remaining underparts (somewhat more rufescent in *duidae* of s. Amazonas).

SIMILAR SPECIES: Generally occurs at higher elevations than other *Automolus* in its range. Olive-backed, the most similar, is duller generally with superciliary obscure or lacking, cheeks concolor, and little or no contrast on underparts.

HABITAT AND BEHAVIOR: Uncommon to locally common in lower and middle growth of humid forest and stunted woodland. Tends to be less skulking and to forage higher above ground than other *Automolus* foliage-gleaners, thus often easier to see; usually seen singly or in pairs accompanying mixed flocks. Sometimes forages by hitching along limbs and briefly even up trunks. We do not know its voice. Small numbers can be seen along the Escalera road in e. Bolívar.

RANGE: Tepuis of s. Venezuela (Bolívar and Amazonas) and adjacent extreme n. Brazil (Roraima); likely occurs in adjacent Guyana as well. Mostly 1100–2400 m.

NOTE: R. W. Dickerman et al. (*Auk* 103[2]: 431–432, 1986) showed that it was the juvenal plumage of *A. roraimae* (with more ochraceous superciliary and throat, etc.) that had been described under the name of *Philydor hylobius* (Neblina Foliage-gleaner). Although our field experience with the species is relatively limited, so far as we know *roraimae*'s behavior seems more reminiscent of a *Philydor* foliage-gleaner than an *Automolus*. Originally described in the genus *Philydor* (as *P. albigularis*), it is possible that the species will ultimately better be placed in *Philydor*.

Automolus dorsalis

DUSKY-CHEEKED FOLIAGE-GLEANER   PLATE: II
Other: Crested Foliage-gleaner

DESCRIPTION: 18.5 cm (7¼"). Local in w. Amazonia, mainly in *bamboo thickets.* Rather stout bill. Above rufescent brown with *narrow buffy whitish superciliary* and faint eye-ring, and *dusky cheeks;* rump and tail rufous-chestnut. *Throat creamy whitish;* remaining underparts pale brownish gray, deepest on sides.

SIMILAR SPECIES: Olive-backed Foliage-gleaner, which sometimes occurs with Dusky-cheeked, is similar, though duller overall; Olive-backed differs mainly in its more olivaceous (not so rufescent) upperparts, lack of an obvious superciliary, and concolor olivaceous cheeks.

HABITAT AND BEHAVIOR: Rare to uncommon and seemingly local in lower growth of humid forest and secondary woodland and borders, in many areas found primarily or entirely inside bamboo thickets. Usually found singly or in pairs and generally even shier and more difficult to see than its congeners. Its most frequent vocalization is a quite loud, measured "tcho-tcho-tcho-tcho-tcho-tcho-tcho" (the number of notes varying) with quality similar to Ferruginous Pygmy-Owl's (*Glaucidium brasilianum*); excited birds give a variety of other calls, among them a very lengthy (sometimes for a minute or more without pause!) chattering.

RANGE: Foothills and adjacent lowlands of se. Colombia (north to w. Caquetá), e. Ecuador, e. Peru (Loreto south locally to Madre de Dios), and extreme nw. Bolivia (n. La Paz at Alto Madidi); w. Amaz.

Brazil (near Cachoeira Nazaré in Rondônia; Alta Floresta in n. Mato Grosso). To 1200 m.

NOTE: We do not know the derivation of the totally misleading English name Crested Foliage-gleaner, used in most recent literature. *A. dorsalis* never shows any semblance of a crest. Accurate and useful descriptive names are difficult to coin in a group as obscure and uniform as the *Automolus* foliage-gleaners; we opt to emphasize its rather prominent dusky cheeks.

Automolus infuscatus

OLIVE-BACKED FOLIAGE-GLEANER

DESCRIPTION: 19 cm (7½"). One of the more common Amaz. foliage-gleaners. *Uniform brownish olive above* with *indistinct* whitish eye-ring and streaking on ear-coverts; rump and tail rufous-chestnut. *Throat white* (often puffed out); remaining underparts pale drab grayish, darker on sides and flanks. See V-20, C-26.

SIMILAR SPECIES: Much less numerous Dusky-cheeked Foliage-gleaner differs in its more rufescent (less olivaceous) upperparts, prominent superciliary, and dusky (not concolor) cheeks. Buff-throated Foliage-gleaners in Amazonia have buff (not white) throat and pale flammulation on breast.

HABITAT AND BEHAVIOR: Fairly common to common in undergrowth of humid forest (especially in terra firme, smaller numbers in várzea). Usually seen singly or in pairs accompanying mixed flocks of *Myrmotherula* antwrens and other understory birds. Clambers about actively and often acrobatically (frequently upside down) in tangled lower growth, occasionally working upward in vine tangles into mid-levels, inspecting suspended dead leaves and other nooks and crannies for its mainly invertebrate prey. The song is a fast, loud, ringing chatter on an even pitch, "chü-chü-chü-chü-chü-chü-chü-chü-chü"; foraging birds also give a 2-noted "chík-wah" as a contact note.

RANGE: Guianas, s. Venezuela (Bolívar and Amazonas), e. Colombia (north to Meta and Guainía), e. Ecuador, e. Peru, nw. Bolivia (Pando at Camino Mucden, La Paz at Alto Madidi), and Amaz. Brazil (east to Maranhão, and south to se. Mato Grosso). To 700 m.

GROUP B   *Throat buff to rich ochraceous.*

Automolus ochrolaemus

BUFF-THROATED FOLIAGE-GLEANER   PLATE: 11

DESCRIPTION: 18.5–19 cm (7¼–7½"). Widespread in tropical lowland forests. *Iris dark.* Nominate group (including *turdinus;* east of Andes) is olive brown above with *buff eye-ring,* indistinct superciliary, and streaking on ear-coverts; rump and tail rufous-chestnut. *Throat pale buff;* remaining underparts dull brownish, *flammulated with pale buff on breast.* Nominate race (e. Peru south of the Amazon, nw. Bolivia, and sw. Amaz. Brazil) has throat brighter buff. Birds found west of Andes (*pallidigularis*) differ in having *throat whitish* and less flammulation on breast; see P-20.

SIMILAR SPECIES: Regularly occurs with similar Olive-backed Foliage-gleaner; Olive-backed differs in area of overlap in its white throat and

grayer underparts which lack any of Buff-throated's distinctive flammulated effect. Brown-rumped and Chestnut-crowned Foliage-gleaners have buff to ochre throats much like sympatric Buff-throateds, but they have bright-colored eyes with *no* eye-ring and lack flammulation below.

HABITAT AND BEHAVIOR: Uncommon to fairly common in undergrowth of humid forest (in Amazonia mainly in terra firme) and mature secondary woodland. Usually found singly or in pairs, clambering about actively in dense tangled growth, rummaging in dead leaves and thick vegetation where often difficult to see well. Frequently accompanies mixed understory flocks, in Amazonia occasionally even with Olive-backed Foliage-gleaner. Buff-throated's presence is frequently made known at dawn and just before dusk by its distinctive song, a short series of well-enunciated, descending notes, "kee-kee-krr-krr" or "ki, ki, ki-ki-kekekrrr"; the number of notes varies, but despite the species' wide range, there is no evident geographic variation.

RANGE: N. and w. Colombia (east in humid Caribbean lowlands to middle Río Magdalena valley in Tolima) and w. Ecuador (south to w. Guayas and Los Ríos); Guianas, s. Venezuela (Bolívar and Amazonas), e. Colombia (north to Meta and Vaupés, likely in Guainía as well), e. Ecuador, e. Peru, n. Bolivia (south to La Paz, Cochabamba, and Santa Cruz), and Amaz. Brazil (east to the lower Rio Tapajós and Amapá, south to s. Mato Grosso). Also Mexico to Panama. To about 1300 m.

Automolus rufipileatus

CHESTNUT-CROWNED FOLIAGE-GLEANER

DESCRIPTION: 19.5 cm (7¾"). Local in Amazonia and Guianas. *Iris bright yellow-orange.* Uniform rufescent brown above with *slightly contrasting rufous-chestnut crown;* rump and tail rufous-chestnut. Throat pale buffyish; remaining underparts drab pale olivaceous brown. See V-20, C-26. *Maynanus* (Bolivia and Peru from at least Junín southward) is more ochraceous below (and hence more uniform).

SIMILAR SPECIES: Buff-throated Foliage-gleaner has a dark eye surrounded by a buff eye-ring and an obviously flammulated breast. Brown-rumped Foliage-gleaner also has a brightly colored eye but it has a notably shorter bill, uniform rufescent brown upperparts (with no chestnut crown), and a brighter, more orange ochraceous throat (particularly on its sides). Cf. also Ruddy Foliage-gleaner.

HABITAT AND BEHAVIOR: Uncommon to locally fairly common in thick undergrowth of várzea and riparian forest (especially in areas with dense stands of *Gynerium* cane), and on river islands; in some areas favors *Guadua* bamboo patches in terra firme forest. Behavior similar to other *Automolus* foliage-gleaners' but even more skulking and often difficult even to glimpse (partly because of the dense nature of its habitat), and seems less inclined to join mixed flocks. Heard far more often than seen. Its song resembles Olive-backed Foliage-gleaner's, though somewhat faster and usually with a descending effect, "kee-ee-ee-rr-rr-rrrrrrrr."

RANGE: Locally in sw. Venezuela (north to w. Barinas), e. Colombia (near base of Andes; away from them only in the Leticia area of Amazonas), ne. Ecuador, e. Peru, n. Bolivia (south to La Paz and Cochabamba), Amaz. Brazil (apparently absent from much of cen. Amaz. Brazil, both north and south of the Amazon; in e. Amazonia south to n. Mato Grosso at Alta Floresta and east to n. Maranhão), s. Venezuela (w. Bolívar and s. Amazonas), and Guianas (where evidently absent from coastal areas). To 1300 m (but mostly below 500 m).

Automolus melanopezus

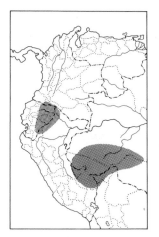

BROWN-RUMPED FOLIAGE-GLEANER PLATE: II

DESCRIPTION: 18.5 cm (7¼"). Local in w. Amazonia. *Iris red to orange.* Uniform dark rufescent brown above; tail rufous-chestnut. *Throat ochraceous orange, brightest on its sides;* remaining underparts drab pale olivaceous brown.

SIMILAR SPECIES: Resembles Buff-throated Foliage-gleaner (especially that species' nominate race of sw. Amazonia), but Buff-throated differs in its dark eye, buff eye-ring and faint superciliary, and flammulated breast. Chestnut-crowned Foliage-gleaner, also with a brightly colored eye, differs in its rufous-chestnut crown and duller throat. Cf. also Ruddy Foliage-gleaner.

HABITAT AND BEHAVIOR: Rare to locally uncommon in undergrowth of terra firme and transitional forest, in sw. Amazonia especially or entirely in stands of *Guadua* bamboo. A reclusive and infrequently encountered *Automolus,* tending to forage inside very thick cover, occasionally mounting to about 5 m above the ground; sometimes accompanies mixed flocks. Its song is a distinctive, fast, and rhythmic "whit, whit, whididididit-wrrrrrrr." Can be found at Tambopata Reserve in Madre de Dios, Peru.

RANGE: Se. Colombia (w. Putumayo), e. Ecuador, and adjacent ne. Peru (n. Loreto at the mouth of the Río Curaray); se. Peru (s. Ucayali, Madre de Dios, and adjacent Cuzco), extreme nw. Bolivia (Pando at Camino Mucden), and sw. Amaz. Brazil (upper Rios Purus and Juruá, and at Cachoeira Nazaré in Rondônia). To 500 m.

Automolus rubiginosus

RUDDY FOLIAGE-GLEANER PLATE: II

DESCRIPTION: 18–19 cm (7–7½"). *Disjunct* in n. and w. South America. Birds from west of Andes, except on Santa Marta Mts. (*nigricauda* group), are *very dark overall:* dark rufescent brown above becoming more chestnut on head and neck; *tail black; throat and upper chest rich rufous,* becoming olivaceous brown on remaining underparts and umber brown on lower belly and crissum. Birds of w. Amazonia (*brunnescens* group) are somewhat larger; they are slightly paler above with a concolor crown and are quite markedly paler below (with throat and chest orange-rufous); crown is concolor with back except in *watkinsi* (se. Peru and w. Bolivia), in which contrastingly chestnut; and tail is *rufous-chestnut.* Birds from ne. South America (*obscurus* group) resemble W. Amaz. birds in color but are smaller (about the size

of *nigricauda* group) and have a shorter bill. Santa Marta birds (*rufipectus*) are the palest and most "ruddy" race.

SIMILAR SPECIES: Very dark trans-Andean races should not be confused, but cf. very differently shaped (but equally dark) *Sclerurus* leaftossers. East of Andes, Ruddy most resembles Brown-rumped Foliage-gleaner, which has a shorter bill, a brightly colored eye, and is less rufescent below with a contrasting ochraceous orange throat. Cf. also Chestnut-crowned Foliage-gleaner.

HABITAT AND BEHAVIOR: Uncommon to fairly common in undergrowth of humid and montane forest, in Amaz. lowlands mainly or entirely in terra firme; apparently scarcer in ne. South America. Perhaps the most skulking *Automolus* (with the Chestnut-crowned), Ruddy Foliage-gleaner usually forages in pairs independently of mixed flocks, rummaging through dense tangles generally very close to the ground, sometimes on the ground itself. It often advertises its presence with its distinctive and persistently given calls. Birds from west of Andes and w. Amazonia give a similar querulous and ascending "kweeeeahhh." Birds from ne. South America (at least in Surinam) give a quite different sharp and emphatic 2-noted "chuk-kwihhh?" (T. Davis).

RANGE: W. and n. Colombia (Pacific lowlands, and humid Caribbean lowlands east to the middle Río Magdalena valley in w. Cundinamarca) and w. Ecuador (south locally to El Oro); lower slopes of Santa Marta Mts. in n. Colombia; extreme sw. Venezuela (w. Apure), e. Colombia (locally along base of Andes), e. Ecuador, and ne. Peru (locally in San Martín and Loreto); se. Peru (Cerros del Sira in Huánuco, and in Madre de Dios and Puno), w. Bolivia (La Paz), and extreme sw. Amaz. Brazil (Acre); Guianas, s. Venezuela (Bolívar and Amazonas), and n. Amaz. Brazil (north of the Amazon and west to the Rio Negro). Also Mexico to Panama. To about 1300 m.

NOTE: More than one species may be involved. In particular, *A. obscurus* (with *venezuelanus*) of ne. South America may, by virtue of its different voice, be worthy of specific separation.

Hylocryptus Foliage-gleaners

A pair of foliage-gleaners found in deciduous and semihumid woodlands in two widely separated regions: on the Pacific slope of s. Ecuador and n. Peru, and in s.-cen. Brazil and adjacent Paraguay. The distribution pattern of this pair of species recalls that of the *Conothraupis* tanagers and the *Melanopareia* crescentchests. Both *Hylocryptus* have rather long, almost decurved bills (especially *erythrocephalus*) and are large with bright orange-rufous on the head. R. A. Paynter, Jr. (*Bull. B. O. C.* 92[6]: 154–155, 1972) proposed merging the genus *Hylocryptus* into *Automolus,* and Vaurie (1980) followed this suggestion. However, we prefer to continue to separate them generically, in part because of their very different, mainly terrestrial feeding behavior. The voice of the Henna-hooded Foliage-gleaner is also distinctly different from that of any *Automolus.*

Hylocryptus erythrocephalus

HENNA-HOODED FOLIAGE-GLEANER   PLATE: II

DESCRIPTION: 21 cm (8¼"). An unmistakable, boldly patterned foliage-gleaner found locally in *sw. Ecuador and nw. Peru*. Iris orange-brown to hazel. *Head, neck, wings, rump, and tail orange-rufous;* back contrastingly brownish olive. *Throat pale orange-rufous;* remaining underparts pale brownish gray, tinged olive brown on lower flanks and with rufous crissum.

HABITAT AND BEHAVIOR: Rare to uncommon and very local in undergrowth of deciduous forest, secondary woodland, and borders; favors ravines and occasionally occurs in very narrow strips of remnant woodland along watercourses and in adjacent, often very disturbed, scrub. This striking foliage-gleaner forages singly or in pairs, frequently with small flocks, usually remaining close to or on the ground. It tends to be noisy when feeding, flicking aside dried leaves with the bill or rummaging actively in vegetation; often it can be located by tracking down these rustling sounds. Its far-carrying calls are even better at drawing attention to its presence; the most common vocalization is a very distinctive ringing and staccato "tok-tok-tok-tok-tok-tok-tok" with an odd mechanical quality. Although it is by no means numerous, its numbers having declined in recent decades because of deforestation and woodland degradation, intensive recent field work in Ecuador has revealed considerably larger numbers persisting in more areas (some of them surprisingly degraded) than had been expected. Nonetheless the species probably deserves threatened status. Small numbers occur in several regions of southern Loja, notably around Sozoranga, east of Celica, and south of Sabanilla.

RANGE: Sw. Ecuador (mainly in e. El Oro and w. Loja, but in the early 1990s found also in the coastal cordillera of sw. Manabí and w. Guayas east to the Chongon Hills) and extreme nw. Peru (Tumbes, Piura, and Lambayeque). 400–1900 m.

Hylocryptus rectirostris

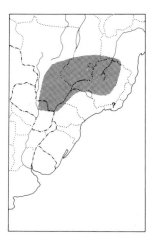

HENNA-CAPPED FOLIAGE-GLEANER   PLATE: II
Other: Chestnut-capped Foliage-gleaner

DESCRIPTION: 20.5 cm (8"). *Interior s. Brazil and adjacent Paraguay.* Iris brownish yellow. *Crown and nape orange-rufous* contrasting with *golden brown back;* wings and tail orange-rufous. *Bright pale ochraceous below,* whiter on throat and tinged olive brown on lower flanks.

SIMILAR SPECIES: Planalto Foliage-gleaner is also rather bright and pale overall but is smaller and shorter-billed and has a more pronounced superciliary without the contrasting crown.

HABITAT AND BEHAVIOR: Rare to uncommon in undergrowth of gallery forest and woodland and in patches of deciduous woodland. Poorly known. Birds seen in Emas Nat. Park in Goiás were foraging singly on or near the ground, mainly in leaf litter; they were not associated with mixed flocks. Vocalizations described by Sick (1985) include a loud "wat" and "ka, ka, ka" and a chicken-like "có-có-có-réc."

RANGE: Interior s. Brazil (s. Bahia and cen. Minas Gerais west through s. Goiás to s. Mato Grosso and Mato Grosso do Sul, and south to n. São Paulo and nw. Paraná) and ne. Paraguay (south of Concepción in San Pedro); a published report from Rio de Janeiro in Brazil (Sick 1985) remains uncorroborated. To about 1000 m.

NOTE: In the recent literature (e.g., Meyer de Schauensee 1966, 1970), *H. rectirostris* has been called the Chestnut-capped Foliage-gleaner. This name causes much confusion with the name of another species, the Chestnut-crowned Foliage-gleaner (*Automolus rufipileatus*) of Amazonia. Given that *H. rectirostris's* closest relative, the geographically distant *H. erythrocephalus,* is called the Henna-hooded Foliage-gleaner, and that the color of their crowns and napes is the same, we feel "Henna-capped" to be an appropriate and certainly much less confusing name.

Sclerurus Leaftossers

A uniform genus of cryptic, mainly dark brown furnariids with short black tails which are found solitarily on or near the ground inside humid forest, favoring damp places. Their legs are short, their bills slender; in all but one species (the aptly named Short-billed), bills are also quite long. Identification to species is often difficult, partly because all are so similar, partly because they are shy and usually hard to see well; note especially throat and chest patterns. Leaftossers never seem to be very numerous and are always encountered only infrequently, most often just by stumbling onto them; mist-netting sometimes reveals that they are more numerous than had been supposed, but even extensive netting programs rarely capture very many. Nests are placed at the end of long tunnels dug into earth banks. The misleading group name of "leafscraper" has often been used for the genus (e.g., Meyer de Schauensee 1966, 1970), but for several decades the far more accurate group name of "leaftosser" has come into increasing use, and it is employed here.

Sclerurus mexicanus

TAWNY-THROATED LEAFTOSSER   PLATE: 11

DESCRIPTION: 16–16.5 cm (6¼–6½"). Bill quite long and *slightly drooped at tip.* Dark brown above with rufous-chestnut to chestnut rump and black tail. *Throat and chest rich tawny-rufous,* becoming dark brown on remaining underparts.

SIMILAR SPECIES: The similar Short-billed Leaftosser differs most markedly in its shorter and straighter bill; it also has a paler (buffier) throat, buffyish lores, and the suggestion of a superciliary. Cf. also other leaftossers and *Cyphorhinus* wrens.

HABITAT AND BEHAVIOR: Rare to locally uncommon on or near the ground in humid forest, in Amazonia almost exclusively in terra firme, also ranging locally up into foothill forest. Furtive, mainly terrestrial, and usually solitary, Tawny-throated Leaftosser hops and shuffles in the leaf litter, using the bill to toss leaves and other debris to the side or probing into damp soil. When disturbed, it flushes a short distance giving a sharp, squeaky "tseeeét," then usually perches on a low branch, motionless except for periodically flicking the wings. Its song is a descending series of 4 or 5 high, wheezy notes, each progressively a little shorter, often ending in an accelerating chatter, "peéeeee-peéeee-peéee-peee-chrrrrr."

RANGE: N. and w. Colombia (Pacific lowlands, and east in humid Caribbean lowlands to Santander and the lower slopes of the Sierra de Perijá), extreme nw. Venezuela (lower slopes of the Sierra de Perijá), and w. Ecuador (south mainly to Pichincha and Manabí; an old record from El Oro); se. Colombia (north to w. Meta), e. Ecuador, e. Peru, n. Bolivia (south to w. Santa Cruz), and sw. Brazil (south of the Amazon east to Rondônia at Cachoeira Nazaré, and south of Tefé); Guianas, s. Venezuela (Bolívar and n. Amazonas), and e. Amaz. Brazil (north of the Amazon west to the lower Rio Negro in the Manaus area, south of it from the lower Rio Tapajós area east to Maranhão, and south locally to ne. Mato Grosso); e. Brazil (Alagoas south to ne. São Paulo). Also Mexico to Panama. Mainly below 1500 m, in small numbers to 2000 m.

Sclerurus albigularis

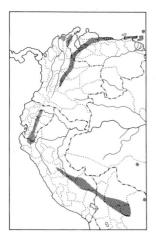

GRAY-THROATED LEAFTOSSER   PLATE: 11

DESCRIPTION: 17–18 cm (6¾–7"). Local in *foothill* forests from Venezuela to Bolivia. Above dark brown with rufous-chestnut rump and black tail. *Chin white, becoming pale ashy gray on lower throat, contrasting with rufous chest band;* lower underparts dull grayish brown.

SIMILAR SPECIES: No other leaftosser in its range has pale throat contrasting with rufous chest. Cf. Rufous-breasted Leaftosser (no overlap).

HABITAT AND BEHAVIOR: Rare to uncommon and local on or near the ground in humid and montane forest, favoring shady dank ravines. Behavior much like other leaftossers' (see Tawny-throated). Gray-throated's song is a complex and often lengthy series of often trebled notes, e.g., "kwee-kwee-kwee, kwu-kwu-kwu, kwee-kwee-kwee . . . ," repeated rapidly with a variable pattern and long musical trills interspersed (G. Diller, in Costa Rica). Perhaps most easily seen on the slopes of Trinidad's Northern Range.

RANGE: Locally on coastal mts. of n. Venezuela (east to Sucre on the Paria Peninsula), and on Andean slopes and adjacent ridges in w. Venezuela, Colombia (e. slope of E. Andes south to w. Meta), e. Ecuador, e. Peru, and Bolivia (south to w. Santa Cruz, where also known from the isolated Serranía de Huanchaca in the northeast); sw. Amaz. Brazil (n. Rondônia at Cachoeira Nazaré); Sierra de Perijá on Venezuela-Colombia border and Santa Marta Mts. in n. Colombia; Trinidad and Tobago. Also Costa Rica and w. Panama. Mostly 1000–2000 m, locally down to about 500 m.

Sclerurus scansor

RUFOUS-BREASTED LEAFTOSSER

DESCRIPTION: 18–18.5 cm (7–7¼"). *E. Brazil and adjacent areas.* Resembles Gray-throated Leaftosser (no overlap), but nominate race (most of range) has *throat whitish scaled with dusky,* with no gray on lower throat. *Cearensis* (ne. Brazil) lacks dusky scaling on throat.

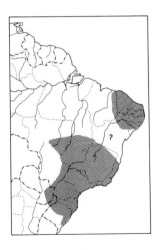

SIMILAR SPECIES: Sympatric *umbretta* race of Black-tailed Leaftosser is similar but generally darker and duller, without any rufous on chest or any rufous-chestnut on rump. Tawny-throated Leaftosser has entirely tawny-rufous throat and chest with *no* white on throat.

HABITAT AND BEHAVIOR: Rare to locally fairly common on or near ground in humid and montane forest. Behavior much like other leaftossers' (see Tawny-throated). Rufous-breasted's song is a simple, sharp descending chippered trill lasting 2–3 seconds and sometimes ending in a chatter, e.g., "chee-ee-ee-ee-ee-ee-ee-ee-ee-eu, cht, cht." Seems especially numerous at Boracéia in the Serra do Mar of São Paulo (D. Stotz).

RANGE: E. Brazil (Ceará south locally to Rio Grande do Sul and west through s. Goiás and s. Mato Grosso; apparently absent from much of Bahia and from coastal lowlands of the southeast from Espírito Santo to at least São Paulo), e. Paraguay (west to Paraguarí), and ne. Argentina (Misiones and ne. Corrientes). To about 1500 m.

Sclerurus rufigularis

SHORT-BILLED LEAFTOSSER   PLATE: 11

DESCRIPTION: 16 cm (6¼"). Amazonia. *Bill short* for the genus. Dark brown above with buffyish lores, rufous-chestnut rump, and black tail; usually a suggestion of a buffyish superciliary. *Throat cinnamon-buff* becoming more rufous on chest; remaining underparts dark brown. Foregoing applies to nominate race from south of the Amazon; birds north of the Amazon (*fulvigularis* group) are somewhat more mottled or scaled on foreneck and have less rufous on chest.

SIMILAR SPECIES: Closely resembles Tawny-throated Leaftosser. Tawny-throated differs most obviously in its longer and slightly decurved bill (Short-billed's bill is straighter); it also has a more deeply colored throat, grayish lores, etc. Cf. also other *Sclerurus*.

HABITAT AND BEHAVIOR: Rare to uncommon on or near ground in terra firme forest. Behavior much like other leaftossers' (see Tawny-throated). We do not know its voice.

RANGE: Guianas, s. Venezuela (Bolívar and Amazonas), se. Colombia (north to Meta and Vaupés), e. Ecuador (known only from 2 specimens in ANSP and MECN, taken at "Río Suno Abajo" and "Río Corrientes"; both had been confused with *S. mexicanus peruvianus*), ne. Peru (locally in Loreto and Amazonas), n. Bolivia (locally in Beni and ne. Santa Cruz on the Serranía de Huanchaca), and Amaz. Brazil (east to n. Maranhão, and south to n. Mato Grosso). Mostly below 500 m, but recorded to 900 m in Venezuela and once to 1800 m in Colombia.

Sclerurus caudacutus

BLACK-TAILED LEAFTOSSER   PLATE: 11

DESCRIPTION: 18.5 cm (7¼"). Amazonia. Above dark brown with rump slightly more chestnut; tail black. *Throat white, feathers faintly scaled darker;* remaining underparts dark brown. Foregoing applies to birds from w. and s. Amazonia (*brunneus* group). Nominate race (with

insignis) of the Guianas, s. Venezuela, and n. Brazil south to the Amazon in the Manaus area differs in having throat and chest buffier with only chin whitish, *no* dusky scaling on throat, and brighter and more contrasting rump; see V-20. Birds from e. Brazil (*umbretta*) resemble *brunneus* group but are darker generally.

SIMILAR SPECIES: Larger than the other leaftossers inhabiting Amaz. lowlands, and the only species there with whitish on throat. Confusion is most likely in range of nominate group of Black-tailed (ne. South America), especially with the potentially sympatric Tawny-throated, but latter is somewhat smaller and shows *no* white on throat.

HABITAT AND BEHAVIOR: Uncommon on or near ground in terra firme forest. Behavior similar to other leaftossers' (see Tawny-throated). Black-tailed's song (in Surinam) is a series of loud, emphatic, ringing notes which at first accelerate and then end with several rising ones, e.g., "kweet, kweet, kweet-kweet-kweet-kweet-kweekweekweekweekwee, kweet-kwee-kweet?" (T. Davis recording).

RANGE: Guianas, s. Venezuela (Bolívar and Amazonas), se. Colombia (north to Meta and Vaupés), e. Ecuador, e. Peru, extreme n. Bolivia (Pando), and Amaz. Brazil (east to n. Maranhão, and south to Rondônia); e. Brazil (Alagoas south locally to Espírito Santo). Mostly below 500 m, but recorded to 1100 m in Venezuela.

Sclerurus guatemalensis

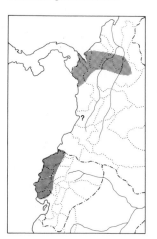

SCALY-THROATED LEAFTOSSER

DESCRIPTION: 18 cm (7″). *N. Colombia and w. Ecuador.* Resembles Black-tailed Leaftosser (no overlap). Differs from *brunneus* group of that species in having *white throat feathers conspicuously margined with black,* giving an *almost spotted effect,* and in a somewhat more rufescent chest with paler shaft streaking. See C-26.

SIMILAR SPECIES: Only sympatric leaftosser is the very different Tawny-throated, differing in its uniform tawny-rufous throat and chest and its rufous-chestnut rump.

HABITAT AND BEHAVIOR: Uncommon on or near ground in humid forest and mature secondary woodland. Behavior much like other leaftossers' (see Tawny-throated). Scaly-throated's song (in Panama) is a fast series of about 12 sharp, clear, whistled notes, often repeated many times in succession.

RANGE: Nw. and n. Colombia (Pacific lowlands in Chocó, and east in humid Caribbean lowlands to middle Río Magdalena valley in Santander; seems possible farther south in Pacific lowlands, but as yet unrecorded) and w. Ecuador (Esmeraldas south locally to w. and n. Guayas). Also Mexico to Panama. To 900 m.

Lochmias Streamcreepers

A single species of distinctively spotted, mainly terrestrial furnariid found in association with rapidly running water. Vaurie (1980) associated the genus with the behaviorally very different *Margarornis* because of their somewhat similar plumage patterns and certain tail similarities, but D. W. Rudge and R. J. Raikow (*Condor* 94[3]: 760–766, 1992) have shown that, based on anatomical characters, they cannot be considered closely related. Despite differences in nesting and plumage pattern, in our view *Lochmias* is likely closely related to the *Sclerurus* leaftossers (which have similar shape and behavior). The streamcreeper's nest is placed, like all leaftossers', at the end of a burrow dug into an earthen bank. The species' English name has been the subject of some discussion in recent years; we prefer the usual Sharp-tailed Streamcreeper, though its tail is actually rather soft (not "sharp").

Lochmias nematura

SHARP-TAILED STREAMCREEPER   PLATE: 11
Other: Streamside Lochmias

DESCRIPTION: 14.5–15 cm (5¾–6"). Local in undergrowth *along streams,* mainly in *montane* areas. Bill long and slender, somewhat decurved; *legs dull grayish pink. Dark brown above* with *irregular ("spotted") white superciliary,* mantle more rufescent; tail black. Below dark brown *profusely spotted with white.* Foregoing applies to nominate race of se. South America, with *castanonota* and *chimantae* of tepuis of s. Venezuela similar. Birds from mts. of n. Venezuela and the Andes (*obscurata* and *sororia*) are somewhat larger and longer-billed and have *black legs;* they differ further in *lacking* the white superciliary and are a darker, more chestnut brown on mantle and *less densely spotted below* (especially so on sides and flanks, which are quite uniform brown).
SIMILAR SPECIES: Shaped much like a *Sclerurus* leaftosser, but none of those show prominent spotting below. Otherwise the streamcreeper is essentially unmistakable, but cf. Spotted Barbtail.
HABITAT AND BEHAVIOR: Rare to locally fairly common on or near the ground or among rocks in humid and montane forest and mature secondary woodland, always along streams and rivers. Considerably more numerous and widespread in se. South America than elsewhere, there more often in the semiopen, regularly hopping on mossy rocks along the edge or even out in the middle of rushing streams. Behaves much like a leaftosser, and in many areas equally difficult to see; the streamcreeper almost always forages alone, hopping and shuffling quietly on the ground, probing in damp vegetation and flicking aside leaves with its bill. In se. South America its rather frequently heard song, usually delivered from a low perch, is a series of very dry unmusical notes, lasting about 5 seconds, which start slowly with a sharply accented note, then gradually accelerate until ending in a run-together chipper. The voice of Andean birds is apparently similar (P. Coopmans).
RANGE: Locally in mts. of n. Venezuela (Yaracuy east to the Distrito Federal), and in Andes of Colombia, e. Ecuador, e. Peru, w. Bolivia, and nw. Argentina (Jujuy and Salta); tepuis of s. Venezuela (locally in Bolívar and Amazonas); se. Brazil (Espírito Santo, Minas Gerais, s. Goiás, and s. Mato Grosso south to Rio Grande do Sul), e. Paraguay (west to Paraguarí), Uruguay, and ne. Argentina (south to Entre Ríos);

seems likely in w. Guyana and in nw. Colombia on Cerro Tacarcuna. Also e. Panama. Mostly below 1700 m, locally up to 2400 m or even higher.

NOTE: More than one species is perhaps involved. If split, *L. nematura* (with *castanonota* and *chimantae*) should become the Eastern Streamcreeper, *L. obscurata* (with *sororia* and *nelsoni*) the Western Streamcreeper.

<table>
<tr><td>Dendrocolaptinae</td><td colspan="2"># WOODCREEPERS</td></tr>
</table>

Dendrocolaptinae # WOODCREEPERS

THE woodcreepers form a uniform group of small to midsized scansorial birds whose stiffened tails have their exposed shafts sharply curved inwards. Until recently they were considered to represent a separate family (Dendrocolaptidae), but the consensus now seems to be to treat them as a subfamily within the Furnariidae (see Feduccia 1973). Almost all the woodcreepers are some shade of brown to rufescent brown (a few are more olivaceous), most with wings and tail rufous. There is marked variation in bill shape, ranging from short and wedge-shaped to long and sickle-shaped. The majority occur in humid and montane forests, with species diversity being highest in Amazonia. Woodcreepers are arboreal birds which forage almost entirely by hitching along trunks and branches at varying heights above the ground, probing into crevices and epiphytes and under bark. A few range in more deciduous woodland or savanna, whereas one species, the Scimitar-billed, does some of its foraging on sandy ground.

Identification to species is often based on very subtle characters, and there are still many taxonomic problems to be resolved, with species limits uncertain in several groups. Most species are quite vocal, and woodcreeper songs are often a conspicuous element of dawn and dusk choruses. Nests are usually placed inside natural cavities or woodpecker holes.

The songs and some calls of virtually all species of woodcreepers are presented in a very useful, commercially available tape recording: *Voices of the Woodcreepers* by J. W. Hardy, T. A. Parker III, and Ben B. Coffey, Jr. (ARA-17). Beware, however, of certain errors in its accompanying notes.

Dendrocincla Woodcreepers

A group of midsized, relatively unpatterned woodcreepers with straight bills found in the lower growth of humid forests, all but one species (the Tyrannine) mainly in the lowlands. Their crown feathers often look distinctively ruffled or shaggy. All the lowland *Dendrocincla* are inveterate "professional" followers of army antswarms, with several (White-chinned, Ruddy) rarely being seen away from them. Their nests are placed in holes or cavities of tree trunks which, if deep, are usually partially filled with moss.

GROUP A *Large Dendrocincla of the Andes.*

Dendrocincla tyrannina **TYRANNINE WOODCREEPER** PLATE: 12

DESCRIPTION: 24–26.5 cm (9½–10½″). A *large, uniform* woodcreeper of *Andean forests* from Venezuela to Peru. Iris brownish gray. *Essentially uniform olive brown*, throat very slightly paler and with faint buff shaft streaking on forecrown, throat, and (on some individuals) upper

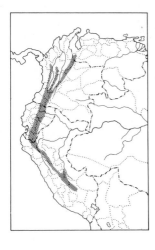

chest; wings and tail rufous-chestnut. There seems to be substantial individual size variation; females average smaller.

SIMILAR SPECIES: Cf. other *Dendrocincla* woodcreepers, all equally plain in appearance, though markedly smaller. Tyrannine occurs at *higher* elevations than other *Dendrocincla;* other sympatric montane woodcreepers show at least some obvious streaking.

HABITAT AND BEHAVIOR: Rare to locally uncommon in lower and middle growth of montane forest and forest borders, occasionally out into trees in adjacent clearings. Not well known and generally infrequently encountered. Usually found singly, often while foraging with mixed flocks; hitches up trunks and along larger lateral branches. Unlike other *Dendrocincla,* Tyrannine has not been found at army antswarms (which are scarce in its preferred elevation zone). Its song, a series of musical notes which start slowly with a few stuttered chips but quickly accelerate into a loud, ringing crescendo, lasts about 5 seconds (P. Coopmans recording).

RANGE: Andes of extreme w. Venezuela (sw. Táchira), Colombia, Ecuador (south locally on w. slope to El Oro and w. Loja), and e. Peru (south to n. Cuzco on the Cordillera Vilcabamba). Mostly 1500–3000 m, locally down to 900 m on w. slope of Andes in Cauca, Colombia.

NOTE: *Macrorhyncha,* described on the basis of two large specimens taken on the e. slope of the Andes in n. Ecuador (Pun) near the Colombian border, apparently represents individual variants of *D. tyrannina* (see Fjeldså and Krabbe 1986).

GROUP B   *"Typical" Dendrocincla of the lowlands.*

Dendrocincla fuliginosa

PLAIN-BROWN WOODCREEPER   PLATE: 12

DESCRIPTION: 19.5–21.5 cm (7¾–8½"). The most common and most widespread *Dendrocincla* woodcreeper; Plain-winged Woodcreeper of se. South America is considered by us as a separate species. Iris brownish gray (quite pale in some birds). *Meruloides* group *essentially uniform brown with paler grayish lores and auricular area* and *fairly prominent dusky malar stripe;* flight feathers and tail rufous-chestnut. *Meruloides* (n. Venezuela and Trinidad/Tobago) is more rufescent generally, whereas *ridgwayi* and *lafresnayei* (extreme w. Venezuela, n. and w. Colombia, and w. Ecuador) are more olivaceous generally. Birds from Amazonia (nominate group) and ne. Brazil (*taunayi*) are larger with a pale, often whitish, throat which merges into faint pale shaft streaking on chest, and a usually distinct, though often broken, buff postocular stripe.

SIMILAR SPECIES: The only basically uniform brown woodcreeper across most of its range. In Amazonia cf. less numerous White-chinned Woodcreeper; in nw. South America cf. more rufescent Ruddy Woodcreeper. Replaced by closely related Plain-winged Woodcreeper in se. South America and by larger Tyrannine Woodcreeper at higher elevations in Andes.

HABITAT AND BEHAVIOR: Fairly common in lower growth of humid forest and mature secondary woodland, locally and in smaller numbers also in more deciduous forest and woodland; in Amazonia found both in terra firme and várzea. Plain-brown Woodcreepers are most often seen at army antswarms; usually only a few birds are present, but occasionally up to a dozen, or even more, individuals gather. Less often they are found foraging alone, or with mixed flocks. At antswarms Plain-browns usually perch on vertical trunks but also sometimes "normally" across a horizontal branch, thence sallying out or dropping to the ground in pursuit of invertebrates attempting to flee the ants. The most common call is an abrupt, loud "sweeach," but they also give various rattles, especially at antswarms. What is evidently the song is a rapid series of sharp, high-pitched notes followed by several that gradually fade away, e.g., "keé-keé-keé-kee-kee-kee-kew-kew-kew."

RANGE: Guianas, Venezuela, Colombia, w. and e. Ecuador (west of Andes south to w. Loja), e. Peru, n. Bolivia (south to La Paz, Cochabamba, and Santa Cruz), and Amaz. Brazil (south to s. Mato Grosso and Goiás, and east to Maranhão); ne. Brazil (Pernambuco and Alagoas); Trinidad and Tobago. Also Honduras to Panama. Mostly below about 1300 m.

NOTE: Behavioral details are given by E. O. Willis (*Ecology* 47:667–672, 1966).

Dendrocincla turdina

PLAIN-WINGED WOODCREEPER
Other: Thrush-like Woodcreeper, Plain Woodcreeper

DESCRIPTION: 21 cm (8¼″). *Se. Brazil area;* formerly considered conspecific with Plain-brown Woodcreeper (no known overlap), which it resembles. *Essentially uniform brown* with faint buff shaft streaking on crown; tail rufous-chestnut (but wings basically uniform brown, *not* contrastingly rufous on flight feathers as in Plain-brown); throat plain pale buff.

SIMILAR SPECIES: The only uniform brown woodcreeper in its range. Plain-brown Woodcreeper of Amazonia northward has grayer auricular area with dusky malar stripe and contrastingly rufous flight feathers. The ranges of Plain-brown and Plain-winged Woodcreepers come closest in ne. Bahia.

HABITAT AND BEHAVIOR: Fairly common in lower and middle growth of humid forest and mature secondary woodland. Behavior, including its strong predilection for following army antswarms, similar to Plain-brown Woodcreeper's. The song, often protracted for a minute or more, is a simple series of "kik" or "keek" notes which gradually fade and then become stronger, almost at random.

RANGE: Se. Brazil (se. Bahia south to n. Rio Grande do Sul), e. Paraguay (Canendiyu to Itapúa), and ne. Argentina (Misiones). To 850 m.

NOTE: We follow E. O. Willis (*Ciencia y Cultura* 35[2]: 201–204, 1983) in considering *D. turdina* as a species separate from the widespread *D. fuliginosa*. The name "Thrush-like" Woodcreeper has been suggested (*Birds of the Americas*, vol. 13, part 4; Meyer de Schauensee 1966) for this taxon. As there is nothing more thrush-like about *D. turdina* than many other woodcreepers, we prefer to emphasize a character separating it from the similar *D. fuliginosa*, the plain wings (without rufous) being the most striking.

Dendrocincla merula

WHITE-CHINNED WOODCREEPER   PLATE: 12

DESCRIPTION: 19–20 cm (7½–8″). Amazonia; perhaps 2 species involved. *Iris bluish gray* in most of range but *rufous brown* in nominate/*obidensis* of Guianas and n. Amaz. Brazil. Above uniform rufescent brown; wings and tail rufous-chestnut. *Small, sharply contrasting white throat patch;* remaining underparts brown to olivaceous brown, crissum rufous. Nominate/*obidensis* similar but somewhat larger.

SIMILAR SPECIES: Resembles generally more numerous Plain-brown Woodcreeper. Plain-brown has brownish gray iris, grayish auriculars and dusky malar (White-chinned's sides of head look plain), and less extensive rufous on wings (only flight feathers); Plain-brown's throat may appear paler than rest of underparts, but it is never as discrete and contrastingly whitish as in White-chinned.

HABITAT AND BEHAVIOR: Rare to locally fairly common in undergrowth of humid forest, mainly in terra firme. Behavior similar to Plain-brown Woodcreeper's, but White-chinned's foraging is even more tied to army antswarms; E. O. Willis, in months of studying this bird, never saw one away from a swarm! More than a pair or family group of White-chinneds is almost never present together; they forage closer to the ground than Plain-browns. The song near Manaus (*obidensis*) is a simple, fast "kew-kew-kew-kew-kew-kew-kew-kew-kuup" (E. O. Willis recording); we do not know the voice elsewhere in its range.

RANGE: Guianas, s. Venezuela (Bolívar and Amazonas), se. Colombia (north locally to Meta and Vaupés), ne. Ecuador, e. Peru, n. Bolivia (south to Santa Cruz), and Amaz. Brazil (south to s. Mato Grosso on the Serra dos Parecís, and east to Maranhão). Mostly below 300 m (recorded to 500 m in Colombia).

NOTE: E. O. Willis (*Pap. Av. de Zool. São Paulo* 33[2]: 27–66, 1979) presents much information on this species' behavior. He also suggests that more than one species may be involved, with birds from the Guianas and n. Brazil differing vocally and in somewhat larger size. Recent information also demonstrates that the brown iris color of *obidensis* (R. Bierregaard photos in VIREO) and nominate race (Cardoso da Silva and Oren 1990) differs from the bluish of birds from elsewhere (*castanoptera* group). We too suspect that two species are involved, but we are reluctant to split them in the absence of tape recordings of the song of any of the *castanoptera* group. If split, *D. castanoptera* could be called Blue-eyed Woodcreeper.

Dendrocincla homochroa

RUDDY WOODCREEPER

DESCRIPTION: 20.5 cm (8″). Local in *n. Colombia and nw. Venezuela*. Resembles Plain-brown Woodcreeper (potentially sympatric) but *essentially uniform reddish brown* with *rufous crown,* grayish lores, and rufous-chestnut wings and tail; shows *no* grayish on auricular area and *no* dusky malar stripe. See C-23, P-18.

SIMILAR SPECIES: The most generally rufescent woodcreeper, but bear in mind that *all* woodcreepers have rufous at least on wings and tail.

HABITAT AND BEHAVIOR: Apparently rare to uncommon in undergrowth of humid and semihumid forest and secondary woodland, es-

pecially in foothills (not lowlands). Not well known in South America, though from the number of specimens it may be more numerous in Venezuela than Colombia. In Middle America, Ruddy Woodcreeper is a furtive and generally seldom-encountered bird that forages almost entirely at army antswarms, sometimes with the mainly lowland-inhabiting Plain-brown Woodcreeper. The seldom-heard song is a series of up to 10–15 rather soft, melancholy "wheep" notes, sometimes gradually fading at the end (B. Spencer recording).

RANGE: Locally in n. Colombia (n. Chocó; e. slope of Santa Marta Mts. and lower slope of Sierra de Perijá; east of Andes in extreme n. Arauca) and w. Venezuela (east to w. Lara, Mérida, w. Barinas, and w. Apure). Also Mexico to Panama. Mostly 300–800 m, rarely up to 1800 m in Venezuela.

Deconychura Woodcreepers

A pair of dull-plumaged and obscure woodcreepers, notable for their long tails and striking sexual dimorphism in size, found inside humid lowland forests.

Deconychura longicauda

LONG-TAILED WOODCREEPER   PLATE: 12

DESCRIPTION: 19–21.5 cm (7½–8½"). Bill straight and slender, moderately long. Males considerably larger than females. Brown above with faint buff streaks on crown and (somewhat wider) on sides of head, and *indistinct buff postocular stripe;* wings, uppertail-coverts, and tail rufous-chestnut, *the tail proportionately longer than in other woodcreepers* (except Spot-throated). Throat dull buffyish with faint dusky streaking; remaining underparts dull olivaceous brown, *breast narrowly streaked with buff.* Foregoing applies to nominate/*pallida* of Amazonia. *Connectens* (foothills and lower subtropical zone on e. slope of Andes in Ecuador and Peru) and *minor/darienensis* (n. Colombia) similar but tending to have *a more spotted or chevroned pattern on breast;* see P-19. Note that birds found in s. Venezuela and se. Colombia (illustrated on V-18 and C-23) appear to be more typical of *pallida,* and not, as labeled, *connectens.*

SIMILAR SPECIES: Easily confused, though its slim appearance, accentuated by the long tail, is helpful. Confusion is especially likely with Spot-throated Woodcreeper, which in some Amaz. forests is sympatric with Long-tailed Woodcreepers of the nominate/*pallida* type. Spot-throated is smaller, but because of sexual dimorphism in size, large male Spot-throateds approach small female Long-taileds in length. In such situations, check for Spot-throated's virtual absence of crown streaking, less extensive rufous on wings, rufous rump, more spotted or chevroned (not so streaked) effect on breast, and shorter and more slender bill. Cf. also various *Xiphorhynchus* woodcreepers (none of which, however, shows such an obvious postocular; cf. especially Spotted) and Plain-brown Woodcreeper (with heavier bill, pale auriculars, little or no streaking on crown or upperparts).

HABITAT AND BEHAVIOR: Rare to locally uncommon in lower and middle growth of humid forest, in Amazonia mainly or entirely in terra firme, on e. slope of Andes in montane forest. Unobtrusive and seldom encountered, the Long-tailed Woodcreeper usually is found singly or in pairs, regularly accompanying mixed flocks. It forages by hitching up trunks and sidling along larger horizontal limbs and is not usually attracted to army antswarms. Although in our experience generally quiet, several strikingly different songs are known. In e. Peru, *pallida* gives a very distinctive, *strongly descending* series of 8–12 well-separated, clear penetrating whistled notes with almost the quality of a *Microcerculus* wren; in Costa Rica (birds ranging south into n. Colombia are likely similar) *typica* gives a much faster and shriller series of notes more recalling a White-bellied Antbird (J. Arvin recording); the voice of *connectens* appears unknown.

RANGE: N. Colombia (n. Chocó east in humid Caribbean lowlands to the middle Río Magdalena valley in Santander); e. slope of Andes in Ecuador (Napo southward) and Peru (south locally to Ayacucho); Guianas, extreme s. Venezuela (s. Amazonas), extreme se. Colombia (e. Guainía and e. Vaupés), e. Peru (e. Loreto south locally to Madre de Dios), n. Bolivia (south to La Paz), and Amaz. Brazil (east to n. Maranhão and south to n. Mato Grosso). Also Honduras to Panama. Lowland forms occur up to about 1300 m; *connectens* mostly 1200–1700 m.

NOTE: More than one species seems likely involved, as indicated (in part) by the striking geographic variation in songs.

Deconychura stictolaema

SPOT-THROATED WOODCREEPER   PLATE: 12

DESCRIPTION: 16.5–17.5 cm (6½–7″). Males considerably larger than females. Bill straight, fairly short. Brown above with indistinct buff postocular stripe and streaking on sides of head; inner flight feathers (*only*) rufous; tail rufous-chestnut, this color *extending up over rump; tail proportionately longer than in other woodcreepers* (except Long-tailed). Upper throat dull buffyish; remaining underparts dull olivaceous brown, *lower throat and breast with small chevron-shaped spots.*

SIMILAR SPECIES: Cf. similar Long-tailed Woodcreeper. Otherwise this small, obscure woodcreeper is most likely confused with much more numerous and widespread Wedge-billed which, though similar in color and overall pattern, differs in its much shorter wedge-shaped bill.

HABITAT AND BEHAVIOR: Rare to locally uncommon in undergrowth of terra firme forest. Its unobtrusive behavior is similar to Long-tailed's, and likewise it usually occurs with mixed flocks, though Spot-throated tends to forage lower. Its song is a simple, colorless, and rapidly delivered trilled series of rather shrill notes, "pee-ee-ee-ee-ee-ee-ee-ee-ew" (P. Donahue recording).

RANGE: S. Venezuela (Amazonas), extreme s. Colombia (w. Putumayo; probably more widespread), ne. Ecuador (a few records from

w. Napo), ne. Peru (south locally to n. Ucayali), Amaz. Brazil (south to Rondônia and nw. Mato Grosso, and east locally to n. Maranhão), and French Guiana. To 400 m.

Glyphorynchus Woodcreepers

A monotypic genus of very small and short-billed woodcreeper which is numerous and widespread in humid forests. The nest is placed in a cavity or hole, usually close to the ground.

Glyphorynchus spirurus

WEDGE-BILLED WOODCREEPER PLATE: 12

DESCRIPTION: 14–15 cm (5½–6″). A widespread and numerous *small* woodcreeper with *distinctive short, wedge-shaped bill*. Above rufescent brown with indistinct buff postocular stripe and buff to whitish streaking on sides of head; wings somewhat more rufescent (in flight a conspicuous buff stripe on flight feathers shows); rump and tail rufous-chestnut, tail with very long protruding spines (proportionately the longest of any woodcreeper). Throat pale to rich buff; remaining underparts dull olivaceous brown, breast with chevron-shaped pale buff to whitish spots.

SIMILAR SPECIES: In Amazonia cf. larger and rarer Spot-throated Woodcreeper. Otherwise not likely to be mistaken, but in a quick look confusion is possible with the differently shaped *Xenops* (which have a similar wing-stripe) or Spotted Barbtail.

HABITAT AND BEHAVIOR: Fairly common to very common in lower growth of humid forest (in Amazonia favoring terra firme) and mature secondary woodland, sometimes coming out into tall trees of adjacent clearings. Although inconspicuous, in many forests this is one of the most numerous birds, as attested to by the large number often mistnetted. The Wedge-bill is usually found singly, and though regularly with mixed flocks, at least as often it forages alone. It characteristically forages by hitching slowly up trunks of larger trees (presumably why it has such long tail spines), only occasionally working out onto lateral branches. It seems nervous, rarely holding still for long, constantly flicking the wings and moving its head. Attention is often drawn to it by its frequently given, abrupt "cheeyf!" call, with a sneezing effect. The more warbled and patterned songs appear to vary geographically.

RANGE: Nw. Venezuela (Maracaibo basin), n. and w. Colombia (humid Caribbean lowlands south in middle Río Magdalena valley to w. Boyacá, and in Pacific lowlands) and w. Ecuador (south to Guayas and El Oro); Guianas, ne. and s. Venezuela (Bolívar and Amazonas, north in the east to the Paria Peninsula, and along base of Andes north to w. Barinas), e. Colombia, e. Ecuador, e. Peru, n. Bolivia (south to La Paz, Cochabamba, and Santa Cruz), and Amaz. Brazil (south to s. Mato Grosso, and east to n. Maranhão); coastal e. Brazil in se. Bahia and n. Espírito Santo. Also Mexico to Panama. Most common below about 1000 m, in decreasing numbers up to about 2000 m.

NOTE: More than one species may be involved (*fide* A. Capparella).

Sittasomus Woodcreepers

Presently recognized as a single species of small, short-billed, plain, and unstreaked woodcreeper, *Sittasomus* more probably consists of a complex of several allospecies with rather different appearances and dramatically different voices. The genus has a wide distribution across the forested neotropics, mainly in the lowlands.

Sittasomus griseicapillus

OLIVACEOUS WOODCREEPER   PLATE: 12

DESCRIPTION: 14.5–16 cm (5¾–6¼″). Widespread but *very variable in appearance;* more than one species is almost certainly involved. Nominate group (including *amazonus;* most of range) has *head, neck, and most of underparts grayish to olive-grayish;* back more rufescent, and flight feathers and tail contrastingly bright rufous (when spread, a conspicuous buff stripe on flight feathers is exposed). *Aequatorialis* (w. Ecuador and nw. Peru) is similar to more olive birds, but its flight feathers and tail are paler, more cinnamon-rufous. More strikingly different are birds of se. Brazil north to se. Bahia, e. Paraguay, and ne. Argentina (*sylviellus* and *olivaceus*): these are the "true" "Olivaceous" Woodcreepers, being *bright ochraceous olive* where the previous races are grayish; they are slightly smaller with more slender bills and deeper rufous wings and tails. Even more different is *reiseri* of ne. Brazil (s. Maranhão and n. Goiás east), which is also small and is washed with rufous on crown and (strongly) on back, has entire wing (including coverts) bright rufous, and is *strongly tinged buff below.*
SIMILAR SPECIES: Despite the striking geographic variation, Olivaceous Woodcreepers as a group can be easily recognized by their small size and (depending on area) *unstreaked* grayish, bright olive, or rufous/buff bodies. The only other equally small woodcreeper is the very different Wedge-billed.
HABITAT AND BEHAVIOR: Uncommon to common at all levels (but most often rather high) in both humid and deciduous forest, woodland, and borders; most numerous in se. South America, in Amazonia found mainly in várzea or transitional forest. Usually seen singly, less often in pairs, foraging on more or less open trunks and branches, sometimes sallying out in pursuit of prey that has been flushed. At times accompanies mixed flocks, but at least as often forages independently. Songs vary geographically and quite strikingly. In w. Ecuador *aequatorialis* gives a fast, rolling, semimusical trilled "tr-r-r-r-r-r-r-r-r-r-r-r-r-eu" lasting about 3 seconds. In Amazonia (e.g., se. Peru) *amazonus* gives a very different series of about 6–8 distinctly rising and gradually louder notes, e.g., "pu-pu-pew-pew-peh-peh-peé-peh." In se. Brazil *sylviellus* gives an equally different series of about 8–10 well-enunciated "weep" notes which descend in pitch, speed up slightly, and end in a slight stutter. We do not know the voice of ne. Brazil's *reiseri.*
RANGE: W. Ecuador (north to w. Esmeraldas) and nw. Peru (Tumbes); n. Colombia (south in the middle Río Magdalena valley to Caldas) and n. Venezuela (east to Sucre, and along e. base of Andes in Barinas and Táchira); French Guiana, w. Guyana, s. Venezuela (Bolí-

var and Amazonas), e. Colombia (north to Meta and Vichada), e. Ecuador, e. Peru, n. and e. Bolivia, virtually all of Brazil (absent only from the lower Amazon region and s. Rio Grande do Sul), Paraguay, and n. Argentina (in the northwest south to Catamarca; in the northeast south to ne. Santa Fe and Corrientes); Tobago. Seems likely in Surinam. Also Mexico to Panama. Mostly below 1500 m, in smaller numbers up to 2000 m or slightly higher.

NOTE: Based on vocal and plumage differences, as well as other criteria, *Sittasomus griseicapillus*, though long considered a single species, seems likely to consist of a complex of three or four allospecies in South America; there may be additional species in Middle America. If the species is split, we suggest that *S. sylviellus* of se. South America retain the English name of Olivaceous Woodcreeper and that the wide-ranging *S. griseicapillus* be called the Grayish Woodcreeper. *S. reiseri* of ne. Brazil would be the Reiser's Woodcreeper, and *S. aequatorialis* of w. Ecuador and nw. Peru would be the Pacific Woodcreeper.

Nasica Woodcreepers

A single species of large and long-billed woodcreeper found in Amazonia, perhaps the finest of all the woodcreepers.

Nasica longirostris

LONG-BILLED WOODCREEPER   PLATE: 12

DESCRIPTION: 35–36 cm (13¾–14¼"). A spectacular and unmistakable *large* woodcreeper of várzea forests in Amazonia. *Bill very long, slightly decurved, yellowish white to ivory.* Looks small headed. Crown and upper cheeks blackish narrowly streaked with buff, separated by a broken white postocular stripe; *above otherwise bright rufous-chestnut. Throat contrastingly white;* remaining underparts brown with broad black-edged white lanceolate streaks on sides of neck and breast.
HABITAT AND BEHAVIOR: Uncommon to fairly common in canopy and middle levels of várzea and riparian forest, often out to forest borders. Usually found singly or in pairs, often foraging in the semiopen along edges of lakes or streams, probing into bromeliads and inspecting crevices in bark. Its song is an unmistakable series of usually 3 or 4 eerie whistled notes, loud and far-carrying, e.g., 'twoooooóoo . . . twoooooóoo . . . twoooooóoo," followed by a pause before another series; agitated birds also give various chuckled calls. Birds respond strongly to tape playback and even crude whistled imitations of this song.
RANGE: Sw. Venezuela (Amazonas), e. Colombia (north to Meta and Vichada), ne. Ecuador, e. Peru, n. Bolivia (south locally to La Paz and Santa Cruz), Amaz. Brazil (south to ne. Mato Grosso and Goiás, and east to n. Maranhão), and French Guiana. Mostly below 300 m, locally up to 500 m.

Drymornis Woodcreepers

A monotypic genus of striking, large woodcreeper found in the chaco woodlands of s.-cen. South America, where it is unique among the woodcreepers in being partially terrestrial while foraging.

Drymornis bridgesii

SCIMITAR-BILLED WOODCREEPER   PLATE: 12

DESCRIPTION: 30–31 cm (11¾–12¼″). A spectacular and virtually unmistakable, *partially terrestrial* woodcreeper of *chaco woodlands and scrub*. Very long and rather slender decurved, mainly blackish bill, "sickle-shaped." Crown chestnut, *long superciliary and malar stripe white*, latter bordered below by a rufous submalar stripe; above otherwise sandy rufescent brown; wings duskier, rump and tail rufous. Throat white; remaining underparts pale brown with *conspicuous broad and black-edged white streaks*.

SIMILAR SPECIES: Only possible confusion, however improbable, is with Red-billed Scythebill.

HABITAT AND BEHAVIOR: Uncommon in chaco woodland and scrub, sometimes coming out into nearby clearings but never too far from cover. Forages both on trunks and larger limbs, like other members of its family, as well as on ground where it tends to hop about somewhat awkwardly with tail splayed out. On the ground it feeds by probing loose soil with its long bill. Scimitar-billed Woodcreeper usually occurs singly or in pairs and is generally independent of mixed flocks. The most distinctive vocalization is a fast series of loud, shrieking notes ending in a jumble, e.g., "wreey! wreey! wreé-wreé-wree-wree-jehjehjeh." Perhaps more numerous toward the s. end of its range, e.g., in Córdoba.

RANGE: S. Bolivia (extreme sw. Santa Cruz at Estancia Perforación), w. Paraguay (west of the Río Paraguay), extreme s. Brazil (sw. Rio Grande do Sul), w. Uruguay, and n. and cen. Argentina (south to La Pampa and extreme sw. Buenos Aires). Below about 500 m.

Dendrexetastes Woodcreepers

A fairly large woodcreeper with a stout but rather short bill, found quite widely in Amazonia.

Dendrexetastes rufigula

CINNAMON-THROATED WOODCREEPER   PLATE: 13

DESCRIPTION: 24–25 cm (9½–9¾″). *Bill rather heavy, horn colored to greenish horn*. Mostly brown, more cinnamon-buff on throat and with *conspicuous "collar" of white, black-edged elongated spots ("ocellations") on nape and upper back and across breast*; flight feathers and tail rufous. Foregoing applies to nominate race of Guianas, s. Venezuela, and n. Brazil north of the Amazon. *Paraensis* (e. Pará around Belém) similar, but evidently (we have not seen specimens) it also has a white postocular. *Devillei* (with *monileger;* remainder of range) less striking, with *no* spotting above, and below reduced to *narrow streaks on breast;* see C-24.

SIMILAR SPECIES: Compared to other large sympatric woodcreepers, Cinnamon-throated looks rather pale and plain overall with an obviously pale bill; this is especially true of the widespread w. race *devillei*

in which the breast streaking is so fine it is often hard to discern in the field. Cf. especially Plain-brown Woodcreeper (dark billed and generally darker in coloration).

HABITAT AND BEHAVIOR: Uncommon to locally fairly common in borders of humid forest, both in terra firme and várzea. Hitches along trunks and major branches much like many other woodcreepers, sometimes foraging out onto slender terminal twigs. Generally remains high above the ground; regularly accompanies mixed flocks. Most apt to be recorded once its distinctive and oft-given song is recognized; in some parts of Amazonia this woodcreeper's song is one of the first to be heard in the predawn darkness, and it also calls frequently at, and even after, dusk. That song is a fast series of loud, ringing notes, often starting with a sputter and always ending with a characteristic, lower-pitched "tchew" or "tchu"; there seems to be no geographic variation.

RANGE: Se. Venezuela (many recent records from e. Bolívar, especially at Río Grande), Guianas (not recorded from Guyana but surely occurs), Amaz. Brazil (south to n. Mato Grosso on the Rio do Cágado and east to n. Mato Grosso at Alta Floresta and e. Pará in the Belém region), n. Bolivia (south to La Paz and Cochabamba), e. Peru, e. Ecuador, and se. Colombia (north to Caquetá). Mostly below 500 m, but recorded to 950 m in Ecuador and Peru.

Hylexetastes Woodcreepers

Large and very heavy-bodied woodcreepers with stout, dark red bills found locally and rarely (but perhaps are just under-recorded) in forests of Amazonia. The genus has been considered "weakly differentiated" from the genus *Dendrocolaptes* (E. O. Willis, *Rev. Brasil. Biol.* 42[4]: 657, 1982).

Hylexetastes uniformis

UNIFORM WOODCREEPER
Other: Red-billed Woodcreeper (in part)

PLATE: 13

DESCRIPTION: 26.5–27.5 cm (10½–10¾"). *Cen. Amaz. Brazil south of the Amazon;* formerly considered conspecific with Red-billed Woodcreeper (found *north* of the Amazon). *Very heavy but rather short, dark red bill. Mostly uniform brown,* somewhat paler below, especially on belly; rump, wings, and tail rufous-chestnut.

SIMILAR SPECIES: Not known to overlap with other *Hylexetastes* woodcreepers; Bar-bellied's range comes closest (replacing it westward), but Bar-bellied has boldly barred lower underparts, etc. Cf. also the *concolor* form of Barred Woodcreeper.

HABITAT AND BEHAVIOR: Rare to uncommon in humid forest, primarily if not entirely in terra firme. Not a well-known bird, but behavior probably differs little from Red-billed's; neither we nor D. Stotz (pers. comm.), however, have ever seen Uniform at an army antswarm. The song (in Rondônia) is a distinctive series of 4–6 loud, piercing, whistled notes, e.g., "wreeeeeét, wreeeeeét, wreeeeeét, wreeeeeét," its ringing quality reminiscent of Long-billed Woodcreeper's; as with so many woodcreepers, Uniform sings mainly in semidarkness of dawn and dusk.

RANGE: Cen. Amaz. Brazil (both sides of lower Rio Tapajós west to south of Tefé, thence southward to s. Mato Grosso on the Serra dos Parecís and Serra das Araras) and ne. Bolivia (ne. Santa Cruz on the Serranía de Huanchaca). To about 500 m.

NOTE: Although usually regarded as a subspecies of *H. perrotii* from north of the Amazon River, in plumage *uniformis* differs as much or more from *perrotii* as the latter differs from *H. stresemanni*, and it is smaller and shorter-billed than either. We believe recognizing three allospecies is a more accurate representation of morphological variation in the complex. The songs of all members of the genus are similar.

Hylexetastes perrotii

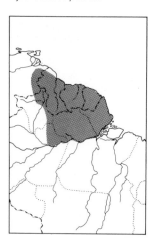

RED-BILLED WOODCREEPER

DESCRIPTION: 28–29 cm (11–11½"). *Guianas and se. Venezuela to n. Brazil.* Resembles Uniform Woodcreeper (south of the Amazon; often considered conspecific) but somewhat larger with *longer bill*. Red-billed differs most strikingly in its facial pattern, with *contrasting whitish lores, broad supramalar stripe, and throat;* about 50% of individuals show faint blackish barring on belly. See V-18.

SIMILAR SPECIES: This large, obviously red-billed woodcreeper is unlikely to be confused, but cf. Barred Woodcreeper (its sympatric nominate race also has a distinctly reddish bill).

HABITAT AND BEHAVIOR: Rare to uncommon in terra firme forest. Found singly or in pairs, foraging at all levels, both at army antswarms and in mixed flocks where it tends to remain well above the ground and is generally difficult to detect. At army antswarms it tends to perch close to the ground on trunks, thence most often dropping to the ground in pursuit of fleeing prey; it is dominant over virtually all other birds at the swarms. We are not familiar with its song, though from the description of E. O. Willis (*Rev. Brasil. Biol.* 42[4]: 655–666, 1982) it appears to be similar to Uniform Woodcreeper's; Willis (op. cit.) provides much information on foraging behavior.

RANGE: Guianas, se. Venezuela (e. Bolívar), and n. Brazil (Amapá west to the Manaus area, and to Roraima at the Maracá Ecological Station). To 500 m.

NOTE: See comments under Uniform Woodcreeper.

Hylexetastes stresemanni

BAR-BELLIED WOODCREEPER   PLATE: 13

DESCRIPTION: 28–29 cm (11–11½"). *W. Amaz. Brazil to nw. Bolivia and se. Peru. Very heavy dark reddish bill.* Mostly uniform brown with whitish lores; wings and tail rufous-chestnut. Throat and breast brown, broadly streaked with whitish on throat, more narrowly and sparsely on breast; *lower breast and belly buffy whitish boldly barred with blackish.* A few birds have barring extending up over chest.

SIMILAR SPECIES: Even larger Strong-billed Woodcreeper has longer and horn-colored bill, more blackish crown with buff shaft streaking (not plain brown), and its barring on lower underparts never is as

bold. Bills of both Barred and Black-banded Woodcreepers are much less heavy. Barred's bill is reddish, especially in ne. South America, but it has barring on *all* of underparts as well as crown and neck. Black-banded's overall pattern is more similar, but its crown and nape are streaked and its breast is more conspicuously buff-streaked.

HABITAT AND BEHAVIOR: Rare in humid forest, probably mainly in terra firme. Poorly known, but behavior probably differs little from Red-billed Woodcreeper's. Its song is also similar, especially in its loud, ringing quality, but the individual notes may be shorter and more "clipped" (T. A. Parker III recording).

RANGE: Locally in w. Amaz. Brazil (north of the Amazon from w. bank of the lower Rio Negro west through the upper Rio Negro drainage, and along the Amazon to Benjamin Constant, south of it from the Rio Purus drainage westward), extreme nw. Bolivia (Pando at Camino Mucden), and se. Peru (s. Ucayali and Madre de Dios). Doubtless occurs in extreme se. Colombia around Leticia. Below 300 m.

Dendrocolaptes Woodcreepers

Fairly large woodcreepers with strong, straight bills found mainly in humid forests, *Dendrocolaptes* tend to have complex patterns with streaking and some barring. They are frequently seen at antswarms. The taxonomy of several members of the genus remains controversial. E. O. Willis (*Condor* 84[3]: 272–285, 1982) suggests that "sleek"-headed individuals, which are dominant, are females and that "ruffed"-headed individuals, which are subordinate, are males.

GROUP A

Northern South America through Amazonia.

Dendrocolaptes certhia

BARRED WOODCREEPER
Includes: Concolor Woodcreeper

PLATE: 13

DESCRIPTION: 27–28 cm (10½–11″). Bill varies from blackish west of Andes, to brownish or reddish brown in w. Amazonia, to decidedly reddish in e. Amazonia. *Prominently and uniformly barred in most of range. Radiolatus* group (with similar *juruanus* and *polyzonus*) from w. Amazonia is mostly brown to buffy brown *evenly barred with blackish across back and on entire underparts;* rump, wings, and tail rufous-chestnut. *Colombianus* group (with very similar *hyleorus* and *punctipectus*) from west of Andes is more densely barred; see P-19. Eastern races differ more. Nominate (Guianas and s. Venezuela to n. Brazil north of the Amazon and east of the Rio Negro) is *much less conspicuously barred* and has a decidedly reddish bill; see V-18. *Concolor* (cen. Amaz. Brazil from Rio Madeira east to Rio Tocantins, and south to ne. Bolivia) is so dramatically different that it has often been regarded as a separate species: it *loses all barring* (except for a few individuals that have some scaling on crown and faint barring on belly); *medius* (east of Rio Tocantins) regains the barring, but it is much less extensive than in typical birds, with none on back.

SIMILAR SPECIES: Easily recognized in most of its range by the obvious dense barring, shared by no other woodcreeper. Problems crop up where barring is lost, particularly in cen. Amaz. Brazil where in some areas the *concolor* Barred, Hoffmanns', and Black-banded Woodcreepers are all sympatric. In this area Barred (*lacking* streaking and barring) is much more uniform than the others, to the extent that it also resembles the heavier and decidedly red-billed Uniform Woodcreeper.

HABITAT AND BEHAVIOR: Uncommon to locally fairly common in lower and middle growth of humid forest, mature secondary woodland, and (less often) borders; favors várzea in w. Amazonia, but in the east more wide ranging. This often rather stolid woodcreeper forages mainly at army antswarms, where it tends to perch quite low, chasing away smaller woodcreepers and pursuing prey that flushes from or moves on the ground; usually no more than 1 or 2 are present at a swarm. Less often it forages with mixed flocks, or alone. Songs, given mainly at dawn and just before dusk, vary geographically. West of Andes a series of loud, clear, whistled notes which gradually become louder is given, "oowít, oowít, oowít, OOWIT, OOWIT!" East of Andes a very different, fast series of run-together, ringing, and whistled notes which fade toward the end is given, "tewtewtewtewtewtewtew-tewtutu-tu-tu." Various snarling calls are given while feeding.

RANGE: W. Venezuela (humid Maracaibo basin), n. and w. Colombia (humid Caribbean lowlands, and Pacific lowlands), and nw. Ecuador (south to Pichincha); Guianas, s. Venezuela (Delta Amacuro, Bolívar, and Amazonas), e. Colombia (north to Meta and Vichada), e. Ecuador, e. Peru, n. Bolivia (south to La Paz, Cochabamba, and Santa Cruz), and Amaz. Brazil (south to s. Mato Grosso, and east to Maranhão); ne. Brazil (Pernambuco and Alagoas). Also Mexico to Panama. Mostly below 900 m (recorded to 1400 m in s. Venezuela).

NOTE: *D. concolor* (Concolor Woodcreeper), which has a range parapatric with that of *D. certhia,* has often been given full species status (most recently by Meyer de Schauensee 1966, 1970). However, recent recordings of its song, which seem very similar to those of *D. certhia* from elsewhere in Amazonia, appear to confirm the contention of E. O. Willis and Y. Oniki (*Ann. Rev. Ecol. Syst.* 9: 243–263, 1978) that *concolor* is best considered only a subspecies of *D. certhia.* However, as described above, the songs of cis- and trans-Andean populations of *D. certhia* differ so strikingly that, despite their close plumage similarity, two separate species are probably involved. If split, *D. certhia* from east of Andes could be called the Amazonian Barred-Woodcreeper, and trans-Andean and Middle American *D. sanctithomae* (named for the northernmost subspecies, whose name has priority) could be called the Northern Barred-Woodcreeper.

Dendrocolaptes picumnus

BLACK-BANDED WOODCREEPER   PLATE: 13

DESCRIPTION: 25.5–28 cm (10–11"). Maxilla blackish to dusky; lower mandible horn, often blue-tinged. Above brown, somewhat darker on crown, narrowly streaked with pale buff on head and, more sparsely, on back; rump, wings, and tail rufous-chestnut. Throat pale buff streaked with brown, breast brown with broad pale buff streaking; belly buff *boldly barred with blackish.* Foregoing applies to nominate

group (with *validus*) of Amazonia. Montane birds of Colombia and n. and w. Venezuela (*multistrigatus* group) similar but somewhat smaller, with less prominent barring below and back streaking sparser or obsolete; see V-18, C-23. Birds from Santa Cruz, Bolivia, and Mato Grosso, Brazil, southward (*pallescens* group; with *casaresi*) are quite different: smaller with *bill pale bluish horn*, overall color *much more rufescent* with concolor crown, and barring on belly nearly *obsolete*.

SIMILAR SPECIES: Combination of streaking on foreparts and barring on lower underparts is distinctive in most of its range. Barred Woodcreeper lacks any streaking, and various superficially similar *Xiphorhynchus* woodcreepers (e.g., Buff-throated) lack belly barring. In cen. Amaz. Brazil south of the Amazon, cf. Hoffmanns' Woodcreeper. In s. part of range, cf. "rufous" *pallescens/casaresi* to Planalto Woodcreeper (mainly found eastward, but perhaps with some overlap) and to the substantially larger but similarly colored Great Rufous Woodcreeper. Strong-billed Woodcreeper has somewhat similar pattern (including some belly barring) but is larger with much longer and heavier bill.

HABITAT AND BEHAVIOR: Rare to uncommon in lower and middle growth of humid and montane forest, in Amazonia primarily in terra firme; *pallescens* group inhabits more deciduous forest and woodland. Behavior similar to Barred Woodcreeper's, foraging almost exclusively at army antswarms and seldom with mixed flocks. The song in Amazonia is a fast series of liquid "winh" notes on the same pitch which start slowly, then accelerate before slowing again at the end; it is given almost entirely at dawn and dusk. Various other calls are given while feeding. We do not know the vocalizations of the *pallescens* group.

RANGE: Guianas, Venezuela (generally in the south; in the north mostly montane, on slopes of n. coastal mts. east to Paria Peninsula, and in Andes), Colombia (mainly on slopes of Andes; also on slopes of Sierra de Perijá and Santa Marta Mts.; also in lowlands of extreme southeast), e. Ecuador, e. Peru, n. and e. Bolivia, much of Amaz. Brazil (also in sw. Mato Grosso), Paraguay (mainly along Río Paraguay itself, locally in better-developed chaco woodland), and nw. Argentina (south to Tucumán). Also Costa Rica and Panama. Mostly below 2000 m, but in small numbers to 2500 m or even higher in Colombia and Venezuela.

NOTE: E. O. Willis (*Condor* 84[3]: 272–285, 1982) suggests that *platyrostris* and *hoffmannsi* might be only subspecifically related to *D. picumnus*. However, *D. hoffmannsi* and *D. picumnus* apparently are sympatric in a limited area near the lower Rios Madeira and Tapajós in Brazil, and *D. platyrostris* and *D. picumnus* are nearly sympatric along the Río Paraguay in Paraguay. Pinto (1978) suggests that *pallescens* and *hoffmannsi* be considered conspecific. We consider it possible that *pallescens* itself might represent a separate species (Pale-billed Woodcreeper), as it was treated in *Birds of the Americas*, vol. 13, part 4. For more behavioral information on *D. picumnus* in Amazonia, see E. O. Willis (op. cit.).

Dendrocolaptes hoffmannsi

HOFFMANNS' WOODCREEPER

DESCRIPTION: 28 cm (11"). *Cen. Amaz. Brazil south of the Amazon*. Bill blackish. Mostly brown above with *crown more rufescent* (looks "*rusty-capped*"), feathers with faint and fine black edging and fine buff shaft

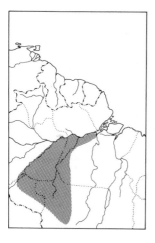

streaks; rump, wings, and tail rufous-chestnut. Underparts brown, throat and breast with *narrow* buff shaft streaking and faint dusky barring on belly.

SIMILAR SPECIES: Confusing. The sympatric *concolor* race of Barred Woodcreeper has a more reddish (not so black) bill, more uniform brown crown, plain throat *without* any streaking, and virtually *lacks* barring on belly. The generally more boldly patterned Black-banded Woodcreeper is much more coarsely streaked on crown and foreneck, lacks rufescence on crown, and has coarser belly barring.

HABITAT AND BEHAVIOR: Apparently rare in lower and middle growth of humid forest. The behavior of this little-known woodcreeper resembles that of the Barred and Black-banded, and it also appears to be a professional antswarm follower; its voice (T. A. Parker III recording) seems similar to the latter's. Small numbers occur in Amazonia Nat. Park southwest of Itaituba on w. bank of the Rio Tapajós.

RANGE: Cen. Amaz. Brazil (south of the Amazon from lower Rio Xingu at Tapará west to the Rio Madeira, thence south locally to Rondônia and sw. Mato Grosso at Tangará da Serra). Below 300 m.

NOTE: See comments under Black-banded Woodcreeper.

GROUP B   *Eastern* South America.

Dendrocolaptes platyrostris

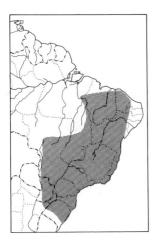

PLANALTO WOODCREEPER   PLATE: 13

DESCRIPTION: 25–26 cm (9¾–10¼″). *E. Brazil to e. Paraguay and ne. Argentina. Bill black.* Mostly olive brown, *crown more blackish* (quite contrasting) and prominently streaked buff, the streaking becoming finer on back and scapulars; wings and tail dull chestnut. Throat buffy whitish *indistinctly streaked with dusky;* remaining underparts brown, breast streaked with pale buffy whitish, belly irregularly barred with buffy whitish and black. Foregoing applies to nominate race (se. Brazil southward); *intermedius* (n. part of range south to Bahia and n. Paraguay) has less contrasting and browner crown, almost no streaking on mantle, paler and brighter rufous wings and tail, and slightly paler underparts.

SIMILAR SPECIES: Confusing. Nominate race overlaps widely with very similarly patterned White-throated Woodcreeper; White-throated is larger with notably longer and heavier bill (black in both species) and has pure white unstreaked throat bordered by obvious black malar. Race (*pallescens*) of Black-banded Woodcreeper that is nearly sympatric with Planalto near the Río Paraguay is much more rufescent generally and is *pale*-billed and *brown*-crowned. Farther north there is no known overlap between Planalto and either Hoffmanns' or Black-banded Woodcreepers. In this area, Planalto (*intermedius*) has more belly barring than Hoffmanns', less than Black-banded; Black-banded differs further from Planalto (*intermedius*) in its blackish crown and boldly streaked back.

HABITAT AND BEHAVIOR: Uncommon to fairly common in lower and middle growth of humid forest, mature secondary woodland, and borders. Usually found singly or in pairs, sometimes following mixed flocks but at least as often moving independently of them; though sometimes at army antswarms, seems much less dependent than other *Dendrocolaptes* on them (doubtless in part because in most of its range there are so few). The song of nominate Planalto is a fast series of sharp "whik" or "week" notes, slightly fading toward the end, recalling Black-banded's but more often protracted and usually shriller and less musical.

RANGE: E. Brazil (se. Pará at Marabá, Maranhão, Piauí, and Ceará south to n. Rio Grande do Sul, and west to s. Mato Grosso and Mato Grosso do Sul), e. Paraguay (east of the Río Paraguay), and ne. Argentina (Misiones and ne. Corrientes). To about 1300 m.

Xiphocolaptes Woodcreepers

Perhaps the heaviest of all the woodcreepers, *Xiphocolaptes* have entirely allopatric ranges in both lowland and montane forests throughout much of South America. The genus is characterized by its massive, long, surprisingly narrow, and somewhat decurved bill. The taxonomy of several species presents serious difficulties, as discussed below.

GROUP A

Typical *Xiphocolaptes,* with streaking on foreparts.

Xiphocolaptes albicollis

WHITE-THROATED WOODCREEPER   PLATE: 13

DESCRIPTION: 28–29 cm (11–11½"). *Se. Brazil area. Long, stout, somewhat decurved black bill.* Above olivaceous brown, head contrastingly blackish with bold buffy whitish superciliary and supramalar stripe and streaking on crown and sides of head; streaking finer and sparser on back; wings and tail dull chestnut. *Throat contrastingly white,* bordered by *conspicuous blackish malar stripe;* remaining underparts pale olivaceous brown, breast streaked buffy whitish and belly irregularly barred pale buff and blackish. *Bahiae* (s. Bahia, Brazil) differs from nominate (remainder of range) in having reduced barring on belly; *villanovae* of cen. Bahia is apparently similar (*fide* D. Stotz).

SIMILAR SPECIES: Often sympatric Planalto Woodcreeper is similarly patterned and colored but has a shorter and less decurved bill, a duskystreaked throat, and no obvious malar stripe. Cf. also the browner Moustached Woodcreeper (no known overlap).

HABITAT AND BEHAVIOR: Uncommon to fairly common in lower and middle growth of humid forest, mature secondary woodland, and borders; in Goiás also in gallery woodland. Usually found singly or in pairs, perching stolidly with large feet splayed outward, generally not far above the ground; regularly forages in bromeliads. Often astonishingly tame. The distinctive song, given mainly near dawn and dusk, is a leisurely series of far-carrying, piercing notes, each note slightly lower in pitch than its antecedent (so the effect is of going downscale) and preceded by a slight hiccuping, the latter audible only at close range: "mc-wheer, mc-wheer, mc-wheer, mc-wheer, mc-wheer" (Belton 1984; RSR). Also has several whining or snarling calls, e.g., a rising "wheee" or "wheee-chuck," regularly given during day.

RANGE: E. Brazil (cen. Bahia at Bonfim south to s. Rio Grande do Sul, and west to s. Goiás and s. Mato Grosso do Sul), e. Paraguay (east of the Río Paraguay), and ne. Argentina (Misiones and ne. Corrientes). Mostly below 1500 m.

NOTE: The little-known *villanovae* of cen. Bahia in Brazil has been regarded as a separate species (Bonfim Woodcreeper; see discussion in Meyer de Schauensee 1966), but we suspect it is more likely only a northern race of *X. albicollis*.

Xiphocolaptes falcirostris

MOUSTACHED WOODCREEPER

Includes: Snethlage's Woodcreeper

DESCRIPTION: 28—29 cm (11—11½"). *Ne. Brazil;* includes Snethlage's Woodcreeper. Resembles a pale, faded, browner (less olivaceous) White-throated Woodcreeper; no known overlap. Differs in its *paler horn-colored bill;* brown crown *concolor* with back, and with finer and faded pale streaking; *less contrasting head pattern* (superciliary, supramalar, and throat tinged buff); rufous wings and tail; and obsolete belly barring. *Franciscanus* (nw. Minas Gerais) differs in its almost unstreaked crown and is more olivaceous brown below.

SIMILAR SPECIES: Not likely confused in its range.

HABITAT AND BEHAVIOR: Rare to uncommon in better-developed caatinga woodland, semideciduous woodland, and riparian woodland. Behavior similar to White-throated Woodcreeper's, as are its calls. The continued existence of *franciscanus* near the type locality was recently confirmed (M. Antonio de Andrade, M. V. de Freitas, and G. T. de Mattos, *An. Soc. Sul-Riogran. de Ornitol.* 7: 18—20, 1986). The nominate race is now quite local because of habitat destruction; both races of the species probably deserve threatened status.

RANGE: Ne. Brazil (e. Maranhão, Piauí, Ceará, w. Paraíba, and w. Pernambuco south locally through w. Bahia and extreme e. Goiás to extreme nw. Minas Gerais at Brejo do Amparo and Itacarambi). To at least 550 m.

NOTE: *X. franciscanus* (Snethlage's Woodcreeper) was long known from only the type specimen, obtained early in the 20th century. It was thought to be most closely related to *X. albicollis* (e.g., Pinto 1978), perhaps only a race of that species. However, we follow D. Teixera (*Bol. Mus. Nac.,* Zool., nov. sér., no. 337, 1990), who has recently presented evidence suggesting that it is better regarded as a subspecies of *X. falcirostris.*

Xiphocolaptes promeropirhynchus

STRONG-BILLED WOODCREEPER   PLATE: 13

DESCRIPTION: 28—30.5 cm (11—12"). Wide-ranging and variable (many subspecies have been described, at least 16 in South America alone!). Occurs in both highlands and lowlands (separate species?). *Long, heavy, somewhat decurved bill,* dusky to horn-colored (generally paler in lowlands). Highland forms (*lineatocephalus* is typical) are brown above with narrow buffy whitish streaking on crown and head and *buffy whitish postocular, lores, and supramalar;* wings, rump, and tail rufous-chestnut. Throat whitish *bordered by usually prominent blackish malar*

stripe; remaining underparts brown, streaked with buffy whitish on breast and usually irregularly barred with blackish on belly. Most highland races have brownish streaking on throat, and in some the crown is blackish and more broadly streaked than in *lineatocephalus;* the small birds of sw. Ecuador and nw. Peru (*crassirostris*) have a whitish, unstreaked throat. Birds of Santa Marta Mts. (*sanctaemartae*) have an especially long bill, narrow breast streaking, and seem never to show any barring on belly. Lowland forms (*orenocensis* group) are typically larger with longer and heavier bills; have blackish crowns with pronounced streaking and a *pale supramalar stripe usually obliterated by narrow buff streaking;* and they tend to be more rufescent generally, especially on breast.

SIMILAR SPECIES: The variation is confusing, though in most of its range this is the *largest woodcreeper,* often identifiable on that basis alone. In Andes, particularly long-billed individuals might be confused with Greater Scythebill which, in addition to having a longer, narrower, and pale bill, has a dark throat with a contrasting whitish malar. In lowlands, confusion is most likely with sympatric large form (*guttatoides*) of Buff-throated Woodcreeper; the latter is slightly smaller than Strong-billed, lacks the dark malar stripe, never shows belly barring, etc. Cf. also Black-banded Woodcreeper (with slimmer, straighter bill, etc.).

HABITAT AND BEHAVIOR: Rare to locally fairly common in humid and montane forest, in w. Amazonia primarily in várzea forest. Found singly or in pairs, foraging at all levels but rarely in the canopy; often follows mixed flocks and sometimes accompanies army antswarms, where it is almost always dominant over other birds present. In some areas (e.g., Santa Martas; Hilty and Brown 1986) reported often to feed in bromeliads. As with White-throated Woodcreeper, frequently seems almost oblivious to the presence of an observer, even when very close. The distinctive, far-carrying song, a regular feature of dawn choruses throughout its range, seems not to vary geographically: it is a leisurely series of 3–5 loud, paired whistled notes, each pair at a slightly lower pitch than the preceding, e.g., "pt-teeu, pt-teeu, pt-teeu, pt-tuuu." Often each phrase's initial short "pt" is inaudible at a distance.

RANGE: Venezuela (in the north mainly in coastal mts. from Paria Peninsula westward, also on Andean slopes and the Sierra de Perijá; in the south locally in Amazonas and s. Bolívar), w. Colombia (mainly on slopes of Andes; also locally in humid Caribbean lowlands and on slopes of Santa Marta Mts. and the Sierra de Perijá), Ecuador (both slopes of Andes, and in eastern lowlands), Peru (Andean slopes and in eastern lowlands; on w. slope of Andes only in Piura), Bolivia (Andean slopes south to w. Santa Cruz, also in adjacent lowlands), w. and cen. Amaz. Brazil (south of the Amazon east to both sides of lower Rio Tapajós), s. French Guiana, and s. Guyana (Acary Mts.). Also Mexico to Panama. To about 2800 m (montane forms mostly above 1500 m, lowland forms mainly below 900 m).

NOTE: The lowland forms have been considered (e.g., *Birds of the Americas,* vol. 13, part 4) to comprise a separate species under the name of *X. orenocensis* (with *berlepschi, obsoletus, paraensis, tenebrosus,* and *neblinae* as subspecies). This may well prove to be correct, but given the complex geographic variation, we feel it premature to split them without additional study. At least along parts of the e. slope of the Andes, there appears to be an elevational gap between the two forms. The suggested (Meyer de Schauensee 1966) English name for *X. orenocensis* is Rusty-breasted Woodcreeper, this despite the fact that many of its races are no more rufescent on the breast than are highland forms. We suggest, instead, using the name of Great-billed Woodcreeper should *X. orenocensis* be treated as a full species.

GROUP B

Distinctive overall *bright rufous coloration*.

Xiphocolaptes major

GREAT RUFOUS WOODCREEPER

PLATE: 13

DESCRIPTION: 28–30.5 cm (11–12"). *An unmistakable large and almost uniformly rufous woodcreeper. Long, heavy, somewhat decurved horn-colored bill. Above mostly bright rufous,* browner on crown and with dusky lores. Below somewhat paler rufous. Some individuals have indistinct pale shaft streaking on breast and a little dusky barring on belly. Foregoing applies to nominate race (Paraguay and n. Argentina). Birds of Bolivia and sw. Brazil (*castaneus*) are somewhat darker generally, whereas those from Tucumán, Argentina (*estebani*; J. M. Cardoso da Silva and D. C. Oren, *Bull. B.O.C.* 111[3]: 147–149, 1991), are described as being slightly paler.

SIMILAR SPECIES: Cf. only the smaller *pallescens* race of Black-banded Woodcreeper, with much less massive bill, etc.

HABITAT AND BEHAVIOR: Uncommon in deciduous forest and woodland, gallery woodland, and occasionally in clearings with scattered trees. As with other *Xiphocolaptes* woodcreepers, the impressive Great Rufous is almost always seen singly or in pairs, foraging on trunks of larger trees, sometimes even dropping to the ground. Like the others, it often seems quite fearless. The loud and far-carrying song, a series of double-stopped whistled notes, each pair dropping a little in pitch, is similar to its congeners', though typically there are more notes (up to about 12) per song. Widespread though never really numerous in wooded habitats through pantanal of Mato Grosso and Paraguay.

RANGE: N. and e. Bolivia (west to Beni and n. La Paz), sw. Brazil (sw. Mato Grosso and w. Mato Grosso do Sul), w. and cen. Paraguay (not ranging far to the east of the Río Paraguay), and n. Argentina (south mainly to Tucumán, Santiago del Estero, and n. Santa Fe, rarely to n. Córdoba). To 1500 m.

Xiphorhynchus Woodcreepers

A very confusing and difficult group of midsized to fairly large woodcreepers found primarily in lowland forests, though a few species range in montane areas and one (the Straight-billed) also occurs in scrubbier habitats. All are streaked or spotted at least to some degree (in some species quite pronounced), and bills are usually more decurved than in *Dendrocolaptes* but stouter and less decurved than in *Lepidocolaptes*. Several species pairs, notably the Straight-billed/Zimmer's and Ocellated/Spix's complexes, continue to present major identification and taxonomic challenges.

GROUP A   Bill rather *short, straight, and pale;* mainly várzea and scrub.

Xiphorhynchus picus   **STRAIGHT-BILLED WOODCREEPER**   PLATE: 14

DESCRIPTION: 21 cm (8¼″). *Bill straight, ivory colored, sometimes with a pinkish tinge.* Above mostly rufous, crown and sides of head contrastingly dusky with narrow buff streaks extending to upper mantle and an indistinct and broken whitish superciliary; wings and tail rufous-chestnut. Throat buffy whitish with faint dusky scaling, *chest with large black-edged pale buff squamate spots;* lower underparts brown with a little narrow pale buff streaking. Foregoing applies to the widespread nominate group of Amazonia and ne. Brazil, Guianas, and Trinidad. *Picirostris* group of n. Colombia and n. Venezuela differs in having upperparts paler and brighter rufous with lighter dusky crown, *wider and whiter superciliary,* and *more extensive and purer white throat* extending down over upper chest; see V-18.

SIMILAR SPECIES: This usually numerous woodcreeper can generally be known by its pale and dagger-shaped bill. In n. part of its range this, in conjunction with the white on face and throat, is diagnostic, but in Amazonia confusion is possible with several other woodcreepers. Cf. the virtually identical Zimmer's Woodcreeper. Also similar is the Striped, whose bill is only slightly darker and more decurved; Striped is best distinguished by its more extensive streaking, both on back and underparts, and its duller (not so rufous) overall coloration. Cf. also Ocellated Woodcreeper.

HABITAT AND BEHAVIOR: Fairly common to common and widespread in a variety of wooded or lightly forested habitats, near the Caribbean regularly in arid desert scrub (sometimes foraging even on cacti) and in mangroves, in Amazonia primarily in várzea forest, forest borders, and secondary woodland. Forages singly or in pairs, regularly accompanying mixed flocks, hitching up trunks and along branches mainly at low and middle levels; usually quite conspicuous, often fully in the open and rather tame. The song is a fast series of semimusical whistled notes with a general descending effect though often with a slight upturn at the end; it seems not to vary appreciably across its vast range. Unlike many other woodcreepers, the Straight-billed does not sing mainly at dawn and dusk.

RANGE: Guianas, Venezuela (including Margarita Is.), n. and e. Colombia (west to n. Chocó, and south in Río Magdalena valley to Huila), ne. Ecuador, e. Peru, n. Bolivia (south to La Paz, Cochabamba, and Santa Cruz), and Amaz. and e. Brazil (south to Mato Grosso do Sul, Goiás, Bahia, and n. Espírito Santo); Trinidad. Also Panama. Mainly below 600 m, but recorded to 1100 m in n. Peru and 1400 m in Venezuela.

Xiphorhynchus necopinus   **ZIMMER'S WOODCREEPER**

DESCRIPTION: 21 cm (8¼″). Mainly *Amaz. Brazil.* Exceedingly similar to nominate group of Straight-billed Woodcreeper and not certainly

distinguishable in the field, at least on presently recognized characters. The 2 species are known to be sympatric. We noted the following differences in AMNH specimens: duller (less rufescent) brown upperparts; brown (not rufous) lesser wing-coverts; slightly more streaked (less spotted or ocellated) effect on chest; fulvous tinge on belly; longer tail with more protruding spines. Bill shape is similar. *Contra* Meyer de Schauensee (1970, p. 197), bill color does *not* appear to be "darker," and the back of Zimmer's is *not* "more prominently streaked."

HABITAT AND BEHAVIOR: Unknown in life. D. Stotz (pers. comm.) believes Zimmer's is probably restricted to várzea forest. From the number of specimens obtained, Zimmer's would appear to be at least locally not uncommon, but no one has as yet separated it with certainty from Straight-billed Woodcreeper in the field.

RANGE: Amaz. Brazil (along the Amazon from near the mouth of the Rio Tapajós west to the lower Rio Negro and the Rios Madeira and Juruá, and south to Rondônia); seems likely in n. Bolivia. The ANSP specimen recorded from "the vicinity of Belém, Pará" (Meyer de Schauensee 1966, p. 232) is actually a *X. o. obsoletus.* Below about 200 m.

NOTE: Although some doubt has been raised regarding the validity of this species (e.g., Pinto 1978), the constancy of the characters ascribed to it by its describer, J. T. Zimmer, are evident in the ample series at AMNH. Thus, despite the failure of subsequent workers definitely to locate it in recent years, we believe that it is a valid species-level taxon.

Xiphorhynchus obsoletus

STRIPED WOODCREEPER   PLATE: 14

DESCRIPTION: 20–20.5 cm (7¾–8″). Bill pale grayish horn, duskier toward base (especially on maxilla). Above brown, the crown duskier, with prominent black-edged pale buff streaks extending from crown *down over back;* wings, rump, and tail rufous-chestnut. Throat buff, feathers scaled blackish; remaining underparts dull brown *prominently streaked with buffy whitish* except on belly.

SIMILAR SPECIES: Amaz. forms of Straight-billed Woodcreeper differ in their straighter, paler bills; lack of back streaking; more ocellated effect on chest; and overall more rufescent (not so olivaceous) tone. Lineated Woodcreeper is similar below (though its streaking is narrower), but Lineated is *un*streaked above, has a more decurved bill, and forages mainly in canopy. Chestnut-rumped Woodcreeper is more fulvous below with blurrier streaking.

HABITAT AND BEHAVIOR: Uncommon to locally fairly common in lower and middle levels of várzea forest and forest borders; like Straight-billed Woodcreeper, often along edges of lakes and sluggish streams, but unlike it seems quite tied to várzea. Behavior similar to Straight-billed's, though Striped is less often in the open and on the whole less confiding. Its song is distinctly different, being a short series of staccato notes that distinctly rise in pitch (Straight-billed's falls).

RANGE: Guianas, s. Venezuela (Delta Amacuro, Bolívar, and Amazonas, and in s. Táchira, s. Barinas, and w. Apure), e. Colombia, e.

Ecuador, e. Peru, n. Bolivia (south to n. La Paz and ne. Santa Cruz), and Amaz. Brazil (south to s. Mato Grosso and east to Pará in the Belém area). To 500 m.

GROUP B

Typical *Xiphorhynchus* with *long bills;* mainly *lowland* forest.

Xiphorhynchus ocellatus

OCELLATED WOODCREEPER

PLATE: 14

DESCRIPTION: 21.5 cm (8½″). *Maxilla blackish, lower mandible pale grayish.* Above brown, duskier on crown and nape, crown and nape with guttate buff spots and *back with sparse but very fine buff streaking* (back looks virtually uniform at any distance); rump, wings, and tail rufous-chestnut. Throat buff, feathers of lower throat scaled blackish; remaining underparts brown, *chest with large squamate black-edged buff spots,* lower underparts obscurely streaked buffyish. Foregoing applies to *napensis* of s. Colombia, e. Ecuador, and n. Peru. Eastward, nominate race and *perplexus* are similar but have back essentially *un*streaked; see C-23. *Chunchotambo* (e.-cen. Peru south of the Río Marañón to at least Junín) similar but with paler (buffy whitish) throat and narrow but distinct black moustachial streak. *Brevirostris* (se. Peru and Bolivia) also shows the moustachial streak but differs in its decidedly shorter and *paler* bill, and its throat is not only paler (buffy whitish) but also plainer (*lacking* any scaling).

SIMILAR SPECIES: *Very* confusing, partly because of geographic variation. Straight-billed and Striped Woodcreepers both are paler billed and are not found in the terra firme forest Ocellated favors; confusion is especially likely with pale-billed *brevirostris* Ocellated, but Striped is more broadly streaked on back than Ocellated ever is, whereas Straight-billed is *un*streaked on back. The potential for confusion is even greater with Spix's Woodcreeper, which can occur in the same terra firme forest as does Ocellated (the two are even locally syntopic). In most of its range, Spix's is more broadly streaked on back than Ocellated ever is, and this easily seen character is the mark to look for. However, *juruanus* Spix's of sw. Amazonia have sparse or no back streaking (thus pattern and extent are similar to Ocellated's); these differ from *chunchotambo* Ocellateds in their whiter throats and smaller chest spots, and from *brevirostris* Ocellateds in their longer and darker bills and smaller chest spots. Sympatric Buff-throated Woodcreeper is considerably larger, etc.; cf. also Chestnut-rumped Woodcreeper (possible overlap in extreme sw. Venezuela).

HABITAT AND BEHAVIOR: Uncommon to fairly common in lower and middle growth of terra firme forest, rarely at borders; on e. slope of Andes ranges up into montane forest. Usually found singly or in pairs, hitching up trunks or working along lateral branches, probing into crevices and among epiphytic vegetation. Often accompanies mixed flocks of understory birds but only infrequently attends army ant-swarms. The song, heard mainly at dawn and dusk but also sometimes when with flocks (especially as a shortened version), is a fast series of nasal notes with a descending effect, ending with several sharply emphasized notes, e.g., "whe-whe-whe-whe-whe-chéchécheow"; either the descending series or the emphasized notes may be given alone, the latter especially when excited (as by tape playback).

RANGE: Extreme sw. Venezuela (sw. Amazonas), se. Colombia (north to Caquetá, Vaupés, and Guianía), e. Ecuador, e. Peru, n. Bolivia (south to La Paz, Cochabamba, and w. Santa Cruz), and Amaz. Brazil (north of the Amazon mainly from the Rio Negro westward, also locally near the lower Amazon; south of the Amazon east mainly to the Rio Purus drainage, but also recorded near the lower Rios Madeira, Tapajós, Xingu, and Tocantins). To about 1500 m.

Xiphorhynchus spixii

SPIX'S WOODCREEPER

PLATE: 14

Includes: Elegant Woodcreeper

DESCRIPTION: 21.5 cm (8½"). *Complex* variation; we include Elegant Woodcreeper, formerly considered a separate species. Bill bluish gray or bluish horn, often duskier on maxilla or blackish toward base. There are 3 "types."

1. Birds from se. Colombia, e. Ecuador, and e. Peru north of the Ríos Marañón and Amazon (*ornatus; buenavistae* of Colombia is essentially identical, the characters mentioned in Hilty and Brown [1986] *not* separating it), and (*elegans*) in cen. Amaz. Brazil from the lower Rio Purus east to the lower Rio Tapajós and south to Rondônia and ne. Santa Cruz, Bolivia, are brown above, somewhat duskier on crown and nape, with guttate buff spotting on crown and nape becoming *rather wide, black-edged buff streaks on back;* rump, wings, and tail rufous-chestnut. Throat buffy whitish; remaining underparts pale dull brown with *large, slightly elongated black-edged pale buff spots on breast,* fading to faint dull streaks on upper belly.

2. Birds from e. Peru south of the Ríos Marañón and Amazon, nw. Bolivia, and w. Brazil east to around Tefé and south to Acre and the upper Rio Madeira (*juruanus; insignis* should probably be synonymized) have *streaking on back much narrower or virtually obsolete,* and *much smaller and less contrasting breast spots.*

3. Birds from lower Amaz. Brazil east of the Rio Tapajós (nominate *spixii*) differ dramatically, with *very broad streaking on back* and *broad and extensive streaking on entire breast and belly.*

SIMILAR SPECIES: In most of its range Spix's Woodcreeper can be known from the similar Ocellated by its *prominent back streaking* (lacking or weak in Ocellated). This distinction breaks down in sw. Amazonia, where *juruanus* Spix's show little or no back streaking. Here look especially for Ocellated's larger and buffier breast spots; Ocellateds from s. Peru and n. Bolivia (*brevirostris*) also have a shorter and paler bill. Nominate Spix's (lower Amazon) are so dramatically different (with their very extensive streaking) from other races that confusion is more likely with Striped Woodcreeper (with paler bill, etc.).

HABITAT AND BEHAVIOR: Uncommon to fairly common in lower and middle growth of terra firme and várzea forest; rarely at edge. In Ecuador, where scarce, favors blackwater várzea forest. Behavior much like Ocellated Woodcreeper's. Spix's voice, however, differs quite markedly and has a clearer, more musical quality though it still descends in pitch, e.g., "tchip-tchip-tchip-tchip-tchup-tchup, tchweu, tchweu"; sometimes this song may be long continued and slide back up in pitch at the end. As far as we are aware, there is no geographic variation, but we do not know the song of nominate *spixii*.

RANGE: Se. Colombia (north to w. Meta and Amazonas; we regard the record from the upper Río Magdalena valley at Moscopán as unverified), e. Ecuador (few records), e. Peru, n. Bolivia (south to La Paz, and in ne. Santa Cruz on the Serranía de Huanchaca), and Amaz. Brazil south of the Amazon (south to s. Mato Grosso and east to n. Maranhão). To 1400 m.

NOTE: Although possibly an oversimplification, after much study we consider all forms in this complex as a single species, following J. T. Zimmer (*Am. Mus. Novitates* 756, 1934). Up to three species, *X. spixii, X. juruanus,* and *X. elegans,* have been recognized in the complex (Pinto 1978), but more usually only two, *X. spixii* and *X. elegans* (e.g., Meyer de Schauensee 1966, 1970). The voices of all forms appear similar, though we do not know the voice of nominate *spixii;* the latter is in plumage the most divergent of the group, and it remains possible that it deserves to be separated as a monotypic species. Plumage variation amongst the several races appears to be "random," or "leap-frog," with the ranges of similar-appearing *elegans* and *ornatus* being separated by the range of the very different *juruanus. X. elegans* (with the similar *ornatus*) was specifically separated (e.g., *Birds of the World,* vol. 7) from *X. spixii* (with *juruanus,* etc.) subsequent to the discovery of the supposed sympatry of *juruanus* and *ornatus* at São Paulo de Olivença, on the s. bank of the Amazon in w. Brazil. We await modern field confirmation of their actual sympatry and suspect that a problem in specimen labeling was involved. Otherwise the distributions of all forms in *X. spixii* are parapatric. We should specifically note that, contrary to what was done in *Birds of the World* (vol. 7), *buenavistae* of Colombia should also have been separated from *X. spixii* when *X. elegans* was recognized as a separate species (with *ornatus* as a subspecies); *buenavistae* is essentially identical to *ornatus,* into which it should probably be synonomized. As a result of this error, in subsequent publications (e.g., Hilty and Brown 1986) both the species *X. spixii* (*buenavistae*) and *X. elegans* (*ornatus*) were treated as occurring in Colombia.

Xiphorhynchus pardalotus

CHESTNUT-RUMPED WOODCREEPER   PLATE: 14

DESCRIPTION: 21.5 cm (8½"). *Ne. South America.* Bill dusky. Brown above, somewhat duskier on crown and nape, with fine guttate buff spotting on crown and sparse buff streaking on back; rump, wings, and tail rufous-chestnut. *Throat fulvous,* lower throat faintly streaked dusky; remaining underparts dull brown, *breast quite prominently streaked fulvous.*

SIMILAR SPECIES: Note that a number of *Xiphorhynchus* woodcreepers, including several of Chestnut-rumped's look-alikes, have identical rufous-chestnut rumps. Ocellated differs in its less streaked back, somewhat paler throat, and (especially) its more spotted effect on breast; it overlaps with Chestnut-rumped only in sw. Venezuela. Nominate Spix's differs in being more broadly streaked both above and below and in having a paler throat; it and Chestnut-rumped are basically allopatric (north and south of the Amazon). Cf. also the larger Buff-throated Woodcreeper.

HABITAT AND BEHAVIOR: Fairly common to common in lower and middle growth of humid forest, occasionally out to forest borders. Behavior similar to Ocellated Woodcreeper's. Chestnut-rumped's song, given mainly at dawn and dusk, is a distinctive "chup, chup, chup, cheh-cheh-chee-chee-ee-ee"; several other sharp, somewhat stuttered call notes are also given.

RANGE: Guianas, s. Venezuela (Bolívar and Amazonas), and n. Amaz. Brazil (north of the Amazon and west to the Rio Negro; south of it recorded only from Aramanaí on e. side of the lower Rio Tapajós, but D. Stotz suggests that the Aramanaí locality may be the result of mislabeling). Mostly below 500 m, but recorded to 1800 m in Venezuela.

Xiphorhynchus guttatus

BUFF-THROATED WOODCREEPER   PLATE: 14
Includes: Dusky-billed Woodcreeper

DESCRIPTION: 26−27 cm (10¼−10½"). A *large* woodcreeper of Amazonia and e. Brazil. Includes Dusky-billed Woodcreeper of e. Amaz. Brazil (often considered a separate species), but does not include Cocoa Woodcreeper of n. Colombia, n. Venezuela, and Trinidad. *Bill long*, horn to dusky in most of range, but *blackish* in *eytoni* of lower Amaz. Brazil. Above brown, duskier on crown and nape, with guttate buff spotting on crown and buff streaking on nape and upper back (variable in width, and in some birds extending down over much of back); rump, wings, and tail rufous-chestnut. Throat pale buff; remaining underparts brown with buff streaking, becoming plain on lower belly. *Dorbignyanus* (n. Bolivia and sw. Brazil) has finer streaking on nape and upper back. *Eytoni* (with *vicinalis*) of Amaz. Brazil west to Rondônia and the Rio Madeira, in addition to its blackish bill, differs mainly in its whiter crown spotting, whiter and consistently wide back streaking, and whiter streaking on throat and breast. *Eytoni* is a striking, "contrasty" bird, though many apparent intergrades with typical *guttatoides* of the rest of Amazonia occur.

SIMILAR SPECIES: This species' *large size* distinguishes it from all other *Xiphorhynchus* woodcreepers in its range and results in its more often being confused with one of the (more similarly sized) *Dendrocolaptes* or even *Xiphocolaptes* woodcreepers. Note that none of these is ever as numerous as the Buff-throated almost always is. Cf. Black-banded Woodcreeper (whose lower underparts are barred, and whose throat as well as breast are streaked) and Strong-billed Woodcreeper (Amaz. forms of which are quite similar in color and pattern, though Strong-billed's bill is *much* heavier). Planalto Woodcreeper can also be confused.

HABITAT AND BEHAVIOR: Fairly common to common in humid forest (both terra firme and várzea), second-growth woodland, and (toward s. end of range) gallery woodland; sometimes at borders. Behavior much like Ocellated Woodcreeper's but more conspicuous on the whole, more apt to forage in the open and at higher levels on open trunks and large branches; often bolder. Frequently rummages in dead palm fronds and other dead leaves. Its most common song, heard at intervals throughout the day, is an evenly paced and pitched series of whistled notes which start softly, gradually become louder, and last 3 or 4 seconds; also gives a shorter series of descending notes with a laughing quality, "wheer, wheer, whip-whip-wip-wip," and other calls.

RANGE: Guianas, s. Venezuela (Delta Amacuro, Bolívar, and Amazonas), se. Colombia (north to Meta and e. Vichada), e. Ecuador, e. Peru, n. Bolivia (south to La Paz, Cochabamba, and Santa Cruz), and Amaz. Brazil (east to Maranhão, n. Piauí, and n. Ceará, and south to Mato Grosso do Sul and Goiás); e. Brazil (Paraíba south to Rio de Janeiro). To about 1100 m.

NOTE: *X. eytoni* (Dusky-billed Woodcreeper) has often been considered a separate species from *X. guttatus* (e.g., Meyer de Schauensee 1966, 1970), and indeed typical examples of that form do appear strikingly different from typical *guttatoides* Buff-throateds. However, as noted above (and detailed by J. T. Zimmer [*Am. Mus. Novitates* 756, 1934]), there exists much individual variation and apparent intergradation between it and the neighboring races of *X. guttatus, guttatoides* and *dorbignyanus;* this, in conjunction with the apparent similarity in their vocalizations, makes us conclude that the best treatment is to consider them conspecific. We have not found that the supposed "ecological" overlap between the two exists. Yet, as noted by E. O. Willis (*Rev. Brasil. Biol.* 43[2]: 125–131, 1983), "Buff-throated Woodcreepers" of Middle and n. South America differ strikingly in their smaller size and also differ vocally—and it thus seems reasonable to separate them as a full species, *X. susurrans* (Cocoa Woodcreeper).

Xiphorhynchus susurrans

COCOA WOODCREEPER
Others: Buff-throated Woodcreeper (in part)

DESCRIPTION: 21.5–22 cm (8½–8¾"). *N. Colombia, n. Venezuela, and Trinidad;* here considered a species separate from Buff-throated Woodcreeper of Amazonia and eastward. Resembles that species in plumage pattern but is *markedly smaller.* Nominate race (Trinidad and Tobago) has whiter throat and more spotted breast pattern; *jardinei* (ne. Venezuela) is buff-throated but is intermediate in breast pattern (i.e., more streaked). See C-23, P-19.

SIMILAR SPECIES: Not many similar woodcreepers occur in its *non-Amazonian range.* Cf. especially Streak-headed Woodcreeper (similar plumage pattern, but smaller with slimmer and more decurved bill).

HABITAT AND BEHAVIOR: Fairly common to common in lower and middle growth of humid and to a lesser extent deciduous forest (including mangroves), second-growth woodland, and borders, sometimes also foraging in trees out in clearings. Behavior much like Buff-throated Woodcreeper's, though Cocoa forages high above the ground less often and perhaps attends army antswarms somewhat more often. Its often-heard song, delivered especially in early morning and late afternoon, is a fast series of loud, clear, whistled notes that start rapidly and then slow and fade away, e.g., "kuwi, kwee-kwee-kwee-kwee-kwee, kwee, kwu kwu."

RANGE: N. Colombia (humid Caribbean lowlands, and south in Río Magdalena valley to Tolima; east of Andes in nw. Arauca) and n. Venezuela (east to Paria Peninsula, and south along e. base of Andes to s. Táchira and w. Apure; Margarita Is.); Trinidad and Tobago. Also Guatemala to Panama. Mostly below 700 m.

NOTE: See comments under Buff-throated Woodcreeper. The English name of Cocoa Woodcreeper for *X. susurrans* was suggested in *Birds of the Americas*, vol. 13, part 4.

Xiphorhynchus lachrymosus

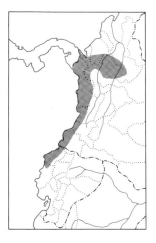

BLACK-STRIPED WOODCREEPER

DESCRIPTION: 24 cm (9½"). *N. and w. Colombia and nw. Ecuador.* Maxilla black, lower mandible gray. *Head and mantle black, head streaked with pale buff and mantle boldly striped with pale buff;* rump and wings rufous, tail rufous-chestnut. Throat pale buff; *remaining underparts boldly streaked pale buff and blackish,* becoming more mottled on lower belly. See C-23. *Alarum* (n. Colombia east of Gulf of Atrato) is less boldly streaked on mantle and underparts.

SIMILAR SPECIES: This handsome woodcreeper is unlikely to be confused, but the somewhat less striking *alarum* might possibly be confused with Cocoa Woodcreeper.

HABITAT AND BEHAVIOR: Fairly common in middle growth and subcanopy of humid forest, to a lesser extent also in forest borders. Routinely forages higher than other *Xiphorhynchus* woodcreepers, hitching along large horizontal limbs often well above the ground; 1 or 2 often accompany mixed flocks. Its loud and distinctive call is a brief series of 3 or 4 rapidly uttered semimusical notes with a laughing quality, e.g., "whee-hew-hew." Less often heard is its true song, a fairly fast series of about 10 musical notes that distinctly descend in pitch and whose tempo accelerates.

RANGE: N. and w. Colombia (Pacific lowlands and humid Caribbean lowlands east to e. Antioquia) and nw. Ecuador (Esmeraldas and n. Manabí). Also Nicaragua to Panama. Mostly below 1000 m, occasionally to 1400 m.

GROUP C

More *olive* coloration with *spotted pattern;* mainly foothills and montane forest.

Xiphorhynchus triangularis

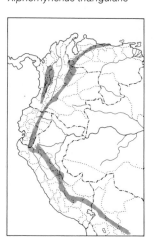

OLIVE-BACKED WOODCREEPER   PLATE: 14

DESCRIPTION: 23 cm (9"). *Subtropical zone of Andes.* Bill mainly bluish horn, with black ridge and base of maxilla. *Above mostly brownish olive,* duskier on crown, the back with at most very faint pale streaking, the *crown lightly spotted with yellowish buff,* and with indistinct buffy whitish eye-ring and postocular stripe; wings and tail rufous. Throat and upper chest *dull yellowish buff scalloped with dusky;* remaining underparts olivaceous boldly spotted with buffy whitish. Foregoing applies to nominate race (*hylodromus* is similar). *Bangsi* and *intermedius* (Junín, Peru, south into Bolivia) have rump more rufous, throat more whitish, and fewer and smaller spots on underparts.

SIMILAR SPECIES: In its *montane* range there are only a few other woodcreepers (e.g., Tyrannine, Montane, Long-tailed), none of them particularly similar. Cf. Spotted Woodcreeper (only on *west* slope of Andes, and only at elevations *below* those of Olive-backed).

HABITAT AND BEHAVIOR: Uncommon to fairly common in montane forest and forest borders. Usually seen singly or in pairs, often accompanying mixed flocks; feeds in typical woodcreeper fashion by hitching up trunks and larger limbs, and for the most part stays well above ground. Unlike many other woodcreepers (including the apparently closely related Spotted), Olive-backed seems a relatively quiet bird; we have never knowingly heard it, but it is known to give a rather sharp, slurred but penetrating "keeweeeeu" call (T. A. Parker III and M. Robbins recordings).

RANGE: Coastal mts. of n. Venezuela (Yaracuy east to Miranda), and Andes of w. Venezuela, Colombia (south on w. slope of W. Andes only to Cauca), e. Ecuador, e. Peru, and w. Bolivia (south to w. Santa Cruz). Mostly 1000–2500 m, occasionally lower (recorded down to 400 m on e. slope of Andes in s. Colombia).

Xiphorhynchus erythropygius

SPOTTED WOODCREEPER

DESCRIPTION: 23 cm (9"). *W. Colombia and w. Ecuador,* where it is the only woodcreeper with *obvious and extensive spotting below.* Resembles the nearly sympatric Olive-backed Woodcreeper, which replaces it at higher elevations on w. slope of Colombia's W. Andes. Differs in its *plainer crown with much less spotting* (only a little on forecrown), buffier eye-ring, slightly more pronounced streaking on back, more extensive rufous on wings and rump, and *spotted* (not scaled) *effect on throat.* See C-23.

SIMILAR SPECIES: Long-tailed Woodcreeper also shows a vague postocular stripe and is spotted on breast but differs in being much less olivaceous overall, etc.

HABITAT AND BEHAVIOR: Fairly common to common in humid and montane forest and second-growth woodland, sometimes also at borders and even out into trees in adjacent clearings. Behavior similar to Olive-backed Woodcreeper's, but Spotted seems considerably more vocal, its distinctive and far-carrying series of high-pitched but descending whistled notes ("d-d-drrreuw, d-d-drreuw, d-d-drreuw," sometimes adding 1 or 2 more clipped final notes at the end) often being heard, even during midday.

RANGE: W. Colombia (Pacific slope, and at n. end of Cen. Andes south in Río Magdalena drainage to Caldas) and w. Ecuador (south to w. Guayas and w. Loja). Also Mexico to Panama. Mostly below 1500 m, but locally higher (to about 2000 m) in s. Ecuador.

Lepidocolaptes Woodcreepers

A rather uniform group of slender, fairly small woodcreepers with distinctive pale, slender, decurved bills; they are almost always well streaked below, though many are unstreaked above. Depending on the species, they are found in a variety of habitats ranging from tall montane forest high in the Andes, to the subcanopy of humid lowland forest, to fairly open scrub and cerrado.

GROUP A

Standard *Lepidocolaptes;* note patterns, but *subspecific variation complex in some species.*

Lepidocolaptes lacrymiger

MONTANE WOODCREEPER
Other: Spot-crowned Woodcreeper (in part)

DESCRIPTION: 19–19.5 cm (7½–7¾"). Mainly *Andes. Slender, decurved bill,* mostly bluish horn with some blackish on maxilla. Above rufescent brown, crown duskier and *spotted with buff* and with broken white postocular stripe. Throat and lower face white, feathers scaled and edged with black; remaining underparts pale dull brown with *bold black-edged buffy whitish elongated spots.* Foregoing applies to *lacrymiger* group of most of Colombia (all but Nariño) and Venezuela; see V-18, C-23; there called Spot-crowned Woodcreeper. *Warscewiczi* group (Nariño, Colombia, southward) have somewhat plainer throat and less striking, more streaked pattern on underparts.
SIMILAR SPECIES: Other *Lepidocolaptes* woodcreepers, some of which are quite similar, do not normally occur in Andean highlands (but see under Lineated). The only other woodcreepers with which Montane regularly occurs are the dissimilar and larger Tyrannine (plain and *un*-streaked) and Olive-backed (olivaceous and comparatively dull overall). Cf. also the smaller Pearled Treerunner, whose overall color and pattern are quite similar (especially to n. races of Montane with their especially bold "lacrimose" pattern), and which often behaves in a similar fashion; their bill shapes differ dramatically.
HABITAT AND BEHAVIOR: Uncommon to fairly common in montane forest, secondary woodland and borders, and trees in adjacent clearings. Forages in typical woodcreeper fashion, hitching up trunks and along larger lateral limbs (most often on their undersides), picking at cracks in bark and into epiphytes. Frequently 1 or 2 will accompany mixed flocks. Although foraging at all forest levels, most often it does not range close to the ground. The rather infrequently heard song is a series of thin, sibilant, whistled notes with a distinctive rhythm, e.g., "tsip, ts-ts-tseeéu, tseu-tsu-tsu-tsu" (D. Wolf recording) or "tseu, tseu, tsip-tsee-tsee-tsee-tsee-tsee" (J. Cartright recording).
RANGE: Coastal mts. of n. Venezuela (east to Sucre), and Andes of w. Venezuela, Colombia, Ecuador (south on w. slope to w. Loja), e. Peru, and w. Bolivia (south to w. Santa Cruz); Sierra de Perijá on Venezuela-Colombia border and Santa Marta Mts. of n. Colombia. Mostly 1500–3000 m, but in small numbers down to 1100 m in w. Ecuador and w. Colombia.

NOTE: We consider the birds of South America (*L. lacrymiger,* Montane Woodcreeper) as a separate species from the birds of Middle America (*L. affinis,* Spot-crowned Woodcreeper). The latter are larger, buff throated, streaked on the back, etc. They were separated in *Birds of the Americas,* vol. 13, part 4 on this basis, and their very different primary vocalizations would appear to confirm their specific separation. The correct spelling of the species name is *lacrymiger*, not *lachrymiger* (*contra* Meyer de Schauensee 1966). It should be noted that an unfortunate error crept into the notes accompanying the commercially available tape *Voices of the Wood-creepers* (J. W. Hardy et al. 1991). As confirmed by G. Budney (pers. comm.), the first cut on this tape given under "*Lepidocolaptes affinis*, Spot-crowned Woodcreeper" was made in Peru by J. Cartright and is *L. lacrymiger*, and the second cut was made by W. Thurber in El Salvador and is true *L. affinis*.

Lepidocolaptes albolineatus

LINEATED WOODCREEPER

PLATE: 14

DESCRIPTION: 19 cm (7½"). *Amazonia to Guianas. Bill slender and decurved,* pale pinkish horn. *Above uniform brown to rufescent brown, including crown* (nominate race of Guianas, se. Venezuela, and n. Brazil north of the Amazon and east of the Rios Negro and Branco has crown with small pale buff spots); wings, rump, and tail rufous. Throat buffy whitish; remaining underparts brownish with *conspicuous crisp black-edged buff to whitish streaking.*
SIMILAR SPECIES: The only *Lepidocolaptes* in its Amaz. range and humid forest habitat. Striped Woodcreeper is somewhat similar but has a heavier bill, broader and blurrier streaking below, and is streaked on head and back; it inhabits várzea and forages lower.
HABITAT AND BEHAVIOR: Uncommon in middle growth and subcanopy of humid forest, primarily in terra firme. Doubtless much overlooked because it almost always remains well above the ground, where usually difficult to see well; its weak and relatively infrequently delivered song also does not attract attention. Usually noted singly as it forages with a mixed-species canopy flock, most often as it hitches along the underside of a large horizontal limb. The song in Ecuador and (D. Delaney recording) sw. Venezuela is a pretty, soft series of melodic notes with a becard-like quality which gradually drop in pitch and accelerate, e.g., "ti, ti, ti-ti-tee-tee-teh-teh-tutututututu." In se. Peru it gives a much faster, run-together trill, also descending (T. A. Parker III recording).
RANGE: Guianas, s. Venezuela (Bolívar and Amazonas), e. Ecuador, e. Peru, n. Bolivia (south to La Paz, Cochabamba, and Santa Cruz), and Amaz. Brazil (south to s. Mato Grosso and Goiás, and east to Maranhão); surely occurs in se. Colombia as well. Mostly below 1000 m, but recorded to 1400 m in Venezuela, and once to 2200 m in Peru (an AMNH specimen taken by J. Weske on the Cerros del Sira in Huánuco).

Lepidocolaptes souleyetii

STREAK-HEADED WOODCREEPER

DESCRIPTION: 19–20 cm (7½–8"). *Bill rather long, slender, and decurved,* pale pinkish to grayish horn. Above rufescent brown, crown and nape duskier with distinct buff streaking, and with *fairly prominent broken whitish superciliary* and streaking on sides of head; rump, wings, and tail rufous. *Throat buffy whitish;* remaining underparts brown *with prominent black-edged buffy whitish streaking.* Foregoing applies to nominate race (with *esmeraldae*) of w. Ecuador and adjacent Colombia

and Peru. *Lineaticeps* and *littoralis* of n. Colombia, n. Venezuela, extreme n. Brazil, and Trinidad similar but smaller with proportionately much smaller bill and have finer crown streaking, a less obvious superciliary, *smaller pale area on throat,* and narrower (more linear) streaking below; see V-18, C-23.

SIMILAR SPECIES: In n. part of range confusion most likely with often-sympatric Straight-billed Woodcreeper, but note differences in bill shape (much heavier and straighter in Straight-billed); Straight-billeds there have extensive white on face and throat. In w. part of range readily known by the combination of its slender decurved bill and whitish superciliary. Cf. also Montane Woodcreeper (no known elevation overlap).

HABITAT AND BEHAVIOR: Fairly common in deciduous woodland and forest, borders of more humid forest, clearings and agricultural areas with scattered trees or dense hedgerows, and (in sw. Ecuador and nw. Peru) arid scrub with scattered cacti and shrubby vegetation. Avoids humid regions and areas with extensive unbroken forest. General behavior similar to Montane Woodcreeper's, though Streak-headed is more apt to forage close to the ground and independently of mixed flocks; it also is much less forest dependent and is actually most frequent in semiopen areas or second-growth. The song is a simple semimusical descending trill lasting 2–3 seconds; it seems not to vary appreciably throughout the species' wide range.

RANGE: N. Colombia (Caribbean lowlands, and south in Río Cauca valley to Valle and in Río Magdalena valley to Tolima; east of Andes along their e. base south to w. Meta), Venezuela (widely north of the Orinoco, south of it locally in e. Bolívar), and extreme n. Brazil (locally in n. Roraima); Pacific slope of sw. Colombia (north to sw. Cauca), w. Ecuador, and nw. Peru (south to Lambayeque); Trinidad. Also Mexico to Panama. Seems likely in Guyana. Mostly below 1000 m, but recorded to 1800 m in sw. Ecuador.

Lepidocolaptes squamatus

SCALED WOODCREEPER   PLATE: 14

DESCRIPTION: 19 cm (7½"). *Se. Brazil area. Slender, decurved bill,* mostly *pinkish* with duskier maxilla. *Above rather bright rufous brown,* crown lightly spotted with buff, and with broken whitish superciliary and streaking on sides of head; rump, wings, and tail rufous. Throat whitish; *remaining underparts brown with bold black-edged whitish streaks.* Foregoing applies to nominate race (n. São Paulo to s. Bahia). *Falcinellus* (s. São Paulo southward) similar but with dusky crown and nape showing more prominent buff streaking, and buffier-tinged underparts. *Wagleri* (seemingly isolated in s. Piauí and nw. Bahia) also similar but much brighter rufous above, including crown (which is essentially unspotted).

SIMILAR SPECIES: Somewhat smaller Lesser Woodcreeper is buffier and more blurrily streaked below (less "crisp" and lacking the black), and its back is lightly streaked (Scaled's is *plain*); the two are sympatric in some areas. Scaled does not overlap with Lineated Woodcreeper of Amazonia.

HABITAT AND BEHAVIOR: Uncommon to fairly common (more numerous southward?) in humid and montane forest, forest borders, and secondary woodland, mainly in canopy and subcanopy; in Rio Grande do Sul, Brazil, regularly ranges in *Araucaria*-dominated forests. Behavior much like Montane Woodcreeper's, usually found singly or in pairs, often with mixed flocks. Its complex and distinctive song is an abrupt, loud musical chatter, "peédeedir," followed by several softer, high-pitched whimpering notes and then an equally loud, syncopated "peetu-peetu-pyeer" (T. A. Parker III recording); also gives a simpler but equally vigorous "pyeer-pyeer."

RANGE: E. Brazil (s. Piauí and nw. Bahia; s. Bahia south to Rio Grande do Sul), se. Paraguay (Canendiyu south to Itapúa), and ne. Argentina (Misiones and ne. Corrientes). Mostly below about 1600 m.

Lepidocolaptes fuscus

LESSER WOODCREEPER PLATE: 14

DESCRIPTION: 17–18 cm (6¾–7"). *E. Brazil to e. Paraguay and ne. Argentina. Slender, decurved bill,* blackish above and pinkish below. Above brown, crown somewhat duskier and spotted with buff and with yellowish buff superciliary; *back lightly streaked with buff;* rump, wings, and tail rufous. *Throat buffyish; remaining underparts broadly and blurrily streaked dusky-olive and buffyish.* Foregoing applies to nominate group (with *tenuirostris* and *brevirostris*), found north to Bahia. *Atlanticus* (ne. Brazil from Ceará to Alagoas) has a longer bill and is more ochraceous below with much blurrier and more faded streaking.

SIMILAR SPECIES: Scaled Woodcreeper's black-edged streaking below has a crisper look, and its back is always plain; from s. São Paulo southward the crown of Scaled is streaked (whereas in Lesser it is always spotted). The larger Narrow-billed Woodcreeper has a longer bill, much more prominent superciliary, and is much brighter rufous above; it favors more open terrain.

HABITAT AND BEHAVIOR: Uncommon to fairly common in humid forest, secondary woodland, forest borders. Behavior similar to Montane Woodcreeper's; tends to remain at lower levels than Scaled Woodcreeper, with which it sometimes occurs. Lesser's song is a series of stuttered notes followed by a faster trill followed by some more stuttered notes, the overall effect quite distinctive, e.g., "chit, chit, chit, chee-ee-ee-ee-ee-ee-ee, chit, chit-chit."

RANGE: E. Brazil (Ceará and Pernambuco south to s. Mato Grosso do Sul, Santa Catarina, and ne. Rio Grande do Sul), e. Paraguay (west to Paraguarí), and ne. Argentina (Misiones). To 1300 m.

GROUP B

Distinctive, with *longer bill* and *broad white superciliary.*

Lepidocolaptes angustirostris

NARROW-BILLED WOODCREEPER PLATE: 14

DESCRIPTION: 19.5–21 cm (7¾–8¼"). *Widespread in semiopen areas of e. and s.-cen. South America. Long, narrow, somewhat decurved bill mostly pinkish,* with base of maxilla dusky. Crown and nape dusky streaked

with buffy whitish, *broad superciliary buffy whitish*, and *auriculars plain blackish;* above otherwise rufous brown. Throat whitish; remaining underparts buffy whitish with diffuse dusky streaking. Foregoing applies to nominate group of e. Bolivia, Paraguay, and n. Argentina. More southerly birds (north to n.-cen. Argentina, Uruguay, and Rio Grande do Sul, Brazil; *praedatus* and *dabbenei*) similar but somewhat duller and browner above and more prominently streaked with blackish below. More northerly birds (lowlands of n. Bolivia and s.-cen. Brazil northward; *bivittatus* group) similar to nominate group but brighter rufous above and *essentially unstreaked buffy whitish below.*

SIMILAR SPECIES: The distinctively bold head pattern together with the long bill should preclude confusion of this handsome and *rather pale* woodcreeper. Cf. Lesser Woodcreeper (also shows blurry streaking below).

HABITAT AND BEHAVIOR: Uncommon to locally common in gallery woodland, chaco and caatinga woodland, cerrado, and agricultural areas with scattered trees. One of the more conspicuous woodcreepers in its range, usually found singly or in pairs, hitching up trunks and larger branches of trees and shrubs, also often investigating wooden fence posts, probing into crannies and flaking off pieces of loose bark. Although sometimes with loose mixed flocks, at least as often it forages independently. The song is a series of loud, sharp, well-enunciated notes which gradually accelerate, fade away, and drop in pitch, e.g., "peeé, pee-pee-pee-pee-peepeepeepeepupupu"; sometimes the individual notes are more rolled or trilled.

RANGE: E. and interior Brazil (s. Maranhão, Ceará, and Paraíba south to São Paulo and west to sw. Pará, s. Mato Grosso, and Mato Grosso do Sul; also in w. Rio Grande do Sul), n. and e. Bolivia (west to Beni), Paraguay, Uruguay, and n. and cen. Argentina (south to Mendoza, La Pampa, and sw. Buenos Aires); locally in campinas and other naturally open vegetation along the lower Amazon from Marajó Is. and s. Amapá upriver to near the mouth of the Rio Tapajós; s. Surinam (Sipaliwini). To at least 2300 m in Bolivia.

NOTE: This species is in need of a thorough racial revision.

Campylorhamphus Scythebills

A distinct genus of woodcreepers marked by their strikingly long, slender, and deeply decurved bills. Despite this unmistakable generic character, most scythebill species are confusingly similar to each other, and we should emphasize that in most cases the English modifier names that have long been applied are not particularly helpful in identification and in some cases are actually misleading. Scythebills are found widely in forested or wooded areas throughout much of South America, both in lowland and montane regions. In most areas only one species occurs, a fact that does greatly aid identification. Note that bill lengths are measured as the chord.

GROUP A

Rare, *large* scythebill with *Andean* distribution.

Campylorhamphus pucherani

GREATER SCYTHEBILL

PLATE: 14

DESCRIPTION: 29 cm (11½"); bill 6.5 cm (2½"). A *large* scythebill found locally in the *Andes from Colombia to Peru. Long and strikingly decurved bill dull pinkish horn* with blackish base of maxilla. *Essentially uniform rufescent brown* with *narrow white superciliary and somewhat broader malar streak;* faint narrow buff streaking on head and neck; wings and tail rufous.

SIMILAR SPECIES: Other scythebills are smaller and proportionately longer billed; none is found at elevations as high as the Greater favors. Strong-billed Woodcreeper has more massive and darker bill, prominent breast streaking, etc.

HABITAT AND BEHAVIOR: Rare in montane forest, foraging mainly in middle levels. Very poorly known in life; single individuals have been seen with mixed flocks. Its voice remains unknown.

RANGE: Locally in Andes of s. Colombia (W. Andes in Valle and Cauca, mainly on their w. slope; above upper Río Magdalena valley in Huila), nw. (w. Pichincha) and e. Ecuador (few records), and e. Peru (locally in Amazonas, San Martín, Huánuco, Ayacucho, and Cuzco). The published record for Puno at "Hacienda Cadena" (=Cadena) (Meyer de Schauensee 1966) is in error for Cuzco. Mostly 1500–3000 m.

NOTE: The species name is apparently correctly spelled *pucherani* (B. L. Monroe, Jr., pers. comm.), not *pucheranii* (as in Meyer de Schauensee 1966, 1970).

GROUP B

Standard scythebills; all more or less *streaked*.

Campylorhamphus trochilirostris

RED-BILLED SCYTHEBILL

PLATE: 14

DESCRIPTION: 24–28 cm (9½–11"); bill 6.5–9 cm (2½–3½"). *The most widespread scythebill,* ranging south to n. Argentina, though absent from Guianas and much of Amazonia. *Very long, decurved (sickle-shaped) bill reddish or reddish brown,* in some birds quite *bright.* Above brown to rufescent brown, somewhat duskier on crown; head and *back narrowly but prominently streaked with buff,* the streaks sometimes margined with dusky; rump, wings, and tail rufous-chestnut. Brown below with buff streaking on throat and breast (variable in extent and sometimes dusky edged). Extent of back streaking varies (*though some is always present*); *napensis* of e. Ecuador and ne. Peru is average. Nominate group of ne. and cen. Brazil (west to Goiás) is longer billed and more pallid (generally more olivaceous, less rufescent). More dramatically different are birds from sw. Brazil (s. Mato Grosso and Mato Grosso do Sul), e. Bolivia, and most of Paraguay (*lafresnayanus*), and n. Argentina and s. Paraguay (*hellmayri*); these are larger and *longer-billed,* especially the truly spectacular *hellmayri,* and are generally *more rufescent* with narrow streaking.

SIMILAR SPECIES: In most of its range Red-billed is the only scythebill present, and hence, on account of its remarkable bill, is instantly unmistakable. In Amazonia it overlaps locally with Curve-billed, which see. Brown-billed Scythebill occurs mainly on Andean slopes *above* range of Red-billed (though there may be some overlap); it differs in being considerably less prominently streaked than the races of Red-billed found in closest proximity below it.

HABITAT AND BEHAVIOR: Uncommon to locally fairly common in lower and middle growth of forest (both humid and deciduous), mature secondary woodland, gallery forest, and chaco and caatinga woodland. Although generally catholic in its habitat requirements, in Amazonia it seems mainly confined to várzea forest. Despite its extraordinary bill, the Red-billed Scythebill feeds much like the many other woodcreepers with "normal" bills, hitching up trunks and along major branches and probing into crevices, under pieces of bark, and in epiphytes (especially bromeliads). One or 2 often accompany mixed flocks, foraging at all levels from near the ground to the subcanopy. The song is a series of quite musical notes with an antbird-like quality, e.g., a somewhat descending "tuwee-tuwee-toowa-tew-tew" or an ascending "twee-twee-twee-twi-twi?," sometimes starting with a trill; agitated birds give a loud, descending, fairly musical chipper.

RANGE: Venezuela (east to Sucre and Bolívar) and n. Colombia (more humid Caribbean lowlands and south in Río Magdalena valley to Huila; east of Andes south along base of Andes to w. Meta; Pacific lowlands of Chocó); extreme sw. Colombia (w. Nariño), w. Ecuador, and nw. Peru (south to Piura); e. Ecuador (north locally to Napo), e. Peru, n. and e. Bolivia, Brazil (quite locally in Amazonia, ranging from the Rio Purus drainage east to the lower Rio Tapajós, north of it near the Amazon in the same region; more widespread in the northeast and interior, ranging from Ceará and Pernambuco south to s. Bahia and n. Minas Gerais, thence westward through s. Mato Grosso and Mato Grosso do Sul), Paraguay (widely west of the Río Paraguay, east of it only in the north and southwest), and n. Argentina (south to La Rioja, Santiago del Estero, n. Santa Fe, and Entre Ríos). Also Panama. Published sightings from French Guiana (Tostain et al. 1992) are regarded as uncertain. Mostly below 1000 m, but recorded to 2000 m in n. Venezuela and 1900 m in sw. Ecuador.

Campylorhamphus procurvoides

CURVE-BILLED SCYTHEBILL

DESCRIPTION: 22.5–24 cm (8¾–9″); bill 6 cm (2¼″). Amazonia. Resembles Red-billed Scythebill, with *bill also reddish* but slightly shorter. *North* of the Amazon relatively easy to distinguish from Red-billed on the basis of its *essentially unstreaked back;* in addition, its streaking below is somewhat finer, with more of a spotted effect especially on throat. See V-18, C-24. Nominate race (French Guiana west to near the lower Rio Negro) is larger than *sanus* (remainder of species' range north of Amazon). *South* of the Amazon (*multostriatus* and *probatus*) more difficult, for these Curve-billeds have pronounced streaking below (comparable to Red-billed's) and also are variably streaked with buff on back (much as in Red-billed). These and the locally sympatric races

of Red-billed (*snethlageae* and *notabilis*) are probably distinguishable only in the hand, on the basis of Curve-billed's slightly shorter and perhaps darker bill, greater contrast between olivaceous brown back and rufous rump, and more olivaceous tinge to ground color of underparts (more rufescent in Red-billed). Habitat and voice also help; see below.

HABITAT AND BEHAVIOR: Rare to locally uncommon in lower and middle growth of terra firme forest. Behavior much like Red-billed Scythebill's, which Curve-billed seems to replace in terra firme (Red-billed in Amazonia being found mainly in várzea). In Venezuela the song, given mainly at dawn, is a series of fairly musical, evenly pitched notes, the first note longest, "keeee, keee, kee-kee-kee-kee-kee" (P. Schwartz recording); it resembles Red-billed's song but tends to be slower and does not seem to slide up or down in pitch.

RANGE: Guianas, e. and sw. Venezuela (e. Bolívar and s. Amazonas), Amaz. Brazil (south to Rondônia at Cachoeira Nazaré and n. Mato Grosso at Alta Floresta, and east to the lower Rio Tocantins), ne. Peru (n. Loreto near e. bank of the lower Río Napo [unpublished LSUMZ specimens, *fide* G. Rosenberg]), extreme ne. Ecuador (Cuyabeno in Sucumbios, *fide* B. Whitney; published records for Limoncocha, Napo, are in error for Red-billed Scythebill), and se. Colombia (recorded only from w. Meta and w. Caquetá, but likely more widespread). We regard the record (Hilty and Brown 1986) from Norte de Santander, Colombia, as uncorroborated. Seems likely in n. Bolivia. To 500 m.

Campylorhamphus falcularius

BLACK-BILLED SCYTHEBILL

PLATE: 14

DESCRIPTION: 25.5 cm (10″); bill 6.5 cm (2½″). *Se. Brazil area. Very long, decurved (sickle-shaped) bill black.* Olivaceous brown above, crown and nape blackish and streaked with whitish; wings, lower rump, and tail rufous-chestnut. Throat whitish; remaining underparts pale olivaceous brown with narrow whitish streaking on chest.

SIMILAR SPECIES: With its long bill, unmistakable in range; does not overlap with Red-billed Scythebill (in area of overlap in s. Bahia, Red-billed occurs at *lower* elevations).

HABITAT AND BEHAVIOR: Rare to locally uncommon in lower and middle growth of humid forest and mature secondary woodland. Behavior much like Red-billed Scythebill's. Black-billed's song, however, is distinctly different, being a series of 8–12 notes which descend slightly in pitch with a throaty or raspy quality very unlike other scythebills', e.g., "jreet, jreet, jreet, jreet, jree-jree-jree-jrew."

RANGE: Se. Brazil (s. Bahia south to n. Rio Grande do Sul), e. Paraguay (Alto Paraná and Itapúa), and ne. Argentina (Misiones and ne. Corrientes). To about 1500 m.

Campylorhamphus pusillus

BROWN-BILLED SCYTHEBILL

DESCRIPTION: 24 cm (9½″); bill 6.5 cm (2½″). *Mainly Andean slopes. Very long, decurved (sickle-shaped) bill dull reddish brown to dusky-brown,* often paler below. Resembles Red-billed Scythebill (found in lowlands

below range of this species; some overlap is possible), but bill color is never as bright; the bill is also proportionately shorter; *streaking on both back and underparts is deeper buff, narrower, and without dusky margins;* throat buffier (not so whitish). See C-24.

SIMILAR SPECIES: Curve-billed Scythebill, also very similar and also conceivably overlapping along e. base of Andes, differs in its *unstreaked* back. Cf. also the larger and darker Greater Scythebill.

HABITAT AND BEHAVIOR: Rare to uncommon in lower and middle growth of montane forest and forest borders; strictly avoids drier regions, and thus rarely or perhaps never actually sympatric with Red-billed Scythebill, even in sw. Ecuador where the 2 species almost overlap. Behavior much like Red-billed's. The song has a sweet, almost tremulous quality but otherwise varies substantially in pattern, being a series of "tuwee" or "teeur" notes which either rise or fall in pitch or are intermixed with trills, e.g., "teeurrrrr, teeur-teeur-tutututututu."

RANGE: Mainly in Andes of extreme w. Venezuela (sw. Táchira), Colombia (mostly on slopes of W. Andes, but locally in Cen. and E. Andes as well; likely overlooked, or locally extirpated because of deforestation), Ecuador (south on w. slope to El Oro), and n. Peru (south to Cajamarca and San Martín); Sierra de Perijá on Venezuela-Colombia border. Also Costa Rica and Panama. The record from Guyana (Meyer de Schauensee 1966) seems to be in error. Recorded mostly 600–1700 m, in small numbers up to 2100 m, and locally down to near sea level in sw. Colombia.

Thamnophilidae   # TYPICAL ANTBIRDS

A LARGE and varied group of very small to midsized birds (a few are fairly large, culminating in the improbable but magnificent Giant Antshrike) found in a range of forested and wooded habitats across much of South America, though absent from much of Argentina and all of Chile. By a wide margin, species diversity is greatest in Amazonia, where upwards of 30 or even 40 species may be syntopic at certain localities. Recent evidence (summarized in Sibley and Ahlquist 1990) has demonstrated conclusively that what was once considered an even larger and more diverse antbird family (Formicariidae) is more properly divided into two families; the Thamnophilidae incorporates about 75% of the species. All genera seem to fall clearly into one family or the other; the correct placement of *Myrmornis* was long debated, but it is now clear that it belongs in the Thamnophilidae.

The Thamnophilidae and Formicariidae differ in their preferred foraging levels and the degree of sexual plumage dimorphism shown. Unlike the Formicariidae, only a very few members of the Thamnophilidae are mainly terrestrial; the vast majority are arboreal, feeding at varying heights above the ground, from the undergrowth to the subcanopy. Most forage by gleaning in foliage, and none habitually eats ants, the name being derived from the characteristic habit of certain species (see especially the species depicted on Plate 25) of following swarms of army ants, capturing arthropod (and sometimes small vertebrate) prey as it attempts to flee. Also unlike the Formicariidae, in which almost all species are monomorphic or virtually so, all but a few members of the Thamnophilidae show strong sexual dimorphism in plumage. Males tend to be gray, black, and white, whereas females tend to be brown, buff, or rufous; females often are more strikingly patterned (and hence are sometimes easier to identify). Females also often show more geographic variation than do males, a pattern that has been called heterogynism. The various genera of typical antbirds vary markedly in size, and some groups have been named (e.g., antwren, antvireo, etc.) for their superficial overall similarity (and similarity in bill shape) to groups of birds that were familiar to the people naming them. Some antshrikes and antbirds show expressive, bushy crests. Many typical antbirds favor dense growth, seem shy, and are hard to see well. Almost all vocalize a great deal, and once you begin to learn and track down their songs you will see and identify many more antbirds than if you simply rely on spotting them. Typical antbirds that have been studied are notably sedentary, and many species (perhaps most or even all) apparently mate for life. Nests are open cups typically placed in the fork of a branch.

Cymbilaimus Antshrikes

A pair of boldly barred antshrikes found in humid lowland forests, only recently shown to be separate species. Their closest generic relative appears to be *Thamnophilus*, especially that genus' "Barred" group (see N. Pierpont and J. W. Fitzpatrick, *Auk* 100[3]; 645–652, 1983), though *Cymbilaimus* is larger and heavier-billed.

Cymbilaimus lineatus

FASCIATED ANTSHRIKE

PLATE: 15

DESCRIPTION: 17–18 cm (6¾–7″). Heavy hooked bill with base of mandible pale. *Iris red.* Male *black narrowly barred with white;* in *intermedius* (most of Amazonia) the crown is basically solid black. *Below narrowly barred black and white.* Nominate race (Guianas, e. Venezuela, and n. Brazil west to the Rio Negro) shows fine white barring on crown as does, to a variable extent, *fasciatus* (west of Andes). Female blackish above *narrowly barred with pale buff;* crown rufous-chestnut, forehead barred buff and black. *Below buff narrowly barred with black.*
SIMILAR SPECIES: Much more of a forest bird than any of the "Barred" *Thamnophilus* antshrikes, all of which are *more coarsely* barred and have yellow irides. The much rarer Undulated Antshrike is considerably larger; males have much fainter, wavier white barring and a black throat, and females are much more rufous generally. In sw. Amazonia cf. also the similar Bamboo Antshrike.
HABITAT AND BEHAVIOR: Uncommon to fairly common in vine-tangled borders and openings in humid forest (e.g., treefalls or along forest streams) and second-growth woodland. Usually in pairs which forage deliberately at all levels, most frequently in midstrata and less often low, but generally remain within heavy cover and often are hard to see. Sometimes accompanies mixed flocks of understory birds. The song is a series of 6–8 steadily repeated, soft whistled notes, "cü, cü, cü, cü . . . ," with ventriloquial quality.
RANGE: W. Venezuela (slopes of Sierra de Perijá and east to Mérida, w. Barinas, and w. Apure), n. and w. Colombia (humid Caribbean lowlands east to Norte de Santander, and south in Río Magdalena valley to e. Antioquia; Pacific lowlands), and w. Ecuador (south to Pichincha and n. Manabí); Guianas, s. Venezuela (Bolívar and Amazonas), e. Colombia (north to Meta and Guainía), e. Ecuador, e. Peru, n. Bolivia (south to n. La Paz, and in ne. Santa Cruz on the Serranía de Huanchaca), and Amaz. Brazil (south to sw. Mato Grosso, and east to the lower Rio Tocantins). Also Honduras to Panama. Mostly below 1000 m, occasionally a bit higher.

Cymbilaimus sanctaemariae

BAMBOO ANTSHRIKE

DESCRIPTION: 17 cm (6¾″). *Limited area in sw. Amazonia.* Both sexes resemble respective sexes of Fasciated Antshrike but have *considerably longer crests* (often with a shaggy effect) and brown eyes. Male Bamboo further differs in having all its white barring somewhat broader and more sharply defined, and in having white barring on tail confined to the sides. Female Bamboo has darker brown crown with *black feathers posteriorly* and is *brighter buff below* with black barring confined to sides, flanks, and crissum.
HABITAT AND BEHAVIOR: Uncommon to locally fairly common in and near *Guadua* bamboo thickets in humid lowland forest (in most areas especially in transitional forest), sometimes at treefalls or borders. Usually in pairs which forage within dense cover in middle strata and are

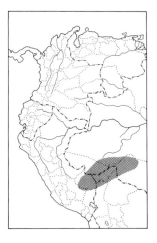

often difficult to see clearly; they regularly accompany mixed flocks of antwrens, furnariids, tanagers, etc. Like the Fasciated, the Bamboo Antshrike is much more apt to be noted once its characteristic song is recognized: a rather fast series of sharply enunciated, far-carrying, clear notes, "cheeyt-cheeyt-cheeyt-cheeyt . . ." (up to 12 or more "cheeyt"s). Quite numerous at the Tambopata Reserve in Madre de Dios, Peru (where often more in evidence than Fasciated; at times both can be heard singing simultaneously), and also around Hacienda Amazonia in adjacent Cuzco.

RANGE: Locally in se. Peru (Madre de Dios and Cuzco), extreme nw. Bolivia (Pando), and sw. Amaz. Brazil (Acre, and Rondônia at Cachoeira Nazaré). 300–1200 m.

NOTE: *C. sanctaemariae* was shown to be a separate species from *C. lineatus* by N. Pierpont and J. W. Fitzpatrick (*Auk* 100[3]: 645–652, 1983).

Frederickena Antshrikes

A pair of very large, proportionately short-tailed, crested antshrikes with massive bills found in humid forests of Amazonia and the Guianas. Both are rare and infrequently encountered.

Frederickena unduligera

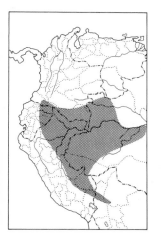

UNDULATED ANTSHRIKE　　　　　　PLATE: 15

DESCRIPTION: 23 cm (9″). W. Amazonia. Somewhat crested. Iris variably colored, usually brownish to pale orange (consistently pale yellow in *diversa*); bill very heavy, bluish to horn below. Male *black with uniform very narrow wavy grayish white barring;* throat blacker. See C-XIII. *Pallida* (se. Peru, nw. Bolivia, and w. Brazil from the Rio Juruá to w. bank of the lower Rio Madeira) similar but with wider gray barring, so that whole effect is paler. Female *evenly barred rufous and black above* (with wavy pattern as in male), more chestnut and black on crown; tail black barred with gray. *Below rich rufous-buff with narrow wavy black barring.* Immature males require considerable time before attaining full adult plumage and are black with variable amount of wavy rufous-buff to white barring. *Diversa* (e. Peru south of the Amazon and Río Marañón) and *pallida* females have narrower black barring above (resulting in paler effect) and are *much less heavily barred below,* with belly an unmarked rich rufous-buff.

SIMILAR SPECIES: So much larger than other antshrikes in its range that confusion is unlikely; does not occur with congeneric Black-throated Antshrike. Cf. especially *Cymbilaimus* antshrikes.

HABITAT AND BEHAVIOR: Rare to locally uncommon in undergrowth of humid forest, primarily in terra firme and especially in dense viny growth around treefalls. Found singly or in pairs, skulking in heavy cover, sometimes hopping somewhat jay-like from branch to branch, and rarely associating with mixed flocks. The song in Ecuador and Colombia is a steadily repeated series of notes (usually 11–16), "uué, uué, uué . . . ," somewhat like Fasciated Antshrike's but higher pitched, faster, and with more notes (Hilty and Brown 1986; RSR); vocalizing birds may raise crest with each call and wag tail. Also has a nasal snarling alarm call much like that of *Mackenziaena* antshrikes. The song of a bird in Bolivia differed in pattern and quality from the songs of more northern birds, being "a rising series of 6–8 short whistles" (Parker et al. 1991).

RANGE: Se. Colombia (north to w. Caquetá and Amazonas in the Leticia area), e. Ecuador, e. Peru, nw. Bolivia (n. La Paz at Alto Madidi and se. Beni at Serranía Eva Eva), and w. Amaz. Brazil (north of the Amazon only in upper Rio Negro region, south of it east to the lower Rio Madeira). Mostly below 700 m (recorded up to 1050 m in s. Peru).

NOTE: It has been suggested that more than one species may be involved (Parker et al. 1991).

Frederickena viridis

BLACK-THROATED ANTSHRIKE　　　　PLATE: 15

DESCRIPTION: 20.5 cm (8"). Ne. South America. Somewhat crested. Iris red (both sexes); very heavy bill bluish to horn below. Male *uniform plumbeous gray,* blacker on head and *blackest on throat and midchest.* Female *uniform rufous-chestnut above,* darkest on crown; tail black barred with gray. *Forehead, sides of head and neck, and entire underparts uniformly barred grayish white and black.* See V-21.

SIMILAR SPECIES: Larger and heavier-billed than other sympatric antshrikes. Female is quite striking and somewhat recalls females of smaller and yellow-eyed Lined and Chestnut-backed Antshrikes (but no range or habitat overlap).

HABITAT AND BEHAVIOR: Uncommon to rare in undergrowth of humid forest, mainly in low tangled viny growth in small openings and at treefalls. Usually in pairs, very skulking and hard to see. Wags its tail like Undulated Antshrike (E. O. Willis). Its song is a steadily repeated series of clear, melancholy notes, "teeü, teeü, teeü, teeü . . ." (usually 9–11 notes), reminiscent of Fasciated Antshrike's song but faster and a longer series of notes.

RANGE: Guianas, se. Venezuela (Bolívar and extreme n. Amazonas at Junglaven), and ne. Brazil (north of the Amazon from Amapá west to the lower Rio Negro in the Manaus area). To at least 500 m.

Mackenziaena Antshrikes

A pair of large and spectacular, but exceptionally shy and skulking, antshrikes found only in the forests of se. Brazil and adjacent areas. Both species are long-tailed, the Large-tailed notably so, but for their size are not particularly large billed.

Mackenziaena severa

TUFTED ANTSHRIKE　　　　PLATE: 15

DESCRIPTION: 24 cm (9½"). *Se. Brazil area.* Iris rufous. *Prominently crested.* Male *mostly dark sooty gray,* blacker on crown, sides of head, and

throat. Female has *rufous crown;* above otherwise blackish brown, *boldly banded with rufous-buff;* tail solid gray. *Below uniformly barred pale buff and blackish.*

SIMILAR SPECIES: On account of its crest, confusion is unlikely. Female Large-tailed Antshrike is spotted (not barred), lacks crest.

HABITAT AND BEHAVIOR: Fairly common in dense lower growth of humid forest, second-growth woodland, and thickets, especially where there is an understory of bamboo. Usually in pairs which skulk about sneakily in dense undergrowth, almost never with mixed flocks and heard far more often than seen. Male's song is a series of 6–8 loud, sharply enunciated, and piercing whistled notes, "pseuw, pseeee, psee, pseee, psee, psee." It is far carrying, and males will often respond readily to tape playback, though seldom perching for long in the open. Females, however, rarely come in; when they do, they usually remain concealed, content merely to voice their concern with a nasal "squeeeyahh" call as they hop around inside cover.

RANGE: Se. Brazil (Espírito Santo and s. Minas Gerais south to Santa Catarina and n. Rio Grande do Sul), ne. Argentina (Misiones), and extreme e. Paraguay (Alto Paraná). To about 1300 m.

Mackenziaena leachii

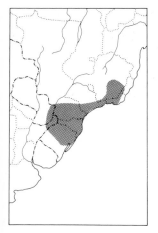

LARGE-TAILED ANTSHRIKE

PLATE: 15

DESCRIPTION: 26.5 cm (10½"). *Se. Brazil area. Tail very long.* Male entirely black with *profuse small white spots on head, neck, back, wings, and* (to a lesser extent) *belly.* Female has crown and neck black *spotted with rufous;* otherwise black above *with prominent but sparse buff spots,* many chevron- or diamond-shaped; tail blackish. *Below black thickly spotted with buffy whitish.*

SIMILAR SPECIES: This striking antshrike is the only large, basically black antbird that is conspicuously spotted. Cf. Spot-backed Antshrike (also spotted with white above, but *mostly white below*).

HABITAT AND BEHAVIOR: Uncommon to fairly common in lower growth of humid forest, second-growth woodland, and thickets at forest borders, often where there is a dense understory of bamboo. Regularly occurs with Tufted Antshrike (e.g., in the Iguazú Falls area), though in much of s. Brazil the Large-tailed tends to be found at higher elevations. Its behavior is much like Tufted's; though Large-tailed tends to be less skulking, it too is heard far more often than seen. The song, basically similar, consists of more notes (usually 15 or so) which are more rapidly delivered; they gradually but distinctly rise in pitch before falling off on the last 2 or 3. Its "squehh" call note is much the same as Tufted's. Unlike the latter, pairs of Large-taileds often respond to tape playback together. This spectacular but prosaically named antshrike (a better name would be "Great Spotted Antshrike"!) is perhaps most readily seen at upper levels of Itatiaia Nat. Park in Brazil.

RANGE: Se. Brazil (Espírito Santo and s. Minas Gerais south to Rio Grande do Sul), e. Paraguay (a few records from Alto Paraná and Itapúa), and ne. Argentina (Misiones). To about 2100 m.

Hypoedaleus Antshrikes

A monotypic genus confined to se. South America, the Spot-backed Antshrike is distinctively patterned and, unlike most of its presumed closest relatives, is arboreal.

Hypoedaleus guttatus

SPOT-BACKED ANTSHRIKE   PLATE: 15

DESCRIPTION: 20.5 cm (8″). *Se. Brazil area.* Male black above *with profuse bold white spots,* tail black boldly banded with white. *Below mostly white,* feathers on sides of chest outlined in black producing a spotted effect, becoming ochraceous on flanks and crissum. Female similar, but spots on upperparts tinged buff and all of underparts tinged ochraceous. *Leucogaster* (Bahia south to Espírito Santo and e. Minas Gerais) males lack ochraceous below; in females it is restricted to belly.

SIMILAR SPECIES: Distinctively and boldly patterned, this antshrike is not likely to be confused.

HABITAT AND BEHAVIOR: Uncommon to locally fairly common in canopy and borders of humid forest and mature second-growth woodland, often in mid-strata viny tangles. Forages solitarily or in pairs and is usually hard to spot, remaining in dense leafy cover; sometimes 1 or a pair will accompany a canopy flock and may come lower and more out into the open, occasionally even dropping down into tangled understory. Much more often recorded once its voice is recognized. The distinctive song, lasting 4–5 seconds, is a fast musical trill which gradually builds into a crescendo; though much louder and more piercing, it recalls the song of Long-billed Gnatwren. Both sexes also give 2 very different calls, a piercing "pyeeeeeeeeeeyeuw" and an abrupt and startling "chrrrrrt!" Seems especially numerous at the Mbaracayu Reserve in e. Paraguay.

RANGE: Se. Brazil (s. Bahia, Minas Gerais, and s. Goiás south to Santa Catarina), e. Paraguay (north to Amambay in Cerro Corá Nat. Park), and ne. Argentina (Misiones). To about 800 m.

Batara Antshrikes

By far the largest antbird, the spectacular Giant Antshrike is a rarely seen inhabitant of subtropical forests in s.-cen. South America. Its very loud voice can be heard for well over a kilometer.

Batara cinerea

GIANT ANTSHRIKE   PLATE: 15

DESCRIPTION: 30.5–35.5 cm (12½–14″). Nominate race (se. Brazil area) considerably larger than *argentina* and *excubitor* (Andes and adjacent chaco). *Unmistakable: a spectacularly large antshrike with long tail* and massive, rather pale bill. Somewhat crested (crest normally protruding only to rear, not upward). Male with solid black crown; otherwise *black above narrowly banded with white. Below uniform gray.* Female has

chestnut crown becoming black on hindcrown; otherwise *broadly banded black and ochraceous buff above* (banding wider than male's). Below uniform dull buff to grayish buff. Female *excubitor* (Santa Cruz, Bolivia) has much less black on hindcrown.

SIMILAR SPECIES: So much larger than any other antbird that confusion is virtually impossible; almost the size of a Squirrel Cuckoo, *Piaya cayana.*

HABITAT AND BEHAVIOR: Rare to locally fairly common in lower and middle growth of humid forest and forest borders; locally also in dense thickets of terrestrial bromeliads in chaco woodland and scrub. Usually in pairs, very shy and exceptionally difficult to see (especially for a bird its size!), skulking in heavy cover, almost never coming into the open, usually slipping away at your approach. Its very loud, ringing song routinely calls attention to its presence but is ventriloquial; calling birds are hard to track down, and even tape playback often seems ineffective. The song is a fast series of musical notes, usually starting with a trill and ending with several "ch" notes, thus, "tredede-deh!-deh!-deh!-deh!-deh!-deh!-deh!-deh!-ch-ch." Its alarm call is similar to that of the 2 *Mackenziaena* antshrikes. Pairs seem to maintain large territories. Especially numerous in Calilegua Nat. Park in Jujuy, Argentina.

RANGE: E. slope of Andes in s. Bolivia (north to w. Santa Cruz, with a single record from the chaco in s. Santa Cruz at Estancia Perforación), nw. Argentina (south to Tucumán), and w. Paraguay (a few records from Boquerón and Presidente Hayes); se. Brazil (Espírito Santo south to Rio Grande do Sul), and ne. Argentina (Misiones). Further work will likely show that its distribution in the chaco is more continuous than shown. To about 3000 m in Bolivia.

Taraba Antshrikes

A single species of widespread and fairly well known antshrike found in shrubby clearings and scrub.

Taraba major

GREAT ANTSHRIKE

PLATE: 15

DESCRIPTION: 20 cm (8″). Heavy hooked bill; slight bushy crest. *Iris bright red.* Male *black above* with variable amount of white tipping on wing-coverts forming 2 or 3 wing-bars; tail varies from essentially all black above in n. and w. races (including *semifasciatus*), with white showing at most on outer feathers, to rather boldly banded with white in s. and e. races. *Below all white,* flanks and lower belly tinged grayish. Female with similar pattern, but *rufous-chestnut to rufous replaces male's black,* and flanks and crissum tinged buff; wings and tail *lack* white; see V-21, C-27.

SIMILAR SPECIES: The bicolored pattern and conspicuous red eye make recognition of this widespread antshrike easy.

HABITAT AND BEHAVIOR: Fairly common in dense undergrowth and thickets in clearings, second-growth woodland, and forest borders,

both in humid and arid regions. Usually in pairs which hop about low to the ground, generally remaining out of sight because of the nature of their habitat, not because they are particularly shy. On Trinidad frequently found at antswarms, but elsewhere this is much less common. The song is a series of slightly accelerating hooting notes, rather trogon-like except for the distinctive nasal or snarled ending, "nyaah," seemingly added almost as an afterthought.

RANGE: Widespread in lowlands south to n. Argentina (south to Córdoba, Santa Fe, and Entre Ríos) and s. Brazil (south to Paraná, São Paulo, Minas Gerais, and Espírito Santo); west of Andes south to extreme nw. Peru (Tumbes and n. Piura); Trinidad. Also Mexico to Panama. Mostly below 1500 m.

Biatas Antshrikes

A very distinct, monotypic genus found mainly in the mountains of se. Brazil; its relationships remain obscure. Its heavy bill is unusual for an antshrike in that it is *not* hooked.

Biatas nigropectus

WHITE-BEARDED ANTSHRIKE   PLATE: 16

DESCRIPTION: 18 cm (7"). *A little-known, rare endemic of se. Brazil and adjacent Argentina.* Bill stout, unhooked. Male with *black crown* (sometimes a bit of white in front of and behind eye) contrasting with *creamy white nuchal collar extending from around neck forward across cheeks (which are purer white) and onto chin;* above otherwise pale olive reddish brown, rufous on wings and tail. *Large pectoral shield black;* lower underparts pale olivaceous brown. Female has crown rufous-chestnut with white superciliary; *buffy whitish nuchal collar much as in male;* above olive brown, wings and tail rufous. Below pale olivaceous brown.

SIMILAR SPECIES: Not likely confused, though White-bearded's pattern of contrasting collar, especially female's, is reminiscent of White-collared Foliage-gleaner.

HABITAT AND BEHAVIOR: Rare in lower and middle growth of humid forest and forest borders; apparently confined to areas where bamboo stands are both extensive and relatively tall. Poorly known and very infrequently encountered; seen singly or in pairs, most often while accompanying mixed flocks, regularly in the company of White-collared Foliage-gleaner. The antshrike's song is a series of 6–8 soft, fairly melodic but querulous and high-pitched notes, "kiu-kiu-kiu-kiu-kiu-kiu-kiu," delivered at a rate of about two "kiu"s per second and with pauses of 5–15 seconds between songs; both members of a pair give much the same song (D. Finch recording). This species, which seems always to have been scarce, likely deserves formal threatened status because of forest clearance and fragmentation. Small numbers occur at lower elevations of Itatiaia Nat. Park and at least on the Brazilian side of Iguazú Falls.

RANGE: Se. Brazil (s. Minas Gerais and Rio de Janeiro south to ne. Santa Catarina at Blumenau; published records from Espírito Santo require confirmation) and ne. Argentina (Misiones). Probably occurs in adjacent Paraguay. To 1300 m.

Sakesphorus Antshrikes

A rather heterogeneous group, the *Sakesphorus* antshrikes may not form a natural unit, for no character seems truly to unite them. Some species are prominently crested, others are not; some are characteristic of semiopen woodland and scrub, others are found inside humid forest; some have complex plumage patterns, others notably simple. At least vocally, however, all are fairly similar.

GROUP A

Black-hooded effect in males; wings prominently *spotted and margined in both sexes.*

Sakesphorus bernardi

COLLARED ANTSHRIKE

PLATE: 16

DESCRIPTION: 16.5–17 cm (6½–6¾"). *Sw. Ecuador and nw. Peru. Expressive bushy crest (male's longer). Head, throat, and center of chest black* with variable amount of white speckling on face and, to a lesser extent, on throat (apparently more in younger birds), contrasting with *white nuchal collar, sides of chest, and lower underparts.* Back brown, wings dusky with conspicuous white spotting on coverts, 2 white wing-bars, and white and rufous edging on flight feathers; tail black with feathers tipped white. Female has *rufous crown* with pale buffyish forehead, *sides of head black speckled white* contrasting with *buff to ochraceous nuchal collar and entire underparts.* Back rufous brown, wings duskier with 2 white to deep buff spotted wing-bars and edging on flight feathers, *tail all rufous.* Birds of s. Ecuador (El Oro and Loja) and Peru (*cajamarcae* group) are slightly larger than nominate race (Ecuador south to Guayas); males are richer brown on back with more rufescent edging on wings.
SIMILAR SPECIES: In its range nothing really similar.
HABITAT AND BEHAVIOR: Common in undergrowth of deciduous forest, lighter woodland, desert scrub, and thickets; found only in arid regions. A bold and relatively easily observed antshrike which often seems almost inquisitive but at other times may remain inside cover for protracted periods. Then often its habit of nearly continuously slowly wagging its tail will identify it even if only a silhouette is visible. The song is a characteristic "ánk, ar-r-r-r-r-r"; both sexes also give a deliberate series of "ank" notes.
RANGE: Sw. Ecuador (north to Manabí, and inland through s. Loja) and nw. Peru (on Pacific slope south to La Libertad, also in Río Marañón valley in Cajamarca). To 1500 m.

Sakesphorus canadensis

BLACK-CRESTED ANTSHRIKE

DESCRIPTION: 16 cm (6¼"). *Semiopen parts of n. South America* (also very locally in Amazonia). Resembles Collared Antshrike (no overlap)

but *notably smaller*. Male differs in having black bib on throat and mid-chest extending down median underparts to midbreast, and in many races is more rufous brown on back and grayer on lower underparts (darkest in *fumosus* of s. Venezuela and adjacent Colombia). Birds of n. Colombia and nw. Venezuela east to cen. Falcón (*pulchellus* and *paraguanae*) have face and throat speckled white (not solid black) and are as white below as Collared Antshrike. Female differs from female Collared in having *throat and (usually) breast finely but distinctly streaked black*, and *tail black tipped white* (not all rufous). See V-21, C-27.

SIMILAR SPECIES: Male's striking pattern and conspicuous crest make it easily recognizable; female is more obscure, but its rufous crown and crest and its streaking below should help (and as the species tends to move about in pairs, there usually is a male nearby for confirmation). In n. Colombia and n. Venezuela, cf. much less numerous Black-backed Antshrike.

HABITAT AND BEHAVIOR: Fairly common to common in lighter woodland, arid scrub and savannas with scattered taller trees, gallery forest, and mangroves; in w. Amazonia, where *much* less numerous and more local, favors shrubbery and trees around the margins of blackwater lakes. Ranges locally (e.g., in French Guiana) into gardens and even city parks (Tostain et al. 1992). Usually in pairs, hopping about in lower and middle growth, generally not too difficult to see; both sexes frequently wag their tails, even when not singing. Sometimes with mixed flocks but at least as often forages independently. The song is a series of notes that start slowly and then rise and accelerate distinctively, "woh, woh, woh-woh-wehwehwehweh?"; the female often echoes the male. The song of Eastern Slaty-Antshrike is quite similar.

RANGE: N. and ne. Colombia (west to n. Chocó in lower Río Atrato valley, and south in Río Magdalena valley to Santander; llanos region south to Meta and Vichada), virtually all of Venezuela (except humid forested regions, and thus somewhat local, especially south of the Orinoco), Guianas, and n. Brazil (Rio Negro region); very locally in se. Colombia (Leticia area at Loretoyacu), and ne. Peru (a few localities near the lower Río Ucayali and lower Río Marañón in Loreto); s. Amaz. Brazil (n. Mato Grosso at Serra do Cachimbo); Trinidad. To 400 m.

Sakesphorus cristatus

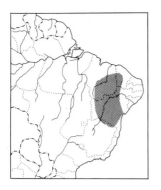

SILVERY-CHEEKED ANTSHRIKE   PLATE: 16

DESCRIPTION: 14.5 cm (5¾"). *Ne. Brazil*. Male has *foreface, crest, and bib extending down over throat and chest black* contrasting with *silvery white cheeks and sides of neck* (grayer in some birds), becoming gray on hindneck. Otherwise rufous brown above; wings black with 2 white-spotted wing-bars and rufous edging on flight feathers; tail black *boldly barred with white*. Lower underparts grayish white. Female *pale rufous above, brighter on crown, crest, and tail;* wings dusky with *2 spotted buffy whitish wing-bars,* flight feathers edged rufous. Below drab buffy whitish.

SIMILAR SPECIES: Dapper male of this small antshrike is easily known in its limited range. Female is more uniform rufous above than female Rufous-winged Antshrike, which also lacks wing-bars.

HABITAT AND BEHAVIOR: Locally fairly common in lower growth and borders of deciduous woodland and arid scrub. Usually in pairs, moving about close to the ground, often skulking for long periods but quite responsive to tape playback. The song is a gravelly but fairly musical "chup, chup, chup, chup, chuh-chuh-chuh-ch-ch-ch-chah," often given by both members of the pair in partial syncopation; also has a very different and, unusual for an antshrike, quite musical call note, "too," steadily repeated at 1- to 2-second intervals. This species is readily found at a number of s. Bahia localities, notably in the Jequié and Boa Nova region.

RANGE: Ne. Brazil (Piauí and Ceará south to Bahia and extreme n. Minas Gerais). Mostly 500–1200 m.

Sakesphorus melanonotus

BLACK-BACKED ANTSHRIKE PLATE: 16

DESCRIPTION: 15.5–16 cm (6–6¼"). *N. Colombia and n. Venezuela.* Much less crested than the previous *Sakesphorus* antshrikes. Male *mainly black above and on throat and breast,* black ending in a point on upper belly; rump gray; scapulars, 2 spotted wing-bars, and edging on flight feathers conspicuously white; tail feathers broadly tipped white. Sides of lower breast and belly white; crissum black, feathers tipped white. Female has *blackish crown;* otherwise dull buffy brown above, wings duskier with 2 spotted whitish wing-bars, *tail rufous-chestnut,* feathers narrowly tipped whitish. Below uniform dull ochraceous. See V-21.

SIMILAR SPECIES: Pattern of black and white male vaguely recalls that of smaller White-fringed Antwren. Female somewhat resembles female Black-crested Antshrike, which has a rufous (not blackish) crown and fine black streaking on throat and chest.

HABITAT AND BEHAVIOR: Rare to locally uncommon in lower growth of deciduous woodland and scrub, frequently in thickets near perennial streams. Less numerous and conspicuous than Black-crested Antshrike. Pairs often forage together, usually independently of mixed flocks. Their tails, almost constantly lowered and then raised, are sometimes also wagged. The song is reported to be a short, throaty roll, "rrrrrrr" (P. Schwartz recording, *in* Hilty and Brown 1986); the call, more often heard, is a nasal "hoo-ráh."

RANGE: Caribbean n. Colombia (west to the Barranquilla area in Atlántico) and n. Venezuela (east locally, in more arid areas, to Miranda; also in nw. Táchira). To 500 m.

GROUP B

Males *mainly black* with white tail-tipping; females distinctive.

Sakesphorus melanothorax

BAND-TAILED ANTSHRIKE PLATE: 16

DESCRIPTION: 17 cm (6¾"). *Ne. South America.* Male *uniform deep black;* wing-coverts with small white spots, *tail with broad white band at tip.* Female *uniform bright rufous-chestnut above. Sides of head, throat, and breast contrastingly black,* becoming brownish gray on lower underparts; lower flanks and crissum rufous.

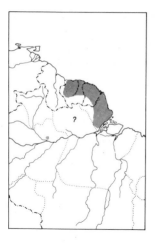

SIMILAR SPECIES: Few other medium-sized antbirds in this species' limited range are so lustrous black, and none shows the conspicuous white terminal tail band. Female's simple, 2-toned rufous and black pattern is distinctive. Unlike most other *Sakesphorus,* Band-tailed shows no crest.

HABITAT AND BEHAVIOR: Rare in undergrowth of humid forest, primarily associated with viny tangles and treefalls. Not a well-known bird. Its song is a slow-paced, rather hollow "kaw, kaw, kaw, kaw, kü-kü" (T. Davis recording). Perhaps most numerous and widespread in French Guiana.

RANGE: Surinam, French Guiana, and lower Amaz. Brazil (mainly in Amapá; also seen by E. O. Willis at Balbina, north of Manaus). E. O. Willis (*Ciencia y Cultura* 40[3]: 280–284, 1988) believes the record from south of the Amazon near the lower Rio Tapajós is in error. To about 500 m.

Sakesphorus luctuosus

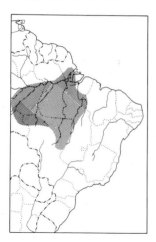

GLOSSY ANTSHRIKE

PLATE: 16

DESCRIPTION: 17.5 cm (7"). *Riparian thickets of lower and cen. Amaz. Brazil south to Goiás. Long, shaggy crest* often fully raised when agitated. Male *uniform deep black,* with scapulars edged white and outer tail feathers tipped white. Female similar but duller and sootier black, somewhat grayer on flanks, and with *chestnut crown.*

SIMILAR SPECIES: In its range and habitat this prominently crested antshrike is distinctive. Castlenau's Antshrike might overlap with this species in cen. Amazonia, and its habitat is similar, but Castlenau's is larger and has no crest.

HABITAT AND BEHAVIOR: Common in riparian thickets (often on islands) and in lower growth of seasonally flooded várzea woodland. Usually in pairs which hop about slowly in tangles and bushes, occasionally mounting well up into trees; the tail is often slowly wagged. The song, a series of slow, measured notes on 1 pitch, starts slowly and then speeds up at the end, "caw, caw, caw, caw-caw-caw-ca-ca-ca-cacaca." Numerous on Amazon River islands near Santarém.

RANGE: Lower and cen. Amaz. Brazil (Amapá west along n. bank of the Amazon to the lower Rio Negro, south of it west to the lower Rio Purus, and south to Rondônia, n. Mato Grosso, and s. Goiás). Below about 300 m.

Xenornis Antshrikes

The Speckled Antshrike has streaked plumage, unique among the antshrikes, and short bristles in front of and below the eye; its bill is fairly heavy and hooked.

Xenornis setifrons

SPECKLED ANTSHRIKE

PLATE: 16

Other: Gray-faced Antbird, Speckle-breasted Antshrike, Spiny-faced Antshrike

DESCRIPTION: 16 cm (6¼"). *Nw. Colombia*. Iris gray. Male *dark brown above with tawny-buff streaks;* wings with 2 prominent buff-spotted wing-bars; tail blackish, outer feathers narrowly tipped whitish. *Sides of head and entire underparts dark slaty gray.* Birds in full adult male plumage seem to be rare. See P-40. Female like male above but with buff streaking narrower (essentially reduced to shaft streaks); tail lacks pale tipping. *Throat streaked whitish and dusky;* breast and belly brown, *breast flammulated with buff.*

SIMILAR SPECIES: Overall color and pattern are much more like a furnariid's than an antshrike's. Most similar foliage-gleaners have a contrasting rufous tail and behave rather differently.

HABITAT AND BEHAVIOR: Rare in undergrowth of humid forest (but perhaps in part overlooked?). Not very well known, and with a very limited range. Forages mostly in pairs, usually with mixed understory flocks (especially *Myrmotherula* antwrens), and favoring dense viny tangled growth. Foraging birds usually perch more or less erectly (recalling a *Thamnomanes* antshrike), often remaining motionless for extended periods, then abruptly sallying after small insect prey, usually to leaves. Foraging birds are often quiet and inconspicuous. The song is a series of 3–9 (most often 5) high-pitched and evenly spaced notes which rise steadily in pitch; the call is a fairly loud, fast "chak-chak-chak" (sometimes only 1 or up to 5 or more syllables). Song and call are given by both sexes. Behavior and vocalization data are summarized from B. M. Whitney and G. H. Rosenberg (*Condor* 95[1]: 227–231, 1993).

RANGE: Nw. Colombia (n. and cen. Chocó). Also e. Panama. To about 600 m.

NOTE: Several English names have been proposed for this distinctive antshrike. E. Eisenmann (*Trans. Linn. Soc. New York* 6, 1955) suggested Gray-faced Antbird, but this has not been used since. Meyer de Schauensee (1966, 1970) employed Speckle-breasted Antshrike, apparently before the plain gray underparts of fully adult males were known. Wetmore's (1972) Spiny-faced Antshrike was employed by the 1983 AOU Check-list; *Xenornis* does indeed have short bristles from the loral area down to the upper chin, but these are virtually impossible to discern in the field. We feel the name Speckled Antshrike, seemingly first proposed by Ridgely (1976) and also used by Hilty and Brown (1986) and Sibley and Monroe (1990) to be the best choice, because *Xenornis* is the most generally speckled of the antshrikes.

Thamnophilus Antshrikes

A large and rather diverse genus of antbirds found throughout tropical and subtropical South America, reaching their highest diversity in humid lowland forests but also with representatives (usually from Group A) in many semiopen, even scrubby, habitats. They are small to midsized antbirds with well-hooked, usually quite stout, bills. *Thamnophilus* antshrikes typically occur in pairs, the more forest-based species frequently occurring with mixed understory flocks. Plumage patterns are most complex in the "Barred" group (though note that in some species only males are barred). The predominant color of all other male *Thamnophilus* is gray to slaty black, usually with black and white accenting; females are brownish to chestnut, many with white to buff accenting. Vocalizations, often given, are a useful identification aid and also assist in locating these otherwise quite unobtrusive birds.

GROUP A

Males more or less *barred below*.

Thamnophilus doliatus

BARRED ANTSHRIKE   PLATE: 16

DESCRIPTION: 16–16.5 cm (6¼–6½"). *The widespread, familiar black and white (male) or rufous (female) antshrike of lowland thickets.* Iris yellow. Expressive loose crest, raised when excited. Male *above black coarsely barred with white* except for *solid black crown* (some races have some semiconcealed white) and more streaked sides of head and neck. *Below white evenly barred with black* except for black-streaked throat. Some racial variation: *nigrescens* of Venezuela's Maracaibo basin is the blackest (with very wide black barring below), whereas *albicans* (Colombia's upper Río Magdalena valley), *capistratus* (ne. Brazil), and *radiatus* (e. Bolivia and se. Brazil southward) are relatively pale, with narrow black barring below; *cadwaladeri* (known only from Tarija, Bolivia) is the whitest below, with almost no barring on belly. Female *bright cinnamon-rufous above* with wings, tail, and especially crown darker rufous; *sides of head and hindneck narrowly streaked buffy whitish and black.* Below pale buff to rather deep ochraceous buff, whiter on throat. *Capistratus* has some black speckling or faint barring across breast; *cadwaladeri* is almost white below, tinged buff only on sides and flanks.

SIMILAR SPECIES: Resembles, to varying degrees, several other more or less "barred" antshrikes in this Group, none of which is as common or wide ranging as this well-known species. Cf. especially Chapman's (sw. Ecuador and nw. Peru) and Bar-crested (mainly Colombia) Antshrikes.

HABITAT AND BEHAVIOR: Common in thickets and dense lower growth of forest borders, lighter woodland, clearings, gardens, and scrub; occurs in both humid and arid regions. Usually in pairs, slowly hopping about in vegetation, peering intently into foliage, usually remaining within cover but not very shy, at times moving unconcernedly in the semiopen. Its frequently heard song, given by both sexes (female often echoes male), is a fast accelerating series of nasal notes, "hah-hah-ha-ha-hahahahahahahaha-hánh," always with a strongly emphasized final note; also has several other growling or guttural calls.

RANGE: Widespread east of Andes south to Bolivia, Paraguay, n. Argentina (south locally to Santiago del Estero and Formosa), and s. Brazil (south to Paraná and São Paulo; not found in e. coastal lowlands); apparently absent from parts of Amazonia (the upper Rio Negro drainage, and part of s. Pará and n. Mato Grosso); west of Andes in n. Colombia and nw. Venezuela (including Margarita Is.); Trinidad and Tobago. Also Mexico to Panama. Mostly below 1500 m, locally up to 2000 m or slightly higher.

NOTE: Does not include *T. zarumae* (Chapman's Antshrike) of sw. Ecuador and nw. Peru. *Cadwaladeri* is so different from the surrounding form of Barred Antshrike (*radiatus*) that its status as a subspecies of *T. doliatus* could be questioned; if split, *T. cadwaladeri* could be called the Tarija Antshrike.

Thamnophilus zarumae

CHAPMAN'S ANTSHRIKE
Other: Barred Antshrike (in part)

DESCRIPTION: 15.5 cm (6"). *Sw. Ecuador and nw. Peru.* Resembles Barred Antshrike. Iris brownish to grayish yellow (only rarely straw yellow as in Barred). Male differs in having ground color of back mixed with gray, rump tinged buff (but still barred), *faint barring below on breast only,* and *buff flanks and lower belly.* Female differs from female Barred in having grayer upper back and faint dusky speckling on pale dull ochraceous breast.

SIMILAR SPECIES: Does not occur with any other member of the "Barred" antshrike group.

HABITAT AND BEHAVIOR: Fairly common in lower growth of scrub, secondary woodland, and forest borders; occurs in both arid and semihumid regions. Behavior similar to Barred Antshrike's, but vocalizations quite different. Male's song, a fast series of 8–10 "chup" notes, ends with several distinctly higher-pitched and more nasal ones (thus is clearly 2-parted, and lacking the final accented note of Barred and Lined). Easily found in woodland and scrub below Celica, in w. Loja, Ecuador.

RANGE: Sw. Ecuador (e. El Oro and s. Loja) and nw. Peru (south to Lambayeque). Mostly 500–1500 m, recorded to 2300 m in Ecuador.

NOTE: Here regarded as a species distinct from *T. doliatus*, with *palamblae* included as a race. *T. zarumae*'s plumage and vocalizations seem quite different.

Thamnophilus multistriatus

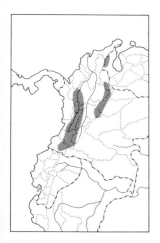

BAR-CRESTED ANTSHRIKE

DESCRIPTION: 16.5 cm (6½"). *W. Colombia and adjacent Venezuela.* Male resembles evenly barred races of male Barred Antshrike but has *black crown barred with white* (not solid black, the white quite prominent in the field); see C-XIII. Female closely resembles female Lined Antshrike (the 2 species are not known to occur together) but appears whiter below because its black barring is narrower; see C-27.

HABITAT AND BEHAVIOR: Fairly common in shrubby thickets at forest borders and in clearings, gardens, and hedgerows in agricultural areas; occurs both in arid and fairly humid regions. Behavior and vocalizations very similar to Barred Antshrike's. Common in parks and gardens in and around Cali.

RANGE: Valleys and lower Andean slopes in w. Colombia south to n. Nariño (on w. slope of W. Andes only in arid upper Río Dagua and upper Río Patía valleys, on e. slope of E. Andes in Norte de Santander and n. Boyacá) and in adjacent nw. Venezuela (lower slopes of Sierra de Perijá). Mostly 900–2200 m, locally down to 400 m.

Thamnophilus tenuepunctatus

LINED ANTSHRIKE

PLATE: 16

DESCRIPTION: 16.5 cm (6½"). *Along e. base of Andes south to ne. Peru;* here regarded as a separate species from Chestnut-backed Antshrike (*T. palliatus*) from farther south and east. Iris yellow. Male *black above with narrow white barring,* except crown solid black. *Below evenly barred black and white,* except streaked on throat. Female *bright rufous-chestnut above except for black and white streaked nuchal collar. Below evenly barred black and white,* except streaked on throat and tinged buff on flanks.

SIMILAR SPECIES: Male resembles Barred Antshrike but is blacker generally, with only very narrow white barring above and with black and white bars on underparts about equal in width; they are not known to occur sympatrically. Females of the 2 species are markedly different. Cf. also (in Colombia) Bar-crested Antshrike.

HABITAT AND BEHAVIOR: Uncommon to fairly common in thickets and dense undergrowth of humid and montane forest borders, shrubby regenerating clearings, and plantations and gardens; mostly in foothills and on lower Andean slopes. Behavior and vocalizations much like Barred Antshrike's, though Lined seems rarely to be as numerous and skulks more. Readily found at various localities in e. Ecuador, notably above Archidona.

RANGE: Along e. slope of Andes in e. Colombia (north to Norte de Santander at Petrólea north of Cúcuta), e. Ecuador, and ne. Peru (south to San Martín); probably occurs in extreme sw. Venezuela. Mostly 500–1400 m.

NOTE: Here *T. tenuepunctatus* (with *tenuifasciatus* and *berlepschi*) is regarded as a species distinct from *T. palliatus* (with *puncticeps* and *similis*). There seems to be no evidence of intergradation between the strikingly different *T. tenuepunctatus berlepschi* of San Martín, Peru (males black-mantled with narrow white barring), and *T. palliatus similis* of Huánuco and Junín, Peru (males chestnut-mantled). Until such intergradation is actually demonstrated, we feel the best course is to treat *T. tenuepunctatus* and *T. palliatus* as separate species, following *Birds of the Americas,* vol. 13, part 3. J. T. Zimmer (*Am. Mus. Novitates* 646, 1933), with no such evidence, treated them as conspecific, and this was followed by Meyer de Schauensee (1966, 1970). We employ the English names suggested by Hellmayr in *Birds of the Americas,* vol. 13, part 3.

Thamnophilus palliatus

CHESTNUT-BACKED ANTSHRIKE

PLATE: 16

Other: Lined Antshrike (in part)

DESCRIPTION: 16.5 cm (6½"). *Along e. base of Andes from cen. Peru south to Bolivia, thence eastward locally to e. Brazil.* Sometimes considered conspecific with Lined Antshrike. Iris yellow. Male has *black crown* and black- and white-streaked sides of head and neck; *mantle and tail rufous-chestnut. Below narrowly and evenly barred black and white.* Female like male but with *rufous-chestnut crown,* and underparts whiter with narrower black barring.

SIMILAR SPECIES: Male Lined Antshrike (no overlap) is barred black and white above and below; females of the 2 species are very similar. Male Rufous-capped Antshrike (regardless of race) always has much duller, grayish or brownish, back (not the uniform bright rufous-chestnut of both sexes of Chestnut-backed), lacks streaked effect on sides of head and nape, and has rufous crown.

HABITAT AND BEHAVIOR: Uncommon to fairly common in humid and montane forest borders, thickets, regenerating clearings, lighter woodland, and gardens. Behavior, including vocalizations, similar to Barred and Lined Antshrikes'. Fairly numerous around Rio de Janeiro, Brazil. RANGE: Along e. slope of Andes in cen. and s. Peru (north to Huánuco) and w. Bolivia (south to Santa Cruz), thence east locally through s. Amaz. Brazil to e. Pará, Maranhão, and Piauí; coastal e. Brazil (Paraíba south to Rio de Janeiro). Mostly 500–2000 m in Andes (occasionally higher); in e. Brazil to about 800 m.

NOTE: See comments under Lined Antshrike.

Thamnophilus ruficapillus

RUFOUS-CAPPED ANTSHRIKE   PLATE: 16

DESCRIPTION: 16.5 cm (6½″). Andean slopes from n. Peru to nw. Argentina, and (nominate race) in se. South America. Confusingly variable. Nominate male *reddish brown above, brightest on crown,* with sides of head and neck grayer; tail dusky brown, outer feathers barred white (visible mainly from below). Below dull whitish with *broad band of black barring across breast. Cochabambae* (s. Cochabamba in Bolivia south to nw. Argentina) similar but back distinctly grayer. *Marcapatae* (Cuzco and Puno, Peru) is radically different: *much darker generally,* with chestnut crown and wings, otherwise dark olivaceous gray above, tail blackish with white barring as in nominate; *below smoky grayish with black and white barring from chest to midbelly. Subfasciatus* (La Paz and n. Cochabamba, Bolivia) is intermediate toward *cochabambae* (and somewhat variable); the isolated *jaczewskii* (n. Peru) is much like *subfasciatus.* Female olivaceous gray to brown above with *contrasting rufous crown, wings, and tail;* below dingy whitish. Again, *marcapatae* is strikingly different, being darker above and *uniform rather bright fulvous below; subfasciatus* and *jaczewskii* are intermediate in color.

SIMILAR SPECIES: Males, regardless of how extensively barred they are below, never show the contrast between uniform bright rufous upperparts and barred underparts of Chestnut-backed (and female Lined) Antshrikes. Pattern of nominate females rather recalls that of various *Synallaxis* spinetails. Cf. also Rufous-winged Antshrike.

HABITAT AND BEHAVIOR: Fairly common in lower growth at edge of forest, secondary scrub and regenerating clearings, monte, and semi-open country with hedgerows and groves of trees; seems less numerous in Andes. Usually in pairs, rather unobtrusive and not too often seen; forages independently of mixed flocks. The song, rather high-pitched for an antshrike, is nasal and comparatively weak (lacking the vigor of "Barred" and "Lined" groups), "renh, renh, renh, reh-reh-reh-reh, rénh."

RANGE: E. slope of Andes in Peru (in the north in Cajamarca north to Cutervo, and in Amazonas; in the southeast from Cuzco southward), Bolivia (La Paz to Tarija), and nw. Argentina (south to Tucumán); se. Brazil (Espírito Santo and cen. Minas Gerais south through Rio Grande do Sul), e. Paraguay, Uruguay, and ne. Argentina (south to n. Buenos Aires). To about 2100 m (in Brazil and Bolivia); recorded to almost 2800 m in s. Peru.

NOTE: Short (1975) suggested that *T. marcapatae* (Marcapata Antshrike), with *jaczewskii*, should be treated as an allospecies of *T. ruficapillus*. However, as noted above, various intermediate forms (especially *subfasciatus*) seem to intergrade along a north-south cline. Given this and the vocal similarity (so far as we are aware) of all forms, we prefer to consider *T. ruficapillus* as a single, notably variable, species.

Thamnophilus torquatus

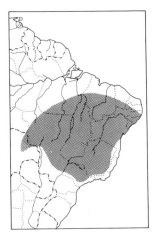

RUFOUS-WINGED ANTSHRIKE

DESCRIPTION: 14 cm (5½"). *Mainly e. and cen. Brazil.* Resembles nominate Rufous-capped Antshrike (limited overlap at most) but *markedly smaller.* Male differs in having *crown black* (not rufous) and in its brighter and more contrasting rufous-chestnut wings and its black tail with white barring. Rufous-winged and nominate Rufous-capped females are very similar, apart from the size difference; Rufous-winged is somewhat buffier below.
SIMILAR SPECIES: Because of its smaller size, female Rufous-winged Antshrike recalls various *Synallaxis* spinetails even more than Rufous-capped does, but shape and behavior of the 2 genera are quite different.
HABITAT AND BEHAVIOR: Uncommon to locally fairly common in arid scrub, lower growth of lighter woodland, and agricultural areas (even in manioc plantations). Behavior and vocalizations much like Rufous-capped Antshrike's. Numerous in second-growth around Santo Amaro, Bahia; in smaller numbers near Brasília.
RANGE: E. and cen. Brazil (s. Pará, s. Maranhão, Ceará, and Pernambuco south to Mato Grosso do Sul, São Paulo, and n. Rio de Janeiro; absent from coastal southeast from se. Bahia southward) and e. Bolivia (locally in ne. Santa Cruz on the Serranía de Huanchaca and at Guarayos). To at least 1000 m.

GROUP B

Rather large and dark. Males with *wings obviously white-fringed;* females variable.

Thamnophilus nigrocinereus

BLACKISH-GRAY ANTSHRIKE   PLATE: 17

DESCRIPTION: 16.5 cm (6½"). Local from e. Colombia to e. and cen. Amaz. Brazil. Rather heavy bill. Male of nominate group (lower Amaz. Brazil west to lower Rio Tapajós) *slaty black above,* blackest on crown and grayer on rump, with semiconcealed dorsal patch white; outer scapulars, bend of wing, and *wing-coverts tipped white giving fringed effect,* and tail feathers narrowly tipped white. *Throat and chest blackish,* becoming gray on lower underparts. *Cinereoniger* (e. Colombia and s. Venezuela to nw. Brazil) is grayer on back and uniform gray below; see V-22, C-29. One or, more probably, 2 males photographed by J. Dunning near Puerto Inirida in Vichada, Colombia, had conspicuous white lores and a partial eye-ring (albinism?). *Tschudii* (cen. Amaz. Brazil from lower Rio Madeira south to Rondônia) is deeper black below, extending down over breast. Female rufescent brown above with *contrasting slaty gray crown and gray sides of head; wings essentially plain* (coverts narrowly tipped cinnamon-rufous). *Below uniform cinnamon-rufous.* Female *tschudii* is *much darker generally,* with black crown, deeper umber brown mantle and lower underparts, and sooty throat and chest.

SIMILAR SPECIES: There are many other similar, essentially gray and black male antshrikes in or near this species' range, but this is the only one with obviously white-*fringed* wing-coverts (others are more *spotted*); but cf. Castlenau's Antshrike. Female can be known by her rufescent overall appearance in conjunction with the gray on head; female Spot-winged and Caura Antbirds have similar overall patterns but show white spotting on wing-coverts. Female White-shouldered Antshrike lacks gray on head.

HABITAT AND BEHAVIOR: Locally fairly common to common in undergrowth of gallery woodland, deciduous forest, and borders of more humid forest; recorded at least locally from river islands (e.g., in the lower Rio Tapajós and lower Rio Negro) and in French Guiana also from mangroves. Seems absent from upland terra firme forest, and therefore quite local in some areas. Usually in pairs, regularly with mixed understory flocks. Slowly wags its tail while foraging, shivering it when calling. Male's song (*cinereoniger*) is a distinctive bouncing "kyoh, kyoh, kyoh, kyuh-kuh-kuh," with female often chiming in with a faster and higher-pitched version of her own, "chook, chook, chook, chuchuchu chu-chu"; both sexes give a low, complaining "caw" and a churring growl "urr-r-r-r-r." Numerous in the Anavilhanas Archipelago in the Rio Negro north of Manaus, and at Junglaven Lodge in Amazonas, Venezuela.

RANGE: Ne. Colombia (w. Meta east through Vichada and Guainía), s. Venezuela (Amazonas and nw. Bolívar), locally in Amaz. Brazil (north of the Amazon in the Rio Negro drainage and east through Amapá, south of it from the Rio Madeira east to the lower Rio Tocantins, and south to Rondônia and n. Mato Grosso), and French Guiana. To 400 m.

NOTE: *T. cryptoleucus* (Castlenau's Antshrike) was formerly considered conspecific with this species.

Thamnophilus cryptoleucus

CASTLENAU'S ANTSHRIKE

DESCRIPTION: 18 cm (7″). Along the Amazon and some of its tributaries from w. Brazil to ne. Peru and e. Ecuador. Heavy bill. Male *all deep lustrous black* with semiconcealed dorsal patch white; outer scapulars, bend of wing, and *wing-coverts tipped white with fringed effect;* see C-29 (but iris *in*correctly colored). Female similar but *lacks white on closed wing;* like male, it has white underwing-coverts and dorsal patch.

SIMILAR SPECIES: Male is much more uniformly black than even the *tschudii* race of Blackish-gray Antshrike, but pattern otherwise very similar. The unrelievedly black female Castlenau's differs greatly from any race of Blackish-gray; it rather resembles male White-shouldered Antbird, but latter usually shows some white on bend of wing and always some bare blue skin around eye (their typical habitats also differ). Cf. also male of nominate White-shouldered Antshrike; its plumage quite closely resembles female Castlenau's, though habitat differs markedly.

HABITAT AND BEHAVIOR: Locally fairly common in lower growth of várzea forest and riparian woodland on river islands. Usually in pairs which often forage together but seem normally not to join flocks. Regularly wags its tail slowly. The song is a short, rapidly delivered, nasal "keoh, keoh, kuh-kuh-kuhkuhkuhkuh"; other "kawh" call notes are given, sometimes in series, sometimes singly. Can be found on islands near Leticia, Colombia, and near the Explornapo Camp below Iquitos, Peru.

RANGE: Locally along Amazon River in w. Brazil (east to near the lower Rio Negro at Manacupurú), extreme se. Colombia (Leticia area), ne. Peru (Loreto and n. Ucayali south to Lagarto), and ne. Ecuador (Río Napo islands downstream from near Pompeia, and in islands in the lower Río Aguarico). To 300 m.

NOTE: Formerly regarded as a race of *T. nigrocinereus*.

GROUP C

Males gray to black, *with or without wing-spots;* females *all distinctive.*

Thamnophilus nigriceps

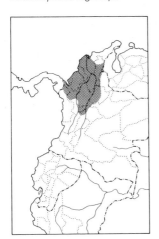

BLACK ANTSHRIKE

PLATE: 17

DESCRIPTION: 16 cm (6¼"). *N. Colombia.* Male *entirely deep black;* white underwing-coverts normally not visible in the field; see C-27. Female has *head, neck, throat, and chest black streaked with buffy whitish,* becoming plain buff on lower flanks and crissum. *Remaining upperparts contrastingly rufous brown.*

SIMILAR SPECIES: No other black antshrike or antbird in this species' range *lacks* visible white on the closed wing; cf. Immaculate Antbird (with bare blue ocular area, etc.). The strikingly patterned female is easily identified in range. Cf. Cocha Antshrike (no overlap).

HABITAT AND BEHAVIOR: Fairly common to common in shrubby overgrown clearings and tangled borders of woodland and forest. Usually forages in pairs, hopping methodically through lower growth. The song is a nasal and slightly accelerating "kuok, kuok, kuok, kuok-ku-ku-ku-ku" (G. Rosenberg; Hilty and Brown 1986).

RANGE: N. Colombia (n. Chocó east across Caribbean lowlands to the Santa Marta area, lower slopes of Sierra de Perijá, and Santander; south in Río Magdalena valley to n. Tolima). Also e. Panama. To 600 m.

NOTE: See comments under Cocha Antshrike.

Thamnophilus praecox

COCHA ANTSHRIKE

DESCRIPTION: 16 cm (6¼"). *Known only from ne. Ecuador.* The recently discovered male is virtually identical to male Black Antshrike (no overlap) but with smaller area on greater underwing-coverts white (as in Black Antshrike, not visible in the field). Female has *head, throat, and chest black* with faint white shaft streaks, especially on throat (but virtually lacking in some birds); *upperparts otherwise bright cinnamon-rufous;* lower underparts somewhat paler cinnamon-rufous.

SIMILAR SPECIES: Both sexes of this range-restricted antshrike uncan-

nily resemble the White-shouldered Antbird, but the antbird is larger with a heavier bill, and in both sexes some bare blue skin shows around eye. Male White-shouldereds differ further in showing white on bend of wing (usually apparent in life, and never shown by male Cocha), and female White-shouldereds are somewhat less brightly colored overall.

HABITAT AND BEHAVIOR: Uncommon to fairly common but (so far as known) very local in lower growth and borders of frequently flooded várzea forest, primarily in thickets along small streams and apparently entirely in blackwater drainages. For more than 50 years this antshrike was known only from a single museum specimen, but in Dec. 1990 it was rediscovered by RSR and P. Greenfield et al. close to the presumed type locality near Imuyacocha in the Río Lagarto drainage. Here several pairs were found along certain creeks, though they were inconspicuous unless calling. Cocha Antshrikes forage mostly within 4 m of the ground or water, gleaning sluggishly in foliage, usually well concealed within tangles. Pairs are usually found together, though sometimes well separated; generally they do not associate with flocks, though a pair sometimes moves in loose association with antbirds such as the Black-chinned or Plumbeous. The male's song is a hollow-sounding, evenly paced "ko-ko-ko-ko-ko-ko-ko-ko-ko-ko," usually given as the bird is motionless except for its vibrating, often somewhat spread tail; females may follow with a slightly higher-pitched, shorter version of the same song. Females (and perhaps males) also give a mellow "pyow-pyow." Unlike virtually all other antbirds, Cocha Antshrikes usually do not vocalize prior to about 0900 or 1000 hours.

RANGE: E. Ecuador (locally in e. Napo along the Río Lagarto, an affluent of the Río Aguarico; in Jan. 1991 also found by P. Greenfield and G. Budney et al. at and near La Selva, on n. side of the Río Napo). Perhaps also occurs in adjacent Colombia and Peru. 200–250 m.

NOTE: J. T. Zimmer described this species on the basis of a single female (*Am. Mus. Novitates* 917, 1937), and for years it remained known only from the type specimen. Zimmer was prescient in recognizing *praecox*'s close relationship to the geographically distant *T. nigriceps*, this having recently been borne out by the now known similarity of their male plumages and vocalizations. They could even be considered conspecific, but given their great range disjunction and certain plumage differences, we do not believe this would be the correct course.

Thamnophilus aethiops

WHITE-SHOULDERED ANTSHRIKE   PLATE: 17

DESCRIPTION: 16 cm (6¼"). Iris variable (individually?), bright red to reddish brown in males, darker red to brown in females. Heavy bill. Male dark gray (slightly paler below) with blackish crown; *wing-coverts with small but distinct white spots* and white on bend of wing. The shade of gray varies geographically, in general being paler eastward, slatier westward (with *injunctus* more or less intermediate). By far the blackest race is nominate *aethiops* (e. Ecuador and adjacent Nariño in s. Colombia), in which male is basically *lustrous black;* curiously, the race occurring just to the north, *wetmorei,* reverts to being similar to "typical" gray Amaz. birds. The extent of wing-spotting also varies, with

nominate, *incertus* and *atriceps* (e. Amaz. Brazil west to e. bank of lower Rio Tapajós), and *kapouni* (e. Peru, n. Bolivia, and extreme w. Brazil) showing very little or none (mostly restricted to shoulders). *Incertus* (e. bank of lower Rio Tocantins east to Maranhão) lacks black on crown. Female looks *uniform* (with *plain* wing): *rufous-chestnut above, below somewhat paler*. Nominate's tail is dusky. W. races are generally more richly colored, e. races paler (buff on belly).

SIMILAR SPECIES: The variation, especially in males, is confusing. Male Plain-winged Antshrike presents the greatest problem, especially in areas where White-shouldered shows few or no spots on wing-coverts (wing of Plain-winged is *always* plain). Plain-winged is smaller and has less heavy bill; only its nw. race, *capitalis,* has a black cap (whereas all White-shouldereds except the all-black nominate race and *incertus* of e. Amazonia *have* a contrasting black cap). Cf. also male Spot-winged Antshrike (markedly shorter tailed, etc.). Male Blackish-gray and Castlenau's Antshrikes show white *fringing* (not spotting) on wing-coverts; female Blackish-gray has contrasting gray head, whereas female Castlenau's is all black. Cf. also Bicolored Antvireo.

HABITAT AND BEHAVIOR: Uncommon in lower growth of terra firme forest, ranging up locally into montane forest, usually inside or at small treefalls. Rather sedentary, generally foraging in pairs and not with mixed flocks. The song of nominate males is a distinctive series of nasal notes, delivered evenly and slowly, "anh, anh, anh, anh, anh," with somewhat forest-falcon-like effect; birds in s. Venezuela (*polionotus*) and Rondônia, Brazil (probably *injunctus*), deliver a markedly faster and higher-pitched "kah-kah-kah-kah-kah-kah-kah." Calling birds of both sexes give a slurred "keyurrr" call.

RANGE: S. Colombia (north to w. Meta) and e. Ecuador (south to Morona-Santiago; not found any distance east of Andes); s. Venezuela (Amazonas and Bolívar), extreme e. Colombia (e. Guainía south to Amazonas in the Leticia area), e. Peru (e. Loreto southward; the record from the mouth of the Río Curaray in n. Loreto likely involved a mislabeled specimen), n. Bolivia (south to La Paz, Cochabamba, and Santa Cruz), and Amaz. Brazil (south to s. Mato Grosso and east to n. Maranhão; mostly absent from north of the Amazon and east of the Rio Negro); coastal ne. Brazil (Pernambuco and Alagoas). To 1700 m on e. slope of Andes in Ecuador.

NOTE: More than one species is perhaps involved; nominate *aethiops,* in particular, stands out in plumage, and its primary song appears to differ as well (though we admit to not being familiar with the songs of all races). If split, a monotypic *T. aethiops* would be called the White-shouldered Antshrike, with *T. polionotus* (the name having priority), encompassing the remaining taxa, becoming the White-dotted Antshrike.

GROUP D

Males *like Group C* (but never black); females rather *dull* (see also Plate 16).

Thamnophilus unicolor

UNIFORM ANTSHRIKE   PLATE: 17

DESCRIPTION: 15.5–16 cm (6–6¼"). *Andes from Colombia to e. Peru. Iris gray* (sometimes pale). Male *uniform slaty gray*. Female rufous brown

above, somewhat brighter on crown, *contrasting with gray face* and upper throat. Below uniform ochraceous brown. Nominate race of w. Ecuador slightly smaller.

SIMILAR SPECIES: There are few other similar antbirds in the *montane forests* this species inhabits. Male White-streaked Antvireo has white spots on wing-coverts; male of very rare Bicolored Antvireo is basically slaty black, not gray, and shows white on wing.

HABITAT AND BEHAVIOR: Uncommon in lower growth of montane forest, less often out to forest borders. Usually in pairs; inconspicuous and rarely accompanies mixed flocks. The song is a short series of nasal notes, evenly and rather deliberately delivered, "anh, anh, anh, anh" (sometimes 3 or 5 notes). Perhaps easiest to see in forest west of Piñas in El Oro and along the Zamora road in Zamora-Santiago, both areas in s. Ecuador.

RANGE: Andean slopes of Colombia (north in E. Andes to Cundinamarca, in Cen. and W. Andes to Antioquia), Ecuador (south on w. slope to El Oro and w. Loja), and e. Peru (south to Pasco). Mostly 1400–2300 m, but regularly ranges lower (to 700 m) on Pacific slope in Ecuador.

Thamnophilus aroyae

UPLAND ANTSHRIKE

DESCRIPTION: 14.5–15 cm (5¾–6"). *Andean slopes of s. Peru and w. Bolivia.* Iris color unusually variable, everything from "dusky straw" and "buffy white" to "brown" being recorded with no apparent correlation to age or sex. Male resembles male Uniform Antshrike (no overlap) but is somewhat paler gray below and has *wing-coverts edged white* and *tail feathers tipped white.* Female like female Uniform but paler generally (more tawny ochraceous below) with *more contrasting rufous crown* and somewhat less contrasting grayish face.

SIMILAR SPECIES: Mainly occurs *above* range of other "gray" antshrikes. Male White-shouldered of *kapouni* race is darker gray generally with less white on wings and tail; female White-shouldered is much more rufescent. Male Eastern Slaty-Antshrike of *sticturus* race is paler gray generally, almost white on belly, with contrasting black crown and even more white on wings and tail; female *sticturus* is very different, with much white on wing and belly, etc. Female Plain-winged Antshrike is notably smaller and drabber generally, and lacks the tawny-ochraceous tone below. Mouse-colored Antshrike does not occur near the range of Upland (males are quite similar).

HABITAT AND BEHAVIOR: Uncommon to locally fairly common in shrubby lower growth of borders of montane forest and secondary woodland. Usually in pairs and generally not associating with mixed flocks. Its song, a series of 5–7 well-enunciated nasal notes, "wunh-wanh-wanh-wanh-wanh-wanh-wháyaah," somewhat recalls songs of Mouse-colored and Plain-winged Antshrikes and is longer than Uniform's. Apparently spreading by way of the second-growth that springs up along newly constructed roads (Parker et al. 1991).

RANGE: Lower Andean slopes and foothills in extreme s. Peru (Puno) and w. Bolivia (La Paz, Cochabamba, and s. Beni on the Serranía Pilón). 800–1700 m.

NOTE: For the first published information on this until recently poorly known species, see J. V. Remsen, Jr., et al. 1982.

Thamnophilus schistaceus

PLAIN-WINGED ANTSHRIKE

PLATE: 17

Other: Black-capped Antshrike

DESCRIPTION: 14 cm (5½″). *Iris reddish brown to red.* Male *uniform gray,* somewhat slatier on crown and slightly paler below; *wings entirely unmarked. Capitalis* (se. Colombia to ne. Peru and extreme w. Brazil) has fairly contrasting *black crown;* see C-29. Female olivaceous to rufescent brown above with fairly contrasting *rufous crown* and somewhat grayer face; *wings entirely unmarked.* Below uniform pale and drab olivaceous buff.

SIMILAR SPECIES: Resembles Mouse-colored Antshrike (with which locally sympatric), but Mouse-colored's wing-coverts are white tipped, its wings have a brown tinge, and its eye is grayish. Male Plain-winged (except its black-capped *capitalis* race) closely resembles male of broadly sympatric Cinereous Antshrike, but Cinereous has a slighter bill, and its vertical posture and vocalizations differ markedly.

HABITAT AND BEHAVIOR: Fairly common to common in lower growth and middle levels of terra firme forest and second-growth woodland, also to some extent in várzea and out to forest borders. Usually in pairs, hopping about methodically in thickets and tangles, less often in more open understory of unbroken forest. Rarely associates with mixed flocks. The male's far-carrying song, one of the characteristic sounds of Amaz. forests, is often given persistently through the day, when most other birds are silent. This song is a series of nasal notes, rather rapidly uttered, "anh-anh-anh-anh-anh-anh-anh-anhanh," with a distinctive doubled note at end; sometimes female chimes in, midway through male's delivery, with a somewhat higher-pitched version. Male also gives a very slow, barking "arr . . . arr . . . arr . . . ," the effect quite like a forest-falcon (*Micrastur*).

RANGE: Se. Colombia (north to Meta and Vaupés), e. Ecuador, e. Peru, n. Bolivia (south to La Paz, Cochabamba, and w. Santa Cruz); and Amaz. Brazil (almost entirely south of the Amazon; east to e. Pará on the lower Rio Tocantins, and south to s. Mato Grosso). To about 1300 m (along e. base of Andes in Ecuador).

NOTE: In all recent literature this species has been called the Black-capped Antshrike, an unfortunate choice because only one race of the species actually has a black cap, whereas many other male *Thamnophilus* antshrikes *do* have black caps. Hellmayr (*Birds of the Americas,* vol. 13, part 3) selected Black-capped Antshrike as the name for *T. schistaceus capitalis* (*only*), and later this name was incorrectly expanded to encompass the entire species. We feel that this error and the subsequent confusion it has caused should not be further perpetuated and suggest emphasizing this species' plain wings, the male's best distinguishing character from its close relative the Mouse-colored Antshrike, *T. murinus.*

Thamnophilus murinus

MOUSE-COLORED ANTSHRIKE

DESCRIPTION: 14 cm (5½"). Resembles Plain-winged Antshrike. *Iris gray* (not reddish). Male differs in its *narrow white tipping on wing-coverts* and, in most of range, its *decidedly brownish wings*. However, males of *canipennis* (e. Ecuador, e. Peru, and w. Brazil east to the Rio Madeira) *lack* brownish tinge on wings. Female differs only subtly from female Plain-winged but is less rufescent above (crown only tinged rufous) and slightly whiter below, especially on belly. See V-22, C-29.
SIMILAR SPECIES: Female is so much like female Plain-winged Antshrike that in the field, unless eye color can be discerned (often not easy in the dim light of the forest interior), it will usually best be identified by its (usually accompanying) mate.
HABITAT AND BEHAVIOR: Fairly common to common in lower and middle levels of humid forest and in woodland of savanna-dominated regions; less numerous westward in Amazonia, where largely confined to forest areas with sandy soil and blackwater streams. Behavior similar to Plain-winged Antshrike's, usually in pairs foraging independently of mixed flocks. Vocalizations, too, are similar, though song of male Mouse-colored usually has fewer notes and is more slowly delivered; Mouse-colored also gives the *Micrastur*-like call.
RANGE: Guianas, s. Venezuela (Bolívar and Amazonas), se. Colombia (mostly in far east in Guainía and Vaupés, also recorded from Amazonas), e. Ecuador (local), e. Peru (south locally to Madre de Dios at Hacienda Amazonia), and Amaz. Brazil (throughout north of the Amazon, south of it east only to Rondônia and the Rio Madeira); seems likely in n. Bolivia. Mostly below 500 m (recorded to 1300 m in Venezuela).

GROUP E

Both sexes with pronounced white wing markings (except female Variables in Peru).

Thamnophilus punctatus

EASTERN SLATY-ANTSHRIKE   PLATE: 17
Other: Slaty Antshrike (in part)

DESCRIPTION: 14.5–15 cm (5¾–6"). Excludes trans-Andean birds, Western Slaty-Antshrike. Iris dark in most subspecies, but usually pale (yellowish to hazel to pale grayish) in whiter-bellied subspecies (see below). Male gray above with black crown, mixed black and gray back with semiconcealed white dorsal patch; wings black, with outer scapulars, wingcoverts, and inner flight feathers *boldly spotted and edged with white;* tail and uppertail-coverts black, all feathers tipped white. Below uniform gray (slightly paler than upperparts). Female olivaceous brown above with crown more rufous to chestnut; *wings and tail marked with white much like male's.* Below pale olivaceous brown. Both sexes of *leucogaster* (extreme s. Ecuador and nw. Peru in Cajamarca), *sticturus* and *pelzelni* (n. Bolivia east across interior Brazil to Alagoas and n. São Paulo), and to a lesser extent *ambiguus* (coastal se. Brazil) are *markedly whiter on belly.*

SIMILAR SPECIES: Western Slaty-Antshrike does not occur with this species. Male Eastern Slaty- and male Amazonian Antshrike are *very* similar, though Eastern Slaty- has grayer back; females, however, differ strikingly (Amazonian with orange-rufous head and underparts). In s. Brazil cf. also the similar Variable Antshrike, and in Amazonia the Pearly Antshrike.

HABITAT AND BEHAVIOR: Common in lower growth of a variety of wooded and forested habitats: in lower and middle growth of terra firme forest borders (rarely or never in forest interior), deciduous woodland, and even in rather low scrubby woodland on Amaz. campinas, caatinga, and the n. fringe of the chaco. Usually quite inconspicuous, in many areas (notably s. Brazil) easily known by its habit of almost perpetually quivering or wagging its tail, particularly when alarmed or calling. Song is a rather leisurely series of well-enunciated notes: nominate gives a rising "anh, anh, anh-anh-anh-anh-ah?"; *ambiguus* (*leucogaster* similar) a slightly faster "anh-anh-anh-anh-ah-ah-ahahah," dropping a bit, with *saturatus* (near Santarém, Brazil) and *sticturus* (near Corumbá, Brazil) similar but with more rolled effect at end.

RANGE: Near e. base of Andes in w. Venezuela (north to Barinas) and n. Colombia (south to w. Meta); foothills and near e. base of Andes in extreme s. Ecuador (s. Zamora-Chinchipe near Zumba; ANSP) and n. and cen. Peru (Cajamarca south to Huánuco); Guianas, e. and s. Venezuela (e. Sucre south through Bolívar and n. Amazonas), e. Amaz. and cen. and e. Brazil (west in Amazonia to the lower Rio Negro and nw. Mato Grosso, and south to Mato Grosso do Sul, São Paulo, and Rio de Janeiro), and ne. Bolivia (east to Cochabamba and Beni). Mostly below 1100 m.

NOTE: We follow the suggestion of E. O. Willis (*Pap. Avuls. Zool.* 35[17]: 177–182, 1982) that *T. atrinucha* (with *subcinereus* and *gorgonae*) be regarded as a species separate from *T. punctatus*, primarily on the basis of its different vocalizations and behavior. The expanded species was called the Slaty Antshrike. We favor continuing to associate the two species through the English group name of Slaty-Antshrike, and "Western" and "Eastern" seem the best modifiers.

Thamnophilus atrinucha

WESTERN SLATY-ANTSHRIKE

Other: Slaty Antshrike (in part)

DESCRIPTION: 14.5–15 cm (5¾–6"). *West of Andes from nw. Venezuela to w. Ecuador.* Resembles Eastern Slaty-Antshrike (formerly considered conspecific). Male differs from male nominate Eastern Slaty- in having *feathers on sides of head edged black giving somewhat scaly or grizzled effect* (not smoothly gray). Female likewise has scaly or grizzled look on sides of head, and further differs from nominate female Eastern Slaty- in being less brownish above *with only a tinge of rufous on crown* and in having wing markings pale buff (not white). See P-20.

SIMILAR SPECIES: Although there are many similar antshrikes east of Andes, confusion is unlikely to their *west,* where no other antshrike similar to the Western Slaty- is present.

HABITAT AND BEHAVIOR: Common in lower growth of humid forest, second-growth woodland, and borders. Widespread and often more conspicuous and less shy than other *Thamnophilus* antshrikes; regularly accompanies mixed flocks of *Myrmotherula* antwrens and other understory birds, and sometimes attends army antswarms. Male's song is a fast, rolling "anhanhanhanhanhanhanhanhanhánh," with a distinctive snarling, accented terminal note.

RANGE: Nw. Venezuela (Maracaibo basin), n. and w. Colombia (south in Río Magdalena valley to Huila), and w. Ecuador (south to El Oro); Gorgona Is. off s. Colombia. Also Guatemala and Belize to Panama. Mostly below 1100 m.

NOTE: See comments under Eastern Slaty-Antshrike.

Thamnophilus amazonicus

AMAZONIAN ANTSHRIKE   PLATE: 17

DESCRIPTION: 14–15 cm (5½–6″), with *cinereiceps* (nw. Brazil, adjacent Colombia and Venezuela, and ne. Ecuador) markedly smaller. Males of most races (nominate group) closely resemble male Eastern Slaty-Antshrike (of gray-bellied nominate group) but have blacker back; in the absence of a female, probably not distinguishable in the field. *Cinereiceps* differs, apart from its smaller size, in having a concolor gray crown (not black), and usually shows less black on back than male Amazonian; see V-22, C-29. Female Amazonian differs radically from female Eastern Slaty-: *head, neck, and underparts quite bright orange-rufous,* slightly fading to cinnamon-buff on belly; back olive brown, with some black intermixed; wings and tail black, feathers marked with white as in Eastern Slaty-. Female *cinereiceps* similar but with *belly contrastingly buffy whitish* (not almost uniform with rest of underparts). SIMILAR SPECIES: Cf. Eastern Slaty-Antshrike.

HABITAT AND BEHAVIOR: Nominate group is uncommon in lower and middle growth and viny borders in várzea forest, and, at least locally (e.g., at Alta Floresta in Brazil), around *Guadua* bamboo thickets in terra firme forest; *cinereiceps* is uncommon to locally common in lower growth and borders of sandy-belt forest and woodland in savanna regions and along swampy creeks. Both groups are usually found in pairs, often accompanying mixed flocks including Gray Antbird and various antwrens; in some areas they regularly range higher above the ground than most *Thamnophilus* antshrikes. Male's song (of both groups) is an accelerating series of trogon-like notes, "kuh, kuh, kuh-kuh-kuh-kuhkuhkuh-kuh," with female sometimes chiming in with her higher-pitched rendition during the beginning; the birds tremble their spread tails vigorously as they sing. One call is a repeated "heeuh." *Cinereiceps* is especially numerous at Junglaven Lodge in Amazonas, Venezuela.

RANGE: Guianas, s. Venezuela (e. Bolívar and Amazonas), e. Colombia (w. Meta and Vichada southward), extreme ne. Ecuador (Río Lagarto drainage of e. Sucumbios; ANSP, MECN), e. Peru (Loreto south locally to Madre de Dios), n. Bolivia (Pando, Beni, and n. Santa Cruz), and Amaz. Brazil (south to s. Mato Grosso and n. Goiás, and east to n. Maranhão). To 1300 m (*cinereiceps* in Venezuela).

NOTE: *T. cinereiceps* (Gray-capped Antshrike) of sw. Venezuela (Amazonas), e. Colombia (e. Vichada south to Vaupés), extreme ne. Ecuador, and nw. Amaz. Brazil (Rio Negro drainage, and recorded south to the Amazon at Manacupuru) may prove to be a species distinct from *T. amazonicus*. They were long so regarded until J. T. Zimmer (*Am. Mus. Novitates* 647, pp. 14–20, 1933) treated them as conspecific. We could not see the "much individual variation" that he mentioned, and the markedly smaller size of *cinereiceps* seems consistent. Pinto (1978) reiterated his belief that *cinereiceps* and nominate *amazonicus* exist in virtual sympatry (on the basis of the Manacupuru record). As vocally they are quite similar, we continue to treat them as conspecific. The situation in the Guianas appears especially to warrant investigation: apparently both black- and gray-crowned birds occur, in a confusing range of habitats (coastal swampy forest to borders of interior terra firme forest).

Thamnophilus insignis

STREAK-BACKED ANTSHRIKE   PLATE: 17

DESCRIPTION: 16.5–17 cm (6½–6¾"). *Tepuis of s. Venezuela.* Resembles Eastern Slaty- and Amazonian Antshrikes but appreciably *larger.* Male has crown black with *considerable white showing on rear; back intermixed with gray, black, and white* (the white from a semiconcealed dorsal patch), with somewhat streaked effect; wings and tail marked with white as in Eastern Slaty- and Amazonian Antshrike. Below uniform and rather dark gray. Female *much like male* but with *midcrown chestnut;* white shows on rear of crown as in male.

SIMILAR SPECIES: Mainly occurs *above* the range of other similar "gray" *Thamnophilus*, all of which are smaller, lack white on hindcrown, and have much less white visible on back.

HABITAT AND BEHAVIOR: Uncommon to locally fairly common in lower and middle growth of relatively stunted forest and forest borders. Usually in pairs, sometimes small (presumed family) groups, which often hop about rather boldly; they may accompany small mixed flocks with other tepui specialties such as Roraiman Barbtail and White-throated Foliage-gleaner. The song, reminiscent of Barred Antshrike's, is a somewhat leisurely, nasal "anh, anh, anh, anh, anh-anh-anh-anh-ánh"; the tail is wagged downward with each note, as if for emphasis. Small numbers can be found in the dense low woodland along the Escalera road in e. Bolívar.

RANGE: Tepuis of s. Venezuela (Bolívar and Amazonas south to Cerro de la Neblina); seems almost certain to occur in adjacent Guyana and Brazil. 900–2000 m.

Thamnophilus caerulescens

VARIABLE ANTSHRIKE   PLATE: 17

DESCRIPTION: 14.5 cm (5¾"). This rather small antshrike found from e. South America to the Peruvian Andes is appropriately named, for it is *exceptionally variable in appearance.* We thus break the species into its 2 basic component groups.

Nominate group males (*e. South America west to s. Bolivia*, e.g., *gilvigaster* of ne. Argentina and Uruguay north to s. São Paulo) are gray above with black crown, back with some black and a semiconcealed white dorsal patch; wings and tail black, wing-coverts spotted and edged with white, and tail feathers and uppertail-coverts tipped white.

Below somewhat paler gray, fading to whitish on belly, with *some tawny on flanks and crissum*. Various other races, including nominate and *pernambucensis,* of e. Brazil (north to Ceará and Pernambuco) and e. Paraguay, are gray bellied with no tawny. *Dinellii* (se. Bolivia to n. Argentina) has *more extensive tawny below,* extending up over breast. Female most resembles female Eastern Slaty-Antshrike: olivaceous brown above, crown tinged rufous and with semiconcealed white dorsal patch; wings and tail dusky, wing-coverts spotted white, tail feathers tipped white. Throat and chest grayish olive, becoming *rather bright tawny on remaining underparts. Pernambucensis* (Pernambuco and Alagoas in ne. Brazil) female is grayer above with much more contrasting rufous crown and less white on wing; below uniform dull buffyish (without any tawny).

Completely different are males of *e. slope of Andes in Peru* (*subandinus* and *melanochrous*), which are *entirely black* except for white wing and tail markings like nominate group's. *Aspersiventer* (w. Bolivia in La Paz and Cochabamba) similar but with white mottling on belly. Clearly intermediate to nominate group is the variable *connectens* of w. Santa Cruz, Bolivia, in which upperparts, aside from black crown, become mostly grayish; throat and chest grayish *with variable amount of black,* and breast and belly buffy whitish to tawny. Females from Peru are dark olivaceous gray above with dusky crown and *plain wings;* throat and breast dusky olive, *contrasting with bright tawny belly.* Female *aspersiventer* similar but slightly paler above and with white wing-bars; *connectens* even paler, basically uniform pale tawny below.

SIMILAR SPECIES: Across much of its range both sexes can be known by the usually quite bright tawny on belly. Gray-bellied males (occurring in parts of e. Brazil) are easily confused with Eastern Slaty-Antshrike, though in area of overlap Variable usually occurs in montane regions; females are relatively straightforward (no female Eastern Slaty- *ever* shows the tawny on belly shown by almost all races of Variable). Black male Variables from Peru and Bolivia can be confused with other antbird genera in which males are mostly black (e.g., *Cercomacra*) but differ in shape and behavior. Pattern of female Variables from Peru and Bolivia is much like female Cinereous Antshrike's.

HABITAT AND BEHAVIOR: Fairly common to common in lower growth of montane and humid forest and second-growth woodland, often at borders. In much of its range one of the more numerous and conspicuous antbirds (though perhaps less common in Peru), and often confiding and easy to see (especially for an antbird). Usually in pairs which routinely accompany mixed flocks, but at least as often found independent of them. Unlike Eastern Slaty-Antshrike, Variable does not almost perpetually quiver its tail, merely occasionally and slowly lowering and raising it. Song of male, one of the most frequent bird sounds in many forested or wooded areas, is a fairly fast, evenly pitched and paced "cow-cow-cow-cow-cow-cow-cow," lacking the nasal tone of so many antshrikes. Both sexes also give single "caw" or more querulous "cuwah?" calls. Rather different is the song of *pernambucensis,* which is slower and more nasal, with fewer (usually 4 or 5) notes, "cwah, cwah, cwah, cwah." We are not familiar with voice of Peruvian birds.

RANGE: E. slope of Andes in Peru (north to s. Amazonas) and Bolivia, thence east in lowlands through Paraguay, n. Argentina (south to n. La Rioja, Córdoba, and extreme n. Buenos Aires), and Uruguay to e. Brazil (north to sw. Mato Grosso, Goiás, Minas Gerais, and Espírito Santo; also from Ceará to Pernambuco and Alagoas). To about 2000 m in Brazil, higher (to about 2500 m) in Peru and Bolivia.

NOTE: More than one species may be involved, though as noted above, *connectens* appears to form a link between the two dramatically differently plumaged groups. If split, *T. aspersiventer* could be called the Andean Antshrike, leaving *T. caerulescens* as the Variable Antshrike. *T. pernambucensis* (Pernambuco Antshrike, presumably with *cearensis*) may also deserve full species status.

Megastictus Antshrikes

A monotypic genus, *Thamnophilus*-like but with a slender bill, fairly short tail, no dorsal patch, and exceptionally large and bold spots on wing-coverts.

Megastictus margaritatus

PEARLY ANTSHRIKE

PLATE: 17

DESCRIPTION: 13.5–14 cm (5¼–5½"). A scarce antshrike found locally in Amazonia. Iris gray. Male bluish gray above; wings and tail black, *wing-coverts and tips of tertials with very large round white spots,* uppertail-coverts and tail feathers broadly tipped white. Below somewhat paler gray, whiter on throat. Female brown above, more olivaceous on crown; *wings and tail like male's, but spotting bright buff.* Below uniform ochraceous buff, whiter on throat. See C-29.

SIMILAR SPECIES: Many other antshrikes have spots on their wing-coverts but none as large and prominent as this species'. Note especially the spotted *tertials,* unique among antshrikes.

HABITAT AND BEHAVIOR: Rare to locally uncommon (perhaps more numerous in a few places; no less than 17 specimens were collected at Lagarto on the upper Río Ucayali in Peru) in lower and middle growth of terra firme forest and mature secondary woodland, in some areas primarily where there is sandy soil. Usually forages in pairs or small family groups, generally not associating with mixed flocks. Birds sometimes change perches frequently, mainly by hopping short distances, then settle down to scan for prey; sallies are made mainly to leaves. The tail is often pumped up and down sharply. Behavioral information from B. M. Whitney and G. H. Rosenberg (*Condor* 95[1]: 229, 1993). Its very distinctive 2-parted song commences with 2 or 3 querulous introductory "whee?" notes, then follows with a series of rapidly delivered "jrr" notes which have a very different raspy, guttural quality, thus "whee? whee? jrr-jrr-jrr-jrr-jrr-jrr" (G. H. Rosenberg).

RANGE: S. Venezuela (s. Bolívar and Amazonas), se. Colombia (w. Caquetá east locally to Vaupés), e. Ecuador (scarce and local), e. Peru (locally in Loreto, and recorded from Lagarto in s. Ucayali), and w. Amaz. Brazil (upper Rio Negro region, and in upper Rio Purus and Rio Madeira drainages). To 400 m.

Pygiptila Antshrikes

A canopy-inhabiting, heavy-billed, and short-tailed antshrike found widely in Amazonia.

Pygiptila stellaris

SPOT-WINGED ANTSHRIKE   PLATE: 17

DESCRIPTION: 13.5 cm (5¼"). *Bill heavy* for size of bird; *strikingly short tail*. Male has black crown, otherwise gray upperparts with some black intermixed on back and a semiconcealed white dorsal patch; *wing-coverts with several rows of small but conspicuous white spots*. Below uniform gray, slightly paler than upperparts. Female above mainly gray with *plain, mostly rufous brown wings* (*no spots*); foreface and entire underparts uniform pale dull ochraceous.

SIMILAR SPECIES: This canopy-inhabiting antshrike is usually identified on the basis of its short-tailed, heavy-billed, stocky shape; male's wing-spotting and female's uniform brown wings provide further clues. Shape and coloration of both sexes are reminiscent of various *Myrmotherula* antwrens, which often occur in the same flock but are much smaller with more slender bills. The species really should have been called the "Short-tailed Antshrike," as so many antbirds have spots on their wings.

HABITAT AND BEHAVIOR: Fairly common in canopy and middle levels and borders of humid forest, both in várzea and terra firme, to a lesser extent in secondary woodland; especially favors viny tangles. Apparently less numerous in the Guianas. Usually in pairs, often with mixed flocks which include various tanagers, foliage-gleaners, and other antbirds; often forages in terminal leafy branches, making it relatively easy to see. The song is a distinctive musical trill "t-t-t-t-t-t-t-teéuw," often repeated several times in quite rapid succession (even going on for several minutes). Also has a much sharper "chét" call, sometimes followed by a "keeeuw."

RANGE: S. Venezuela (e. Bolívar and Amazonas), s. Colombia (north to Caquetá and Vaupés), e. Ecuador, e. Peru, n. Bolivia (Pando, Beni, and n. Santa Cruz), and Amaz. Brazil (south to n. Mato Grosso and s. Pará, and east to n. Maranhão; north of the Amazon not recorded east of Roraima and the Rio Negro); Surinam and French Guiana (seems likely in Guyana). To about 500 m.

Thamnistes Antshrikes

An arboreal antshrike found mainly in forests on Andean slopes. It is unusual among the antshrikes in that sexes are much alike, with males lacking gray or black.

Thamnistes anabatinus

RUSSET ANTSHRIKE

DESCRIPTION: 14.5–15 cm (5¾–6″). A stocky, arboreal, dull-patterned antshrike of Andean foothill forests; note its *heavy bill* (though less stout in *rufescens* of Peru and Bolivia). *Rufescens* is brown above, more grayish on crown, both crown and back with fine pale shaft streaks; wings and tail rufous. *Superciliary, most of face, and all of underparts rather bright ochraceous,* becoming duller and more olivaceous on belly. Male has a usually concealed orange-rufous dorsal patch. N. races (south to Ecuador, the nominate group) are smaller and somewhat shorter-tailed; they are more rufescent on crown and olivaceous on back (lacking shaft streaks on both), paler on superciliary (a duller yellowish buff), and markedly less ochraceous below (more olivaceous generally; brightest on throat); see V-21, C-27.

SIMILAR SPECIES: Russet Antshrike's pattern and coloration more resemble a foliage-gleaner's than most other antshrikes'; of the latter, female Spot-winged, a lowland bird of Amazonia with at most limited overlap, is the most similar. Cf. especially various *Philydor* foliage-gleaners (e.g., Buff-fronted and Rufous-rumped), which may be found in the same flock as the antshrike.

HABITAT AND BEHAVIOR: Uncommon to locally fairly common in canopy and borders of humid forest, mainly in foothills and adjacent lowlands. Usually found singly or in pairs, frequently accompanying mixed flocks including various tanagers, flycatchers, and furnariids. Forages rather actively, hopping about and peering among smaller branches and on limbs, sometimes probing into clusters of dead leaves, usually easy to see (*rufescens* may remain more under cover?). Usually quiet, but n. birds give a high, sibilant "wee-tsip," easily overlooked but occasionally lengthened and strengthened into a quite powerful "weet, see-see-see-tsip" or "teeeo, tseu-tseu-tseu-tseu-tseu-tseu" which can be given repeatedly. We do not know if the voice of *rufescens* is similar. Numerous just above the Tinalandia Hotel in w. Ecuador.

RANGE: Pacific lowlands and foothills of w. Colombia (Chocó to Nariño) and w. Ecuador (south to El Oro); a sighting (W. Brown) from n. Colombia (Tayrona Nat. Park on n. slope of Santa Marta Mts.); e. slope of Andes in extreme w. Venezuela (Táchira), Colombia (w. Meta southward), Ecuador (south to Zamora-Chinchipe), Peru (south of the Río Marañón from Amazonas southward), and w. Bolivia (Cochabamba). Also s. Mexico to Panama. To about 1700 m.

NOTE: More s. birds (mainly from south of the Río Marañón in Peru and Bolivia) are perhaps a separate species from the group of races found farther north. However, a 1992 specimen (ANSP) from Panguri in extreme s. Zamora-Chinchipe in s. Ecuador seems somewhat intermediate: while closely resembling *rufescens*, in certain characters it shows some evidence of intergradation toward *aequatorialis* found farther north in e. Ecuador. If split, *T. rufescens* could be called the Peruvian Russet-Antshrike and *T. anabatinus* the Northern Russet-Antshrike.

Thamnomanes Antshrikes

Four rather plain antshrikes found inside Amazonian forests, often with understory flocks. The genus is similar morphologically to the *Dysithamnus* antvireos—indeed various species have been transferred from one genus to the other, and the affinities of one (*occidentalis*) until very recently remained unclear; it is now being placed in *Dysithamnus*). The two genera behave quite differently, *Thamnomanes* perching erectly and sallying flycatcher-like to foliage and into the air, *Dysithamnus* merely hopping about and gleaning from foliage. Much information on the genus was presented by T. S. Schulenberg (*Wilson Bull.* 95[4]: 505–521, 1983), and the behavior of the flocks in which they figure so prominently was described by C. A. Munn and J. W. Terborgh (*Condor* 81[4]: 338–347, 1979).

Thamnomanes saturninus

SATURNINE ANTSHRIKE PLATE: 18

DESCRIPTION: 14.5 cm (5¾"). W. and cen. Amazonia *south* of the Amazon. Male *essentially dark bluish gray* with *black patch on throat and upper chest*, some whitish on belly, and very narrow white fringing on tail tips (latter hard to see in the field); *large white dorsal patch* (normally concealed except when bird is excited). Female mostly olive brown above, face vaguely mottled with buffy whitish, wings (especially) and tail more rufescent; *large white dorsal patch* (like male's usually hidden). Throat whitish, breast mottled with olive brown, becoming buffy ochraceous on lower underparts (deepest on crissum).
SIMILAR SPECIES: Cf. very similar Dusky-throated Antshrike. Males of somewhat longer-tailed Cinereous and Bluish-slate Antshrikes have concolor gray throats (without black). Female of latter is contrastingly gray and rich rufous-chestnut below, whereas females of most races of former are also richer ochraceous below (palest female Cinereous occur in e. Amaz. Brazil south of the Amazon, mainly east of Saturnine's range).
HABITAT AND BEHAVIOR: Fairly common in lower growth of humid forest, especially in terra firme. Usually in pairs, sometimes in small family groups, often accompanying mixed understory flocks of *Myrmotherula* antwrens, various furnariids, and very often Cinereous or (depending on range) Bluish-slate Antshrikes. Saturnine tends to perch more horizontally than Cinereous or Bluish-slate, usually remains lower, and less often perches prominently. Its song is a series of raspy but nonetheless somewhat musical notes that obviously rise in pitch and speed up, "grr, grr-grr-grr-gee-gee-gee-geegeegeegigigigi?" Numerous in Amazonia Nat. Park west of the Rio Tapajós south of Itaituba, Brazil.
RANGE: Ne. Peru (Loreto south of the Amazon, and south to Sarayacu on the Río Ucayali), w. and cen. Amaz. Brazil (east to w. bank of the Rio Tapajós, and south to Acre, Rondônia, and n. Mato Grosso), and extreme ne. Bolivia (ne. Santa Cruz). Below 300 m.

NOTE: Perhaps conspecific with *T. ardesiacus*, and so treated by Hilty and Brown (1986). Behavior and vocalizations of both forms are very similar, and their ranges are, so far as known, entirely allopatric. Their reported sympatry at Tonantins, on the n. bank of the Amazon in w. Brazil, apparently was based on a single misidentified specimen, and despite "ample opportunity" for them to come into contact in w. Brazil south of the Amazon, there is no evidence of intergradation (T. S. Schulenberg, pers. comm.).

Thamnomanes ardesiacus

DUSKY-THROATED ANTSHRIKE

DESCRIPTION: 14 cm (5½"). W. Amazonia to Guianas. Closely resembles Saturnine Antshrike; they are not known to occur together. Nominate male (se. Colombia south to se. Peru) typically has *concolor gray throat*, though especially in n. portion of range, some black may show. Black is always present on throat of *obidensis* (Brazil, Venezuela, and Guianas) but *is never as extensive as in male Saturnine*. Male Dusky-throated is also somewhat paler (less bluish) gray, and it lacks Saturnine's white dorsal patch (at most very small) and whitish on belly. Females are very similar, though Dusky-throated lacks white dorsal patch and shows less whitish on throat. See V-22, C-29.

SIMILAR SPECIES: Male of nominate Dusky-throated Antshrike (which lacks black on throat) also closely resembles male Cinereous Antshrike, but the latter is slightly larger with a somewhat longer tail with no white tipping (its absence is hard to see in the field). Dusky-throated and Cinereous are thus often best distinguished by voice and shape, Dusky-throated looking "dumpier" and perching less vertically. Females of the two are comparatively easy, Cinereous with considerably richer ochraceous on belly.

HABITAT AND BEHAVIOR: Fairly common in lower growth of humid forest, especially in terra firme. Behavior, including vocalizations, similar to Saturnine Antshrike's.

RANGE: Guianas, s. Venezuela (Delta Amacuro south through Bolívar and Amazonas), Amaz. Brazil (mostly north of the Amazon from Amapá westward; south of it only along lower Rio Purus and at Tefé), se. Colombia (north to Meta and Vaupés, probably also in e. Guianía), e. Ecuador, e. Peru (though not south of the Amazon nor east of the lower Río Ucayali), and extreme nw. Bolivia (Pando at Camino Mucden). Mostly below 500 m (recorded to 1100 m in Venezuela).

NOTE: See comments under Saturnine Antshrike.

Thamnomanes caesius

CINEREOUS ANTSHRIKE　　　　　　　　　　PLATE: 18

DESCRIPTION: 14.5 cm (5¾"). Rather long tailed. Male *uniform slaty gray*. Female olivaceous brown above, somewhat more rufescent on wings and tail and more grayish on face, usually showing an indistinct buffyish eye-ring and lores. Throat dull whitish, chest grayish olive; *remaining underparts rather rich cinnamon-rufous;* see C-29. Both sexes of *glaucus* and *persimilis* (all of range north of the Amazon, south of it from the Rio Purus east to the Rio Tapajós) have a usually hidden white dorsal patch. Female of nominate race (coastal e. Brazil) is duller below, with breast olivaceous gray, only the crissum being rich ochra-

ceous; *hoffmannsi* (Amaz. Brazil south of the Amazon east of the Rio Tapajós) is intermediate.

SIMILAR SPECIES: Male of nominate Dusky-throated Antshrike (lacking black throat) is very similar to Cinereous but has shorter tail. Cf. also Bluish-slate Antshrike (no known overlap; males quite similar, females rather different). Male Plain-winged Antshrike closely resembles male Cinereous (both are uniform gray), but their behavior and vocalizations differ markedly.

HABITAT AND BEHAVIOR: Fairly common to common in lower growth of humid forest (especially in terra firme) and mature secondary woodland. Usually in pairs or small family groups, around which mixed understory flocks of other antbirds and furnariids often form. Cinereous usually perches erectly on horizontal limbs, scanning nearby foliage and airspace, then abruptly sallies to pick off an insect; its foraging strategy is thus similar to certain tyrannids', e.g., the *Rhynchocyclus* flatbills. Vocalizations are distinctive and often heard, carrying far and often drawing attention to forest flocks. The song commences with several wheezy whistled notes and then rapidly accelerates before ending in a bubbling trill, "whee, whee, whee-whee-whee-wheep-wheepwhipwhipwhip-p-p-p-p-p-p-pr"; a frequent call is a staccato "wer-chicory."

RANGE: Guianas, s. Venezuela (Bolívar and Amazonas), e. Colombia (north to Meta and Vichada), e. Ecuador, ne. Peru (Loreto north of the Amazon and west of the lower Río Ucayali), Amaz. Brazil (throughout north of the Amazon, south of it from the lower Rio Purus and Rondônia east to Maranhão), and ne. Bolivia (ne. Santa Cruz on the Serranía de Huanchaca); e. Brazil (Paraíba and Alagoas south to Rio de Janeiro). To 800 m.

NOTE: *T. glaucus* (with *persimilis,* Glaucous Antshrike) has been considered a separate species (e.g., Pinto 1978). See also comments under Bluish-slate Antshrike.

Thamnomanes schistogynus

BLUISH-SLATE ANTSHRIKE

DESCRIPTION: 14.5 cm (5¾"). *Sw. Amazonia.* Male resembles male Cinereous Antshrike (no overlap) but is slightly more bluish gray with a larger (but still usually hidden) white dorsal patch. Female more distinctive: *uniform bluish gray above,* sometimes showing a faint buffyish eye-ring; large dorsal patch white. Throat and chest bluish gray (some indistinct whitish streaking on throat), *contrasting with rich rufous-chestnut lower underparts.*

SIMILAR SPECIES: Does not occur in range of Cinereous Antshrike. Races of male Saturnine and Dusky-throated Antshrikes in Bluish-slate's range have black throats.

HABITAT AND BEHAVIOR: Fairly common to common in lower growth of humid forest, both in terra firme and várzea. Behavior, including vocalizations, similar to Cinereous Antshrike's. Numerous at Tambopata Reserve in Madre de Dios, Peru.

RANGE: E. Peru (from Loreto south of the Amazon and east of the lower Río Ucayali south to Madre de Dios), n. Bolivia (south to La

Paz and Cochabamba), and w. Amaz. Brazil (south of Amazon only, ranging east to Tefé and upper Rio Juruá and upper Rio Purus regions). To about 800 m.

NOTE: Possibly conspecific with *T. caesius;* the two are very similar in behavior and vocalizations. However, both species were apparently taken at São Paulo de Olivença, on the s. bank of the Amazon in w. Brazil; further, their ranges are nearly in contact along the upper Rio Purus, with no sign of intergradation.

Dysithamnus Antvireos

Antvireos are small, chunky, and bull-headed antbirds found in forest undergrowth. They are larger and heavier-billed than *Myrmotherula* antwrens and have more sluggish behavior, and they are shorter tailed than *Thamnophilus* antshrikes (which they rather more resemble in behavior). The genus is apparently closely related to *Thamnomanes,* but antvireos are stouter and shorter-tailed, and they perch more horizontally and glean in foliage rather than sally out. *Thamnomanes* antshrikes are found exclusively in Amaz. lowland forests, whereas *Dysithamnus* antvireos range almost entirely in foothill or subtropical forests.

GROUP A

"Plain" and "fancy" antvireos; females with *rufescent crowns.*

Dysithamnus mentalis

PLAIN ANTVIREO   PLATE: 18

DESCRIPTION: 11.5 cm (4½"). A small and chunky antbird, rather variable, widespread in foothill and subtropical forests (but *not* in Amazonia). Male above gray to olive grayish, grayest on head (sometimes with vaguely paler superciliary), purest olive on back (especially in nominate race of se. Brazil, e. Paraguay, and ne. Argentina), with *darker, usually contrasting, dusky auriculars;* wing-coverts narrowly edged whitish. Below mostly somewhat paler gray, with whiter throat and belly; nominate race and *aequatorialis* (w. Ecuador) have considerable pale yellow on belly, whereas races on tepuis (*spodionotus* and *ptaritepui*) and in n. Andes (e.g., *extremus;* see C-28) are darker gray. Female mostly olive to olive brown above with *contrasting rufous to chestnut crown,* whitish eye-ring, and *dusky auriculars.* Below variable, usually mostly pale olive grayish with throat and midbelly whitish to grayish white, some races (especially nominate) considerably yellower on lower underparts.
SIMILAR SPECIES: Undistinguished looking but often encountered; it is thus important to learn the Plain Antvireo well as a basis of comparison with other, less frequently seen antbirds. Males usually look quite dull and gray, but their distinctive darker cheeks can usually be discerned. Females, because of their rufous crowns, are often more readily recognized than their consorts. *Myrmotherula* antwrens are smaller and behave more actively; *Thamnophilus* antshrikes are larger and longer-tailed. Female of nominate race bears a striking resem-

blance to Rufous-crowned Greenlet (the two are widely sympatric), but greenlet's behavior and more slender, longer-tailed shape are quite different.

HABITAT AND BEHAVIOR: Fairly common to common in lower growth of montane forest, less frequently out to borders and in second-growth woodland, usually in humid areas but also locally (at least in w. Ecuador) in deciduous forest and in interior Brazil in gallery forest. Especially numerous in se. Brazil area. Most often in pairs which forage rather sluggishly (rather like a *Vireo* vireo, in fact), hopping along small branches or perching stolidly for extended periods; regularly accompanies mixed understory flocks with antwrens, small flycatchers, and others. Male's song is a short series of rapidly repeated notes which accelerate into a roll with a clipped, staccato effect; it somewhat recalls a *Thamnophilus* antshrike but is higher pitched than most. Both sexes also give several nasal or churring calls.

RANGE: N. and w. Venezuela (Paria Peninsula west through n. mts. and the Andes, and on Sierra de Perijá), w. Colombia (mostly on slopes of Andes; also in nw. Chocó), w. Ecuador (both slopes of Andes, and in w. lowlands down locally to near sea level), nw. (Tumbes and Piura) and e. Peru (e. slope of Andes), and w. Bolivia (La Paz, Cochabamba, w. Santa Cruz and s. Beni); extreme e. and s. Venezuela (s. Sucre south through Bolívar and Amazonas); ne. Brazil (e. Pará on the lower Rio Tocantins east to Paraíba, Pernambuco, and Alagoas); locally in cen. Brazil (extreme s. Piauí, Goiás, and s. Mato Grosso); se. Brazil (s. Bahia and Minas Gerais south to Rio Grande do Sul, inland to s. Mato Grosso do Sul), e. Paraguay, and ne. Argentina (Misiones); Trinidad and Tobago. Seems likely in Guyana. Also Mexico to Panama. Mostly below 2000 m.

Dysithamnus puncticeps

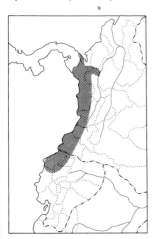

SPOT-CROWNED ANTVIREO

DESCRIPTION: 11.5 cm (4½"). *W. Colombia and nw. Ecuador. Iris whitish to grayish.* General form recalls Plain Antvireo, but both sexes lack dusky auriculars. Male additionally differs in having *crown vaguely streaked black and gray* (*flemmingi* of Ecuador and Nariño, Colombia); crown is *lightly dotted whitish* in *intensus* of w. Colombia (see C-28) and *even more boldly spotted* in nominate race of n. Chocó, Colombia (see P-21). Further, male's wing-coverts are *dotted* with white (without forming wing-*bars*), and it has *blurry gray streaking on throat and breast.* Female has *crown streaked rufous and blackish;* above otherwise olive brown, wing-coverts dotted with buff; *below mostly pale buffy ochraceous, faintly streaked dusky on throat and chest* and more olivaceous on flanks.

SIMILAR SPECIES: Plain Antvireo has dark eye, *plain* crown lacking streaks or dots, dusky auriculars, and lacks streaking below.

HABITAT AND BEHAVIOR: Uncommon to locally fairly common in lower growth of humid forest. Behavior much like Plain Antvireo's. Male's song is a rather long series of soft, minor-keyed whistled notes, longer and with a more even cadence and less abrupt delivery than Plain Antvireo's.

RANGE: Pacific slope of w. Colombia (Chocó to Nariño, and around n. end of Cen. Andes in Antioquia) and nw. Ecuador (south to Pichincha). Also Panama. To about 1000 m.

Dysithamnus stictothorax

SPOT-BREASTED ANTVIREO   PLATE: 18

DESCRIPTION: 12 cm (4¾"). *Se. Brazil and ne. Argentina.* Male mostly dusky olive above, grayer on head and with *postocular "stripe" of white spots arching behind ear-coverts;* wings dusky, coverts edged with white. Throat whitish, *remaining underparts pale apricot yellow with gray spotting on breast.* Female similar but with *rufous crown.*

SIMILAR SPECIES: Plain Antvireo, often found with this species, is smaller and lacks spotting below and on face.

HABITAT AND BEHAVIOR: Fairly common in lower growth of humid forest and second-growth woodland. General behavior similar to Plain Antvireo's, and in some places pairs of both forage in the same flock. Spot-breasted's song is a rather loud and vigorous series of mellow musical notes, accelerating somewhat but without Plain Antvireo's abrupt effect, and longer and not so run together at the end. Its call is unusual (for an antbird), a somewhat burry and querulous "wurr," steadily repeated, often for extended periods. Numerous at lower elevations in Itatiaia Nat. Park, and not uncommon in Tijuca Nat. Park above city of Rio de Janeiro.

RANGE: Se. Brazil (Espírito Santo and e. Minas Gerais south to Paraná; perhaps also in s. Bahia) and ne. Argentina (Misiones in Iguazú Nat. Park). To 1100 m.

Dysithamnus xanthopterus

RUFOUS-BACKED ANTVIREO   PLATE: 18

DESCRIPTION: 12.5 cm (5"). *Higher mts. of se. Brazil.* Male has head and upper back gray, *feathers of face with white spots* (imparting a grizzled effect); *above otherwise bright rufous-chestnut,* tail feathers blackish edged rufous. Pale grayish below, darkest on sides of breast and olivaceous on flanks. Female similar but with *rufous crown;* facial spotting and underparts yellowish buff, sides clouded olivaceous.

SIMILAR SPECIES: Unlikely to be confused.

HABITAT AND BEHAVIOR: Uncommon in middle levels and subcanopy of montane forest. This striking antvireo characteristically forages in higher forest strata than its congeners; pairs often accompany mixed flocks including various furnariids, other antbirds, tanagers, and warbling-finches. Its song is a fast series of 10–12 minor-keyed whistled notes, slightly descending or simply fading away. Small numbers can be seen along upper part of the "jeep trail" in Itatiaia Nat. Park and at the Boracéia Reserve in São Paulo.

RANGE: Se. Brazil (Rio de Janeiro to e. Paraná; published records from Espírito Santo require confirmation). 900–1700 m.

GROUP B

"Plumbeous" antvireos (males *slaty*); females dissimilar.

Dysithamnus plumbeus

PLUMBEOUS ANTVIREO   PLATE: 18

DESCRIPTION: 12.5 cm (5"). *Local in e. Brazil;* White-streaked Antvireo of Andes is considered a separate species. Male uniform slaty gray, *blacker on chest;* bend of wing white and *small white spots on wing-coverts.* Female dull olive brown above with faint whitish eye-ring and *whitish tipping on wing-coverts.* Throat grayish white; remaining underparts dull grayish olive brown, somewhat more ochraceous on lower belly and crissum.

SIMILAR SPECIES: In its limited range, most likely confused with Cinereous Antshrike which is somewhat larger with both sexes *lacking* any markings on wing; further, male Cinereous is uniform gray below with no black on chest. *Myrmotherula* antwrens are smaller.

HABITAT AND BEHAVIOR: Uncommon and local in lower growth of humid forest. An inconspicuous bird, usually noted in pairs foraging alone close to the ground, but occasionally with mixed flocks including various other antbirds. Its song is a series of about 10 rather slow, melancholy whistled notes with an even cadence, at first slightly rising, then fading away and lasting 2–3 seconds. Plumbeous Antvireo is now greatly reduced in overall range and numbers because of deforestation across most of its former range; it deserves threatened (if not endangered) status. Small numbers continue to be found in the Sooretama Reserve in n. Espírito Santo.

RANGE: E. Brazil (s. Bahia south to e. Minas Gerais and n. Rio de Janeiro). Below 100 m.

NOTE: Placed in the genus *Thamnomanes* by Meyer de Schauensee (1966, 1970); recent information on vocalizations and behavior place it clearly with *Dysithamnus* (see T. S. Schulenberg, *Wilson Bull.* 95[4]: 505–521, 1983). We regard *D. leucostictus* (with *tucuyensis*) of the Andes as a separate species.

Dysithamnus leucostictus

WHITE-STREAKED ANTVIREO   PLATE: 18
Other: White-spotted Antvireo, Plumbeous Antvireo (in part)

DESCRIPTION: 12.5 cm (5"). *Local in mts. from Venezuela to Ecuador.* Male uniform slaty gray, *blacker on chest;* bend of wing white and *small white spots on wing-coverts.* Female has rufous crown and *otherwise uniform rufous brown upperparts. Sides of head and neck and underparts gray boldly streaked with white. Tucuyensis* (Venezuela) is somewhat paler generally than nominate race (Ecuador and Colombia), and its streaking below is blurrier.

SIMILAR SPECIES: Male virtually identical in plumage to male of geographically distant Plumbeous Antvireo, but females of the two are very different. Male Plain Antvireo is smaller, lacks black below, has dark auriculars; cf. also male Uniform Antshrike (larger, with plain wings, no black below, and obvious pale iris). Female is easily recognized, but cf. rare Bicolored Antvireo.

HABITAT AND BEHAVIOR: Uncommon to locally fairly common in

lower and middle growth of montane forest. Usually found in pairs, foraging quietly and methodically, almost invariably with mixed flocks of understory birds. The song is a well-enunciated series of 7 or 8 soft, minor-key whistled notes which gradually but distinctly descend in pitch. Small numbers can be found in forest patches above Zamora in s. Ecuador.

RANGE: Coastal mts. of n. Venezuela (Monagas west to Lara); e. slope of E. Andes in Colombia (recorded only from w. Meta and e. Nariño, but likely more widespread); e. Ecuador (e. slope of Andes from Napo to Zamora-Chinchipe). Mostly 1300–1800 m.

NOTE: *D. leucostictus* has usually been considered conspecific with *D. plumbeus* of se. Brazil (e.g., by Meyer de Schauensee 1966, 1970), mainly because of the close resemblance of the males. However, their very wide range disjunction, very different elevation preferences, strikingly dissimilar female plumages, and rather different behavior and songs suggest that they are better treated as separate species. The usual English name for *D. leucostictus* has been White-spotted Antshrike (Meyer de Schauensee 1966, Hilty and Brown 1986), in reference to the female's ventral pattern. As this pattern is actually one of streaks (not spots), we have modified it slightly. B. Whitney (pers. comm.) suggests that *tucuyensis*, endemic to the n. Venezuela mts., may itself be worthy of specific rank (its song differs from that of nominate *leucostictus;* we are not familiar with it); if split, it should be called the Venezuelan Antvireo.

Dysithamnus occidentalis

BICOLORED ANTVIREO

Other: Western Antvireo, Western Antshrike

DESCRIPTION: 13.5 cm (5½"). *Sw. Colombia and ne. Ecuador.* Male *uniform sooty black*, slightly paler below and browner on primaries; small white spots on wing-coverts and a concealed white dorsal patch. *Punctitectus* (e. Ecuador) somewhat paler (grayer) than nominate race (w. Colombia). Female has *crown chestnut; upperparts otherwise dark chestnut brown*, wing-coverts with small buffy whitish spots. Sides of head and underparts dull grayish with sparse narrow whitish shaft streaks; umber brown on lower belly.

SIMILAR SPECIES: White-streaked Antvireo is smaller. Females of these 2 species are very different (Bicolored being much darker generally and much less boldly patterned below), but males are similar except that Bicolored is slightly blacker generally, lacking the black-chested, gray-bellied effect characteristic of White-streaked. Male of nominate White-shouldered Antshrike is larger, glossier black generally, and has white on bend of wing only (not spots on wing-coverts). Cf. also Uniform Antshrike.

HABITAT AND BEHAVIOR: Until recently unknown in life. B. M. Whitney (*Auk* 109[2]: 302–308, 1992) presented the first information on the behavior and vocalizations of this enigmatic antbird, which he located in 1991 on the lower slopes of Volcán Sumaco in e. Ecuador; all of what follows is based on his observations. Rare to perhaps locally uncommon in understory of montane forest, with an apparent predilection for thicker growth found around openings such as those created by treefalls and landslides. Found singly or in pairs, moving independently of mixed flocks, with gleaning foraging behavior much like other antvireos' (and quite *un*like those of *Thanomanes* antshrikes). Its most commonly heard call (heard only from males) is a distinctive low throaty scold, "jeér-deer-dur" or "jeér-deer-dur-dr"; also heard are "peer" and "peeur" calls similar to those of other antvireos'. Its song was not definitely heard. Both forms of the species appear to be threatened by deforestation.

RANGE: Locally on w. slope of W. Andes in sw. Colombia (Valle at Finca Hato Viejo, near Farallones de Cali Nat. Park, and w. Cauca); e. slope of Andes in ne. Ecuador (w. Napo). 900–2200 m in Colombia; about 1500–2000 m in Ecuador.

NOTE: The nomenclatural history of this species is convoluted. *Occidentalis* was originally described by Chapman in the genus *Thamnophilus* as a subspecies of *T. aethiops.* Chapman later described *punctitectus* as well, as a separate species, this time in the genus *Dysithamnus.* J. T. Zimmer (*Am. Mus. Novitates* 646, 1933) then concluded that *occidentalis* was not a race of *Thamnophilus aethiops* but was most closely related to *punctitectus,* which he accepted as a *Dysithamnus.* The name *occidentalis* had priority, so *punctitectus* became a subspecies of *D. occidentalis;* this treatment was followed in *Birds of the World,* vol. 7. Meyer de Schauensee (1964) continued to place *occidentalis* in *Dysithamnus,* but he later (1966, 1970) transferred it to *Thamnomanes,* together with various other of its purported relatives (e.g., *plumbeus*), and Hilty and Brown (1986) retained it there. We believe that on distributional grounds (and plumage pattern of females) its placement in *Thamnomanes* is incorrect, and we agree with Zimmer (op. cit.) and E. O. Willis (*Pap. Avuls. Zool.* 35[18]: 183, 1984) that it is best placed in *Dysithamnus.* Whitney (op. cit.) also concluded that the species was best placed in *Dysithamnus,* based on his observations of the behavior and vocalizations of *punctitectus.* He also suggested the new English name of Bicolored Antvireo for the species, based on the female plumage.

Herpsilochmus Antwrens

Quite long-tailed antwrens found mainly in the canopy and borders of humid forest, some species in more deciduous woodland and forest. Almost all have a bold white superciliary, wing-bars, and broad tail-tipping. Many species, particularly those in our Group B, are difficult to distinguish in the field (particularly as most are so often seen only high overhead in the canopy). Females are often easier to identify than males. *Herpsilochmus* antwrens' oft-repeated vocalizations, though all basically similar, frequently reveal their presence. Nesting is poorly documented, though the nest of a Large-billed Antwren was recently described by F. C. Straube, M. R. Bornshein, and D. M. Teixera (*Bull. B.O.C.* 112[4]: 277–279, 1992).

GROUP A

Males with *patterned breast;* females have *crowns and underparts ochraceous to buff.* Brazil.

Herpsilochmus longirostris

LARGE-BILLED ANTWREN   PLATE: 18

DESCRIPTION: 12.5 cm (5"). *Mainly interior Brazil.* Rather heavy bill. Male has black crown, long broad white superciliary, narrow black postocular line, and gray ear-coverts; back gray mottled with black and

white; wings and tail black, wings with bold white wing-bars, tail feathers broadly tipped white. Below white, *throat and (especially) breast with numerous gray spots.* Female has *bright orange-rufous head and neck* contrasting with gray back; wings and tail as in male. *Below bright cinnamon-buff,* paling somewhat on belly.

SIMILAR SPECIES: Very striking and pretty female is unlikely to be confused, but compare to female of much smaller and shorter-tailed Streaked Antwren. Male's overall pattern is much like numerous other *Herpsilochmus* antwrens', including several that are sympatric (e.g., Black-capped), but Large-billed is considerably larger and is the only one with spotting below.

HABITAT AND BEHAVIOR: Uncommon to locally fairly common in middle levels and subcanopy of gallery forest and deciduous woodland. Usually in pairs, gleaning in foliage and along branches; generally remains well above the ground except at forest borders and openings, where sometimes lower. Male's song is a series of about 15 evenly delivered chippering notes, then slightly slowing toward end, "wh-chchchchchchchchchchchch-chu-chu," usually delivered as it vibrates its tail; often female echoes her mate, on a slightly higher pitch. Although fast, the tempo is slightly slower than the songs of many other *Herpsilochmus* antwrens. Can be seen in woodland north of Cuiabá, Mato Grosso, along the road to Chapada.

RANGE: Interior Brazil (s. Piauí and Goiás south to São Paulo and Mato Grosso do Sul, and west to s. Mato Grosso) and ne. Bolivia (Beni at Río Iténez, Cerro San Simón, and Espíritu; ne. Santa Cruz on Serranía de Huanchaca). 200–1000 m.

Herpsilochmus pectoralis

PECTORAL ANTWREN

PLATE: 18

DESCRIPTION: 11.5 cm (4½"). *Very local in ne. Brazil.* Male resembles male of larger Large-billed Antwren but has *conspicuous black crescent across chest* and no throat or breast spotting. Female has *crown rufous;* otherwise brownish olive above, uppertail-coverts tipped white; wings and tail black, wings with bold white wing-bars, tail feathers broadly tipped white. *Uniform dull buff below, richest on breast.*

SIMILAR SPECIES: Female Pectoral could be confused with female of considerably larger and more brightly colored Large-billed Antwren; they are not known to occur together but could be found to do so. Male virtually unmistakable.

HABITAT AND BEHAVIOR: Uncommon and local in gallery forest and relatively tall caatinga woodland, where there are numerous trees above 10 m in height. Recently found in e.-cen. Bahia (near Itaberaba and Santa Bárbara) by B. Whitney, who provided the behavioral information that follows. General behavior much as in other *Herpsilochmus* antwrens, gleaning in foliage and along limbs, but on several occasions seen foraging close to the ground (and once actually on it—unusual for a *Herpsilochmus*). Male's song is a fast and slightly rising series of 14–20 evenly spaced chippered notes which steadily become louder before leveling on the last 4 or 5, the whole lasting about 2 seconds;

female's song is similar but higher pitched and usually shorter. Foraging males also frequently give a short, barking "ehrrk." Although still poorly known, Pectoral Antwren is believed to be threatened by the removal of woodland across much of its range.

RANGE: Ne. Brazil (recorded from a few localities in ne. Maranhão, e. Rio Grande do Norte, Sergipe, and ne. Bahia). Below 200 m.

GROUP B

Males *plain grayish white* below; females with *spotted or streaked crown* and buff-tinged *breast*.

Herpsilochmus sticturus

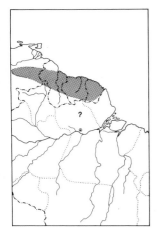

SPOT-TAILED ANTWREN

PLATE: 18

DESCRIPTION: 11 cm (4¼"). *Ne. South America*. Male has black crown with inconspicuous small white spots on forehead, long white superciliary, black postocular line, and grayish ear-coverts; back gray with large but usually concealed white dorsal patch and some black mottling; wings black with bold white wing-bars (with almost a spotted effect); tail black, feathers broadly tipped white and *central feathers with large white spots on inner webs (visible from above)*. Below uniform grayish white. Female has *crown black with elongated streaks of rufous-chestnut*; above otherwise much like male except more brownish tinged. Below uniform dingy grayish white.

SIMILAR SPECIES: *Closely* resembles Spot-backed and Todd's Antwrens; for distinctions see under those species. Dugand's Antwren of w. Amazonia does not occur sympatrically with Spot-tailed.

HABITAT AND BEHAVIOR: Uncommon in canopy and borders of humid forest, especially forest that grows on sandy or impoverished soils. Usually in pairs, gleaning among leaves and on outer branches, most often encountered while accompanying canopy flocks; has occasionally been found foraging in the same flock as Todd's Antwren near the Voltzberg in Raleigh Falls Nature Park, Surinam (B. Whitney). Male's song is an accelerating series of fast chippered notes, the first several given slightly slower, e.g., "ch, ch, ch-chchchchchchchch," slightly dropping in pitch (B. Whitney; RSR). It is much like Pygmy Antwren's song. Calls include a burry, throaty "greep!" and (as an alarm) a rapid, sharp "tyu-tyu" (B. Whitney).

RANGE: Guianas, s. Venezuela (Bolívar west to the lower Río Caura), and n. Brazil (recorded only from Óbidos in Pará north of the Amazon, but probably more widespread). Below 400 m.

NOTE: Does not include *H. dugandi* (Dugand's Antwren) of upper Amazonia, sometimes considered conspecific.

Herpsilochmus dugandi

DUGAND'S ANTWREN

Other: Spot-tailed Antwren (in part)

DESCRIPTION: 11 cm (4¼"). Local in *w. Amazonia*. Closely resembles Spot-tailed Antwren (sometimes considered conspecific); no overlap. Males would be indistinguishable in the field; back of Dugand's may be plainer gray. Females also similar, but Dugand's has *crown uniform*

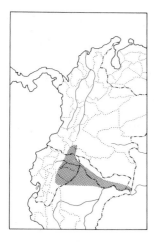

rufous (showing little or no black) and is somewhat more tinged with buff below.

SIMILAR SPECIES: The only *Herpsilochmus* antwren in its range, and as such should be readily recognizable.

HABITAT AND BEHAVIOR: Uncommon and local in canopy of humid forest, mainly in terra firme but sometimes in várzea. This is a very rare bird in collections, and until its vocalizations are recognized, it is usually overlooked because it usually remains so high above the ground. Its song and general behavior are similar to Spot-tailed Antwren's (RSR; B. Whitney). Has been seen at La Selva Lodge in e. Ecuador and at both Explorama Lodge and Explornapo Camp near Iquitos, Peru.

RANGE: Locally in se. Colombia (w. Caquetá, and seen near Leticia in Amazonas by E. O. Willis), e. Ecuador (Napo south to Morona-Santiago), and ne. Peru (Loreto north of the Río Marañón and Amazon River). To 400 m.

NOTE: Often considered a race of *H. sticturus* of ne. South America. We treat it as a full species because of the great range disjunction and the differences in female plumage.

Herpsilochmus stictocephalus

TODD'S ANTWREN

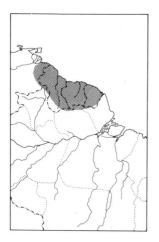

DESCRIPTION: 11.5 cm (4½"). *Guianas and adjacent Venezuela and Brazil.* Male very similar to male of slightly smaller Spot-tailed Antwren, and essentially indistinguishable in the field; the spots on upper side of its tail are slightly smaller. Female differs from female Spot-tailed in having *crown black spotted with white (showing no rufous or buff)* and in having *a wash of fairly rich buff across breast* (almost like a pectoral band). See V-21.

SIMILAR SPECIES: Both sexes of Spot-backed Antwren have rather extensive black and white spotting on back, and in addition female shows ochraceous spotting on black forecrown. Cf. also the larger Roraiman Antwren.

HABITAT AND BEHAVIOR: Uncommon in canopy and borders of humid forest. General behavior similar to Spot-tailed Antwren's; pairs of both species have occasionally been seen in the same mixed flock at the Voltzberg in Surinam's Raleigh Falls Nature Park (B. Whitney). The somewhat different song of male Todd's is an often shorter series of slower-paced, soft chippered notes which slow markedly (rather than speeding up; B. Whitney, RSR) and fall slightly in pitch. This is the only *Herpsilochmus* found at Surinam's Brownsberg Nature Park.

RANGE: Guianas, extreme e. Venezuela (e. Bolívar), and extreme n. Brazil (female in Goeldi Museum from Cabeceiras do Rio Paru de Oeste in n. Pará). To about 500 m.

Herpsilochmus dorsimaculatus

SPOT-BACKED ANTWREN   PLATE: 18

DESCRIPTION: 11.5 cm (4½"). *Drainages of upper Orinoco River and Rio Negro.* Both sexes resemble Spot-tailed Antwren (the 2 species overlap locally) but differ in having *back broadly striped and spotted with black,*

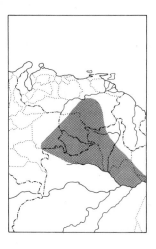

gray, and white and a longer tail. See V-21, C-28. Female further differs from female Spot-tailed in having *ochraceous spots on forecrown*, white spots on black mid- and hindcrown, and *more buff on loral area and sides of head, throat, and chest.*

SIMILAR SPECIES: Roraiman Antwren occurs only at higher elevations. Todd's Antwren is not known to overlap with this species, though their ranges approach in cen. Bolívar, Venezuela; male Todd's shows fewer black and white markings on back, whereas female has crown spotting all white (not buffyish on forecrown).

HABITAT AND BEHAVIOR: Uncommon in canopy and borders of humid forest, both in terra firme and várzea. General behavior similar to that of other lowland forest-inhabiting *Herpsilochmus,* and like them difficult to see well enough for positive identification. Its song (given by both sexes, female usually following male) is a soft, simple, evenly paced chippered trill, slightly dropping in pitch and fading toward the end; one call is an oft-repeated, soft "kuít, kuít, kuít. . . ." Can be seen north of Manaus, often best from the WWF/INPA canopy tower; also present at Junglaven Lodge in Amazonas, Venezuela.

RANGE: S. Venezuela (w. and cen. Bolívar, and Amazonas), extreme e. Colombia (e. Guainía and e. Vaupés), and n. Brazil (Rio Negro drainage south to Faro and just north of Manaus). A sighting from French Guiana requires further corroboration. To about 300 m.

Herpsilochmus roraimae

RORAIMAN ANTWREN

DESCRIPTION: 12.5 cm (5"). *Tepuis of s. Venezuela and adjacent areas.* Resembles Spot-backed Antwren, but Roraiman is *larger* and *substantially longer-tailed,* tail with *more spots* which extend over both inner and outer webs. Back of both sexes is, like Spot-backed's, quite extensively spotted and streaked with black and white. See V-21. Female has black crown spotted with white (no rufous or buff) and buff wash across breast similar to Todd's.

HABITAT AND BEHAVIOR: Uncommon in canopy and borders of humid forest and more stunted woodland. General behavior similar to other *Herpsilochmus* antwrens' of this Group. Song of male is a fast, rather musical chippering of 10–15 notes, slowing slightly and dropping toward the end; often female echoes male with a slightly higher-pitched call. Can be seen along the Escalera road in e. Bolívar, Venezuela, mainly with mixed flocks along edge of taller forest toward the Soldier's Monument.

RANGE: Tepuis of s. Venezuela (Bolívar and Amazonas), and adjacent Guyana (Mt. Twek-quay) and n. Brazil (Roraima). 900–2000 m.

Herpsilochmus atricapillus

BLACK-CAPPED ANTWREN   PLATE: 18

DESCRIPTION: 12 cm (4¾"). Widespread through much of interior central South America. (Note recent changes in species-level taxonomy; see below.) Male has *crown black, long broad white superciliary,* and *black postocular line;* back gray with semiconcealed dorsal patch

white; wings black with white wing-bars and spotting on shoulders; tail black, feathers broadly tipped white. *Below pale grayish,* whitest on throat and midbelly. Female patterned much like male but forehead buff, *crown black broadly streaked with white,* back tinged more olivaceous, and buff tinge on breast, flanks, and crissum.

SIMILAR SPECIES: See similar Pileated Antwren, now known to be syntopic with Black-capped. Creamy-bellied and Ash-throated Antwrens of Peru do not occur with this species. The previous 5 *Herpsilochmus* species are all forest-based antwrens of n. South America which have white spotting on central rectrices (absent in this and the next 3 species).

HABITAT AND BEHAVIOR: Fairly common in deciduous woodland, gallery woodland, and borders of more humid forest and woodland. Usually in pairs, foraging at all levels, lowest at borders; generally not difficult to see, in part because it regularly gleans in outer foliage in the semiopen. Its song is a distinctive semimusical chippered trill, usually with an introductory note (sometimes with an almost hiccuping effect), then accelerating with notes becoming more sputtered and louder toward the end. The song is given by both sexes, usually the male echoed by the female; the tail is rapidly vibrated.

RANGE: Interior e. and cen. Brazil (s. Maranhão, Ceará, and Pernambuco south and west to São Paulo and Mato Grosso do Sul, and west very locally to Rondônia at Cachoeira Nazaré), e. and nw. Paraguay, e. Bolivia (Santa Cruz south to Tarija), and nw. Argentina (Salta and Jujuy). To about 1100 m.

NOTE: Does not include *H. pileatus* (Pileated Antwren), *H. motacilloides* (Creamy-bellied Antwren), or *H. parkeri* (Ash-throated Antwren), following T. J. Davis and J. P. O'Neill (*Wilson Bull.* 98[3]: 337–352, 1986).

Herpsilochmus pileatus

PILEATED ANTWREN
Other: White-browed Antwren, Black-capped Antwren (in part)

DESCRIPTION: 11 cm (4¼"). *Interior ne. Brazil.* Resembles Black-capped Antwren (until recently considered conspecific with it); smaller, with *markedly shorter tail.* Male further differs in having superciliary grayish (not nearly so pure white, especially behind eye) and in *lacking* Black-capped's thin black postocular line. Female differs more strikingly from female Black-capped: her black crown *lacks white streaks,* though there is some gray scaling (particularly on sides of crown); her forehead is more grayish (less buffyish); and her *entire face is essentially plain buffy grayish* with no superciliary or postocular line, resulting in a quite different effect.

HABITAT AND BEHAVIOR: Uncommon in caatinga scrub and deciduous woodland. Behavior similar to Black-capped Antwren's, and recently found to occur at some localities with it; Pileated favors scrubbier and less wooded habitats and therefore often forages closer to the ground. Pileated's song is generally similar to Black-capped's but is faster and more evenly paced, with a gradual crescendo reaching its peak at middle, then becoming softer toward the end; as with Black-capped, female often chimes in right after male. Can be seen around Boa Nova and Morro do Chapeu, both small towns in e.-cen. Bahia. RANGE: Locally in interior ne. Brazil; recorded from cen. Maranhão at Barra do Corda (FMNH), s. Pará on the Serra do Cachimbo (MZUSP, *fide* D. Stotz; these specimens were formerly identified as *H. atricapillus*), Ceará at Chapada de Aripe (Rio Museum) and Várzea Formosa (FMNH), and several localities in cen. and s. Bahia (AMNH and Rio Museum). To about 1000 m.

NOTE: Here regarded as a species distinct from *H. atricapillus*, following T. J. Davis and J. P. O'Neill (*Wilson Bull.* 98[3]: 337–352, 1986) and Schulenberg and Ridgely (in prep.). The English name for this taxon, first suggested by Hellmayr (*Birds of the Americas*, vol. 13, part 3) and also used by Davis and O'Neill (op. cit.), was White-browed Antwren; evidently none of these authors realized that the brow of this species is actually much grayer than that of, particularly, *H. atricapillus*. Rather than continue to use this misleading name, we suggest calling it the Pileated Antwren, taken directly from its Latin species name.

Herpsilochmus motacilloides

CREAMY-BELLIED ANTWREN

Other: Yellow-bellied Antwren, Black-capped Antwren (in part)

DESCRIPTION: 12 cm (4¾"). *E. slope of Andes in cen. and s. Peru.* Closely resembles Black-capped Antwren and until recently considered conspecific with it; no overlap. Both sexes differ in having a black loral spot (this area whitish in Black-capped) and are tinged creamy yellowish on midbelly (this area white in male Black-capped, buff-tinged in female). SIMILAR SPECIES: Not known to occur with other *Herpsilochmus* antwrens other than the very different Rufous-winged and Yellow-breasted. HABITAT AND BEHAVIOR: Uncommon to locally fairly common in canopy and borders of montane forest. Occurs in pairs, usually foraging with canopy mixed flocks, tending to remain in crown and on outer limbs of tall trees (T. J. Davis). The song is reported to be similar to Ash-throated Antwren's, though seemingly without that species' introductory component. All behavioral information from T. J. Davis and J. P. O'Neill (*Wilson Bull.* 98[3]: 337–352, 1986). RANGE: E. slope of Andes in e. Peru (Junín to n. Cuzco). At least 1000–2200 m.

NOTE: Here regarded as a species distinct from *H. atricapillus*, following T. J. Davis and J. P. O'Neill (op. cit.). These authors suggested the English name of Yellow-bellied Antwren for *H. motacilloides*. We find this unsatisfactory, for its ventral yellow is decidedly pale and faded (they describe it as only a "yellowish wash"), quite different from the brighter yellow ventral color of *H. axillaris*, well named the Yellow-breasted Antwren. We feel that our name of Creamy-bellied Antwren much more accurately conveys the ventral color and is less likely to cause confusion.

Herpsilochmus parkeri

ASH-THROATED ANTWREN

DESCRIPTION: 12 cm (4¾"). *One locality in San Martín, n. Peru.* Resembles Black-capped Antwren (no overlap). Both sexes differ in having a black loral spot (this area whitish in Black-capped). Male further differs in having somewhat darker gray underparts, especially on throat

(which is not whitish), female in having *buff* (not white) *superciliary,* darker buff throat, white (not buffyish) lower belly, and buffy grayish (not plain buff) flanks.

SIMILAR SPECIES: Male Creamy-bellied Antwren of cen. and s. Peru is not as gray below, and Ash-throated lacks any creamy tinge on belly. Females of the two look quite different: superciliary of Creamy-bellied is white (not buff), anterior underparts not nearly so buffy, etc. The two are not known to range close to each other, but this gap may well be due to inadequate field work at the requisite elevations.

HABITAT AND BEHAVIOR: Common in canopy and mid-levels of montane forest, and somewhat less numerous in stunted forest forming a transition between savanna-like vegetation found in lower part of Moyobamba valley and taller forest above. General behavior similar to that of other *Herpsilochmus,* usually noted foraging in pairs in association with mixed flocks of other antwrens, furnariids, and flycatchers. Male's song is an accelerating and slightly descending chippered trill with several well-spaced introductory notes, frequently echoed by female whose song is similar but softer, shorter, and perhaps slightly higher pitched. Given the species' extremely limited known distribution, the Ash-throated Antwren would appear to be potentially threatened by deforestation.

RANGE: Known only from the type locality on e. slope of Andes in n. Peru (San Martín, ca. 15 km northeast of Jirillo on the trail to Balsapuerto). 1350 m.

NOTE: A recently described species: T. J. Davis and J. P. O'Neill (*Wilson Bull.* 98[3]: 337–352, 1986). All data presented here are from this paper.

GROUP C

Both sexes *mainly yellowish below;* females with rufous crown.

Herpsilochmus rufimarginatus

RUFOUS-WINGED ANTWREN   PLATE: 18

DESCRIPTION: 11–11.5 cm (4¼–4½"). Male has black crown, long white superciliary, and black postocular line; back mixed gray and black; wings black with bold white wing-bars and *conspicuous rufous-chestnut edging on flight feathers* forming an almost solid patch; tail blackish, feathers broadly tipped white (visible mainly from below). *Below mainly pale creamy yellowish,* throat whitish. Female similar but with *crown rufous-chestnut,* postocular line and back brownish olive; see V-21, C-28. Foregoing applies to *frater* of most of range and *scapularis* of ne. Brazil. *Exiguus* of n. Colombia is similar but smaller, whereas nominate race (se. Brazil south to Paraguay and Argentina) is brighter yellow below, this yellow extending up over the throat.

SIMILAR SPECIES: The prominent rufous edging on the wing of both sexes is easy to see in the field and renders this species virtually unmistakable provided you get a decent view. Cf. especially Yellow-breasted Antwren (also yellow below but brighter in area of overlap) and Rufous-winged Tyrannulet.

HABITAT AND BEHAVIOR: Uncommon to locally fairly common in

canopy and borders of forest (both humid and deciduous, the latter mainly in Colombia and Venezuela). Usually in pairs, most often accompanying mixed flocks, gleaning in dense foliage and especially viny tangles. Heard much more often than seen; the song, a fast, accelerating series of nasal, almost gravelly notes, "chu, chu, chu-chu—ch-ch-chchchch-chúp," with an accented last note, is usually given first by the male, followed by the female's softer version. Singing birds rapidly shiver their tail. Perhaps most numerous around Iguazú Falls and in adjacent Paraguay.

RANGE: Locally in Venezuela (north of the Orinoco mainly on lower slopes of Andes and n. mts. east to Monagas; south of it in Bolívar and Amazonas) and Colombia (humid Caribbean lowlands, and very locally along e. base of Andes), and slopes of Sierra de Perijá on Venezuela-Colombia border; locally in nw. Ecuador (w. Esmeraldas at Cerro San Mateo, s. Pichincha at Río Palenque, and n. Los Ríos at Jauneche); along e. base of Andes in e. Ecuador, e. Peru, and n. Bolivia (south to w. Santa Cruz), in s. Peru and Bolivia occurring locally out into adjacent lowlands (in Bolivia north to Pando at Puerto Remanso) and east into sw. Amaz. Brazil (locally in Rondônia and Mato Grosso); near the Rio Urucu south of Tefé in w. Amaz. Brazil; e. Amaz. Brazil from the lower Rio Tapajós east into n. Maranhão; e. Brazil (e. Pernambuco south to Paraná), e. Paraguay (west to Canendiyu and Paraguarí), and ne. Argentina (Misiones). Also e. Panama. To 1000 m.

Herpsilochmus axillaris

YELLOW-BREASTED ANTWREN   PLATE: 18

DESCRIPTION: 12 cm (4¾"). *Local on lower Andean slopes from Colombia to Peru.* Male has crown black *spotted with white* and long white superciliary composed of dense white spots, sides of head blackish with white speckling; back uniform grayish olive; wings black with bold white wing-bars and grayish olive edging on flight feathers; tail blackish, feathers broadly tipped white (visible mainly from below). *Below uniform pale clear yellow,* clouded with olive on sides. Female like male but *crown uniform rufous;* upperparts more brownish, underparts more clouded with olive. *Senex* (W. Andes of Colombia) similar, but both sexes have throat whitish.

SIMILAR SPECIES: Both sexes of Rufous-winged Antwren show prominent rufous in wings; its male lacks white spotting on crown, whereas its female lacks speckled effect on face. Otherwise Yellow-breasted is not likely to be confused, though from below it looks somewhat warbler-like (e.g., *Basileuterus*). Cf. also *Xenerpestes* graytails.

HABITAT AND BEHAVIOR: Rare to locally fairly common in canopy and borders of humid and montane forest. Behavior similar to Rufous-winged Antwren's but tends to favor more humid regions. Yellow-breasted also is heard much more often than seen; its song is more musical than Rufous-winged's, an evenly descending chippered trill, "tree-ee-ee-ee-ee-ee-ew"; like the Rufous-winged, the female often sings immediately after the male, and both sexes shiver their tail.

RANGE: W. slope of W. Andes in w. Colombia (Caldas south to Cauca); e. slope of Andes in s. Colombia (sightings from w. Caquetá), e. Ecuador, and e. Peru (south to Puno). 900–1800 m.

Microrhopias Antwrens

A distinctive antwren of humid lowland forest and woodland, its rather long and often fanned and cocked tail showing much white.

Microrhopias quixensis

DOT-WINGED ANTWREN

PLATE: 18

DESCRIPTION: 11.5–12.5 cm (4½–5″). Variation complex, especially in females. Male *uniform glossy black* with large white dorsal patch, *white spotting on wing-coverts, a broad single white wing-bar*, and *white tipping to tail feathers*. Female of most races like male above but duller, sootier black to slaty (grayest above in *bicolor*, of w. Amaz. Brazil south of the Amazon and east to the Rio Tapajós); *below uniform rufous-chestnut*. *Consobrina* (west of Andes in Colombia and Ecuador) and *microsticta* (French Guiana and probably adjacent Brazil) similar but markedly smaller. Female of nominate race (se. Colombia to ne. Peru north of the Amazon and Río Marañón) has *black throat* (see C-28); female of *nigriventris* (e. Peru from San Martín and s. Loreto to Cuzco) has not only a black throat but a *black belly*, and darker chestnut breast; female of geographically distant *emiliae* (a large dark form from lower Amaz. Brazil south of the Amazon and east of the lower Rio Tapajós) has *throat and breast deep chestnut, belly black*. White tail-tipping varies in both sexes, being most extensive in *albicauda* of se. Peru in s. Cuzco, Puno, and Madre de Dios (in which outer 2 or 3 pairs of rectrices are mostly white) and narrowest in *emiliae*.

SIMILAR SPECIES: Despite geographic variation in the amount of white in tail and in female plumages, this attractive antwren is not likely to be confused. Cf. male White-flanked Antwren.

HABITAT AND BEHAVIOR: Uncommon to locally common in lower growth and borders of humid forest and mature second-growth woodland, in some areas favoring extensive stands of bamboo; seems relatively scarce in upper Amazonia, more numerous west of Andes and, at least locally, in lower Amazonia (e.g., in Amazonia Nat. Park on w. side of the lower Rio Tapajós). Usually in pairs or small groups, often foraging in mixed flocks including various *Myrmotherula* antwrens, but sometimes moving independently. Regularly cocks its often-fanned tail, as if to show off all the white. Its song (e.g., in w. Ecuador and se. Peru) is a series of 5–10 somewhat musical whistled notes, often dropping on the last note or 2 (e.g., "wee, tsee-tsi-tsi-tu-tu"), sometimes interspersed with rough "zhait" notes (which may be given alone).

RANGE: W. Colombia (Pacific lowlands, and in humid Caribbean lowlands east to middle Río Magdalena valley in Antioquia) and w. Ecuador (south to nw. Azuay); se. Colombia (w. Caquetá to e. Nariño, probably also in Amazonas), e. Ecuador, e. Peru, n. Bolivia (Beni), Amaz. Brazil (south of the Amazon east to the lower Rio Tocantins, and south to s. Mato Grosso on the Serra dos Parecís; north of it only in Amapá), and Guianas. Also Mexico to Panama. To 900 m.

NOTE: More than one species may be involved, as noted by Pinto (1978) and others. The lower Rio Tapajós region would seem particularly to warrant further investigation: its w. bank is inhabited by *bicolor* (fairly typical of the species), its e. bank by the very different *emiliae* (whose English name, if split, could be the Emilia's Antwren).

Myrmotherula Antwrens

One of the larger and more complex neotropical bird genera; we recognize 32 species of *Myrmotherula* antwrens, and some additional forms may in due course be raised to full species status. One species, the Black-hooded, has recently been transferred from *Myrmotherula,* in which it was long placed, to the genus *Formicivora*—but *after* our plate had been completed, hence its species account is retained here.

Myrmotherula antwrens are small, rather short-tailed antbirds, most found in humid forest in tropical lowlands, some at borders or in secondary growth (especially near water), but only a very few in foothills or the subtropical zone. Most are difficult to become familiar with, not only because of their size and the dense nature of their habitats, and because so many closely resemble each other and thus are hard to identify, but also because they tend to be shy, often permitting only brief views. Many *Myrmotherula* habitually accompany mixed flocks in forest understory—in fact they are often an important component of such flocks (especially in Amazonia, where four or five species may be in the same group). A few species, notably those in the "Pygmy"/"Streaked" assemblage, do not follow flocks so often. None habitually follows army antswarms.

The two basic divisions within the genus are reflected in our Groups. The first division is the "Pygmy"/"Streaked" Group, 8 species found in forest borders and canopy (sometimes lower in shrubbery but rarely or never inside forest or woodland). These are often very small with such short tails that they look tail-less under normal viewing conditions. Both sexes are prominently streaked above, and some are also streaked below. The second division, encompassing our Groups B through E, is even more complex and variable and contains 24 species. Many are very hard to identify. Points especially to watch for include:

    1. overall color (whether essentially brownish or gray/black);

    2. whether a black bib is present (in males);

    3. whether checkered on throat with black and white;

    4. pattern on wing-coverts (whether plain or with wing-bars, and if latter, whether with spotted or fringed effect); and

    5. whether there is rufous on back, rump, or tail.

The assistance of D. Stotz in helping RSR to better comprehend certain plumage and behavioral subtleties is acknowledged.

GROUP A   *"Pygmy"/"Streaked"* assemblage. Both sexes *prominently streaked above.*

Myrmotherula brachyura   **PYGMY ANTWREN**   PLATE: 19

DESCRIPTION: 7.5–8.5 cm (3–3¼"). *Very small* and *virtually tail-less.* Male *black streaked with white above,* with pale auriculars and semiconcealed white dorsal patch; wings black with 2 broad white wing-bars. *Throat white* bordered by *narrow* black malar stripe; *remaining underparts pale yellow* with a few black streaks on sides of chest. *Ignota* (west of Andes in Colombia) is smaller with a wider black malar stripe; see P-21. Female resembles male but has white streaking on crown, and face tinged buff; throat and breast also often tinged buff.

SIMILAR SPECIES: Cf. generally scarcer and more local Short-billed, Sclater's, and Yellow-throated Antwrens.

HABITAT AND BEHAVIOR: Fairly common but inconspicuous in canopy and middle levels of borders of humid forest and second-growth woodland, favoring viny tangles at edge and often at treefalls. Reportedly less numerous in w. Colombia (Hilty and Brown 1986). Usually in pairs, remaining in dense foliage and often difficult to observe; sometimes accompanies mixed flocks but at least as often forages independently. Most often located by its frequently given song. Song of nominate (east of Andes) is a fast, accelerating, slightly husky "chree, chree-chree-chee-chee-ee-ee-ee-ee"; that of *ignota* (west of Andes) is slower (less acceleration) and clearer, and the notes have a more musical quality (more resembling song of Short-billed Antwren).

RANGE: W. Colombia (Pacific lowlands south to w. Nariño, and east in humid Caribbean lowlands to lower Río Cauca region); Guianas, s. Venezuela (Bolívar and Amazonas), e. Colombia (north to Meta and Guainía), e. Ecuador, e. Peru, n. Bolivia (south to La Paz, Cochabamba, and n. Santa Cruz), and Amaz. Brazil (south to s. Mato Grosso and se. Pará, and east to the lower Rio Tocantins). Also Panama. Mostly below 500 m, in small numbers to 1000 m.

NOTE: Trans-Andean *ignota* probably does not belong with this species. Morphologically it almost falls "between" *M. brachyura* and *M. obscura;* vocally it more resembles the latter (RSR, M. and P. Isler). If considered subspecifically related to *M. obscura,* then the name of that species would have to become *M. ignota,* as the latter name has priority. The best course may be to recognize *M. ignota* as a monotypic species (Griscom's Antwren).

Myrmotherula obscura   **SHORT-BILLED ANTWREN**   PLATE: 19

DESCRIPTION: 7.5 cm (3"). W. Amazonia. Resembles Pygmy Antwren; the 2 species are regularly sympatric. Bill slightly shorter (but this not discernible in the field). Male differs in being *substantially blacker above* (white streaks much narrower) and in having a *wider and more conspicuous black malar stripe.* Female, also *blacker above* and with a *wider black malar stripe* than female Pygmy, further differs in having *throat and chest buff to orange-buff,* contrasting somewhat with pale yellow lower underparts.

SIMILAR SPECIES: Male Sclater's Antwren is streaked with yellow

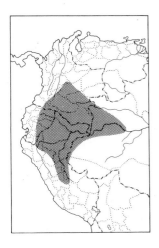

above and does not look nearly so black; female is much yellower below with no orange-buff and usually shows prominent black streaking at least across breast. Sclater's and Short-billed may range together locally in ne. Peru. Male Yellow-throated Antwren (no known overlap, but comes close in far e. Colombia) has yellow streaking above and all-yellow underparts with no white throat; females are very similar, but Yellow-throated shows less orange-buff on throat and chest.

HABITAT AND BEHAVIOR: Uncommon to fairly common but always inconspicuous in canopy and borders of humid forest and second-growth woodland. How this species differs in its habitat requirements from the more widespread Pygmy Antwren remains uncertain; in e. Ecuador they have repeatedly been found in precisely the same forest edge habitat, though in general Short-billed favors openings (treefalls and the like) in taller and more continuous forest and is most numerous in terra firme. Behavior much like Pygmy Antwren's, perhaps even less often with mixed flocks. Male's song similar to Pygmy Antwren's but more musical, slower, and with notes less run-together (little acceleration), e.g., "chew-chew-chew-che-che-che-che-che-che."

RANGE: Se. Colombia (north to Meta and e. Guainía; the latter an ANSP specimen from Colombian bank of Río Negro opposite San Carlos, establishing virtual sympatry with Yellow-throated Antwren; Short-billed possibly occurs in adjacent w. Venezuela), e. Ecuador, ne. Peru (south to upper Río Ucayali valley in Ucayali), and locally in w. Amaz. Brazil (east to Tefé on s. bank of the Amazon). To 600 m.

Myrmotherula sclateri

SCLATER'S ANTWREN

PLATE: 19

DESCRIPTION: 8.5 cm (3¼"). Male *above black streaked with pale yellowish,* with semiconcealed dorsal patch also pale yellowish; wings black with 2 white wing-bars. Below, *including throat,* entirely pale yellow. Female above like male, though in some individuals the pale streaks on head are more ochraceous. Below pale yellow with *variable amount of black streaking, usually quite prominent* especially across breast, but in some birds reduced to sides.

SIMILAR SPECIES: Pygmy and Short-billed Antwrens are both white-throated. Male Pygmy is streaked with white (not yellowish) above, female shows much less streaking below. Male Short-billed is much blacker above, female has buff on throat and chest. Cf. also Yellow-throated Antwren.

HABITAT AND BEHAVIOR: Uncommon to fairly common but always inconspicuous in canopy and borders of humid forest, both in terra firme and várzea, favoring viny tangles and dense foliage. Tends to occur higher above the ground than Pygmy Antwren; Pygmy is mainly an edge bird, whereas Sclater's occurs regularly in the canopy of continuous forest. Sclater's often forages with mixed flocks. The song of Sclater's is very different from Pygmy's, being a slow (about 1 note per second) series of 4–6 rather soft, melancholy "peeu" notes; it recalls the louder song of Fasciated Antshrike. Regularly found at the Tambopata Reserve in Madre de Dios, se. Peru.

RANGE: E. Peru (Loreto, south of the Amazon along Río Manití, south to Madre de Dios), n. Bolivia (locally in Pando, La Paz, and ne. Santa Cruz), and Amaz. Brazil south of the Amazon (south to s. Mato Grosso at Rio do Cágado, and east to Alta Floresta in n. Mato Grosso and to the lower Rio Tapajós). To 700 m.

NOTE: Evidently (see Parker and Remsen 1987) what was called *M. kermiti* is the less heavily marked extreme of the variation shown by females (see above); D. Stotz (pers. comm.) suspects that *kermiti* may prove to be a recognizable subspecies. For additional natural history information, see Parker (1982).

Myrmotherula ambigua

YELLOW-THROATED ANTWREN

DESCRIPTION: 8.5 cm (3¼"). *Limited area in sw. Venezuela, nw. Brazil, and adjacent Colombia.* Male much like male Pygmy Antwren but *underparts all pale yellow* (no white throat); semiconcealed dorsal patch pale yellow. Female probably indistinguishable from female Pygmy, but throat slightly yellower (not whitish) and crown streaking more rufescent.

SIMILAR SPECIES: The similar Sclater's Antwren does not overlap with Yellow-throated, occurring only *south* of the Amazon. Short-billed Antwren male (like Pygmy) has white throat, female is much buffier on throat and chest.

HABITAT AND BEHAVIOR: Fairly common in canopy and borders of humid terra firme forest. Behavior very much like Sclater's Antwren's; voice also similar, but series of notes longer, usually 10–15. All information from D. Stotz (pers. comm.).

RANGE: Sw. Venezuela (s. Amazonas), n. Brazil (upper Rio Negro drainage east into Roraima [2 males taken by D. Stotz near Rio Mucujaí, about 60 km west of the Rio Branco; MZUSP]), and extreme e. Colombia (e. Guainía). Below 200 m.

Myrmotherula surinamensis

STREAKED ANTWREN   PLATE: 19

DESCRIPTION: 9.5 cm (3¾"). By far the most *widespread* of the "Streaked" antwren subgroup; *pacifica* (west of Andes in Colombia and Ecuador) has a long bill. Male of all forms *black above streaked with white* with *semiconcealed white dorsal patch;* wings black with 2 broad white wing-bars; *white below streaked with black.* Female of *multostriata* (much of range east of Andes, but see below) has *crown and nape orange-rufous streaked with black;* otherwise above like male. *Below mostly ochraceous with extensive fine black streaking,* especially across breast, whiter on belly. Female *pacifica* and nominate (Guianas, n. Amaz. Brazil north of the Amazon and east of the Rio Negro, and s. Venezuela except in sw. Amazonas) *basically lack black streaking on head and underparts* (although retaining it on hindcrown); thus their head and sides of neck are uniform bright orange-rufous, underparts plain ochraceous. See P-21, V-21.

SIMILAR SPECIES: Along e. base of Andes cf. somewhat larger Stripe-chested Antwren, males of which have streaking below confined to breast, females of which are unstreaked below. Cf. also Cherrie's and Klages' Antwrens.

HABITAT AND BEHAVIOR: Uncommon to locally common in shrubby humid forest and woodland borders, gallery forest, and overgrown clearings; more widespread and often more numerous west of Andes (even occurring in gardens), east of them nearly confined to shrubbery near water and várzea forest borders. Usually in pairs, generally not foraging high above the ground, often in the semiopen; usually does not accompany mixed flocks. Vocalizations vary geographically. West of Andes, song of *pacifica* males is a fast, spritely, somewhat rising chipper, "chee-chee-chi-chi-ch-ch-ch-ch-ch-ch"; female may follow with a shorter but similar version. East of Andes, *multostriata* males give an evenly pitched, dry, rattled trill, "dr-r-r-r-r-r-r-r" (so different from *pacifica*'s song as to be virtually unrecognizable), often "answered" by female's more musical "pur-pur-peé-peé-peé-pur" with variable, almost lilting phraseology (K. Zimmer recording; RSR). Throughout, both sexes often voice various soft contact notes, among which a "chee-pu" or "chee-cher" figures prominently.

RANGE: W. and n. Colombia (Pacific lowlands, and east in humid Caribbean lowlands to middle Río Magdalena valley in Santander) and w. Ecuador (south to nw. Azuay); Guianas, s. and extreme e. Venezuela (Delta Amacuro, Bolívar, and Amazonas), e. Colombia (north locally to Meta), e. Ecuador, e. Peru (south to Madre de Dios), n. Bolivia (Pando and ne. Santa Cruz on the Serranía de Huanchaca), and Amaz. Brazil (south to s. Mato Grosso and n. Goiás, and east to n. Maranhão). Also Panama. To 1300 m (in nw. Ecuador).

NOTE: More than one species is almost certainly involved, as indicated primarily by the very striking difference in songs west and east of the Andes. If split, trans-Andean *M. pacifica* should be called the Pacific Streaked-Antwren, while *M. surinamensis* (with *multostriata*) from east of the Andes should be called the Amazonian Streaked-Antwren.

Myrmotherula cherriei

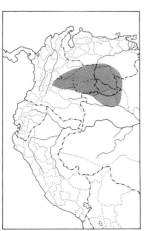

CHERRIE'S ANTWREN

DESCRIPTION: 10 cm (4"). *Ne. Colombia to sw. Venezuela and n. Brazil.* Closely resembles slightly smaller, locally sympatric Streaked Antwren. Male differs in being *more coarsely streaked with black below* and in lacking the white dorsal patch. Female differs in having underparts *more uniformly ochraceous* (not whitish on belly) *with coarse black streaking* (coarser than in female *multostriata* Streaked). See C-28.

SIMILAR SPECIES: Female of sympatric (nominate) race of Streaked Antwren is unstreaked below. Cf. very similar Klages' Antwren.

HABITAT AND BEHAVIOR: Locally fairly common in shrubby borders of gallery forest, canopy and borders of várzea forest, and savanna woodland and scrub; in many areas occurs mostly in vegetation growing on sandy soils. Behavior similar to that of cis-Andean forms of Streaked Antwren, but may not associate with mixed flocks as much, seems more often to forage closer to the ground, and is not as tied to presence of water. Its song is a distinctive, almost mechanical-sounding and rattled "trrrrrrrrrrrrrrrrrr" lasting about 3 seconds; various more musical "cheeyp" and "chee-du" call notes are also given. Easily seen at Junglaven Lodge in Amazonas, Venezuela.

RANGE: Ne. Colombia (w. Meta east to Vichada and Guainía), sw. Venezuela (Amazonas), and nw. Brazil (upper Rio Negro region). To 500 m.

Myrmotherula klagesi

KLAGES' ANTWREN

DESCRIPTION: 10 cm (4"). *Limited area along lower Amazon.* Male closely resembles slightly smaller Streaked Antwren, and probably not distinguishable in the field; it lacks Streaked's semiconcealed dorsal patch. Female Klages' differs from *multostriata* race of Streaked in having *crown essentially black with narrow buffyish streaking* (not orange-rufous with bold black streaking); it seems to show *no* black streaking on throat (but this is only faintly indicated in Streaked).

SIMILAR SPECIES: So closely resembles Cherrie's Antwren (no known overlap) that they could be distinguished in the field only with difficulty. Streaking on underparts of male Cherrie's is somewhat coarser and more extensive. This is even more the case in females: in female Klages' the streaking below is comparatively fine (with more of a spotted effect) and is more restricted to the breast.

HABITAT AND BEHAVIOR: Fairly common but very local in canopy and borders of várzea forest, especially on islands. Long known only from a few specimens taken near Santarém. In Apr. 1990 Klages' Antwren was rediscovered on the Anavilhanas Archipelago in the Rio Negro above Manaus (RSR and GT et al.; Mario Cohn-Haft, who also has collected several examples). Their behavior resembles that of Cherrie's Antwren, though, at least there, Klages' tends to remain higher above the ground. The male's song is a repeated soft musical "cheedi-cheedi-cheedi . . . ," similar to Stripe-chested Antwren's song but usually with fewer notes, generally only 5−7.

RANGE: Along both banks of the lower Amazon in Brazil near the mouth of the Rio Tapajós, and on Anavilhanas Archipelago in the Rio Negro north of Manaus. Below 100 m.

Myrmotherula longicauda

STRIPE-CHESTED ANTWREN   PLATE: 19

DESCRIPTION: 10.5 cm (4"). *Along e. base of Andes.* Male *black above streaked with white;* wings black with 2 broad white wing-bars. Below white, *with black streaking confined to broad band across breast.* Female *black above streaked with buff;* wings black with 2 broad, buffy whitish wing-bars. *Below uniform ochraceous buff* with, *no* streaking. More n. birds (*soderstromi* and *pseudoaustralis;* south to Huánuco, Peru) have whiter belly.

SIMILAR SPECIES: Both sexes lack Streaked Antwren's white dorsal patch and have slightly shorter tails. Male Streaked has black streaking below from throat to belly; female of potentially sympatric race of Streaked, *multostriata*, has prominent blackish streaking on breast and is not so uniformly ochraceous below (being whiter on belly and throat).

HABITAT AND BEHAVIOR: Uncommon to locally fairly common in secondary woodland, shrubby clearings, and forest borders in foothill zone, mainly above range of Streaked Antwren. Unlike Streaked, the Stripe-chested Antwren is *not* associated with water. Behavior similar to Streaked's; also usually in pairs which forage independently of mixed flocks. Male's song is distinctively different, a quite rapidly repeated musical "chidu-chidu-chidu-chidu . . ." with up to 11 or 12 notes. Seems especially numerous at Hacienda Amazonia and along lower part of road above Atalaya in Cuzco, Peru.

RANGE: E. base of Andes in s. Colombia (north at least to w. Putumayo), Ecuador, Peru, and w. Bolivia (La Paz and Cochabamba). Mostly 400–1300 m.

GROUP B

Large spots on tertials (both sexes), throat concolor. On or near ground, usually not in mixed flocks.

Myrmotherula hauxwelli

PLAIN-THROATED ANTWREN   PLATE: 19

DESCRIPTION: 10 cm (4"). *Short tail.* Male *uniform gray, only slightly paler below,* with semiconcealed white dorsal patch; wings blackish with 2 wing-bars and *tipping on tertials white;* uppertail-coverts and rectrices narrowly tipped white. Female olive brown above with dorsal patch like male's; wing pattern as in male but *with buff replacing white;* uppertail-coverts and rectrices narrowly tipped buff. *Below mostly bright cinnamon-rufous,* more olivaceous on lower belly. See C-28.

SIMILAR SPECIES: Most other *Myrmotherula* antwrens do not habitually remain so close to the ground; Plain-throated does not overlap with similar-behaving Rufous-bellied Antwren. Cf. the *Hypocnemoides* antbirds (males both with black throats and white-tipped tails, females whitish below) and especially male Scale-backed Antbird (note similarity in behavior and even song, but Scale-backed is larger and scaled on back).

HABITAT AND BEHAVIOR: Uncommon to locally fairly common near the ground (almost always within 1 m of it) inside humid forest, both in terra firme and várzea, frequently near streams or swampy places. Usually in pairs (less often singly or in small, presumably family, groups), generally foraging independently of mixed flocks but sometimes with *Thamnomanes* antshrike–led groups. Behavior reminiscent of a miniature *Hylophylax* antbird, even often clinging to small vertical stems. Male's song is a series of high-pitched, loud, and very penetrating "chweeé" notes, usually starting softly, then increasing in volume.

RANGE: Se. Colombia (north to Meta and Vaupés), e. Ecuador, e. Peru, n. Bolivia (Beni, Pando, and n. Santa Cruz), and Amaz. Brazil (only south of the Amazon; east to n. Maranhão and south to s. Mato Grosso). To 600 m.

Myrmotherula guttata

RUFOUS-BELLIED ANTWREN   PLATE: 19

DESCRIPTION: 9.5 cm (3¾"). *Ne. South America. Short tail.* Male has head and upperparts mostly gray, becoming more olive brown on lower back, with a semiconcealed white dorsal patch; wings blackish

with 2 bold wing-bars and tipping on tertials buff; uppertail-coverts and rectrices also tipped buff. Underparts gray (slightly paler than above) with *contrasting cinnamon-rufous lower belly*. See V-21. Female olive brown above with dorsal patch like male's; wings and tail as in male, but wing-spotting and tipping slightly deeper buff. Throat and breast dingy olivaceous brown, *becoming cinnamon-rufous on belly*.

SIMILAR SPECIES: Both sexes of this handsome antwren are readily known by the contrasting and conspicuous rufous on lower underparts, as well as by their bold buff markings on wings.

HABITAT AND BEHAVIOR: Uncommon near ground inside humid forest, mainly in terra firme, but near streams and swampy spots. Behavior much like Plain-throated Antwren's. Song of male, also much the same, is a repetition of a single penetrating whistled note, usually gradually increasing in intensity, "tueee, tueee, tueee, tueee . . ." (up to 10–15 notes).

RANGE: Guianas, s. Venezuela (Bolívar and Amazonas), and ne. Amaz. Brazil (north of the Amazon, and west to the Rio Negro). To 900 m.

GROUP C

"Stipple-throated" assemblage. Males generally *browner-backed*, though *may or may not have a chestnut saddle*; both sexes show wing-spotting.

Myrmotherula gularis

STAR-THROATED ANTWREN   PLATE: 19

DESCRIPTION: 9.5 cm (3¾"). *Se. Brazil. Above rufescent brown;* forehead grizzled with gray; wing-coverts blackish, tipped buff forming 2 wing-bars. *Throat black spotted with white;* remaining underparts gray, rufescent on lower flanks and crissum. Female similar to male but *white spots on throat larger*.

SIMILAR SPECIES: Star-throated Antwren, unlike other members of Group C, tends to forage *close to ground in humid forest* much like the 2 species comprising Group B, neither of which is found in se. Brazil. Star-throated resembles the other members of the "Stipple-throated" group in overall plumage pattern, but none of these is found in se. Brazil, where all other *Myrmotherula* antwrens are more arboreal. Cf. the various *Drymophila* antbirds (all of which are larger and longer-tailed) and the small *Myrmeciza* antbirds in Star-throated's range.

HABITAT AND BEHAVIOR: Locally fairly common near the ground and in lower growth inside humid forest, often in ravines or near streams. Usually found singly or in pairs, foraging independently of mixed flocks. Male's song is a series of up to 12 or so well-enunciated, penetrating, sibilant notes, much like the songs of Plain-throated and Rufous-bellied Antwrens, to which Star-throated seems to be related, despite its different plumage. Also often gives a harsh, chattered alarm call.

RANGE: Se. Brazil (Espírito Santo south to w. Paraná and ne. Rio Grande do Sul). 300–1200 m.

Myrmotherula haematonota

STIPPLE-THROATED ANTWREN

DESCRIPTION: 11 cm (4¼″). Amazonia; does not include Foothill Antwren of Andean foothills. Iris varies from white to hazel or pale orange. Male brown above with *rufous-chestnut back;* wings blackish, coverts tipped with white forming 2 spotted wing-bars, tail brown. *Throat black spotted with white;* face and remaining underparts gray, browner on lower flanks and crissum. Female above much like male, including the *rufous-chestnut back* (only faintly indicated in some individuals), but coverts spotted with buff. Sides of head and underparts uniform ochraceous to pale brownish, *usually with some flammulation on throat;* some individuals have a whiter throat strongly checkered with black.

SIMILAR SPECIES: Male's combination of checkered throat and rufous-chestnut back is usually distinctive, but note that the throat pattern sometimes is not conspicuous in the field. Throats of both Brown-bellied and White-eyed Antwrens are also checkered, but these have concolor brownish backs (not contrastingly rufous). *Phaeonota* race of White-eyed (which has a rufous lower back) is very similar to Stipple-throated but has buff-edged (not white-spotted) wing-coverts and a more rufescent tail. Male Ornate Antwren always has a solid black throat and looks grayer above than Stipple-throated (except Ornates from Colombia to n. Peru have chestnut saddles). Female Ornates in the Colombia to n. Peru portion of their range have throat black spotted with white (when female Stipple-throateds show a checkered throat, it is obviously white spotted with black) and wing-coverts spotted with white (not buff). Female Stipple-throated most resembles female of rufous-backed *phaeonota* White-eyed Antwren (limited area in Amaz. Brazil west of lower Rio Tapajós); *phaeonota* differs only in its brighter buff underparts which lack the "messy" streaky appearance of virtually all female Stipple-throateds. There is no known overlap (*phaeonota* occurring just to east of Stipple-throated's range).

HABITAT AND BEHAVIOR: Uncommon in lower growth of humid forest, primarily in terra firme. Usually in pairs or small groups, almost always foraging with mixed understory flocks including other *Myrmotherula* antwrens, *Thamnomanes* antshrikes, various woodcreepers and foliage-gleaners; often probes into suspended dead curled leaves. The song is a very high, thin "zee-ee-ee-ee-ee-ee" which drops somewhat and recalls a piculet (*Picumnus*). Its alarm call is a fast, thin rattle (D. Stotz).

RANGE: S. Venezuela (Bolívar and Amazonas), se. Colombia (north to Meta and Vaupés), e. Ecuador (very local; WFVZ, ANSP), e. Peru (recorded rather widely in Loreto, and from Cuzco Amazonico in Madre de Dios), extreme nw. Bolivia (Pando at Camino Mucden), and w. and cen. Amaz. Brazil (north of the Amazon east to the Rio Negro and Rio Branco, south of it east to the lower Rio Madeira, and south to Acre and Rondônia). A recent sighting from French Guiana (Tostain et al. 1992) requires further corroboration. Mostly below 500 m (recorded to 1300 m in Venezuela).

NOTE: See comments under Foothill Antwren.

Myrmotherula spodionota

FOOTHILL ANTWREN

Other: Ecuadorian Antwren, Stipple-throated Antwren (in part)

DESCRIPTION: 11 cm (4¼"). *Foothill zone along e. base of Andes in Ecuador and Peru,* well above range of Stipple-throated Antwren, with which formerly considered conspecific. Iris white to pale grayish or hazel. Both sexes resemble Stipple-throated but *have no rufous-chestnut on back.* Male's head and upperparts essentially gray (slightly browner on crown); female's head and underparts olive brown with *no* flammulation or any "checkers" on throat.

SIMILAR SPECIES: Male is only *Myrmotherula* antwren in its *foothill* range with a checkered throat. White-eyed Antwren is quite similar, but male is browner above with buff edging (not white spots) on wing-coverts, whereas female has ochraceous edging (not buff spots) on wing-coverts and is not so dark overall. Females of some races of Ornate Antwren (e.g., *atrogularis* of Peru) also have olive brown backs without a chestnut saddle, but these always have throat boldly checkered (lacking in female Foothill).

HABITAT AND BEHAVIOR: Uncommon in lower growth of montane forest. Behavior much like Stipple-throated and Ornate Antwrens', and it likewise most often occurs with mixed flocks in understory; Slaty Antwrens are often in the same flock.

RANGE: E. slope of Andes in s. Colombia (sightings by E. O. Willis in w. Caquetá), Ecuador, and Peru (south to Cuzco in Río Cosñipata valley; FMNH). Mainly 700–1300 m.

NOTE: *M. spodionota* is here considered a species separate from *M. haematonota* (Stipple-throated Antwren), following Hilty and Brown (1986) and Parker and Remsen (1987), with the race *sororia* included. We employ the English name suggested by the latter. Ecuadorian Antwren, the name used by Hilty and Brown (1986), seems an inappropriate choice given that the species ranges also in Peru, and actually was the name given by Hellmayr (*Birds of the Americas,* vol. 13, part 3) for nominate *spodionota* only.

Myrmotherula leucophthalma

WHITE-EYED ANTWREN

PLATE: 19

DESCRIPTION: 11.5 cm (4½"). Primarily *south of the Amazon from se. Peru east to Pará, Brazil.* Despite its name, this species' iris is *not* always pale, sometimes (in both sexes, perhaps younger birds?) being brown, even reddish brown; note that iris color, even when pale, is *not* a useful character as irides of both Stipple-throated and Foothill Antwrens are *also* sometimes whitish. Male olive brown above with 2 buff wing-bars. *Throat checkered black and white; sides of head and breast gray,* becoming brownish on belly and crissum. Female similar above; sides of head and underparts (*including throat*) ochraceous buff. Both sexes of *phaeonota* (limited area south of the Amazon in Brazil between the lower Rio Madeira and lower Rio Tapajós) have *lower back rufous.*

SIMILAR SPECIES: Stipple-throated Antwren male also has a checkered throat, but it is rufous-backed (back of sympatric race of White-eyed is uniform olive brown). In the small range of *phaeonota* White-eyed, that race is best distinguished from the *very* similar Stipple-throated by its more flammulated throat (not crisply checkered white on black), slightly less extensive rufous on back, somewhat paler gray breast, more rufescent tail, and (especially) more edged (not so spotted) effect on wing-coverts. Male White-eyed resembles male Foothill Antwren, but latter is gray (not olive brown) above and is found mainly in foothill zone above range of this species. The rather dull female White-eyed lacks a checkered throat and, except for *phaeonota*, any rufous on back and can be quite tricky to identify. Female Foothill and Stipple-throated both have streaky throats (clear ochraceous in White-eyed), are less warm buff below, and have less rufescent tails. Female White-eyed especially resembles female *hoffmannsi* race of Ornate, differing in its more edged (not so spotted) effect on wing-coverts and shorter grayish (less rufescent) tail.

HABITAT AND BEHAVIOR: Uncommon in undergrowth of humid forest, both in terra firme and transitional forest, often in areas with stands of bamboo. Usually in pairs, less often small groups, which regularly accompany mixed flocks including other *Myrmotherula* antwrens and *Thamnomanes* antshrikes; most often forages quite close to the ground, especially investigating curled-up dead leaves in viny or bamboo tangles. Territorial males sometimes posture a few feet apart, puffing out their throats and loudly calling a repeated "tsip-tsip-tsip. . . ." The song is a descending "seee, seee, seeu, seeu" much like Checker-throated Antwren's, whereas its alarm call is a fast rattle much like Stipple-throated's (D. Stotz). Can be found at the Tambopata Reserve and Manu Lodge, both in Madre de Dios, Peru.

RANGE: Se. Peru (Ucayali, Madre de Dios, and Puno), n. Bolivia (south locally to La Paz and n. Santa Cruz), and Amaz. Brazil (south of the Amazon east to e. Pará and Marajó Is., and south to n. Mato Grosso); a male in the MECN was taken in e. Ecuador at "Río Bufeo" (which cannot be located). Mostly below 800 m (rarely up to 1000 m).

NOTE: J. T. Zimmer (*Am. Mus. Novitates* 523, 1932) points out that *M. phaeonota* may prove to be a separate species from *M. leucophthalma*, for both *phaeonota* and another race of *leucophthalma* (*sordida*) have been recorded from Igarapé Brabo on the w. bank of the Rio Tapajós. However, as he points out, the amount of rufescence on the back of *phaeonota* is somewhat variable, and specimen mislabeling remains a possibility, so additional proof of sympatry would seem desirable. If split, *M. phaeonota* could be called the Rufous-backed Antwren.

Myrmotherula gutturalis

BROWN-BELLIED ANTWREN

DESCRIPTION: 11 cm (4¼"). *Ne. South America.* Iris whitish or pale grayish (male) to pale mauve (female). Male closely resembles male White-eyed Antwren (no overlap) but has lesser wing-coverts olive brown like back (not dusky) and *tips of wing-coverts minutely spotted with whitish* (not with broad buff wing-bars). See V-21. Female resembles male, but like White-eyed, lacks checkered throat and has buff tips on wing-coverts.

SIMILAR SPECIES: Male is only *Myrmotherula* in its range with *checkered throat*. Female is dull and rather featureless, best known by her brown overall appearance with buff-tipped wing-coverts. Female

Stipple-throated Antwren (no recorded overlap, though the two come close in s. Venezuela, with Stipple-throated found west of Brown-bellied's range) has rufous on back.

HABITAT AND BEHAVIOR: Uncommon in lower growth of humid forest. Behaves much like other antwrens in the "Stipple-throated" Group, also frequently probing into suspended dead leaves. Male's song is a high, thin, chippered trill which slowly descends, "see-ee-ee-ee-ee-ee-ee-ee-eu."

RANGE: Guianas, se. Venezuela (e. Bolívar), and ne. Amaz. Brazil (north of the Amazon from Amapá west to the Rio Branco and lower Rio Negro). Mostly below 400 m (recorded to 1000 m in Venezuela).

Myrmotherula fulviventris

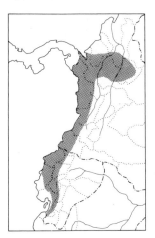

CHECKER-THROATED ANTWREN

DESCRIPTION: 10 cm (4"). *W. Colombia and w. Ecuador. Iris pale,* buffy or hazel (usually) to grayish. Resembles somewhat larger White-eyed Antwren (no overlap). Male is much less gray (more brownish) on face and especially breast. Females are much alike aside from the size difference. See C-28, P-21.

SIMILAR SPECIES: Easily identified male is the only *Myrmotherula* in its range with a checkered throat. Female resembles female White-flanked Antwren (and they often are in the same flock), but White-flanked has a dark (not usually pale) iris and whiter throat and flank plumes (not so uniform ochraceous below). Cf. also female Slaty Antwren.

HABITAT AND BEHAVIOR: Fairly common to common in lower growth of humid forest and more mature secondary woodland. Behavior much like White-eyed Antwren's, like that species seeming to specialize in investigating curled-up hanging dead leaves (often crawling completely inside!). Checker-throated males also sometimes display at each other in much the same way as White-eyeds. The song is a sharp, squeaky, high-pitched, somewhat descending "tseek-seek-seek-seek."

RANGE: W. Colombia (Pacific lowlands, and east in humid Caribbean lowlands to middle Río Magdalena valley in e. Antioquia) and w. Ecuador (south to El Oro). Also Honduras to Panama. Mostly below 1100 m (recorded to 2000 m in Colombia).

Myrmotherula erythrura

RUFOUS-TAILED ANTWREN   PLATE: 19

DESCRIPTION: 11.5 cm (4½"). *W. Amazonia.* Male olive brown above with *rufous back* and *rufous tail;* wings olive brown, coverts tipped with buffy whitish forming 2 spotted wing-bars. *Throat and breast gray* (sometimes with some faint black speckling on throat), becoming olive brown on belly. Female above like male; *throat and chest rather bright ochraceous buff,* becoming duller on lower underparts.

SIMILAR SPECIES: All other similar male *Myrmotherula* have throats either checkered or solid black (not essentially uniform gray); Rufous-tailed's black throat speckling, if present, is so slight as not usually to be noticeable. Female's brightly colored throat is distinctive (in other

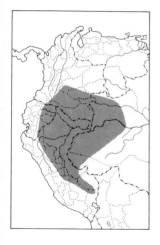

similar species either dull or checkered). The rufous tail is usually not particularly obvious in the field. White-eyed Antwren in area of overlap with Rufous-tailed has no rufous on back.

HABITAT AND BEHAVIOR: Uncommon to locally fairly common in lower growth of humid forest, mainly in terra firme but also in várzea. General behavior similar to other antwrens' in the "Stipple-throated" Group, often with understory flocks and like them regularly inspecting curled-up dead leaves, but tending to forage somewhat higher above ground. The song is a high, almost squeaky "seep-seep-seep" (T. A. Parker III, *in* Hilty and Brown 1986).

RANGE: Se. Colombia (north to Meta and Vaupés), e. Ecuador, e. Peru (south locally to Puno), and w. Amaz. Brazil (north of the Amazon in the upper Rio Negro area, south of it east to around Tefé). To about 900 m.

Myrmotherula ornata

ORNATE ANTWREN   PLATE: 19

DESCRIPTION: 11 cm (4¼″). *Variable; more than 1 species is perhaps involved.* In se. Colombia and e. Ecuador (nominate and *saturata*), male gray above with *chestnut lower back and rump*; wings blackish with white *spotting* on wing-coverts forming 2 wing-bars. *Throat black,* sharply set off from *gray remaining underparts.* See C-28. Female like male above but with gray replaced by olive brown. *Throat black boldly spotted with white,* sharply set off from dull brownish remaining underparts. Both sexes of *atrogularis* and *meridionalis* (Peru and Bolivia) differ in *lacking* chestnut saddle; females are also richer ochraceous below but still have boldly checkered throat. *Hoffmannsi* (Brazil) reverts to having *chestnut saddle* (though somewhat smaller, especially in females); these females differ strikingly in *lacking* the checkered throat (underparts entirely rich ochraceous).

SIMILAR SPECIES: The variation is confusing. Ignoring the chestnut saddle, male Ornates more resemble male "typical" slaty/gray antwrens with black throats than they do the "Stipple-throated" Group; they lack white tail-tipping, their throat patch is less extensive and does not end in a point on chest, and their wing-coverts are more spotted with white (not edged or barred). Except for *hoffmannsi,* most helpful for female Ornates is their conspicuous and contrasting checkered throat. *Hoffmannsi* resembles female Rufous-tailed Antwren, though that has a longer, more rufous tail. Most female White-eyed Antwrens have no rufous on back; the race *phaeonota* (which does) differs from Ornate in its edged (not spotted) wing-coverts.

HABITAT AND BEHAVIOR: Locally fairly common in lower growth of humid forest, mainly in terra firme but also in transitional forest and várzea. In areas with bamboo, Ornate Antwren is usually restricted to it, whereas in areas without it Ornate favors dense tangles and openings (D. Stotz). Usually in pairs, most often foraging while accompanying mixed understory flocks; like so many other *Myrmotherula* in the "Stipple-throated" Group, Ornate frequently probes into hanging dead leaves; it tends to range higher above ground than the others.

Song of *meridionalis* and *hoffmannsi* is a short, high, thin "whee-zee-zee-zee-zee." Quite numerous at the Tambopata Reserve in Madre de Dios, se. Peru.

RANGE: Along e. base of Andes and in adjacent lowlands in se. Colombia (north to w. Meta) and e. Ecuador; lowlands of e. Peru, n. Bolivia (south to La Paz and Cochabamba), and s. Amaz. Brazil (south of the Amazon from the upper Rio Madeira drainage east to the lower Rio Tocantins, and south to s. Mato Grosso). To 1250 m.

NOTE: More than one species may be involved. *Atrogularis* (with *meridionalis*) was long considered a full species until being placed in *M. ornata* by J. T. Zimmer (*Am. Mus. Novitates* 524, 1932); no intergradation between these rather different forms has been shown, but there are specimens in FMNH of *meridionalis* from Cuzco and Madre de Dios with at least some rufous on their backs (D. Stotz). If split, *M. atrogularis* could be called the Inornate Antwren. *Hoffmannsi* is also quite distinct and could also prove to be a separate species (Hoffmanns' Antwren).

GROUP D

Silky white flank feathers (but grayer in e. Brazil race of White-flanked). Recent evidence shows that Black-hooded Antwren belongs in genus *Formicivora*.

Myrmotherula axillaris

WHITE-FLANKED ANTWREN   PLATE: 19

DESCRIPTION: 10–10.5 cm (4–4¼"). *Widespread and usually numerous in lowland forest.* Male blackish to gray above, wing-coverts tipped white forming 2 spotted wing-bars, rectrices tipped white. Throat and breast black, often in contrast to gray of remaining underparts (sometimes all blackish in *albigula* and *melaena,* of w. Colombia and w. Ecuador, and n. Colombia and w. Venezuela south to ne. Peru, respectively), with axillars and *long silky plumes on flanks* white (often quite conspicuous but sometimes hidden behind wing). Male *luctuosa* (e. Brazil) differs strikingly in having its shorter *flank plumes silvery gray;* it is a gray-backed form. Female olive to grayish brown above, wings and tail somewhat browner with 2 rather faint buff-dotted wing-bars. Mostly ochraceous below, with whiter throat and *long white flank plumes* (also sometimes concealed) as in male.

SIMILAR SPECIES: Learn this numerous species well as a basis of comparison with other *Myrmotherula.* No other member of the genus shows white on flanks (sometimes hidden, though rarely for long as it is often exposed while wings are flicked). Female Long-winged Antwren is more uniform below, lacking whitish throat and white flank plumes. Band-tailed Antwren of e. Brazil is sympatric with much more numerous *luctuosa* race of White-flanked, but both sexes differ in having broader white tail-tipping, and males have more contrasting black bib (Band-tailed male is rather pale gray overall, so its bib stands out more). In e. Bahia, Brazil, cf. scarce and very local Narrow-billed Antwren (in genus *Formicivora*).

HABITAT AND BEHAVIOR: Fairly common to common in lower and middle growth of humid forest and more mature secondary woodland. Forages through lower and middle levels inside forest, sometimes at borders, actively gleaning in foliage and inspecting viny tangles, often flicking its wings. A pair or family group will regularly accompany understory mixed flocks including other antwrens and various antshrikes and foliage-gleaners. Songs vary: west of Andes it is a series of up to 10 or 12 rather high whistled notes which distinctively drop in pitch (similar but faster and more run-together in se. Peru); in e. Brazil *luctuosa*'s song is also a series of notes, but each is substantially burrier and, though slowing somewhat, without the descending effect, "drew-drew-dree-dree-dree-dree-dree." Call notes include a querulous "chee-poo" or "cheep, chee-poo."

RANGE: Nw. Venezuela (Maracaibo basin), n. and w. Colombia (humid Caribbean lowlands and Pacific lowlands), and w. Ecuador (south to nw. Azuay); s. Venezuela (Delta Amacuro, widely south of the Orinoco in Bolívar and Amazonas, and along base of Andes north to Mérida and w. Barinas), e. Colombia (except in llanos of northeast), e. Ecuador, e. Peru, n. Bolivia (south to La Paz, Cochabamba, and w. Santa Cruz), and Amaz. Brazil (south to s. Mato Grosso, and east to n. Maranhão); e. Brazil (Pernambuco south to Rio de Janeiro); Trinidad. Also Honduras to Panama. To about 900 m.

NOTE: More than one species may be involved. The divergent (and vocally somewhat different) form of e. Brazil perhaps deserves recognition as a full species (*M. luctuosa*, Gray-flanked Antwren). In addition, E. O. Willis (*Rev. Brasil. Zool., São Paulo* 2[3]: 153–158, 1984) suggests that *melaena* and the nominate group may not be conspecific.

Formicivora erythronotos

BLACK-HOODED ANTWREN · PLATE: 19

DESCRIPTION: 11.5 cm (4½"). Rediscovered in 1987 in *Rio de Janeiro, Brazil;* long considered a *Myrmotherula* antwren but now returned to the genus *Formicivora*, in which it was described. Male has *head, neck, and breast slaty black* contrasting with *rufous-chestnut back* and *silky white flanks;* median belly slaty gray; wings and tail black, wing-coverts fringed white forming narrow wing-bars. Female has pattern of male including *rufous-chestnut back* and *white flanks,* but slaty black replaced by olive brownish, becoming pale ochraceous on breast.

SIMILAR SPECIES: Distinctive in its very restricted range and habitat. White-flanked Antwren lacks chestnut back and in area of overlap is gray-flanked. Cf. various *Formicivora* antwrens.

HABITAT AND BEHAVIOR: Known presently from near the coast west of Angra dos Reis and (*fide* Collar et al. 1992) along the w. side of the Baía da Ribeira in s. Rio de Janeiro, in lower growth of secondary woodland and adjacent shrubby clearings. Usually in pairs, foraging within a few meters of the ground, inconspicuous and not with mixed flocks. Male's song is a rapid repetition of a single semimusical note, "tcho-tcho-tcho-tcho-tcho . . ."; both sexes also utter a characteristically doubled, rather nasal and sharp "jeer-jeer" call. Until its recent rediscovery, Black-hooded Antwren had long been feared extinct; early records supposedly from the hilly interior of Rio de Janeiro at Nova Friburgo are now thought unlikely. The Black-hooded Antwren remains an extremely localized and endangered bird, and at least some of the habitat in which it was rediscovered is under threat of development.

RANGE: Coastal se. Brazil (s. Rio de Janeiro; published records of this species from Espírito Santo are believed unlikely).

NOTE: See F. Pacheco (*Bull. B. O. C.* 108[4]: 179–182, 1988) for an account of the dramatic rediscovery of this striking antwren and for the rationale, with which we agree, for returning it to the genus *Formicivora*. Unfortunately, the plate on which we depict it had already been prepared, forcing us to retain its text account here.

GROUP E

"*Slaty*"/"*Gray*" assemblage. Most males have *throat black*, concolor in some. Females often difficult.

Myrmotherula longipennis

LONG-WINGED ANTWREN   PLATE: 19

DESCRIPTION: 10–10.5 cm (4–4¼"). Male mostly gray, slightly paler below, with *contrasting black bib on throat and middle of chest* and *lower face often with some whitish frosting* (sometimes extending to fore-crown); scapular fringes white (usually inconspicuous but diagnostic in the hand) and wing-coverts black, tips fringed or barred with white forming 2 wing-bars; tail feathers narrowly tipped white (inconspicuous in field). Females vary geographically. In most of range *brown above*, nearly rufous in *ochrogyna* (south of the Amazon between lower Rio Madeira and lower Rio Tapajós); wings almost unmarked (coverts inconspicuously tipped rufescent). Below uniform pale ochraceous to ochraceous buff. *Garbei* (e. Peru and w. Amaz. Brazil) *uniform olive grayish above*, whereas *zimmeri* (e. Ecuador and adjacent ne. Peru) is *nearly blue-gray above*. Nominate race (north of the Amazon west to se. Colombia and extreme ne. Peru) and *transitiva* (n. Mato Grosso) have whitish midbelly, whereas *ochrogyna* and *zimmeri* are strongly ochraceous below.

SIMILAR SPECIES: *Very confusing* (especially females). Male resembles several other "black-bibbed" *Myrmotherula;* often the best mark, not shared by the others except for an occasional Ihering's, is the whitish on face, most pronounced east of the Rio Madeira in Brazil. The white on wing-coverts usually looks fringed or barred (not spotted as in Slaty and Rio Suno Antwrens). Both Slaty and Rio Suno are darker gray generally (especially Slaty), hence their black bibs stand out less; Slaty occurs mainly in foothills or above (not in Amaz. lowlands). Often sympatric Gray Antwren (except its race *berlepschi*) is easy to distinguish from Long-winged because it shows much less black on throat. Female Long-winged is difficult. Rio Suno Antwren is slightly smaller; it differs from nominate Long-winged in having belly uniform dull ochraceous (not whitish) and from *zimmeri* and *garbei* Long-winged in being browner above. Female Gray Antwren is usually gray above (Long-winged is usually brown); where Long-winged races (*zimmeri* and *garbei*) are gray above, they and Gray are very difficult to distinguish, but Gray is perhaps more intense ochraceous below. Especially in the latter situation, behavioral differences are perhaps the best clue: Long-winged (but not Gray) flicking wings, Gray (but not Long-winged) twitching tail. Cf. also female White-flanked and Ihering's Antwrens.

HABITAT AND BEHAVIOR: Uncommon to fairly common in lower and middle growth of humid forest, especially in terra firme but also in transitional forest. Like so many other *Myrmotherula*, Long-winged is almost always seen as it forages while accompanying mixed understory flocks including *Thamnomanes* antshrikes and other antwrens, most often gleaning while hovering in front of foliage 4–10 m above ground. It often flicks its wings. The song in Peru is a high, thin, rising "chewey-chewey-chewey-chewee-chewee-chee" (T. A. Parker III, *in* Hilty and Brown 1986), and in e. Ecuador it is similar (RSR).

RANGE: Guianas, s. Venezuela (Bolívar and Amazonas), se. Colombia (north to Caquetá and Guainía), e. Ecuador, e. Peru (but seemingly absent from lower Río Marañón and lower Río Ucayali drainages), extreme nw. Bolivia (Pando at Camino Mucden), and Amaz. Brazil (east to Amapá and n. Maranhão, and south to Rondônia and n. Mato Grosso). Mostly below 500 m (along base of Andes), but recorded higher (to 1300 m) in Venezuela.

NOTE: More than one species may be involved. For example, female of nominate race (with brown upperparts and white belly) and female *zimmeri* (with gray upperparts and uniform ochraceous underparts) differ strikingly. No intergradation between them is known, though they may come into contact along the Colombia-Ecuador border.

Myrmotherula schisticolor

SLATY ANTWREN

DESCRIPTION: 10 cm (4″). Mainly *foothills and lower montane slopes* from Venezuela to Peru. Male resembles male Long-winged Antwren (they are not known to be sympatric, with Long-winged in Amaz. lowlands *below* range of Slaty). Minor differences: Slaty's somewhat darker gray general coloration, slightly larger black bib (extending lower on breast) which contrasts less with lower underparts, and tendency toward spotting on wing-coverts (rather than fringing or barring); also, it never shows Long-winged's white frosting on face. Female much like female Long-winged, differing in its deeper fulvous underparts. Back of nominate race (w. Colombia and w. Ecuador) is grayish olive, whereas back of *interior* (e. Andean slopes above Long-winged's range) is *pure gray* (not grayish olive), as is *sanctaemartae*'s (n. and w. Venezuela, and Colombia's Santa Marta Mts.). See V-21, C-28.

SIMILAR SPECIES: The only gray, black-bibbed *Myrmotherula* in most of its foothill range. Slaty closely resembles Rio Suno Antwren (which, like Long-winged, is found in lowlands *below* range of Slaty, with no known overlap though they come close). See full discussion under Rio Suno Antwren. Female Slaty is notably plain aside from its richly colored underparts; female Checker-throated Antwren has buff wingbars. Female Slaty Antwren of sympatric *interior* race differs in its uniform blue-gray mantle and much brighter ochraceous underparts.

HABITAT AND BEHAVIOR: Uncommon to fairly common in lower growth of montane forest and mature second-growth woodland. Most often in pairs, gleaning from foliage and in tangles, regularly accompanying mixed understory flocks including other *Myrmotherula* antwrens, *Basileuterus* warblers, and foliage-gleaners. A call often given by both sexes while foraging is a nasal, complaining "skeeuh-skur" or "skeeur"; we are not familiar with any true song.

RANGE: Coastal mts. of n. Venezuela (east to Paria Peninsula), and Andean slopes of Colombia, Ecuador (south on w. slope to w. Loja; also locally out into humid Pacific lowlands and on slopes of coastal cordillera in sw. Manabí and w. Guayas), and e. Peru (south to Puno); Sierra de Perijá on Venezuela-Colombia border, Santa Marta Mts. of n. Colombia, and Cerro Tacarcuna in extreme nw. Colombia. Also Mexico to Panama. Mostly 900–1800 m, lower (locally to 200 m) on Pacific slope, especially in Ecuador.

Myrmotherula sunensis

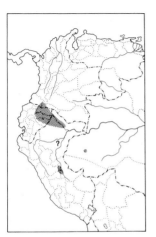

RIO SUNO ANTWREN

DESCRIPTION: 9 cm (3½"). Local from se. Colombia to cen. Peru. Both sexes closely resemble Long-winged Antwren (sympatric at some localities), but Rio Suno is *substantially smaller* (this discernible in the field, given a good view) with proportionately *shorter tail*. Male further differs in being somewhat darker gray generally, never shows any white facial grizzling, lacks white on outer scapulars, and its white on wing-coverts gives effect of *spotting* (not fringing or barring). See C-28. Female, aside from its smaller size and shorter tail, virtually identical to brown-backed races of Long-winged, though Rio Suno averages drabber below.

SIMILAR SPECIES: Slaty Antwren (which occurs on Andean slopes *above* range of Rio Suno, with no known overlap) male very closely resembles male Rio Suno and would probably not be distinguishable in the field; females are easier, for female Slaty Antwrens of nearly sympatric races are pure gray (not olive brown) above.

HABITAT AND BEHAVIOR: Rare to locally uncommon (perhaps somewhat overlooked because of identification difficulties) in lower growth of humid forest, mainly if not entirely in terra firme. Not a well-known bird, but general behavior seems similar to Long-winged Antwren's, though Rio Suno tends to forage lower. One vocalization is a clear, melodic "wi-weedy-weedy-weedy" (P. Coopmans).

RANGE: Extreme se. Colombia (Río Churuyaco and Estación de Bombeos de Guamez in w. Putumayo), ne. Ecuador (Napo), and extreme ne. Peru (mouth of Río Cururay into Río Napo); cen. Peru (locally in Huánuco and Pasco; AMNH and ANSP); w. Âmaz. Brazil (a single male specimen in MZUSP from the middle Rio Juruá). To 900 m (FMNH specimens from Colombia).

Myrmotherula iheringi

IHERING'S ANTWREN   PLATE: 19

DESCRIPTION: 9 cm (3½"). Local in sw. and cen. Amazonia. A *small* and *short-tailed* antwren. Male mostly gray, slightly paler below, with

contrasting black bib on throat and middle of breast, sometimes with some white on lower face; wing-coverts black with 2 bold white wing-bars, underwing-coverts white; tail black. Female *pale grayish above;* wing-coverts black, feathers tipped with large pale buff spots, *forming wing-bars.* Below rather pale ochraceous buff.

SIMILAR SPECIES: Male resembles male Long-winged Antwren, but latter is larger, has narrow white tail-tipping (tail all black and shorter in Ihering's), and gray underwing-coverts. Females differ more strikingly: Ihering's has a bold, "male-type" wing pattern (female Long-winged's wing is virtually plain) and considerably drabber underparts. Long-winged does not twitch tail. Ihering's is not known to occur with similarly sized Rio Suno Antwren.

HABITAT AND BEHAVIOR: Rare to locally uncommon in lower growth of humid forest, both in terra firme and transitional forest. In some areas (e.g., the Tambopata Reserve in se. Peru) apparently restricted to stands of *Guadua* bamboo, but elsewhere more widespread (D. Stotz). Behavior similar to many other *Myrmotherula* antwrens', tending to glean in foliage at heights 3–8 m above the ground, often with mixed understory flocks. Twitches tail from side to side almost constantly (D. Stotz). Its song is a series of fairly musical "peeu" notes, usually 6–12 (but sometimes as many as 25 in a series; Parker 1982); in quality it resembles the song of Sclater's Antwren, though the series of notes is longer and usually more rapidly delivered, and they are more musical and less melancholy.

RANGE: Se. Peru (Madre de Dios) and w. and cen. Amaz. Brazil (south of the Amazon from the upper Rio Juruá east to the lower Rio Tapajós); should occur in extreme n. Bolivia. To 650 m.

NOTE: For more natural history information, see Parker (1982).

Myrmotherula fluminensis

RIO DE JANEIRO ANTWREN

DESCRIPTION: 9.5 cm (3¾"). Recently described from a single male specimen from *Rio de Janeiro, Brazil.* Closely resembles geographically distant Ihering's Antwren but is slightly larger and has more slender bill and longer and more graduated tail. The gray is more tinged with bluish, and the black of the bib extends down farther, over upper belly. Female unknown.

SIMILAR SPECIES: Male Salvadori's Antwren's black bib is distinctly smaller (extending barely to chest). The sympatric race of White-flanked Antwren is basically gray-flanked (showing little or no white); it thus resembles the Rio de Janeiro Antwren but shows much more black below. Cf. also Band-tailed Antwren.

HABITAT AND BEHAVIOR: The specimen was mist-netted "in a partially isolated and very disturbed woodlot located in the foothills of Serra dos Órgãos" (L. P. Gonzaga, *Bull. B.O.C.* 108 [3]: 132, 1988). It has been suggested that the bird may have straggled down from the slopes of that mountain range (encompassed in a national park), where a population might in time be located.

RANGE: Se. Brazil (Rio de Janeiro). 20 m.

NOTE: A recently described species: L. P. Gonzaga, *Bull. B. O. C.* 108(3): 132–135, 1988.

Myrmotherula minor

SALVADORI'S ANTWREN

DESCRIPTION: 9 cm (3½"). *Se. Brazil* (apparently all the w. Amaz. records are uncertain). Resembles Ihering's Antwren (no overlap, if one excludes the Amaz. records). Male has a smaller black bib (barely extending down over midchest), crissum barred blackish and white (hard to see in the field but not shared by any other *Myrmotherula*); adult male has narrow blackish subterminal tail-band, with feathers very narrowly fringed whitish (tail not all black). Female has *crown ashy gray* merging into brownish olive back; wing-coverts dusky brown narrowly tipped with olivaceous buff; tail feathers edged russet. Throat whitish; *remaining underparts bright olivaceous buff,* deepest on flanks and crissum.

SIMILAR SPECIES: In se. Brazil, cf. *luctuosa* race of White-flanked Antwren (with silvery gray flanks and more extensive black bib in male, contrastingly paler flanks in female), Band-tailed Antwren (with more broadly white-tipped tail in both sexes, especially from below), and the recently described Rio de Janeiro Antwren. Female Unicolored Antwren lacks the obviously gray crown, is not so bright buff below, has a shorter tail. Only doubtfully identifiable in Amazonia (from whence the few specimens are questionable; see below).

HABITAT AND BEHAVIOR: Uncommon in lower and middle growth of humid forest and mature secondary woodland. Behavior not well known to us, vocalizations not at all. Birds seen in s. Rio de Janeiro have been foraging singly with small flocks (regularly with *luctuosa* White-flanked Antwrens), sometimes at forest edge or openings. Probably threatened by deforestation.

RANGE: Se. Brazil from Espírito Santo (recorded from Reserva Florestal Rio Doce by D. Stotz) south locally through Rio de Janeiro to ne. São Paulo, with old specimens also from e. Santa Catarina; possibly also in w. Amazonia (see below). To 500 m.

NOTE: The records from Amazonia present a vexing problem. There are only a few purported specimens, none recent. One, a male in ANSP labeled as having been taken at Iquitos, Peru, seems to be correctly identified, but we regard the locality as suspect. ANSP has another *M. minor* male labeled as from Cayenne, which we also regard as of dubious provenance. The immature male from the Rio Purus in w. Brazil seems to have been studied only by Hellmayr, who considered it correctly identified but thought its locality might be incorrect. There remains the AMNH immature male from Sarayacu, Peru, discussed in detail by J. T. Zimmer (*Am. Mus. Novitates* 524, 1932), but which we suspect may actually be *M. sunensis.*

Myrmotherula urosticta

BAND-TAILED ANTWREN   PLATE: 19

DESCRIPTION: 9.5 cm (3¾"). *E. Brazil.* Male pale gray, usually with some whitish frosting on lower face, and black bib on throat and middle of chest; wing-coverts black with 2 bold white wing-bars; tail

black, *rather broadly tipped white* (especially below). Female rather pale gray above; wings gray with 2 fairly prominent whitish wing-bars; tail blackish, *tipped white as in male*. Throat whitish, becoming creamy buff below, narrowly pure pale gray on sides.

SIMILAR SPECIES: The tail-band, reasonably prominent in the field, easily marks this distinctive species. Salvadori's Antwren male lacks obvious white in tail, as does female; latter also is much more ochraceous below and more olivaceous on back. Sympatric *luctuosa* White-flanked Antwren shows much less white on tail (though a little tipping is present), and male is darker generally so its black bib stands out less.

HABITAT AND BEHAVIOR: Uncommon to fairly common but very local in lower growth of humid forest. Usually seen in pairs, most often accompanying mixed understory flocks, usually foraging within 4–5 m of the ground. Its alarm call is a nasal, descending "beer bin," similar to call of Long-winged Antwren. Band-tailed can be seen at the Sooretama Reserve and the nearby Reserva Florestal Rio Doce, both in the lowlands of n. Espírito Santo and now vital refuges for a species that has seen most of its forest habitat destroyed over the past half century.

RANGE: E. Brazil (se. Bahia and Espírito Santo). To 100 m.

Myrmotherula menetriesii

GRAY ANTWREN   PLATE: 19

DESCRIPTION: 9.5–10 cm (3¾–4"). Male *mostly rather pale gray*, somewhat paler below; wing-coverts gray, feathers with *black subterminal band* and white tip forming bars; tail mostly slaty, very narrowly tipped white. Birds from e. Peru and n. Bolivia east into Amaz. Brazil south of the Amazon to the lower Rio Tapajós (nominate race and *berlepschi*) have a variable but usually obvious black patch on middle of throat and upper chest; elsewhere males are *all gray below*. Female *gray to olive grayish above* (*berlepschi* browner), with *wings unmarked*. Below rather bright ochraceous. See V-21, C-28.

SIMILAR SPECIES: Male in most of range is only "gray" antwren combining all-gray underparts (no black on throat) with bold wing markings, but remember that young males of other species may lack black on throat; female is grayer above than most other female *Myrmotherula* with plain wings. Gray Antwrens with black on throat can be recognized by the *small extent* of the bib and the complex pattern on wing-coverts (*gray, black, and white*) with a *fringed* (rather than spotted) effect. Gray Antwren typically forages *higher* than other *Myrmotherula*, though there is overlap. Cf. especially Leaden Antwren (restricted to várzea woodland along Amazon and major tributaries); Plain-throated Antwren has very different habitat near ground in forest interior.

HABITAT AND BEHAVIOR: Fairly common to common in middle levels and canopy of humid forest and forest borders and openings, mostly in terra firme, also to some extent in transitional forest. Pairs accompany flocks including *Thamnomanes* antshrikes, other *Myrmotherula* antwrens, and various furnariids and woodcreepers but tend to remain higher than most other members of the flock, and sometimes are with canopy flocks of mainly different composition (e.g., with Gray Antbird, Spot-winged Antshrike, and various tanagers). Forages by gleaning actively in foliage and viny tangles; tail is often twitched from side to side. The song is a weak, thin, wavering series of about 12 "ree" or "shree" notes that rise in pitch and accelerate slightly.

RANGE: Guianas, s. Venezuela (Bolívar and Amazonas), e. Colombia (north to w. Meta and e. Vichada), e. Ecuador, e. Peru, n. Bolivia (south to La Paz, Cochabamba, and n. Santa Cruz), and Amaz. Brazil (east to Amapá and n. Maranhão, and south to n. Mato Grosso). Mostly below 900 m.

Myrmotherula assimilis

LEADEN ANTWREN   PLATE: 19

DESCRIPTION: 9.5–10 cm (3¾–4"). *Restricted to várzea woodland along the Amazon and its major tributaries.* Male *essentially uniform gray,* somewhat paler below (palest on belly), with semiconcealed white dorsal patch; wings slaty, wing-coverts with 2 white wing-bars; tail slaty, very narrowly tipped white. Female pale olivaceous gray above; wing feathers edged brownish, wing-coverts with *2 buffyish wing-bars;* tail slaty. Below pale cinnamon-buff, white on upper throat.

SIMILAR SPECIES: In its habitat usually the only "gray" *Myrmotherula* present. Male Gray Antwren is basically a terra firme bird; in most of its races male has a small black bib, and it always has a different pattern on wing-coverts and *lacks* the dorsal patch (quite large in Leaden). Female Gray Antwren has no wing markings and is more richly colored below.

HABITAT AND BEHAVIOR: Uncommon to locally common in várzea woodland and forest along the Amazon and certain of its major tributaries, often in the extensive stands of fairly mature *Cecropia* trees found on older islands. Usually in pairs which forage at all levels, and often is markedly tamer and easier to see that most other *Myrmotherula;* sometimes with mixed flocks. The song is a fast, descending musical trill which lasts 2–3 seconds, given mainly (perhaps only) by male. Particularly numerous at Anavilhanas Archipelago in the Rio Negro above Manaus, Brazil.

RANGE: Along the Amazon in ne. Peru, extreme se. Colombia (Leticia region), Amaz. Brazil, and n. Bolivia (Pando, Beni, and ne. Santa Cruz); ranges up to about where the Ríos Marañón and Ucayali separate in Peru, and down to around Santarém; also ranges along the lower Rio Negro and along the Rios Juruá, Purus, and Madeira. To about 175 m.

Myrmotherula unicolor

UNICOLORED ANTWREN   PLATE: 19

DESCRIPTION: 9.5 cm (3¾"). Local in *se. Brazil;* does not include *M. snowi* of ne. Brazil. Male *uniform gray,* somewhat paler below, most individuals with *a small blackish patch on throat* (inconspicuous, the feathers often fringed with gray). Female *fulvous brown above,* becoming *russet on tail;* crown and nape tinged olivaceous. Throat whitish, *remaining underparts pale olivaceous buff.*

SIMILAR SPECIES: In its range, both sexes can be known by their *plain wing-coverts*. Female Salvadori's Antwren (whose wings are only faintly marked) is much less rufescent above and has gray crown, brighter underparts, shorter tail. Female *luctuosa* White-flanked Antwren has pale flank plumes.

HABITAT AND BEHAVIOR: Rare to locally fairly common in lower growth of humid forest and mature secondary woodland. Seems capable of persisting in quite degraded second-growth (D. Stotz). Behavior much like many other *Myrmotherula* antwrens', pairs usually foraging in forest understory, gleaning in foliage, often with mixed flocks and regularly with *luctuosa* White-flanked Antwrens (which usually forage higher). Male's song is a short, high, plaintive "eeeeeeee" (Belton 1985). Numerous near Peruibe in coastal s. São Paulo.

RANGE: E. Brazil (Espírito Santo south to ne. Rio Grande do Sul). To 800 m, but mostly below 200 m in s. part of range.

NOTE: See comments under Alagoas Antwren.

Myrmotherula snowi

ALAGOAS ANTWREN

DESCRIPTION: 9.5 cm (3¾"). *Ne. Brazil in Alagoas.* Closely resembles Unicolored Antwren (of which originally described as only a race) but with slightly longer bill and shorter tail. Female more rufescent below than female Unicolored.

HABITAT AND BEHAVIOR: Uncommon in lower growth and middle levels of humid forest and mature secondary woodland. Behavior much like Unicolored Antwren's, but evidently its [undescribed] vocalizations are "very different" (Collar et al. 1992, p. 662). Thus far known only from the type locality, the Alagoas Antwren is seriously endangered by continuing deforestation; we hope that the recent initiative to protect at least some of what remains will succeed.

RANGE: Ne. Brazil (Alagoas near Murici on the Pedra Branca). 400–550 m.

NOTE: A recently described species: D. M. Teixera and L. P. Gonzaga, *Bol. Mus. Nac.*, Zool., nov. sér., no. 310, 1985. These authors described *snowi* as only a subspecies of *M. unicolor,* but we follow Collar et al. (1992) in treating *M. snowi* as a full species.

Myrmotherula behni

PLAIN-WINGED ANTWREN

DESCRIPTION: 9.5 cm (3¾"). *Very local* in n. South America, mainly in *foothills*. Resembles Unicolored Antwren of Brazil (no overlap). Plain-winged male is darker gray and has *much larger black bib;* see V-21. Female *olivaceous brown above,* slightly duskier on tail, with *plain* wing-coverts. Mostly olivaceous buff below, with throat whitish. *Yavii* (Amazonas and nw. Bolívar, Venezuela) is more olivaceous above and darker below.

SIMILAR SPECIES: Overlaps with very few other *Myrmotherula* in its *foothill* range, and both sexes of all these show wing markings. In Guyana, where Plain-winged evidently occurs in lowlands, cf. female

Long-winged and Gray Antwrens, both of which are markedly *grayer* (not so rufescent) above and more strongly colored below.

HABITAT AND BEHAVIOR: Rare to perhaps locally uncommon in lower growth of humid foothill and montane forest. Not well known. A pair seen by RSR and P. Greenfield above Archidona in Ecuador foraged with a mixed flock of understory birds, gleaning in foliage 4–6 m above ground. One vocalization, heard on the Escalera in Venezuela, is a "keeeur-kerr" (P. Coopmans).

RANGE: French Guiana (sight reports from several interior localities); Guyana, s. Venezuela (tepuis of Bolívar and Amazonas south to Cerro de la Neblina), and extreme n. Brazil (Roraima); e. Colombia (known only from Macarena Mts. in w. Meta); e. Ecuador (locally in foothills of w. Napo and Morona-Santiago; specimens AMNH, MCZ, ANSP, and WFVZ). Mostly 900–1800 m, lower in Guianas.

Myrmotherula grisea

YUNGAS ANTWREN

Other: Ashy Antwren

DESCRIPTION: 10 cm (4"). *Foothills and lower Andean slopes of w. Bolivia.* Male *uniform gray* with *plain* wing-coverts. Female *olivaceous brown above,* wings and *tail more rufescent,* wing-coverts *unmarked.* Below uniform bright ochraceous.

SIMILAR SPECIES: The uniform plain gray male is the most unmarked member of its genus. Female is also plain but is quite brightly colored below. Note *foothill* range, above that of most of its congeners. Does overlap with somewhat longer-tailed nominate race of Gray Antwren, males of which show a black throat patch and prominent wing markings, females of which are markedly grayer on back and tail.

HABITAT AND BEHAVIOR: Not well known; apparently rare to uncommon in middle growth of humid foothill forest and mature second-growth woodland. Pairs forage actively with mixed flocks which may include other *Myrmotherula* antwrens (at least at lower edge of its elevational range), Tawny-crowned Greenlets, Golden-crowned Warblers, and Red-crowned Ant-Tanagers. Frequently flicks wings. Calls are similar to Gray Antwren's (Parker et al. 1992). Apparently threatened by deforestation.

RANGE: W. Bolivia (foothills of La Paz, Cochabamba, and w. Santa Cruz). 600–1400 m.

NOTE: As many other male *Myrmotherula* antwrens are equally "ashy," it seems preferable to emphasize this species' very small range by employing a geographical epithet in its English name: *M. grisea* is endemic to the yungas of Bolivia. See Remsen et al. (1982) and Parker et al. (1992) for additional natural history information.

Terenura Antwrens

Small antbirds, rather like wood-warblers or tyrannulets, with allopatric or parapatric distributions in the canopy of lowland and subtropical forest. Compared to *Myrmotherula* antwrens, *Terenura* are thin-billed and relatively slim in shape, long-tailed and small-bodied. All but one sex of one species (the male of the newly described Orange-bellied Antwren) have a patch of rufous (usually) or yellow on lower back and rump. Until recently *Terenura* antwrens were believed rare, but this turns out to be more a reflection of how difficult they are to see and collect than of actual rarity.

GROUP A

Streaked head (both sexes); most also with *rufous back*. E. Brazil region.

Terenura maculata

STREAK-CAPPED ANTWREN   PLATE: 20

DESCRIPTION: 10 cm (4″). *Se. Brazil area.* Male has *crown, sides of head, and nape black streaked with white,* contrasting with *bright rufous back;* wings blackish with 2 white wing-bars, tail dusky. Below mainly white with a faint black malar streak, some fine black streaking across breast, and yellow-tinged belly. Female like male but streaking on head buffyish (rather than white), wing-coverts more olive brown, and throat tinged buffyish.

SIMILAR SPECIES: Nothing really similar in range (no "pygmy" or "streaked" *Myrmotherula* antwren is sympatric). Cf. Orange-bellied Antwren (no overlap). Female especially might be confused with larger and longer-tailed Rufous-winged Antwren.

HABITAT AND BEHAVIOR: Uncommon to locally fairly common in canopy and borders of humid forest. Usually seen singly or in pairs, gleaning quite actively in foliage and viny tangles, often accompanying mixed flocks of insectivorous birds, including Rufous-winged Antwrens. Its song is a simple, evenly-pitched, semimusical trill lasting about 2 seconds, but more often heard is its call, a more distinctive "picheeé-picheeé-picheeé-picheeé," sometimes "picheeéya"; sometimes a singing bird ends with this call. Foraging birds also give a loud "chip" note. Seems especially numerous in coastal São Paulo northeast of Ubatuba.

RANGE: Se. Brazil (se. Bahia south to Santa Catarina, and inland through much of s. Minas Gerais, São Paulo, and Paraná), ne. Argentina (Misiones), and e. Paraguay (Canendiyu south to Caazapá and Alto Paraná). To 800 m.

Terenura sicki

ORANGE-BELLIED ANTWREN
Other: Alagoas Antwren

DESCRIPTION: 10 cm (4″). *Ne. Brazil.* Male *mostly black above,* crown and nape narrowly streaked white, with some very sparse streaking on back as well; wings black with 2 white wing-bars; tail dusky. *Below pure white.* Female has crown black streaked with white, *back and rump rufous;* wings black with 2 white wing-bars, tail dusky. Throat buffy whitish becoming *rich orange-rufous on remaining underparts.*

SIMILAR SPECIES: This species' closest relative is the Streak-capped Antwren; Orange-bellied is much more strongly sexually dimorphic, with females quite orange below (Streak-capped only tinged yellow)

and males quite black above (lacking any rufous); they do not occur together. In its very limited range (where there are no "pygmy" or "streaked" *Myrmotherula* antwrens), Orange-bellied Antwren is thus virtually unmistakable.

HABITAT AND BEHAVIOR: Locally fairly common in canopy and borders of humid forest and secondary woodland. Behavior much like Streak-capped Antwren's, like that species (but unlike their other congeners) rarely or never fluttering or momentarily hanging upside down. Vocalizations also seem similar; in Oct. 1987 at Pedra Branca, RSR and T. Schulenberg heard only what sounded equivalent to Streak-capped's "call" (and no semimusical trill), a fairly loud, rollicking, and fast "picheecheechee-picheecheechee-picheecheechee." The remnant forests where this bird is found are being constantly reduced in extent and quality; one area has recently received protection as the Pedra Talhada Biological Reserve.

RANGE: Ne. Brazil in ne. Pernambuco (seen at Agua Azul, south of Timbaúba; E. O. Willis) and Alagoas (Pedra Branca above Murici, Pedra Talhada Biological Reserve, and Novo Lino). 300–700 m.

NOTE: A recently described species: D. M. Teixera and L. P. Gonzaga, *Bull. B. O. C.* 103(4): 133–135, 1983. See also D. M. Teixera (*Bol. Mus. Par. Emílio Goeldi*, Zool. 3[2]: 241–251, 1987) for additional notes on this well-marked bird, including the first written description of the male and the first described nest for any *Terenura*. We follow Teixera and Gonzaga (op. cit.) in using the English name of Orange-bellied Antwren for this species, even if it is applicable only to the female. Alagoas Antwren has also been suggested (e.g., Sibley and Monroe 1990), but that name seems better reserved for *Myrmotherula snowi* (e.g., Collar et al. 1992).

GROUP B

Standard *Terenura;* females lack males' *black crown.*

Terenura spodioptila

ASH-WINGED ANTWREN

PLATE: 20

DESCRIPTION: 10 cm (4"). Mainly *ne. South America.* Male has *black crown* and narrow line through eye, separated by *white superciliary;* sides of head and upper back ashy gray, contrasting with *rufous lower back and rump;* wings and tail blackish, wings with *2 white wing-bars. Below uniform grayish white.* Female has rufescent brown crown with faint buffyish superciliary, becoming olivaceous brown on upper back and *rufous on lower back and rump;* wings and tail as in male. Throat and breast dingy buffy whitish, becoming whiter on belly.

SIMILAR SPECIES: Rufous-rumped Antwren probably never occurs with this species (ranging in foothills *above* Ash-winged, which is found in lowlands), but they could overlap marginally. Both sexes of Rufous-rumped differ in being quite bright yellow below, in having rufous above only on rump, and in having an olive back and edging on wings. Cf. also Chestnut-shouldered Antwren. Some *Myrmotherula* antwrens (e.g., Stipple-throated, Rufous-tailed, Ornate) have vaguely similar color patterns with rufous on back, but none shows black crown and white superciliary of male Ash-winged or pale underparts of female Ash-winged; their behavior also differs markedly. None of the (similarly shaped) greenlets shows wing-bars.

HABITAT AND BEHAVIOR: Uncommon to locally fairly common (generally overlooked until vocalizations are recognized) in canopy and borders of humid forest, largely confined to terra firme. Found singly or in pairs, usually ranging high above ground and hard to see clearly; frequently associates with mixed flocks. Male's song is a trill which starts slowly and then ends with several well-enunciated and separated notes, "tee-tee-tee-ti-ti-ti-titititititititititititi-tsíp-tsíp-tsíp." Can be seen in forest north of Manaus, Brazil (often to good advantage from the INPA/WWF tower), and in the Río Grande forests in e. Bolívar, Venezuela.

RANGE: Guianas, s. Venezuela (Bolívar and Amazonas), se. Colombia (Vaupés and w. Caquetá [female in ANSP taken at Morelia]), ne. Ecuador (sightings at Sucumbios at Cuyabeno and north of Lumbaquí), and n. Amaz. Brazil (north of the Amazon from the upper Rio Negro region eastward, south of it only near e. bank of the lower Rio Tapajós). To 1100 m.

Terenura callinota

RUFOUS-RUMPED ANTWREN

PLATE: 20

DESCRIPTION: 11 cm (4¼″). Local in *foothills and subtropics*. Male has *black crown* and thin dark line through eye, separated by *grayish white superciliary;* sides of head and neck gray and back olive, contrasting with *large area of rufous on rump; shoulders bright yellow,* wing-coverts black with *2 pale yellowish wing-bars,* flight feathers with olive edging; tail dusky. Throat and chest pale grayish, becoming *bright pale yellow on belly.* See C-28. Female similar but has crown grayish or brownish olive barely contrasting with back, faint superciliary, no yellow on shoulders, and duskier wing-coverts.

SIMILAR SPECIES: Not known to occur with any other *Terenura* antwren, but this species and Chestnut-shouldered have been recorded from almost the same elevations along e. base of Andes in s. Peru. They (especially females) would be difficult to differentiate under normal field conditions; males differ in shoulder color. Cf. also Ash-winged Antwren (with whitish underparts, etc.). Certain tyrannulets (e.g., Sulphur-bellied) have a similar pattern (with wing-bars, superciliary, etc.) and rather long-tailed shape, though the antwren's posture and rufous rump are distinctive.

HABITAT AND BEHAVIOR: Uncommon to locally fairly common but inconspicuous in canopy and borders of montane forest, coming lower at borders and in openings. Seen most often in pairs accompanying mixed flocks of insectivorous birds, gleaning actively in foliage, regularly amongst outer branches. Habitually turns upside down to search the underside of leaves, and then the rufous on the rump may flash out. Male's song is a high-pitched but still semimusical, somewhat descending trill.

RANGE: Andes of Colombia (north in E. Andes to Cundinamarca, in W. Andes to Valle), Ecuador (south on w. slope to El Oro), and e. Peru (south to Cuzco, in vicinity of Hacienda Amazonia and Atalaya); slopes of Sierra de Perijá in nw. Venezuela; s. Guyana (Acary Mts.)

and adjacent s. Surinam. Also Costa Rica and Panama. Mostly 800–2000 m, occasionally somewhat higher or lower.

Terenura humeralis

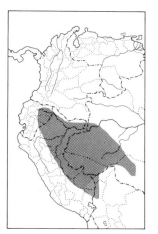

CHESTNUT-SHOULDERED ANTWREN

DESCRIPTION: 11 cm (4¼″). W. Amazonia. Male resembles male Rufous-rumped Antwren (no recorded overlap, with Chestnut-shouldered in lowlands, Rufous-rumped montane), differing in its *chestnut (not yellow) shoulders,* darker more rufous-chestnut rump, and *whitish belly* (with pale yellow restricted to flanks and crissum). Female so like female Rufous-rumped they would be barely distinguishable in the field. Female Chestnut-shouldered has *buffyish throat* (not whitish) and, like male, a slightly darker rump; at least some females have a bit of chestnut on shoulders.

SIMILAR SPECIES: Ash-winged Antwren (no known overlap, though their ranges come close in s. Amazonia), particularly female, is also similar; it differs in lacking chestnut shoulders (at most obscure in female Chestnut-shouldered) and in its whiter underparts (especially on breast).

HABITAT AND BEHAVIOR: Uncommon in canopy and borders of humid forest, mainly in terra firme but also in transitional forest. Until recently a poorly known bird, recent observations have revealed that the behavior of this inconspicuous antwren is much like its congeners' and that it is considerably more numerous and widespread than the paucity of earlier records had indicated. Recorded much more often once its frequently given song, a simple series of high-pitched chippering notes which speed into a terminal trill, is recognized. In fact, the canopy flocks with which this antwren almost invariably travels are often themselves most easily followed by listening for the *Terenura*'s song. Can be found at the Tambopata Reserve and Manu Lodge, both in Madre de Dios, Peru.

RANGE: E. Ecuador (Napo south locally to Morona-Santiago), e. Peru (recorded only from Loreto and Madre de Dios, but probably more widespread), extreme nw. Bolivia (Pando at Camino Mucden and n. La Paz at Alto Madidi), and w. Amaz. Brazil (recorded east to São Paulo de Olivença, the upper Rio Purus, and Rondônia at Cachoeira Nazaré and Pimenta Bueno). Either this species or *T. spodioptila* likely occurs in cen. Amaz. Brazil south of the Amazon between the Rios Tapajós and Madeira. To 650 m.

NOTE: For further notes on this species, see Parker (1982) and Remsen and Parker (1987).

Terenura sharpei

YELLOW-RUMPED ANTWREN   PLATE: 20

DESCRIPTION: 11 cm (4¼″). *Subtropical zone of s. Peru and w. Bolivia,* replacing Rufous-rumped Antwren southward. Male resembles male Rufous-rumped but has *lower back and rump bright yellow.* Female likewise differs from female Rufous-rumped in having *lower back and rump yellowish olive.*

SIMILAR SPECIES: No other member of the genus has yellow on the rump.

HABITAT AND BEHAVIOR: Uncommon in canopy and borders of montane forest. Behavior much like other *Terenura*, likewise seen most often with mixed flocks, gleaning actively in foliage, frequently in outer branches and usually high above ground. Hangs upside down while searching underside of leaves, exposing the yellow on the rump. Its song is a high-pitched, somewhat accelerating trill, the last few notes rapidly descending in pitch. Can be found in the Serranía Bellavista north of Caranavi in La Paz, but overall numbers have declined substantially because of deforestation, and the species likely deserves threatened status.

RANGE: E. slope of Andes in s. Peru (Puno) and w. Bolivia (La Paz and Cochabamba). 1100–1680 m.

NOTE: For further natural history notes, see Remsen et al. (1982).

Drymophila Antbirds

Small antbirds with quite long, markedly graduated tails, found mainly in se. South America where six of the eight species range; a single species occurs in the Andes and another in w. Amazonia. All are found in forest or woodland undergrowth, with all but two species (Scaled and Dusky-tailed) showing a decided preference for bamboo. They are boldly and handsomely patterned, most with prominent streaking or spotting, many sporting a conspicuous superciliary. The genus is less sexually dimorphic than many other antbird genera, with most females duller overall but having a pattern similar to the male's. The genus may be most closely related to the shorter-tailed *Hypocnemis* whose overall plumage patterns are similar, as are their vocalizations.

GROUP A

Se. Brazil and adjacent areas.

Drymophila squamata

SCALED ANTBIRD   PLATE: 20

DESCRIPTION: 11.5 cm (4¾"). E. Brazil. Male *black above with bold white spotting and white superciliary;* wings and tail black, wings with 2 white wing-bars, *tail boldly banded with white.* Below white *boldly spotted with black.* Males of nominate race (Bahia, and presumably Alagoas) have crown solid black, whereas those from farther south (*stictocorypha*) have some white spotting on midcrown. Female brown above with pale buff superciliary and *large buff spots on back;* wings and tail dusky, with 2 buff wing-bars, tail *boldly banded with buff.* Below whitish with *elongated dusky spots or streaks,* flanks dull ochraceous. Females of *stictocorypha* have small buff spots on midcrown.

SIMILAR SPECIES: Both sexes are easily recognized by their obvious spotted or ocellated effect (despite its English name, this species is not really "scaled").

HABITAT AND BEHAVIOR: Fairly common to locally common in undergrowth of humid forest, forest borders, and mature secondary woodland; not associated with bamboo but (D. Stotz) does seem to be inordinately fond of *Heliconia*. Usually in pairs, hopping about near ground, often not particularly shy (especially for an antbird). Male's often-heard and distinctive song is a raspy, quite high-pitched "pseey-pseeu, pseeu, pseeu, psew" with decided descending effect; often female echoes male with a softer but similar song. Both sexes also frequently give a "dee-deét" call (D. Stotz, RSR). Occurs in Tijuca Nat. Park above Rio de Janeiro; particularly numerous in coastal forests of São Paulo.

RANGE: E. Brazil (Alagoas; se. Bahia south to e. Santa Catarina, inland to e. Minas Gerais). Mostly below 600 m (recorded to 980 m in Bahia).

Drymophila ferruginea

FERRUGINOUS ANTBIRD   PLATE: 20

DESCRIPTION: 14 cm (5½"). Se. Brazil; does not include Bertoni's Antbird (see below). Male has *crown and sides of head black, long white superciliary,* and mainly white lower cheeks; otherwise brown above, becoming chestnut on rump, back mixed with black, and semiconcealed white dorsal patch; wings black with 2 bold white wing-bars; *tail black,* feathers broadly tipped white. *Below uniform bright ferruginous.* Female similar in overall pattern but paler and duller below, tail duskier, and crown blackish *streaked olive-gray especially on forecrown.*

SIMILAR SPECIES: Cf. Bertoni's Antbird; otherwise this handsome antbird is essentially unmistakable, especially because of its brightly colored underparts.

HABITAT AND BEHAVIOR: Fairly common in lower growth of humid forest and second-growth woodland, particularly in stands of bamboo (thus often especially at forest edge). Usually in pairs, sometimes with small flocks of understory birds, generally fairly easy to observe. Its frequently heard call is a distinctive, basically bisyllabic "jee, jeweé," sometimes followed by several other notes of similar quality. Numerous at lower levels of Itatiaia Nat. Park.

RANGE: Se. Brazil (se. Bahia south to e. Santa Catarina). Mainly below 1200 m (small numbers up to 1600 m).

NOTE: See comments under Bertoni's Antbird.

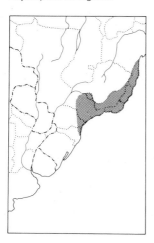

Drymophila rubricollis

BERTONI'S ANTBIRD

Other: Ferruginous Antbird (in part)

DESCRIPTION: 14 cm (5½"). *Ne. Argentina north locally into higher mts. of se. Brazil.* Recently shown to be a separate species from Ferruginous Antbird. Bertoni's is slightly longer-tailed. Male differs in being more pallid generally, with *belly distinctly duller and paler than throat and breast,* little or no black mixed into back, and *tail dusky* (but feathers tipped white like Ferruginous). Female Bertoni's differs from female

Ferruginous in much the same ways, and in addition has *a more rufescent forecrown,* with hindcrown streaked the same color.

SIMILAR SPECIES: Although both sexes are slightly duller than Ferruginous Antbird, they still can be readily differentiated from other similar species by their ferruginous throats and breasts.

HABITAT AND BEHAVIOR: Fairly common in much the same habitats as Ferruginous Antbird, and likewise with a strong predilection for bamboo. The 2 species have similar behavior and even occur together locally, e.g., at 1500–1600 m on slopes of Itatiaia Mts. (Bertoni's occurs from there *up*wards, Ferruginous from there *down*wards). However, their voices differ strikingly, Bertoni's giving a series of 5–8 rather nasal notes which descend distinctively, "jeep, ji-ji-jee-jee-jew."

RANGE: Se. Brazil (from high on Itatiaia Mts. in w. Rio de Janeiro south to n. Rio Grande do Sul), extreme e. Paraguay (e. Canendiyu and Alto Paraná), and ne. Argentina (Misiones). To 1800 m (much lower in s. part of range); on Itatiaia Mts. mainly 1500–1800 m, in Serra do Mar of São Paulo at 800–1000 m (*fide* D. Stotz).

NOTE: E. O. Willis (*Rev. Brasil. Biol.* 48[3]: 431–438, 1988) presented evidence showing that the form named by Bertoni as *rubricollis* from se. Paraguay is a species separate from *D. ferruginea* of mainly coastal se. Brazil. Willis suggested Bertoni's Antbird as the English name for the species.

Drymophila genei

RUFOUS-TAILED ANTBIRD   PLATE: 20

DESCRIPTION: 14 cm (5½"). *Higher mts.* of se. Brazil. Male has crown and sides of head black, a long white superciliary, and lower cheeks grizzled white; above otherwise olive brown, back marked with black and with usually concealed white dorsal patch, *becoming rufous on rump and entire tail;* wing-coverts blackish with 2 white-spotted wing-bars, *flight feathers mainly rufous.* Below mainly whitish, throat faintly streaked black and *feathers of breast with black centers giving a scaly look,* becoming olive brown on flanks and crissum. Female mostly olivaceous brown above, crown and neck streaked with black and with buffy whitish superciliary; *rump, wings, and tail as in male.* Below buffy whitish, *almost unmarked* (only a few fine black streaks on breast, these perhaps mostly on immatures).

SIMILAR SPECIES: The only *Drymophila* antbird with a rufous tail. Ochre-rumped Antbird occurs at lower elevations, and both sexes differ in being prominently streaked below and in having white-tipped dusky-olive tail.

HABITAT AND BEHAVIOR: Common in bamboo-dominated lower growth of montane forest and secondary woodland. Usually in pairs, often with flocks of other small understory birds, hopping about in undergrowth where sometimes hard to see without tape playback. Its song is a distinctive nasal, almost snarling, "pi-jzzz-jzzz-jzzz-jzzz-jzzz," without the descending effect of Bertoni's Antbird's (the 2 species are frequently found together at upper levels of Itatiaia Nat. Park).

RANGE: Higher mts. of se. Brazil (s. Espírito Santo, se. Minas Gerais, Rio de Janeiro, and ne. São Paulo). Mostly 1200–2200 m.

Drymophila ochropyga

OCHRE-RUMPED ANTBIRD

DESCRIPTION: 13.5 cm (5¼″). Se. Brazil. Male patterned much like male Rufous-tailed Antbird above, but back much grayer with no (or much smaller) dorsal patch, wings blackish *with no rufous, ochraceous rump brighter and paler* (thus more prominent than the rufous of Rufous-tailed's), and *tail blackish with feathers tipped white.* Throat and breast white *boldly streaked black; flanks and crissum rufous.* Female much like male but crown streaked blackish and buffy whitish, back not so gray, rump as in male, and more buffy whitish below (not so pure white but *distinctly streaked on throat and breast*).

SIMILAR SPECIES: Dusky-tailed Antbird lacks this species' bold superciliary and rufous on rump and flanks. Rufous-tailed Antbird has rufous tail and a more scaly look below.

HABITAT AND BEHAVIOR: Uncommon to locally fairly common in bamboo-dominated understory of forest, second-growth woodland, and borders. Behavior much like other members of genus, hopping through lower growth and often shy and difficult to see without tape playback. Its song is a sharp, nasal, snarling "pur, jeeeeéu." Readily found in Serra dos Órgãos Nat. Park, and small numbers are found at lower levels of Itatiaia Nat. Park, especially along the road below the Moromba bridge.

RANGE: Se. Brazil (Espírito Santo and se. Minas Gerais south to se. São Paulo). Mostly 600–1300 m.

Drymophila malura

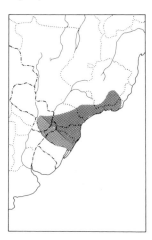

DUSKY-TAILED ANTBIRD

PLATE: 20

DESCRIPTION: 14.5 cm (5¾″). Se. Brazil area. Male has *head black streaked with pale gray,* becoming grayish olive on remaining upperparts, back with semiconcealed white dorsal patch and black feather tips; wings and *tail brownish,* wing-coverts blackish with 2 white-spotted wing-bars. *Throat and breast white streaked with black,* becoming dull olivaceous brown on flanks and crissum. Female patterned like male but more olivaceous brown generally, buffier below with dusky streaking on breast.

SIMILAR SPECIES: Both sexes of Ochre-rumped Antbird show an obvious superciliary, much rufous on flanks and rump, and have a blackish white-tipped tail. Female Rufous-tailed Antwren has rufous tail and shows less streaking on breast.

HABITAT AND BEHAVIOR: Uncommon to locally common in lower growth of humid forest, forest borders, and secondary woodland; unlike most *Drymophila, not* particularly associated with bamboo. Behavior much like other *Drymophila* antbirds'. Male's song is a series of chippered notes which descend in pitch, accelerate, and become harsher toward the end, "chew, chew, chee-chee-chi-chi-ch-ch-chchchch"; sometimes female chimes in with a similar but briefer and weaker song. Perhaps more numerous in Rio Grande do Sul than elsewhere in its range (through much of which it seems to have declined).

RANGE: Se. Brazil (s. Minas Gerais south to n. Rio Grande do Sul), se. Paraguay (west to Paraguarí), and ne. Argentina (Misiones). To 1100 m.

GROUP B   Mostly *Andes* and *Amazonia*.

Drymophila caudata

LONG-TAILED ANTBIRD   PLATE: 20

DESCRIPTION: 15 cm (6″). *Mts. from Venezuela to w. Bolivia*. Male has *head and back black streaked with white,* becoming *rufous-chestnut on rump;* wing-coverts black with 2 white-spotted wing-bars, flight feathers dusky edged rufous; *long tail* dusky olive, feathers broadly white-tipped. *Throat and breast white with fine black streaking,* becoming *bright rufous on flanks and crissum.* Female has similar pattern, but *upperparts streaked cinnamon-buff and black* and all of underparts buff-tinged. *Klagesi* (Venezuela) similar but with streaking below somewhat finer and more restricted to sides (see V-21).
SIMILAR SPECIES: This attractive antbird is the only *Drymophila* in its Andean range. Cf. similarly patterned Striated and Warbling Antbirds, both found mainly in Amaz. lowlands.
HABITAT AND BEHAVIOR: Uncommon to locally fairly common in lower growth of montane forest borders, around treefalls and landslides, and in second-growth woodland; in many areas its presence seems tied to the existence of dense stands of bamboo, where always most numerous. Usually in pairs, most often not with mixed flocks; often shy and difficult to locate, especially until its distinctive voice is known. Male's song, very different from most other Andean bird songs, has the raspy quality typical of its congeners and is a quite frequently uttered "chit-chit, wheezh, wheezh." Sometimes the female chimes in with a few "chit"s.
RANGE: Mts. of n. Venezuela (east to Paria Peninsula), and Andes of w. Venezuela, Colombia (north in W. and Cen. Andes to Antioquia), Ecuador (south on w. slope to e. Guayas), e. Peru, and w. Bolivia (La Paz); Sierra de Perijá on Venezuela-Colombia border, and Santa Marta Mts. of n. Colombia. 1200–2700 m.

Drymophila devillei

STRIATED ANTBIRD

DESCRIPTION: 13.5–14 cm (5¼–5½″). *Local in bamboo patches of w. and s. Amazonia.* Resembles larger and somewhat longer-tailed Long-tailed Antbird. Both sexes show *sparser black streaking below* (only on sides of chest), less extensive and less rich rufous on lower underparts, brighter rufous (more ochraceous) on rump, and *large white spots on middle tail feathers* (visible from above). Both sexes of *subochracea* (cen. Amaz. Brazil and ne. Bolivia) have underparts more uniformly buff, deepest on breast and flanks.
SIMILAR SPECIES: Not known to occur with any other *Drymophila* antbird, although it might overlap with Long-tailed Antbird along e. base of Andes. The chunkier and much shorter-tailed Warbling Antbird is often sympatric and has a similar overall pattern, but (regardless of subspecies) its tail feathers are never white-tipped, its rump is not bright rufous, and it is less boldly and evenly streaked on upperparts; also, their voices differ characteristically.
HABITAT AND BEHAVIOR: Locally uncommon to fairly common in

stands of *Guadua* bamboo, its presence in an area being strictly tied to the existence of bamboo, and absent from the wide areas where bamboo is scarce or nonexistent. Usually in pairs (less often small family groups) which hop about through the understory, gleaning mainly from foliage, uttering soft "chit" contact notes. Male's often-heard song is a series of 4 or 5 wheezy "dzzrrip" notes ending with a slightly more musical trill; often female echoes with a softer and shorter version. Readily found at Tambopata Reserve in Madre de Dios, Peru.

RANGE: Locally in extreme s. Colombia (w. Putumayo) and ne. Ecuador (a few specimens from w. Napo; no recent reports); se. Peru (north to Pasco and s. Ucayali), n. Bolivia (south to La Paz and Cochabamba, and in ne. Santa Cruz on the Serranía de Huanchaca), and s. Amaz. Brazil (east to the upper Rio Xingu drainage, and south to s. Mato Grosso). Published records from ne. Peru in n. Loreto (Pebas; mouth of Río Curaray) are either in error (Pebas, *fide Birds of the Americas,* vol. 13, part 3) or are believed by us likely to have been mislabeled (Curary). To 1050 m (in s. Peru).

NOTE: For more behavioral details, see Parker (1982).

Formicivora Antwrens

A small genus of attractively patterned antwrens found in light woodland and scrubby areas (not in tall forest), most species in s. South America; they tend to occur in habitats where few other antbirds are found. Males of most species have a distinctive pattern featuring a stripe of white separating the black of the underparts from the upperparts, which are some shade of brown; the two exceptions are the Narrow-billed and Black-hooded (both endemic to e. Brazil), in which this pattern is either absent (Narrow-billed) or reduced to the flanks (Black-hooded). Females are often more distinctive than their respective mates. Nests are open cups placed in a fork within a few meters of the ground. One species, *F. erythronotos* (Black-hooded Antwren), has only recently been transferred back into this genus; it had long been classified as a *Myrmotherula* antwren, and the paper in which it is concluded that it is a *Formicivora* appeared after both of our plates had been completed, hence its incorrect placement (Plate 19 and p. 279).

GROUP A

Aberrant: slaty with "white fringe" *restricted to flanks.*

Formicivora iheringi

NARROW-BILLED ANTWREN

PLATE: 20

DESCRIPTION: 11.5 cm (4½"). *Local in interior e. Brazil.* Both sexes closely resemble respective sexes of White-flanked Antwren (*Myrmotherula*) but have a *much longer tail* (also wider) and indeed a narrower bill. Uniform dark gray above; wings blackish with 2 white wing-bars, *tail rather long,* outer feathers narrowly white-tipped. *Throat and midbreast black,* becoming gray on sides; *flanks white* (sometimes hidden

by wings). Female's plumage closely resembles female White-flanked Antwren's, but uppertail-coverts more rufescent and underparts more uniformly ochraceous (showing little white on flanks).

SIMILAR SPECIES: Cf. White-flanked Antwren, especially its *luctuosa* race of coastal e. Brazil. Narrow-billed and White-flanked, so uncannily similar in plumage (though differing structurally), appear not to occur together.

HABITAT AND BEHAVIOR: Locally fairly common in deciduous forest and woodland (sometimes even where quite patchy). Arboreal, foraging singly or in pairs, sometimes with flocks, gleaning in foliage and along limbs (sometimes peering underneath them like a *Tangara* tanager), generally some 3–8 m above ground. Often pumps its tail while feeding, raising it slowly, then dropping it rapidly. Male's song is a distinctive, quite musical series of 7–12 "peer" notes delivered at a rate of about 2 per second; female often follows with a softer, shorter version. A descending chipper is sometimes given as a contact note or in alarm. Substantial deforestation has taken place across much of this species' small range, such that though it remains numerous where habitat remains, the Narrow-billed Antwren must be regarded as a threatened species; none of its habitat presently receives protection. Can be seen in woods above Boa Nova and south of Jequié.

RANGE: Interior e. Brazil (cen. Bahia to ne. Minas Gerais). 500–900 m.

GROUP B

Typical *Formicivora*.

Formicivora grisea

WHITE-FRINGED ANTWREN

PLATE: 20

DESCRIPTION: 12–12.5 cm (4¾–5″). The most widespread *Formicivora*. Male *grayish brown above* (more rufescent in *orenocensis* of s. Venezuela from n. Amazonas through Bolívar to s. Monagas) with *white superciliary;* wings blackish with a bold white wing-bar and extensive spotting on coverts; tail blackish, feathers broadly tipped white. *Below mostly black, broadly outlined with white on sides and flanks* (extending back from superciliary). Female above much like male but with grayish cheeks. *Below uniform cinnamon-buff* (deepest in *rufiventris* of sw. Venezuela and adjacent Colombia), whiter on throat. Foregoing description of female applies to nominate group (with *deluzae*) of Guianas to e. Brazil. Female *hondae* (Colombia west of Andes except Santa Marta/Guajira area) similar but paler creamy buff below. Females of *intermedia* group (with *fumosa, orenocensis,* and *tobagensis;* n. Colombia in Santa Marta region and ne. Colombia east through much of Venezuela to Tobago) *white below with dusky or black streaking across breast* (see V-21), most extensive in *orenocensis.*

SIMILAR SPECIES: Male *Formicivora* antwrens, of which White-fringed is typical and generally the most numerous, are readily recognized by the white outline (or "fringe") to their black underparts. Cf. male Rusty-backed and Black-bellied Antwrens, whose patterns are similar. Females vary geographically, but in area of overlap with Rusty-backed and Black-bellied they are cinnamon-buff below (Rusty-backed boldly streaked below, Black-bellied whitish below).

HABITAT AND BEHAVIOR: Fairly common to common in low shrubby woodland, gallery woodland, dense thickets in dry scrub, mangroves (at least in the Guianas), and (especially in Amazonia) young second-growth. Usually in pairs, moving methodically through lower growth, gleaning in foliage, often swiveling the partially fanned tail from side to side. Quite tame but sometimes difficult to see because of the usually dense nature of its habitat. Birds from w. Venezuela (*intermedia*) give a mellow "tu" often repeated in a series of 3 or more notes, sometimes followed by a soft descending trill of similar quality. In Guianas and e. Brazil (nominate group) we have heard only a much sharper, more penetrating "chup-chup-chup-chup . . ." (up to 20 or more times), sometimes lengthened into an equally incisive "chedep-chedep-chedep."

RANGE: N. and ne. Colombia (n. Antioquia and Córdoba eastward, and south in Río Magdalena valley to Huila; east of Andes from Meta to Vaupés and northward), Venezuela, Guianas (coastal areas), Amaz. and e. Brazil (north of the Amazon only in Amapá; south of it west locally to the Rio Madeira and south to s. Mato Grosso and Goiás; in the east from Rio Grande do Norte south to Rio de Janeiro), and ne. Bolivia (extreme e. Beni and ne. Santa Cruz); Margarita Is. off Venezuela, Chachacare Is. off Trinidad, and Tobago. Also Panama (Pearl Is.). Mostly below 1000 m (recorded to 1500 m in Venezuela).

NOTE: More than one species could be involved. Females show dramatic geographic plumage variation (uniform buff below vs. white below with breast streaking), and the substantial difference in primary vocalizations of males is apparently associated with the two "types" of females. More work is needed.

Formicivora rufa

RUSTY-BACKED ANTWREN

PLATE: 20

DESCRIPTION: 12.5 cm (5"). Mainly *interior s.-cen. South America*. Male *rufous brown above;* wings blacker with 2 dotted wing-bars; tail dusky brown, feathers broadly tipped white. *Throat, breast, and middle of belly black broadly margined with white,* becoming *buff on flanks* and white on center of lower belly. Female above like male; *below white conspicuously streaked with black on throat and breast,* becoming buff on flanks and white on center of lower belly.

SIMILAR SPECIES: In area of overlap, male White-fringed Antwren has less rufescent upperparts and its white "fringe" extends down over flanks (flanks buff in male Rusty-backed), whereas female White-fringed has uniform buff underparts (with *no* streaking). Cf. also Black-bellied Antwren.

HABITAT AND BEHAVIOR: Uncommon to locally fairly common in thickets and low shrubby areas, gallery woodland, and shrubby ce-rrado. Favors more sparsely vegetated areas than White-fringed or Black-bellied Antwrens; sometimes near water. Behavior similar, though less likely to be with small flocks of birds. The song is a fast, gravelly "chedede, chedede, chedede . . . ," repeated rapidly up to 12–15 times; also gives a long, run-together "chchchchchchchchchch." Locally numerous in the pantanal of w. Mato Grosso do Sul, Brazil.

RANGE: S. Surinam (Sipaliwini Savanna) and locally in Amaz. Brazil (Amapá west to the lower Rio Tapajós area around Santarém, and at Humaitá on the Rio Madeira); e. and cen. Brazil (Maranhão and Piauí south to Minas Gerais, São Paulo, and Mato Grosso do Sul; has also recently spread locally into deforested parts of coastal southeast, e.g., into n. Espírito Santo [*fide* D. Stotz]), e. Paraguay (south locally and in small numbers to near Asunción), and n. and e. Bolivia (Santa Cruz west to Beni and La Paz); very locally in valleys on e. slope of Andes in Peru (San Martín and Cuzco). To 1450 m (in Peru).

Formicivora melanogaster

BLACK-BELLIED ANTWREN

PLATE: 20

DESCRIPTION: 12.5 cm (5″). Mainly *e. and interior s. Brazil.* Both sexes resemble slightly smaller and shorter-tailed White-fringed Antwren. Male Black-bellied is somewhat darker above, has a *broader white superciliary,* shows *less white on flanks* (more intermixed with gray, and often hidden under wings) and has white edging on inner secondaries (absent in White-fringed). Female differs more strikingly, showing a *broader white superciliary, distinctly blackish cheeks,* and uniform *whitish underparts* (at most tinged with cinnamon-buff).

SIMILAR SPECIES: Cf. also Serra Antwren.

HABITAT AND BEHAVIOR: Uncommon in lower growth of woodland and dense scrub. Behavior seems similar to other *Formicivora* antwrens'; its voice is not known to us. Can be seen in the woodland patches south of Jequié and above Boa Nova in se. Bahia, Brazil.

RANGE: E. and s.-cen. Brazil (Maranhão and Ceará south to se. Bahia and São Paulo, thence westward through Mato Grosso do Sul and s. Mato Grosso), e. Bolivia (Santa Cruz south to Tarija), and extreme n. Paraguay (near Cerro León in Chaco, where seen and photographed [VIREO] in June–July 1990; A. Madroño et al.). Mostly 500–1000 m.

Formicivora serrana

SERRA ANTWREN

DESCRIPTION: 12.5 cm (5″). *Limited area in se. Brazil.* Male resembles male Black-bellied Antwren but differs in its *much richer, more rufescent crown and back* (not dark grayish brown), *rufescent tertial edging* (not white), and slightly grayer flanks (with even less white than shown by Black-bellied). Foregoing applies to nominate race of e.-cen. Minas Gerais and Espírito Santo. *Interposita* (of n. Rio de Janeiro and adjacent s. Minas Gerais) is much darker (less rufescent) brown above and has less prominent white superciliary and reduced white on wing-coverts. Female Serra Antwren (which does not vary geographically) is very similar to female Black-bellied, differing only in being somewhat buffier (not so whitish) below.

SIMILAR SPECIES: Male White-fringed Antwren is grayish brown above and shows prominent white flanks; female lacks the blackish cheeks and is deeper buff below. Male Rusty-backed Antwren has buff flanks and white midbelly; female has throat and breast black-streaked (female Serra is *un*streaked below). Cf. also Black-hooded Antwren (now considered a *Formicivora* antwren, though long placed in the genus *Myrmotherula* [Plate 19 and p. 279]).

HABITAT AND BEHAVIOR: Uncommon to locally fairly common in dry scrub, shrubby areas, and low secondary woodland. Behavior similar to other typical *Formicivora* antwrens', as is its voice, a series of rapidly delivered soft notes, "ch-ch-ch-ch-ch-ch-ch-ch-ch."

RANGE: Se. Brazil (s. Espírito Santo, s. Minas Gerais, and n. Rio de Janeiro). To 1000 m.

NOTE: See comments under Restinga Antwren. The subspecies *interposita* was recently described by L. P. Gonzaga and J. F. Pacheco (*Bull. B. O. C.* 110[4]: 187–193, 1990). It has been suggested that *F. serrana* might be conspecific with *F. melanogaster* (e.g., Meyer de Schauensee 1966), though actual intergradation has never been recorded. We suspect that Meyer de Schauensee's calling (1966, 1970) this species the Serra Antbird, when all other members of the genus *Formicivora* are called antwrens, was merely a *lapsus calami*.

Formicivora littoralis

RESTINGA ANTWREN

DESCRIPTION: 12.5 cm (5″). *Se. Brazil on coast of Rio de Janeiro.* Resembles Serra Antwren (and described as only a race of that species; see below). Male differs in being dark brown above (less rufescent than Serra), *lacking the white superciliary* and also *lacking white spots on wing-coverts,* and in having much narrower white tips to tail feathers. Female resembles female Serra Antwren.

SIMILAR SPECIES: Cf. also White-fringed Antwren.

HABITAT AND BEHAVIOR: Locally fairly common in restinga scrub on or very near coast. Behavior similar to that of other *Formicivora* antwrens'; we do not know Restinga's voice. The species is considered seriously at risk because much of its extremely limited range is threatened by development for seaside homes (L. P. Gonzaga and J. F. Pacheco).

RANGE: Se. Brazil in coastal cen. Rio de Janeiro. Near sea level.

NOTE: A recently described species: L. P. Gonzaga and J. F. Pacheco, *Bull. B. O. C.* 110(4): 187–193, 1990. These authors described *littoralis* as only a subspecies of *F. serrana* but suggested that it might be worthy of specific rank. We follow Collar et al. (1992) in considering it a separate species, based on the taxon's clear morphological differences from *F. serrana* and its distinctly different (and highly restricted) habitat.

Myrmorchilus Antbirds

An attractive, scrub-inhabiting antbird found in two distinct arid regions of South America, the chaco and caatinga. The relationships of the genus have been debated; Remsen et al. (1986) suggest that it may be closest to *Formicivora* and *Drymophila*, though we note that *Myrmorchilus* is much more terrestrial than either. Its nest is an open cup composed mainly of grasses and hidden on the ground (S. M. Caziani and J. J. Protomastro, *Condor* 93[2]: 445–446, 1991).

Myrmorchilus strigilatus

STRIPE-BACKED ANTBIRD

PLATE: 20

DESCRIPTION: 16 cm (6¼"). *An essentially terrestrial antbird of the chaco and caatinga.* Male *boldly streaked rufous and black above* with a narrow white superciliary (pale buff in *suspicax* of chaco region); wing-coverts black with bold white spotting and tipping; central tail feathers rufous, lateral ones broadly tipped black and edged with white. *Throat and chest black,* contrasting sharply with white lower face and sides of neck; lower underparts whitish, tinged buff on flanks and lower belly. Female above similar to male but superciliary more buffyish; below entirely buffy whitish (no black), *streaked with dusky across breast* (especially on sides).

SIMILAR SPECIES: Readily recognized in its range and habitat (where there are few other antbirds) by its terrestrial behavior and prominent streaking above. Cf. various *Formicivora* antwrens (especially Rusty-backed, in which both sexes have similar pattern but are *unstreaked above*); no *Formicivora* is nearly so terrestrial.

HABITAT AND BEHAVIOR: Locally fairly common to common in chaco and caatinga woodland and scrub. Usually found singly or in pairs, hopping on or near the ground in dense undergrowth where often difficult to see well; generally found independently of mixed flocks. Male's song is a loud, wheezy "cheem, cheery-gweér" or "chree, chree-cho-weé" with distinctive cadence; sometimes it is followed by female's "pur, cheer-cheer-chur-chur-chr-chr." A repeated "pee-yeér" is also given, apparently by either sex. Readily found (at least by voice) at various points in its notably disjunct range, e.g., in se. Bahia, Brazil, between Feira de Santana and Boa Nova, and in w. Paraguay around Filadelfia.

RANGE: Se. Bolivia (Santa Cruz south to Tarija), extreme sw. Brazil (w. Mato Grosso do Sul), w. Paraguay (mainly west of the Río Paraguay, east of it only in Concepción), and n. Argentina (Salta east through Formosa and Chaco, and south to n. Santa Fe); interior ne. Brazil (Piauí, Ceará, and Pernambuco south through Bahia to extreme n. Minas Gerais). To 1100 m.

NOTE: For more details on distribution and behavior, see Remsen et al. (1986).

Cercomacra Antbirds

Midsized and rather slim antbirds with slender bills and quite long, graduated tails. *Cercomacra* antbirds are found in lower growth of forest (primarily at edge) and woodland in tropical lowlands, especially in Amazonia but with a series of species (in our Group C) found only around its periphery. Both sexes are simply patterned, males black or gray, usually with white spotting or fringing on wing-coverts, females with underparts some shade of ochraceous to rufous, or gray below with white streaking or mottling at least on throat. All *Cercomacra* species are rather inconspicuous and are most often found by tracking down their distinctive vocalizations.

GROUP A

Canopy vine tangle habitat unique in genus; note *bold white tail-tips.*

Cercomacra cinerascens

GRAY ANTBIRD

PLATE: 21

DESCRIPTION: 16 cm (6"). Male *uniform gray* (slightly paler below); usually concealed dorsal patch white (sometimes small or lacking); tail feathers with *broad* white tipping. Female olive brown above, grayer on rump and tail; *below mostly dull ochraceous,* dingier and more olivaceous on belly; tail feathers broadly tipped white. Both sexes from north of the Amazon (nominate group) have wing-spotting on wing-coverts vestigial or absent (*essentially invisible in the field*), whereas those from south of it (*sclateri* group) have fairly prominent white wing-covert spotting.
SIMILAR SPECIES: This species forages *higher* than other *Cercomacra* antbirds (*not* in undergrowth). In plumage, male Gray closely resembles male Dusky Antbird, though the latter species is proportionately shorter-tailed and has much narrower white tail-tipping. Spot-winged Antshrike, often found with Gray Antbird, is much shorter-tailed and heavier-billed, etc.
HABITAT AND BEHAVIOR: Fairly common to common (though generally overlooked until its often-heard song is known) in canopy and middle levels of terra firme forest and taller second-growth woodland, especially around treefalls and at borders. Usually in pairs, difficult to see as they creep about within viny tangles and dense vegetation, only rarely emerging into the open. Gray Antbirds sometimes accompany mixed flocks but more often are found apart from them. Male's frequently given and distinctive song is a gravelly "ch-kr, ch-kr, ch-kr, ch-kr, ch-kr" (can also be transcribed as "cruk-shank, cruk-shank . . .").
RANGE: Guianas, s. Venezuela (Bolívar and Amazonas), e. Colombia (north to Meta and Guianía), e. Ecuador, e. Peru, n. Bolivia (south to La Paz and n. Santa Cruz), and Amaz. Brazil (east to Amapá and n. Maranhão, and south to s. Mato Grosso and se. Pará). Mostly below 700 m (recorded to 1150 m in s. Peru).

GROUP B

Males *gray to dark slaty,* females *bright ochraceous to rufous below; no* tail-tipping (or at most faintly fringed).

Cercomacra brasiliana

RIO DE JANEIRO ANTBIRD

PLATE: 21

DESCRIPTION: 14.5 cm (5½"). *Se. Brazil.* Male *uniform gray,* somewhat paler and duller below; rather large white semiconcealed dorsal patch; wing-coverts darker and *fringed* with white, tail feathers *narrowly* tipped with white. Female olive brown above with white dorsal patch smaller than male's; *below quite bright ochraceous tawny,* duller and more olivaceous on lower belly; wing-coverts very narrowly fringed buff, tail feathers very narrowly tipped buff (both *essentially invisible* in the field).

Cercomacra tyrannina

SIMILAR SPECIES: The only *Cercomacra* antbird in its limited range. Cf. Eastern Slaty- and Variable Antshrikes (both differently shaped and with much more prominent wing and tail markings).

HABITAT AND BEHAVIOR: Apparently rare and local in undergrowth of humid forest borders, secondary woodland, and caatinga scrub. Poorly known, perhaps threatened by habitat loss in its small range, though Sick (1985) believed it adapted well to secondary habitats. Its apparent song is a bizarre, ringing "prkárnk" note repeated 4–6 times (D. W. Finch recording).

RANGE: Se. Brazil in s. Bahia, e. Minas Gerais (Muriaé and Felisburgo), Rio de Janeiro, and (apparently) Espírito Santo; probably also in adjacent ne. São Paulo. To 1000 m.

NOTE: Although it has long been considered allied to *C. cinerascens* (e.g., in *Birds of the Americas*, vol. 13, part 3), we believe *C. brasiliana* is more closely related to *C. tyrannina*, and indeed that it replaces the latter in se. Brazil. The wing and tail patterns of *C. brasiliana* are closer to *C. tyrannina* than they are to *C. cinerascens*, as is the color of the female *C. brasiliana*'s underparts. We are not familiar with *C. brasiliana*'s song, but its behavior, as described by Sick (1985), also appears to be more like that of *C. tyrannina* than of *C. cinerascens*.

DUSKY ANTBIRD

DESCRIPTION: 14.5 cm (5½"). N. South America south locally to ne. Brazil. Both sexes so closely resemble Rio de Janeiro Antbird (though Dusky's tail is shorter) that they would be indistinguishable in the field were they to occur together. See V-22, C-29. Female *laeta* of lower Amaz. Brazil has cheeks grayish like upperparts (rather than buffyish like underparts). Female *sabinoi* of coastal ne. Brazil differs (*fide* the type description) from females of other races (and from female Rio de Janeiro Antbird) in being generally paler, especially below (where buffy rather than rich ochraceous tawny).

SIMILAR SPECIES: Male Blackish Antbird (limited overlap in cen. Amaz. Brazil) is very similar to male Dusky, differing only in being slightly darker generally and in lacking Dusky's pale wash on midbelly and its narrow white tail-tipping. Female Blackish is markedly brighter orange-rufous below and on forehead than female Dusky (not merely an ochraceous tawny) and is browner (not so olivaceous) above.

HABITAT AND BEHAVIOR: Fairly common to common in undergrowth of forest borders, second-growth woodland, and shrubby clearings; *laeta* of lower Amaz. Brazil (likely a distinct species, see below) favors thickets at edges of streams (*fide* R. Bierregaard); the perhaps endangered form *sabinoi* of coastal ne. Brazil is much less numerous (*fide* D. Teixera). Usually in pairs, generally remaining hidden in thick lower growth, though often not really shy and can at times be observed closely. Usually not with mixed flocks. Male's distinctive and often-heard song, in most of the species' range, is a series of whistled notes, the first 2 given rather slowly, the remaining ones more rapidly and usually rising sharply in pitch, e.g., "pü, pü, pí-pipipi?"; often female chimes in with a softer, shorter version of her own as male's song is ending. Song of *laeta* is very different, a loud and musical "pur, peéter, peéter, peéter."

RANGE: N. and w. Colombia (Pacific lowlands and humid Caribbean lowlands east to the middle Río Magdalena valley in w. Cundina-marca) and w. Ecuador (south, at least formerly, to El Oro; in recent years not south of Guayas); e. Colombia (south to w. Caquetá and e. Vaupés), w. and s. Venezuela (Maracaibo basin, north along base of Andes to n. Barinas, and widely south of the Orinoco), Guianas, and n. Amaz. Brazil (south to the Rio Negro and the Amazon; west of the Rio Negro only in the Manacupuru region; south of the Amazon in e. Pará in the Belém area and n. Maranhão); ne. Brazil (locally in Pernambuco and Alagoas). Also Mexico to Panama. Mainly below 1000 m (in smaller numbers up to 1800 m or even higher).

NOTE: Apparently more than one species is involved. Recent work by R. Bier-regaard, M. Cohn-Haft, and others in the Manaus area has revealed that the taxon *laeta* has an entirely different voice from *M. tyrannina* elsewhere in its range (see above). *Laeta* ranges from the Manaus area (Balbina) east locally to around Belém in e. Pará and in n. Maranhão, and around Manaus it occurs syntopically with *C. tyrannina* (the race *saturatior*). If split, *C. laeta* might best be called simply the Laeta Antbird. The voice of the disjunct *sabinoi* form remains unknown, at least to us; it too could represent a distinct species, or it may be allied to *laeta*.

Cercomacra nigrescens

BLACKISH ANTBIRD   PLATE: 21

DESCRIPTION: 15 cm (6″). Male *mostly slaty gray* with rather large semi-concealed white dorsal patch; bend of wing white, and with small white spots or fringes on blackish wing-coverts. Nominate race of Guianas blacker above than subspecies elsewhere. Female mostly olive to rather rufescent brown above with semiconcealed white dorsal patch. *Forehead, sides of head, and entire underparts deep orange-rufous*, more olive brownish on lower flanks.

SIMILAR SPECIES: *Closely* resembles both Dusky and Black Antbirds. Male Black is blacker below (not slaty gray); female Black differs from female Blackish only in being slightly grayer above (not so brownish), especially on crown, with less rufous on forehead. Dusky Antbird male is about the same overall color as male Blackish but has some white fringing on tail feathers (never shown by male Blackish, but not very conspicuous in Dusky either); female Dusky is much less richly colored below and on face than female Blackish.

HABITAT AND BEHAVIOR: Fairly common in undergrowth of humid forest borders, secondary woodland, and shrubby regenerating clearings. Behavior much like Dusky Antbird's, also heard much more often than seen. Male's most common vocalization is a distinctive "wor, chíh-chih-ch-ch-ch-ch," sometimes followed by its mate's clearly enunciated rising series of 4 or 5 notes, "pur, pu-puh-peh-pih-pi?" The overall effect is strongly reminiscent of Dusky Antbird (not distinctly rising as in Black Antbird, and notes more slurred together). Also gives a "wor-chík," a low nasal "chaw," and a vaguely thrush-like "jee-jee-jee-jee-jut."

RANGE: Extreme se. Colombia (e. Nariño, and around Leticia in Amazonas), e. Ecuador, e. Peru, n. Bolivia (south to La Paz, Cochabamba, and n. Santa Cruz), and Amaz. Brazil (mainly south of the Amazon east to extreme n. Goiás and se. Pará, and south to cen. Mato Grosso;

north of the Amazon locally along its n. bank); Surinam and French Guiana. To 1600 m (occasionally up to 2000 m).

Cercomacra serva

BLACK ANTBIRD

DESCRIPTION: 15 cm (6"). *W. Amazonia. Closely* resembles Blackish Antbird and sometimes found with it. Male differs in being *considerably blacker below* (not uniform slaty gray), the black extending down at least to the median breast. See C-29. Female differs in being somewhat grayer above (not so brownish), especially on crown, and in having less rufous on forehead. However, the 2 species (especially females) so closely resemble each other that, unless singing, they are often not distinguishable in the field.

HABITAT AND BEHAVIOR: Uncommon to fairly common in dense undergrowth at borders of humid forest and secondary woodland (both terra firme and várzea), also regularly at treefalls inside forest. Usually in pairs, foraging separately from mixed flocks. Male's song is a series of loud, distinctly *rising* notes, quite deliberately given (speeding up a bit toward end), "wor, chur, cheh-cheh-che-che-chi-chi-chi?"; sometimes its mate chimes in with a shorter, softer version.

RANGE: Extreme se. Colombia (north to w. Caquetá), e. Ecuador, e. Peru, n. Bolivia (south to n. La Paz), and w. Amaz. Brazil (east to Rio Juruá). To at least 1100 m.

GROUP C

Black males much alike; females *blackish to ashy gray below,* most with *whitish streaking/mottling* on throat. Tail *boldly white-tipped.* Most species *range-restricted; all allopatric.*

Cercomacra nigricans

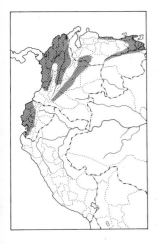

JET ANTBIRD   PLATE: 21

DESCRIPTION: 15 cm (6"). *Venezuela to w. Ecuador.* Male *deep black* with large but semiconcealed white dorsal patch; bend of wing and *prominent wing-bars white; tail feathers broadly tipped white.* See P-21. Female *mostly dark slaty, throat and breast with fine white streaking;* wings and tail as in male. What appear to be immatures are more boldly streaked and scaled with white below, in some birds this extending down to midbelly.

SIMILAR SPECIES: Male Dusky Antbird is much grayer (not black) and shows much less white on wings and tail; female Dusky is very different (ochraceous below, etc.).

HABITAT AND BEHAVIOR: Uncommon to locally common in tangled, often viny undergrowth of secondary woodland, forest borders (humid and, especially, deciduous), and dense shrubby clearings. Usually in pairs, foraging independently of mixed flocks; skulking, and infrequently seen unless vocalizing. Song of male is often heard and easily recognized (though it resembles Gray Antbird's; note that the 2 species are never sympatric), being a fairly loud, measured series of harsh "tchker" notes (usually 4 or 5 of them, occasionally more). Numerous along the entrance road into Tayrona Nat. Park in n. Colombia and around the Laguna de Sonso near Cali.

RANGE: W. and n. Colombia (Pacific lowlands in s. Chocó and Valle, Caribbean lowlands south in Río Cauca valley to Valle and in Río Magdalena valley to e. Tolima, and along e. base of Andes south to w. Caquetá) and extreme w. Venezuela (s. Táchira and w. Apure); w. Ecuador (w. Esmeraldas south locally to El Oro); ne. Venezuela (Aragua east to Paria Peninsula, thence south to Delta Amacuro and upriver along the Orinoco to e. Apure). The record from Caracarahí in Roraima, extreme n. Brazil (*Birds of the World*, vol. 7; Meyer de Schauensee 1966, 1970) is in error for *C. carbonaria*, whereas that for Balta in s. Ucayali, Peru (O'Neill 1974), refers to *C. manu* (J. W. Fitzpatrick and D. E. Willard, *Auk* 107[2]: 239–245, 1990). Also Panama. Mostly below 500 m, but recorded to 1500 m in Colombia.

Cercomacra ferdinandi

BANANAL ANTBIRD

DESCRIPTION: 16 cm (6¼"). *Found only on and near Bananal Is. in cen. Brazil.* Male *closely* resembles male of slightly smaller Jet Antbird (no overlap) and would not be distinguishable in the field. Female gray above; *below gray with fine white streaking on throat and breast.*

SIMILAR SPECIES: Nothing really similar in its limited range. Female Mato Grosso Antbird (no overlap) is *un*streaked below.

HABITAT AND BEHAVIOR: Uncommon in lower growth of deciduous and gallery woodland and in riparian thickets; almost always near water, often in seasonally flooded areas. Generally in pairs, foraging mostly between 3 and 6 m above ground, frequently more in the open (and thus easier to see) than other *Cercomacra* antbirds. Sometimes accompanies small flocks including Glossy Antshrikes, Band-tailed Antbirds, and Rusty-backed Spinetails. Calls include a nasal, repeated "cawh!," sometimes in series and regularly accelerated into a jumbled "caw-cuh-didi-cuhdidi-cuhdidi-cúh-chuk-chuk," with many variations though apparently never with the regular cadence of Jet Antbird's song.

RANGE: Cen. Brazil (n. Goiás on Bananal Is. and north to Araguatins, and in adjacent ne. Mato Grosso near the Rio Araguaia). 200 m.

Cercomacra melanaria

MATO GROSSO ANTBIRD

PLATE: 21

DESCRIPTION: 16.5 cm (6¼"). *N. and e. Bolivia, sw. Brazil, and extreme n. Paraguay.* Male *glossy black* with large but semiconcealed white dorsal patch; *bend of wing and prominent wing-bars white; tail feathers tipped white.* Female gray above, *uniform paler gray below* (palest on throat and midbelly but *unstreaked*); dorsal patch, wings, and tail as in male.

SIMILAR SPECIES: Does not occur with any other *Cercomacra* antbird. Female Bananal Antbird (no overlap) is unstreaked below. Cf. female of smaller Band-tailed Antbird.

HABITAT AND BEHAVIOR: Fairly common in thickets in gallery and deciduous woodland, usually near water. Almost always in pairs, generally quite vocal and fairly easy to see. Male's song is a very distinctive, guttural "ker-cheeeér-chk, ker-cheeeér-chuk, ker-cheeeér," delivered at a deliberate pace; both sexes also give a low "churk" call, sometimes in series. Readily found at various sites in the pantanal of w. Mato Grosso do Sul, Brazil.

RANGE: N. and e. Bolivia (Beni to Santa Cruz), extreme n. Paraguay (Bahía Negra in n. Alto Paraguay), and sw. Brazil (s. Mato Grosso and w. Mato Grosso do Sul). The record mentioned by Pinto (1978, p. 382) from Bananal Is. in Goiás is in error for *C. ferdinandi* (*fide* D. Stotz). Below 500 m.

Cercomacra carbonaria

RIO BRANCO ANTBIRD

DESCRIPTION: 15 cm (6"). *Limited area in Roraima, extreme n. Brazil.* Male virtually identical to male Jet Antbird (no overlap) and would not be distinguishable in the field. Female quite different, with throat white streaked with dark gray and *breast, sides, and lower belly washed with ochraceous.*

SIMILAR SPECIES: Does not occur with any other *Cercomacra* antbird.

HABITAT AND BEHAVIOR: Fairly common in dense thickets in gallery forest. Calls include a deliberate "pook-pook-pook . . ." (up to 20 notes) and a faster, syncopated "kikuk-kikuk-kikuk . . ." (also up to 20 notes); vocal mainly in early morning. Numerous in vicinity of Boa Vista. All information from D. Stotz (pers. comm.).

RANGE: Extreme n. Brazil (Roraima along the Rio Branco and lower Rio Mucujaí). Probably occurs in adjacent Guyana. About 100 m.

Cercomacra manu

MANU ANTBIRD

DESCRIPTION: 15 cm (6"). Recently described from *sw. Amazonia.* Male closely resembles male Jet Antbird (no overlap) but is more sooty black than deep black, and has narrower white tips to tail feathers (usually not noticeable in the field). Female differs more: *olivaceous brown above,* duskier on wings and tail; wing-coverts fringed with white and tail feathers tipped white. *Below uniform gray* (*un*streaked), tinged olivaceous on flanks.

SIMILAR SPECIES: The only *Cercomacra* antbird of its Group in its range; *largely confined to bamboo thickets.* Cf. Blackish and Black Antbirds (both with very different females).

HABITAT AND BEHAVIOR: Locally uncommon to fairly common in thickets of *Guadua* bamboo, locally in both transitional and riparian forest as well as in terra firme (e.g., at Alta Floresta). Usually in pairs, foraging through dense lower and middle growth where often difficult to see (in part because it is shy, in part because of habitat). Occasionally accompanies mixed flocks, but more often pairs move about alone. Its presence is most often made known by male's easily recognized harsh, guttural song with a distinctive cadence, "ker-chérrr-chik, ker-chérrr-chek, ker-cherr."

RANGE: Locally in se. Peru (Madre de Dios and adjacent s. Ucayali and e. Cuzco), nw. Bolivia (Pando and La Paz), and s. Amaz. Brazil (Alta Floresta in n. Mato Grosso). To 1200 m.

NOTE: A recently described species: J. W. Fitzpatrick and D. E. Willard, *Auk* 107(2): 239–245, 1990.

Rhopornis Antbirds

A quite large and slender antbird restricted to a small area in e. Brazil. *Rhopornis* apparently is most closely related to the *Pyriglena* fire-eyes, but it has a graduated and longer tail and male is much grayer.

Rhopornis ardesiaca

SLENDER ANTBIRD   PLATE: 21

DESCRIPTION: 19 cm (7½"). *Limited area in interior s. Bahia, Brazil.* Bright red iris in both sexes; bill rather long and slender. Male *plumbeous gray above;* wings and *rather long and graduated tail blackish,* wing-coverts narrowly but prominently fringed white. *Throat black, contrasting with gray of remaining underparts.* Female has *crown and nape russet* contrasting with gray back; wings and tail as in male. *Throat white,* becoming pale gray on remaining underparts, whitish on midbelly.

SIMILAR SPECIES: No other similar antbird occurs in its small range. Cf. White-shouldered Fire-eye (male of which is mainly black, female rufescent above).

HABITAT AND BEHAVIOR: Locally fairly common to common in lower growth of surviving patches of deciduous woodland and woodland borders, especially where there are stands of large terrestrial bromeliads. Usually in pairs, hopping on or near the ground, often disappearing into bromeliad patches but otherwise not too hard to observe and not especially shy. Male's song is a loud, far-carrying, and rather shrill "peer, peer-peer-peer-peer-peer-peer-peer-peer" with much the quality of a *Pyriglena* fire-eye; sometimes female follows with a shorter and less vigorous version. Calling birds slowly wag their long slim tails. Slender Antbird appears to be fairly numerous wherever wooded cover remains in its small range; however, woodland gradually continues to be cleared, and much of what persists was apparently once much more luxuriant and taller. The species deserves formal threatened status, in part because none of its habitat presently receives formal protection. Quite readily seen in woods above Boa Nova and south of Jequié.

RANGE: E. Brazil (locally in interior s. Bahia). 700–1000 m.

NOTE: For more details on this interesting antbird, until recently very poorly known, see E. O. Willis and Y. Oniki (*Wilson Bull.* 93[1]: 103–107, 1981) and D. M. Teixera (*Rev. Brasil. Biol.* 47[3]: 409–414, 1987).

Pyriglena Fire-eyes

A uniform genus of quite large, long-tailed antbirds with relatively short bills found in humid forest and woodland undergrowth. Probably most closely related to *Myrmeciza*. Note the extreme racial variation in female White-backed Fire-eyes; some of these forms may prove to represent separate species.

Pyriglena leucoptera

WHITE-SHOULDERED FIRE-EYE

PLATE: 21

DESCRIPTION: 18 cm (7"). *Se. Brazil area. Bright red iris.* Male *mostly glossy black* with semiconcealed white dorsal patch, *white on bend of wing, and white tipping on wing-coverts.* Female *uniform rufescent brown above* with blackish tail. Throat whitish, becoming *dingy buffy brownish on remaining underparts,* more olivaceous on flanks and dusky on crissum.

SIMILAR SPECIES: The only fire-eye in its range. Similar Fringe-backed Fire-eye occurs just to the north in coastal Bahia. In Mato Grosso do Sul, Brazil, and ne. Paraguay, White-shouldered's range approaches that of *maura* race of White-backed Fire-eye; male White-backed differs in *lacking white on wing,* whereas females are brighter ochraceous below and have a pronounced white supraloral and (lacking in female White-shouldered) a semiconcealed white dorsal patch. Female White-shouldered Fire-eye could be confused with various sympatric tanagers (e.g., female Red-crowned Ant-Tanager or female Ruby-crowned Tanager), though none of these have red eyes, and their bill shapes differ.

HABITAT AND BEHAVIOR: Fairly common to common in lower growth of humid forest, more mature second-growth woodland, and borders, often where there is bamboo but by no means restricted to it. Usually in pairs which forage independently of mixed flocks, and not often seen because of the dense nature of the species' typical habitat; sometimes small groups gather at army antswarms. Its frequently heard song is a loud, penetrating "peer-peer-peer-peer-peer-peer" with slightly descending effect. On the whole this species is quite widespread in its range for a forest-based bird.

RANGE: E. Brazil (Bahia south to n. Rio Grande do Sul, and west into s. Mato Grosso do Sul), e. Paraguay (Canendiyu south to Itapúa), and ne. Argentina (Misiones). To 1250 m.

NOTE: See comments under Fringe-backed Fire-eye.

Pyriglena atra

FRINGE-BACKED FIRE-EYE

DESCRIPTION: 17.5 cm (6¾"). *Very limited area in coastal Bahia, Brazil.* Closely resembles White-shouldered Fire-eye (no known overlap); tail slightly shorter. Male Fringe-backed differs in *lacking* white on wing, and its white dorsal patch is patterned differently: the feathers are extensively white at their base, and they have a *black subapical band* and *broad white "fringe."* The white dorsal patch (larger than in White-shouldered) is always visible, and the "fringed" pattern (sometimes quite "laddered") is usually evident. Females are so similar that they cannot be distinguished in the field.

HABITAT AND BEHAVIOR: Rare to locally uncommon in the few remaining patches of secondary woodland left in its always extremely limited range. The Fringe-backed Fire-eye has declined drastically in recent decades because of the near total removal of forest and woodland, caused mainly by local expansion of sugar cane cultivation. A few pairs survive around Santo Amaro, all on private property which remains vulnerable to forest clearance. This severely endangered bird is in dire need of a formally protected area, although we suspect it, like other fire-eyes, may be capable of persisting in quite small and degraded areas of second-growth. Behavior, including voice, very similar to White-shouldered Fire-eye's.

RANGE: E. Brazil (coastal cen. Bahia). Below 100 m.

NOTE: *Atra* is perhaps only a subspecies of *P. leucoptera;* though all recent authors have listed it as a full species, the two are certainly very closely related. We continue to regard *P. atra* and *P. leucoptera* as distinct species because no intergrades are known and because we suspect that the males' different back patterns serve as a reproductive isolating mechanism.

Pyriglena leuconota

WHITE-BACKED FIRE-EYE   PLATE: 21

DESCRIPTION: 17.5–18 cm (6¾–7″). *Iris bright red.* Male *all glossy black* with semiconcealed white dorsal patch. See C-27. Females *vary strikingly. Maura* group (s. Peru, Bolivia, and sw. Brazil; with *hellmayri* and *marcapatensis*) is rufescent brown above with semiconcealed white dorsal patch and *prominent white supraloral stripe surmounting dusky area through eyes;* tail blackish. *Throat and breast ochraceous buff,* becoming olivaceous brown on lower underparts, dusky on crissum. Nominate race (lower Amaz. Brazil from about the Rio Xingu eastward) and *pernambucensis* (ne. Brazil) are similar but lack the white supraloral. *Similis* (lower Amaz. Brazil between the lower Rio Tapajós and Rio Xingu; eastern limit uncertain) is radically different, being *mostly rich umber brown with contrasting sooty black head. Picea* is remarkably similar to *similis* given its very disjunct range (e. slope of Andes from Huánuco [also northward?] to n. Cuzco) but is slightly duller brown. *Castanoptera* (e. slope of Andes from Colombia south to Cajamarca, Peru) again differs radically, with *head and entire underparts sooty black* (with only the mantle chestnut brown); see C-27. Finally, *pacifica* (w. Ecuador and extreme nw. Peru), is also entirely different (and duller and more uniform), being *more olivaceous brown above, drab grayish buff below;* its bill is longer and tail shorter.

SIMILAR SPECIES: The only fire-eye in most of its range (range approaches White-shouldered's in sw. Brazil and n. Paraguay, and Fringe-backed's and White-shouldered's in ne. Brazil; cf. those species). Various large *Myrmeciza* antbirds (e.g., Immaculate and Sooty) are similar but have bare blue skin around eyes, and their irides are not bright red (this is particularly helpful in distinguishing the otherwise dull female *pacifica*).

HABITAT AND BEHAVIOR: Fairly common in lower growth of humid forest and mature secondary woodland, to a lesser extent also at borders, and in w. Ecuador also in more deciduous forest and woodland. General behavior similar to White-shouldered Fire-eye's. White-backed's voice is, however, somewhat different, the song being more rapidly delivered and tending to have more notes (most often 8–15), e.g., "chee-chee-chee-chee-chee-chee-chee-chee-chee-chee," usually a bit less loud toward the end. In our experience, the songs of the various forms of White-backed Fire-eye all seem similar.

RANGE: W. Ecuador (Esmeraldas south locally to El Oro and w. Loja) and extreme nw. Peru (Tumbes); e. slope of Andes in s. Colombia (north to upper Río Magdalena valley in Huila), Ecuador, Peru, and w. Bolivia (south to w. Santa Cruz), and extending east through lowlands of Santa Cruz, Bolivia, to sw. Brazil (s. Mato Grosso and w. Mato Grosso do Sul) and ne. Paraguay (Retiro Potrerito in Amambay); lower Amaz. Brazil (e. bank of the lower Rio Tapajós east to n. Maranhão); ne. Brazil (Pernambuco and Alagoas). Mostly below 600 m, but on e. slope of Andes mainly 1000–2000 m (recorded to 2700 m in Colombia).

NOTE: More than one species may be involved. In particular, the isolated form *pacifica* stands out by virtue of its longer bill, shorter tail, and very distinct female plumage; it would be called the Pacific Fire-eye.

Neoctantes Bushbirds

Found locally in upper Amazonia, this monotypic genus is characterized by its distinctive upturned lower mandible.

Neoctantes niger

BLACK BUSHBIRD   PLATE: 21

DESCRIPTION: 16 cm (6¼″). W. Amazonia. Bill mainly black above, bluish gray below, *lower mandible strongly upturned*. Male *all deep black* with large semiconcealed dorsal patch white. Female also *mainly black* (somewhat sootier than male) with *breast contrastingly chestnut,* dorsal patch as in male.

SIMILAR SPECIES: Male could be confused with other black antbirds found in Amaz. forests, though its bill is different from any except the larger Rondonia Bushbird's, which is even heavier. Black Bushbird also lacks any obvious bare skin around eye, unlike several other superficially similar antbirds. Female's pattern is unique.

HABITAT AND BEHAVIOR: Rare to locally uncommon in dense lower growth of humid forest and second-growth woodland, perhaps mostly at forest borders (or treefalls) and along watercourses. In general a scarce, infrequently recorded bird whose reclusive, skulking habits make it even harder to find. Usually found in pairs, hopping near ground; has been seen probing into fallen rotting logs (Hilty and Brown 1986). Male's rather infrequently heard song is a series of somewhat musical notes "werk-werk-werk-werk . . . ," steadily repeated for 10 seconds or more (M. Robbins); this may continue for up to several minutes without pause (Hilty and Brown 1986).

RANGE: Se. Colombia (north to Caquetá and Vaupés), e. Ecuador, e. Peru (mainly in Loreto but also recorded south locally to Madre de Dios and adjacent Cuzco), and w. Amaz. Brazil (recorded from São Paulo de Olivença, along the Rio Juruá at João Pessoa, and near w. bank of the lower Rio Tapajós). To 500 m.

Clytoctantes Bushbirds

Found disjunctly in n. Colombia and adjacent Venezuela and in s. Amaz. Brazil, the very distinct genus *Clytoctantes* is marked by its large, compressed, and strikingly upswept bill and very long, curved hindclaw.

Clytoctantes alixii

RECURVE-BILLED BUSHBIRD   PLATE: 21

DESCRIPTION: 16.5 cm (6½"). *Local in n. Colombia and adjacent Venezuela. Unique large bill laterally compressed with lower mandible very strongly upturned.* Male *mostly dark gray* with *black forehead, foreface, throat, and breast;* small semiconcealed white dorsal patch; wing-coverts with small white tips. Female *mostly rufous-chestnut,* slightly brighter on forehead, face, and underparts; wing-coverts with small buff tips; tail dusky; dorsal patch as in male. See C-27.

SIMILAR SPECIES: Essentially unmistakable in its small range.

HABITAT AND BEHAVIOR: Apparently rare in dense lower growth of humid forest borders, second-growth woodland, and shrubby overgrown clearings. Poorly known in life. M. A. Carriker, Jr. (*in* Hilty and Brown 1986) once saw it at an army antswarm. It has also been seen pecking at dead stems, then ripping them outward with sharp upward movements of the bill and peering into each gash, evidently searching for insects (Willis 1988). How it uses its very long hindclaw remains undescribed. A female has been heard giving a "ke'e'e'ew" chir vaguely like an Ocellated Antbird's (Willis 1988). The species seems likely to be threatened by forest clearance.

RANGE: N. Colombia (humid Caribbean lowlands from Córdoba and w. Antioquia east to s. Cesar and Santander, and south in Río Magdalena valley to n. Caldas) and extreme w. Venezuela (slopes of Sierra de Perijá). Although the type series was supposedly collected in Ecuador, based on what is now known of the species' range, we consider it unlikely that the birds were actually obtained there. To 1200 m.

NOTE: The correct spelling of the species name is *alixii,* not *alixi* (Sibley and Monroe 1990).

Clytoctantes atrogularis

RONDONIA BUSHBIRD

DESCRIPTION: 17 cm (6¾"). Recently described from a single female specimen from *Rondônia, Brazil.* That bird resembles female of geographically distant Recurve-billed Bushbird but is slightly larger and has a *large black bib on throat and upper chest,* plain wing-coverts (lacking small buff tips), and dark gray uppertail-coverts and crissum dark gray (not chestnut). Sight records of the male indicate it is *entirely black* (not mainly dark gray).

SIMILAR SPECIES: Male Black Bushbird is somewhat smaller with significantly less heavy (though still upturned) bill.

HABITAT AND BEHAVIOR: Rare and apparently local in lower growth of terra firme forest, especially in dense vine tangles. Very poorly

known in life. The few birds that have been seen were foraging in thick vegetation around treefalls, up to 5 m above ground. A very loud, trilled whistle given at irregular intervals, "tree-tree-tree," has been heard.

RANGE: Sw. Amaz. Brazil in Rondônia (Cachoeira Nazaré) and n. Mato Grosso (sighting from Alta Floresta). About 400 m.

NOTE: A recently described species: S. M. Lanyon, D. F. Stotz, and D. E. Willard, *Wilson Bull.* 102(4): 571–580, 1990. Virtually all the information presented above has been derived from this article. Lanyon et al. (op. cit.) question whether the Alta Floresta birds were actually this species, mainly because the song ascribed to it differed from that given in Rondônia. However, it was later determined by RSR et al. that the song ascribed to *Clytoctantes* at Alta Floresta was actually the voice of *Myrmornis torquata* (Wing-banded Antbird); a male *Clytoctantes* was actually *seen* there by a very experienced observer, T. A. Parker III.

Myrmoborus Antbirds

Four rather short-tailed and plump antbirds found in undergrowth of Amaz. forests and woodlands, for the most part segregated by habitat. In two species (Black-faced and Ash-breasted), geographic variation in female plumage is striking (particularly in Black-faced) but is much less marked in males: these are excellent examples of what has been termed "heterogynism," which seems to occur unusually often among the thamnophiline antbirds.

GROUP A

Wings *plain* (males), or only lightly dotted (females).

Myrmoborus leucophrys

WHITE-BROWED ANTBIRD   PLATE: 22

DESCRIPTION: 13.5 cm (5¼"). *Secondary habitats and forest borders.* Male has *broad snowy white superciliary extending back from forehead* (a "diadem") and black face and throat; *otherwise uniform dark bluish gray* (wing-coverts *unmarked*). Female has *broad cinnamon-buff superciliary* (richest on forehead) *contrasting with black mask;* otherwise brown above (including crown), wing-coverts tipped buff. *Below white,* sides and flanks washed with brown. Immature females have some blackish scaling or spotting on sides.

SIMILAR SPECIES: No other *Myrmoborus* has such a bold and conspicuous brow. Both sexes of Black-faced Antbird have more prominent markings on wing-coverts and weaker eyebrows. Cf. Ash-breasted Antbird (strictly limited to várzea).

HABITAT AND BEHAVIOR: Fairly common in undergrowth of humid forest borders and second-growth woodland, sometimes surprisingly young and low in stature, often along streams; seldom within extensive unbroken forest, and not in terra firme forest except in bamboo patches. Generally in pairs which forage close to the ground, often perching on slender vertical saplings; sometimes with understory flocks but at least as often moving independently. Song of male is a fast series of loud, ringing notes, "pee-pee-pee-pee-pee-pee-pee-pee-pee-pee-ee-ee-u" (usually 10–20 "pee"s, sometimes up to 30 or so, lasting 3 or 4 seconds), at first increasing in volume, fading away at end. Female gives a weaker version, and both sexes also have nasal calls, e.g., a slowly repeated "syeéyr."

RANGE: Guianas, s. and w. Venezuela (south of the Orinoco in Bolívar and Amazonas, also along e. base of Andes north to nw. Barinas and Mérida), e. Colombia (locally throughout east of Andes, except in extensive llanos), e. Ecuador, e. Peru, n. Bolivia (south to La Paz, Cochabamba, and Santa Cruz), and Amaz. Brazil (south to s. Mato Grosso and east to Amapá and the lower Rio Tocantins). Mostly below 900 m (recorded to 1400 m in Colombia).

Myrmoborus lugubris

ASH-BREASTED ANTBIRD

PLATE: 22

DESCRIPTION: 13.5 cm (5¼"). *Várzea and island forests along the Amazon and its major tributaries.* Iris red. Male uniform bluish gray above (whiter on forehead; wings *plain*) and uniformly paler gray below, with *contrasting black sides of head and throat.* Female of nominate race (lower Amazon upriver to above mouth of the Rio Tapajós) *plain dull rufous above* (brightest on sides of head) with buff dotting on wing-coverts; mostly white below, washed with buff on sides and flanks. Females from upper Amazon region (*berlepschi*) are very different, above browner (less rufescent) with *contrasting black mask through eyes;* throat white, remaining underparts pale gray, with faint thin black "necklace" separating the gray and white. "Intermediate"-plumaged females found in the lower Rio Madeira/Rio Negro region (e.g., *stictopterus* of the lower Rio Negro) are rufescent above with black cheeks.

SIMILAR SPECIES: The only *Myrmoborus* antbird in its restricted habitat; rarely occurs with any of its congeners. Lacks bold eyebrow of both sexes of White-browed Antbird, and prominent wing markings of both sexes of Black-faced Antbird. Nominate female has pattern somewhat like female Silvered Antbird, but latter is less rufescent above, lacks red eye, and has longer pink legs.

HABITAT AND BEHAVIOR: Fairly common in undergrowth of várzea and riparian forest, mainly on river islands, along the Amazon and the lower part of its major tributaries, to a lesser extent in similar habitat on "mainland" along larger rivers. Usually in pairs which remain close to the ground, seeming to favor *Heliconia* thickets, but regularly emerging into more open areas. Vocally Ash-breasted is similar to White-browed Antbird. Numerous on various islands near Iquitos, Peru, and Leticia, Colombia.

RANGE: Along the Amazon and its tributaries in extreme ne. Ecuador (island in the Río Napo at the mouth of the Río Aguarico; ANSP, MECN), ne. Peru (along the Amazon, Río Napo, and up the Río Ucayali to Sarayacu), extreme se. Colombia (Leticia area), and Brazil (east to the lower Rio Tocantins). Below 125 m.

GROUP B Wings *boldly fringed white (or buff)* in *both* sexes.

Myrmoborus myotherinus

BLACK-FACED ANTBIRD PLATE: 22

DESCRIPTION: 13 cm (5″). *Terra firme forest* of Amazonia. Iris red. Male uniform bluish gray above with *contrasting black face and throat* outlined above by *whitish border,* and semiconcealed white dorsal patch; *wing-coverts black fringed with white forming 3 wing-bars.* Below pale gray. Males from nw. part of range (Venezuela southward into w. Brazil west of the Rio Madeira, and westward through ne. Peru into se. Colombia and e. Ecuador; *elegans, ardesiacus,* and *proximus*) are darker gray below than birds from elsewhere. Female olive brown above with *contrasting black mask* and semiconcealed white dorsal patch; *wing-coverts black fringed with buff forming 3 wing-bars. Throat white, contrasting with ochraceous remaining underparts,* with a few blackish spots along their border forming a partial necklace (best developed in w. Amazonia, less so eastward, with *none* in *ochrolaema* from east of the Rio Madeira in lower Amaz. Brazil). *Ochrolaema,* quite different, is *uniform intense ochraceous below.* Females from a limited area north of the Amazon and west of the lower Rio Negro (*ardesiacus* and "*incanus*") are paler below, some almost whitish.

SIMILAR SPECIES: Males of this often numerous antbird are best known by their contrasting black face and the white wing-fringing, females by their white throat (usually accented by a partial necklace), black mask, and 3 buff wing-bars. Cf. the rare and range-restricted Black-tailed Antbird.

HABITAT AND BEHAVIOR: Fairly common to common in undergrowth of terra firme forest and mature secondary woodland. Generally found in pairs or small family groups, foraging on or close to the ground; usually fairly easy to observe. Male's song is a loud, fairly fast series of notes, becoming somewhat nasal toward the end, "chee-chee-chee-chee-chee-chee-chee-chew-chew-che-chu-chu" with slight descending effect; it is not as rapidly paced as the songs of White-browed or Ash-breasted Antbirds.

RANGE: S. Venezuela (Amazonas and w. Bolívar), se. Colombia (north to Meta and Vaupés), e. Ecuador, e. Peru, n. Bolivia (south to La Paz, Cochabamba, and Santa Cruz), and Amaz. Brazil (north of the Amazon east only to the Rio Negro and Rio Branco, south of it east to e. Pará and south to s. Mato Grosso). Mostly below 700 m, in smaller numbers up to 1200 m along e. base of Andes.

NOTE: This species' racial variation was discussed by J. Haffer and J. Fitzpatrick (*Neotropical Ornithology,* AOU Monograph no. 36, pp. 152–157, 1985).

Myrmoborus melanurus

BLACK-TAILED ANTBIRD PLATE: 22

DESCRIPTION: 12.5 cm (5″). *Limited area in ne. Peru; rare.* Iris red or orange. Male *mostly dark slaty gray* with slightly blacker face and throat; wings and tail black, wing-coverts fringed white forming 3 wing-bars.

Some (all?) males have a semiconcealed white dorsal patch. Female *brown above* (including tail) with *indistinct dusky mask;* wing-coverts black, fringed as in male. *Whitish below with buff tinge across breast* and some brown on sides.

SIMILAR SPECIES: Male Black-faced Antbird has much more contrasting black face surmounted by a narrow white brow; female Black-faced (in area of overlap) has conspicuous black mask and mostly ochraceous underparts with partial necklace and white only on throat.

HABITAT AND BEHAVIOR: Poorly known; evidently rare (or just overlooked?). A pair seen at Yarinacocha (RSR and E. Eisenmann) was in várzea forest (to which it may be largely or totally restricted, with Black-faced taking over in terra firme). Its song is described as a loud, fast series of clear descending "tew" notes, much like an Ash-breasted Antbird (T. A. Parker III, *in* Hilty and Brown 1986).

RANGE: Ne. Peru (known from a few localities south of the Amazon and east of the Río Ucayali in Loreto and south to n. Ucayali at Yarinacocha). To 125 m.

Dichrozona Antbirds

A distinctive, monotypic genus of small antbird with a long bill and very stubby tail found in upland forests of w. and cen. Amazonia.

Dichrozona cincta

BANDED ANTBIRD

PLATE: 22

DESCRIPTION: 10 cm (4"). *Very small.* Long slender bill and *very short tail.* Male has crown and back chestnut brown with indistinct narrow whitish superciliary and grayish sides of head; lower back and rump black, *rump crossed by conspicuous white band;* wings mainly black with lesser-coverts broadly tipped whitish and *greater-coverts broadly tipped buff;* outer rectrices white. *Below white,* with *conspicuous band of black spots across chest,* sides washed grayish. Female similar but with shoulder spots and *rump band buff,* underparts slightly tinged buff, and somewhat less chest spotting.

SIMILAR SPECIES: Pattern vaguely reminiscent of somewhat larger and longer-tailed Spot-backed Antbird, but Spot-backed is less terrestrial and has back *spots* instead of a rump *band.* Banded Antbird's buff wing-band appears more or less continuous with the rump band, giving a unique effect. Cf. also Wing-banded Wren (similarly shaped and with comparable wing-band) and Collared Gnatwren.

HABITAT AND BEHAVIOR: Rare to locally uncommon on or near ground in terra firme forest. Often in pairs, the territories of which are large. Foraging birds walk on ground, frequently wagging their tails and spreading the outer rectrices as if to display the white. Its unmistakable song is a series of up to 12–15 loud "pueeeeée" notes, steadily delivered at a rate of about 1 note per second, with an odd ringing quality and a slight crescendo effect.

RANGE: Extreme sw. Venezuela (sw. Amazonas), se. Colombia (north to Meta and e. Guainía), e. Ecuador, e. Peru, n. Bolivia (south to n. La Paz), and Amaz. Brazil (north of the Amazon only in the upper Rio Negro region, south of it east to the lower Rio Tapajós and south to Rondônia). To about 900 m (in s. Peru).

Hylophylax Antbirds

Small and plump antbirds with attractive and rather ornate plumage patterns; their tails are short and are often fanned. They range in humid lowland forests and are quite vocal; several species regularly follow army antswarms.

GROUP A　　　"Spot-backed" Group; both sexes with *breast boldly spotted.*

Hylophylax naevia

SPOT-BACKED ANTBIRD　　　PLATE: 22

DESCRIPTION: 11.5 cm (4½"). Amazonia. Legs pinkish; iris grayish. Male has crown and upper back brownish gray, grayest on forecrown and with *distinctly gray lower face, black lower back with large tear-shaped buff spots,* brownish *unmarked* rump, and semiconcealed white dorsal patch; wing-coverts black prominently tipped white or buffy white, forming 3 distinct wing-bars, and with buff tertial tipping; tail brownish tipped white. Throat black; remaining underparts white with *conspicuous band of large black spots across breast;* flanks and lower belly buff. Birds from north of the Amazon west to Vaupés, Colombia (nominate and *consobrina*), have crown and upper back brown; see V-24, C-32. Female like male above but with wing markings buff. Throat white bordered by a prominent black malar stripe; *remaining underparts mostly ochraceous buff* (deepest on lower belly) with breast spots as in male. *Ochracea* (lower Amaz. Brazil south of the Amazon and east of the Rio Tapajós) has deeper ochraceous underparts and less breast spotting (reduced to a few on sides).

SIMILAR SPECIES: Cf. much scarcer Dot-backed Antbird, and Banded Antbird (latter with rump band rather than back spots, etc.). Somewhat similar Spotted Antbird is found west of Andes (no overlap).

HABITAT AND BEHAVIOR: Fairly common to common in undergrowth of humid forest, mainly in terra firme but also in várzea. Usually in pairs, foraging close to the ground, often clinging to vertical stems. Generally not found at army antswarms, unlike Spotted and Scalebacked Antbirds. Male's song is a distinctive, fast, high-pitched and somewhat wheezy "chr, weéper-weéper-weéper-weéper-weéper-weéper-weéper-weépur," loudest toward the middle and fading at end.

RANGE: Guianas, s. Venezuela (Bolívar and Amazonas), se. Colombia (north to Meta and Vaupés), e. Ecuador, e. Peru, n. Bolivia (south to Cochabamba and n. Santa Cruz), and Amaz. Brazil (east to Amapá and the Rio Tocantins and south to n. Mato Grosso). To 1100 m.

Hylophylax punctulata

DOT-BACKED ANTBIRD

PLATE: 22

DESCRIPTION: 11 cm (4¼"). Local in Amazonia. Resembles much more common Spot-backed Antbird; Dot-backed is somewhat shorter-tailed and has *gray* (not pink) *legs* and brown (not gray) iris. Both sexes differ further in their *whitish* (not gray) *lower face, white* (not buff) *spots on lower back* (*and these are smaller, less tear-shaped, and extend down over rump*), whiter lower underparts (showing only a tinge of buff), and *black tail* (not brown). Male and female Dot-backeds are similar, differing only in the solid black throat of male (see V-24), reduced to a wide black malar stripe in female. *Subochracea* (Amaz. Brazil south to n. Bolivia) differs in having a buff tinge to the white spots above and in being washed with buff across belly; it thus even more closely resembles the Spot-backed Antbird, with the best distinguishing characters being differences in soft-part colors and face patterns.

HABITAT AND BEHAVIOR: Rare to locally uncommon in undergrowth of várzea forest, sometimes where trees are of short stature and almost always near streams; perhaps most numerous in s. Venezuela. Usually in pairs, often rather tame, foraging independently of mixed flocks. Male gives an endlessly repeated, emphatic "whee-wheéyr, whee-wheéyr, whee-wheéyr. . . ." Often very responsive to tape playback, but unlike many other antbirds, Dot-backed tends to fly in directly and then remain almost motionless on an open perch, rather than continuing to hop around in agitation.

RANGE: Locally in s. Venezuela (w. Bolívar and Amazonas), Amaz. Brazil (locally in Rio Negro/Rio Branco region, and south of the Amazon from the Rio Xingu westward, ranging south to Rondônia and n. Mato Grosso), n. Bolivia (Pando, Beni, and ne. Santa Cruz), ne. Peru (locally in Loreto, where recorded south along Río Ucayali to Sarayacu), e. Ecuador (local), and se. Colombia (male in FMNH taken in Macarena Mts. of w. Meta, formerly misidentified as *H. naevia*); French Guiana (seen at Koulé-Koulé and Saut Pararé). Mostly below 300 m.

Hylophylax naevioides

SPOTTED ANTBIRD

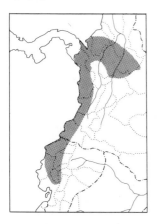

DESCRIPTION: 11.5 cm (4½"). *W. Colombia and w. Ecuador.* Legs dull pinkish gray; iris grayish. Male has *head ashy gray* contrasting with *plain rufous-chestnut back* and semiconcealed white dorsal patch; wings black with white dots on coverts and *2 broad rufous wing-bars and tertial tipping;* tail olive brown with blackish subterminal band and buff tip. Throat black; *remaining underparts white with band of large black spots across breast,* flanks washed with grayish. Female similar but duller generally and buffier below, with browner head, buff dots on coverts, white throat, and less distinct band of dusky spots across breast. See C-32, P-22.

SIMILAR SPECIES: This attractive small antbird is virtually unmistakable in its trans-Andean range; it does not overlap with any congener.

HABITAT AND BEHAVIOR: Uncommon in lower growth of humid forest and mature secondary woodland. Behavior much like Spot-backed Antbird's, but unlike that species Spotted frequently attends army antswarms. Spotted's song is also similar, a series of high wheezy notes which drop in pitch and gradually fade away, "peezee, wheezee, wheezee, wheezee, wheeya."

RANGE: W. Colombia (Pacific lowlands, and east in humid Caribbean lowlands to middle Río Magdalena valley in e. Antioquia) and w. Ecuador (at least formerly south to e. Guayas; recent reports only from Esmeraldas). Also Honduras to Panama. To 900 m.

NOTE: For more information on behavior, see E. O. Willis, *The Behavior of Spotted Antbirds,* Ornithol. Monogr., no. 10, 1972.

GROUP B

"Scale-backed": females highly *variable,* some races *lacking* fringing.

Hylophylax poecilinota

SCALE-BACKED ANTBIRD   PLATE: 22

DESCRIPTION: 13 cm (5"). Male *mostly gray with midback and wings black, feathers prominently tipped white giving conspicuous scaly effect,* and with semiconcealed white dorsal patch; tail black with large white spots toward base and white tip. *Nigrigula* (lower Amaz. Brazil south of the Amazon from just west of the lower Rio Tapajós east to the Rio Tocantins) and *gutturalis* (south of the Amazon in ne. Loreto, Peru, east into extreme w. Brazil in the Rio Juruá drainage) have *contrasting black throat.* Geographic variation in females is extensive. *Lepidonota* and *gutturalis* (se. Colombia, e. Ecuador, most of e. Peru except far southeast, and extreme w. Brazil) patterned like male (including *conspicuous white scaling across back and wings*) but rufous brown above and ochraceous buff below; *duidae* (e. Colombia to extreme sw. Venezuela and nw. Brazil south to west of the lower Rio Negro) similar but brighter, almost rufous, below (see C-28). Nominate race (s. Venezuela through Guianas to n. Brazil north of the Amazon and west to the lower Rio Negro) quite different, with *buff scaling above* and (except for buffy to whitish chin) *entirely gray underparts;* see V-22. Birds from extreme se. Peru, n. Bolivia, and all of Amaz. Brazil south of the Amazon except the far west (*griseiventris, nigrigula,* and *vidua*) are *unscaled uniform rufous brown above* and *uniform gray below* except for white throat, the gray extending up over cheeks except in *griseiventris* (which ranges east to the Rio Madeira and s. Mato Grosso) in which cheeks are rufous.

SIMILAR SPECIES: Variation in females is confusing, but this attractive antbird is usually seen in pairs (and *males are always "scale-backed"*). Basically, females in w. Amazonia and north of the Amazon are also *scale-backed* (with either white or buff) and thus are not likely confused. Females south of the Amazon (except in Peru and adjacent Brazil) are *plain-backed;* their underparts are *rufescent* in w. birds (east to the Rio Negro and the Rio Juruá in westernmost Brazil), *gray* elsewhere.

HABITAT AND BEHAVIOR: Uncommon to fairly common in lower growth of humid forest, primarily in terra firme. Like its congeners generally in pairs, foraging close to but usually not on the ground, often perching on slender vertical stems, from which it pursues prey by briefly dropping to the ground or sallying to nearby foliage. A pair is frequently found at army antswarms. The song, apparently the same throughout its range, is a series of 5–6 upslurred whistled notes, "tew, tueeé? tueeé? tueeé? tueeé? tueeé?"

RANGE: Guianas, s. Venezuela (Bolívar and Amazonas), se. Colombia (north to Meta and Guainía), e. Ecuador, e. Peru, n. Bolivia (south to La Paz and ne. Santa Cruz), and Amaz. Brazil (east to Amapá and n. Maranhão, and south to s. Mato Grosso). To about 1100 m, occasionally a bit higher.

NOTE: The correct spelling of the species name is evidently *poecilinota* and not *poecilonota* (*fide Birds of the Americas,* vol. 13, part 3, and Willis [1988]). The striking geographic variation in female plumages might make one suspect that more than one species is involved, though vocalizations and behavior of all forms are similar. Indeed Pinto (1978) regarded *H. lepidonota* (with *duidae*) as a distinct species, mainly because both *duidae* and nominate *poecilinota* are recorded from east of the lower Rio Negro at Itacoatiara near Manaus, Brazil. However, as E. O. Willis (*Wilson Bull.* 94[4]: 447–462, 1982) points out, recent records of Scale-backed Antbirds from east of the Rio Negro refer solely to the nominate form, and likely the explanation for the supposed sympatry is that the *duidae* specimens were mislabeled. Willis (op. cit.) also provides much information on Scale-backed's behavior and further suggests that behaviorally it resembles the two *Hypocnemoides* antbirds more than the others classified in *Hylophylax.* Possibly the genera should be merged, or *poecilinota* should be removed to *Hypocnemoides.*

Hypocnemis Antbirds

A pair (possibly a trio) of antbirds found in the lower growth of forests and borders in Amazonia. They recall the *Drymophila* antbirds (and are sometimes found with Striated) but are considerably shorter-tailed.

Hypocnemis cantator

WARBLING ANTBIRD

PLATE: 22

DESCRIPTION: 12 cm (4¾"). Geographically variable. Bill black above, whitish below. Nominate group (including *peruviana*) has head black with white streaks and *white superciliary;* back mixed black, grayish brown, and white, with semiconcealed white dorsal patch, becoming rufescent brown on rump; wing-coverts black tipped with white forming 3 bold wing-bars; tail brown narrowly tipped buff. Throat and breast white, *feathers scalloped with black especially on sides of breast; flanks contrastingly bright rufous,* center of belly pale yellow. Female much like male except streaks on upperparts and wing-bars buffyish and dorsal patch reduced or lacking. Nominate race (Surinam, French Guiana, and n. Brazil west to the lower Rio Negro and Rio Branco) has back unstreaked and grayer. *Flavescens* (far e. Colombia, extreme nw. Brazil, and sw. Venezuela east to w. Bolívar) is *tinged with yellow below;* see V-21. Dramatically different are *subflava* and *collinsi* of se. Peru and nw. Bolivia; these are quite yellow below (even more so than *flavescens*), have black *streaking* (instead of scalloping) on sides of breast, and have greatly *reduced* rufous on flanks.

SIMILAR SPECIES: The *Herpsilochmus* antwrens are forest canopy dwellers not found in Warbling's habitat; Yellow-breasted Antwren is most similar. The *Drymophila* antbirds, though also generally streaked, have much longer tails whose feathers are white-tipped; cf. especially the often syntopic Striated Antbird. Cf. also Yellow-browed Antbird (but note that regardless of the amount of yellow below, all races of Warbling have *white* brow).

HABITAT AND BEHAVIOR: Fairly common to common in lower growth of humid forest borders and second-growth woodland (sometimes in bamboo and often near water or in swampy places). Usually in pairs which usually but not always forage low, sometimes ranging up to 8 m above ground in viny tangles. The song, seemingly similar throughout its wide range, is a raspy, almost snarling "peér, peer-peer-peer-peer-pur-pur-pyur"; sometimes female chimes in with a shorter, higher-pitched version about halfway through male's. Also often given (by both sexes) is a distinctive simpler call, "wur-cheeé."

RANGE: Guianas, s. Venezuela (Bolívar and s. Amazonas), se. Colombia (north to Meta and Guainía), e. Ecuador, e. Peru, n. Bolivia (south to La Paz, Cochabamba, and Santa Cruz), and Amaz. Brazil (east to Amapá and the lower Rio Tocantins, and south to s. Mato Grosso). To about 1100 m.

NOTE: The abrupt and striking shift in s. Peru from the nominate type (ssp. *peruviana*) to *subflava* and *collinsi* deserves further study; possibly separate species are involved. No definite intermediates seem to be known, but the voices of both "types" seem very similar. Further, T. Schulenberg (in litt.) has seen an apparent pair at the Tambopata Reserve in Madre de Dios, Peru, in which one bird was a "typical *peruviana*-type" and the other a "good *collinsi*-type."

Hypocnemis hypoxantha

YELLOW-BROWED ANTBIRD

DESCRIPTION: 12 cm (4¾"). W. Amazonia. Bill all black. Male has crown black with white streaks in midcrown, *a long bright yellow superciliary,* and *back mainly olive* with sparse black streaking; wing-coverts black with bold white tipping, forming 3 wing-bars; tail dusky tipped whitish. *Below mainly bright yellow,* sides of breast *streaked* with black, and some olive on flanks. See C-28. Female much like male but with yellowish midcrown streaks. *Ochraceiventris* (e. Amaz. Brazil between the lower Rios Tapajós and Xingu) has some rufous on flanks (but much less than typically shown by Warbling Antbird).

SIMILAR SPECIES: Warbling Antbird always shows *white* (not yellow) superciliary. Note that the yellow-breasted races of Warbling that range in s. Peru, *subflava* and *collinsi,* may occur sympatrically with Yellow-browed; in addition to eyebrow difference, these Warblings show a streaked (not plain olive) back; recall that they have relatively little rufous on flanks.

HABITAT AND BEHAVIOR: Rare to locally uncommon in lower growth of humid forest, primarily in terra firme, where it shows a predilection for the dense tangled vegetation found around treefalls. Usually found in pairs, foraging mostly between 2 and 4 m above the ground; generally not with mixed flocks. The song is very similar to Warbling Antbird's, with the same raspy, guttural effect. Small numbers occur south of the Río Napo near La Selva in Ecuador.

RANGE: Se. Colombia (north to Caquetá and Vaupés), e. Ecuador, ne. Peru (Loreto south to the lower Río Ucayali), and nw. Brazil (north of the Amazon east to the lower Rio Negro); lower Amaz. Brazil (south of the Amazon between the lower Rios Tapajós and Xingu). Below 400 m.

Myrmochanes Antbirds

A small black-and-white antbird found exclusively on islands in w. Amazonia. Its virtual lack of sexual dimorphism is unusual among thamnophiline antbirds.

Myrmochanes hemileucus

BLACK-AND-WHITE ANTBIRD PLATE: 22

DESCRIPTION: 11.5 cm (4½"). *A small, bicolored antbird found locally on islands in upper Amazon system. Long slender bill* (grayish below in female); quite short tail. *Black above* with large semiconcealed white dorsal patch (conspicuous when bird is excited), becoming gray on rump; wing-coverts spotted with white, tail feathers tipped white. *Below white*. Female differs from male in having slightly more white on lores and in being tinged with buff on flanks and crissum.

SIMILAR SPECIES: This small black-and-white (well named!) antbird is unlikely to be confused in its limited range and restricted habitat. Male Great Antshrike is well over twice its size, with much heavier bill, etc. Male Black-and-white Tody-Tyrant is similarly sized and colored but shows pale edging on tertials (not spotting on wing-coverts); the two would be unlikely ever to occur together.

HABITAT AND BEHAVIOR: Fairly common in younger successional growth on river islands, primarily in stands of the low shrub *Tessaria* but also in shrubby *Cecropia*-dominated woodland. Necessarily rather local because of the ephemeral nature of its habitat, but often rather easily found once that habitat is located. Usually in pairs which glean quite actively in lower growth; not shy, and generally fairly easy to see. The song is an often-given, fast "tu-tu-u-u-u-u-u-u" with a distinctive odd "tooting" or chortling quality. Excited birds often ruffle crown feathers. Good numbers are found on islands in the Río Napo in ne. Peru and Ecuador.

RANGE: Locally along the middle and upper Amazon (downriver to the Manaus area and near the mouth of the Rio Madeira) and a few of its major tributaries in w. Brazil, n. Bolivia (along the Río Madeira in Beni), extreme se. Colombia (Leticia area), ne. Peru (in Loreto, and up the Río Ucayali as far as Lagarto in Ucayali), and e. Ecuador (islands in the Río Napo in Napo). To 300 m.

Hypocnemoides Antbirds

A pair of closely related, small, fairly long-billed antbirds found around swampy backwaters and streams in Amazonia; for the most part they separate by range, though there is apparently some geographic overlap.

Hypocnemoides maculicauda

BAND-TAILED ANTBIRD

PLATE: 22

DESCRIPTION: 12 cm (4¾"). *South* of the Amazon. Iris pale grayish. Male mostly gray, somewhat paler below (especially on belly), with black throat patch; *rather large semiconcealed white dorsal patch;* wing-coverts black fringed with white forming 2 or 3 wing-bars; tail also black, *quite broadly tipped white.* Female above like male (including the *dorsal patch*); *below whitish, mottled with grayish* especially across breast and down flanks.

SIMILAR SPECIES: Cf. very similar Black-chinned Antbird (found mainly north of the Amazon but with considerable overlap with Band-tailed). Band-tailed is such a small antbird that confusion is possible with certain of the "gray" *Myrmotherula* antwrens; note their very different habitats and behavior, and Band-tailed's broad white tail-tips. Female somewhat resembles male Silvered Antbird in w. part of its range (*argentata*), and they are regularly sympatric; Silvered is considerably larger with pink (not grayish) legs and lacks white on tail-tip.

HABITAT AND BEHAVIOR: Uncommon to locally fairly common in undergrowth of várzea or swampy forest, around wooded margins of lakes and sluggish streams, and in gallery woodland; the requirement is the proximity of water. Usually found in pairs, hopping on or near the ground in the tangles of branches so common in such situations; not particularly shy. The song is a loud series of notes that gradually accelerate and turn raspy toward the end, "pee-pee-pi-pi-pipipipipi-pipi-pe-pe-peh-pez-pez-pzz."

RANGE: E. Peru (from south of the Amazon and Río Marañón in Loreto south to Madre de Dios), n. Bolivia (south to La Paz, Cochabamba, and n. Santa Cruz), and Amaz. Brazil south of the Amazon (east to n. Maranhão, and south to n. Mato Grosso do Sul and n. Goiás). To 500 m.

Hypocnemoides melanopogon

BLACK-CHINNED ANTBIRD

DESCRIPTION: 11.5 cm (4½"). Mainly *north* of the Amazon (but occurs south of it in Brazil and Peru). So closely resembles the slightly larger and longer-tailed Band-tailed Antbird that field discrimination is often not easy. Both sexes *lack* Band-tailed's white dorsal patch and have slightly *narrower* white tail-tipping. See V-22, C-28.

HABITAT AND BEHAVIOR: Uncommon to locally fairly common in much the same sort of terrain as Band-tailed Antbird; seems equally tied to water, usually stagnant or slow moving. Behavior is so similar

that a study of how they segregate in the few areas (e.g., along the lower Rio Tapajós in Brazil) where they evidently come into contact would be of interest. The song, also similar, is often shorter with an overall effect not unlike Warbling Antbird's.

RANGE: Guianas, s. Venezuela (Delta Amacuro, Bolívar, and Amazonas; also locally north of the Orinoco in Guárico), e. Colombia (north to Meta and Vichada), ne. Ecuador (along the lower Río Yasuní, near Imuyacocha on the Río Lagarto, and Cuyabeno; ANSP, MECN), ne. Peru (locally in Loreto, mainly or entirely north of the Amazon and Río Marañón), and Amaz. Brazil (east to Amapá and along the lower Rio Tocantins in e. Pará, and south to n. Mato Grosso; not found south of the Amazon west of the Rio Purus). To 500 m.

Sclateria Antbirds

A midsized antbird with a notably long bill and quite long legs, found in swampy places across much of Amazonia. Probably most closely related to *Percnostola* and *Schistocichla*.

Sclateria naevia

SILVERED ANTBIRD

PLATE: 22

DESCRIPTION: 14.5–15 cm (5¾–6"). *Long bill;* rather long, *pinkish legs.* Two rather different "types." Male of nominate race (with *diaphora;* Trinidad and e. Venezuela south to lower Amaz. Brazil) gray above, wings and tail blackish, wing-coverts with small but prominent white spots. *Below prominently streaked gray and white,* whitest on throat and grayest on flanks. Female patterned much the same, but *brown above* with buff spots on wing-coverts; *below streaked brown and buffy white,* whitest on throat and midbelly. *Argentata* (w. Amazonia east to sw. Venezuela and the Rio Madeira in Brazil) male is *essentially unstreaked white below,* with gray restricted to mottling on sides and flanks; female somewhat darker and more grayish brown above than nominate race, and *mainly white below* (no streaking) with *sides and flanks extensively orange-rufous;* see C-30. *Toddi* (lower Amaz. Brazil in the Rio Tapajós area) resembles *argentata* but is somewhat more streaked below (thus intermediate toward nominate).

SIMILAR SPECIES: The "types" look very different, but both are distinctive and should be readily known. Cf. females of Band-tailed and Black-chinned Antbirds (which especially resemble male *argentata* Silvereds), and in s. Venezuela also note similarity to the rare and range-restricted Yapacana Antbird.

HABITAT AND BEHAVIOR: Fairly common to common in undergrowth of swampy and várzea forest and along edges of lakes and sluggish streams; also found locally in mangroves (e.g., in Trinidad). Usually found in pairs, hopping on the ground in damp leaf litter or along muddy margins of a stream or lake; not too shy, and generally responsive to tape playback. The song (which does not appear to vary throughout range) is a loud and ringing "jyip; ji-ji-ji-ji-ji-ji-jíjíjíjíjí-ji-ji-jew," gradually speeding up and reaching a crescendo in the middle, then fading off, and always with the distinctive initial and separated note.

RANGE: E. and s. Venezuela (e. Sucre and Delta Amacuro, Bolívar, and Amazonas), e. Colombia (north to ne. Meta and Vichada), e. Ecuador, e. Peru, n. Bolivia (Pando, Beni, and ne. Santa Cruz), and Amaz. Brazil (east to Amapá and n. Maranhão, and south to n. Mato Grosso); Trinidad. To 500 m.

Percnostola Antbirds

A pair of possibly unrelated antbirds found in Amazonia, males with bold white fringing on wing-coverts; we have resurrected the genus *Schistocichla* for three species that recently have been placed in *Percnostola*. The Black-headed Antbird seems close to *Myrmeciza;* the White-lined looks superficially like a *Sakesphorus* antshrike, mainly because of its long, expressive crest, though they likely are not closely related.

Percnostola lophotes

WHITE-LINED ANTBIRD   PLATE: 23

Includes: Rufous-crested Antbird

DESCRIPTION: 14.5 cm (5¾"). *Se. Peru and adjacent Bolivia. Long, shaggy crest in both sexes.* Male mostly dark slaty gray, *blacker on head and crest, throat, and breast; bend of wing and wing-coverts boldly fringed with white,* and underwing-coverts also white. Female has *cinnamon-rufous crown,* dusky cheeks, and rufescent brown back; *wings mostly cinnamon-rufous,* coverts edged paler, and tail rufous-chestnut. *Mostly white below,* tinged grayish on cheeks and sides, and olivaceous on flanks.

SIMILAR SPECIES: The crest is usually apparent (though at times laid flat), and its shape recalls certain dissimilarly plumaged *Sakesphorus* antshrikes. Crest should readily separate it from various other superficially similar species (e.g., Black Antbird); somewhat similar Black-tailed Antbird of ne. Peru (possible overlap?) lacks crest, has red iris, etc. Female White-lined is strongly *bicolored;* cf. female of larger Great Antshrike (with bold red iris, shorter crest, etc.).

HABITAT AND BEHAVIOR: Uncommon to locally fairly common in dense lower growth of transitional and várzea forest and forest borders, especially in or near stands of *Guadua* bamboo and *Gynerium* cane. Usually in pairs, hopping through undergrowth within 2 m of ground, frequently pounding tail downward and slowly raising it back up again, also often raising and lowering crest. Hard to see, in part because of its dense preferred habitat. Male's song is a distinctive, loud series of accelerating notes, "kew, kew-kew-kew-ku-ku-ku-kukukuku," which female often follows with a similar but shorter song; calls include a loud "chéwf," often repeated several times in succession, and a nasal "wraa." Can be found at the Tambopata Reserve in Madre de Dios, Peru, but especially numerous at Hacienda Amazonia in Cuzco. RANGE: Se. Peru (Ucayali to Madre de Dios) and extreme nw. Bolivia (Pando at Camino Mucden and west of Porvenir, and La Paz at Alto Madidi); extreme se. Colombia (near Mitu in e. Vaupés; Hilty and Brown 1986). Mostly below 700 m, locally to 1050 m.

NOTE: Parker (1982) showed that what was described as *P. macrolopha* was the male of *P. lophotes*. Prior to this (e.g., Meyer de Schauensee 1966, 1970), *P. lophotes* (which until the 1970s was known only from female specimens) had gone by the English name of Rufous-crested Antbird. Parker (1982) and Parker and Remsen (1987) present additional behavioral information.

Percnostola rufifrons

BLACK-HEADED ANTBIRD   PLATE: 23

DESCRIPTION: 14.5–15 cm (5¾–6″). Local from Guianas to ne. Peru. *Iris red* in e. nominate group (with *subcristata;* Guianas to lower Rio Negro area), *gray* in w. *minor* group (nw. Brazil and sw. Venezuela to ne. Peru). Male of nominate group mostly dark gray with *black crown and throat* and fairly long crown feathers (sometimes showing as a short, bushy crest); wings blackish, bend of wing and fringing on coverts white. Female olivaceous dusky above with *crown blackish to sooty-chestnut;* wing-coverts with *broad tawny fringing. Sides of head and underparts rich orange-rufous,* becoming olivaceous on flanks. *Minor* is somewhat smaller and has shorter crown feathers (no crest); males of *minor* differ in having narrow gray tipping on crown feathers, whereas females differ in having *crown dull chestnut* and contrastingly paler ochraceous belly (see C-30, but note that iris color there is wrong). SIMILAR SPECIES: All superficially similar *Schistocichla* antbirds have *spots* (not fringes) on wing-coverts; none ever shows lengthened crown feathers. Male Black-chinned Antbird is smaller (even than *minor*), has no black on crown, shows white tail-tipping, etc. Cf. also female of rare Black-tailed Antbird. HABITAT AND BEHAVIOR: Uncommon to locally common in undergrowth at edge of humid forest (also at treefalls) and mature second-growth woodland. Usually found singly or in pairs, rarely with mixed flocks, often accompanying army antswarms. Frequently pounds tail downward. Song of nominate and *subcristata* an even, loud "peer-peer-peer-peer-peer-peer"; voice of *minor* not known to us. Numerous at Surinam's Brownsberg Nature Park and north of Manaus, Brazil. RANGE: Guianas, n. Amaz. Brazil (north of the Amazon from Amapá west locally to drainage of the Rio Negro), extreme s. Venezuela (s. Amazonas), and extreme e. Colombia (e. Guainía to e. Vaupés); ne. Peru (locally in ne. Loreto). To 500 m.

NOTE: Birds from ne. Peru appear to represent an undescribed form (G. H. Rosenberg and A. P. Capparella, pers. comm.).

Schistocichla Antbirds

A trio of quite uniform-looking antbirds found in forests of Amazonia, males mainly some shade of gray, females rich orange-rufous below, both sexes with spots on wing-coverts. We have here resurrected the genus *Schistocichla* for this group, the species of which are readily separated from true *Percnostola* by their rounder and uncrested heads and in having spots, not fringing, on their wing-coverts. *Schistocichla* was evidently last used by J. T. Zimmer (*Am. Mus. Novitates* 500, 1931) but subsequently was sunk into *Percnostola* (e.g., *Birds of the World*, vol. 7; Meyer de Schauensee 1966, 1970). The possible relationship of both genera to *Myrmeciza* (or some part of it) remains to be elucidated.

Schistocichla leucostigma

SPOT-WINGED ANTBIRD   PLATE: 23

DESCRIPTION: 14.5–15 cm (5¾–6"). Legs *bluish gray* (*subplumbea* group, with *intensa* and *brunneiceps,* of w. Amazonia from Colombia to s. Peru; also *obscura* and *saturata* of tepui region in e. Bolívar, Venezuela) or *pinkish* (nominate group, with *infuscata, humaythae,* and *rufifacies,* of Amaz. Brazil and Guianas west to far e. Colombia). Lower mandible bluish gray. Males of *subplumbea* group are *uniform dark gray,* duskier on wings and tail, *wing-coverts with small white dots.* Females have *head dark gray* contrasting with rufous brown upperparts; wings and tail dark brown, *wing-coverts with rufous-buff dots. Below uniform deep orange-rufous.* Males of nominate group have underparts noticeably paler gray than upperparts (showing contrast) and usually have larger white wing-spots; see C-30. Females are paler orange-rufous below than females of *subplumbea* group; *infuscata* (far e. Colombia, adjacent Venezuela, and extreme w. Brazil north of Amazon) has gray restricted to crown, whereas *humaythae* (limited range in Amaz. Brazil, north of the Amazon just west of the lower Rio Negro, south of it from the Rio Juruá to the lower Rio Madeira) has entire head brown.

SIMILAR SPECIES: Generally the most numerous *Schistocichla* antbird; cf. similar Slate-colored and Caura Antbirds. Both sexes of similarly plumaged Plumbeous Antbird have conspicuous bare pale blue skin around eye. Both sexes of Black-headed Antbird have fringing (not spotting) on wing-coverts. Two *Thamnophilus* antshrikes, though with different behavior and voices, are also somewhat similar to Spot-winged. Males of some races of White-shouldered Antshrike, a heavier billed and somewhat larger bird with blacker crown, show similar spotting on wing-coverts. Female Blackish-gray Antshrike has more or less uniform wing (lacking female Spot-winged's spots on coverts).

HABITAT AND BEHAVIOR: Uncommon to locally fairly common in lower growth inside terra firme forest, primarily along small forest streams and in damp places (seems not to occur in várzea forest). Usually in pairs or small groups, generally shy and difficult to see well; does not associate with mixed flocks and only rarely follows army antswarms. Song of nominate race (e.g., in Surinam) is an evenly pitched, fairly musical trill lasting 2–3 seconds (T. Davis), whereas *subplumbea*'s (e.g., in Ecuador) is similar but somewhat more musical and forceful, fading a bit toward the end. Song of *humaythae* (in Rondônia and n. Mato Grosso) is, however, entirely different, being a series of strident "chee" notes followed by a descending churring, "chee-chee-chee-chee-chee-chee-ch-ch-ch-ch-ch-chr."

RANGE: Guianas, s. and extreme sw. Venezuela (Bolívar and Amazonas; also in sw. Táchira), e. Colombia (north along e. base of Andes to Arauca, and from e. Guainía southward), e. Ecuador, e. Peru, extreme nw. Bolivia (Pando at Camino Mucden), and Amaz. Brazil (east to Amapá and the lower Rio Tocantins, and south to Rondônia and n. Mato Grosso). Mostly below 1000 m, but recorded to 1500 m in Venezuela and to 1660 m in Peru.

NOTE: The striking shift in leg color from bluish gray to pinkish suggests the possibility that more than one species is involved, and *humaythae*'s distinctly different song suggests that it too may be a separate species. However, the situation is complex, and some forms remain poorly known, so for the present we continue to treat all forms as conspecific.

Schistocichla schistacea

SLATE-COLORED ANTBIRD   PLATE: 23

DESCRIPTION: 14.5 cm (5¾"). W. Amazonia. Resembles *subplumbea* group of Spot-winged Antbird; they occur sympatrically. *Bill usually all black* (sometimes some gray at base of lower mandible); *iris grayish* (not brown as in *subplumbea* Spot-winged); legs bluish gray. Males are hard to distinguish, but Slate-colored's mainly black bill is also somewhat shorter than Spot-winged's; Slate-colored is more bluish (less leaden) gray. See C-30. Females are readily distinguished because they *lack gray on head* (crown rufous-chestnut with pale shaft streaks); crown, especially, and breast look somewhat *flammulated*.

HABITAT AND BEHAVIOR: Rare to locally fairly common in undergrowth of terra firme forest. Not well known, but behavior seems similar to Spot-winged Antbird's. At Santa Cecilia, south of the Amazon in Loreto, Peru (near mouth of the Río Napo), both species were present, though Slate-colored was substantially more numerous; it was not clear how or if they segregated in habitat. Slate-colored's song is distinctly different: a more leisurely series of penetrating but quite melodic notes, "teuw, teuw, teuw, teuw, teep-teep-teep," sometimes only 1 or 2 "teep"s at end (M. Robbins; RSR).

RANGE: E. Ecuador (locally in Sucumbios; ANSP), e. Peru (Loreto south locally to Puno), Amaz. Colombia (Leticia area), and extreme w. Amaz. Brazil (east only to Tonantins on n. bank of the Amazon, and in nw. Acre); s. Colombia (Puerto Umbría in w. Putumayo). To 300 m.

Schistocichla caurensis

CAURA ANTBIRD   PLATE: 23

DESCRIPTION: 17.5 cm (7"). *S. Venezuela*. Resembles Spot-winged Antbird but *substantially larger; legs slaty gray*. Male's *iris red* (*fide* D. Delaney), this received subsequent to the completion of our plate

(in which shown as grayish). Male *dark slaty gray* with feathers of crown edged blackish giving a faint scaly effect; wing-coverts with large white spots. Female mostly brown above, feathers of crown darker with scaly look like male's, and with dark gray sides of head; wings and tail duskier, wing-coverts with large rufous-buff spots. Below rich orange-rufous, becoming duller on lower belly and crissum. SIMILAR SPECIES: Males of partially sympatric nominate race of Spot-winged Antbird are smaller and paler below than Caura (and thus look *less uniform*) and have pinkish (not slaty) legs; female nominate Spot-winged is less uniform orange-rufous below, being paler on belly. Male Caura also closely resembles male White-shouldered Antshrike (its sympatric *polionotus* race), but that is smaller and has a shorter and heavier bill. Female Caura also resembles female Blackish-gray Antshrike, but Blackish-gray has an entirely gray head (including crown), lacks spotting on wing-coverts, and has heavier bill. HABITAT AND BEHAVIOR: Poorly known but presumably similar to Spot-winged Antbird's. Judging from the number of specimens that have been taken, Caura must be locally not uncommon. Meyer de Schauensee and Phelps (1978, p. 216) record it from "high dense rain forest," where it apparently occurs primarily on "the slopes of the tepuis"; Spot-winged may mainly occur lower. Caura's voice is not known. RANGE: S. Venezuela (w. Bolívar and Amazonas) and extreme n. Brazil (headwaters of the Rio Padauari in nw. Amazonas). To 1300 m.

NOTE: Based on AMNH specimens, we cannot see that the race *australis* is worthy of recognition; we thus consider the species monotypic.

Myrmeciza Antbirds

A heterogeneous and probably polyphyletic genus of midsized to fairly large antbirds found mainly in humid forests of Amazonia, with outlying species or species groups in e. Brazil and west of the Andes. The formerly recognized genus *Myrmoderus*, which itself may contain unrelated elements (in particular our first two species and the trio from e. Brazil), comprises a group of smaller and usually more colorful and strongly patterned species than are found in "typical" *Myrmeciza*.

GROUP A

Two aberrant, dissimilar *Myrmeciza*.

Myrmeciza griseiceps

GRAY-HEADED ANTBIRD   PLATE: 23

DESCRIPTION: 13.5–14 cm (5¼–5½"). *Limited area in montane sw. Ecuador and nw. Peru. Head and neck gray,* back olive brown with semi-concealed but usually large white dorsal patch; wing-coverts mostly black with bold white fringing; graduated tail dusky, *feathers tipped white.* Chin dark gray, *lower throat and midbreast black;* upper belly gray, becoming olive brown on flanks and crissum. Female above like male but head paler gray and dorsal patch smaller; *throat and breast pale gray*

with mottled whitish streaking, becoming olive brown on lower flanks.
SIMILAR SPECIES: Nothing similar (certainly no antbird) occurs in its small range. Cf. Speckle-breasted Wren and various *Synallaxis* spinetails.
HABITAT AND BEHAVIOR: Rare to locally uncommon in lower growth of montane forest and second-growth woodland, especially where there is an understory of bamboo. Usually found singly or in pairs, moving inconspicuously through undergrowth, generally remaining 2–4 m above ground (rarely dropping to the ground itself). Regularly accompanies mixed understory flocks with Line-cheeked Spinetails, Gray-breasted Wood-Wrens, Three-banded Warblers, Rufous-naped Brush-Finches, and others. A regularly given call is a nasal, somewhat querulous "squee-squirt" steadily repeated every 2–5 seconds; sometimes only a "squeey?" is given. Its song is a simple, short, descending trill lasting about a second, "trrrrrrrrrr." Can be found in patches of woodland west of Celica, in s. Loja, Ecuador, but this is now a very scarce and infrequently recorded bird, declining because of the widespread deforestation that has occurred and the trampling of undergrowth by livestock in what woodland remains. It certainly deserves threatened or endangered status.
RANGE: Locally in sw. Ecuador (El Oro and w. Loja) and nw. Peru (Piura and Lambayeque). 600–2500 m.

NOTE: The generic allocation of this species remains uncertain. Originally described in the then-recognized genus *Myrmoderus,* it was subsequently usually placed in the genus *Myrmeciza.* Various authors have suggested that it may not belong therein, though none has gone so far as to actually shift its allocation. J. T. Zimmer (*Am. Mus. Novitates* 545, 1932, p. 21) commented that "except for the more slender bill there is nothing to argue strongly against inclusion of this species in *Cercomacra.*" RSR's field experience indicates that it behaves more like a *Cercomacra* than any *Myrmeciza;* its graduated, white-tipped tail also is more typical of *Cercomacra* than of other *Myrmeciza.* The best solution may be to erect a monotypic genus for this distinctive species.

Myrmeciza disjuncta

YAPACANA ANTBIRD   PLATE: 23

DESCRIPTION: 13.5 cm (5¼"). *Limited area in sw. Venezuela and adjacent Colombia. Legs pinkish;* lower mandible pale pinkish at least basally. Male *dark gray above* with semiconcealed white dorsal patch; wings and tail blackish, wing-coverts narrowly edged white. *Below white,* tinged with creamy buff and with gray on sides and flanks. Female above like male but with wing-coverts unmarked; *most of underparts* (except throat) *strongly washed with ochraceous-buff.*
SIMILAR SPECIES: Silvered Antbird of sympatric *argentata* race (unstreaked below) is superficially quite similar (both show pink legs, etc.) but somewhat larger and longer-billed. Male Silvered differs further in having white spotting (not fringing) on wing-coverts, whereas female Silvered is basically brown (not gray) above and white below with only sides and flanks ochraceous. Female Black-throated Antbird is much browner above with spotted wing-coverts. Female of sympatric *rufiventris* race of slightly smaller White-fringed Antwren is also rufescent below but has prominent white on wing-coverts and a white superciliary.

HABITAT AND BEHAVIOR: Essentially unknown in life; recorded from "scrubby sandy-belt forest undergrowth" (Hilty and Brown 1986).
RANGE: Sw. Venezuela (w. Amazonas, at bases of Cerro Yapacana and Cerro de la Neblina) and adjacent e. Colombia (e. Guainía). 100 m.

NOTE: This little-known species may not belong in the genus *Myrmeciza* and perhaps is more closely allied to *Sclateria*.

GROUP B

Typical "*Myrmoderus*": males *brown-backed* with black bib, females usually *rufous below;* both sexes with *wing-spotting.*

Myrmeciza hemimelaena

CHESTNUT-TAILED ANTBIRD PLATE: 23

DESCRIPTION: 12 cm (4¾"). A *small,* short-tailed antbird of terra firme forest in Amazonia. Male has *head and neck dark gray* (feathers with black centers, resulting in faint scaly look); otherwise mostly reddish brown above with semiconcealed white dorsal patch, becoming *rufous-chestnut on tail;* wing-coverts mainly black, tipped with white or buffy white. *Throat and breast black,* becoming gray on sides (with variable amount, sometimes extensive, of white on midbelly) and brown on lower flanks and crissum. Female patterned above like male (including *rufous-chestnut tail*) but paler gray on head and neck and paler brown on back; *throat and breast rufous to cinnamon-buff,* usually quite strongly demarcated from *buffy white belly;* lower flanks tinged brownish.
SIMILAR SPECIES: Both sexes of Black-throated Antbird have somewhat longer, blackish (not chestnut) tail; males show no white on belly, whereas females lack female Chestnut-tailed's obvious 2-toned effect below.
HABITAT AND BEHAVIOR: Fairly common to common in undergrowth of terra firme forest and secondary woodland, also to some extent at forest borders (e.g., around treefalls); scarcer at n. end of range. Usually seen singly or in pairs, hopping about on or near the ground; rarely with mixed flocks and seldom attends army antswarms. Male's frequently given song, one of the characteristic forest sounds where the species is numerous (e.g., at the Tambopata Reserve in Madre de Dios, se. Peru) is a far-carrying, descending series of ringing, clear notes, "klee-klee-kli-kli-kli-klu."
RANGE: S. Colombia (recorded only from Puerto Umbría in w. Putumayo), e. Ecuador (few records), e. Peru, n. Bolivia (south to La Paz, Cochabamba, and n. Santa Cruz), and Amaz. Brazil (only south of the Amazon; east to the lower Rio Xingu, and south to s. Mato Grosso). Mostly below 1000 m (often numerous in foothills; recorded to 1480 m in Peru).

Myrmeciza atrothorax

BLACK-THROATED ANTBIRD PLATE: 23

Includes: Spot-breasted Antbird

DESCRIPTION: 14 cm (5½"). Male dark olive brown above with semi-concealed white dorsal patch; wings and *tail blackish,* wing-coverts

tipped with white dots. *Throat and breast black, sides of head, neck, and lower underparts dark gray. Tenebrosa* (w. Brazil west of the lower Rio Negro west locally to ne. Peru and ne. Ecuador) quite different, being *much more uniform slaty blackish* (including upperparts) with wing-spotting reduced to minute dots. Female above like male, except browner on wings and with buffier wing-dots (but *tail still blackish*); *throat white, breast orange-rufous,* becoming paler on belly and olivaceous on flanks. Female *tenebrosa* unknown.

SIMILAR SPECIES: Chestnut-tailed Antbird is smaller, and both sexes have a shorter, chestnut (not blackish) tail. Female Black-throated superficially resembles female of larger Spot-winged Antbird, but that is uniform orange-rufous below (no white throat). Female Yapacana Antbird is gray (not brown) above, lacks spotting on wing-coverts, etc. Cf. also Gray-bellied Antbird.

HABITAT AND BEHAVIOR: Uncommon to locally common (seemingly less numerous in nw. Amazonia) in dense undergrowth at borders of humid forest and especially in second-growth woodland and savanna woodland, most often in swampy areas or near water. Usually in pairs or small groups, foraging close to the ground, generally not with mixed flocks and rarely following army antswarms; not particularly shy and, for an antbird, not hard to see. Male's song is an incisive, sharp, high-pitched "chee-chi-chi-chi-chi, see, see, seé"; both sexes also give various "chit-chit" and "cheeyt" calls.

RANGE: Guianas, s. Venezuela (Bolívar and Amazonas), ne. Ecuador (few records), e. Peru, n. Bolivia (south to La Paz, Cochabamba, and Santa Cruz), and Amaz. Brazil (east to Amapá and the Rio Tocantins [though seemingly local east of the Rio Madeira], and south to s. Mato Grosso and n. Goiás). Mostly below 500 m (recorded to 1200 m in Venezuela).

NOTE: The two specimens from which *Myrmeciza stictothorax* (Spot-breasted Antbird) was described, a male and a female taken at Apacy on the lower Rio Tapajós in e. Amaz. Brazil, are here regarded as localized variants of *M. atrothorax,* following T. S. Schulenberg and D. F. Stotz (*Auk* 108[3]: 731–733, 1991). The male differs in having white spotting on its black breast, but several specimens of *M. atrothorax* from elsewhere in its range also show this, albeit to a lesser degree. The female has more extensively white underparts than any female *M. atrothorax,* so these authors suggest that *stictothorax* perhaps deserves recognition as a subspecies of *M. atrothorax.*

Myrmeciza pelzelni

GRAY-BELLIED ANTBIRD

DESCRIPTION: 13.5–14 cm (5¼–5½"). *Sw. Venezuela and adjacent Colombia and Brazil.* Resembles Black-throated Antbird (and no more "gray-bellied"). Male differs in being more rufescent above, with *tail rufous-chestnut* (not blackish); *wing-coverts with large buff spots* (not smaller white ones); and *sides of head and neck grizzled grayish and whitish.* See V-22. Female above like male (likewise with *grizzled sides of head and neck* and *large buff spots on wing-coverts*); *below mostly white,* scaled with black across breast, lower flanks and crissum olive brown.

HABITAT AND BEHAVIOR: Virtually unknown in life. Recorded from "shady humid rain forest" with "habits like those of Dull-mantled Antbird" (Meyer de Schauensee and Phelps 1978, p. 217).

RANGE: Sw. Venezuela (s. Amazonas), extreme e. Colombia (e. Guainía),and extreme nw. Brazil (upper Rio Negro drainage in n. Amazonas). 200–400 m.

GROUP C   *Ornately* patterned "*Myrmoderus*"; mainly terrestrial.

Myrmeciza ferruginea

FERRUGINOUS-BACKED ANTBIRD   PLATE: 23

DESCRIPTION: 15 cm (6″). Ne. South America. *Large, bare orbital area bright blue; legs and lower mandible bluish. Above mostly chestnut,* wing-coverts black with *2 bold buff wing-bars. Cheeks, throat, and breast black* boldly outlined by *white stripe back from eye and down sides of neck to sides of breast;* upper belly mottled gray and white, lower belly rufescent brown. Female like male but with *white throat.*

SIMILAR SPECIES: This exceptionally attractive antbird is virtually unmistakable.

HABITAT AND BEHAVIOR: Common on or near the ground inside humid forest, mainly in terra firme, and at forest borders; to a lesser extent also in lower stature forest growing in regions with sandy soil and savannas. Usually in pairs which walk and hop on forest floor, reminiscent of an antpipit (*Corythopis*); almost always independent of mixed flocks. Male's frequently heard song is a rather fast-paced and loud "weehee-weehee-weehee-weehee-weehee," with variations but the basic pattern normally the same.

RANGE: Guianas, extreme e. Venezuela (e. Bolívar), and ne. Amaz. Brazil (north of the Amazon west to the lower Rio Negro, south of it only between the lower Rio Tapajós and lower Rio Madeira). To 500 m.

Myrmeciza ruficauda

SCALLOPED ANTBIRD   PLATE: 23

DESCRIPTION: 14.5 cm (5¾″). *A scaly-looking antbird of e. Brazil.* Legs pinkish. Male mostly olive brown above, grayer on crown, *feathers of midback black tipped buff,* rump and tail dark rufous; wings blackish, coverts tipped buff forming wing-bars. Cheeks, throat, and chest black; *sides of neck and chest black fringed gray, breast feathers black broadly tipped gray,* belly ochraceous. Female above like male; throat white, *breast whitish boldly scalloped and spotted with black,* belly ochraceous.

SIMILAR SPECIES: Squamate and White-bibbed Antbirds are both longer-tailed, and both sexes of each show a bold white superciliary. Squamate only occurs south of Scalloped's range; Scalloped not known to overlap with White-bibbed, which is found only at higher elevations.

HABITAT AND BEHAVIOR: Uncommon to fairly common in undergrowth of humid forest, forest borders, and secondary woodland. Usually found singly or, more often, in pairs, foraging inconspicuously on or near ground, flicking leaves with its bill. Usually not associated with other birds. Its song, a semimusical, almost trilled "tree-ee-ee-ee-ee-ee-ee-ee" lasting about 2 seconds, is delivered at about 5-second intervals. Small numbers occur at Sooretama Reserve in n. Espírito Santo, and also at Pedra Branca above Murici in Alagoas. Scalloped Antbird deserves threatened status because of deforestation across much of its small range.

RANGE: E. Brazil (Paraíba to Alagoas, and in s. Bahia, extreme e. Minas Gerais, and Espírito Santo). To 500 m.

Myrmeciza squamosa

SQUAMATE ANTBIRD   PLATE: 23

DESCRIPTION: 15.5 cm (6"). *Se. Brazil.* Legs pinkish. Male *appears to combine head pattern of White-bibbed with underparts of Scalloped.* Brown above, feathers of midback with intermixed black, and a large white dorsal patch; wing-coverts black boldly tipped white forming prominent spotted wing-bars. *Long superciliary white,* outlining black face and throat; *feathers of breast black broadly tipped white* (producing a *bold scaly effect*); lower underparts whitish, flanks tinged brownish. Female above like male but lacks black bib (black reduced to cheeks); *throat and breast white,* feathers of throat tipped black producing faint scaly effect, feathers of breast variably mottled with black and with some olivaceous on sides; lower underparts like male's.

SIMILAR SPECIES: Male White-bibbed Antbird has white "bib" separating black throat from scaly breast; female has ochraceous buff throat and buff (not white) spotting on wing-coverts.

HABITAT AND BEHAVIOR: Fairly common on or near the ground inside humid forest and second-growth woodland. Behaves much like Scalloped Antbird, walking and hopping on or near the ground, rarely moving far and often quite tame. Male's song is a distinctive, somewhat shrill and wheezy "wheesee-wheesee-wheesee-wheesee-wheesee" gradually descending in pitch (sometimes up to 7 or only 4 "wheesee"s); female's is even shriller and higher-pitched. Both sexes also give a hard rattle in alarm (D. Stotz).

RANGE: Se. Brazil (Rio de Janeiro to ne. Rio Grande do Sul). To 1000 m.

NOTE: It has been suggested (e.g., Pinto 1978) that *squamosa* is conspecific with *M. loricata.* Although vocally they are very close, there is no evidence of intergradation in AMNH specimens, and we continue to follow most authorities (e.g., Meyer de Schauensee 1966, 1970) in treating it as a separate species.

Myrmeciza loricata

WHITE-BIBBED ANTBIRD   PLATE: 23

DESCRIPTION: 15.5 cm (6"). *Se. Brazil.* Legs pinkish. Male above much like male Squamate Antbird but *white superciliary even wider and hence more prominent,* and spotting on greater-coverts buff. Sides of head and upper throat black; remaining underparts, including *white "bib" on lower throat,* white with *band of black, white-tipped feathers across chest,* flanks brownish. Female above like male except spotting on all wing-coverts buff. *Throat ochraceous buff;* remaining underparts whitish with

some black scaling and olivaceous mottling on sides of breast, flanks brownish.

SIMILAR SPECIES: Dapper males are unlikely to be confused; females are unique among the 3 e. Brazil *Myrmeciza* in having a buffy throat (white in others).

HABITAT AND BEHAVIOR: Uncommon to fairly common on or near the ground inside humid forest and mature secondary woodland. Behavior similar to Squamate Antbird's, and its voice is virtually identical. Can be found at lower levels of Itatiaia Nat. Park.

RANGE: Se. Brazil (s. Bahia to Rio de Janeiro and in adjacent Minas Gerais and São Paulo). 700–1300 m.

GROUP D

Large and robust, with *heavy bill;* most show a *bare blue orbital patch.* Males *slaty to black* (only Plumbeous with wing-spots); all females *dissimilar.*

Myrmeciza hyperythra

PLUMBEOUS ANTBIRD   PLATE: 24

DESCRIPTION: 18 cm (7"). W. Amazonia. *Bare pale blue skin around eye* (mainly an elongated tear-shaped patch behind eye). Male basically *uniform slaty gray,* more blackish on wings and tail; *wing-coverts with small but conspicuous white spots.* Female above like male (*including the wing-spots*); *below uniform bright orange-rufous.*

SIMILAR SPECIES: Spot-winged and Slate-colored Antbirds are similar but have no bare blue skin on ocular area. Female Spot-winged is *brown* above except on head and has *buff* wing-spots; female Slate-colored is generally rufescent above. Sooty, White-shouldered, and Goeldi's Antbird males *lack* wing-spots.

HABITAT AND BEHAVIOR: Fairly common to common in undergrowth and borders of várzea and transitional forest. Usually in pairs, hopping through lower growth, generally not with mixed flocks and rarely or never in attendance at army antswarms. Among its near relatives, Plumbeous is the least shy and easiest to see. Pounds tail downward, especially when disturbed. In appropriate habitat its distinctive song is a characteristic sound: a fast, accelerating, slightly rising series of notes, "wo-wu-wr'wr'wr'wr'wr'wr'wr'wr'wr'wr" (Hilty and Brown 1986; RSR) given by both sexes and lasting about 3 seconds. The call is an equally characteristic, fast "wo-pur" or "wo-pur-chur," often rapidly repeated several times in succession. Seems particularly numerous at various points near the Río Napo in Ecuador and ne. Peru.

RANGE: Se. Colombia (north to w. Caquetá; probably also in s. Amazonas in Leticia area), ne. Ecuador (so far only in Napo), e. Peru, n. Bolivia (south to Beni and n. La Paz), and south of the Amazon in w. Brazil (east only to around Tefé, and south through Acre). To about 400 m.

Myrmeciza fortis

SOOTY ANTBIRD   PLATE: 24

DESCRIPTION: 18.5 cm (7¼"). W. Amazonia. *Extensive bare blue skin around eye.* Male *uniform sooty gray,* somewhat blacker on crown, re-

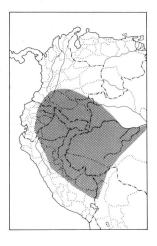

lieved only by (sometimes concealed) white along bend of wing; see C-30. Female has *crown rufous-chestnut;* otherwise brown above, more rufous on wings and rufous-chestnut on tail, with bend of wing as in male. *Sides of head, neck, and underparts uniform gray,* brown on flanks.
SIMILAR SPECIES: Male White-shouldered Antbird is very similar but is more uniformly black, shows less bare blue skin around eye (the best mark), and has slightly more white on shoulders; females of the two are very different. Cf. the mostly trans-Andean Immaculate Antbird (not known to overlap with Sooty, though their ranges come close in e. Colombia and they could occur together in the Macarena region). Females are very different, but male Immaculate differs from male Sooty only in being glossy black (not sooty).
HABITAT AND BEHAVIOR: Uncommon to locally fairly common in undergrowth of terra firme forest and mature secondary woodland. A shy antbird of deep forest interior, most often seen, and a little bolder, at army antswarms, where sometimes small groups are present. Pounds tail downward, especially when disturbed. Male's song is a rather infrequently heard, loud and penetrating, evenly delivered "teeuw-teeuw-teeuw-teeuw-teeuw-teeuw-teeuw-teeuw-teeuw," lasting about 3 seconds.
RANGE: Se. Colombia (north to w. Caquetá and Vaupés), e. Ecuador, e. Peru, extreme nw. Bolivia (Pando at Camino Mucden and La Paz at Alto Madidi), and w. Amaz. Brazil (north of the Amazon only at Tonantins; south of it east to the lower Rio Madeira). Mostly below 600 m (but recorded to 1050 m in s. Peru).

Myrmeciza immaculata

IMMACULATE ANTBIRD

DESCRIPTION: 18.5 cm (7¼"). *W. Venezuela to w. Ecuador. Extensive bare blue skin around eye* (paler, sometimes almost whitish, behind eye). Male *uniform black* with white (sometimes concealed) along bend of wing; see P-22. Female *uniform rich dark brown,* slightly paler below, with *blackish face and upper throat* and blackish tail; see C-27, P-22.
SIMILAR SPECIES: Occurring mostly west of Andes, the Immaculate Antbird is not known to range with any other large *Myrmeciza* antbird, though on Andes' e. slope in n. Colombia there is the possibility of overlap with Sooty Antbird. Chestnut-backed Antbird (which also has bare blue skin around eye and occurs with Immaculate) is substantially smaller.
HABITAT AND BEHAVIOR: Fairly common in undergrowth of humid forest, forest borders, and mature secondary woodland. A shy antbird, most often seen at army antswarms. Like Plumbeous and Sooty Antbirds, Immaculate often pounds its tail downward, especially when agitated or singing. Its presence is often made known by its loud song, a distinctive series of clear whistled notes, delivered rapidly and with slight emphasis on first note, "peer-peer-peer-peer-peer-peer-peer-peer," slowing somewhat toward the end.
RANGE: W. Venezuela (north locally to s. Lara), w. Colombia (Pacific lowlands, and slopes of Andes south in Río Cauca valley to Valle, in

Río Magdalena valley to Cundinamarca and Tolima; east of Andes south locally along their base to w. Meta on Macarena Mts.), and w. Ecuador (south to w. Loja). Also Costa Rica and Panama. Mostly below 1300 m (small numbers locally up to 2000 m).

Myrmeciza melanoceps

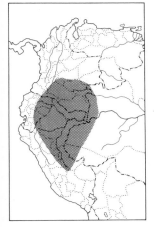

WHITE-SHOULDERED ANTBIRD PLATE: 24

DESCRIPTION: 18 cm (7″). W. Amazonia. *Limited* area of bare blue skin around eye. Male *uniform black* with white on shoulders and along bend of wing. Female has *head, throat, and chest black* contrasting with *rufous remaining upperparts* and *cinnamon-rufous remaining underparts.*
SIMILAR SPECIES: Male closely resembles male Sooty Antbird (which is grayer with more bare blue skin around eye). The striking female White-shouldered, with its black hood and basically rufous body, is virtually unmistakable. Both sexes are, however, remarkably similar to Cocha Antshrike (found only in a limited area of ne. Ecuador). The antshrike is smaller with a less robust bill, and both sexes lack any bare blue skin around eye; male has no white on bend of wing.
HABITAT AND BEHAVIOR: Fairly common in dense shrubby or viny growth at borders of humid forest (both terra firme and várzea) and in secondary woodland; rarely found far inside extensive terra firme forest. Usually in pairs which forage by hopping through lower growth, at times ranging higher above ground than the preceding 3 species are apt to. Sometimes with mixed flocks, and occasionally at army antswarms, but more often independent. Male's song is loud, very distinctive, and frequently heard, a ringing "pur, peeur-peeur-peeur-peeur"; sometimes female echoes with a softer version of her own. Alarmed or excited birds give an abrupt, loud "cheedo-cheeo-cheeo-cheeo-cheeyo" with almost a nunbird (*Monasa*)-like quality.
RANGE: Se. Colombia (north to Meta and Vaupés), e. Ecuador, ne. Peru (south to Lagarto on the upper Río Ucayali in Ucayali), and w. Amaz. Brazil (north of the Amazon along the lower Rio Putumayo, south of it along the upper Rio Juruá). To about 500 m.

Myrmeciza goeldii

GOELDI'S ANTBIRD PLATE: 24

DESCRIPTION: 18 cm (7″). *Se. Peru and adjacent Bolivia and Brazil. Iris bright red.* Male closely resembles male White-shouldered Antbird (no overlap) but with red (not dark) eye, only a little bluish gray bare skin around eye, almost *no* white on bend of wing, but *with* semiconcealed white dorsal patch (lacking in White-shouldered). Female is very different from female White-shouldered: above mostly rufous with *dusky gray crown and cheeks;* throat white, remaining underparts bright ochraceous cinnamon.
SIMILAR SPECIES: Male is also much like male of equally black White-backed Fire-eye, but the fire-eye has a smaller bill, more slender build, and longer tail; females are quite different in plumage.
HABITAT AND BEHAVIOR: Uncommon to locally fairly common in dense lower growth of transitional and várzea forest, especially favor-

ing thickets of *Heliconia* and bamboo. Behavior (including its loud "pur, peeur-peeur-peeur-peeur" song and other vocalizations) much like White-shouldered Antbird's. Goeldi's Antbird, until recently a very poorly known bird, is now readily found both at the Tambopata Reserve and at Hacienda Amazonia in se. Peru.

RANGE: Se. Peru (s. Ucayali at Balta south to Madre de Dios and adjacent Cuzco), extreme nw. Bolivia (Pando and n. La Paz at Alto Madidi), and extreme sw. Brazil (upper Rio Purus drainage). To 550 m.

NOTE: For additional behavioral information, see Parker (1982).

GROUP E

Smaller *Myrmeciza;* most *lack* prominent orbital patch.

Myrmeciza longipes

WHITE-BELLIED ANTBIRD

PLATE: 24

DESCRIPTION: 14.5–15 cm (5¾–6"). Local in deciduous and semihumid woodland and forest from Colombia to n. Brazil. Legs pinkish; narrow eye-ring bluish. Male *mostly bright rufous-chestnut above*, crown intermixed with some gray, and with *prominent gray superciliary wrapping around cheeks;* wings often, but not always, with black spots (sometimes large) on coverts. *Lower face, throat, and chest black* contrasting with gray breast; belly white, washed with rufous on lower flanks and crissum. Female similar but with duller foreparts: crown browner, cheeks dusky, and *throat and breast ochraceous.* Foregoing applies to *griseipectus* of Venezuela south of the Orinoco, e. Colombia, and Brazil; nominate race and *panamensis* of n. Venezuela and n. Colombia similar but with whiter breast (meeting the black bib) and no wingspots in male; see V-22, P-22. *Boucardi* males, of Colombia's upper Río Magdalena valley, have fully gray crown, gray breast, and no wingspots; females have more ochraceous belly.

SIMILAR SPECIES: There are relatively few other more or less terrestrial antbirds in the deciduous woodlands/forests this antbird favors, none of them with such bright rufous upperparts. Cf. Bicolored and female Chestnut-backed Antbirds (both inhabitants of humid forest.

HABITAT AND BEHAVIOR: Fairly common to common (recorded mostly by voice) in the often thick undergrowth of deciduous and semi humid forest, second-growth woodland, and borders. Usually in pairs, hopping about on or near the ground; generally shy and seldom seen without tape playback. Sometimes follows army ants. Ants (not necessarily army ants) constitute, at least in Panama, "a regular source of food" (Wetmore 1972, p. 199); despite the name "antbird," this is unusual in the family, originally named for their habit of following, not eating, ants. Male's loud, far-carrying, and often-heard song is a fast, ringing crescendo of notes which trail off toward the end, e.g., "cheer, cheer, cheer-cheer-cheer-cheercheercheercheer-chew-chew, chew, chew."

RANGE: N. Colombia (Caribbean lowlands from e. Córdoba eastward, up Río Magdalena valley to Huila, and east of Andes south along their e. base to w. Meta), much of Venezuela (though absent from much of the llanos area), w. Guyana, and locally in n. Brazil (Roraima, and along n. bank of the Amazon from Amapá west to Óbidos); French Guiana (sightings at Saül); Trinidad. Also Panama. Mostly below 700 m, in smaller numbers up locally to 1700 m.

Myrmeciza exsul

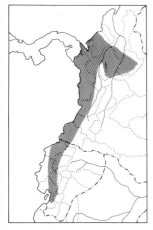

CHESTNUT-BACKED ANTBIRD PLATE: 24

DESCRIPTION: 13.5 cm (5¼″). *W. Colombia and w. Ecuador. Bare ocular region pale blue;* iris brown. In most of S. Am. range (*maculifer* and *cassini*) male has *head, neck, and underparts slaty black* contrasting with *dark chestnut back, wings, and tail;* wing-coverts with white spots; flanks and crissum brown. Female above much like male but duller; upper throat slaty gray, remaining underparts brown, brightest and most rufescent on breast. See C-29. Both sexes of *niglarus* (extreme nw. Colombia) lack wing-spotting, and females are duller below; they resemble P-22 (2a).

SIMILAR SPECIES: Among trans-Andean antbirds, neither Dull-mantled nor Esmeraldas Antbird shows a bare blue ocular area, and both of these have red eyes.

HABITAT AND BEHAVIOR: Fairly common to common (recorded mostly by voice, though not especially shy) in undergrowth of humid forest and secondary woodland. Usually in pairs which forage close to, but generally not on, the ground, often perching sideways on small vertical saplings. Sometimes attracted to army antswarms, though not a persistent follower. Best known from its easily recognized and often-heard song, 2 or 3 emphatic whistled notes, "peh, peeea" or "peh, peh, peeéa" (sometimes aptly paraphrased, e.g., by F. Chapman, as "come-here" or "come-right-hére"); also gives a soft nasal chirring note and a sharper, fast "quit-it" (Willis and Oniki 1972).

RANGE: W. Colombia (humid Caribbean lowlands east across n. base of Andes to middle Río Magdalena valley in Antioquia, and Pacific lowlands) and w. Ecuador (south to El Oro). Also Honduras to Panama. To about 900 m.

Myrmeciza nigricauda

ESMERALDAS ANTBIRD PLATE: 24

DESCRIPTION: 14 cm (5½″). Formerly called *Sipia rosenbergi* (the female of "*rosenbergi*" turns out to be the same as the female of *Myrmeciza laemosticta nigricauda;* see below). *Sw. Colombia and w. Ecuador. Iris bright red.* Male *mostly dark leaden gray* with semiconcealed white dorsal patch; wing-coverts blacker with small but conspicuous white spots. Female similar to male but back, rump, and wings mostly dark brown, spotting on wing-coverts sometimes buffier, *throat lightly spotted with white,* and flanks and lower belly dark brown.

SIMILAR SPECIES: Female Dull-mantled Antbird (no known overlap) closely resembles female Esmeraldas but has rufous tail, is brighter and more rufescent (not so dark) brown above, and has more extensive white markings on throat. Male Chestnut-backed Antbird differs from female Esmeraldas in showing a bare blue ocular area and in lacking throat flecking. Both sexes of Stub-tailed Antbird are blacker generally and have brown eyes, and female is prominently spotted white below. HABITAT AND BEHAVIOR: Uncommon in undergrowth of humid forest and mature secondary woodland, especially favoring shady damp ravines, and mainly in foothills. Seems to be the southern replacement for Dull-mantled Antbird, with very similar general behavior and vocalizations. Usually in pairs, hopping about close to, but usually not on, ground; sometimes attends army antswarms. The song is a short series of high, thin, sharp notes, "psee-pseé-psee-psee-psee-pseé," with some variation in the number of notes but usually the second and always the last accented. Can be found along lower sections of the Chiriboga road in Pichincha, Ecuador.

RANGE: W. Colombia (Chocó from Baudó Mts. southward) and w. Ecuador (south to El Oro). Mostly 500–1100 m.

NOTE: M. Robbins and RSR (*Bull. B. O. C.* III[1]: 11–18, 1991) are followed in considering *Sipia rosenbergi* as a synonym of *M. laemosticta nigricauda* and in merging the genus *Sipia* into *Myrmeciza*. *Nigricauda* was described on the basis of a single female, and the type has been shown to be identical to what were long considered to be female "*rosenbergi*." The taxa *nigricauda* and *rosenbergi* are thus one and the same; the name *nigricauda* has priority. Recent field work indicates that there is no fundamental difference between *Sipia* and certain members of the genus *Myrmeciza*, and indeed the long-standing confusion between "*rosenbergi*" and *nigricauda* demonstrates just how similar they are.

Myrmeciza laemosticta

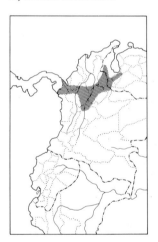

DULL-MANTLED ANTBIRD

DESCRIPTION: 14 cm (5½"). *N. Colombia and nw. Venezuela. Iris red.* Male has head, neck, and most of underparts gray with *back olive brown* and rump, most of wings, and tail more rufescent; wing-coverts with white spots, and a semiconcealed white dorsal patch; *throat black;* flanks and lower belly brown. Female much like male but *throat checkered black and white* and spots on wing-coverts buff; it closely resembles female Esmeraldas Antbird (see that species). See C-29, P-22.

SIMILAR SPECIES: Both sexes of the much more common Chestnut-backed Antbird have a prominent bare blue ocular area and a dark eye; male Chestnut-backed has a brighter back which contrasts more with its slaty head, and a less discrete black throat patch. Cf. also Esmeraldas Antbird.

HABITAT AND BEHAVIOR: Poorly known in South America; the information given by Hilty and Brown (1986) actually refers to *M. nigricauda, not* to true *M. laemosticta*. Better known in Panama (see Ridgely and Gwynne 1989); there, local and uncommon in undergrowth of humid forest, mainly in foothills and especially favoring shady streamsides and dark ravines. General behavior, including occasional presence at army antswarms, similar to Chestnut-backed Antbird's. Male's song, a series of about 6 very high, penetrating notes, "beet, beet, beet-beet-beet-beet" with female occasionally following with a softer "beet-beet, chutu" (B. Whitney; RSR), is very similar to Esmeraldas Antbird's.

RANGE: N. Colombia (humid Caribbean lowlands from n. Chocó east along n. base of Andes into Río Magdalena valley in Caldas and Norte de Santander) and nw. Venezuela (east locally to Mérida and Táchira, and on slopes of Sierra de Perijá). Also Costa Rica and Panama. To 1100 m.

NOTE: *Nigricauda* is no longer considered a race of *M. laemosticta;* until recently it was treated as a blackish-tailed subspecies of that species, but it was then shown to be the same as "*Sipia rosenbergi*" (see M. Robbins and RSR, *Bull. B. O. C.* 111[1]: 11–18, 1991). Dull-mantled Antbird thus does not occur in sw. Colombia or w. Ecuador.

Myrmeciza berlepschi

STUB-TAILED ANTBIRD   PLATE: 24

DESCRIPTION: 13.5 cm (5¼″). *W. Colombia and nw. Ecuador.* Tail short (the shortest-tailed *Myrmeciza,* but only by a small margin). Iris reddish brown. Male *all black* with semiconcealed white dorsal patch. Female similar but wing-coverts with tiny white dots; *throat and breast thickly dotted with white.*

SIMILAR SPECIES: Esmeraldas Antbird favors somewhat higher elevations (though with some overlap). Both sexes have red (not brown) eye; male is basically slaty (not black), female is gray and brown (not essentially black) with white flecking on throat only.

HABITAT AND BEHAVIOR: Uncommon and perhaps local in lower growth of humid forest, secondary woodland, and dense overgrown borders; possibly mainly a bird of disturbed areas, not extensive primary forest. Usually in pairs which forage close to, but usually not on, the ground in thick undergrowth, where often hard to see (though not especially shy); pumps tail downward. Male's song is a series of notes which start slowly, then rise, "chi, chu-chu-chu-chew-chéw-chéw-chéw," with accented final note; the call is a high, sharp "chít" or "ch-dit." Small numbers occur in lower growth along lower Buenaventura road in Valle, Colombia.

RANGE: W. Colombia (Pacific lowlands from s. Chocó southward) and nw. Ecuador (Esmeraldas). To 650 m.

NOTE: Formerly placed in the genus *Sipia.* See comments under Esmeraldas Antbird.

Gymnocichla Antbirds

A monotypic genus which seems closely related to the "large" *Myrmeciza* antbirds; it likely should be merged into that genus. Males have a unique bare crown, possibly just an "extension" from the bare ocular areas of so many other antbirds, including several *Myrmeciza.*

Gymnocichla nudiceps

BARE-CROWNED ANTBIRD   PLATE: 24

DESCRIPTION: 16 cm (6¼″). *N. Colombia.* Male *black* with *entire crown and ocular area bare and bright blue,* and semiconcealed white dorsal patch; wing-coverts narrowly fringed white and tail feathers narrowly tipped white (sometimes abraded off). Female has only *orbital area bare and bright blue;* otherwise olivaceous brown above with semiconcealed white dorsal patch, wing-coverts fringed rufous (more broadly

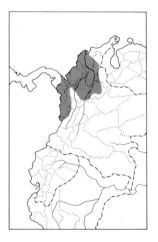

than in male); *below uniform rufous.* See C-27. Female of nominate race, which just enters n. Chocó from Panama, differs from *sanctamartae* (remainder of Colombian range) in being more rufescent above and richer rufous below.

SIMILAR SPECIES: Male virtually unmistakable as no other antbird has *entire crown* featherless and bright blue. Female Chestnut-backed Antbird (also with bare blue orbital area) is smaller, has gray head, and not as bright underparts. Female Immaculate Antbird is darker brown generally with no rufous edging on wing-coverts.

HABITAT AND BEHAVIOR: Uncommon to locally fairly common in lower growth at borders of humid forest, second-growth woodland, and shrubby overgrown clearings. Usually in pairs, often skulking and difficult to see except when it attends army antswarms (which it frequently does); often pounds tail downward. Male's song is a series of about 8 loud, ringing notes on same pitch but with some acceleration during second half, "chew-chew-chew-chew-cheep-cheep-cheep-cheep," delivered with quivering tail; recalls song of Immaculate Antbird.

RANGE: N. Colombia (Pacific lowlands south to s. Chocó, and humid Caribbean lowlands east locally to Guajira Peninsula and south in Río Magdalena valley into Antioquia). Also Guatemala and Belize to Panama. To 400 m.

Myrmornis Antbirds

An oddly proportioned antbird found locally in humid lowland forests. Its systematic position was long debated, but it now seems well established that it is not especially close to the antthrushes and antpittas but rather is closest to several thamnophiline genera, perhaps especially *Hylophylax* (E. O. Willis, *Rev. Brasil. Zool.,* São Paulo 2: 159–164, 1984). The voice is typically thamnophiline (P. Schwartz and M. Lentino, *Serie Informes Científicos* DGSIIA/IC/24, 1984), and the placement of its nest in a fork and its white egg also indicate this relationship (O. Tostain and J.-L. Dujardin, *Condor* 90[2]: 236–239, 1988).

Myrmornis torquata

WING-BANDED ANTBIRD

PLATE: 24

DESCRIPTION: 15.5–16 cm (6–6¼"). A *short-legged, short-tailed, and* long-billed antbird found on the floor of humid lowland forests. Dark gray eye-ring. Male brown above mottled with chestnut and dusky and with semiconcealed white dorsal patch; wings blackish, coverts and outer flight feathers edged buff; tail rufous-chestnut. *Throat and chest black,* bordered by *wide area of scaled black and white from behind eye down sides of neck to sides of chest;* remaining underparts gray, crissum rufous. Female similar but with *throat and upper chest rufous,* only lower cheeks black. *Stictoptera* (n. Colombia) differs in having a more prominent bare blue eye-ring, the scaled black and white area restricted to sides of neck, duller chestnut tail, no rufous on crissum, and richer buff

banding on wing-coverts; female has rufous, decidedly deeper, only on throat. See P-22.

SIMILAR SPECIES: This chunky terrestrial antbird has such a distinctive shape that confusion is improbable: it is short-tailed like an antpitta but has short legs, and its behavior is much closer to various thamnophiline antbirds'.

HABITAT AND BEHAVIOR: Rare to uncommon and seemingly local (from specimens perhaps most numerous in Amaz. Brazil south of the Amazon) on and near the ground inside humid forest. Usually in pairs, and quite tame for an antbird, sometimes hopping (*not* walking) and feeding unconcernedly almost at one's feet. Forages on the ground, probing into leaf litter, industriously flicking aside leaves, sometimes almost disappearing "inside" or under leaves. Seems not to be attracted to army antswarms. A nasal "chirr" call, frequently given in alarm, sometimes reveals its presence. Less often heard is its song, a long series (lasting up to 8–10 seconds) of insistent emphatic whistled notes very gradually ascending in pitch and increasing in intensity, "tueee, tueee-tueee-tueee-tueee . . . tweetweetwee"; this is often given from a perch some 3–6 m above ground. Nominate and *stictoptera* give similar songs.

RANGE: N. Colombia (n. Chocó east along humid n. base of Andes to middle Río Magdalena valley in w. Boyacá); se. Colombia (w. Caquetá and w. Putumayo), e. Ecuador (local), and ne. Peru (ne. Loreto); Guianas, s. Venezuela (Bolívar and Amazonas), and e. and cen. Amaz. Brazil (north of the Amazon west to the lower Rio Negro, south of it to Rondônia and n. Mato Grosso, and east to n. Maranhão); there is also an uncertain 19th-century record supposedly from Bahia, Brazil. Also Nicaragua and Panama. To about 1200 m.

NOTE: Trans-Andean *stictoptera* is perhaps a separate species from *M. torquata:* its plumage differences are quite marked, but the similarity of its song suggests that it may not have attained reproductive isolation. If split, it could be called the Western Wing-banded Antbird, and *M. torquata* the Eastern Wing-banded Antbird. Calling *stictoptera* the Buff-banded Antbird, as suggested by Meyer de Schauensee (1966), seems unhelpful as *both* forms have similar buff wing-bands.

Pithys Antbirds

A pair of striking and attractively patterned antbirds found in Amazonian and Guianan forests. The White-plumed Antbird, one of the most widely recognized members of its family, in its range is perhaps the most frequently seen "professional" follower of army antswarms. The status of the White-masked Antbird, however, remains a complete enigma.

Pithys albifrons   **WHITE-PLUMED ANTBIRD**   PLATE: 25

DESCRIPTION: 12–12.5 cm (4¾–5"). Legs yellow-orange. Unmistakable, with *unique ornate facial plumes: conspicuous long white plumes* on either side of forehead *almost always held straight up in a bifurcated*

point, and *shorter white plumes on chin forming a "beard."* Head and throat black; mantle and wings dark blue-gray. *Nuchal collar, underparts, rump, and tail chestnut.* Nominate race (s. Venezuela and Guianas south to the Rio Negro and Amazon in n. Brazil) has a narrow white postocular streak which *brevibarba* and *peruviana* of w. portion of range lack. Juvenile duller with no white plumes or rufous collar.

SIMILAR SPECIES: Cf. the rare and range-restricted White-masked Antbird.

HABITAT AND BEHAVIOR: Fairly common to common in undergrowth of terra firme forest, less often into adjacent second-growth woodland and at forest borders; less numerous in w. Amazonia. A confirmed follower of army antswarms, seldom seen elsewhere; a dozen or more may gather at large swarms where, in correct habitat, they are usually the most numerous antbird. Even then they are normally wary, retreating to dense cover when disturbed, there skulking and chirring in alarm until satisfied that danger is past. Like so many other forest understory antbirds, the White-plumed likes especially to cling to slender vertical saplings; at swarms it quickly drops to the ground to snap up prey, then goes to another branch. Foraging birds utter sharp chipping notes interspersed with a listless whistled note, e.g., "seeeee . . . seeeee . . . tchíp . . . seeeee . . . tchíp-tchip."

RANGE: Guianas, s. Venezuela (Bolívar and Amazonas, and in s. Táchira), Amaz. Brazil (only north of the Amazon), e. Colombia (north along base of Andes to Arauca), e. Ecuador, and e. Peru (south to n. Cuzco on the Cordillera de Vilcabamba; not recorded south of the Amazon or east of the Río Ucayali). Mostly below 1100 m (recorded to 1360 m in Venezuela).

Pithys castanea

WHITE-MASKED ANTBIRD

DESCRIPTION: 14 cm (5½"). *Known from only a single female specimen from n. Peru.* Recalls White-plumed Antbird but larger and *lacking plumes. Mostly chestnut* (including all of upperparts; *no gray mantle*) with *contrasting black head and throat* and *white face (including triangular area back from eye) and upper throat.*

SIMILAR SPECIES: Overall coloration and pattern somewhat recall female White-shouldered Antbird, but White-masked is much smaller.

HABITAT AND BEHAVIOR: Unknown in life. E. O. Willis (*Rev. Brasil. Zool.,* São Paulo 2[3]: 165–170, 1984) searched unsuccessfully for this bird at the type locality, as have we in nearby Ecuador.

RANGE: Recorded from a single specimen taken in 1937 at Andoas on the Río Pastaza in extreme n. Loreto, Peru. 250 m.

NOTE: E. O. Willis (op. cit.) suggests that what is known as *Pithys castanea* may represent only a hybrid between *P. albifrons* and some other antbird species.

Gymnopithys Antbirds

A small group of plump and short-tailed antbirds found in undergrowth inside humid lowland forest, where they are among the more numerous of the "professional" attendants at army antswarms. Bicolored and Rufous-throated Antbirds form a closely related pair of species (Bicolored may itself be composed of two species), and White-throated and Lunulated form another such pair.

Gymnopithys leucaspis

BICOLORED ANTBIRD

PLATE: 25

Includes: White-cheeked Antbird

DESCRIPTION: 14–14.5 cm (5½–5¾″). Populations of this species found east and west of Andes, sometimes considered as 2 species, are here considered conspecific. Leg color variable, apparently always plumbeous to bluish gray in trans-Andean birds, rarely pinkish in cis-Andean birds. *Pale bluish ocular area striking in birds east of Andes, dusky* (and less conspicuous) *in birds west of Andes. East* of Andes, nominate group (including *castanea*) *uniform chestnut brown above. Below mostly white* (extending up to include lower cheeks below eye), with black band extending from face down to sides of breast; flanks broadly black to brown. Female (only) has semiconcealed dorsal patch cinnamon-rufous. *West* of Andes, *bicolor* group similar but has *gray border above and behind black cheeks* (*ruficeps* of ne. Antioquia, Colombia, lacks this), and white throat does *not* reach eye; *daguae* and *aequatorialis* (Pacific w. Colombia from s. Chocó southward, and in w. Ecuador) have paler, *rufous crown. Bicolor* group female's back feathers lack cinnamon-rufous. See C-27, P-22.

SIMILAR SPECIES: The geographic variation is confusing, but this well-named antbird is indeed "*bicolored*" (essentially brown above and white below).

HABITAT AND BEHAVIOR: Uncommon to fairly common in undergrowth of humid forest (east of Andes mainly or entirely in terra firme) and mature secondary woodland. Almost always noted at army antswarms, where often the most numerous species (sometimes 12 or more individuals are present); frequently clings to vertical stems. Usually wary at such swarms, though at times its eagerness to feed overcomes its natural shyness and it becomes wonderfully bold. In Costa Rica (elsewhere?) Bicolored Antbirds have even been recorded accompanying a person walking through forest, evidently feeding on flushed insects, much as they feed on arthropods attempting to flee ants at antswarms. Rather noisy and vocal; the Bicolored's calls are often the first indication of a nearby antswarm. Its song is a series of semimusical whistled notes, at first rising and more musical, then descending and more nasal, characteristically ending with a nasal snarl or "chrrrr"; also often gives a separate "chrrrr" call. Birds east and west of Andes have similar vocalizations.

RANGE: W. Colombia (east in humid Caribbean lowlands to middle Río Magdalena valley in e. Antioquia) and w. Ecuador (south, at least formerly, to El Oro; few recent records south of Pichincha); e. Colombia (north to Meta and Guainía), e. Ecuador, ne. Peru (Amazonas, n. San Martín, and Loreto; not recorded east of the Río Ucayali or south of the Amazon), and nw. Amaz. Brazil (north of the Amazon and west of the Rio Negro). Also Honduras to Panama. West of Andes up to 900 m, east of them to 750 m.

NOTE: Trans-Andean birds have sometimes been considered a separate species from birds east of Andes; if split, the former would be *G. bicolor* (Bicolored Antbird), the latter *G. leucaspis* (White-cheeked Antbird). E. O. Willis (*Univ. Cal. Publ. Zool.* 79: 1–127, 1967) suggested that the *bicolor* and *leucaspis* groups might not be conspecific; this was followed by Hilty and Brown (1986), though not by Meyer de Schauensee (1970) or the 1983 AOU Check-list. As all forms in the complex are so morphologically and vocally similar, we prefer to treat them as a single specific unit.

Gymnopithys rufigula

RUFOUS-THROATED ANTBIRD   PLATE: 25

DESCRIPTION: 14.5–15 cm (5¾–6″). *Ne. South America*. Legs pinkish. *Striking large ocular area pale bluish*. Uniform brown above with blackish forehead; semiconcealed dorsal patch white in male, cinnamon-rufous in female. *Throat and lower cheeks rich rufous-chestnut*, becoming ochraceous on remaining underparts, broadly more olive brown on sides and flanks.

SIMILAR SPECIES: Combination of bold ocular area, mostly brown coloration, and rufous throat distinctive.

HABITAT AND BEHAVIOR: Fairly common in undergrowth of humid forest, primarily in terra firme. Behavior very similar to Bicolored Antbird's and, like it, almost always encountered following an army antswarm, often with larger numbers of White-plumed Antbirds. At a swarm Rufous-throated gives chirring calls much like those given by Bicolored and White-plumed Antbirds.

RANGE: Guianas, s. Venezuela (Bolívar and Amazonas), and n. Amaz. Brazil (north of the Amazon and west to the Río Negro). To 900 m.

Gymnopithys salvini

WHITE-THROATED ANTBIRD   PLATE: 25

DESCRIPTION: 14.5 cm (5¾″). *Sw. Amazonia*. Male *mostly gray with contrasting white throat and broad supraloral* and some white on ear-coverts; tail blackish *barred with white*. Female has *blackish crown contrasting with rufous sides of head, throat, and chest*; otherwise brown above, *feathers of mantle and wing-coverts with black subterminal band and rufous tip* (imparting an obvious barred effect); *tail rufous barred black*. Lower underparts brown.

SIMILAR SPECIES: Cf. the similar Lunulated Antbird (no overlap). Female is colored much like females of longer-tailed Blackish and Black Antbirds (*Cercomacra*), neither of which shows any barring.

HABITAT AND BEHAVIOR: Uncommon in undergrowth of terra firme and transitional forest. Like its congeners, the White-throated Antbird is an inveterate follower of army antswarms and is seldom seen elsewhere. Typically only a few are found at a swarm, where they are often quite easy to observe, being relatively tame. Vocalizations, though generally not so vigorous, recall those of Bicolored Antbird. Can be found at the Tambopata Reserve in Madre de Dios, Peru.

RANGE: South of the Amazon in e. Peru (s. Loreto south to Madre de Dios and Puno; not recorded west of the Río Ucayali), n. Bolivia (south to n. La Paz and Cochabamba), and w. Amaz. Brazil (east to the Río Madeira). To 500 m.

NOTE: For more information on this and the following species, see E. O. Willis (*Condor* 70[2]: 128–148, 1968).

Gymnopithys lunulata

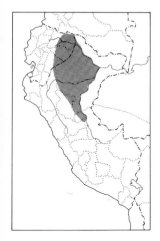

LUNULATED ANTBIRD

DESCRIPTION: 14.5 cm (5¾″). *Local in e. Ecuador and ne. Peru.* Male resembles male White-throated Antbird (no overlap) but has *plain blackish tail* with no white barring. Female is less like female White-throated: it *lacks rufous-chestnut* (being mainly olive brown) and has *throat and supraloral white* (recalling male); further, its dusky tail has 3 inconspicuous white bars on inner web of rectrices (showing mostly on central pair; *no black barring*), and feathers on back and wing-coverts are tipped with buff (not rich rufous).

HABITAT AND BEHAVIOR: Rare to uncommon in undergrowth of, so far as known, várzea forest. Behavior similar to White-throated Antbird's; the 2 species have parapatric ranges. Reportedly numerous at Yarinacocha, near the Río Ucayali in Loreto, Peru (E. O. Willis, *Condor* 70[2]: 128–148, 1968). We do not know its voice.

RANGE: Locally in e. Ecuador (a few localities in Sucumbios, Napo, and Pastaza) and ne. Peru (Loreto and Ucayali; recorded only west of the Río Ucayali). 200–300 m.

Rhegmatorhina Antbirds

A group of five (possibly six) species, all with allopatric ranges, of rather plump and short-tailed antbirds found in Amaz. forests. They are among the more spectacular antbirds on account of their wide, bare ocular areas (which impart an odd, goggle-like effect) and their striking coloration or bold patterning. Most species' crown feathers are elongated, shiny, and pointed; those of Hairy-crested Antbird are shorter, decomposed, and more filamentous. All are confirmed followers of army antswarms. E. O. Willis (*Wilson Bull.* 81[4]: 363–395, 1969) described the behavior of the genus; this paper included a color illustration depicting both sexes of each species.

GROUP A

Elongated crest feathers "*normal.*"

Rhegmatorhina gymnops

BARE-EYED ANTBIRD   PLATE: 25

DESCRIPTION: 14–14.5 cm (5½–5¾″). *Limited area east of the Rio Tapajós in lower Amaz. Brazil. Wide bare ocular area pale glaucous green.* Long crown feathers usually held depressed but at times elevated into a *spiky crest.* Male's *head and most of underparts sooty black*, becoming brown on belly; back, wings, and tail uniform umber brown. Female similar but most of breast brown.

SIMILAR SPECIES: Not likely to be confused in its limited range. Sooty Antbird male is vaguely similar but larger and all black (with no brown), lacks crest, has differently shaped ocular area, etc.; it only occurs farther west in Amazonia.

HABITAT AND BEHAVIOR: Uncommon in undergrowth of terra firme forest. Usually quite shy and encountered mainly at army antswarms; generally only a few birds are present at a swarm. Forages close to the ground, often clinging to vertical saplings, less often on logs or horizontal branches, from there dropping briefly to the ground in pursuit of fleeing arthropod prey. Overall behavior and vocalizations closely resemble those of *Gymnopithys* antbirds, though *Rhegmatorhina* frequently raise their long crest feathers in aggressive displays and flick their tail upward (E. O. Willis). A typical song is a descending "wheeeeu, whew-whew-whew-whew-wrr," sometimes with several more nasal snarling notes at the end; these more nasal notes are also often given independently.

RANGE: E. Amaz. Brazil (mainly between e. bank of the lower Rio Tapajós and w. bank of the lower Rio Xingu, south to n. Mato Grosso at Alta Floresta). To 400 m.

Rhegmatorhina hoffmannsi

WHITE-BREASTED ANTBIRD   PLATE: 25

DESCRIPTION: 15 cm (6"). *Limited area east of the Rio Madeira in central Amaz. Brazil. Wide bare ocular area yellowish green.* Long crown feathers, usually held depressed, sometimes elevated into a *spiky crest*. Male has crown black; otherwise plain olive brown above. *Cheeks, throat, and breast white;* remaining underparts dull grayish. Female like male but crown dark chestnut with fine black streaking; feathers of back and wing-coverts with broad black subterminal band and buff tip (*imparting a bold scaly appearance*), and *lower underparts irregularly banded black and dull buff.*

SIMILAR SPECIES: Nearly unmistakable in its small range. Female Harlequin Antbird (no recorded overlap) has similar overall color and pattern, but its face is black and its chest rufous-chestnut.

HABITAT AND BEHAVIOR: Uncommon to locally common in undergrowth of terra firme forest. Behavior and vocalizations very like Bare-eyed Antbird's. Small numbers can be seen on Fazenda Rancho Grande south of Ariquemes in Rondônia.

RANGE: Cen. Amaz. Brazil (e. bank of the lower Rio Madeira south and east through Rondônia to w. Mato Grosso on the Serra dos Parecís and Serra das Araras). To 300 m.

Rhegmatorhina berlepschi

HARLEQUIN ANTBIRD   PLATE: 25

DESCRIPTION: 15 cm (6"). *Very limited area west of the lower Rio Tapajós in e. Amaz. Brazil. Wide bare ocular area yellowish to glaucous green.* Long crown feathers usually held depressed but at times elevated into a *spiky crest*. Male has chestnut crown (crest feathers darker, almost blackish), *black face and upper throat,* and *rufous-chestnut nape, lower throat, and chest;* otherwise olive brown above; *sides of neck and chest, and remaining underparts, gray.* Female patterned much like male but feathers of back and wing-coverts with black subterminal band and

narrow buff tip, and *lower underparts irregularly banded black and dull buff.*

SIMILAR SPECIES: Boldly patterned male is essentially unmistakable. Female resembles female White-breasted Antbird (no recorded overlap) but has black and rufous (not white) throat and chest.

HABITAT AND BEHAVIOR: Uncommon in undergrowth of terra firme forest. Behavior much like Bare-eyed Antbird's; vocalizations are also much alike (E. O. Willis). Small numbers are found in Amazonia Nat. Park west of Itaituba along the Trans-Amazon Highway.

RANGE: E. Amaz. Brazil (near w. bank of the lower Rio Tapajós). 150 m.

Rhegmatorhina cristata

CHESTNUT-CRESTED ANTBIRD

DESCRIPTION: 15 cm (6″). *Very limited area in Vaupés, Colombia, and adjacent nw. Brazil. Wide bare ocular area pale bluish.* Long crown feathers usually held depressed but at times elevated in a *spiky crest.* Male has *bright rufous-chestnut crown, sides of neck, and underparts,* becoming brown on belly; face and upper throat black, crest feathers somewhat darker than crown; above otherwise olive brown. See C-30. Female similar but back with scattered small black bars.

SIMILAR SPECIES: Combination of conspicuous ocular area and bright rufous-chestnut on crown, neck, and breast makes this species virtually unmistakable.

HABITAT AND BEHAVIOR: Uncommon in undergrowth of terra firme forest. Behavior very like Bare-eyed Antbird's; vocalizations are also much alike (E. O. Willis).

RANGE: Se. Colombia (Vaupés and extreme n. Amazonas near Apaporis, *fide* H. Brodkin) and extreme nw. Brazil (along the upper Rio Uaupés). About 200 to 250 m.

GROUP B

Elongated crest feathers *decomposed* (pale ashy or golden in color).

Rhegmatorhina melanosticta

HAIRY-CRESTED ANTBIRD

PLATE: 25

DESCRIPTION: 15 cm (6″). W. Amazonia. *Wide bare ocular area pale bluish. Crown feathers rather filamentous and hair-like,* sometimes raised as a bushy crest. Male has *pale smoky gray crown* and black face and upper throat; otherwise brown above, more rufescent on wings and tail. Below grayish olive brown. Female similar but feathers of back and wing-coverts with black subterminal band and narrow buff tipping (*imparting an irregular scaly look*). *Brunneiceps* (along e. base of Andes in Peru from San Martín south to n. Cuzco at Hacienda Luisiana) looks strikingly different, with *golden buff crown.*

SIMILAR SPECIES: Conspicuous pale ocular area and gray or golden crown are distinctive.

HABITAT AND BEHAVIOR: Uncommon to locally fairly common in undergrowth of humid forest, primarily in terra firme forest away from

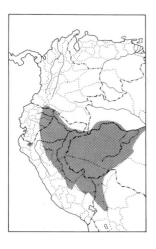

rivers. Behavior much like Bare-eyed Antbird's; vocalizations are also much alike.

RANGE: Extreme s. Colombia (w. Putumayo), e. Ecuador (rather local), e. Peru, n. Bolivia (south to n. La Paz and sw. Beni), and w. Amaz. Brazil (east to the Rio Madeira, and recorded mainly south of the Amazon; north of it known only from Tonantins). To 1050 m.

NOTE: *Brunneiceps* perhaps deserves full species status for it differs dramatically from races of *R. melanosticta* found to its east; as far as we are aware, no intergradation between the two types has been shown. If split, *R. brunneiceps* could be called the Golden-crested Antbird, with *R. melanosticta* called the Gray-crested Antbird, retaining the name Hairy-crested Antbird for the expanded species.

Skutchia Antbirds

A medium-sized ant-following antbird found in a small part of Amaz. Brazil. The recently erected genus *Skutchia* is apparently most closely related to the *Phlegopsis* bare-eyes, from which it differs in lacking extensive bare red skin around the eye.

Skutchia borbae

PALE-FACED ANTBIRD   PLATE: 25
Other: Pale-faced Bare-eye

DESCRIPTION: 16.5–17 cm (6½–6¾"). *Limited area in cen. Amaz. Brazil.* Small triangle of pale grayish bare skin behind eye. *Large patch of elongated white feathers on forehead and lores;* small patch of stiffened black feathers above eye. Head brown, becoming dull rufescent brown with scattered black bars on back, and brownish on rump; wings rufescent brown, coverts fringed black, and tail blackish. *Throat and chest cinnamon-rufous,* bordered below by *narrow band of black and white barring;* lower underparts dull brownish. Sexes virtually alike (female a little smaller).

SIMILAR SPECIES: Somewhat recalls female Reddish-winged Bare-eye, which also has limited bare skin around eye; they are not known to occur together (replacing each other across the Rio Madeira). Reddish-winged female has bold buff wing-bands, no band across chest, no white plumes on lores, etc. All *Rhegmatorhina* antbirds show conspicuous pale ocular areas.

HABITAT AND BEHAVIOR: Rare to uncommon in undergrowth of forest, primarily in terra firme. Almost always found at an army antswarm, with general behavior much like that of *Gymnopithys* and *Rhegmatorhina* antbirds, but somewhat less active and more apt to spend time on the ground. Its somewhat different song is shorter and simpler, usually merely a pair of thin, whistled notes, "heeeeeeeee, heeee!," lacking the descent into nasal snarling notes found in most closely related antbirds. All behavioral information from E. O. Willis (*Auk* 85[2]: 253–264, 1968). Small numbers are found in Amazonia Nat. Park west of Itaituba along the Trans-Amazon Highway.

RANGE: Cen. Amaz. Brazil (between w. bank of lower Rio Tapajós and e. bank of lower Rio Madeira; recorded south to Aripuanã in nw. Mato Grosso). 100–200 m.

NOTE: Called the Pale-faced Bare-eye by Meyer de Schauensee (1966, 1970). Willis (op. cit.) pointed out that because the species shows so much less bare skin around the eye than the members of the genus *Phlegopsis*, in which *borbae* was formerly placed, that it should not be called a bare-eye. He suggested calling it simply the Pale-faced Antbird.

Phlegopsis Bare-eyes

A pair of rather large and ornately patterned antbirds characterized especially by their bold red ocular areas, found in the understory of Amaz. forests. *Phlegopsis* bare-eyes are persistent followers of army ant-swarms. What was described as *P. barringeri* (Argus Bare-eye), known from a single male specimen taken in 1951 at Río Rumiyaco in e. Na-riño, Colombia, has been shown to represent only a hybrid between the Reddish-winged and Black-spotted Bare-eyes (G. R. Graves, *Proc. Biol. Soc. Wash.* 105[4]: 834–840, 1992).

Phlegopsis erythroptera

REDDISH-WINGED BARE-EYE

PLATE: 25

DESCRIPTION: 18.5 cm (7¼"). W. Amazonia. *Large bare ocular area bright red in male,* but much reduced (little more than a small triangle behind eye) in female. Male *mostly black,* feathers of back, wing-coverts, and rump with *narrow but striking white fringes* (giving a scaly effect); *wings with bold rufous markings* (2 broad wing-bars, tipping on tertials, and large patch on flight feathers). Female very different: dark rufes-cent brown above; wings and tail blackish, *wings with 2 bold buff bands on coverts and another across flight feathers. Below rich rufous,* becoming browner on belly.

SIMILAR SPECIES: The beautiful male is unmistakable; female can easily be known by its large size, rich brown overall coloration, and buff bands on wing.

HABITAT AND BEHAVIOR: Uncommon in undergrowth of humid for-est, primarily in terra firme of uplands away from rivers, sometimes following army antswarms into adjacent secondary woodland. Almost always encountered at swarms, where it is dominant over other antbird species; usually only 1 or 2 birds are present. Its song is a series of descending notes, becoming more nasal toward the end.

RANGE: Sw. Venezuela (s. Amazonas), e. Colombia (north to Caquetá and Vaupés), e. Ecuador, ne. Peru (mainly in Loreto; also recorded uncertainly from Lagarto in Ucayali), extreme nw. Bolivia (Pando at Camino Mucden), and w. Amaz. Brazil (east to the lower Rio Negro and lower Rio Madeira). To 600 m.

NOTE: For more behavioral information, see E. O. Willis (*Rev. Brasil. Zool.,* São Paulo 2[3]: 165–170, 1984).

Phlegopsis nigromaculata

BLACK-SPOTTED BARE-EYE   PLATE: 25

DESCRIPTION: 17–18.5 cm (6¾–7¼"). *Large bare ocular area bright red in adults of both sexes* (blackish in immatures). *Head, neck, and most of underparts black,* becoming brown on flanks; back and wing-coverts olive brown with *scattered large tear-like black spots* encircled with buff; flight feathers and tail rufous-chestnut, tertials with large black spot at tip. Foregoing applies to nominate race of w. Amazonia south of the Amazon (east to the Rio Madeira in Brazil); *bowmani* (Amaz. Brazil from e. bank of the Rio Madeira east to the Rio Xingu) similar but dorsal spots rounder. The 2 easternmost races (east of the Rio Xingu) are both smaller and have *bare red eye-ring even more extensive; confinis* (east to the lower Rio Tocantins) has dorsal spots like nominate race, but those of *paraensis* (from the Rio Tocantins east into Maranhão) are sparser and *much smaller,* resulting in a quite different effect. Sexes similar.

SIMILAR SPECIES: Confusion possible only with Reddish-winged Bare-eye, which see.

HABITAT AND BEHAVIOR: Uncommon to fairly common in undergrowth of humid forest, sometimes following army antswarms out into adjacent secondary woodland. In w. part of range occurs mainly in várzea and floodplain forest, with Reddish-winged Bare-eye "replacing" it in upland terra firme; in e. part of range (where Reddish-winged does not occur) also found regularly in terra firme. Like the Reddish-winged, Black-spotted Bare-eye is only rarely encountered away from army antswarms, but unlike it up to 12 or more birds may congregate at swarms. Very occasionally both bare-eye species may be present at the same swarm. Black-spotted's frequently heard song is a distinctive, simple "zhweé, zhwu," the second note characteristically lower pitched (sometimes an additional even lower, weaker note is given); also often heard, especially at antswarms or in alarm, is a rough raspy "zhheeeuw."

RANGE: Se. Colombia (north to Meta and Amazonas), ne. Ecuador (Napo and Sucumbios), e. Peru, n. Bolivia (south to La Paz, Cochabamba, and w. Santa Cruz), and Amaz. Brazil (mainly south of the Amazon, where recorded south to s. Mato Grosso and east to n. Maranhão; north of it recorded only from s. Amapá). To 500 m.

NOTE: For more behavioral details, see E. O. Willis (*Rev. Brasil. Biol.* 39: 117–159, 1979).

Phaenostictus Antbirds

A spectacular and large antbird found in wet lowland forests west of the Andes. The genus seems most closely related to the *Phlegopsis* bare-eyes (though it is longer-tailed and has a dramatically different colored bare ocular area). In fact, if any antbird deserves to be called a "bare-eye," this would be it—but unfortunately the more prosaic name "Ocellated Antbird" seems well established.

Phaenostictus mcleannani

OCELLATED ANTBIRD

PLATE: 25

DESCRIPTION: 19.5 cm (7¾″). *W. Colombia and nw. Ecuador.* Unmistakable. *Very large area of bare bright blue skin around eye.* Crown grayish; otherwise mostly olive brown above with *large buff-rimmed black spots on back and wing-coverts;* tail blackish. Ear-coverts, throat, and upper chest black; *nape, sides of neck, and remaining underparts rufous-chestnut, with large black spots on breast and upper belly;* lower belly brown. Sexes alike.

SIMILAR SPECIES: Nothing even remotely like it in its *Pacific slope range.*

HABITAT AND BEHAVIOR: Uncommon in undergrowth of humid forest. Infrequently seen away from army antswarms, and on the whole encountered even less often in S. Am. portion of its range than in Middle America. Usually only a few, almost always wary, are at a swarm, and they tend to dominate the other antbirds (Bicolored and Spotted) regularly found with them. The tail is frequently jerked upward and then slowly lowered. Its song is an infrequently heard series of high, penetrating whistles which rise rapidly, "peee-peee-pee-pee-peepee-ee-ee-ee-ee-ee-ee-ee-eer-eer," usually dropping on the last several notes. Sometimes gives a subdued version of this at antswarms, but its "dzerrr" call notes are more often heard there (B. Whitney; RSR).

RANGE: W. Colombia (Pacific lowlands, and in humid Caribbean lowlands east to lower Río Cauca valley) and nw. Ecuador (Esmeraldas). Also Honduras to Panama. To 900 m.

Formicariidae   # GROUND ANTBIRDS

THE ground antbirds were formerly united with what are now considered to be the typical antbirds (Thamnophilidae), but recent evidence (see Sibley and Ahlquist 1990) indicates that they are more closely related to the tapaculos (Rhinocryptidae) and the gnateaters (Conopophagidae). Antthrushes and antpittas are somberly colored, mainly in shades of brown, rufous, and gray, though many are attractively patterned. Antthrushes are, despite their name, actually more reminiscent of land rails than thrushes, and antpittas are clearly convergent in shape (if not in bright coloration) with the pittas (Pittidae) of the Old World. The ground antbirds range in both lowland and montane forests and are basically solitary, walking or hopping on or near the ground; antthrushes tend to walk, antpittas to hop. Maximum species diversity is reached in the Andes, where series of species (especially *Grallaria* antpittas) replace each other with changes in elevation. Shy and elusive, they are all too rarely seen, though their far-carrying and often quite melodic (but usually simple) songs are frequently heard.

Formicarius Antthrushes

Dark and plainly patterned antbirds of the forest floor, *Formicarius* antthrushes are shy and infrequently seen, but all members of the genus have persistently given vocalizations. Most species show some bare skin around eyes; the sexes are much alike in plumage. *Formicarius* antthrushes walk about deliberately in a jaunty manner, usually holding their heads high and cocking their fairly short tails; they can look uncannily rail-like. Nests are cups placed in upward-opening stumps or stubs.

Formicarius analis   ### BLACK-FACED ANTTHRUSH   PLATE: 26

DESCRIPTION: 17–18 cm (6¾–7″). Bare ocular area bluish white, widest in front of and behind eye. Brown above (*including crown*), more rufescent on uppertail-coverts, with small white loral spot; tail blackish. *Lower cheeks and throat contrastingly black;* breast gray, becoming paler grayish on belly, somewhat browner on flanks; crissum rufous. More n. races (*panamensis, virescens, saturatus,* and *crissalis,* of n. Colombia east to the Guianas and Amapá, Brazil) have patch of rufous on sides of neck (see V-23); in other races this area is more clay-colored. Juveniles have throat whitish flecked or scaled with dusky.
SIMILAR SPECIES: The most widespread and numerous *Formicarius;* cf. the next 4 species. *Chamaeza* antthrushes are obviously streaked or scalloped below, etc.
HABITAT AND BEHAVIOR: Fairly common to common (by voice; infrequently seen) on or near the ground in humid forest and secondary

woodland; in Amazonia occurs mainly in second-growth or várzea, with Rufous-capped replacing it in upland terra firme forest, though in some areas Black-faced also occurs in terra firme. Usually seen walking slowly and deliberately, almost like a little rail, over the forest floor, generally with tail cocked (sometimes high); occasionally pauses to sing, with head thrown back and tail depressed. Turns over leaves with its bill, searching for various insects and other invertebrate prey (rarely will also take a small snake, frog, or lizard). Sometimes forages at edge of army antswarms (this may occur especially often on Trinidad, where there are few other competing ant-following birds). The song, heard far more often than bird is seen, is one of the characteristic avian sounds in many lowland forests and is given throughout the day, at least at some seasons. Across the vast majority of its S. Am. range this is a fast "tü, títititetu," fading away at the end; in Panama (and presumably also at least in adjacent nw. Colombia: *panamensis*) gives a very different, much more deliberate "pee; pü, pü, pü . . ." (with up to 10–15 "pü"s), with characteristic hesitation after the initial note. Also often heard is a sharp, harsh "kwik" or "kwik-whik" alarm note.

RANGE: N. and e. Colombia (more humid Caribbean lowlands east to Venez. border, south in Río Magdalena valley to e. Antioquia; absent from Pacific lowlands south of n. Chocó; e. lowlands from Meta and Vaupés southward, and north along base of Andes to Arauca), much of humid-forested Venezuela (Maracaibo basin east along bases of Andes and n. cordilleras to Paria Peninsula, and in e. Bolívar), e. Ecuador, e. Peru, n. Bolivia (south to La Paz, Cochabamba, and n. Santa Cruz), Amaz. Brazil (south to s. Mato Grosso and east to n. Maranhão), and Guianas; absent from entire llanos region of Venezuela and ne. Colombia and, more surprisingly, from much of the Río Orinoco/Rio Negro drainage; Trinidad. Also Mexico to Panama. Mostly below 1000 m (recorded to 1300 m in n. Venezuela, likely in response to the absence of any congeners).

NOTE: More than one species may be involved: the abrupt shift in song type (occurring in n. Colombia?) deserves further attention. A comparable shift occurs in Central America with the different-singing *monileger* group (with *pallidus* and *intermedius*) from Honduras northward (S. Howell).

Formicarius nigricapillus

BLACK-HEADED ANTTHRUSH

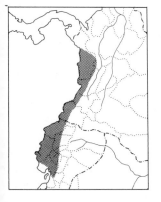

DESCRIPTION: 17 cm (6¾"). *Pacific w. Colombia and w. Ecuador.* Ocular area similar to Black-faced's, but *lacks* white loral spot. *Entire head, neck, throat, and chest black,* becoming rich dark brown on remaining upperparts and shading into slaty gray on breast and slightly paler gray on belly; uppertail-coverts and crissum rufous-chestnut. Female tinged olivaceous brown on belly. See P-22.

SIMILAR SPECIES: Resembles a dark Black-faced Antthrush (no known overlap in South America), though all of foreparts are obviously black.

HABITAT AND BEHAVIOR: Uncommon to locally fairly common on or near the ground in humid forest and mature secondary woodland, favoring ravines and other areas with very dense undergrowth. Behavior similar to Black-faced Antthrush's but even harder to see, not so much because it is shyer as because of its often almost impenetrable habitat. Its distinctive and frequently heard song, which lasts about 5 seconds, is a series of 10–20 slightly accelerating short whistled "hü" notes, gradually becoming a little louder and then stopping abruptly. Seems especially numerous at Río Palenque, Ecuador.

RANGE: W. Colombia (north to cen. Chocó) and w. Ecuador (south to sw. Manabí, e. Guayas, and nw. Azuay). Also Costa Rica and Panama. Mostly below 900 m (recorded to 1800 m in Colombia).

Formicarius rufifrons

RUFOUS-FRONTED ANTTHRUSH

DESCRIPTION: 18 cm (7"). *Local in se. Peru.* Resembles Black-faced Antthrush; bare skin around eye less extensive. Above like Black-faced but with *prominent orange-rufous forecrown;* sooty gray below *with no black bib* and no rufous crissum; underwing-coverts cinnamon-rufous as in Rufous-capped Antthrush (not black as in Black-faced).

HABITAT AND BEHAVIOR: Rare to locally uncommon (and very hard to see) on or near the ground in swampy transitional forest, especially favoring dense thickets of *Heliconia* or *Guadua* bamboo. Behaves much like Black-faced Antthrush, which regularly occurs in the same habitat; how they segregate ecologically remains unknown. Rufous-fronted's song is a distinctive series of musical notes given with an even, regular cadence, the first notes somewhat lower in pitch, the last sliding off, "pü-pü-pü-pü-pee-pee-pee-pee-pu-pu-peh-peh." A few are found near Manu Lodge at the edge of Manu Nat. Park.

RANGE: Se. Peru (Madre de Dios). Seems possible in adjacent Bolivia and Brazil. 350–400 m.

NOTE: For more information on this until recently little-known species (it was not even described until 1957), see T. A. Parker III (*Gerfaut* 73: 287–289, 1983).

Formicarius colma

RUFOUS-CAPPED ANTTHRUSH   PLATE: 26

DESCRIPTION: 18 cm (7"). *Crown and nape bright rufous* (paler laterally), contrasting with otherwise brown upperparts; tail blackish. *Sides of head and neck, throat, and breast sooty black,* becoming dull grayish on lower underparts. Foregoing applies to very similar *ruficeps* (coastal e. Brazil) and *amazonicus* (Amaz. Brazil from Rio Madeira eastward); nominate/*nigrifrons* pair (remainder of range) differ in having a *black forehead* and less bright crown, especially laterally; see V-23, C-31. Many females have a *white throat* (usually speckled with black); these apparently are younger birds, as some (older?) females have the throat black. Males never have white throat.

SIMILAR SPECIES: Other *Formicarius* show a bare ocular area. Widely sympatric Black-faced Antthrush has dull brown (not bright rufous) crown and contrasting black bib on throat *only* (not extending down over breast).

HABITAT AND BEHAVIOR: Uncommon to fairly common (but hard to see) on or near the ground in humid forest (in Amazonia mainly in terra firme); seems most numerous in s. Venezuela and the Guianas. Behaves much like Black-faced Antthrush, which tends to replace

Rufous-capped in várzea forest and second-growth, though sometimes the two can be heard calling from the same spot. Rufous-capped's often-heard and distinctive song is a rapidly delivered series of trilled musical notes which falter and drop at the beginning, then gradually rise, "tr-r-r-ew-u-u-u-u-u-u-u-u-u-u-u-u-u?"; it usually lasts 4 or 5 seconds.

RANGE: Guianas, s. Venezuela (Bolívar and Amazonas), e. Colombia (north to Meta and Guainía), e. Ecuador, e. Peru, n. Bolivia (Pando, n. La Paz, and n. Santa Cruz), and Amaz. Brazil (south to s. Mato Grosso, and east to n. Maranhão); e. Brazil (Pernambuco south to ne. Rio Grande do Sul). Mostly below 500 m (recorded to 1100 m in Venezuela).

Formicarius rufipectus

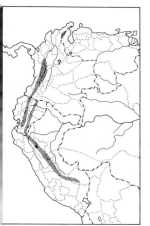

RUFOUS-BREASTED ANTTHRUSH   PLATE: 26

DESCRIPTION: 19 cm (7½"). *Mainly on Andean slopes.* Narrow bare ocular area bluish white, broadest in front of and behind eye. *Head and throat black,* not quite so dark on crown; remaining upperparts brown, more rufescent on uppertail-coverts; tail blackish. *Breast rich rufous-chestnut,* becoming olivaceous brown on flanks; crissum also rufous-chestnut. Foregoing applies to *thoracicus* of e. slope of Andes in Ecuador and Peru. *Carrikeri* and *lasallei* of w. Venezuela, Colombia, and w. Ecuador have *entire crown and nape chestnut,* resulting in the face looking darker, and are larger-billed; see V-23, C-31.

SIMILAR SPECIES: Occurs at higher elevations than other *Formicarius,* with limited or no overlap; can easily be known by its obvious rufous breast.

HABITAT AND BEHAVIOR: Uncommon to fairly common on or near the ground in montane forest and secondary woodland, particularly in dense low vegetation in ravines, adjacent to landslides, and on steep slopes. A devilishly hard bird to see (even after tape playback) but with general behavior similar to Black-faced Antthrush's. Heard far more often than seen; its distinctive song is a simple, fast, flat, 2-noted whistle, "hü-hü," with second note (often seeming slightly shorter) either a semitone above the first or on same pitch.

RANGE: Andes of extreme w. Venezuela (sw. Táchira), w. Colombia (locally on slopes of W. and Cen. Andes), Ecuador (south on w. slope to El Oro), and e. Peru (south to Cuzco); Sierra de Perijá on Venezuela-Colombia border. Also Costa Rica and Panama. Mostly 1100–2200 m (but regularly down to 850 m in w. Ecuador).

Chamaeza Antthrushes

Fairly large, terrestrial antbirds found in humid and montane forests, *Chamaeza* resemble *Formicarius* antthrushes but are plumper and shorter-billed. All species are basically similar, with brown upperparts, a prominent whitish postocular, and boldly patterned underparts (streaked, scalloped, or barred). The sexes are alike. Plumage differences between the species are minor, and they are usually best distinguished by their songs (and will in any case be heard much more often than seen). Species-level systematics have recently changed substantially, with two "new" species now being recognized.

GROUP A   Typical *Chamaeza, streaked to scalloped below.* All very much *alike.*

Chamaeza ruficauda

RUFOUS-TAILED ANTTHRUSH   PLATE: 26

DESCRIPTION: 19–19.5 cm (7½–7¾"). *Mts. of se. Brazil* (birds from Venezuela and Colombia are now considered a separate species). Bill rather short, blackish. Rufescent brown above (*including tail,* which is rather long and *lacks* pale tip), with buffy white loral spot, postocular streak, and patches on sides of neck. Below whitish to buff (deepest on breast), *coarsely streaked and speckled across breast and down flanks;* crissum buff barred with blackish.
SIMILAR SPECIES: Resembles Short-tailed Antthrush; where they overlap, Rufous-tailed occurs mainly at *higher elevations.* Further subtle differences include Short-tailed's larger size, longer bill, and black subterminal band and pale tip on tail. Their *differing voices* are usually the biggest help. Cf. also the recently differentiated Cryptic Antthrush, which also occurs sympatrically with Rufous-tailed, though usually at slightly lower elevations; Cryptic's voice also differs markedly from Rufous-tailed's.
HABITAT AND BEHAVIOR: Fairly common to common (but heard far more often than seen) on or near the ground in montane forest, forest borders, and mature secondary woodland, mostly where undergrowth is dense. Usually shy, encountered singly or in pairs walking slowly on the forest floor, often pumping their somewhat cocked tail (normally held lower than in *Formicarius*). Singing birds generally take a somewhat elevated perch, standing high with head raised and neck arched. The distinctive song, a short, fast series of bubbling musical notes which characteristically ascend in pitch, lasts about 2 or 3 seconds (sometimes up to 5). Numerous at upper elevations of Itatiaia Nat. Park, but seeing it will require patience or luck unless you use a tape recorder.
RANGE: Se. Brazil (e. Minas Gerais and Espírito Santo south to n. Rio Grande do Sul); also reported, without details, from ne. Argentina (*fide* E. Chebez, *in* E. O. Willis, *Condor* 94[1]: 110–116, 1992). Mainly 1000–2200 m, but lower southward.

NOTE: *C. turdina* (with *chionogaster*) of n. Venezuela and w. Colombia is here regarded as a species separate from monotypic *C. ruficauda* of se. Brazil, in accord with Willis (op. cit.). Their voices are entirely different and their ranges widely disjunct; ventral plumage patterns also differ.

Chamaeza turdina

SCALLOPED ANTTHRUSH
Other: Schwartz's Antthrush, Rufous-tailed Antthrush (in part)

DESCRIPTION: 19–19.5 cm (7½–7¾"). *Local in mts. of n. Venezuela and Andes of Colombia.* Resembles the geographically distant Rufous-tailed

Antthrush, with which formerly considered conspecific. Differs in its *markedly scalloped (not streaked or speckled) pattern below,* especially pronounced on breast; the ground color of underparts is purer white (with little or no buff tinge, even on breast and crissum). See V-23, C-31.

SIMILAR SPECIES: Short-tailed Antthrush is very similar, but in Venezuela (the only area of sympatry) Short-tailed occurs at somewhat lower elevations. Short-tailed differs in its larger bill, streaked pattern on breast (with underparts less heavily marked overall), and black subterminal band and white tipping on tail. The 2 species are best distinguished by their utterly different songs.

HABITAT AND BEHAVIOR: Fairly common (but hard to see) on or near the ground in montane forest and forest borders. Behavior similar to Rufous-tailed Antthrush's, and likewise heard much more often than seen. Scalloped has a memorably beautiful song, usually delivered from a slightly elevated perch but also while walking on the ground. It is a *very long* series of "cu" notes which start softly but gradually increase in strength and slightly accelerate; the song routinely lasts for 30 seconds or longer. Frequently heard in Henri Pittier Nat. Park north of Maracay, particularly along the Ocumare road.

RANGE: Mts. of n. Venezuela (Yaracuy east to Miranda); w. Colombia (mainly around head of Río Magdalena valley in Huila; also recorded from w. slope of Cen. Andes in Valle above Palmira). 1400–2600 m.

NOTE: See comments under Rufous-tailed Antthrush. E. O. Willis (*Condor* 94[1]: 110–116, 1992) suggested the English name of Schwartz's Antthrush for this species, in honor of the late ornithologist. We prefer, however, to emphasize the difference in breast pattern from its Brazilian relative in the descriptive modifier "Scalloped."

Chamaeza meruloides

CRYPTIC ANTTHRUSH

Other: Such's Antthrush, Rufous-tailed Antthrush (in part)

DESCRIPTION: 19–19.5 cm (7½–7¾"). *Mts. of se. Brazil;* recently specifically separated from Rufous-tailed Antthrush. They are *very* similar and will normally be distinguished in the field only by their very different songs. Cryptic differs from Short-tailed in being somewhat smaller and in having a slightly shorter and dark bill; it lacks Short-tailed's small black blotch on forehead, and its blackish subterminal tail band is usually indistinct; the throat is plain white or pale buff (*not speckled*). Cryptic differs from Rufous-tailed in being more olivaceous (less rufescent) brown above with a pale tail tip, and in being much less strongly patterned below with an *unbarred crissum.*

HABITAT AND BEHAVIOR: Uncommon on or near the ground in montane forest and forest borders; heard far more often than seen. Behavior much like Rufous-tailed Antthrush's, but Cryptic's song is very different, being almost exactly like that of the geographically distant Scalloped Antthrush, a very long series of beautiful "cu" notes which gradually increase in loudness. Readily heard at middle elevations of Itatiaia Nat. Park.

RANGE: Se. Brazil (e. Minas Gerais and Espírito Santo south to ne.

Santa Catarina at Corupá). M. A. Raposo and D. M. Teixera (*Bol. Mus. Nac.,* Zool., nov. ser., no. 350, 1992) state that *C. meruloides* occurs in Bahia, but they provide no details. 200–1500 m.

NOTE: Since the 1970s field workers have been aware that geographic differences in primary vocalizations of certain *Chamaeza* antthrushes did not match their generally accepted species-level systematics (as given, e.g., in Meyer de Schauensee 1966, 1970). Some Rufous-tailed Antthrushes in se. Brazil sang very differently from supposedly conspecific birds of n. Venezuela, but some *Chamaeza* there seemed to sound virtually identical to Venezuelan birds. E. O. Willis (*Condor* 94[1]: 110–116, 1992) clarified the situation, demonstrating that there are three altitudinally segregated *Chamaeza* on the mountain slopes of se. Brazil: Rufous-tailed highest, Cryptic at middle levels, and Short-tailed on lower slopes. The specific name to be applied to the "middle" species (which sings like the geographically distant Venezuelan and Colombian birds) is shrouded in antiquity, and the type specimens appear to be lost, but *meruloides* was determined by Willis (op. cit.) to be applicable. Willis (op. cit.) suggested the English name of Such's Antthrush for *C. meruloides* to honor the species' first collector. Although we would usually endorse such a proposed patronym with enthusiasm, in English the name "Such's" seems so likely to be misunderstood that we hesitate to employ it. We thus highlight the species' highly cryptic nature: it was long confused with not just one but *two* species!

Chamaeza campanisona

SHORT-TAILED ANTTHRUSH

DESCRIPTION: 19–20 cm (7½–8"). Disjunct range in Andes, on the tepuis, and in e. Brazil area. Bill larger than in previous *Chamaeza,* and lower mandible (at least) *pale.* Olivaceous brown above with crown tinged rufescent and a *small black blotch on forehead;* white loral spot, postocular streak, and patch on sides of neck; *tail with blackish subterminal band and whitish tip* (neither easy to see in the field). Below whitish to buffy, coarsely streaked with blackish brown except on throat and midbelly, *throat variably speckled with black,* crissum buff with sparse black markings. See V-23, C-31. Birds from e. Brazil southward (nominate race and the doubtfully separable *tshororo*) are larger. *Olivacea* and *berlepschi* (e. Peru from Junín to Cuzco) are richer and almost ochraceous on breast, with buff reaching the throat, flanks, and crissum, and even invading the postocular.

SIMILAR SPECIES: Overlaps with similar Cryptic Antthrush in se. Brazil, and with Scalloped Antthrush in n. Venezuela; in both countries Short-tailed occurs at somewhat *lower* elevations. Their different and often-heard songs are usually the best distinction. In se. Brazil, Cryptic differs in its smaller size and shorter bill, and it lacks Short-tailed's forehead blotch and throat speckles. In Venezuela, Scalloped and Short-tailed are about the same size but differ in pattern of underparts (Scalloped with bolder and markedly scalloped, not streaked, breast and tail. In Colombia they do *not* occur together, as Scalloped ranges only *west* of E. Andes, Short-tailed only on e. slope of E. Andes. Cf. also the larger Noble Antthrush of Amaz. lowlands (at most limited overlap).

HABITAT AND BEHAVIOR: Uncommon to locally fairly common on or near the ground in humid and montane forest and mature secondary woodland. Behavior much like other *Chamaeza* antthrushes' (see under Rufous-tailed), likewise not an easy bird to see, though often heard. Almost always delivers its distinctive song from a slightly elevated perch (occasionally a surprising 5 or 6 m above the ground). The song, a series of usually 10–20 hollow "cow" notes which slightly accelerate and rise in pitch, ends with a shorter series of more guttural and strongly descending "cuh" or "wok" notes. The "wok" notes are sometimes omitted, and the number of "cow" notes seems to vary (perhaps individually?), W. Belton (1985) having counted as many as 128! Its voice seems not to vary across the species' large range.

RANGE: Mts. of n. Venezuela (east to Distrito Federal and Aragua), and e. slope of Andes in w. Venezuela, Colombia, Ecuador, Peru, and w. Bolivia (south to w. Santa Cruz); tepuis of s. Venezuela (Bolívar and Amazonas south to Cerro de la Neblina) and adjacent Guyana; e. Brazil (locally in Ceará and Alagoas, more widely from s. Bahia south to Rio Grande do Sul), e. Paraguay (west to Paraguarí), and ne. Argentina (Misiones). Mostly 500–1800 m, but usually not above about 1200 m in n. Venezuela and se. Brazil, or below about 900 m on e. slope of Andes.

Chamaeza nobilis

NOBLE ANTTHRUSH

PLATE: 26

Other: Striated Antthrush

DESCRIPTION: 22.5 cm (8¾"). The only *Chamaeza* in *Amaz. lowlands*. Above dark rufescent brown with white loral spot, postocular streak, and patch on sides of neck; tail with *black subterminal band* and *narrow white tipping*. White below (*no buff tinge*) with *bold blackish scalloping especially across breast, down flanks, and on crissum*.

SIMILAR SPECIES: Resembles Short-tailed Antthrush but larger (particularly than Andean races of Short-tailed, which occur on slopes *above* range of Noble); further differences include Short-tailed's paler upperparts and streaked (not scalloped) pattern on breast. *Both* species have inconspicuous white tail-tipping (*contra* Hilty and Brown 1986).

HABITAT AND BEHAVIOR: Uncommon on or near the ground in humid forest, especially in terra firme in which undergrowth is relatively sparse. Behavior similar to Short-tailed Antthrush's, as is its often-heard song (though the song is often somewhat higher-pitched and faster; Parker [1982] and RSR). In our experience, this is a shyer and more difficult bird to see, even with tape playback.

RANGE: Se. Colombia (north to Meta and Vaupés), e. Ecuador, e. Peru, extreme nw. Bolivia (Pando at Camino Mucden and La Paz at Alto Madidi), and w. Amaz. Brazil (south of the Amazon east locally to Rondônia and the lower Rio Tapajós near Santarém). Mostly below 700 m, locally up to 1000 m in Ecuador.

NOTE: Although long called the Striated Antthrush, this species actually is one of the *least* "striated" of the genus; in fact the pattern on this species' underparts is one of scalloping. We favor referring to this largest and finest *Chamaeza* as the Noble Antthrush, taken directly from its Latin name.

GROUP B

Chamaeza mollissima

Dense *barring below.*

BARRED ANTTHRUSH   PLATE: 26

DESCRIPTION: 20.5 cm (8"). *A superb, rare antthrush found locally in Andean forests.* Above rich chestnut brown with buffy whitish loral spot and *dusky brown and white barred postocular stripe and stripe on sides of neck. Below densely barred dusky brown and white.* Foregoing applies to nominate race of most of range; *yungae* (Cuzco, Peru, south into Bolivia) has throat with more streaked pattern, breast with *chevroned* pattern, and belly with wavy coarse barring—in all, lending it a slightly more spotted effect.
SIMILAR SPECIES: Virtually unmistakable; other *Chamaeza* are streaked or scalloped, not barred, below, and none occurs at such high elevations. Various antpittas are also barred below, but these are all *very* differently shaped, etc.
HABITAT AND BEHAVIOR: Rare and local on or near the ground in montane forest. Behavior similar to other *Chamaeza* antthrushes' (see under Rufous-tailed) but seems more secretive and is definitely scarcer. Its song, a beautiful, long series of rapidly repeated musical "cuh" notes which become increasingly emphasized and louder, ends suddenly (with no descending "wok" notes at end), the whole lasting 15–22 seconds; it resembles Scalloped Antthrush's song but is shorter.
RANGE: Locally in Andes of Colombia (W. Andes in Valle and Cauca; Cen. Andes from Quindío southward), Ecuador (few records), Peru (recorded only from Cerro Chinguela in Piura, Cordillera de Vilcabamba in Cuzco [AMNH], and Puno), and w. Bolivia (La Paz and Cochabamba). Mostly 1800–3000 m.

Pittasoma Antpittas

A pair of quite large and boldly patterned antpittas found only in Pacific nw. South America. Like other antpittas they are plump, long-legged, and very short-tailed; unlike *Grallaria* their bills are rather long and straight. Both species are somewhat sexually dimorphic.

Pittasoma rufopileatum

RUFOUS-CROWNED ANTPITTA   PLATE: 26

DESCRIPTION: 16–17.5 cm (6¼–6¾"). *W. Colombia and nw. Ecuador,* showing complex geographical variation despite its small range. Nominate race (nw. Ecuador) has *rufous-chestnut crown* and *long, broad, black superciliary reaching back to nape;* otherwise olive brown above with broad black stripes; wing-coverts and tertials dotted whitish. *Cheeks, sides of neck, and throat pale to rather deep ochraceous* sparsely dotted with black; *remaining underparts evenly barred black and white.* Female has the black superciliary spotted with whitish and is *mostly ochraceous below* with only sparse and irregular black spotting and speckling. *Rosenbergi* (Chocó, Colombia) is smaller and plainer overall, with *plain dull buffy*

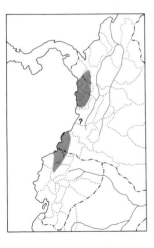

whitish underparts in both sexes. *Harterti* (sw. Colombia) is intermediate in both size and plumage: both sexes are basically ochraceous below, deepest (most orange) on throat, and males show *variable amount of black barring on underparts* (ranging from nearly complete to almost none); see C-31.

SIMILAR SPECIES: This spectacular and beautifully patterned antpitta is easily recognized in its limited range. Cf. Black-crowned Antpitta (no known overlap).

HABITAT AND BEHAVIOR: Rare to locally uncommon on or near the ground in humid forest. Usually encountered singly or in pairs, bounding rapidly on its long legs, then pausing, sometimes remaining motionless for long periods; flushed birds sometimes fly to low branches. At least in some areas encountered most often at army antswarms, where it may be quite bold and tame, hopping about unconcernedly only a few meters away. Tends to dominate other antbirds and woodcreepers at an antswarm. Its alarm call is an abrupt and loud series of harsh notes much like the Black-crowned Antpitta's; its true song, however, seems still to be unknown.

RANGE: W. Colombia (Pacific lowlands from n. Chocó southward) and nw. Ecuador (mainly in Esmeraldas, but a few records south to Pichincha). To 1100 m.

Pittasoma michleri

BLACK-CROWNED ANTPITTA

DESCRIPTION: 18 cm (7"). *Nw. Colombia.* Lower mandible flesh-colored. Male has *crown and nape glossy black* contrasting with *chestnut cheeks* and a black-and-white grizzled loral spot; otherwise brown above with indistinct broad black streaks; wing-coverts and tertials dotted buff. Throat mostly black; *remaining underparts white boldly and broadly scalloped with black.* See P-22. Female similar but throat rufous marked with black, underparts with sparser scalloping and variably tinged buffyish.

SIMILAR SPECIES: Essentially unmistakable in its limited range.

HABITAT AND BEHAVIOR: Poorly known in Colombian portion of its range. In Panama (see Ridgely and Gwynne 1989) rare to locally uncommon (more numerous eastward) on or near the ground in humid forest. Behavior much like Rufous-crowned Antpitta's and like it most often encountered when attending an army antswarm. The most often heard call, apparently given mainly in alarm, is a loud, sudden series of 10–16 harsh notes, slowing toward the end, "wakwakwakwakwakwak-wak-wak-wak-wak." The true song is a long, level series of high, clear, penetrating "tu" notes which start rapidly and gradually slow down, the sequence sometimes lasting a minute or longer.

RANGE: Nw. Colombia (n. Chocó). Also Costa Rica and Panama. To 400 m (but regularly to 1000 m in Panama).

Grallaria Antpittas

A wonderful, large group of uniformly shaped antbirds: all have extremely short tails, are plump and round with feathers often fluffed making them look even rounder, and have very long, bluish gray legs (pinkish in Watkins' Antpitta). Bills are fairly stout. Antpittas are attractively patterned in shades of brown, rufous, and gray, some with obvious barring, streaking, or scaling; sexes are alike. All are essentially terrestrial birds which range inside forest where they run or hop but do not walk, sometimes moving rapidly with springing bounds. Unlike many other antbirds, *Grallaria* antpittas do not regularly attend army antswarms. They are notoriously shy and secretive. A few sometimes forage along forest edges in early morning and late afternoon; the Tawny and Stripe-headed regularly occur in the semiopen. Virtually all antpittas have distinctive and often-heard vocalizations, almost invariably the primary indication of their presence. Nests are sloppily constructed shallow cups or saucers of sticks and leaves, often lined with moss, rootlets, or other finer material, generally placed 1–2 m above the ground, often on fallen decaying tree trunks (see D. A. Wiedenfeld, *Wilson Bull.* 94[4]: 580–582, 1982).

Although virtually any S. Am. forest (aside from Fuegian forests of the far south, where they are replaced by tapaculos) supports at least 1 species of *Grallaria,* the genus is basically montane in distribution, reaching its greatest diversity in the Andes. There numerous altitudinal "replacement species," up to seven or eight in Colombia's Cen. Andes (G. R. Graves, *Wilson Bull.* 99[3]: 313–321, 1987), occur. Numerous *Grallaria* are thought to be rare or to have very small ranges, though some may have been under-recorded because of their reclusive habits. Remarkably, 4 new species have been described since the late 1960s.

We divide the genus into five Groups, based upon the subgeneric classification proposed by G. H. Lowery and J. P. O'Neill (*Auk* 86[1]: 1–12, 1969).

GROUP A   *"Barred"* and *"scaled"* antpittas; *malar streaks* often evident.

Grallaria gigantea   **GIANT ANTPITTA**   PLATE: 26

DESCRIPTION: 24 cm (9½"). *A rare, very large antpitta found locally in Andes of s. Colombia and Ecuador. Hylodroma* (w. Ecuador) has *rufous forehead* grading into gray crown and nape, which contrasts with olive brown upperparts. *Sides of head and neck and entire underparts orange-rufous with narrow wavy black barring.* Nominate race (e. Ecuador) similar but shows *paler* ochraceous buff ground color below, and has broader and sparser ventral barring. *Lehmanni* (s. Colombia) is described as resembling nominate but with heavier barring below (*contra* Hilty and Brown 1986; note that the race depicted on Plate 30 is *hylodroma* and *not,* as labeled, *lehmanni.*). Juveniles show narrow ochraceous tipping on wing-coverts.

SIMILAR SPECIES: Undulated Antpitta always shows a prominent

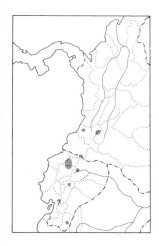

blackish submalar stripe and never has rufous on forehead (showing a white or buff loral spot instead). Undulated and Giant Antpittas are most similar in Colombia and e. Ecuador, where their ventral ground colors are about the same; in w. Ecuador the Giant is more richly colored below. Cf. Great Antpitta of Venezuela (no overlap).

HABITAT AND BEHAVIOR: Apparently rare on or near the ground in montane forest and secondary woodland (sometimes where there is extensive *Chusquea* bamboo) and adjacent overgrown, usually muddy clearings. Poorly known; *hylodroma*, despite having been collected in reasonable numbers in the early 20th century, and despite much searching, has not been found at all in recent decades. A population of nominate *gigantea* was, however, discovered in 1992 at Hacienda Aragon in western Napo (ANSP). Here birds seemed to favor areas of secondary growth, and according to ranch employees regularly emerged to feed in rough cattle pastures near forest. The Giant's song, delivered from perches 1–4 m above the ground, resembles the Undulated Antpitta's, being a similar but even faster series of quavering notes on an even pitch lasting about 5 seconds, starting somewhat faintly, then abruptly increasing in strength, usually given at 10- to 15-second intervals (M. Robbins recording). The near absence of recent records has led to speculation that the Giant Antpitta deserves formal threatened status, though a great deal of seemingly suitable habitat remains (at least in Ecuador).

RANGE: Locally in Andes of s. Colombia (known only from head of Río Magdalena valley in Huila) and Ecuador (on w. slope only in Pichincha, on e. slope in Napo and Tungurahua; there are also two ANSP specimens of *hylodroma* which are labeled as having been taken at El Tambo in Loja, a locality which [*fide* N. Krabbe] most likely lies on the slopes of Urutisinga, just west of the actual continental divide). The supposed Giant Antpitta specimen from Cerro Munchique in Cauca, Colombia (see Collar et al. 1992, pp. 695–697) proves, on examination, to be only an example of the Undulated Antpitta (*Grallaria squamigera*). Mostly 2200–3000 m, but *hylodroma* seemingly recorded only 1200–2000 m.

Grallaria excelsa

GREAT ANTPITTA

DESCRIPTION: 24 cm (9½″). *A rare, very large antpitta found locally in mts. of Venezuela.* Mostly olive brown above (including forehead) with contrasting gray crown and nape. *Sides of head and neck and entire underparts tawny with bold wavy black barring;* midthroat white. See V-23.

SIMILAR SPECIES: Undulated Antpitta is slightly smaller with less contrasting gray crown and shows a distinct dusky submalar stripe. Giant Antpitta, the nominate race of which resembles Great except for its lack of white midthroat, does not occur in Great's range.

HABITAT AND BEHAVIOR: Poorly known in life. Recorded from "dense cloud forest . . . on the highest ridges. . . . [Its song] sounds like the low, vibrant note created by blowing over the neck of an empty bottle" (Meyer de Schauensee and Phelps 1979, p. 222).

RANGE: Locally in mts. of n. Venezuela (known only from Colonia Tovar in Aragua), and in Andes of w. Venezuela (Lara south to Táchira); Sierra de Perijá (recorded only from its Venezuelan side but probably in Colombia as well). 1700–2300 m.

NOTE: *G. excelsa* may prove to be conspecific with *G. gigantea*, as its Venezuelan representative. Nominate *gigantea* (e. Ecuador), *lehmanni* (s. Colombia), and *excelsa* and *phelpsi* (Venezuela) are more similar to each other than any is to the ventrally much more richly colored *hylodroma* (w. Ecuador). Possibly the best arrangement will be to consider the first four taxa as one species (*G. gigantea*, Giant Antpitta), with *G. hylodroma* (Pichincha Antpitta) as another.

Grallaria squamigera

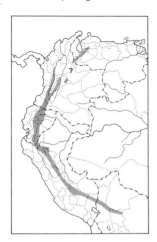

UNDULATED ANTPITTA   PLATE: 26

DESCRIPTION: 21.5–22.5 cm (8½–8¾"). A *large* antpitta of Andes. *Uniform gray above* with whitish loral area. *Sides of head and neck and most of underparts ochraceous with wavy black barring;* midthroat white bordered by *prominent black submalar stripe*. Foregoing applies to *canicauda* of se. Ecuador (ANSP specimen from Cordillera de Cutucú) southward. Nominate race (n. Ecuador northward) has upperparts more olivaceous, sometimes with a gray tinge (but pure gray only on crown and nape), and loral spot buffyish; see C-30. Juveniles show narrow ochraceous tipping on wing-coverts.

SIMILAR SPECIES: Giant Antpitta never shows a submalar stripe and has a rufescent forehead.

HABITAT AND BEHAVIOR: Rare to locally fairly common on or near ground in montane forest and secondary woodland; occasionally hops out into adjacent grassy clearings, especially in early morning or when light levels are low (e.g., in foggy conditions). A shy and retiring bird, infrequently seen even in prime habitat, but locally heard more often. The song, usually given from a somewhat elevated perch, is a fast series of quavering notes lasting about 3 or 4 seconds, "hohohohohohohohoho-ho-ho-ho-ho," with last few notes more clearly enunciated; the effect is very screech-owl- (*Otus-*)like, and as the antpitta often sings in predawn or postdusk darkness (when screech-owls often vocalize), it can easily be mistaken for one.

RANGE: Locally in Andes of w. Venezuela (north to Mérida), Colombia, Ecuador (south locally on w. slope to Azuay and w. Loja), e. Peru, and w. Bolivia (La Paz and Cochabamba). Mostly 1800–3700 m.

Grallaria varia

VARIEGATED ANTPITTA   PLATE: 26

DESCRIPTION: 18–20.5 cm (7–8"). Above olive brown with gray hindcrown and nape (more "frosty" on rearmost feathers), the feathers of all of upperparts edged black giving a *scaly look* and with *scattered pale shaft streaks;* wing-coverts tipped buff, tail rufous. Throat, cheeks, and breast brown with semiconcealed *patch* of white on center of lower throat and with *broad white malar stripe extending downward from white lores;* lower underparts buffy with *blurry dusky barring or scaling*. Foregoing applies to large *imperator* and *intercedens* of e. Brazil southward; races from elsewhere in range (nominate group) are markedly smaller.

The latter lose the pronounced barred effect below (*reduced to dark speckling on flanks*), have reduced or no covert spots, somewhat narrower shaft streaks on back, and some *whitish streaks* below the throat patch; *cinereiceps* (nw. Brazil and adjacent Venezuela) has more ochraceous belly.

SIMILAR SPECIES: Birds from e. Brazil region are so much larger than other antpittas there that confusion is improbable. Confusion is quite likely, however, between the small forms of Variegated found in n. part of its range and the Scaled Antpitta. By and large, Variegated is a bird of lowland forest, whereas Scaled is found in foothills and higher; Scaled has also recently been found in the lowlands of e. Ecuador, and they could eventually be found to overlap. Scaled is a bit smaller and always lacks pale shaft streaking on back; it also has more of a transverse white crescent (not a patch) on lower throat, its belly is more tawny to rufous (not pale buff), and it lacks Variegated's flank speckling.

HABITAT AND BEHAVIOR: Uncommon to rare on or near the ground in humid forest and mature secondary woodland; slightly more numerous in e. Brazil than elsewhere. A shy and retiring inhabitant of dense forest undergrowth, almost always difficult to see. Usually encountered singly as it hops rapidly on forest floor, pausing to flick aside leaves with its bill, probing into the soft, often-damp ground for earthworms and other invertebrates. In the very early morning occasionally emerges to feed at the edge of little-traveled roads, especially when these are wet. Startled birds flush abruptly and may fly strongly to a perch (sometimes 3 or 4 m or more above ground), there pausing to ascertain the source of the disturbance, then usually diving back into heavy cover. The song in e. Brazil is a series of deep, hollow, mournful notes which swell in volume, "whoo-doo-doo-doo, WHOO-WHOO-WHOO-WHOO-WHOO-whoo," often given from an elevated perch up to about 5 m above ground. Birds in Surinam have a similar song, though it usually is shorter and delivered more slowly.

RANGE: Guianas and lower Amaz. Brazil (north of the Amazon west to the lower Rio Negro, south of it west locally to the Rio Madeira, Rondônia, and n. Mato Grosso); nw. Brazil (upper Rio Negro region) and adjacent sw. Venezuela (sw. Amazonas); ne. Peru (on n. bank of the lower Río Napo in Loreto); e. Brazil (Pernambuco; s. Bahia south to n. Rio Grande do Sul), e. Paraguay (Canendiyu to Itapúa), and ne. Argentina (Misiones and ne. Corrientes). To about 1400 m in se. Brazil; to 600 m in ne. South America.

NOTE: Two species may be involved: *G. imperator* (with *intercedens*) of e. Brazil southward (Imperial Antpitta) and *G. varia* of n. South America.

Grallaria guatimalensis

SCALED ANTPITTA

PLATE: 26

DESCRIPTION: 16–16.5 cm (6¼–6½"). Above olive brown with gray hindcrown and nape, the feathers of all of upperparts edged black giving a *scaly look;* tail dark rufous. Throat and chest brownish olive with semiconcealed *crescent* of white across upper chest and with *buffyish to white malar stripe extending downward from whitish lores* (the crescent and stripe almost touch); *remainder of underparts rich rufous to tawny*

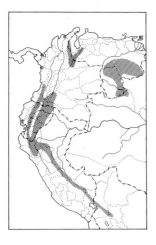

buff. Some individuals (especially of *regulus* and *carmelitae* of w. Venezuela to Ecuador) show extensive white streaking on breast below crescent (see V-23, C-31). *Aripoensis* (Trinidad) is *deep unstreaked rufous below; sororia* (Peru and Bolivia) is pale ochraceous buff below.

SIMILAR SPECIES: Scaling on upperparts is often not obvious in the field and can be narrow in birds with worn plumage. Better marks are the prominent pale malar stripe, crescent across upper chest, and the rich ochraceous lower underparts. Scaled closely resembles n. races of Variegated Antpitta; see discussion under that species. Plain-backed Antpitta has white throat, lacks the chest crescent, and shows little or no scaly pattern on upperparts. Cf. also the range-restricted Tachira and Moustached Antpittas.

HABITAT AND BEHAVIOR: Uncommon and somewhat local on or near the ground in humid and montane forest and secondary woodland, mainly in foothills and subtropical zone (but also out locally into adjacent lowlands); generally under-recorded (except by voice) because of its secretive behavior, which resembles Variegated Antpitta's. Favors ravines or areas with dense growth near water. Scaled's song is a series of low-pitched hollow and resonant notes which gradually slide up in pitch and become louder, lasting 4 or 5 seconds; compared to Variegated's, Scaled's song consists of many more individual notes and is delivered much more rapidly, almost with a tremolo effect.

RANGE: Locally on lower Andean slopes and in foothills in w. Venezuela (north to Mérida), Colombia, Ecuador (where also found locally in e. lowlands out to Zancudococha, and on slopes of the coastal cordillera in sw. Manabí and w. Guayas), Peru (south on w. slope to Lambayeque), and w. Bolivia (La Paz and Cochabamba); Sierra de Perijá on Venezuela-Colombia border and Colombia's Santa Marta Mts.; tepuis of s. Venezuela (Bolívar and Amazonas) and adjacent n. Brazil (Serra do Curupira in n. Amazonas), probably occurring also in adjacent Guyana; Trinidad (where scarce). Also Mexico to Panama. Mostly 500–1500 m, locally down to 200 m in e. Ecuador and up to about 2500 m in sw. Ecuador and nw. Peru.

NOTE: There appears to be some geographic variation in songs and more than one species may be involved (P. Coopmans and N. Krabbe).

Grallaria chthonia

TACHIRA ANTPITTA

DESCRIPTION: 17 cm (6¾"). Known only from the type locality in Andes of *sw. Táchira, Venezuela.* Resembles Scaled Antpitta but slightly larger. Differs in having dull whitish (not ochraceous) lower underparts, the *breast and flanks lightly but distinctly barred with gray.*

HABITAT AND BEHAVIOR: Virtually unknown in life. Recorded from "mossy undergrowth of high, dense cloud forest . . . where basically terrestrial and hard to see" (Meyer de Schauensee and Phelps 1978, p. 222). The species has not been recorded since the type series was obtained in the 1950s. Its voice is unknown.

RANGE: Andes of w. Venezuela (sw. Táchira at Hacienda La Providencia on the Río Chiquito). 1800–2100 m.

Grallaria alleni

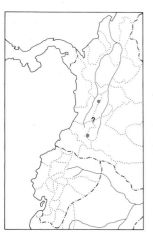

MOUSTACHED ANTPITTA

DESCRIPTION: 16.5 cm (6½"). Very local and rare in *Andes of Colombia*. Resembles Scaled Antpitta, but *belly creamy whitish* (not ochraceous) and darker above; the degree of scaling on the upperparts is about the same (*contra* Hilty and Brown 1986). Moustached further differs in its uniformly dark brown cheeks and in showing black scaling in the white malar stripe. See the fine L. A. Fuertes painting in Chapman (1917).

HABITAT AND BEHAVIOR: Very poorly known. Recorded from "undergrowth of very humid montane forest" (Hilty and Brown 1986, p. 419). Probably deserves threatened or endangered status, though doubtless under-recorded; known from only 2 specimens.

RANGE: Very local in Andes of Colombia (recorded only from Salento in Quindío, and at Cueva de los Guácharos Nat. Park in Huila). 2000–2130 m.

NOTE: J. Hernández-C. and J. V. Rodríguez (*Caldasia* 12[60]: 573–580, 1979) suggest that *alleni* might only be a race of *G. guatimalensis*. We suggest that perhaps *G. chthonia* of Venezuela may be even more closely related to *G. alleni*. Both have very limited ranges, at almost precisely the same elevations, and they share the paler lower underparts. *Chthonia* and *alleni* also agree in their elongated, rather slender bills (see A. Wetmore and W. H. Phelps, *Proc. Biol. Soc. Wash.* 69: 1–12, 1956).

Grallaria haplonota

PLAIN-BACKED ANTPITTA

DESCRIPTION: 16.5–17 cm (6½–6¾"). Local and disjunct in *n. Venezuela and Ecuador. Uniform olive brown above,* crown at most slightly grayer, with whitish lores; tail rufescent. *Midthroat white* bordered by *dusky submalar stripe* and *pale buffy malar stripe;* remaining underparts ochraceous, somewhat darker on chest. See V-23. *Chaplinae* (M. Robbins and RSR, *Bull. B.O.C.* 106[3]: 101–104, 1986) of e. Ecuador is similar but with feathers of crown and back edged blackish giving faint scaly effect, and somewhat less richly colored below with more olivaceous mottling on breast.

SIMILAR SPECIES: Recalls Scaled Antpitta. Plain-backed Antpittas even from e. Ecuador (the "scaliest" race of the species) are much less scaled dorsally than Scaled, and they have median throat contrastingly white instead of having a pale crescent on upper chest.

HABITAT AND BEHAVIOR: Uncommon to locally fairly common (heard much more often than seen) on or near ground in montane forest and forest borders, especially in foothills; under-recorded (except by voice) because of its secretive behavior, which is much like Variegated Antpitta's. Plain-backed's song is a series of 10–18 low, hollow, mournful whistled notes which gradually become louder and rise slightly in pitch, then fall at the end. Seems most numerous at various sites in n. Venezuela (especially below Colonia Tovar and in Henri Pittier Nat. Park above Maracay).

RANGE: Coastal mts. of n. Venezuela (Lara east to Paria Peninsula); locally in Ecuador (on w. slope in Imbabura and Pichincha, and in El Oro; on e. slope in w. Napo and Morona-Santiago). Seems likely to occur in Colombia (has possibly been heard in Valle and w. Nariño; Hilty and Brown 1986). Mostly 800–1600 m.

GROUP B

Simply patterned Grallaria found mainly in temperate zone of Andes.

Grallaria quitensis

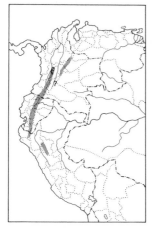

TAWNY ANTPITTA   PLATE: 27

DESCRIPTION: 16–18 cm (6–7"). *A plain, essentially olive brown and ochraceous antpitta found in páramo and adjacent scrub from Colombia to n. Peru.* Olive brown above with paler sides of head and *whitish lores and eye-ring.* Below dull buffy ochraceous, often slightly flammulated with olive, whitest on throat and midbelly. *Alticola* (E. Andes of Colombia) is notably smaller.

SIMILAR SPECIES: A rather dull-plumaged antpitta, *much less skulking than the others.* Rufous Antpitta is much more uniformly rufous or rufescent. Plain-backed Antpitta is a forest bird found at lower elevations. Cf. also the very rare Brown-banded Antpitta of Colombia.

HABITAT AND BEHAVIOR: Fairly common to common in páramo with scattered low bushes and/or *Espeletia,* and in scrub and hedgerows in mainly agricultural terrain; most numerous near and just above treeline. Unusually conspicuous for an antpitta, frequently seen hopping about in the open, sometimes on roadsides or perching conspicuously on bushes and low trees, even fence posts. Regularly flicks its wings and tail and bobs on its long legs. Its often-heard song is a loud, far-carrying "took, tu-tu," with a slightly hollow quality; birds sometimes vocalize from an exposed elevated perch, their heads thrown back, bills wide open, and white throats puffed out. Apparently birds in Colombia's E. Andes (*alticola*) sing differently (F. G. Stiles). Also frequently heard is a very loud call note, "keeyurt!," quite similar to one of the common calls of Great Thrush. Tawny Antpitta seems especially numerous in various páramo areas near Quito, Ecuador (e.g., in the Papallacta pass region); the Latin species epithet is thus singularly appropriate.

RANGE: Andes of Colombia (north in E. Andes to Boyacá, in Cen. Andes to Caldas), Ecuador, and Peru (south to Piura and e. La Libertad). Mostly 2800–4000 m (recorded down to 2200 m in Colombia).

Grallaria erythrotis

RUFOUS-FACED ANTPITTA   PLATE: 27

DESCRIPTION: 18.5 cm (7¼"). *Andes of w. Bolivia.* Olive brown above with grayer crown and *contrasting orange-rufous sides of head and neck.* Dingy whitish below, whitest on throat and midbelly, suffused with orange-rufous across breast and with olivaceous on flanks.

SIMILAR SPECIES: White-throated Antpitta has entire head (not just face) rufous and has grayer underparts (aside from its white throat); it occurs at lower elevations.

HABITAT AND BEHAVIOR: Fairly common to common at borders of montane forest and in regenerating shrubby areas; often along roads or at edges of landslides. Usually on or near the ground, and like Tawny not a particularly difficult antpitta to see (though rarely as confiding as that species). Its often-heard song is much like Tawny Antpitta's, a loud "heelo-hee-hee" or "heeo, hee-hee"; also has a loud, descending call.

RANGE: W. Bolivia (La Paz, Cochabamba, and w. Santa Cruz). 2000–3050 m.

NOTE: For more information on this species, see J. V. Remsen, Jr., et al. 1982.

Grallaria milleri

BROWN-BANDED ANTPITTA

DESCRIPTION: 16.5 cm (6½"). *Very limited area in Cen. Andes of Colombia. Dark brown above;* lores, throat, and midbelly grayish white; *breast band* and flanks brown. See C-31.

SIMILAR SPECIES: A *dark* and relatively unpatterned antpitta, lacking a malar streak and any scaling on upperparts. Far more numerous Tawny Antpitta is paler and more ochraceous below and does not show an obvious breast band. Rufous Antpitta is generally *rufous* (not *brown*).

HABITAT AND BEHAVIOR: Virtually unknown in life. Brown-banded Antpitta has not been found since K. von Sneidern obtained 2 specimens (ANSP) at Laguneta in Quindío in Apr. 1942; these 2 birds are labeled as having been taken in "forest." The region has mostly been deforested (Hilty and Brown 1986), and though it is believed very likely that the species survives in areas that still have forest (some of them protected; Collar et al. 1992), the species must be considered endangered.

RANGE: W. slope of Cen. Andes of Colombia (Caldas and Quindío). 2700–3100 m.

Grallaria rufula

RUFOUS ANTPITTA   PLATE: 27

DESCRIPTION: 14.5–15 cm (5¾–6"). *Uniform and rather rich rufous,* slightly paler below, with an indistinct pale buffyish eye-ring (widest to rear); some birds have whitish midbelly (this apparently especially well marked in *spatiator* of Colombia's Santa Marta Mts.). Foregoing applies to nominate group of sw. Venezuela, Colombia, Ecuador, extreme n. Peru, and se. Peru and Bolivia. Birds from most of n. and cen. Peru (Amazonas to Junín; *cajamarcae* and *obscura*) are much less rufous overall, being *duller and more olivaceous brown above* and *paler almost ochraceous below.* A few examples from Colombia's W. Andes are especially deeply colored and show a suggestion of dark barring on belly, thus resembling the newly described Chestnut Antpitta; these may represent an undescribed subspecies of Rufous Antpitta (G. R. Graves). *Saltuensis* (Sierra de Perijá) is very different: olivaceous brown above and pale drab buffy brownish below, with no hint of rufous anywhere.

SIMILAR SPECIES: In most of its range this handsome, uniformly rufescent, small antpitta should be easily recognized. In n. and cen. Peru cf. the similar Chestnut Antpitta.

HABITAT AND BEHAVIOR: Uncommon to fairly common on or near the ground in montane forest and forest borders, favoring boggy areas, seepage zones, and undergrowth near streams, particularly where there is a dense undergrowth of *Chusquea* bamboo. Shy and unobtrusive, hopping mainly on forest floor, and unlikely to be noted unless it is vocalizing, when it may perch up to 4 m above ground. The most frequently heard vocalization (in Colombia and Ecuador, at least) is a penetrating, fast, 3-noted "píh, pipee" or "peé, pipipee" with a clear ringing quality, the last note slightly longer and lower in pitch; at a distance the song can sound 2-noted. A trill is also given, at least in Peru (Fjeldså and Krabbe 1990).

RANGE: Andes of extreme sw. Venezuela (sw. Táchira), Colombia, Ecuador (south on w. slope to Azuay), e. Peru, and w. Bolivia (La Paz and Cochabamba); Sierra de Perijá on Venezuela-Colombia border and Colombia's Santa Marta Mts. Mostly 2300–3600 m, locally down to 2100 m in e. Ecuador.

NOTE: *Saltuensis* may deserve full species status (Perija Antpitta). Information on its vocalizations—still apparently unknown, as for all the numerous Perijá endemics—would be instructive. If *saltuensis* is not a distinct species, then we suggest it might be a subspecies of *G. quitensis* and not of *G. rufula*.

Grallaria blakei

CHESTNUT ANTPITTA

DESCRIPTION: 14.5 cm (5¾"). Known very locally from Andes of n. and cen. Peru. Resembles nearly sympatric races of Rufous Antpitta, but *distinctly darker and more chestnut in coloration*. Recall that the races of Rufous Antpitta found there (*cajamarcae* and *obscura*) are much paler and more olivaceous than other races of the species. Chestnut Antpitta further differs in having indistinct dark barring on belly feathers (lacking in most Rufous) and in having *no eye-ring* (latter quite distinct in pale races of Rufous). Where both species occur, Chestnut is found at *lower elevations*.

SIMILAR SPECIES: Cf. also larger Bay Antpitta.

HABITAT AND BEHAVIOR: Uncommon on or near the ground in montane forest and secondary woodland, often where there is a dense understory of bamboo. Behavior much like Rufous Antpitta's. The song of birds in Pasco is a steadily repeated single "toop" note, continued several times at about 1-second intervals (T. J. Davis).

RANGE: Locally on e. slope of Andes in n. and cen. Peru in Amazonas (Cordillera de Colán and 30 [road] km northeast of Florida), Huánuco (Cordillera Carpish), and Pasco (Cordillera de Yanachaga and Playa Pampa [south of Millpo; unpublished LSUMZ specimens]). The Pasco birds may represent an undescribed subspecies of *G. blakei*, differing in lacking barring on belly (T. J. Davis). 2150–2475 m.

NOTE: A recently described species: G. R. Graves, *Wilson Bull.* 99(3): 313–321, 1987.

Grallaria griseonucha

GRAY-NAPED ANTPITTA   PLATE: 27

DESCRIPTION: 16 cm (6¼"). *Andes of w. Venezuela*. Above chestnut brown with *dark gray band extending back from eye and around nape*. Below bright rufous.

SIMILAR SPECIES: Does not occur in the range of any basically similar antpitta.

HABITAT AND BEHAVIOR: Uncommon on or near the ground inside montane forest. Behavior much like other *Grallaria* antpittas' (see under Scaled). Its song is a short but fast series of hollow notes of typical antpitta quality which become emphatically louder, "ho-ho-ho-ho-hó-hó-hóhóhó" (T. Meyer recording). Can be found along the Pico Humboldt Trail near Mérida (city), Venezuela; here it replaces Chestnut-crowned Antpitta above about 2400 m (T. Meyer).

RANGE: Andes of w. Venezuela (Mérida and n. Táchira). 2300–2800 m.

Grallaria rufocinerea

BICOLORED ANTPITTA   PLATE: 27

DESCRIPTION: 15.5–16 cm (6–6¼"). *Local in Andes of Colombia. Rufous brown above and on throat. Remaining underparts contrastingly dark gray.* At least some females (immatures?) have a "messy" admixture of slate feathers on face and throat.

SIMILAR SPECIES: Handsome and distinctive, this scarce antpitta is not likely to be confused. Cf. substantially larger Chestnut-naped Antpitta.

HABITAT AND BEHAVIOR: Uncommon on or near the ground in montane forest, smaller numbers in secondary growth and at borders. Reclusive behavior apparently similar to that of other montane *Grallaria*. Its song is a high, clear, whistled "treeeee" or more doubled "treeeeeaaaa" with the latter part slurred lower; it is given at 2½- to 3-second intervals (Hilty and Brown 1986). Overall numbers have unquestionably declined because of deforestation, especially in the Cen. Andes; a substantial population is found in the Alto Quindío Acaime Natural Reserve in Quindío (L. M. Renjifo).

RANGE: Locally in Andes of Colombia (both slopes of Cen. Andes from Antioquia south to extreme w. Huila in Puracé Nat. Park, and on e. slope of E. Andes in w. Putumayo [seen 20 km east of San Francisco; S. Hilty]). 2400–3150 m.

Grallaria nuchalis

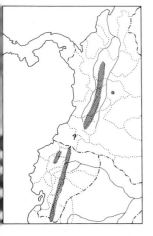

CHESTNUT-NAPED ANTPITTA   PLATE: 27

DESCRIPTION: 19.5–20 cm (7¾–8"). *Mainly in Andes of Colombia and Ecuador.* Iris usually gray, but apparently more whitish in some (older?) birds; triangular patch of bare whitish skin behind eye, much as in a *Formicarius* antthrush. *Crown, nape, and sides of head chestnut-rufous* (brightest on nape and darkest on auriculars), becoming dark reddish brown on remaining upperparts. *Below dark gray,* slightly blacker on throat. Foregoing applies to nominate race of e. Ecuador and n. Peru. *Ruficeps* (of Colombia) is a bit bigger, slightly paler gray below, and brighter rufous on nape (see C-30); *obsoleta* (nw. Ecuador) is darker above (only the nape is chestnut-rufous) and much darker and sootier below.

SIMILAR SPECIES: This handsome dark antpitta can be readily known by its large size and basically dark gray underparts; it will usually be identified by its distinctive voice (see below). In Colombia, cf. smaller Bicolored Antpitta (with rufous on throat, etc.).

HABITAT AND BEHAVIOR: Uncommon to locally fairly common on or near the ground in montane forest, secondary woodland, and borders; especially favors dense damp tangled thickets and areas with a thick growth of *Chusquea* bamboo. Mainly because of its preference for almost impenetrable habitats, Chestnut-naped is hard to see; though it often responds to tape playback, often it remains invisible if heavy cover is nearby. The distinctive and far-carrying song, heard most often soon after dawn, is a series of musical but somewhat metallic notes which hesitate at first and then gradually accelerate before ending in a short series of rapidly rising tinkling notes, "tew; tew, tew, tew-tew-tew-teh-te-ti-ti-titititi?" Seems especially numerous (and unusually easy to see, regularly hopping on trails through the forest) in the Cajanuma sector of Podocarpus Nat. Park in s. Ecuador.

RANGE: Locally in Andes of Colombia (Cen. Andes from Antioquia south to Cauca and Huila; an old record from E. Andes south of Bogotá in Cundinamarca), Ecuador (on w. slope recorded only from Imbabura and Pichincha; on entire east slope), and extreme n. Peru (Cerro Chinguela in Piura). 2200–3000 m.

Grallaria carrikeri

PALE-BILLED ANTPITTA

DESCRIPTION: 19 cm (7½"). *Very local on e. slope of Andes in n. Peru.* Resembles slightly larger Chestnut-naped Antpitta (replacing that species south of the Río Marañón) but with *striking ivory-colored bill* and *red iris,* and apparently lacking Chestnut-naped's bare postocular patch; further differs in having a black crown, face, and throat.

SIMILAR SPECIES: No other antpitta is so obviously whitish-billed.

HABITAT AND BEHAVIOR: Recorded on or near ground in montane forest, usually where the undergrowth is dense and most often in or near thickets of *Chusquea* bamboo. The song consists of 6 notes with a staccato effect and a slightly irregular tempo (longer pauses between the first and second, and the fifth and sixth notes); the entire song lasts 3 seconds (T. S. Schulenberg and M. D. Williams, *Wilson Bull.* 94[2]: 105–113, 1982).

RANGE: E. slope of Andes in n. Peru (Amazonas on the Cordillera de Colán and 33 [road] km northeast of Ingenio; La Libertad at Cumpang, above Utcumamba on the trail to Ongón). 2350–2900 m.

NOTE: A recently described species: T. S. Schulenberg and M. D. Williams, op. cit.

GROUP C

Simply patterned Grallaria found mainly in subtropical zone of Andes. All allopatric; the G. hypoleuca superspecies.

Grallaria flavotincta

YELLOW-BREASTED ANTPITTA   PLATE: 27

Other: Bay-backed Antpitta (in part)

DESCRIPTION: 17 cm (6¾"). *W. slope of W. Andes in w. Colombia and nw. Ecuador. Above uniform rufous brown,* lores slightly paler, and a bit duskier on cheeks. *Below pale yellowish;* sides, flanks, and crissum mottled with rufous brown.

SIMILAR SPECIES: The only antpitta of its group on *west* slope of Andes, and the only *Grallaria* with *yellowish* underparts.

HABITAT AND BEHAVIOR: Rare to locally uncommon on or near the ground in montane forest and forest borders, favoring ravines, steep hillsides, and vicinity of streams. Behavior similar to that of other montane forest-based antpittas, being shy and difficult to see except through tape playback, though not infrequently heard in appropriate habitat. Usually found singly, most often hopping on ground, pausing to probe in litter or to flick aside leaves. The song is a musical "pi-püüü-puuh," with first note so short it is inaudible at any distance; similar to song of Rufous-breasted Antthrush but less sharp in quality (and antthrush's is never 3-noted).

RANGE: W. slope of W. Andes in Colombia (north to Antioquia) and nw. Ecuador (a few recent records from Carchi and Pichincha). 1300–2350 m.

NOTE: Sometimes considered conspecific with *G. hypoleuca*, in which case the enlarged species (including these two and the next four species) would be called the Bay-backed Antpitta. We prefer to treat all of these as allospecies in a superspecies complex, following Hilty and Brown (1986) and the suggestion of Parker and O'Neill (1980).

Grallaria hypoleuca

WHITE-BELLIED ANTPITTA

Other: Bay-backed Antpitta (in part)

DESCRIPTION: 17 cm (6¾"). Mainly *e. slope of Andes* from Colombia to extreme n. Peru. Resembles Yellow-breasted Antpitta (no overlap), but *very pale gray below* except for pure white throat and midbelly; cheeks and sides of head somewhat rustier red than rest of upperparts. See C-30. Nominate race (of Colombia) is slightly brighter above than *castanea* (of Ecuador).

SIMILAR SPECIES: Much whiter (less yellowish) below than Yellow-breasted Antpitta and lacks rufous on breast shown by Rusty-tinged Antpitta; none of these 3 closely related species occur together.

HABITAT AND BEHAVIOR: Uncommon to locally fairly common on or near the ground in montane forest, especially in tangles at or near forest borders, at treefalls and landslides, etc. Behavior similar to Yellow-breasted Antpitta's, like it often heard but rarely seen. White-bellied's far-carrying song is a fast, comparatively high-pitched "too, tew-tew," the second pair of notes higher than the initial note, repeated at rather long intervals (usually 15 or more seconds).

RANGE: Andes of Colombia (w. slope of E. Andes north to Virolín in Santander, Cen. Andes north to Antioquia, and e. slope of Andes in e. Nariño), e. Ecuador, and extreme n. Peru (Cerro Chinguela in Piura, and at Chaupe in Cajamarca). 1500–2225 m.

NOTE: See comments under Yellow-breasted Antpitta.

Grallaria przewalskii

RUSTY-TINGED ANTPITTA
PLATE: 27

Other: Bay-backed Antpitta (in part)

DESCRIPTION: 17 cm (6¾"). *E. slope of Andes in n. Peru.* Above uniform rufous brown with *crown dark sooty* and lores pale grayish. *Throat*

rufous-buff, merging into *deeper rufous on breast and on sides of head and neck,* contrasting with pale gray belly; flanks and crissum rufous brown.

SIMILAR SPECIES: White-bellied Antpitta (which replaces this species northward) has white throat and gray breast (not rufous). Cf. also Bay Antpitta (which replaces this species southward).

HABITAT AND BEHAVIOR: Poorly known, but habitat and behavior likely similar to Yellow-breasted (and White-bellied) Antpitta's. Rusty-tinged's song resembles White-bellied's (Parker and O'Neill 1980), though Fjeldså and Krabbe (1990) describe the middle note as lower pitched.

RANGE: E. slope of Andes in n. Peru (Amazonas south to e. La Libertad). 2200–2750 m.

NOTE: See comments under Yellow-breasted Antpitta.

Grallaria capitalis

BAY ANTPITTA

Other: Bay-backed Antpitta (in part)

DESCRIPTION: 17 cm (6¾"). *E. slope of Andes in cen. Peru.* Resembles a "saturated" Rusty-tinged Antpitta (which replaces this species northward; no overlap), but *throat, breast, and flanks rufous-chestnut* and midbelly paler rufous-buff with a vaguely streaked look.

SIMILAR SPECIES: This is essentially a *uniform rufous-chestnut* antpitta with a sooty crown and somewhat paler belly. The smaller Chestnut Antpitta is similar in overall coloration but lacks sooty-black crown and has proportionately smaller bill. The races of Rufous Antpitta found in cen. Peru (and which might be sympatric with Bay) are duller and more olivaceous brown.

HABITAT AND BEHAVIOR: Uncommon to locally fairly common on or near the ground in montane forest and second-growth woodland, especially at borders and treefalls. General behavior similar to Yellow-breasted Antpitta's, and equally secretive. Bay's song, moderately different from those of others in this superspecies, consists of 4 (sometimes 5) notes, the first *higher* pitched than the others, thus "tew, too-too-too." Can be found along the Paty Trail in the Carpish Mts. of Huánuco.

RANGE: E. slope of Andes in cen. Peru (Huánuco to Junín). 2600–3000 m.

NOTE: See comments under Yellow-breasted Antpitta.

Grallaria erythroleuca

RED-AND-WHITE ANTPITTA   PLATE: 27

Other: Bay-backed Antpitta (in part)

DESCRIPTION: 17.5 cm (7"). *E. slope of Andes in s. Peru. Above uniform bright rufous red.* Below white, *the bright rufous red extending down onto sides, flanks, and crissum,* in some birds almost reaching across breast, with *some feathers tipped white giving distinct spotted effect.*

SIMILAR SPECIES: Perhaps the most handsome antpitta, Red-and-white is easily recognized in its limited range. Cf. White-throated Ant-

pitta (replacing Red-and-white southward); White-throated and Red-and-white share the bright rufous head and white throat, but former is mainly olive brown above and has gray on sides and flanks.

HABITAT AND BEHAVIOR: Uncommon to locally fairly common on or near the ground in montane forest and second-growth woodland, favoring tangled borders and bamboo stands. General behavior similar to Yellow-breasted Antpitta's; often seems less shy, however. The song is a far-carrying "too, teh-too," the second note softer and not audible at a distance. Can be found along the upper part of the Shintuya-Paucartambo road in Cuzco, Peru.

RANGE: E. slope of Andes in Peru (Cuzco). 2150–2970 m.

NOTE: See comments under Yellow-breasted Antpitta.

Grallaria albigula

WHITE-THROATED ANTPITTA PLATE: 27

DESCRIPTION: 18.5 cm (7¼"). *E. slope of Andes from s. Peru to nw. Argentina. Head bright chestnut-rufous* contrasting with olive brown upperparts; *narrow but prominent white eye-ring. Throat pure white*, becoming grayish white on remaining underparts, grayest on sides and flanks.

SIMILAR SPECIES: Rufous-faced Antpitta has dark crown contrasting with rufous face (not an all-rufous head) and shows less gray on underparts; it inhabits higher elevations. In se. Peru, cf. Red-and-white Antpitta (which replaces White-throated northward).

HABITAT AND BEHAVIOR: Uncommon to locally common on or near the ground in montane forest and forest borders, in Argentina also in more deciduous forest and alder-dominated forest. Behavior similar to Yellow-breasted Antpitta's. The song is a pair of mellow whistled notes, "hu-hooo," the first note shorter and lower-pitched; alarmed or excited birds also utter a more trilled short series of notes. Numerous in Calilegua Nat. Park in Jujuy, Argentina.

RANGE: Locally on e. slope of Andes in s. Peru (s. Madre de Dios on Cerro de Pantiacolla [FMNH], and Puno), w. Bolivia (recorded only from Cochabamba and w. Santa Cruz, but doubtless more widespread), and extreme nw. Argentina (Jujuy and Salta). 800–1700 m.

NOTE: See comments under Yellow-breasted Antpitta. Although *G. albigula* has not heretofore been associated with the *G. hypoleuca* superspecies, we suspect that it belongs here; it appears most closely related to *G. erythroleuca*.

GROUP D

Montane *Grallaria* with *conspicuous streaking*.

Grallaria bangsi

SANTA MARTA ANTPITTA PLATE: 27

DESCRIPTION: 18 cm (7"). *Colombia's Santa Marta Mts.* Above olive brown to grayish olive with whitish lores and eye-ring. *Throat ochraceous buff; remaining underparts streaked whitish and brownish olive*, more solidly brownish olive on flanks and with midbelly white.

SIMILAR SPECIES: The only antpitta on the Santa Martas with streaking.

HABITAT AND BEHAVIOR: Common on or near the ground in montane forest, mature secondary woodland, and tangled borders. Behavior much like that of other *Grallaria*, though generally not so shy; sometimes, especially in early morning, feeds along edges of roads and tracks. Much more often heard than seen, its call being a hollow, far-carrying "whow-whoit." Frequent along the road up the San Lorenzo ridge.

RANGE: Santa Marta Mts. of n. Colombia. 1200–2400 m (mostly above 1600 m).

Grallaria kaestneri

CUNDINAMARCA ANTPITTA

DESCRIPTION: 15.5 cm (6"). *E. slope of Andes in Cundinamarca, Colombia.* Resembles Santa Marta Antpitta (no overlap) but considerably *smaller* and *darker generally* (both above and below); *throat dull whitish* (not buff); *breast grayish olive with very narrow white shaft streaking.*

SIMILAR SPECIES: Not likely to be confused in its very limited range; cf. Chestnut-crowned Antpitta (with obvious orange-rufous on head, etc.).

HABITAT AND BEHAVIOR: Fairly common but very local on or near the ground in montane forest and mature secondary woodland. Behavior reported to be similar to that of other *Grallaria*. Its song consists of 3 sharp, clear whistled notes (occasionally the last is omitted), "wirt, wiirt-weert!" (F. G. Stiles, *Wilson Bull.* 104[3]: 389–399, 1992).

RANGE: E. slope of E. Andes in Cundinamarca, Colombia (thus far known only from the type locality, ca. 3 km east-northeast of Monterredondo, just north of the main Bogotá-Villavicencio highway). 1800–2300 m.

NOTE: A recently described species: F. G. Stiles, op. cit.

Grallaria ruficapilla

CHESTNUT-CROWNED ANTPITTA   PLATE: 27

DESCRIPTION: 18.5–19 cm (7¼–7½"). *A generally widespread and numerous antpitta of Andes from Venezuela to n. Peru.* Legs grayish blue (brighter than in other *Grallaria*). *Head and nape orange-rufous;* otherwise olive brown above. Throat white; remaining underparts white with *bold blackish brown to olive brown streaking,* especially pronounced on sides and flanks. Birds from sw. Ecuador (El Oro and Loja; *connectens*) and nw. Peru (*albiloris* and *interior*) have whitish lores (lores are rufous or buff in nominate group from elsewhere in species' range; see V-23, C-31) and some whitish streaking on ear-coverts and malar area; they are somewhat more pallid generally with duller crown and are less streaked below.

SIMILAR SPECIES: In sw. Ecuador and extreme nw. Peru, cf. the similar Watkins' Antpitta, and in Cundinamarca, Colombia, the smaller and much duller Cundinamarca Antpitta. Otherwise this beautiful and distinctive antpitta is unlikely to be confused.

HABITAT AND BEHAVIOR: Fairly common to common on or near the ground in montane forest, secondary woodland, and borders; seems more tolerant than other *Grallaria* of habitat degradation and often occurs in decidedly small patches of regenerating woodland, sometimes even in densely overgrown hedgerows. Although shy and secretive like most other antpittas, the Chestnut-crowned is more likely than most to hop on the ground in the open (though never far from cover), especially at the edge of clearings with short grass or at roadsides. Its song, sometimes delivered from a slightly elevated perch, is distinctive and often heard, a loud, whistled "whee, whuu-whoou"; an onomatopoeic local name for this species, at least in Venezuela and Colombia, is a very accurate *compra pan* ("buy bread").

RANGE: Coastal mts. of n. Venezuela (Aragua to Miranda), and Andes of w. Venezuela (north to s. Lara), Colombia, Ecuador, and n. Peru (south to Cajamarca and n. San Martín); Sierra de Perija on Venezuela-Colombia border. Mostly 2000–2900 m, locally down to 1700 m and up to 3250 m.

Grallaria watkinsi

WATKINS' ANTPITTA

Other: Chestnut-crowned Antpitta (in part), Scrub Antpitta

DESCRIPTION: 18 cm (7"). *Sw. Ecuador and adjacent nw. Peru;* here regarded as a species separate from Chestnut-crowned Antpitta, with *very different habitat and voice* (see below). Resembles Chestnut-crowned, especially that species' nearly sympatric race *connectens,* but with somewhat longer *striking pinkish legs* (not grayish blue). Further differs in its slightly smaller size, more pallid and less extensive rufous on crown and nape, more white on auriculars, and tendency toward whitish shaft streaking on crown and nape.

HABITAT AND BEHAVIOR: Fairly common on or near the ground in dense vegetation in deciduous woodland and regenerating secondary scrub; seems quite capable of persisting in the latter, in numbers roughly equal to those found in less disturbed woodland. Behavior similar to Chestnut-crowned Antpitta's, and equally vocal. Its distinctively different song is a series of well-enunciated and emphatic whistled notes, the first 4–6 similar, the last longer and sharply upslurred, "wheeu, wheeu, wheeu, wheeu, whuu-u-e-e-e-e"; also has shorter calls, usually consisting of fewer initial notes and the upslurred final one, sometimes the upslurred note alone. Readily found in the scrub and patchy woodland near Arenillas in El Oro, and between El Empalme and Celica in sw. Loja, both in Ecuador.

RANGE: Sw. Ecuador (mainly in El Oro and w. Loja, with an isolated population on the coastal cordillera of sw. Manabí and w. Guayas) and extreme nw. Peru (Tumbes). To 1700 m.

NOTE: We consider *G. watkinsi* as a species separate from *G. ruficapilla;* its morphological differences and strikingly different voice surely serve to isolate it reproductively from *G. ruficapilla.* They replace each other altitudinally, *G. watkinsi* found lower (locally down to near sea level) and *G. ruficapilla connectens* higher; near Celica in sw. Ecuador their elevational ranges almost meet (or may even overlap).

Grallaria andicola

STRIPE-HEADED ANTPITTA

PLATE: 27

DESCRIPTION: 16–16.5 cm (6¼–6½"). *High elevation woodland, mainly in Peru.* Above olive brown, darker on crown, *crown and mantle with*

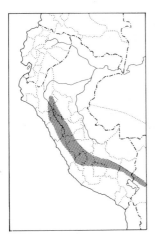

black-edged whitish streaks; white eye-ring and whitish lores. Below buffy whitish, *feathers margined black giving a bold scaly or streaked appearance;* midthroat and midbelly almost unmarked. *Punensis* (Cuzco, Peru, southward) resembles nominate race (remainder of range) but is much less streaked above (streaking *restricted to forecrown*) and is usually even more densely and coarsely marked below.

SIMILAR SPECIES: This coarsely streaked antpitta is not likely to be confused in its restricted habitat and range.

HABITAT AND BEHAVIOR: Uncommon to locally fairly common on or near the ground in groves of *Polylepis*-dominated woodland and in stunted woodland just below treeline; sometimes forages out into adjacent areas with tall grass and boulders. Usually shy and furtive, though in the morning one may hop about more or less in the open, even perching nonchalantly on logs or low limbs. For the genus not very vocal, but does have a truly unusual and strange voice: a purring or reeling, somewhat frog-like, "prree-prree, rrréeeeu" (T. Meyer recording). Can be found along w. side of Abra Málaga road above Ollantaytambo in Cuzco, Peru.

RANGE: Andes of Peru (north to Amazonas and Cajamarca) and extreme w. Bolivia (La Paz; AMNH specimen from "Alaska Mine" [= near Pongo]). Mostly 3000–4200 m.

GROUP E

Large; restricted to *w. Amaz. lowlands.* Note white streaks on rump and very short tail. The *Thamnocharis* subgenus.

Grallaria dignissima

OCHRE-STRIPED ANTPITTA   PLATE: 27

DESCRIPTION: 19 cm (7½"). *A strikingly patterned antpitta found locally in nw. Amazonia.* Above brown, grayer on crown and with pale buffyish lores; long plumes on lower back and rump with white shaft streaks. *Throat and chest rich orange-ochraceous,* chest feathers with white shaft streaks, becoming white on lower underparts (with long plumes on flanks); *sides and flanks broadly striped black and white.*

SIMILAR SPECIES: No other lowland antpitta shares the rich foreneck color and prominently striped flanks. Cf. Elusive Antpitta (no known overlap).

HABITAT AND BEHAVIOR: Rare to locally uncommon on the ground inside terra firme forest, primarily in upland areas and especially favoring vicinity of shady forest streams. Almost exclusively terrestrial, hopping or bounding rapidly, pausing occasionally to sing with head thrown back and throat puffed out. Ranging singly or in pairs, usually shy and very difficult to see. The song is a distinctive, far-carrying, low and mournful "whü, whüüw" or "whü, whaöw" repeated slowly at 5- or 10-second intervals. Small numbers occur near La Selva in e. Ecuador.

RANGE: Extreme se. Colombia (a single specimen from w. Putumayo at San Miguel), e. Ecuador, and ne. Peru (Loreto, east to near the mouth of the Río Napo). To at least 400 m.

Grallaria eludens

ELUSIVE ANTPITTA

DESCRIPTION: 19 cm (7½"). *Lowlands of se. Peru.* Generally resembles Ochre-striped Antpitta but somewhat paler and more olivaceous brown above (with crown concolor) and *lacking the orange-ochraceous on foreneck* (breast only tinged buff, and throat pure white).

HABITAT AND BEHAVIOR: Not known to us, the Elusive Antpitta, like the closely related Ochre-striped, probably inhabits interior of upland terra firme forest. In their description of the species, G. H. Lowery and J. P. O'Neill (*Auk* 86[1]: 1–12, 1969) mention that its local Indian name at and near the type locality is *du xau,* which sounds strikingly like the song of Ochre-striped Antpitta; a comparable call was described from Manu Nat. Park (Terborgh, Fitzpatrick, and Emmons 1984).

RANGE: Se. Peru in Ucayali (Balta, and on Cordillera Divisor), and probably Madre de Dios (Manu Nat. Park). Seems likely in adjacent Brazil. 300 m.

Myrmothera Antpittas

A pair of dull brownish antpittas, one species found in Amaz. lowlands, the other on the tepuis. In shape much like *Grallaria,* but smaller than most and with more slender bills. The genus is probably most closely related to *Hylopezus.* The nest, a shallow cup of twigs and leaves placed less than 1 m above the ground on a rosette of leaves of an undergrowth plant, is similar to the nests of *Grallaria* (O. Tostain and J.-L. Dujardin, *Condor* 90[1]: 236–239, 1988).

Myrmothera campanisona

THRUSH-LIKE ANTPITTA   PLATE: 28

DESCRIPTION: 15 cm (6"). *A relatively numerous, plainly attired antpitta of Amaz. and Guianan lowlands.* Above rufous brown to dark olivaceous brown with buffy whitish lores and white postocular spot (or triangle). Below white with variable amount of *blurry brown to grayish brown streaking on breast and down flanks.*

SIMILAR SPECIES: Cf. various cis-Andean *Hylopezus* antpittas. Tepui Antpitta lacks streaking below and has more montane range.

HABITAT AND BEHAVIOR: Uncommon to locally fairly common on or near the ground in humid forest, both in terra firme and várzea, favoring areas with dense undergrowth, e.g., around treefalls and along streams. Usually found singly or in pairs; shy and difficult to see, and heard much more often than seen. Its song, a series of 5 or 6 hollow, whistled notes, "whoh-whoh-whoh-whoh-whoh," with middle notes slightly louder, is often heard. Birds may vocalize for many minutes while remaining absolutely motionless on a slightly elevated perch.

RANGE: Guianas, s. Venezuela (e. Bolívar and Amazonas), e. Colombia (north to Meta and Guainía), e. Ecuador, e. Peru, extreme nw. Bolivia (Pando at Camino Mucden), and Amaz. Brazil (widely north of the Amazon; south of it east to both sides of the lower Rio Tapajós, and south to Rondônia). To 1200 m in s. Ecuador.

Myrmothera simplex

TEPUI ANTPITTA

Other: Brown-breasted Antpitta

DESCRIPTION: 16 cm (6¼″). *Slopes of tepuis in s. Venezuela.* Above chestnut brown. Throat white, *breast and flanks unstreaked olivaceous gray;* midbelly also white. *Duidae* (s. Amazonas) differs from other described races (all very similar) in being a warmer olivaceous brown on breast and flanks.

SIMILAR SPECIES: Thrush-like Antpitta is obviously streaked across breast; it occurs at lower elevations than Tepui (though possibly with local overlap). Note superficial similarity to Brown-banded Antpitta of Colombian Andes.

HABITAT AND BEHAVIOR: Uncommon to fairly common on or near ground inside humid forest and woodland. Behavior much like Thrush-like Antpitta's, though usually not as shy and difficult to see. The song is a series of 7−10 hollow, whistled notes on the same pitch, "wh-wh-wh-whoh-whoh-whoh-whoh-whoh-whoh," gradually building to a crescendo. Quite numerous in stunted woodland along the Escalera road in e. Bolívar.

RANGE: S. Venezuela (Bolívar and Amazonas south to Cerro de la Neblina) and extreme n. Brazil (n. Roraima on Cerro Uei-tepui); probably occurs in adjacent Guyana. 600−2400 m.

NOTE: Although this species has long been called the Brown-breasted Antpitta, this name is very misleading because only one geographically restricted race of *M. simplex* has brown on the breast, all the others being decidedly gray. As *Myrmothera simplex* is the only species of antpitta endemic to the tepui region, we suggest it is better called the Tepui Antpitta. Furthermore, *Grallaria milleri* of the Colombian Andes has the confusingly similar name of Brown-banded Antpitta; *G. milleri* is actually more "brown-breasted" than *M. simplex*.

Hylopezus Antpittas

Fairly small antpittas similar in general configuration to the *Myrmothera* antpittas, and likewise found mainly in lowland forests. All *Hylopezus* have streaking or spotting on the breast, conspicuous in some, and ochraceous underwing-coverts; most species, especially the Speckle-breasted and White-browed Antpittas, have a buffy "speculum" at the base of their primaries. Like the *Grallaria* and *Myrmothera* antpittas, *Hylopezus* frequently give their distinctive and fairly loud songs. They were formerly (e.g., *Birds of the World,* vol. 7, and Meyer de Schauensee 1966) placed in the genus *Grallaria* but were generically separated, mainly on anatomical evidence, by G. H. Lowery and J. P. O'Neill (*Auk* 86[1]: 1−12, 1969).

GROUP A

Wide ochraceous eye-ring; very bold spotting/streaking on breast.

Hylopezus macularius

SPOTTED ANTPITTA

PLATE: 28

DESCRIPTION: 14 cm (5½″). *Guianas west locally to w. Amazonia. Crown and nape gray* with *bold ochraceous eye-ring* and buff lores; otherwise olive brown above, wing-coverts tipped with tawny. *Mostly white below*

with black submalar streak and *conspicuous band of black spotting across breast,* which is also tinged buff; flanks buff.

SIMILAR SPECIES: The similar Streak-chested Antpitta occurs only west of Andes. Other *Hylopezus* antpittas occurring in Amazonia show little or no eye-ring and have finer streaking on breast.

HABITAT AND BEHAVIOR: Uncommon on or near the ground in humid forest, mainly in terra firme and especially in dense lower growth at borders and treefalls. Usually found singly, less often in pairs, hopping or running on ground, feeding mainly by flicking aside leaves; frequently fluffs out its feathers, then looking very round. Usually shy and difficult to see, though not as hard as most *Grallaria.* The song of birds in Guianas and e. Venezuela (nominate race) is a series of deep and beautifully modulated whistled notes, "koh, koh, ko-wóh, ko, ko-woh-ko," with an unmistakable rhythm. The song of birds south of the Amazon in Brazil and Bolivia (*paraensis/auricularis*) differs strikingly, being a short series of 4–6 fast, hollow notes, e.g., "ko-ko-ko-ko-ko." The song of birds in ne. Peru (*diversa?*) is also very different, a more musical "kuhlo-kuhlo-kuhlo, klu, klu." When alarmed (and sometimes in response to tape playback) this species, and also other *Hylopezus,* gives a low, fast, more guttural "kokokoko."

RANGE: Guianas, s. Venezuela (e. Bolívar and s. Amazonas), extreme se. Colombia (s. Amazonas near Leticia), ne. Peru (locally in Loreto west to the Pacaya-Samiria Reserve), extreme n. Bolivia (Pando), and Amaz. Brazil (south to Rondônia and east to e. Pará in the Belém region). To 500 m.

NOTE: Despite the close plumage similarity among what are presently considered to be its subspecies, *H. macularius* may actually consist of more than a single species, so striking is the geographical variation shown in its vocalizations.

Hylopezus perspicillatus

STREAK-CHESTED ANTPITTA

Other: Spectacled Antpitta

DESCRIPTION: 14 cm (5½"). *W. Colombia and w. Ecuador.* Resembles Spotted Antpitta (which occurs only east of Andes). Differs in having back with sparse buff streaking, slightly paler spotting on wing-coverts, more extensive white on throat, only a black malar streak (not a black submalar and a white malar streak), and bold breast markings which are more extensive and *obviously streaks* (not spots). See P-22.

SIMILAR SPECIES: Fulvous-bellied Antpitta has a plainer face (without the wide buff eye-ring), plain wings lacking buff spots on wing-coverts, and mostly buffy underparts (not nearly so white) with much finer and blurrier streaking on breast.

HABITAT AND BEHAVIOR: Uncommon on or near the ground in humid forest, unlike the Fulvous-bellied (and other *Hylopezus*) *not* favoring places with particularly dense undergrowth, and thus not excessively difficult to see (at least for an antpitta). Usually solitary, hopping on the forest floor, often freezing when alarmed but sometimes flushing to a low perch; there it may remain motionless for a protracted period, or it may dive back to the ground and disappear by running away rapidly. Heard much more often than seen. The song is a slow series of melancholy whistled notes, rising slightly at first, the last 3 lower pitched and fading away, "deh, dee-dee-dee-dee-dee-dee, deu, deu deu." Often vocalizes from a slightly elevated perch (a log, or a branch up to 3 or 4 m above ground), puffing out throat; singing birds can sometimes be approached, with caution, quite closely.

RANGE: W. Colombia (Pacific lowlands, and humid Caribbean lowlands east to Río Magdalena valley in Santander) and w. Ecuador (south to El Oro). Also Honduras to Panama. To 1200 m (mostly below 900 m).

NOTE: Although this species had long been called the Streak-chested Antpitta, the 1983 AOU Check-list opted to call it the Spectacled Antpitta, and this was followed by Ridgely and Gwynne (1989) and by Stiles, Skutch, and Gardner (1989). We have concluded that it is best to retain the name Streak-chested (also used by Hilty and Brown 1986), as that name draws attention to the most important character separating *H. perspicillatus* from the closely related and similar Spotted Antpitta.

GROUP B

More "*plain-faced*"; streaking/spotting on breast typically *finer*.

Hylopezus fulviventris

WHITE-LORED ANTPITTA   PLATE: 28
Other: Fulvous-bellied Antpitta (in part)

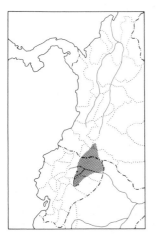

DESCRIPTION: 14.5 cm (5¾"). *E. Ecuador and adjacent Colombia;* here considered a species distinct from Fulvous-bellied Antpitta, found *west* of Andes. Above olive, *much darker and slatier on head and nape* and with *prominent white lores* and a small white triangle behind eye. Throat and partial nuchal collar white; remaining underparts tinged buffy ochraceous, strongly so on chest and especially down sides and flanks, and with coarse dusky streaking across breast and on flanks.

SIMILAR SPECIES: Amazonian Antpitta (no known overlap) is uniform olive brown above (no slaty on crown) and has plainer face, lacking the conspicuous white lores. Cf. Fulvous-bellied Antpitta (only west of Andes).

HABITAT AND BEHAVIOR: Uncommon on or near the ground in very dense lower growth at edge of humid forest (both terra firme and várzea) and in regenerating clearings. Exceptionally difficult to see, in part because of its habitat. Sometimes decoys in well to a tape playback of its song, a short series of 3 or 4 fairly fast, abrupt, hollow notes, "kyo, kwoh-kwoh-kwoh," the first note soft and inaudible at a distance, repeated numerous times with 5- to 7-second pauses between songs.

RANGE: Amaz. lowlands of extreme s. Colombia (north to w. Caquetá), e. Ecuador (Napo and Pastaza), and extreme n. Peru (near Pantoja on the Río Napo; RSR). To 600 m.

NOTE: We consider Amaz. birds, *H. fulviventris* (with *caquetae*), a species separate from trans-Andean *H. dives* (true Fulvous-bellied Antpitta). Not only are there marked plumage differences (bright white lores in *fulviventris*, richer ochraceous underparts in *dives*, etc.) but most importantly, their primary songs are utterly dissimilar. In fact, the song of *H. fulviventris* bears a strong resemblance to that of *H. berlepschi;* it is even conceivable that it is those two forms that should be considered conspecific.

Hylopezus dives

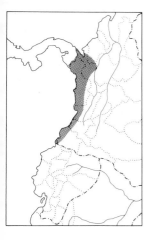

FULVOUS-BELLIED ANTPITTA

DESCRIPTION: 14 cm (5½″). *W. Colombia*. Resembles White-lored Antpitta of east of Andes, and long considered conspecific with it. Differs in being slightly smaller and in having *less conspicuous buffyish lores* (not boldly white), a grayer (much less dark and slaty) crown and nape, somewhat finer ventral streaking, and *deeper orange-rufous on flanks*. See C-31, P-22.

SIMILAR SPECIES: Streak-chested Antpitta (locally sympatric, though favoring more mature and open forest) has a conspicuous ochraceous eye-ring, buff spotting on tips of wing-coverts, and whiter underparts with coarser, wider streaking.

HABITAT AND BEHAVIOR: Fairly common to locally common on or near the ground in dense lower growth at forest borders and in regenerating clearings. Behavior similar to White-lored Antpitta's; equally difficult to see, and much more often heard than seen. Decoys readily to tape recordings (and also quite easy to whistle in) but often remains obscured by thick vegetation. A singing bird frequently rocks back and forth on its perch without moving its head and puffs out its throat feathers. The song is a series of 6–8 whistled notes, "oh-oh-ou-ou-ou-uu-uu-uu," the quality similar to Streak-chested Antpitta's (or Black-headed Antthrush's) but the tempo faster; it gradually becomes a little louder and ends abruptly (not fading away as in Streak-chested). Numerous near Buenaventura, Colombia.

RANGE: Pacific lowlands of w. Colombia (Chocó south to w. Nariño); perhaps occurs in adjacent nw. Ecuador. Also Honduras to Panama. To 900 m.

NOTE: See comments under White-lored Antpitta.

Hylopezus berlepschi

AMAZONIAN ANTPITTA

DESCRIPTION: 14.5 cm (5¾″). *Local in s. Amazonia*. Resembles White-lored Antpitta (no known overlap, replacing it southward) but has *comparatively plain face* (lores only slightly buffyish) and is *uniform olive brown above* (not slatier on crown and nape); also somewhat less richly colored below.

SIMILAR SPECIES: Spotted Antpitta has bold ochraceous eye-ring, gray crown, spotted (not streaked) breast.

HABITAT AND BEHAVIOR: Uncommon on or near the ground in very dense undergrowth at forest borders and in dense overgrown clearings. General behavior similar to White-lored and Fulvous-bellied Antpittas', and just as hard to see. Amazonian's song has the hollow guttural quality of White-lored's, but consists of more (usually 5–7) and slower notes (about 1 note per second), "kho, kho, kho, kho, kho, kho"; the overall effect is quite like the advertising song of Zigzag Heron (*Zebrilus undulatus*)! Quite numerous at Hacienda Amazonia near Shintuya in Cuzco, Peru.

RANGE: Se. Peru (north to Junín), n. Bolivia (south to La Paz, Cochabamba, and Santa Cruz), and south of the Amazon in Amaz. Brazil (south to s. Mato Grosso and east to the lower Rio Xingu in e. Pará). To 500 m in se. Peru.

NOTE: See comments under White-lored Antpitta.

Hylopezus ochroleucus

WHITE-BROWED ANTPITTA   PLATE: 28
Other: Speckle-breasted Antpitta (in part)

DESCRIPTION: 13.5 cm (5¼"). *Local in interior ne. Brazil.* Mostly olive gray above, grayest on crown, and with *white lores and prominent white postocular stripe;* an ochraceous speculum shows at base of primaries and wing-coverts are vaguely tipped buff. White below, breast boldly spotted with dusky; sides and flanks washed with buff.
SIMILAR SPECIES: Cf. Speckle-breasted Antpitta of se. Brazil (no overlap); it lacks the postocular stripe, etc.
HABITAT AND BEHAVIOR: Uncommon on or near the ground in better-developed, lusher caatinga woodland and forest. Behavior much like that of better-known Speckle-breasted Antpitta of se. Brazil. White-browed's song, however, differs distinctly, being a 2-parted series of whistled notes, e.g., "du-DU-du-DU-du-du, DU-DU-DU-DU-DU-DU-DU" (B. Whitney and J. F. Pacheco). As with Speckle-breasted Antpitta, White-browed delivers its song from a somewhat elevated perch in a dense tangled thicket of vegetation.
RANGE: Interior ne. Brazil (Piauí south locally to s. Bahia). About 500–1000 m.

NOTE: We regard *H. nattereri* (Speckle-breasted Antpitta) and *H. ochroleucus* (White-browed Antpitta) as separate species, and indeed are uncertain why these two taxa were ever considered conspecific as their plumage differences are so striking, their distributions so widely disjunct, and their habitats so different. In addition, it is now known that their songs differ dramatically.

Hylopezus nattereri

SPECKLE-BREASTED ANTPITTA   PLATE: 28

DESCRIPTION: 13.5 cm (5¼"). *Se. Brazil area;* does not include the White-browed Antpitta of ne. Brazil. Above olive brown with *buffy white lores and partial eye-ring* (broadest in front of and behind eye); an ochraceous speculum shows at base of primaries. Below pale ochraceous buff, whiter on throat and midbelly, and *profusely speckled with black especially across breast and down flanks.*
SIMILAR SPECIES: White-browed Antpitta of ne. Brazil (no overlap) is grayer above (especially on crown), has a prominent white postocular stripe, and is less profusely marked below. Speckle-breasted is substantially smaller than the large race of Variegated Antpitta that occurs with it.
HABITAT AND BEHAVIOR: Fairly common on or near the ground in lower growth of humid and montane forest, mature secondary woodland, and borders. Tends to remain in very dense tangled growth, often bamboo, and therefore difficult to observe, even with the aid of tape playback. The song, usually delivered from a slightly elevated perch, is a distinctive, fairly fast series of 7–10 penetrating whistled notes which gradually slide upscale and become more emphatic, "teeu-teeu-teeu-

teeu-teeu-téw-téw-téw-téw!" Numerous at higher levels of Itatiaia
Nat. Park.

RANGE: Se. Brazil (w. Rio de Janeiro in Itatiaia Nat. Park south to n.
Rio Grande do Sul), e. Paraguay (1 old record from Alto Paraná), and
ne. Argentina (Misiones). To 1600 m.

NOTE: See comments under White-browed Antpitta.

Grallaricula Antpittas

Attractively patterned and very small antpittas (smaller than any *Grallaria*), the various *Grallaricula* antpittas are exceptionally elusive and
seldom-seen inhabitants of montane forest undergrowth. Unlike *Grallaria,* they only rarely descend to the ground. *Grallaricula* antpittas are
found only on the slopes of the Andes south to Bolivia and in the mts.
of Venezuela, mainly in the subtropical zone; their absence from the e.
Brazil region is notable. Several species with very small known ranges
are believed to be genuinely rare within those restricted ranges. As a
whole, they remain poorly known birds, and there are several species-
level taxonomic problems yet to be resolved. Most *Grallaricula* have a
partially concealed white crescent, more obvious in study skins than in
life, across the lower throat; singing birds with their heads thrown
back may expose it.

GROUP A

Typical small *Grallaricula;* note the wide variation in the commonest
species (even to bill color).

Grallaricula cucullata

HOODED ANTPITTA

PLATE: 28

DESCRIPTION: 10 cm (4"). *Local in Andes of Colombia and adjacent Venezuela. Bill orange-yellow. Entire head and throat orange-rufous;* otherwise olive brown above. Mostly pale gray below with a small white
crescent on lower throat and white midbelly.

SIMILAR SPECIES: No other *small* antpitta has a completely bright rufous head. Hooded Antpitta's color pattern, and indeed its shape, are
vaguely reminiscent of Rufous-headed Pygmy-Tyrant.

HABITAT AND BEHAVIOR: Uncommon to locally fairly common
(probably overlooked) in undergrowth of montane forest. Usually
found singly, hopping through lower growth just off ground. We do
not know its voice. Numerous in Cueva de los Guácharos Nat. Park in
Huila, though even there difficult to see, despite being regularly mist-
netted. Its overall numbers have doubtless declined because of deforestation, and the species likely deserves threatened status.

RANGE: Locally in Andes of extreme sw. Venezuela (sw. Táchira and
extreme w. Apure) and Colombia (Cen. Andes north to Antioquia, W.
Andes in Valle [west of Cali], and around head of Río Magdalena
valley in Huila). Mostly 1800–2150 m.

Grallaricula flavirostris

OCHRE-BREASTED ANTPITTA   PLATE: 28

DESCRIPTION: 10 cm (4″). Andes from Colombia to Bolivia, showing *complex variation. Bill usually bicolored,* with upper mandible dark and lower yellow, but usually *all yellow* in *zarumae* of El Oro, Ecuador. Olive brown above, somewhat grayer on crown, and with *prominent ochraceous eye-ring and lores. Throat and breast ochraceous,* breast with variable, usually extensive, *blackish streaking,* becoming whitish on belly. Foregoing applies to nominate group of most of Ecuador and Colombia (see C-31); some examples of *zarumae* have breast streaking obsolete and less obvious pale lores and eye-ring. Birds from Peru (south of the Río Marañón) and Bolivia, the *boliviana* group (with *similis*), have darker lores and a less prominent eye-ring, are *much more boldly scalloped with blackish across breast and down flanks,* and have a black submalar streak.

SIMILAR SPECIES: In n. Peru and adjacent Ecuador, cf. somewhat similar (also boldly marked below) Peruvian and Ochre-fronted Antpittas; these species are not known to occur with Ochre-breasted.

HABITAT AND BEHAVIOR: Uncommon to locally fairly common (probably overlooked) in lower growth of montane forest. Behavior similar to other *Grallaricula* antpittas', of which this is generally the most numerous. Nonetheless, Ochre-breasted Antpitta is seldom seen because of its dense favored habitat and relative inactivity. Hops singly or in pairs through thick tangled undergrowth usually within 1 m of (but only briefly on) ground, regularly flicking its wings. Does not associate with mixed flocks. One commonly given call in sw. Ecuador and e. Peru is a melancholy whistled "peeeu" repeated at 8- to 10-second intervals (M. Robbins and T. Schulenberg recordings). This likely is not its primary vocalization; a rattling trill reported from Costa Rica (Stiles, Skutch, and Gardner 1989) is more probably the true song. The song ascribed to this species by Hilty and Brown (1986) is apparently incorrect (B. Whitney, pers. comm.).

RANGE: Locally in Andes of Colombia (in W. Andes north to s. Chocó, in E. Andes north to w. Meta), Ecuador (south locally on w. slope to El Oro; on e. slope not recorded south of nw. Pastaza), e. Peru, and w. Bolivia (La Paz and Cochabamba). Also Costa Rica and Panama. 800–2200 m.

NOTE: More than a single species may be involved. Birds from Peru and Bolivia differ dramatically in plumage from those found farther north in the Andes, and the break in their distribution, the upper Río Marañón, is a frequent one for allospecies pairs. If separated, *G. boliviana* (with *similis*) could be called the Bolivian Antpitta (as in *Birds of the Americas,* vol. 13, part 3).

Grallaricula peruviana

PERUVIAN ANTPITTA   PLATE: 28

DESCRIPTION: 10 cm (4″). *Very local on e. slope of Andes in s. Ecuador and n. Peru.* Bill all blackish. Male has *rich rufous crown and nape* and buff lores and partial eye-ring (broad in front of and behind eye); otherwise olive brown above. *White below* with broad black submalar streak and *extensive heavy black scalloping or streaking on breast and down*

flanks. Female similar but with brown crown (virtually no rufous) and blackish forecrown.

SIMILAR SPECIES: Ochre-breasted Antpitta, regardless of subspecies, never has rufous crown and always has some ochraceous on breast. Cf. also Ochre-fronted Antpitta.

HABITAT AND BEHAVIOR: Rare in "dense to moderately open" (Parker et al. 1985, p. 179) lower growth of montane forest. Seemingly unknown in life; recent specimens have all been obtained as the result of intensive mist-netting efforts.

RANGE: Locally on e. slope of Andes in se. Ecuador (a few recent specimens from the Cordillera de Cutucú in Morona-Santiago, and Podocarpus Nat. Park in Zaruma-Chinchipe) and extreme n. Peru (Chaupe in Cajamarca, and Cerro Chinguela in Piura). 1680–2100 m.

Grallaricula loricata

SCALLOP-BREASTED ANTPITTA

DESCRIPTION: 10 cm (4″). *Mts. of n. Venezuela*. Resembles Peruvian Antpitta, differing only in its yellowish lower mandible, pale buff throat, and not quite so heavy black scalloping below. See V-23.

SIMILAR SPECIES: Other *Grallaricula* antpittas in its n. Venezuelan range are buff or rufescent below, not coarsely marked.

HABITAT AND BEHAVIOR: Rare in lower growth of montane forest. Not well known, but behavior probably differs little from congeners'. We do not know its voice. Small numbers occur at higher levels of Henri Pittier Nat. Park in Aragua.

RANGE: Mts. of n. Venezuela (Yaracuy east to Distrito Federal). 1440–2100 m.

Grallaricula ochraceifrons

OCHRE-FRONTED ANTPITTA

DESCRIPTION: 10.5 cm (4¼″). *Very local on e. slope of Andes in n. Peru*. Resembles Peruvian Antpitta. Male differs from male Peruvian in having *ochraceous buff forecrown and eye-ring*, olive brown hindcrown (crown not uniform rich rufous), sides and flanks tinged buff, and less extensive markings below (*black streaking more or less confined to breast*). Female lacks the buff forecrown; it differs from female Peruvian in lacking buff lores.

SIMILAR SPECIES: Ochre-breasted Antpitta (of potentially sympatric *boliviana* group) resembles female Ochre-fronted but shows an ochraceous loral spot (lacking in female Ochre-fronted), is more scalloped (not streaked) below, and has ground color of throat and breast buffy (not white).

HABITAT AND BEHAVIOR: Rare in dense undergrowth of stunted montane forest, where recorded mainly from mist-net captures. Its voice is not known.

RANGE: E. slope of Andes in n. Peru (below Abra Patricia in San Martín, and at Cordillera de Colán in Amazonas). 1890–1980 m.

NOTE: A recently described species: G. R. Graves, J. P. O'Neill, and T. A. Parker III, *Wilson Bull.* 95(1): 1–6, 1983.

Grallaricula ferrugineipectus

RUSTY-BREASTED ANTPITTA

DESCRIPTION: 10–10.5 cm (4–4¼″). *Disjunct* range, in Venezuela and n. Colombia, and in Peru and w. Bolivia. Northerly birds (nominate race and *rara*) are brownish olive above with *whitish lores and bold but partial white eye-ring* (wide in front of and behind eye). *Below ochraceous*, with white midbelly. See V-23, C-31 (note that the white crescent across lower throat is much too prominent). Birds from Peru and Bolivia (*leymebambae*) are slightly larger, buffier on lores, have eye-ring reduced to a triangular patch behind eye, and are indistinctly mottled with olive on breast.

SIMILAR SPECIES: Slate-crowned Antpitta has crown slaty gray (not concolor brownish olive) and is more richly colored below. Rusty-breasted lacks the obvious dusky to black streaking on underparts shown by virtually all Ochre-breasted Antpittas.

HABITAT AND BEHAVIOR: Uncommon and local (but probably mostly just overlooked) in undergrowth of montane forest, less often at forest borders; the number of specimens taken in recent decades at various Peruvian sites by LSUMZ workers indicates that at least there Rusty-breasted can be locally more numerous. Behavior similar to other *Grallaricula* antpittas'. The song in n. Venezuela is a fast series of soft, slightly nasal notes which accelerate and become a bit louder, "kwi-kwi-kwi-kwi-kwi-kwi-kwi-kwi-kwi-kwu," the last note characteristically dropping and weaker (T. Meyer recording; RSR). The song in Peru differs quite markedly, being a series of sharper, more enunciated and separated notes which characteristically end with a faint and *higher*-pitched note, e.g., "kee-kee-kee-kee-kee-kee-kee-kee-ki?" (T. Schulenberg recording).

RANGE: Mts. of n. Venezuela (east to Distrito Federal), and Andes of w. Venezuela (north to Lara) and ne. Colombia (w. slope of E. Andes south locally to Cundinamarca); Sierra de Perijá on Venezuela-Colombia border and Santa Marta Mts. of n. Colombia; Andes of Peru (mainly on e. slope from Amazonas southward, on w. slope only in Piura) and w. Bolivia (La Paz). 600–2200 m in n. part of range; 1750–3350 m in s. part.

NOTE: The widely disjunct distribution of the southern population, together with its higher elevation preference, plumage differences, and quite distinct song, all point to its specific distinctness from northerly birds. If considered a full species, *G. leymebambae* could be called the Leymebamba Antpitta, after its type locality (and for several decades the only site from which the taxon was known), leaving *G. ferrugineipectus* (with *rara*) as the Rusty-breasted Antpitta.

GROUP B   Somewhat larger than Group A; share *slaty gray crown*.

Grallaricula nana

SLATE-CROWNED ANTPITTA   PLATE: 28

DESCRIPTION: 11–11.5 cm (4¼–4½″). *Local in mts. from Venezuela to extreme n. Peru.* Bill dark. *Crown slaty gray*, with lores and eye-ring buffy ochraceous; otherwise olive brown above. *Below rich orange-rufous*, white on center of lower belly. Foregoing applies to nominate

group (including *occidentalis*) of most of range. Birds from ne. Venezuela (*cumanensis* and *pariae*) have yellow or flesh-colored lower mandible and are paler above with more extensive and clearly demarcated white on median belly.

SIMILAR SPECIES: Rusty-breasted Antpitta lacks the gray crown, is not so richly colored below, and is a little smaller.

HABITAT AND BEHAVIOR: Uncommon to locally fairly common (though usually overlooked) in undergrowth of montane forest, often in thickets of *Chusquea* bamboo. Behavior much as in other *Grallaricula,* tending to be sedentary and to move very little, hence hard to see even though often in areas with a fairly open understory. Generally stays a bit above ground, but also descends to forest floor, hopping about and stopping abruptly like a *Catharus* thrush (T. A. Parker III et al. 1985). Like other members of genus, regularly flicks both wings simultaneously. The song in n. Venezuela and e. Ecuador is a short, pretty, quite melodic trill with descending effect, "tree-ee-ee-ee-ee-ee-ee," reminiscent of Long-billed Gnatwren's; it sometimes, though with similar effect, is less trilled, with more discrete notes. Fairly numerous near Colonia Tovar in n. Venezuela, and around the Cabañas San Isidro near Baeza in e. Ecuador.

RANGE: Locally in mts. of n. Venezuela (Paria Peninsula west to Aragua), and in Andes of w. Venezuela (Trujillo to Táchira), Colombia (in E. Andes recorded only from Norte de Santander, in W. Andes only from Valle and Cauca), e. Ecuador, and extreme n. Peru (Cerro Chinguela in Piura); tepuis of se. Venezuela (e. Bolívar). Probably occurs in adjacent Guyana. Mostly 2000–2900 m, lower (to 1300 m) in w. Colombia, and recorded even lower (to 700 m) in Venezuela.

NOTE: The birds of ne. Venezuela may warrant being treated as a separate species, *G. cumanensis* (with *pariae*). Vocally, however, they seem similar (T. Meyer recording) to birds from the rest of the species' range. If split, the English name of Paria Antpitta would seem appropriate.

Grallaricula lineifrons

CRESCENT-FACED ANTPITTA

PLATE: 28

DESCRIPTION: 11.5 cm (4½"). *A strikingly patterned antpitta found locally in Andes of s. Colombia and e. Ecuador. Head mostly dark slaty,* blacker on auriculars, and with *conspicuous white crescent in front of eye* which becomes ochraceous on its lower part, white postocular spot, and *ochraceous patch on sides of neck;* otherwise brownish olive above. *Most of underparts heavily streaked black and ochraceous buff,* becoming browner on flanks with whitish streaking; center of throat white bordered by broad black malar streak.

SIMILAR SPECIES: No other antpitta shows such a spectacular facial pattern.

HABITAT AND BEHAVIOR: Rare to locally uncommon in undergrowth of montane forest and adjacent secondary woodland. Virtually unknown in life until recently, but since 1991 there have been several encounters with this species in Ecuador (RSR and F. Sornoza; N. Krabbe, M. B. Robbins, and G. Rosenberg). Almost invariably found in pairs which hop quietly through undergrowth; shy and difficult to see. Does not join mixed flocks. Its song is a series of ascending, piping notes, the last several rather shrill, "pu-pu-pe-pe-pee-pee-pi-pi-pi?" (N. Krabbe and M. B. Robbins recordings). This fanciest of the antpittas can be found on w. slope of Cerro Mongus in se. Carchi, Ecuador.

RANGE: Andes of s. Colombia (e. Cauca in Puracé Nat. Park) and on e. slope of Andes in Ecuador (known from the type specimen from Oyacachi in w. Napo and from 1991 and 1992 specimens [ANSP, MECN] obtained in se. Carchi on w. slope of Cerro Mongus, in Cañar at Hacienda La Libertad, and in n. Loja south of Saraguro). 2900–3400 m.

Conopophagidae

GNATEATERS

THE gnateaters, small and round birds found in the understory of humid forest, are found exclusively in South America. Ames et al. (1968) presented anatomical evidence for considering the gnateaters to belong to the antbird family (Formicariidae), and this merger was followed by Meyer de Schauensee (1970). More recently, however, Sibley and Ahlquist (1990) concluded that, based on DNA hybridization data, the Conopophagidae still should be recognized as a full family.

Conopophaga Gnateaters

The gnateaters are small, plump, short-tailed, and long-legged birds resembling small antpittas, particularly *Grallaricula;* gnateaters are notably less vocal. They are found in the undergrowth of humid forest and borders, where they are elusive and seldom seen. Although most species are Amazonian in distribution, a few are found in the subtropical zone of the Andes, and a few others range in e. Brazil and adjacent countries. Except for the relatively uniform Rufous, males are boldly and attractively patterned, and all except Black-cheeked have a striking silvery white postocular tuft. Agitated birds spread and flare these tufts laterally. Females usually differ from males, and their tufts are often grayer; most species are more rufescent below.

GROUP A

Andes; mainly subtropical zone. Males gray below.

Conopophaga castaneiceps

CHESTNUT-CROWNED GNATEATER   PLATE: 28

DESCRIPTION: 13–13.5 cm (5–5¼"). *Local in Andes from Colombia to Peru. Lower mandible pale;* legs bluish gray. Male of *brunneinucha* (Peru from Huánuco to Cuzco) is *mostly chestnut brown above,* paler and more *rufous on forecrown,* and has a long silvery white postocular tuft. *Below dark slaty gray,* becoming paler gray on lower breast and whitish on lower midbelly. Female like male above but paler, with *orange-rufous forecrown. Throat and breast orange-rufous,* becoming grayish on belly, whiter in middle. Both sexes of nominate race (Cen. and E. Andes of Colombia south to n. Ecuador) are similar but have brighter and more extensively rufous rearcrown and grayer mantle (some feathers edged blackish giving a slightly fringed effect); see C-31. *Chapmani* (s. Ecuador and Peru in San Martín) and *chocoensis* (w. Colombia) are intermediate (crown like nominate and back like *brunneinucha*).
SIMILAR SPECIES: The only gnateater in its *Andean* range; replaced southward by Slaty Gnateater (which see). Chestnut-belted Gnateater

of adjacent Amaz. lowlands (limited overlap) has distinctive male but rather similar female; Chestnut-belted's bill is all dark and it lacks the contrasting orange-rufous forecrown (entire crown concolor). Cf. also Ash-throated Gnateater, both sexes of which always show buff spots on wing-coverts.

HABITAT AND BEHAVIOR: Uncommon and local (easily overlooked) in undergrowth of montane forest and forest borders, favoring the dense tangles that spring up at treefalls. Usually found singly or in pairs, perching very low (often on vertical saplings), hopping or jumping short distances in pursuit of prey, only rarely dropping to the ground. Rarely follows mixed flocks but is sometimes stimulated to greater activity by their passage. Although infrequently seen, does not seem especially shy. Both sexes give a raspy chipping rattle, "chit, chit-it, chit-it-it" (S. L. Hilty, *Condor* 77[4]: 513–514, 1975), and in alarm a sharp, raspy "zhweeík."

RANGE: Andes of Colombia (in W. Andes from Chocó and Córdoba south to Cauca, near n. end of Cen. Andes in Caldas, and around head of Río Magdalena valley; also in Baudó Mts. of cen. Chocó), e. Ecuador, and e. Peru (south to Cuzco on the Cordillera Vilcabamba; AMNH). Mostly 1200–2000 m, but in Colombia regularly down to 700 m on w. slope of W. Andes in Valle, and also recorded to 500 m in w. Meta.

Conopophaga ardesiaca

SLATY GNATEATER

DESCRIPTION: 13–13.5 cm (5–5¼"). *E. slope of Andes in s. Peru and Bolivia.* Lower mandible *pale.* Male olive brown above, feathers of back irregularly margined with black, and with long silvery white postocular tuft. *Below plumbeous gray,* becoming whitish on belly. Female much like male but with *orange-rufous forecrown,* virtually no postocular tuft, and brown tinge to lower flanks.

SIMILAR SPECIES: Male Chestnut-crowned Gnateater of next race to the north (*brunneinucha;* no overlap) differs from male Slaty in its orange-rufous forecrown, more rufescent upperparts with no black feather margins on back, and considerably darker throat and breast. Female Chestnut-crowned differs dramatically from female Slaty in its orange-rufous (not gray) throat and breast and prominent postocular tuft. Male Ash-throated Gnateater of Amaz. lowlands (no known overlap) also resembles male Slaty but has buff-tipped wing-coverts and a grayer back with more blackish scaling; its bill is all black. Female Ash-throated, with its orange-rufous underparts, is quite different from female Slaty.

HABITAT AND BEHAVIOR: Uncommon in undergrowth of montane forest and forest borders. Behavior, so far as known, much like Chestnut-crowned Gnateater's (Remsen 1984).

RANGE: E. slope of Andes in s. Peru (north to s. Cuzco) and Bolivia (south to s. Tarija). 800–2075 m (mostly 1000–1700 m).

NOTE: For more natural history information on this species, see Remsen (1984).

GROUP B   *E. Brazil area;* females much more alike than males.

Conopophaga lineata   **RUFOUS GNATEATER**   PLATE: 28

DESCRIPTION: 13 cm (5″). *E. Brazil, e. Paraguay, and ne. Argentina.*
Lower mandible flesh to yellowish; legs flesh to dull yellowish horn.
Nominate group (with *vulgaris;* most of range, and north to Pernambuco at Brejão) is rufescent brown above with *gray superciliary*
merging into silvery white postocular tuft (postocular tuft silvery gray
in female). *Throat and breast orange-rufous* with semiconcealed white
crescent across lower throat, becoming more olive brown on flanks and
white on midbelly. *Cearae* (local in ne. Brazil in Ceará, w. Pernambuco,
and n. Bahia) is quite different, with *no* gray superciliary (though
males have a similar white postocular tuft) and brighter cinnamon-
rufous crown, throat, breast, and flanks. Female *cearae* has gray restricted to lores and *postocular stripe pale cinnamon-rufous.* Neither sex
of *cearae* ever shows a white crescent across lower throat.
SIMILAR SPECIES: Female Black-cheeked Gnateater is a little smaller
and has an all-black bill, small buff dots on tips of wing-coverts, and
black fringing on back feathers.
HABITAT AND BEHAVIOR: Fairly common to common in undergrowth
of humid forest, second-growth woodland, and borders. *Cearae* is
much less well known and seems less numerous; all the following information refers to the s. nominate group. Found singly or in pairs,
usually perching close to the ground, sometimes on the ground when
foraging. Sedentary and not very shy, at times even approaching a
quiet observer. Occasionally follows a mixed understory flock. The
song is a series of 8–10 fairly high whistled notes which hesitate at first
and become higher pitched, "tew; tew; tew, tew, tew-tew-tiw-tiw-ti-
ti"; also often gives a sneezing "chiff" or "cheff." Sick (1985) also describes a crepuscular flight in which the wings make an apparently mechanical buzzing sound. Numerous at Itatiaia Nat. Park and in general
the easiest gnateater to see.
RANGE: E. Brazil (Ceará and Pernambuco south to Rio Grande do
Sul, and inland locally to s. Goiás, sw. Mato Grosso on Serra das
Araras, and s. Mato Grosso do Sul), e. Paraguay (east to Amambay
and Misiones), and ne. Argentina (Misiones and ne. Corrientes). To
2400 m.

NOTE: The rather different *cearae* may prove to be specifically distinct. Both nominate *lineata* and *cearae* have been recorded from Pernambuco, *cearae* in e. Pernambuco at Dois Irmãos and nominate in cen. Pernambuco at Brejão. This, combined
with the record of *cearae* at Bonfim in Bahia, would seem to establish sympatry of
the two forms. However, the region remains relatively poorly known ornithologically, and the possibility that the two forms may intergrade cannot be totally dis-
counted. Meyer de Schauensee (1966) suggested Caatinga Gnateater as the English
name for *C. cearae* if it is regarded as a separate species, but recent information
indicates that it is not actually found in caatinga but rather in humid and dry forest
(D. Teixera, pers. comm.). We thus favor reverting to the English name originally
suggested by Hellmayr in *Birds of the Americas,* vol. 13, part 3: Ceara Gnateater.

Conopophaga melanops

BLACK-CHEEKED GNATEATER

PLATE: 28

DESCRIPTION: 11.5 cm (4½"). *E. Brazil from Paraíba to Santa Catarina. Bill all black;* legs pinkish. Male of nominate race (se. Bahia southward) has *bright orange-rufous crown and nape* contrasting with *black face and sides of neck;* otherwise brown above, back feathers fringed black and scapulars tinged rufescent; wings with buff dots on coverts. Throat white; remaining underparts gray, whiter on midbelly and tinged buff on lower flanks. Males of ne. Brazil south to e. Bahia (*perspicillata* and *nigrifrons*) have a black frontlet, gray upper back with more rufous on scapulars, and usually lack buff tipping on wing-coverts. Female rufescent brown above with *long narrow white superciliary, black fringing on back feathers,* and *buff dots on wing-coverts.* Below mostly orange-rufous, whiter on throat and midbelly. Occasional males of all races have a rudimentary white postocular tuft.

SIMILAR SPECIES: Handsome male is distinctive, but female resembles the slightly larger Rufous Gnateater. Rufous differs in having a pale lower mandible, gray superciliary with silvery postocular tuft, and in lacking dots on wing-coverts and black fringing on back feathers.

HABITAT AND BEHAVIOR: Uncommon to locally fairly common in undergrowth of humid forest and mature secondary woodland. Behavior similar to Rufous Gnateater's, though Black-cheeked seems more terrestrial and less likely to accompany mixed understory flocks. Its song is an ascending series of short musical whistled notes (Sick 1985), apparently similar to Rufous Gnateater's; its frequently heard call is a similar sharp wheezy "chef" or "chif." Small numbers can be found above Rio de Janeiro in Tijuca Nat. Park and near Ubatuba in coastal ne. São Paulo.

RANGE: E. Brazil (Paraíba south to e. Santa Catarina). To 1000 m.

GROUP C

Amazonian lowlands east to ne. Brazil.

Conopophaga peruviana

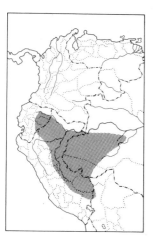

ASH-THROATED GNATEATER

PLATE: 28

DESCRIPTION: 11.5–12 cm (4½–4¾"). *W. Amazonia. Bill all black;* legs pinkish to horn. Crown dark brown, with pale grayish lores and *conspicuous long silvery white postocular tuft;* otherwise brownish gray above, feathers of back conspicuously but irregularly margined with black; wings and tail chestnut brown, *coverts tipped with buff. Below gray,* paler on throat and (especially) midbelly, lower flanks browner. Female patterned above much like male but paler and browner generally, with rufous crown. Throat and midbelly whitish, breast orange-rufous and flanks browner.

SIMILAR SPECIES: Female distinguished from female Chestnut-belted Gnateater mainly by its wing-covert dotting (wings plain in Chestnut-belted), also its more prominent black margins on back feathers. Cf. also Chestnut-crowned and Slaty Gnateaters (at most limited overlap along base of Andes).

HABITAT AND BEHAVIOR: Uncommon in undergrowth of humid forest, in both terra firme and transitional forest, the main requirement apparently being dense, often tangled, habitat such as regenerating growth at treefalls and viny tangles on ridges. Behavior similar to other gnateaters', like them usually inconspicuous, solitary or in pairs, most often not associating with flocks. A sharp "cheff" or "chink" has been heard; we know no true song.

RANGE: E. Ecuador (Napo south to Morona-Santiago; no records from north of the Río Napo), e. Peru, extreme nw. Bolivia (La Paz at Alto Madidi), and w. Amaz. Brazil south of the Amazon (east to the middle and upper Rio Purus). To 850 m.

Conopophaga aurita

CHESTNUT-BELTED GNATEATER   PLATE: 28

DESCRIPTION: 11.5–12 cm (4½–4¾"). *Bill all black;* legs pale bluish. Crown chestnut brown with *conspicuous long white postocular tuft;* otherwise brown above, mantle feathers faintly scaled black. *Narrow frontlet, sides of head, and throat black,* contrasting with rufous breast; lower underparts olivaceous brown, midbelly whiter. *Australis* (e. Peru east to the Rio Madeira in w. Amaz. Brazil, south of the Amazon) has black of throat extending down over chest, reducing the rufous; in *snethlageae* (Amaz. Brazil along both banks of the Rio Tapajós) it extends over *entire* breast, completely *obliterating* the rufous "belt," with lower underparts dull buffy brownish. Female above like male, including postocular tuft; sides of head, throat, and breast orange-rufous, becoming olivaceous brown on lower underparts (buffier in *snethlageae*).

SIMILAR SPECIES: Male distinctive. Female very like female Ash-throated Gnateater except for that species' buff dotting on wing-coverts and more prominent black scaling and margins to back feathers. In e. Amaz. Brazil cf. also Hooded Gnateater.

HABITAT AND BEHAVIOR: Rare to uncommon in undergrowth of humid forest, mainly in terra firme. In e. Ecuador found mainly in relatively flat upland forests. Behavior similar to other gnateaters'. Like other members of the genus, Chestnut-belted gives an abrupt sneezing "cheff" call; no true song is known to us.

RANGE: Guianas, Amaz. Brazil (widely north of the Amazon except in the upper Rio Branco drainage; south of it east to the lower Rio Tocantins, and south to Rondônia), se. Colombia (north to Putumayo; probably also in Vaupés and Amazonas), ne. Ecuador (apparently only north of the Río Napo), e. Peru (Loreto south locally to Ucayali). To 700 m.

Conopophaga roberti

HOODED GNATEATER

DESCRIPTION: 12 cm (4¾"). *E. Amaz. Brazil. Lower mandible pale;* legs bluish gray. Male has *head, throat, and breast black* with *conspicuous white postocular tuft;* above otherwise rufous brown. Lower underparts gray, white on midbelly. Female rufous brown above with *white postocular tuft. Below ashy gray* with white midbelly.

SIMILAR SPECIES: Male Chestnut-belted Gnateater of *snethlageae* race

(which may overlap with this species) has similar pattern but its crown is chestnut brown, mantle more olivaceous, and lower underparts buffy brownish. Female Chestnut-belted, with its orange-rufous anterior underparts, is very different. Female Hooded has pattern similar to female Black-bellied Gnateater, which is substantially larger, has all-dark bill, and is duller on crown which contrasts with much brighter chestnut mantle.

HABITAT AND BEHAVIOR: Rare to uncommon in undergrowth of humid forest and mature second-growth woodland. Not well known, but behavior likely does not differ much from other gnateaters'.

RANGE: Ne. Brazil (Pará in Belém area and along e. bank of the lower Rio Tocantins, thence east to Ceará and s. Piauí). To about 300 m.

Conopophaga melanogaster

BLACK-BELLIED GNATEATER

PLATE: 28

DESCRIPTION: 14.5 cm (5¾"). A *large* gnateater found locally in *s. Amazonia;* rather longer-tailed than its congeners. Bill black; legs bluish gray. Male has *entire head and most of underparts black* with *conspicuous long white postocular tuft; otherwise bright rufous-chestnut above;* flanks and lower belly grayish. Female has forecrown dark gray becoming dark brown on hindcrown and nape, *postocular tuft silvery gray,* and auriculars gray; *otherwise bright rufous-chestnut above. Mostly pale gray below,* whiter on throat and midbelly.

SIMILAR SPECIES: This strikingly plumaged gnateater is so much larger than its congeners that confusion is improbable.

HABITAT AND BEHAVIOR: Rare to uncommon in undergrowth of humid forest, apparently mainly, if not entirely, in terra firme. The behavior of this fine bird is not known to us.

RANGE: Locally in Amaz. Brazil south of the Amazon (w. bank of the lower Rio Tocantins west to the Rio Madeira drainage, and south to Rondônia and n. Mato Grosso) and n. Bolivia (Beni). To 400 m.

Rhinocryptidae

TAPACULOS

THE tapaculos form an interesting New World family of obscure small to midsized birds which are found primarily in s. South America, though a number of species range northward in the Andes and one reaches the mountains of Costa Rica in Central America. Amazingly, two recent (Quaternary) bones of some small tapaculo, probably a *Scytalopus,* were recently found in Cuba (S. L. Olson and E. N. Kurochin, *Proc. Biol. Soc. Wash.* 100[2]: 353–357, 1987). Their plumage is lax and soft and colors usually muted (though some species have rather bold barring or spotting); there is little or no sexual dimorphism in most species. Bills tend to be short and heavy, with the nostrils covered by a movable flap (or operculum). The feet are strong, and in some species the hindclaw is very well developed, presumably for scratching in loose soil and leaf litter. A majority of tapaculos are essentially terrestrial inhabitants of montane forests and woodlands. Only a few species occur in more open, scrubbier habitats. Many run and hop on the ground and through dense low undergrowth much more than they actually fly; flight always is weak and brief. The vast majority (even those inhabiting more open terrain, such as the *Melanopareia* crescent-chests) are secretive and not often seen, though many species vocalize persistently and loudly. Tails (which vary in length) are often held cocked, and this is the usual explanation for the English name *tapaculo,* adapted from an impolite way of saying "cover your posterior" in Spanish—though, as noted below, a Chilean species also has a call readily transcribed as "ta-pa-cu-lo." Nests are artfully hidden globular structures placed in a hole, crevice, or at the end of a burrow; some species dig long burrows in the ground.

Recent biochemical evidence (summarized in Sibley and Ahlquist 1990) indicates that the tapaculos are a distinct family whose closest relative is the gnateaters (Conopophagidae); they are also quite closely related to the ground antbirds (Formicariidae). A. Fedducia and S. L. Olson (*Smiths. Contr. Zool.* no. 366, 1982) suggested, based on certain morphological characters, a close relationship of the Rhinocryptidae to an oscine family, the lyrebirds and scrub-birds (Menuridae) of Australia; to date, however, this has not been confirmed by biochemical data (Sibley and Ahlquist 1990). It should be emphasized that species-level taxonomy within the family's largest genus, *Scytalopus,* is far from being adequately resolved, and also that whether several genera (e.g., *Psilorhamphus* and *Melanopareia*) are actually tapaculos still remains uncertain.

Pteroptochos Huet-huets and Turcas

Magnificent and very large tapaculos found primarily in Chile and characterized especially by their long legs with strong feet and long claws. Their large legs and feet are used to good advantage when scratching the ground, as they regularly do; we have repeatedly seen both the Moustached Turca and Black-throated Huet-huet perform this (despite the skepticism voiced by Fjeldså and Krabbe 1990, p. 419). Nests are placed at the end of very long burrows which the birds dig into banks or (in the case of the turca) on hillsides.

Pteropotochos tarnii

BLACK-THROATED HUET-HUET

PLATE: 29

DESCRIPTION: 24--25 cm (9½—9¾″). *A very large tapaculo of forests of s. Chile and adjacent Argentina.* Crown rufous-chestnut; *remainder of head, entire throat and neck, and back slaty black with conspicuous wide bare buffyish eye-ring;* rump rufous-chestnut; wings and tail blackish. *Lower underparts rufous-chestnut* with variable amount of dusky and buff barring on belly.

SIMILAR SPECIES: Cf. similar Chestnut-throated Huet-huet (no overlap, Chestnut-throated occurring north of Black-throated's range in Chile). Chucao Tapaculo is considerably smaller, etc.

HABITAT AND BEHAVIOR: Uncommon to locally common on or near the ground in humid *Nothofagus*-dominated forest, forest borders, and secondary woodland; seems less numerous in Argentina than in Chile. This spectacular large tapaculo is, unlike the turca, only infrequently seen without the aid of tape playback, mainly because of its dense favored habitat; in the early morning the huet-huet does sometimes emerge to feed in the semiopen, but it never strays far from cover, to which it quickly retreats if disturbed. It is mainly terrestrial except when singing, walking on the damp forest floor, usually proceeding slowly (though capable of running rapidly when the occasion demands it), from time to time pausing to scratch the ground litter with a single foot, sometimes leaning sideways while doing so. The rather long tail is often held cocked, though usually not at such an acute angle as the Moustached Turca's. The group name *huet-huet* is onomatopoeic, derived from its frequently heard call note, a sharp and loud "whet!" (often doubled or trebled), which seems to be used primarily as a contact note between members of a pair. Also given is a descending series of hollow notes, e.g., "wok-wok-wok-wok-wok-wu," reminiscent of one of the turca's calls. During the breeding season, also heard is its low, sonorous song, a fast series of 20–25 "whoo" notes which start softly but gradually become considerably louder; the effect is strikingly owl-like.

RANGE: S. Chile (Arauco and Bío-Bío south to n. Magallanes) and adjacent s. Argentina (Neuquén, w. Río Negro, w. Chubut, and nw. Santa Cruz). To about 1000 m.

NOTE: See comments under Chestnut-throated Huet-huet.

Pteropotochos castaneus

CHESTNUT-THROATED HUET-HUET

DESCRIPTION: 24–25 cm (9½–9¾″). *S.-cen. Chile,* replacing Black-throated Huet-huet northward (north of the Río Bío-Bío); the two are perhaps conspecific. Differs in having a solid chestnut foreneck and throat contrasting with gray on sides of neck, less extensive and darker chestnut on crown, buff tipping on wing-coverts (not shown by Black-throated), and more pronounced barring on belly. It has a similar bold eye-ring (S. Howell and S. Webb).

SIMILAR SPECIES: Moustached Turca occurs in more arid and open habitats (not forest) and has conspicuous white on sides of throat.

HABITAT AND BEHAVIOR: Fairly common on or near the ground in humid forest, forest borders, and secondary woodland. Behavior, including vocalizations, similar to Black-throated Huet-huet's (Johnson 1967; S. Howell and S. Webb, pers. comm.).

RANGE: S.-cen. Chile (Colchagua south to Ñuble and Concepción). To 1500 m.

NOTE: It has been suggested that *P. tarnii* and *P. castaneus* are conspecific (e.g., *Birds of the World*, vol. 7; Johnson 1967). Although this remains possible, and indeed the similarity of their vocalizations is certainly indicative of a close relationship (they are unquestionably sister taxa), there as yet is no definitive evidence of any intergradation in the plumage characters that differentiate them. Their ranges are largely, if not entirely, separated by the Río Bío-Bío. Agreeing with Vuilleumier (1985), we prefer to treat them as allospecies. If considered conspecific, the enlarged species can be called simply the Huet-huet.

Pteroptochos megapodius

MOUSTACHED TURCA   PLATE: 29

DESCRIPTION: 23–24 cm (9–9½"). *Matorral and semiopen mt. slopes in cen. Chile.* Above pale grayish brown, becoming more rufescent on wings, rump, and tail; *narrow superciliary, and very broad moustachial streak extending from chin down the sides of throat and neck, white.* Breast rufescent brown; lower underparts whitish with variable amount (usually extensive) of coarse black and rufescent brown barring. *Atacamae* (n. edge of range, in Atacama) is smaller, much paler overall, and has much reduced black and rufescent barring on lower underparts.

SIMILAR SPECIES: The conspicuous white moustache of this magnificent large tapaculo is unique. White-throated Tapaculo is considerably smaller, etc.

HABITAT AND BEHAVIOR: Fairly common to common in matorral and on scrubby and semiopen slopes, often where there are scattered rocks and boulders. Unlike the huet-huets, the primarily terrestrial Moustached Turca is often quite conspicuous, walking and standing freely in the open (sometimes even on roadsides, especially early and late in the day) or perching atop a boulder or shrub. The long tail is usually held sharply cocked, often at such an acute angle as to almost touch the back; the result can at times be almost comical. Although it flies only rarely (and then not far), the turca can run very rapidly. The strong feet are used for scratching the ground, and the turca is capable of moving surprisingly large stones. At least during the nesting season (Oct.–Jan., perhaps longer), the turca is very vocal, and in good habitat its distinctive loud calls may resound from all around. The most memorable is a slow series of 10–15 semimusical "wook" notes, given at a rate of no more than about 1 note per second, which gradually go downscale; also given is a much faster series of short "wok" notes. The turca is numerous in a number of areas around Santiago, notably along the road to the Farallones ski area.

RANGE: Cen. Chile (s. Atacama south to Concepción). To 2300 m.

Scelorchilus Tapaculos

A pair of distinctive, medium-sized tapaculos found mainly in Chile, where one species (the Chucao) inhabits the Southern Beech (*Nothofagus*) forests of the south, the other (the White-throated) matorral scrublands of the central sector. In shape both species are reminiscent of *Chamaeza* antthrushes, though their long tails (especially long in the White-throated) are usually held cocked at an acute angle.

Scelorchilus rubecula

CHUCAO TAPACULO   PLATE: 29

DESCRIPTION: 18.5–19 cm (7¼–7½″). *Forests of s. Chile and adjacent Argentina.* Legs grayish flesh. Above dark to rufescent brown (reportedly more rufescent in older birds) with *lores and short postocular stripe orange-rufous,* gray intermixed on forecrown, and gray sides of neck. *Throat and breast orange-rufous; median lower underparts boldly barred black and white,* flanks broadly gray. *Mochae* (Mocha Is. off Chile) slightly larger.

SIMILAR SPECIES: This handsome, boldly patterned, and relatively colorful tapaculo is unlikely to be confused. Huet-huets are much larger and show a large bare eye-ring.

HABITAT AND BEHAVIOR: Fairly common to locally very common on or very near the ground in *Nothofagus*-dominated humid forest, forest borders, and secondary woodland; seems less numerous in Argentina than in Chile. The Chucao seems more capable than the huet-huets of persisting in and colonizing relatively young and small woodland patches, and in most (perhaps all?) regions is mainly or entirely confined to the often very extensive thickets of *Chusquea* bamboo that spring up when the forest or woodland is disturbed. Basically terrestrial (frequently even singing from the ground as it walks around), the Chucao occurs singly or in dispersed pairs; the tail is almost invariably held cocked, often at an acute angle, unless the bird is vocalizing. Heard much more often than seen, though it occasionally is encountered feeding in the semiopen adjacent to cover, especially in the early morning. During the breeding season, the Chucao's loud and unmistakable song often reverberates from all around: a startlingly abrupt and obviously onomatopeic "chuu, chu-chu-chu-caoow," with some variation.

RANGE: S.-cen. and s. Chile (Colchagua south to Aysén) and adjacent Argentina (Neuquén, w. Río Negro, and w. Chubut). To about 1500 m.

Scelorchilus albicollis

WHITE-THROATED TAPACULO   PLATE: 29

DESCRIPTION: 18.5–19.5 cm (7¼–7¾″). *Matorral of cen. Chile.* Above rufous brown with *white lores and superciliary;* wings and tail more purely rufous. *Throat pure white;* remaining underparts creamy whitish *boldly barred with dusky brown especially on sides and flanks* (females perhaps more extensively barred than males). *Atacamae* (n. end of range

from Antofagasta to n. Coquimbo) similar but smaller, paler and grayer above, and with more ventral bars.

SIMILAR SPECIES: Moustached Turca is substantially larger, has white on throat confined to sides, browner upperparts, etc.

HABITAT AND BEHAVIOR: Uncommon to fairly common on or near the ground in dense matorral. Usually found singly or in pairs, often together with Moustached Turca though not ascending as high in the mts.; White-throated Tapaculo is, however, a much more difficult bird to see, almost always remaining within dense cover (except sometimes after tape playback). Except when calling, mainly terrestrial; the long tail is usually cocked up at a sharp angle (though generally is held depressed when calling). A vocalizing bird usually perches a few meters up in a shrub or small tree, generally remaining hidden. The song is an unmistakable loud "tá-pa, tá-pa-ku-lo, tá-pa-ku-lo, tá-pa-ku, tá-pa-ku, tá-pa-ku, tá-ku, tá-ku" with a variable cadence but always the accent on the first syllable of each phrase. Also sometimes given is an interminable "whha-poo, whha-poo, whha-poo, wha-poo . . ." or a repeated "poo-poo-poo-poo-poo-pah." One phrase of the song is clearly a possible onomatopoeic source for the family name *tapaculo*.

RANGE: N.-cen. Chile (s. Antofagasta at Quebrada Paposo south to Curicó). Mostly below 1000 m, in small numbers to 1500 m.

Rhinocrypta Gallitos

A large tapaculo sporting a large bushy crest and found in the dense scrub of interior s.-cen. South America. The nest is a bulky, untidy structure of sticks, bits of bark, and grasses with its entrance on the side, placed about 1 m above the ground in a dense thorny bush (Wetmore 1926). Despite its group name (*gallito* means "small chicken" in Spanish), any resemblance to a chicken is at best marginal!

Rhinocrypta lanceolata

CRESTED GALLITO
PLATE: 29

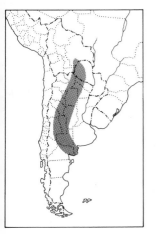

DESCRIPTION: 21.5 cm (8½"). *A large and virtually unmistakable, bushy-crested tapaculo of the chaco and n. Patagonia.* Bill fairly short. *Entire head (including conspicuous crest) rufous brown narrowly streaked with white;* above otherwise olive brown, the wings browner and the fairly long full tail dusky. Below mostly pale grayish, *the sides and flanks contrastingly bright rufous;* crissum grayish brown. Juvenile duller.

HABITAT AND BEHAVIOR: Uncommon to locally fairly common in chaco scrub and woodland, and in Patagonian scrub, preferring areas where the thorny undergrowth is dense. Although it can be quite bold, especially when calling, the Crested Gallito is often elusive and generally is only infrequently seen. Mainly terrestrial, the gallito is capable of running very rapidly, though when feeding it walks along at a more sedate pace; it flies very little, often preferring to proceed by hopping from branch to branch. The tail is held cocked high above the back when on the ground, though it is usually depressed when perched. A calling bird generally mounts up into a bush or small tree where it sometimes perches fully in the open (especially during the early morning). The most common vocalization is a loud but semimusical, far-carrying "cholloh . . . cholloh . . . cholloh . . ." repeated steadily at a rate of about 1 call every 2–3 seconds. The Crested Gallito is particularly numerous and easy to see at Lihue Callel Nat. Park in La Pampa, Argentina.

RANGE: Extreme s. Bolivia (sw. Santa Cruz at Guanacos and Estancia Perforación), w. Paraguay, and n. and cen. Argentina (south to n. Río Negro and extreme sw. Buenos Aires). Mostly below 800 m, but recorded up to 1800 m in Mendoza, Argentina.

Teledromas Gallitos

A plainly attired, sandy-fawn tapaculo of w. Argentina whose "look," accentuated by the short bill and large dark eye, is unlike that of any other neotropical bird (and somewhat recalls certain of the Australian *Amytornis* grasswrens). The nest is placed at the end of a burrow dug about ⅓ m into the loose soil of a bank (Wetmore 1926).

Teledromas fuscus

SANDY GALLITO

PLATE: 29

DESCRIPTION: 19 cm (7½"). *A pallid tapaculo of arid scrublands in w. Argentina.* Bill rather stubby. *Above pale sandy brown* with eye-ring and short superciliary whitish; all but central pair of rectrices mainly blackish with pale tip, central pair sandy brown. *Buffy whitish below,* somewhat browner on flanks.

SIMILAR SPECIES: Not likely confused: paler and more uniform than virtually any other bird with which it occurs, and with distinctive behavior as well (sprinting on the ground with tail cocked high). Cf. White-throated Cacholote and various miners.

HABITAT AND BEHAVIOR: Uncommon on or near the ground in sparse, arid scrub, usually where the soil is sandy or gravelly, perhaps especially in association with washes or small quebradas. The Sandy Gallito is very shy, elusive, and hard to see well (at least without tape playback): almost exclusively terrestrial, it runs extremely rapidly when in the open, seeming to appear out of nowhere, disappearing just as quickly. It flies only rarely, and then but for short distances. On the ground the long slender tail is almost always cocked up almost vertically, sometimes being held so far forward that it almost touches the back. Calling birds perch on low branches inside bushes, and the tail then is held more "normally." The song in Salta and Tucumán is a rather fast series of about 10 "cho" or "chu" notes, the first several a bit softer and the series lasting about 3 seconds; in quality it is reminiscent of the songs of several *Melanopareia* crescent-chests. Reportedly in Río Negro the song is shorter, consisting of only 3–5 notes (B. Whitney, *in* Fjeldså and Krabbe 1990).

RANGE: W. and cen. Argentina (w. Salta south to Neuquén and Río Negro). To 2500 m.

Merulaxis Bristlefronts

A pair of medium-sized, rather long-tailed tapaculos confined to the forests of e. Brazil. Both species have unique stiff "bristles" on the forehead and are unusual among the tapaculos in showing striking sexual plumage dimorphism.

Merulaxis ater

SLATY BRISTLEFRONT   PLATE: 29

DESCRIPTION: 18.5 cm (7¼"). *Forests (mainly montane) of se. Brazil. Both sexes have stiff pointed plumes springing from the sides of the forehead.* Male *mostly bluish slate* with lower back, rump, and flanks dark rufescent brown. Female brown above, tail duskier. *Below cinnamon-rufous,* browner on flanks.

SIMILAR SPECIES: Cf. very rare Stresemann's Bristlefront (no known overlap). Otherwise not likely confused. *Scytalopus* tapaculos are considerably smaller and shorter-tailed.

HABITAT AND BEHAVIOR: Uncommon to locally fairly common on or near the ground in humid and montane forest and mature secondary woodland. Heard much more often than seen, though at least when breeding sometimes strongly responsive to tape playback. Usually found singly, walking and running on the ground, occasionally hopping up into low tangled vegetation or onto logs. The extraordinary frontal plumes are quite conspicuous, and the rather long tail is often held slightly elevated with the feathers somewhat spread (but it seems never actually to be cocked). The Slaty Bristlefront's enchanting song is one of the most memorable bird sounds of the se. Brazil mountains: a cascading series of rich musical notes that start very loudly and then tumble downward and become softer toward the end, the series lasting 7–10 seconds. Foraging birds keep in contact through a repeated semi-musical "tink" call note, from which males periodically break out into the marvelous song. The bristlefront is not scarce at Itatiaia Nat. Park, though as noted above, a lot of luck is needed to see one unless tape playback is employed.

RANGE: Se. Brazil in s. Bahia (only 1 19th-century record, the type, from Belmonte), Espírito Santo (few records), Rio de Janeiro, e. São Paulo, and e. Paraná). 400–1300 m, locally down to 100 m.

Merulaxis stresemanni

STRESEMANN'S BRISTLEFRONT

DESCRIPTION: 19.5 cm (7¾"). *Se. Bahia, Brazil.* Closely resembles Slaty Bristlefront (no known overlap), with *similar plumes on forehead,* but somewhat larger. Males are very similar in plumage, as are females, though female Stresemann's is somewhat brighter cinnamon-rufous below.

HABITAT AND BEHAVIOR: Unknown in life, but presumed to occur in undergrowth of humid forest in lowlands. Stresemann's is known from only 2 specimens and is almost certainly threatened by widespread deforestation in its very small range.

RANGE: E. Brazil (e. Bahia). Known from only 2 specimens, the first obtained early in the 19th century near Salvador at Recôncavo, the other in May 1945 at Ilhéus. Near sea level.

Liosceles Tapaculos

A distinctive, monotypic genus of tapaculo, the only member of its family to inhabit the forests of Amazonia.

Liosceles thoracicus

RUSTY-BELTED TAPACULO   PLATE: 29

DESCRIPTION: 19–19.5 cm (7½–7¾"). A fairly large tapaculo of *Amaz. forests*. Iris dark (*contra* Hilty and Brown 1986 and C-41; all recent evidence indicates that *Liosceles*'s iris is never yellow). Brown above, grayer on head and sides of neck, and more rufescent on back, rump, and wings; eye-ring and short narrow superciliary white; wing-coverts with a few elongated tawny spots tipped dusky. *Throat and breast white* with *band of orange-rufous across chest* (somewhat variable in extent; broadest in *dugandi* of se. Colombia), variably bordered above with yellowish; belly heavily barred blackish, brown, and white.
SIMILAR SPECIES: Not likely to be confused, though overall pattern and coloration somewhat recall a *Thryothorus* wren, perhaps especially the Coraya.
HABITAT AND BEHAVIOR: Uncommon to fairly common on or near the ground inside humid forest, mainly in terra firme but also small numbers in várzea. Heard far more often than seen, the Rusty-belted Tapaculo forages singly while walking and hopping on the ground, usually where the vegetation is dense and often around fallen logs. The tail seems rarely or never actually to be cocked (*contra* Hilty and Brown 1986 and C-41). The song is a characteristic sound in some areas (notably e. Ecuador, where the species is widespread); it consists of a series of low, mellow whistled notes on a nearly even pitch, "puu-puu-puu-puu-puu-puu-pu," seeming to get faster and trail off toward the end; in quality it somewhat resembles a Ferruginous Pygmy-Owl (*Glaucidium brasilianum*). Easily attracted by imitating this easily whistled song (or by a tape recording), but even if one comes close, it often will remain frustratingly difficult to actually see, continuing to sneak furtively in heavy vegetation with head bowed low, almost never remaining long in the open unless it happens to pause to sing back.
RANGE: Se. Colombia (north to w. Putumayo and Amazonas around Leticia), e. Ecuador, e. Peru (south locally to Madre de Dios), and Amaz. Brazil (mainly south of the Amazon east to the lower Rio Tapajós and south to Rondônia; north of the Amazon only in the ex-

treme west at Tonantins). Seems likely to occur in n. Bolivia. To about 1000 m.

Acropternis Tapaculos

A spectacular large tapaculo found in the n. Andes, well known for its unique boldly spotted appearance. It has notably large feet with an exceptionally long, straight, and sharp hindclaw (the function of which remains unknown) and a heavy bill with a coot- (*Fulica-*) like frontal shield.

Acropternis orthonyx

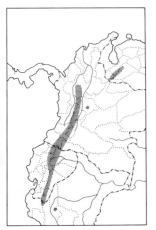

OCELLATED TAPACULO

PLATE: 29

DESCRIPTION: 21.5–22 cm (8½–8¾″). *An unmistakable, large, ornately patterned tapaculo of n. Andes. Mostly black to blackish with large round white spots,* spots on hindcrown buffier, and tail unspotted; *face (including forehead) and throat contrastingly cinnamon-rufous;* rump and upper-tail-coverts rufous, as are lower flanks. Nominate race (w. Venezuela and Colombia) is browner where *infuscata* (Ecuador and n. Peru) is black; see V-23.

HABITAT AND BEHAVIOR: Uncommon in undergrowth of montane forest, forest borders, and (locally) secondary woodland; often favors stands of *Chusquea* bamboo. Although not infrequently heard in some areas, the Ocellated Tapaculo is, most unfortunately, a shy and only rarely seen bird. It ranges singly or in pairs, walking, running, and hopping through dense tangled undergrowth, usually 1–3 m above the ground. At least in our experience, the species only rarely actually drops to the ground (though perhaps this is where it feeds, using its amazing hindclaw?). The tail is not normally held cocked. The most frequently heard song, evidently given by males, is a distinctive, loud, and penetrating jay-like "KEEEUW" repeated at varying intervals (usually every 2–4 seconds, the interval becoming shorter when the bird is agitated). Females give a less penetrating (but still fairly loud) "queeu-queeu-queeu-queeu" or a long-continued repetition (at 5- to 7-second intervals) of the same "queeu" note.

RANGE: Locally in Andes of w. Venezuela (north to Mérida), Colombia, Ecuador (south on w. slope to w. Cotopaxi), and extreme n. Peru (Cerro Chinguela in Piura, and Cordillera de Colán in Amazonas). Although it has been under-recorded in the past because of its reclusive habits, with knowledge of its voice the Ocellated Tapaculo has in recent years begun to be found more widely. 1900–3650 m.

Eugralla Tapaculos

A gray tapaculo found mainly in s. Chile. It is seemingly closely related to *Scytalopus* but has a heavy bill with a coot- (*Fulica-*)like frontal shield and yellow legs.

Eugralla paradoxa

OCHRE-FLANKED TAPACULO

PLATE: 30

DESCRIPTION: 14.5 cm (5¾"). *Forests of s.-cen. Chile and adjacent Argentina. Legs yellow.* Uniform medium gray with *rather bright and contrasting rufous flanks and lower belly* and uppertail-coverts, and white median belly. Immature browner and more scaled above.

SIMILAR SPECIES: Magellanic Tapaculo is notably smaller and proportionately shorter-tailed, lacks the bright rufous on flanks, and has dark legs and (usually) at least some white on crown.

HABITAT AND BEHAVIOR: Uncommon to locally fairly common on or near the ground in dense undergrowth of *Nothofagus*-dominated forest and mature secondary woodland, favoring areas with a bamboo understory; apparently less numerous (though perhaps mainly just overlooked) in Argentina than in Chile. Heard far more often than seen, the Ochre-flanked is even more secretive than most of the other tapaculos and is rarely seen without tape playback. Creeps around, mouse-like, in dense undergrowth near the ground, usually running very rapidly across any spot outside dense cover; the tail is normally held only slightly cocked, though the angle is more acute when the bird is scampering on the ground. Usually in pairs (though often well separated, keeping in contact through calling). Its song is a sharp staccato "cheh" note repeated for sometimes protracted periods, usually starting as 2- or 3-note phrases, then with each phrase gradually getting longer, each after a minute or so with up to 8 or more "cheh" notes. Frequently heard below Antillanca in Chile's Puyehue Nat. Park.

RANGE: S.-cen. Chile (mostly Maule south to Chiloé, with 1 sighting north to s. Santiago) and adjacent Argentina (known only from w. Río Negro [near Angostura and Lago Espejo], but likely occurs in sw. Neuquén and nw. Chubut as well). To at least 900 m.

Myornis Tapaculos

A monotypic genus of rather long-tailed tapaculo found in temperate zone forests of the n. Andes. *Myornis* has sometimes been merged into the genus *Scytalopus* (e.g., Hilty and Brown 1986), but we maintain it as distinct (in agreement with Fjeldså and Krabbe 1990), based especially on its markedly longer tail and very different, virtually unbarred juvenal plumage.

Myornis senilis

ASH-COLORED TAPACULO

PLATE: 30

DESCRIPTION: 14–14.5 cm (5½–5¾"). A *comparatively long-tailed* tapaculo of Andes from Colombia to Peru. *Uniform gray, somewhat paler below;* at least a tinge of cinnamon on lower belly and crissum. Juvenile very different: rufous brown above and buffy ochraceous below, with only faint dusky barring on wings and tail (none elsewhere).

SIMILAR SPECIES: The several *Scytalopus* tapaculos that occur sympatrically with the Ash-colored Tapaculo are all markedly shorter-tailed. Otherwise is not likely to be confused.

HABITAT AND BEHAVIOR: Fairly common (by voice) in undergrowth of montane forest and forest borders, favoring extensive dense stands of *Chusquea* bamboo; often most numerous just below treeline. Inconspicuous and not likely to be noticed unless it is vocalizing, the Ashcolored Tapaculo creeps and hops through dense low undergrowth; it is usually solitary. The rather long tail is frequently held partially cocked. The song is a distinctive long (sometimes continuing for over a minute) mechanical-sounding trill or churr on an even pitch, sometimes given as a series of shorter such trills; it is nearly always introduced by a series of sharp single or doubled "chef!" or "chedef!" notes.
RANGE: Locally in Andes of Colombia, Ecuador (south on w. slope to Azuay), and Peru (south to Carpish Mts. in Huánuco). Must surely occur on Venezuelan side of the Páramo de Tamá, but thus far recorded there only from Colombian territory. The secretive nature of this species doubtless accounts for the wide scatter of records in many areas (notably Colombia). Mostly 2300–3700 m.

Scytalopus Tapaculos

Probably the most complicated and difficult of all neotropical bird genera, the *Scytalopus* tapaculos have been called "feathered mice" by those frustrated in their repeated inability to obtain a decent view of one. Although they reach their maximum diversity in the Andes, there are outlying species in the e. Brazil region and others in various mts. of n. South America (though, somewhat surprisingly, none occurs on the tepuis). They are skulking and barely capable of flight, and the various species (no one knows how many there are!) are often nearly impossible to tell apart on morphological characters, all being essentially some shade of gray or blackish, usually with some shade of rufous brown on the flanks and rump. Young birds of all species are browner and more barred with dusky or blackish, and they apparently require several years to attain full adult plumage; they usually cannot be identified to species. To identify even the adults you must carefully study their vocalizations, which fortunately are usually given frequently and often are readily distinguishable. Each species may have several voices, various alarm calls as well as a territorial song; the latter is the most distinctive and usually is the only one mentioned in these accounts. Most *Scytalopus* are readily attracted by tape playback, and at least some can also be lured into view by artful "pishing."

It must be emphasized that *Scytalopus* taxonomy is still in a very active state of development, primarily through the research of N. Krabbe and T. S. Schulenberg, both of whom have graciously aided RSR in his attempts to understand the complexities involved. Note that the *Scytalopus* taxonomy used in older works (even as recent as Hilty and Brown 1986) is now out of date and will differ greatly from that found here; Fjeldså and Krabbe's (1990) *Scytalopus* taxonomy is roughly the same insofar as Andean species are concerned. Several additional new species should soon be described (these will not be mentioned here), and several existing ones are likely to be further split into additional full species. For more information, refer to Fjeldså and Krabbe (1990).

GROUP A   Mainly in *Andes*.

Scytalopus unicolor

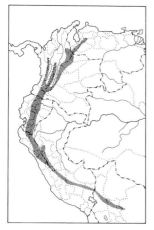

UNICOLORED TAPACULO   PLATE: 30

DESCRIPTION: 12–12.5 cm (4¾–5″). Andes of Venezuela to Bolivia. N. birds (Venezuela, Colombia, most of Ecuador, and extreme n. Peru on Cerro Chinguela; *latrans*) are *uniform blackish slate* in both sexes, with *no* rufous or barring. S. birds (including *subcinereus* of sw. Ecuador on w. slope and inter-Andean ridges north to Azuay, and nw. Peru; *parvirostris* of e. slope of Andes south of the Río Marañón; and nominate *unicolor* of nw. Peru) are *paler uniform gray*, females and younger males with flanks and rump rufous brown with blackish barring.
SIMILAR SPECIES: The blackish northern birds are relatively distinctive. More southern birds resemble Rufous-vented Tapaculo, though that is slightly larger and has a different song.
HABITAT AND BEHAVIOR: Fairly common to common (by voice) in undergrowth of montane forest, forest borders, secondary woodland, and even in quite young regenerating low scrub. Occurs in both humid and comparatively dry regions; sometimes occurs in stands of *Chusquea* bamboo, but by no means restricted to it. Forages solitarily within 1 m of the ground in dense vegetation (though agitated birds will sometimes creep a bit higher), hopping and scurrying about and usually remaining nearly invisible. The presumed song of *latrans* (in Ecuador) is a series of rather low-pitched "pir" notes, sometimes almost with a pygmy-owl- (*Glaucidium-*)like quality, which are repeated steadily for long periods (often 15 or more seconds); *latrans* also gives a distinctive hollow "wiur" or "huir" call note, often repeated endlessly (sometimes doubled) at a rate of about 1 call per second. The song of *parvirostris* is a higher-pitched trill which can last up to about 15 seconds.
RANGE: Andes of w. Venezuela (north to Mérida), Colombia, Ecuador, Peru (south on w. slope to s. Cajamarca), and w. Bolivia (south to w. Santa Cruz). Mostly 2000–3500 m, locally down to 1700 m and (in w. Ecuador at least) up to 3900 m; *parvirostris* of e. Peru and Bolivia apparently only 2000–2500 m.

NOTE: Based on the marked plumage differences and apparent geographic variation in vocalizations, at least two species are likely involved in what is now called *S. unicolor;* one difficulty concerns the allocation of nominate *unicolor* itself, which remains unknown in life (Fjeldså and Krabbe 1990). If separated from *S. unicolor,* northern birds would be called *S. latrans* (Blackish Tapaculo).

Scytalopus macropus

LARGE-FOOTED TAPACULO   PLATE: 30

DESCRIPTION: 14.5 cm (5¾″). A *large Scytalopus* found locally on *e. slope of Andes in Peru. Uniform slate to blackish gray.* Somewhat younger birds show a bit of rufous and black barring on the rump, lower flanks,

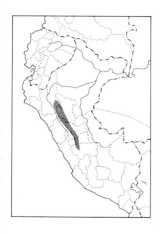

and thighs. Although it is not a field character, this species does have markedly large feet!

SIMILAR SPECIES: Rufous-vented Tapaculo is somewhat smaller and shows considerably more rufous on rump and flanks.

HABITAT AND BEHAVIOR: Uncommon and local in undergrowth of montane forest and elfin woodland, especially where mossy conditions prevail; favors boulders and rocky areas along streams. Secretive behavior much like that of other *Scytalopus,* though reportedly even shyer than most, and perhaps more terrestrial. The song is a monotonous series of low-pitched notes given at a rate of about 3 per second and sometimes continuing for a minute or more (Fjeldså and Krabbe 1990). RANGE: Locally on e. slope of Andes in Peru (Amazonas to Junín). 2400–3500 m.

Scytalopus femoralis

RUFOUS-VENTED TAPACULO   PLATE: 30

DESCRIPTION: 13.5 cm (5¼"). E. slope of Andes from s. Colombia to Peru; does not include a lower elevation species (*S. bolivianus,* White-crowned Tapaculo) or *S. sanctaemartae* (Santa Marta Tapaculo), both formerly considered conspecific. Comparatively long-tailed. Above *dark* slaty gray. Below slightly paler gray, with lower flanks and crissum rufous brown with wavy blackish barring.

SIMILAR SPECIES: White-crowned Tapaculo has a white crown patch (which may be small and hard to see); it occurs at lower elevations and has a different song. Brown-rumped Tapaculo has a similar overall pattern but is somewhat smaller, shorter-tailed, and paler gray generally with brighter and more contrasting rufous on flanks.

HABITAT AND BEHAVIOR: Fairly common to common (by voice) in undergrowth of montane forest, forest borders, and secondary woodland. Secretive behavior much like that of other *Scytalopus* (see under Unicolored). The song in Ecuador is a long series of notes which start slowly but then quickly accelerate, "chu-dok, chu-dok, chudók, chudók, chudók, chudók-chudók-chudók-chudók . . ." continued for ½ minute or more.

RANGE: E. slope of Andes in s. Colombia (north to head of Río Magdalena valley in Huila; perhaps north to Cundinamarca), Ecuador, and Peru (south to Ayacucho). Mostly 1500–2200 m, locally down to 1200 m in Ecuador.

NOTE: In 1984, on an expedition on the Cordillera de Cutucú in Ecuador, T. S. Schulenberg and M. B. Robbins confirmed that *S. bolivianus* (White-crowned Tapaculo) and *S. femoralis* occurred sympatrically at around 1600–1700 m and that the two differed markedly in their vocalizations. Unfortunately, details on this discovery have not been published, but we have no hesitation in regarding them as separate species. *Micropterus* is included as the more northerly race of *S. femoralis.*

Scytalopus bolivianus

WHITE-CROWNED TAPACULO   PLATE: 30
Other: Rufous-vented Tapaculo (in part)

DESCRIPTION: 12.5 cm (5"). Mainly Andes from extreme w. Venezuela to Bolivia, at *relatively low elevations.* Resembles Rufous-vented Tapaculo (with which long confused and long considered conspecific), but

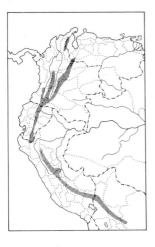

differs in having a *small white crown patch,* and often also shows whitish tipping on some breast feathers. Females are slightly paler overall than males, tend to be tinged with brownish, and often have smaller crown patches. Fjeldså and Krabbe (1990, p. 430) state that "white [on crown] possibly sometimes absent." Both sexes of nominate race (extreme s. Peru southward) have somewhat larger crown patches. Note that on C-41 what was there called *S. femoralis confusus* apparently actually refers to *S. vicinior.*

SIMILAR SPECIES: Rufous-vented Tapaculo occurs at higher elevations (with some overlap, at least in Ecuador) and never has any white on crown (which, among Andean *Scytalopus,* is found only in White-crowned).

HABITAT AND BEHAVIOR: Uncommon to fairly common (by voice) in undergrowth of montane forest, forest borders, and secondary woodland. Secretive behavior much like that of other *Scytalopus* (see under Unicolored). The song is a fast series of strikingly frog-like notes (therefore easily passed over as not belonging to a bird!), e.g., in Ecuador, "wr-wr-wr-wr-wr" or "wrt, wr-wr-wr-wr." Although all songs seem basically similar, there is apparently some geographic variation in pitch and speech (see Fjeldså and Krabbe 1990).

RANGE: Andes of extreme w. Venezuela (sw. Táchira), Colombia (fairly widely on lower slopes of E. and Cen. Andes; in W. Andes apparently only on their e. slope in Cauca), e. Ecuador, e. Peru, and w. Bolivia (south to w. Santa Cruz); Sierra de Perijá on Venezuela-Colombia border. Mostly 900–1800 m (though apparently locally occurs higher in Colombia).

NOTE: *S. bolivianus* (with, proceeding from the north, *nigricans, atratus, confusus,* and nominate as its component races) is here regarded as a species separate from *S. femoralis.* Fjeldså and Krabbe (1990) suggest that *S. bolivianus* may itself be comprised of more than one species, but the morphological and vocal similarity of its constituent forms makes us reluctant to do so, at least for now. If split further, *S. atratus* (with *nigricans* and *confusus* as races) could be called the Northern White-crowned Tapaculo, and a monotypic *S. bolivianus* could be called the Southern White-crowned Tapaculo.

Scytalopus sanctaemartae

SANTA MARTA TAPACULO

Other: Rufous-vented Tapaculo (in part)

DESCRIPTION: 11.5 cm (4½"). *Colombia's Santa Marta Mts.* Resembles White-crowned Tapaculo; like it, Santa Marta has long been considered only a subspecies of Rufous-vented Tapaculo. Santa Marta differs in its *smaller size,* smaller white crown patch (such that it likely would not be noticeable in the field), and paler gray general coloration (especially in females).

SIMILAR SPECIES: The only other tapaculo on the Santa Martas is the Brown-rumped, which is slightly paler generally with rustier and less barred flanks; it occurs mainly (entirely?) at higher elevations.

HABITAT AND BEHAVIOR: Fairly common (by voice) in undergrowth of montane forest and forest borders. Secretive behavior much as in other *Scytalopus* (see under Unicolored). The song is reported to be a "rapid trill lasting 7 seconds" (S. Hilty, *in* Fjeldså and Krabbe 1990, p. 432).

RANGE: Santa Marta Mts. of n. Colombia. 1350–1700 m.

NOTE: See comments under Rufous-vented and White-crowned Tapaculos, with which the Santa Marta has usually been considered conspecific.

Scytalopus vicinior

NARINO TAPACULO

DESCRIPTION: 12.5 cm (5"). *W. slope of Andes in sw. Colombia and nw. Ecuador.* Closely resembles Rufous-vented Tapaculo, and almost certainly not distinguishable on plumage characters. See C-41. The 2 species are not known to overlap, with Rufous-vented being found only on the *east* slope of Andes. Their voices differ strikingly (see below).

HABITAT AND BEHAVIOR: Fairly common to common (at least in Ecuador) in undergrowth of montane forest and forest borders; sometimes occurs in areas with very mossy forest, but rarely or never in *Chusquea* bamboo. Status in Colombia uncertain because of confusion with Rufous-vented Tapaculo. Secretive behavior much as in other *Scytalopus* (see under Unicolored). The song in Ecuador is a fast, well-enunciated, and ringing "pü-ü-ü-ü-ü-ü-ü-ü-ü . . . ," continuing for 10–30 or even more seconds.

RANGE: W. slope of Andes in sw. Colombia (north to Valle) and nw. Ecuador (south at least to Pichincha, but probably ranging as far south as w. Chimborazo). Mostly 1600–2000 m (locally to 2300 m in Ecuador).

NOTE: As discussed by Fjeldså and Krabbe (1990, p. 433), several Colombian specimens identified as *S. vicinior* have been taken at various Andean sites away from the W. Andes. Whether these birds are in fact *S. vicinior* remains to be determined (their voice remains unknown); though some may be valid, the possibility of confusion with *S. femoralis micropterus* remains likely, and we have not included any of these sites as verified for *either* species. Fjeldså and Krabbe (op. cit.) also suggest that the tapaculo found on Cerro Pirre in e. Panama, though previously identified as *S. vicinior,* cannot be that species, based on its different voice (lower pitched and with a slower tempo); the Pirre birds evidently have no valid name.

Scytalopus panamensis

TACARCUNA TAPACULO

Other: Pale-throated Tapaculo

DESCRIPTION: 12 cm (4¾"). *Cerro Tacarcuna in extreme nw. Colombia.* Resembles Rufous-vented and Narino Tapaculos but has *distinctive whitish superciliary,* slightly paler gray throat, and some pale gray mottling on breast. See C-41.

SIMILAR SPECIES: The only tapaculo in its range.

HABITAT AND BEHAVIOR: Apparently common (by voice) in undergrowth of montane forest and forest borders. Secretive behavior much like that of other *Scytalopus* (see under Unicolored). The song is described as a strident "tuh tu-tu-tu-t" lasting about 1½ seconds and repeated at several-second intervals (M. Pearman).

RANGE: Extreme nw. Colombia (slopes of Cerro Tacarcuna in nw.

Chocó). Also occurs on Panama side of the same mt., to which, as far as known, it is endemic. 1100–1500 m.

NOTE: As pointed out by Ridgely and Gwynne (1989), despite its usually employed English name the throat of this species is barely "paler" than that of the remaining underparts, or than that of other *Scytalopus*. We consider it preferable to employ a geographic epithet for *S. panamensis,* as it is restricted to the Cerro Tacarcuna massif.

Scytalopus latebricola

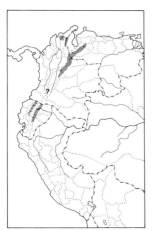

BROWN-RUMPED TAPACULO   PLATE: 30

DESCRIPTION: 12 cm (4¾"). Local in Andes from w. Venezuela to Ecuador; does not include *S. caracae* (Caracas Tapaculo) of n. Venezuela. Tail comparatively short. *Rather pale gray overall,* with *quite contrasting and bright rufous flanks, crissum, and rump* with variable amount of dark barring. Despite the range disjunctions, the various forms presently placed in this species are morphologically much alike.
SIMILAR SPECIES: Rufous-vented and Narino Tapaculos, though similar overall, are darker gray generally, with less contrasting rufous-chestnut flanks which show more blackish barring. Andean Tapaculos, regardless of race, all are smaller and have shorter bills.
HABITAT AND BEHAVIOR: Fairly common to common (by voice) in undergrowth of montane forest and forest borders. Skulking behavior similar to that of other *Scytalopus* (see under Unicolored). The song in Ecuador (*spillmanni*) is a long, very fast, and high-pitched trill, lasting 10–15 seconds and, though basically even-pitched, rising slightly toward the end. In Colombia (except the Santa Marta Mts.) and w. Venezuela, *meridanus* apparently gives a similar but sometimes shorter trill (Fjeldså and Krabbe 1990). The voice of nominate *latebricola* of the Santa Marta Mts. remains unknown (N. Krabbe).
RANGE: Andes of w. Venezuela (north to s. Lara at Anzoátegui), and very locally in Colombia (known definitely from E. Andes south to Cundinamarca; records from the remainder of the Colombian Andes are uncertain, *fide* N. Krabbe); n. Ecuador (on w. slope south to w. Cotopaxi, on e. slope south to nw. Morona-Santiago on the Río Upano), perhaps also in adjacent s. Colombia; Sierra de Perijá on Venezuela-Colombia border, and Colombia's Santa Marta Mts. Records from extreme n. Peru on Cerro Chinguela (Parker et al. 1985) are, *fide* N. Krabbe, in error for a still-undescribed species. Mostly 2100–3200 m, at least in Ecuador locally a little lower, and there and on the Santa Martas recorded up to about 3700 m.

NOTE: More than one species may be involved (N. Krabbe). See comments under Caracas Tapaculo.

Scytalopus caracae

CARACAS TAPACULO
Other: Brown-rumped Tapaculo (in part)

DESCRIPTION: 12 cm (4¾"). *Mts. of n. Venezuela.* Formerly considered a subspecies of Brown-rumped Tapaculo, which in plumage it very closely resembles.

SIMILAR SPECIES: No other tapaculo occurs in the range of this species.

HABITAT AND BEHAVIOR: Fairly common to common (by voice) in undergrowth of montane forest, forest borders, and secondary woodland; tends not to be found in *Chusquea* bamboo. Seems less secretive in behavior than other *Scytalopus,* regularly visible even without aid of tape playback. The song is a rhythmic "pur-chee, chí, chi-pur" with variations but never trilled like all forms presently considered races of Brown-rumped Tapaculo. Easily seen at various sites in the mts. above Caracas (e.g., around Colonia Tovar).

RANGE: Mts. of n. Venezuela (Aragua to Miranda, and in w. Sucre on Cerro Turumiquire). Mostly 1200–1800 m.

NOTE: Here considered a species distinct from *S. latebricola* (Brown-rumped Tapaculo) because of its very different voice.

Scytalopus magellanicus

MAGELLANIC TAPACULO

PLATE: 30

Other: Andean Tapaculo (in part)

DESCRIPTION: 11 cm (4¼"). Here considered a monotypic species of *cen. and s. Chile and adjacent Argentina;* more northerly forms are treated as a separate species (*S. griseicollis,* Andean Tapaculo), with *S. fuscus* (Dusky Tapaculo) of Chile also regarded as a full species. Bill rather small; legs yellowish horn. Mostly gray with a limited amount of rufous on lower flanks and (especially) thighs; a small silvery white patch, often with a scaly effect, is found on the crown feathers of some birds (apparently individual variation).

SIMILAR SPECIES: The only *Scytalopus* in most of its range; cf. similar Dusky Tapaculo.

HABITAT AND BEHAVIOR: Fairly common to common in undergrowth of humid forest (including *Nothofagus*-dominated forest), forest borders, woodland, and scrub; often most numerous in areas overgrown with *Chusquea* bamboo, and frequently along streams. At n. end of its range in Chile, the Magellanic Tapaculo seems to occur only at comparatively high elevations; here it inhabits, apparently exclusively, extensive areas of loose boulders. At and near Cape Horn it is found in tall grass, scrub, and the few patches of low woodland that can survive in this windswept region. Secretive behavior much like that of other *Scytalopus* tapaculos (see under Unicolored), but (*fide* S. Howell) the Magellanic often responds readily to "pishing" (more so than other species?). The frequently heard and very distinctive song is an endlessly repeated, rhythmic "ka-chéw, ka-chéw, ka-chéw, ka-chéw . . ." which may go on for several minutes without a pause, the phrases being given at a rate of about 2 per second. Somewhat surprisingly, the birds of cen. Chile's screeslopes sound very much like birds of the wettest Fuegian forest, and they respond vigorously to tapes of s. birds (though not to the song of *S. fuscus*).

RANGE: Cen. and s. Chile (mainly from Arauco and Malleco southward, but small numbers occur north on mt. slopes to Aconcagua at Portillo) and w. Argentina (north to Neuquén) south to Cape Horn; in 19th century recorded from Falkland Is. (where apparently extirpated by habitat changes induced by sheep overgrazing). Mostly below 1000 m, but to at least 2300 m in cen. Chile.

NOTE: Because of clear-cut vocal differences, we recognize the Fuegian *S. magellanicus* as a separate species from the many Andean forms that were formerly treated as subspecies under *S. magellanicus* and are now called *S. griseicollis* (Andean Tapaculo). We have also recognized the Chilean *S. fuscus* as a separate species from *S. magellanicus*, again based primarily on their different songs; it and *S. magellanicus* are locally sympatric. The English name of Magellanic Tapaculo, derived directly from the specific epithet, seems suitable.

Scytalopus griseicollis

ANDEAN TAPACULO   PLATE: 30
Includes: White-browed Tapaculo

DESCRIPTION: 11–11.5 cm (4¼–4½"). A *small, short-tailed* tapaculo with a *fine bill* found at *high elevations* in Andes, usually *near or above treeline,* from w. Venezuela to nw. Argentina. Two austral forms (*S. fuscus* and *S. magellanicus*) are here considered to constitute full species, and the latter necessitates the change in the specific name for what we consider to be the Andean Tapaculo. Further, what was formerly considered a separate species, *S. superciliaris* (White-browed Tapaculo), is here treated as the southernmost race of *S. griseicollis*. The species *S. griseicollis* shows very complex geographic variation, as follows.

Birds from Ecuador to w. Bolivia south to w. Santa Cruz (*simonsi* is typical) are mainly clear gray, often showing a vague paler "silvery" superciliary; rump and lower flanks rufous brown with blackish barring. Females are more brown-tinged dorsally. *Opacus* of Ecuador is slightly darker. *Urubambae* (known only from 2 specimens taken in Cuzco, Peru) lacks barring on its rather bright and rich rufous lower flanks and rump, and also lacks any trace of a superciliary.

Birds from s. Bolivia (*zimmeri*) have a *pale grayish superciliary and throat* and are clearly intermediate toward *superciliaris* (and *santabarbarae*) of nw. Argentina, which are similar but have an even sharper and more distinct head pattern, with *white superciliary and throat*. All three of these races are quite brown-backed, even in males.

Birds from W. and Cen. Andes of Colombia (*canus*) are entirely gray, without any rufous on flanks or rump; they thus start to resemble the larger and also all-dark *latrans* race of Unicolored Tapaculo, with which sympatric. See C-41.

Birds from E. Andes of Colombia (*griseicollis*) and Andes of w. Venezuela (*fuscicauda*) are comparatively pale gray and have *bright and contrasting rufous flanks and rump* with no barring and a whitish midbelly. See C-42.

SIMILAR SPECIES: The variation is confusing, but bear in mind that this is a small, slender-billed, and short-tailed *Scytalopus* found near treeline; most of the other species are larger, and virtually all tend to be found in taller forest at lower elevations.

HABITAT AND BEHAVIOR: Fairly common (by voice) in undergrowth of low stunted woodland at and near treeline, in patches of *Polylepis* or (*superciliaris* and *zimmeri*) *Alnus* woodland and shrubby areas with tall grass and boulders; usually, but not always, in humid regions. Some races favor areas near streams, and *superciliaris* can regularly be seen hopping on boulders in such situations. In general Andean Tapaculo is not quite so skulking as are many other *Scytalopus,* doubtless in part because of the more open nature of its favored habitats. Vocalizations vary geographically. Ecuador birds (*opacus*) sing a fast dry trill, "trrrrrrrrrrrrr," lasting 5–10 seconds. Birds from E. Andes of Colombia (*griseicollis*) give a lower-pitched, crake- (*Laterallus-*)like trill. Birds from Tucumán, Argentina (*superciliaris*), have a very different song with a gravelly quality, "tzit-tzeeeu, tzit-tzeeeu, tzit-tzeeeu . . ." repeated at intervals of about 1 call per 1½ seconds for long periods. We are not familiar with the songs of other races currently placed in this species; for a more ample discussion, see Fjeldså and Krabbe 1990.

RANGE: Andes of w. Venezuela (north to s. Lara), Colombia (where seemingly local, but probably just under-recorded), Ecuador (on w. slope only in Carchi), Peru, w. Bolivia, and nw. Argentina (south to La Rioja near El Cantadero). Elevation ranges vary: e.g., 2500–3200 m in w. Venezuela and E. Andes of Colombia, 3000–4000 m in the rest of Colombia and in Ecuador and Peru, and mainly 1800–2800 m in s. Bolivia and Argentina.

NOTE: Here *S. griseicollis* (Andean Tapaculo) is considered a separate species from *S. magellanicus* (Magellanic Tapaculo) of extreme s. South America, and *S. superciliaris* (White-browed Tapaculo) is considered as only subspecifically related to it. Several full species are probably involved in what we have called *S. griseicollis,* but much more study is needed (N. Krabbe). In addition, *fide* N. Krabbe, the all-gray form *acutirostris* of cen. Peru (Huánuco) to w. Bolivia (Cochabamba) from about 2400–3400 m, though traditionally classified as a subspecies of the Andean Tapaculo, also likely represents a separate species.

Scytalopus fuscus

DUSKY TAPACULO

Other: Andean Tapaculo (in part)

DESCRIPTION: 11.5 cm (4½"). Mainly in *cen. Chile,* also Mendoza, Argentina; formerly considered a subspecies of *S. magellanicus* (Andean Tapaculo). *Uniform blackish slate* with little or no rufous brown on flanks or rump.

SIMILAR SPECIES: Magellanic Tapaculo is not as black and sometimes shows a white crown spot; it and Dusky Tapaculo are best distinguished by their readily differentiated songs.

HABITAT AND BEHAVIOR: Uncommon to locally fairly common in undergrowth of woodland and dense matorral, showing a strong predilection for ravines. Secretive behavior much like other *Scytalopus* tapaculos (see under Unicolored). Its song is an easily recognized "j-reeén . . . j-reeén . . . j-reeén . . ." which is repeated steadily, sometimes for minutes on end, at a rate of slightly more than once per second.

RANGE: Cen. Chile (Atacama south to Bío-Bío) and w. Argentina (a few old records from w. Mendoza which would appear to need modern confirmation [actually *magellanicus?*]). Up to at least 800 m.

NOTE: Here considered a species separate from *S. magellanicus* (Magellanic Tapaculo), on the basis of its very different song and the local sympatry of the two (see discussion in Johnson 1967; there are a number of subsequent reports of sympatry as well).

GROUP B

E. Brazil region.

Scytalopus speluncae

MOUSE-COLORED TAPACULO   PLATE: 30

DESCRIPTION: 11.5 cm (4½″). *Se. Brazil and ne. Argentina.* Male *uniform dark gray.* Female similar, but at least some are tinged with brown above and with rufescent lower flanks. Immatures, as with all *Scytalopus,* are browner generally (especially above) and are variably barred with dusky on wings and underparts.

SIMILAR SPECIES: The only essentially *all-dark* tapaculo in its range; all other *Scytalopus* in e. Brazil region show some white or whitish on underparts.

HABITAT AND BEHAVIOR: Uncommon to fairly common in undergrowth of montane forest, forest borders, and secondary woodland; often, but not always, found in stands of *Chusquea* bamboo. Creeps about, mouse-like, in dense vegetation near (but not usually actually on) the ground, favoring very dense tangles and hard to see without tape playback. Its often-heard song is a long-continued and simple series of rapidly repeated "chif" notes. The series may go on for several minutes without a pause, with its pace appearing to vary depending on the degree to which the bird is agitated; in natural song the notes are given at 1–2 notes/second, but stimulated birds may rev up to 4–5 notes/second. Numerous at higher levels of Brazil's Itatiaia Nat. Park.

RANGE: Se. Brazil (s. Minas Gerais and Espírito Santo south to Rio Grande do Sul) and ne. Argentina (Misiones); seems likely in extreme se. Paraguay. To 2500 m; exclusively above 1000 m in n. part of range.

Scytalopus indigoticus

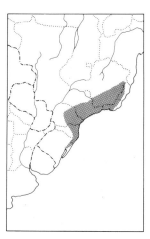

WHITE-BREASTED TAPACULO   PLATE: 30

DESCRIPTION: 11.5 cm (4½″). *E. Brazil.* Lower mandible yellowish. Above bluish slate, becoming reddish brown on lower back and rump. *Throat and median underparts contrastingly white;* sides bluish slate, with flanks and thighs barred rufous and blackish. Immature brown above; coarsely barred buff and dusky below.

SIMILAR SPECIES: Brasilia Tapaculo's anterior underparts, though pale, are not as pure white as White-breasted's; the 2 species do not occur together and have very different songs.

HABITAT AND BEHAVIOR: Rare to locally fairly common in undergrowth of humid forest, forest borders, and secondary woodland. Behavior much like Mouse-colored Tapaculo's, and certainly equally difficult to see; in their area of overlap, White-breasted occurs at lower elevations than Mouse-colored. White-breasted's unique song is an extraordinarily frog-like and guttural "rrrrrrrrrrrrrrrroowww," lasting 2–3 seconds and usually with a slight upturn at the end. Numerous around the Caraça Monastery in Minas Gerais, also found at lower levels of Itatiaia Nat. Park.

RANGE: Se. Brazil (Espírito Santo and s. Minas Gerais south to e. Santa Catarina and extreme ne. Rio Grande do Sul). To about 1300 m.

NOTE: Does not include the recently described *S. psychopompus* (Bahia Tapaculo) of the coastal lowlands of Bahia.

Scytalopus psychopompus

BAHIA TAPACULO

DESCRIPTION: 11.5 cm (4½"). Recently described from *se. Bahia, Brazil*. Closely resembles White-breasted Tapaculo (of which it may be only a northern representative); Bahia differs only in its *unbarred rufous flanks* and bluish slate thighs.

HABITAT AND BEHAVIOR: Barely known in life. Two recent specimens were obtained in "flooded areas [with] thick vegetation [in] lowland forest" (D. M. Teixera and N. Carnevalli). Its voice remains unknown. Deforestation has been so extensive in and around this species' tiny range that, despite the absence of definite information, it must be judged almost certainly at risk.

RANGE: E. Brazil (se. Bahia, where known from Valença and Ilhéus). 45 m.

NOTE: A recently described species: D. M. Teixera and N. Carnevalli, *Bol. Mus. Nac.,* Zool., no. 331, 1989. Although the taxon may prove to be only a subspecies of the similar *S. indigoticus,* the fact that it is found in the lowlands is probably significant; in the n. part of its range *S. indigoticus* is found exclusively in the foothill zone.

Scytalopus novacapitalis

BRASILIA TAPACULO

DESCRIPTION: 11.5 cm (4½"). *Very local in interior s. Brazil*. Legs yellowish. Resembles White-breasted Tapaculo (no overlap) but *throat and breast pale gray to whitish* (not pure white).

HABITAT AND BEHAVIOR: Rare to uncommon and seemingly very local in undergrowth of gallery forest, often where swampy. Described only in 1958, the Brasilia Tapaculo, with very inconspicuous behavior similar to its congeners', is probably more numerous and widespread than the few available records would seem to indicate. Its simple song is a steady repetition of a single, rather high-pitched "chet" note (somewhat insect-like in quality); this may be continued in an almost monotonous manner for a minute or more. Has occasionally been found near the swimming pool in Brasília Nat. Park.

RANGE: Very locally in interior s. Brazil (s. Goiás at Formosa; Brasília in the Distrito Federal; a few localities in w. Minas Gerais, including Serra da Canastra Nat. Park). 800−1000 m.

NOTE: Although *S. novacapitalis* was originally described by H. Sick as a subspecies of *S. indigoticus,* we agree with Sick's subsequent publications, and with J. Vielliard (*Ararajuba* 1: 5−18, 1990), in which *S. novacapitalis* is deemed worthy of full species status; *inter alia,* their voices are utterly unlike.

Psilorhamphus Bamboowrens

Unique among the tapaculos, the distinctive bamboowren is a scarce and local (perhaps overlooked?) inhabitant of bamboo stands in se.

South America. We suspect that ultimately the genus' affinities will be shown to be other than with the Rhinocryptidae.

Psilorhamphus guttatus

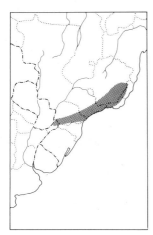

SPOTTED BAMBOOWREN   PLATE: 30

DESCRIPTION: 13.5 cm (5¼″). A strange, *minutely dotted* tapaculo found locally from *se. Brazil to ne. Argentina*. Bill rather long and slender, lower mandible pale; iris apparently whitish. *Above mostly gray with small white dots,* somewhat browner on lower back; wings mostly rufous brown, the coverts with large white tips; tail dusky and "notched" along sides with buff and tipped white. *Throat and chest pale grayish* becoming buff on lower underparts, *all of underparts with small black dots* except somewhat more barred on lower flanks and crissum. Female lacks all the gray; thus its ground color above is brown, below buff, but *its spotting is like male's*.

HABITAT AND BEHAVIOR: Rare to locally uncommon in lower growth of humid forest and secondary woodland; heard far more often than seen. The bamboowren, as its English name indicates, is almost entirely confined to large stands of bamboo. Found singly or in pairs, it works through dense stands of bamboo some 2–5 m above the ground and rarely consorts with mixed flocks. The fairly long and somewhat graduated tail is usually held slightly cocked. The bamboowren's song is a fairly fast series of hollow, resonant notes on an even pitch and cadence of about 2 notes per second, and with an unusual ringing bell-like quality, the whole lasting for 15 seconds or sometimes even more, e.g., "to-to-to-to-to . . ."; the series usually commences with several notes with a more querulous quality. Small numbers can be found on the Argentinian side of Iguazú Falls.

RANGE: Se. Brazil (locally from Espírito Santo and s. Minas Gerais south to Paraná) and ne. Argentina (Misiones); probably also occurs in adjacent Paraguay. To 800 m.

Melanopareia Crescent-chests

A distinct genus of uncertain affinities, the four species of crescent-chests bear little or no resemblance to any other group of tapaculos. They are boldly and attractively patterned and occur allopatrically in semiopen, usually arid habitats from Ecuador to Argentina. The genus was formerly sometimes placed with either the Thamnophilidae (typical antbirds) or Furnariidae (ovenbirds), but more recently it has usually been placed with the Rhinocryptidae (e.g., Meyer de Schauensee 1966, 1970). We have not seen a description of its nest; the eggs of *M. torquata* have been described (Sick 1985) as being antbird-like. *Melanopareia*'s eventual familial allocation thus remains a matter for speculation (its biochemical relationships have not yet been analyzed in detail; Sibley and Ahlquist 1990); we suspect that ultimately it will be shown to have affinities other than with the Rhinocryptidae.

Melanopareia torquata

COLLARED CRESCENT-CHEST

PLATE: 30

DESCRIPTION: 14.5 cm (5¾"). *Mainly in the cerrado of cen. Brazil.* Crown rufous brown, long and narrow superciliary white, and sides of head black; *wide nuchal collar bright rufous;* upperparts, including tail, otherwise russet brown, with a semiconcealed white dorsal patch. Throat buff, *contrasting sharply with a neat black pectoral band across the chest,* the band edged with white above; remaining underparts tawny-buff. Foregoing applies to *rufescens* (most of range). Nominate race (ne. Brazil) similar but with crown grayish brown; *bitorquata* (e. Bolivia) differs more radically from *rufescens,* having the entire upperparts (aside from nuchal collar) brownish olive, a dusky brown tail, and a deeper and more ochraceous throat and lower underparts.

SIMILAR SPECIES: Olive-crowned Crescent-chest, which otherwise is rather similar, lacks this species' prominent rufous nuchal collar; they do not overlap.

HABITAT AND BEHAVIOR: Uncommon in grassy cerrado with scattered low bushes. Inconspicuous and heard much more often than seen, the Collared Crescent-chest occurs singly or (less often) in pairs, creeping and hopping about near the ground, usually under the cover of tall grass. Singing males are sometimes more obvious, for they tend to mount to near the top of a low shrub. Their far-carrying and distinctive song is a monotonous repetition of a single, melodic "tü" note given at a rate of about 1 call per second for up to 20 or even 30 seconds. Readily found in Brasília Nat. Park; there often is a pair near the main entrance.

RANGE: Interior Brazil (s. Pará and cen. Piauí south through Goiás and w. Bahia to w. Minas Gerais, n. São Paulo, and Mato Grosso do Sul), e. Bolivia (Santa Cruz), and extreme ne. Paraguay (UMMZ specimen from Cerro Amambay in Amambay). To about 1000 m.

Melanopareia maximiliani

OLIVE-CROWNED CRESCENT-CHEST

PLATE: 30

DESCRIPTION: 15 cm (6"). *Bolivia to n. Argentina. Uniform olivaceous above,* with long and narrow superciliary yellowish white and sides of head black, and a large semiconcealed white dorsal patch. Throat pale buff, *contrasting sharply with a neat black pectoral band across chest;* remaining underparts rich tawny-buff, deepest (more chestnut) near the pectoral band. Foregoing applies to *argentina* (found mainly at higher elevations, Bolivia to Argentina); nominate *maximiliani* (found mainly in lowlands of Bolivia, w. Paraguay, and n. Argentina) differs in having a whiter throat and darker, more chestnut lower underparts.

SIMILAR SPECIES: Generally similar Collared Crescent-chest (no overlap) always shows a prominent rufous nuchal collar.

HABITAT AND BEHAVIOR: Uncommon to locally fairly common in grassy areas with scattered small bushes (nominate race), and also in arid scrub (especially *argentina*). Behavior similar to Collared Crescent-chest's; forages principally on or near the ground within cover, and inconspicuous unless vocalizing. The song of *argentina* is a fast trill lasting 3 or 4 seconds, e.g., "tree-ee-ee-ee-ee-ee-ee-ee-ee," whereas that of the nominate race (e.g., in w. Paraguay) is a repetition of about 15–20 more separated "tee" notes, given at a rate of 2–3 notes per second. Can be found around Filadelfia in w. Paraguay (nominate *maximiliani*), and at various spots in Andean foothills of Salta and Córdoba, Argentina (*argentina*).

RANGE: Intermontane valleys and slopes of s. Bolivia (west locally to La Paz) and w. Argentina (south to n. San Luis), and east across lowlands of s. Bolivia, w. Paraguay, and n. Argentina (south to n. Santa Fe). Mostly below 2200 m, but recorded to 2950 m in Cochabamba Bolivia.

NOTE: Although similar morphologically, the two forms presently considered to comprise this species perhaps will prove to be specifically distinct. Their songs differ characteristically, and the pattern of altitudinal replacement by representative taxa is usually one shown by separate species. If split, *M. maximiliani* should continue to be called the Olive-crowned Crescent-chest, with *M. argentina* becoming the Montane Crescent-chest (it being the only *Melanopareia* whose entire range is at higher elevations).

Melanopareia elegans

ELEGANT CRESCENT-CHEST   PLATE: 30

DESCRIPTION: 14.5 cm (5¾"). *Sw. Ecuador and nw. Peru.* Male has head black with *long buffy white superciliary;* back grayish olive; wing-coverts and tertials broadly edged rufous, primary coverts and outer primaries edged silvery; tail blackish with outer web of outermost rectrix whitish. *Throat buffy white, contrasting sharply with black pectoral band across chest,* bordered below by a chestnut band which shades into pale cinnamon-buff of lower underparts. Female similar but duller above, with sootier crown, and lacking the chestnut below the pectoral band; its lower underparts are somewhat paler. Foregoing applies to nominate race of Ecuador. *Paucalensis* of Peru similar, but female's crown sooty olive nearly concolor with black.

SIMILAR SPECIES: This handsome bird is unlikely to be confused in its range; cf. Maranon Crescent-chest (no overlap).

HABITAT AND BEHAVIOR: Uncommon to locally fairly common in dense scrub, usually where there is at least some tall grass, and in thick undergrowth of low woodland; favors more arid regions (sometimes ranging into scrub in actual desert), but with deforestation seems gradually to be spreading into more humid, formerly forested areas as well. Inconspicuous unless vocalizing (which it fortunately often does virtually throughout the year), the Elegant Crescent-chest forages by hopping in low vegetation on or near the ground; it almost always remains concealed within dense cover, even when singing rarely taking a prominent perch. The distinctive and far-carrying song is a measured chortling "cho-cho-cho-cho-cho-cho-cho-cho."

RANGE: Sw. Ecuador (north to cen. Manabí and extreme s. Pichincha at Río Palenque) and nw. Peru (south to La Libertad). To about 2000 m in Loja, Ecuador.

NOTE: See comments under Maranon Crescent-chest.

Melanopareia maranonica

MARANON CRESCENT-CHEST

DESCRIPTION: 16 cm (6¼"). *Upper Río Marañón valley of nw. Peru and adjacent Ecuador.* Resembles Elegant Crescent-chest (no overlap) but distinctly larger with a longer tail. Additional differences include the absence of rufous edging on most of wing feathers (rather, Maranon's *wing-coverts are conspicuously edged silvery white,* with tertials only edged dull buff), and the more richly colored ochraceous lower underparts. Both sexes have a glossy black crown; as in female Elegant Crescent-chest, female Maranon lacks the chestnut band below the black pectoral band.

HABITAT AND BEHAVIOR: Uncommon in dense scrub and low woodland. Not well known, but behavior apparently differs little if at all from Elegant Crescent-chest's. The song is not definitely known, but a song similar to Elegant Crescent-chest's has been heard where the Maranon Crescent-chest was recently found in s. Ecuador (F. Sornoza and T. J. Davis).

RANGE: Nw. Peru (locally in upper Río Marañón valley of Cajamarca) and extreme s. Ecuador (Zumba region of s. Zamora-Chinchipe). 200–750 m.

NOTE: Although *M. maranonica* is occasionally considered conspecific with *M. elegans* (e.g., Sibley and Monroe 1990), the morphological differences between the two indicate that they are better considered as allospecies.

Tyrannidae

MANY aspects of the taxonomy of the Tyrannidae remain contro-
versial; this involves both the subdivision and hierarchical level of the higher-order units and
the allocation of certain genera among the subfamilies and families. Until recently (e.g., 198:
AOU Check-list; *Birds of the World,* vol. 8; Meyer de Schauensee 1966, 1970), the Cotingidae
(cotingas) and Pipridae (manakins) were considered separate full families. We have opted, however, to follow Sibley and Ahlquist (1990) in considering both as subfamilies in an expanded
Tyrannidae. Additional complications are presented by what has been termed the "*Schifforni,*
group" (Prum and Lanyon 1989). Although considered united on various morphological characters, this group contains members from the tyrant flycatchers (*Pachyramphus* and *Xenopsaris*)
manakins (*Schiffornis*), and cotingas (*Laniisoma, Laniocera,* and *Iodopleura*). Because of continuing uncertainties, we have retained these genera in their traditional subfamilies.

Tyranninae

TYRANT FLYCATCHERS

ALTHOUGH strictly American in distribution, the tyrant fly
catchers have radiated into every neotropical habitat, and from the bleak windswept plains of
Patagonia to the lush forests of Amazonia and the Andes they rank among the most numerou
and conspicuous birds. Doubtless because of the propensity of certain genera for long-distance
migration, some tyrant flycatchers (unlike any of the cotingas and manakins) have spread into
North America, but the overwhelming preponderance of species are found in the neotropics
They are exceptionally diverse in form, so much so that generalizations are difficult. There reall
is no such thing as a "typical" tyrant flycatcher, though small gleaning species are certainly mor
numerous than the sallying species which North Americans tend to think of as the norm. Ty
rannids of more open terrain are often terrestrial, running rapidly on the ground; one genu
(*Corythopis*) is even terrestrial inside humid forests. Most tyrant flycatchers are small, drabl
colored, and monomorphic, though sexual dimorphism in plumage does occur in some, and
few species are colorful. Field identification of many genera (and even their identification in th
hand) can be a major challenge, especially among the elaenias and many tyrannulets. Man
tyrant flycatchers have a semiconcealed coronal patch of some bright color, this reaching a

extreme in the unique transverse crest of the Royal Flycatcher (*Onychorhynchus*). The vast majority are mostly or entirely insectivorous, but some species do consume fruit, especially when not breeding. Many tyrant flycatchers are very vocal, and their various songs and calls are often an important identification aid. Although most species are monogamous, males of some have persistently used singing perches (a few even in dispersed leks) and do not aid in the rearing of young. Nest form is exceptionally varied, ranging from simple open cups to very large hanging constructions suspended from a drooping branch; a few groups (e.g., *Myiarchus* and related genera) nest in cavities, and one species, the Piratic Flycatcher, usurps the nests of other birds.

It is possible, indeed perhaps likely, that the Tyranninae subfamily should be subdivided. Traylor (*in Birds of the World*, vol. 8) broke the tyrant flycatchers (Tyrannidae) into four subfamilies (Elaeniinae, Fluvicolinae, Tyranninae, and Tityrinae), but Sibley and Ahlquist (1990) concluded that there were only three (Pipromorphinae, Tyranninae, and Tityrinae), and some recent work (e.g., Prum 1990) does not support the monophyly of the Tityrinae. Given the continuing uncertainty, we concluded that it was preferable not to break them up.

The following genera whose familial placements have been debated have been placed by us in the Tyranninae: *Rhytipterna, Attila, Casiornis, Pachyramphus, Xenopsaris,* and *Tityra.*

Suiriri Flycatchers

A midsized flycatcher found in lighter woodlands of e. and s. South America; two species are sometimes recognized. The genus has traditionally been allied with *Elaenia*, from which it differs most notably in its all-black bill (lower mandible not pale as in *Elaenia*) and distinctive juvenal plumage, with conspicuous white spotting above unique in the Tyrannidae. Lanyon (1988a), however, suggests that, based on syringeal morphology, *Suiriri* may be closer to a group containing *Ornithion, Camptostoma,* and others. Its nest is a simple cup (Lanyon 1988a).

Suiriri suiriri

SUIRIRI FLYCATCHER

PLATE: 31

DESCRIPTION: 15.5–16 cm (6–6¼″). Often slightly bushy-crested. Nominate race (Argentina north to e. Bolivia) *mostly gray above* with small white supraloral spot; wings and tail blacker with *bold grayish white wing-bars and edging*, and prominent white vanes and pale tipping on tail feathers. *Whitish below*, tinged pale gray on breast. *Affinis* (mainly in Brazilian portion of range and n. Bolivia) slightly larger and longer-billed and more olive on back with *distinctly paler buffy yellowish rump and base of tail;* wing markings more yellowish and less crisp; throat whitish, becoming pale grayish on chest and *pale yellow on belly.* What are apparently intergrades between the 2 distinctly different "types" have been recorded from ne. Paraguay and adjacent Brazil, and in Santa Cruz, Bolivia. Additionally, some birds of ne. Brazil (east to s. Piauí) have the rump and base of tail brownish, not paler; these birds ("*bahiae*") are otherwise like *affinis.* A shorter-billed form is also known from a limited area in cen. Brazil.

SIMILAR SPECIES: Gray and white nominate type readily recognized in its range (*essentially the chaco*). N. *affinis* type is more easily confused, especially with a *Sublegatus* scrub-flycatcher or small *Myiarchus,* though none of these ever show the contrasting, usually quite conspicuous, pale rump.

HABITAT AND BEHAVIOR: Southern nominate type is fairly common to common in chaco woodland, lighter scrub, and monte woodland; northern *affinis* is uncommon to fairly common in open cerrado and campos with scattered trees, less often at edge of gallery woodland and in cerrado with denser tree growth. Nominate generally perches quite upright, recalling a small *Myiarchus,* usually in the open, gleaning and making short sallies to foliage; often in small groups. It frequently gives an abrupt harsh nasal scold, a slowly repeated "dyyr," sometimes given more rapidly in succession and then vireo- or antbird-like, "dya-dya-dya-dya," or speeded up into a higher-pitched chatter. *Affinis* behaves somewhat differently, tending to perch on low branches, from there dropping to grass or the ground, often hovering and frequently exposing the pale rump and fanning its tail; most often in pairs. Pairs deliver a fast, jumbled, exuberant song as a duet.

RANGE: Ne. and cen. Brazil (Maranhão, Ceará, and Pernambuco south and west to s. Mato Grosso, Mato Grosso do Sul, and n. São Paulo; absent from coastal southeast), n. and e. Bolivia (west to Beni), Paraguay (except in the extreme east), Uruguay, adjacent s. Brazil (w. Rio Grande do Sul), and n. and cen. Argentina (south to La Pampa and s. Buenos Aires); isolated populations in lower Amaz. Brazil (in Amapá, and around Santarém and Monte Alegre) and s. Surinam (Sipaliwini). All populations are basically resident; an Aug. specimen of nominate race from Minas Gerais, Brazil, may indicate that a few birds move north during austral winter. To about 2500 m (in e. Bolivia).

NOTE: Two species (*S. suiriri* and *S. affinis,* if split best known as the Chaco Suiriri and Campo Suiriri, respectively) were recognized in the genus *Suiriri* until J. T. Zimmer (*Am. Mus. Novitates* 1749, 1955) pointed out that AMNH had a variable series of *Suiriri* from three localities in ne. Paraguay which appeared to be intermediate in several characters. Meyer de Schauensee (1966, 1970) followed Zimmer (op. cit.) in considering *Suiriri* to consist of only one species, but Short (1975) disagreed and felt recognition of two species was warranted. *Contra* Sibley and Monroe (1990), we opt to continue to treat the two forms as conspecific because of the apparently intermediate specimens. However, having repeatedly seen and heard both "types" in the field, we continue to suspect that two biological species are probably involved. There are additional complications in Brazil. Two AMNH specimens from Gilbués in e. Piauí resemble (*affinis*) *bahiae* but have white bellies (like the geographically distant nominate race); the explanation for this variation is unknown. Further, Zimmer (op. cit.) found five additional AMNH specimens that resembled *affinis* but had shorter, broader bills and broad pale tipping on their rectrices. Traylor (1982) discusses an additional specimen with these characters in the FMNH (and there also appears to be one in the ANSP); these specimens also all had broad central tail feathers with no pale edging. Traylor (op. cit.) suspects (and we concur) that an undescribed sibling species is involved.

Elaenia Elaenias

Notoriously difficult, the elaenias represent perhaps the most confusing tyrannid group. Probably no other causes one to throw up one's hands in frustration so often. The task is *not*, however, hopeless, and we hope that with the information presented below, careful observers will be able to make some accurate diagnoses. Nevertheless, we do not wish to minimize the difficulties: it simply will *not* be possible to identify some elaenias in the field. As a group, *Elaenia* elaenias are relatively easy to recognize: they perch upright, are of medium size, are mostly olive with belly paler (yellow or white), and have bold wing-bars. Many have a slight crest (conspicuous in a few species); a white coronal streak or patch is sometimes visible in certain species. Aside from a very few forest-based species, elaenias are relatively conspicuous; they will be seen often, whether or not one wants to deal with them. Assuming one does, look especially at the following.

1. Size.

2. Size, presence, and shape of crest (remember that these crests are "expressive," i.e., they tend to be raised when a bird is alert or agitated; many elaenias are "round-headed").

3. Presence of white (rufous in 1 species) in crown; this is often hidden, so except in the hand it is difficult to be certain it is *not* present—but the converse can be very helpful if confirmed.

4. Number of wing-bars (several species have 3 instead of the usual 2, but beware of wear and molt stage).

5. Color of belly (whether whitish or pale yellow).

6. Voice (many vocalize a lot, and this is often the best clue of all).

GROUP A

"Typical," confusing elaenias.

Elaenia flavogaster

YELLOW-BELLIED ELAENIA PLATE: 31

DESCRIPTION: 16–16.5 cm (6¼–6½"). The most widespread and familiar elaenia but does *not* always look particularly yellow-bellied. Generally shows a *conspicuous upstanding bushy crest,* parted in the center to reveal a *white coronal patch.* Brownish olive above, wings and tail duskier, wings with 2 prominent whitish wing-bars and yellowish white edging; faint eye-ring whitish. Throat pale gray merging into grayish olive breast and sides; belly pale yellow to yellowish white.
SIMILAR SPECIES: A good elaenia to learn well, as in its range it is usually the most numerous member of its genus. Cf. especially Lesser Elaenia (slightly smaller, with smaller crest and more uniform below) and Large Elaenia (larger, with less of a crest which reveals almost no white at base of feathers, and usually showing a third wing-bar).
HABITAT AND BEHAVIOR: Fairly common to common in lighter woodland and scrub, clearings and gardens; occurs in both arid and humid regions. An animated and conspicuous bird, usually found singly or in pairs, though larger numbers may gather in fruiting trees. When Yellow-bellied Elaenias are excited (which seems to be often), their crest is especially noticeable and the birds are particularly vocal. Noisy, with a variety of calls, most with a slightly hoarse quality, e.g., "breeeer" or "wreek-kreeup," the latter often repeated several times; often both members of a pair call in a jumbled manner.
RANGE: Widespread south to n. Argentina (south to Jujuy and Salta,

ne. Santa Fe, and Corrientes) and s. Brazil (south to Rio Grande do Sul) but absent from a large part of cen. and w. Amazonia; west of Andes south to sw. Ecuador (El Oro and w. Loja), with a sight report from extreme n. Chile (1 seen near Arica in Sept. 1986; M. Sallaberry et al.); Trinidad and Tobago, and Margarita Is. off Venezuela. Also Middle America and the Lesser Antilles. Mostly below 1500 m, but to 2000–2500 m in clearings on e. slope of Andes.

Elaenia spectabilis

LARGE ELAENIA

DESCRIPTION: 18 cm (7″). Resembles Yellow-bellied Elaenia, and their ranges overlap broadly (though whether they actually breed at the same site is unknown). Large is somewhat *larger* and *less crested* (usually no crest shows), with little or no white showing at base of crest; usually shows a *third whitish wing-bar* on lesser coverts; and throat and chest slightly purer gray. Vocalizations of the 2 species also differ characteristically (see below).

SIMILAR SPECIES: Besides Yellow-bellied, cf. Mottle-backed and Highland Elaenias; other possibly confusing elaenias are smaller. Cf. also Short-crested and Swainson's Flycatchers.

HABITAT AND BEHAVIOR: Locally fairly common in forest borders, shrubby clearings, and groves of trees around buildings; during austral winter found mainly in riparian growth across w. and cen. Amazonia. Less conspicuous and more of a woodland bird than Yellow-bellied Elaenia. Seems much less excitable and vocal, with its most frequently heard call being a soft, melancholy "cleeur" or "wheeo." Its dawn song, however, is reported to be a shrill, repetitious, 3-syllabled "twee-wee-tweet" (Belton 1985).

RANGE: Breeds across cen. Brazil (Bahia and Goiás west through s. Mato Grosso and Mato Grosso do Sul) and in e. Bolivia (Santa Cruz to Tarija), Paraguay, and n. Argentina (south in the northwest to Tucumán and Santiago del Estero, in the northeast south in very small numbers to extreme n. Buenos Aires), and in extreme s. Brazil (w. Rio Grande do Sul); during austral winter migrates northward (mostly June–Aug.) to w. and cen. Amaz. Brazil, se. Colombia (Amazonas), e. Ecuador (a few records from Napo), and e. Peru. Likely occurs in Uruguay. Exact breeding range still somewhat uncertain, but there seems no doubt that across Amazonia the Large Elaenia occurs only as an austral migrant.

Elaenia ridleyana

NORONHA ELAENIA

DESCRIPTION: 17 cm (6¾″). *Restricted to Fernando de Noronha,* an isolated island off coast of ne. Brazil. Resembles Large Elaenia but somewhat smaller with shorter tail, longer bill.

SIMILAR SPECIES: The only elaenia on Fernando de Noronha, indeed the only suboscine bird resident on the island; the only other passerine resident is the vastly different Noronha Vireo.

HABITAT AND BEHAVIOR: Apparently uncommon in scrub, woodland,

and around houses. Reportedly the least numerous of the 3 resident landbirds on Noronha, with a population something over 100 individuals. Its calls are reported to be varied, including a short, strong "thiu-thiu-thiu . . ."; also gives a monotonous "üuu . . . üuu . . . üuu" (J. B. Nacinovic and D. M. Teixera, *Rev. Brasil. Biol.* 49[3]: 720–723, 1989).
RANGE: Fernando de Noronha Is., off coast of ne. Brazil.

NOTE: Here, following Sick (1985), *E. ridleyana* is regarded as a species distinct from *E. chiriquensis* (with which considered conspecific by Hellmayr in *Birds of the Americas*, vol. 13, part 5) and from *E. spectabilis* (with which considered conspecific by J. T. Zimmer, *Am. Mus. Novitates* 1108, 1941). The voice of *E. ridleyana* seems to bear little resemblance to either of these species.

Elaenia gigas

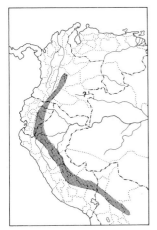

MOTTLE-BACKED ELAENIA

PLATE: 31

DESCRIPTION: 18 cm (7"). *A large elaenia found mainly along e. base of Andes. Prominent crest with unmistakable bifurcated shape*, often protruding straight up from forehead (*sometimes looking "horned"*), and *almost always exposing considerable white in center*. Olive brown above, feathers edged paler olive giving a distinct mottled effect; wings with 2 whitish wing-bars and edging; eye-ring very faint. Throat gray, becoming flammulated with olive on breast and flanks; belly pale yellow.
SIMILAR SPECIES: No other elaenia has a similar crest (its shape is reminiscent of a Harpy Eagle's!), and as it is conspicuous and almost invariably raised, confusion is unlikely.
HABITAT AND BEHAVIOR: Rare to locally fairly common in clearings with scattered trees and bushes and (at least in Ecuador) also locally in riparian scrub on river islands. General behavior much like other elaenias', and like Yellow-bellied seems active and excitable. Its most frequently heard call is a sharp "direeet," almost martin-like; what apparently functions as a dawn song is a loud "wurdít" or "purdíp," given repeatedly from atop a bush or low tree. Although not often encountered, Mottle-backed may be increasing in numbers because of the spread of clearings across its formerly mostly forested range. Presumably its ancestral habitats were natural riparian growth and perhaps also small clearings formed by landslides.
RANGE: Se. Colombia (w. Meta south to Caquetá, with 1 report also from e. Vaupés), e. Ecuador, e. Peru, and w. Bolivia (south to w. Santa Cruz). Mostly 250–1000 m.

Elaenia obscura

HIGHLAND ELAENIA

PLATE: 31

DESCRIPTION: 18 cm (7"). *Subtropical and temperate zones in Andes and se. Brazil area. A large* and *dark-looking* elaenia, *round-headed*, and with *bill notably short and stubby for its size* (imparting a distinctive snub-nosed effect). *Uniform dark olive above* with yellowish eye-ring and *no crest or coronal patch*; wings and tail duskier, wings with 2 yellowish wing-bars and edging. Throat pale yellowish, *breast and flanks dull olive*, belly clear pale yellow.
SIMILAR SPECIES: Sierran Elaenia is obviously smaller with coronal

patch usually showing, and has less pure olive below and more yellow on belly. Large Elaenia is much less olive, is notably grayer on throat and chest, and almost always shows a third wing-bar.

HABITAT AND BEHAVIOR: Uncommon to fairly common in borders and undergrowth of montane and humid forest and secondary woodland (sometimes where quite patchy and young). A rather inconspicuous elaenia, tending to remain within cover more than most others. A frequent call (at least in Andes) is a fast, burry "burrrr" or "burrreep"; the full song in nw. Argentina (R. Straneck recording) is a more complex and melodic, almost thrush-like, phrase, e.g., "chee-chooit, chu-wheeo-chu-whee?"

RANGE: E. slope of Andes in s. Ecuador (very locally in Azuay and Loja [including MCZ], Peru, Bolivia, and nw. Argentina (south to Tucumán); se. Brazil (Rio de Janeiro, Minas Gerais, extreme s. Goiás, and s. Mato Grosso do Sul south to Rio Grande do Sul), e. Paraguay (west to Canendiyu and Paraguarí), and ne. Argentina (Misiones and Corrientes; a single old record from ne. Santa Fe at Ocampo). Mostly 1700–3000 m in Andes, ranging lower (down to 1000 m) in nw. Argentina; up to 2000 m in se. South America.

Elaenia pallatangae

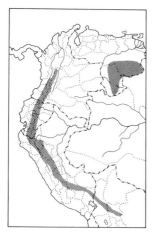

SIERRAN ELAENIA   PLATE: 31

DESCRIPTION: 14.5 cm (5¾"). *Andes of Colombia to Bolivia, and on tepuis.* Olive above with *narrow white coronal stripe* (which usually is visible; but shows little or no crest) and prominent yellowish eye-ring; wings and tail duskier, wings with 2 conspicuous yellowish white bars and edging. Chin pale grayish; lower throat and breast *yellowish* olive, becoming *pale yellow on belly. Olivina* (of tepuis) tends to be browner above and is darker and more uniformly olive yellow below.

SIMILAR SPECIES: In Colombian Andes most likely confused with Mountain Elaenia, which lacks white in crown and is not as yellow below; Sierran tends to occur at higher elevations. Elsewhere in Andes confusion is most likely with White-crested Elaenia, though that species lacks the relatively uniformly yellow underparts of Sierran. Cf. also Small-billed Elaenia (an austral migrant to lowlands *below* range of Sierran).

HABITAT AND BEHAVIOR: Fairly common to common at borders of forest and second-growth woodland and in shrubby clearings. Behavior similar to many other elaenias', though less active and less conspicuous than some, often perching quietly for protracted periods. The call in Andes is a fairly sharp, clear "wheeu," lacking the burry quality of many other elaenias.

RANGE: Andes of s. Colombia (north in W. Andes to Valle, in Cen. Andes to Tolima), Ecuador (south on w. slope to El Oro), e. Peru, and w. Bolivia (La Paz and Cochabamba); tepuis of s. Venezuela (Bolívar and Amazonas) and adjacent Guyana and extreme n. Brazil. Mostly 1500–3000 m.

NOTE: May hybridize with White-crested Elaenia (*griseigularis*) in the Ecuadorian Andes (*fide Birds of the World,* vol. 8).

Elaenia frantzii

MOUNTAIN ELAENIA

DESCRIPTION: 14 cm (5½"). *Highlands of Colombia and Venezuela.* Resembles Sierran Elaenia but has *no* white coronal stripe; likewise shows no crest (usually looking rather *round-headed*). Above dull brownish olive with prominent yellowish white eye-ring; wings and tail duskier, wings with 2 prominent yellowish white bars and edging. *Below uniformly pale yellowish olive,* becoming *yellowish white on midbelly.* See C-37, P-24.

SIMILAR SPECIES: Sierran Elaenia is yellower below, especially on belly, and has white usually visible in crown. Small-billed Elaenia is much grayer below (especially on throat and chest) and has white in crown much like Sierran. Lesser Elaenia usually shows a slight crest (not the "rounded" effect of Mountain) which reveals white in crown, and is grayer (not so olive) below.

HABITAT AND BEHAVIOR: Fairly common to common in overgrown clearings, forest and woodland borders, and cultivated areas with hedgerows and scattered shrubby areas and trees. Behavior similar to other elaenias', though seems more frugivorous than most. Calls include a whistled "peeee-oo" or "twee-oo" and a more drawn out "peeee-err."

RANGE: Coastal mts. of n. Venezuela (east to Paria Peninsula) and Andes of w. Venezuela and Colombia (south to Cauca); Santa Marta Mts. of n. Colombia and Sierra de Perijá on Venezuela-Colombia border. Also Guatemala to Panama. Mostly 1500–2500 m, locally and in smaller numbers somewhat higher and lower.

Elaenia cristata

PLAIN-CRESTED ELAENIA

PLATE: 31

DESCRIPTION: 14.5 cm (5¾"). *Savannas of e. and s.-cen. South America.* Generally appears *crested* (feathers rather long and narrow) but with *no white in crown,* the absence of which is often noticeable because the crest is so frequently raised. A *very dull* elaenia. Above dull olive brown with narrow pale eye-ring; wings and tail duskier, wings with 2 broad whitish bars and edging. Throat grayish white, becoming grayish olive on breast and pale yellowish on belly.

SIMILAR SPECIES: Most resembles White-crested/Small-billed Elaenia complex, though these have white in crown (*lacking* in Plain-crested) and appear much less crested. Lesser Elaenia is also quite similar and can occur with Plain-crested, but Lesser shows white in crown. Cf. also Rufous-crowned Elaenia. No other elaenia is so tied to *natural savanna vegetation;* Plain-crested rarely or never occurs outside this habitat.

HABITAT AND BEHAVIOR: Fairly common to locally common in savannas with scattered bushes and in cerrado. Often quite conspicuous, in part because its habitat is so open. The call, rather infrequently heard, is a fast, gravelly "jer-jéhjeh," sometimes repeated.

RANGE: Venezuela (widespread in appropriate habitat but absent from the northwest and all forested regions), Guianas, e. and cen. Brazil (locally in isolated savannas along the lower Amazon upriver almost to the Manaus area, and south to s. Mato Grosso, s. Goiás, n. São Paulo, and Minas Gerais), and ne. Bolivia (ne. Santa Cruz on Serranía de Huanchaca); a single record from se. Peru (Cuzco, a specimen from Santa Ana, in an arid rain-shadow valley of Andes). The species appears to be partially migratory, or at least is nomadic. To about 1000 m.

Elaenia chiriquensis

LESSER ELAENIA

DESCRIPTION: 13.5 cm (5¼"). *Not* appreciably smaller than many other elaenias, despite its English name. An easily confused elaenia with *no fully confirmatory field mark;* often best identified by voice (see below). Usually slightly crested (at times giving back of head a *squared-off* look), which *often exposes some white in crown.* Grayish olive above with narrow whitish eye-ring; wings and tail duskier, wings with 2 broad whitish bars and edging. Throat grayish, becoming grayish olive on breast, and whitish tinged pale yellow on belly. See C-37, P-24.

SIMILAR SPECIES: Most resembles a small Yellow-bellied Elaenia, but that species has a more conspicuous crest (often somewhat parted down the middle) and shows more contrast between breast and belly colors. Small-billed Elaenia is more clean-cut, with a sharply defined eye-ring, more contrast between olive upperparts and gray throat and chest, and a round-headed look with white showing as a stripe down midcrown. Mountain Elaenia also tends to look round-headed, but it lacks white in crown and is more uniformly yellowish olive below. Cf. also Sierran and White-crested Elaenias.

HABITAT AND BEHAVIOR: Uncommon to fairly common in open grassy areas with scattered shrubs and trees, regenerating clearings, cultivated areas with hedgerows and brushy patches, and cerrado (interior and e. Brazil). Behavior similar to Yellow-bellied Elaenia's but on the whole less conspicuous and noisy. Lesser's usual calls are a burry "chíbur" or "jwebü," a longer "freeeee" (much like a vocalization of Yellow-bellied), and a softer, sometimes repeated "weeb" or "beezb."

RANGE: Widespread in lowlands and on lower slopes south to n. and e. Bolivia (south to La Paz, Cochabamba, and Santa Cruz), n. Argentina (locally in e. Jujuy and Misiones), e. Paraguay (few records), and s. Brazil (south to Paraná and São Paulo), but absent or very local in extreme ne. Brazil and the Amazon basin (where apparently largely or entirely restricted to isolated patches of natural savanna), and not recorded from most of e. Ecuador or w. Amaz. Brazil; west of Andes only in nw. Venezuela, w. Colombia (Santa Marta region south to upper Río Magdalena valley, and Río Cauca valley), and nw. Ecuador (locally in valleys on w. slope of Andes in Imbabura and Pichincha); Trinidad and Netherlands Antilles (either as migrant or with small resident population). Also Costa Rica and Panama. Southernmost breeders apparently migrate northward during austral winter, but as the subspecies *albivertex* occurs across all of cis-Andean South America, their wintering range is hard to delineate. Mostly below 2000 m, but locally to 2800 m.

Elaenia martinica

CARIBBEAN ELAENIA

DESCRIPTION: 15 cm (6"). *Netherlands Antilles. Closely* resembles Lesser Elaenia, which has also been recorded on these islands (though it is *much* less numerous). Generally looks more crested, with more white in crown; slightly larger.

SIMILAR SPECIES: The only numerous elaenia on the Netherlands Antilles; cf. Lesser and Small-billed Elaenias (both of which have been recorded only infrequently there). Northern Scrub-Flycatcher has a shorter bill, fairly prominent pale supraloral, no white in crown, and shows more contrast on underparts.

HABITAT AND BEHAVIOR: Uncommon to locally fairly common in deciduous woodland, scrub, cultivated land with scattered trees and shrubs, and mangroves; evidently rare on Aruba, however. Behavior is typical of various elaenias; not an especially conspicuous or noisy species, often perching quietly in foliage for long periods. Its call, a whistled "wee-weew" or "wee-wee-weew," often reveals its presence; dawn song is a clear, loud "pee-wee-reereeree" or "peeweetprrr" (Voous 1983).

RANGE: Netherlands Antilles. Also on smaller islands in West Indies, and on islands off Yucatán Peninsula. Below 100 m.

Elaenia albiceps

WHITE-CRESTED ELAENIA   PLATE: 31

DESCRIPTION: 14.5–15 cm (5¾–6"). At most only slightly crested, but white coronal stripe often visible (especially in *chilensis*); *chilensis* (breeding in s. Andes, migrating far to north) is dark olive with bold whitish eye-ring; wings and tail duskier, wings with 2 prominent yellowish white wing-bars and edging. Throat and breast pale gray, tinged olive especially on sides, becoming white on center of belly; crissum tinged pale yellow. More n. races (resident from s. Colombia to w. Bolivia and n. Chile) are dingier, more grayish or brownish olive above and more olivaceous on breast, and have a less well marked eyering (or none at all) and less prominent wing-bars (latter especially so in *modesta* of Pacific-slope Peru and n. Chile).

SIMILAR SPECIES: Exceedingly like Small-billed Elaenia; go by range when possible, and recognize that many birds will not be identifiable in the field, especially across their vast (and overlapping) wintering ranges. In Andes the situation is less confusing, mainly because Small-billed occurs mostly or entirely in lowlands *east* of them. In Andes, cf. especially Sierran Elaenia (similar to White-crested but much yellower below) and Lesser Elaenia. In se. South America confusion is also likely with Olivaceous Elaenia (which see).

HABITAT AND BEHAVIOR: *Chilensis* is common to abundant as a breeder in *Nothofagus-* (Southern Beech-) dominated forest, humid and more deciduous woodland, borders, shrubby clearings, and cultivated areas with scattered trees and bushes; during austral winter it occurs mainly in low shrubbery and woodland. More northerly breeding races seem to be less numerous; they favor scrub and woodland borders, perhaps mostly in more arid, nonforested areas (with Sierran Elaenia replacing them at forest borders in more humid regions). *Modesta* is common in gardens and shrubby areas around Arica in north-ernmost Chile but seems less numerous in Peru. White-crested Elaenia is the most numerous and conspicuous bird in and near *Nothofagus* forests during austral summer (Oct.–Mar.), but it then disperses over such a wide area during austral winter that it seems much less nu-merous (one problem is that in the field many probably are not rec-ognized). The call of breeding birds from throughout their range is a burry "feeur" or "feeeo," often given interminably; also has a faster, clearer "peeur-peer." Wintering birds are mostly silent, and birds breeding in n. Andes seem less vocal generally. These vocalizations give rise to the species' local name in Argentina, Chile, and coastal Peru, *fio-fio*.

RANGE: Nominate group is resident in Andes from s. Colombia (Na-riño) south to w. Bolivia (La Paz and Cochabamba); *modesta* is resi-dent on the Pacific slope down to sea level in w. Peru (north to Lam-bayeque) and n. Chile (Tarapacá); *chilensis* breeds from cen. and s. Chile (north to Atacama) and cen. Argentina (north to La Rioja, Córdoba, Santa Fe, and Corrientes) south to Tierra del Fuego. The n. limit of the breeding range of *chilensis* is uncertain; in *Birds of the World*, vol. 8, it is given as north to Chuquisaca in s. Bolivia, but we are not certain whether this has been verified, and recent observations by Ar-gentinian field workers suggest that more northerly records during the "breeding" season are attributable to early and late migrants (*fide* R. Straneck). *Chilensis* is entirely migratory, and during austral winter occurs north to Peru (possibly even e. Colombia) and Amaz. and e. Brazil, but the relatively few records are very scattered, doubtless be-cause of its huge wintering range relative to the small size of its breed-ing area. Vagrants have been recorded twice on Falkland Is., and R. Straneck has even seen one flying south half-way to S. Shetland Is. off Antarctica! *Modesta* may also migrate, or at least disperse to some extent; FMNH has specimens from se. Peru taken in Nov. (*fide* D. Stotz). Mostly below 3000 m (an errant migrant once to 5100 m).

NOTE: Despite their close plumage similarity, the distribution of *chilensis* and the n. nominate group makes us wonder whether a pair of biological species are in-volved. *E. modesta* (Peruvian, or Modest, Elaenia) has also sometimes been accorded full species rank (e.g., Koepcke 1970), though it is not strikingly different from *E. al-biceps* vocally. See also comments under Small-billed Elaenia.

Elaenia parvirostris

SMALL-BILLED ELAENIA

DESCRIPTION: 14.5 cm (5¾"). *Very* closely resembles *chilensis* race of White-crested Elaenia. Small-billed's only differences are its slightly stubbier bill and purer gray throat and chest; a *third wing-bar* (on lesser coverts) is usually present. These (subtle) distinctions may hold best for birds in fresh plumage; *many elaenias in this group are not identifi-able in the field.* See V-29, C-37.

SIMILAR SPECIES: Besides White-crested, Small-billed is very similar

to Olivaceous Elaenia, with which it broadly overlaps in se. South America. Olivaceous has no coronal stripe (or at most shows only a trace—but remember that this is sometimes hidden in Small-billed), shows relatively little contrast between upper- and underparts, has a dull olive wash across breast, and has 2 (not 3) wing-bars. Cf. also Lesser Elaenia.

HABITAT AND BEHAVIOR: Common as a breeder (mostly Sept.–Mar.) in woodland (including monte), forest borders, and adjacent shrubby clearings; during austral winter occurs mostly in lighter woodland, shrubbery, and gardens, but has also been observed in canopy of humid forest (where it doubtless often passes unnoticed). Small-billed Elaenia seems to be a much more numerous austral winter visitor to Amazonia than White-crested, at least based on frequency of specimen records. The most frequent song appears to be a burry "chi-brr," quite similar to White-crested's. Belton (1985) also describes a song (given mostly at dawn?) that he transcribes as "weedable-we." Also has several sharp, quick call notes; birds wintering in Amazonia give a repeated sharp "cheeu."

RANGE: Breeds in e. Bolivia (Cochabamba and Santa Cruz southward, possibly north into Beni), Paraguay, extreme s. Brazil (Rio Grande do Sul, and north at least locally to São Paulo; D. Stotz has seen it in Jan. at the Boracéia Reserve, and E. O. Willis and Y. Oniki have found breeding birds in Jan. near Itararé), Uruguay, and n. Argentina (south to San Luis and Buenos Aires); during austral winter moves north widely across w. and cen. Amazon basin to ne. Colombia, Venezuela, and Guianas, with a few records from as far north as Trinidad and Netherlands Antilles. Mostly below 1000 m, locally higher on e. slope of Andes.

NOTE: Closely related to *E. albiceps*. Traylor (1982, p. 15) found extensive hybridization between the two in a limited area on the e. slope of the Andes in s. Bolivia, though in nw. Argentina they behave as good sympatric species (*albiceps* mostly on Andean slopes above the range of *parvirostris,* but with some overlap). He continues to regard them as full species but admits that this is a "subjective opinion."

Elaenia mesoleuca

OLIVACEOUS ELAENIA

DESCRIPTION: 14.5 cm (5¾"). *A dull olive elaenia of woodland and forest in se. Brazil area.* Olive above with little or no white in crown; wings and tail duskier, wings with 2 yellowish white bars and edging. Throat pale grayish, breast dull grayish olive (sometimes with the effect of a dull olive pectoral band), becoming white on center of belly; flanks and crissum tinged greenish yellow.

SIMILAR SPECIES: So closely resembles Small-billed Elaenia that many individuals cannot be distinguished. The 2 species frequently occur together; when breeding, though, Olivaceous tends to be more a bird of woodland and forest (with Small-billed more in semiopen areas). Olivaceous is drabber and more uniform, with a more olivaceous breast; it has little or no white in crown (but as Small-billed's white is often at least partially hidden, this is of little help in the field) and has only 2 wing-bars (Small-billed usually shows 3).

HABITAT AND BEHAVIOR: Locally fairly common to common in forest canopy and borders, woodland, gallery forest, and adjacent clearings. Perhaps more numerous in Rio Grande do Sul, Brazil, than elsewhere, for Belton (1985) considered it "abundant" there. He also considered it only an austral summer visitor (Sept.–Apr.) to that state, but the extent of its migration is uncertain (s. birds may simply move north into range of more northerly, resident populations?). Also numerous at higher elevations in Itatiaia Nat. Park. Olivaceous is rather more forest-based than most other elaenias. Its song is a harsh, fast, and abrupt "whik-whikiur"; also commonly gives a "chirr" call.

RANGE: Se. Brazil (s. Goiás and s. Bahia south to Rio Grande do Sul), e. Paraguay (west to Paraguarí), and ne. Argentina (e. Formosa, e. Chaco, ne. Santa Fe, Corrientes, and Misiones). To over 2000 m (in Itatiaia Nat. Park, Brazil).

GROUP B

Relatively distinctive elaenias. Coloration decidedly brownish or gray.

Elaenia strepera

SLATY ELAENIA   PLATE: 31

DESCRIPTION: 15.5 cm (6"). *Breeds in Andes of s. Bolivia and n. Argentina, migrating north to Venezuela.* Male unmistakable (for an elaenia), being *mostly slaty gray.* Coronal streak white, but this is often hidden (visible especially when bird calling); usually looks round-headed (at most only slightly crested); narrow white eye-ring. Male above slaty gray, wings with *2 indistinct pale gray bars* and edging. Below somewhat paler gray, becoming white on midbelly and crissum. Female similar but tinged olive above, wing-bars more prominent and *more ochraceous.* Throat and breast olive grayish, grayest on throat, contrasting with yellowish white to white belly.

SIMILAR SPECIES: Male unlike any other *Elaenia;* its color recalls Smoke-colored Pewee's (sometimes found with it); cf. male Gray Elaenia (with much bolder wing-bars, etc.) and Suiriri Flycatcher. Female usually looks gray enough to be recognizable (no other *Elaenia* is so gray), and its ochraceous wing-bars are also distinctive.

HABITAT AND BEHAVIOR: Locally common in woodland and forest borders when breeding; in shrubby clearings and forest borders during austral winter. Rather inconspicuous, tending to remain in dense foliage; easiest to see when males are vocalizing. At times their unmistakable call is heard from all around: it is utterly unlike any other elaenia's, being a frequently repeated, dry gravelly "eh-eh-ehhhhh?" Its peculiar mechanical quality is difficult to transcribe, in part because it sounds more like a frog than a bird. Slaty Elaenia is common during the nesting season (at least Oct.–Feb.) along the Abra Santa Laura between Salta and Jujuy (cities), and in Finca El Rey Nat. Park, Argentina. It seems much less numerous northward on its winter range (where recorded mainly May–July), doubtless because it then fans out over a wide area compared with its restricted breeding range.

RANGE: Breeds on e. slope of Andes in s. Bolivia (w. Santa Cruz, Chuquisaca, and Tarija) and nw. Argentina (south to ne. La Rioja); winters north to n. Venezuela (north and east to Sucre and Bolívar), with records of apparent transients from e. Colombia (recorded in w. Putumayo, w. Meta, and Amazonas) and e. Peru (recorded from several localities in Loreto, and in Madre de Dios), but few records overall (and still unreported from both w. Brazil and e. Ecuador, in both of which it must surely occur as a transient). Mostly 500–2000 m when breeding, in lowlands to about 400 m during austral winter.

NOTE: Distributional details, particularly regarding migration, are given by C. A. Marantz and J. V. Remsen, Jr. (*J. Field Ornithol.* 62[2]: 162–172, 1991).

Elaenia pelzelni

BROWNISH ELAENIA   PLATE: 31

DESCRIPTION: 18 cm (7″). *A large, dull brownish elaenia found locally on islands in Amazon River system.* Head usually looks rounded; males have a small, usually concealed white coronal patch, but females usually lack it. *Dull brown above,* wings with 3 obscure grayish white to buffyish wing-bars. *Below mostly pale dingy grayish brown,* grayest on throat, becoming whitish on midbelly and crissum.
SIMILAR SPECIES: *Shows no olive.* Among elaenias, most likely to be confused with Large and Mottle-backed (both of which can occur with this species) but *much browner than either.*
HABITAT AND BEHAVIOR: Locally fairly common in riparian growth on islands in the Amazon and its larger tributaries. Around Iquitos, Peru, found especially in canopy of uniform stands of taller *Cecropia* trees that grow on certain older islands (G. H. Rosenberg; M. Robbins). Hilty and Brown (1986) suggest it may move locally in response to seasonal fluctuations in river levels. We do not know its voice.
RANGE: Along the Amazon in Brazil downriver to the Rio Xingu, se. Colombia (a single sight report from the Leticia area), and ne. Peru (near Iquitos, and up the Río Napo from its mouth to the mouth of the Río Curaray); also recorded along various of the Amazon's major northward-flowing tributaries (Rios Juruá, Madeira, Tapajós, and Xingu), and up the Rio Madeira as far as extreme n. Bolivia (Pando). To 200 m.

Elaenia dayi

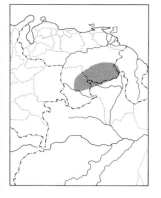

GREAT ELAENIA

DESCRIPTION: 20 cm (8″). *A very large, dark elaenia of the tepuis.* Above mostly dark sooty brown, blacker on crown (no semiconcealed white coronal patch); narrow eye-ring white; wings with 2 prominent whitish bars. Below mostly dull olive grayish, becoming pale yellowish on middle of belly. See V-29.
SIMILAR SPECIES: No likely confusion in its restricted range. *Much larger and darker than other elaenias (Sierran, Plain-crested, Rufous-crowned) with which possibly sympatric. Cf. also various* Myiarchus *flycatchers (which Great Elaenia equals in size).*
HABITAT AND BEHAVIOR: Not well known. Recorded from forest and forest edge habitats on slopes and summits of tepuis (Meyer de Schauensee and Phelps 1978). We do not know its voice. A few pairs

reside in the shrubbery and low woodland near the Soldier's Monument at the beginning of the Gran Sabana south of the Escalera in e. Bolívar.

RANGE: S. Venezuela (Bolívar and n. Amazonas). 1500–2600 m.

Elaenia ruficeps

RUFOUS-CROWNED ELAENIA

PLATE: 31

DESCRIPTION: 14.5 cm (5¾"). *Savannas of ne. South America.* At most slightly crested (usually looks round-headed) but with *rufous patch on rearcrown usually visible;* narrow white eye-ring. Above dark brownish olive, wings and tail duskier, wings with 2 whitish bars and edging. Below mostly pale yellowish, with *blurry but obvious grayish olive streaking on throat, breast, and flanks.*

SIMILAR SPECIES: Distinct from other elaenias on the basis of its rufous coronal patch and the streaking on underparts. Cf. especially Lesser and Plain-crested Elaenias (Rufous-crowned can occur with both).

HABITAT AND BEHAVIOR: Uncommon to locally common on savannas with scattered bushes and spiny palms and at edge of woodland, almost always in regions with sandy soil. Behavior much like other elaenias'; usually conspicuous. Its call in Surinam is a low growling burry "d-rr-rr-rr" (B. Whitney), with trogon-like quality.

RANGE: Locally in n. Surinam and n. French Guiana, and in adjacent extreme n. Brazil (n. Amapá); w. Guyana, s. Venezuela (Bolívar and Amazonas), and se. Colombia (Guainía and Vaupés west to Meta); very locally in Amaz. Brazil (recorded only from n. Roraima at Maracá Ecological Station, Faro along the lower Amazon, the lower Rio Madeira, and along the Rio Cururu in s. Pará). To 1400 m (on tepuis in s. Venezuela).

Sublegatus Scrub-Flycatchers

A small genus of elaenia-like flycatchers, but with much more retiring habits; they are characterized by their short, all-dark bill and lack of white in crown. Species-level taxonomy within *Sublegatus* remains controversial. We here consider the three main groups as full species, mainly because recent evidence shows that, in addition to plumage differences, they differ vocally. Because all three are so similar, we suggest using the group name "scrub-flycatcher" for all three, and then applying a geographical species epithet.

Sublegatus arenarum

NORTHERN SCRUB-FLYCATCHER

PLATE: 31

Other: Scrub Flycatcher (in part)

DESCRIPTION: 14 cm (5½"). *N. South America. Bill short and all black.* Olive brown above with *narrow but distinct whitish supraloral* and incomplete eye-ring; wings and tail duskier, wings with 2 brownish

white bars and edging. *Throat and breast gray, contrasting with pale yellow lower underparts.*

SIMILAR SPECIES: Cf. the confusingly similar Amazonian Scrub-Flycatcher, overlapping only in e. Venezuela and Guianas. Otherwise, Northern Scrub-Flycatcher is most likely confused with several *Elaenia* elaenias (e.g., Yellow-bellied and Lesser), but it differs in its short, all-black bill (elaenia bills are almost always pale on basal mandible), supraloral stripe (more distinct than in any elaenia), absence of white coronal patch, and more contrasty clear gray and yellow underparts. Northern Scrub- also somewhat resembles various *Myiarchus* flycatchers, but they are larger with much longer bills and no supraloral stripe.

HABITAT AND BEHAVIOR: Uncommon to fairly common in mangroves, dry scrub, and lighter deciduous woodland. Rather inconspicuous and quiet, the Northern Scrub-Flycatcher perches upright in low trees or shrubs (usually not out in the open), sallying after insects, either into the air or to a leaf. Often in pairs. Although generally quiet, occasionally gives several soft calls, among them a plaintive "peee," often doubled. Particularly numerous and easy to see in mangroves at Colombia's Salamanca Nat. Park.

RANGE: N. Colombia (Caribbean lowlands west to Sucre, and south in Río Magdalena valley to Bolívar, also in ne. llanos south to Meta), n. Venezuela, and Guianas; Trinidad and various small islands off n. coast of Venezuela (including Margarita and the Netherlands Antilles). Also Costa Rica and Panama. To about 500 m.

NOTE: See comments under Amazonian and Southern Scrub-Flycatchers.

Sublegatus obscurior

AMAZONIAN SCRUB-FLYCATCHER

Other: Scrub Flycatcher (in part)

DESCRIPTION: 14 cm (5½"). Resembles Northern Scrub-Flycatcher (overlapping that species only marginally) but *decidedly dingier below*, with duller gray throat *blending* into yellow belly (*lacking obvious contrast*).

SIMILAR SPECIES: Over most of South America, simply identifying to the genus *Sublegatus* will suffice, because for the most part the 3 species are allopatric. Southern Scrub-Flycatcher does migrate north into range of the Amazonian during austral winter; it is shorter-billed and has bolder and whiter wing-bars and edging, as well as more contrast between its grayish olive breast and pale yellow belly. In Guianas, Amazonian Scrub- occurs inland in clearings and forest edge situations, whereas Northern Scrub- is found mainly along coast, primarily in mangroves (presumably this is also the situation in ne. Venezuela); they may also occur together in Meta, Colombia.

HABITAT AND BEHAVIOR: Rare to uncommon and local (overlooked?) in borders of terra firme forest and adjacent clearings. Rather quiet and inconspicuous, at least in Ecuador tending to occur as sedentary pairs. The song (in Ecuador) is a repeated, rather sweet "chwedeé . . . chwedeé . . . , chuweeé . . . ," often continuing for several minutes without pause (M. B. Robbins recording).

RANGE: Guianas, e. and s. Venezuela (north to Sucre and Delta Amacuro), e. Colombia (north to Meta), e. Ecuador (recent specimens [ANSP] from Morona-Santiago and Napo, and an undated "Ecuador" specimen in FMNH [*fide* M. Traylor, Jr.]), e. Peru, n. Bolivia (Beni), and Amaz. Brazil (east to e. Pará in the Belém region). To at least 400 m.

NOTE: This taxon was raised to species rank by M. A. Traylor, Jr., in *Birds of the World*, vol. 8, but was then subsequently (Traylor 1982) considered a subspecies of *S. modestus*. Recent information on vocal differences leads us to give it species rank, though the possibility of limited intergradation between *S. obscurior* and *S. m. modestus* in Amaz. Brazil remains (see Traylor 1982).

Sublegatus modestus

SOUTHERN SCRUB-FLYCATCHER
Other: Short-billed Flycatcher, Scrub Flycatcher (in part)

DESCRIPTION: 14 cm (5½"). Widespread in s.-cen. South America *mainly south of range of Amazonian Scrub-Flycatcher* (but with some overlap during austral winter). Resembles Northern Scrub-Flycatcher but *bill even shorter* and *wing-bars bolder and whiter* (not so brownish).
SIMILAR SPECIES: Amazonian Scrub-Flycatcher has somewhat longer bill, decidedly less conspicuous wing markings, and is dingier below with less contrast between breast and belly (in this, Northern and Southern Scrub-Flycatchers are quite similar).
HABITAT AND BEHAVIOR: Uncommon in scrub and lighter woodland, usually in quite arid areas (at least when breeding). General behavior similar to Northern Scrub-Flycatcher's, equally quiet and inconspicuous most of the time. The song is rather similar to Northern Scrub-'s, though sharper and more penetrating; it is a slowly repeated, rather high-pitched single note, "pseeeu . . . pseeeu . . . pseeeu. . . ."
RANGE: N. and e. Bolivia (northwest to La Paz and Beni), much of cen. and s. Brazil (s. Mato Grosso, s. Pará, s. Maranhão, and Pernambuco south to Paraná; absent from the coastal southeast, and all but extreme w. Rio Grande do Sul), Paraguay (except the southeast), Uruguay, and n. and cen. Argentina (south to Mendoza, La Pampa, and sw. Buenos Aires). The s. population (*brevirostris*) is at least partially migratory, with a few records from as far north as se. Peru (s. Ucayali and Madre de Dios) and w. Amaz. Brazil; apparently, however, some birds remain in Argentina throughout the year (e.g., Wetmore 1926, Nores et al. 1983). Mostly below 1000 m, locally to over 2000 m in arid intermontane valleys on e. slope of Andes in Bolivia.

NOTE: See comments under Amazonian Scrub-Flycatcher. "Short-billed Flycatcher," sometimes suggested as an English name for this species (e.g., Hilty and Brown 1986), is accurate for this species (*sensu stricto:* when the relatively long-billed *obscurior* is excluded), but we prefer to use the group name "scrub-flycatcher" for all members of the genus.

Myiopagis Elaenias

A confusing, difficult genus of fairly small flycatchers, closely related to *Elaenia* but so far considered distinct. The five species now assigned to it are a rather diverse lot, though all have either white or yellow in the crown and, unlike *Elaenia,* tend to be dark-capped. Some have strong wing-bars, others have quite plain wings. Some perch vertically, others usually more horizontally. No *Myiopagis* is as conspicuous or noisy as most *Elaenia* elaenias, as *Myiopagis* elaenias tend to remain in heavy foliage and have softer, often overlooked calls.

GROUP A

Prominent yellowish to white wing-bars; usually in forest.

Myiopagis gaimardii

FOREST ELAENIA   PLATE: 31

DESCRIPTION: 12.5 cm (5″). A widespread but inconspicuous small tyrannid of lowland forest canopy and edge; note its *rather narrow short bill* and *usually quite horizontal posture.* Head brownish gray, darker on crown, with indistinct whitish supraloral and *white to yellowish white coronal stripe* (often concealed). Otherwise olive to brownish olive above, wings and tail duskier, wings with *2 prominent yellowish bars.* Throat whitish, *breast pale yellow mottled with olive* (often looking *streaky*); belly and crissum fairly bright pale yellow. *Macilvainii* (n. Colombia) similar but with coronal stripe bright pale yellow.

SIMILAR SPECIES: Frequently confused; often its distinctive voice (see below) is the best clue to its identity. Occurs regularly with certain *Tolmomyias* flycatchers (Yellow-margined and Gray-crowned); these have broader, flatter bills, no coronal stripe, etc. Also occurs with similar but smaller Slender-footed Tyrannulet; Slender-footed further differs in having a pale (not dark) iris and no coronal stripe. Cf. also Yellow-crowned Tyrannulet and female Gray Elaenia.

HABITAT AND BEHAVIOR: Fairly common in canopy and borders of humid and (to a reduced degree) deciduous forest and woodland, less often in younger secondary woodland. Generally remains well above ground, where hard to see well or become very familiar with. Often forages with mixed flocks, gleaning in foliage, cocking its tail slightly. The frequently heard, distinctive call is a sharp, emphatic "pitchweét," usually with a long pause between repetitions; learn this call well, for many birds will be heard for every one seen.

RANGE: Widespread south to n. and e. Bolivia (south to La Paz, Cochabamba, and Santa Cruz) and cen. Brazil (south to Mato Grosso do Sul, n. São Paulo, and Goiás); ne. Brazil (Alagoas); west of Andes only in n. Colombia and nw. Venezuela; Trinidad. Also Panama. To about 1000 m along e. base of Andes.

Myiopagis flavivertex

YELLOW-CROWNED ELAENIA

DESCRIPTION: 13 cm (5″). *Guianas to w. Amazonia.* Resembles Forest Elaenia, from which it differs by its slightly larger *bright golden yellow coronal patch* (whitish in sympatric Forest Elaenias); brownish olive sides of crown (no gray tone); slightly yellower wing-bars; and *no vaguely streaked effect on breast* (more of an olive *wash*). Behavior also markedly different.

SIMILAR SPECIES: Greenish Elaenia is also similar (its coronal patch is much the same) but has no wing-bars. Cf. also female Gray Elaenia.

HABITAT AND BEHAVIOR: Uncommon (but inconspicuous and usually overlooked until its distinctive voice is recognized) in lower and middle growth of várzea forest and in swampy forest in sandy-soil regions. Usually found singly or in pairs, perching upright, and only rarely with mixed flocks. Its call is a distinctive loud and sharp "jéw, jee-jee-jew," repeated at fairly long (5- to 10-second) intervals, sometimes varied to a faster and more involved "jéw-jijijijijijijijew-jew."

RANGE: Locally in s. and e. Venezuela (Amazonas and Delta Amacuro); Surinam and French Guiana (not recorded from Guyana but seems likely to occur) and Amaz. Brazil (upriver to near the mouth of the Rio Juruá); e. Peru (Loreto and Ucayali), ne. Ecuador (recorded from various sites in the Ríos Napo and Aguarico drainages [ANSP]), and extreme w. Brazil (upper Rio Juruá). To 300 m.

Myiopagis caniceps

GRAY ELAENIA   PLATE: 31

DESCRIPTION: 12.5 cm (5"). *Sexually dimorphic: males very gray overall,* females olive and yellow. Male of more n. and w. *cinerea* (with *parambae* from west of Andes) is *blue-gray above* with white coronal streak (often concealed); wings black with *2 prominent white bars and broad edging. Throat and breast paler gray,* becoming grayish white on belly. Female (and some males, perhaps young?) *mostly bright olive above,* with only head gray and coronal streak pale yellow (white in *parambae*); wings as in male but with *markings bright pale yellow.* Throat grayish white, with remaining underparts pale greenish yellow, brightest on belly. More s. and e. nominate race similar, but male duller gray (not so blue and often suffused with olive, especially on back), female with grayish chest and only a wash of yellow on belly; both sexes have somewhat less bold wing markings.

SIMILAR SPECIES: In pattern vaguely reminiscent of some becards, but shape and behavior markedly different. Gray males are distinctive, but females are more difficult and are unlikely to be identified away from attendant males; they especially resemble Forest Elaenia but have a brighter olive back which contrasts more with gray crown, bolder wing markings, and lack mottling on breast. Cf. also chaco form (nominate) of Suiriri Flycatcher.

HABITAT AND BEHAVIOR: Rare to locally uncommon in canopy and borders of humid forest (in both terra firme and várzea). Not well known, but specimen numbers seem to indicate that the nominate race (of s. and e. part of range) is more numerous than *cinerea.* Behavior generally like Forest Elaenia's, usually perching horizontally, often with tail somewhat cocked; usually feeds by gleaning in outer foliage. Because it normally forages so high above the ground, Gray Elaenia is probably often overlooked. A male in ne. Argentina perched rather upright as it gave a vocalization very different from Forest Elaenia's, a fast, loud, chippering trill, introduced by a longer note, then gradually dropping in intensity. Around Manaus a very different, 2- or 3-noted buzzy call has been heard regularly (D. Stotz).

RANGE: Pacific w. Colombia and nw. Ecuador (recorded locally south to w. Cañar, but few records); lower slopes of Sierra de Perijá in nw.

Venezuela; s. Venezuela (w. Bolívar and Amazonas), w. Amaz. Brazil (east to the Manaus area and south into Rondônia), e. Ecuador (few records), e. Peru (recorded locally from Loreto and Ucayali, with a recent FMNH specimen and other sightings from Madre de Dios; D. Stotz et al.), n. and e. Bolivia (recorded mainly along base of Andes from La Paz to Tarija, with 1 record from extreme e. Santa Cruz at Santiago de Chiquitos), nw. Argentina (Jujuy and Salta), locally in s. and e. Brazil (s. Mato Grosso east and north to Maranhão, Ceará, and e. Bahia, and south to n. Rio Grande do Sul), e. Paraguay (west to Paraguarí), and ne. Argentina (Misiones and ne. Corrientes); French Guiana (few records). Also Panama. To 1200 m.

NOTE: J. M. Cardoso da Silva (*Goeldiana*, Zoología, Núm. 1, 1990) showed that what was known as *Serpophaga araguayae* (Bananal Tyrannulet), known from a single specimen taken on Bananal Is. in Goiás, Brazil, is actually an example of *Myiopagis c. caniceps*.

GROUP B

Wing-bars obscure or lacking, pale brownish to whitish; typically in drier habitats than Group A.

Myiopagis subplacens

PACIFIC ELAENIA   PLATE: 31

DESCRIPTION: 13.5 cm (5¼"). *W. Ecuador and nw. Peru.* Crown grayish brown with yellow coronal stripe; *broad superciliary grizzled whitish, arching around blackish ear-coverts.* Otherwise dull and rather pale brownish olive above, wings and tail somewhat duskier, wings with prominent pale yellowish edging (but wing-bars obscure or absent). Throat and breast pale grayish, blurrily streaked with white; belly pale yellow.

SIMILAR SPECIES: Resembles Greenish Elaenia. Compared to sympatric race of that species (*implacens*), Pacific is more brownish on head (not so gray), grayer across breast (with little or no olive), and in particular has a longer and wider superciliary (not just a white supraloral).

HABITAT AND BEHAVIOR: Fairly common in lower growth and borders of deciduous woodland and secondary scrub. Quiet and inconspicuous, usually perching rather upright. Seldom joins mixed flocks. The song is a sharply enunciated "cheet! woorrr-it" repeated at 3- to 4-second intervals.

RANGE: W. Ecuador (north to w. Esmeraldas and Manabí) and nw. Peru (Tumbes, Piura, and Lambayeque). To 1500 m.

Myiopagis viridicata

GREENISH ELAENIA

DESCRIPTION: 13.5 cm (5¼"). *A small, plain elaenia of deciduous woodland.* Resembles Pacific Elaenia. Mostly olive above with crown grayer in more n. races (more uniform farther south); *short supralorai stripe and eye-ring white;* coronal stripe yellow (often hidden). Wings and tail duskier, *wings with yellowish edging* (but *wing-bars obscure or lacking*). Throat pale grayish, blending into grayish olive breast; belly pale yellow. See V-29, C-37.

SIMILAR SPECIES: Forest Elaenia shows obvious wing-bars and has

whitish (not yellow) coronal patch over most of its range; it tends to perch more horizontally and to occur in more humid habitats. Cf. also range-restricted Pacific Elaenia. All *Tolmomyias* flycatchers have broader bills and more definite wing markings (usually bold bars). Sooty-headed Tyrannulet has a similar pattern but is much smaller, more yellow on breast, etc. Greenish Elaenia is also easily confused with the *Neopelma* tyrant-manakins, but they have a much plainer facial area, show less wing-edging, etc.

HABITAT AND BEHAVIOR: Fairly common but inconspicuous in lower growth of deciduous woodland, forest borders, gallery woodland, and clearings with scattered trees and shrubs; mostly in drier areas (thus avoiding much of Amazonia). Tends to remain within cover, perching quietly, and doubtless often overlooked. Its posture is usually vertical but during foraging may be more horizontal. The call is a slurred, buzzy "cheerip," less emphatic than the distinctly 2-noted call of Forest Elaenia.

RANGE: Venezuela (except absent from the extreme east and south); Colombia (east of Andes south to Guainía and w. Putumayo; absent from Pacific lowlands); w. Ecuador (w. Esmeraldas to El Oro and w. Loja); lower Amaz. Brazil (s. Amapá west to the lower Rio Tapajós area and the middle Rio Xingu); se. Peru (north to Cuzco and Ucayali), n. and e. Bolivia, e. Paraguay, n. Argentina (south in the northwest to Catamarca, in the northeast in Misiones and ne. Corrientes), and s. and e. Brazil (Ceará and Goiás south to n. Rio Grande do Sul, and west through Mato Grosso do Sul and s. Mato Grosso to Rondônia; absent from coastal se. lowlands). Also Mexico to Panama. Sight reports from French Guiana (Tostain et al. 1992) require verification. To 1300 m.

Phaeomyias and *Pseudelaenia* Tyrannulets

Phaeomyias is a monotypic genus now that the superficially similar *leucospodia* has been transferred out of it, first into *Myiopagis* (Traylor 1977), more recently (Lanyon 1988a) with a new monotypic genus, *Pseudelaenia,* having been created for it. W. E. Lanyon (*Condor* 86[1]: 42–47, 1984) concluded that *Phaeomyias* is most closely related to *Capsiempis;* however, the two genera have decidedly dissimilar behavior and appearance. Lanyon (1988a) also suggests that, based on cranial and syringeal characters, the closest relative of *Pseudelaenia* is the very dissimilar *Stigmatura* (wagtail-tyrants). Because in the field the widespread and drab Mouse-colored and the range-restricted Gray-and-white Tyrannulets are so similar, we opt to treat them together here. Both species build cup nests, the Gray-and-white's being deep, "barrel-shaped," and notably "neat" (S. Marchant, *Ibis* 102[3]: 375, 1960).

Phaeomyias murina

MOUSE-COLORED TYRANNULET   PLATE: 32

DESCRIPTION: 12 cm (4¾"). *Notably nondescript.* Rather thick bill with mandible flesh-colored at least at base. *Brownish olive to dull brown above*

with *weak whitish superciliary;* wings duskier with *2 brownish white to buffy ochraceous wing-bars.* Throat whitish becoming dull olive grayish on breast; belly pale yellow to whitish. Birds of Venezuela and Colombia (*incomta*) are the brownest above; see V-30, C-36. Birds of w. Peru from Piura to Lima (*inflava*) are the whitest below and have the strongest ochraceous wing-bars; *tumbezana* (sw. Ecuador to nw. Peru) and *maranonica* (upper Río Marañón valley of n. Peru) have similar wing-bars but are slightly more yellowish below. The s. nominate group (with *ignobilis*) has wing-bars more whitish.

SIMILAR SPECIES: Readily confused. Smaller Southern Beardless-Tyrannulet usually shows a bushy crest and often cocks its tail; it has little or no superciliary. Slender-billed Tyrannulet is even smaller; where their ranges overlap, Mouse-colored is browner above with buffier wing-bars. Plain Tyrannulet is smaller and slimmer, grayer (not so brown) above, and is more active. In sw. Ecuador and nw. Peru, cf. Gray-and-white Tyrannulet. *Sublegatus* scrub-flycatchers have stubbier and all-black bills, and their underparts show more contrast.

HABITAT AND BEHAVIOR: Fairly common to common in scrub, lighter woodland, hedgerows, and parks and gardens. More widespread and numerous in arid to semiarid areas; in Amazonia and Guianas more or less restricted to várzea and river-edge habitats and natural savannas. Usually perches fairly upright except when gleaning for insects in foliage; also regularly eats fruit. Likely to be overlooked until its distinctive dry gravelly call, a fast chattering "jejejejejéjew" (varied to "jejeje-jejéw"), is learned. In sw. Ecuador *tumbezana* gives a very different, sharp and squeaky "squeéky, squeey-kit!"

RANGE: Widespread in semiopen areas south to n. Argentina (in the northwest south to La Rioja, in the northeast only in nw. Corrientes), Paraguay, and se. Brazil (south to São Paulo and Minas Gerais), though unrecorded from part of nw. Amazonia; west of Andes in sw. Ecuador (north to Manabí) and nw. Peru (south to Lima); Trinidad. Also Panama. Mostly below 1000 m, but locally up in intermontane valleys of Andes to about 2000 m.

NOTE: More than one species is perhaps involved. The strikingly different vocalization of birds from sw. Ecuador and nw. Peru needs more investigation, especially in the arid upper Río Marañón valley. If split, *P. tumbezana* (with *inflava* and probably *maranonica*) could be called the Tumbes Tyrannulet.

Pseudelaenia leucospodia

GRAY-AND-WHITE TYRANNULET

DESCRIPTION: 12.5 cm (5"). *Sw. Ecuador and nw. Peru.* Pale base of lower mandible. Mostly grayish brown above with *nearly always exposed white showing in crest* (usually conspicuous, often with somewhat bifurcated effect) and a faint whitish supraloral; wings with *dull grayish to whitish edging. Below whitish,* sometimes faintly tinged yellow on belly.

SIMILAR SPECIES: Dull-plumaged, but the distinctive white in crest is always obvious. Mouse-colored Tyrannulet lacks any white in its crown, and in sympatric races its wing-bars are rufescent (not grayish). Southern Beardless-Tyrannulet is smaller and, though obviously

bushy-crested, also lacks white in crown; its wing markings are more pronounced than Gray-and-white's.

HABITAT AND BEHAVIOR: Uncommon to locally fairly common in scrub and low trees in arid regions, favoring desert washes and dry streambeds. Gleans actively in foliage, usually perching horizontally, sometimes with the tail partially cocked; at times the tail is even slowly wagged. Its call is a simple, short, sharp "chevit" or "chevit-chet." Frequent on the Santa Elena Peninsula of w. Guayas, Ecuador, and numerous on Isla de la Plata.

RANGE: Sw. Ecuador (locally in w. Guayas, and on Isla de la Plata off s. Manabí) and nw. Peru (Tumbes south to La Libertad). Mostly below 300 m.

Camptostoma Beardless-Tyrannulets

A widespread, small tyrannulet of semiopen lowlands; an additional species occurs in Middle America. In plumage the Southern Beardless- is much like the Mouse-colored Tyrannulet, though the animated behavior and perky crest of Southern Beardless- are decidedly different. The nest is a globular structure with a side entrance, notably different from nests of the superficially similar Mouse-colored and Gray-and-white Tyrannulets.

Camptostoma obsoletum

SOUTHERN BEARDLESS-TYRANNULET   PLATE: 32

DESCRIPTION: 9.5–10.5 cm (3¾–4¼"). *A widespread, usually common tyrannulet of semiopen areas and borders.* Usually looks distinctly *bushy-crested;* bill rather thick, with lower mandible at least basally pale. Southern nominate group (north to w. Ecuador, se. Peru, and cen. and ne. Brazil) is dull olive to grayish olive above, grayest on crown with weak whitish supraloral and narrow eye-ring; wings duskier with *2 well-marked pale ochraceous to cinnamon wing-bars.* Throat whitish, becoming pale olive grayish on breast, and whitish to yellowish white on belly. Northern races (south to ne. Peru and along the Amazon in Brazil) are yellower below (clear yellow on belly), have wing-bars whitish to pale yellowish, and usually look dark-capped; they tend to be smaller than the more s. and w. nominate group.

SIMILAR SPECIES: Learning to recognize this numerous tyrannulet is vital. Confusion is most likely with less-active Mouse-colored Tyrannulet; cf. also in n. Colombia and nw. Venezuela the Slender-billed Tyrannulet, in w. Ecuador and nw. Peru the Gray-and-white Tyrannulet, and in the south various *Serpophaga* and *Phyllomyias* tyrannulets. None of these shows this species' mannerisms, and voices of many will help.

HABITAT AND BEHAVIOR: Fairly common to very common and widespread in scrub, lighter woodland, gardens and clearings, even forest borders and (in Amazonia) the canopy of várzea forest. Southern Beardless-Tyrannulet tolerates a wide variety of ecological conditions and occurs in both arid and humid regions. It is absent only from extensively forested regions, and even there it seems able quickly to colonize newly cleared areas. Usually confiding, foraging actively in foliage at all levels, gleaning much like a vireo or warbler; its perky crest is nearly continuously raised, and its tail is usually held slightly cocked. Occurs regularly with mixed flocks but also often moves about independently. The call is a distinctive, melancholy (minor-keyed) series of quite loud notes, "plee-plee-pee-pee" (often slightly descending, sometimes 3 or 5 notes). Also often gives a usually doubled "toreé-toreé," or a simple, slightly huskier "feeee."

RANGE: Widespread south to n. Argentina (south to San Juan, San Luis, Córdoba, Santa Fe, and Entre Ríos) and Uruguay; west of Andes in w. Ecuador (north to w. Esmeraldas) and w. Peru (south to Lima); Trinidad. Also Costa Rica and Panama. Mostly below 2000 m, locally to over 2500 m in arid intermontane valleys of Andes.

NOTE: More than one species could be involved. The variation in vocalizations seems worthy of investigation, particularly if it can be correlated with distribution. This variation actually seems to exceed the minor vocal differences shown between the northwesternmost race (*flaviventre*) of *C. obsoletum* and *C. imberbe* (Northern Beardless-Tyrannulet) of Middle America.

Tyrannulus Tyrannulets

A monotypic genus, rather weakly defined, probably most closely related to *Myiopagis*. It looks most like various *Zimmerius* tyrannulets but differs in its yellow coronal patch, stronger wing-bars, and posture. Found widely in semiopen and edge areas in tropical lowlands.

Tyrannulus elatus

YELLOW-CROWNED TYRANNULET   PLATE: 32

DESCRIPTION: 10.5 cm (4¼"). *Stubby black bill*. Above olive with slaty crown and *gray superciliary* above dusky line through eye; coronal stripe yellow, often hidden or barely showing (most evident when bird is calling). Wings duskier with 2 distinct yellowish white wing-bars and edging. *Throat and sides of head pale grayish*, with remaining underparts clear yellow, clouded olive on breast.

SIMILAR SPECIES: Usually best recognized either by its *characteristic voice* or its *gray-faced look*. Resembles a small Forest Elaenia, but bill shape differs (elaenia's is longer), and the Yellow-crowned lacks the elaenia's blurry breast streaking (more an olive wash). Slender-footed Tyrannulet lacks the coronal patch and strong wing-bars, and its normal posture is horizontal with partially cocked tail (not more or less vertical). Cf. also Sooty-headed Tyrannulet (similar except for its wing pattern).

HABITAT AND BEHAVIOR: Fairly common to common in shrubby clearings and gardens, lighter woodland, and forest borders. Usually found singly, perching vertically; rarely accompanies mixed flocks. This inconspicuous bird, heard far more often than seen, is hard to spot even when calling as it usually remains within dense foliage. Its call is a distinctive clear whistled "pray-téer," constantly repeated at fairly long intervals, often even in the heat of the day.

RANGE: Colombia, Venezuela (except much of cen. part), Guianas, w. and e. Ecuador (south on w. slope to se. Guayas), e. Peru, n. Bolivia (south to La Paz and Cochabamba), and Amaz. Brazil (east to n. Maranhão, and south to Rondônia and n. Mato Grosso). Also Costa Rica and Panama. To about 1000 m.

Ornithion Tyrannulets

Very small, inconspicuous tyrannulets found in forest canopy and edge in tropical lowlands. Both species in South America have a well-marked superciliary. Two species (one of them wholly Middle American in distribution, the Yellow-bellied Tyrannulet) are notably short-tailed; the White-lored, however, is not.

Ornithion brunneicapillum

BROWN-CAPPED TYRANNULET   PLATE: 32
Other: Yellow-bellied Tyrannulet

DESCRIPTION: 8 cm (3¼"). *N. Venezuela to w. Ecuador.* A tiny, plain tyrannulet with a *very short tail* and bold but simple face pattern. Bill relatively thick, black. Olive above with *dark brown crown* and *prominent short white superciliary;* wings duskier with inconspicuous greenish edging (*no wing-bars*). *Entirely bright yellow below,* faintly tinged olive on breast. Birds from w. Ecuador (apparently unnamed) have grayer crown.
SIMILAR SPECIES: Most tyrannulets in its range, other than Sooty-headed, have wing-bars. Does not occur with (nor does it particularly resemble) congeneric White-lored Tyrannulet.
HABITAT AND BEHAVIOR: Uncommon to fairly common in canopy and borders of humid forest and secondary woodland, and in adjacent clearings and plantations. Inconspicuous and apt to be overlooked until its distinctive call is learned. Forages by gleaning in foliage and on smaller branches at all heights but usually high; quite often with mixed flocks. Does not cock tail. Its call is a series of fast, high, piping whistled notes with a characteristic pause after the first note, "peee, pih-pey-peh-puh," the cadence unmistakable.
RANGE: N. and nw. Venezuela (east on lower slopes of coastal mts. to Miranda), n. and w. Colombia (north of Santa Marta Mts., Pacific lowlands, and humid Caribbean lowlands east along n. base of Andes to middle Río Magdalena valley in Antioquia), and w. Ecuador (south to nw. Guayas and El Oro). Also Costa Rica and Panama. Mostly below 700 m, locally to 1200 m in Venezuela.

NOTE: *O. brunneicapillum* is considered a species distinct from *O. semiflavum* (the true Yellow-bellied Tyrannulet of Middle America), following *Birds of the World*, vol. 8, and the 1983 AOU Checklist (see also Stiles and Smith 1980).

Ornithion inerme

WHITE-LORED TYRANNULET   PLATE: 32

DESCRIPTION: 8.5 cm (3½"). Olive above with dark gray crown; *prominent, though narrow and short, superciliary and narrow eye-ring (producing a spectacled look);* wings duskier with *2 rows of large yellowish white*

spots on wing-coverts, forming "white-spotted wing-bars." Throat grayish white, becoming yellowish olive on breast and clear yellow on belly. SIMILAR SPECIES: Numerous other tyrannulets show solid wing-bars, but White-lored is unique in having wing-bars obviously made up of a series of discrete spots.

HABITAT AND BEHAVIOR: Uncommon to fairly common but inconspicuous in canopy and borders of humid forest and woodland, both in terra firme and várzea but especially near water (margins of oxbow lakes, rivers, etc.). Generally remains high above the ground and thus is difficult to observe; occurs singly or in pairs, regularly with mixed flocks. Most apt to be seen well when a canopy flock comes lower, e.g., along edge of a lake or road. White-lored Tyrannulet will often be overlooked until its call, a persistently repeated, high-pitched, and rather sharp "pee, dee-deet" or "pee, dee-dee-deet," is recognized.

RANGE: Guianas, s. Venezuela (Bolívar and Amazonas), se. Colombia (few records, but known north to e. Vichada), e. Ecuador, e. Peru (south to Madre de Dios), n. Bolivia (south to La Paz and cen. Santa Cruz), and Amaz. Brazil (east to n. Maranhão, and south locally to Rondônia and n. Goiás); e. Brazil (Alagoas south locally to Rio de Janeiro). To about 900 m.

Zimmerius Tyrannulets

This newly erected genus (Traylor 1977) comprises seven stubby-billed tyrannulets formerly in the now suppressed genus *Tyranniscus.* They are united by a wing pattern with well-marked yellow edging on the coverts and flight feathers (though there are no wing-bars) and a long, black, wedge-shaped patch along the inner primaries. Note that certain other tyrannulets, now placed in the genus *Phyllomyias,* share this pattern to some extent (e.g., the Sooty-headed, Gray-crowned, and Plumbeous-crowned). So far as known, the *Zimmerius* tyrannulets are mostly frugivorous; some specialize in eating mistletoe berries. They are found mainly in montane areas, with only one (the Slender-footed) occurring widely in the lowlands. All are forest-based birds, often very hard to identify.

GROUP A

Contrasting supraloral and *dark* iris; subtropical.

Zimmerius chrysops

GOLDEN-FACED TYRANNULET   PLATE: 32

DESCRIPTION: 11–11.5 cm (4¼–4½"). Mainly mts. from n. Venezuela to n. Peru. *Distinctively golden yellow on face.* Mostly olive above with *narrow frontlet, broad supraloral, and lower eyelid yellow;* wings and tail dusky, *wing-coverts and most flight feathers crisply edged yellow.* Throat yellowish white, becoming grayish white on remaining underparts. *Minimus* of Santa Marta Mts. is slightly smaller.

SIMILAR SPECIES: Venezuelan Tyrannulet has much the same pattern (including the wing markings) but has crown darker than back (either

gray or brown, but *not* concolor olive) and facial area white. The 2 species may occur together.

HABITAT AND BEHAVIOR: Common in canopy and borders of humid and montane forest, secondary woodland, and clearings and gardens with scattered trees and shrubbery. An active, conspicuous tyrannulet which gleans among outer foliage and often perches fully in the open, regularly on top of leaves. Sometimes with mixed flocks but at least as often away from them. Usually perches horizontally, its tail "half-cocked." Particularly numerous and widespread in Colombian Andes, where its frequently given clear call, "cleeuw," is one of the dominant sounds; also has other less distinctive vocalizations, but none resembles the common call of Peruvian Tyrannulet (with which formerly often considered conspecific). Birds in sw. Ecuador have an entirely different call, a rather loud and sharp, drawn out "truuu-eeét."

RANGE: Coastal mts. of ne. Venezuela (Sucre, n. Monagas, ne. Anzoátegui); Andes of w. Venezuela (north to Mérida and w. Barinas), Colombia, Ecuador (south on w. slope to El Oro and w. Loja; also locally out into more humid adjacent lowlands, on both sides of Andes), and n. Peru (south to San Martín); Sierra de Perijá on Venezuela-Colombia border, and Santa Marta Mts. of n. Colombia. Mostly 300–2400 m.

NOTE: We regard *Z. chrysops* of Venezuela to n. Peru as a species distinct from *Z. viridiflavus* of cen. Peru. J. T. Zimmer (*Am. Mus. Novitates* 1109, 1941) treated them as separate species. As far as we are aware, there is no evidence to justify Meyer de Schauensee's (1966, 1970) subsequent merging of these; in plumage they are quite different (for tyrannulets), their voices differ, and no intergradation between them has been shown. In addition, the primary vocalization of birds in El Oro and w. Loja, Ecuador, is strikingly different, and they show somewhat less facial yellow. They may prove to be a separate species (*Z. flavidifrons,* Loja Tyrannulet).

Zimmerius viridiflavus

PERUVIAN TYRANNULET

Other: Tschudi's Tyrannulet, Golden-faced Tyrannulet (in part)

DESCRIPTION: 11.5 cm (4½"). *Andes of cen. Peru;* formerly considered conspecific with Golden-faced Tyrannulet, *Z. chrysops*. Above mostly rather bright olive, but *crown distinctly gray; narrow frontlet, supraloral, and lower eyelid yellowish white;* wings and tail dusky, *wing-coverts and most flight feathers crisply edged yellow. Mostly pale yellow below,* heavily clouded with olive especially on breast and flanks.

SIMILAR SPECIES: Golden-faced Tyrannulet (no overlap) is obviously yellow on face, is whitish (not yellow) below, and has crown concolor with olive back (not contrastingly gray). Peruvian Tyrannulet most resembles Red-billed Tyrannulet, but latter occurs at lower elevations (mostly in foothills), has a yellow (not dark) iris, and has a much plainer face (lacking the whitish supraloral, etc.). Other montane tyrannulets in Peruvian's range that have a similar pattern show distinct wing-bars.

HABITAT AND BEHAVIOR: Fairly common in canopy and borders of montane forest and secondary woodland. Behavior similar to Golden-faced Tyrannulet's, which it replaces to the south. Its oft-repeated call is, however, distinctly different, a clear, fast, whistled "kleederoweéoo."

Can be found regularly in the Carpish Mts., along the road between Huánuco and Tingo María in Huánuco, Peru.

RANGE: E. slope of Andes in cen. Peru (Huánuco to Junín). Mostly 1000–2500 m.

NOTE: See comments under Golden-faced Tyrannulet. Given its restricted range, we feel *P. viridiflavus* should be called the Peruvian Tyrannulet, rather than the previously suggested (*Birds of the Americas*, vol. 13, part 5) Tschudi's Tyrannulet.

Zimmerius improbus

VENEZUELAN TYRANNULET

Other: Paltry Tyrannulet (in part)

DESCRIPTION: 11.5 cm (4½"). *Mts. of n. Venezuela and adjacent Colombia;* formerly considered conspecific with Paltry Tyrannulet, *Z. vilissimus*. Above mostly olive, with crown and lores dark brown, and *conspicuous narrow white frontlet, supraloral, and lower eyelid;* wings and tail dusky, with wing-coverts and most flight feathers crisply edged yellow. Throat whitish, becoming olive grayish on breast and pale yellowish on belly. *Petersi* (coastal mts. of n. Venezuela from Lara eastward) similar but with crown slaty; see V-30.

SIMILAR SPECIES: Golden-faced Tyrannulet has yellow on face and crown concolor with its olive back. Paltry Tyrannulet (no overlap) is smaller with a pale iris, much less clean-cut facial pattern, and more whitish underparts.

HABITAT AND BEHAVIOR: Uncommon to locally fairly common in canopy and borders of montane forest and secondary woodland, and in adjacent clearings. Found singly or in pairs, regularly foraging with mixed flocks. Its loud call consists of 3 or 4 notes given in succession, "wheeyr, wheeyr, wheeyr, wheeyr," then often with a long pause before being given again, usually at intervals of 2 or 3 minutes; being far-carrying, this call regularly heralds the approach of a bird flock (K. Zimmer).

RANGE: Coastal mts. of n. Venezuela (east to Miranda), and Andes of w. Venezuela and adjacent ne. Colombia (Norte de Santander); Sierra de Perijá on Venezuela-Colombia border and Santa Marta Mts. of n. Colombia. Mostly 1200–2400 m.

NOTE: We consider the montane *improbus* group of n. South America (with *tamae* and *petersi*) as a species distinct from *Z. vilissimus* (Paltry Tyrannulet), which is mainly found in Middle America. The two differ in size as well as coloration, and their vocalizations are very different; further, their ranges are disjunct and seemingly unassociated, *improbus* being subtropical, *vilissimus* basically tropical. As no English name seems to have been suggested since Hellmayr's (*Birds of the Americas*, vol. 13, part 5) "Mountain Tyrannulet"—which we regard as overly vague—and as its range falls primarily within Venezuela, we opt to call it the Venezuelan Tyrannulet.

GROUP B   *Weak* facial pattern with *pale* iris; most in tropical zone.

Zimmerius bolivianus

BOLIVIAN TYRANNULET   PLATE: 32

DESCRIPTION: 12 cm (4¾"). *E. slope of Andes in s. Peru and w. Bolivia.* Iris pale grayish. Uniform dark olive above (*including crown*) with *little or no facial pattern;* wings and tail duskier, *wing-coverts and most flight*

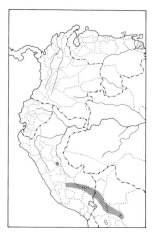

feathers narrowly and sharply edged yellow. Throat dull yellowish white, becoming pale yellowish olive on breast and flanks and clear pale yellow on belly.

SIMILAR SPECIES: A drab tyrannulet with no outstanding field marks but relatively easy to recognize in its range on the basis of its dull pattern and *olive* (not gray) crown. Other tyrannulets in its range and habitat all have wing-bars and stronger facial patterns.

HABITAT AND BEHAVIOR: Fairly common to common in canopy and borders of montane forest, secondary woodland, and adjacent clearings with scattered trees. Usually found singly, most often not with mixed flocks. Apparently feeds to a large extent on mistletoe berries. Vocalizes frequently, its most characteristic call being a rapid, whistled "whee-whee-whee-wheéoo" similar to the primary call of Peruvian Tyrannulet (Remsen et al. 1982). Readily seen in the yungas of Bolivia, and along the Shintuya-Paucartambo road in Cuzco, Peru.

RANGE: E. slope of Andes of s. Peru (on Cerros del Sira in e. Huánuco, and from Cuzco and n. Ayacucho southward) and w. Bolivia (La Paz and Cochabamba). 1000–2600 m.

NOTE: For more information on this species, see Remsen et al. (1982).

Zimmerius gracilipes

SLENDER-FOOTED TYRANNULET   PLATE: 32

DESCRIPTION: 10.5 cm (4″). *Guianas to Amazonia* (where the only *Zimmerius* tyrannulet present). Iris pale grayish. Above mostly olive with *gray crown, short whitish supraloral* (mainly just above eye), and grizzled gray and white lores; wings and tail dusky, *wing-coverts and most flight feathers edged yellow.* Throat grayish white, becoming grayish olive on breast and flanks and clear pale yellow on belly.

SIMILAR SPECIES: Often confused. Yellow-crowned Tyrannulet has dark (not pale) iris; grayer face with yellow coronal stripe (sometimes concealed, but conclusive if visible); much broader, whiter wing-bars; and more upright posture. Sooty-headed Tyrannulet has dark iris and much duller wing markings; its posture is also typically quite upright. Plumage of somewhat larger Forest Elaenia is similar (and the two often occur together, even foraging in the same flock); besides size, look for the elaenia's stronger wing-bars, blurry breast streaking, and (if visible) its coronal patch; the tail is relatively short. Cf. also the rare Red-billed Tyrannulet, and Golden-faced Tyrannulet (which usually occurs at higher elevations, though Golden-faced and Slender-footed may overlap along base of Andes).

HABITAT AND BEHAVIOR: Fairly common in canopy and borders of humid forest (both terra firme and várzea) and in adjacent clearings with scattered trees. Forages much like its congeners, tending to remain high above the ground and thus usually hard to see well, coming lower only at edge or in clearings. Its call in Surinam is a strident, measured "peeu, peeu, peeu, peeu . . ." (T. Davis recording); in Rondônia a series of 4–5 slurred, rising, whistled notes have been heard (D. Stotz); one common call (around Manaus at least) is a simple, soft "chef," often given as a bird perches on a high exposed branch or leaf in the canopy (RSR, A. Whittaker).

RANGE: Guianas, s. Venezuela (Bolívar and Amazonas), se. Colombia (north to Putumayo and e. Vichada), e. Ecuador (thus far only in Napo, but likely more widespread), e. Peru, n. Bolivia (south to La Paz, Cochabamba, and n. Santa Cruz), and Amaz. Brazil (east to n. Maranhão and n. Ceará, and south to Rondônia and n. Mato Grosso); ne. Brazil (Alagoas). Mostly below 500 m, though recorded higher in Venezuela and to 850 m in s. Peru.

Zimmerius vilissimus

PALTRY TYRANNULET

DESCRIPTION: 10 cm (4"). *Extreme nw. Colombia.* Iris pale grayish. Above mostly olive with gray crown and whitish supraloral; wings and tail dusky with *wing-coverts and most flight feathers crisply edged yellow. Below pale grayish,* slightly tinged pale yellowish on lower flanks and crissum. See P-25.

SIMILAR SPECIES: The only tyrannulet in its limited S. Am. range with the *Zimmerius* wing pattern and that lacks virtually all yellow below. Cf. Venezuelan Tyrannulet (with which formerly considered conspecific; no overlap) and Sooty-headed Tyrannulet (with dark iris and much less edging on wings).

HABITAT AND BEHAVIOR: Not well known in Colombia. In Panama (Ridgely and Gwynne 1989) common in canopy and borders of humid forest and secondary woodland and in adjacent clearings. Perky in appearance, though not very conspicuous; eats mainly mistletoe berries. Most likely noted by its characteristic call, an interminably repeated (though often at long intervals), whistled "peeayik."

RANGE: Nw. Colombia (nw. Chocó). Also Mexico to Panama. In Panama ranges up to about 1000 m, but in Colombia (so far) recorded only to 100 m.

NOTE: See comments under Venezuelan Tyrannulet. Traylor (1982) suggests that nominate *vilissimus* (s. Mexico, Guatemala, and El Salvador) and *parvus* (the form found from Honduras to nw. Colombia) may themselves not be conspecific.

Zimmerius cinereicapillus

RED-BILLED TYRANNULET

DESCRIPTION: 12 cm (4½"). *Local in foothills along e. base of Andes in Ecuador and Peru. Iris straw yellow;* bill blackish above, purplish flesh below. Closely resembles Slender-footed Tyrannulet but with *facial pattern essentially plain,* with no whitish supraloral and gray crown contrasting more with brighter olive back; *brighter and clearer yellow below* (though breast is distinctly flammulated with olive). The 2 species usually segregate by range and elevation.

SIMILAR SPECIES: Bill color is usually difficult to discern in the field. Besides the Slender-footed, Red-billed could be confused with Peruvian Tyrannulet which, however, has a dark iris, conspicuous yellowish white supraloral, and less pronounced wing-bars. Bolivian Tyrannulet has olive (not gray) crown and shows less pronounced wing-bars.

HABITAT AND BEHAVIOR: Rare to locally fairly common in humid foothill forest and forest borders; though probably often overlooked, this species seems genuinely more numerous in s. Peru than in Ecuador. Usually found singly, foraging with mixed flocks high above the ground; active and often hover-gleaning. Its call is a fast, somewhat musical "chirchedededede-whét-whét." Can be seen along lower part of the Shintuya-Paucartambo road in Cuzco, Peru.

RANGE: E. slope of Andes in e. Ecuador (known definitely only from w. Napo; probably also in Zamora-Chinchipe and likely elsewhere) and e. Peru (Huánuco south locally to e. Cuzco and Madre de Dios; in Cuzco and Madre de Dios known from recently obtained FMNH specimens and from sight records, *fide* D. Stotz). 750–1200 m.

Phyllomyias Tyrannulets

A diverse genus of tyrannulets whose short bills are either all dark or have a pale lower mandible (four species, formerly in the genera *Acrochordopus* and *Xanthomyias*, have the latter). Unlike *Zimmerius*, most *Phyllomyias* have well-marked wing-bars, though the wings of the Sooty-headed are quite plain. Most lack the crisp yellow wing edging of *Zimmerius*, though two species (Gray-capped and Plumbeous-crowned), formerly in the genus *Oreotriccus*, have it but to a reduced degree. *Phyllomyias* tyrannulets are found mostly in the Andes or other highland areas (with many species in se. South America), where they range primarily in humid forest.

They are a confusing, difficult lot. Among the genera most apt to be confused with *Phyllomyias* are typical *Phylloscartes* (which have longer bills and usually a longer, often cocked tail), the *Pogonotriccus* subgenus of *Phylloscartes* (though these tend to perch more upright), *Mecocerculus* (which tend to have very bold wing-bars and superciliaries), and *Zimmerius* (which tend to cock their shorter tails).

Various species have been transferred by taxonomists between these genera, and this has resulted in confusing systematics. In the most recent revision (Traylor 1977, 1978, and 1982), *Xanthomyias*, *Tyranniscus* (except for some that were placed in the new genus *Zimmerius*), *Oreotriccus*, and *Acrochordopus* were all subsumed into *Phyllomyias*. We follow Traylor in these generic mergers.

GROUP A

Wing-bars *obscure*.

Phyllomyias griseiceps

SOOTY-HEADED TYRANNULET   PLATE: 32

DESCRIPTION: 10 cm (4"). *A very plain tyrannulet found locally in n. South America.* Iris dark gray to brown. *Crown sooty brownish,* becoming grayer on sides of head, and with narrow white supraloral stripe; otherwise olive above, duskier on wings and tail with *obscure narrow whitish edgings* (*no evident wing-bars*). Throat grayish white; remaining underparts pale yellow, breast clouded with olive.

SIMILAR SPECIES: Has the *plainest wings* of any similar tyrannulet. All

other *Phyllomyias* have wing-bars; *Zimmerius* have no wing-bars but, rather, sharp wing-edging (much more pronounced than in this species). Greenish Elaenia has a somewhat similar pattern and is also plain-winged but is notably larger, etc. Cf. also Yellow-crowned Tyrannulet.

HABITAT AND BEHAVIOR: Uncommon to locally fairly common in forest borders and clearings with scattered trees; occurs mostly in humid regions. Usually in pairs, perching upright and foraging independently of mixed flocks, but sometimes comes to fruiting trees; overall appearance and comportment resemble the better-known Yellow-crowned Tyrannulet's. Frequently overlooked (there are relatively few specimens), especially until its characteristic voice, a rather loud, bright, rhythmic (even rollicking) "whip, whip-dip-irip" or "whit, whit-wheeu" (with a distinctive cadence somewhat like Yellow Tyrannulet's), is learned. Frequent in Colombia's Tayrona Nat. Park and around the Tinalandia Hotel in w. Ecuador.

RANGE: Locally in w. Colombia (Santa Marta region, Río Magdalena and Río Cauca valleys, and nw. Chocó), w. and e. Ecuador (in the west recorded from w. Esmeraldas south to El Oro and w. Loja; in the east known locally from w. Napo, Morona-Santiago, and Zamora-Chinchipe, mainly along base of Andes), e. Peru (along base of Andes from San Martín south to Junín and Ayacucho at Hacienda Luisiana); slopes of Sierra de Perijá on Colombia-Venezuela border, locally in n. and e. Venezuela, and w. Guyana (Annai; other published specimens prove to be Slender-footed Tyrannulets); locally along lower Amazon in n. Brazil (near Manaus and Óbidos). Also Panama. To about 1800 m.

GROUP B

Mainly *se. South America,* with all but Gray-capped having basically *concolor crowns.*

Phyllomyias griseocapilla

GRAY-CAPPED TYRANNULET

PLATE: 32

DESCRIPTION: 11 cm (4¼"). An attractive, *brightly marked* tyrannulet of *se. Brazil. Crown, nape, and sides of head gray* contrasting with *bright olive back;* quite conspicuous area around eye whitish; wings duskier, *feathers sharply edged with yellow* but wing-bars rather narrow. Throat pale gray, becoming grayish white on middle of remaining underparts, with *sides and flanks bright greenish yellow.*

SIMILAR SPECIES: Other similar tyrannulets in range show more obvious wing-bars, and none has contrasting bright yellow on sides. This species resembles geographically distant Paltry Tyrannulet.

HABITAT AND BEHAVIOR: Uncommon to fairly common in forest borders and shrubby clearings with scattered trees. Usually found singly, tending to forage low, and often hover-gleaning; sometimes with flocks but at least as often apart from them. Frequently eats mistletoe berries. A quiet bird, though individuals sometimes give a soft, whistled "wheeuw-wheeuw-wheeuw-wheeuw," sometimes only 1 or 2 notes (D. Stotz; RSR). Small numbers can be seen at Itatiaia Nat. Park.

RANGE: Se. Brazil (e. Minas Gerais and Espírito Santo south to e. Santa Catarina). To about 1600 m.

NOTE: Formerly classified in the genus *Oreotriccus. Griseocapilla* may be as close, perhaps even closer, to *Zimmerius* as it is to *Phyllomyias,* but we nonetheless follow *Birds of the World,* vol. 8, in transferring it to the latter.

Phyllomyias fasciatus

PLANALTO TYRANNULET   PLATE: 32

DESCRIPTION: 11–11.5 cm (4¼–4½"). *Dull and easily confused.* Brownish olive above, darker and more grayish on crown, with short supraloral and eye-ring white; wings and tail duskier, wings with *2 dull olive whitish wing-bars* and edging. Throat whitish; remaining underparts clear yellow but clouded grayish olive on breast. Nominate race and *cearae* (n. part of range south to Goiás and s. Mato Grosso) are slightly smaller and duller than *brevirostris,* with somewhat grayer crowns, more whitish wing-bars, and paler yellow lower underparts.

SIMILAR SPECIES: *Closely* resembles Rough-legged Tyrannulet (which see). Greenish Tyrannulet is also quite similar but is brighter olive above with crown concolor (not darker and duskier), brighter yellow below, and has bolder yellow wing-bars and somewhat longer tail; cf. also Reiser's and Mottle-cheeked Tyrannulets. Southern Beardless-Tyrannulet has more ochraceous wing-bars and tends to look bushy-crested (Planalto always round-headed). Cf. also White-crested Tyrannulet (grayer above with crisper and whiter wing-bars and, if showing, a white coronal patch).

HABITAT AND BEHAVIOR: Fairly common to locally common in canopy and borders of humid and (to a lesser degree) deciduous forest and woodland, including gallery forests in cen. Brazil. Usually remains well above the ground, foraging singly or in pairs, often with tail partially cocked. Frequently accompanies mixed forest flocks. The distinctive call of *brevirostris* is a soft, clear, minor-keyed "pee, puu, puuit?," sometimes lacking the final "puuit?"; we are not familiar with the voice of nominate/*cearae* (the same?).

RANGE: E. Brazil (s. Maranhão, Piauí, and Ceará south to Rio Grande do Sul, and west locally across much of Goiás to s. Mato Grosso), extreme ne. Bolivia (ne. Santa Cruz on the Serranía de Huanchaca), e. Paraguay (Canendiyu and Alto Paraná), and ne. Argentina (Misiones); an isolated population on the Serranía Pilón in s. Beni, Bolivia. Reported to be only a summer resident in Rio Grande do Sul, Brazil (Belton 1985), but there seems as yet no actual evidence of long-distance migration. To about 1800 m.

Phyllomyias virescens

GREENISH TYRANNULET

DESCRIPTION: 12 cm (4¾"). *Se. Brazil area. A brighter, somewhat longer-tailed version of Planalto Tyrannulet;* the two are often found together. Brighter, purer olive above with *crown concolor* (not duskier or grayer); *wing-bars bolder* (wider and more sharply defined) and paler yellow. Below brighter clear yellow, with breast flammulated with olive (not clouded grayish olive).

SIMILAR SPECIES: Cf. *very* similar Reiser's Tyrannulet. Greenish also

closely resembles Mottle-cheeked Tyrannulet, but Mottle-cheeked is shorter-billed and lacks the grizzled facial effect. Rough-legged Tyrannulet has the dullest wing-bars of any of this group of tyrannulets (not nearly as discrete as in Greenish), and its throat and breast are rather uniform dull olive.

HABITAT AND BEHAVIOR: Uncommon in canopy and borders of humid forest. Not well known, though behavior apparently differs little from its congeners'. Numbers may have declined toward s. edge of its range, as in the past numerous specimens were taken near Iguazú Falls and in Rio Grande do Sul, though there are only a few recent records from either area, even in the areas where forest habitat remains. Its call is a rapid series of staccato, almost stuttered "ch" sounds, at first rising in pitch, then dropping at end and slowing, quite unlike calls of Planalto, Rough-legged, and Mottle-cheeked Tyrannulets.

RANGE: Se. Brazil (Espírito Santo south to Rio Grande do Sul and west to s. Mato Grosso do Sul), e. Paraguay (west to Paraguarí), and ne. Argentina (Misiones and ne. Corrientes). To at least 1400 m.

NOTE: Formerly placed in the genus *Xanthomyias*. See comments under Reiser's Tyrannulet.

Phyllomyias reiseri

REISER'S TYRANNULET

DESCRIPTION: 11.5–12 cm (4½–4¾"). *Very local in interior s.-cen. Brazil and ne. Paraguay, and in ne. Venezuela.* Closely resembles Greenish Tyrannulet (with which it has been considered conspecific). Differs only in its slightly smaller size, paler yellow underparts and even brighter olive upperparts, *grayer crown* (not bright olive uniform with back), *whiter wing-bars* (not so yellow), and *plainer facial pattern* (yellowish ear-coverts and yellowish white lores and cheeks, lacking the grizzling found in Greenish). *Urichi* (ne. Venezuela) similar but slightly larger; see V-30 (there called Greenish Tyrannulet).

HABITAT AND BEHAVIOR: Not certainly known in life. Believed likely to inhabit gallery forest in cerrado region; has been collected at Brasília.

RANGE: Very locally in interior e. Brazil (recorded from a few localities in s. Piauí, s. Goiás, Distríto Federal, and e. Mato Grosso do Sul) and ne. Paraguay (Concepción at Zanja Morotí; likely also in Amambay); extreme ne. Venezuela (sw. Sucre, nw. Monagas, and ne. Anzoátegui). To 1000 m.

NOTE: This form has enjoyed a checkered taxonomic history, having at various times been regarded as a full species (e.g., Meyer de Schauensee 1966, 1970) or as a subspecies of *P. virescens* (e.g., *Birds of the Americas*, vol. 13, part 5; and Traylor 1982). D. F. Stotz (*Bull. B. O.C.* 110[4]: 184–187, 1990), having discovered several unrecognized specimens in the MZUSP, reviewed its status and concluded that it was best regarded as a separate species, with Venezuelan *urichi* as a subspecies of it (and not of *P. virescens*). Given the extreme range disjunction, *P. urichi* seems likely to prove to be a separate species in its own right (Urich's Tyrannulet).

Phyllomyias burmeisteri

ROUGH-LEGGED TYRANNULET

DESCRIPTION: 11.5 cm (4½"). Closely resembles Planalto Tyrannulet. Differs only in its slightly heavier bill with *pale grayish or pinkish lower*

mandible (bill all black in Planalto), brighter olive back with crown duller olive (but not darker and more grayish), and in showing less contrast between throat and breast (which are more or'less grayish olive). Their voices also differ (see below).

SIMILAR SPECIES: Various long-tailed tyrannulets (some of them sympatric) are very similar to the Rough-legged, and as a result their separation is often difficult, particularly as so many remain high in trees and are rarely seen closely. Greenish Tyrannulet has bolder wing-bars and shows more olive on breast (which contrasts with its throat); voices differ. Mottle-cheeked Tyrannulet has longer bill and a grizzled face.

HABITAT AND BEHAVIOR: Not well known; likely overlooked, as once its voice is recognized it proves to be locally not uncommon in canopy and borders of humid forest. Its call in se. South America is a high-pitched "psee-psee-psee-psee-psee-psee-psee-psee," falling slightly toward the end (T. A. Parker III; RSR). Small numbers can be found at lower elevations of Brazil's Itatiaia Nat. Park, though here as elsewhere it is more easily heard than seen.

RANGE: E. slope of Andes in Bolivia (recorded locally in La Paz, s. Beni, w. Santa Cruz, and Chuquisaca) and nw. Argentina (south to Tucumán); se. Brazil (Espírito Santo south to Rio Grande do Sul), ne. Argentina (Misiones), and e. Paraguay (west to Paraguarí; few records). To about 1300 m.

NOTE: Formerly placed in the genus *Acrochordopus*. We consider *P. zeledoni* (White-fronted Tyrannulet) of w. and n. South America (and Panama and Costa Rica) as a species distinct from *P. burmeisteri* of s. and e. South America, though recent sightings from w. Bolivia (see Parker et al. 1991) leave open the possibility of intergradation there.

GROUP C

Mainly *Andean* Group, with more or less *contrasting gray to dusky crowns.* A few have a dark auricular patch like *Phylloscartes.*

Phyllomyias zeledoni

WHITE-FRONTED TYRANNULET
Other: Rough-legged Tyrannulet (in part)

DESCRIPTION: 11.5 cm (4½"). *Local from n. South America to s. Peru.* Bill black above, mainly flesh or whitish below. Olive above with *slaty crown and white superciliary distinctly broader in front of eye and on forehead;* narrow line through eye dusky and lower face grizzled gray and white; wings dusky with 2 broad yellowish wing-bars and edging. Throat whitish, remaining underparts pale yellow, vaguely streaked with olive on breast. See P-25. Birds of coastal mts. of n. Venezuela (*viridiceps*) have crown olive with only forehead gray.

SIMILAR SPECIES: An obscure bird, often hard to identify. Most resembles Sclater's Tyrannulet but has a slatier crown and more white on forehead; they overlap only in s. Peru, with Sclater's occurring at higher elevations. Slender-footed Tyrannulet is also very similar but differs in its lack of definite wing-bars and grizzling on lower face, and in its all-dark bill; Slender-footed occurs mostly at lower elevations (though overlap is possible). White-fronted *lacks the dark cheek patch* of many other potentially confusing tyrannulets (e.g., Plumbeous-crowned and Ashy-headed). Rough-legged Tyrannulet's range is not known to overlap with White-fronted's (though they approach each other in s. Peru or Bolivia); Rough-legged differs in its olive crown and lack of a superciliary.

HABITAT AND BEHAVIOR: Rare in canopy and borders of montane forest, mostly in foothills and on lower slopes. Relatively few specimens have been taken; this species may be genuinely scarce, rather than merely difficult to collect. Birds seen have usually been foraging actively in middle and upper levels, often with mixed flocks; they perch rather horizontally but tend not to cock their tails, though they occasionally flick up their wings (one at a time). The call in Venezuela is a high-pitched "tzee-yeep" repeated at 2- to 3-second intervals for long periods (T. Meyer recording). Small numbers can be seen in Venezuela's Henri Pittier Nat. Park.

RANGE: Locally in coastal mts. of n. Venezuela (Carabobo to Miranda), Sierra de Perijá on Venezuela-Colombia border, and Andes of Colombia (known only from e. slope of E. Andes: a specimen from w. Meta and a sighting from w. Caquetá), se. and sw. Ecuador (a specimen and a sighting from Zamora-Chinchipe; a specimen from e. Guayas and a sighting from nw. Azuay), and e. Peru (single specimens from San Martín, Cuzco, and Madre de Dios); 1 tepui in se. Venezuela (Cerro Chimantátepui, Bolívar). Also Costa Rica and Panama. 600–1600 m.

NOTE: Formerly placed in the genus *Acrochordopus*. We consider *P. zeledoni* a species distinct from *P. burmeisteri* of s. South America, following *Birds of the Americas* (vol. 13, part 5) and J. T. Zimmer (*Am. Mus. Novitates* 1126, 1941) but not Meyer de Schauensee (1966, 1970) or *Birds of the World*, vol. 8. Plumage differences between the two are greater than in many other sympatric tyrannulets. The possible contact zone between the two in s. Peru or w. Bolivia needs to be evaluated.

Phyllomyias sclateri

SCLATER'S TYRANNULET

PLATE: 32

DESCRIPTION: 12 cm (4¾"). *E. slope of Andes from s. Peru to nw. Argentina.* Mostly olive above with gray crown and with short whitish superciliary; wings and tail dusky with *2 bold wing-bars and edging yellowish white.* Auricular area slightly grizzled; throat and breast pale grayish white, breast tinged olive; *belly yellowish white.*

SIMILAR SPECIES: Confusing. Most like Buff-banded Tyrannulet (and they occur sympatrically), whose wing-bars are at best pale buffy ochraceous and thus not very different; Buff-banded is smaller and has a darker gray crown. Sclater's is also easily confused with Plumbeous-crowned Tyrannulet (recorded overlap only in Cuzco, Peru), which is yellower below and has a distinct dark patch on ear-coverts and a slightly different wing pattern. Mottle-cheeked Tyrannulet is considerably yellower below and has more olive (not so gray) crown.

HABITAT AND BEHAVIOR: Uncommon to fairly common in canopy and borders of montane forest, occasionally out into adjacent clearings with scattered trees; also recorded from alder-dominated woodland. Usually found singly or in pairs, most often foraging with mixed flocks of tanagers and other birds. Sclater's hover-gleans actively in foliage, generally in the upper or outer part of trees, frequently shivering and sometimes even briefly lifting its wings. Its call is a series of 10—15 distinctively harsh (unpleasant-sounding) and emphatic sputtering notes. Can be seen near the base of Machu Picchu, Peru.

RANGE: E. slope of Andes in s. Peru (Cuzco) and from s. Bolivia (north to Cochabamba) to nw. Argentina (south to Tucumán). 1000—2200 m.

NOTE: Includes *Tyranniscus australis* (Olrog's Tyrannulet), which Traylor (1982) determined to be a synonym of *Phyllomyias sclateri*. *Sclateri* was formerly placed in the genus *Xanthomyias*.

Phyllomyias plumbeiceps

PLUMBEOUS-CROWNED TYRANNULET   PLATE: 32

DESCRIPTION: 11.5 cm (4½"). *Andes of Colombia to Peru*. Short, all-black bill. *Crown gray*, back rather bright olive; superciliary white, bordered below by a dusky streak through eye; *sides of head whitish with dusky crescent on ear-coverts*. Wings and tail dusky, wings with *2 prominent pale yellow bars and edging*. Throat grayish white, becoming yellow on remaining underparts, clouded olive on breast, brightest yellow on belly. SIMILAR SPECIES: Often confused. Ecuadorian Tyrannulet is especially similar but is a bit smaller with slightly longer bill and lacks any pale area behind the dark ear crescent; it occurs primarily at lower elevations. Also closely resembles Ashy-headed Tyrannulet, but has crown duller gray (not as blue), ear-crescent duskier (not as black), wings with edging on coverts (*lacking* in Ashy-headed), and lacks Ashy-headed's streaky effect on breast (more of a wash). Cf. also Marble-faced Bristle-Tyrant and slightly larger Slaty-capped Flycatcher. Sclater's Tyrannulet is less yellow below and lacks the dark spot on ear-coverts. HABITAT AND BEHAVIOR: Uncommon to locally fairly common (though usually overlooked because of identification difficulties) in subcanopy and canopy of montane forest and forest borders. Usually forages with mixed flocks of insectivorous birds, sallying to leaves and twigs but often remaining motionless for protracted periods. Occasionally lifts a wing up above its back. Its song, a series of 5—8 short hard notes with the quality of a furnariid (e.g., *Anabacerthia*), is delivered at long intervals. All behavioral information is based on observations by B. Whitney (pers. comm.). RANGE: Locally in Andes of Colombia (in E. Andes north to Cundinamarca, in W. Andes north to Cauca), e. Ecuador (w. Napo, Tungurahua, and Zamora-Chinchipe), and e. Peru (south to Cuzco). Mostly 1300—2200 m.

NOTE: Formerly placed in the genus *Oreotriccus*.

Phyllomyias cinereiceps

ASHY-HEADED TYRANNULET   PLATE: 32

DESCRIPTION: 11 cm (4¼"). *Andes of Colombia to Peru*. Short, all-black bill; dark red iris. *Crown bluish gray contrasting with bright olive back;*

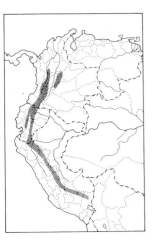

lores and area around eyes white grizzled with black; sides of head *yellowish* white with *large black crescent on wing-coverts;* wings with 2 yellowish white bars and edging on flight feathers (but *not* on coverts). *Mostly yellow below,* flammulated with olive on throat and breast (giving *faintly streaked effect*).

SIMILAR SPECIES: Plumage pattern is much like that of Plumbeous-crowned Tyrannulet, several bristle-tyrants (especially Marble-faced), and even notably larger Slaty-capped Flycatcher, but Ashy-headed can be distinguished from all of these by the bluer tone of its crown and its brighter yellow underparts with their suggestion of fine but blurred breast streaking.

HABITAT AND BEHAVIOR: Rare to locally fairly common in middle levels and canopy of montane forest, sometimes lower at borders. Looks plumper than many of its congeners and tends to perch more upright. Regularly forages with mixed flocks. Generally a scarce bird, perhaps most numerous in the now partially deforested subtropical zone of Colombia's upper Río Magdalena valley, and still relatively common in and near Cueva de los Guácharos Nat. Park.

RANGE: Andes of Colombia (local; in E. Andes recorded from Santander southward, in Cen. Andes from Antioquia southward, in W. Andes in Cauca and Nariño), Ecuador (recorded south on w. slope to Chimborazo, though in recent years only to Pichincha), and e. Peru (south to Puno [LSUMZ]). Mostly 1400–2700 m.

NOTE: Formerly placed in the genus *Tyranniscus.*

Phyllomyias nigrocapillus

BLACK-CAPPED TYRANNULET

DESCRIPTION: 11 cm (4¼"). *Andes of Venezuela to Peru.* Short, all-black bill. In most of range (nominate race) *crown black* bordered below by narrow white superciliary; otherwise dark olive above, wings blackish with *2 bold yellowish white wing-bars* and ochraceous yellow edging on secondaries. Throat grayish, with remaining underparts yellow, breast heavily clouded olive. See C-36. Venezuelan birds (*aureus*) and those of Santa Marta Mts. (*flavimentum*) have *crown dark sepia brown* with a pale yellow superciliary, are yellower below (the yellow extending up onto throat), and have breast less clouded with olive; see V-30.

SIMILAR SPECIES: Much like Tawny-rumped Tyrannulet but yellower below with whitish rather than buff wing-bars, not nearly as brownish above, and with no trace of that species' tawny rump. Cf. also smaller *Mecocerculus* tyrannulets.

HABITAT AND BEHAVIOR: Rare to fairly common in forest borders, low woodland, and clearings with scattered trees and bushes, often up to timberline. Seems more numerous in Venezuela and Colombia than in Ecuador and Peru. Usually seen singly or in pairs, gleaning actively in foliage at various levels, often nervously twitching its wings. Regularly accompanies mixed flocks. Its call is a clear, high "peeeep," often persistently repeated (Hilty and Brown 1986).

RANGE: Andes of w. Venezuela (north to s. Lara), Colombia, Ecuador (where seemingly rather local, south on w. slope only to Pichincha), and e. Peru (south to Cuzco); Santa Marta Mts. of Colombia. Mostly 1800–3300 m, but recorded down to 950 m in Colombia.

NOTE: Formerly placed in the genus *Tyranniscus*.

Phyllomyias uropygialis

TAWNY-RUMPED TYRANNULET

PLATE: 32

DESCRIPTION: 11.5 cm (4½"). *Andes of Venezuela to Bolivia.* Short, all-black bill. Crown dark sepia brown with short white superciliary; *back olive brown,* shading into *tawny on rump and uppertail-coverts;* wings blackish with *2 buff wing-bars* and buff edging on secondaries. Throat and breast grayish, tinged with olive brown on breast, becoming yellowish white on belly.

SIMILAR SPECIES: Black-capped Tyrannulet has much more yellow on underparts, is more olive above (not so brownish on back and with no tawny on rump), and has whiter wing-bars (not as buff). Tawny-rumped's pattern also like White-banded and White-tailed Tyrannulets', but neither of these is so brown, and both have a bolder and longer superciliary.

HABITAT AND BEHAVIOR: Rare to locally uncommon in borders of montane forest and woodland, sometimes in adjacent shrubby clearings. Usually found singly, less often in pairs, gleaning in foliage and frequently hovering while searching for insects on leaf surfaces, exposing the distinctive tawny rump. Often accompanies mixed foraging flocks. Its infrequently heard call is a soft "tseep-tseep," sometimes repeated several times in succession.

RANGE: Locally in Andes of w. Venezuela (Mérida), Colombia (very local; recorded in E. Andes south to Cundinamarca and in W. Andes in Cauca and Nariño), Ecuador (south on w. slope to El Oro and w. Loja), e. Peru (also 3 west-slope records, from Piura, Lima, and Arequipa), and w. Bolivia (south to Tarija). Mostly 1800–3100 m.

NOTE: Formerly placed in the genus *Tyranniscus*.

Mecocerculus Tyrannulets

The *Mecocerculus* tyrannulets, found mainly in the Andes, have bold wing-bars and simple facial patterns with a usually prominent superciliary. The six species vary in shape and posture; one, the White-throated, differing strikingly in being larger and having a vertical posture. A small black patch at the base of the inner remiges (recalling a kinglet's, *Regulus*) is present in all species. All but the atypical White-throated have the lower mandible flesh-colored at least at its base. Based on syringeal morphology, Lanyon (1988a) suggested that the genus was polyphyletic, but in this case he refrained from naming new genera pending the acquisition of more natural history information. He placed the Rufous-winged and Sulphur-bellied in one group; the White-banded, White-tailed, and Buff-banded in a second; and the White-throated in a third.

GROUP A

Typical *horizontal* posture; usually grayish below, 2 species with white underside of tail.

Mecocerculus calopterus

RUFOUS-WINGED TYRANNULET   PLATE: 32

DESCRIPTION: 11 cm (4¼"). *Mainly on lower Andean slopes of Ecuador and n. Peru.* Virtually unmistakable by virtue of its *conspicuous rufous edging on flight feathers*, forming a large patch. Mostly olive above with dark gray crown, long white superciliary, and blackish area from lores back through eyes and over ear-coverts; wings blackish with, in addition to the rufous edging, 2 prominent buffy white wing-bars; *tail with outer 2 pairs of feathers white*. Throat and breast pale gray, becoming white on belly, slightly yellowish on crissum.

SIMILAR SPECIES: Pattern bears a superficial resemblance to Rufous-winged Antwren's.

HABITAT AND BEHAVIOR: Locally uncommon to fairly common in canopy and borders of both humid and deciduous forest and in adjacent clearings and plantations with scattered trees. Seems more numerous on w. slope of Andes than on e. slope. A dapper, easily recognized tyrannulet, usually seen singly or in loosely associated pairs foraging in leafy branches at middle and upper levels, often accompanying mixed flocks of other insectivorous birds. In general comportment resembles better-known White-tailed Tyrannulet; Rufous-winged occurs at lower elevations.

RANGE: W. slope of Andes in Ecuador (mainly in El Oro and w. Loja, smaller numbers north to Pichincha with 1 sighting from Imbabura; an isolated population on the coastal cordillera in sw. Manabí) and nw. Peru (south to Lambayeque); e. slope of Andes in se. Ecuador (Zamora-Chinchipe) and ne. Peru (south to e. La Libertad). Mostly 400–1500 m.

Mecocerculus poecilocercus

WHITE-TAILED TYRANNULET

DESCRIPTION: 11 cm (4¼"). *Andes of Colombia to Peru.* Mostly olive above with gray crown and narrow white superciliary; *rump and upper-tail-coverts pale greenish yellow*, often quite conspicuous, even in flight; wings blackish with 2 prominent whitish to buffy whitish wing-bars and yellowish edging on secondaries; tail dusky but with *outer 2 feathers mostly white* (conspicuous from below and in flight). Throat and breast pale gray, becoming yellowish white on belly. See C-36.

SIMILAR SPECIES: White-banded Tyrannulet is notably larger and longer-tailed, with bolder superciliary and pure white wing-bars, and lacks white in tail; it usually occurs at higher elevations than White-tailed. Cf. also Rufous-winged Tyrannulet.

HABITAT AND BEHAVIOR: Uncommon to fairly common in canopy and borders of montane forest. Seemingly more numerous in Ecuador than elsewhere, and easily seen along the Mindo and Chiriboga roads west of Quito. Forages actively, alone or in separated pairs, usually with mixed flocks; generally conspicuous, tending to remain among outer branches. The characteristic white in the tail and the pale rump are often visible during its active flitting. Its easily recognized call, a series of 4 (sometimes 3) minor-keyed notes, descending in pitch and fading in volume, "pee, pee-pee-pee," is often heard.

RANGE: Andes of Colombia (north in E. Andes to Norte de Santander, in Cen. Andes north to Caldas, in W. Andes only in Cauca and Nariño), both slopes of Ecuador (on w. slope south to El Oro and w. Loja), and e. Peru (south [locally?] to Cuzco). Mostly 1500–2500 m.

Mecocerculus hellmayri

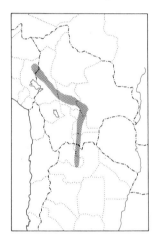

BUFF-BANDED TYRANNULET

DESCRIPTION: 11 cm (4¼"). *Andes of s. Peru to n. Argentina.* Mostly olive above with *gray crown* and long white superciliary, rump and uppertail-coverts slightly paler, more ochraceous olive; wings blackish with 2 prominent pale buff wing-bars and buffy yellowish edging. Throat pale gray, becoming olive grayish on breast and yellowish white on belly.

SIMILAR SPECIES: Closely resembles better-known White-tailed Tyrannulet (replacing it southward), but rump not as pale and with *no white in tail.* Sclater's Tyrannulet is quite similar but larger with somewhat whiter wing-bars. White-banded Tyrannulet is larger with pure white wing-bars, etc.

HABITAT AND BEHAVIOR: Uncommon in canopy and borders of montane forest, foraging mostly in middle and upper strata. Usually found singly, associating with mixed flocks of other insectivorous birds. A regularly heard call is a series of 4 clear whistled notes, each inflected upward (Remsen 1984).

RANGE: E. slope of Andes in s. Peru (Puno at Sandia), w. Bolivia (La Paz to Tarija), and n. Argentina (Jujuy on Cerro Santa Bárbara). Mostly 1100–2600 m.

NOTE: For additional information on this until recently poorly known species, see Remsen (1984).

Mecocerculus stictopterus

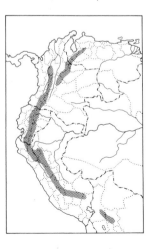

WHITE-BANDED TYRANNULET   PLATE: 32

DESCRIPTION: 12.5 cm (5"). *Andes of Venezuela to Bolivia.* Olive above with gray head and *long broad white superciliary;* wings blackish with *2 broad white wing-bars* and buffy yellowish edging on flight feathers. Throat and breast pale gray, becoming yellowish white on belly. Nominate race and *albocaudatus* (south to n. Peru) have back more brownish olive and edging on wings slightly more rufescent than in *taeniopterus* (remainder of range).

SIMILAR SPECIES: White-tailed and Buff-banded Tyrannulets are smaller, shorter-tailed, and have less bold superciliaries and less pure white wing-bars; they occur at lower elevations (being essentially subtropical, not temperate, zone birds).

HABITAT AND BEHAVIOR: Uncommon to locally common in canopy and borders of montane forest and woodland and out into adjacent clearings with scattered trees and bushes; sometimes up to near timberline and in regenerating scrub. Seems especially numerous where alder stands are prevalent. Forages actively, perching horizontally (warbler-like), most often with mixed flocks. Usually conspicuous, remaining among outer branches and regularly not far above ground. Its frequently given and characteristic call is a somewhat raspy, upward-slurred "squeeyh?," sometimes repeated 3–5 times in succession, or lengthened (perhaps as full "song") to a "squeeee-e-e-eyh? squeh-deh-deh-deh-deh," the first note very high pitched, the latter ones descending.

RANGE: Andes of w. Venezuela (north to Trujillo), Colombia (in W. Andes not recorded north of Cauca), Ecuador (on w. slope south to Azuay and w. Loja), e. Peru, and w. Bolivia (La Paz and Cochabamba). Mostly 2300–3300 m, occasionally to about 2000 m.

Mecocerculus minor

SULPHUR-BELLIED TYRANNULET   PLATE: 32

DESCRIPTION: 11.5 cm (4½"). *Mainly on e. slope of Andes from Venezuela to Peru;* unique among *Mecocerculus* tyrannulets in having *extensively yellow underparts.* Mostly dark olive above with *gray crown* and narrow whitish superciliary, lower face grizzled gray and white; wings blackish with *2 broad buff wing-bars* and edging on flight feathers. *Mostly clear yellow below* with chin whitish and lower throat and breast somewhat clouded olive.

SIMILAR SPECIES: As the only *Mecocerculus* with much yellow below, Sulphur-bellied is more likely confused with certain tyrannulets of other genera (e.g., *Phyllomyias,* "*Pogonotriccus*" portion of *Phylloscartes,* etc.). It is perhaps most similar, at least in plumage, to Variegated Bristle-Tyrant, which has a more complex facial pattern (including a patch on ear-coverts), more vertical posture, and entirely orange-yellow lower mandible (in Sulphur-bellied pale flesh color is found only at base of lower mandible).

HABITAT AND BEHAVIOR: Rare to uncommon in canopy and borders of montane forest, nearby second-growth, and clearings with scattered trees. Seems primarily an edge bird. Although infrequently recorded in the past and still rare in collections, Sulphur-bellied Tyrannulet is now being found with greater frequency; it may be undergoing an actual increase, perhaps in response to the opening up of more terrain because of deforestation. Forages singly or in pairs, often with mixed flocks; like most *Mecocerculus,* perches quite horizontally. The only call we have heard is a fairly sharp, fast "chew-chew-chew-chew-chew." Regularly encountered along the Gualaceo-Limón road in Morona-Santiago, Ecuador.

RANGE: Andes of extreme w. Venezuela (Táchira), Colombia (seemingly very local [perhaps overlooked?], recorded only from Norte de Santander to Boyacá in E. Andes, around upper Río Magdalena valley in Huila, and on e. slope of E. Andes in e. Nariño), nw. and e. Ecuador (though first found only in the 1960s, now known to be reasonably widespread and numerous on Andes' e. slope; on w. slope recorded above Maldonado in Carchi), and e. Peru (south to Huánuco in Carpish ridge area). 1600–2700 m.

GROUP B

Upright posture; contrasting *white throat*.

Mecocerculus leucophrys

WHITE-THROATED TYRANNULET

PLATE: 32

DESCRIPTION: 14 cm (5½"). *Widespread at higher elevations in Andes and on the tepuis.* Bill all black. Olive brown to deep umber brown above with faint whitish superciliary; wings blackish with 2 whitish to deep rufous wing-bars and edging on flight feathers. *Prominent puffy white throat,* contrasting with dull brownish to olive grayish breast; belly whitish to pale yellow. Birds with darkest upperparts and deepest rufous wing-bars are *rufomarginatus* and *brunneomarginatus* of s. Colombia to se. Peru; birds from Bolivia and Argentina (nominate race) and ne. Venezuela (*palliditergum* and *nigriceps*) are more olive above and have the whitest wing-bars (see V-30).

SIMILAR SPECIES: The conspicuous white throat of this familiar small tyrannid is not shared by any similar species. In most of its range the long tail is accentuated by its *vertical posture* (very different from other *Mecocerculus*).

HABITAT AND BEHAVIOR: Uncommon to common in forest borders, low woodland (including groves of *Polylepis* and low trees near tree-line), and in regenerating pastures, clearings with scattered bushes and trees, and hedgerows; perhaps more numerous in Colombia and w. Venezuela than elsewhere. Usually perches vertically with tail held straight down, most often at no great height and frequently in the open. Typically several are loosely associated with a mixed flock. Forages both by gleaning and by making short sallies. A frequent contact note is a short "pit"; in nw. Argentina gives a short series of notes, e.g., "chif-chif-chef-chef-chúf." The dawn song (in Ecuador) is a fast, jumbled "whichiry, whichiry, whichiry-chéw," with variations. Birds from nw. Argentina, at least in Salta and Tucumán, often forage differently and more actively, more often in a horizontal posture like other members of genus.

RANGE: Coastal mts. of n. Venezuela (east to Paria Peninsula in Sucre), and Andes of w. Venezuela (north to s. Lara), Colombia, Ecuador, Peru (south on w. slope to Ancash), w. Bolivia, and nw. Argentina (south to La Rioja); Sierra de Perijá on Venezuela-Colombia border and Santa Marta Mts. in n. Colombia; tepuis of s. Venezuela (Bolívar and Amazonas south to Cerro de la Neblina) and adjacent n. Brazil (Roraima). Seems likely in adjacent Guyana. Mostly 2500–4000 m; locally much lower (to 1500 m or even lower), both in Venezuela and in s. part of Andean range.

Stigmatura Wagtail-Tyrants

A pair of flycatchers with long, graduated, white-tipped tails, short bills, and perky mannerisms. One is found on islands in the Amazon system, the other in chaco woodland and scrub, with isolated populations of both in ne. Brazil where the nature of their apparent overlap remains uncertain. Lanyon (1988a) suggests that, based on cranial and syringeal evidence, the genus *Stigmatura* is most closely related to his newly erected genus *Pseudelaenia* (Gray-and-white Tyrannulet), an externally and behaviorally very different bird. *Stigmatura*'s nest is a shallow cup.

Stigmatura budytoides

GREATER WAGTAIL-TYRANT

PLATE: 33

DESCRIPTION: 14.5–15 cm (5½–6″). *A distinctive, slender tyrannid with a long graduated tail found mainly in interior s.-cen. South America* (also locally in ne. Brazil). Mostly grayish olive with *broad yellow superciliary;* wings and tail duskier, wings with *a broad longitudinal patch; tail feathers broadly tipped and edged white* and with broad white band at base (visible from below). Below yellow, tinged buff across breast. *Flavocineria* (cen. Argentina) is duller and less patterned generally, with brownish olive shading on breast and no basal white tail-band; *gracilis* (ne. Brazil) resembles nominate race but is *smaller.*
SIMILAR SPECIES: Cf. Lesser Wagtail-Tyrant (limited overlap in ne. Brazil).
HABITAT AND BEHAVIOR: Fairly common to common in arid scrub and chaco woodland. A lively, attractive, and often bold little bird, usually in pairs, and though generally in undergrowth, easy to observe as it moves about incessantly. The tail is held partially cocked, often with feathers fanned exposing their white tips; despite the bird's name, its tail is never exactly "wagged." The most common call is a clipped "chirt" (with quality of Pectoral Sandpiper), sometimes doubled or given in series; this is sometimes varied to "chirt, wuri-tit, chirt." Occasionally pairs perched side by side sing a syncopated duet, swiveling their bodies rapidly and giving a rollicking, vigorous "whidididitdeh, whidididitdeh, whidididitdeh," altogether a charming performance.
RANGE: S. Bolivia (Cochabamba south to Tarija), w. Paraguay, and w. and cen. Argentina (south to Río Negro and extreme s. Buenos Aires); ne. Brazil (Pernambuco and n. Bahia). Apparently does not migrate. To about 2700 m in arid intermontane valleys of Bolivia, but mostly below 1000 m.

Stigmatura napensis

LESSER WAGTAIL-TYRANT

DESCRIPTION: 13 cm (5″). Local on *river islands in Amazonia* (also local in ne. Brazil). Resembles slightly larger Greater Wagtail-Tyrant, but *Lesser is only member of its genus in Amazon basin,* so easily recognized there. See C-38. The race (*bahiae*) of Lesser found in ne. Brazil closely resembles sympatric race (*gracilis*) of Greater; *bahiae* is slightly smaller, browner (not so grayish) above, and duller and buffier yellow below. Recall that *gracilis* is a *small* race of Greater.
HABITAT AND BEHAVIOR: Locally fairly common on islands in the Amazon and some of its tributaries, and in arid scrub in ne. Brazil (where not well known). Amazonian birds show a decided preference for uniform stands of young *Tessaria* trees (one of the first plants to

colonize newly exposed sand and mudbars), rarely being found away from them. Vocalizations and general behavior similar to Greater Wagtail-Tyrant's.

RANGE: Amaz. Brazil (upriver from about the mouth of the Rio Tapajós, also up the Rios Madeira and Juruá, and perhaps other Amaz. tributaries), s. Colombia (along the Amazon near Leticia), ne. Peru (along the Amazon and lower Río Ucayali, and up the Río Napo), and e. Ecuador (numerous recent records from several islands in the Río Napo upstream to near La Selva, and on the lower Río Aguarico below Lagartococha; ANSP, MECN); ne. Brazil (w. Pernambuco and w. and cen. Bahia). Below 500 m.

Inezia Tyrannulets

The three *Inezia* tyrannulets are a superficially diverse lot. The Pale-tipped somewhat resembles *Stigmatura,* the Slender-billed recalls *Camptostoma,* and the Plain is very much like a *Serpophaga* (in which genus it was long placed). We follow the most recent treatments of the genus (K. C. Parkes, *Condor* 75[4]: 249–250, 1973; *Birds of the World,* vol. 8), in which all were considered congeneric. Lanyon (1988a) also concluded that, despite their external dissimilarities, the three species form a monophyletic unit, based on their similar skulls and syringes.

Inezia subflava

PALE-TIPPED TYRANNULET PLATE: 33

DESCRIPTION: 11.5 cm (4½"). Above olive to brownish olive with *bold white supraloral and narrow eye-ring;* wings and tail duskier, wings with *2 prominent white bars, tail feathers tipped and outer vane edged whitish* (usually not conspicuous, often most evident from below). Below mostly pale yellow, with upper throat whitish and breast clouded olive (especially in *obscura* of s. Venezuela and adjacent Colombia and Brazil). Iris color variable; age may play a role (paler in older birds?), but it seems consistently yellow in n. Colombia and n. Venezuela, dark in s. Venezuela and the Guianas.

SIMILAR SPECIES: Southern Beardless- and Slender-billed Tyrannulets are smaller, not as yellow below, and lack the spectacled look and pale tail-tipping; they tend to be more arboreal than this species (which usually forages quite low). Cf. also Mouse-colored Tyrannulet.

HABITAT AND BEHAVIOR: Uncommon to fairly common in shrubbery along margins of gallery woodland, rivers, and lakes, lighter woodland and scrub generally, and (at least in Guianas) mangroves. Most numerous near water, and especially common on the Venezuelan llanos. Usually forages singly or in pairs, independent of mixed flocks. Frequently holds tail partially cocked (reminiscent of a wagtail-tyrant, though feathers usually not spread). Vocalizes frequently, the most common call being a characteristic clear, soft, melancholy "teep, ti-ti-tu."

RANGE: Caribbean lowlands of n. Colombia (west to Sucre, and south in middle Río Magdalena valley to Santander) and nw. Venezuela (Maracaibo basin east to Falcón); e. and s. Venezuela, ne. Colombia (south to Vaupés and Guainía), Guianas (mainly near coast), and Amaz. Brazil (Rio Negro drainage and along the middle and lower Amazon east to the Rio Tocantins drainage, where it occurs south to Bananal Is. on Rio Araguaia); locally in n. Bolivia (ne. Beni near Costa Márques; Serranía de Huanchaca in ne. Santa Cruz). To about 400 m.

Inezia tenuirostris

SLENDER-BILLED TYRANNULET

DESCRIPTION: 9 cm (3½"). *A very small, nondescript, thin-billed tyrannulet of arid scrub in ne. Colombia and nw. Venezuela.* Bill all black. Above mostly dull olive brown with short whitish superciliary; wings and tail duskier, wings with 2 whitish wing-bars and edging on flight feathers. Throat and chest grayish white, becoming yellowish white on lower underparts. See V-30, C-36.

SIMILAR SPECIES: Note this species' limited range, mostly near the Caribbean. There most likely confused with Southern Beardless-Tyrannulet, which is slightly larger with a stouter bill showing orange-yellow on lower mandible, more olive upperparts, and a distinctive bushy-crested look with slightly darker crown (crown and back more or less concolor in Slender-billed). Their voices also differ characteristically.

HABITAT AND BEHAVIOR: Fairly common to common in arid scrub and dry woodland. Usually forages in outer foliage and twigs of small trees (not in thickety lower growth), thus not hard to see. Slender-billed's mannerisms are not dissimilar from Southern Beardless-Tyrannulet's, and the two often occur together; both regularly cock their tails. Slender-billed's characteristic call is a fast, dry trill, "bzz-zee-ee-ee-ee-ee-eep," ending abruptly, utterly different from the simple plaintive calls of Southern Beardless-. Readily seen in scrub in lowlands just west of the Santa Marta Mts., and numerous through much of Falcón, Venezuela.

RANGE: Ne. Colombia (n. Magdalena east through the Guajira Peninsula, but avoiding humid areas) and nw. Venezuela (n. Zulia, Falcón, and n. Lara). To 600 m.

Inezia inornata

PLAIN TYRANNULET

DESCRIPTION: 10 cm (4"). *Interior s.-cen. South America.* Extremely similar to White-crested and White-bellied Tyrannulets (*Serpophaga*), both of which can occur with it; they sometimes cannot be distinguished in the field. Plain Tyrannulet often has some pale color on lower mandible (whereas bill is all black in White-crested and White-bellied); *it lacks a white coronal patch* (though this is often hidden in White-crested and White-bellied) and has *smoothly gray crown* (lacking White-crested and White-bellied's black streaking; this may be the best field character); and it generally is *tinged pale yellow on belly* (this helps to distinguish it from White-bellied, though some White-bellied immatures may have yellow-tinged belly).

HABITAT AND BEHAVIOR: Not well known in life, in part doubtless

because of confusion with more widespread and numerous White-crested and White-bellied Tyrannulets. Favors chaco woodland and scrub, and forest borders. In se. Peru, where believed only an austral migrant, recorded in willow groves along rivers; at Cachoeira Nazaré in Rondônia, where also only an austral migrant, found in low forest growing on sandy soil. Foraging behavior and posture similar to Southern Beardless-Tyrannulet's, often partially cocking its tail. Its call, "pseee, tee-ee-ee-ee-ee," is similar to Slender-billed Tyrannulet's in pattern but is perhaps more musical.

RANGE: Se. Peru (Madre de Dios, where apparently present only during austral winter), n. and e. Bolivia, sw. Brazil (recorded only from upper Rio Juruá in Amazonas, Rondônia, s. Mato Grosso, and w. Mato Grosso do Sul; in Amaz. Brazil believed to be only an austral migrant, *fide* D. Stotz), w. and ne. Paraguay, and nw. Argentina (Salta and Jujuy). N. limit of breeding uncertain, but it is believed to be resident in Beni, Bolivia (*fide* J. V. Remsen, Jr.), and a Nov. specimen (AMNH) on the Río Iténey suggests nesting along the Beni-Rondônia border. To about 500 m.

Serpophaga Tyrannulets

The genus *Serpophaga* contains two behaviorally and ecologically distinct "types":

1. active, foliage-gleaning species, and
2. stockier species, closely associated with water.

All are at least united by their predominantly or entirely gray plumage, with a semiconcealed white coronal patch. They are found in habitats as divergent as rocky Andean streams and arid Patagonian scrub.

Two previously recognized species (Meyer de Schauensee 1966, 1970) turn out not to be valid taxa. *S. araguayae* (Bananal Tyrannulet), described from a single specimen from Bananal Is. in Goiás, Brazil, is actually an example of the nominate subspecies of the Gray Elaenia, *Myiopagis caniceps* (J. M. Cardoso da Silva, *Goeldiana*, Zoología, Núm. 1, 1990). *S. griseiceps* (Gray-crowned Tyrannulet), described from Cochabamba, Bolivia, is a synonym of the White-bellied Tyrannulet, *S. munda* (*Birds of the World*, vol. 8).

GROUP A

More slender species; elongated but flat, blackish crest feathers.

Serpophaga subcristata

WHITE-CRESTED TYRANNULET   PLATE: 33

DESCRIPTION: 11 cm (4¼"). *Widespread in s. South America.* Above grayish olive to olivaceous gray, grayest on head and neck; short white superciliary and *long blackish crown feathers somewhat concealing a white coronal patch;* wings and tail blackish, wings with 2 bold whitish to pale buff wing-bars. Throat whitish, becoming pale gray on breast and pale yellow on belly (slightly brighter in birds from se. Brazil, *straminea*).
SIMILAR SPECIES: Look for the white in the crown; even if not fully exposed, it often shows as a narrow stripe, reminiscent of some of the

smaller elaenias. No other really similar tyrannulet, aside from the very close White-bellied (which see), shows this; cf. especially the Plain Tyrannulet. White-crested's black crown streaking is also distinctive and reasonably apparent given a close study.

HABITAT AND BEHAVIOR: Fairly common to common in forest borders, gallery woodland and monte, shrubbery and groves of trees in agricultural regions, and deciduous scrub. An active and spritely tyrannulet, seemingly quite fearless, usually in the semiopen, where it often forages low. The most frequent call is a soft chippering trill introduced by 1 or more rising notes, e.g., "pseee? pseee? psee-ee-ee-ee-ee-ee." One bird responding to tape playback at Brasília gave a fast "chi-di-di-di-dit" (RSR).

RANGE: Lowlands of e. and s. Bolivia (northeast to n. La Paz), Paraguay, s. and e. Brazil (north mainly to Mato Grosso do Sul, s. Goiás, Minas Gerais, and s. Bahia, with isolated records from s. Piauí and Pernambuco), Uruguay, and n. and cen. Argentina (south to ne. Chubut). Migratory status still uncertain; some birds may withdraw from the southernmost part of range during austral winter, and the species may not breed along the n. edge of range. To at least 2000 m (in se. Brazil), but in Bolivia and Argentina rarely or never above 500–700 m.

NOTE: We continue to recognize both *S. subcristata* and *S. munda* as full species, though some authorities have considered them conspecific (e.g., J. T. Zimmer, *Am. Mus. Novitates* 1749, 1955; *Birds of the World*, vol. 8). Sympatry seems established, though actual breeding overlap is still uncertain; J. V. Remsen, Jr., confirms (pers. comm.) that at least in Bolivia their voices differ.

Serpophaga munda

WHITE-BELLIED TYRANNULET PLATE: 33

DESCRIPTION: 11.5 cm (4½″). Resembles White-crested Tyrannulet, generally replacing it in w. Bolivia and w. Argentina (but with some overlap especially during austral winter). *Grayer above* (not so olivaceous on back), with *belly white* (not pale yellow). As in White-crested, *bill black*. In Bolivia and w. Argentina, White-crested occurs only in lowlands, with White-bellied breeding mainly in foothills and highlands, though descending some in austral winter.

SIMILAR SPECIES: Aside from White-crested Tyrannulet, this species must also be distinguished with great care from Plain Tyrannulet, with which it is widely sympatric. Plain Tyrannulet's head is "plainer" (lacking White-bellied's white coronal patch and black crown streaking), and it often shows some pale color on lower mandible (bill all black in White-bellied); Plain also usually shows a tinge of yellow on belly.

HABITAT AND BEHAVIOR: Fairly common to common in arid deciduous scrub and woodland, and forest borders. In Bolivia and w. Argentina breeds mainly in foothills and highlands, then descending to some extent during austral winter. General behavior similar to White-crested Tyrannulet's, but White-bellied's voice differs characteristically, being more syncopated and spitting, e.g., "tsi, tsu-tsu, tsu-tsu, tsu-tsu" or "sit, sit-dit-su" (J. V. Remsen, Jr.).

RANGE: Breeds in foothills and highlands of w. Bolivia (La Paz and Cochabamba south to Tarija) and w. Argentina (south to w. Río Negro); more southerly breeders apparently migrate north during austral winter into the chaco of n. Argentina, w. Paraguay, s. Bolivia, and extreme sw. Brazil (sw. Mato Grosso do Sul) and occasionally stray as far east as coastal Uruguay and Rio Grande do Sul, Brazil. To about 2800 m.

NOTE: Closely allied to *S. subcristata;* see discussion under that species. Included in *S. munda* is *Serpophaga griseiceps* (Gray-crowned Tyrannulet), described in 1959 from four specimens from Cochabamba, Bolivia. This form was synonymized without comment in *S. munda* in *Birds of the World,* vol. 8. Although we have not seen the specimens, from the taxon's 1959 description we would suppose that they were juvenile *S. munda,* for these tend to have the wing-bars more ochraceous.

Serpophaga hypoleuca

RIVER TYRANNULET

PLATE: 33

DESCRIPTION: 11 cm (4¼″). *A slender, small tyrannulet found locally on islands in the Amazon and Orinoco systems. Uniform grayish brown above, crown feathers elongated and blackish* and partially concealing a white coronal patch; plain wings and tail somewhat duskier. Below whitish, tinged gray across breast.

SIMILAR SPECIES: Drab Water-Tyrant is markedly larger and behaves very differently. Cf. much grayer Torrent Tyrannulet (found mainly along Andean streams above range of River, though there may be some overlap).

HABITAT AND BEHAVIOR: Uncommon to fairly common but local in sparse, semiopen, early succession growth on river islands. Usually encountered in pairs, foraging independently of other birds; generally gleans in foliage of shrubs and small trees, sometimes sallying quickly into the air. Posture is typically horizontal, but when resting may perch more upright. A restless and seemingly shy bird, seldom remaining long in an area and often flying for considerable distances between feeding bouts.

RANGE: S. Venezuela (along the Orinoco and its tributaries in Apure, n. Bolívar, and Anzoátegui); e. Ecuador (locally along the Río Napo), e. Peru (Loreto south locally to Cuzco), extreme se. Colombia (along the Amazon near Leticia), and n. Bolivia (Pando); lower Amaz. Brazil (along the Amazon and lower Rio Tapajós, and along the Rios Tocantins and Araguaia upriver to n. Goiás on Bananal Is.). To 600 m in e. Peru.

GROUP B

Plumper species with *contrasting black tail.* Both *closely associated with water.*

Serpophaga nigricans

SOOTY TYRANNULET

PLATE: 33

DESCRIPTION: 11.5 cm (4½″). *A virtually unmistakable, uniform grayish and black-tailed tyrannulet found near water from s. Brazil to n. Argentina.* Above dark brownish gray, below paler and purer gray; usually concealed white coronal patch; wings duskier, coverts with 2 vague grayish bars and flight feathers edged grayish; *tail uniform black* (contrasting with gray of remaining plumage).

Serpophaga cinerea

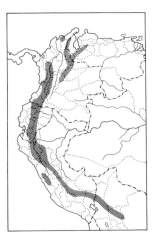

HABITAT AND BEHAVIOR: Uncommon in shrubbery and semiopen areas but *always near water* (both still and flowing), sometimes in agricultural areas or around farmyards. Found in pairs, foraging on or near the ground, perching at water's edge, on floating vegetation, or on rocks or logs in the middle of a stream or irrigation ditch. Restless and nervous, Sooty Tyrannulets seem constantly on the move, flitting into the air or ahead a short distance. The often somewhat fanned tail is characteristically jerked upwards.

RANGE: S. Brazil (north to s. Goiás, cen. Minas Gerais, and Espírito Santo), e. Paraguay, Uruguay, n. and cen. Argentina (south to Mendoza and Río Negro), and extreme se. Bolivia (Tarija). Apparently mostly resident, though it may withdraw from southernmost part of range during austral winter; some of the records from n. edge of its range may pertain to migrants. To 1000 m (in Bolivia).

TORRENT TYRANNULET

DESCRIPTION: 11.5 cm (4½"). *Fast-flowing streams and rivers in Andes.* Virtually unmistakable. *Mostly pale gray,* paler below (whitest on throat and lower belly), with *crown and sides of head black;* usually concealed white coronal patch; wings and tail blackish, wing coverts with indistinct pale grayish edging. See V-30.

SIMILAR SPECIES: The perfectly named Torrent Tyrannulet has much the same colors as White-capped Dipper, with which it shares its mountain streams. In e. Peru, cf. much browner River Tyrannulet of lowlands; these species generally separate by elevation, but limited overlap is possible.

HABITAT AND BEHAVIOR: Usually common and conspicuous along fast-flowing and usually rocky rivers and streams (sometimes quite narrow). Although it occasionally forages a short distance from water, especially venturing out onto pastures, this is preeminently a bird of rushing torrents. Here it can be seen on rocks out in streams, or on branches overhanging the water, almost always low. Usually in pairs, though they may be well separated. Occasionally flicks tail upward. Often gives a sharp "chip," sometimes repeated in a short series, loud enough to be heard over the roar of rushing water.

RANGE: Andes of w. Venezuela (north to Trujillo), Colombia, Ecuador, Peru (south on w. slope to Lima), and w. Bolivia (La Paz and Cochabamba); Sierra de Perijá on Venezuela-Colombia border and Santa Marta Mts. of n. Colombia. Also Costa Rica and Panama. Mostly 700–2500 m, occasionally higher (rarely to treeline or even slightly above), and locally lower (to 300 m in w. Ecuador; this low only where swift-flowing stream conditions exist).

Polystictus Tachuris

This still poorly known genus contains a pair of species, one found locally in savannas with tall grass, the other in grassy campos on certain serras in e. Brazil. The Bearded Tachuri is basically brown and buff and has narrow tail feathers; the Gray-backed Tachuri is gray and cinnamon and has a more normal tail. We are not convinced the two are congeneric, but they were so treated by the most recent revisers of the group (J. T. Zimmer, *Am. Mus. Novitates* 1749, 1955; and *Birds of the World*, vol. 8).

Polystictus pectoralis

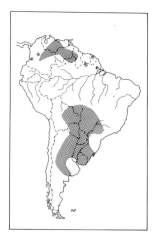

BEARDED TACHURI

PLATE: 33

DESCRIPTION: 9.5–10.5 cm (3¾–4¼″). *A tiny, buffy flycatcher found very locally in tall grass areas.* Above mostly brown, rump more ochraceous; crown gray, with elongated blackish feathers (though not appearing crested) partially concealing a white coronal patch; white supraloral, bordered below by *finely streaked black-and-white lower face and chin* (the "beard"). Wings and tail duskier, edged cinnamon-buff, wings with *2 cinnamon-buff bars.* Below pale yellowish white, *washed with cinnamon across breast and down flanks.* Female similar but with brown crown and no "beard." *Brevipennis* (lowlands of ne. Colombia to ne. Brazil) markedly smaller than either *bogotensis* (w. Colombia) or nominate race (s. South America).

SIMILAR SPECIES: Males are quite distinctive, but females are easily confused with the even scarcer Rufous-sided Pygmy-Tyrant (which see).

HABITAT AND BEHAVIOR: Rare to uncommon and very local in savannas, tall grass in cerrado, lightly grazed fields, and adjacent shrubbery. As a result of overgrazing and too-frequent fires, habitats favored by this species have mostly disappeared or persist only at very scattered sites. The Bearded Tachuri may well deserve threatened status (*bogotensis* has not been found at all in over 50 years). It is usually seen clinging to a grass stem, sallying within grass to pick off insects, frequently changing perches but rarely flying far. Inconspicuous and small, it is probably often overlooked. Usually seen singly, less often in pairs, tachuris sometimes accompany flocks of other grassland birds such as seedeaters, Black-masked Finches, and Sharp-tailed Grass-Tyrants. Usually quiet, but displaying males have a plaintive "wheee? whididi-drrr" with a distinctive low, guttural ending, sometimes given during a short display flight.

RANGE: Very locally in w. Colombia (Valle in arid upper Río Dagua valley, and Cundinamarca on the Bogotá savanna; no recent records from either area); locally in ne. Colombia (Meta), Venezuela (primarily in south from Barinas to Bolívar, also a record from near Valencia, Carabobo), Guyana, s. Surinam (Sipaliwini), n. French Guiana (Sinnamary), and extreme n. Brazil (Roraima, n. Pará, and Amapá); e. Bolivia (Santa Cruz), Paraguay, s. Brazil (s. Mato Grosso, Mato Grosso do Sul, s. Goiás, São Paulo, and Rio Grande do Sul), Uruguay, and n. Argentina (south to Mendoza, La Pampa, and w. Buenos Aires). Mostly below 1300 m, at 2600 m in Colombia.

Polystictus superciliaris

GRAY-BACKED TACHURI

PLATE: 33

DESCRIPTION: 9.5 cm (3¾″). *Serras of e. Brazil. Above brownish gray,* with crown purer gray and feathers elongated (though at least nor-

mally not appearing crested), partially concealing a white coronal patch; *short superciliary and eye-ring white.* Wings and tail duskier, with 2 faint brownish gray wing-bars and edging on flight feathers. *Below mostly uniform pinkish buff,* whitish on midbelly.

SIMILAR SPECIES: This tiny, basically bicolored (gray above, buff below) tyrannid does not at all resemble the congeneric Bearded Tachuri. Its color pattern is actually more reminiscent of some Emberizine finches (e.g., certain seedeaters and warbling-finches).

HABITAT AND BEHAVIOR: Uncommon and very local in shrubby and rocky grasslands on certain serras in interior e. Brazil. Usually forages in pairs, clinging to grass stems or perching on branches and gleaning for insects, occasionally dropping to the ground. Generally does not fly long distances. The song is an infrequently given and rather weak, lilting, fast musical trill that stutters at the start, rises slightly, then trails off quickly, "prrrrdududidídídídidudu"; another distinctive call is a bisyllabic "teé kpujj," and a frequent contact call is a quiet, musical "purp" (B. Whitney). Can be found on the Serra do Cipó north of Belo Horizonte, Minas Gerais.

RANGE: E. Brazil (very locally from the Morro do Chapéu in cen. Bahia south through cen. Minas Gerais to the Serra do Bocaina in n. São Paulo). 1100–1600 m.

Culicivora Grass-Tyrants

A monotypic genus and a peculiar tyrannid indeed, with a very long, narrow, frayed-looking tail and a rather thick bill for its body size. Restricted to grasslands of interior s. South America.

Culicivora caudacuta

SHARP-TAILED GRASS-TYRANT   PLATE: 33

Other: Sharp-tailed Tyrant

DESCRIPTION: 10.5 cm (4¼"). *A small tyrannid found locally in grasslands of s.-cen. South America. Tail very long and narrow,* with feathers pointed and barbs stiff and decomposed like a *Synallaxis* spinetail's. Essentially unmistakable. Above mostly buffy brown, *broadly streaked with blackish;* crown blackish, with *long broad superciliary white.* Below mostly yellowish white, broadly washed with cinnamon-buff on sides and flanks.

HABITAT AND BEHAVIOR: Locally fairly common in savannas and cerrado with tall grass, occasionally near water. The grass-tyrant is now very local because of overgrazing and excessive burning over much of its range; it probably deserves threatened status. Numbers are greatest where these human activities are controlled or prevented, as in Brazil's Brasília and Emas Nat. Parks. The grass-tyrant is found singly or in pairs, mostly moving through tall grass, sometimes perching in low bushes; once located, it is often relatively tame. Has been reported (Traylor and Fitzpatrick 1982) to feed to some extent on seeds of grass and other forbs—the only tyrannid known to do so—but RSR has only seen it foraging for insects. The call is an odd, weak, somewhat nasal "wree? wree? wree? wree?," the number of notes variable.

RANGE: Locally in e. Bolivia (from Santa Cruz northwest to n. La Paz), interior s. Brazil (s. Mato Grosso, Mato Grosso do Sul, and cen. Goiás south to w. Paraná), e. Paraguay, and ne. Argentina (south to ne. Santa Fe and Corrientes). To about 1100 m.

NOTE: Formerly called the Sharp-tailed Tyrant, but as *Culicivora* is so typical of the fast-disappearing natural grasslands in its range, we opt to call it a "grass-tyrant."

Euscarthmus Pygmy-Tyrants

A pair of small, brownish, open-country flycatchers. Although both have rufous crown patches, they otherwise seem quite different, with the rare Rufous-sided having a very different, long narrow tail. The two species are possibly not congeneric.

Euscarthmus meloryphus

TAWNY-CROWNED PYGMY-TYRANT　　　　PLATE: 33

DESCRIPTION: 10–10.5 cm (4–4¼"). *Above dull brown* with semiconcealed rufous coronal patch and dull buffy whitish lores and eye-ring; *wings virtually plain* (rufous bars and edging faint or lacking). Throat and breast grayish white, becoming pale yellowish on belly. *Fulviceps* of sw. Ecuador and w. Peru is quite different and virtually unmistakable in its range, with *conspicuous bright buff facial area* and rufescent-tinged forecrown (but rufous coronal patch reduced) and 2 prominent buff wing-bars.

SIMILAR SPECIES: Over most of its range a dull-plumaged pygmy-tyrant which can be known by its overall brown coloration with plain wings, semiopen habitat, and distinctive call. The distinctive western birds are easily recognized.

HABITAT AND BEHAVIOR: Fairly common to common in weedy regenerating clearings, shrubby thickets, arid scrub, and woodland edges. Usually remains close to the ground, where it moves about restlessly but often stays hidden. Most likely to be recorded once its frequently repeated call, a rapid, explosive "plee-ti-re-tik," with several variations, is recognized. Even then you will still have to work hard to actually see it, as vocalizing birds rarely perch in the open. Calls are similar throughout its range.

RANGE: N. Colombia (drier parts of Río Magdalena valley south to Huila) and n. Venezuela (east to n. Bolívar); sw. Ecuador (north to w. Esmeraldas, and in Río Marañón drainage in s. Zamora-Chinchipe) and w. Peru (on Pacific slope south to Lima, and also in upper Río Marañón valley of Amazonas, Cajamarca, and La Libertad); n. and e. Bolivia (northwest to Pando at Humaita), s. and e. Brazil (s. Mato Grosso, Goiás, Piauí, and Ceará south to w. Rio Grande do Sul), e. Paraguay, nw. and ne. Argentina (south to n. Córdoba in the west, to Entre Ríos and extreme n. Buenos Aires in the east), and n. Uruguay. Mostly below 1500 m, but locally to 2000 m in s. Ecuador.

Euscarthmus rufomarginatus

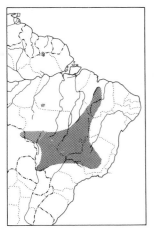

RUFOUS-SIDED PYGMY-TYRANT

DESCRIPTION: 11 cm (4¼"). Very local in savannas of e. South America. Above brown with semiconcealed cinnamon-rufous coronal patch and small white supraloral; wings and *long* tail duskier, *wings with 2 ochraceous wing-bars. Throat white, contrasting with pale yellow of remaining underparts;* sides and flanks rich ochraceous.

SIMILAR SPECIES: Resembles female Bearded Tachuri, and the two are sympatric at several localities. The tachuri has a shorter and thicker bill, not so long and narrow tail feathers, and shows less contrast between the white throat and the yellow of the rest of underparts. Tawny-crowned Pygmy-Tyrant in this species' range is duller generally with virtually plain wings, is not as yellow below, and has *no ochraceous on sides*.

HABITAT AND BEHAVIOR: Rare in cerrado and savannas with very scattered trees and bushes. Usually inconspicuous, foraging alone or in pairs near (sometimes even on) the ground. We do not know its voice. The species is threatened by the conversion of much of its habitat to more intensive agricultural use; a substantial population does, however, apparently exist in Bolivia's Noel Kempff Mercado Nat. Park (which encompasses much of the Serranía de Huanchaca).

RANGE: Very locally in interior s.-cen. Brazil (e. Maranhão at Ponto and s. Piauí at Corrente south and west to cen. Minas Gerais [1990 sightings by A. Whittaker near Belo Horizonte], n. São Paulo [few records], Mato Grosso do Sul, and s. Mato Grosso), extreme ne. Bolivia (ne. Santa Cruz on the Serranía de Huanchaca), and extreme ne. Paraguay (Zanja Morotí in Concepción); s. Surinam (Sipaliwini). To about 1000 m.

Pseudocolopteryx Doraditos

A distinctive group of four generally rather scarce, small, marsh-inhabiting flycatchers, all basically olive above and uniform yellow below, with some additional pattern on head (most marked in Crested). In males of all species except Warbling, some of the primaries are narrow, pointed, or shortened; presumably these are used in as yet undescribed displays. Nests of all species are loosely woven small cups placed in a fork of a bush or small tree growing amidst or at the edge of a reedbed or marsh (de la Peña 1988).

Pseudocolopteryx flaviventris   **WARBLING DORADITO**   PLATE: 33

DESCRIPTION: 11.5 cm (4½"). *Marshes* of s. South America. Dull olive brown to brownish olive above, *more rufescent on crown* (especially forecrown), and with *lores and cheeks dusky;* wing-coverts and flight feathers narrowly tipped and margined buffyish. *Below entirely yellow.*

SIMILAR SPECIES: Cf. similar Subtropical and Dinelli's Doraditos. Warbling Doradito also resembles female Masked Yellowthroat in

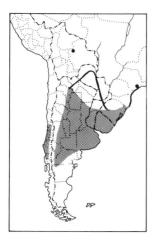

overall coloration (and they often occur together), but their behavior and attitudes differ.

HABITAT AND BEHAVIOR: Locally fairly common in reedbeds in freshwater marshes, to a lesser extent also in bordering shrubbery. Generally shy and inconspicuous, moving about in reedbeds and not often noticed, though it can be excited and lured in by squeaking. The "song" of males in the breeding season is remarkable (though it certainly cannot be described as "warbling"!): a series of odd, disjointed, sharp, squeaky, almost hiccuping, notes, not at all loud and apt to be overlooked, but very distinctive once you recognize it. Its pattern varies, but one sequence frequently heard, at least in Buenos Aires, is "u-eet-u, u-eét!" or simply "u-eét!"

RANGE: Extreme s. Brazil (Rio Grande do Sul), Uruguay, and n. and cen. Argentina (Salta, Córdoba, Santa Fe, and Entre Ríos south to Río Negro and nw. Chubut; n. limit of breeding uncertain); cen. Chile (Aconcagua south to Valdivia). Migratory status still unclear. Apparently only an austral summer resident in Chile, much of Argentina, and Uruguay (Gore and Gepp 1978), but considered a permanent resident in Rio Grande do Sul, Brazil (Belton 1985). Apparently occurs only during austral winter in extreme n. Argentina (e.g., Corrientes) and w. and cen. Paraguay (where records extend from Mar.–Oct.); there are also single records (presumably of overshoots) from Buenavista in Santa Cruz, Bolivia (May), and s. São Paulo, Brazil (June). Mostly below 500 m.

Pseudocolopteryx acutipennis

SUBTROPICAL DORADITO

DESCRIPTION: 11.5 cm (4½"). *Marshes in Andean valleys and adjacent areas. Uniform bright olive green above,* with *cheeks dusky;* wings duskier, with coverts obscurely edged grayish olive. *Below entirely bright yellow.* See C-38. Immature has pale lower mandible and somewhat more prominent wing-bars.

SIMILAR SPECIES: Resembles Warbling Doradito, which is duller and more brownish olive above, has a rufescent tone on crown, and is less bright yellow below. Dinelli's Doradito is also similar but has a rufescent tinge to crown and cheeks.

HABITAT AND BEHAVIOR: Locally fairly common in reedbeds in marshes, sedgy areas, and shrubbery near water, less often in grain fields or tall grassy areas some distance from water. Behavior similar to Warbling Doradito's, which it generally replaces in Andes, though Subtropical seems more catholic in choice of habitat. We do not know its voice. Locally quite numerous in Tucumán and Salta, Argentina, and has recently been found to be resident in a few small sedge-dominated marshes near the Hacienda Cienega, north of Latacunga in Ecuador.

RANGE: Locally in Andes of Colombia (E. Andes in Cundinamarca, Cen. Andes in Antioquia and Caldas), Ecuador (Imbabura south to e. Guayas), Peru, Bolivia, and nw. Argentina (south to La Rioja; also in the hills of Córdoba). Records from Andes of Colombia to Peru have been considered (e.g., C. C. Olrog, *Op. Lill.* 9, 1963) to pertain to austral migrants, but there are numerous recent records from the austral summer, and a nest has been found in Ecuador (J. C. Matheus); we consider austral migration this far north to be unproven and unlikely. Status away from Andes still unclear, with austral migration still a possibility (it is, for instance, thought to be only a summer resident in some parts of Argentina). A scatter of records exist from the lowlands of se. Peru (Madre de Dios) and ne. and e. Bolivia; most are from the austral winter, but one in Oct. from s. Beni causes us to suspect local nesting there. However, a small population is apparently resident in w. Paraguay (locally in Presidente Hayes), where there are 2 records from the austral summer, implying local breeding. To about 3500 m.

Pseudocolopteryx dinellianus

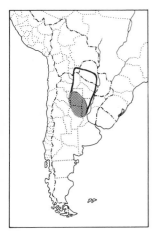

DINELLI'S DORADITO

DESCRIPTION: 11.5 cm (4½"). *Very local in n. Argentina and adjacent Bolivia and w. Paraguay.* Olive above with *rufescent tinge on crown, lores, and cheeks;* wings duskier, narrowly edged buffyish. Below entirely bright yellow.

SIMILAR SPECIES: The least numerous, or at least the most local, of the doraditos. It closely resembles Warbling Doradito, though that is browner above (not so pure olive) with a less rufescent tone on head and distinctly dusky cheeks (lacking in Dinelli's). Subtropical has dusky (not rufescent) lores and cheeks and an olive crown.

HABITAT AND BEHAVIOR: Not well known. Nores et al. (1983) consider it a "more or less common, though not abundant, resident" in 2 places near the Laguna Mar Chiquita in ne. Córdoba, where it frequents reedbeds, grassy marsh vegetation, and adjacent shrubbery. These observers have apparently not found Dinelli's to be sympatric with the other doraditos—in fact, no 2 species in the genus have ever been found to breed together. Its song is an odd, soft but decidedly twangy "redek-redek-redídek" (R. Straneck recording).

RANGE: Breeds very locally in n. Argentina (Tucumán, Santiago del Estero, ne. Córdoba, and Santa Fe); during austral winter moves north to extreme s. Bolivia (Apr. and May specimens from Villa Montes) and w. Paraguay (2 specimens and a few sightings from Presidente Hayes, May–Aug.). To at least 500 m.

Pseudocolopteryx sclateri

CRESTED DORADITO   PLATE: 33

DESCRIPTION: 11 cm (4¼"). *Very local in marshes, mostly in s. South America.* Mostly olive above, mottled with dusky on back; *facial area blackish* and with *long blackish crest feathers usually raised and parted enough to reveal narrow yellowish coronal stripe.* Wings duskier, with 2 pale grayish wing-bars and edging a little more prominent than in other doraditos. Below entirely bright yellow. Apparently females also have a narrow white superciliary.

SIMILAR SPECIES: No other doradito has the crest, feathers of which are usually raised, often imparting a ruffled look.

HABITAT AND BEHAVIOR: Rare to uncommon and very local in marshes and adjacent shrubby vegetation. Usually rather inconspicuous, moving about singly or in pairs in dense reedy or sedgy growth. Responsive to squeaking, when it may perch in the open for fairly long periods. The song is described as a squeaky "tsik-tsik-tsee-lee" and the call as a high, thin, very soft "sik" (R. Andrews and T. Manolis, in Trinidad). May be most numerous in pantanal of Paraguay and n. Argentina, but even there decidedly local, favoring less disturbed marshes with permanent water and seemingly absent from the far more extensive seasonally inundated grasslands. In Venezuela believed to move into ephemeral habitat when conditions are optimal, breeding opportunistically, then disappearing as conditions deteriorate (*fide* C. Parrish).

RANGE: Very locally to w. Venezuela (2 localities in e. Falcón [R. Rivero et al., *fide* C. Parrish]; also seen once in n.-cen. Apure by R. Andrews, *fide* C. Parrish) and Guyana; locally in s. Brazil (a few scattered records from s. Mato Grosso, Rio Grande do Sul, and from Rio de Janeiro north to s. Bahia), Paraguay, and n. Argentina (south to Córdoba and n. Buenos Aires); recorded once from n. Bolivia (Beni); Trinidad. Almost surely occurs in Uruguay. *Contra* several older sources, evidence now available indicates that Crested Doradito is not an austral migrant: it is not known to leave the s. part of its range during austral winter, and is now known to breed in Venezuela and Trinidad (*fide* C. Parrish).

Tachuris Rush-Tyrants

The most colorful of all the flycatchers, the rush-tyrant is found widely in marshes across s. South America. It is characterized by a colorful and complex plumage pattern and long legs (well suited for grasping a pair of reed stalks). The rush-tyrant has an unusual and distinctive nest: attached to a single stem, it is cone-shaped and constructed of dried bits of reed, bound together by an odd, glue-like substance that leaves the outside of the nest remarkably smooth. The genus probably is most closely related to *Pseudocolopteryx,* though nest shapes differ.

Tachuris rubrigastra

MANY-COLORED RUSH-TYRANT   PLATE: 33

DESCRIPTION: 11–11.5 cm (4¼–4½"). *An unmistakable, colorful little flycatcher of marshes in s. South America.* Male has crown black with a partially concealed *red coronal stripe;* conspicuous *long golden superciliary,* with *sides of head glossy blue-black.* Back bright moss green; wings and tail mostly black, wings with single broad white bar and edging on tertials forming stripe; outer tail feathers also white. Below bright yellow, almost orange-yellow on breast, with *broad partial black band across lower breast* and *orange-red to rose-pink crissum.* Female similar but slightly duller with a smaller coronal patch. *Alticola* of altiplano from Peru to nw. Argentina is slightly larger and has wider superciliary;

libertatis of coastal Peru can be whiter below, especially on throat and belly (apparently when plumage is worn), and has less prominent, greener superciliary.

HABITAT AND BEHAVIOR: Locally common in reedbeds and marshes; unlike doraditos, the rush-tyrant seems strictly confined to reedbeds and rarely or never leaves them, even for bordering shrubbery or grassy areas. The marvelous little *siete colores,* as it is locally called (though actually there are 8 or 9 colors), is quite conspicuous as it moves about reedbeds, often flying from patch to patch or perching in the open. It forages mostly by gleaning insects from reed stems or vegetation floating on water, less often by sallying. Constantly on the move, and rather acrobatic, often even hanging upside-down, it is an altogether charming little bird. Even the voice is more musical than that of most flycatchers, with a rich, gurgled effect, e.g., "treetu-tu, teetu-tu-tu."

RANGE: Cen. and s. Peru (along coast from La Libertad to Arequipa, and in altiplano from Junín to Puno), w. Bolivia (La Paz to Potosí), Chile (south to Aysén, but very local in the north), Argentina (altiplano in Jujuy and Salta, and in lowlands from Córdoba and Santa Fe south to Santa Cruz), s. Paraguay (a few recent sightings from Neembucú, *fide* F. Hayes), Uruguay, and s. Brazil (mostly Rio Grande do Sul, also s. São Paulo). Migratory status unclear: it evidently leaves the southernmost part of its breeding range during austral winter, and at least some of the few records from Paraguay, Misiones, Corrientes, and São Paulo may pertain to migrants (though the MZUSP has a specimen taken 12 Dec. 1896 at Iguape in São Paulo which appears to be a juvenile, *fide* D. Stotz). One was recorded 170 km out in the Atlantic Ocean off Rio Grande do Sul on 23 Mar. 1960 (Sick 1985). To 4100 m (*alticola*).

Anairetes Tit-Tyrants

A distinctive group of small flycatchers found in scrub and low woodlands in the Andes and Patagonia. All but one rare species are prominently streaked, and all have obviously bifurcated crests: thin, wispy, and recurved in a few species, long and straight in the others.

Anairetes parulus

TUFTED TIT-TYRANT   PLATE: 33

DESCRIPTION: 11 cm (4¼"). *A tiny, conspicuously crested tit-tyrant of the Colombian Andes south to Tierra del Fuego.* Bill all black; *iris white or pale yellow. Long, thin, recurved crest black,* usually parted with 2-horned effect. Head blackish with narrow white superciliary, streaking on forecrown, and small spot below eye; above otherwise dull grayish brown, wings duskier with 2 narrow whitish wing-bars, outer tail feathers pale-edged. Throat and breast white *conspicuously streaked black,* becoming pale yellow on belly. Nominate race (Chile and adjacent s. Argentina) has wing-bars reduced or absent.

SIMILAR SPECIES: Cf. Yellow-billed Tit-Tyrant. Agile and Unstreaked

Tit-Tyrants are larger with longer tails and have flatter crests with no forward curl, more prominent superciliaries, and dark irides.

HABITAT AND BEHAVIOR: Uncommon to locally common in shrubbery and borders of low forest and woodland, including *Polylepis,* often right up to or even above treeline. In Peruvian and Bolivian Andes tends to favor more humid areas, and thus mainly occurs on east slope; in Chile favors monte, in Argentina scrub and low woodland. Usually in pairs or small groups, foraging rather low in dense bushes and trees, often shivering wings nervously. Seldom with mixed flocks. The song is a fairly loud, fast "chuit-chuit-chuit-chuit-chuit-chuit-chuit-chidi-didi"; it also has other chattering or trilled calls.

RANGE: Andes of s. Colombia (north in Cen. Andes to Cauca), Ecuador (south on w. slope to Azuay), e. Peru (also recorded on w. slope in *Polylepis* groves at Pampa Galeras in Ayacucho), w. Bolivia, and Chile (north to s. Antofogasta; also in lowlands of cen. and s. Chile) and w. Argentina (also ranging east to Córdoba and across Patagonia to extreme s. Buenos Aires) south to Tierra del Fuego. Apparently only a summer visitant in southernmost part of range; the race *patagonicus* is recorded north during austral winter to nw. Argentina in Tucumán and Salta, where it locally overlaps with resident *aequatorialis.* To about 3500 m (rarely to 4000 m) in n. part of range; in cen. Chile up only to about 2000 m.

Anairetes fernandezianus

JUAN FERNANDEZ TIT-TYRANT

DESCRIPTION: 12.5 cm (5"). *Restricted to Juan Fernández Is. off Chile.* Resembles Tufted Tit-Tyrant but considerably larger and longer-crested and with heavier breast streaking and whiter belly.

SIMILAR SPECIES: The only small insectivorous bird on Isla Robinson Crusoe, the island to which it is now restricted.

HABITAT AND BEHAVIOR: Until recently feared extinct (Traylor and Fitzpatrick 1982), but now known to be common in all wooded habitats, including those with natural, disturbed, and more or less exotic vegetation (M. de L. Brooke, *Birds of the Juan Fernández Islands, Chile,* ICBP Study Report no. 16, 1987). Behavior apparently much like Tufted Tit-Tyrant's.

RANGE: Juan Fernández Is. on Isla Robinson Crusoe (formerly Isla Masatierra) off s. Chile. To 900 m.

NOTE: Usually considered most closely related to *A. parulus* of the adjacent mainland, but Vuilleumier (1985) suggests that a relationship with *A. reguloides* is just as likely.

Anairetes flavirostris

YELLOW-BILLED TIT-TYRANT

DESCRIPTION: 11.5 cm (4½"). *Peruvian Andes south to Argentina.* Resembles Tufted Tit-Tyrant. Differs in its *dark iris* (pale in Tufted), *mostly pale lower mandible* (varying from yellowish to pale orange; bill all black in Tufted), less black face (with more white streaking in crown

and on cheeks), less recurved crest, bolder wing-bars, and *broader black breast streaking ending abruptly at yellow belly.*

SIMILAR SPECIES: Tufted Tit-Tyrant favors more humid areas, whereas Yellow-billed tends to occur in more xeric areas and is often found in shrubbery out on the altiplano. Yellow-billed also resembles Pied-crested Tit-Tyrant, but the latter is slightly larger with a blacker face and throat and has an even longer black crest showing more white in its center, a black-and-white streaked back (not plain dull grayish), and whiter belly.

HABITAT AND BEHAVIOR: Fairly common to common in low thickets and shrubbery, often quite sparse, and in hedgerows in partially cultivated areas; usually found in more arid regions, though regular in streamside vegetation in such areas. Behavior similar to Tufted Tit-Tyrant's. Usually quiet; its infrequently heard song is a series (sometimes long) of high, thin wiry notes.

RANGE: Andes of Peru (north to Piura and Cajamarca), w. Bolivia, extreme n. Chile (n. Tarapacá), and w. Argentina (south to Mendoza and Río Negro, ranging out onto Patagonian lowlands from La Pampa to Chubut; during austral winter recorded east rarely to Buenos Aires and Entre Ríos). Extent of migration remains uncertain, but it is apparently absent from southernmost part of range during winter and at that season certainly occurs farther east in Argentina. To about 4000 m.

Anairetes reguloides

PIED-CRESTED TIT-TYRANT

PLATE: 33

DESCRIPTION: 11.5 cm (4½"). *Mainly w. Peru;* Black-crested Tit-Tyrant is regarded as a separate species. Lower mandible yellowish flesh. Long, thin, bifurcated crest mainly black, usually parted to reveal *extensive white in crown and on nape.* Male has *face and throat black; back broadly streaked black and white;* wings and tail blackish, wings with 2 bold white bars, outer tail feathers with white outer web, others with narrow white tips. *Breast coarsely streaked black and white,* belly white. Belly of nominate race of sw. Peru (north to s. Ayacucho and Arequipa) and n. Chile is tinged very pale yellow. Birds with full black faces, presumably older adult males, form a distinct minority of specimens. Female has throat indistinctly streaked black and white.

SIMILAR SPECIES: Cf. Black-crested Tit-Tyrant. Otherwise this striking flycatcher is likely to be confused only with Yellow-billed Tit-Tyrant, which is slightly smaller with much less black on face and no streaks on back.

HABITAT AND BEHAVIOR: Fairly common on shrubby hillsides and thick hedgerows in partially cultivated areas. General behavior similar to Tufted and Yellow-billed Tit-Tyrants'; found with the latter in shrub zone above Huinco, in the Río Santa Eulalia valley of Lima, Peru. Often gives a series of loud whistled notes which descend in pitch, vaguely reminiscent of Southern Beardless-Tyrannulet (Fjeldså and Krabbe 1990).

RANGE: Pacific slope of w. Peru (north to w. Ancash) and extreme n. Chile (n. Tarapacá). To about 3000 m (occasionally to 3300 m).

NOTE: See comments under Black-crested Tit-Tyrant.

Anairetes nigrocristatus

BLACK-CRESTED TIT-TYRANT

Other: Pied-crested Tit-Tyrant (in part)

DESCRIPTION: 13 cm (5″). *Mainly n. and cen. Peru.* Resembles Pied-crested Tit-Tyrant (and formerly often considered conspecific with it) but *notably larger* and with *much longer crest;* tail feathers are more broadly tipped white; and both sexes have throat mottled or streaked with white, thus lacking the black-gorgeted effect of male Pied-crested.
SIMILAR SPECIES: This most spectacular of the tit-tyrants is so much larger and longer-crested than any of the others (including even Pied-crested) that confusion is unlikely.
HABITAT AND BEHAVIOR: Uncommon in *Polylepis* woodland and low shrubby montane vegetation. Behavior much like other tit-tyrants', gleaning and sallying among foliage; sometimes occurs with Tufted Tit-Tyrant. One call is an explosive, rapid series of notes, "wheek-titititttttiti," lasting about 3 seconds (T. A. Parker III et al. 1985). Can be found in *Polylepis* woodland near La Quinua, along the road between Huánuco and Lake Junín in Peru.
RANGE: Andes of extreme s. Ecuador (near Utuana in extreme s. Loja; B. Best et al. and ANSP) and w. Peru (Piura and Cajamarca south to e. Ancash, w. Huánuco, and w. Pasco). 2300–3500 m.

NOTE: Although this species was considered conspecific with *A. reguloides* by Meyer de Schauensee (1966, 1970) and most other recent authors, we believe that the markedly larger and longer-crested *nigrocristatus* deserves recognition as a full species until intergradation between *A. nigrocristatus* and the less montane *A. reguloides* can be shown. Fjeldså and Krabbe (1990, p. 471) also treat *A. nigrocristatus* as a full species; they indicate that *A. nigrocristatus* and *A. reguloides* are "perhaps sympatric" in the Cordillera Blanca of Ancash, Peru.

Anairetes alpinus

ASH-BREASTED TIT-TYRANT

DESCRIPTION: 13.5 cm (5¼″). *Very local in isolated high Polylepis woodlands of Peru and w. Bolivia. Mostly dark ashy gray with no streaking;* long, narrow, bifurcated crest, usually parted to reveal a white patch on hindcrown; wings black with 2 broad white wing-bars and edging on inner flight feathers; tail black with outer feathers mostly white. Unstreaked belly is yellowish white (nominate race; Ancash, Peru) or white (*bolivianus;* s. Peru and w. Bolivia).
SIMILAR SPECIES: Other tit-tyrants with long bifurcated crests have prominent streaking on breast. Unstreaked Tit-Tyrant is found at lower elevations than this species (in temperate zone forests on e. slope of Andes), lacks the long recurved crest (its crest is basically flat), and has a white superciliary and gray breast vaguely streaked whitish.
HABITAT AND BEHAVIOR: Very local and rare in isolated groves of *Polylepis* woodland with an understory of *Gynoxys* shrubs, at and somewhat above treeline. Behavior similar to other *Anairetes* tit-tyrants' (Parker and O'Neill 1980). Usually quiet, though sometimes giving a

complaining "eeeh" (Fjeldså and Krabbe 1990). Occurs within Peru's Huascarán Nat. Park, but even there hard to find; the species is threatened by the continued destruction of *Polylepis*.

RANGE: Very locally in high Andes of Peru (Ancash on the Cordillera Blanca; southeast of Abancay in ne. Apurímac, and in Cuzco on the Cordillera Vilcanota, e.g., at Abra Málaga) and w. Bolivia (known only from a 1935 specimen from north of La Paz [city] in La Paz; possible Cochabamba sightings). 3700–4600 m.

Uromyias Tit-Tyrants

A pair of small flycatchers found in the high Andes from extreme w. Venezuela to Peru. Both species have flat, black crests showing no tufts (unlike the *Anairetes* tit-tyrants) and fairly long tails. Although Traylor (1977) placed both species in *Anairetes*, Lanyon (1988a) suggests that certain anatomical characters, as well as its external morphology and behavior, argue for the retention of *Uromyias* as a separate genus.

Uromyias agilis

AGILE TIT-TYRANT   PLATE: 33

DESCRIPTION: 13–13.5 cm (5–5¼"). *Andes from w. Venezuela to Ecuador.* Lower mandible basally orange-yellow. *Long flat crest blackish,* usually protruding slightly to rear, bordered below by *long, narrow, "raised" white superciliary.* Above brown, broadly streaked blackish on back; wings and tail dusky. Below yellowish white, *narrowly streaked brown on throat, breast, and flanks;* belly pale yellow.

SIMILAR SPECIES: Tufted Tit-Tyrant is markedly smaller and shorter-tailed, has a narrow but obviously bifurcated and recurved crest, and shows wing-bars. Cf. also Unstreaked Tit-Tyrant (no overlap).

HABITAT AND BEHAVIOR: Fairly common in lower growth and especially borders of montane forest and woodland, favoring stands of *Chusquea* bamboo; can occur in shrubbery and low trees up to treeline, but mostly found a little lower. Usually moves in small groups of up to 5–6 individuals (less often only pairs) which almost always accompany mixed flocks (a marked behavioral difference from *Anairetes* tit-tyrants). Forages actively by gleaning from foliage and twigs; both *Uromyias* tit-tyrants behave much more like chickadees (*Parus* spp.) than do the *Anairetes* tit-tyrants. Agile's call is a simple, short, soft trill, with various "conversational" notes also given while foraging.

RANGE: Andes of extreme w. Venezuela (n. Táchira at Páramo Zumbador), Colombia (E. Andes from Boyacá southward; Cen. Andes north to Cauca), and Ecuador (south on w. slope to w. Cotopaxi, on e. slope to n. Loja on the Cordillera Cordoncillo [ANSP, MECN]). Mostly 2700–3400 m, but recorded down to 1800 m in Colombia.

Uromyias agraphia

UNSTREAKED TIT-TYRANT   PLATE: 33

DESCRIPTION: 13 cm (5"). *Local on e. slope of Andes in Peru.* Bill black. *Crown and nape sooty black contrasting with plain brown back, wings, and*

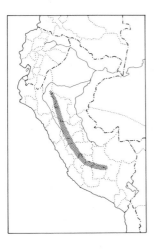

tail; superciliary mottled gray and white. *Sides of head, neck, throat, and breast gray* with vague whitish streaking; pale yellow belly. *Plengei* (Cordillera de Colán in Amazonas) similar but more olivaceous above, belly whiter.

SIMILAR SPECIES: Clearly the s. replacement for Agile Tit-Tyrant (no overlap); Unstreaked is less streaked overall and has a "normal" super-ciliary (not "raised" above the usual superciliary placement, as is Agile's). Cf. also Tufted and Ash-breasted Tit-Tyrants.

HABITAT AND BEHAVIOR: Uncommon and local in lower growth and borders of montane forest and woodland, especially where there are dense stands of *Chusquea* bamboo. Behavior much like Agile Tit-Tyrant's. Can be seen along the Abra Málaga road in Cuzco, Peru (on the "far" side of the pass). Vocally it seems similar to Agile Tit-Tyrant.

RANGE: Locally on e. slope of Andes in Peru (Amazonas on the Cordillera de Colán; e. La Libertad on the Mashua-Ongón trail; Huánuco in the Carpish Mts.; Cuzco on the Cordillera Vilcanota). Mostly 2700–3100 m.

Capsiempis Tyrannulets

A small, very yellow tyrannulet found locally in lower growth of wood-land and borders. Its affinities have been disputed. Traylor (1977) sank it into *Phylloscartes,* but W. E. Lanyon (*Condor* 86[1]: 42–47, 1984) argued against this merger. He suggested, based on its nasal septum and syrinx, that *Capsiempis* is much closer to *Phaeomyias,* and that these genera, with *Nesotriccus* from Cocos Is. off Costa Rica, form a distinct natural grouping.

Capsiempis flaveola

YELLOW TYRANNULET   PLATE: 34

DESCRIPTION: 11.5 cm (4½"). Slender and rather long-tailed. Mostly *yellowish* olive above with *bold yellow superciliary;* wings dusky with yel-lowish edging and *2 broad yellow wing-bars. Below entirely yellow.* Birds of Caribbean lowlands in n. Colombia and nw. Venezuela (*leucophrys*) have *white* superciliary and chin.

SIMILAR SPECIES: No other similar tyrannulet gives such a yellow overall impression.

HABITAT AND BEHAVIOR: Fairly common to common in woodland borders and shrubby clearings and in forest and woodland lower growth, often where there is much bamboo. Forages in pairs or small groups, usually apart from mixed flocks, gleaning actively much like a warbler, also regularly perching quite upright. The frequently given call is rather pleasant-sounding and rollicking; it usually starts slowly but then speeds up rapidly and seems to lack any recognizable pattern. Also often gives a short dry trill, "tr-r-r-r-r."

RANGE: Colombia (Caribbean lowlands from Sucre east to Santa Marta Mts., and south in Río Magdalena valley to Cundinamarca; also east of Andes south to Nariño and Vaupés), ne. Ecuador (w. Napo),

Venezuela, Guianas, and n. and e. Amaz. Brazil (upper Rio Negro drainage east locally to lower Amazon area and n. Maranhão, and south to n. Mato Grosso at Alta Floresta); w. Ecuador (Pichincha south to El Oro); se. Peru (recent FMNH specimen from Cuzco at Hacienda Amazonia, and sightings from adjacent Madre de Dios, *fide* D. Stotz), and ne. Bolivia (n. Beni at San Joaquin [ANSP]; Santa Cruz at Guarayos) and adjacent sw. Brazil (s. Mato Grosso at Porto Limão); e. Brazil (Paraíba south to n. Rio Grande do Sul, and west locally into s. Goiás), e. Paraguay (west to Paraguarí), and ne. Argentina (Misiones). Also Nicaragua to Panama. To 1500 m.

Phylloscartes Tyrannulets and Bristle-Tyrants

This large and diverse group of small tyrannids was until recently separated into three genera: *Phylloscartes* for a large group of slender, long-tailed tyrannulets; *Leptotriccus,* a single species with similar general configuration; and *Pogonotriccus* for a group of mainly Andean tyrannids called bristle-tyrants. All three genera were combined into a single genus by Traylor (1977), and we follow his taxonomic lead. All are united by their relatively long slender bills. There are, however, distinct differences between what was formerly called *Pogonotriccus* and the typical *Phylloscartes* tyrannulets. *Pogonotriccus* are less active and perch vertically, whereas true *Phylloscartes* (including *Leptotriccus*) move about very energetically, perch horizontally, and often hold their long tail cocked up; they often droop and shiver their wings, and they also sometimes lift them upward. No species combines these behavioral differences. Recent field work has identified three species that were formerly placed in the wrong group. *P. gualaquizae* and *P. flaviventris* were formerly placed with the bristle-tyrants but are actually typical true *Phylloscartes* tyrannulets, whereas *P. chapmani* was previously considered a typical *Phylloscartes* tyrannulet but is actually by behavior a bristle-tyrant. When the various species of the two groups are separated correctly and then analyzed for various morphological and anatomical characters, we suspect that differences formerly obscured by their misallocation will emerge; this may result in the need to resurrect the genus *Pogonotriccus.*

Not only is there confusion within the genus *Phylloscartes,* there remains the likelihood of confusion between certain of its species and various other tyrannulet genera, notably *Phyllomyias* (despite the latter's shorter bill).

Phylloscartes tyrannulets and bristle-tyrants are found in humid forests, with many true *Phylloscartes* favoring the canopy and upper levels, whereas bristle-tyrants range at lower and middle levels inside forest. Most species are found in montane areas, and there exists a notable diversity in se. South America; equally notable is their absence from all but the fringes of Amazonia. A number of species are rare or have extremely small ranges; no less than three new species have been described in recent years, and a fourth awaits formal description.

Nesting appears to be unreported in the literature, but an almost completed nest of the Mottle-cheeked Tyrannulet found in Nov. 1991 in nw. Argentina (RSR) was a rather large cup with a domed roof (the nest lining and roof with considerable moss) placed close to the ground in a clump of dead vegetation on a steep, almost inaccessible bank.

GROUP A

"True" *Phylloscartes* with *rather weak facial pattern,* but wing-bars *prominent.*

Phylloscartes ventralis

MOTTLE-CHEEKED TYRANNULET   PLATE: 34

DESCRIPTION: 12 cm (4¾"). *E. slope of Andes from Peru to n. Argentina, and in se. Brazil area. Slender and quite long-tailed.* Bill black. Uniform olive above with *whitish supraloral and eye-ring,* dusky line from lores through eye onto ear-coverts, and some dusky mottling (despite the species' name, *not* very conspicuous) on whitish cheeks; wings and tail duskier, wings with *2 bold pale yellow bars* and edging on flight feathers. *Mostly pale yellow below,* more whitish on throat and clouded with buffy olive on breast.

SIMILAR SPECIES: This tyrannulet is rather common over most of its range; use it as the basis of comparison with various other (usually rarer) species. Confusion is most likely with various *Phyllomyias* tyrannulets; cf. especially Sclater's (in Andes), Rough-legged, and (in the southeast) Planalto, Greenish, and Restinga Tyrannulets. The generic characters of *Phylloscartes* (relatively long slender bill, horizontal posture, and partially cocked tail) are often more helpful than any specific plumage differences.

HABITAT AND BEHAVIOR: Fairly common to common in canopy and borders of montane and humid forest and older secondary woodland, less often out into adjacent clearings with scattered trees. Usually noted singly or in pairs, foraging quickly and restlessly, generally with mixed flocks but sometimes apart. Easy to see as it most often gleans partially or fully in the open, usually on terminal twigs and leaves. The call in se. Brazil is a loud, somewhat musical "chididididit" (D. Stotz; RSR), in nw. Argentina a distinctive, spritely "whík-whík-whi-i-i-i-r, whik-whik" (RSR).

RANGE: E. slope of Andes in Peru (north to San Martín), Bolivia, and nw. Argentina (south to Tucumán and Catamarca); se. Brazil (north to s. Minas Gerais and se. Mato Grosso do Sul), e. Paraguay (west to Paraguarí), ne. Argentina (south to n. Buenos Aires), and Uruguay. Mostly 1000–2200 m in Andes; up to about 1500 m in se. South America.

Phylloscartes ceciliae

ALAGOAS TYRANNULET
Other: Long-tailed Tyrannulet

DESCRIPTION: 12 cm (4¾"). *Ne. Brazil in Alagoas.* Dark olive above with *prominent whitish superciliary,* also a less conspicuous eliptical whitish area extending from below eye onto ear-coverts, the latter out-

lined with dusky; wings and tail duskier, wings with *2 bold pale yellowish bars. Below uniform whitish.*

SIMILAR SPECIES: *The only Phylloscartes tyrannulet in its range,* and thus readily recognizable on the basis of genus characters alone, especially its long and usually cocked tail. Mottle-cheeked Tyrannulet (no overlap) is the most similar but is yellower below with a less complex facial pattern. Cf. sympatric Slender-footed Tyrannulet (different wing pattern, shorter bill).

HABITAT AND BEHAVIOR: Locally fairly common in canopy and borders of humid forest and secondary woodland. Recently discovered on the slopes of Pedra Branca, a range of low coastal mts. north of Murici in Alagoas, where it is quite numerous; an additional population has since been located in the Quebrangulo area, some of which has recently been incorporated into the Pedra Talhada Biological Reserve. With its very limited total range, much of which continues to be under threat of deforestation, the species clearly qualifies for formal endangered status. Behavior similar to Mottle-cheeked Tyrannulet's. Seems not very vocal; the only call RSR has heard is an occasional fast "sweek! sweek-a-dee-deek."

RANGE: Ne. Brazil (Alagoas). 400–550 m.

NOTE: A recently described species: D. M. Teixera, *Bull. B. O. C.* 107(1): 37–41, 1987. Although he considered it closest to *P. difficilis,* in plumage and behavior we find it much more like *P. ventralis.* Teixera (op. cit.) suggested the English name of Long-tailed Tyrannulet for the species, although its tail is in fact not especially long for the genus. We prefer to emphasize its extremely limited range by employing a geographical epithet.

Phylloscartes kronei

RESTINGA TYRANNULET

DESCRIPTION: 12 cm (4¾"). *Restinga woodlands of coastal se. Brazil.* Closely resembles Mottle-cheeked Tyrannulet (found inland in montane forest) but differs in its *yellow* (not whitish) *supraloral, quite bright yellow cheeks and throat* (but with similar dusky mottling as Mottle-cheeked), and olive mottling on chest with no buff tinge.

SIMILAR SPECIES: Not known to overlap with similar Mottle-cheeked Tyrannulet, with which it was confused until very recently; in se. Brazil Mottle-cheeked is exclusively a bird of the highlands.

HABITAT AND BEHAVIOR: Fairly common in scrubby restinga woodland and second-growth near the coast, often just back from the beach. Behavior similar to Mottle-cheeked Tyrannulet's, usually in pairs or small groups, sometimes accompanying mixed flocks; apparently somewhat less active, and does not tend to cock tail as much. Its frequently heard call is a short "feesee" or "plea"; also gives a fast twittering song, e.g., "sit-it-it-it-it-it-it-it-it-it-sitit-sitit." Can be seen on Ilha Comprida along the se. São Paulo coast, but there and probably elsewhere threatened by coastal development.

RANGE: Coastal se. Brazil (se. São Paulo south to Joinville in ne. Santa Catarina). Near sea level.

NOTE: A recently described species: E. O. Willis and Y. Oniki, *Bull. B. O. C.* 112(3): 158–165, 1992. All of the above information is derived from this article.

Phylloscartes virescens

OLIVE-GREEN TYRANNULET

DESCRIPTION: 12 cm (4¾"). *Mainly in Guianas.* Rather closely resembles geographically distant Mottle-cheeked Tyrannulet. Differs mainly in having no yellowish supraloral and no dusky line through eye; a pale yellow eye-ring is quite prominent; not quite as bright yellow below.

SIMILAR SPECIES: Typical *Phylloscartes* shape and posture should be distinctive in its range. Confusion most likely with Slender-footed Tyrannulet (which has a very different wing pattern, showing obvious yellow edging even on coverts but *no bars;* it also has a gray crown), and Forest and female Gray Elaenia.

HABITAT AND BEHAVIOR: Rare (perhaps in reality more difficult to see or collect) in canopy and borders of humid forest. Not well known. Pairs and single birds have been noted accompanying mixed canopy flocks; behavior (including wing-lifting) seems to differ little from congeners'. Has been seen at Brownsberg Nature Park, Surinam, and from the INPA/WWF tower north of Manaus.

RANGE: Guianas; recently (1988 onwards) also seen by various observers (including RSR and M. Cohn-Haft) north of Manaus in Amazonas, Brazil. To about 500 m.

NOTE: Yellow-green Tyrannulet, *P. flavovirens,* was seen virtually on the Colombian boundary on Cerro Quía, Darién, in July 1975 (RSR) and almost certainly ranges on the Colombian side of that mountain. This Panama "endemic" closely resembles Olive-green Tyrannulet (and Mottle-cheeked as well), but it shows mainly an eye-ring (no supraloral) and also has an obscure dark crescent on the ear-coverts.

Phylloscartes gualaquizae

ECUADORIAN TYRANNULET

Other: Ecuadorian Bristle-Tyrant

DESCRIPTION: 11.5 cm (4½"). *Foothills at e. base of Andes in Ecuador and n. Peru.* Bill black. *Crown gray; indistinct superciliary and narrow eye-ring white; cheeks whitish, indistinctly outlined with blackish.* Above otherwise olive; wings and tail blackish, wings with 2 pale yellow bars and narrow edging on flight feathers. Throat whitish; breast mottled olive and pale yellow; belly clear yellow.

SIMILAR SPECIES: Easily confused. So closely resembles Plumbeous-crowned Tyrannulet that the two are barely distinguishable in the field. Plumbeous-crowned is slightly larger overall with a slightly shorter bill and has a pale area behind the dark ear-crescent; it is found mostly, if not entirely, at higher elevations. Spectacled Bristle-Tyrant's behavior is different (it is a typical "*Pogonotriccus*"), but its plumage is quite similar; it differs in its bolder eye-ring, yellower underparts, and pale lower mandible. Cf. also White-fronted Tyrannulet, which has a shorter bill with at least a partially pale lower mandible, as well as different facial pattern details.

HABITAT AND BEHAVIOR: Rare to uncommon in canopy and borders of montane forest in foothills, occasionally out into tall trees in adjacent clearings. Perhaps more numerous than the few records seem to indicate; birds recently collected (ANSP) in the Cordillera de Cutucú,

Ecuador, were for a while misidentified as White-fronted Tyrannulets even after they were in the hand! There the Ecuadorian was seen to forage singly in foliage and on limbs, almost always with mixed flocks of tanagers, other tyrannids, etc. Its vocalizations include a thin "feeee" and a more spitting, rattled "sp-i-i-i-i-i-i" somewhat reminiscent of the common call of Cinnamon Flycatcher.

RANGE: Foothills along e. slope of Andes in Ecuador (north to w. Sucumbios and w. Napo; ANSP) and n. Peru (n. San Martín). Mostly 800–1200 m.

NOTE: Formerly called the Ecuadorian Bristle-Tyrant and placed in the genus *Pogonotriccus*. For more information on this species, see M. B. Robbins et al. (*Proc. Acad. Nat. Sci. Phila.* 139: 243–259, 1987).

GROUP B

"True" *Phylloscartes* with *obvious black or rufous on brow or lores;* all scarce or "range-restricted."

Phylloscartes nigrifrons

BLACK-FRONTED TYRANNULET   PLATE: 34

DESCRIPTION: 12 cm (4¾"). *Tepuis of s. Venezuela. Forehead and lores black,* with indistinct short whitish superciliary and gray crown; *cheeks mottled whitish, narrowly outlined with black.* Above otherwise olive; wings and tail duskier, wings with 2 prominent pale yellow bars and edging on flight feathers. *Below mostly pale grayish,* whiter on belly, tinged pale yellow on flanks and crissum.
SIMILAR SPECIES: Nothing really similar in its limited range, but cf. Chapman's Bristle-Tyrant (with very different vertical posture, plumage).
HABITAT AND BEHAVIOR: Fairly common in canopy and borders of humid forest on slopes of the tepuis. Usually seen singly, less often in pairs, as it forages with mixed flocks, actively gleaning from foliage. Its horizontal posture resembles that of other typical *Phylloscartes* tyrannulets. We do not know its voice. Regularly seen in tall forest along upper part of the Escalera road in e. Bolívar.
RANGE: S. Venezuela (Bolívar and Amazonas south to Cerro de la Neblina, the last based on a USNM specimen formerly identified as a Slaty-capped Flycatcher, *fide* G. R. Graves). Probably occurs in adjacent Brazil and Guyana, but as yet unrecorded. 900–1800 m.

Phylloscartes superciliaris

RUFOUS-BROWED TYRANNULET

DESCRIPTION: 11.5 cm (4½"). *Very local in n. Colombia, nw. Venezuela, and se. Ecuador.* Crown and nape slaty with *narrow rufous frontal band and superciliary;* spot at base of bill and *ear-coverts white, latter narrowly encircled by black.* Otherwise mostly olive above, wings and tail duskier edged with yellowish green. Throat and breast pale grayish, becoming white on belly. See C-36.
SIMILAR SPECIES: The rufous superciliary is dark and rather inconspicuous, but the rest of the complex facial pattern should preclude confusion of this scarce, local species.

Phylloscartes flaviventris

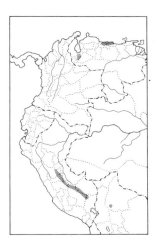

HABITAT AND BEHAVIOR: Uncommon and very local in canopy and borders of montane forest. Forages actively in foliage, almost bringing to mind a gnatcatcher (an impression further enhanced by the tyrannulet's long, often partially cocked tail). Usually seen accompanying mixed flocks of tanagers, other tyrannids, etc. Its call in Ecuador is a spritely "spee-ee-ee-ee-ee, spee-didi-dee."

RANGE: Very locally on slopes of Sierra de Perijá on Venezuelan side, w. slope of E. Andes in ne. Colombia (se. Santander at Virolín; there is also an old "Bogotá" skin without precise locality, and the species may occur in nw. Chocó on Colombian side of Cerro Tacarcuna), and e. slope of Andes in se. Ecuador (Cordillera de Cutucú in Morona-Santiago and Cordillera del Condor in Zamora-Chinchipe). Also Costa Rica and Panama. 1650–2000 m.

RUFOUS-LORED TYRANNULET   PLATE: 34

Other: Yellow-bellied Bristle-Tyrant

DESCRIPTION: 11.5 cm (4½"). *Highly disjunct range in mts. of n. Venezuela and foothills of e. Peru* (2 species are almost certainly involved). *Lores and eye-ring rufous,* with short pale yellowish superciliary; *ear-coverts mostly black,* with small yellowish area in center. Above otherwise olive; wings and long tail duskier, wings with 2 prominent pale yellow bars and edging on flight feathers. *Below entirely bright yellow.* Foregoing applies to Venezuelan birds. The still unnamed birds from Peru and Bolivia are similar but have *more extensive and deeper rufous* (more a *chestnut* tone) *on face,* extending back as a supraloral; sides of head buffier and crown *slaty.*

SIMILAR SPECIES: Other tyrannulets with rufous on face are grayish or whitish (not yellow) below; none is found in the range of this one. Note that this species was long considered a *Pogonotriccus* bristle-tyrant, though observations of living birds of both forms (in Venezuela and Peru) confirm that they are typical *Phylloscartes* tyrannulets.

HABITAT AND BEHAVIOR: Rare to locally uncommon in canopy and borders of humid forest, especially in foothill areas. Behavior similar to others' in the genus, foraging singly or in pairs, most often with mixed flocks. Horizontal perching posture and long, partially cocked tail are typical of the true *Phylloscartes* tyrannulets; the wings are often shivered and occasionally raised. Peruvian form frequently gives a fast, spritely "chit, chit, tr-ree-e-e-e-e"; voice in Venezuela not known to us. Venezuelan birds are regularly found at Rancho Grande and along the Choroni road in Henri Pittier Nat. Park in Aragua; Peruvian birds can be seen along the lower part of the Shintuya-Paucartambo road in Cuzco.

RANGE: Coastal mts. of n. Venezuela (Aragua, Distrito Federal, and Miranda), and Andes of w. Venezuela (Mérida); locally on e. slope of Andes in cen. and s. Peru (Huánuco, Pasco, and Cuzco) and n. Bolivia (Serranía Pilón in s. Beni). 750–1500 m.

NOTE: Although formerly called the Yellow-bellied Bristle-Tyrant, this species is not a bristle-tyrant (using the restricted sense we employ, based on the posture and behavior of living birds), but rather a typical *Phylloscartes* tyrannulet. *Ornithion semiflavum* of Middle America is already named the Yellow-bellied Tyrannulet, and thus a new name for *P. flaviventris* is needed. We opt to emphasize its most distinctive feature, the rufous on its lores. When the Peruvian form is formally named, we suggest the English name Chestnut-lored Tyrannulet.

Phylloscartes roquettei

MINAS GERAIS TYRANNULET

DESCRIPTION: 11.5 cm (4½"). *Interior se. Brazil;* known from only a single specimen. Very closely resembles the geographically remote Rufous-lored Tyrannulet but apparently lacks that species' pale yellowish superciliary (at least it is not figured in the color illustration accompanying the bird's description) and has a yellower rump (*fide* D. Stotz).
SIMILAR SPECIES: Nothing really similar in range. Bay-ringed Tyrannulet has pale grayish, not bright yellow, underparts.
HABITAT AND BEHAVIOR: Very poorly known. In Sept. 1977, E. O. Willis and Y. Oniki observed this species in the canopy of deciduous forest near the type locality, but apparently it has not been observed there since. At that time the tyrannulets foraged mainly in pairs. The region has undergone considerable deforestation, and it is to be hoped that at least some remnants can be permanently protected. All the above information is summarized from Collar et al. (1992).
RANGE: Se. Brazil (n. Minas Gerais at Brejo Januária, near the Rio São Francisco). 450 m.

GROUP C

"True" *Phylloscartes endemic to se. Brazil region;* all with *distinctive facial patterns,* but *no wing-bars.*

Phylloscartes sylviolus

BAY-RINGED TYRANNULET

PLATE: 34

DESCRIPTION: 11 cm (4¼"). *Se. Brazil area.* Iris whitish. Mostly rather bright yellowish olive above, with *lores and especially eye-ring rufouschestnut;* wings and tail duskier, wing feathers edged yellowish olive (but no bars). Throat pale buffy yellow, becoming *whitish on remaining underparts,* crissum tinged buffy yellow.
SIMILAR SPECIES: No other similar tyrannulet in range has rufous on face.
HABITAT AND BEHAVIOR: Uncommon in canopy and borders of humid forest. Usually found singly or in pairs, less often 3–5 birds associating together, accompanying mixed flocks of other insectivorous birds through upper strata. Its active, spritely behavior and characteristic silhouette, especially the long, slender, usually half-cocked tail, bring to mind a gnatcatcher. Regularly found in forest near Iguazú Falls (on both Argentinian and Brazilian sides), but overall numbers must have declined substantially because of destruction of much forest within its range. Its song is a complex, fast, spritely "swit-swi-swi-swi-swi-sweédeédeédeédeé-swi-swi."
RANGE: Se. Brazil (Espírito Santo and s. Minas Gerais south to Santa Catarina), e. Paraguay (Canendiyu south to Itapúa), and ne. Argentina (Misiones). Below 300 m.

NOTE: Formerly placed in the monotypic genus *Leptotriccus*. We follow Traylor (1977) in merging this into *Phylloscartes*.

Phylloscartes oustaleti

OUSTALET'S TYRANNULET   PLATE: 34

DESCRIPTION: 13 cm (5"). *Se. Brazil.* Mostly olive above with *conspicuous wide yellow eye-ring, large blackish auricular patch with bright yellow both in front and behind,* and small blackish patch below eye; wings and tail duskier, wing feathers with yellowish olive edging. Dull pale yellow below, heavily clouded olive on breast. Often most easily recognized by its *constantly quivering tail.*

SIMILAR SPECIES: Sao Paulo Tyrannulet is markedly smaller and has a less fancy facial pattern, with a yellow superciliary (but *almost no eye-ring*) "wrapping around" a deep black auricular patch; its posture is less horizontal, and its tail is not quivered.

HABITAT AND BEHAVIOR: Locally uncommon to fairly common in canopy, subcanopy, and borders of humid forest, primarily on slopes of the Serra do Mar. Behavior typical of genus, and usually noted foraging actively with mixed flocks. Constantly quivers its long cocked tail. Regularly seen in Nova Lombardia Reserve above Santa Teresa in Espírito Santo, and at Boracéia in São Paulo. Its call is a fairly soft "ku-dut" or "ku-dut-dut" (D. Stotz).

RANGE: Se. Brazil (Espírito Santo south to e. Santa Catarina). To about 800 m.

Phylloscartes paulistus

SAO PAULO TYRANNULET

DESCRIPTION: 10.5 cm (4"). *Se. Brazil area.* General form resembles Oustalet's Tyrannulet but *smaller* (the smallest *Phylloscartes*). Mostly olive above with *narrow yellow superciliary extending back to wrap around deep black auricular patch;* wings and tail duskier, wings with *2 vague yellowish bars* and edging on flight feathers. Dull pale yellow below, heavily clouded olive on breast.

SIMILAR SPECIES: Oustalet's Tyrannulet is larger and shows a conspicuous yellow eye-ring (not a true superciliary), with yellow reappearing behind its duskier (less black) auricular patch; it *lacks* wing-bars. Mottle-cheeked Tyrannulet is also larger, has mottled (not solidly black) cheeks, and shows much more prominent wing-bars. Cf. also Yellow Tyrannulet (also with wing-bars).

HABITAT AND BEHAVIOR: Rare to uncommon in lower and middle growth and borders of humid forest. Usually seen singly or in pairs, regularly with mixed flocks; forages very actively, often with rapid, almost jerky, movements. Its usual posture is less horizontal than Oustalet's Tyrannulet's, and it only rarely cocks tail. The call is a rather insignificant, quiet, whistled "swhee-eet" or "swhee-ee-eet" (D. Stotz; RSR). Fairly numerous on Ilha do Cardoso on the São Paulo coast, but on the whole the Sao Paulo Tyrannulet is a scarce and infrequently encountered bird whose overall numbers have declined substantially because of deforestation across a major portion of its range; it may deserve threatened status.

RANGE: Se. Brazil (Espírito Santo south to ne. Santa Catarina, and west to se. Mato Grosso do Sul at Campanário), e. Paraguay (Canendiyu, Caaguazú, and Alto Paraná), and ne. Argentina (recently recorded from Misiones, in Iguazú Nat. Park). To about 900 m.

Phylloscartes difficilis

SERRA DO MAR TYRANNULET
PLATE: 34

DESCRIPTION: 11.5 cm (4½"). *Se. Brazil. Mostly uniform bright olive above* with *prominent white eye-ring* (partially interrupted in front) *and supraloral*, lores and area below eye blackish, and gray cheeks bordered behind by blackish crescent; wings without bars, but flight feathers edged greenish yellow. *Below mostly grayish,* more whitish on throat and lower belly.

SIMILAR SPECIES: This species' colors, and even shape, may remind N. Am. observers of a nonbreeding Chestnut-sided Warbler. Eyeringed Tody-Tyrant has similar pattern but is yellowish (not so gray) below and has broad whitish margins to tertials; behavior of the 2 species differs markedly. Drab-breasted Bamboo-Tyrant is duller, more brownish (not so pure) gray below, and has whitish tertial edging; its shape and preferred habitat differ.

HABITAT AND BEHAVIOR: Uncommon in lower growth and shrubbery at borders of montane forest. Usually encountered singly, less often in pairs, generally not with mixed flocks; seems less active than most of its congeners. Perches horizontally, usually cocking its long tail and often drooping its wings. Often gives a fast, harsh chipper and sometimes also snaps bill. Regularly found along the Agulhas Negras road high in Itatiaia Nat. Park.

RANGE: Se. Brazil (Espírito Santo and s. Minas Gerais south to ne. Rio Grande do Sul). Mostly 900–2100 m.

GROUP D

Subgenus "*Pogonotriccus,*" the bristle-tyrants. Most show *auricular patch* and *gray crown.*

Phylloscartes poecilotis

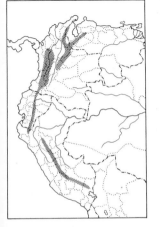

VARIEGATED BRISTLE-TYRANT
PLATE: 34

DESCRIPTION: 11.5 cm (4½"). *Andes from Venezuela to Peru.* Maxilla black, *lower mandible yellow to orange-yellow.* Crown gray; facial area and indistinct superciliary grizzled gray and white, with blackish crescent on ear-coverts bordered with white. Otherwise olive above, wings and tail duskier, *wings with 2 bright cinnamon bars* and greenish yellow edging on flight feathers. Chin grayish white, becoming olive yellowish on lower throat and breast and bright pale yellow on belly.

SIMILAR SPECIES: Resembles Marble-faced Bristle-Tyrant, which has all-blackish (not bicolored) bill and yellowish (not cinnamon) wingbars. Variegated is also often confused with Slaty-capped Flycatcher, which is larger with a longer, *all-dark* bill; note that over large portions of its range the flycatcher has cinnamon or buff wing-bars *much like Variegated's.* Sulphur-bellied Tyrannulet has a distinct superciliary, no crescent on the ear-coverts, and very different posture and behavior.

HABITAT AND BEHAVIOR: Uncommon to locally fairly common in lower and middle growth of montane forest and forest borders. Behavior similar to Marble-faced Bristle-Tyrant's; regularly occurs with it in the same flock. Its call is a clear, thin "whee-see" (Miller 1963, *in* Hilty and Brown 1986).

RANGE: Andes of w. Venezuela (Mérida), Colombia (but not in w. Nariño), e. Ecuador (the single old record from w. slope of Andes in Pichincha requires modern confirmation), and e. Peru (south locally to Puno [LSUMZ]). 1500–2300 m.

Phylloscartes chapmani

CHAPMAN'S BRISTLE-TYRANT

Other: Chapman's Tyrannulet

DESCRIPTION: 12 cm (4¾"). *Tepuis of s. Venezuela.* Resembles slightly smaller Variegated Bristle-Tyrant of Andes (no overlap) but has *crown olive* concolor with back (not contrastingly gray). See V-30 (but note that posture depicted is incorrect).

SIMILAR SPECIES: Confusion is unlikely as Chapman's is *the only bristle-tyrant found on the tepuis.* The similar Slaty-capped Flycatcher does not occur on the tepuis. Cf. Black-fronted Tyrannulet (which is a true *Phylloscartes* tyrannulet with horizontal posture).

HABITAT AND BEHAVIOR: Apparently locally not uncommon in lower growth inside montane forest. Not a well-known bird in life, despite the substantial number of specimens taken. Recently found to occur in small numbers in forest at the top of the Escalera in e. Bolívar. Its behavior is much like that of a typical bristle-tyrant (B. Whitney). We do not know its voice.

RANGE: S. Venezuela (Bolívar and Amazonas south to Cerro de la Neblina). Probably occurs in immediately adjacent Brazil and Guyana, but as yet unrecorded. 1000–2000 m.

Phylloscartes ophthalmicus

MARBLE-FACED BRISTLE-TYRANT   PLATE: 34

DESCRIPTION: 11.5 cm (4½"). Bill blackish. Crown gray; *facial area grizzled gray and white,* with *blackish crescent on ear-coverts bordered with white.* Otherwise olive above; wings and tail duskier, *wings with 2 yellowish bars and edging.* Chin grayish white, becoming yellowish olive on lower throat and breast and bright pale yellow on belly. *Purus* (coastal mts. of n. Venezuela) similar but with yellowish in front of the blackish crescent on ear-coverts; see V-30. *Ottonis* (Bolivia and s. Peru north to Cuzco) is strikingly different, with a basically *gray throat and breast,* white belly with only a slight yellow tinge, and whiter wing-bars.

SIMILAR SPECIES: Easily confused; bear in mind that this is often *the most numerous* of the several small montane flycatchers with more or less similar head patterns. Cf. Variegated Bristle-Tyrant. Ashy-headed Tyrannulet has crown more bluish gray, no yellowish edging on wing-coverts (it shows only wing-*bars*), and faint narrow streaky effect on breast (not the solid olive clouding of Marble-faced). Very similar Plumbeous-crowned Tyrannulet is less grizzled on face, and its crescent on ear-coverts is not as dark; its different posture and behavior provide the best clues. Slaty-capped Flycatcher is larger, with a proportionately longer bill, and in most areas where they overlap it has ochraceous or buffy (not yellowish) wing-bars. These 2 species are especially similar in n. Venezuela, where *both* have yellowish wing-bars; rely on size to distinguish them here. (In n. Venezuela one must also contend with Venezuelan Bristle-Tyrant, which see.) In Bolivia and s. Peru the 2 species are again very similar, and here *both* have rather grayish throats and breasts (more an olivaceous gray in Slaty-capped); the main difference is Marble-faced's whiter belly.

HABITAT AND BEHAVIOR: Fairly common in lower and middle growth of montane forest and forest borders. Usually seen singly (sometimes up to 3 or 4 birds) while accompanying a mixed flock of other insectivorous birds. Perches vertically, frequently flicking a wing up over back, and sallying out short distances to pick prey off foliage. Generally forages in slightly higher strata than Slaty-capped Flycatcher (and as a result is captured less often in mist-nets). The song (in n. Venezuela, Ecuador, and s. Peru) is a high, thin "psee-ee-ee-ee, titititi."

RANGE: Coastal mts. of n. Venezuela (Yaracuy east to Distrito Federal), and Andes of w. Colombia (W. Andes north to Valle, Cen. Andes north to Tolima), nw. and e. Ecuador (south on w. slope to Pichincha), e. Peru, and w. Bolivia (La Paz, Cochabamba, and w. Santa Cruz). Mostly 800–2200 m, ranging a bit lower on Pacific slope (to 600 m in Colombia).

Phylloscartes orbitalis

SPECTACLED BRISTLE-TYRANT
PLATE: 34

DESCRIPTION: 11 cm (4¼"). *E. slope of Andes from s. Colombia to Bolivia.* Maxilla black, *lower mandible flesh. Crown gray* contrasting with otherwise olive upperparts; *prominent eye-ring yellowish white, facial area mottled yellowish* with indistinct dusky crescent on ear-coverts; wings and tail duskier, wings with 2 bold yellowish white bars and narrow edging on flight feathers. Below rather bright yellow, clouded olive on throat and breast.

SIMILAR SPECIES: Has a more conspicuous eye-ring than other bristle-tyrants. Ecuadorian Tyrannulet has similar plumage but different posture and an all-dark bill. Cf. also Venezuelan and Antioquia Bristle-Tyrants (no overlap).

HABITAT AND BEHAVIOR: Generally rare and perhaps local in lower and middle growth of forest and forest borders in foothills, but locally fairly common in se. Peru (D. Stotz). Birds seen in Ecuador behave much like other bristle-tyrants but are rather more active when foraging; they perch upright and make frequent short sallies to the underside of leaves and frequently lift or twitch their wings. The call is a series of dry "tic" notes run together rapidly (D. Stotz).

RANGE: E. slope of Andes in extreme s. Colombia (sw. Putumayo), e. Ecuador, e. Peru, and w. Bolivia (locally in La Paz, extreme s. Beni, and Cochabamba). Mostly 700–1200 m, occasionally down to 500 m or up to 1425 m.

Phylloscartes lanyoni

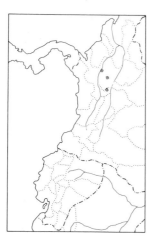

ANTIOQUIA BRISTLE-TYRANT

DESCRIPTION: 11 cm (4¼"). *Foothills at n. end of Cen. Andes in Antioquia, Colombia.* Resembles Spectacled Bristle-Tyrant (no overlap) but with an incomplete eye-ring, wider yellow wing-bars, and brighter yellow underparts.

HABITAT AND BEHAVIOR: Very poorly known. Recorded from lower growth of tall secondary forest and adjacent clearings and treefalls; F. G. Stiles (*Bol. Soc. Antioq. Ornitol.* 1[2]: 12–13, 1990) observed a group of 4 foraging together. Much of this species' limited range has been extensively deforested in recent decades, and it clearly deserves formal threatened status. A population of undetermined size does inhabit the small Río Claro Natural Reserve.

RANGE: N. end of Cen. Andes of Colombia in Antioquia (El Pescado, 12 km below Puerto Valdivia; Río Claro Natural Reserve, 10 km east of El Doradal) and e. Caldas (1 km west of La Victoria). 450–750 m.

NOTE: A newly described species: G. R. Graves, *Wilson Bull.* 100(4): 529–534, 1988.

Phylloscartes venezuelanus

VENEZUELAN BRISTLE-TYRANT

DESCRIPTION: 10.5 cm (4"). *N. Venezuela mts.* Closely resembles Marble-faced Bristle-Tyrant and often occurs with it. *Smaller,* with *lower mandible pale* (flesh to dull yellowish). Venezuelan's wing-bars are somewhat different, with more of a *spotted* effect, and the greater-coverts are blacker and lack edging (they thus contrast more with the pale bars). Entire throat, including chin, uniform pale greenish yellow (not grayish white). See V-30.

SIMILAR SPECIES: Confusion most likely with Marble-faced Bristle-Tyrant (see above). Cf. also the quite similar Spectacled Bristle-Tyrant (no overlap). Slaty-capped Flycatcher is markedly larger.

HABITAT AND BEHAVIOR: Uncommon in lower and middle growth of montane forest and forest borders. General behavior similar to Marble-faced Bristle-Tyrant's, with which it sometimes occurs in the same flock. Venezuelan's frequently given call is a spritely "tree-ee-ee-ew, tee-tee-tee," with a characteristic cadence (but Marble-faced's call is similar). Found regularly around Rancho Grande in Henri Pittier Nat. Park.

RANGE: Coastal mts. of n. Venezuela (Carabobo east to Distrito Federal). 850–1400 m.

Phylloscartes eximius

SOUTHERN BRISTLE-TYRANT   PLATE: 34

DESCRIPTION: 11 cm (4¼"). *The only bristle-tyrant in se. Brazil area;* easily recognized by its *fancy facial pattern.* Maxilla black, lower mandible pinkish at base. Crown gray, diffused with olive in center; *broad white superciliary grizzled with gray;* facial area yellowish with blackish lores and conspicuous ear-crescent, bordered behind by yellowish. Above otherwise bright olive; wings and tail duskier, edged with olive yellowish. Throat whitish, breast yellowish olive becoming *bright yellow on belly.*

SIMILAR SPECIES: Cf. much smaller Eared Pygmy-Tyrant.

HABITAT AND BEHAVIOR: Uncommon to locally fairly common in lower and middle growth of humid forest and forest borders, including forest dominated by araucarias. Found singly or in pairs, perching very upright, usually some 5–10 m above the ground; generally not with mixed flocks. The frequently given call, a simple chippering trill with a slight acceleration and often ending abruptly (quite reminiscent of the call of Cinnamon Flycatcher), draws attention to what is otherwise a rather inconspicuous bird. Can be found in woodland near Iguazú Falls, especially on the Argentinian side; overall numbers must have declined substantially because of deforestation across much of range.

RANGE: Se. Brazil (Espírito Santo and cen. Minas Gerais south to n. Rio Grande do Sul, and west to s. Mato Grosso do Sul), e. Paraguay (west to Paraguarí), and ne. Argentina (Misiones). To about 600 m.

Leptopogon Flycatchers

Slender, rather long-tailed flycatchers with fairly long, narrow bills found in forest lower growth, three of the four species in the Andes. All have a dark patch on the ear-coverts and a grizzled face, both characters reminiscent of the bristle-tyrants (which are smaller). *Leptopogon* flycatchers perch erectly; they quickly lift a wing up over their back more often than any of the other flycatchers with a similar mannerism.

Leptopogon amaurocephalus

SEPIA-CAPPED FLYCATCHER   PLATE: 34

DESCRIPTION: 13.5–14 cm (5¼–5½"). *Crown brown,* with *facial area dull buff grizzled dusky, and dusky patch on ear-coverts;* otherwise mostly olive above, tail decidedly brownish; wings dusky with 2 broad tawny-buff bars and yellowish buff edging on flight feathers. Throat pale grayish, becoming dull olive on breast and pale yellow on belly. Nominate race (e. Bolivia and s. Brazil southward) slightly larger and with more pronounced black auricular patch further emphasized by paler yellowish area to its rear.

SIMILAR SPECIES: Slaty-capped Flycatcher is similar but has a gray (not brown) crown and grizzled gray and *white* (not buff) facial area; it is basically a foothill and subtropical bird (Sepia-capped occurs in *lowlands*).

HABITAT AND BEHAVIOR: Uncommon to locally fairly common in lower growth of shady woodland and forest (both humid and deciduous), less often out to borders; in Amazonia mostly in várzea and more open forest, infrequent or absent from extensive terra firme. Usually found singly, and generally rather unobtrusive; sometimes with mixed flocks in understory, but also regularly forages independently. Its call is a fast gravelly chatter which trails off toward the end, "dret-deedee-deedeeduw" (sometimes with several additional introductory "dret" notes).

RANGE: Colombia (except in Pacific lowlands), w. and s. Venezuela,

Guianas, ne. Brazil (Amapá, perhaps elsewhere), e. Ecuador, e. Peru, n. and e. Bolivia, e. Paraguay (west to near the Río Paraguay), nw. and ne. Argentina (in the west in Jujuy and Salta, in the east in Misiones, Corrientes, and e. Chaco), and s. Brazil (extreme w. Amaz. Brazil east through Rondônia and much of Mato Grosso and Mato Grosso do Sul to s. Maranhão, Bahia, and Pernambuco, and south to Rio Grande do Sul). Also Mexico to Panama. Mostly below 1100 m.

Leptopogon superciliaris

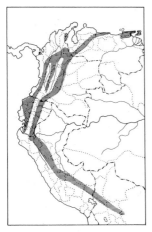

SLATY-CAPPED FLYCATCHER

DESCRIPTION: 13.5 cm (5¼"). *Bill all black. Crown slaty gray,* with *facial area whitish grizzled with gray* and a *dusky patch on ear-coverts;* otherwise olive above, tail more brownish; wings dusky with *2 prominent ochraceous to yellowish buff bars* (sometimes varying in color in the same population) and buffy yellowish edging on flight feathers. Throat pale grayish, becoming olive on breast and pale yellow on belly. Birds from Venezuela (*venezuelensis* and *pariae*) have pale yellowish wing-bars; see V-30. Birds from s. Peru (s. Cuzco southward) and Bolivia (*albidiventer*) also have yellowish wing-bars and have grayer breast and belly yellowish white.

SIMILAR SPECIES: Marble-faced Bristle-Tyrant has very similar pattern but is smaller with proportionately shorter bill. In most of their extensive area of overlap (Colombia to Peru), Marble-faced has yellowish (not ochraceous) wing-bars. In Venezuela and again in s. Peru and Bolivia this distinction breaks down as both species have yellowish wing-bars there. In these areas one must differentiate mostly by size, but in s. Peru and Bolivia Marble-faceds are also decidedly grayer below. Variegated Bristle-Tyrant always has ochraceous wing-bars and thus can be confused with Slaty-capped from Colombia to Peru, but Variegated is smaller and always shows an orange-yellow lower mandible (bill all black in Slaty-capped). Sepia-capped Flycatcher is patterned much like Slaty-capped but has a brown (not gray) crown; it is basically a lowland (not montane) bird.

HABITAT AND BEHAVIOR: Fairly common to locally common in lower and middle growth of montane forest, somewhat less often out to forest borders. Found singly or in pairs, almost always with a mixed flock; usually perches erectly on an unobstructed branch, sallying out to pick insects off the underside of leaves. Generally more active and conspicuous than Sepia-capped. Its distinctive and often-heard call is a sharp "skeeéy, di-i-i-i-i-ir."

RANGE: Coastal mts. of n. Venezuela (east to Paria Peninsula), and Andes of Venezuela, Colombia, Ecuador (south on w. slope to El Oro and w. Loja; an isolated population on the coastal cordillera in sw. Manabí and w. Guayas), e. Peru, and w. Bolivia (south to w. Santa Cruz); Sierra de Perijá on Venezuela-Colombia border; Trinidad. Also Costa Rica and Panama. The published record from extreme s. Venezuela (in s. Amazonas near the Brazilian frontier) is based on a misidentified USNM specimen (*fide* G. R. Graves). Mostly 500–1800 m (occasionally up to 2400 m), but regularly lower (virtually to sea level) in Pacific lowlands of Colombia and Ecuador, and occasionally up to 2400 m.

Leptopogon rufipectus

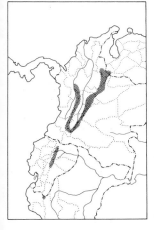

RUFOUS-BREASTED FLYCATCHER

PLATE: 34

DESCRIPTION: 13 cm (5¼″). *Andes of w. Venezuela to n. Peru.* Bill all dark. Crown dark gray; *facial area, sides of head, throat, and breast rufous* with obscure grizzling and dusky patch on ear-coverts. Upperparts otherwise olive, tail decidedly brownish; wings dusky with 2 broad dark rufous bars and strong buff edging especially on inner flight feathers. Belly pale yellow.

SIMILAR SPECIES: Handsome Flycatcher is smaller with buffier throat and breast (not such a deep rufous) and no rufous on facial area; its lower mandible is pale, and its wing-bars paler and thus more conspicuous.

HABITAT AND BEHAVIOR: Uncommon to locally fairly common in lower and middle growth of montane forest, less often out to forest borders and in second-growth. Behavior similar to Slaty-capped Flycatcher's. Frequently utters an explosive "skwee!" (which has been likened to squeezing a baby's bath toy!), often repeated several times in succession. Seen regularly in forest patches near Cuyuja in Ecuador.

RANGE: Andes of extreme w. Venezuela (Táchira), Colombia (except in W. Andes), e. Ecuador (seemingly local), and extreme n. Peru (Cerro Chinguela in Piura). Mostly 1500–2400 m.

Leptopogon taczanowskii

INCA FLYCATCHER

DESCRIPTION: 13 cm (5¼″). *E. slope of Andes in Peru.* Resembles Rufous-breasted Flycatcher, which it replaces south of the Río Marañón. Differs in having *facial area and sides of head grizzled gray and white,* grayish throat, and *breast dull tawny-olive* (not rufous).

SIMILAR SPECIES: Slaty-capped Flycatcher has a purer olive breast and paler, more tawny-buff (not so rufous) wing-bars and edging; it mostly occurs at elevations below Inca, though there is some overlap.

HABITAT AND BEHAVIOR: Uncommon to fairly common in lower and middle growth of montane forest, sometimes out to forest borders. Behavior similar to Slaty-capped Flycatcher's, but in Pasco, Peru, was usually not seen with mixed flocks (D. Stotz). Regularly found along the Paty Trail in the Carpish Mts., Huánuco, Peru. We do not know its voice.

RANGE: E. slope of Andes in Peru (Amazonas to Cuzco). Mostly 1700–2800 m.

Mionectes Flycatchers

Plain flycatchers with slender bills and slim builds, found widely and often numerous in forest and woodland lower growth. Traylor (1977) subsumed the genus *Pipromorpha* in *Mionectes,* and Lanyon (1988a) concurred, based on anatomical considerations. All are predominantly olive, the "*Pipromorpha*" group with ochraceous lower underparts. The genus is well known for "wing-flashing," raising a single wing up over its back, either alternately or the same one repeatedly, especially during display but also at other times. All members of the genus consume considerable fruit, the two true *Mionectes* being among the most frugivorous flycatchers.

GROUP A

"True" *Mionectes;* mainly *dark olive* with *streaking below, white postocular spot.*

Mionectes striaticollis

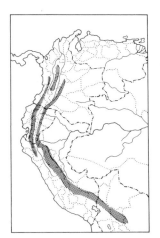

STREAK-NECKED FLYCATCHER   PLATE: 34

DESCRIPTION: 13–13.5 cm (5–5¼"). *Andes from Colombia to Bolivia. Head and neck gray,* with *small but prominent white spot behind eye;* otherwise rather bright olive above, wings duskier edged with yellowish olive (no wing-bars). *Throat and chest olive gray finely streaked white;* breast and flanks finely streaked olive and yellow, becoming pale clear yellow on midbelly. *Viridiceps* (w. Ecuador and adjacent sw. Colombia) has hood dull grayish olive, *not* looking distinctly gray; see C-37.

SIMILAR SPECIES: Cf. similar Olive-striped Flycatcher, which mostly occurs at lower elevations. Otherwise this obscure, inconspicuous flycatcher of shady woodland and forest is not likely to be confused.

HABITAT AND BEHAVIOR: Fairly common to common in lower and middle growth of montane forest and secondary woodland, less often out to borders and in adjacent clearings even to isolated trees, especially when these are bearing fruit. Found singly, perching quietly, occasionally flying out to pick off a small fruit while hovering, then moving on to another perch; sometimes joins mixed tanager flocks. Its posture is typically vertical, though it often leans forward or even nods its head. Sometimes, but less often than in true *Pipromorpha,* twitches a wing up over its back. Phlegmatic and quiet, this small flycatcher is numerous (many are caught in mist-nets) but not too often seen. Singing males have been heard to give a series of thin, wiry notes (Miller 1963, *in* Hilty and Brown 1986).

RANGE: Andes of Colombia (E. Andes north to Cundinamarca, Cen. and W. Andes north to Antioquia), Ecuador, nw. and e. Peru (south on w. slope to Lambayeque), and w. Bolivia (La Paz, Cochabamba, and w. Santa Cruz). Mostly 1200–2700 m, less often (more frequently southward?) down to 600 m, sometimes up to 3400 m.

Mionectes olivaceus

OLIVE-STRIPED FLYCATCHER

DESCRIPTION: 13–13.5 cm (5–5¼"). Closely resembles Streak-necked Flycatcher; *they generally replace each other altitudinally,* with Olive-striped at lower elevations than Streak-necked. In most of their respective ranges, Olive-striped can be distinguished by its *olive* (not gray) *hood;* note too that Olive-striped's white postocular spot is a little

larger and thus more prominent, and that *only* Olive-striped is found in ne. Colombia and Venezuela. See V-30. Race of Olive-striped found in w. Ecuador (*hederaceus;* see C-37) is *very* difficult to tell from nearly sympatric olive-crowned race of Streak-necked (*viridiceps*), but it has *more completely olive-streaked belly* (Streak-necked's midbelly is unstreaked and brighter yellow, with olive streaking confined to flanks) and somewhat paler throat.

HABITAT AND BEHAVIOR: Fairly common to common in lower growth of humid forest, and shady secondary woodland and plantations. Behavior similar to Streak-necked Flycatcher's, also solitary, quiet, and inconspicuous, and perhaps most often noted at fruiting trees. In e. Panama small groups of displaying males give a high, sibilant call with a hummingbird-like quality, "ts-ts-ts-tsu," repeated several times, then a pause before another series.

RANGE: Lower slopes and adjacent lowlands of coastal mts. of n. Venezuela (east to Paria Peninsula) and of Andes in w. Venezuela, Colombia, Ecuador (south on w. slope to w. Loja), e. Peru, and w. Bolivia (La Paz at Alto Madidi); Santa Marta Mts. of n. Colombia and Sierra de Perijá on Colombia-Venezuela border; Trinidad. Also Costa Rica and Panama. Mostly 500–1600 m, but recorded much higher (to 3000 m) in Venezuela, and locally down to sea level at least in nw. South America.

GROUP B   Subgenus "*Pipromorpha*"; *lower underparts ochraceous or rufous.*

Mionectes oleagineus

OCHRE-BELLIED FLYCATCHER   PLATE: 34

DESCRIPTION: 13 cm (5"). *Very plain.* Olive above, wings and tail brownish, wings with ochraceous edging and 2 indistinct bars; sides of head and throat olive grayish, becoming ochraceous olive on chest and *rich ochraceous on remaining underparts.*

SIMILAR SPECIES: Cf. more local McConnell's Flycatcher and (in se. Brazil area) Gray-hooded Flycatcher. Ruddy-tailed Flycatcher is smaller with stubbier bill, largely rufous wings and tail.

HABITAT AND BEHAVIOR: Common in lower growth of forest (both humid and deciduous), secondary woodland, borders, and adjacent clearings with scattered trees and shrubbery. Usually seen singly, though regularly found with mixed flocks; generally inconspicuous and retiring, with quick furtive movements. Eats both insects and fruit, including much mistletoe. Almost continually flashes a wing up over back. During the breeding season males "sing" in a dispersed lek, perching in fairly open undergrowth within earshot of each other, interminably giving a variable series of chirps and twitters, some quite fast and sharp (e.g., "twich-twich . . ." or "tit-twich, tit-twich . . ."), all the while flicking or flashing wings and ruffling crown feathers.

RANGE: Widespread south to n. Bolivia (south to Cochabamba and Santa Cruz) and Amaz. Brazil (south to s. Mato Grosso and Maranhão); e. Brazil (Alagoas south to n. Rio de Janeiro); on Pacific slope south to sw. Ecuador (w. Loja) but absent from wettest Pacific lowlands of w. Colombia (s. Chocó to Nariño); Trinidad and Tobago. Also Mexico to Panama. Mostly below 1000 m, occasionally or in smaller numbers up to 1800 m.

Mionectes macconnelli

MCCONNELL'S FLYCATCHER

DESCRIPTION: 13 cm (5″). Closely resembles Ochre-bellied Flycatcher, with which sympatric from Guianas to sw. Amazonia. Differs in having *plain wings* with *no* wing-bars (but remember that these are obscure in some Ochre-bellieds) and *no pale edging on tertials* (this conspicuous in Ochre-bellied). The 2 species usually occupy different habitats (see below). In the hand, mouth lining of McConnell's is blackish, that of Ochre-bellied yellowish (T. Lovejoy).

HABITAT AND BEHAVIOR: Uncommon to locally common in lower growth of humid forest, primarily in terra firme. General behavior similar to Ochre-bellied Flycatcher's. Within the range of McConnell's, Ochre-bellied is mostly restricted to second-growth and edge habitats, with McConnell's taking over in undisturbed terra firme forest. Outside the range of McConnell's, Ochre-bellied is regularly found in primary forest as well as secondary habitats. Displaying males "sing" nearer the ground than do Ochre-bellieds, often near the base of a buttressed tree, where they give a series of rough, thrush-like "wiib" notes, sometimes varied with an odd, nasal, nuthatch- (*Sitta-*)like "riu-tiu-tiu-tiu-tiu . . ." (E. O. Willis).

RANGE: S. Venezuela (Amazonas and Bolívar, mainly on tepui slopes), Guianas, and e. Amaz. Brazil (west on both sides of the Amazon to near the mouth of the Rio Negro, and southwest locally to n. Mato Grosso at Aripuanã); se. Peru (north to Junín and s. Ucayali) and w. Bolivia (Pando and s. Beni south to La Paz, Cochabamba, and w. Santa Cruz). Mostly in lowlands below 500 m, but mainly 1000–2000 m in s. Venezuela, and recorded up to 2400 m in Bolivia.

NOTE: For more information on the behavior (including nesting) of this species and its ecological relationship with *P. oleaginea,* see E. O. Willis, D. Wechsler, and Y. Oniki, *Auk* 95(1): 1–8, 1978.

Mionectes rufiventris

GRAY-HOODED FLYCATCHER   PLATE: 34

DESCRIPTION: 13.5 cm (5¼″). *Se. Brazil area. Hood gray;* otherwise olive above, wings essentially plain. Gray throat merges into olive-tinged chest; *lower underparts rich ochraceous.*

SIMILAR SPECIES: Not found in range of other *Mionectes,* though Ochre-bellied, which lacks the gray hood, comes close in the lowlands of Espírito Santo and n. Rio de Janeiro (in this area Gray-hooded is more montane).

HABITAT AND BEHAVIOR: Uncommon to fairly common in lower growth of humid forest, secondary woodland, and borders. General behavior similar to Ochre-bellied Flycatcher's, but displaying males seem more solitary and less animated. Their "song," a series of odd nasal notes that start slowly and then accelerate before abruptly stop-

ping, sounds rather like a foliage-gleaner's (D. Stotz, RSR). It is usually given from a perch 3–8 m above the ground. Seems especially numerous around Iguazú Falls.

RANGE: Se. Brazil (Espírito Santo and s. Minas Gerais south to Rio Grande do Sul), e. Paraguay (west to Paraguarí), and ne. Argentina (Misiones). To about 1000 m.

Myiornis Pygmy-Tyrants

A small group of four tiny, round-looking tyrannids, two of them (Short-tailed and Black-capped) being virtually tail-less and ranking among the world's smallest birds—indeed they may be the smallest passerines. All are found along the borders of humid tropical and subtropical forests. Lanyon (1988c) suggests that, based on their very similar syringes, the genus *Myiornis* is very closely related to *Hemitriccus*.

Myiornis ecaudatus

SHORT-TAILED PYGMY-TYRANT   PLATE: 35

DESCRIPTION: 6.5 cm (2½″). A *tiny* and *virtually tail-less* tyrannid found in Guianas and Amazonia. *Head gray* with *prominent white supraloral and eye-ring* (giving a "spectacled" look); otherwise bright olive above, wings duskier with rather prominent yellowish edging and vague wing-bars. *Below white,* tinged pale yellow on crissum.

SIMILAR SPECIES: Virtually unmistakable because of its minute size; cf. Black-capped Pygmy-Tyrant, though that is found only *west* of Andes (no overlap). Overall color pattern is reminiscent of considerably larger (though still small), longer-tailed Slate-headed Tody-Flycatcher, though that species' behavior and shrubby edge habitat are entirely different.

HABITAT AND BEHAVIOR: Uncommon to fairly common in lower and middle growth of forest borders and secondary woodland. Apt to be overlooked, both because of its very small size and because its voice is so insect- or frog-like. Its usual foraging behavior doesn't help, for typically it perches motionless for a long period, darts suddenly to pick an insect off the underside of a leaf, then moves on to a new perch; these motions are so abrupt and quick, almost cicada-like, that they are hard to follow. Its call is a series, usually short, of weak squeaky notes.

RANGE: Locally in Venezuela (along e. base of Andes north to Barinas, with 1 record from Lake Maracaibo basin in Mérida at Santa Elena; more widely south of the Orinoco, and probably also in Delta Amacuro), e. Colombia (known only from w. Meta and e. Guainía, but probably more widespread), e. Ecuador (a few recent records from several sites in Napo and Morona-Santiago), e. Peru, n. Bolivia (south to Cochabamba and w. Santa Cruz), Amaz. Brazil (south to s. Mato Grosso on the Serra dos Parecís and at Rio do Cagado, and east to e. Pará in the Belém region), and Guianas; Trinidad. To about 900 m.

NOTE: See comments under Black-capped Pygmy-Tyrant.

Myiornis atricapillus

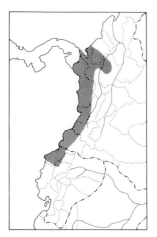

BLACK-CAPPED PYGMY-TYRANT

DESCRIPTION: 6.5 cm (2½"). *W. Colombia and nw. Ecuador;* formerly considered conspecific with Short-tailed Pygmy-Tyrant. The *smallest* flycatcher west of Andes. Resembles that species (found *east* of Andes), but male with *prominent black crown* (gray, with only forehead black, in female), and both sexes with *belly pale yellow* (not white). See C-36, P-25.

SIMILAR SPECIES: Diminutive size should preclude confusion in range. Cf. Black-headed Tody-Flycatcher.

HABITAT AND BEHAVIOR: Locally fairly common in lower and middle growth at borders of humid and wet forest, sometimes out into shrubbery and trees in adjacent clearings. Behavior similar to Short-tailed Pygmy-Tyrant's but call more apt to be extended into a longer series of sometimes quite rapid "tseeyp" notes. Regularly encountered along the lower Buenaventura road in Valle, Colombia.

RANGE: W. Colombia (Pacific lowlands, and east along n. base of Andes to Bolívar) and nw. Ecuador (Esmeraldas, w. Imbabura, and n. Pichincha). Also Costa Rica and Panama. To about 900 m.

NOTE: Often considered conspecific with cis-Andean *M. ecaudatus* (e.g., Meyer de Schauensee 1966, 1970), but treated as a full species in the 1983 AOU Check-list, and this is followed here.

Myiornis auricularis

EARED PYGMY-TYRANT   PLATE: 35

DESCRIPTION: 7.5 cm (3"). *Se. Brazil area.* Above mostly bright olive, tinged brown on crown (especially forecrown); *ocular area cinnamon-buff,* with remainder of sides of head, neck, and nape gray, and *large black spots below eye and on ear-coverts.* Wings and tail dusky, wings with bright olive yellow edging and 2 indistinct wing-bars. Throat white, *sharply streaked black; remaining underparts bright yellow,* streaked olive on breast and sides.

SIMILAR SPECIES: This strikingly marked pygmy-tyrant is unlikely to be confused in its range. None of the *Hemitriccus* tody-tyrants shows such an ornate facial pattern, nor is any sympatric member of that genus so boldly streaked below or so short-tailed.

HABITAT AND BEHAVIOR: Fairly common in lower and middle growth of humid forest and woodland borders, usually where dense and shrubby; much less frequent inside forest itself or in adjacent clearings. Unlike Short-tailed and Black-capped Pygmy-Tyrants, Eared is relatively easy to see as it tends to perch more in the open and its calls are louder and more noticeable. Its most frequent vocalization is a somewhat musical trill, often preceded by several "pic" notes, e.g., "pic, pic, pic, pree-ee-ee-ee-ee." The wings make a whirring noise in flight.

RANGE: Se. Brazil (se. Bahia south to Rio Grande do Sul), e. Paraguay (west to Paraguarí), and ne. Argentina (Misiones and ne. Corrientes). To about 1300 m.

NOTE: See comments under White-bellied Pygmy-Tyrant.

Myiornis albiventris

WHITE-BELLIED PYGMY-TYRANT

Other: Eared Pygmy-Tyrant (in part)

DESCRIPTION: 7 cm (2¾"). *E. slope of Andes in s. Peru and w. Bolivia.* Plumage pattern similar to Eared Pygmy-Tyrant's (no overlap); somewhat shorter-tailed. Ocular area paler, more buffy whitish; *auricular patch less conspicuous and grayer* (not so black); *lower underparts white* (not bright yellow), with tinge of yellowish olive only on flanks and crissum, and streaked with gray (not olive) on breast.

SIMILAR SPECIES: Tiny size, distinctive facial pattern, and basically white underparts should preclude confusion in its limited range. Short-tailed Pygmy-Tyrant is even smaller, lacks auricular patch and streaking below.

HABITAT AND BEHAVIOR: Uncommon in lower and middle growth at borders of humid forest, primarily in foothill zone. Behavior similar to Eared Pygmy-Tyrant's. Easily found along lower part of the Villa Tunari road in Cochabamba, Bolivia.

RANGE: E. slope of Andes in cen. and s. Peru (north to Huánuco) and w. Bolivia (south to w. Santa Cruz). 400–1200 m.

NOTE: Considered a race of *M. auricularis* by Meyer de Schauensee (1966, 1970), though other authors have treated it as a full species. In some respects *M. albiventris* seems intermediate between *M. auricularis* and the *M. ecaudatus* superspecies.

Oncostoma Bentbills

A small genus of only one or two species, the bentbills seem most closely related to the *Hemitriccus* tody-tyrants (see Traylor and Fitzpatrick 1982), though they differ strikingly in their heavy, bent-downward bills. The genus ranges mainly in Middle America.

Oncostoma olivaceum

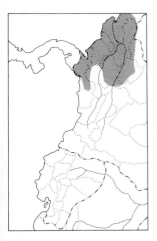

SOUTHERN BENTBILL

PLATE: 35

DESCRIPTION: 9 cm (3½"). *N. Colombia.* Easily recognized by its *odd, rather thick, peculiarly bent-downward bill.* Iris usually pale yellowish. Plain olive above with lores whitish; wings duskier with 2 narrow greenish yellow wing-bars and edging. Mostly olive yellow below, with some darker olive clouding on breast, becoming clear pale yellow on belly. A few individuals are more whitish below.

SIMILAR SPECIES: This species' nondescript plumage resembles that of several *Hemitriccus* tody-tyrants, but no *Hemitriccus* has anything like the bentbill's peculiar bill. Aside from the very different Pearly-vented Tody-Tyrant (with whitish underparts, etc.), no *Hemitriccus* occurs in the bentbill's range.

HABITAT AND BEHAVIOR: Fairly common in lower growth of secondary woodland and shrubby clearings, and at borders of humid forest; occurs mostly in humid regions. Generally secretive and hard to see, perching in dense cover and making short, abrupt flights which are hard to follow; usually does not associate with mixed flocks. Its call is given more or less continuously, a soft guttural purring trill, sometimes preceded by a single note, thus "grrrrrr" or "pt-trrrrrrrr."

RANGE: Caribbean lowlands of n. Colombia (east to Santa Marta region, and south in Río Magdalena valley to n. Cundinamarca). Also Panama. To 1000 m.

NOTE: A specimen tentatively identified as the Northern Bentbill, *O. cinereigulare*, was taken in nw. Antioquia, Colombia, in April 1965 (Z. H. Romero and J. V. Rodríguez, *Lozania* 31: 5–6, 1980). The Northern Bentbill is otherwise known only from Middle America, with no certain records south of w. Panama. As the color of *O. olivaceum*'s underparts is somewhat variable, and as this is the primary difference distinguishing the two species (*O. cinereigulare* has a whitish throat and chest), we consider the record as too uncertain to include *O. cinereigulare* as a definitely occurring species in South America. The two forms may actually prove to be conspecific, under the name of *O. cinereigulare* (Bentbill).

Lophotriccus Pygmy-Tyrants

Four small flycatchers found in lower growth of forest and woodland, mostly in the lowlands of Amazonia and the Guianas, with one ranging on lower Andean slopes. All have broad transverse crests (slightly narrower in Helmeted), with the feathers edged rufous, gray, or olive; these crests are erected when birds are displaying or are excited.

Lophotriccus pileatus

SCALE-CRESTED PYGMY-TYRANT   PLATE: 35

DESCRIPTION: 10 cm (4"). *Montane areas* from Venezuela to Peru. Iris straw yellow. Above mainly olive, with brown forecrown and buffyish facial area; *lengthened* feathers of mid- and hindcrown are *black with broad rufous edging* and are *sometimes erected as a broad transverse crest* but more often are laid flat over nape. Wings and tail dusky, wings with 2 yellowish wing-bars and edging. Below mainly whitish to pale yellowish with blurry dusky-olive streaking on throat and breast.

SIMILAR SPECIES: Note the unusual crown feathers, the colors of which are always apparent even when the crest is flat. This is the only *Lophotriccus* found on Andean slopes.

HABITAT AND BEHAVIOR: Fairly common to common in lower growth of humid forest, secondary woodland, and borders. Except for its remarkable voice, Scale-crested Pygmy-Tyrant is a quite inconspicuous bird, perching motionless in the shadows, then darting out to pluck an insect off a nearby leaf surface and continuing on to a new perch. Male's voice often draws attention: its calls are astonishingly loud for so small a bird and are persistently given throughout the day, though often with long pauses between bouts. Most frequently given is a series of sharp, enunciated "preek" notes, sometimes accelerating and slightly rising in pitch; a softer purring call is also uttered.

RANGE: Coastal mts. of n. Venezuela (east to Miranda), and Andes of w. Venezuela, Colombia, Ecuador (south on w. slope to w. Loja), and e. Peru (south to Puno); Sierra de Perijá on Venezuela-Colombia border. Also Costa Rica and Panama. The record from the upper Río

Juruá in w. Brazil, based on 2 specimens in MZUSP (Pinto 1944; Meyer de Schauensee 1966, 1970), is in error; 1 of the specimens is a *L. vitiosus congener,* the other a *Hemitriccus minor* (D. F. Stotz, *Condor* 92[4]: 1078, 1990). Mostly 500–1500 m, locally down to near sea level (especially in w. Ecuador), and occasionally up to 2300 m.

Lophotriccus vitiosus

DOUBLE-BANDED PYGMY-TYRANT   PLATE: 35

DESCRIPTION: 10 cm (4"). *Local from Guianas to w. Amazonia.* Iris straw yellow. Above olive, with *lengthened* feathers of mid- and hind-crown *black with gray edging,* occasionally (less often than Scale-crested) erected as a transverse crest but usually laid flat over nape. Wings and tail dusky, wings with 2 dull greenish yellow wing-bars and edging. Below pale yellowish to whitish, with blurry dusky-olive streaking on throat and breast. *Congener* (south of the Amazon in w. Amaz. Brazil and in e. Peru east of the Río Ucayali) is the whitest race below and also differs strikingly in having *crown feathers edged with buff-yellow.* Female's crown feathers are slightly shorter than male's.

SIMILAR SPECIES: See Scale-crested Pygmy-Tyrant, which Double-banded replaces in the lowlands (possibly with some overlap along e. base of Andes). They resemble each other except for the difference in color of edging on crown feathers (rufous in Scale-crested, gray in Double-banded). Double-banded's *congener* race's crown feather edging looks much like Scale-crested's (slightly paler), but its range, *w. Amazonia well away from Andes,* should preclude confusion. When crest colors and shape are not apparent, Double-banded can be confused with various *Hemitriccus* tody-tyrants. Cf. also Helmeted Pygmy-Tyrant.

HABITAT AND BEHAVIOR: Uncommon to fairly common in lower and middle growth of borders of humid forest and secondary woodland. Behavior much like Scale-crested Pygmy-Tyrant's. However, its voice, a buzzy trill, "turrrrrrrrr," sometimes several in series, is distinctly different, much more like a bentbill's and not nearly as loud as Scale-crested's. We do not know *congener*'s voice.

RANGE: Guianas, n. and w. Brazil (locally in Amapá, the Manaus area, and the upper Rio Negro and Rio Juruá drainages), se. Colombia (north to Meta and Guainía), e. Ecuador, e. Peru (south to Huánuco). To about 500 m.

Lophotriccus eulophotes

LONG-CRESTED PYGMY-TYRANT

DESCRIPTION: 10 cm (4"). *Limited range in sw. Amazonia.* Resembles Double-banded Pygmy-Tyrant (no known overlap, though they come close). Differs in its *plain wings* (*no* wing-bars) and whitish underparts with no yellow tinge, streaked throughout with gray.

SIMILAR SPECIES: All other more or less similar small tyrannids have wing-bars.

HABITAT AND BEHAVIOR: Uncommon to fairly common but local in shady bamboo-dominated undergrowth in swampy riverine forest, second-growth woodland, and borders; occasionally at treefalls. Usu-

ally seen singly, but sometimes with mixed flocks; mainly forages 4–10 m above the ground. The call is a frequently uttered series of 5–8 "tic" notes; also occasionally gives a short, slightly descending trill. A few have been found recently near the Pakitza guard station at the edge of Manu Nat. Park.

RANGE: Locally in sw. Amaz. Brazil (upper Rio Purus drainage at Huitanaã), se. Peru (se. Ucayali at Balta, and Madre de Dios at Altamira and in Manu Nat. Park), and extreme nw. Bolivia (Pando in Cobija area). 300–400 m.

NOTE: Parker and Remsen (1987) provide more information on this until recently poorly known species.

Lophotriccus galeatus

HELMETED PYGMY-TYRANT

DESCRIPTION: 10 cm (4″). *Ne. South America.* Resembles Double-banded Pygmy-Tyrant, differing in its slightly narrower elongated crown feathers *edged with grayish olive* (not pure gray) and *very obscure wing-bars.* See V-30, C-36. In the hand, note that both sexes have outer 3 primaries greatly shortened and narrowed.

SIMILAR SPECIES: As its crest is less conspicuous than Double-banded Pygmy-Tyrant's, Helmeted can also be confused with White-eyed Tody-Tyrant and other allied *Hemitriccus* tody-tyrants. None of these has *any* crest.

HABITAT AND BEHAVIOR: Fairly common to common in lower and middle growth of humid forest, secondary woodland, and borders; favors areas with sandy soils, though by no means confined to them. Behavior similar to Double-banded Pygmy-Tyrant's, though tending to remain in higher strata; like that species, usually overlooked until its characteristic call is recognized. Its most frequent vocalization is a series of dry, staccato "pik" notes, sometimes ending with a short warbled or trilled phrase; birds vocalize, sometimes interminably, through the heat of the day. In pattern this call is reminiscent of Scale-crested Pygmy-Tyrant's, though not nearly as loud.

RANGE: E. and s. Venezuela (e. Monagas and Sucre, and south of the Orinoco in Bolívar and Amazonas), extreme e. Colombia (e. Vichada to e. Vaupés, also a single sight report from near Leticia, on the Amazon), Guianas, and Amaz. Brazil (mostly north of the Amazon, south of it west only to the lower Rio Tapajós and south to the Serra da Cachimbo in sw. Pará). To 1100 m.

NOTE: Formerly separated in the monotypic genus *Colopteryx* (e.g., Meyer de Schauensee 1966, 1970). Its inclusion in *Lophotriccus* (Traylor 1977), which it closely resembles, seems reasonable, despite the modification of its outer primaries.

Atalotriccus Pygmy-Tyrants

A monotypic genus characterized by its small bill and greatly shortened and narrowed outer four primaries. The function of the latter, present in both sexes, remains uncertain, though it probably serves in display.

Behaviorally and vocally, the Pale-eyed Pygmy-Tyrant recalls the *Lophotriccus* pygmy-tyrants, though it lacks their distinctive crests. Indeed, Lanyon (1988c) recommends its merger in *Lophotriccus,* but he also suggests that both genera may best be merged into *Oncostoma;* because of the uncertainty, we elect to maintain all three genera for the present.

Atalotriccus pilaris

PALE-EYED PYGMY-TYRANT PLATE: 35

DESCRIPTION: 9.5 cm (3¾"). *A very small tyrannid of scrub and deciduous woodland in Venezuela and ne. Colombia.* Pale yellow iris. Above mostly olive, with whitish lores and narrow buffyish eye-ring and sides of head; wings dusky with 2 narrow yellowish wing-bars and edging. Below mostly whitish, with *indistinct brownish streaking on throat and breast;* flanks and crissum tinged pale yellow. Birds from Venezuela (except Maracaibo basin) and Guyana, *venezuelensis* and *griseiceps,* have crown more grayish.
SIMILAR SPECIES: An often-confused little flycatcher without any really characteristic marks. In its range and habitat most likely confused with Pearly-vented Tody-Tyrant, which is larger with a proportionately longer bill, is duller and browner above and more prominently streaked below, and has a pure white belly with no yellow tinge. Note that Pearly-vented also has a pale iris. Cf. also Slate-headed Tody-Flycatcher.
HABITAT AND BEHAVIOR: Fairly common in lower growth of deciduous woodland and in arid scrub. Inconspicuous and apt to be overlooked until its calls are recognized. Usually in pairs, perching upright and motionless within cover, but sometimes moving about frequently; makes short upward sallies to foliage, often hovering for a second, then moves on to a new branch. The loud and strident call is reminiscent of Scale-crested Pygmy-Tyrant's; it is variable, but typical phrases are "kip-kip, t-t-trrr" or "kip-kip, t-t-t-tr-tr-r-rreép."
RANGE: N. Colombia (lower Río Magdalena valley east through Guajira Peninsula, and south in upper Río Magdalena valley to Huila; east of Andes south to w. Meta and Vichada), Venezuela (south to n. Amazonas and n. Bolívar), w. Guyana (Quonga), and extreme n. Brazil (n. Roraima near Contão, where seen in July 1992; B. Forrester et al.). Also Panama. Mostly below 800 m (recorded to 2000 m in Colombia).

Hemitriccus Tody-Tyrants

A difficult group of obscure, usually drab, small flycatchers found virtually throughout tropical and subtropical South America, with the most species in the Andes and e. Brazil. All have relatively broad, somewhat flattened, short bills, more or less "intermediate" between certain of the pygmy-tyrants (e.g., *Lophotriccus* and *Atalotriccus*) and the *Todirostrum* tody-flycatchers. *Hemitriccus* usually inhabit lower and middle growth of humid forest and woodland, to a lesser extent edge, but the

Pearly-vented is found mainly in arid scrub, and the Stripe-necked and Johannes' are typical of riparian growth.

Many species are confusing and very hard to identify, especially the drab White-eyed Tody-Tyrant group. Others are somewhat more distinctive, particularly the group of species found in e. Brazil, which share unusual broad pale edging to tertials (also present in one Andean species, Cinnamon-breasted, and in certain of the *Poecilotriccus* todytyrants).

Behavior is relatively uniform. Most are inconspicuous, with even their "tic-tic . . ." or trilled calls being easily passed over as the songs of insects. They perch more upright than *Todirostrum* tody-flycatchers and unlike many *Todirostrum* do not cock their tails; most do not accompany mixed flocks (Black-throated being a notable exception). Vocalizations, despite being weak, are often persistently given and thus usually provide the best means of locating the birds. All build pendant nests.

Traylor (1977) merged the large *Idioptilon* genus into *Hemitriccus* (which name had priority); we follow this, as well as his merger of three former monotypic genera (*Snethlagea, Microcochlearius,* and *Ceratotriccus*) into the enlarged *Hemitriccus*. Note that this change in generic names has forced a change in the ending of some species names, e.g., *rufigulare* to *rufigularis*, etc.

GROUP A

Lowland Group. Most *flammulated below* to some extent; most with pale iris.

Hemitriccus margaritaceiventer

PEARLY-VENTED TODY-TYRANT

PLATE: 35

DESCRIPTION: 10–10.5 cm (4–4¼"). *A numerous and widespread but quite nondescript tody-tyrant of semiopen, usually arid areas,* both north and south of the Amazon. Iris pale, straw to hazel. Brownish olive above, somewhat grayer on crown, with whitish lores and narrow eyering; wings and tail duskier, with 2 buffy whitish to yellowish wingbars and edging. Below white, streaked with grayish on throat and breast. Birds from Colombia and n. Venezuela (*septentrionalis* and *impiger*) are paler and browner above and slightly smaller; see V-30, C-36. Nominate group (south of the Amazon) is more olive above with more contrasting gray crown; *wuchereri* (ne. Brazil) is intermediate. *Duidae* (restricted to Cerro Duida in s. Venezuela) is the most distinctive race, being dark brown above with a buffy belly.

SIMILAR SPECIES: Pale-eyed Pygmy-Tyrant is smaller with a more slender bill, has brighter and more olive upperparts, and is less streaked below. Cf. also Slate-headed Tody-Flycatcher.

HABITAT AND BEHAVIOR: Generally fairly common though often inconspicuous in lower growth of dry woodland and scrub, including both the chaco and caatinga, and in gallery woodland. Usually in pairs, perching vertically and flitting up to underside of leaves or twigs; does not cock tail. Usually not at all shy but not often in the open, thus more often recorded once its frequently given voice is recognized. Its most common call is a series of several sharp staccato notes followed by a fast, descending, more musical trill; sometimes the staccato notes are given alone.

RANGE: N. Colombia (Santa Marta area east to Guajira Peninsula, and in upper Río Magdalena valley south to Huila) and Venezuela (widely north of the Orinoco, including Margarita Is., south of it locally on some tepuis); locally in arid intermontane valleys on e. slope of Andes in Peru (north to Junín), and widely in e. and s. Bolivia, Paraguay, n. Argentina (south to e. Catamarca, Córdoba, Santa Fe, and Entre Ríos), and s. and e. Brazil (s. Mato Grosso and Mato Grosso do Sul east and north to Maranhão, Ceará, and Pernambuco; absent from the coastal southeast). To about 2000 m (on tepuis in Venezuela and in arid valleys and Andean slopes of Bolivia).

Hemitriccus inornatus

PELZELN'S TODY-TYRANT

DESCRIPTION: 9 cm (3½"). Known only from a single 19th-century specimen taken in *nw. Brazil*. Resembles Pearly-vented Tody-Tyrant, especially its *impiger* race of n. Venezuela and ne. Colombia, but slightly smaller, darker above, and with whitish wing-bars (not pale buffyish to yellowish). Description from P. L. Sclater (*Catalogue of the Birds in the British Museum*, 1888).

HABITAT AND BEHAVIOR: Unknown.

RANGE: Nw. Brazil (Rio Içana, in upper Rio Negro drainage).

NOTE: Perhaps only a subspecies of *H. margaritaceiventer*.

Hemitriccus striaticollis

STRIPE-NECKED TODY-TYRANT   PLATE: 35

DESCRIPTION: 11 cm (4¼"). *Mainly n. Bolivia to ne. Brazil*. Iris whitish to pale yellow. Above mainly olive with crown tinged dull grayish brown; *usually large spot on lores and narrow eye-ring white; wings essentially plain olive* (with *no* wing-bars, and only weak yellowish edging on flight feathers). *Throat white sharply streaked dusky;* remaining underparts yellow, breast broadly streaked olive.

SIMILAR SPECIES: Cf. very similar Johannes' Tody-Tyrant. Stripe-necked also resembles Spotted Tody-Flycatcher, but that species has narrower and crisper streaking on throat and breast, is grayer on crown contrasting more with olive back, lacks the eye-ring (but supralorals about the same), and has fairly prominent yellowish wing-bars; Stripe-necked tends to perch more horizontally.

HABITAT AND BEHAVIOR: Uncommon to locally fairly common in riparian growth of shrubbery and low trees, especially in savanna-dominated regions. Usually found singly, less often in pairs, perching in tangles at low and mid-heights and usually not very conspicuous. Its call in Brazil is a fast "pit-pit-pit-pit, whi-didit," sometimes without the introductory "pit" series.

RANGE: Se. Peru (Cuzco and Madre de Dios) and n. Bolivia (south to La Paz and n. Santa Cruz) east across Brazil south of the Amazon to Ceará and Bahia, and south to the pantanal region of the upper Rio

Paraguay basin in n. Mato Grosso do Sul; isolated populations in ne. Peru (Moyobamba in San Martín) and ne. Colombia (n. Meta, at Carimagua and Laguna Mozambique). To about 1000 m in ne. Peru.

NOTE: See comments under Johannes' Tody-Tyrant.

Hemitriccus iohannis

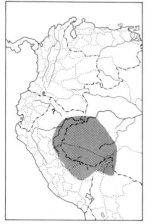

JOHANNES' TODY-TYRANT

DESCRIPTION: 11 cm (4¼"). Found only in *w. Amazonia;* formerly considered conspecific with Stripe-necked Tody-Tyrant. Resembles that species apart from the following: ocular area and lores brownish (*lacking Stripe-necked's usually prominent white lores and narrow eye-ring*); throat not as pure white, with the dark streaking on throat finer, and that on breast blurrier and less distinct; narrow yellow edging on wing-coverts forming *slight wing-bars* (wings plain in Stripe-necked). SIMILAR SPECIES: Johannes' and Stripe-necked Tody-Tyrants are very similar, but fortunately they do not normally occur together. Johannes' also resembles Spotted Tody-Flycatcher but has blurrier (not so crisp) throat and breast streaking and olive (not gray) crown; behavior also differs. Cf. also White-eyed Tody-Tyrant (especially nominate race), which is much less yellow below and has more prominent wing-bars; its preferred habitat also differs (White-eyed inside forest). HABITAT AND BEHAVIOR: Rare to locally fairly common in secondary woodland and riparian areas, foraging at all levels though less often low; found in mostly forested regions, though absent from actual tall forest. Ranges singly or in pairs, usually remaining inside viny tangles and thus inconspicuous and not often seen until its voice is learned. Its most common vocalization is a simple, fast, semimusical trill introduced by an emphasized note, "tik-trrrrrrrrrrrrree," usually sliding up a bit at end. Numerous around Hacienda Amazonia in Madre de Dios, Peru. RANGE: Locally in se. Colombia (w. Putumayo at San Antonio; Pto. Nariño on the Amazon), e. Peru (e. Loreto south to Madre de Dios), n. Bolivia (south to La Paz and Beni), and w. Amaz. Brazil (east at least to the upper Rio Purus). Seems likely in e. Ecuador. To about 500 m.

NOTE: We follow Traylor (1982) in considering *H. iohannis* as a full species distinct from *H. striaticollis*. Both have been collected in n. Bolivia, at Victoria in Beni; Traylor (op. cit.) found no evidence of intergradation in specimens from either that region or from se. Peru, where *H. iohannis* and *H. striaticollis* also come into contact.

Hemitriccus zosterops

WHITE-EYED TODY-TYRANT   PLATE: 35

DESCRIPTION: 11 cm (4¼"). Amazonia. Iris not "white" but pale grayish or straw yellow; lower mandible pinkish at least at base. Plain olive above with whitish supraloral; wings with *2 fairly prominent yellowish wing-bars* and edging on flight feathers. Throat pale grayish, lightly streaked dusky; breast olive flammulated with yellow, becoming pale yellow on belly, tinged olive on flanks. Foregoing applies to nominate race (*flaviviridis* is similar) of north of the Amazon. *Griseipectus* (south

of the Amazon) is quite different, grayer on breast (less olive) with a *whitish belly; naumburgi* (ne. Brazil) is similar.

SIMILAR SPECIES: A confusing, widespread, and locally numerous tody-tyrant. Its 2 forms (nominate with yellow below, *griseipectus* whiter below) segregate along much of the length of the Amazon. Cf. especially the very similar Snethlage's and Zimmer's Tody-Tyrants. More southerly *griseipectus* can also be confused with Flammulated Bamboo-Tyrant, but that has plain wings (*no* wing-bars), a dark iris, and a pale lower mandible (not a mostly dark bill); it is mainly confined to bamboo thickets. More northerly nominate race resembles Double-banded and Helmeted Pygmy-Tyrants but lacks their lengthened crown feathers.

HABITAT AND BEHAVIOR: Locally fairly common in lower and middle growth of humid forest, both in terra firme and transitional forest. Inconspicuous, usually not noted until the interminably given, if insignificant, song of territorial males is recognized. That of *griseipectus* is a staccato "kwidíp" or "kwididíp," given at 2- to 3-second intervals even into the heat of day; *naumburgi* (ne. Brazil) has similar call. Calling birds usually perch 5–10 m up, often on a more or less unobstructed limb, but are usually hard to spot as they tend not to fly much; they are numerous at the Tambopata Reserve in Madre de Dios, Peru. Nominate birds in se. Ecuador give a rather different song, a "tic, tic, tic, tididídidit" repeated at rather fast intervals off and on through day; sometimes birds repeat only the "tic" note.

RANGE: Surinam and French Guiana, s. Venezuela (Amazonas), se. Colombia (north to Caquetá and Vaupés), e. Ecuador, e. Peru, n. Bolivia (south to La Paz and w. Santa Cruz), and Amaz. Brazil (south to se. Pará and s. Mato Grosso on the Serra dos Parecís, and east in the lower Amazon basin to the lower Rio Tocantins area; absent from much of the Rio Negro/Rio Branco drainages); ne. Brazil (Paraíba to Alagoas). Usually below 1000 m, but recorded to 1500 m in Venezuela.

NOTE: More than one species is likely involved, in which case *H. griseipectus* (with *naumburgi*) could be known as the White-bellied Tody-Tyrant.

Hemitriccus minor

SNETHLAGE'S TODY-TYRANT

DESCRIPTION: 10 cm (4"). *Mainly e. Amaz. Brazil.* Iris white to pale yellow. Very like White-eyed Tody-Tyrant but slightly smaller; lacks its whitish supraloral, and with somewhat less well marked wing-bars. Females are evidently brighter olive above and yellower below than males (*fide* J. T. Zimmer, *Am. Mus. Novitates* 1066, p. 17, 1940). Thus male Snethlage's resembles white-bellied *griseipectus* White-eyed, whereas female Snethlage's resembles yellow-bellied nominate White-eyed. Snethlage's occurs sympatrically mainly with *griseipectus* White-eyed. In the hand note that bill of Snethlage's is somewhat shorter and also wider basally; nostrils are rounder and more exposed. Further, its crown feathers are slightly longer than in other *Hemitriccus,* recalling *Lophotriccus.*

SIMILAR SPECIES: See also Zimmer's Tody-Tyrant. Zimmer's, Sneth-

lage's, and *griseipectus* form of White-eyed are exceedingly similar, so much so as to be almost indistinguishable in the field. Remarkably, all are known from the lower Rio Tapajós area in Brazil.

HABITAT AND BEHAVIOR: Locally fairly common in vine tangles and other dense vegetation at edge of humid forest, mostly in terra firme. Usually found singly or in pairs, independent of flocks, perching 3–8 m up. Inconspicuous, most often noted when calling. Vocalizations include a gravelly trill much like Double-banded Pygmy-Tyrant's call, but this is often preceded by a long, irregular series of "tic" notes.

RANGE: Amaz. Brazil (north of the Amazon locally in the Rio Negro drainage, south of it from the Rio Juruá east to the lower Rio Tocantins, and south to s. Mato Grosso) and ne. Bolivia (ne. Santa Cruz and e. Beni); a single record from Amazonas (Puerto Yapacana) in s. Venezuela (Meyer de Schauensee and Phelps 1978). The reported Surinam specimen proves to be a nominate White-eyed Pygmy-Tyrant (*fide* E. R. Blake, in litt. to R. Meyer de Schauensee); in light of this, the identity of the Venezuela bird should also be confirmed. Recent sight reports from French Guiana (Tostain et al. 1992) also await confirmation.

NOTE: Formerly separated in the monotypic genus *Snethlagea* based on slight differences in its bill and nostrils. We follow *Birds of the World,* vol. 8, in merging it with *Hemitriccus.*

Hemitriccus minimus

ZIMMER'S TODY-TYRANT

DESCRIPTION: 10 cm (4"). *Very local in the lower Amazon area and ne. Bolivia. Closely* resembles slightly larger and relatively longer-tailed nominate form (yellow-bellied) of White-eyed Tody-Tyrant. Fortunately, the form of White-eyed that ranges with Zimmer's is whitish-bellied; belly of Zimmer's is *pale yellow.* In addition, lores of Zimmer's are buffyish (not whitish), its crown darker, and its whole auricular region browner; the throat is more finely streaked dusky. Its rather strong wing-bars are yellow, and *inner flight feathers are edged yellow, whereas outers are not,* producing a distinct 2-toned effect. *All* of White-eyed's flight feathers are edged yellow, producing a uniform look.

SIMILAR SPECIES: Snethlage's Tody-Tyrant is also exceedingly similar but shows less crisp dusky streaking on throat and is somewhat paler olive above (including the crown, feathers of which lack the indistinct dark central stripes of Zimmer's). Snethlage's typically shows yellow edging on all flight feathers, so it (like White-eyed) lacks the 2-toned effect so prominent in Zimmer's; some Snethlage's do, however, seem to show less edging on inner flight feathers, producing somewhat the same effect.

HABITAT AND BEHAVIOR: Apparently uncommon and very local; birds in ne. Bolivia were found in canopy of stunted forest on sandy soil. Usually in pairs. Its loud but ventriloquial vocalizations include "a variety of short trills and twittering notes reminiscent of the calls of the Eared Pygmy-Tyrant" (J. M. Bates et al. 1992, p. 91).

RANGE: E. Amaz. Brazil (specimens from e. bank of the lower Rio

Tapajós at Tauary and Fôrdlandia; AMNH, ANSP, and MZUSP); ne. Bolivia (n. Beni at Versalles, and ne. Santa Cruz on the Serranía de Huanchaca). To 450 m in Bolivia.

NOTE: D. F. Stotz (*Auk* 109[4]: 916–917, 1992) determined that the correct species name for Zimmer's Tody-Tyrant was *H. minimus* and not *H. aenigma* (as it long was called; e.g., Meyer de Schauensee 1966, 1970).

Hemitriccus josephinae

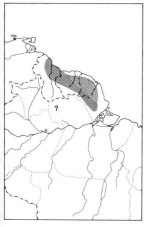

BOAT-BILLED TODY-TYRANT

PLATE: 35

DESCRIPTION: 11 cm (4¼″). Local from *Guianas to n. Brazil. Iris reddish brown;* lower mandible pale at base. *Plain olive above* (wings with no bars or even edging) with *pale grayish lores and area behind eye;* tail browner. Throat grayish white; remaining underparts *uniform* pale yellowish.

SIMILAR SPECIES: White-eyed and Snethlage's Tody-Tyrants both have pale irides, wing-bars, and some streaking below. Superficially resembles Ochre-bellied Flycatcher.

HABITAT AND BEHAVIOR: Rare in middle strata of humid forest and forest borders. Shows a distinct preference for viny tangles and lianas at the edge of forest or in small openings, where it tends to perch, often motionless for extended periods, usually 5–10 m above the ground. Its voice is a falling, dry "pic-pic-pic" (P. Donahue, *Am. Birds* 39[2]: 229–230, 1985). A very rare bird in collections.

RANGE: Locally in Guianas (Guyana at Supenaam River; Surinam at Raleigh Falls Nature Park; several localities in interior French Guiana) and n. Brazil (Amapá; in 1988 found in Amazonas at Balbina north of Manaus [VIREO; A. Whittaker et al.]). Below 200 m.

NOTE: Formerly separated in the monotypic genus *Microcochlearius* based on its wider bill and more rounded tail than in *Idioptilon* (= *Hemitriccus*). We follow *Birds of the World*, vol. 8, in merging it with *Hemitriccus*.

GROUP B

Montane and e. Brazil groups. More distinctive than Group A, many showing *buff to ochraceous on face.*

Hemitriccus spodiops

YUNGAS TODY-TYRANT

DESCRIPTION: 11 cm (4¼″). *A dark, drab tody-tyrant of foothills in Bolivia. Iris pale yellow.* Above olive with grayish buff preocular area; wings with *2 vague yellowish olive wing-bars. Throat and breast grayish olive* vaguely streaked with whitish, becoming unstreaked yellowish white on belly.

SIMILAR SPECIES: Confusing. Similar White-eyed Tody-Tyrant (*griseipectus*) is grayer on throat and breast and has bolder, paler wing-bars; it and Yungas are not known to overlap altitudinally (White-eyed in *lowlands*) but they could; they differ in behavior. Yungas is even more apt to be confused with Flammulated Bamboo-Tyrant, with which it definitely does overlap; Flammulated differs in having a brown iris, not showing any wing-bars at all, and having a distinctly brown wash on breast (showing little or no olive).

HABITAT AND BEHAVIOR: Uncommon in shrubby forest borders, dense low growth of regenerating clearings and landslides, and roadside second-growth. Usually found singly, perching low and making short upward sallies to foliage; occasionally perches fully in the open, allowing a close approach. The call, a short harsh trill, is usually given 3–4 times in succession; it resembles the primary call of Scale-crested Pygmy-Tyrant (T. A. Parker III, *in* Remsen et al. 1982).

RANGE: W. Bolivia (foothills and lower Andean slopes in La Paz, Cochabamba, and s. Beni). Mainly 800–1600 m.

NOTE: For more information on this species, see Remsen et al. (1982).

Hemitriccus granadensis

BLACK-THROATED TODY-TYRANT
PLATE: 35

DESCRIPTION: 10.5 cm (4″). *Mts. from Venezuela to Bolivia;* virtually unmistakable *fancy facial pattern*. Birds from Santa Marta Mts. (*lehmanni*) and in Andes from s. Ecuador to Bolivia (*pyrrhops*) are uniform olive above with *prominent buff lores and ocular area;* wings without bars. *Upper throat blackish* (with almost a gorgeted effect), contrasting sharply with whitish lower throat; breast grayish, becoming white on belly, tinged yellow on lower flanks and crissum. Birds from n. Venezuela to extreme n. Ecuador (nominate group) have *lores and ocular area whitish;* see V-30, C-36.

HABITAT AND BEHAVIOR: Uncommon to fairly common in borders of montane forest and secondary woodland. Generally found in lower growth, sometimes up to 10 m above ground; usually quiet and rather inactive but relatively easy to see as it often perches in the open. Like many of its congeners, flight typically is buzzy and direct, often with an audible whirr. Regularly associates with mixed foraging flocks. The most common call (of *pyrrhops*) is a fast but rather soft "whididik"; when excited, a sharper "wheép-wheép-wheép-wheép." Rather different calls are described (Hilty and Brown 1986) for the nominate race in Colombia, including a gravelly "dut't't, dut't't," a nasal "tip-buuuuu," and a sharp "pik, peet, peet."

RANGE: Coastal mts. of n. Venezuela (Distrito Federal), and Andes of extreme w. Venezuela (Táchira), Colombia, locally in Ecuador (on w. slope known only from extreme north in Carchi; on e. slope in extreme north in Napo, and from Morona-Santiago southward), e. Peru, and w. Bolivia (La Paz); Sierra de Perijá on Venezuela-Colombia border, and Santa Marta Mts. in n. Colombia. Mostly 1500–2800 m.

NOTE: Possibly more than one species is involved.

Hemitriccus rufigularis

BUFF-THROATED TODY-TYRANT
PLATE: 35

DESCRIPTION: 12 cm (4¾″). *Very local on e. slope of Andes from Ecuador to Bolivia.* The *largest of the tody-tyrants* (but hardly "big"). Iris whitish to straw yellow; lower mandible grayish flesh. Above olive, grayer on crown; *ocular area, sides of head and neck, and breast pale dull buff,* vaguely streaked with gray; throat buffy whitish streaked with gray,

belly whitish, somewhat mottled with gray on flanks. *Wings plain,* with no bars or obvious edging.

SIMILAR SPECIES: Cinnamon-breasted Tody-Tyrant is much brighter cinnamon on face and breast and pale yellow (not whitish) on belly.

HABITAT AND BEHAVIOR: Uncommon and very local in humid forest of foothill zone. Birds seen (RSR and R. A. Rowlett) on the Cordillera de Cutucú in Ecuador perched 6–8 m above ground in fairly open forest along ridge crests in a narrow elevation zone around 1300 m. Here presumably territorial males called "kw-díp, kw-díp, kw-díp, kw-díp . . ." more or less interminably, even during midday. Can also be seen on slopes above Hacienda Amazonia in Cuzco, Peru.

RANGE: Locally on e. slope of Andes in Ecuador (recent records from w. Napo along the road to Loreto [N. Krabbe] and on the slopes of Volcán Sumaco [B. Whitney], slopes of the Cordillera del Cutucú in Morona-Santiago, and slopes of the Cordillera del Condor at Pachicutza in Zamora-Chinchipe [WFVZ]), Peru (San Martín, and from Huánuco southward), and w. Bolivia (La Paz, extreme sw. Beni, and w. Santa Cruz on Cerro Hosane). 800–1450 m.

Hemitriccus
cinnamomeipectus

CINNAMON-BREASTED TODY-TYRANT

DESCRIPTION: 10 cm (4"). *Known only from a few remote, isolated mt. ranges in n. Peru and adjacent Ecuador.* Iris light reddish brown. Uniform dark olive above, somewhat browner on crown, with *broad pale yellowish edging on tertials. Ocular area, cheeks, throat, and breast bright cinnamon,* darkest around eye; belly pale clear yellow.

SIMILAR SPECIES: Geographically far-distant Kaempfer's Tody-Tyrant has dull ochraceous brown face and breast, and these contrast less with its olive crown. In Cinnamon-breasted's Andean range most likely to be confused with Buff-throated Tody-Tyrant, but that species is larger with much duller buff face and breast, whitish belly, and *no* stripe along tertials.

HABITAT AND BEHAVIOR: Apparently uncommon in undergrowth of thick mossy montane forest. Poorly known. One briefly observed bird appeared to be accompanying a small understory flock of antbirds and warblers; it made short, quick sallies to nearby foliage (T. Schulenberg). Others have been noted foraging independently (B. Whitney; RSR). We do not know its voice.

RANGE: Locally in extreme s. Ecuador (specimens taken near Chinapinza on the Cordillera del Condor in Zamora-Chinchipe; ANSP, MECN) and n. Peru (Cordillera del Condor in Cajamarca; Cordillera de Colán in Amazonas; Abra Patricia in San Martín). 1700–2200 m.

NOTE: A recently described species: J. W. Fitzpatrick and J. P. O'Neill, *Auk* 96(3): 443–447, 1979. See comments under Kaempfer's Tody-Tyrant.

Hemitriccus mirandae

BUFF-BREASTED TODY-TYRANT   PLATE: 35

DESCRIPTION: 10 cm (4"). *Ne. Brazil.* Uniform olive above, with *broad creamy edging on tertials. Ocular area, cheeks, and entire underparts uniform pale creamy buff,* slightly whiter on belly.

SIMILAR SPECIES: Not found with other members of its superspecies, Cinnamon-breasted and Kaempfer's; neither of these is nearly as uniform pale buff below. Buff-breasted should be easily distinguished from other potentially sympatric *Hemitriccus* tody-tyrants by its tertial stripes and lack of streaking below.

HABITAT AND BEHAVIOR: Uncommon and very local in understory and middle strata of semihumid and secondary woodland, often where there are dense tall vine tangles; apparently occurs exclusively on slopes of various serras in its range. Little known. Birds forage individually, sallying short distances upward to foliage or vines. We do not know its voice. Seems always to have been local, and continued deforestation in ne. Brazil clearly imperils it; a population does occur in the recently created Pedra Talhada Biological Reserve in Alagoas. All information from Collar et al. (1992).

RANGE: Very locally in ne. Brazil (Ceará on the Serra de Ibiapaba and Serra de Baturité; Pernambuco at Brejão; and Alagoas near Quebrangulo). 700–1000 m.

NOTE: See comments under Kaempfer's Tody-Tyrant.

Hemitriccus kaempferi

KAEMPFER'S TODY-TYRANT

DESCRIPTION: 10 cm (4"). *Known only from Santa Catarina, Brazil;* formerly considered conspecific with Buff-breasted Tody-Tyrant. Uniform olive above; wings with broad pale yellowish edging on tertials and 2 narrow buffy-olive wing-bars. *Orbital area and cheeks buffyish, becoming dull ochraceous on throat and breast;* belly pale clear yellow.

SIMILAR SPECIES: Buff-breasted Tody-Tyrant, found well to north of this species in ne. Brazil, is more uniform creamy buff below. Eye-ringed Tody-Tyrant also has a tertial stripe, but it has a conspicuous white eye-ring and is olive (not ochraceous) on throat and chest. Cf. also Brown-breasted Bamboo-Tyrant.

HABITAT AND BEHAVIOR: Virtually unknown in life. For many years known only from the type specimen, taken by E. Kaempfer in 1929; an only recently recognized specimen was obtained in 1950. In 1991 M. Pearman found a lone individual within 1 km of the type locality at Salto Piraí; it was foraging in the middle strata of secondary woodland and had a "distinctive" call (undescribed). Forested habitats in and around the type locality, though somewhat degraded by logging, are still in reasonably good condition, and some are protected within a forest reserve surrounding a hydroelectric plant; nonetheless, given its highly restricted range, the species must be judged potentially at risk (nothing is known about current habitat conditions at Brusque).

RANGE: Se. Brazil (e. Santa Catarina, at Salto Piraí near Joinville, and Brusque). 150 m.

NOTE: Described as a race of *H. mirandae,* and so treated by Meyer de Schauensee (1966, 1970). J. W. Fitzpatrick and J. P. O'Neill (*Auk* 96[3]: 443–447, 1979), however, suggest that *H. kaempferi* is best treated as a full species and that it and *H. cinnamomeipectus* are best considered as part of the *H. mirandae* superspecies.

Hemitriccus furcatus

FORK-TAILED TODY-TYRANT   PLATE: 35

Other: Fork-tailed Pygmy-Tyrant

DESCRIPTION: 11 cm (4¼"). *Very rare and local in se. Brazil;* virtually unmistakable, with *colorful facial pattern* and *long, boldly patterned tail. Head and throat cocoa brown with paler buff ocular area* and vague streaking on throat; above otherwise bright olive, wings with rather bright chestnut edging on inner flight feathers. White spot on center of chest; *breast gray* with somewhat flammulated effect extending down over flanks; midbelly white. Tail olive with *prominent white tipping and black subterminal band,* quite long and *obviously forked* and often spread; tail may be somewhat more forked in males.

HABITAT AND BEHAVIOR: Rare to locally uncommon in lower growth of humid forest borders and secondary woodland, especially where there are dense thickets of bamboo (particularly large-leaved species?). Behavior similar to many other tody-tyrants'; rather sedentary, generally foraging independently of mixed flocks (though may briefly join them when a flock passes through its small territory). Its usual posture is quite vertical; makes upward strikes to vegetation, most often to the underside of bamboo leaves. The primary vocalization is a fast, sharp, staccato "chídididik" or "kikky-tutu," delivered at 3- to 8-second intervals; often quite responsive to tape playback. Long considered very rare, but there has been a spate of recent sightings of this attractive small flycatcher from a number of sites within much of its range, and the fact that it appears to favor secondary growth and borders presumably operates in its favor; nonetheless it probably deserves formal threatened status. Can be seen north of Ubatuba in ne. São Paulo.

RANGE: Se. Brazil (Rio de Janeiro, adjacent s. Minas Gerais on the Serra da Mantiquiera, and ne. São Paulo). Its reported occurrence in Espírito Santo remains unconfirmed. To 1200 m.

NOTE: Formerly separated in the monotypic genus *Ceratotriccus* on the basis of its lengthened outer rectrices, but recent authorities (e.g., Traylor 1977) have merged it into *Hemitriccus.* Although we agree that it likely does not deserve generic separation, we would emphasize that *H. furcatus* is a very distinct species, not clearly associated with any other *Hemitriccus.* It was formerly called a pygmy-tyrant, but given its present generic association, it should now be called a tody-tyrant.

Hemitriccus orbitatus

EYE-RINGED TODY-TYRANT   PLATE: 35

DESCRIPTION: 11.5 cm (4½"). *Se. Brazil.* Iris dark. Above uniform olive with *prominent white supraloral and eye-ring* and dusky area below eye; wings with *broad white edging on tertials.* Mostly yellowish below, streaked with olive on throat and with solid wash of olive across chest; *belly clear yellow.*

SIMILAR SPECIES: Most likely confused with Serra do Mar Tyrannulet, whose overall plumage and facial pattern are quite similar (though its typical horizontal posture differs radically). Besides posture, the best distinguishing points are Serra do Mar's mostly grayish (not yellowish)

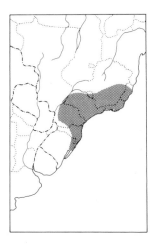

underparts and *lack* of the long white stripe on tertials. Kaempfer's and Hangnest Tody-Tyrants both lack the eye-ring and have differently colored underparts.

HABITAT AND BEHAVIOR: Locally uncommon to fairly common in lower and middle growth of humid forest and mature secondary woodland, mainly remaining inside, less often at edge. Behavior similar to many other forest-interior tody-tyrants'; tends to perch vertically and to make short, abrupt flights during which the wings whir audibly, manakin-like. Usually solitary or in pairs, apart from mixed flocks. Its primary vocalization is a short, snappy, trilled "tr-r-r-r-r-r-r." Can be found in Tijuca Nat. Park above Rio de Janeiro (city), e.g., in the Retiro area; overall numbers have doubtless declined substantially as so much of its original range has been deforested.

RANGE: Se. Brazil (Espírito Santo, s. Minas Gerais, and São Paulo south to ne. Rio Grande do Sul). To about 1000 m.

Hemitriccus nidipendulus

HANGNEST TODY-TYRANT

PLATE: 35

DESCRIPTION: 9.5–10 cm (3¾–4"). *Se. Brazil;* small and *relatively unpatterned. Iris whitish;* mandible grayish flesh. *Above bright uniform olive green,* wing-coverts and flight feathers rather prominently edged yellowish olive. *Whitish below,* vaguely streaked pale grayish olive on throat and breast. *Paulistus* (all of range except Bahia) slightly larger.

SIMILAR SPECIES: Cf. Eye-ringed Tody-Tyrant (with different facial pattern and dark eye, much yellower underparts) and Serra do Mar Tyrannulet.

HABITAT AND BEHAVIOR: Uncommon in lower growth at edge of humid forest and in secondary woodland, mostly in foothills (e.g., the Serra do Mar). Usually forages singly, perching upright in shrubbery and making short, abrupt, manakin-like flights. Call is a fast "weet-weet-weet" (D. Stotz). Small numbers occur at lower levels in Itatiaia Nat. Park and in remnant woodland at Boa Nova in s. Bahia. It should be noted that, so far as known, all *Hemitriccus* build "hanging" globular nests.

RANGE: Se. Brazil (s. Bahia south to São Paulo; probably in adjacent Paraná). To about 900 m.

GROUP C

"True" *Hemitriccus* bamboo-tyrants. Confined to *bamboo thickets;* iris dark. The three members of this group have large dark eyes which impart a wide-eyed look, unpatterned wings, "drab" underparts lacking yellow on belly, and a pale flesh lower mandible. They are the "original" *Hemitriccus* (formerly separated from *Idioptilon* on the basis of minor wing and tail characters), into which *Idioptilon* was recently merged (Traylor 1977). When these three species were the sole members of the *Hemitriccus* genus, they were called pygmy-tyrants. With the merger of *Idioptilon* into *Hemitriccus,* all theoretically became known as tody-tyrants, the long-accepted group name for *Idioptilon.* That, however, would lead to *H. flammulatus* being called the Flammulated Tody-Tyrant. Although that species is slightly flammulated on the breast, it is markedly less so than many of its new congeners. We propose to solve this potentially confusing situation by calling the three "true" *Hemitriccus* bamboo-tyrants, for all are closely associated with bamboo. That having been done, Flammulated Bamboo-Tyrant stands as a good name for *H. flammulatus,* for it is a bit more flammulated below than its two closest relatives.

Hemitriccus diops

DRAB-BREASTED BAMBOO-TYRANT   PLATE: 35

Other: Drab-breasted Pygmy-Tyrant

DESCRIPTION: 11 cm (4¼"). *Se. Brazil area.* Above plain olive with *conspicuous whitish supraloral spot and eye-ring. Throat and breast dull mauve grayish,* with indistinct white crescent across lower throat; belly whitish, tinged yellow on crissum.

SIMILAR SPECIES: Cf. Brown-breasted Bamboo-Tyrant. There are several more or less similar tody-tyrants found in Drab-breasted's range, but none is quite so dull and dark or has the whitish supraloral; most have a conspicuous pale tertial stripe, which all bamboo-tyrants lack.

HABITAT AND BEHAVIOR: Uncommon to fairly common in undergrowth of humid forest and mature secondary woodland, especially in bamboo tangles at forest edge. An unobtrusive little bird, usually found in pairs, rarely perching in the open; does not seem to move with mixed flocks. The call is a short, somewhat dry trill, often doubled, e.g., "tr-r-r-r-r, tr-r-r-r-r." Quite numerous at lower elevations in Itatiaia and Serra dos Órgãos Nat. Parks.

RANGE: Se. Brazil (se. Bahia south to nw. Rio Grande do Sul), e. Paraguay (west to Canendiyu, Caaguazú, and Caazapá), and ne. Argentina (Misiones). To about 1300 m.

Hemitriccus obsoletus

BROWN-BREASTED BAMBOO-TYRANT

Other: Brown-breasted Pygmy-Tyrant

DESCRIPTION: 11 cm (4¼"). *Se. Brazil.* Resembles Drab-breasted Bamboo-Tyrant, differing in its *buff supraloral spot and eye-ring, dingy buff throat and breast,* and slightly more brownish olive upperparts.

SIMILAR SPECIES: Cf. also Kaempfer's Tody-Tyrant. Both species are basically dull buffy ochraceous below, but Kaempfer's shows obvious pale edging on tertials and a clear yellow belly.

HABITAT AND BEHAVIOR: Uncommon to fairly common in undergrowth of montane forest and more mature secondary woodland, particularly favoring shady bamboo thickets. Behavior similar to Drab-breasted Bamboo-Tyrant's, remaining under cover, flying abruptly from one low perch to another, often with an audible whir of its wings. The call is a short, fast series of sharp staccato notes, typically 4 or 5, "tic-tic-tic, tic," not as run-together or trilled as in Drab-breasted. Regularly encountered at higher elevations in Itatiaia Nat. Park, Drab-breasted replacing it below about 1200 m.

RANGE: Se. Brazil (Rio de Janeiro to n. Rio Grande do Sul). To about 2300 m.

Hemitriccus flammulatus

FLAMMULATED BAMBOO-TYRANT PLATE: 35
Other: Flammulated Pygmy-Tyrant

DESCRIPTION: 11 cm (4¼"). *Bamboo thickets of w. Amazonia.* Above uniform plain olive with dull whitish supraloral spot and eye-ring. Throat whitish streaked with dull brownish gray; *breast somewhat flammulated with pinkish buffy brown;* belly whitish.

SIMILAR SPECIES: Occurs far from the other two bamboo-tyrants, though it is similar in appearance and behavior. In range most likely confused with White-eyed Tody-Tyrant, which differs in its pale eye, mostly dark bill, wing-bars, and lack of any brownish cast to breast. Unlike the bamboo-tyrant, the tody-tyrant is not confined to bamboo thickets, though it may occur in their vicinity. Cf. also the quite similar Yungas Tody-Tyrant.

HABITAT AND BEHAVIOR: Fairly common but localized in bamboo stands in humid forest, both in terra firme and transitional forest. Usually found in pairs, foraging mainly inside dense thickets of spiny bamboo and thus not easy to see without a tape recorder. Its calls consist of a variety of sharp "tic" notes and fast trills, e.g., "tik-trrrrrrríp" or "tik-tik," all quite similar to the calls of White-cheeked Tody-Tyrant, found with it in the same bamboo stands. Quite frequent at the Tambopata Reserve in Madre de Dios, Peru.

RANGE: E. Peru (north locally to San Martín), n. Bolivia (south to La Paz, Cochabamba, and n. Santa Cruz), and adjacent sw. Brazil (w. Mato Grosso at Rio Mequenez). To 1300 m.

Pseudotriccus Pygmy-Tyrants

A trio of forest-inhabiting flycatchers found in the Andes. They forage actively near the ground, frequently making mechanical sounds. Recent authors (Traylor 1977; Traylor and Fitzpatrick 1982) have suggested that, based on external morphology and behavior, the genus *Pseudotriccus* is most closely related to *Corythopis* (the antpipits); this association has been further supported by cranial and syringeal evidence (Lanyon 1988a). We retain the genus in its present position, close to *Hemitriccus,* because of its superficial similarity to various members of that genus.

Pseudotriccus pelzelni

BRONZE-OLIVE PYGMY-TYRANT PLATE: 35

DESCRIPTION: 11–11.5 cm (4¼–4½"). *A small, dark, uniform flycatcher of subtropical Andean forest undergrowth.* Iris reddish brown to dark red. Above uniform dark olive. Throat whitish, breast and flanks olive (paler than upperparts), midbelly dull creamy yellowish. Birds from W. Andes of Colombia and w. Ecuador (*berlepschi* and *annectens*) are considerably browner above, especially on mantle and tail, and buffier

below; see C-38. *Contra* some references, this species does *not* normally look crested in the field, though its long crown feathers may be slightly raised in alarm.

SIMILAR SPECIES: Overall coloration recalls a *Myiobius* flycatcher, but the pygmy-tyrant lacks that group's yellow rump and behaves very differently. Some female manakins are similar in color, especially to more olive races of the pygmy-tyrant, but the pygmy-tyrant's slender shape and behavior are quite different.

HABITAT AND BEHAVIOR: Fairly common in undergrowth of montane forest and forest borders, but on the whole inconspicuous and not very vocal, hence often overlooked (mist-netting better reveals its true numbers). Often active, making short, "nervous" flights between branches, jumping upwards to snap at insects on the underside of leaves. Its wings whir audibly as it flies, and it also frequently makes a sharp snapping noise, sometimes in series, presumably with its bill. Usually forages independently of mixed flocks, though sometimes associating with *Basileuterus* warblers and other understory species.

RANGE: Andes of Colombia (where now apparently local because of deforestation), Ecuador (south on w. slope to El Oro), and e. Peru (south locally to Cuzco; published records from Puno seem unverified); Cerro Tacarcuna on the Colombia-Panama border. Also e. Panama. Mostly 700–2000 m.

Pseudotriccus simplex

HAZEL-FRONTED PYGMY-TYRANT

DESCRIPTION: 11 cm (4¼"). Resembles Bronze-olive Pygmy-Tyrant, which it replaces in *s. Peru and w. Bolivia.* Differs mainly in having *forecrown and sides of head dull rufous;* wing and tail feathers are more broadly edged rufous.

SIMILAR SPECIES: Rather closely resembles regularly encountered immatures of Rufous-headed Pygmy-Tyrant. Rufous feathers on head of that species come in first on forecrown and face (causing a resemblance to Hazel-fronted), but usually there will also be a scatter of rufous feathers elsewhere on the head, and it is generally more rufous on wings and tail. The 2 species mainly separate out by elevation, with Rufous-headed occurring higher.

HABITAT AND BEHAVIOR: Uncommon in undergrowth of montane forest and forest borders. Not well known, though its behavior is probably similar to Bronze-olive Pygmy-Tyrant's. Birds seen in Cochabamba whirred their wings in flight in much the same way.

RANGE: E. slope of Andes in s. Peru (Puno, and on Cerro de Pantiacolla in s. Madre de Dios; FMNH) and w. Bolivia (La Paz and Cochabamba). 1300–2000 m.

NOTE: Perhaps conspecific with *P. pelzelni* (*fide* D. Stotz).

Pseudotriccus ruficeps

RUFOUS-HEADED PYGMY-TYRANT   PLATE: 35

DESCRIPTION: 11 cm (4¼"). *Andes from Colombia to Bolivia. Entire head and throat bright rufous;* otherwise dark olive above with *contrasting*

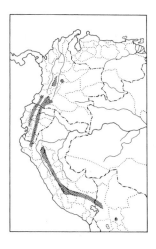

mostly chestnut wings and tail. Breast and flanks grayish olive, center of belly creamy yellowish. Young birds gradually acquire the rufous and chestnut; very young individuals show only a little color, usually especially on the foreface.

SIMILAR SPECIES: Nothing really resembles this "cute," perky little flycatcher of high-elevation Andean forests; closest is perhaps Rufous-crowned Tody-Tyrant, though its head pattern is quite different.

HABITAT AND BEHAVIOR: Fairly common in dense undergrowth of montane forest and shrubby forest borders. General behavior similar to Bronze-olive Pygmy-Tyrant's, though Rufous-headed appears to be a plumper, "fluffier," shorter-tailed bird. Makes soft snapping noises, sometimes in series, with (presumably) its bill, and also periodically emits a louder, almost explosive "tzzzzzzzzzzzzzeuw" lasting almost 2 seconds and sometimes ending with a snap.

RANGE: Andes of Colombia (north in E. Andes to Cundinamarca, in W. Andes to Valle), Ecuador (south on w. slope to e. Guayas; in recent years not recorded south of Pichincha), e. Peru, and w. Bolivia (La Paz and Cochabamba). Mostly 2000–3300 m.

Todirostrum Tody-Flycatchers

A diverse, perhaps polyphyletic group of often boldly patterned small flycatchers characterized by their broad, flat, and rather long bills. They have even more spatulate bills than the *Hemitriccus* tody-tyrants, and their posture is more horizontal, typically with tail partially cocked. Tody-flycatchers are found mainly in the lowlands, with only a few ranging in hilly or montane regions. Almost all occur primarily in edge or scrub habitats, and (unlike *Hemitriccus*) none is found inside humid forest, though a few are found in forest canopy and borders. They move about in foliage and along branches (many are difficult to see well), typically foraging by making short upward strikes to the underside of leaves. Three fairly obvious "species groups" can be discerned (these groups were first suggested by Fitzpatrick 1976). With rare exceptions, *only one member from each group is found in any area.*

  1. The *T. sylvia* group: six relatively dull species with mainly whitish underparts and usually some rusty on face; these range low in shrubbery and forest edge habitats.

  2. The *T. cinereum* group: six brighter species with mainly yellow underparts; although more arboreal than the preceding, they still tend to be found in semiopen places such as clearings and riparian growth.

  3. The *T. pictum* group: three small, brightly patterned species found high in trees in forest edge situations; these have the shortest tails and widest bills.

  Lanyon (1988c) has suggested that, based on syringeal morphology, some species long classified in *Todirostrum* be transferred to the genus *Poecilotriccus* or that they should be placed in a separate genus. These species include our entire *T. sylvia* Group, plus the Golden-winged and Black-backed Tody-Flycatchers.

We have been unable to correlate the unusual, and puzzling, variation in iris color of the Slate-headed, Golden-winged, Yellow-browed, and Painted Tody-Flycatchers with sex, age, or geography. More information on this point is needed.

GROUP A

T. sylvia Group. Lacking bright yellow below, but *usually with rusty on face.* Found in *undergrowth,* difficult to see. Iris usually dark.

Todirostrum plumbeiceps

OCHRE-FACED TODY-FLYCATCHER   PLATE: 36

DESCRIPTION: 9.5–10 cm (3¾–4″). *A bright-faced tody-flycatcher of forest undergrowth in s. South America.* Crown gray, *outlining cinnamon-buff sides of head and throat,* with auriculars more or less dusky; otherwise olive above, wings duskier with 2 ochraceous wing-bars. Below mostly grayish white, whitest on midbelly. Andean races (not nominate, which is found in se. South America) have somewhat grayer breasts.
SIMILAR SPECIES: Should be easily recognized. No other similar tyrannid shows the bright face.
HABITAT AND BEHAVIOR: Fairly common in dense shrubbery and bamboo thickets at borders of humid and montane forest and in secondary woodland. Usually in pairs (often loosely associated) which often are quite bold; less difficult to see than many other undergrowth flycatchers. Generally does not accompany mixed flocks. The call is a sharp, low, rattled trill, "tr-r-r-r-r," sometimes with a preceding "tik" note.
RANGE: E. slope of Andes in s. Peru (Puno), Bolivia, and nw. Argentina (Salta and Jujuy); se. Brazil (s. Minas Gerais and Espírito Santo southward), e. Paraguay (west to Paraguarí), and ne. Argentina (Misiones and ne. Corrientes); ne. Brazil (Alagoas at Quebrangulo). To about 2000 m in Bolivian Andes, but only to about 1300 m in Brazil.

Todirostrum russatum

RUDDY TODY-FLYCATCHER

DESCRIPTION: 9.5 cm (3¾″). *Tepuis of se. Venezuela.* Virtually unmistakable: a dark, *richly colored* relative of Ochre-faced Tody-Flycatcher. Crown slatier, with *forehead and facial area a deeper cinnamon-rufous,* slightly paler on throat, and *extending down over breast; wing-bars also rufous;* back darker olive green. See V-30.
HABITAT AND BEHAVIOR: Uncommon in dense thickets at borders of montane forest and in undergrowth of secondary woodland. Behavior and voice resemble Ochre-faced Tody-Flycatcher's; a typical call is a "tik-tik-tr-r-r-r-r" sometimes followed by a fast "tik-a-doo." Small numbers can be seen along the Escalera road, particularly at edge of patches of dense, stunted woodland.
RANGE: Se. Venezuela (Bolívar) and adjacent extreme n. Brazil (Cerro Uei-tepui in Roraima). Seems likely in adjacent Guyana. 1200–2500 m.

Todirostrum fumifrons

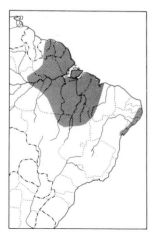

SMOKY-FRONTED TODY-FLYCATCHER   PLATE: 36

DESCRIPTION: 9 cm (3½"). *Ne. South America.* Forecrown smoky grayish, with *dull buff ocular area and short supraloral;* otherwise olive above, wings duskier with 2 buffy yellowish wing-bars. Throat whitish, becoming *pale yellowish on remaining underparts,* clearest yellow on midbelly.

SIMILAR SPECIES: Rusty-fronted Tody-Flycatcher is slightly larger, has more extensive and richer ochraceous on face, and *lacks yellow on underparts.* Cf. also the very rare Buff-cheeked Tody-Flycatcher. Slate-headed Tody-Flycatcher lacks any buff around eye (it has a *white* supraloral) and also is whitish below.

HABITAT AND BEHAVIOR: Uncommon in dense shrubbery and thickets in overgrown clearings and woodland borders. Usually in pairs, foraging low, and difficult to see well. Its call is typical of the Group, a low throaty trill usually preceded by 1 or several "tic" notes, e.g., "tic-tic-tr-r-r-r." Can often be found along the airstrip at Foengoe Is. at Raleigh Falls Nature Park, Surinam.

RANGE: Surinam, French Guiana, and lower Amaz. Brazil (west to the Manaus area and lower Rio Tapajós, and south to s. Maranhão, n. Goiás on Bananal Is., and ne. Mato Grosso); coastal ne. Brazil (Paraíba south to ne. Bahia). To about 400 m.

Todirostrum latirostre

RUSTY-FRONTED TODY-FLYCATCHER

DESCRIPTION: 9.5 cm (3¾"). *Upper Amazonia to cen. Brazil.* Above olive with slightly browner crown and *dull pale buff forehead and facial area;* wings dusky with 2 ochraceous wing-bars. *Below dull grayish white,* whitest on median belly. *Caniceps* of w. Amazonia has darker gray crown and slightly richer ochraceous facial area. See C-36.

SIMILAR SPECIES: Smoky-fronted Tody-Flycatcher is mainly pale yellow (not whitish) below and has more yellowish (not ochraceous) wing-bars. Slate-headed Tody-Flycatcher has no buff on face and bright yellow wing-bars; it and Rusty-fronted do not overlap. Pearly-vented Tody-Tyrant shows streaked effect below, has pale iris, and perches more vertically.

HABITAT AND BEHAVIOR: Fairly common in dense thickets in clearings and in undergrowth of young secondary woodland and borders of humid forest. Stays low and seldom emerges from its almost impenetrable habitat. Rarely noted but for its call, which is given at intervals throughout day. This call resembles those of others in this Group, but typically the throaty trill is doubled, thus "tik, tr-r-r-r, tr-r-r-r."

RANGE: Se. Colombia (north to Caquetá and Vaupés), e. Ecuador, e. Peru, n. and e. Bolivia (south to La Paz, Cochabamba, and Santa Cruz), and mainly south of the Amazon in Amaz. and s.-cen. Brazil (east to the lower Rio Tapajós area, and south to Goiás and w. São Paulo; north of it only in the extreme west). Published records from Paraguay (Meyer de Schauensee 1966, 1970) appear to be unsubstantiated, though the species could occur in the northeast in Concepción or Amambay. To about 1000 m.

Todirostrum senex

BUFF-CHEEKED TODY-FLYCATCHER

DESCRIPTION: 9 cm (3½"). *Known only from the type specimen taken on the lower Rio Madeira in Amaz. Brazil.* Apparently resembles Smoky-fronted Tody-Flycatcher, differing in its *extensively pinkish cinnamon face and throat,* darker olive back, and more yellowish white wing-bars. Bill shorter than in any other *Todirostrum.*

HABITAT AND BEHAVIOR: Unknown. The type specimen was taken in 1830.

RANGE: Recorded only from Borba, on e. bank of lower Rio Madeira, in Amazonas, Brazil. Under 100 m.

NOTE: The status of this form remains in doubt, but it has been considered "a very distinct species" (*Birds of the Americas,* vol. 13, part 5, p. 308). It has been suggested (Fitzpatrick 1976) that *senex* might belong in the *Hemitriccus mirandae* superspecies, though its short, wide bill and Amaz. distribution argue against this. For now we maintain it in its traditional position.

Todirostrum sylvia

SLATE-HEADED TODY-FLYCATCHER   PLATE: 36

DESCRIPTION: 9.5–10 cm (3¾–4"). *N. South America;* the only tody-flycatcher in this Group with *no rusty or buff on face.* Iris color variable, brown to whitish or pale yellow. *Crown slaty gray* with *contrasting white supraloral and eye-ring* (broken in front by dark lores). Otherwise bright olive above, wings blackish with 2 prominent yellow wing-bars and edging. Below grayish white, grayest across breast. *Schulzi* of ne. Brazil is notably darker generally, with much grayer breast and more ochraceous wing-bars.

SIMILAR SPECIES: Cf. similarly colored but much smaller and shorter-tailed Short-tailed Pygmy-Tyrant; the pygmy-tyrant is arboreal, not found in the thickets that Slate-headed favors. Pale-eyed Pygmy-Tyrant resembles pale-eyed examples of Slate-headed Tody-Flycatcher, but the pygmy-tyrant is generally duller, has some vague streaking on throat and breast (Slate-headed's underparts are unstreaked), and never has a slaty crown.

HABITAT AND BEHAVIOR: Fairly common in dense thickets at borders of forest and woodland and in shrubby regenerating clearings; tends to favor drier regions. General behavior similar to that of other members of its Group, and usually equally hard to observe, hopping about inside cover within a few feet of the ground. The most frequent call is a soft "tk, tr-r-r-t," easily passed over as an insect or frog.

RANGE: N. Colombia (south in Río Cauca valley to Valle, in Río Magdalena valley to Huila, and east of Andes to Meta and Vichada) and Venezuela (east to n. Bolívar); s. Guyana and adjacent n. Brazil (Roraima); French Guiana; ne. Brazil (e. Pará, extreme n. Goiás, Maranhão, and n. Piauí). Also Mexico to Panama. To about 800 m.

GROUP B

T. cinereum Group. *More or less bright yellow below.* More arboreal than Group A.

Todirostrum maculatum

SPOTTED TODY-FLYCATCHER

PLATE: 36

DESCRIPTION: 9.5–10 cm (3¾–4″). *Amazonia to Guianas.* Iris orange-yellow. Head mostly gray, often with some blackish and white streaking on crown (crown more uniformly blackish in *amacurense* of e. Venezuela, Guyana, and Trinidad), and with small white supraloral spot; remaining upperparts olive. Wings blackish with narrow yellow wing-bars and edging. Throat white, remaining underparts yellow, brightest on midbelly; *throat, breast, and flanks with narrow but sharp and dense black streaking.* Immatures are more narrowly and lightly streaked.

SIMILAR SPECIES: Most resembles Stripe-necked and Johannes' Tody-Tyrants, and regularly found with one or the other. Their streaking below is much broader and blurrier, and they are duller, more olive on head (less gray); have dull whitish irides; have faint or no wing-bars; and usually perch more upright. Cf. also Common and Painted Tody-Flycatchers.

HABITAT AND BEHAVIOR: Fairly common to common in riparian areas with thickets and groves of taller trees and light woodland; also regularly in shade trees around houses or in towns (including some larger cities such as Belém, Brazil), and at least in Guianas and on Trinidad in mangroves. Usually in pairs, foraging in dense foliage and thus often not easy to see, though usually quite fearless once located. Most easily found by tracking down its calls; the most common vocalization is a series of sharp, loud "peek" notes, often given as a syncopated duet by a pair, thus "pik-peek, pik-peek, pik-peek. . . ."

RANGE: Extreme e. Venezuela (e. Sucre south through Delta Amacuro), Guianas, Amaz. Brazil (south to n. Mato Grosso, n. Goiás, and Maranhão), se. Colombia (Caquetá and Amazonas), ne. Ecuador (islands in the Río Napo upriver to near La Selva, and in the Río Aguarico up to Lagartococha; ANSP), e. Peru, and n. Bolivia (Pando and Beni); Trinidad (local). To about 500 m.

Todirostrum cinereum

COMMON TODY-FLYCATCHER

PLATE: 36

DESCRIPTION: 9–9.5 cm (3½–3¾″). *The most widespread and often-seen tody-flycatcher. Iris usually conspicuously pale,* contrasting with *black fore-crown and face,* shading to *slaty on nape* and gray on back and rump. Wings blackish conspicuously edged yellow; tail black with outer feathers tipped white. Below yellow. *Peruanum* shows a dark iris (at least in Ecuador), whereas *sclateri* (sw. Colombia to nw. Peru, on Pacific slope) has whitish throat and numerous individuals have dark eyes; the latter and *cearae* (ne. Brazil) are slightly smaller than most races. *Coloreum* (se. Brazil west across n. Bolivia) has paler gray nape, more olive back and rump, and usually a small yellow spot at the base of the maxilla.

SIMILAR SPECIES: Cf. Yellow-lored and Maracaibo Tody-Flycatchers (both range-restricted). Black-headed Tody-Flycatcher is smaller with dark eye, white throat, and all-black head.

HABITAT AND BEHAVIOR: Fairly common to common in shrubby clearings, lighter woodland and forest borders, and hedgerows and gardens. Absent from many extensively forested regions (e.g., much of the heart of Amazonia), even in seemingly suitable habitat. Often looks almost comical, standing on long legs, fluttering and hopping about with its long tail held cocked up over back and perpetually in motion, flipping from side to side or quivering. In a frequent display it also hitches along a branch. Typically bold and active, Common is much easier to see than most other tody-flycatchers. Calls frequently, most often a short trill quickly repeated several times, or a repeated ticking note.

RANGE: Widespread south to n. and e. Bolivia (south to La Paz and Santa Cruz), extreme n. Paraguay (Alto Paraguay and n. Concepción), and e. Brazil (south to Mato Grosso do Sul, n. Paraná, and São Paulo), west of Andes south to nw. Peru (Lambayeque); absent from nw. Venezuela and from a wide area across w. and cen. Amazonia (though found along e. base of Andes, and in Guianas and lower Amazon region). Also Mexico to Panama. Mostly below 1200 m, in decreasing numbers up to about 2000 m.

Todirostrum poliocephalum

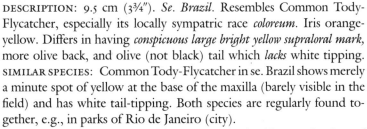

YELLOW-LORED TODY-FLYCATCHER
Other: Gray-headed Tody-Flycatcher

DESCRIPTION: 9.5 cm (3¾"). *Se. Brazil.* Resembles Common Tody-Flycatcher, especially its locally sympatric race *coloreum*. Iris orange-yellow. Differs in having *conspicuous large bright yellow supraloral mark*, more olive back, and olive (not black) tail which *lacks* white tipping.
SIMILAR SPECIES: Common Tody-Flycatcher in se. Brazil shows merely a minute spot of yellow at the base of the maxilla (barely visible in the field) and has white tail-tipping. Both species are regularly found together, e.g., in parks of Rio de Janeiro (city).
HABITAT AND BEHAVIOR: Fairly common in shrubbery at borders of humid forest and in adjacent clearings and gardens. Behavior similar to Common Tody-Flycatcher's, though more a forest-associated bird. Yellow-lored's call is usually not so run-together, most often a simple and sharply emphatic "cheep, chip-chip."
RANGE: Se. Brazil (s. Minas Gerais and Espírito Santo south to e. Santa Catarina). To about 1200 m.

NOTE: The head color of this species differs little from Common Tody-Flycatcher's (it is *not* any more "gray-headed"). The main point of distinction is its obvious yellow loral area, which we opt to highlight in our English name.

Todirostrum viridanum

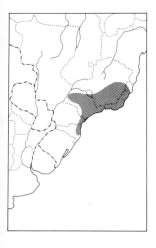

MARACAIBO TODY-FLYCATCHER
Other: Short-tailed Tody-Flycatcher

DESCRIPTION: 9 cm (3½"). A *pallid* and *markedly shorter-tailed* version of Common Tody-Flycatcher, which it replaces in *nw. Venezuela.* Usu-

ally shows *some yellowish white on forehead and above lores;* hindcrown paler gray and back paler olive; wings more broadly edged with buffy yellow; paler buffyish yellow below.

HABITAT AND BEHAVIOR: Fairly common in shrubbery and arid woodland. Behavior and voice similar to Common Tody-Flycatcher's. RANGE: Nw. Venezuela (coastal Zulia and Falcón). To about 100 m.

NOTE: Considered a full species by Meyer de Schauensee and Phelps (1978), whom we follow, though actual sympatry with *T. cinereum* seems not yet to have been established. *T. viridanum*'s tail is indeed short, shorter than that of *T. cinereum* but no shorter than tails of tody-flycatchers in the *T. pictum* complex. Therefore, we prefer to emphasize its small range, employing the English name long ago suggested by Hellmayr in his description of the form (*Birds of the Americas*, vol. 13, part 5) and used at first even by Meyer de Schauensee (1966).

Todirostrum pulchellum

BLACK-BACKED TODY-FLYCATCHER   PLATE: 36

DESCRIPTION: 9.5 cm (3¾"). *Foothills of se. Peru;* formerly treated as conspecific with Golden-winged Tody-Flycatcher. Iris usually dark. Above mostly black with a small whitish spot behind eye, *conspicuous broad golden-yellow band on greater wing-coverts,* pale yellow edging on tertials, and dull chestnut shoulders (inconspicuous); outer web of outer pair of tail feathers pale yellowish. Throat and malar stripe white, partially separated by a *black submalar streak;* remaining underparts bright yellow. Female has whitish loral spot and sooty olive back, otherwise like male.

SIMILAR SPECIES: Nothing similar in its limited range; cf. Golden-winged Tody-Flycatcher (no overlap).

HABITAT AND BEHAVIOR: Rare to uncommon in dense low shrubbery at edge of humid foothill forest. Behavior, including voice, similar to closely related Golden-winged Tody-Flycatcher's. Small numbers can be found along the lower part of the Shintuya-Paucartambo road in Cuzco, Peru.

RANGE: Se. Peru (Cuzco and Puno). 300–1000 m.

NOTE: Here considered a species separate from *T. calopterum;* we believe that the two forms are better treated as members of a superspecies. Although vocalizations and behavior are similar, they differ strikingly in plumage (especially in facial pattern), and their ranges are widely disjunct.

Todirostrum calopterum

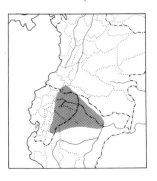

GOLDEN-WINGED TODY-FLYCATCHER

DESCRIPTION: 9.5 cm (3¾"). *E. Ecuador and adjacent Colombia and Peru.* Resembles Black-backed Tody-Flycatcher (they were formerly considered conspecific) but *back bright olive* (both sexes); *no whitish spot behind eye or black submalar streak* (thus head solidly black down to white throat); and larger area of brighter maroon-chestnut on shoulders (usually quite conspicuous). See C-36.

SIMILAR SPECIES: Common Tody-Flycatcher has gray nape and lacks the prominent yellow wing-band and white throat. Cf. also Yellow-browed Tody-Flycatcher.

HABITAT AND BEHAVIOR: Rare to locally uncommon in shrubbery

and low trees at borders of humid forest and in secondary woodland. Usually in pairs, foraging close to the ground, almost always independent of mixed flocks; often hard to see, remaining in dense cover. The call is a distinctive dry, gravelly, almost sputtering "drededeuw," often repeated rapidly several times in succession. This attractive tody-flycatcher is found in a number of areas near Tena in e. Ecuador.

RANGE: Extreme se. Colombia (w. Putumayo and e. Nariño), e. Ecuador, and ne. Peru (drainage of the Río Napo, downriver to near its mouth in the Amazon). To 1100 m.

NOTE: See comments under Black-backed Tody-Flycatcher.

GROUP C

T. pictum Group. *Smaller and shorter-tailed* than Group B; olive back contrasting with *black crown*.

Todirostrum chrysocrotaphum

YELLOW-BROWED TODY-FLYCATCHER   PLATE: 36

DESCRIPTION: 9 cm (3½"). *W. Amazonia to lower Amaz. Brazil (but only south of the Amazon).* Formerly sometimes considered conspecific with Painted Tody-Flycatcher. Variable geographically (some streaked below, others not), but all races are united by their *prominent golden yellow postocular stripe.* Iris color also variable, but usually dark. *Neglectum* (most of e. Peru, w. Amaz. Brazil) has head glossy black with broad yellow postocular stripe; upperparts otherwise bright olive, wings black with 2 yellow wing-bars and edging. Below entirely bright yellow. *Similis* (limited area near the lower Rio Tapajós, Brazil) similar but with white supraloral spot; *illigeri* (lower Amazon region east to Maranhão) reverts to having no supraloral spot but shows a prominent black submalar streak. Nominate *chrysocrotaphum* and *guttatum* (nw. Amazonia south to ne. Peru, and east to sw. Venezuela and Brazil north of the Amazon to the lower Rio Negro) similar but have *black streaks on malar area and across breast* (bolder and heavier in more northerly *guttatum*) and also show white supraloral spot; see C-36.

SIMILAR SPECIES: Nominate/*guttatum* type (with streaks below) resembles Painted Tody-Flycatcher except for Painted's lack of yellow brow; the two replace each other along the Rio Negro. Neither Common nor Spotted Tody-Flycatcher has a yellow brow, and their tails are notably longer.

HABITAT AND BEHAVIOR: Uncommon to locally fairly common in canopy and borders of humid forest (both terra firme and várzea) and taller secondary woodland, sometimes out into adjacent clearings with scattered large trees. Inconspicuous and often overlooked because of its size and habit of remaining high, generally hidden in foliage. Usually in pairs, most often not with mixed flocks. Most readily noted through its loud call, a series of sharp, enunciated, evenly spaced "pik" notes, usually given in a series of 8–12 notes.

RANGE: Extreme sw. Venezuela (sw. Amazonas), se. Colombia (north to Meta and Guainía), e. Ecuador, e. Peru, n. Bolivia (south to La Paz, Cochabamba, and w. Santa Cruz), and Amaz. Brazil (north of the Amazon east only to w. bank of the Rio Negro; south of it east to

n. Maranhão, and south to Rondônia and n. Mato Grosso). Mostly below 1000 m, in small numbers up to 1400 m.

NOTE: Here considered a species distinct from *T. pictum* of ne. South America, following most recent authors (e.g., *Birds of the World*, vol. 8). These species are parapatric along either side of most of the Rio Negro (*pictum* to the east, *chrysocrotaphum* to the west) and along the lower Amazon (*pictum* to the north, *chrysocrotaphum* to the south). No intermediates are known.

Todirostrum pictum

PAINTED TODY-FLYCATCHER　　　　　PLATE: 36

DESCRIPTION: 9 cm (3½"). *Ne. South America.* Resembles nominate/*guttatum* type of Yellow-browed Tody-Flycatcher (no overlap) but *lacks yellow postocular stripe;* iris apparently always yellow. *Head glossy black* with white spot above lores; above otherwise bright olive, wings black with 2 yellow wing-bars and edging. Mostly bright yellow below, with *black streaks on malar area and across breast;* lower facial area and sides of throat white.
SIMILAR SPECIES: Cf. Yellow-browed Tody-Flycatcher, which replaces this species westward and southward. Spotted Tody-Flycatcher is slightly larger and longer-tailed and is duller with mainly gray (not black) crown; their habitats differ.
HABITAT AND BEHAVIOR: Uncommon to fairly common in canopy and borders of humid forest and in adjacent clearings and plantations with scattered large trees. Behavior and voice much like Yellow-browed Tody-Flycatcher's, though Painted's most common call is typically doubled, e.g., "pi-pik, pi-pik . . ." (D. Stotz).
RANGE: S. Venezuela (Amazonas and Bolívar), Guianas, and n. Brazil (north of the Amazon from e. bank of the Rio Negro east through Amapá). To about 400 m.

NOTE: See comments under Yellow-browed Tody-Flycatcher.

Todirostrum nigriceps

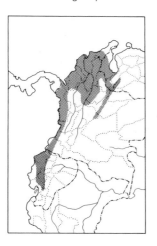

BLACK-HEADED TODY-FLYCATCHER

DESCRIPTION: 8.5 cm (3¼"). *Nw. Venezuela to w. Ecuador.* Iris dark brown. *Entire head glossy black,* contrasting sharply with bright yellowish olive back; wings and tail black, wings with 2 yellow wing-bars and edging. *Throat white; remaining underparts bright yellow.* See V-30, C-36.
SIMILAR SPECIES: This species basically replaces Yellow-browed and Painted Tody-Flycatchers *west of Andes.* However, Black-headed also occurs *east* of Andes along their base in ne. Colombia, where its range almost or actually overlaps with Yellow-browed's. Here Yellow-browed can be distinguished by its yellow postocular stripe, white loral spot, and black streaking on breast. Common Tody-Flycatcher is larger and longer-tailed and has grayish rearcrown which merges into a grayish olive back (with no contrast).
HABITAT AND BEHAVIOR: Fairly common in canopy and borders of humid forest, secondary woodland, and adjacent clearings with scat-

tered tall trees. Behavior much like Yellow-browed and Painted Tody-Flycatchers', and like them not often noted unless vocalizing. Its main vocalization is a repetition of a single "pik" note, much like Yellow-browed's.

RANGE: W. Venezuela (Maracaibo basin and also along e. base of Andes in Barinas, and probably southward), n. and w. Colombia (widespread in more humid parts of Caribbean lowlands, more local on Pacific slope; south in Río Magdalena valley to e. Caldas; also locally along e. base of Andes from Boyacá to Cundinamarca), and w. Ecuador (south to e. Guayas and nw. Azuay). Also Costa Rica and Panama. To about 900 m.

Poecilotriccus Tody-Tyrants

Plump, boldly patterned flycatchers found locally in shrubbery and forest thickets; none is very numerous. Until recently the genus had as its sole member the subtropical-ranging *P. ruficeps*. Traylor (1977), however, removed two species (*capitale* and *albifacies*) from *Todirostrum* and placed them in *Poecilotriccus*. Although we agree that they do not belong in *Todirostrum*, neither are we entirely convinced that they belong in *Poecilotriccus*, for they are so different from *P. ruficeps*. They are sexually dimorphic (*ruficeps* is not); differ in bill shape and color (all black in *ruficeps*; an orange-yellow lower mandible in the others); and have very different wing patterns ("standard" wing-bars and edging in *ruficeps*; plain with broad tertial edging, much like that of certain *Hemitriccus*, in the others). Lanyon (1988c), however, did conclude that, based on their syringes, the genus *Poecilotriccus* (with *capitalis*, *albifacies*, and *ruficeps* examined) indeed was distinct and uniform.

Poecilotriccus capitalis

BLACK-AND-WHITE TODY-TYRANT   PLATE: 36

Other: Black-and-white Tody-Flycatcher

DESCRIPTION: 9.5 cm (3¾"). *Local from s. Colombia to sw. Brazil;* includes Tricolored Tody-Tyrant, formerly considered a separate species. Bill black above, orange-yellow below. Male *glossy black above* with small white spot on lores; tertials broadly edged pale yellow. *Below mainly white,* with black intruding onto sides of throat and (particularly) the chest, sometimes with the effect of a partial pectoral collar; flanks tinged pale yellow. *Tricolor* (sw. Brazil) is very similar, its "black pectoral band" (Meyer de Schauensee 1970, p. 307) being solely due to variation in specimen preparation (*fide* D. Stotz). Female mostly olive above with gray head and neck and *chestnut crown;* wings and tail black, feathers narrowly edged olive and with broad pale yellow edging on tertials. Below like male but grayish on chest. See C-38.

SIMILAR SPECIES: This striking little tody-tyrant is not likely to be confused. Female, with its chestnut crown, might carelessly be mistaken for a female Plain Antvireo, though that species has very different bill, lacks pale edging on tertials, etc.

HABITAT AND BEHAVIOR: Rare and local in tangled thickets (sometimes but not always in bamboo) at edge of humid forest, and along streams; *tricolor* is found mainly in bamboo stands but also occurs in dense shrubby growth at forest borders (D. Stotz). Seems a genuinely scarce bird; the species is not, for a bird of such dense habitats, particularly hard to see. Forages singly, independently of mixed flocks, moving through undergrowth up to about 3 m above the ground. We do not know its voice.

RANGE: Locally in s. Colombia (w. Putumayo and e. Nariño), e. Ecuador, e. Peru (south to Pasco on the Cordillera Yanachaga; also recorded from a few localities on the lower Río Napo and from a single sighting on the Río Javarí, south of Leticia), and sw. Brazil (Rondônia on the Rio Jamarí, and recently recorded at Cachoeira Nazaré). To about 1350 m.

NOTE: Formerly placed in the genus *Todirostrum*, but transferred to *Poecilotriccus* by Traylor (1977). Because of the change in genera, the correct spelling of the species name becomes *capitalis*, not *capitale* (Sibley and Monroe 1990). The generic change also mandates a switch in its English name from tody-flycatcher to tody-tyrant, so as to be in accord with other members of the genus. We include *tricolor* (Tricolored Tody-Tyrant) in *P. capitalis;* this form, long known from only a single (male) specimen, was found recently by FMNH personnel at Cachoeira Nazaré in Rondônia. D. Stotz and T. Schulenberg (pers. comm.) suggest that not only should it not be regarded as a separate species from *P. capitalis,* but that indeed it may not even be worthy of subspecific recognition.

Poecilotriccus albifacies

WHITE-CHEEKED TODY-TYRANT   PLATE: 36

Other: White-cheeked Tody-Flycatcher

DESCRIPTION: 9.5 cm (3¾"). A *boldly patterned* little flycatcher with a *very limited range in bamboo thickets of se. Peru.* Bill black above, orange-yellow below. *Crown bright rufous-chestnut* with *sides of head white,* both contrasting sharply with *black nuchal collar* which in turn contrasts with bright yellowish olive back; wings and tail jet black, wings with prominent white edging on tertials. Below mainly white, with black malar area and black on sides of chest. Female somewhat duller overall with cheeks and neck gray and wings broadly edged olive.

SIMILAR SPECIES: Strikingly colored and patterned, hardly to be confused in its small range.

HABITAT AND BEHAVIOR: Uncommon and very local in dense thickets of bamboo found in humid forest (mainly transitional), to which it is quite strictly confined. Here it forages in pairs, generally independently of other birds, usually in the upper levels of bamboo thickets some 2–8 m above the ground, only occasionally coming out into adjacent areas of forest. Its call is a fast series of sharp "pik" notes, often with some hesitation at first but then run together, e.g., "pik, pik-pik-pik-pik-pik," similar to but less trilled than the call of Flammulated Bamboo-Tyrant, regularly found with it. White-cheeked Tody-Tyrant is one of the most special birds found at the Tambopata Reserve in Madre de Dios, Peru, but even here it is not numerous and various bamboo patches may have to be searched carefully before it is found; has also been found above Hacienda Amazonia in Cuzco.

RANGE: Se. Peru (s. Madre de Dios and adjacent ne. Cuzco). To 1050 m.

NOTE: Described in the genus *Todirostrum* and thus long called a tody-flycatcher (e.g., Meyer de Schauensee 1966, 1970). With its transfer to *Poecilotriccus*, it should be called a tody-tyrant. For more natural history information on this species, see Parker (1982).

Poecilotriccus ruficeps

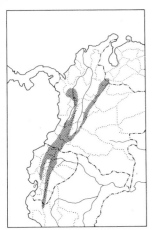

RUFOUS-CROWNED TODY-TYRANT   PLATE: 36

DESCRIPTION: 9.5–10 cm (3¾–4"). *Mainly Andes of Colombia and Ecuador. Crown bright rufous* bordered behind by black line and then by gray nape; supraloral spot and cheeks buff to rufous; otherwise bright olive above, wings black with 2 pale yellowish wing-bars and edging on flight feathers. *Throat and upper chest white to buffy whitish,* bordered by some black in malar area, and separated from bright yellow of lower underparts by *diffuse dusky band across breast. Melanomystax* (w. Colombia south in W. Andes to Cauca, and in Cen. Andes to Tolima) is quite different, with *much broader black facial markings encircling whitish cheeks*.

SIMILAR SPECIES: Despite its similar-sounding name, Rufous-headed Pygmy-Tyrant, with its *solid rufous* head and throat, is actually quite dissimilar in appearance.

HABITAT AND BEHAVIOR: Uncommon to locally fairly common in shrubby overgrown clearings and at edge of humid forest. Usually very inconspicuous, foraging inside bushes and low trees. Found singly or in pairs, generally not accompanying mixed flocks. Its call is a short, weak (and thus easily overlooked) gravelly stutter, "patreer-pít" or "put-put-prréer-put."

RANGE: Andes of extreme w. Venezuela (Táchira), Colombia (north in both W. and Cen. Andes to Antioquia), Ecuador (south on w. slope to Chimborazo), and extreme n. Peru (Piura and Cajamarca). Mostly 1500–2500 m.

NOTE: An as yet unnamed form, related to *P. ruficeps* but perhaps a distinct species, has been found in Amazonas, Peru (south of the Río Marañón). It differs in having its entire head and throat bright rufous, with black areas vestigial.

Taeniotriccus Tyrants

A very striking flycatcher found only in ne. South America, where seemingly rare and local. The genus was subsumed into *Poecilotriccus* by Traylor (1977), and this merger was supported implicitly by Lanyon (1988c). We, however, consider that its several very distinctive features (large size, different bill shape, crest, and radically different facial and wing patterns) continue to argue for generic separation.

Taeniotriccus andrei

BLACK-CHESTED TYRANT

PLATE: 36

DESCRIPTION: 11.5 cm (4½"). *Ne. South America. Conspicuously bushy-crested.* Above mostly black with *rufous-chestnut face* (throat a bit paler) and *black crest;* wings with *broad pale yellow band along base of flight feathers and broad edging on tertials.* Breast sooty black, becoming gray on belly. Female similar but with more restricted, paler rufous-buff face (forehead blackish and throat gray), more olive on back, grayish on breast, and whitish on belly.

SIMILAR SPECIES: Virtually unmistakable; no other similar tyrannid has such a bold wing-band or the crest.

HABITAT AND BEHAVIOR: Poorly known, the spectacular Black-chested Tyrant must be presumed rare and/or very local. A mist-netted pair was taken in secondary woodland near Belém, Pará, Brazil (Novaes 1978). South of Altamira along e. bank of the lower Rio Xingu it was "occasionally observed in bamboo-dominated understory in terra firme forest, and in rank understory of *Cecropia*-dominated second-growth near the river" (G. R. Graves and R. L. Zusi, pers. comm.). There are more specimen records from s. Venezuela than elsewhere.

RANGE: Locally in se. Venezuela (Delta Amacuro and Bolívar; probably also in Amazonas) and very locally in n. Brazil (nw. Amazonas and n. Roraima; south of the Amazon recorded from Pará at Itaituba on w. bank of the lower Rio Tapajós, south of Altamira on the lower Rio Xingu, near Belém, and in n. Maranhão); recorded from Surinam (Donahue and Pierson 1982), but details unknown. To 350 m in Venezuela.

Corythopis Antpipits

A very distinct genus of long-legged, long-tailed, basically terrestrial flycatchers found in humid lowland forest. Until recently the antpipits were placed with the gnateaters in a separate family, the Conopophagidae. P. L. Ames, M. A. Heimerdinger, and S. L. Warter (*Postilla* 114: 1–32, 1968) presented anatomical evidence indicating that *Corythopis* was actually a tyrannid genus, and this contention was supported by Lanyon (1988c), who felt that it was most closely related to the *Pseudotriccus* tody-tyrants. Both genera share their most frequent foraging technique, an upward strike to the underside of leaves, as well as frequent bill snapping. The nest of the Ringed Antpipit is a moss-covered oven-shaped structure with a side entrance, placed on the forest floor (Y. Oniki and E. O. Willis, *Wilson Bull.* 92[1]: 126–127, 1980).

Corythopis torquata

RINGED ANTPIPIT

PLATE: 36

DESCRIPTION: 13.5–14 cm (5¼–5½"). *Amazonia to Guianas.* Bill blackish above, flesh-colored below, more yellowish near base; legs pale flesh. *Pipit-like shape* (long-tailed, with horizontal posture). Above uniform dark olive brown, somewhat grayer on crown, often whitish be-

hind eye. Throat white, *breast with broad band of bold black streaks* (often coalescing into a more solid band); belly whitish, somewhat browner on lower flanks and crissum. W. Amaz. races are darker, especially on belly which is essentially grayish. Immatures with *brown breast streaking* are fairly often encountered.

SIMILAR SPECIES: Distinctive shape and behavior, together with the conspicuous necklace, render this species virtually unmistakable (but cf. very similar Southern Antpipit; minimal overlap). Color pattern resembles that of certain *Hylopezus* antpittas, but their round and short-tailed shape is utterly different.

HABITAT AND BEHAVIOR: Uncommon to fairly common on or near the ground in humid forest, particularly inside terra firme near streams. Antpipits walk on the ground with a mincing gait reminiscent of an Ovenbird or waterthrush (*Seiurus* spp.), nodding the head and pumping the tail up and down; they also perch on fallen logs or low branches. Their presence is often first revealed by their *frequent bill snapping*. Unlike many terrestrial birds, antpipits do not feed by picking up insects from the leaf litter; rather, they make short sallies up from the ground to snatch insects from the underside of leaves. They do not associate with mixed flocks. Antpipits typically are found only by accident, but they often permit a close approach once located, and can often be followed by listening for the bill snapping. The song is a distinctive shrill, whistled "peeeur, peeeur- peépit," with some variation in phraseology.

RANGE: Guianas, s. Venezuela (Bolívar and Amazonas), e. Colombia (north to Meta and Vaupés), e. Ecuador, e. Peru, n. Bolivia (south to La Paz, Cochabamba, and w. Santa Cruz), and Amaz. Brazil (south to n. Mato Grosso and n. Goiás on Bananal Is., and east to n. Maranhão). Mostly below 500 m, in small numbers to 1300 m.

Corythopis delalandi

SOUTHERN ANTPIPIT

DESCRIPTION: 13.5 cm (5¼"). Closely resembles Ringed Antpipit, *which it replaces in s. Brazil and adjacent areas* (with only very limited overlap). Paler and more olive (not so brown) above; slightly creamier on throat (not as pure white); underwing-coverts whitish (not grayish).

SIMILAR SPECIES: So close to Ringed Antpipit in plumage that it is best to go by range and voice.

HABITAT AND BEHAVIOR: Fairly common on or near the ground in humid forest and secondary woodland. Seems more tolerant of disturbed conditions than Ringed Antpipit, and often found in quite small and seriously degraded woodlots. Behavior very like Ringed Antpipit's. Although of same quality, its song does differ characteristically, the most common phrase being a "peee, peeur-pi-pi-peépit," which sometimes can be paraphrased as "3 cheers for the pípit!" Regularly encountered around Iguazú Falls.

RANGE: S. Brazil (s. Mato Grosso, s. Goiás, s. Maranhão, Minas Gerais, and Espírito Santo south to nw. Rio Grande do Sul; perhaps also in s. Bahia), e. Bolivia (e. Santa Cruz), e. Paraguay (west to Paraguarí), and ne. Argentina (Misiones and ne. Corrientes). Mostly below 800 m, rarely to 1000 m.

NOTE: *C. delalandi* is so close morphologically to *C. torquata* that they could be considered conspecific. However, as they differ vocally, and as Sick (1985) found them together in the upper Rio Xingu drainage of Brazil, we prefer to maintain them as full species until evidence of intergradation is obtained.

Platyrinchus Spadebills

A well-defined, homogeneous group of small, stub-tailed flycatchers found in undergrowth inside forest. Their hallmark is the broad flat bill, proportionately wider than in any other flycatcher genus. Spadebills forage mostly alone, obtaining their insect prey almost invariably by making short upward strikes to the underside of leaves. Their movements, sudden and hard to follow, combine with their small size to make them difficult to see. Nests are small, almost hummingbird-like cups placed in a crotch within a few meters of the ground. The relationships of the genus have been debated. Despite their radically different nests, Lanyon (1988c) considered the genera *Platyrinchus* and *Onychorhynchus* (Royal Flycatcher) to be sister taxa, based on anatomical evidence. *Rhynchocyclus* flatbills and *Tolmomyias* flycatchers, also with dissimilar nests, were likewise considered quite closely related to the spadebills.

GROUP A

Relatively simple facial patterns. Bills average *broader* than next Group.

Platyrinchus platyrhynchos

WHITE-CRESTED SPADEBILL   PLATE: 36

DESCRIPTION: 10.5 cm (4″). *Amazonia to Guianas;* the *largest* spadebill found in tropical forests, and the one with the *widest bill.* Flat bill blackish above, whitish to pale flesh below. *Crown dark gray,* somewhat *paler gray on rest of head,* with white coronal patch (usually mostly concealed) and buffy loral spot; upperparts otherwise contrastingly bright brown, wings and tail duskier. Throat white, *becoming uniform bright rich ochraceous below* (in nominate race and *senex*). Races (*nattereri* and *amazonicus*) south of the Amazon in Brazil (west to Rio Purus) have ochraceous on underparts duller and more restricted to breast, with belly more yellowish.

SIMILAR SPECIES: Cinnamon-crested Spadebill is smaller, lacks gray on head, is not as richly colored below, and has a rufous crown patch. White-crested Spadebill also vaguely resembles certain female manakins.

HABITAT AND BEHAVIOR: Generally rare in understory of humid forest; in w. Amazonia quite local, perhaps mostly in forest on sandy soil. Not very active, though because it often perches more in the open and somewhat higher than other spadebills, usually 3–5 m above ground, it is sometimes easier to see than other spadebills, which tend to remain in denser lower growth. Forages alone, not joining mixed flocks. Its call, given from an often fairly open perch, is a sharp, loud, explosive "skeeuw!," repeated every second or two. The full song, heard much less often, is a sharp and somewhat burry "bree-ee-ee-ee-ee-ee-ee-ee-euw," with a gradual crescendo before falling off on the last note; singing birds also have a display flight in which they angle steeply downward to another perch with a manakin-like wing-whirring.

RANGE: Guianas, s. Venezuela (Bolívar and Amazonas), extreme e. Colombia (e. Vaupés; perhaps more widespread), e. Ecuador (few records), e. Peru, n. Bolivia (south to La Paz, sw. Beni, and ne. Santa Cruz on the Serranía de Huanchaca), and Amaz. Brazil (south to Rondônia and nw. Mato Grosso; east to n. Maranhão). Mostly below 500 m, but recorded to 900 m in s. Peru.

Platyrinchus flavigularis

YELLOW-THROATED SPADEBILL PLATE: 36

DESCRIPTION: 9.5 cm (3¾"). *A rare, yellow-throated spadebill of subtropical Andean forests.* Wide flat bill blackish above, dull whitish to pale flesh below. *Head bright rufous brown* with large coronal patch (usually mostly concealed) of white, black-tipped feathers; above otherwise olive, duskier on wings and tail. *Below mostly pale yellow, brightest on throat;* distinct band of olive across breast.
SIMILAR SPECIES: White-throated Spadebill has much more prominent facial pattern, no rufous on head, and is much less yellow below.
HABITAT AND BEHAVIOR: Generally rare and local in lower growth of montane forest, but locally (e.g., in se. Ecuador) seems somewhat more numerous. Favors fairly open areas in mature forest, perhaps especially on ridges where the soil is thin and vegetation less well developed. Tends to perch more or less in the open, but seldom moves, making short, rapid, difficult-to-follow flights. Does not forage with mixed flocks. Its call is a sharp "peeeyr!," repeated slowly at intervals of 4–5 seconds.
RANGE: Very locally in Andes of w. Venezuela (north to s. Lara), Colombia (recorded only from w. Cundinamarca and at head of Río Magdalena valley in sw. Huila), e. Ecuador, e. Peru (south to n. Cuzco on the Cordillera Vilcabamba); Sierra de Perijá on Venezuela-Colombia border. 750–2300 m.

Platyrinchus saturatus

CINNAMON-CRESTED SPADEBILL

DESCRIPTION: 9.5 cm (3¾"). *A small, dull-looking spadebill.* Wide flat bill all blackish. Dark rufous brown above with whitish lores and inconspicuous eye-ring, and orange-rufous coronal patch (usually mostly concealed); wings edged rufescent. *Mostly whitish below,* breast washed with olive brown, slightly yellower on belly.
SIMILAR SPECIES: Looks most like a White-throated Spadebill lacking the facial pattern and also with orange-rufous (not white) coronal patch. They are not known to occur together, though their ranges come close in the tepui region (with White-throated found at higher

elevations). White-crested Spadebill is larger with mostly gray head and is brighter ochraceous below.

HABITAT AND BEHAVIOR: Rare in undergrowth of humid forest, mainly or entirely in terra firme. In w. Amazonia perhaps mostly found in forest growing on sandy soil. Not well known, but behavior seems to differ little from its congeners' except that it may associate with small understory flocks somewhat more frequently; we once have even seen it in attendance at an army antswarm. Its call is a distinctively 2-noted "chip-it" (K. Zimmer).

RANGE: Guianas, s. Venezuela (Bolívar and Amazonas), extreme e. Colombia (recorded only from Vaupés, but probably more widespread), ne. Peru (a single old record from Puerto Indiana on the lower Río Napo in n. Loreto), and Amaz. Brazil (north of the Amazon in the upper Rio Negro region, Roraima, and from n. Pará east through Amapá; south of it from the lower Rio Tapajós region east to around Belém in e. Pará, and recently found in Rondônia at Cachoeira Nazaré and Fazenda Rancho Grande). To 900 m.

GROUP B

Bolder, more complex facial patterns.

Platyrinchus mystaceus

WHITE-THROATED SPADEBILL   PLATE: 36

DESCRIPTION: 9.5–10 cm (3¾–4″). The common, *mostly montane* spadebill (though also found locally in lowlands, especially in se. South America). Two rather different "types," the *albogularis* group (with *zamorae*) in Andes and the nominate group of e. South America west to n. Bolivia (including the tepuis and *insularis* of n. Venezuela, Trinidad, and Tobago). Andean group has wide, flat, *mostly dark bill (including lower mandible)* and is mostly olive brown above, somewhat darker on crown with yellow coronal patch (usually mostly concealed, and smaller or absent in females); rather bold facial pattern, with whitish supraloral and *buffy yellowish eye-ring, arching postocular stripe, and patch on ear-coverts. Throat white,* contrasting with olive brown breast and sides, becoming pale yellowish on midbelly. Nominate group has *lower mandible pale* and is more uniform below with throat tinged yellowish and *breast and belly brighter and more ochraceous buff.* Birds from Andes of Bolivia and adjacent Puno, Peru (*partridgei*), are essentially intermediate in plumage between the 2 groups but have an all-dark bill as in Andean group. On the tepuis the situation is confused: *ptaritepui* (found on several tepuis in e. Bolívar) has an all-black bill like Andean group, but *duidae* and *ventralis* (s. Bolívar and Amazonas) have mandible pinkish at least at tip and more ochraceous underparts like the eastern group.

SIMILAR SPECIES: Besides the very different Yellow-throated, other spadebills are found strictly in lowlands. Golden-crowned is the most similar to White-throated in its facial pattern. In se. Brazil area, cf. larger and much scarcer Russet-winged Spadebill.

HABITAT AND BEHAVIOR: Fairly common but inconspicuous in undergrowth of montane forest and secondary woodland, sometimes in tangles and bamboo thickets at forest borders. Tends to remain in dense growth and often remains motionless for protracted periods, then darts off rapidly, hard to follow. Usually found singly, and seems not to accompany mixed flocks. Numbers are better revealed by mist-netting (it may be one of the more frequently captured birds) and through its vocalizations. The most characteristic of these is an abrupt, sharp "squeep!" or "squip," sometimes doubled or in series, and a fast chipper. The true song of birds from se. Brazil (*cancromus*) is a fast series of semimusical descending notes ending with an accented "whik."

RANGE: Venezuela (mostly on mt. slopes and the tepuis south to Cerro de la Neblina, also locally in lowlands) and adjacent Guyana and extreme n. Brazil (Roraima); Andes of w. Venezuela, Colombia, Ecuador (south on w. slope to El Oro; an isolated population on the coastal cordillera in sw. Manabí and w. Guayas), e. Peru, and w. Bolivia (south to w. Santa Cruz); French Guiana (numerous recent records); e. Brazil (Maranhão and Ceará south to n. Rio Grande do Sul, and west across s. Mato Grosso and Mato Grosso do Sul), ne. Bolivia (locally in Beni), e. Paraguay (west to Concepción and Paraguarí), and ne. Argentina (ne. Corrientes and Misiones); Sierra de Perijá on Venezuela-Colombia border and Santa Marta Mts. of n. Colombia; Trinidad and Tobago. Also Costa Rica and Panama. Mostly 600–2000 m, but lower in n. Venezuela, w. Ecuador, n. Bolivia, and se. South America.

NOTE: Does not include *P. cancrominus* (Stub-tailed Spadebill) of Middle America south to Costa Rica, following the 1983 AOU Check-list; it and *P. mystaceus* occur in near sympatry in Costa Rica, and have different calls. Certain features of the *albogularis* (essentially Andean) and nominate (essentially eastern and lowland) groups are comparable to that situation, but the recently described *partridgei* of Bolivia (L. Short, *Auk* 86[2]: 262–270, 1969) seems intermediate in some characters. This, combined with the general similarity in the calls of all populations, leads us to conclude that probably a single species is involved, though it remains possible that additional work will require modifying this conclusion. The distribution and plumage variation of *P. mystaceus*, particularly within Bolivia, was discussed by J. V. Remsen, Jr., O. Rocha O., C. G. Schmitt, and D. C. Schmitt (*Ornitol. Neotrop.* 2[2]: 77–83, 1991).

Platyrinchus coronatus

GOLDEN-CROWNED SPADEBILL

DESCRIPTION: 9 cm (3½"). Wide, flat bill dark above and pale flesh below. Mostly brownish olive above with *black-bordered rufous crown patch* (male also with a partially concealed yellow coronal streak); facial pattern striking, with *lores, arching postocular stripe, and patch on ear-coverts buffy yellowish*. Dull yellowish below, washed with olive on breast and flanks. See V-30, C-36.

SIMILAR SPECIES: White-throated Spadebill has a similar bold facial pattern, but it lacks the black-bordered rufous crown, and in area of possible sympatry along e. slope of Andes it has a contrasting white throat; White-throated here occurs at higher elevations than Golden-crowned. Overlap is also possible at the base of the tepuis in s. Venezuela. Cinnamon-crested Spadebill lacks the bold facial pattern.

HABITAT AND BEHAVIOR: Uncommon to fairly common in undergrowth (usually within 2 m of ground) inside humid forest, very infrequent at borders. Like other spadebills, Golden-crowned is inconspicuous, despite its favoring areas with a fairly open understory. It tends to perch quietly and motionless, often for long periods; doubtless one often walks by without noticing it. Its weak, thin, buzzy trill, "bzee-eee-eép," slightly ascending at end, sometimes draws attention, but as it is often barely audible, this too is easily overlooked.

RANGE: N. and w. Colombia (humid Caribbean lowlands east along n. base of Andes to middle Río Magdalena valley in w. Santander, and in Pacific lowlands) and nw. Ecuador (south to Manabí); Guianas, s. Venezuela (Bolívar and Amazonas), se. Colombia (north to w. Caquetá and ne. Amazonas at Estación Kaparu), e. Ecuador, e. Peru, n. Bolivia (south to La Paz), and Amaz. Brazil (south of the Amazon south to nw. Mato Grosso, and east to Rio Xingu area). Also Honduras to Panama. Mainly below 500 m (recorded to 1300 m in Venezuela).

Platyrinchus leucoryphus

RUSSET-WINGED SPADEBILL

PLATE: 36

DESCRIPTION: 12.5 cm (5"). *A large, long-tailed spadebill of se. Brazil area.* Very wide, flat bill mostly rather bright yellow with some dusky on ridge; legs also yellowish. Above mainly uniform olive brown with usually mostly concealed white coronal patch; whitish supraloral spot and eye-ring, arching postocular stripe, and buffy yellowish patches on ear-coverts. *Wing-coverts and flight feathers broadly edged rufous.* Throat white, contrasting with olive brown breast, becoming dull yellowish white on belly.

SIMILAR SPECIES: By far the largest spadebill. In its range likely confused only with White-throated Spadebill, which has similar facial pattern but is markedly smaller and lacks the rufous in wing.

HABITAT AND BEHAVIOR: Rare and perhaps local in undergrowth inside humid forest. The solitary behavior of this striking spadebill is much like that of its congeners. Its vocalizations, though similar to the geographically distant White-crested's, are quite different from those of the sympatric White-throated. Russet-winged Spadebill is threatened by the extensive deforestation that has occurred across much of its range. Belton (1985, p. 84) comments grimly that his sole Rio Grande do Sul record came from "since-destroyed wet coastal forests." It has been seen recently along the Pozo Preto road in Iguaçú Nat. Park, Brazil, and in Paraguay's Mbaracayú Reserve.

RANGE: Se. Brazil (Espírito Santo south to ne. Rio Grande do Sul), e. Paraguay (recorded from Canendiyu and Paraguarí), and ne. Argentina (n. Misiones). To at least 900 m.

Tolmomyias Flycatchers

Large-headed, broad- and flat-billed flycatchers found across most of the lowlands. *Tolmomyias* are arboreal, usually inconspicuous, and among the most difficult tyrannids to identify: each of the four known species (there may be several more) is basically olive and yellow with strong wing markings. As might be expected from their bills, based on anatomical evidence their closest relative is the even wider-billed flatbill genus *Rhynchocyclus* (Lanyon 1988c). Nests are purse-shaped hanging bags with a downward-projecting entrance spout, often suspended over a stream or small road (with Gray-crowned and Yellow-breasted's often near wasp nests).

Tolmomyias sulphurescens

YELLOW-OLIVE FLYCATCHER PLATE: 37

DESCRIPTION: 14–14.5 cm (5½–5¾″). Iris color variable but typically rather pale, either grayish or brownish; maxilla black but *mandible pale,* grayish white to pale flesh. Mostly olive to bright olive above, most races with more or less gray crown and whitish supraloral and narrow eye-ring; wings blackish with 2 yellowish wing-bars and prominent edging. Throat whitish, becoming olive on breast and flanks and pale yellow on belly. Nominate race (se. Brazil and adjacent Argentina and Paraguay) has a distinct dusky patch on auriculars and is usually dark-eyed. Birds from n. tier of South America (east to Trinidad) tend to be more olive-crowned, whereas *aequatorialis* (w. Ecuador and nw. Peru) and *peruvianus* (foothills on e. slope of Andes in Ecuador and Peru) have the most contrasting gray crowns; these latter 2 taxa are also usually dark-eyed.

SIMILAR SPECIES: Often difficult to distinguish from Yellow-margined Flycatcher; see the full discussion under that species. Forest Elaenia has more slender shape, much narrower bill, and a sometimes hidden yellow or white coronal streak; its voice and typical posture also differ. Olivaceous Flatbill is larger, more streaked but much less yellow below, and has an even wider bill.

HABITAT AND BEHAVIOR: Uncommon to fairly common in a variety of wooded habitats ranging from the subcanopy and borders of humid foothill and montane forest to rather dry woodland, isolated woodlots, and plantations with scattered tall trees; in Amazonia apparently also on river islands and in other riparian habitats. Yellow-olive generally is not found in humid lowland forest, where Yellow-margined and Gray-crowned Flycatchers take over; however, in se. Brazil area and on e. slope of Andes in Ecuador and Peru it does range into tall forest (note that in both areas Yellow-margined and Gray-crowned are absent). Typically forages at middle heights, tending to perch more upright than Yellow-margined and Gray-crowned; unlike them it rarely cocks its tail. Generally found singly or in pairs and often sluggish, despite regularly accompanying mixed flocks. Its call is a short, deliberate series of sharp, emphatic, somewhat sibilant notes, "dzeeyp, dzeeyp, dzeeyp"; the series may be longer (up to 6 or so notes), sometimes with a pause between the first and following notes. Geographic variation in vocalizations may exist.

RANGE: Widespread south to n. Argentina (south to Catamarca, ne. Santa Fe, and Corrientes) and s. Brazil (south to Rio Grande do

Sul); on Pacific slope south to nw. Peru (Tumbes and Piura); Trinidad. Also Mexico to Panama. Mostly below 1200 m, but found in smaller numbers on Andean slopes up to about 1800 m.

NOTE: An apparently undescribed species of *Tolmomyias* exists on river islands and in várzea forests near the mouth of the Río Napo into the Amazon in ne. Peru (T. A. Parker III), and it also has been found at least once in e. Ecuador (P. Greenfield). It has an orange iris, somewhat ochraceous breast, etc. In addition, the relationship between the gray and olive-crowned forms remains to be worked out, and regional variation in vocalizations also appears to exist. It seems likely that more than a single species is involved among the forms now united in *T. sulphurescens*.

Tolmomyias poliocephalus

GRAY-CROWNED FLYCATCHER   PLATE: 37

DESCRIPTION: 12 cm (4¾″). Humid forests of Amazonia to Guianas. Iris typically rather pale, straw yellow to pale grayish or pale brownish; *bill mostly dark,* pale only at base of lower mandible. Mostly olive above with usually contrasting gray crown, and whitish lores and partial narrow eye-ring; wings blackish with 2 yellowish wing-bars and edging, and sometimes a faint pale speculum at base of primaries. Throat grayish yellow, becoming olive on breast and flanks and pale yellow on belly.

SIMILAR SPECIES: A difficult identification challenge. Gray-crowned is most apt to be confused with Yellow-margined Flycatcher, with which it often occurs in the canopy of Amazonian forests, sometimes even in the same flock. At close range Yellow-margined may be distinguished by its larger size, pale lower mandible, and distinct pale speculum on primaries. Voice also helps (see below). Yellow-olive Flycatcher is markedly larger and, like Yellow-margined, has a pale lower mandible; it does not occur in terra firme Amazonian forests, only in lower stature, often secondary habitats.

HABITAT AND BEHAVIOR: Uncommon to fairly common in canopy and borders of humid forest, both in várzea and terra firme; often overlooked because of identification difficulties. Usually forages at middle levels or higher, where regularly with mixed flocks of tanagers, furnariids, and other flycatchers; generally remains higher than Yellow-margined Flycatcher. Somewhat more active than Yellow-olive Flycatcher, tending to perch more horizontally, sometimes partially cocking its tail. Gray-crowned's most characteristic call is a fairly fast series of 2–3 somewhat wheezy, high-pitched notes, "fweee? fweee? fweee?" with somewhat the inflected quality of Rufous-tailed Jacamar (*Galbula ruficauda*).

RANGE: Guianas, s. Venezuela (Bolívar and Amazonas), se. Colombia (north to Meta and e. Vichada), e. Ecuador, e. Peru, nw. Bolivia (Pando and at Serranía Eva Eva in sw. Beni), and Amaz. Brazil (south to Rondônia and se. Pará, and east to n. Maranhão); e. Brazil (Pernambuco south to Espírito Santo). Mostly below 600 m (recorded to over 900 m in Venezuela).

Tolmomyias assimilis

YELLOW-MARGINED FLYCATCHER

DESCRIPTION: 13.5 cm (5¼"). Iris typically dark, brownish to grayish; color of lower mandible variable but usually brownish, *paler* than blackish maxilla. *Closely* resembles both Yellow-olive and Gray-crowned Flycatchers, seeming almost "intermediate" between them. From Yellow-olive best distinguished by its pale speculum at base of primaries, though this is sometimes hard to discern in the field; note that in many areas they separate by habitat, with Yellow-margined more in mature forest, Yellow-olive more at edge and in clearings. In the hand they differ in wing formulae, Yellow-margined having 10th (outer) primary longer than 4th (the reverse in Yellow-olive). Even harder to distinguish from Gray-crowned; these 2 species are routinely together in Amazonia, but *west* of Andes only Yellow-margined occurs. Yellow-margined is slightly larger, has a slightly paler lower mandible (Gray-crowned's bill looks mostly dark, with at most a little paleness at base of lower mandible), and shows a distinct pale speculum at base of primaries (Gray-crowned's is faint or, more often, absent). Voice is often the best clue (see below). See P-24.

HABITAT AND BEHAVIOR: Fairly common in the canopy and borders of humid forest, in Amazonia both in terra firme and várzea. Behavior similar to Gray-crowned Flycatcher's, occasionally even with it in the same flock. Yellow-margined is generally less of a canopy bird and more often forages at middle levels. Its call is distinctly different, being markedly harsher, buzzier, and more emphatic, "zhweek, zhweek-zhweek-zhweek"; typically there is a pause after the first note. The call is often given only at long intervals, and sometimes several minutes may pass between repetitions.

RANGE: W. Colombia (east in Caribbean lowlands to lower Río Cauca valley) and w. Ecuador (recorded south to Guayas, but no recent reports from south of Pichincha and Manabí); Guianas, s. Venezuela (Bolívar and Amazonas), se. Colombia (north to Meta and e. Vichada), e. Ecuador, e. Peru, n. Bolivia (south to La Paz, Cochabamba, and n. Santa Cruz), and Amaz. Brazil (south to Rondônia and nw. Mato Grosso, and east to n. Maranhão). Also Costa Rica and Panama. Mostly below 1000 m.

Tolmomyias flaviventris

YELLOW-BREASTED FLYCATCHER PLATE: 37

DESCRIPTION: 12 cm (4¾"). Iris dark brown to grayish brown; bill usually all dark, but base of lower mandible sometimes paler. Rather different from other *Tolmomyias: brighter and with no gray on crown. Uniform yellowish olive above,* yellower above lores and on eye-ring; wings blackish with 2 prominent yellow wing-bars and edging. *Below yellow,* slightly clouded olive on breast and sides. Foregoing applies to birds from lower Amaz. and e. Brazil, extreme s. Venezuela, and ne. Bolivia, the "intermediate" nominate group. Races found in w. Amazonia (the *viridiceps* group) are duller and darker olive above with little or no yellow on face and are more clouded olive on breast. Birds

from n. Colombia to Amapá, Brazil (the *aurulentus* group), are brighter yellowish olive above with *loral area and eye-ring ochraceous;* throat and chest also tinged ochre. See V-29, C-37.

SIMILAR SPECIES: Birds found in w. Amazonia are rather drab and can be confusing if the wide bill is not noted; no tyrannulet has a comparable bill. Yellow Tyrannulet is perhaps the most similar in plumage. More easterly birds, particularly the *aurulentus* group, are more distinctive.

HABITAT AND BEHAVIOR: Fairly common to common in lighter woodland, gardens and groves of trees, gallery woodland, and mangroves (at least in Guianas and on Trinidad); in Amazonia found mainly in riparian growth and in edge and canopy of várzea forest. Especially widespread on Trinidad and Tobago, where it occurs in virtually all wooded habitats; particularly numerous on Tobago. Usually found singly or in pairs, foraging at various heights but coming low mainly in clearings or borders. The call of the bright nominate group (e.g., *dissors* in s. Venezuela) is a characteristic loud, shrill "shreeeép," usually given singly at long intervals, less often in series of 2 or 3; the voice of *aurulentus* is similar. The call of the duller *viridiceps* group (e.g., in e. Ecuador) is a faster series of 3–4 "cheeyp" notes which gradually rise in a crescendo.

RANGE: Widespread south to n. Bolivia (La Paz and ne. Santa Cruz on the Serranía de Huanchaca) and s. Brazil (s. Mato Grosso, Goiás, Bahia, and Espírito Santo); west of Andes only in nw. Venezuela and n. Colombia; Trinidad and Tobago. Recently also found in e. Panama (P. Coopmans). To about 1000 m.

NOTE: More than one species may be involved. The dull and olive *viridiceps* group of w. Amazonia seems distinct both in plumage and voice from the brighter nominate group of n. and e. South America.

Rhynchocyclus Flatbills

Four large-headed, very wide-billed flycatchers found inside humid or montane forest. All are basically dull olive with some olive flammulation on underparts. They are stolid and inconspicuous birds which perch quietly at the edge of mixed flocks of other understory birds.

Rhynchocyclus olivaceus

OLIVACEOUS FLATBILL

PLATE: 37

DESCRIPTION: 15 cm (6"). The most widespread *Rhynchocyclus*. Dull and unpatterned, appearing large-headed. *Very wide, flat bill,* pale yellowish to flesh below. Dark olive above with indistinct whitish eye-ring; wings duskier, margined with yellowish to ochraceous and with 2 dull yellowish wing-bars. Throat dull grayish, breast dull grayish olive with flammulated effect on lower breast and flanks, becoming pale yellowish on belly.

SIMILAR SPECIES: Compare to the smaller *Mionectes* and *Tolmomyias* flycatchers; the latter are unflammulated below and usually forage higher above ground. In nw. Colombia, cf. also Eye-ringed Flatbill and Broad-billed Sapayoa.

HABITAT AND BEHAVIOR: Uncommon to fairly common in lower growth of humid forest (both terra firme and várzea) and taller secondary woodland. Perches erectly, slowly looking around with a "dazed" expression (Hilty and Brown 1986, p. 485), suddenly darting up to the underside of a leaf or twig, then dropping off to another perch. Regularly accompanies mixed flocks of *Myrmotherula* antwrens and various antshrikes and furnariids in the understory. Occasionally gives a surprisingly loud, harsh "tsheet" or "breeyp" call.

RANGE: Guianas, Venezuela, n. and e. Colombia (more humid Caribbean lowlands east to the Santa Marta area and the middle Río Magdalena valley in Santander; east of Andes from Norte de Santander and Arauca southward), e. Ecuador, e. Peru, n. Bolivia (south to La Paz and Cochabamba), and Amaz. Brazil (south to Rondônia and s. Pará, east to n. Maranhão); e. Brazil (e. Pernambuco south to Rio de Janeiro). Also Panama. Seemingly absent from much of black water/sandy soil region of the upper Río Negro and Orinoco River drainages. To about 1000 m.

Rhynchocyclus brevirostris

EYE-RINGED FLATBILL

DESCRIPTION: 15 cm (6"). *Nw. Colombia on Cerro Tacarcuna;* Pacific Flatbill of w. Colombia and nw. Ecuador is regarded as a separate species. Eye-ringed resembles Olivaceous Flatbill (no known overlap, though their ranges come close, with Olivaceous at *lower* elevations), but it has a *much bolder white eye-ring* and more yellowish olive wingbars. See P-24.

SIMILAR SPECIES: Pacific Flatbill has a very indistinct grayish eye-ring, more prominent fulvous wing-bars, and more ochraceous olive wingedging; it does not overlap with Eye-ringed.

HABITAT AND BEHAVIOR: Little known in its extremely limited range in South America. In Panama uncommon to fairly common in lower growth of humid forest, less often at forest borders, with a special predilection for shady ravines (Ridgely and Gwynne 1989). Behavior, including voice, much like Olivaceous Flatbill's.

RANGE: Extreme nw. Colombia (slopes of Cerro Tacarcuna). Also Mexico to Panama. 700–1500 m.

NOTE: See comments under Pacific Flatbill.

Rhynchocyclus fulvipectus

FULVOUS-BREASTED FLATBILL   PLATE: 37

DESCRIPTION: 15 cm (6"). *Andes from Venezuela to Bolivia. Very wide, flat bill,* pale flesh below; indistinct grayish eye-ring. Above uniform dark olive, wings and tail duskier with *fairly prominent tawny-fulvous edging on wing-coverts and flight feathers. Lower throat and breast dull tawny-fulvous;* belly pale yellowish streaked with olive on flanks.

SIMILAR SPECIES: Pacific Flatbill shows *no* tawny below, but note that the tawny of Fulvous-breasted can be hard to discern in the dim light of forest interior. The 2 species may overlap in the foothills, but whether they occur together in the same forest is unknown.

HABITAT AND BEHAVIOR: Uncommon in lower growth of montane forest, perhaps especially in the vicinity of streams. Behavior much like Olivaceous Flatbill's.

RANGE: Andes of extreme w. Venezuela (Táchira), Colombia (locally), Ecuador (south on w. slope to Pichincha), e. Peru, and w. Bolivia (La Paz and Cochabamba). Mostly 800–2000 m.

Rhynchocyclus pacificus

PACIFIC FLATBILL

Other: Eye-ringed Flatbill (in part)

DESCRIPTION: 15 cm (6"). *W. Colombia and nw. Ecuador.* Here regarded as a separate species from Eye-ringed Flatbill. Resembles Fulvous-breasted Flatbill, which apparently replaces it at somewhat higher elevations (with limited or no overlap), *but has virtually no fulvous on throat and breast.* The edging on wing feathers is more olivaceous-tinged and, like Fulvous-breasted, Pacific shows only an indistinct grayish eye-ring.

SIMILAR SPECIES: Eye-ringed Flatbill (in South America found only in extreme nw. Colombia; no overlap) has a bold white eye-ring and olivaceous (not fulvous) wing-bars.

HABITAT AND BEHAVIOR: Uncommon in lower growth of humid forest and mature secondary woodland. Behavior much like Olivaceous Flatbill's. Small numbers occur in the forest patches above the Tinalandia Hotel in Pichincha, Ecuador.

RANGE: W. Colombia (Pacific lowlands and lower slopes from Chocó southward) and nw. Ecuador (south to w. Esmeraldas and s. Pichincha). Below about 1000 m.

NOTE: We follow J. T. Zimmer (*Am. Mus. Novitates* 1045, 1939) in considering *R. pacificus* as a species distinct from *R. brevirostris*. He considered *pacificus* to be allied more closely to *R. fulvipectus* than to *R. brevirostris.* Meyer de Schauensee (1966, 1970), however, treated *pacificus* as a race of the actually rather different *R. brevirostris,* without explaining why he differed from Zimmer; it has been so regarded since (e.g., in *Birds of the World,* vol. 8, and Hilty and Brown 1986).

Ramphotrigon Flatbills

Three species of forest-inhabiting flycatchers with broad wing-bars and fairly wide bills. The *Ramphotrigon* flatbills have traditionally been associated with the genera *Rhynchocyclus, Tolmomyias,* and *Cnipodectes* on account of their overall similarity. *Ramphotrigon*'s bill, however, is not as proportionately wide and flat as in at least the first two, and various anatomical features, as well as its recently discovered habit of nesting in tree cavities, all point toward it not being closely related to the other flatbills. Rather, it is now believed to be more closely related to *Myiarchus* (W. E. Lanyon, *Neotropical Ornithology,* AOU Monograph no. 36, pp. 360–380, 1985). Nonetheless, because they "look" and even behave somewhat alike, we continue to associate the "flatbill" genera together and *Ramphotrigon* is presented here. Much information on their be havior (including nesting) is given by T. A. Parker III (*Auk* 101[1]: 186–188, 1984).

Ramphotrigon megacephala

LARGE-HEADED FLATBILL　　　　　　　PLATE: 37

DESCRIPTION: 13 cm (5″). *Local in humid forests with bamboo understory.* Dull dark olive above with prominent *yellowish supraloral and eye-ring* contrasting with dusky lores; wings and tail duskier, wings with *2 prominent ochraceous wing-bars* and yellowish edging. Throat yellowish, breast ochraceous olive vaguely streaked paler; belly pale yellow. SIMILAR SPECIES: Bamboo habitat and distinctive voice (see below) are the keys to identifying this obscure small flycatcher; note, too, its *fairly bold facial pattern*. Dusky-tailed Flatbill is larger, lacks the supraloral (it has only an eye-ring), and is a darker bird generally. HABITAT AND BEHAVIOR: Fairly common but very local in bamboo thickets in lower growth of humid forest and forest borders. In Amazonia seems largely or entirely confined to thickets of bamboo, whereas in se. Brazil it seems to be found where bamboo is a dominant component of the forest understory. This inconspicuous bird tends to remain motionless for long periods; sometimes it moves with mixed flocks but at least as often alone. Generally the Large-headed Flatbill is encountered by tracking down its distinctive, mournful call. In Peru and Ecuador this is an even, fairly fast "whoo-whoo," whereas in se. Brazil it is a somewhat burrier (especially first note) "wheeu . . . whoo," typically with a *long* interval, often several seconds or more, between notes. At least in Peru it also has a more involved dawn call of similar quality, but its characteristic call (which can almost be paraphrased as "bam-boo"), given at intervals through much of the day, is much better known and more often heard. Readily found at the Tambopata Reserve in Madre de Dios, se. Peru. RANGE: Locally in w. and cen. Venezuela (recorded from Yaracuy, Barinas, w. Apure, and Amazonas) and e. Colombia (not recorded north of Meta and Vaupés, though it probably occurs along base of Andes); west of Andes in n. Colombia (an until recently unrecognized specimen in USNM taken at Simití, Bolívar, in middle Río Magdalena valley [G. R. Graves]); e. Ecuador (near Paquisha in Zamora-Chinchipe, and numerous recent sightings and several WFVZ and ANSP specimens from north of Archidona and west of Coca, in w. Napo); se. Peru (Ucayali and Madre de Dios), n. Bolivia (south to La Paz, Cochabamba, and ne. Santa Cruz on the Serranía de Huanchaca), and w. Amaz. Brazil (recorded from upper Rio Juruá east to near Tefé in Amazonas, and at Cachoeira Nazaré in Rondônia and at Alta Floresta in n. Mato Grosso); se. Brazil (e. Minas Gerais south to São Paulo), ne. Argentina (Misiones), and se. Paraguay (Alto Paraná and recently in Canendiyu at Mbaracayú [F. Hayes]). To about 1300 m along base of Andes, to at least 1400 m in se. Brazil.

Ramphotrigon fuscicauda

DUSKY-TAILED FLATBILL

DESCRIPTION: 15.5 cm (6″). *Rare and very local in w. Amazonia.* Above dull brownish olive, crown somewhat darker, with narrow incomplete

eye-ring whitish; wings and *tail dusky*, with *2 cinnamon wing-bars* and cinnamon-buff edging on flight feathers, tail feathers edged cinnamon-rufous. *Below mostly dark olive streaked with yellow*, unstreaked yellow on midbelly.

SIMILAR SPECIES: Large-headed Flatbill is smaller, has a prominent supraloral as well as an eye-ring, and lacks conspicuous streaking below. Cf. also Rufous-tailed Flatbill. Olivaceous Flatbill is more uniform olive and lacks bold wing-bars.

HABITAT AND BEHAVIOR: Rare to locally uncommon in lower growth of humid forest. In se. Peru favors bamboo thickets and viny tangles, sometimes at forest edge and up into foothills; in e. Ecuador it has been found in dense undergrowth near ravines in hilly terra firme forest. Behaves much like Large-headed Flatbill but seems less numerous and even less inclined to join mixed foraging flocks than that species. On the whole a quiet bird, with calls including a mellow, down-slurred whistle that ends with a distinct upward inflection, "peeyooo-wheé" (T. A. Parker III).

RANGE: Locally in extreme s. Colombia (sw. Putumayo) and ne. Ecuador (w. Napo); se. Peru (Junín and Ucayali south to Madre de Dios) and n. Bolivia (south to La Paz, and in ne. Santa Cruz on the Serranía de Huanchaca); recently found at Alta Floresta in n. Mato Grosso, Brazil. Mostly below 600 m (recorded to 900 m in se. Peru).

Ramphotrigon ruficauda

RUFOUS-TAILED FLATBILL   PLATE: 37

DESCRIPTION: 16 cm (6¼"). Above mainly uniform dull olive green with *bright rufous tail;* wings duskier with *2 broad wing-bars and very broad edging on flight feathers bright rufous;* narrow supraloral and eye-ring yellowish. Throat grayish and breast olive, both vaguely streaked paler, becoming pale clear yellow on belly with olive streaking on sides.

SIMILAR SPECIES: Virtually unmistakable, as the rufous tail and rufous in wing are contrasting and conspicuous.

HABITAT AND BEHAVIOR: Uncommon to locally fairly common in lower growth of humid forest, both in terra firme and várzea. Found singly or in pairs, most often foraging independently of mixed flocks; unlike the previous 2 species, Rufous-tailed Flatbill tends to occur in forests with a relatively open understory and thus is easier to observe. One's attention is most often drawn to it by its characteristic mournful call, "preeeee-yoú," first a drawn-out rising note, then a shorter, lower, more abrupt note (as if in reply).

RANGE: Guianas, s. Venezuela (Bolívar and Amazonas), se. Colombia (north to Meta and Guainía), ne. Ecuador (a few recent records from Napo and Sucumbios; ANSP, MECN), e. Peru, n. Bolivia (south to La Paz and Santa Cruz), and Amaz. Brazil (south to s. Mato Grosso and n. Goiás on Bananal Is., east to n. Maranhão). Mostly below 300 m.

Cnipodectes Twistwings

The male Brownish Twistwing has uniquely modified outer primaries, a feature we opt to highlight in its English name, as suggested by

Traylor and Fitzpatrick (1982, p. 30). The plumage of this rather large forest-inhabiting flycatcher is soft and lax. A nest in Panama was a 1-m-long mass of tangled fibers attached to an aerial root about 2 m above the ground, generally similar to a Royal Flycatcher's (A. Skutch, *in* Wetmore 1972).

Cnipodectes subbrunneus

BROWNISH TWISTWING   PLATE: 37

Other: Brownish Flycatcher

DESCRIPTION: Male 18 cm (7"); female 15.5 cm (6"). Fairly broad bill black above, flesh-colored below; iris orange to grayish buff. Tail rather long. *Mostly dull brown, more rufous on rump and tail;* wings duskier, with *rufous-buff wing-bars and edging*. Throat pale brownish, breast brown, becoming dingy whitish to pale yellowish buff on belly (always buff at least on crissum). Adult male has stiffened and peculiarly twisted outer primaries with thick shafts (difficult to discern in the field); their function is uncertain, but presumably they are used in display.

SIMILAR SPECIES: In size and overall coloration resembles Royal Flycatcher, and the two are frequently found together, but Royal's head is uniquely shaped with hammerhead effect, and it has spots on wings. Somewhat similar Thrush-like Mourner has *plain* wings. Neither of . these species lifts its wings in display.

HABITAT AND BEHAVIOR: Rare to uncommon in lower growth of humid forest and shady secondary woodland, locally also in deciduous forest; in Pando, Bolivia, found associated with bamboo (Parker and Remsen 1987), but elsewhere this is not the case. Usually seen singly, rarely or never accompanying mixed flocks; favors areas with a relatively viny or tangled understory. Frequently raises a wing up over its back, slowly and almost casually, almost seeming to stretch it. Displaying males are very sedentary. Their song is a distinctive, sharp, emphatic "keeéuw-keeéuw," sometimes given as only a single "keeéuw," often preceded by bill snapping and sometimes accompanied by wing-lifting. What is evidently a foraging call, given by both sexes, is an arresting "kuuuu-wít!, kuuuu-wít!," sometimes single or trebled. Birds may vocalize on and off throughout the day.

RANGE: N. and w. Colombia (humid Caribbean lowlands east along n. base of Andes to middle Río Magdalena valley in e. Antioquia, and Pacific lowlands south to Valle [southward?]) and w. Ecuador (w. Esmeraldas south to El Oro, but only a few recent reports); se. Colombia (north to w. Meta), e. Ecuador (numerous recent records from Sucumbios, Napo, and Pastaza; ANSP, MECN), e. Peru (south to Ucayali at Balta), extreme nw. Bolivia (Pando in the Cobija area), and w. Amaz. Brazil (east to lower Rio Negro). Also Panama. To about 1200 m (in w. Colombia).

Onychorhynchus Flycatchers

One of the most remarkable flycatchers, with no apparent close relative, the Royal Flycatcher has a spectacular, unique crest. Other characters of the genus are its exceptionally long rictal bristles (almost as long as the long bill) and unusually short legs. Based on cranial and syringeal characters, Lanyon (1988c) concluded that its closest relative is the very different *Platyrinchus* (spadebills). The Royal Flycatcher is widespread, though never especially common, in lowland forests. The nest, a very long (up to almost 2 m), loose structure with a low side entrance, is suspended over a shady stream or sometimes a little-used road or track.

Onychorhynchus coronatus

ROYAL FLYCATCHER

PLATE: 37

DESCRIPTION: 16–16.5 cm (6–6½"). *Spectacular crest only rarely seen.* Very long, flat bill; legs yellowish-flesh. Nominate/*castelnaui* (Amazonia) uniform dull brown above with small buff spots on wing-coverts; *rump cinnamon-rufous, becoming rufous on tail* (darker toward tip). Throat whitish, becoming ochraceous-buff on remaining underparts; duller breast narrowly barred with brown. The fully expanded crest, a *large semicircular fan of shiny scarlet feathers (yellow-orange in female) with scattered black spots and broad shiny steel-blue tips,* is held perpendicular to the axis of body. Other races are somewhat larger and have proportionately longer bills and tails. *Fraterculus* (n. Colombia) has a less marked breast (more mottled) and *much paler bright cinnamon tail. Swainsoni* (se. Brazil) is paler generally, with *bright ochraceous-buff underparts* and no breast markings; *occidentalis* (w. Ecuador) is similar but even brighter and paler, almost orange-ochraceous below (especially on breast). Immatures of both sexes show broad and irregular pale and dark barring on upperparts and tips of flight feathers, with females' crests a paler orange.

SIMILAR SPECIES: The remarkable crest renders this species unmistakable when it is extended—which, sadly, it usually is not. Even when closed the lengthened feathers protrude to the rear, imparting a *distinct hammerheaded effect;* occasionally a bit of color shows through. Cf. Brownish Twistwing.

HABITAT AND BEHAVIOR: Uncommon in lower growth of forest, mature secondary woodland, and borders; found both in humid and deciduous forest and woodland, in Amazonia mainly in várzea or near streams; *swainsoni* of se. Brazil seems rare (D. Stotz), and *occidentalis* of w. Ecuador is now scarce and local because of habitat destruction. Generally inconspicuous, foraging quietly rather close to ground, most often alone or in pairs and not often with mixed flocks. Usually rather quiet but sometimes draws attention to itself with a clear, repeated "preé-o," sounding rather like a *Manacus* manakin or a jacamar. The still uncertain functions of its remarkable and beautiful crest have been reviewed by G. R. Graves (*Condor* 92[2]: 522–524, 1990). Only rarely has it been seen fully expanded under normal conditions (during courtship and agonistic displays); Graves (op. cit.) concludes that there is no evidence to indicate that it is used in antipredator defense. Those working with mist-nets are the most likely to see the crest in its full glory: when handled the bird raises it and then rhythmically twists its head from side to side, almost contorting its neck, while slowly opening and closing its bill—altogether a mesmerizing performance.

RANGE: N. Colombia (Caribbean lowlands) and adjacent nw. Venezuela (lower slopes of Sierra de Perijá); w. Ecuador (w. Esmeraldas south to El Oro) and extreme nw. Peru (Tumbes); s. and e. Venezuela (north along e. base of Andes to w. Barinas, in Amazonas and Bolívar, and north through Delta Amacuro to Paria Peninsula in Sucre), Guianas, e. Colombia (north to Meta and Guainía, and along base of Andes in Arauca), e. Ecuador, e. Peru, n. Bolivia (south to La Paz, Cochabamba, and n. Santa Cruz), and Amaz. Brazil (south to Rondônia and n. Mato Grosso, and east to n. Maranhão); se. Brazil (e. Minas Gerais south to Paraná). Also Mexico to Panama. To about 1200 m (recorded to 2000 m in Venezuela).

NOTE: Two species are sometimes recognized (e.g., 1983 AOU Check-list): trans-Andean *O. mexicanus* (Northern Royal-Flycatcher) and cis-Andean *O. coronatus* (Amazonian Royal-Flycatcher). However, the plumage of *swainsoni* (isolated in se. Brazil; Swainson's Royal-Flycatcher) is as different from Amaz. populations as is the *mexicanus* group, whereas *occidentalis* (isolated in w. Ecuador and nw. Peru; Pacific Royal-Flycatcher) is also distinctly divergent from other geographically close forms. We conclude that perhaps four species should be recognized, or all should be combined into one polytypic species—but that recognizing *two* does not accord with the variation observed. In part because the voice and behavior of all the royal-flycatchers, so far as known, appear to be similar, we continue to treat all taxa in the genus as a single species.

Myiotriccus Flycatchers

A striking, easy to recognize little flycatcher of Andean forest borders. Its closest relative is uncertain, though its cup-shaped nest, set in a bank or tree cavity, would seem to indicate that it is not very close to the superficially similar *Myiobius* flycatchers.

Myiotriccus ornatus

ORNATE FLYCATCHER

PLATE: 37

DESCRIPTION: 12 cm (4¾"). *A pert and attractive little flycatcher found at montane forest borders in Andes of Colombia to Peru.* Virtually unmistakable. Head and throat mostly gray, becoming black on face and crown, with *conspicuous large white preocular patch* and semiconcealed yellow coronal patch; back deep olive, *rump bright golden yellow,* wings dusky, and *tail rufous.* Breast olive, belly bright golden yellow. Foregoing applies to *phoenicurus* of e. slope range. Birds from Colombia (except on e. slope of Andes) and w. Ecuador (nominate race and *stellatus*) have tail dusky, with rufous only toward base; see C-37.

HABITAT AND BEHAVIOR: Fairly common to common at borders and openings, often at treefalls or along streams, in montane forest and secondary woodland. Usually in pairs, perching upright quite in the open at low or middle levels, rarely higher; seems very sedentary and does not move with mixed flocks. Makes sudden sallies into the air, often flying out only a short distance, usually going on to a different perch. The call is a sharp, high-pitched, emphatic "peek!" repeated at frequent intervals, occasionally in a rapid series. Particularly numerous in Ecuador.

RANGE: Andes of Colombia (where somewhat local, seemingly absent from slopes above upper Río Magdalena valley; north in E. Andes to Santander), Ecuador (south on w. slope to El Oro; an isolated population on the coastal cordillera in w. Guayas), and e. Peru (south to Puno). Mostly 600–2000 m, locally down to 300 m in humid areas on Pacific slope.

Myiobius Flycatchers

An attractive trio of acrobatic, forest- or woodland-inhabiting flycatchers with fairly broad bills, long rictal bristles, and rather large black eyes surrounded by a pale eye-ring, broadest to the rear. The species resemble each other closely, and all have a conspicuous sulphur yellow rump and broad black tail. None is very vocal. Nests, messy bell-shaped structures with a low side entrance, are suspended from a branch, most often over a stream.

Myiobius barbatus

SULPHUR-RUMPED FLYCATCHER   PLATE: 37

DESCRIPTION: 12.5 cm (5″). Underparts variable in color, but always with *conspicuous sulphur yellow rump* and somewhat rounded *black tail*. Above mostly olive, male with usually concealed yellow coronal patch; wings duskier, unmarked. Throat and breast grayish olive to brownish olive, contrasting with pale yellow belly. Foregoing applies to nominate group of Amazonia. *Aureatus* (n. and w. Colombia, w. Ecuador) quite different, with *bright tawny breast, extending down over flanks;* see C-37. Geographically distant *mastacalis* (s.-cen. and e. Brazil) resembles *aureatus* but is not quite as bright tawny on breast, and the tawny does not extend down over flanks.

SIMILAR SPECIES: The *Myiobius* flycatchers present a vexing identification challenge; for specifics, see under Black-tailed and Tawny-breasted Flycatchers. In general, west of Andes Sulphur-rumped is bright tawny across breast and is easily confused with the more montane Tawny-breasted Flycatcher but readily distinguished from Black-tailed. In e. Brazil, where Black-tailed is *uniform* plain yellow or yellowish buff below, it is Sulphur-rumped that has tawny on breast. In Amazonia it gets more complicated; see under Black-tailed Flycatcher.

HABITAT AND BEHAVIOR: Uncommon to fairly common in lower growth of humid forest and mature secondary woodland, in cen. Brazil also in gallery woodland. Usually remains inside forest where it forages animatedly, fanning and closing its tail and drooping its wings as if to show off its yellow rump, often pivoting on its perch. Continually on the move, sallying into the air for short distances or clinging momentarily to trunks; sometimes begins a sally by knocking an insect off a leaf, then following it in rapid aerial pursuit. One or 2 regularly accompany mixed foraging flocks of *Myrmotherula* antwrens, various antshrikes, furnariids, and others.

RANGE: N. and w. Colombia (east along n. base of Andes to middle Río Magdalena valley in Santander) and w. Ecuador (south to El Oro and w. Loja); Guianas, s. Venezuela (Bolívar and Amazonas), e. Colombia (north to Meta and Guainía), e. Ecuador, e. Peru (south to Madre de Dios at Manu Nat. Park and Cerro de Pantiacolla), and Amaz. Brazil (south to Rondônia, n. Mato Grosso, and s. Goiás, and east to e. Pará in the Belém area); e. Brazil (Paraíba south to e. Santa Catarina). Probably occurs in extreme n. Bolivia. Also Mexico to Panama. To about 1000 m.

NOTE: More than a single species may be involved. Trans-Andean *M. sulphureipygius* (with *aureatus*) has often been separated specifically from cis-Andean *M. barbatus,* e.g., by the 1983 AOU Check-list. However, *mastacalis* of e. Brazil is almost equally different from *barbatus,* and it is equally geographically isolated from the *barbatus* group of Amazonia. We feel that if *M. sulphureipygius* is specifically separated, then *M. mastacalis* should also be considered a distinct species. Although this may ultimately prove to be the correct treatment, for now we prefer to consider all forms as conspecific. If split, the English name of Sulphur-rumped Flycatcher would remain with *M. sulphureipygius,* with *M. barbatus* becoming the Whiskered Flycatcher and *M. mastacalis* the Yellow-rumped Flycatcher, as originally suggested by Hellmayr in *Birds of the Americas,* vol. 13, part 5.

Myiobius atricaudus

BLACK-TAILED FLYCATCHER

DESCRIPTION: 12.5 cm (5"). *Closely* resembles Sulphur-rumped Flycatcher. Also always has a *conspicuous sulphur yellow rump* and somewhat rounded *black tail. Throat and breast drab buff to olive buff,* with belly pale yellow. Foregoing applies to the *modestus* group (with *adjacens* and *connectens*) of Amazon/lower Orinoco region and to trans-Andean birds (nominate race and *portovelae*). The 2 races of e. Brazil are, however, quite different, both being *more uniform below:* plain yellow with no buff in *snethlagei* (s. Maranhão east to Pernambuco and south to Goiás) or plain yellowish buff in *ridgwayi* (Espírito Santo south to São Paulo).

SIMILAR SPECIES: The variation vis-à-vis Sulphur-rumped Flycatcher is *very* confusing. Perhaps the easiest course is to *consider each area of actual or potential overlap separately* (bear in mind, too, that habitat differences do exist and can be helpful; see below). *West of Andes,* where Sulphur-rumped is extensively bright rich tawny on breast, Black-tailed is merely drab olive-buff; here they are comparatively easy to distinguish. In the *upper Amazon area* it switches, with Sulphur-rumped being drabber and more *olive* on breast, Black-tailed more a dull *buff.* In the *lower Amazon area and Guianas* differentiation is especially difficult, for here *both* species are dull buff across breast, but in Black-tailed a tinge of buff extends to flanks (this lacking in Sulphur-rumped). In *e. Brazil* it is again relatively easy: Black-tailed is, depending on locale, *uniform* yellow or yellowish buff below, whereas Sulphur-rumped has tawny on breast *contrasting* with yellow belly. Here Sulphur-rumped usually occurs in the lowlands, Black-tailed on lower mountain slopes (D. Stotz).

HABITAT AND BEHAVIOR: Uncommon to locally fairly common in lower growth of lighter woodland (deciduous or humid) and forest borders, often near water; in Amazonia usually in várzea forest. Tends not to be found inside terra firme forest, where Sulphur-rumped takes over. Behaves much like Sulphur-rumped Flycatcher, but not quite so spritely or acrobatic.

RANGE: N. and w. Colombia (east to Santa Marta area and middle Río Magdalena valley in e. Antioquia, south in Río Cauca valley to around Cali, and locally in arid intermontane valleys on Pacific slope of Valle; also in sw. Nariño), w. Ecuador, and extreme nw. Peru (Tumbes); e. Venezuela (locally in n. Bolívar); e. Ecuador (north to Napo) and e. Peru (south to Madre de Dios); Amaz. Brazil (south of the Amazon from the lower Rio Madeira drainage east to n. Maranhão); ne. Brazil (s. Maranhão and Piauí east to Pernambuco); se. Brazil (Espírito Santo and s. Minas Gerais south to São Paulo and ne. Paraná). Also Costa Rica and Panama. To 1400 m (in arid valleys of w. Colombia).

Myiobius villosus

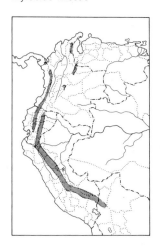

TAWNY-BREASTED FLYCATCHER   PLATE: 37

DESCRIPTION: 14 cm (5½"). *Montane forests, mainly in Andes, mostly above ranges of its 2 smaller congeners.* Above mostly *dark* brownish olive, brownest on head and slightly grayer on face, male with usually concealed yellow coronal patch (cinnamon-rufous or lacking in female); *conspicuous sulphur yellow rump* and somewhat rounded black tail. Throat whitish; *breast tawny brown, the brown extending down broadly over sides and crissum,* with only midbelly dull yellowish.

SIMILAR SPECIES: Often confused with more numerous Sulphur-rumped Flycatcher, particularly west of Andes where that species is also tawny on breast. Tawny-breasted is larger (but this is usually hard to ascertain in the field) and darker above and *much darker and more uniformly brown below;* Sulphur-rumped is paler and brighter on breast, its tawny is not nearly as extensive on sides, and its crissum is yellow (not brown). Sulphur-rumped generally occurs at lower elevations, though there is local overlap. There is less of a problem on e. slope of Andes (though again there is some overlap), for here Sulphur-rumped is dull brownish olive on breast (with *no* tawny).

HABITAT AND BEHAVIOR: Rare to locally fairly common in lower growth of montane forest, especially in the vicinity of streams. Apparently a montane replacement of Sulphur-rumped Flycatcher, Tawny-breasted is generally a much less numerous and less often seen bird. Their behavior is similar, though Tawny-breasted tends to forage higher above ground. Particularly numerous at El Placer in Esmeraldas, nw. Ecuador.

RANGE: Andes of extreme w. Venezuela (Táchira), Colombia (very locally: mostly on w. slope of W. Andes, but also recorded from e. slope of E. Andes in Arauca and on Cerro Tacarcuna in nw. Chocó), Ecuador (south on w. slope to e. Guayas), e. Peru, and w. Bolivia (La Paz); Sierra de Perijá on Colombia-Venezuela border. There is also a highly questionable specimen (almost surely mislabeled) in AMNH from the mouth of the Río Cururay in the lowlands of ne. Peru. Also e. Panama. Mostly 900–2000 m, smaller numbers down locally to about 600 m.

Terenotriccus Flycatchers

A small, perky, mainly cinnamon-rufous flycatcher of humid lowland forests; it has exceptionally long rictal bristles. The nest, a pear-shaped pouch with an often covered side entrance near the bottom, is suspended from a small branch fairly close to the ground. Despite its striking external and behavioral dissimilarities, *Terenotriccus*'s closest relative is apparently the genus *Myiobius*; indeed Lanyon (1988b) argued for its merger into *Myiobius*.

Terenotriccus erythrurus

RUDDY-TAILED FLYCATCHER
PLATE: 37

DESCRIPTION: 10 cm (4"). *A small, mainly rufous-looking flycatcher of humid lowland forests.* Head and neck olive gray, more fulvous on forecrown, becoming more olive brown on back, cinnamon on rump, and *rufous on tail;* wings dusky, broadly edged cinnamon-rufous, *looking mostly rufous at a distance. Below uniform cinnamon-buff* (richness varying racially), more whitish on throat.

SIMILAR SPECIES: Rare Cinnamon Tyrant-Manakin's color pattern is remarkably similar. Cf. also Ochre-bellied Flycatcher.

HABITAT AND BEHAVIOR: Fairly common to common and widespread in lower and middle strata of humid forest (both terra firme and várzea) and secondary woodland. Usually found singly, most often as it perches erectly more or less in the open, sometimes with mixed flocks though at least as often independent of them. Tends to fly abruptly, sallying out to capture a small insect from foliage or, less often, the air, continuing on to a new perch. Often it twitches both wings simultaneously up over its back. Although most often quiet, this usually inconspicuous bird does have thin calls which are given at intervals throughout the day; the most common is a distinctive but rather faint "psee-ee-ee-tseét."

RANGE: Widespread south to n. Bolivia (south to La Paz, Cochabamba, and n. Santa Cruz) and Amaz. Brazil (south to Rondônia and s. Mato Grosso, and east to n. Maranhão); west of Andes south to sw. Ecuador (nw. Azuay); apparently absent from much of ne. and cen. Venezuela. Also Mexico to Panama. To 1000 m.

Pyrrhomyias Flycatchers

A small, mainly rufous flycatcher found in the Andes and which, unlike the superficially similar genus *Mitrephanes*, shows no crest. Traylor and Fitzpatrick (1982) argued that the genus is most closely related to the considerably larger *Hirundinea*, and Lanyon (1986), based on certain additional anatomical considerations, agreed.

Pyrrhomyias cinnamomea

CINNAMON FLYCATCHER

PLATE: 38

DESCRIPTION: 13 cm (5″). *An attractive, mainly cinnamon-rufous flycatcher of Andes.* Olive brown above with semiconcealed yellow coronal patch and narrow cinnamon rump band (usually hidden); wings and tail blackish, with *broad cinnamon-rufous wing-bars and a large patch on inner flight feathers. Below rich cinnamon-rufous,* slightly paler on belly. Birds of most of Venezuela (except Táchira and Sierra de Perijá) and Colombia's Santa Marta Mts. are *rufous to rufous-chestnut above* with dusky tail feathers edged rufous-chestnut (tail mainly rufous in *assimilis* of Santa Martas); see V-29.
SIMILAR SPECIES: No other montane flycatcher is so rufous overall; cf. Ruddy-tailed Flycatcher of lowlands and Cliff Flycatcher.
HABITAT AND BEHAVIOR: Common in shrubby borders of montane forest and secondary woodland; often along roads and trails. Generally conspicuous, usually in pairs which perch upright atop a bush or small tree, making short sallies into the air, often returning to the same perch. Confiding birds, Cinnamon Flycatchers are notably sedentary, pairs frequenting the same restricted areas almost constantly. An often-heard call is a distinctive low-pitched dry rattling, "tr-r-r-r-r-r."
RANGE: Coastal mts. of n. Venezuela (east to Paria Peninsula) and Andes of w. Venezuela, Colombia, Ecuador, nw. and e. Peru (south on w. slope to Cajamarca), w. Bolivia, and nw. Argentina (south to Tucumán); Sierra de Perijá on Venezuela-Colombia border and Santa Marta Mts. of n. Colombia. Mostly 1200–3000 m, occasionally somewhat lower (especially in w. Colombia) or higher.

Myiophobus Flycatchers

Many *Myiophobus* flycatchers superficially resemble *Empidonax* flycatchers, though they show a coronal patch (never present in *Empidonax*), and most have quite prominent buff to ochraceous wing-bars (whitish in adult *Empidonax*). The resemblance is most marked in the forest understory species (our Group A), which are all basically olive. Our second Group (B) is more arboreal and active, as well as more brightly marked, whereas our third Group (C), the Bran-colored group, differs in being usually streaked below and browner above and in favoring more open habitats. Many species are scarce and/or local, with ranges mainly centering on the Andes; only the Bran-colored is at all wide-ranging. All *Myiophobus* are relatively inconspicuous; only members of Group C are particularly vocal.

Lanyon (1986) suggests that the genus is polyphyletic, and argues for removing the Orange-crested, Roraiman and Ochraceous-breasted Flycatchers on the basis of their different nasal septa, but he does not suggest an alternative generic placement. We would, however, be surprised if further work did not demonstrate that the Orange-crested and Roraiman do indeed belong in *Myiophobus,* so very similar are they morphologically, behaviorally, and ecologically to (for example) the Flavescent Flycatcher. Yet we agree that the rather different Ochraceous-breasted (and perhaps the Orange-banded as well) may ultimately deserve to be separated generically; possibly the Handsome Flycatcher will also belong here.

GROUP A

Solitary, *forest understory* species, all found in the *Andes*. Underparts *yellowish to grayish olive*.

Myiophobus flavicans

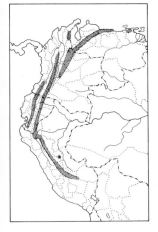

FLAVESCENT FLYCATCHER

PLATE: 38

DESCRIPTION: 12–12.5 cm (4¾–5″). Bill all dark. Uniform olive above with *prominent yellow supraloral and eye-ring, latter broken in front and behind;* semiconcealed yellow coronal patch (lacking in females, and orange in a few males of nominate race, found from Colombia to extreme n. Peru); *wings virtually plain* (in *superciliosus* of Peru south of the Río Marañón), *or with ochraceous wing-bars* (in nominate group, found elsewhere in species' range; see V-29, C-37), often with only the lower one at all prominent. Below mostly yellow, brightest on belly, and washed with olive on breast and sides.

SIMILAR SPECIES: Generally the most numerous and widespread of the forest-inhabiting *Myiophobus* flycatchers. Cf. the scarcer Orange-crested, Unadorned, and Roraiman Flycatchers. None of the *Empidonax* flycatchers is nearly so yellow below, and none shows this species' broken eye-ring or crown patch.

HABITAT AND BEHAVIOR: Fairly common in lower and middle strata of montane forest and forest borders, but rather inconspicuous and not too often seen. Perches erectly, rather like an *Empidonax*, sallying short distances either into the air or to foliage. Most often in pairs or small groups but usually does not accompany mixed flocks. Surprisingly unvocal for a forest understory bird.

RANGE: Coastal mts. of n. Venezuela (east to Sucre), and Andes of w. Venezuela (north to Lara), Colombia (though not recorded north of Valle in W. Andes), Ecuador (south on w. slope to El Oro and w. Loja), and e. Peru (south to Cuzco); Sierra de Perijá on Venezuela-Colombia border. Mostly 1200–2700 m.

Myiophobus phoenicomitra

ORANGE-CRESTED FLYCATCHER

DESCRIPTION: 11.5–12 cm (4½–4¾″). *Very local in Andean foothills from s. Colombia to n. Peru.* Closely resembles nominate group of more numerous Flavescent Flycatcher, and the two may perhaps be sympatric locally though in general *Orange-crested occurs at lower elevations.* Differs in being slightly smaller, darker olive above with blacker wings showing somewhat less edging on flight feathers (but with ochraceous wing-bars about the same), and in having a *very narrow* yellow eyering (sometimes lacking altogether, though if present it tends *not* to be broken as in Flavescent), with *no* supraloral. The semiconcealed *coronal patch of male is usually orange-rufous* (but occasionally yellow, so this is of little help in distinguishing the two). *Lower mandible mainly flesh-colored* (not all dark as in Flavescent). See C-37.

HABITAT AND BEHAVIOR: Uncommon to fairly common but seemingly very local (perhaps mostly with narrow ecological and elevational tolerances) in lower growth of montane forest and forest borders *in foothill zone*. Behavior similar to Flavescent Flycatcher's. Can occasionally be found near the Tinalandia Hotel and along the lower Chiriboga road in Pichincha, Ecuador, but much more numerous at El Placer, in e. Esmeraldas. The call in nw. Ecuador is a weak, thin, high-pitched "tsut, tseép-tsu."

RANGE: W. slope of W. Andes in w. Colombia (north to s. Chocó) and w. Ecuador (south to Pichincha); locally on e. slope of Andes in e. Ecuador (north to w. Napo) and ne. Peru (San Martín). Mostly 500–1300 m.

Myiophobus inornatus

UNADORNED FLYCATCHER

DESCRIPTION: 11.5 cm (4½"). *E. slope of Andes in s. Peru and Bolivia.* Closely resembles sympatric race (*superciliosus*) of Flavescent Flycatcher, and the two are perhaps locally sympatric (though Unadorned seems generally to occur at lower elevations). Differs in being slightly smaller, more brownish olive above with *wing-bars and wing-edging much broader and cinnamon-rufous* (some dull rufescent edging even shows on tail), and *much less bright yellow below* (quite pale and washed-out on belly, more yellowish white on throat). Lower mandible mainly flesh-colored (not all dark, as in Flavescent).

HABITAT AND BEHAVIOR: Rare to uncommon in lower and middle strata of montane forest and forest borders. Usually seen singly or in pairs, often more in the open and higher above ground than Flavescent. Can be seen along the Shintuya-Paucartambo road in Cuzco, Peru.

RANGE: E. slope of Andes in s. Peru (north to Cuzco on Cordillera Vilcabamba) and w. Bolivia (La Paz and Cochabamba). 1000–2000 m.

Myiophobus roraimae

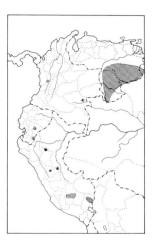

RORAIMAN FLYCATCHER

PLATE: 38

DESCRIPTION: 13.5 cm (5¼"). *Disjunctly on tepuis and very locally on e. slope of Andes in Ecuador and Peru.* Lower mandible pale dull orange. Above olive brown with semiconcealed orange-rufous coronal patch (lacking or small in female) and narrow pale yellowish eye-ring; wings and tail blackish with *2 bold broad cinnamon-rufous wing-bars and edging.* Throat dull grayish white, becoming dull grayish olive on breast and flanks, pale yellow on midbelly.

SIMILAR SPECIES: The largest of the forest-inhabiting *Myiophobus* flycatchers, with browner upperparts and much duller underparts (not as yellow) than any of the others; note also its very conspicuous rufous wing markings. Cf. also Euler's Flycatcher (quite similar but never with as bright rufous wing-bars).

HABITAT AND BEHAVIOR: Rare to uncommon in lower and middle strata of montane forest and forest borders. At least in Andes, where it seems to be very local, apparently confined mainly to areas with impoverished soil, either along ridges or in places with pockets of sandy soil. In s. Venezuela and adjacent areas occurs both in "sandy-belt forest" (or woodland) and in better-developed forest on slopes of tepuis. Behavior similar to Flavescent Flycatcher's.

RANGE: S. Venezuela (Bolívar and Amazonas) and adjacent Guyana (Mt. Twek-quay), extreme n. Brazil (Cerro de la Neblina), and e. Colombia (around Mitú in Vaupés); locally on e. slope of Andes in s. Ecuador (Cordillera de Cutucú in Morona-Santiago and Cordillera del Condor in Zamora-Chinchipe; ANSP) and Peru (scattered localities in San Martín, Huánuco, Pasco, Ayacucho, Cuzco, and Puno). Recorded to 2000 m on the tepuis (also in adjacent lowlands), but in Andes mostly 1100–1700 m.

GROUP B

Flock-associated, *forest canopy and edge* species, all found in the *Andes*. Underparts *clear yellow to ochraceous.*

Myiophobus pulcher

HANDSOME FLYCATCHER
PLATE: 38

DESCRIPTION: 10.5–11 cm (4–4¼"). *Mainly Andes of Colombia and n. Ecuador* (also s. Peru). Lower mandible flesh-yellow. *Crown olive gray* with whitish supraloral spot and narrow broken eye-ring and semiconcealed orange-rufous coronal patch (reduced or absent in females); back olive, wings and tail dusky with *2 bold buffy whitish wing-bars and prominent edging on flight feathers. Throat and breast ochraceous contrasting with pale yellow lower underparts. Bellus* (E. and Cen. Andes of Colombia, and e. slope of Andes in n. Ecuador) is slightly larger and has deeper ochraceous wing-bars, throat, and breast. Despite the huge range disjunction, *oblitus* of Peru hardly differs from nominate race of sw. Colombia and nw. Ecuador (but is a little bigger).
SIMILAR SPECIES: Cf. Orange-banded and Ochraceous-breasted Flycatchers, both of which are considerably larger and notably longer-tailed. In n. part of its range most likely confused with Rufous-breasted Flycatcher, which shares Handsome's overall color pattern but is notably larger and proportionately longer-tailed, has rufous of throat and chest extending up over face, etc.
HABITAT AND BEHAVIOR: Uncommon to fairly common in montane forest and forest borders. Forages at varying levels, most often quite high though coming lower at forest edge. Sometimes in small groups of 3–5 birds, often associated with mixed flocks of tanagers, other flycatchers, etc.; tends to perch more horizontally than does the Flavescent Flycatcher group and to be more active, making short sallies to foliage (less often into air).
RANGE: Locally in Andes of Colombia (in E. Andes north to Santander near Bucaramanga; not recorded in W. Andes north of Valle) and n. Ecuador (south on w. slope to Pichincha, and on e. slope in w. Napo, with a recent sighting from near Sabanilla in Zamora-Chinchipe [D. Wolf]); e. slope of Andes in s. Peru (Cuzco at Huasampilla, and recently taken in Cosñipata valley [FMNH]; Puno at Oconeque). Mostly 1500–2500 m, locally lower on w. slope (at least in Colombia).

Myiophobus ochraceiventris

OCHRACEOUS-BREASTED FLYCATCHER
PLATE: 38

DESCRIPTION: 13.5–14 cm (5¼–5½"). *Andes of Peru and w. Bolivia.* Bill all black. Above *dark* brownish olive with short stripe of orange-ochraceous above eye and on its lower lid, and semiconcealed yellow

to reddish-orange coronal patch (apparently yellow in most males and juveniles, redder in adult males from cen. Peru southward; always a duller reddish chestnut in females); wings and tail dusky, *wings with 2 bold buffy whitish wing-bars and edging. Throat and breast pale orange ochraceous, this extending back over ear-coverts and sides of neck;* belly bright yellow.

SIMILAR SPECIES: Orange-banded Flycatcher apparently replaces this species north of the Río Marañón; the two are generally similar, but the smaller Orange-banded lacks the ochraceous tone on throat and breast. Handsome Flycatcher is much smaller (and proportionately much shorter-tailed), not as dark above, and has quite different color pattern on head.

HABITAT AND BEHAVIOR: Locally common in montane forest and woodland, mainly in a narrow zone just below timberline. Most often in small groups of 3–5 birds which frequently are associated with a mixed flock containing various high-elevation tanagers, etc. Usually forages in middle and upper strata (lower at edge), habitually perching on top of large leaves, from which it sallies out for short distances to capture insects from foliage; also eats some fruit (Remsen 1984). Regularly seen in yungas of La Paz, Bolivia (e.g., in the Chuspipata area) and along the Shintuya-Paucartambo road in Cuzco, Peru.

RANGE: E. slope of Andes in Peru (Amazonas south to Puno) and w. Bolivia (La Paz). Mostly 3000–3300 m, occasionally or locally down to 2500 m.

NOTE: For more information on this species, see Remsen (1984).

Myiophobus lintoni

ORANGE-BANDED FLYCATCHER

DESCRIPTION: 13 cm (5"). *E. slope of Andes in s. Ecuador and extreme n. Peru. Iris grayish yellow to yellow* (dark in all other *Myiophobus*); lower mandible dull orange. Mostly dark brownish olive above, darker and duskier on crown and with semiconcealed ochraceous orange to yellow coronal patch (reduced or lacking in females and juveniles); wings and tail dusky, wings with *2 bold pale cinnamon wing-bars* and rather narrow ochraceous edging (wing-bars deeper rufous-buff in juveniles). *Mostly greenish yellow below,* becoming clearer yellow on belly.

SIMILAR SPECIES: Lacks any hint of the ochraceous tone below shown by both Handsome and Ochraceous-breasted Flycatchers; also, those both have dark irides and whiter wing-bars. The range of this species seems to be sandwiched between the ranges of the other two, though Orange-banded is apparently more closely related to Ochraceous-breasted: the latter two are united in having a proportionately long tail, dark upperparts with brown-capped look, etc.

HABITAT AND BEHAVIOR: Uncommon and local in canopy and borders of montane forest and secondary woodland. Behavior similar to Ochraceous-breasted Flycatcher's, though consistently found at lower elevations than that species. Readily found on the Cordillera Cordoncillo south of Saraguro in n. Loja, Ecuador; also occurs in Podocarpus Nat. Park near Loja (city).

RANGE: E. slope of Andes in s. Ecuador (north to Morona-Santiago on the Gualaceo-Limon road, spreading west into Azuay at El Portete) and extreme n. Peru (Cerro Chinguela in Piura). 2250–2800 m.

NOTE: For more information on this species, see Parker et al. (1985).

GROUP C

In *more open, shrubby habitats* than previous Groups, found in *lowlands*. Underparts *usually streaked*.

Myiophobus fasciatus

BRAN-COLORED FLYCATCHER   PLATE: 38

DESCRIPTION: 12–12.5 cm (4¾–5″). *The most widespread Myiophobus. Reddish brown above* with semiconcealed coronal patch yellow to orange-rufous (but faint or lacking in females); wings and tail dusky with 2 broad buff wing-bars. Below mainly dull whitish, *breast and sides with broad blurry brown streaking;* belly pale yellowish in some races. S. birds slightly larger. *Crypterythrus* (Pacific sw. Colombia to nw. Peru) similar but with duller, more grayish brown upperparts. *Rufescens* (w. Peru from La Libertad south, and in extreme n. Chile) differs notably in having *uniform plain cinnamon underparts* (with streaking faint at best).

SIMILAR SPECIES: Cf. very similar Olive-chested Flycatcher. Otherwise most likely confused with Euler's or Fuscous Flycatchers, neither of which shows streaking below or is as rufescent above. Female/immature Vermilion Flycatcher is larger and lacks wing-bars, most often shows at least a tinge of red on lower underparts, differs in behavior and habitat, etc. Cf. also females of various *Knipolegus* black-tyrants.

HABITAT AND BEHAVIOR: Fairly common in shrubby clearings and pastures, lighter woodland, forest borders, and dense hedgerows in mostly agricultural terrain; *rufescens* seems less numerous and more local. Although found in more open terrain than most of its congeners, Bran-colored Flycatcher is still an inconspicuous bird, tending to perch low and usually not fully in the open. Occurs mostly in pairs; eats some fruit in addition to the usual flycatcher fare of insects, procured by short sallies both to the air and to foliage. Its most common vocalization is a "weeeb" or "weeub" note, often extended in a fairly fast series; we do not have vocal data for *rufescens*.

RANGE: Widespread south to extreme n. Chile (Tarapacá), n. and e. Bolivia, and n. Argentina (south to San Luis, Córdoba, and Buenos Aires), but absent from a broad swath of Amazonia (except in its w. and extreme e. sectors) as well as much of the llanos of e. Colombia and Venezuela; Trinidad. Also Costa Rica and Panama. Though data is scanty, there is increasing evidence that the species departs the s. part of its breeding range (north to about Paraguay and Rio Grande do Sul, Brazil) during austral winter; it is regarded as definitely migratory into se. Peru (where it becomes locally numerous during austral winter in bamboo and second-growth between 500 and 1000 m; D. Stotz). Mostly below 1500 m, higher (to about 2500 m) in drier Andean valleys.

NOTE: *Rufescens* of w. Peru and n. Chile stands apart strikingly from all the other subspecies of *M. fasciatus* and may represent a separate species. The single AMNH specimen from Pacasmayo referred to by J. T. Zimmer (*Am. Mus. Novitates* 1043, p. 6, 1939) as evidence for considering the two as conspecific in fact does not look very "intermediate" to us, being very close to typical *rufescens*. However, M. Koepcke (*Am. Mus. Novitates* 2028, pp. 17–18, 1961) also obtained two specimens from "Yantán" (= Yaután), in the Río Casma valley of Ancash, which she felt were "intermediate between *crypterythrus* and *rufescens*"; we have not seen these specimens. We thus continue to treat *rufescens* as a race of *M. fasciatus*, while harboring the suspicion that additional work may show that these apparent intermediates may be isolated cases and that *M. rufescens* will ultimately be shown to represent a full species (Rufescent Flycatcher).

Myiophobus cryptoxanthus

OLIVE-CHESTED FLYCATCHER

DESCRIPTION: 12 cm (4¾"). *Local in e. Ecuador and n. Peru*. Resembles the dull w. race (*crypterythrus*) of Bran-colored Flycatcher, but ranges only with brighter races of Bran-colored (*saturatus* and nominate). Dull brown above with semiconcealed yellow coronal patch in both sexes (slightly smaller in female); wings and tail dusky with 2 broad pale buff wing-bars. Throat whitish, *breast with broad blurry grayish olive streaking, belly pale yellow*.

SIMILAR SPECIES: Bran-colored Flycatchers of upper Amazonia are more rufescent above, have somewhat more discrete and grayer breast streaking, and are not as yellow on belly (with dorsal color probably the best distinction). Cf. also Fuscous and Euler's Flycatchers.

HABITAT AND BEHAVIOR: Uncommon to locally fairly common in shrubby clearings and borders of humid and montane forest and woodland. Behavior and vocalizations similar to Bran-colored Flycatcher's. Olive-chested tends to occur at somewhat higher elevations, mostly along e. base of Andes, though there is overlap. Frequent above Archidona in e. Ecuador.

RANGE: E. Ecuador (Sucumbios south to Zamora-Chinchipe) and ne. Peru (San Martín). There is also an AMNH specimen supposedly taken well out in the Amaz. lowlands at the mouth of the Río Curaray into the Río Napo; we suspect it was mislabeled. Mostly 300–1100 m, but recorded to 1600 m in s. Ecuador.

NOTE: Despite their close similarity, it does not appear that this species and *M. fasciatus* can be considered conspecific. Specimens of both have been taken at two localities, "San José Abajo" in e. Ecuador, and at the mouth of the Río Curaray in ne. Peru (though, as noted above, mislabeled specimens may be involved at the latter locality). More importantly, in July 1989, M. Robbins found both *cryptoxanthus* and nominate *fasciatus* to be resident in the same clearings at Santiago, Morona-Santiago, Ecuador (ANSP).

Mitrephanes Tufted-Flycatchers

A pair of pewee-like flycatchers found locally in the Andes, mainly at the edge of humid forest. Both are best known by their prominent, somewhat bushy crests; this character provided Lanyon (1986) with the strongest argument for maintaining the genus as distinct from *Contopus* (though we would note that some *Contopus* are almost as crested). We feel it is preferable to unite the two species with a group name, tufted-flycatcher, so as to better demonstrate their close relationship.

Mitrephanes phaeocercus

COMMON TUFTED-FLYCATCHER PLATE: 38
Other: Tufted Flycatcher

DESCRIPTION: 12.5 cm (5"). *W. Colombia and nw. Ecuador. Fairly conspicuous crest.* Above mostly olive, more brownish on crest and with whitish loral spot and inconspicuous eye-ring; wings and tail dusky with indistinct grayish olive wing-bars. Throat and chest buffy olive, contrasting with bright yellow lower underparts.

SIMILAR SPECIES: No other even vaguely similar flycatcher in its range shows the crest.

HABITAT AND BEHAVIOR: Uncommon at borders of humid forest and around treefalls and in adjacent shrubby clearings, mostly in foothill zone. A perky and attractive little flycatcher whose mannerisms recall a pewee's. It perches upright more or less in the open, usually at lower and middle levels, sallying short distances into the air, often repeatedly returning to the same perch, characteristically shivering its tail upon realighting. Generally found in sedentary pairs, remaining independent of flocks. Frequently gives a fast piping series of "pee" or "pik" notes. Can be seen along the lower Buenaventura road in Valle, Colombia.

RANGE: W. Colombia (Cerro Tacarcuna, and on w. slope of W. Andes) and nw. Ecuador (Esmeraldas). Also Mexico to Panama. To 1200 m.

Mitrephanes olivaceus

OLIVE TUFTED-FLYCATCHER
Other: Olive Flycatcher

DESCRIPTION: 13 cm (5¼"). *E. slope of Andes in Peru and Bolivia;* formerly often considered conspecific with Common Tufted-Flycatcher. Resembles that species (no overlap) but slightly larger and with less whitish on face; wing-bars slightly broader; *underparts more or less uniform buffy-olive,* only slightly more yellowish on belly.

SIMILAR SPECIES: As with Common Tufted-Flycatcher, this species' tufted crest is its best mark; otherwise it is a rather drab, uniform olive, undistinguished-looking little flycatcher.

HABITAT AND BEHAVIOR: Rare to uncommon in lower and middle strata of montane forest and borders. Behavior seems similar to Common Tufted-Flycatcher's. Small numbers can be seen along the Shintuya-Paucartambo road in Cuzco, Peru.

RANGE: E. slope of Andes in Peru (north to Cerro Chinguela in Piura) and w. Bolivia (La Paz and Cochabamba). Seems possible in extreme s. Ecuador. Mostly 1000–2000 m.

NOTE: We follow J. D. Webster (*Auk* 85[2]: 287–303, 1968) and *Birds of the World,* vol. 8, in considering *M. olivaceus* as a species distinct from *M. phaeocercus.*

Lathrotriccus, Empidonax, and *Aphanotriccus* Flycatchers

The *Empidonax* flycatchers are known in North America for being among the most difficult of that continent's birds to identify. Only three members of the genus *Empidonax* occur in South America, all of them nonbreeding visitors from North America. Two other species resident in South America were long placed in the genus *Empidonax*. W. E. Lanyon and S. Lanyon (*Auk* 103[2]: 341–350, 1986) erected a new genus, *Lathrotriccus,* for what had been called *E. euleri* (Euler's Flycatcher). Although *E. griseipectus* (Gray-breasted Flycatcher) was excluded from their paper because of a lack of data, recent information from Ecuador suggests that it is closely related to *euleri,* and we have no hesitation in also placing that species in *Lathrotriccus*. A sixth species, Black-billed, is more or less similar to *Empidonax* (though placed in the genus *Aphanotriccus*), differing in its all-black bill (the lower mandible is pale in all *Empidonax* and in *Lathrotriccus*). All are treated together here because of their overall general similarity; they are relatively drab, olive to olive grayish flycatchers with a more or less upright posture which inhabit forest and woodland lower growth and also (in the migrant species) shrubby areas.

Lathrotriccus euleri

EULER'S FLYCATCHER

PLATE: 38

DESCRIPTION: 13–13.5 cm (5–5¼"). Above brownish olive with very narrow whitish eye-ring and vague supraloral; wings dusky with 2 pale buffyish wing-bars, tail olive brown. Throat grayish white, breast brownish olive, belly pale yellow. S. nominate group (with *argentinus,* both of these also migrating north into range of n. *lawrencei* group, which includes *bolivianus*) slightly larger and browner above (especially on crown), with wing-bars a bit more rufescent and whiter (less yellow) belly.

SIMILAR SPECIES: A difficult, drab bird. Easily mistaken for one of the migrant *Empidonax* flycatchers, though those are never as brown above, nor do they show such buffy wing-bars. Voice (see below) may be the most help. Also resembles Fuscous Flycatcher but lacks that species' fairly distinct whitish superciliary. Cf. also various *Myiophobus* flycatchers.

HABITAT AND BEHAVIOR: Uncommon to locally common in lower growth of humid forest, forest borders, and secondary woodland (sometimes in areas dominated by bamboo). More numerous and much more widespread in s. South America than it is northward; it is, for instance, decidedly scarce and local in Colombia and Ecuador. Usually found perching inconspicuously in shady undergrowth, generally alone or in pairs, sallying out to foliage, not returning repeatedly to the same perch. Rarely follows mixed flocks. The frequently heard song does not seem to vary across the species' wide range, usually being a fast, burry "peeeur, peer-per-per-peeur," sometimes varied to just the initial "peeeur" or an even faster "peeeur, peepiti" or "bew-bewee."

RANGE: Widespread east of Andes south to n. and e. Bolivia and n. Argentina (south to La Rioja, e. Santa Fe, Entre Ríos, and n. Buenos Aires), but apparently absent from the llanos of Venezuela and from much of e. Colombia, as well as most of Guianas (aside from a few Surinam records and 1 from French Guiana); Trinidad. Also Grenada.

S. breeding birds (*argentinus* and nominate; north through Paraguay and s. Brazil, and perhaps farther) migrate north into Amazonia during austral winter, when they are, for example, locally numerous in se. Peru (D. Stotz). To at least 1500 m.

Lathrotriccus griseipectus

GRAY-BREASTED FLYCATCHER   PLATE: 38

DESCRIPTION: 13 cm (5"). *W. Ecuador and nw. Peru.* Grayish olive above, grayer on crown, with *wide broken eye-ring and supraloral white;* wings dusky with *2 well-marked white wing-bars.* Throat pale gray, *breast darker gray,* contrasting with white to yellowish white belly.

SIMILAR SPECIES: Obviously grayer in the field than any other *Empidonax* or near relative. However, the sympatric race (*punensis*) of Tropical Pewee is similar in appearance and actually is even more uniformly gray above than the flycatcher. The pewee is somewhat larger, lacks the spectacled look (though its lores are white), and has less bold wing-bars; typically its behavior differs as well.

HABITAT AND BEHAVIOR: Rare to locally fairly common in lower growth of humid and deciduous forest and woodland. Behavior much like Euler's Flycatcher, likewise inconspicuous and usually encountered singly or in pairs, perching low in dense and often viny undergrowth. In some areas occurs most often near streams; we have also seen it at army antswarms. Its song is very similar to Euler's, being a fast, burry "peeéur, peer-per-per-pur," with variations. Although now very local because of destruction of much of its habitat, Gray-breasted Flycatcher persists in substantial numbers in Machalilla Nat. Park of Manabí, Ecuador. The species deserves formal threatened status.

RANGE: Locally in w. Ecuador (w. Esmeraldas and Pichincha south to El Oro and Loja) and nw. Peru (south to n. Lambayeque); upper Río Marañón valley in drainage of Río Chinchipe in n. Cajamarca, Peru (near San José de Lourdes and Jaen) and extreme s. Ecuador in s. Zamora-Chinchipe (near Zumba). Mostly below 1700 m, locally to 2200 m in s. Ecuador (at least formerly); most numerous below 700 m.

Aphanotriccus audax

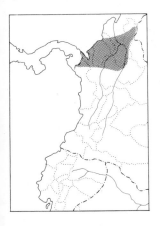

BLACK-BILLED FLYCATCHER

DESCRIPTION: 13.5 cm (5¼"). *N. Colombia. Short, all-black bill.* Above bright olive, somewhat grayer on crown, with *whitish supraloral and narrow eye-ring broken in front and behind;* wings duskier, with 2 pale buff wing-bars. Throat whitish, sides of chest clouded olive, becoming clear yellow on lower breast and belly. See C-37.

SIMILAR SPECIES: Size and plumage recall a migrant *Empidonax* (especially Acadian), but note all-black bill (lower mandible pale in *Empidonax*) and white supraloral (only an eye-ring in Acadian); Black-billed does not perch as erectly. Shape and posture resemble Sepia-capped Flycatcher's, but that species' facial pattern (especially the black auricular spot) is quite different. Might also be confused with a *Tolmomyias* flycatcher (e.g., Yellow-olive), but Black-billed's bill is not as wide, its overall shape is more slender, and it is less gray on crown. Cf.

also Euler's Flycatcher (not known to overlap, with pale lower mandible, etc.).

HABITAT AND BEHAVIOR: Uncommon in lower growth of humid forest and mature secondary woodland, mostly near streams or in swampy places. Inconspicuous, found singly or in pairs, perching quietly then sallying out a short distance, usually to foliage, and continuing to a new perch. The distinctive but infrequently given call is a sharp but burry "jee-jee-jew."

RANGE: N. Colombia (humid Caribbean lowlands east to w. base of Sierra de Perijá in Cesar at Casacará and middle Río Magdalena valley in Santander). Also e. Panama. To about 700 m.

Empidonax traillii
and *E. alnorum*

"TRAILL'S" FLYCATCHER

DESCRIPTION: 14 cm (5½"). N. Am. migrants mainly to w. Amazonia. Includes both Willow (*E. traillii*) and Alder (*E. alnorum*) Flycatchers; these are so similar as to be indistinguishable (even in the hand) unless they are vocalizing, which they regularly do (see below). Brownish olive to grayish olive above with *inconspicuous narrow whitish eye-ring* (often altogether lacking), sometimes with some whitish on lores; wings and tail dusky, wings with *2 bold whitish to pale buff wing-bars* (buffier in juveniles). Throat whitish; breast grayish to brownish olive; belly pale yellowish white (yellowest in juveniles). Alder tends to show a slightly more prominent eye-ring than Willow and to be somewhat greener above (but variation occurs, and certainly neither character is definitive).

SIMILAR SPECIES: Besides the extreme problem differentiating Willow and Alder Flycatchers, both are hard to distinguish from Acadian Flycatcher. Note, however, that for the most part their ranges in South America are separated; further, that Acadian tends to have a more obvious eye-ring and to be greener above and yellower on belly, and that preferred habitats and vocalizations do differ. "Traill's" also closely resembles Euler's Flycatcher, though that species always shows deeper buff, almost rufescent, wing-bars (rarely or never matched by "Traill's," even in fresh-plumaged immatures).

HABITAT AND BEHAVIOR: Fairly common n.-winter resident (mostly Sept.–April, a few Aug. and May records) in shrubby clearings, pastures, and lighter woodland; favors areas near water, and in Amazonia regularly on river islands with early-successional growth. Quite conspicuous on their wintering grounds, where territorial. Both species most often give just their calls, a short, dry "whit" for Willow and a low, flat "peep" or "tip" for Alder. Wintering birds also sometimes give a more or less full song (especially when on their winter territory or during northward passage). For Willow this is a sharp, snappy "fitz-bew," for Alder a burrier "free-breéo;" at times these can sound similar, but *the accent differs* (on first syllable for Willow, on second for Alder).

RANGE: Nonbreeding visitor to n. and e. Colombia (not recorded from Pacific lowlands south of n. Chocó), w. Venezuela, e. Ecuador, e. Peru, n. and e. Bolivia, and nw. Argentina (south to Tucumán); vagrants have been found in Amaz. Brazil (a specimen from Santarém and a sighting of a singing Alder Flycatcher in Manaus) and ne. Argentina (Misiones). Willow Flycatcher tends to winter northward, with e. Ecuador appearing to be as far south as it has definitely been recorded. Alder winters southward (all in se. Peru appear to be this), but of course is also found northward on migration. Because of the difficulty in separating the 2 species, we have mapped their distributions together. Both species breed in North America; Willow winters also in Middle America. Mostly below 1000 m, but on migration occasionally higher (once to 3500 m in Ecuador).

NOTE: Until recently *E. alnorum* was considered conspecific with *E. traillii.*

Empidonax virescens

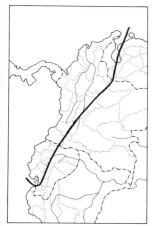

ACADIAN FLYCATCHER

DESCRIPTION: 14 cm (5½″). N. Am. migrant to nw. South America. Olive above with fairly prominent yellowish white eye-ring and whitish lores; wings and tail dusky, wings with 2 bold whitish wing-bars. Throat grayish white, becoming pale olive gray on breast, white on midbelly, and pale yellow on flanks and crissum. Juveniles have buffier wing-bars and are often yellower below, especially on belly.

SIMILAR SPECIES: Closely resembles Willow and Alder Flycatchers, and often not safely separated in the field. Acadian tends to have a bolder eye-ring and to be yellower below; it favors more wooded habitats, and calls differ (see below). In the hand, Acadian has difference between the longest and the 6th primary of 6 mm or more; Traill's usually has less than 6 mm.

HABITAT AND BEHAVIOR: Uncommon to locally fairly common n.-winter visitor (Sept.–April) in lower growth of humid forest and especially forest borders, secondary woodland, and shady plantations (e.g., cacao); favors areas near water. Unlike either Willow or Alder Flycatcher, Acadian rarely is found in the open. Its rather loud call is a sharper, more inflected "wheep!" or "peet!"; unlike Willow and Alder, it rarely seems to sing in South America (perhaps sometimes on northward migration?).

RANGE: Nonbreeding visitor to w. Colombia (mostly west of E. Andes, also a few records along their e. base), nw. Venezuela (Zulia and Táchira), and w. Ecuador (south to nw. Azuay). Breeds in North America, migrating through Middle America, wintering from Costa Rica south. To about 1500 m, but on migration occasionally recorded higher (to 2700 m in Colombia).

Contopus Pewees and Flycatchers

A group of drab, small to midsized flycatchers, conspicuous at forest edges. Their specialty is aerial hawking, typically from an exposed perch to which they often return repeatedly. Three species are migratory from North America, whereas two small, dark resident species have very restricted ranges; only two resident species, Smoke-colored and Tropical Pewees, are at all widespread. The pewees tend to be more bushy-crested than the *Empidonax* flycatchers, though there is some variation; the two small, dark species (Blackish and White-throated) have the least, the two wood-pewees and Tropical are about average, Olive-sided is somewhat more "crested," and Smoke-colored is quite "shaggy."

GROUP A   *Smaller pewees.*

Contopus nigrescens

BLACKISH PEWEE   PLATE: 38

DESCRIPTION: 13 cm (5″). *Rare and local.* Lower mandible yellowish. *Uniform dark gray* with some pale gray on lores and an obscure, very narrow whitish eye-ring (more pronounced to rear); blackest on crown, wings, and tail. Immature apparently has narrow whitish wing-bars, but adult's wings are almost plain blackish.

SIMILAR SPECIES: Virtually identical in coloration to the sympatric race, *ardosiacus,* of *much* more common Smoke-colored Pewee (*ardosiacus* being the darkest, most uniform race of that species) but *much* smaller and does not have Smoke-colored's bushy crest. Many over-enthusiastic observers have incorrectly turned "small-looking" Smoke-coloreds into this species. White-throated Pewee has an obvious white throat patch. Even the darkest race (nominate) of Tropical Pewee is never as dark as Blackish; nominate Tropical is not found sympatrically with Blackish, and it has more prominent wing-bars and a dull yellowish midbelly.

HABITAT AND BEHAVIOR: Rare to locally fairly common high in canopy and borders of humid forest; there are rather few records overall, though we suspect this mostly is due to the species often being overlooked. Birds from w. portion of range are found mainly in foothills at base of Andes; Guyanan and Brazilian birds also range in hilly areas, though the forest is not so humid. Ecuadorian birds occur almost invariably in pairs, perching very high in trees, often along streams or at other openings in tall forest. They make long sallies into the air, often returning to the same perch over and over again, shivering the tail just after realighting. The call, given by both sexes, is a repeated sharp "pip" or "peep," usually given in series (but typically not trebled, unlike Smoke-colored). Male's song is a snappy but somewhat burry "chí-bew" repeated at 3- to 4-second intervals.

RANGE: Locally on e. slope of Andes in Ecuador (north to w. Sucumbios; ANSP) and e. Peru (San Martín, Amazonas, Huánuco, and Cuzco); very locally in s. Guyana (Acary Mts.) and e. Amaz. Brazil in se. Pará (Itupiranga along the Rio Tocantins [MZUSP specimen, *fide* D. Stotz]), and sightings from Serra das Carajás [P. Roth]) and Maranhão (pair seen in Rio Pindaré area in Nov. 1977; RSR). To 1200 m (along e. base of Andes only above 400 m).

Contopus albogularis

WHITE-THROATED PEWEE

DESCRIPTION: 13 cm (5″). *Guianas and Amapá, Brazil. Mostly dark gray.* Much like Blackish Pewee but with *large white throat patch.*

SIMILAR SPECIES: Tropical Pewee is not nearly so dark, lacks the contrasting white throat, and has different vocalizations.

HABITAT AND BEHAVIOR: Uncommon but very local at edge of humid forest and in adjacent small clearings. Perches on high exposed snags at forest edge or on branches just beneath forest canopy, sallying out into the air, repeatedly returning to the same branch, shivering its tail upon alighting. Persistently gives a dry "pip-pip-pip" call note, reminiscent of a Smoke-colored Pewee or Olive-sided Flycatcher. Easily seen at Brownsberg Nature Park, Surinam, particularly along the various roads on top of the plateau.

RANGE: Locally in Guianas (Surinam and French Guiana) and extreme ne. Brazil (Amapá). Mainly 400–500 m.

Contopus cinereus

TROPICAL PEWEE   PLATE: 38

DESCRIPTION: 14 cm (5½″). Lower mandible yellowish. Grayish olive above with *whitish lores* (sometimes indistinct) and usually a darker crown; wings and tail dusky, wings with 2 whitish to pale gray wing-bars. Throat whitish, breast and flanks olive grayish, with midbelly whitish to pale yellowish. Nominate race (se. Brazil area) is *darker and dingier generally* and lacks the pale lores; it is more uniformly olivaceous grayish below and has weaker wing-bars.

SIMILAR SPECIES: Cf. the wood-pewees; both are *very* similar to Tropical but are slightly larger, lack the whitish lores, and have different calls. In the hand note that Tropical Pewee's 10th (outermost) primary is shorter than 6th; in the wood-pewees it is distinctly longer. Easily confused also with various *Empidonax* flycatchers, especially Alder and Willow ("Traill's"), which are about the same size and have generally similar coloration. Best distinguishing marks are the pewee's blurrier wing-bars and grayer overall coloration; voice is also often helpful. Note that "Traill's" often flicks the tail upward, a mannerism not shared by Tropical Pewee. Gray-breasted Flycatcher (w. Ecuador and nw. Peru) resembles sympatric race of Tropical Pewee (*punensis*) but differs in its bolder and whiter wing-bars and its spectacled look (with white supraloral and eye-ring, vs. only the lores in the pewee); its behavior also differs.

HABITAT AND BEHAVIOR: Uncommon to locally common in forest borders, shrubby clearings, lighter woodland, and locally even in mangroves; perhaps most numerous in drier areas (though in some areas found at edge of humid forest). Absent from most of Amazonia. Generally not very conspicuous, though regularly perching on exposed branches; from these it sallies out to the air, often for a long distance, repeatedly returning and usually shivering its tail just after landing. Its rather soft call differs from that of either of the wood-pewees', in most of its range being a distinctive fast dry "seerip," but with some geographic variation (e.g., birds in e. Brazil frequently give a "pip-pip-pip" call not heard elsewhere, whereas in w. Ecuador the song is a very different, clear "peee, pidit").

RANGE: N. Colombia (mostly west of E. Andes, but not in Pacific

lowlands south of s. Chocó; also along e. base of Andes south to
w. Caquetá) and n. Venezuela; w. Ecuador (north to Manabí and Pichincha; east of Andes only in Río Marañón drainage at Zumba in
s. Zamora-Chinchipe) and w. Peru (south to Ica); nw. Brazil (Rio Pa-
duari in upper Rio Negro drainage); Guianas to mouth of the Amazon
(Mexiana and Marajó Is.); s. and e. Brazil (s. Mato Grosso, Goiás,
s. Maranhão, and Pernambuco south to Rio Grande do Sul), e. Paraguay (west about to the Río Paraguay), ne. and nw. Argentina (in
Misiones, and Salta and Jujuy), n. and e. Bolivia (west to La Paz), and
extreme se. Peru (Madre de Dios at Cuzco Amazonico); Trinidad. Also
Mexico to Panama. Mostly below 1500 m (occasionally higher).

NOTE: More than one species is probably involved. In particular, *C. punensis* (Pacific pewee) of w. Ecuador and w. Peru stands apart at least vocally.

Contopus virens

EASTERN WOOD-PEWEE

DESCRIPTION: 14.5 cm (5¾"). Lower mandible yellowish, sometimes
tipped dusky. Dark grayish olive above, wings and tail duskier with
2 distinct pale gray to whitish wing-bars. Throat whitish, more grayish
on sides; breast and flanks olive grayish, becoming whitish on midbelly
and often pale yellowish on crissum. Juveniles have buffier wing-bars
and tend to be yellower below, especially on belly; they may have an
all-dark bill.
SIMILAR SPECIES: *Drab and easily confused;* voice is often the only way
to confirm identification; fortunately it vocalizes often. Problems are
greatest with several other N. Am. migrants, notably Western Wood-
Pewee (which see) and "Traill's" (Willow and Alder) Flycatchers. The
latter have subtly different shapes (less crested, shorter wings), are generally less grayish (tending toward olive or brown) with bolder and
whiter wing-bars (buffier in juveniles), and may show an eye-ring
(which Eastern Wood-Pewee never has). See also Olive-sided Flycatcher. Among resident S. Am. species, Eastern Wood-Pewee most
resembles Tropical Pewee, but Eastern is a bit larger and lacks Tropical's whitish lores. Tropical's call differs characteristically, and note that
Eastern does *not* seem to shiver its tail upon alighting.
HABITAT AND BEHAVIOR: Fairly common to common n.-winter resident (mostly Sept.–April, a few earlier and later records) in forest borders, shrubby clearings, and lighter woodland; more numerous near
base of Andes (e.g., in Ecuador and Peru) than it is farther east in
Amaz. Brazil. Usually solitary, perching at varying heights but most
often not very high, then sallying out, often for long distances, after
flying insects. Calls quite often, usually a "pee-wee?" with characteristic
sweet plaintive quality; occasionally interspersed with this common
call is a burrier, down-slurred "pee-ur." The full song, "pee-a-wee," is
heard much less often except on northward passage.
RANGE: Nonbreeding visitor to Colombia, w. and cen. Venezuela, Ecuador (south on w. slope to nw. Azuay), e. Peru (south to Cuzco and
Madre de Dios), extreme n. Bolivia (Beni at Tumi Chucua), and locally
(perhaps overlooked?) in w. Amaz. Brazil (recorded from north of

Manaus, Rio Urucu south of Tefé in Amazonas, and Cachoeira Nazaré in Rondônia; the only Brazil specimen is one in the MZUSP from Santa Cruz on the Rio Juruá); 2 sight reports from coastal French Guiana. Breeds in e. North America, migrating mainly through Middle America, wintering mostly in South America. Mostly below 1500 m, a few higher (perhaps mostly on migration).

Contopus sordidulus

WESTERN WOOD-PEWEE

DESCRIPTION: 14.5 cm (5¾"). *Very* closely resembles Eastern Wood-Pewee, so much so that *identification is often impossible unless the bird is vocalizing* (which, fortunately, it often does; see below). Bill usually all or mostly dark, but lower mandible yellowish to horn in juveniles (and some adults?). Plumage virtually identical to Eastern Wood-Pewee's, though tending to be somewhat darker below.

HABITAT AND BEHAVIOR: Fairly common to common n.-winter resident (mostly Sept.–April, with a few earlier and later records) in forest borders, shrubby clearings, and lighter woodland. Behavior identical to Eastern Wood-Pewee's. Calls quite often (*contra* Hilty and Brown 1986), a melancholy, burry "preeer" or "freeer." This has a markedly different quality from the typical clear sweet call of Eastern Wood-Pewee, but note that one of the less frequently given calls of the latter can sound burry.

RANGE: Nonbreeding visitor to Colombia, Venezuela, Ecuador (south on w. slope to El Oro), e. Peru, and w. Bolivia (south to La Paz and Cochabamba); 2 birds collected in Salta in nw. Argentina (G. Hoy, *Hist. Nat.* 2[5]: 43–44, 1981) were reported as *C. virens* but are presumed to have been the geographically more likely *C. sordidulus* (the author may not have considered *C. sordidulus* as a separate species). Breeds in w. North America, migrating mainly through Middle America, wintering mostly in South America. To about 2500 m.

NOTE: *C. virens* and *C. sordidulus* have sometimes been considered conspecific (e.g., by Meyer de Schauensee 1966, 1970), but we follow most recent authorities (e.g., *Birds of the World*, vol. 8, and the 1983 AOU Check-list) in regarding them as full species.

GROUP B

Larger pewees. May show *conspicuous crest*.

Contopus fumigatus

SMOKE-COLORED PEWEE   PLATE: 38
Other: Greater Pewee (in part)

DESCRIPTION: 17 cm (6¾"). Lower mandible orange-yellow. *A large, essentially uniform grayish flycatcher with usually prominent bushy crest, found mainly in Andes.* Color varies from being *uniform dark smoky gray* in n. part of range south to s. Peru (*ardosiacus* is typical) to *paler more olivaceous gray* in nominate group found from extreme s. Peru southward (*brachyrhynchus* of s. Bolivia and Argentina is even slightly paler), with throat and midbelly whitish to yellowish white. Wings are nearly plain in all races, with somewhat more pale feather edging in s. group.
SIMILAR SPECIES: Birds on e. slope of Andes can be confused with the

always rarer Blackish Pewee, which is much smaller and does not show a crest; *the coloration of both species in that region is similar.* Cf. also Olive-sided Flycatcher.

HABITAT AND BEHAVIOR: Fairly common to common in borders of montane forest and clearings with scattered trees. Conspicuous, favoring prominent perches (often snags or exposed branches high above the ground), from there sallying long distances into the air, frequently returning to its original lookout over and over. Its most often heard call is a loud "pip-pip-pip," often repeated more or less interminably. Dawn song of the northern *ardosiacus* group is an emphatic "wheer, wheerit" or "peer-peereét" with quality of Olive-sided Flycatcher (J. Fitzpatrick), whereas that of *brachyrhynchus* in Argentina is a subdued "per-wheeer" with quality of a *Spizaetus* hawk-eagle.

RANGE: Coastal mts. of n. Venezuela (east to Miranda), and Andes of w. Venezuela, Colombia, Ecuador (also an isolated population on the coastal cordillera in sw. Manabí and w. Guayas), nw. and e. Peru (south on w. slope to Cajamarca), w. Bolivia, and nw. Argentina (south to Tucumán, with a single sighting from Córdoba); also Sierra de Perijá on Colombia-Venezuela border and tepuis of s. Venezuela (Bolívar and Amazonas). Mostly 1000–2500 m, but regularly lower on Pacific slope and in s. part of range, locally almost to sea level in sw. Ecuador.

NOTE: We follow the 1983 AOU Check-list in considering the S. Am. forms as a species distinct from birds of Middle America and sw. United States (these latter are divided into two species, Coues' Pewee, *C. pertinax*, and Dark Pewee, *C. lugubris*). Other authorities (e.g., *Birds of the World,* vol. 8) combine all members of the complex into a single species (under the name of Greater Pewee, *C. fumigatus*). J. T. Zimmer (*Am. Mus. Novitates* 1042, 1939) points out that northernmost birds (found in sw. United States and Mexico) rather resemble southernmost birds (found in Argentina and Bolivia), whereas those of Costa Rica and Panama resemble the dark races of the more northerly mountains of South America. This convinced him that merging all forms into one polytypic species was the best course, and that may well be correct. However, there are some sharp morphological breaks between populations, as well as some vocal variation in dawn songs—enough for us to regard *pertinax, lugubris,* and *fumigatus* as allospecies. There could even be a fourth full species, for when the potential contact zone between *ardosiacus* and nominate *fumigatus* in s. Peru is thoroughly analyzed, the former may also deserve to be recognized as distinct (Slate-colored Pewee).

Contopus borealis

OLIVE-SIDED FLYCATCHER

DESCRIPTION: 17.5 cm (6¾"). A rather large flycatcher, resembling s. race of Smoke-colored Pewee in color but with *proportionately short tail.* Lower mandible mostly yellowish. Dark grayish olive above, wings and tail dusky, wings with 2 indistinct pale grayish wing-bars. Throat and median underparts whitish to yellowish white, *sides and flanks olive grayish,* sometimes with a mottled streaky effect, almost extending across breast (suggesting a "dark unbuttoned vest over a white shirt"). *A tuft of white, sometimes hidden, may protrude from behind wing onto sides of rump.* See V-XIII, P-23.

SIMILAR SPECIES: Both wood-pewees are smaller with proportionately longer tails and lack the Olive-sided's often obvious bull-headed

look; they also never show the white protruding onto sides of rump, nor an "open vested" look. Can also be confused with Smoke-colored Pewee, particularly that species' paler southernmost races, but Olive-sided shows *much more contrast below* as well as the white tuft; Smoke-colored is obviously longer-tailed and usually has a prominent bushy crest.

HABITAT AND BEHAVIOR: Uncommon to locally fairly common n.-winter visitor (mostly Sept.–May, a few earlier records) to clearings with scattered tall trees and forest borders and openings. Occurs mainly in montane or foothill areas, especially on Andean slopes, and much less numerous in Amaz. lowlands. Usually conspicuous, perching on high exposed snags or branches, from there sallying out, often very long distances, for flying insects. Habitually returns to the same favored perch over and over, and can sometimes be seen in the same tree for several days or even weeks; winter territories are presumably established. Frequently given is a characteristic loud "pip-pip-pip" call similar to Smoke-colored Pewee's, and on northward passage (especially) also gives its full song, an unmistakable, far-carrying "hic, three-beers."

RANGE: Nonbreeding visitor mainly to Trinidad, n. and w. Venezuela, w. Colombia, Ecuador, e. Peru, and w. Bolivia (La Paz, Cochabamba, and w. Santa Cruz), with smaller numbers in s. Venezuela (Bolívar), Guianas (so far reported from Surinam and French Guiana, but doubtless in Guyana as well), and Amaz. Brazil; vagrants have been seen in São Paulo and Rio de Janeiro, Brazil, and at Mollendo in Arequipa, Peru. Breeds in North America, migrating mostly through Middle America, wintering mainly in South America (a few north to Mexico). Mostly 500–2000 m, but sometimes higher or down into lowlands.

NOTE: Formerly placed in the monotypic genus *Nuttallornis;* all recent authors (e.g., Traylor 1977 and the 1983 AOU Check-list) have advocated its merger into *Contopus.*

Cnemotriccus Flycatchers

A monotypic genus of *Empidonax/Lathrotriccus*-like flycatcher found widely in the lowlands of South America, differing in being larger and in having a fairly well marked superciliary. Its closest relative is probably *Lathrotriccus* (Lanyon 1986).

Cnemotriccus fuscatus

FUSCOUS FLYCATCHER

PLATE: 38

DESCRIPTION: 14.5 cm (5¾″). A drab flycatcher which seems characterless and has few obvious field marks. Bill mostly dark (at most, base of lower mandible pale flesh). Dull grayish to rufous brown above with *long, fairly conspicuous whitish superciliary;* wings dusky with *2 broad tawny-buff wing-bars.* Throat whitish, breast pale olive brown, belly whitish. The dingiest and darkest races (*fuscatior, fumosus,* and *duidae* of Amazonia to the Guianas) also have a shorter and less distinct su-

perciliary and narrower and less bright wing-bars. Nominate race (coastal se. Brazil) has the yellowest belly of any race.

SIMILAR SPECIES: Euler's Flycatcher lacks the superciliary. Mouse-colored Tyrannulet has similar plumage, but its bill is shorter and it has different behavior and vocalizations.

HABITAT AND BEHAVIOR: Fairly common to common in undergrowth of woodland and forest borders, gallery woodland, and (in Amazonia) shrubbery and light woodland on river islands. Usually inconspicuous, remaining in shady recesses, rarely emerging into the open. Perches more or less upright, much like an *Empidonax*. Vocalizations seem to vary geographically (though on the whole a rather quiet bird), usually a fast jumbled series of clear notes, e.g., "chip, weety-weety-weety, cheedip," but *bimaculatus* (interior Brazil south to n. Argentina) reported to give a rather different, single clear whistled "ooooooooeee?" (Belton 1985).

RANGE: Widespread east of Andes south to n. and e. Bolivia, Paraguay, nw. and ne. Argentina (Salta and Jujuy, and from Misiones south to ne. Santa Fe), and s. Brazil (south to Rio Grande do Sul); west of Andes only in n. Colombia and nw. Venezuela; Trinidad and Tobago. May withdraw from s. part of range during the austral winter; though details remain sparse, it is apparently absent from Rio Grande do Sul, Brazil (Belton 1985) at that season. Mostly below 900 m (but recorded to 2400 m in La Paz, Bolivia).

NOTE: Belton (1985) suggests that, despite the only minor morphological variation exhibited, more than one species may be involved. Voices of the two forms occurring in Rio Grande do Sul, Brazil (*bimaculatus* in the west, nominate in the coastal northeast), differ, and he reports that they do not respond to recordings of each other's voice. Nest sites also seem to differ.

Sayornis Phoebes

A single species of *Sayornis* occurs in South America; two others are found in North America. It is a distinctive, mainly black tyrannid found along montane watercourses.

Sayornis nigricans

BLACK PHOEBE

PLATE: 38

DESCRIPTION: 17.5 cm (6¾"). *An unmistakable black and white fly-catcher found along streams, mainly in Andes. Mostly sooty black* with middle of lower belly white; *wing-coverts and flight feathers edged white;* outer tail feathers narrowly edged white. *Latirostris* (Bolivia and Argentina) has broader white edging on wings than *angustirostris* (found south to s. Peru).

HABITAT AND BEHAVIOR: Fairly common and conspicuous in semi-open areas along streams and rivers, almost always where there is a fast current, often near habitations. Confiding and attractive, Black Phoebes usually occur in pairs and are most often spotted perching on a boulder in the water, occasionally jerking their tails upward. They

also regularly perch on fences, wires, even buildings—but never too far from water, toward which they quickly retreat if disturbed. They feed by sallying into the air after flying insects, usually not going very far.

RANGE: Coastal mts. of n. Venezuela (east to Paria Peninsula), and Andes of w. Venezuela, Colombia, Ecuador, Peru (south on w. slope to Lambayeque), w. Bolivia, and nw. Argentina (south to Catamarca); Sierra de Perijá on Venezuela-Colombia border and Santa Marta Mts. in n. Colombia. Also sw. United States to Panama. Mostly 500–2500 m.

NOTE: As there is a north-south cline toward increased white on wing and decreased white on belly throughout this species' range, there seems to be little justification in splitting *S. nigricans* into two or more allospecies, as has sometimes been suggested.

Pyrocephalus Flycatchers

Found widely in more arid or open areas, the male Vermilion Flycatcher is the most dazzling member of its family; among tyrannids the species is unusual in being so strikingly dimorphic in plumage.

Pyrocephalus rubinus

VERMILION FLYCATCHER
PLATE: 38

DESCRIPTION: 14.5–15 cm (5¾–6″). Somewhat bushy-crested. Male unmistakable: *crown, lower face, and entire underparts brilliant scarlet,* contrasting with sooty blackish upperparts and broad mask through eye. Female ashy brown above, sootier on wings and tail, *wings virtually plain*. Throat and breast whitish, *breast with dusky streaking* (variable in extent), becoming *pink to reddish pink on belly and crissum* (*saturatus* of n. South America is the reddest). Females of various w. races (w. Colombia south to n. Chile) may have *lower underparts tinged with yellow* (no pink). Females of nominate race (breeding in s. part of range north to s. Bolivia, Paraguay, and s. Brazil, migrating in austral winter to Amazonia) tend to show no pink below and to have *dusky streaking extending down over belly*. A melanistic morph occurs in both sexes of birds found in w. Peru from Lima southward and in adjacent Chile (*obscurus* and *cocachacrae*): it is *uniform sooty,* males sometimes with a few scattered red feathers. About 50% of Lima birds are melanistic, the proportion decreasing southward.

SIMILAR SPECIES: Males obviously present no problem, but females, if unaccompanied, can be a little confusing, though usually their shape and behavior provide a sufficient clue. Cf. especially Bran-colored Flycatcher (browner above, with wing-bars) and various *Knipolegus* black-tyrants (note Vermilion's *lack* of wing-bars).

HABITAT AND BEHAVIOR: Uncommon to locally common in open areas with scattered trees and bushes, and borders of light woodland. Favors arid areas, though typically does not range too far from a watercourse; during austral winter found in clearings and riparian growth in Amazonia. Conspicuous, usually perching in the open, often along fences or on lower branches of trees, less frequently higher (e.g., on phone wires). The tail is often pumped downward and spread. When feeding, usually drops to the ground for its insect prey, then quickly flutters back up again; aerial sallies are less frequent. The spectacular males, whose red is so intense that they almost seem to glow when seen in good light, are at their best during their display flights. They then ascend with crest raised and breast fluffed, wings flapping furiously but weakly, slowly gaining height until they are 30 or more meters up, there hovering for a few moments before dropping back down to a perch, all the while repeating a series of musical tinkling notes. Males regularly display in predawn darkness but also sometimes in midday sun.

RANGE: Guyana, Venezuela, more arid parts of n. and w. Colombia, w. Ecuador, w. Peru, and extreme n. Chile (Arica); e. Bolivia, s. Brazil, Paraguay, Uruguay, and n. and cen. Argentina (south to Río Negro); during the austral winter southerly breeders (nominate *rubinus*) migrate north as far as Amaz. Brazil, se. Colombia, and se. Ecuador (Morona-Santiago; ANSP). Also sw. United States to Nicaragua, and on Galápagos Is. (where separate species are possibly involved). To about 3000 m in Ecuador.

Colorhamphus Tyrants

A small flycatcher restricted to s. South America. Although Traylor (1977) suggested that it be merged into *Ochthoeca*, Lanyon (1986) concluded that it would be "prudent" to retain it. The nest is a cup-shaped structure of grass and moss placed close to the ground inside *Nothofagus* (Southern Beech) forest (Marin et al. 1989), apparently often attached to a bamboo stem (A. E. Casas, A. T. García, and M. R. de la Peña, *Hornero* 13[2]: 159–160, 1990).

Colorhamphus parvirostris

PATAGONIAN TYRANT   PLATE: 39

DESCRIPTION: 12 cm (4¾"). *Cen. and especially s. Chile and adjacent s. Argentina.* Short bill. *Head and neck gray,* darker on mid- and hindcrown, and with narrow whitish eye-ring and *blackish patch on earcoverts,* gradually becoming olive brown on back and rump; wings and tail dusky, *wings with 2 broad cinnamon-rufous bars. Throat and breast gray,* gradually becoming buffy whitish on belly.

SIMILAR SPECIES: A small, short-billed, gray and brown flycatcher whose wing-bars are not very obvious when it is in dark, shady undergrowth. There are few other arboreal flycatchers in its range, which is well to the south of any *Ochthoeca* chat-tyrant. See White-crested Elaenia.

HABITAT AND BEHAVIOR: Uncommon to rare at borders of humid forest (including tall *Nothofagus* forest) and in shrubby openings. An inconspicuous small flycatcher, usually found singly, perching upright. Forages at varying levels, perhaps remains lower during austral winter. Nesting birds usually feed quite high above the ground, though their nests are placed low. Patagonian Tyrants are most likely to be noted once their distinctive call—a drawn-out, fairly high, quavering, and rather melancholy "pseeeuwww"—is recognized. This call is also occasionally given during migration and in winter.

RANGE: Breeds in s. Chile (north to Valdivia) and adjacent w. Argentina (north to Neuquén) south to Tierra del Fuego (where very scarce); during austral winter migrates north in Chile to Coquimbo. Old records from Buenos Aires, Argentina, have not been verified. Below 1000 m.

Ochthoeca and *Silvicultrix* Chat-Tyrants

The chat-tyrants are attractively patterned midsized flycatchers found in the Andes, some species in forest, others in much more open areas. Most species have a bold wide superciliary (white to yellow or buff), and many also show prominent rufescent wing-bars. The chat-tyrants perch erectly, frequently flicking their tails; unlike so many other Andean tyrants, they tend not to follow mixed flocks. It was recently proposed (Lanyon 1986) that, based on anatomical considerations, a group of four forest understory chat-tyrants (Yellow-bellied, Golden-browed, Crowned, and Jelski's) be separated from *Ochthoeca* and placed in a new genus, *Silvicultrix*. We have accepted this change, but because the two groups at least superficially look so much like each other, we present and discuss them together.

GROUP A

Ochthoeca cinnamomeiventris

Smaller species, favoring forest undergrowth and edge.

SLATY-BACKED CHAT-TYRANT

PLATE: 39

DESCRIPTION: 12–12.5 cm (4¾–5″). *A mainly blackish chat-tyrant (most subspecies with some chestnut below) found near Andean streams.* Geographically variable; perhaps more than 1 species involved. Proceeding from the south: *thoracica* (cen. Peru south to Bolivia) is *mostly slaty blackish* with a short white superciliary and *wide band of dark maroon-chestnut across chest; angustifasciata* (n. Peru) is similar but with somewhat narrower chest band. The northern 2 subspecies are quite different and both have slightly shorter white supraloral: nominate race of Colombia and Ecuador (as well as extreme sw. Venezuela and extreme n. Peru) is *mostly chestnut below,* with only throat and crissum blackish (see C-38), whereas *nigrita* of w. Venezuela is *all blackish below* (see V-29).

SIMILAR SPECIES: Despite the geographic variation, this distinctively patterned and colored species is unlikely to be confused.

HABITAT AND BEHAVIOR: Fairly common in shrubbery at borders of montane forest and secondary woodland and in adjacent clearings, almost always near water (at least the nominate form), typically a rushing mountain stream. Often in pairs, perching rather low just inside forest or at edge, making short sallies into the air. Often inconspicuous because of its dark plumage, though its calls do attract attention. The most common vocalization of nominate form is a sharp and quite loud (easily heard over the sound of rushing water) "dzzweee-yew," often tirelessly repeated; that of *thoracica* is a very different, higher-pitched "tseeeeeyeeee," reminiscent of a *Pipreola* fruiteater though not quite so sibilant; the voice of *nigrita* is not known to us.

RANGE: Andes of w. Venezuela (Mérida, w. Barinas, and Táchira), Colombia, Ecuador (south on w. slope to Chimborazo), e. Peru, and w. Bolivia (La Paz and Cochabamba). Mostly 1600–3000 m.

NOTE: More than a single species is probably involved. Not only are there dramatic plumage differences between the three basic "types," but vocally two of them are quite distinct. If split, *O. thoracica* (with *angustifasciata*) of Bolivia and most of Peru would be known as the Chestnut-belted Chat-Tyrant; *O. nigrita* of w. Venezuela as the Blackish Chat-Tyrant; and *O cinnamomeiventris* of (mostly) Colombia and Ecuador would remain the Slaty-backed Chat-Tyrant. The three were considered full species by Hellmayr (*Birds of the Americas*, vol. 13, part 5) but then were treated as conspecific by J. T. Zimmer (*Am. Mus. Novitates* 930, 1937), who has been followed by all authors since. The break between *nigrita* and *cinnamomeiventris* apparently occurs at the "Táchira Depression" in sw. Venezuela, whereas that between *thoracica* (*angustifasciata*) and *cinnamomeiventris* occurs basically at the "Marañón Depression" in n. Peru (though *angustifasciata* is known from west of the upper Río Marañón at Chira in Cajamarca [ANSP]).

Silvicultrix diadema

YELLOW-BELLIED CHAT-TYRANT   PLATE: 39

DESCRIPTION: 12 cm (4¾″). Venezuela to n. Peru. Above mostly brownish olive, darker on crown, with *prominent yellow frontal area and superciliary* (latter somewhat paler behind eye); wings and tail duskier, wings with 2 fairly prominent rufous wing-bars. *Below yellowish olive*, most strongly olive across breast. Foregoing applies to *gratiosa* group, ranging north to Cen. and W. Andes of Colombia (also on Sierra de Perijá). Nominate group (Venezuela aside from the Perijá, E. Andes and Santa Marta Mts. of Colombia) has wings plain dusky with wing-bars obscure; see V-29.

SIMILAR SPECIES: *The only chat-tyrant with yellowish underparts*. As rear part of superciliary may be pale yellowish, this species can be confused with Crowned or Jelski's Chat-Tyrants, though both of those have gray underparts; Golden-browed Chat-Tyrant, which has superciliary much like Yellow-bellied, likewise has *gray* underparts. Also superficially like Citrine Warbler in plumage (especially those races of chat-tyrant that *lack* rufous wing-bars), but shape and behavior very different.

HABITAT AND BEHAVIOR: Uncommon to locally fairly common in undergrowth inside montane forest, less often at forest borders, but rarely or never out into clearings. Generally avoids areas dominated by bamboo. Inconspicuous, usually in pairs which stay close to the ground in dense undergrowth, making short sallies to foliage. The call in Venezuela is a distinctive, fast, accelerating, and rising trill lasting several seconds and sometimes ending with a separated lower note.

RANGE: Mts. of n. Venezuela (Aragua and Distrito Federal), and Andes of w. Venezuela (north to Trujillo), Colombia (not recorded in W. Andes north of Valle), nw. and e. Ecuador (on w. slope south to Pichincha), and n. Peru (Piura and Cajamarca); Sierra de Perijá on

Colombia-Venezuela border and Santa Marta Mts. of n. Colombia. Mostly 2000–2900 m.

NOTE: Formerly placed in the genus *Ochthoeca*.

Silvicultrix pulchella

GOLDEN-BROWED CHAT-TYRANT

DESCRIPTION: 12 cm (4¾″). *E. slope of Andes in Peru and Bolivia* does not include Jelski's Chat-Tyrant. Above mostly dark brown, grayer on head and neck, more rufescent on lower back and rump, with *frontal area and long superciliary golden yellow;* wings with *2 broad and bright rufous wing-bars.* Below uniform dark gray, whiter on midbelly, with some rufous-buff on lower flanks and crissum.

SIMILAR SPECIES: Crowned Chat-Tyrant is similar but shows yellow on frontal area only (its superciliary is *white*); it and Golden-browed usually segregate by altitude (Golden-browed lower). See also Jelski's Chat-Tyrant.

HABITAT AND BEHAVIOR: Uncommon in lower growth of montane forest and shrubby forest borders. Quiet and unobtrusive, usually found singly or in pairs in shady ravines and tangled places; most often not with flocks. Its call is reported to be a distinctive "te-tirrrr" (Koepcke 1970).

RANGE: E. slope of Andes in Peru (north to Amazonas) and w. Bolivia (La Paz, Cochabamba, and w. Santa Cruz). Mostly 2000–2800 m, occasionally somewhat higher or lower.

NOTE: See comments under Jelski's Chat-Tyrant. Formerly placed in the genus *Ochthoeca*.

Silvicultrix frontalis

CROWNED CHAT-TYRANT ·   PLATE: 39

DESCRIPTION: 12.5 cm (5″). Andes of Colombia to Bolivia. Above mostly dark brown, grayer on head and neck, with *frontal area bright yellow and long white superciliary;* wings and tail dusky. Below uniform dark gray with dull rufous-buff crissum. *Albidiadema* (E. Andes of Colombia) similar but with all-white frontal band and superciliary. *Spodionota* (Bolivia and Peru north to Huánuco) differs from above 2 races (which occur south to La Libertad, Peru) in usually showing fairly prominent rufous wing-bars (sometimes only 1, occasionally none at all) and in having less rufous-buff on crissum (often none at all).

SIMILAR SPECIES: Closely resembles Jelski's Chat-Tyrant, but in area of potential or actual sympatry (s. Ecuador and n. Peru) Crowned Chat-Tyrant has *plain wings* (prominent rufous wing-bars in Jelski's); note too that Jelski's tends to occur at *lower* elevations than Crowned. Golden-browed Chat-Tyrant has an all-yellow superciliary, but otherwise it too resembles Crowned; Golden-browed also occurs mostly at lower elevations than Crowned.

HABITAT AND BEHAVIOR: Uncommon to locally fairly common in lower growth of stunted forest, montane forest borders, and shrubby thickets, mostly just below treeline; at least in Ecuador also occurs in *Polylepis* woodland. An inconspicuous and easily overlooked small flycatcher, usually perching low in undergrowth, most often alone and rarely with mixed flocks. Rather silent, though it has been heard to give a very thin trill (D. Stotz).

RANGE: Andes of Colombia (E. Andes north to Norte de Santander, Cen. Andes north to Caldas, W. Andes on Páramo Frontino in Antioquia and in w. Nariño), Ecuador (south on w. slope to Azuay), e. Peru, and w. Bolivia (La Paz, Cochabamba, and w. Santa Cruz). Mostly 2500–3500 m, but locally up to 4000 m (at least in Ecuador), and at least occasionally down to about 1600 m in Bolivia.

NOTE: Formerly placed in the genus *Ochthoeca*.

Silvicultrix jelskii

JELSKI'S CHAT-TYRANT

DESCRIPTION: 12 cm (4¾"). *S. Ecuador and nw. Peru;* formerly considered conspecific with Golden-browed Chat-Tyrant. Most resembles Crowned Chat-Tyrant but always shows *2 prominent rufous wing-bars* (wings plain in nearly sympatric race of Crowned) and is not as dark brown above or dark gray below.

SIMILAR SPECIES: Jelski's also resembles Golden-browed Chat-Tyrant, but brow of Jelski's is mostly white, with yellow restricted to frontal area. Jelski's Chat-Tyrant is not known to occur on the actual *east* slope of Andes, where in its range Crowned and Golden-browed Chat-Tyrants take over; however, their ranges can come close.

HABITAT AND BEHAVIOR: Uncommon in lower growth of montane forest and secondary woodland and in borders and adjacent shrubby areas. Behavior similar to Crowned Chat-Tyrant's, and probably equally quiet; we have not heard it vocalize.

RANGE: Locally in s. Ecuador (Loja) and w. Peru (south to w. Huánuco and Lima). 1300–2800 m in Ecuador and n. Peru, 2600–3400 m southward.

NOTE: Until recently considered a race of *O. pulchella*, this taxon was raised to full species status by M. E. Traylor, Jr. (*Neotropical Ornithology*, AOU Monograph no. 36, pp. 430–442, 1985). Formerly placed in the genus *Ochthoeca*.

Ochthoeca rufipectoralis

RUFOUS-BREASTED CHAT-TYRANT   PLATE: 39

DESCRIPTION: 13.5 cm (5¼"). Mainly Andes from Colombia to Bolivia. Above sooty brown to brown, darker and grayer on crown, with *long and broad white superciliary;* wings and tail blackish, wings with *single broad rufous bar,* tail with outer web of outermost rectrix white. Upper throat grayish, with *broad orange-rufous band across chest;* lower underparts grayish white to white. Nominate race (s. Peru north to Cuzco and in Bolivia) similar but with plain wings.

SIMILAR SPECIES: Should not be confused; no other similar chat-tyrant has a contrasting rufous pectoral band.

HABITAT AND BEHAVIOR: Fairly common at borders and openings of montane forest and secondary woodland; often along roads. Perky and attractive, usually found singly or in pairs, regularly perching in the open, usually at middle levels to subcanopy, from there making short sallies into the air and to foliage. More conspicuous and easily seen than the preceding several species. Sometimes follows mixed flocks, but at least as often found away from them.

RANGE: Andes of Colombia, Ecuador (south on w. slope to Azuay), e. Peru, and w. Bolivia (La Paz, Cochabamba, and w. Santa Cruz); Sierra de Perijá on Colombia-Venezuela border and Santa Marta Mts. of n. Colombia. Mostly 2500–3400 m.

GROUP B

Larger and rangier species (except *O. piurae*), more conspicuous in *semiopen scrub.*

Ochthoeca leucophrys

WHITE-BROWED CHAT-TYRANT   PLATE: 39

DESCRIPTION: 14.5–15 cm (5¾–6"). *Andes of Peru to nw. Argentina;* overall the *grayest* chat-tyrant. Above uniform brownish gray with *long broad frontal area and superciliary white;* tail dusky with outer web of outermost rectrix white. *Below uniform pale gray,* becoming whitish on belly. Birds from Peru and n. Chile (including *leucometopa*) have *wings plain* or with at most faint rufescent wing-bars; those from Bolivia and Argentina (nominate race and *tucumana*) have *2 broad rufous wing-bars* as well as a browner lower back.

SIMILAR SPECIES: D'Orbigny's Chat-Tyrant is mostly rufous below. Cf. also Piura Chat-Tyrant (found only in nw. Peru). Plain-capped Ground-Tyrant is similarly colored to more northerly White-browed Chat-Tyrants (those lacking wing-bars), but its shape and comportment are very different.

HABITAT AND BEHAVIOR: Uncommon to fairly common in shrubby areas, patches of woodland, and hedgerows, mostly in quite arid regions. Usually in pairs which typically take prominent perches, often along fences or atop a bush or low tree, from which they make short sallies into the air or drop to ground. Their frequently heard call is a sharp "queeuw."

RANGE: Andes of Peru (north to Piura and Cajamarca), extreme n. Chile (Tarapacá), w. Bolivia, and nw. Argentina (south to San Juan). Mostly 2000–3500 m, but in Peru, especially in Arequipa, occurs locally and in smaller numbers down to or near sea level.

Ochthoeca piurae

PIURA CHAT-TYRANT

DESCRIPTION: 12.5 cm (5"). *Nw. Peru.* Very similar to s. races of White-browed Chat-Tyrant (*with broad rufous wing-bars*) but *much smaller.* Note that potentially sympatric Peruvian races of White-browed have *wings plain or virtually so.*

SIMILAR SPECIES: Jelski's Chat-Tyrant also has rufous wing-bars, but its yellow frontal area and darker gray underparts distinguish it.

HABITAT AND BEHAVIOR: Uncommon on shrubby hillsides and at edge of montane woodland patches. Behavior similar to White-browed Chat-Tyrant's, with which it occurs sympatrically at certain localities in Ancash. Small numbers can be found along w. side of the Porculla Pass road in Lambayeque.

RANGE: Locally in Andes of nw. Peru (Piura south to Ancash). 1500–2800 m.

Ochthoeca fumicolor

BROWN-BACKED CHAT-TYRANT   PLATE: 39

DESCRIPTION: 14.5–15 cm (5¾–6"). Andes from Venezuela to Bolivia. Over most of its extensive range the only chat-tyrant with *mainly rufescent underparts*. Above mostly rufous brown, most rufescent on back and rump, with *long broad buffy whitish frontal area and superciliary;* wings and tail blackish, wings with *2 conspicuous rufous wing-bars* (the lower one wider). Throat and lower face grayish; *remaining underparts cinnamon-rufous.* Southernmost race, *berlepschi* (s. Peru and Bolivia), has a narrower and whiter superciliary. Nominate race (E. Andes of Colombia and adjacent Venezuela) is much dingier and less rufescent below, but *superciliosa* (remainder of Venezuelan Andes) is much brighter, with *rufous superciliary and breast,* fading to buff on belly; see V-29.
SIMILAR SPECIES: D'Orbigny's Chat-Tyrant, which is also rufescent below, differs from locally sympatric race (*berlepschi*) of Brown-backed in e. Peru and w. Bolivia in its much less prominent wing-bars, pure white superciliary with no trace of buff, and grayer (not so brown) upperparts.
HABITAT AND BEHAVIOR: Fairly common to common in semiopen shrubby areas, borders of montane woodland, stunted forest near timberline, and groves of *Polylepis* woodland; sometimes out into adjacent páramo, especially where there are a few scattered low trees or bushes. Usually conspicuous, often perching on shrubs or low trees, sallying out a short distance into the air or to the ground, then flitting on to another perch. Generally confiding, though it may flick its tail in alarm; pairs may cover considerable distances while foraging. Most often quiet but occasionally gives a soft "pseeu" call.
RANGE: Andes of w. Venezuela (north to Trujillo), Colombia, Ecuador, Peru (south on w. slope to Lima), and w. Bolivia (La Paz and Cochabamba). Mostly 2600–4200 m.

NOTE: The abrupt shift in w. Venezuela from a very bright form (*superciliosa*) to the dingiest race of the species (nominate *fumicolor*) makes us suspect that separate species may be involved. The break apparently occurs on either side of the "Táchira Depression"; to our knowledge, no intergrades between these two taxa are known. If split, *O. superciliosa* could be known as the Rufous-browed Chat-Tyrant.

Ochthoeca oenanthoides

D'ORBIGNY'S CHAT-TYRANT

DESCRIPTION: 14.5–15 cm (5¾–6"). *Andes of Peru to nw. Argentina.* Above grayish brown with *long broad frontal band and superciliary white;* wings and tail duskier, wings virtually plain, outer web of outermost rectrix white. Throat grayish, *remaining underparts cinnamon-rufous.* S. nominate race (north to southernmost Peru in Puno and Tacna) is slightly smaller and generally paler than *polionota* (of most of Peru), and has more prominent rufous wing-bars.
SIMILAR SPECIES: Brown-backed Chat-Tyrant is browner (not so grayish) above with a buffyish superciliary and much more conspicuous rufous wing-bars. The two species occur together in a few places,

but in general D'Orbigny's favors more open and arid areas, Brown-backed more densely vegetated and humid ones mainly at or near edge of timberline on *east* slope of Andes.

HABITAT AND BEHAVIOR: Uncommon to fairly common in shrubby areas and patches of low woodland such as *Polylepis* stands, often near water and regularly along small rushing streams. General behavior similar to White-browed Chat-Tyrant's but less conspicuous and more tied to woodland, less frequently out into semiopen or partially cultivated areas; D'Orbigny's occurs mostly at higher elevations. Not very vocal, but breeding males do have a rollicking and semimusical "reeka-teeekera, reeka-teekera, reeka-teekera . . . ," with variations.

RANGE: Andes of Peru (north to La Libertad and w. Huánuco), extreme n. Chile (Tarapacá), w. Bolivia, and nw. Argentina (south to La Rioja). Mostly 3200–4400 m.

Myiotheretes Bush-Tyrants

Restricted to higher elevations in the Andes, the bush-tyrants are large flycatchers of rather diverse appearance and behavior. All show cinnamon or rufous in the wing (particularly noticeable in flight and from below); most also have some rufous in the tail as well and have some throat streaking and/or rufous on lower underparts.

We follow Lanyon (1986) in his separation of two large species, the Red-rumped and Rufous-webbed, into monotypic genera; these were formerly usually placed in *Myiotheretes*. Note also that what was long called "Jelski's Bush-Tyrant," *Myiotheretes signatus* (see Meyer de Schauensee 1966, 1970), was shown by Traylor (1982) to be a synonym of *Knipolegus cabanisi* (Andean Tyrant).

GROUP A

Smaller, forest-based bush-tyrants.

Myiotheretes fumigatus

SMOKY BUSH-TYRANT

PLATE: 39

DESCRIPTION: 20.5 cm (8"). *A dark, nondescript, almost thrush-like flycatcher of Andean forests. Mostly uniform sooty brown* with short whitish superciliary and some whitish mottling on lower face and throat; wings and tail blackish, wing-coverts very faintly edged buffyish, and with *cinnamon underwing-coverts and band along base of flight feathers* (the band hidden in closed wing but showing as a prominent stripe in flight). *Lugubris* (Venezuelan Andes south to n. Táchira) has a reduced superciliary and an ochraceous crissum; see V-28.

SIMILAR SPECIES: Although relatively patternless, this dark flycatcher should not be confusing as the startling cinnamon in the wing will instantly be seen once it takes flight.

HABITAT AND BEHAVIOR: Uncommon to locally fairly common in montane forest, often at borders, foraging at all levels. Seems less numerous in Peru. Found singly or in pairs, frequently following mixed flocks. Tends to perch just below the canopy, from which it flies out to snap an insect from foliage or a limb. It is relatively quiet.

RANGE: Andes of w. Venezuela (north to Trujillo), Colombia, Ecuador, and Peru (south to Cuzco; on w. slope south to Cajamarca); Sierra de Perijá on Venezuela-Colombia border. Mostly 2000–3200 m, in smaller numbers somewhat lower and higher.

Myiotheretes pernix

SANTA MARTA BUSH-TYRANT

DESCRIPTION: 19 cm (7½″). *Colombia's Santa Marta Mts.* Above dark brown with whitish lores; wings duskier, coverts and inner flight feathers narrowly edged rufous, and with cinnamon wing pattern similar to Smoky Bush-Tyrant's; *tail blackish with only outer web of outermost rectrix rufous.* Throat whitish, narrowly and obscurely streaked black; *remaining underparts deep rich rufous,* tinged olive on chest. See C-38.

SIMILAR SPECIES: In its limited range liable to be confused only with Streak-throated Bush-Tyrant, which is markedly larger and paler (especially below) and shows more cinnamon-rufous on tail and more prominent throat streaking.

HABITAT AND BEHAVIOR: Uncommon at borders of montane forest and woodland, less often out into adjacent shrubby clearings. Behavior similar to Streak-throated Bush-Tyrant's, even though Santa Marta is believed to be more closely related to Smoky Bush-Tyrant. Usually sallies into the air from a prominent perch at edge of forest or atop a bush. Occurs at lower elevations on the San Lorenzo road than Streak-throated and is more closely associated with forest edge. We do not know its voice.

RANGE: Santa Marta Mts. of n. Colombia. 2100–2900 m.

Myiotheretes fuscorufus

RUFOUS-BELLIED BUSH-TYRANT

DESCRIPTION: 19 cm (7½″). *E. slope of Andes in s. Peru and Bolivia.* Above mainly brown with a short whitish superciliary; wings blackish with *2 broad rufous bars and prominent edging on inner flight feathers* and with cinnamon underwing-coverts and wide band along base of flight feathers (the band showing as a prominent stripe in flight); tail mostly blackish with outer web of outermost rectrix, and edging on all inner webs, cinnamon. Throat whitish, remaining underparts cinnamon-rufous, *obscurely* streaked and mottled with brownish olive on lower throat and chest.

SIMILAR SPECIES: This species shows much more rufous on *closed* wing than any of the other bush-tyrants; it is the *only* one with actual wing-bars, and would better have been called the "Rufous-banded Bush-Tyrant" as most of the bush-tyrants have rufous bellies. Cf. especially the larger Streak-throated Bush-Tyrant, which differs in its bold, sharp throat streaking, much more cinnamon-rufous in tail, etc.

HABITAT AND BEHAVIOR: Rare to uncommon at borders of montane forest and secondary woodland, sometimes out into adjacent clearings. Most often in pairs, perching in the understory just inside forest or at edge of clearings, thence sallying to foliage and into the air. Unlike Smoky Bush-Tyrant (with which it is locally sympatric in s. Peru), this species seems less prone to accompany mixed flocks. We do not know its voice. Can be found in forest on n. side of the Abra Málaga road in Cuzco, Peru.

RANGE: E. slope of Andes in s. Peru (north to Pasco) and w. Bolivia (La Paz and Cochabamba). 1900–2900 m.

GROUP B   *Large* bush-tyrant of semiopen areas.

Myiotheretes striaticollis

STREAK-THROATED BUSH-TYRANT   PLATE: 39

DESCRIPTION: 23 cm (9″). Generally *the most numerous and widespread bush-tyrant*. Above mostly brown with whitish supraloral; wings dusky, with varying (depending on molt stage) amounts of cinnamon-rufous edging and with *cinnamon underwing-coverts and wide band along base of flight feathers* (the band showing as a prominent stripe in flight); from above tail looks mostly dusky but with much cinnamon on basal two-thirds of all but central pair of feathers (*from below tail looks cinnamon with terminal third dusky*). Throat and upper chest white *sharply and boldly streaked blackish*, becoming uniform cinnamon-rufous on remaining underparts. *Pallidus* (s. Peru south) somewhat paler generally, with slightly less crisp throat streaking.

SIMILAR SPECIES: Even at a distance the cinnamon in wings and tail and the throat streaking are usually apparent. Cf. smaller and range-restricted Santa Marta and Rufous-bellied Bush-Tyrants, both of which tend to occur in more wooded habitats. At first glance, Streak-throated might be confused with certain *Turdus* thrushes.

HABITAT AND BEHAVIOR: Uncommon to fairly common in semiopen regions, often partially cultivated terrain with shrubby areas and woodland patches; tends to avoid extensively forested regions, where most often around natural openings such as near cliffs or landslides and at roadside cuts. Although conspicuous, Streak-throated Bush-Tyrant is never really numerous and always occurs at low densities. Found alone or in pairs, sallying out from exposed perches, sometimes for great distances; often perches very high above ground, even on high-tension wires. Drops to ground less often. Not very vocal but gives a loud, clear, rising whistle, "pseeeeeee?" with a human quality.

RANGE: Andes of w. Venezuela (north to Mérida), Colombia, Ecuador, Peru (south on w. slope to Arequipa), w. Bolivia, and nw. Argentina (south to Tucumán and Catamarca); Sierra de Perijá on Venezuela-Colombia border and Santa Marta Mts. in n. Colombia. Mostly 2000–3500 m, but occurs lower (to 500–1000 m; seasonally?) in s. Peru, Bolivia, and Argentina.

Polioxolmis Bush-Tyrants

Lanyon (1986) proposed a new monotypic genus for this local, narrow-billed bush-tyrant of high Andean woodlands. It had previously been placed either in *Xolmis* (Meyer de Schauensee 1966, 1970) or *Myiotheretes* (*Birds of the World*, vol. 8).

Polioxolmis rufipennis

RUFOUS-WEBBED BUSH-TYRANT   PLATE: 39

Other: Rufous-webbed Tyrant

DESCRIPTION: 21–21.5 cm (8¼–8½"). *A mostly ashy gray bush-tyrant of high Andes in Peru, Bolivia, and adjacent Argentina.* Above uniform ashy gray with whitish supraloral; closed wing essentially plain, but *underwing-coverts and wide band along base of flight feathers cinnamon* (the band showing as a prominent stripe in flight); from above tail mostly dusky, with outer web of outermost rectrix white and inner web of all but central pair cinnamon with dusky tips. *Below slightly paler ashy gray,* becoming white on lower belly and crissum. *Bolivianus* (Puno, Peru, southward) is slightly smaller and a bit duller gray than nominate race of most of Peruvian range (also w. Oruro, Bolivia).

SIMILAR SPECIES: In overall coloration more reminiscent of a shrike-tyrant, but the rufous patterning in wings and tail is very different.

HABITAT AND BEHAVIOR: Rare to uncommon and local in low woodland and shrubbery near timberline and in *Polylepis* groves and adjacent scrub, usually where there are boulders or cliff faces. Generally alone or in pairs, it perches conspicuously atop a bush or low tree, then drops to the ground in pursuit of insect prey; aerial sallies are made less often. The call is a fairly high-pitched "tree" given at intervals throughout the day (Fjeldså and Krabbe 1990). Small numbers can be seen in Peru in the Cordillera Blanca of Ancash and the upper Santa Eulalia valley of Lima, and in Bolivia along the road between Oruro and Cochabamba.

RANGE: Andes of Peru (north locally to Cajamarca and Amazonas, south on w. slope to Arequipa), w. Bolivia, and nw. Argentina (1 seen near Lago Pozuelos in Jujuy in Nov. 1986; RSR et al.); seems possible in extreme n. Chile. Mostly 3000–4300 m, occasionally somewhat lower.

NOTE: J. Fjeldså (*Bull. B. O. C.* 110[1]: 26–31, 1990) presents more distributional, taxonomic, and natural history information, including the description of *bolivianus*.

Cnemarchus Bush-Tyrants

Lanyon (1986) presented the rationale for separating this attractive bush-tyrant into a monotypic genus apart from *Myiotheretes*. It is a boldly patterned, rather narrow-billed tyrannid of high Andean scrub and semiopen areas.

Cnemarchus erythropygius

RED-RUMPED BUSH-TYRANT   PLATE: 39

DESCRIPTION: 23 cm (9"). Virtually unmistakable. *Forecrown white streaked gray, becoming solid pale gray on hindcrown and nape,* with vague white superciliary; above otherwise brownish slate with *contrasting rufous rump;* wings blackish with *conspicuous white patch on tertials* and cinnamon underwing-coverts; central tail feathers blackish, *others rufous with terminal third black.* Throat streaked gray and white, becoming solid gray on breast and sharply rufous on belly.

HABITAT AND BEHAVIOR: Rare to locally uncommon in mostly open areas with scattered shrubs and low trees (including *Polylepis* groves), regularly foraging out into adjacent open páramo and puna grasslands. Found singly or in pairs, perching on fences, boulders, or bushes and dropping to the ground for prey, less often sallying to the air. Seems always to occur at very low densities; though conspicuous, never frequently recorded. Its call is reported to be similar to Streak-throated Bush-Tyrant's (T. A. Parker III, *in* Hilty and Brown 1986).

RANGE: Locally in Andes of Colombia (recorded only from E. Andes in Norte de Santander and Cundinamarca, and in Nariño), Ecuador (south on w. slope to Azuay), e. Peru, and w. Bolivia (La Paz and Cochabamba); Santa Marta Mts. in n. Colombia. Mostly 3000–4000 m.

Hirundinea Flycatchers

A distinctive flycatcher with a rather long, basally-broad bill and long, pointed, somewhat swallow-like wings, perfectly suited for its extended, graceful sallies after passing insects. Its habitat, cliffs (or their artificial equivalents, the sides of buildings or roadcuts), is equally distinctive. Recent evidence indicates that the closest relative of the genus *Hirundinea* is the much smaller *Pyrrhomias* (Traylor and Fitzpatrick 1982, Lanyon 1986). We have placed *Hirundinea* here, however, next to the *Myiotheretes* bush-tyrants, because of their similar wing and tail coloration, behavior, and habitat.

Hirundinea ferruginea

CLIFF FLYCATCHER   PLATE: 39

DESCRIPTION: 18.5 cm (7¼"). *Almost always on or near cliffs or buildings.* Two quite distinct "types." S. group (*bellicosa* and *pallidior*; Bolivia and Brazil south) mostly brown above with some whitish on lores and *conspicuous cinnamon-rufous rump and basal half of tail;* closed wing dusky with edging on coverts and *most of flight feathers conspicuously rufous;* underwing-coverts cinnamon-rufous. Below mostly cinnamon-rufous, mottled grayish on throat. Andean *sclateri* much darker, more blackish brown above with *whitish grizzling on face and crown;* from below, tail mostly dark with cinnamon-rufous at base, wings blacker with no rufous edging on coverts. Tepui and Guianan *ferruginea* similar to *sclateri* but with whitish grizzling restricted to face, and tail all dark; see V-28.

SIMILAR SPECIES: Habitat and behavior, together with the conspicuous rufous in wing, make this species virtually unmistakable. Overall pattern and behavior reminiscent of much larger Streak-throated Bush-Tyrant (which has streaking on throat, etc.).

HABITAT AND BEHAVIOR: Fairly common but local around cliffs and rocky canyons, exposed granite outcroppings, and roadcuts. At least in s. part of range also frequent around buildings, and now resides in various towns and cities (even in bustling downtown districts), the facades and window ledges of buildings replacing its normal rocky habitat. Southernmost breeders are apparently migratory, and in austral winter migrants are occasionally seen far from rocks or buildings.

Usually in pairs, sometimes family groups, perching on rock ledges or overhanging vegetation or on buildings and adjacent wires, making long swooping sallies far into the air. Nervous and excitable though sometimes quite tame, almost oblivious to passing people and noisy traffic, often keeping up a constant chatter of high-pitched calls, including a "wheeeyp!" or "whee, dee-dee-ee-ee-ee" or "wha-deép, wha-deép . . ."; there seems to be no geographic variation in vocalizations. RANGE: Sierra de Perijá on Venezuela-Colombia border, and locally on e. slope of Andes in w. Venezuela (w. Barinas), Colombia, Ecuador, and Peru (south to Cuzco); tepui region of s. Venezuela (Bolívar and Amazonas), adjacent e. Colombia (Guainía and Vaupés), and very locally in Guianas; w. Bolivia (north to s. La Paz) and w. Argentina (south to Córdoba, San Luis, and Mendoza); cen. and e. Brazil (north to s. Mato Grosso, se. Pará, and Ceará; some n. records may pertain to austral migrants, with actual n. limit of breeding uncertain), e. Bolivia (e. Santa Cruz), Paraguay (few or no records from the chaco), Uruguay, and ne. Argentina (Misiones; recorded west to Formosa and Chaco in nonbreeding season). Mostly below 2000 m, but locally to over 3000 m in Bolivia.

NOTE: Two species may be involved, as suggested by Sibley and Monroe (1990). The distributions of the two groups, which differ markedly in plumage pattern and coloration, approach each other closely in the Andes of s. Peru with no evidence of intergradation, but as yet no specimens are available from the critical intervening area in Puno, Peru. In their absence, and given the general similarity in form and behavior of the two groups, we retain the traditional single-species treatment. Should they be split, *H. ferruginea* (with *sclateri*) might best be called the Northern Cliff-Flycatcher, *H. bellicosa* (with *pallidior*) the Southern Cliff-Flycatcher.

Agriornis Shrike-Tyrants

A distinct group of big, heavy-bodied flycatchers found in open places in the Andes and Patagonia; if lengthened tail feathers are excluded, the Great Shrike-Tyrant is the largest flycatcher. Shrike-tyrants are named for their prominently hooked bills, used to capture relatively large, even vertebrate, prey. One, the Lesser, is much smaller and has a less hooked bill. Lesser, Great, and Gray-bellied Shrike-Tyrants place their bulky cup-shaped stick nests in bushes, whereas Black-billed usually places its nest in crevices (often in walls or roofs of buildings); White-tailed's nest is apparently undescribed.

GROUP A

Small shrike-tyrant. Mainly Argentina.

Agriornis murina

LESSER SHRIKE-TYRANT

PLATE: 40

Other: Mouse-brown Monjita, Mouse-brown Shrike-Tyrant

DESCRIPTION: 18.5 cm (7¼"). Breeds on Patagonian steppes, migrating northward. *Bill rather slender and slightly hooked. Above pale grayish brown* with indistinct whitish supraloral; wings dusky with whitish edging on wing-coverts and inner flight feathers; tail dusky with outer

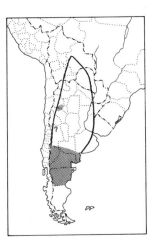

web of outermost pair of feathers whitish. *Throat white with fairly prominent dusky streaking,* becoming very pale grayish brown on breast and creamy whitish on belly, often tinged buff on flanks.

SIMILAR SPECIES: Other shrike-tyrants are markedly larger with thicker bills. Cf. especially Gray-bellied Shrike-Tyrant, with which Lesser is widely sympatric; aside from Gray-bellied's much bolder throat streaking, they are quite similar in coloration.

HABITAT AND BEHAVIOR: Uncommon to fairly common on open Patagonian plains with scattered shrubs during breeding season; at other times found in open scrub, sometimes with a few taller trees, or agricultural areas. Perches on top of shrubs, dropping to the ground for prey, then often running a considerable distance before flying back up to another elevated perch.

RANGE: Breeds in s. and w. Argentina (mainly from Neuquén and extreme sw. Buenos Aires south to s. Chubut; recently a few have also been found nesting in s. La Rioja and Catamarca); in austral winter (about May–Sept.) migrates north through much of the rest of Argentina (except the far northeast) to w. Paraguay and s. Bolivia (north to Cochabamba and w. Santa Cruz). To about 2500 (during austral winter in Bolivia).

NOTE: Formerly placed in the genus *Xolmis* (e.g., Meyer de Schauensee 1966, 1970). Smith and Vuilleumier (1971) suggested that *murina* be transferred to the genus *Agriornis*, which it resembles in plumage color and pattern, and this has been followed by virtually all authors since. However, it must be pointed out that in overall form, relatively fine and pointed bill shape, and behavior *murina* more resembles a *Xolmis* than an *Agriornis*. Further (*fide* R. Straneck), it has an aerial display, like most or all *Xolmis* but unlike any *Agriornis*. In sum, *murina* appears to be intermediate between the two genera and represents an argument for their merger. For the present, however, we opt to continue to place it in *Agriornis*, though doing so creates an English name difficulty. The species was formerly called the Mouse-brown Monjita, fine when it is considered a *Xolmis* (none of which is similarly colored), but very inappropriate when it is considered an *Agriornis* (all of which have similar coloration). Olrog (1984) suggested the name of Lesser Shrike-Tyrant, and this is employed here.

GROUP B

Typical, *large* shrike-tyrants with *strongly hooked bills*.

Agriornis montana

BLACK-BILLED SHRIKE-TYRANT

PLATE: 40

DESCRIPTION: 24 cm (9½"). *Mainly high open places in Andes*, where the *most numerous and widespread shrike-tyrant*. Hooked bill *black*, with yellowish base of lower mandible in juvenile; adult's iris yellowish to ivory, juvenile's dark. Above uniform grayish brown with indistinct whitish supraloral; white edging on inner flight feathers; *tail mostly white* (very noticeable in flight) with central pair of feathers dusky. *Throat and cheeks white streaked with brown*, becoming pale ashy brown on breast and whitish tinged with clay color on belly. Birds of Ecuador and s. Colombia (*solitaria*) are darker generally than *insolens* of Peru, whereas nominate group (of s. Bolivia southward) resembles *insolens* but shows less white on tail (mainly on outer webs of rectrices), with a variable intermediate population in w. Bolivia.

SIMILAR SPECIES: Cf. especially much rarer and stouter-billed White-tailed Shrike-Tyrant. Gray-bellied Shrike-Tyrant has white only on outer web of outermost rectrix, thus showing *much* less white in tail than even the southerly races of Black-billed. All ground-tyrants also show much less white in tail (White-fronted is most similar).

HABITAT AND BEHAVIOR: Uncommon to fairly common in open shrubby or grassy terrain, especially around buildings, walls, or cliffs. Often seen perched atop a low bush or wall or on a rock, from there dropping to the ground after prey. Also runs on ground. Conspicuous and sometimes tame—occasionally bold almost to the point of seeming oblivious to one's presence—but nonetheless never seen in large numbers because territory size is so large. When flushed, often flies for long distances. Unlike ground-tyrants, does not flock. The seldom-heard call is a loud, ringing, far-carrying "wheee, wheeeu" or just "wheeeu." Residents of many areas call this the *gaucho,* a term also used (at least in Argentina) for other shrike-tyrants; also locally called *arreiro* from the call (F. Vuilleumier).

RANGE: Andes of s. Colombia (Nariño), Ecuador, Peru, w. Bolivia, n. and cen. Chile (south to Cautín), and w. Argentina (mostly in Andes south to w. Santa Cruz, also east across Patagonian steppes to sw. Buenos Aires and in w. Córdoba); accidental on Falkland Is. Mostly 2500–4500 m from Bolivia north, locally down to near sea level in cen. Chile and s. Argentina.

Agriornis andicola

WHITE-TAILED SHRIKE-TYRANT

DESCRIPTION: 26.5 cm (10½"). *Very local* in Andes from Ecuador to nw. Argentina and n. Chile. Resembles Black-billed Shrike-Tyrant, which always greatly outnumbers it. White-tailed differs in its larger size, dark iris, *heavier bill with pale yellowish lower mandible,* and *markedly sharper and blacker throat streaking.* Its tail, despite the English name, shows the *same* amount of white as Black-billed's in n. part of latter's range; in Chile and Argentina, White-tailed's tail does show more white than sympatric races of Black-billed. Recall that juvenile Black-billed has yellowish at least at base of lower mandible (thus usually best to go by bill *shape*).

HABITAT AND BEHAVIOR: Very rare to rare in open shrubby or grassy areas, especially in vicinity of old adobe buildings and walls. Behavior much like Black-billed Shrike-Tyrant's; presumably their different sizes, and especially bills, permit them to coexist. White-tailed is *much* the rarer species: even in areas where it was earlier reported to be relatively numerous (e.g., above Putre, in Arica, Chile), it is now decidedly scarce. There are surprisingly few recent reports of this species, so few that one has to conclude that it is a threatened species, declining for as yet unascertained reasons. In addition to being seen in Chile's Lauca Nat. Park, a few have been noted recently in the Sierra de Aconquija above Tafi del Valle in Tucumán, Argentina.

RANGE: Andes of Ecuador (north to Imbabura), Peru, w. Bolivia,

n. Chile (Tarapacá and Antofagasta), and nw. Argentina (south to Tucumán and n. Catamarca). Mostly 3000–4500 m.

NOTE: This species' correct name is *A. andicola*, not *A. albicauda* (see *Birds of the World*, vol. 8).

Agriornis microptera

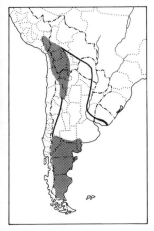

GRAY-BELLIED SHRIKE-TYRANT

DESCRIPTION: 24.5 cm (9¾″). Resembles Great Shrike-Tyrant but smaller and grayer (not so brown) with *much more prominent white supraloral* and lower eyelid, and not nearly as much cinnamon on lower underparts (*merely a tinge of buff on crissum*); outer web of outermost rectrix more sharply and contrastingly white.

SIMILAR SPECIES: Black-billed and White-tailed Shrike-Tyrants have more white on tail. Lesser Shrike-Tyrant is much smaller with less hooked bill and less sharply streaked throat and is generally paler below.

HABITAT AND BEHAVIOR: Uncommon on Patagonian plains with scattered bushes and in puna grasslands with some shrubbery, boulders, etc.; also in open agricultural areas in austral winter. Behavior similar to other shrike-tyrants', like them often perching atop a bush or on a rock or wire, dropping to the ground to pursue prey, sometimes running rapidly. Usually wary, when disturbed often flying away for long distances.

RANGE: Andes of s. Peru (Cuzco and Puno), w. Bolivia, n. Chile (Tarapacá and Antofogasta), and nw. Argentina (south to Catamarca and Tucumán); s. Argentina (Neuquén and s. Buenos Aires south to e. Santa Cruz). S. breeders (nominate race) migrate northward in austral winter (at least June–Oct.), spreading over much of Argentina and occurring north at least casually to Bolivia (Cochabamba), w. Paraguay (where rare but perhaps regular), and s. Uruguay (apparently no recent records). In n. part of range mostly 2000–4000 m, but southward regularly down to sea level.

Agriornis livida

GREAT SHRIKE-TYRANT   PLATE: 40

DESCRIPTION: 26.5–28 cm (10½–11″). *Chile and adjacent s. Argentina;* the *largest* shrike-tyrant, looking very bull-headed. *Heavy and strongly hooked bill* blackish, with at least base of lower mandible yellowish. Mostly dull grayish brown above with some whitish on lores; wings and tail duskier, wing feathers obscurely edged pale brown, outer web of outermost rectrix whitish. *Throat white sharply streaked with black;* remaining underparts slightly paler grayish brown, *lower belly* and especially *crissum washed cinnamon*. Immatures have much less streaking on throat and less cinnamon on lower underparts (F. Vuilleumier). *Fortis* (Argentina and southernmost Chile) somewhat larger than nominate race (rest of Chilean range).

SIMILAR SPECIES: Gray-bellied Shrike-Tyrant is smaller and grayer, has more prominent white supraloral, and lacks cinnamon on lower

underparts. Note that they are more or less allopatric, Gray-bellied out on Patagonian steppes and northward, Great near e. base of Andes and in cen. and s. Chile.

HABITAT AND BEHAVIOR: Rare to uncommon in semiopen shrubby and agricultural regions. Occurs in highly dispersed pairs, perching conspicuously on rocks or atop bushes or fences. Prey items tend to be large, ranging from beetles to lizards and occasionally even nestlings or small birds. M. Rumboll (pers. comm.) has seen it capture and devour a Tufted Tit-Tyrant!

RANGE: Cen. and s. Chile (recorded north to Atacama, but more numerous south of Aconcagua) and s. Argentina (north to w. Neuquén) south to n. Tierra del Fuego (where very rare). Mostly below 1500 m.

Ochthornis Water-Tyrants

A monotypic genus, found along riverbanks across the lowlands of Amazonia. Despite recent suggestions that *Ochthornis* be subsumed into the genus *Ochthoeca* (e.g., Smith and Vuilleumier 1971, Traylor 1977), we favor maintaining it as distinct: its distribution, behavior, and appearance all differ markedly from the *Ochthoeca* and *Silvicultrix* chat-tyrants of the Andes. Recent anatomical evidence (Lanyon 1986) also indicates that the genus *Ochthornis* should be maintained.

Ochthornis littoralis

DRAB WATER-TYRANT   PLATE: 40

DESCRIPTION: 13.5 cm (5¼"). *A nondescript flycatcher of Amaz. riverbanks.* Bill all black. *Mostly pale sandy brown,* palest on rump and underparts, with *white supraloral;* wings and tail plain dusky brown.

SIMILAR SPECIES: Little Ground-Tyrant, sometimes found in same places, is quite similar but has a more slender bill with pale at base of lower mandible, no supraloral, at least indistinct rufescent wing-bars and a white outer rectrix on its otherwise black tail, and a whiter belly (thus not so uniform below). It is more terrestrial than Drab Water-Tyrant. Cf. also Fuscous Flycatcher.

HABITAT AND BEHAVIOR: Fairly common along rivers, especially where there are steep eroding or undercut banks with protruding branches, exposed roots, and accumulated driftwood, but also sometimes on sandbars where there is some vegetation or piles of debris. Absent or rare along grassy river margins or edges of lakes. Usually in pairs which typically perch a few feet above the water, often allowing a close approach, sometimes flushing repeatedly, kingfisher-like, ahead of an approaching boat. Generally quiet, but does give an occasional soft, weak "freee."

RANGE: S. Guyana, s. Venezuela (Bolívar and Amazonas), e. Colombia (north to Meta and Guainía), e. Ecuador, e. Peru, n. Bolivia (south to w. Santa Cruz), and Amaz. Brazil (east to the lower Rio Tapajós area, and south to n. Mato Grosso); n. French Guiana and adjacent n. Amapá, Brazil. To about 500 m.

Muscisaxicola Ground-Tyrants

Slim, terrestrial flycatchers found in open country, often at very high elevations, in the Andes and south to Tierra del Fuego. The genus achieves its highest diversity in s. South America; almost half the species breed only in Chile and Argentina, some of them migrating northward in the austral winter. Ground-tyrants are basically gray or brownish gray, usually with some contrasting color or pattern on the head. All have relatively slender dark or mostly dark bills, long pointed wings, contrasting blackish tails with white outer webs, and long legs. Alert and often wary, they stand erectly between bursts of running on the ground. At other times they may rest motionless facing the wind for long periods, a habit that has earned them the widespread local name *dormilona,* a Spanish vernacular word meaning "sleepy one." All nest in holes, in crevices between rocks, or in stone walls. Most or all breeding ground-tyrants have a display in which the male ascends into the air, flutters more or less in place, then raises its wings high over its back, stalls and drops a few meters, then recovers and repeats the performance. The displaying bird remains silent, or at most utters a simple repeated call; indeed ground-tyrants are quiet birds generally, only seldom making a sound.

GROUP A

Distinctly *small* ground-tyrants with *rufescent wing-edging* (sometimes shown by immatures of other species).

Muscisaxicola maculirostris

SPOT-BILLED GROUND-TYRANT   PLATE: 40

DESCRIPTION: 14–14.5 cm (5½–5¾"). *Base of lower mandible yellow to orange-yellow,* forming the usually inconspicuous "spot." *Above sandy brown* with dusky line through eye and *short white supraloral;* wings duskier, *feathers edged with cinnamon;* tail black with outer web of outermost rectrix whitish. Below *uniform* buffy whitish (in nominate race of Peru southward), or with *breast and belly washed with dull cinnamon-buff* (in n. pair of races in Colombia and Ecuador, *niceforoi* and *rufescens* respectively).

SIMILAR SPECIES: Cf. quite similar Little Ground-Tyrant of Amaz. lowlands, and also female negritos (*Lessonia*). Spot-billed is smaller and markedly browner (not so gray) above than other similar ground-tyrants of Andes and is the only one with cinnamon wing-edging (but beware juveniles of other species, which may also show this).

HABITAT AND BEHAVIOR: Uncommon to fairly common in open barren areas with sparse bushy vegetation (sometimes none at all); seems less numerous in Chile and Argentina. Usually found singly or in pairs, sometimes in small loose groups when not breeding; in particularly favorable habitat nesting pairs may occur in what seem to be loose "colonies." Unlike some other ground-tyrants, Spot-billed shows no particular affinity for water.

RANGE: Andes of n. Colombia (E. Andes in Boyacá and Cundinamarca); Andes of Ecuador (Pichincha to Azuay); and Andes of Peru (north to s. Amazonas and s. Cajamarca), w. Bolivia, Chile (south to Magallanes), and Argentina (south to Santa Cruz; also recorded from w. Córdoba and ne. San Luis), accidentally south to Tierra del Fuego. May withdraw from s. portion of range in austral winter, but no evidence of extensive migration exists. Mostly 2000–4000 m northward, lower in sw. Peru (e.g., the lomas of Arequipa), Chile, and Argentina; occasionally wanders down to sea level.

Muscisaxicola fluviatilis

LITTLE GROUND-TYRANT

DESCRIPTION: 13.5 cm (5¼"). *The only ground-tyrant in Amaz. lowlands.* Resembles Spot-billed Ground-Tyrant of Andes (little or no range overlap). Little's bill (with pale area at base of lower mandible) and rufescent edging on wing feathers are similar; sometimes also shows vague rufescent wing-bars. Little differs in its proportionately shorter tail, virtual lack of a white supraloral, and *contrasting white belly* (underparts of Spot-billed are relatively uniform). See C-38.
SIMILAR SPECIES: Could be confused with Drab Water-Tyrant but differs in its typical ground-tyrant behavior (running on ground, etc.), lack of whitish supraloral and pale rump, white on outer tail feathers, and whiter belly (not relatively uniform below).
HABITAT AND BEHAVIOR: Uncommon and rather local on open or very sparsely vegetated sandbars or river islands; sometimes in adjacent open, grassy areas. Found singly or in pairs, running about in the open; usually rather inconspicuous, so perfectly does its dorsal color match its sandy habitat. Generally quiet. Can be found on some of the younger islands around the mouth of the Río Napo, just down the Amazon from Iquitos, Peru.
RANGE: Amaz. lowlands of se. Colombia (along the Amazon near Leticia), e. Ecuador (a few recent reports of presumed wanderers, mainly along the Río Napo; also a 1992 specimen [ANSP] from Panguri in s. Zamora-Chinchipe), e. Peru (not recorded north of the Amazon or the Río Marañón), n. Bolivia (south to Cochabamba and w. Santa Cruz), sw. Amaz. Brazil (east only to the upper Rio Madeira drainage). Reports from nw. Argentina await confirmation; published records from Tucumán are in fact referable to Spot-billed Ground-Tyrant (Smith and Vuilleumier, 1971), and recent sightings from Jujuy and Salta could also be of that species. Mostly below 800 m, rarely up to 1400 m in Ecuador and 1900 m in Peru. Anomalous (?) specimens were taken on the shores of Lake Titicaca at Desaguadero at 3800 m by M. A. Carriker, Jr., and at 3200 m at Liriuni in Cochabamba, Bolivia, by A. M. Olalla.

GROUP B

Typical ground-tyrants; note *forehead and crown patterns.*

Muscisaxicola alpina

PLAIN-CAPPED GROUND-TYRANT   PLATE: 40

DESCRIPTION: 19 cm (7½"). Andes of Colombia to Bolivia. *Mostly brownish gray above, crown tinged sepia brown,* with *rather broad white superciliary* and small white area below eye; wings duskier but with

some paler edging on coverts, and outer web of outermost rectrix whitish. Below uniform grayish white. *Grisea* (Peru except in the extreme north, and Bolivia) is much purer gray above than birds of Colombia, Ecuador, and extreme n. Peru (*alpina, columbiana,* and *quesadae*), lacking their brownish tinge above and with no sepia on crown. See C-38.

SIMILAR SPECIES: In the Colombian Andes only 1 other groundtyrant, the much smaller and even browner Spot-billed is present. In Ecuador one must also contend with the austral migrant White-browed Ground-Tyrant, which differs in its paler and more rufous crown and (despite its name) a narrower and *less* conspicuous white superciliary. Farther south, where there are more ground-tyrant species, it gets more complicated, but bear in mind that Plain-capped shows the *least* head color of any except for the similar Cinereous (which see).

HABITAT AND BEHAVIOR: Locally fairly common to common in open páramo and puna grasslands, often where rocky but usually avoiding areas where there are many bushes. Like other ground-tyrants, forages on ground or on rocks except for occasional short sallies into the air in pursuit of insects, hopping or running rapidly for a short distance, then abruptly pausing and looking about with erect posture. Sometimes takes slightly elevated perches, e.g., on a rock or wall. In nonbreeding season regularly gathers into loose flocks, occasionally in association with other ground-tyrants or other puna-zone birds, e.g., sierra-finches and miners. Flight is swift and direct, on slim pointed wings; upon landing, and occasionally at other times, may flick open its tail and quiver or partially droop its wings.

RANGE: Andes of Colombia (E. Andes in Boyacá and Cundinamarca, Cen. Andes from Nevado del Ruiz south to Cauca), Ecuador (Carchi south to Azuay at El Cajas), Peru, and w. Bolivia (La Paz and Cochabamba). Mostly 3300–4700 m.

NOTE: *M. cinerea* (Cinereous Ground-Tyrant) is now regarded as a full species (see *Birds of the World*, vol. 8). We further note that *grisea* of Peru and Bolivia, currently treated as the southernmost race of *M. alpina*, differs about as much from the forms of *M. alpina* found in Ecuador and Colombia as it does from *M. cinerea*. *M. grisea* may also warrant full species status; if split, *M. grisea* should retain the name Plaincapped Ground-Tyrant, and *M. alpina* (with *columbiana* and *quesadae*) should be called the Paramo Ground-Tyrant.

Muscisaxicola cinerea

CINEREOUS GROUND-TYRANT

DESCRIPTION: 16.5 cm (6½"). High Andes of s. Peru to cen. Chile and Argentina; formerly considered conspecific with Plain-capped Ground-Tyrant. Resembles most southerly, pale gray race of Plain-capped Ground-Tyrant (*grisea*), overlapping with that form in Peru and w. Bolivia. Cinereous differs in being *markedly smaller* and in having only a *narrow short white supraloral* extending back only to over the eye.

SIMILAR SPECIES: Spot-billed Ground-Tyrant is smaller and browner above with rufescent wing-edging and small yellow area on lower mandible (bill of Cinereous is all black). Otherwise, Cinereous shows *less head pattern* than any other ground-tyrant in its range. Cf. especially Puna Ground-Tyrant, which has the weakest head pattern of the others; it does show a brownish tinge on crown (entirely pure gray in Cinereous) and has a slightly longer white superciliary.

HABITAT AND BEHAVIOR: Fairly common in open puna grasslands and pastures, often where there are many rocks and boulders and often near streams or lakes. Behavior similar to Plain-capped Ground-Tyrant's.

RANGE: Andes of s. Peru (Puno), w. Bolivia, w. Argentina (south to Mendoza), and cen. Chile (Atacama to Talca); s. breeders migrate northward during austral winter (Mar.–Oct.), at which time they are recorded north to Andes of cen. Peru (Junín). Mostly 2500–4500 m.

NOTE: Here regarded as a species distinct from *M. alpina*, following Smith and Vuilleumier (1971) and *Birds of the World*, vol. 8.

Muscisaxicola juninensis

PUNA GROUND-TYRANT   PLATE: 40

DESCRIPTION: 16.5 cm (6½″). Andes of Peru to n. Chile and n. Argentina; a "difficult" ground-tyrant, easy to confuse. Above mostly pale brownish gray, *more strongly tinged brown on entire crown* (but *no discrete coronal patch*), with short narrow white superciliary; wings somewhat duskier, tail black with outer web of outermost rectrix white. Below grayish white, becoming whiter on belly.

SIMILAR SPECIES: Cf. very similar White-browed Ground-Tyrant. Cinereous Ground-Tyrant lacks Puna's tinge of brown on back and especially crown. Rufous-naped Ground-Tyrant is paler and purer gray dorsally with no brown tinge at all, and it has a more conspicuous, discrete, rufous occipital patch.

HABITAT AND BEHAVIOR: Locally fairly common to common in puna grasslands at high elevations, most often close to rock outcroppings, boulders, or cliffs, or around bogs, lakes, or marshes. Apparently resident, though stormy weather may cause brief altitudinal displacement. General behavior similar to other ground-tyrants' (see under Plain-capped).

RANGE: Andes of cen. and s. Peru (north to Junín and Lima), w. Bolivia, extreme n. Chile (Tarapacá), and extreme n. Argentina (south to Tucumán). 3200–5000 m, mostly above 4200 m.

Muscisaxicola albilora

WHITE-BROWED GROUND-TYRANT

DESCRIPTION: 17 cm (6¾″). *Breeds in Chile and Argentina, migrating north to Ecuador.* Closely resembles slightly smaller Puna Ground-Tyrant. Differs in *browner crown which gradually blends into more rufous hindcrown; longer and more prominent, though still quite narrow, white superciliary;* and slightly browner upperparts.

SIMILAR SPECIES: Also readily confused with n. races of Plain-capped Ground-Tyrant (of Colombia and Ecuador), but these show much less rufous on occipital region and have a broader but shorter white superciliary; Plain-capped is also considerably larger. Rufous-naped Ground-Tyrant is purer gray above and has a much more distinct and crisply delineated rufous occipital patch which *contrasts* with gray forecrown.

HABITAT AND BEHAVIOR: Fairly common in open puna grasslands and pastures; when breeding favors relatively barren, often rocky or

sparsely vegetated, slopes near water. When migrating sometimes found in pastures and other open areas in partly wooded terrain. Best known and most numerous in its Chilean nesting grounds, from which it disperses northward over a relatively much greater area during austral winter, when it may often be overlooked or not correctly identified. Seems to occur regularly on various Ecuadorian mountains (e.g., Pichincha and Cotopaxi Volcanos), even at the n. limit of its migratory range. The most numerous nesting ground-tyrant in Andes of Santiago, Chile, but rare at s. end of its breeding range (e.g., in Magallanes). RANGE: Breeds in Andes of cen. and s. Chile (Aconcagua south to n. Magallanes) and adjacent Argentina (Neuquén south to w. Santa Cruz; also apparently nests on Somuncará Plateau in se. Río Negro); during austral winter (Apr.–Sept.) migrates far northward in Andes, when recorded from w. Bolivia, Peru, and Ecuador (north to Pichincha); accidental on Falkland Is., and recently recorded on Gorgona Is. off sw. Colombia (1 collected in Nov. 1987; B. Ortiz-von Halle). Breeds mostly 1600–2600 m, at other seasons mainly 2500–4000 m.

Muscisaxicola rufivertex

RUFOUS-NAPED GROUND TYRANT PLATE: 40

DESCRIPTION: 16.5–18 cm (6½–7″). Peru to Chile and Argentina. *The palest and purest gray ground-tyrant*. Above *mostly pale pure gray with sharply defined orange-rufous occipital patch* (often surprisingly inconspicuous) and short narrow white superciliary; wings somewhat browner, tail black with outer web of outermost rectrix whitish. Below grayish white, becoming whiter on belly. Foregoing applies to nominate race of cen. Chile and adjacent Argentina. *Pallidiceps* (sw. Peru in Arequipa and s. Bolivia south to nw. Argentina and n. Chile) similar but even paler gray above and with slightly paler occipital patch. *Occipitalis* (most of Peruvian range south to w. Bolivia in Cochabamba) is quite different, however: it is notably larger with a darker, *more rufous-chestnut occipital patch;* broader and more prominent white superciliary; and little or no pale edging on tail.
SIMILAR SPECIES: Cf. especially Plain-capped and Cinereous Ground-Tyrants, both of which lack any rufous on crown, and White-browed Ground-Tyrant, which is distinctly browner-tinged above with *entire crown* browner (not just a rufous occipital patch). Occipital patch of the *pallidiceps* race of Rufous-naped is often so pale that confusion is possible with larger Ochre-naped Ground-Tyrant.
HABITAT AND BEHAVIOR: Uncommon to locally common in grasslands and pastures with short-cropped grass and (especially when breeding) on rocky slopes and in quebradas, often feeding on relatively level areas near water. When not breeding regularly gathers in small groups, usually composed only of its own species. General behavior similar to other ground-tyrants' (see under Plain-capped). The most numerous ground-tyrant in much of sw. Peru (R. A. Hughes).
RANGE: Andes of Peru (north to Cajamarca), w. Bolivia, n. and cen. Chile (south to Colchagua), and nw. Argentina (south to La Rioja and in Mendoza, with an isolated population in w. Córdoba). No definite evidence of long-distance migration. Mostly 2200–4500 m, but in aus-

tral winter moves downslope into coastal lowlands of Chile; resident populations occur lower (600–1000 m) in the loma zone of sw. Peru and n. Chile.

NOTE: Two species are perhaps involved, for *occipitalis* seems distinctly different from the *M. rufivertex* group (with *pallidiceps* and *achalensis*). No intergradation between *occipitalis* and the *rufivertex* group has been shown, and indeed they have even been recorded together locally (though this has been attributed to migration of *pallidiceps;* in our view this seems unlikely). If *M. occipitalis* is split as a full species, it could be known as Chestnut-naped Ground-Tyrant.

Muscisaxicola flavinucha

OCHRE-NAPED GROUND-TYRANT
PLATE: 40

DESCRIPTION: 20 cm (8″). A *large* and particularly long-winged ground-tyrant that breeds in Chile and Argentina and migrates north to Peru. Above mostly pale brownish gray with *broad frontal area and short superciliary white; occipital patch buffy yellowish to plain yellow* (perhaps purer yellow when breeding). Wings duskier with coverts and inner flight feathers pale-edged; tail black, outer web of outermost rectrix whitish. Below grayish white, becoming white on lower belly. Juveniles apparently lack the occipital patch.
SIMILAR SPECIES: Should more properly be called Ochre-capped Ground-Tyrant (the *nape* is not colored). Rivaled in size only by the even bigger White-fronted, which lacks the yellowish occipital patch (its entire crown is tinged brown) and has more extensive white edging on coverts and inner flight feathers. Cf. also Rufous-naped Ground-Tyrant.
HABITAT AND BEHAVIOR: Uncommon to locally fairly common on barren mountain slopes with scattered rocks and boulders, but often foraging in lusher situations with short-cropped grass, frequently in bogs or near water. Best known from Andes of cen. Chile, where it is one of the more numerous nesting ground-tyrants. Behavior similar to other ground-tyrants' (see under Plain-capped), though we have also seen it flicking aside litter at base of isolated plants, searching for hidden insects.
RANGE: Breeds in Andes of Chile (north to Tarapacá) and Argentina (north to Mendoza, perhaps farther; also apparently nests on Somuncará Plateau in se. Río Negro) south to Tierra del Fuego in Cape Horn area; a recent Dec. record from Oruro in w. Bolivia makes one suspect local nesting there as well, and apparently there are a few other sightings from during the austral winter in s. Peru (Fjeldså and Krabbe 1990). During austral winter (Mar.–Sept.) migrates north into Andes of w. Bolivia and Peru (once north to La Libertad, regularly to Lima). From n. Chile northward mostly 3000–4500 m, progressively lower southward, in Tierra del Fuego nesting at 500–1000 m but occasionally down to sea level during inclement weather.

Muscisaxicola albifrons

WHITE-FRONTED GROUND-TYRANT

DESCRIPTION: 21.5 cm (8½″). *High Andes from cen. Peru to Bolivia and extreme n. Chile;* the *largest* ground-tyrant. Resembles Ochre-naped Ground-Tyrant but *even larger*. Differs further in having: *no yellow oc-*

cipital patch (entire crown is tinged brown), *more prominent whitish edging on wing-coverts and inner flight feathers* (especially conspicuous in flight but also evident as a *patch* at rest), and more uniformly pale grayish underparts (not so white on belly).

SIMILAR SPECIES: Except for Ochre-naped (which see), White-fronted Ground-Tyrant is easily distinguished from all its congeners on the basis of its large size. Cf. also Black-billed and other shrike-tyrants.

HABITAT AND BEHAVIOR: Uncommon in high puna grasslands, usually where there are many boulders or cliff-faces but little or no shrubbery and often even little grass. Often forages on bogs where flat-topped cushion plants are dominant. Seems more restricted to higher elevations than any other ground-tyrant, though it does occur with others, especially Puna and Plain-capped. Rather solitary, even when not breeding, but otherwise behavior similar to other ground-tyrants' (see under Plain-capped). Can be found at La Cumbre pass north of La Paz, Bolivia, and in Chile's Lauca Nat. Park.

RANGE: Andes of cen. and s. Peru (north to Ancash), w. Bolivia (La Paz), and extreme n. Chile (Tarapacá). Mostly 4100–5200 m.

Muscisaxicola frontalis

BLACK-FRONTED GROUND-TYRANT   PLATE: 40

DESCRIPTION: 18 cm (7″). Breeds in Andes of Chile and Argentina, migrating north to s. Peru. Bill rather long and slim, slightly decurved. Mostly ashy gray above with *conspicuous white lores* and *black forehead extending back on center of crown and ending as blackish chestnut point on occiput;* wings duskier, tail black with outer web of outermost rectrix whitish. Below pale grayish white.

SIMILAR SPECIES: No other ground-tyrant has such striking head markings. Cf. especially Cinereous, which lacks any black on head, and Dark-faced, which has entire foreface black and no white on lores. Black-fronted's white loral spot is so prominent that at a distance it can almost resemble the larger Ochre-naped and White-fronted Ground-Tyrants.

HABITAT AND BEHAVIOR: Rare to uncommon in puna grasslands, usually on stony slopes with sparse shrubby vegetation, or near water when not nesting. Behavior similar to other ground-tyrants' (see under Plain-capped), though on the whole relatively scarce and infrequently seen. Most readily found when breeding in Andes of cen. Chile (e.g., around the Portillo ski resort or at El Yeso Reservoir), but even here outnumbered by various congeners and nesting at higher elevations than any other.

RANGE: Breeds in Andes of n. and cen. Chile (Antofogasta to Colchagua) and cen. Argentina (Mendoza, Neuquén, and w. Río Negro; apparently also nests on Somuncará Plateau in se. Río Negro); during austral winter (Apr.–Sept.) migrates north into the altiplano of w. Bolivia and s. Peru (where apparently rare and recorded only from Arequipa). Breeds mostly 2500–3500 m, sometimes lower (to 1800 m) in Río Negro, Argentina; in austral winter occurs in Bolivia and Peru up to 4300 m.

Muscisaxicola capistrata

CINNAMON-BELLIED GROUND-TYRANT   PLATE: 40

DESCRIPTION: 17.5 cm (7″). Breeds in s. Chile and Argentina, migrating north to s. Peru. Above mostly brownish gray with *black forehead and face* and *bright chestnut mid- and hindcrown;* wings duskier, tail black with outer web of outermost rectrix whitish. Throat whitish, becoming dull pale grayish buff on breast and *cinnamon-rufous on flanks and lower belly.* In the field, the head pattern is usually conspicuous, but belly color often is not.

SIMILAR SPECIES: Dark-faced Ground-Tyrant lacks the conspicuous chestnut on crown and is grayer below with no cinnamon-rufous on belly.

HABITAT AND BEHAVIOR: Uncommon to fairly common on open grassy steppes with scattered bushes and sparse grass, often adjacent to rocky slopes or cliffs; when not breeding, on open grassy or rocky slopes and plains. In Tierra del Fuego sometimes nests in association with rodents or their abandoned burrows (F. Vuilleumier). Behavior similar to other ground-tyrants' (see under Plain-capped), regularly in groups when on its winter quarters.

RANGE: Breeds in s. Chile (Magallanes) and s. Argentina (north to n. Santa Cruz, perhaps farther; may nest on Somuncará Plateau in se. Río Negro) south into n. Tierra del Fuego; during austral winter (Mar.–Oct.) migrates northward into Andes of the rest of Chile and Argentina (where also regular east into Córdoba mts.), and to altiplano of w. Bolivia and s. Peru (Puno and Arequipa); 1 sighting of an extralimital migrant in Sept. 1990 in chaco lowlands at Estancia Perforación in s. Santa Cruz, Bolivia. Mostly below 500 m when breeding, but mainly 2000–4000 m on its winter quarters (recorded at least once to 4700 m in Bolivia).

Muscisaxicola macloviana

DARK-FACED GROUND-TYRANT   PLATE: 40

DESCRIPTION: 16–16.5 cm (6¼–6½″). *Breeds in s. Chile and s. Argentina, migrating north to w. Peru and Uruguay.* Proportionately shorter-billed than other ground-tyrants. Above mostly brownish gray with *black foreface,* becoming dull chestnut-brown on remainder of crown; wings duskier, tail black with outer web of outermost rectrix whitish. *Mostly pale grayish below,* becoming whiter on lower belly and crissum.

SIMILAR SPECIES: The only other ground-tyrant with a conspicuously dark foreface is the Cinnamon-bellied, which also has bright chestnut on crown and cinnamon-rufous on lower belly. See also Black-fronted Ground-Tyrant.

HABITAT AND BEHAVIOR: Common in open grassy areas. In breeding season favors meadows at edge of woodland and forest and above timberline; at other seasons, both on migration and on its winter quarters, frequents grasslands and pastures, especially near the coast. General behavior similar to other ground-tyrants' (see under Plain-capped), but when nesting considerably more arboreal, regularly perching in trees at edge of woodland. The most numerous ground-tyrant in s. part of Isla Grande in austral summer.

RANGE: Breeds in s. Chile (nesting proven only in Magallanes, but possible north to Malleco) and s. Argentina (north to Neuquén and Río Negro) south to Tierra del Fuego; during austral winter (Apr.–Oct.) migrates northward, mainly along either coast, reaching n. Argentina (north to Jujuy, Córdoba, Entre Ríos, and Buenos Aires), Uruguay, remainder of Chile, Peru (north to La Libertad), and extreme s. Ecuador (1 sighting from El Oro; J. Sterling); seems likely then in extreme s. Brazil; Falkland Is. (where resident, *contra* Olrog 1979). Mostly below 2500 m.

Muscigralla Field-Tyrants

An odd little flycatcher, plump and very long-legged, the Short-tailed Field-Tyrant shares so many characteristics with the *Muscisaxicola* ground-tyrants that it has been suggested (Smith and Vuilleumier 1971) that they are congeneric. We agree that similarities exist, but we believe that the differences are striking enough to follow Traylor (1977) in maintaining *Muscigralla* as a separate genus. These differences include *Muscigralla*'s having a coronal patch, its very different scutellation on extremely long and pale (not dark) legs, bare tibia (together with the Golden Pipit, *Tmetothylacus tenellus,* of Africa, unique among passerines), more rounded and differently marked wings, and much shorter and differently marked tail. Lanyon (1986) not only considered *Muscigralla* a valid genus but felt it did not belong in the Fluvicoline assemblage (in which *Muscisaxicola* is placed); he considered its systematic position to be "enigmatic."

Muscigralla brevicauda

SHORT-TAILED FIELD-TYRANT   PLATE: 40

DESCRIPTION: 11 cm (4¼″). A virtually unmistakable *small* and *short-tailed* flycatcher of *sw. Ecuador and w. Peru. Very long legs,* flesh-colored. Above mostly brownish gray with short white supraloral and semiconcealed yellow coronal patch; *band on rump pinkish buff,* becoming *rufous-chestnut on uppertail-coverts.* Wings dusky with *2 broad whitish wingbars;* tail black narrowly tipped rufous-buff. Below creamy whitish, tinged olive grayish on sides of breast.

SIMILAR SPECIES: In a brief view might be confused with Coastal Miner.

HABITAT AND BEHAVIOR: Fairly common but often rather inconspicuous in open barren or sandy areas with or without scattered shrubbery and low trees, and in agricultural fields. Mostly terrestrial, though sometimes perching in bushes and low trees, with behavior strongly reminiscent of the *Muscisaxicola* ground-tyrants', even to the frequent flicking of its wings and tail. Like them the field-tyrant moves in short running or hopping bursts, often almost comical because of its long legs, then pausing to look around. Its song is a weak, sibilant "tizztízzz," sometimes preceded by some "tik" notes, usually delivered from an elevated perch such as the top of a shrub, but periodically the vocalizing bird may mount some 10–20 m into the air while giving much the same song.

RANGE: Sw. Ecuador (north to Guayas, and inland into w. Loja; also on Isla de la Plata off s. Manabí), w. Peru (mostly coastal lowlands, also locally in upper Río Marañón valley in Cajamarca at Shumba), and extreme n. Chile (Arica); an accidental vagrant to Gorgona Is. off coast of sw. Colombia (May 1988 specimen; B. Ortiz-von Halle). To about 1300 m.

Neoxolmis Tyrants

A large, boldly patterned, and very long-winged but mainly terrestrial flycatcher found primarily in Argentina. Traylor (1977) placed another species, *rubetra* (Rusty-backed Monjita), in the genus *Neoxolmis,* but we continue to place that species in *Xolmis.* Lanyon (1986) suggested that, based on syringeal evidence, *Neoxolmis* was close to *Gubernetes* and *Muscipipra,* though in other respects these are extremely different. The nest of *Neoxolmis* is a cup placed on the ground, partially concealed by a low shrub (G. L. Maclean, *Auk* 86[1]: 144–145, 1969).

Neoxolmis rufiventris

CHOCOLATE-VENTED TYRANT   PLATE: 40

DESCRIPTION: 23 cm (9"). *A handsome, large terrestrial flycatcher of Patagonia* (migrating northward). *Above mostly ashy gray* with black foreface and ocular area. *Shoulders contrastingly pale sandy* (often appearing silvery in the field), *inner flight feathers bright cinnamon broadly tipped whitish,* and outer flight feathers black, resulting in a very flashy flight pattern; tail blackish tipped white and with outer web of outermost rectrix whitish. *Throat and breast pure gray* becoming sharply *cinnamon-rufous on lower breast and belly.*

SIMILAR SPECIES: So strikingly colored and patterned that confusion is improbable; in shape and behavior recalls a large *Muscisaxicola* ground-tyrant or even an American Kestrel (*Falco sparverius*).

HABITAT AND BEHAVIOR: Uncommon on semiopen Patagonian steppes with sparse grass and scattered low shrubs while breeding, at other seasons in open grasslands and agricultural fields. Somewhat thrush-like in overall aspect, but this splendid bird's behavior more resembles a *Muscisaxicola* ground-tyrant's. Like them it is primarily terrestrial, though also perching on low bushes; it walks quickly, then pauses and stands erect. The tail is often flicked open, exposing the white. Flight is very swift and direct with pointed wing shape almost like a falcon's; birds often chase each other in the air. Pairs scatter out on the windswept far-southern plains where they breed, but on the pampas of Argentina and Uruguay, where Chocolate-vented Tyrants winter, they usually range in small flocks; here they are known locally as *chorlos* (a Spanish colloquial term for plovers—which in some ways they do resemble). Not very vocal, but breeding males emit a simple, weak "bur-bit" from the ground or a rock (R. Straneck recording).

RANGE: Breeds in extreme s. Chile (Magallanes) and s. Argentina (w. Chubut and Santa Cruz) south to n. Tierra del Fuego (where rare); during austral winter migrates north into e. Argentina (to Córdoba and Entre Ríos) and Uruguay, rarely to extreme s. Brazil (a single May 1973 record from s. Rio Grande do Sul). Mostly below 500 m.

Xolmis and *Heteroxolmis* Monjitas

A distinctive group of fairly large flycatchers found in open county of cen. and s. South America. The group name *monjita* (meaning "little nun") is their colloquial name in Argentina, apparently in reference to their rather simple patterns of white, gray, and black. The monjitas forage mainly by dropping to the ground from a low perch. A few also run on the ground, thus demonstrating a fairly close relationship with other southern/Andean tyrannids that are at least partly terrestrial (e.g., *Agriornis, Muscisaxicola,* and *Neoxolmis*). Nesting seems to have been little described; a White Monjita nest found in Argentina (RSR et al.) was a rather large open cup placed in an open hollow of a tree 3 m above ground. We follow Smith and Vuilleumier (1971) and Traylor (1977) in merging the monotypic genus *Pyrope* into *Xolmis.* Based on anatomical considerations, Lanyon (1986) erected a new genus, *Heteroxolmis,* for Black-and-white Monjita; because of that species' great similarity to the rest of *Xolmis,* we continue to treat it with the other monjitas.

GROUP A

Pair of monjitas found in *Argentina;* both species with *rusty brown back.*

Xolmis rubetra

RUSTY-BACKED MONJITA

PLATE: 41

DESCRIPTION: 19 cm (7½"). *A distinctive and handsome flycatcher of Argentina. Above rusty brown,* most rufescent on crown, with *long broad white superciliary;* wings mostly black, with greater-coverts and inner flight feathers edged buff to grayish white (rather rufescent on lesser-coverts); rump pale, tail mostly black with outer web of outermost rectrix white. Sides of neck and entire underparts white, with *sides of head, neck, and breast streaked with black,* flanks tinged rufous. Female less rufescent and duller overall.

SIMILAR SPECIES: Not likely to be confused except with recently described and range-restricted Salinas Monjita (which see). Shrike-tyrants are not as rufescent above, have streaking on *throat.*

HABITAT AND BEHAVIOR: Uncommon to locally fairly common in shrubby steppe vegetation and sparse grassland with scattered low bushes. Usually in pairs when breeding, but in austral winter reported to gather in bands of up to 20 or 30 birds. Feeds mostly by dropping to the ground from a low perch, e.g., the top of a bush or a fence, but also sometimes runs rapidly with head held erect in the manner of a ground- or shrike-tyrant. Although almost always silent, a pair (doubt-less agitated by our presence near their recently fledged young) gave a simple, soft metallic "pik" call. Small numbers of this handsome monjita breed on the Valdés Peninsula in Chubut.

RANGE: Breeds in s. Argentina (Mendoza and s. Buenos Aires south to n. Santa Cruz); more southerly breeders withdraw northward dur-ing austral winter into n.-cen. Argentina (north to Tucumán, Santiago del Estero, Santa Fe, and Entre Ríos) and extreme w. Uruguay (1 rec-ord from Paysandu). To about 1000 m.

NOTE: The generic relationship of this species (and of *X. salinarum*) is uncertain. Long placed in *Xolmis,* it was considered by Smith and Vuilleumier (1971) to be "intermediate between the other species of *Xolmis* and *Neoxolmis rufiventris*" (Chocolate-vented Tyrant). Traylor (1977) took that one step farther and placed *rub-etra* in the formerly monotypic genus *Neoxolmis;* Lanyon (1986) concurred. *Rubetra* does seem a rather aberrant *Xolmis* (no other species runs on the ground so much), but we question whether it is very close to *Neoxolmis* and in fact suspect that *rubetra* might instead be "intermediate" toward the genus *Agriornis,* perhaps via *A. murina* (Lesser Shrike-Tyrant). Given the uncertainty, we maintain it in its traditional ge-nus, *Xolmis.*

Xolmis salinarum

SALINAS MONJITA

DESCRIPTION: 16.5 cm (6½"). *Nw. Argentina.* Resembles Rusty-backed Monjita but considerably *smaller* and *whiter.* Further differ-ences are: the *virtual absence of streaking on sides of neck and breast;* an almost complete white nuchal collar; *mostly white wing-coverts and scapulars;* whiter rump and grayer tail with broad black terminal band; no rufous on flanks.

HABITAT AND BEHAVIOR: Locally uncommon to fairly common in semiopen scrubby vegetation growing in salt-impregnated soil around the Salinas Grandes and Salinas de Ambargasta. Behavior similar to Rusty-backed Monjita's; like that species, Salinas Monjita is fairly ter-restrial (though often also perching atop bushes). It can occur in flocks of up to about 50 birds during austral winter (J. Clements), but pairs separate out when breeding. Small numbers occur year-round north of San José de las Salinas, near the Salinas Grandes in nw. Córdoba.

RANGE: Nw. Argentina (nw. Córdoba, extreme s. Catamarca, sw. San-tiago del Estero, and e. La Rioja). 100–200 m.

NOTE: A recently described taxon: M. Nores and D. Yzurieta, *Acad. Nac. Córdoba Misc.* 61: 7–8, 1979. *Salinarum* was described as a subspecies of *X. rubetra,* but Olrog (1984) suggested that it might better be considered a distinct species, and we agree. Narosky and Yzurieta (1987) and Canevari et al. (1991) also treat it as a full species.

GROUP B   *Typical* monjitas.

Xolmis pyrope

FIRE-EYED DIUCON   PLATE: 41

DESCRIPTION: 21–21.5 cm (8¼–8½"). *Chile and adjacent s. Argentina. Iris bright red* (sometimes surprisingly hard to see). Uniform dark gray above, wings blacker and virtually plain (some narrow grayish edging); tail gray, outer feathers slightly paler. Below paler ashy gray, throat

whiter with some faint gray streaking, belly grayish white. *Fortis* of Chile's Chiloé Is. is slightly larger.

SIMILAR SPECIES: Uniform gray appearance combined with the red eye is distinctive in range. Shrike-tyrants have much more prominent throat streaking and are larger with heavier and more hooked bills.

HABITAT AND BEHAVIOR: Fairly common to common at edge of *Nothofagus-* (Southern Beech-) dominated forest, woodland, and in shrubby clearings. A conspicuous bird, usually perching in the open, often dropping to the ground to pursue insects, also sometimes sallying into the air for short distances. Eats some fruit, perhaps especially during austral winter. Not very vocal, a soft subdued "pit" or "whit" being the note most often heard.

RANGE: Cen. and s. Chile (resident north to Aconcagua, in austral winter a few north to Atacama) and adjacent s. Argentina (north to w. Neuquén) south to Tierra del Fuego; southernmost breeders are absent during austral winter (e.g., present on Isla Grande only Nov.– May); a few records from Falkland Is. Below 1000 m.

NOTE: We follow Smith and Vuilleumier (1971) and Traylor (1977) in merging the monotypic genus *Pyrope,* in which this species was formerly separated (mostly on the basis of male's rather different, very narrow primaries), into *Xolmis.*

Xolmis cinerea

GRAY MONJITA

PLATE: 41

DESCRIPTION: 23 cm (9"). Iris bright red. *Above ashy gray* with short but broad white supraloral; wings and tail mostly black, wings with *large white speculum at base of primaries* (forming a conspicuous *square patch* of white in flight) and whitish edging on coverts and tertials, tail broadly tipped whitish. Throat white with *broad black malar streak,* breast ashy gray, belly white.

SIMILAR SPECIES: Black-crowned Monjita has black crown encircled by white, shows a white wing stripe (rather than a patch), and is all white below (with no gray on breast and no black malar streak). Cf. various *Mimus* mockingbirds (all longer and rounder-tailed, etc.).

HABITAT AND BEHAVIOR: Uncommon to common in grasslands with scattered trees, cerrado, and around buildings; at times (when not breeding?) even in the outskirts of major cities. Shows no predilection for water. Conspicuous, often perching on fences, phone wires, or tops of bushes, from there dropping to the ground after insect prey, less often sallying to the air; sometimes runs for short distances. Like *Tyrannus* kingbirds, Gray Monjita often remains active and conspicuous during the heat of the day. Its flight is fast and graceful, on pointed wings. Breeding birds often execute an undulating display flight, repeatedly looping into the air and returning to the same perch; at that season, males can occasionally be heard repeating their pretty, whistled song (unexpectedly soft for such a robust bird), "peee, preeu." One of the more numerous birds across much of Brazil's cerrado (e.g., around Brasília), but seems less common southward.

RANGE: Extreme se. Peru (Pampas de Heath in Madre de Dios), n. and e. Bolivia, much of cen. and s. Brazil (lower Amazon area in Amapá and on Marajó Is. upriver locally to around Santarém, and from Maranhão and Ceará south and west through Mato Grosso, Goiás, and Bahia to Rio Grande do Sul; absent from coastal e. Brazil north of Rio de Janeiro), Paraguay, Uruguay, and n. Argentina (south to Tucumán, Santiago del Estero, and n. Buenos Aires; apparently only formerly in Córdoba); s. Surinam (Sipaliwini). Possibly to some extent migratory from s. part of breeding range. To about 1200 m.

Xolmis coronata

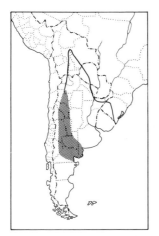

BLACK-CROWNED MONJITA   PLATE: 41

DESCRIPTION: 21–21.5 cm (8¼–8½″). Breeds in s. Argentina, migrating to s. Bolivia and extreme s. Brazil. *Crown black surrounded by broad white frontal band, superciliary, and nuchal band;* ear-coverts blackish, otherwise gray to brownish gray above. Wings blackish, coverts and inner flight feathers edged whitish and with *white wing stripe along base of flight feathers conspicuous in flight;* tail mainly blackish. Below entirely white. Female slightly smaller.

SIMILAR SPECIES: Gray Monjita lacks the black crown and is grayer generally *including breast,* showing a *square* wing patch in flight (rather than a stripe) and obvious white tip to tail.

HABITAT AND BEHAVIOR: Uncommon to fairly common in open and semiopen areas with scattered low trees and bushes. Behavior similar to Gray Monjita's, which it replaces southward; usually perches fully in the open, often atop a shrub or tree or on a wire. Most food is obtained by dropping to the ground, and only rarely does it sally to the air or run on the ground. Tends to be wary. Its song is a soft, melodic "whut-whut, wheeeyr? whut" (R. Straneck recording).

RANGE: Breeds in s. Argentina (mainly in Mendoza, Río Negro, and La Pampa, in small numbers north to w. Tucumán); in austral winter migrates north through most of the remainder of Argentina (except Misiones) and north to s. Bolivia (reaching w. Santa Cruz), w. Paraguay, Uruguay, and extreme s. Brazil (w. Rio Grande do Sul). A single Jan. specimen from w. Paraguay at Orloff suggests possible breeding. To about 1500 m.

Xolmis velata

WHITE-RUMPED MONJITA

DESCRIPTION: 19 cm (7½″). *Mostly cen. and e. Brazil. Head mostly white with pearly gray hindneck;* back brownish gray with *contrasting white rump and basal half of tail,* terminal half of tail black; wings blackish with white band at base of flight feathers (*showing in flight as a stripe*), and patch of white on inner secondaries and tertials. Below all white. Sexes alike.

SIMILAR SPECIES: Gray Monjita is larger and grayer generally, lacks white on rump (though it has white on tip of tail), has bold black malar streak. White-rumped actually more closely resembles female Black-and-white Monjita, though Black-and-white's wings are *solid* black; the 2 species are not known to occur together.

HABITAT AND BEHAVIOR: Fairly common in semiopen areas with scattered bushes and trees and around ranch buildings and outskirts of towns; often, but not always, near water. Usually in pairs, perching conspicuously on fence posts, wires, and tops of bushes. Rather tame and approachable, much more so than Gray Monjita, but not as familiar as White Monjita.

RANGE: Cen. and e. Brazil (lower Amazon area around Tefé and on Marajó Is., and Maranhão south to Mato Grosso do Sul, São Paulo, and Rio de Janeiro), ne. Paraguay (Concepción), and n. and e. Bolivia (west through Santa Cruz to Beni). To about 1000 m.

Xolmis irupero

WHITE MONJITA
PLATE: 41

DESCRIPTION: 17–18 cm (6¾–7″). *Almost entirely pure white;* primaries, primary coverts, and tip of notched tail black. Female tinged gray on back. *Nivea* (ne. Brazil) slightly smaller and with slightly wider black tail-band.

SIMILAR SPECIES: Essentially unmistakable. Even at tremendous distances, this lovely, almost ethereally white, flycatcher need only be compared with the *much rarer and range-restricted* Black-and-white Monjita (though that species is not nearly so white).

HABITAT AND BEHAVIOR: Fairly common to common in open and semiopen country with scattered bushes and trees, often along roads or near houses; occurs in both savannas and artificial pastures as well as more or less cultivated terrain. Often near water but by no means restricted to it. A well-known and very conspicuous bird, both because of its stunning white plumage and because of its habit of so often perching fully in the open, on a wire or atop a bush or tree. Feeds mainly by dropping to the ground in pursuit of insects, sometimes hovering briefly before swooping down. Like most other monjitas, White is usually a very quiet bird, though breeding males have a very distinctive, slowly repeated, and soft "preeeyp . . . tooit . . . preeeyp . . . tooit . . . ," often given well before dawn. One of the most common and most frequently seen birds in the pantanal of Paraguay and adjacent Argentina (where called the *viudita,* or "little widow"); not as numerous elsewhere, seemingly especially scarce in ne. Brazil.

RANGE: Brazil in the northeast (Ceará and Pernambuco south to n. Minas Gerais) and extreme south (w. Mato Grosso do Sul, and in Rio Grande do Sul), e. and s. Bolivia (northwest to Beni), Paraguay, Uruguay, and n. Argentina (south to Mendoza, La Pampa, and n. Río Negro). To about 1300 m (in Bolivia).

Heteroxolmis dominicana

BLACK-AND-WHITE MONJITA
PLATE: 41

DESCRIPTION: 20.5 cm (8″). *Very local in se. South America.* Rather long tail. Male *mostly white* (not as pure a white as White Monjita, often with smudgy pale gray effect especially on head and back) with *very contrasting black wings and tail;* outer third of primaries white, showing especially in flight. Female similar but differing in having crown and back brownish gray, the latter contrasting with *prominent long white scapular stripe* and whitish rump.

SIMILAR SPECIES: White Monjita is smaller, always purer white, and shows less black on wings (only on primaries) and only on tip of tail. White-rumped Monjita is vaguely similar to female Black-and-white, but White-rumped has a white wing-stripe and white at base of tail (both solid black in Black-and-white) and is grayer above; they are not known to occur together.

HABITAT AND BEHAVIOR: Rare to uncommon and very local in or near boggy swales, often with stands of sedges (e.g., *Cyperus* or *Eryngium* spp.), in open rolling or marshy terrain, or just inland from coastal sand dunes; often feeds in adjacent grasslands. Somewhat more numerous locally (e.g., in ne. Rio Grande do Sul, Brazil, and north of Pinamar in e. Buenos Aires, Argentina), but in general this attractive monjita is now extremely scarce. It may merit formal threatened status, for formerly it seems to have been considerably more common and widespread; presumably drainage and other modifications to its specialized habitat have reduced its overall range and numbers. Behavior similar to White Monjita's, usually in pairs, dropping to the ground for prey from a low perch, but rather more restless, seeming constantly to be on the move. At least in Rio Grande do Sul, foraging birds are very often followed by flocks of feeding Saffron-cowled Blackbirds; this unusual association, first noted by Belton (1985), has not been adequately explained. Although almost always quiet, a soft, somewhat querulous "weeyrt" or "wurrt" call is occasionally given, perhaps especially when birds are agitated.

RANGE: Se. Brazil (Paraná south to Rio Grande do Sul, but recent records only from Santa Catarina and Rio Grande do Sul), Paraguay (very locally, with no recent records), Uruguay, and ne. Argentina (south to ne. Buenos Aires, but now very rare or absent from most areas). To about 1000 m.

NOTE: Lanyon (1986) erected a new genus, *Heteroxolmis,* for this species, based on anatomical considerations; it was formerly placed in the genus *Xolmis.*

Satrapa Tyrants

The Yellow-browed Tyrant is a midsized, basically yellow and olive flycatcher of uncertain affinities found in trees in mainly semiopen terrain. Traylor (1977) suggested that it was perhaps closest to *Tumbezia* (Tumbes Tyrant), which it resembles in color; we note at least an equal similarity to *Myiozetetes*, though *Satrapa*'s open cup nest is very different. Lanyon (1986) admitted that he was unable to make any conclusions regarding its relationships.

Satrapa icterophrys

YELLOW-BROWED TYRANT   PLATE: 41

DESCRIPTION: 16.5 cm (6½"). Above dark olive, somewhat grayer on crown and nape, with *contrasting bright yellow superciliary and blackish cheeks;* wings and tail blackish, wings with *2 pale gray bars,* and outer web of outermost pair of rectrices whitish. *Below bright yellow* with

sides of chest olive. Female similar but slightly duller, with paler yellow eyebrow and throat and some obscure olive mottling on breast.

SIMILAR SPECIES: This attractive flycatcher is most likely confused with various *Myiozetetes* flycatchers, all of which it resembles in general conformation and pattern, though most of them have a white (not yellow) superciliary. Lemon-browed Flycatcher (found in Andes, thus limited or no overlap) does also have a yellow brow, but it extends back around nape; Lemon-browed also lacks wing-bars, etc.

HABITAT AND BEHAVIOR: Uncommon to fairly common in semiopen or shrubby areas with scattered trees or groves, monte, and at edge of marshes and gallery woodland; austral migrants to Peru also occur in riparian growth. Usually in pairs, perching erectly and usually more or less in the open; makes short sallies, usually to foliage, less often out into the air. Strikingly unlike the superficially similar but very noisy *Myiozetetes* flycatchers, the Yellow-browed Tyrant is normally quiet.

RANGE: Cen. and s. Brazil (north to s. Mato Grosso, Goiás, and w. and s. Bahia; less numerous northward, and apparently occurring only as an austral migrant farther north, with a few reports from n. Mato Grosso and an Aug. sighting from near Manaus), n. and e. Bolivia (uncertain breeding status in the north), extreme se. Peru (Madre de Dios, north to Manu Nat. Park, and ne. Cuzco at Hacienda Amazonia; apparently only as an austral migrant), Paraguay, Uruguay, and n. Argentina (south to La Rioja, Córdoba, and Buenos Aires; absent from at least the last in austral winter); also recorded locally from Venezuela (Carabobo, Apure, Guárico, Bolívar, and Delta Amacuro). The Venezuela records have been assumed to represent austral migrants (e.g., Meyer de Schauensee 1966), but an AMNH specimen was taken on 19 Nov., an unlikely date for such a migrant, and RSR has seen birds in Feb. in Apure and in early Mar. in Guárico. Recent observations, including nests under construction (*fide* C. Parrish), corroborate the presence of a resident breeding population here; this is further confirmed by the observation of a nest and recently fledged birds in Apure (A. Cruz and R. W. Andrews, *Wilson Bull.* 101[1]: 70–71, 1989). We believe it unlikely that any austral migrant Yellow-browed Tyrants occur in Venezuela. Mostly below 2000 m, but locally higher at least in w. Bolivia, where recorded up to 2900 m.

Machetornis Tyrants

Widespread in open country in tropical lowlands, the Cattle Tyrant is most often seen running about on the ground, frequently in the company of grazing animals. In appearance it strongly recalls a *Tyrannus* kingbird (even its voice is similar), but its wings are notably short and rounded, and anatomical evidence demonstrates that *Machetornis* is not a member of the kingbird assemblage (Lanyon 1984, 1986). Presumably the similarity is due to convergence; its actual systematic position remains unclear.

Machetornis rixosus

CATTLE TYRANT

PLATE: 41

DESCRIPTION: 19.5 cm (7¾"). *Superficially kingbird-like, but often terrestrial, running on long legs.* Iris dark red. *Mostly olive brown above,* notably grayer on crown and nape with usually concealed fiery orange coronal patch, and a narrow dusky stripe through eye; wings and tail plain olive brownish, *tail narrowly tipped paler.* Throat whitish, remaining *underparts mainly bright yellow,* tinged ochraceous olive across breast. Birds from Venezuela and Colombia (*flavigularis* and *obscurodorsalis*) have throat pale yellow.

SIMILAR SPECIES: Cattle Tyrant has no single diagnostic mark, but its combination of terrestrial habits and mainly yellow underparts effectively eliminates other more or less similar tyrannids. Kingbirds do drop to the ground, but they rarely remain there for long. Cattle Tyrant's running behavior is rather reminiscent of the *Muscisaxicola* ground-tyrants, though that group is basically Andean (not lowland) in distribution, and none is yellow below.

HABITAT AND BEHAVIOR: Fairly common to common in semiopen country, agricultural regions, around farmhouses, and sometimes even in city parks; avoids mostly forested or wooded areas. Usually in pairs or small groups, running about on ground with erect stance. Often attends grazing domestic animals (sometimes even capybaras!), frequently hitching a ride on their backs or heads, dropping off to pursue flushed insects. When not feeding, regularly perches in trees or on houses. Calls, the most frequent of which is a brief rising series of squeaky notes, are reminiscent of Tropical Kingbird.

RANGE: N. and e. Colombia (Caribbean lowlands west to n. Chocó, and east of Andes south to Meta and Vichada) and n. Venezuela (widely north of the Orinoco, south of it in n. Bolívar); e. and s. Brazil (Maranhão and s. Mato Grosso southward; 1 Aug. sighting of a wanderer in n. Mato Grosso on Rio Aripuanã by P. Roth), n. and e. Bolivia (west to Beni), Paraguay, Uruguay, and n. Argentina (south to San Luís, Córdoba, and Buenos Aires); a wandering bird was seen in Mar. 1979 at Buenaventura, Valle, Colombia. Also Panama (a few reports of vagrants). To about 800 m.

Tumbezia Tyrants

The little Tumbes Tyrant is found only in a small area in nw. Peru. Attractively patterned, it probably is most closely related to *Ochthoeca* (chat-tyrants), in which it was originally described; the genus *Tumbezia* was created for it several decades later. Smith and Vuilleumier (1971) suggested that it was "possibly congeneric with *Ochthoeca*," and based on syringeal characters, Lanyon (1986) also concluded that it should be returned to the genus *Ochthoeca*. Traylor (1977), however, continued to regard it as a monotypic genus of uncertain affinities (perhaps closest to *Satrapa*). We place it here, well apart from *Ochthoeca*, because of the plumage similarity of *Satrapa* and *Tumbezia*.

Tumbezia salvini

TUMBES TYRANT

PLATE: 41

DESCRIPTION: 13.5 cm (5¼"). *Nw. Peru.* Mostly grayish olive above, grayer on crown and blacker on cheeks, with *frontal band and long superciliary bright lemon yellow;* wings dusky with *2 broad whitish wing-bars* and edging, tail blackish with *outermost pair of feathers edged white.* Below entirely bright lemon yellow.

SIMILAR SPECIES: Nothing really similar in its limited range.

HABITAT AND BEHAVIOR: Uncommon in arid woodland and groves of acacias and mesquite, usually near watercourses (which are often dry). Typically forages within 1 or 2 m of ground, perching fairly erectly, making short sallies to foliage and air; sometimes perches more horizontally and wags its partially spread tail. Generally in pairs and rather confiding. We do not know its voice.

RANGE: Nw. Peru (Tumbes south to La Libertad); has never been found within the present borders of Ecuador. Below about 200 m.

Muscipipra Gray Tyrants

A very distinctive species of uncertain affinities, the Shear-tailed Gray Tyrant ranges locally in forest borders of se. South America. It is superficially like the *Contopus* pewees in behavior, voice, and even (vaguely) appearance. Lanyon (1986) concluded that, based on anatomical characters, the genus was most closely related to *Gubernetes* and (very surprisingly) *Neoxolmis*.

Muscipipra vetula

SHEAR-TAILED GRAY TYRANT

PLATE: 41

DESCRIPTION: 22.5 cm (8¾"). *Se. Brazil area. Mostly gray,* with duskier auriculars, whiter throat, and *contrasting black wings and long slender tail;* tail rather deeply forked, with outer feathers broad and their outer vane mostly pale, but usually folded at rest so the fork is not too apparent except in flight. Juvenile has crown, back, and wing feathers scaled white.

SIMILAR SPECIES: This sleek, elegant flycatcher is virtually unmistakable. Its gray color recalls Crowned Slaty Flycatcher, but Shear-tailed's slender long-tailed shape is very different.

HABITAT AND BEHAVIOR: Rare to uncommon in borders of humid and montane forest and secondary woodland, to a lesser extent out into adjacent clearings or natural grasslands. Usually in pairs but also not infrequently in small loose groups of up to 5–6 birds, this svelte flycatcher generally perches on high exposed branches from which it sallies out after passing insects with graceful undulating flight, often for long distances. Less often perches lower, sometimes even dropping to the ground. Usually silent but occasionally gives a somewhat pewee-like "pup-pup-pup." Overall appearance and mannerisms are reminiscent of the Phainopepla (*Phainopepla*) and silky-flycatchers (*Ptilogonys* spp.) of North and Middle America.

RANGE: Se. Brazil (Espírito Santo and cen. Minas Gerais south to cen. Rio Grande do Sul), ne. Argentina (Misiones and ne. Corrientes), and e. Paraguay (an old record from Alto Paraná, and a recent sighting [P. Scharf] from Mbaracayú in Canendiyu). To about 2200 m; mostly above 1000 m in n. part of its Brazilian range, at least when breeding.

Gubernetes Tyrants

One of the finest flycatchers, the dramatic Streamer-tailed Tyrant is found locally in damp, grassy, and shrubby terrain in s.-cen. South America. Its spectacular long and deeply forked tail is convergent with the similarly shaped tail of the Fork-tailed Flycatcher. Lanyon (1986) concluded that, based on anatomical considerations, its closest relative is the somewhat similar *Muscipipra* (together with the very different *Neoxolmis* of Argentina).

Gubernetes yetapa

STREAMER-TAILED TYRANT   PLATE: 41

DESCRIPTION: 38–40 cm (15–16″). *A splendid, strongly patterned, long-tailed flycatcher of s.-cen. South America.* Rather stout bill. *Above mostly pale gray* with dark brown shaft streaks, palest (almost white) on fore-crown and superciliary; wings blackish with patch of cinnamon-rufous at base of primaries (showing as *conspicuous stripe in flight*) and tertials edged sandy; long tail also blackish, graduated and *very deeply forked. Throat white, sharply outlined on sides of neck and across upper chest by chestnut pectoral collar;* breast and sides pale gray with faint dark shaft streaks, becoming white on belly. Females average smaller and shorter-tailed, and are slightly duller.

HABITAT AND BEHAVIOR: Uncommon to locally fairly common in damp grasslands and marshy terrain near streams, always with some shrubbery nearby. Usually in pairs, less often small (family?) groups, perching conspicuously atop bushes and low trees, often at edges of gallery woodland. A spectacular bird that sallies out, often long distances, after insects, its long flexible tail whipping around. Its calls also attract attention, the most frequent being a very loud, sharp "whee-irt!" or simply "weert!" A pair's display is magnificent: the male perches just above its mate, calling loudly and excitedly "wurreéeper, wurreéeper . . . ," all the while with wings outstretched and flapping, the cinnamon wing-stripe flashing conspicuously. The female usually remains silent but may move her body almost in timing to male's call, and may also flare open her wings. Several pairs reside just below the main entrance to Brasília Nat. Park.

RANGE: S.-cen. and se. Brazil (n. Mato Grosso do Sul, cen. Goiás, and extreme s. Bahia south to w. Rio Grande do Sul), n. and e. Bolivia (northwest to La Paz near Ixiamas), Paraguay (mostly east of the Río Paraguay; seen once west of it in n. Alto Paraguay), and ne. Argentina (south to e. Chaco and n. Corrientes). To about 1100 m.

Colonia Tyrants

A mainly black flycatcher with a small bill and elongated central tail feathers, found widely at forest edge in tropical lowlands but inexplicably absent from parts of the Amazon basin. Its relationships remain obscure.

Colonia colonus

LONG-TAILED TYRANT

PLATE: 42

DESCRIPTION: Male 23–25 cm (9–10″), female 18–20 cm (7–8″). Unmistakable. *Mostly black* with *white forecrown and superciliary* becoming silvery gray (s. races) to ashy gray (n. races) on crown and nape; *central pair of tail feathers greatly elongated* (up to 12 cm [almost 5″] longer than the others); inconspicuous white rump patch. *Leuconotus* (west of Andes in Colombia and Ecuador) and *poecilonotus* (s. Venezuela and Guianas) have an irregular white area on midback. Females and immatures are somewhat paler and grayer on belly; young birds may not have lengthened tail feathers.

SIMILAR SPECIES: Young birds lacking the elongated tail feathers and with little white or gray on crown might be confused with a *Knipolegus* black-tyrant, but note Long-tailed's stubby bill.

HABITAT AND BEHAVIOR: Fairly common to common and often conspicuous in canopy and borders of humid forest and secondary woodland and in small openings and clearings, the main requirement being a few dead trees or exposed snags. Long-tailed Tyrants are almost invariably found in pairs, sometimes family groups; they are quite sedentary and have certain favored perches, from which they sally to the air after passing insects for hours on end. Their most frequent call, a distinctive soft, rising "tuweee?," often accompanied by a flick of the tail, regularly attracts attention.

RANGE: Guianas, s. Venezuela (mainly in Bolívar, with a recent record from Cerro de la Neblina in s. Amazonas), and extreme n. Brazil (Roraima); w. Colombia (Pacific lowlands and east in humid Caribbean lowlands to middle Río Magdalena valley in Tolima and Cundinamarca) and w. Ecuador (south to Manabí); e. Colombia (Casanare south to Nariño), e. Ecuador (few records far from Andes), e. Peru (absent from Loreto), n. Bolivia (south to Cochabamba and n. Santa Cruz), s. and e. Brazil (mainly south of the Amazon basin, but recorded north to Rondônia, Marajó Is., and Maranhão; found south to n. Rio Grande do Sul), e. Paraguay (west to Paraguarí), and ne. Argentina (Misiones). Also Honduras to Panama. Usually below 1200 m.

Knipolegus Tyrants and Black-Tyrants

Distinctive midsized, relatively long-tailed flycatchers found primarily in s. South America, with a few species ranging in the Andes or the Amazon/Orinoco basins. Most are found in forest or woodland, some in more open situations; all are quiet, and some, especially those found inside forest, are very inconspicuous. Nests are open cups placed in shrubs or trees (usually quite low). In all species except the Rufous-tailed Tyrant, at least the male is gray or black. Blue bills, red irides, and crests are features of some species. Females of most are basically brown with rufous rumps and are usually streaked below; two species are monomorphic or virtually so. The genus presents some tricky identification challenges, in part because of intrageneric diversity. In some polytypic species, males of different races resemble other species as much as or even more than they resemble each other; in others, female characters seem not to particularly relate or correspond to their respective males.

Short (1975) and Traylor (1977) merged the monotypic genus *Entotriccus* (Cinereous Tyrant) and *Phaeotriccus* (Hudson's and Amazonian Black-Tyrants) into the genus *Knipolegus;* both had formerly been separated on the basis of wing-shape differences (e.g., Meyer de Schauensee 1966, 1970). Lanyon (1986), on the basis of their syringeal morphology, supported this merger.

GROUP A

Sexes similar (*hen-plumaged*). Andes and tepuis.

Knipolegus poecilurus

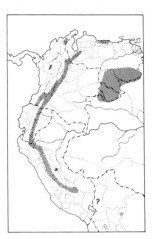

RUFOUS-TAILED TYRANT

PLATE: 42

DESCRIPTION: 14.5 cm (5¾"). *Iris red* (but often not too conspicuous). Mostly grayish to brownish gray above, wings duskier with 2 dull buffyish to pale grayish wing-bars; tail dusky with *inner webs mostly rufous* (prominent in flight). Mostly dull buffy grayish below, grayest on breast, *becoming cinnamon-buff on belly and crissum.* Birds of the tepuis (*salvini* and *paraquensis*) are not as deeply colored below, have a more extensive gray wash on breast, and show little or no rufous in tail.

SIMILAR SPECIES: Somewhat reminiscent of a *Contopus* pewee though with buffier underparts. Female White-winged Black-Tyrant has rufous rump in addition to conspicuous rufous in tail, and in Rufous-tailed's range the White-winged shows some breast streaking. Cf. also female Andean Tyrant.

HABITAT AND BEHAVIOR: Uncommon and local at borders of montane forest and in adjacent shrubby clearings with scattered trees, sometimes out into pastures and in hedgerows. Usually found singly or in pairs, most often alone and not associating with mixed flocks; generally quite conspicuous, perching in the open. Often raises its tail, then slowly lowers it. Seems very quiet.

RANGE: Coastal mts. of n. Venezuela (Distrito Federal), and Andes of w. Venezuela (Mérida and Táchira), Colombia (not recorded in W. Andes north of Valle), e. Ecuador (rather few records), e. Peru, and n. Bolivia (known only from 1 old specimen from w. Santa Cruz); Sierra de Perijá on Venezuela-Colombia border; tepuis of s. Venezuela (Bolívar and Amazonas) and extreme n. Brazil (Roraima). Likely also occurs in adjacent Guyana, but published records from Trinidad and Tobago are apparently in error. Mostly 900–2200 m.

GROUP B

"Standard" *Knipolegus:* males *ashy gray to shiny black;* females either *duller* (1 species) or (more frequently) very different, *mottled or streaked below* with variable amount of *rufous at base of tail.*

Knipolegus striaticeps

CINEREOUS TYRANT

PLATE: 42

DESCRIPTION: 13–13.5 cm (5–5¼"). *Found in the chaco and adjacent areas.* Male has *bright scarlet iris* and is *mostly dark gray,* blacker on foreface, throat, and chest (imparting a *dark-hooded effect*); wings blackish with 2 narrow pale gray wing-bars and edging on inner flight feathers, tail blackish with outer web of outer pair of rectrices paler. Female has pale brown iris and is slightly smaller than male; is mainly olivaceous brown above, more *rufous on crown and nape* with *some dusky streaking,* cinnamon on uppertail-coverts, and whitish on lores; and has wings dusky with 2 prominent white bars, tail blackish with considerable rufous on inner webs. Both sexes are whitish below *prominently but finely streaked dusky.*
SIMILAR SPECIES: Male is smaller than other male *Knipolegus,* most of which are truly black and many of which have white in wing; cf. also Crowned Slaty Flycatcher. Female most resembles female Hudson's Black-Tyrant, though Hudson's is larger and more conspicuously rufous (not merely cinnamon) at base of tail. Female Blue-billed Black-Tyrant is larger and generally richer and darker above, more coarsely streaked below, and has buff wing-bars; its normal habitat and range differ. Cf. also Bran-colored Flycatcher.
HABITAT AND BEHAVIOR: Fairly common to locally common in chaco woodland, borders, and openings. Usually found singly, less often in pairs, perching erectly and alertly, frequently twitching tail; it is often in the open, atop a bush or low tree. Males have an interesting display, presumably territorial (but also given during austral winter when they presumably are not breeding): from an exposed perch they suddenly mount 8–15 m into the air, then fold their wings and drop like a stone before recovering and pulling up to a new perch, giving a sneezy, hiccupping "skidi-ik" (perhaps with wings?) as they bottom out. Displaying males also give a "ts-ip" while perched.
RANGE: E. and s. Bolivia (Santa Cruz southward), extreme sw. Brazil (sw. Mato Grosso do Sul), w. Paraguay (almost entirely west of the Río Paraguay; in east, 1 old April record from Sapucaí in Paraguarí), and nw. Argentina (south to San Luis and Córdoba). Not certainly known to be an austral migrant, though Olrog (1979) and Short (1975) considered it migratory without providing details; the single e. Paraguay record suggests that at least local movements do take place. Mostly below 1000 m, though recorded to 1900 m in Bolivia.

NOTE: Formerly placed in the monotypic genus *Entotriccus* on the basis of its uniformly narrow primaries in both sexes.

Knipolegus signatus

ANDEAN TYRANT

PLATE: 42

Other: Plumbeous Tyrant, Jelski's Bush-Tyrant

DESCRIPTION: 16–16.5 cm (6¼–6½"). *E. slope of Andes from Peru to n. Argentina.* Two quite different races. Males of better-known, more southerly *cabanisi* (Argentina north to Cuzco, Peru) have iris dark red and bill blue-gray with black tip and paler, more flesh-colored lower mandible; females have iris brown and bill blackish. Male *uniform plumbeous gray,* slightly paler on lower belly; wings and tail blackish (inner webs of secondaries and inner half of primaries edged white, but this hard to see in the field). Female mostly dull brown above, becoming bright rufous on uppertail-coverts; wings dusky with 2 buff wing-bars, tail dusky with feathers broadly edged cinnamon-rufous. Below dull buffy whitish, *broadly streaked grayish olive especially on breast* (can look almost uniform), becoming buff on crissum. Nominate *signatus* (n. Peru south to Junín) is larger and has longer bill; both sexes have iris brown or chestnut and bill blackish. Male *uniform dull black.* Female darker, more olive brown above than *cabanisi,* and with *darker, more olive brown streaking below* (can also look quite uniform) and much less cinnamon-rufous in tail (which *looks markedly darker*).

SIMILAR SPECIES: Note its *Andean range.* Male White-winged Black-Tyrant is black with *conspicuous* white in the wing showing in flight (though hidden when perched), whereas female is much more ochraceous below with little or no streaking. White-winged is more a bird of semiopen or woodland edge situations, whereas Andean mainly ranges in forest interior. Cf. also Slaty Elaenia (with shorter bill and orange on mandible, indistinct pale wing-bars, etc.) and male Jet Manakin.

HABITAT AND BEHAVIOR: Uncommon to locally fairly common in lower growth of montane forest and woodland, less often at borders (though often easier to see there than actually inside). Perhaps more numerous in Argentina than it is northward. Inconspicuous and generally quiet, usually found alone and not accompanying mixed flocks. Perched birds often shiver their tail sideways. Breeding males in Argentina (nominate *cabanisi*) have a display flight in which they shoot into the air and describe a high arc (up to 7 m above their display perch) with a short glide at its apex, emitting a brief wing whirr on the way up and a "tec" (perhaps produced by the bill) upon landing; see R. V. Almonacid and M. G. Márquez (*Hornero* 13[3]: 231–232, 1992). Quite readily found in alder woodland in the Río Yala valley above Jujuy [city].

RANGE: E. slope of Andes in Peru (n. Cajamarca on the Cordillera del Condor [FMNH] south to Junín, and in Cuzco and Puno), w. Bolivia, and nw. Argentina (south to Tucumán and adjacent Catamarca). 700–2500 m (*cabanisi*); 1900–3050 m (nominate *signatus*).

NOTE: Traylor (1982) showed that what had long been called *Myiotheretes signatus* (Jelski's Bush-Tyrant; see Meyer de Schauensee 1966), until recently only known from three female-plumaged specimens, actually belonged in the genus *Knipolegus*. This generic transfer had originally been proposed by J. T. Zimmer in an unpublished ms. and during the 1970s was confirmed by the collection of adult male specimens of *signatus*. Traylor (op. cit.) concluded that *signatus* and *Knipolegus cabanisi* (which until then had been considered a monotypic species) were sister taxa, i.e., they were more closely related to each other than they were to any other. He treated *cabanisi* as a subspecies of *K. signatus* (which name had priority) but noted (p. 19) that "the two are quite distinct, and a case can be made for calling them two species." In the absence of any new information on *signatus*, we continue to consider them as conspecific, though we too are struck by their marked dissimilarities. We suspect that further work will result in their being separated specifically. In that case we suggest that *K. signatus* be known as the Black Andean-Tyrant and *K. cabanisi* as the Plumbeous Andean-Tyrant. Regardless, *K. signatus* (*sensu lato*) should *not* be called the Plumbeous Tyrant, because that name is applicable only to one of the species' races (the other is *black*). Further, what was described as *K. subflammulatus* (Berlioz' Tyrant; see Meyer de Schauensee 1966) has proven to be only the immature male of *K. s. cabanisi* (E. Mayr, *J. f. Ornith.* 112: 313, 1971).

Knipolegus orenocensis

RIVERSIDE TYRANT

DESCRIPTION: 15–15.5 cm (6–6¼"), *xinguensis* slightly larger. Locally in semiopen habitat *along Orinoco and Amazon rivers* and some tributaries. Bill blue-gray tipped black; iris brown (*contra* Hilty and Brown 1986). Both sexes of nominate *orenocensis* (Orinoco system) and *xinguensis* (along Rios Xingu and Araguaia in e.-cen. Brazil) are *uniform slaty gray*, the female slightly paler and more olive; see C-38. *Sclateri* (Amazon system downstream to near lower Rio Tapajós) is now known (from ANSP specimens obtained in Ecuador in 1992) to be sexually dimorphic. Male *uniform dull black*. Female dull olive-gray above with rufescent tinge on rump; wings and tail unmarked. Whitish below with coarse blurry olive grayish streaking on breast and down flanks. Juvenile like female but with dull rufous edging on wing-coverts (forming indistinct wing-bars) and rectrices, more rufous on rump, and buff-tinged underparts with more diffused streaking.

SIMILAR SPECIES: Note this species' *restricted habitat and range*. It occurs with only 1 other *Knipolegus*, Amazonian Black-Tyrant, both sexes of which are easily confused, particularly with Riverside's *sclateri* form. Amazonian is somewhat smaller; males are glossier blue-black, whereas females have a clearer and paler belly with little streaking. Amazonian is generally less conspicuous, tending to remain within shady tangled cover.

HABITAT AND BEHAVIOR: Uncommon and quite local in semiopen brushy areas along rivers and near lakes, most often in early-succession growth on river islands. Usually in pairs, sometimes perching conspicuously atop a bush or low tree (*xinguensis*), but *sclateri* seems more often to remain within cover. Often drops to ground in pursuit of prey. Male *sclateri* have a display in which every 10–15 seconds they quickly mount a few meters into the air, then drop back down, accompanied by a (mechanical?) snap; foraging birds give a "tuc" contact note.

RANGE: Locally along the Orinoco and some of its tributaries in s.-cen. Venezuela (s. Anzoátegui and n. Bolívar west to Apure) and ne. Colombia (recorded only from ne. Meta, but probably more widespread); locally along the Amazon and some of its tributaries in extreme ne. Ecuador (found in Sept. 1992 on an island in the Río Napo at the mouth of the Río Aguarico; ANSP), ne. Peru (along the Amazon from the Iquitos area eastward), extreme se. Colombia (Leticia area), and Brazil (downriver to the lower Rios Tapajós and Xingu, and along the Rio Araguaia in Goiás). Below 300 m.

NOTE: More than a single species may be involved. Nominate *orenocensis* is essentially monomorphic, *xinguensis* nearly so, but *sclateri* is now known to be strongly dimorphic. We would favor treating *K. sclateri* and *K. orenocensis* as separate species (under the English names of Black and Slaty River-Tyrant respectively) but for the problem of the *xinguensis* taxon. It seems more to resemble *orenocensis,* though its range is highly disjunct from that form. Until more is known of the complex, we consider it prudent to retain the usual single-species treatment.

Knipolegus cyanirostris

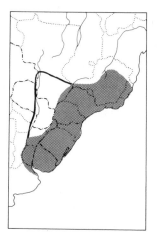

BLUE-BILLED BLACK-TYRANT

PLATE: 42

DESCRIPTION: 14.5–15 cm (5¾–6″). *Se. Brazil area.* Male has *pale blue bill with black tip* and *bright red eye;* female's bill blackish, usually with some bluish on lower mandible, and iris pale brownish red to orange. Male *all glossy black* with *no white on wing evident in the field* (inner web of secondaries and inner primaries edged white, visible only from below or in the hand). Female rufous brown above, *bright rufous on crown and especially rump;* wings blackish with 2 buff wing-bars, tail dusky with feathers broadly edged cinnamon-rufous. Below whitish to yellowish white, *coarsely streaked with dark olive brown especially on breast,* with *cinnamon-rufous crissum.*

SIMILAR SPECIES: In its range, male is only black-tyrant *lacking* conspicuous white in wing. Note, too, that its red iris is much more prominent than in any other *Knipolegus;* as this is the case, and as various *Knipolegus* have similar blue bills, the species would much more usefully have been called the "Red-eyed Black-Tyrant." Dark female is more heavily streaked than any other black-tyrant in range, and its streaks are darker and extend onto belly. It most resembles female Cinereous Tyrant, which is smaller and paler above and has finer breast streaking and no rufous on crissum; the two are not known to occur together, though their ranges do come close (note that preferred habitats differ). Cf. also female Hudson's Black-Tyrant. Bran-colored Flycatcher is smaller, lacks rufous on rump, and is less coarsely streaked below.

HABITAT AND BEHAVIOR: Uncommon to locally very common at borders of humid forest and gallery woodland, less often out into shrubby semiopen areas, usually near water. Normally not found in the interior of extensive forest. Usually in pairs; inconspicuous, tending to remain low, though at times a bird may remain on a high exposed perch for protracted periods. Makes fast sallies into the air and to foliage. Seems most numerous in s. Brazil (e.g., in Rio Grande do Sul). Very quiet; even as experienced an observer as W. Belton has heard its "barely audible" call only once (Belton 1985).

RANGE: Se. Brazil (north to Minas Gerais and Espírito Santo), Uruguay, and ne. Argentina (south to Santa Fe and n. Buenos Aires; an old and uncertain record from n. La Pampa); during austral winter more s. breeders move north into e. Paraguay and Mato Grosso do Sul, Brazil. To about 2200 m in se. Brazil.

Knipolegus poecilocercus

AMAZONIAN BLACK-TYRANT

DESCRIPTION: 13.5 cm (5¼"). *Local in damp thickets and seasonally flooded areas in Amazonia.* Male has blue bill and dark iris; female's bill dusky, iris dark brown. Male *all glossy black* with a slight blue sheen; see C-38. Female dull olive brown above, lores and narrow eye-ring whitish, and more rufescent on uppertail-coverts; wings and tail dusky, wings with 2 broad pale buff bars, tail feathers broadly edged cinnamon-rufous. Below mostly yellowish white, *heavily streaked brownish olive especially across breast,* clearest and palest on belly.

SIMILAR SPECIES: Riverside Tyrant is larger and never as glossy black as male Amazonian (even Riverside's black *sclateri* race of upper Amazon being duller and sootier); it inhabits *more open* riparian areas. Cf. also rather similar male Black Manakin, which is *not* associated with water. Female resembles various other female/immature *Knipolegus* tyrants (besides Riverside, however, none occurs in its range or habitat; see discussion under Riverside). Female's large dark eye imparts a distinctive wide-eyed look. Bran-colored Flycatcher is neither so olive above nor so broadly streaked on breast, and lacks rufous on tail and uppertail-coverts.

HABITAT AND BEHAVIOR: Uncommon and local in lower growth of tangled woodland near water, usually where it is shady, often in seasonally flooded areas. Inconspicuous, perching at or below eye level, sallying to foliage or to the surface of shallow water; its movements are sudden, often manakin-like. Quiet and sedentary, usually in pairs. Males in presumed display jump upward abruptly a short distance and return to their original perch; they sometimes make a soft snapping sound.

RANGE: Locally in w. Guyana (a single specimen from Merume Mts.), s. Venezuela (Amazonas and Apure), ne. Colombia (recorded only from Mozambique in w. Meta and 2 localities in e. Vichada, but likely more widespread), extreme ne. Ecuador (1990–1991 records from along the Río Lagarto in e. Napo; ANSP), e. Peru (Loreto), and Amaz. Brazil (locally in the Rio Negro drainage, and south of the Amazon east to along the Rios Tocantins and Araguaia). Below 300 m.

NOTE: Formerly separated in the genus *Phaeotriccus* on the basis of its extremely narrowed outer three primaries in both sexes.

Knipolegus aterrimus

WHITE-WINGED BLACK-TYRANT   PLATE: 42

DESCRIPTION: 16.5–18 cm (6½/27"). Mainly Peruvian Andes to Argentina. Male's bill blue-gray tipped black, iris dark; female's bill black with some bluish at base of lower mandible, iris also dark. Male *entirely shiny black* with *white band across base of primaries* hidden at rest but *conspicuous in flight.* Female of nominate race (most of Bolivia south through Argentina) mostly grayish brown above, freckled whitish on lores and below eye, becoming *bright cinnamon-rufous on rump and basal half of tail;* wings blackish with 2 broad cinnamon-buff bars; terminal tail-band blackish. *Below unstreaked uniform buffy ochraceous,*

somewhat whiter on throat and midbelly. Female *anthracinus* (Ayacucho, Peru, south to La Paz, Bolivia) somewhat smaller with mottled dusky-olive streaking on breast and reduced rufous on upper tail; *heterogyna* (n. Peru south to Ancash and Huánuco) is also smaller and female is more whitish below (with only a slight buff tinge) and with wing-bars and *rump buffy whitish to whitish*. Female *franciscanus* (interior e. Brazil) apparently similar to female of nominate race.

SIMILAR SPECIES: Males of the various races are essentially alike, but females vary so strikingly that the extremes appear unrelated. Cf. male of much rarer Hudson's Black-Tyrant, and Velvety Black-Tyrant (latter found only in e. Brazil). Female White-winged, aside from its n. *heterogyna* race, is the only *Knipolegus* with mostly ochraceous underparts, rufous on rump, and prominent buff wing-bars.

HABITAT AND BEHAVIOR: Fairly common to common in light scrub, woodland, and forest borders, mostly in arid regions (in Peru also more humid areas). Usually perches erectly in the open, sallying into the air, to foliage, and to the ground; male's white wing-band and female's bright rufous rump are both very noticeable. Generally rather quiet. Breeding males have a display flight in which they repeatedly jump a short distance (usually about 1 m) into the air, describe an arc, and return to the same perch (though often facing the other way); they then sometimes also emit their insignificant, faint song, a thin, wiry "chit-tzzzr." Look for this species around the Machu Picchu train station; it is also generally numerous and widespread in appropriate habitat in nw. Argentina.

RANGE: Andean slopes and valleys in Peru (north to Cajamarca), w. Bolivia, and w. Argentina (where it spreads out onto cen. and Patagonian plains south to Chubut and east to w. Buenos Aires); interior e. Brazil (sw. Bahia south locally to cen. Minas Gerais); in austral winter evidently withdraws from s. part of breeding range, and then recorded north to Entre Ríos in Argentina, with 2 records from w. Paraguay (Fortín General Diaz in Alto Paraguay [July] and Enciso Nat. Park in Nueva Asunción [Sept.]). Mostly 1500–3000 m in Peru and Bolivia, lower in Brazil and Argentina (in Argentina down virtually to sea level).

NOTE: The very isolated Brazilian population (*franciscanus*) may warrant full species status (Caatinga Black-Tyrant).

Knipolegus hudsoni

HUDSON'S BLACK-TYRANT

DESCRIPTION: 15 cm (6"). *A seemingly rare, little-known black-tyrant found mainly in chaco.* Male closely resembles male White-winged Black-Tyrant but *markedly smaller* and with an *indistinct small whitish area on lower flanks* (usually visible on perched birds, but sometimes obscured by wing). Note that the white on the wing of perched male Hudson's and male White-winged is normally *not* visible (though prominent in flight). Female grayish brown above, becoming rufous on rump and basal half of tail, terminal tail-band blackish; wings dusky

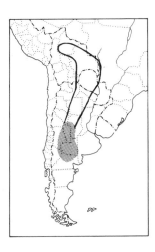

with 2 buff wing-bars. Below mostly buffyish with *mottled dusky-olive streaking across breast,* clear buff on belly.

SIMILAR SPECIES: Male also resembles male Amazonian Black-Tyrant, which is smaller and has no white on wing; they are not known to overlap. Female is easily confused with several other female black-tyrants. Female White-winged (of its potentially sympatric nominate race) is larger and *much more finely streaked below.* Female Blue-billed is more rufescent on crown and *more heavily and extensively streaked below.* Female Cinereous is smaller and markedly more rufescent on crown but only cinnamon on rump.

HABITAT AND BEHAVIOR: Rare to locally uncommon in low woodland and scrub; during austral winter in Bolivia has been found in overgrown pastures and in gardens around towns (S. Davis). Usually much less conspicuous than White-winged Black-Tyrant, tending to remain inside thick cover close to the ground; only displaying males seem to routinely take prominent perches. Males defending territories display almost entirely from a single favored tree, always dead and slightly emergent from surrounding woodland. Here it moves about and jumps restlessly from branch to branch, occasionally launching a short distance into the air (never more than 1–2 m), irregularly uttering short, guttural, hiccuping and snapping sounds, the most distinctive of which can be paraphrased as "tic-tic-titireétic." Readily seen during the breeding season at Lihue Callel Nat. Park in La Pampa, Argentina.

RANGE: Breeds in cen. Argentina (s. Córdoba south to Neuquén, Río Negro, and sw. Buenos Aires); during austral winter migrates north through n. Argentina and w. Paraguay to n. Bolivia (north to Beni, from whence a substantial number of specimens) and extreme sw. Brazil (w. Mato Grosso do Sul and sw. Mato Grosso). N. limit of breeding range in Argentina remains uncertain, perhaps somewhat farther north than indicated; we regard breeding evidence from w. Paraguay (see Short 1976) as equivocal. Mostly below 500 m.

NOTE: Formerly placed in the genus *Phaeotriccus* on the basis of its extremely narrowed outer three primaries in both sexes.

GROUP C

Sexes similar (*cock-plumaged*): *glossy black* with *white in wing;* mainly in s. Brazil.

Knipolegus nigerrimus

VELVETY BLACK-TYRANT   PLATE: 42

DESCRIPTION: 18 cm (7″). *Higher areas in e. Brazil.* Bill pale bluish gray; iris dark red. *Small* bushy crest. Male glossy blue black except for *white band across base of primaries* (hidden or mostly hidden at rest, but conspicuous in flight). Female similar but *throat chestnut streaked black.*

SIMILAR SPECIES: Male Blue-billed Black-Tyrant is smaller, shows *no* conspicuous white wing-stripe, and has a *brighter* red eye. Crested Black-Tyrant, more a bird of basically open terrain, is larger with prominent slender pointed crest and black bill.

HABITAT AND BEHAVIOR: Uncommon to locally fairly common in

grassy or rocky areas at high elevations, usually not far from trees or shrubby cover. Generally in pairs, foraging near the ground, with general behavior similar to most other black-tyrants'; more conspicuous than the often-sympatric Blue-billed. A pair can often be found around the Corcovado Statue above Rio de Janeiro (seemingly not intimidated by the tourist hordes); numerous in the high grasslands of the Serra do Itatiaia.

RANGE: E. Brazil (locally from w. Alagoas south to cen. Bahia on the Morro do Chapeu; mainly from Espírito Santo and s. Minas Gerais south to ne. Rio Grande do Sul). 700–2700 m.

Knipolegus lophotes

CRESTED BLACK-TYRANT
PLATE: 42

DESCRIPTION: 20.5–21 cm (8–8¼"). *A large, conspicuously crested black-tyrant found in open areas mainly in s. Brazil.* Iris dark red to reddish brown; bill black. *Crest long, slender, and pointed.* Entirely glossy blue-black with white band across base of primaries (hidden or barely visible at rest, but conspicuous in flight). Female slightly smaller.

SIMILAR SPECIES: Velvety Black-Tyrant is smaller, has only a small crest, and blue-gray (not black) bill. Otherwise slender Crested Black-Tyrant is virtually unmistakable. Note its remarkable convergence with the unrelated Phainopepla (*Phainopepla nitens*) of sw. United States and Mexico.

HABITAT AND BEHAVIOR: Uncommon to fairly common in open grassy or shrubby areas, often near groves of trees. Although conspicuous, Crested Black-Tyrants usually occur as highly dispersed pairs which appear to have large home ranges, and only locally are they numerous (one such area being below Itatiaia Nat. Park). They mainly capture insects from the air in rapid graceful flight but also eat some fruit. Like other *Knipolegus,* they seem mostly silent.

RANGE: S. Brazil (s. Mato Grosso, Goiás, and Minas Gerais south locally to Rio Grande do Sul), ne. Paraguay (1938 series in UMMZ from Cerro Amambay in Amambay), and Uruguay. To about 1100 m.

Hymenops Tyrants

A striking, marsh-inhabiting tyrannid found in s. South America. *Hymenops* is most closely related to the genus *Knipolegus* (Lanyon 1986) but differs in its longer legs and slender, quite sharply pointed bill, as well as its unique "spectacles" and mostly white primaries (rufous in female). The nest is a deep cup hidden in herbage or at the base of a shrub near the ground.

Hymenops perspicillatus

SPECTACLED TYRANT
PLATE: 42

DESCRIPTION: 15.5–16 cm (6–6¼"). *Near water in s. South America. Both sexes have prominent fleshy yellow wattle around eye* and yellow iris; in nonbreeding birds, male's wattle averages smaller and female's is

virtually obsolete. Male's bill is pale yellow, female's duskier with yellow lower mandible. Male black except for *mainly white primaries* (only their bases and tips are black), extremely conspicuous in flight and visible as a patch even on the folded wing. Female streaked brown and dusky above with buffy superciliary; wings with 2 buff bars and *mostly rufous primaries* (conspicuous in flight but also visible when perched). Below whitish to pale buff, with dusky streaking across chest. *Andinus* (Chile and adjacent s. Argentina; perhaps migratory) slightly larger.

SIMILAR SPECIES: Male shows much more white in wing (not just a white stripe) than any *Knipolegus* black-tyrant, and none of those have anything comparable to Spectacled's contrasty yellow wattle. Female's wattle is smaller and can be harder to discern, but no similar bird has a wattle or the contrasting rufous primaries.

HABITAT AND BEHAVIOR: Fairly common to common in marshes and grassy or shrubby areas, *almost always near water*. Males especially are very conspicuous. Usually seen perched on a fence post or other exposed lookout, though they also run often on the ground. Mainly solitary, pairs not often being seen together even when breeding, though what are apparently migrant groups of female-plumaged birds, many doubtless immatures, are sometimes found. Breeding males have a spectacular display in which they repeatedly rise 5–10 m above their perch, there executing an almost perfect somersault, then dropping head-first back to their perch, alighting with a jerk; at times the wings are flapped so rapidly as to appear to vibrate.

RANGE: Breeds in Argentina (Tucumán, Formosa, and Corrientes south to Chubut, in small numbers to n. Santa Cruz), Chile (Atacama south to Aysén), Uruguay, and extreme se. Brazil (Rio Grande do Sul and s. Santa Catarina); during austral winter migrates north into Paraguay, Bolivia (as far as Beni and Santa Cruz), and s. Brazil (sw. Mato Grosso do Sul with a few records from São Paulo and Rio de Janeiro; numbers also increase in Rio Grande do Sul); a single July report from highlands of Cuzco, Peru. A few may remain to breed in s. Paraguay (and possibly elsewhere in its winter range). To about 2000 m (in Andean valleys of nw. Argentina), occasional vagrants higher.

NOTE: The correct spelling of the species name is *perspicillatus,* not *perspicillata* (Sibley and Monroe 1990).

Lessonia Negritos

A pair of small, plump, basically terrestrial flycatchers of open terrain in the high Andes and far s. South America. The striking males are mainly black, and both sexes have rufous on the back. The bill is short and slender, and the hindclaw is long and pipit-like. Lanyon (1986) considered *Lessonia* to be part of his "*Knipolegus* assemblage" and considered its closest relative to be *Pyrocephalus* (the seemingly very different Vermilion Flycatcher). Until recently the genus was considered monotypic (e.g., Meyer de Schauensee 1966, 1970), but it was separated into a pair of allospecies by Traylor (1977), which seems the best course.

The English name of Rufous-backed Negrito was appropriate under the former broad species concept, but when its component forms are considered distinct, it seems best to highlight their different ranges ("Austral" and "Andean"), reserving "Rufous-backed" for use should they ever again be deemed conspecific.

Lessonia rufa

AUSTRAL NEGRITO   PLATE: 42

Other: Southern Rufous-backed Negrito, Patagonian Negrito

DESCRIPTION: 12 cm (4¾"). Male *mostly black* with contrasting *rufous-chestnut back*. Female has head and nape brownish gray, becoming *rufous brown on back,* contrasting with black wings and tail; outer web of outermost rectrix whitish. *Below dull ashy grayish,* darkest on breast, whitest on belly. Males in mottled immature plumage are frequently seen.
SIMILAR SPECIES: Cf. Andean Negrito. Otherwise males are unmistakable, whereas far drabber females can be known by their distinctive behavior, habitat, and rufous on back (but might be confused with Spot-billed Ground-Tyrant, which see).
HABITAT AND BEHAVIOR: Common to locally abundant (more numerous as a breeder southward) in open, often barren areas with short grass or bare soil, usually near water. Basically terrestrial (though also perching freely on low bushes and fences), negritos are very active and restless, constantly running about in short bursts like a ground-tyrant, and like them pursuing their insect prey mainly by short flutters into the air. In austral summer almost omnipresent in appropriate habitat in Tierra del Fuego and in Santa Cruz, Argentina, and Magallanes, Chile. At other seasons seen mostly in small loose flocks which move north along either coast and spread out across the lowlands. Males evidently depart the nesting grounds early, well before females, which finish caring for the young. At all seasons negritos are usually quiet.
RANGE: Breeds from cen. Chile (north at least to Santiago) and cen. Argentina (north to Mendoza and La Pampa, possibly in small numbers a little farther north) south to Tierra del Fuego; during austral winter migrates north into the remainder of lowland Chile and Argentina and to s. and e. Bolivia (Tarija and Santa Cruz), Paraguay (few records), Uruguay, and extreme se. Brazil (Rio Grande do Sul); accidental on Falkland Is. Mostly below 1000 m.

Lessonia oreas

ANDEAN NEGRITO

Other: Andean Rufous-backed Negrito, White-winged Negrito

DESCRIPTION: 12.5 cm (5"). *Replaces similar Austral Negrito in altiplano of Peru to n. Chile and nw. Argentina.* Slightly larger. Male has slightly paler rufous-chestnut back, and *inner webs of flight feathers whitish* (not dusky) usually visible only in flight. Female differs more markedly from female Austral: in addition to having the whitish on flight feath-

ers, it is more extensively rufous on back and rump, and *much sootier on underparts, with blackish crissum,* and has almost no whitish on outer rectrix.

HABITAT AND BEHAVIOR: Uncommon to locally fairly common in open areas with short grass or barren ground, almost invariably near water; seems less numerous in Chile and Argentina, most common in Peru. Behaves like Austral Negrito but not migratory. Both could occur together during austral winter in n. Chile or Bolivia.

RANGE: Andes of cen. and s. Peru (north to Huánuco), w. Bolivia, n. Chile (south to Coquimbo), and nw. Argentina (south to Catamarca). Mostly 3000–4000 m, occasionally somewhat lower. There are 2 sightings (Aug. and Sept.) of *Lessonia,* the species undetermined in both cases (but more likely the strongly migratory *L. rufa?*), from coast of Peru (Lima and Arequipa).

Fluvicola Water-Tyrants

An attractive trio of basically black and white flycatchers found near water in the lowlands of South America. Their large and often conspicuous ball-shaped nests with a side entrance are usually placed low in a bush or small tree, frequently over water.

Fluvicola albiventer

BLACK-BACKED WATER-TYRANT   PLATE: 42

DESCRIPTION: 14 cm (5½"). *A striking black and white flycatcher found in s. South America, migrating to Amazonia;* formerly considered conspecific with Pied Water-Tyrant. *Above mostly black* except for white forecrown, sides of head, narrow rump band, and with variable amount of white tipping on wing-coverts and tip of tail. *Below entirely pure white.*

SIMILAR SPECIES: Cf. Pied Water-Tyrant (found only in n. South America). Black-backed's basic pattern resembles female White-headed Marsh-Tyrant's, but latter is ashy brown (not black) above and not as pure white below with breast smudged brownish. Masked Water-Tyrant's pattern is quite different.

HABITAT AND BEHAVIOR: Uncommon to locally fairly common in marshes and nearby shrubby vegetation, and in riparian areas along rivers. Forages on or near ground, often moving out onto floating and emergent vegetation, frequently cocking and fanning its tail; flight is fast and low. Usually quite bold, sometimes even inquisitive. Rather quiet (more so than Pied), though it has a soft ticking note.

RANGE: Breeds in e. Bolivia (north to Santa Cruz), e. Brazil (lower Amazon region and Ceará south locally to w. São Paulo and Mato Grosso do Sul; has bred as far west as the Manaus area, *fide* S. Wilson), Paraguay, and n. Argentina (south to n. Córdoba and n. Buenos Aires); in austral winter migrates north into w. Amaz. Brazil and n. Bolivia, with a few records from e. Peru (north to Loreto). Mostly below 1000 m.

NOTE: Formerly usually considered a race of *F. pica*, but we believe its marked plumage differences, the lack of intergradation, and the difference in vocalizations justify treating it as a full species.

Fluvicola pica

PIED WATER-TYRANT

DESCRIPTION: 12.5 cm (5″). Replaces Black-backed Water-Tyrant in *n. South America*. Differs in being smaller and in having *more pied pattern above*, with scapulars broadly white, entire rump white, and some white mottling on back; Pied shows *no* wing-bars. See V–XIII.

SIMILAR SPECIES: Distinctive in its marshy or water-edge habitat; no known overlap with Black-backed Water-Tyrant. Cf. female White-headed Marsh-Tyrant.

HABITAT AND BEHAVIOR: Fairly common to common in and around marshes and freshwater ponds and lakes, sometimes out into adjacent open areas, including corrals and gardens. General behavior similar to Black-backed Water-Tyrant's, also conspicuous and often tame, usually foraging in the open, frequently on floating vegetation. Its frequently given call is a nasal "zhweeoo" or "zhreeo."

RANGE: W. and ne. Colombia (Caribbean lowlands and up Río Cauca valley to Cauca and Río Magdalena valley to Huila, but not in Pacific lowlands; east of Andes south to Meta and Vichada), Venezuela (south through n. Amazonas and Bolívar), Guianas, and extreme n. Brazil (n. Roraima and Amapá); 1 sighting from e. Ecuador (along the upper Río Napo in July 1974); Trinidad. Also Panama. To about 1000 m.

NOTE: See comments under Black-backed Water-Tyrant.

Fluvicola nengeta

MASKED WATER-TYRANT   PLATE: 42

DESCRIPTION: 14.5–15 cm (5¾–6″). *Remarkably disjunct range: e. Brazil, and w. Ecuador and nw. Peru. Mostly white with contrasting narrow black stripe through eye onto ear-coverts* and blackish brown wings and tail, the tail broadly tipped white; back tinged pale grayish. *Atripennis* (w. Ecuador area) has blacker wings with white-fringed tertials.

SIMILAR SPECIES: Black-backed and Pied Water-Tyrants are mostly or entirely black across back with mainly white heads (lacking black stripe through eye). Masked is somewhat longer-tailed than either, and looks vaguely like a wheatear (*Oenanthe* spp.).

HABITAT AND BEHAVIOR: Fairly common in marshes and open or semi-open shrubby areas near water, sometimes ranging out into adjacent areas such as gardens. We have seen Masked and Black-backed Water-Tyrants nesting at the same marsh in e. Bahia, Brazil, together with White-headed Marsh-Tyrant. General behavior similar to congeners'. Call of Masked is a distinctive sharp "kirt!," sometimes doubled. Displaying birds face each other, standing high on their rather long legs, and bob up and down; usually their tails are spread and partially cocked.

RANGE: W. Ecuador (w. Esmeraldas and Pichincha south to El Oro) and extreme nw. Peru (Tumbes); e. Brazil (Maranhão east to Rio

Grande do Norte, and south to e. Minas Gerais, Rio de Janeiro, and ne. São Paulo; has spread into the Rio and São Paulo area only since the 1950s). Mostly below 800 m.

Arundinicola Marsh-Tyrants

The White-headed Marsh-Tyrant is found widely in marshes and shrubby or grassy areas near water across the S. Am. lowlands. It has been suggested that the monotypic *Arundinicola* be merged into the genus *Fluvicola* (e.g., *Birds of the World*, vol. 8), but Lanyon (1986) presented anatomical evidence suggesting that the genera are best kept separate; they also behave quite differently.

Arundinicola leucocephala

WHITE-HEADED MARSH-TYRANT   PLATE: 42

DESCRIPTION: 12.5 cm (5″). Bill blackish with lower mandible yellow basally. Slightly bushy-crested. Male unmistakable, *mostly black with sharply contrasting white head and throat*. Female mostly *plain ashy brown above* with white forecrown and blackish tail. Whitish below, whitest on throat, mottled ashy brown across breast. See V–XIII.

SIMILAR SPECIES: Female might at a glance be mistaken for a Black-backed or Pied Water-Tyrant, but it is nowhere near as sharply black and white, being more brownish above and smudgy whitish below; shape and typical attitudes differ as well.

HABITAT AND BEHAVIOR: Fairly common in marshes and shrubby damp grasslands and on river islands. A conspicuous bird (males are noted far more often than females, doubtless because of their striking coloration), perching erectly on posts or low branches, making short sallies to the air. Unlike the *Fluvicola* water-tyrants, the marsh-tyrant only briefly drops to the ground and rarely spreads or cocks its tail. It is usually quiet.

RANGE: N. and e. Colombia (Caribbean lowlands and south in Río Magdalena valley to Huila, and locally in lowlands east of Andes except in Caquetá and Putumayo), Venezuela, Guianas, Amaz. and e. Brazil (south to Rio Grande do Sul; seemingly absent from sw. Amaz. region), ne. Peru (Loreto and Ucayali south to Pucallpa area), e. Ecuador (a 1990 sighting from along the Río Napo in Napo; G. De Smet et al.), n. and e. Bolivia, Paraguay, and n. Argentina (south to Salta, Chaco, n. Santa Fe, and Corrientes); Trinidad. Seems possible in Uruguay. To about 500 m.

Alectrurus Tyrants

This genus comprises two of the most spectacular flycatchers; they are found very locally in grasslands of s.-cen. South America. The males' outer rectrices are highly modified, twisted, and lengthened; in Strange-tailed even the female's tail is adorned. Strange-tailed shows another almost unique attribute: breeding males lose their throat feathers, one of only a handful of birds in which this occurs. Lanyon (1986) concluded that the genus' closest relatives are *Fluvicola* and *Arundinicola*. The nest is a neat grassy cup hidden on or near the ground.

The Strange-tailed Tyrant was formerly placed in the monotypic genus *Yetapa* (e.g., Meyer de Schauensee 1966, 1970), mostly on the basis of its "strange" tail. However, the basic structure and plumage pattern of both sexes, as well as its modified outer rectrix, are both similar to those found in Cock-tailed Tyrant, and we agree with recent authors (e.g., Short 1975; *Birds of the World*, vol. 8) that the two genera should be merged.

Alectrurus tricolor

COCK-TAILED TYRANT   PLATE: 42

DESCRIPTION: 12 cm (4¾"), but males in full breeding plumage (including lengthened tail feathers) up to 18 cm (7"). Bill mostly yellowish (some dusky on culmen). Male *mostly black above* with gray on rump; shoulders and patch on secondaries white. *Extraordinary tail usually held cocked*, with inner pair of feathers lengthened and very broad and *oriented in a perpendicular position relative to the rest of tail. Face and underparts mostly white*, with black patch on side of chest forming a partial collar. Freshly molted birds have black feathers fringed brown; tail of breeding males apparently becomes quickly frayed. Female mottled brown above, paler and buffer on superciliary, shoulders, secondaries, and rump. Below whitish, often tinged buff, with some brown on sides of chest. Tail normally shaped, and short.

SIMILAR SPECIES: Adult males are unique and unmistakable, but note that subadults or molting adult males with only partially developed tails are often seen. Female-plumaged birds (many doubtless immature males) are often more numerous than full-plumaged males and can be confusing. They are plump, short-tailed birds with large and rather round heads, thus quite differently shaped from the female seedeaters that they vaguely resemble (the two are often found loosely associated with each other, especially when not breeding); bill shape and behavior are, of course, also markedly different.

HABITAT AND BEHAVIOR: Uncommon to locally common in open grassy areas that have not been recently burned or heavily grazed (and thus have *tall* grass), also to a lesser extent in adjacent areas with scattered shrubbery or near water. Because they require relatively undisturbed grasslands, Cock-tailed Tyrants have become extremely local in recent years; overall numbers have declined greatly, and the species deserves formal threatened status. The only areas where the birds remain numerous are where grassland is more or less protected, e.g., in Brazil's superb Emas Nat. Park. Where they occur Cock-tailed Tyrants are conspicuous, generally seen as they perch near the top of a tall, swaying grass stem, less often in a low bush. Even when breeding they seem somewhat gregarious, concentrating in certain particularly favorable areas. They may be partially migratory (or merely nomadic?), as loose flocks of up to 30–40 mostly female-plumaged birds have been seen. Males are at their best when displaying: they launch into the air with fast, fluttery wingbeats which seem singularly ineffective as they progress so slowly. They proceed for up to 100 m or so, wings flapping furiously and with the extraordinary tail cocked so far forward over the back that the tip is almost above the head! This remarkable display is given in Brazil at least Sept.–Nov., but its timing may vary with the onset of rains. The species seems never to make a sound.

RANGE: Very locally in n. and e. Bolivia (La Paz, Beni, and n. Santa Cruz), s. Brazil (s. Mato Grosso, s. Goiás, Minas Gerais, and Espírito Santo south to Paraná, possibly to Rio Grande do Sul; no recent records from the coastal southeast), ne. Paraguay (Concepción and San Pedro), and ne. Argentina (Corrientes and Misiones; no recent records known to us). To about 1100 m.

Alectrurus risora

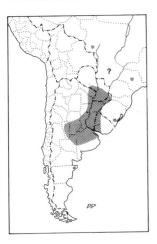

STRANGE-TAILED TYRANT   PLATE: 42

DESCRIPTION: 20 cm (8″), but males in full breeding plumage (including lengthened tail feathers) up to 31 cm (12″). Bill mostly pinkish yellow. Male *mostly black above* with gray on rump; scapulars and edging on wing-coverts and flight feathers whitish. *Extraordinary tail,* with *outer pair of feathers very much lengthened,* reduced to their shaft at base but *with outer two-thirds of inner web becoming very broad;* these feathers *seem to spring from the crissum* and then *twist* so they are held perpendicular to and below the rest of tail. Throat white, but *feathers lost while breeding, exposing pinkish red skin; broad breast band black;* lower underparts white. Freshly molted birds have black feathers fringed brown, and nonbreeding or molting birds may have narrower, shorter tail plumes. Female like female Cock-tailed Tyrant but slightly larger and with *brown on breast forming a complete pectoral band.* Tail, however, quite different: the normal feathers longer and more pointed, and with outer 2 pairs of rectrices quite elongated and essentially reduced to their shafts but *terminating with narrow racquets.*

SIMILAR SPECIES: Male is unique and unmistakable. Female could only be confused with female Cock-tailed Tyrant, which is smaller with differently shaped tail and only a *partial* breast band (just on sides).

HABITAT AND BEHAVIOR: Rare to locally uncommon in less disturbed damp grasslands, marshy areas, and to a lesser extent adjacent shrubby areas. Has declined substantially over most of its range, presumably because of habitat degradation and destruction, and deserves formal threatened status. The Strange-tailed Tyrant has not been reported recently from a large portion of its former range, though it remains locally numerous in Corrientes, Argentina, and in se. Paraguay (e.g., west of San Juan Bautista in Misiones). It is a conspicuous bird, generally perching atop a tall grass stem, post, or shrub, sallying both into the air and to grass. In the nonbreeding season birds may gather into small loose groups, much as in Cock-tailed Tyrant. Flying males present a bizarre appearance, with their 2 long, blade-like plumes carried perpendicular to its axis *beneath* the rest of tail (almost like a weird rudder!); perhaps because of this odd adornment, their flight is usually slow and weak, with the tail slowly whipped up and down. Actual display seems not to have been described. This truly bizarre flycatcher seems to have converged toward certain African whydahs (*Vidua* spp.). RANGE: Locally in s. Brazil (very old records from single sites in s. Mato Grosso, São Paulo, and Rio Grande do Sul; no recent reports known to us), e. Paraguay, Uruguay, and n. Argentina (south to San Luis, Córdoba, and Buenos Aires; not recorded in recent years south of e. Chaco and Corrientes, though likely persists locally in ne. Santa Fe). Possibly migratory to some extent, at least in s. part of range. Below 500 m.

NOTE: Formerly placed in the genus *Yetapa*. The correct spelling of the species name is *risora*, not *risoria* (Sibley and Monroe 1990).

Attila Attilas

Found in wooded habitats in tropical lowlands and on lower mountain slopes, attilas can be readily known by their heavy, straight, and prominently hooked bills and bull-headed appearance. They are generally inconspicuous but often very vocal, perching erectly and stolidly in middle and upper levels of forest, making occasional sallies to snap insects off branches or leaves; they also eat some fruit. Long classified in the Cotingidae (e.g., Meyer de Schauensee 1966), the genus *Attila* is now considered, on several lines of evidence, to belong in the Tyrannidae, allied to the *Myiarchus* flycatchers (Lanyon 1985). We follow Traylor (1977) and *Birds of the World*, vol. 8, in merging the monotypic genus *Pseudattila* into *Attila*.

GROUP A

Head more or less contrastingly gray.

Attila phoenicurus

RUFOUS-TAILED ATTILA   PLATE: 43

DESCRIPTION: 18 cm (7"). *A rare attila, migrating to cen. Amazonia from se. Brazil area.* Smaller than other attilas, with slightly shorter bill blackish to dark brown, usually with some whitish at base of lower mandible. *Head and nape dark gray contrasting with deep rufous upperparts* (only slightly paler on rump), primaries blackish. *Below ochraceous yellow,* tinged rufous across breast.

SIMILAR SPECIES: Most resembles Citron-bellied Attila but with gray head more sharply demarcated from rich rufous back, rump nearly concolor with back (not markedly paler), and bill showing less pale color. Gray-hooded Attila (with which locally sympatric in se. Brazil— though Rufous-tailed seemingly much scarcer) is larger and has throat whitish streaked gray (at least in area of recorded overlap with Rufous-tailed). Female Crested Becard has pattern similar to this attila's but is not so bright overall and is considerably stockier with stouter bill.

HABITAT AND BEHAVIOR: Rare to locally fairly common in canopy and middle levels of humid forest and taller secondary woodland, at least in some areas seems associated with *Araucaria*-dominated forest.

Not a well-known bird, but perhaps merely overlooked, especially when not vocalizing. Its distinctive song is a loud, far-carrying "whee? whee? whee-bit" repeated over and over; sometimes responds to tape playback. The species may be threatened by the loss of much forest habitat in its breeding range. Particularly numerous in the Serra do Mar of São Paulo, where substantial numbers can be heard and seen locally, e.g. at Fazenda Intervales.

RANGE: Breeds in se. Brazil (Rio de Janeiro south to Rio Grande do Sul, and perhaps inland to Goiás and Mato Grosso), e. Paraguay (only sightings, including 1 seen by B. Treiterer in Jan. 1990 at Ybicui Nat. Park in Paraguarí), and ne. Argentina (Misiones); recorded, apparently only during austral winter from May to Oct., in Amaz. Brazil (lower Rio Tapajós area west to Rio Purus drainage) and sw. Venezuela (1 record from Cerro Yapacana in Amazonas); a 1989 report from ne. Bolivia (birds tape-recorded in ne. Santa Cruz at Serranía de Huanchaca in Aug. and Sept.) presumably refers to transient individuals, as likely also was a specimen taken at Fortín Conchitas in Boquerón, w. Paraguay, in Apr. 1962 (Steinbacher 1968). To about 1500 m.

NOTE: Formerly placed in the monotypic genus *Pseudattila* (e.g., Meyer de Schauensee 1966, 1970), but transferred to *Attila* by Traylor (1977).

Attila rufus

GRAY-HOODED ATTILA PLATE: 43

DESCRIPTION: 21 cm (8¼"). *Se. Brazil.* Rather long bill brown above, grayish to whitish below. *Head and nape gray,* becoming *deep rufous on back* and cinnamon-rufous on rump and tail (palest on rump); primaries blackish. *Throat white streaked gray, contrasting sharply with orange-ochraceous breast* and flanks; midbelly yellower. *Hellmayri* (s. Bahia) differs from nominate race (remainder of range) in its mostly rufous throat (whitish only on chin).

SIMILAR SPECIES: Rufous-tailed Attila is smaller and has shorter bill, entirely ochraceous underparts (throat not contrasting), and more contrast between its darker gray head and rufous back. Even the most rufous examples of the variable Bright-rumped Attila show wing-bars, streaking on breast, and whitish on belly.

HABITAT AND BEHAVIOR: Fairly common in humid and montane forest and forest borders, ranging mostly in the subcanopy and middle strata; seems most numerous in foothill and lower montane areas. Found singly or in pairs, and like other attilas heard much more often than seen. Its song is a loud, far-carrying series of 6–9 slowly delivered "whee" notes, gradually rising in pitch and strength before fading on the last note; also gives a shorter, softer "wee, tee-tee-pu," sometimes alternating with primary song. Readily found (at least heard) in lower levels of Itatiaia Nat. Park and at Nova Lombardia Reserve above Santa Teresa in Espírito Santo.

RANGE: Se. Brazil (cen. Bahia south to ne. Rio Grande do Sul). To about 1500 m.

Attila citriniventris

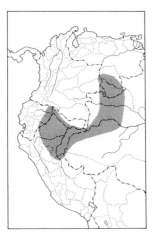

CITRON-BELLIED ATTILA

DESCRIPTION: 18.5 cm (7¼"). *W. Amazonia*. Upper mandible grayish, lower mandible pale horn to pinkish. *Head gray,* becoming rufous brown on back and *paler cinnamon-rufous on rump;* tail rufous; wings duskier *with no wing-bars. Below mostly bright ochraceous,* more whitish on chin, obscurely streaked dusky on lower throat and breast, yellower on belly. See V-27.

SIMILAR SPECIES: Rufous-tailed Attila (apparently only a rare migrant into range of Citron-bellied) has more contrasting gray head but less conspicuous paler area on rump; it has no whitish on throat. Rufous phase of Bright-rumped Attila lacks gray on head, shows wing-bars, and is whitish (not ochraceous yellow) on belly.

HABITAT AND BEHAVIOR: Rare to locally uncommon in canopy of terra firme forest and forest borders. Not a well-known bird but perhaps just overlooked, being difficult to record unless one recognizes its voice. Its song, often tirelessly repeated, is a fast "whee-whee-whee-whee-whee-wheebu"; in quality it resembles common song of Bright-rumped Attila, but its tempo is quicker and the initial notes are single-noted (not doubled).

RANGE: Extreme s. Venezuela (Amazonas), extreme e. Colombia (seen by P. Coopmans and P. Kaestner in Jan. 1990 near Puerto Inirida, Guainía; perhaps more widespread), nw. Amaz. Brazil (mostly in upper Rio Negro drainage, but also recorded from Tefé on the Amazon), ne. Peru (Loreto), and e. Ecuador (few records, including specimens from Chichirota on the lower Río Bobonaza in Pastaza, and Zancudococha on the lower Río Aguarico in Napo; ANSP). Below 500 m.

GROUP B

Head and back rather *uniform*.

Attila cinnamomeus

CINNAMON ATTILA   PLATE: 43

DESCRIPTION: 19.5 cm (7¾"). Amazonia to Guianas. *Bill black;* iris brown. *Mostly cinnamon-rufous,* only very slightly paler on rump; underparts somewhat paler than upperparts; primaries and greater wing-coverts mainly blackish.

SIMILAR SPECIES: Somewhat similar White-eyed Attila regularly occurs with Cinnamon; White-eyed is less rufous above (its crown in particular is more grayish), shows a striking *white* eye, and has lower mandible *pale.* Citron-bellied Attila is similar, especially from below, but has distinctly gray head and obviously paler rump. Cf. also Varzea Mourner (which often occurs with Cinnamon Attila, though differing in comportment, etc.).

HABITAT AND BEHAVIOR: Uncommon to locally fairly common in lower and middle growth of várzea forest, swampy forest around lake margins, and woodland on river islands. Usually in pairs, often perching more in the open and easier to see than many other attilas, though not especially active. Most common and characteristic call, at least in w. Amazonia, is a repeated loud and ringing "tuu-tueeeeeer," rather hawk-like in quality and fading away. Also has other vocalizations that more closely resemble other attilas', e.g., a repeated "whoo-whoo-wheeeyeér."

RANGE: Guianas, e. and s. Venezuela (Sucre south to Bolívar and Amazonas), se. Colombia (north to Casanare and Guainía, but seemingly rather local), e. Ecuador, ne. Peru (Amazonas and Loreto), n. Bolivia (Pando and Beni), and Amaz. Brazil (south to n. Mato Grosso, and east to n. Maranhão). Below 500 m.

Attila torridus

OCHRACEOUS ATTILA

DESCRIPTION: 20.5 cm (8"). *Mainly w. Ecuador.* Pattern similar to Cinnamon Attila's (latter found only *east* of Andes) but *much paler and yellower overall,* essentially pale ochraceous above with yellowish rump and ochraceous yellow underparts (yellowest on belly). As in Cinnamon Attila, primaries and greater wing-coverts are contrastingly blackish.

SIMILAR SPECIES: Nothing really similar in range; Rufous Mourner and Rufous Piha are more truly rufous, not so yellow. Cf. Bright-rumped Attila.

HABITAT AND BEHAVIOR: Rare to locally fairly common in canopy and middle strata of humid forest and secondary woodland, and in adjacent clearings and plantations (e.g., cacao); seems to avoid areas of very wet forest, such as those in n. Esmeraldas. Often in pairs and generally inconspicuous, usually seen perching quietly on an open branch, occasionally raising tail. Recorded most often from its far-carrying calls, the most common being a loud, repeated "whoeeeer," sometimes lengthened into a "whoeeeer, wheéu, whit-whit" or shortened to a sharp "wheerk!" The quality of some of these calls is strikingly similar to Black Hawk-Eagle's (*Spizaetus tyrannus*). This attractive attila is becoming increasingly rare and local because of forest destruction across much of its always small range. Although it seems capable of persisting in partially degraded or patchy habitat (in fact appearing to be more of an "edge bird" than the locally sympatric Bright-rumped Attila), the Ochraceous Attila probably deserves formal threatened status.

RANGE: Extreme sw. Colombia (a 1958 specimen from sw. Nariño at Ricuarte), w. Ecuador (Esmeraldas south to El Oro and w. Loja), and extreme nw. Peru (Tumbes in Tumbes Nat. Forest). Mostly below 1400 m, in small numbers up to 1900 m in s. Ecuador.

Attila bolivianus

WHITE-EYED ATTILA   PLATE: 43
Other: Dull-capped Attila

DESCRIPTION: 19 cm (7½"). Amazonia along and south of the Amazon. *The only attila with a prominent yellowish white iris,* and virtually unmistakable as a result. Lower mandible mostly pinkish horn. Mainly rufous brown above, grayer on crown, becoming bright cinnamon-rufous on rump and tail; primaries and greater wing-coverts mainly

blackish. Below cinnamon-rufous, paler on belly. *Nattereri* (upper Amazonia) is distinctly darker overall than nominate race (n. Bolivia and sw. Brazil).

SIMILAR SPECIES: Cinnamon Attila, with which White-eyed sometimes occurs, is somewhat similar aside from having a dark iris.

HABITAT AND BEHAVIOR: Uncommon to fairly common in várzea forest and forest borders, often on river islands; also in gallery forest in the pantanal of Mato Grosso, Brazil. Usually forages alone, most often in lower and middle strata, and more often heard than seen though it may respond briskly to tape playback. Its song resembles Bright-rumped Attila's but is delivered at a more leisurely pace, almost haltingly at first, "whup; whup, wheep, wheep, wheep, wheeyp, wheeyp, wheebit, wheeeur," the final note distinctly lower in pitch and intensity. Can be found regularly in appropriate habitat at Peru's Tambopata Reserve in Madre de Dios and at Explornapo Camp in Loreto.

RANGE: E. Peru (Loreto south to Madre de Dios; not recorded north of n. bank of the Amazon), n. Bolivia (south to La Paz, Cochabamba, and Santa Cruz), and Amaz. Brazil (from along the Amazon south locally to s. Mato Grosso, and east to e. Pará in the Belém area). Below 300 m.

NOTE: This species' striking white eye is so prominent and unique that we prefer to highlight it in its English name; it previously went by the vague and unhelpful name of Dull-capped Attila.

Attila spadiceus

BRIGHT-RUMPED ATTILA

PLATE: 43

DESCRIPTION: 18–19 cm (7–7½"). A widespread *polymorphic* attila, but all birds are united by showing *strong wing-bars* and *streaking on breast*. Iris reddish brown to hazel or auburn; bill basally pale pinkish. Usually mostly olive above with *contrasting bright yellow rump*, latter sometimes tinged buff or tawny; wings duskier with *rufescent to pale grayish wing-bars. Throat and breast olive streaked yellow,* becoming whitish and unstreaked on belly; crissum pure pale yellow, often tinged rufous. Scarce variants, apparently color morphs, are most frequent in nominate race of Amazonia, but even here each represents at most 5% of the total population (as seen in specimen collections); there are also intermediates. *Gray morph* has solid gray head and neck, olive back, yellow rump, gray throat and breast indistinctly streaked whitish, buffy whitish belly; *rufous morph* has all rufous upperparts except for ochraceous yellow rump (showing little contrast), rufous throat and breast indistinctly streaked whitish, buffy whitish belly.

SIMILAR SPECIES: Perched bird's "bright rump" is usually hidden, but *no other attila is predominantly olive,* and none shows breast streaking or such prominent wing-bars. Confusion is most likely with one of the rufous morph Bright-rumpeds, some of which are uniform enough that they could be mistaken for another of the mainly rufous attilas; cf. especially Citron-bellied and Cinnamon. Gray morph Bright-rumpeds could also be confused with Cinereous Mourner, though the latter's round, dove-like ("cotingid") head shape is very different, as are its bill shape and various plumage details. Note that several other attilas have rumps every bit as "bright" as in this species.

HABITAT AND BEHAVIOR: Uncommon to locally fairly common in forest, forest borders, and secondary woodland, occasionally venturing out into tall trees in adjacent clearings. In Amazonia mainly or entirely in terra firme forest and usually less numerous here than elsewhere. Rather stolid and inconspicuous, tending to perch high, so not too often seen. More apt to be recorded once its frequently given song is recognized (though this resembles in quality that of several other attilas), a loud and far-carrying series of emphatic whistled notes, most of them characteristically doubled, e.g., "wheédip, wheédip, wheédip, wheédip, wheédip, wheeeeur," with a distinctive downward slur at the end. Although often given tirelessly, this song is notably ventriloquial; a calling bird sometimes responds to even a crude whistled imitation.

RANGE: Widespread in humid lowlands and on lower mountain slopes south to n. Bolivia (La Paz, Cochabamba, and n. Santa Cruz) and Amaz. Brazil (south to n. Mato Grosso and east to n. Maranhão); e. Brazil (Alagoas south to Rio de Janeiro); west of Andes south to nw. Ecuador (Pichincha); Trinidad. Also Mexico to Panama. To about 1500 m, occasionally somewhat higher.

Casiornis

A pair of predominantly rufous flycatchers inhabiting lighter woodland across interior South America. The genus is close to *Myiarchus*, both from an anatomical standpoint (see Lanyon 1985) and from behavior.

Casiornis rufa

RUFOUS CASIORNIS   PLATE: 43

DESCRIPTION: 18 cm (7"). Bill basally flesh-pink. *Uniform rufous above,* somewhat duller on back. *Throat and breast cinnamon,* tinged whitish on midthroat, becoming pale buffy yellowish on belly.

SIMILAR SPECIES: Superficially rather like several becards, especially various females, but more slender with longer tail and smaller bill. Cf. also Ash-throated Casiornis (limited overlap).

HABITAT AND BEHAVIOR: Fairly common in deciduous and gallery woodland, more heavily wooded cerrado, chaco woodland and scrub, and, at least in austral winter, riparian woodland and thickets. Usually in pairs, perching erectly and alertly, often raising crown feathers into a bushy crest; also sometimes nods its head in a *Myiarchus*-like manner. A surprisingly quiet bird, though it sometimes gives a brief, weak note, "pssee," occasionally extended into a short series.

RANGE: N. and e. Bolivia (northwest to Beni and La Paz), s.-cen. Brazil (s. Mato Grosso, n. Goiás, and cen. Minas Gerais south to São Paulo and Mato Grosso do Sul), Paraguay, and n. Argentina (south to Tucumán, e. Chaco, and n. Corrientes); during austral winter (May–Sept.) small numbers have been recorded north in s. Amazonia as far in Brazil as Maranhão, north of the Amazon at Porto Alegre, Rondônia at Cachoeira Nazaré, and Acre, and in se. Peru (north to Junín at Río Ene; AMNH). Mostly below 1500 m, occasionally or locally up in arid intermontane valleys of Bolivia to 2000–2500 m.

Casiornis fusca

ASH-THROATED CASIORNIS   PLATE: 43

DESCRIPTION: 18 cm (7″). *Ne. Brazil.* Bill basally flesh-pink. Crown rufous becoming *dull sandy brown on back;* tail rufous, wings dusky *broadly edged with rufous to buff,* more rufous on shoulders. Throat pale grayish, becoming *grayish fawn on breast* and pale creamy yellowish on belly.

SIMILAR SPECIES: The better-known Rufous Casiornis, which replaces this species southward, is much more uniform rufous above (including back and wings), brighter cinnamon (not so dull grayish) across breast, and not so yellowish on belly.

HABITAT AND BEHAVIOR: Uncommon to locally fairly common in caatinga woodland and more heavily wooded cerrado; also probably in campina vegetation in lower Amazon region. Not well known in life; behavior seems similar to that of Rufous Casiornis.

RANGE: Ne. Brazil (lower Amaz. region, south of the Amazon, from near lower Rio Tapajós east locally to the Bélem area, and east to Paraíba and Pernambuco; southeast to ne. Mato Grosso in the upper Rio Xingu drainage, n. Goiás on Bananal Is., and nw. Minas Gerais). To about 500 m.

NOTE: *C. fusca* is possibly conspecific with *C. rufa.* They are not known to be resident at the same locality, the more northerly records of *C. rufa* being ascribed to austral migration. As we have not seen any specimens comparable to the "intermediate birds" referred to by D. Snow (*Birds of the World,* vol. 8, p. 191), we thus retain *C. fusca* as a full species.

Rhytipterna Mourners

The genus *Rhytipterna,* formerly included in the Cotingidae, is now considered closely related to the *Myiarchus* flycatchers (see Lanyon 1985). Note that the superficially somewhat similar *Laniocera* mourners and *Lipaugus* pihas remain with the cotingas. Given that *Rhytipterna* is apparently not closely related to the other mourners, we recognize that members of the genus probably should not continue to have the group name "mourner," but its use seems so well entrenched that we are loathe to change it. The three *Rhytipterna* species are a diverse lot; the Rufous and Grayish are humid forest birds very similar to a pair of piha species (Rufous and Screaming respectively), whereas the Pale-bellied looks remarkably like a *Myiarchus* flycatcher and is found in wooded savannas. Nest placement for the genus remains unrecorded.

Rhytipterna holerythra

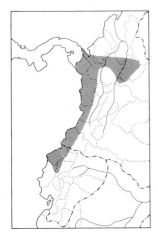

RUFOUS MOURNER

DESCRIPTION: 20 cm (7¾"). *W. Colombia and nw. Ecuador.* Bill mostly blackish, paler toward base. *Uniform rich rufous,* somewhat paler and tawnier on belly and crissum. See C-35. *Rosenbergi* (Pacific slope of Colombia and nw. Ecuador) is darker rufous overall than nominate race (n. Colombia).

SIMILAR SPECIES: *Easily* confused with Rufous Piha. The mourner is somewhat smaller and slimmer with a less heavy and blackish bill; throat and breast more uniform rufous (not paler on throat); and crown and wing-coverts slightly darker rufous than back (not uniform or slightly brighter). These differences are subtle, and identification often is more easily made through vocalizations (see below). Speckled Mourner is also similar but shows rufous spotting on dusky wing-coverts and usually has an eye-ring. Cf. also Cinnamon Becard and female One-colored Becard.

HABITAT AND BEHAVIOR: Uncommon in humid forest and mature secondary woodland. Usually lethargic and inconspicuous, perching alone or in pairs at varying heights in forest, much less often at edge. Frequently hunches far forward on its perch, at the same time raising its tail. Heard more often than seen, with calls including a clear mournful whistle, "wheeeip, wheeeer" (sometimes likened to a minor-key wolf whistle), and a somewhat snappier "wheee-per, wheeéur."

RANGE: W. Colombia (Pacific lowlands, and east in more humid Caribbean lowlands to middle Río Magdalena valley in Santander and e. Antioquia) and nw. Ecuador (mainly in Esmeraldas; sightings south to s. Pichincha). Also Mexico to Panama. To 1000 m.

Rhytipterna simplex

GRAYISH MOURNER   PLATE: 43

DESCRIPTION: 20.5 cm (8"). *Iris dark red to reddish brown;* bill mainly black, sometimes some pink basally. *Uniform plain gray,* slightly paler below, underparts with faint yellowish green cast (evident only at close range; strongest on belly and crissum). Presumed immatures and some females show fairly prominent fulvous edging on wing and tail feathers.

SIMILAR SPECIES: *Confusingly similar to the sympatric Screaming Piha.* Despite the piha's being markedly larger, in the absence of direct comparison (which is infrequent) they sometimes cannot be told apart in the field. Piha often has more grayish (never so red) eye, it lacks the mourner's slight yellowish cast to underparts and is darker and purer (less olivaceous) gray above, and it has a rounder head and all-black and somewhat stouter bill (lacking the basal pink generally shown by the mourner). Their voices are very different (see below), and fortunately both species vocalize a good deal. Cf. also Cinereous Mourner.

HABITAT AND BEHAVIOR: Uncommon to locally fairly common in middle and upper strata of humid forest (especially in terra firme, less frequently in transitional and várzea forest). Rather inconspicuous, especially if not calling. Often in pairs, sometimes alone or in small groups, perching quietly and then sallying out to pick insects off foliage or branches; regularly accompanies mixed flocks. Its distinctive call is a loud, fast "r-t-t-t-t-t-t-tchéw!" with a sneezing effect; sometimes gives 2–3 emphasized notes at the end or repeats the whole phrase several times in succession. The quality of this call is reminiscent of a nunbird (*Monasa*).

RANGE: Guianas, s. and extreme e. Venezuela (Delta Amacuro, Bolívar, and Amazonas), e. Colombia (north to Meta and Vaupés, probably north to Vichada), e. Ecuador, e. Peru, n. Bolivia (south to La Paz, Cochabamba, and n. Santa Cruz), and Amaz. Brazil (south to s. Mato Grosso, n. Goiás, and n. Maranhão); e. Brazil (Alagoas south to e. Minas Gerais and se. São Paulo). Mostly below 800 m, but recorded to 1300 m in Venezuela.

Rhytipterna immunda

PALE-BELLIED MOURNER

PLATE: 43

DESCRIPTION: 18.5 cm (7¼″). A *Myiarchus*-like mourner found *locally in savannas* from *Guianas to e. Amazonia*. Lower mandible pinkish at base. *Grayish olive brown above*, becoming browner on uppertail-coverts and tail; wings duskier with *2 pale grayish wing-bars* and rufous edging on primaries; rectrices also edged rufous with outer web of outermost pair pale. Throat and breast grayish, becoming pale dingy yellowish on belly, with *flanks usually tinged rusty* (merely buff in some birds).

SIMILAR SPECIES: Looks remarkably like a faded, dingy *Myiarchus* flycatcher; even specimens have long gone misidentified. Swainson's Flycatcher's often-sympatric *phaeonotus* race differs in being considerably darker overall (especially on crown) and in having an all-black bill; Short-crested Flycatcher also has an all-black bill. The diagnostic (though usually inconspicuous) rusty on the mourner's flanks is not shown by any *Myiarchus*. The mourner tends to perch more horizontally than do *Myiarchus*, and its head is rounder and eye larger, resulting in a different facial expression. In the field, Pale-bellied Mourner is often best distinguished by its vocalizations (see below).

HABITAT AND BEHAVIOR: Rare to uncommon and decidedly local in patches of woodland and scrub growing on sandy soil, often in savanna-dominated areas and (in Amaz. Brazil) in campinas. Doubtless often overlooked because of its close similarity to various *Myiarchus* flycatchers, and probably not so rare as usually thought; once its presence there was confirmed, Pale-bellied Mourner turned out to be quite numerous at Junglaven Lodge in Amazonas, Venezuela. Unless it is vocalizing, the Pale-bellied Mourner is usually rather inconspicuous, perching quietly in bushes and trees at varying heights, often hidden by foliage, peering about slowly like other mourners and occasionally making short sallies to foliage or for fruit. Its most common call, given at intervals through the day, is a distinctive "pur-treeép, cheeeuu" or "puu-puu-trreeép, cheeeuu," with some variation in phraseology but always with a loud ringing quality somewhat reminiscent of a *Schiffornis;* also gives a plaintive "pueeeer" call similar to Dusky-capped Flycatcher's (W. E. Lanyon; RSR). Male's infrequently heard dawn song is a leisurely "cheeuu . . . purreeéyp . . . cheeuu . . . purreeéyp . . ." (W. E. Lanyon).

RANGE: Locally in Surinam, French Guiana, and extreme ne. Brazil (Amapá); locally in sw. Venezuela (sightings and tape recordings since Feb. 1992 at Junglaven and south of Puerto Ayacucho in n. Amazonas [RSR and K. Zimmer, D. Delaney]; perhaps more widespread), extreme e. Colombia (e. Guainía), and Amaz. Brazil (upper Rio Negro drainage east to the Manaus area and around Santarém, and south to s. Mato Grosso). Below 300 m.

Myiarchus Flycatchers

One of the most difficult genera in a family replete with them, the *Myiarchus* flycatchers are now one of the best-known groups, thanks to the exhaustive work of W. E. Lanyon (Lanyon 1967, 1978). Although his study was basically taxonomic, his research also revealed numerous heretofore unknown facets of their natural history. In particular, Lanyon demonstrated how important it is to know the vocalizations of these similar-appearing birds and that the birds themselves discriminate between calls of their own species and those of other species. This latter realization led to the conclusion that they were not interbreeding and thus that several morphologically very similar forms should be recognized as full species.

Myiarchus flycatchers are widespread in wooded regions but are most numerous in edge situations; some species have restricted ranges, this often an identification aid, and two (Great Crested and Swainson's) are highly migratory. The genus also occurs widely in the West Indies and in Middle and North America. Most *Myiarchus* flycatchers are extremely similar in appearance, being grayish to olive above, often with a darker crown, and gray on throat and breast with contrasting yellow belly. Many species have rufous or white edging or tipping to the tail (and sometimes flight) feathers; note that immatures of *all* species have rufous edging on wings and tail. One species, the Rufous Flycatcher, stands far apart in coloration but otherwise is typical of the genus.

Behavior of all species is basically similar. All often raise their crown feathers, giving them a bushy-crested look; they frequently lean forward on their perches, nodding or pumping their heads in an almost lizard-like manner; and all nest in cavities, rather an unusual habit for flycatchers, characteristically lining their nests with pieces of cast-off snake skin (sometimes, or in some species, mammal fur or insect wings).

GROUP A

The only mostly *rufous Myiarchus.*

Myiarchus semirufus

RUFOUS FLYCATCHER

PLATE: 43

Other: Seaboard Flycatcher

DESCRIPTION: 18 cm (7″). *Nw. Peru.* Bill black. Above mostly dull dark grayish brown, becoming rufous on uppertail-coverts and with mostly rufous tail; *wing-coverts and broad edging on flight feathers rufous. Uniform cinnamon below.*

SIMILAR SPECIES: The most rufescent *Myiarchus,* not likely to be confused in its restricted range.

HABITAT AND BEHAVIOR: Uncommon in patches of thorny scrub and woodland dominated by acacia and mesquite trees, often in areas mainly devoted to agriculture (i.e., river valleys) but also occasionally in isolated groves out in the middle of otherwise desolate sandy desert. Rufous Flycatchers are usually inconspicuous, occurring mostly as well-dispersed pairs, and are now rather local because of the cutting of so many trees for firewood and as a result of increasingly large-scale farming. Their most frequent call is a soft, simple "huit" repeated at intervals; also gives a rasping "brrrt" note (Lanyon 1975).

RANGE: Coastal nw. Peru (Tumbes south to n. Lima); has never been found within the present borders of Ecuador. Below 200 m.

NOTE: For more information on this species, see W. E. Lanyon (*Wilson Bull.* 87[4]: 441−455, 1975).

GROUP B

Conspicuous *rufous in tail;* somewhat larger.

Myiarchus tyrannulus

BROWN-CRESTED FLYCATCHER   PLATE: 43

DESCRIPTION: 19.5 cm (7¾"). *Widespread in semiopen areas, mostly in arid regions.* Bill black, sometimes with a little pink at base of lower mandible. Crown dull brown, becoming dull brownish gray on remaining upperparts; wings dusky with 2 grayish white wing-bars and edging on inner flight feathers, and *primaries edged rufous;* tail blackish with *inner webs of all flight feathers broadly edged rufous* (especially prominent from below). Throat and breast pale gray, contrasting with pale yellow lower underparts.

SIMILAR SPECIES: Great Crested Flycatcher shows even more rufous in tail, is more olivaceous above with less brown on crown, and has darker gray throat and chest. No other *Myiarchus* shows rufous in wings and tail, but bear in mind that Brown-crested's rufous can be hard to see and that juveniles of other species may show some. Voice, habitat, and range are often better clues than morphological characters.

HABITAT AND BEHAVIOR: Fairly common to common in a variety of semiopen to open habitats (ranging from savanna to cerrado, caatinga, and chaco scrub and lighter woodland) and in gallery woodland and mangroves; mainly occurs in drier regions. Often more conspicuous than other *Myiarchus,* Brown-crested frequently perches fully in the open and rather low, peering about intently and often nodding its head and ruffling its crown feathers. Forages mostly by hover-gleaning from foliage, less often sallying to the air or dropping to the ground. One of the noisier *Myiarchus;* Brown-crested's loud and emphatic calls frequently draw attention. The most common vocalization is a short, sharp "peert!" or "weerp!" and a "whip" or "hurrip," sometimes repeated in a short fast series. There are no whistled notes.

RANGE: N. and ne. Colombia (Caribbean lowlands, and east of Andes in lowlands south to Meta and Vichada), Venezuela (except s. Amazonas), Guianas, Brazil in lower and s. Amazonia (west locally along the Amazon to the lower Rio Tapajós area and Faro, also a few records from n. Mato Grosso, Rondônia, and Acre) and much of the east and south (south to São Paulo and Mato Grosso do Sul, also in extreme w. Rio Grande do Sul), Paraguay (except extreme east), n. Argentina (south to La Rioja, Córdoba, Santa Fe, and Corrientes; not in Misiones), n. and e. Bolivia, and very locally in e. Peru (upper Río Marañón valley in Cajamarca and Amazonas; sightings from Madre de Dios at Manu Nat. Park and the Tambopata Reserve); Trinidad and Tobago and other offshore Caribbean islands (including Margarita and the Netherlands Antilles). Seems possible in n. Uruguay. Birds recorded from sw. Amaz. Brazil and Madre de Dios, Peru, are perhaps attributable to austral migration. Also sw. United States to Costa Rica. To about 1700 m (in Bolivia).

Myiarchus crinitus

GREAT CRESTED FLYCATCHER

DESCRIPTION: 20 cm (8″). *N. migrant to w. Colombia, Ecuador, and nw. Venezuela.* Resembles Brown-crested Flycatcher but slightly larger, more olivaceous above (not so brown on crown and less grayish on back), darker gray on throat and chest, deeper yellow on lower underparts, and has *almost entire inner web of tail feathers rufous,* resulting in almost solidly rufous underside to tail. Voice and habitat also help (see below).

HABITAT AND BEHAVIOR: Rare to uncommon n.-winter resident (mostly Oct.–April) in borders and canopy of humid forest and secondary woodland, to some extent also out into adjacent clearings with scattered trees. Usually found singly and not very conspicuous despite regularly giving its characteristic upward-inflected, throaty call, "whreeep?"

RANGE: Nonbreeding visitor to w. Colombia (apparently only west of E. Andes), nw. Venezuela (Zulia and Mérida, with a single record from nw. Amazonas), and ne. Ecuador (a few recent sight reports from Napo). Breeds in e. North America, wintering from s. United States south through Middle America. To 1100 m.

GROUP C

"Typical" *Myiarchus;* many species *extremely similar.*

Myiarchus swainsoni

SWAINSON'S FLYCATCHER   PLATE: 43

DESCRIPTION: 18 cm (7″). Bill blackish above, *pale brown to pinkish below* (sometimes only base of lower mandible is pale); *phaeonotus* has all-black bill. Confusingly *variable. Pelzelni* (Guianas and se. Peru south to s. Brazil in n. São Paulo and Mato Grosso do Sul) and *ferocior* (breeding in Argentina and se. Bolivia, migrating to w. Amazonia) *rather pale* grayish olive above with distinctly darker ear-coverts in *ferocior* (almost recalling the "mask" of a *Coccyzus* cuckoo); wings dusky with 2 whitish wing-bars and edging, tail blackish with pale outer web. Throat and breast pale gray, belly pale yellow. Nominate *swainsoni* (breeding mainly in se. Brazil and Uruguay, migrating north to Venezuela and e. Colombia) similar but somewhat darker olive above, brighter yellow on belly.

Phaeonotus (s. Venezuela and adjacent Guyana and n. Brazil) is *markedly darker above* (almost sooty brown, blackest on crown), with outer rectrix not paler, and *duller creamy yellowish on belly.*

SIMILAR SPECIES: Most apt to be confused with Short-crested Flycatcher, but that species *always has all-black bill.* Most races of Swainson's have at least base of lower mandible pale, but *phaeonotus* Swainson's does have an all-black bill and thus must be distinguished from Short-crested by its pale and dull belly (remember that both species have very dark upperparts). Swainson's, aside from *phaeonotus, looks rather faded and washed-out,* whereas Short-crested is quite dark overall; voices differ (see below). Cf. also Brown-crested and Dusky-capped Flycatchers (latter especially vis-à-vis *phaeonotus*) and Great and Large Elaenias.

HABITAT AND BEHAVIOR: Fairly common to common in a variety of basically forested or wooded habitats or their borders, savannas with scattered trees (especially *pelzelni*), and as an austral migrant also in riparian habitats in Amazonia. Behavior much like that of other members of genus; wintering nominate and *ferocior* are reportedly quite frugivorous. When breeding, song of nominate and *ferocior* is a loud "pút-it-here," often repeated for protracted periods, sometimes varied to "pút-it" or "here-pút-it" (Belton 1985). Other distinctive calls include a short, soft, mournful "whoo" or "poo," sometimes interspersed with other notes. Wintering birds in Amazonia are rather quiet. The dawn song of *phaeonotus* is a whistled "wheeeyr" delivered at several-second intervals, sometimes with a "hic" note interspersed (W. E. Lanyon); *phaeonotus* also gives fast, harsh, raspy notes reminiscent of those of several other *Myiarchus* (but *not* Short-crested).

RANGE: Breeds in s. and extreme e. Venezuela (Amazonas, Bolívar, and Delta Amacuro), Guianas, virtually all of Brazil except the far west, se. Peru (Cuzco; elsewhere?), n. and e. Bolivia, Paraguay, Uruguay, and n. and cen. Argentina (south to n. La Pampa and sw. Buenos Aires); in austral winter (May–Sept.) recorded north through e. Peru, e. Ecuador, e. Colombia, and across most of Venezuela except in the northwest, also on Trinidad. Mostly breeds below 1200 m (*phaeonotus* recorded to 1800 m in Venezuela), migrants mostly in lowlands (but once recorded to 2600 m near Bogotá in Colombia).

NOTE: A confusing species, as W. E. Lanyon commented (*Auk* 99[3]: 581, 1982), "one of those cases that gives taxonomists nightmares." As he had earlier noted (Lanyon 1978, p. 531), "*phaeonotus* and *pelzelni* are about as distinct morphologically as any two *species* in the genus" and yet, on the basis of tape-playback experimentation as well as morphological intergradation, he concluded that all forms were best considered conspecific. G. Mees (*Proc. Kon. Neder. Akad.,* Series C, 88: 75–91, 1985) nonetheless still favored treating *M. pelzelni,* including by inference *phaeonotus* as well, as a separate species (Pelzeln's Flycatcher). In our view, however, the exhaustive evidence presented by Lanyon is persuasive.

Myiarchus ferox

SHORT-CRESTED FLYCATCHER   PLATE: 43

DESCRIPTION: 18–18.5 cm (7–7¼"). *Bill entirely black.* Sooty olivaceous brown above, darkest on crown; wings dusky with 2 indistinct pale grayish wing-bars and edging, tail uniform dusky. Throat and

breast gray, lower underparts pale yellow. *Brunnescens* (llanos of Venezuela and ne. Colombia) and slightly larger *australis* (e. Bolivia and s. Brazil south to ne. Argentina) are similar to nominate race (remainder of range) but paler above and have feathers of tail and uppertail-coverts edged rufous brown (the latter especially in *brunnescens,* which also has lower underparts, especially crissum, often tinged brown).

SIMILAR SPECIES: Cf. very similar Venezuelan and Panama Flycatchers; these and Short-crested are difficult to distinguish except by range, unless they are calling. Swainson's Flycatcher usually has a brown (pale to dark) lower mandible; its race with an all-dark bill, *phaeonotus* of s. Venezuela and nearby, is very similar to Short-crested but is duller and paler on belly; voices also differ. Brown-crested Flycatcher also has a mostly black bill (though it is sometimes paler at base) and thus can resemble Short-crested (especially its races with brownish edging on rectrices). Note that Brown-crested's rufous on tail is on *inner* webs and thus is most conspicuous from below. Rufous also usually shows on Brown-crested's primaries; this is *absent* in Short-crested except in immatures, which also show rufescent wing-bars. Cf. also Dusky-capped Flycatcher.

HABITAT AND BEHAVIOR: Fairly common to common in borders of forest and secondary woodland, riparian and gallery woodland, clearings with scattered trees and shrubs, and plantations. Behavior similar to that of other *Myiarchus.* Its most common call is a distinctive short, soft, rolling or purring "prrrt"; nothing similar is given by other *Myiarchus.*

RANGE: Guianas, Venezuela (Paria Peninsula and llanos southward; absent from n. coastal area and the northwest), e. Colombia, e. Ecuador, e. Peru, n. and e. Bolivia (south to Santa Cruz), virtually all of Brazil except Santa Catarina and with only 1 record from extreme w. Rio Grande do Sul, e. Paraguay (west to along the Río Paraguay), and ne. Argentina (south to ne. Santa Fe and Corrientes). Lanyon (1978, p. 580) states that all records of Short-crested from farther west and south in Argentina are referable to Swainson's Flycatcher; Short-crested's occurrence in w. Paraguay and Uruguay is also regarded as unverified. There is no evidence of migration. Mostly below 1000 m, locally somewhat higher along base of Andes in Peru and Bolivia.

NOTE: Does not include *M. venezuelensis* or *M. panamensis,* following Lanyon (1978).

Myiarchus venezuelensis

VENEZUELAN FLYCATCHER

DESCRIPTION: 18 cm (7″). *N. Venezuela and n. Colombia. Closely* resembles Short-crested Flycatcher (formerly considered conspecific); where sympatric (so far as known, only in e. Venezuela) best identified by voice. Venezuelan shows rufous edging on outer webs of all tail feathers except outer pair (but this hard to see in the field); the race of Short-crested, nominate, found in e. Venezuela is also notably darker above than Venezuelan. See V-28, C-39.

SIMILAR SPECIES: Venezuelan Flycatcher overlaps with Panama Flycatcher in n. Colombia and Venezuela's Maracaibo basin. This pair of

species can probably be distinguished only by voice, though Panama is a bit paler dorsally.

HABITAT AND BEHAVIOR: Uncommon to fairly common in deciduous woodland and borders, plantations, and groves of trees in semiopen areas. Behavior much like that of other *Myiarchus*. Most common call is a distinctive sharp "wheeyr," often repeated steadily; also has a drier "whik." Can be found on wooded ridges of Tobago, where Brown-crested largely replaces it in coastal lowlands; also occurs in cocoa plantations near Ocumare north of Henri Pittier Nat. Park in Aragua, Venezuela.

RANGE: N. Colombia (Caribbean lowlands from n. Sucre east to the Guajira Peninsula, and at Cúcuta in Norte de Santander) and n. Venezuela (Maracaibo basin east to Aragua and Distrito Federal, and locally in ne. Bolívar); Tobago. To about 500 m.

NOTE: *Venezuelensis* was regarded as a race of *M. ferox* by Meyer de Schauensee (1966, 1970); Lanyon (1978) raised it to species rank.

Myiarchus panamensis

PANAMA FLYCATCHER

DESCRIPTION: 18 cm (7"). *W. and n. Colombia and nw. Venezuela.* Closely resembles Venezuelan and Short-crested Flycatchers; formerly considered conspecific with the latter. Overlaps only with the former, from which it can be distinguished in the field only by voice, though Panama is somewhat paler grayish olive above. See P-24.

HABITAT AND BEHAVIOR: Fairly common in semiopen areas, lighter woodland, clearings with scattered trees and shrubbery, and mangroves. Behavior similar to that of other *Myiarchus,* though it favors more open habitats than many. Along Colombia's Pacific coast it seems largely if not entirely restricted to mangroves. Most common call is a short whistled note uttered in pairs or as a fast series; dawn song is a fast whistled "tseeédew" or "wheédeedew," also a semiwhistled, twittering "tee, deedeedeedeedeedee" with variations.

RANGE: W. Colombia (widely in lowlands west of E. Andes; south along coast to sw. Nariño) and nw. Venezuela (Maracaibo basin); possible also in extreme nw. Ecuador. Also Costa Rica and Panama. To 600 m.

NOTE: *Panamensis* was regarded as a race of *M. ferox* by Meyer de Schauensee (1966, 1970); Lanyon (1978) raised it to full species rank.

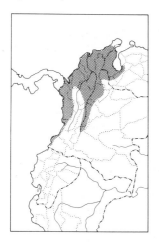

Myiarchus phaeocephalus

SOOTY-CROWNED FLYCATCHER
PLATE: 43

DESCRIPTION: 18–19 cm (7–7¼"). *W. Ecuador and nw. Peru,* mainly in more arid regions. Bill all black. *Forecrown ashy gray, becoming blackish on hindcrown,* contrasting strongly with grayish olive back; wings dusky with 2 indistinct (but sometimes wide) grayish wing-bars, tail blackish with *pale outer web and tip.* Throat and breast gray, lower underparts pale yellow. *Interior* of upper Río Marañón valley has slightly browner crown.

SIMILAR SPECIES: Note its restricted range, in most of which sympat-

ric with only one other similar *Myiarchus,* Dusky-capped. Dusky-capped is somewhat smaller, shows narrow rufous edging on primaries, and is brighter yellow on lower underparts; note that the sympatric races of Dusky-capped, *nigriceps* and *atriceps,* are even blacker-crowned than Sooty-crowned. Dusky-capped tends to occur in more humid areas. Short-crested Flycatcher never shows any pale color on tail.

HABITAT AND BEHAVIOR: Fairly common in light deciduous woodland, arid scrub, and forest borders; sometimes at edge of mangrove forest. Behavior much like other *Myiarchus;* generally quite conspicuous. Most common call is a "freee?" or "whreeee?" with somewhat querulous quality. Numerous in Chongon Hills west of Guayaquil, Ecuador.

RANGE: W. Ecuador (north to w. Esmeraldas, and inland through w. Loja) and nw. Peru (south to Lambayeque); upper Río Marañón valley in nw. Peru (Cajamarca and adjacent Amazonas) and extreme s. Ecuador (s. Zamora-Chinchipe near Zumba; ANSP). To about 1500 m.

Myiarchus cephalotes

PALE-EDGED FLYCATCHER

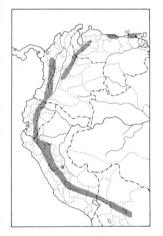

DESCRIPTION: 18–19 cm (7–7¼"). *Subtropical zone of Andes and mts. of n. Venezuela.* Resembles Sooty-crowned Flycatcher but *crown and back uniform brownish olive* (with *no* contrast, and showing no gray, blackish, or brown on crown); also lacks that species' pale tail-tip, though Pale-edged does show *pale buffy whitish outer web* on outer pair of tail feathers (much as in Sooty-crowned). See C-39.

SIMILAR SPECIES: Apical Flycatcher (found only in Colombia) shows wide, pale tail-tipping, in addition to having pale outer webs to outer rectrices. Short-crested Flycatcher (limited overlap along e. base of Andes) has no pale color on tail.

HABITAT AND BEHAVIOR: Uncommon to locally fairly common in canopy and borders of montane forest and secondary woodland and in partially cleared areas with patches of secondary woodland and scattered taller trees. Behavior much like that of other *Myiarchus,* but seems quite flexible in terms of habitat choice; thus although basically forest based, it persists in partially deforested terrain where it is more conspicuous. Its most common call is a fairly distinctive loud and clear but rather spiritless "peeur," repeated over and over.

RANGE: Mts. of n. Venezuela (east to Sucre), and Andes of w. Venezuela, Colombia (in W. Andes south only to Cauca), e. Ecuador, e. Peru, and w. Bolivia (south to w. Santa Cruz). Mostly 1500–2500 m, in smaller numbers down to 800 m in Peru and Bolivia.

Myiarchus apicalis

APICAL FLYCATCHER

DESCRIPTION: 18 cm (7"). *W. Colombia.* Resembles Sooty-crowned Flycatcher (no overlap). Crown somewhat browner though still showing some contrast with back; *slightly graduated tail with feathers broadly tipped whitish* (least so on central pair), with outer web of outer pair also whitish. See C-39.

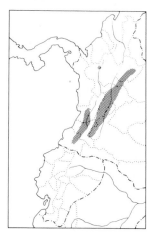

SIMILAR SPECIES: As no other *Myiarchus* shows the conspicuously wide, pale tail-tipping, Apical is a refreshingly easy species to identify. Pale-edged Flycatcher has pale only on *sides* of tail feathers.

HABITAT AND BEHAVIOR: Uncommon to locally fairly common in gallery woodland, deciduous thickets and scrub, and hedgerows and woodland patches in agricultural areas; favors arid regions, though not entirely confined to them. Behavior much like that of other *Myiarchus*. Has a variety of calls, including a "huit" (often in series), a hiccuping note, and a series of whistled notes (Lanyon 1978). Regularly found in upper Río Dagua valley west of Cali in Valle.

RANGE: Locally in w. Colombia (Río Magdalena valley from Santander and Boyacá south to Huila, Río Cauca valley in Valle and Cauca with a single record also from El Pescado in Antioquia, and spilling over onto Pacific slope in arid valleys of upper Río Dagua in Valle and upper Río Patía valley in Nariño). Mostly below 1700 m, a few records up to 2000–2500 m.

Myiarchus tuberculifer

DUSKY-CAPPED FLYCATCHER

DESCRIPTION: 16–17 cm (6¼–6¾"). A widespread *small Myiarchus*. Bill mostly black. Nominate group (all of S. Am. range aside from areas specified below; includes *brunneiceps* and *pallidus*) has *crown sepia brown*, becoming dark olive on back (usually showing some contrast); wings dusky with 2 indistinct grayish to buffyish wing-bars and some rufous edging on primaries, tail all dusky. Throat and breast gray, lower underparts pale clear yellow. See V-28, C-39. *Nigriceps* (w. Ecuador) similar but with *much more contrasting sooty black crown; atriceps* (Andes from s. Ecuador to Argentina) has equally contrasting blackish crown and is *markedly larger* than all other races.

SIMILAR SPECIES: All races of Dusky-capped Flycatcher except *atriceps* are so much smaller than other *Myiarchus* that confusion is unlikely. *Atriceps* can be recognized by its very dark crown, lack of rufous or pale color on tail, and characteristic call (see below); cf. especially Sooty-crowned Flycatcher.

HABITAT AND BEHAVIOR: Fairly common in canopy and borders of forest and secondary woodland (both in humid and more arid regions), clearings with scattered trees, and plantations; in Amazonia primarily in várzea and transitional forest (not terra firme). More apt to be seen in somewhat disturbed situations than in continuous forest. Seems more likely to accompany mixed flocks than many other *Myiarchus* flycatchers, but even so most often seen alone. Its most often heard call, which seems not to vary across its wide range, is a distinctive plaintive whistled "wheeerrr" or "fueeeeerr," fading slightly at end.

RANGE: Widespread south to n. and e. Bolivia, nw. Argentina (south to Tucumán), and Amaz. Brazil (south to s. Mato Grosso, n. Goiás, and n. Maranhão); se. Brazil (se. Bahia south to Rio de Janeiro); west of Andes south to nw. Peru (Lima); Trinidad. Also sw. United States to Panama. Apparently not migratory in South America. Mostly below 1800 m, but *atriceps* of Andes recorded mainly 1000–2500 m, occasionally as high as 3000 m.

NOTE: Two strikingly different taxa come into virtual contact along the e. slope of the Andes from s. Ecuador to w. Bolivia: nominate *tuberculifer* of the lowlands and *atriceps* on the slopes above. Although they are more different in appearance than are many other species in this genus, their vocalizations are much alike, and Lanyon (1978, pp. 470–488) did finally locate an intermediate population in the Chapare of Cochabamba, Bolivia. He thus concluded that they should be considered a single species.

Sirystes

The boldly patterned Sirystes has been shown to be most closely related to the genus *Myiarchus* (W. E. Lanyon and J. W. Fitzpatrick, *Auk* 100[1]: 98–104, 1983; and Lanyon 1985), even to its nesting in natural tree cavities.

Sirystes sibilator

SIRYSTES   PLATE: 43

DESCRIPTION: 18–18.5 cm (7–7¼″). *A distinctive Myiarchus-like black, gray, and white flycatcher of forest canopy.* Nominate race (se. Brazil area) has *crown black* contrasting with mottled olivaceous gray back; wings blackish, coverts and inner flight feathers broadly edged whitish; tail all blackish. Throat and breast gray, becoming grayish white on belly. *Subcanescens* (Guianas to lower Amaz. Brazil) similar but with *whitish rump. Albocinereus* (of upper Amazonia) has a *wider area on rump pure white,* black wings with only very narrow white edging, and is whiter below especially on belly; see V-28, C-39. *Albogriseus* (w. Colombia and nw. Ecuador) shows not only the white rump and underparts, but also has 2 very broad white wing-bars and wing-edging and a *bold white tip on tail;* see P-23.

SIMILAR SPECIES: Note the essentially clinal nature of the geographic variation, with s. and e. birds being more olivaceous above and grayer below with little white on rump; trans-Andean birds are the most striking, with even the addition of tail-tipping. When seen against the light, Sirystes of all races can be easily mistaken for a *Myiarchus* flycatcher, so similar are their attitudes and profiles; even their calls are similar. Otherwise most likely confused with various becards (e.g., male Crested) or even Eastern Kingbird.

HABITAT AND BEHAVIOR: Uncommon to fairly common in canopy of forest and mature secondary woodland, less often at borders where it may come lower; in w. Amazonia perhaps most frequent in várzea and riparian forest. Perhaps most numerous in e. Paraguay and adjacent Brazil, at least where forest cover remains. Often in pairs, with forward-leaning posture much like a *Myiarchus;* also regularly nods its head and raises its crown feathers, then looking bushy-crested. Regularly accompanies mixed flocks. The Sirystes is a vocal bird, and these calls often draw attention to it; the species otherwise is quite easy to overlook. East of Andes most often gives a loud ringing "wheer-péw," sometimes lengthened into an excited-sounding series, "wheer-pe-pe-pew-pew-péw"; west of Andes gives a rather different series of huskier notes, "chup-chup-chup" or "prip-prip-prip," sometimes accelerating into a chatter.

RANGE: Nw. Colombia (Chocó, e. Antioquia, and Córdoba); nw. Ecuador (locally in w. Esmeraldas, s. Pichincha, and n. Manabí); extreme sw. Venezuela (w. Barinas and Táchira), e. Colombia (locally, and to date only recorded fairly close to e. base of Andes), e. Ecuador, e. Peru, n. Bolivia (south to La Paz, Cochabamba, and n. Santa Cruz), Surinam, French Guiana, Brazil in Amazonia (east to Maranhão and south to s. Mato Grosso and n. Goiás; absent from the northwest in the Rio Negro and Rio Branco drainages) and the southeast (s. Goiás, Minas Gerais, and Espírito Santo south to Rio Grande do Sul), e. Paraguay (west to Amambay and Paraguarí), and ne. Argentina (Misiones and ne. Corrientes). Also Panama. Possibly migratory in southernmost Brazil (Belton 1985), but seemingly resident in e. Paraguay. To about 1000 m.

NOTE: Birds of Amazonia (*albocinereus* and *subcanescens*) seem intermediate in plumage between the nominate race of se. South America and trans-Andean *albogriseus,* and thus all are considered conspecific, despite the striking differences in their calls. If split, *S. albogriseus* should be called the Western Sirystes, *S. sirystes* the Eastern Sirystes.

Megarynchus Flycatchers

The widespread Boat-billed Flycatcher is distinguished by its massive broad-based bill and simple cup-shaped nest, the latter quite unlike the large, untidy globular nests of many of its relatives. Based on syringeal anatomy, Lanyon (1984) concluded that its closest relative is *Tyrannopsis* which, though it looks quite different, also builds a cup nest. The correct spelling of the genus name is *Megarynchus* (*contra* Meyer de Schauensee 1966, 1970).

Megarynchus pitangua

BOAT-BILLED FLYCATCHER

PLATE: 44

DESCRIPTION: 23 cm (9"). A *large* flycatcher with *very heavy broad bill, strongly curved on culmen*. Brownish olive above with blackish crown and sides of head, semiconcealed yellow coronal patch, and long broad white superciliary; wings and tail with *little* rufous edging (a bit more in immatures). Throat white, remaining underparts bright yellow. *Chrysogaster* (w. Ecuador and nw. Peru) and *mexicanus* (nw. Colombia) have tawny-orange coronal patch.

SIMILAR SPECIES: Great Kiskadee is browner (less olive) above, and its less massive and essentially straight bill lacks the arched culmen and is not as proportionately wide at base.

HABITAT AND BEHAVIOR: Uncommon to fairly common in a variety of wooded and forested habitats (both in humid and arid regions), usually in the semiopen or at forest borders, and in Amazonia mainly in várzea forest canopy and along rivers and lakes. Although widespread, Boat-billed is rarely as conspicuous or numerous as the fairly similar Great Kiskadee, is more arboreal, and is not nearly so tied to water. It usually is seen in pairs, often remaining high in densely foliaged trees, but at other times perching boldly in the open and low down. Its loud grating calls, usually a rattling "keerrrrrr-eék" or a nasal whining "er-er-er-erk," often attract attention.

RANGE: Widespread south to n. and e. Bolivia, Paraguay, ne. Argentina (south to e. Formosa, Corrientes, and Misiones), and s. Brazil (south to Rio Grande do Sul); west of Andes in nw. Venezuela and n. Colombia (Caribbean lowlands and south in Río Magdalena valley to Huila, but absent from Pacific lowlands south of n. Chocó), and in w. Ecuador (north to w. Esmeraldas) and nw. Peru (Tumbes and n. Piura); Trinidad. Also Mexico to Panama. Mostly below 1500 m.

Pitangus and *Philohydor* Kiskadees

Two superficially similar, boldly patterned flycatchers, both formerly placed in *Pitangus*. Lanyon (1984) erected a new genus for the Lesser Kiskadee because of its different syrinx and its cup-shaped nest, the latter very different from the Great Kiskadee's large globular nest with a side entrance.

Pitangus sulphuratus

GREAT KISKADEE

PLATE: 44

DESCRIPTION: 20.5–23.5 cm (8–9¼"). *Bill quite heavy and straight.* Olive brown to brown above with blackish crown and sides of head, semiconcealed yellow coronal patch, and long broad white superciliary; *wing feathers margined with rufous.* Throat white, remaining underparts bright yellow. Races of n. Colombia and Venezuela (*caucensis, rufipennis,* and *trinitatis*) are smaller, more rufous brown above, and have especially prominent broad rufous edging on wing and tail feathers (see V-28, C-39); s. races (*maximiliani, bolivianus,* and *argentinus*) are considerably larger, paler dorsally, and have little or no rufous edging on wings or tail; nominate race (of Amazonia to Guianas) is intermediate.

SIMILAR SPECIES: In many areas one of the more common and more frequently seen birds; learn it well so as to compare it to the numerous other flycatchers with same overall basic pattern. Larger, more southerly, and less brown races are particularly apt to be confused with Boat-billed Flycatcher, but note latter's different bill shape, voice, and behavior; from Amazonia northward, where kiskadees are more rufescent, the distinctions are more marked. Cf. also Lesser Kiskadee.

HABITAT AND BEHAVIOR: Common to very common and widespread in a variety of habitats ranging from residential areas (even small city parks or plazas) to semiopen agricultural regions and areas near water; less numerous and more local in mostly forested regions, where more or less confined to areas along shores of rivers and lakes. Inexplicably absent from much of Pacific slope. An aggressive, adaptable, and conspicuous bird which eats almost anything (even fish) but most often insects or fruit. Regularly perches low and fully in the open. Often very noisy, with a variety of loud calls, the most frequent of which, "kis-ka-dee!," is reflected in its English name (and in the Spanish *Christo-fué* and Portuguese *Ben-te-ví*).

RANGE: Widespread south to cen. Argentina (south to Neuquén and Río Negro, with a few recent reports from ne. Chubut); west of Andes only in nw. Venezuela and n. Colombia (Caribbean lowlands and south in Río Cauca and Río Magdalena valleys), but with several records of wanderers in n. and cen. Chile; accidental in Falkland Is.; Trinidad. Also Texas and Mexico to Panama, and introduced onto Bermuda. Mostly below 1500 m.

NOTE: For a discussion of racial variation, see Haffer and Fitzpatrick (1985).

Philohydor lictor

LESSER KISKADEE

PLATE: 44

DESCRIPTION: 17 cm (6¾"). *Bill long and slender.* Pattern and coloration much like Great Kiskadee, especially the latter's more northerly races. Best distinguished by very different bill shape, *smaller size* (Lesser is notably smaller than even the smallest races of Great), and more slender proportions. Its very different voice also helps a great deal (see below).

SIMILAR SPECIES: Also resembles White-bearded and Rusty-margined Flycatchers, but these have markedly shorter and broader bills.

HABITAT AND BEHAVIOR: Fairly common in shrubby areas along margins (often marshy) of lakes, ponds, and sluggish rivers; most numerous in Amazonia, but there as elsewhere *invariably near water.* Usually in pairs, not perching too far above ground or water level; often in same areas as Great Kiskadee but not nearly as conspicuous. Lesser's very distinctive nasal calls often attract attention and are completely unlike any of Great's, e.g., "dzáy, dzwee," or "dzáy-dzwee-zwee-zwee," always with first note strongest.

RANGE: Widespread south to n. and e. Bolivia (south to Cochabamba and n. Santa Cruz) and Amaz. and cen. Brazil (south to n. Mato Grosso do Sul, Goiás, and Piauí); e. Brazil (Pernambuco south to Rio de Janeiro); west of Andes only in nw. Venezuela and n. Colombia (Caribbean lowlands and Río Magdalena valley south to e. Antioquia). Recorded from n. Argentina (n. Buenos Aires), but this "requires confirmation" (Narosky and Yzurieta 1987, p. 292) and would appear improbable. Also Panama. To about 500 m.

NOTE: Formerly placed in the genus *Pitangus*.

Phelpsia and *Myiozetetes* Flycatchers

A group of medium-sized flycatchers with stubby bills; three species with bold black and white head patterns, two others with heads mainly gray. The new (Lanyon 1984) genus *Phelpsia* is placed here because it visually resembles certain *Myiozetetes*. *Myiozetetes* nests are untidy ball-like structures made of grass with a side entrance, whereas the White-bearded's nest is a neat open cup. All are relatively conspicuous and noisy birds of semiopen situations and borders, the Dusky-chested being the most forest-based.

GROUP A   Larger, with *clear yellow underparts.*

Phelpsia inornata

WHITE-BEARDED FLYCATCHER   PLATE: 44

DESCRIPTION: 16.5 cm (6½"). *Venezuela.* Rather short black bill. Olive brown above with black crown (with *no* coronal patch) and sides of head, and long broad white superciliary; *wings plain* with *no* rufous edging. Throat white, remaining underparts bright yellow.

SIMILAR SPECIES: Rusty-margined Flycatcher shows prominent rufous edging on wing feathers (especially the Rusty-margined race sympatric with White-bearded) and has a semiconcealed yellow coronal patch; voices also differ notably. Social Flycatcher has duskier (not so black) crown and face and usually shows pale wing-bars. Like Rusty-margined, Social has a normally concealed coronal patch, red in its case (but it is difficult to confirm its *absence,* as in White-bearded). Cf. also Lesser Kiskadee (with longer, narrower bill, rufous on wing).

HABITAT AND BEHAVIOR: Uncommon to locally fairly common in gallery woodland, "hammocks" of woodland in open or semiopen llanos terrain, and trees around ranch buildings. Usually in pairs, less often in small family groups. Rather inconspicuous, and less numerous than its several sympatric near look-alikes on the llanos, White-bearded Flycatcher is often most easily located by listening for its loud, very distinctive vocalizations. These, usually given as an antiphonal duet by a pair, consist of a burst of excited-sounding calls, "cheé-dur, cheé-dur, cheé-dur . . ." or "churup, churup, churup," sometimes varied to "cheedurit, cheedurit, cheedurit. . . ." While calling, birds often fluff their feathers and quiver their wings.

RANGE: N.-cen. Venezuela (Carabobo and Cojedes east locally to Anzoátegui, and south to Apure and Bolívar); probably also occurs in adjacent ne. Colombia. Below 500 m.

NOTE: This species has in the past been transferred between the genera *Myiozetetes* (in which it was described) and *Conopias;* Meyer de Schauensee (1966, 1970) retained it in *Myiozetetes.* Lanyon (1984) proposed placing it in a monotypic genus, *Phelpsia,* on the basis of its different syrinx and its cup-shaped nest, very different from the bulky globular nests of *Myiozetetes* and cavity nests of *Conopias.* For more behavioral information, see B. T. Thomas (*Auk* 96[4]: 767–775, 1979).

Myiozetetes cayanensis

RUSTY-MARGINED FLYCATCHER

DESCRIPTION: 17 cm (6¾"). Olive brown above with black crown and sides of head, semiconcealed *yellow coronal patch,* and long broad white superciliary; *wing feathers narrowly margined with rufous.* Throat white, remaining underparts bright yellow. *Rufipennis* (most of Venezuela and e. Colombia) similar but with broader, more conspicuous rufous

edging on wings, also some on tail; see V-28. *Erythropterus* of se. Brazil also shows much rufous on wing.

SIMILAR SPECIES: Some Social Flycatchers (especially immatures) also show inconspicuous rusty wing-edging. Other, often more helpful, points distinguishing the Rusty-margined are: its blacker (not so dusky) cheeks and crown, resulting in a more contrasty facial pattern; its yellow (not red) coronal patch, most often revealed by vocalizing birds; its lack of pale edging on wing-coverts (shown by virtually all Socials, regardless of age); and its browner (not so olive) back. Vocalizations also help (see below). Cf. also White-bearded Flycatcher and Lesser Kiskadee.

HABITAT AND BEHAVIOR: Fairly common to common in clearings, semiopen areas, and forest borders, most often near water and less frequently around habitations than Social Flycatcher. In some areas occurs sympatrically with Social but is usually less numerous; in other areas they seem to replace each other. Thus Rusty-margined is absent from much of upper Amazonia, Social from Guianas and some of lower Amazonia, and both are plentiful in Venezuela and e. Colombia. Rusty-margined is generally more retiring, somewhat recalling Lesser Kiskadee, and is usually not as noisy as Social. Its most characteristic and frequent call is a thin, whining, almost plaintive "freeeeee" or "wheeeeee," sometimes repeated several times. When excited Rusty-margined also gives various other vocalizations which resemble Social's.

RANGE: N. and w. Colombia and w. Ecuador (south to El Oro); Guianas, Venezuela, e. Colombia, e. Ecuador (few records), e. Amaz. and cen. Brazil (up the Amazon as far as the mouth of the Rio Negro, and south though Pará, Maranhão, and Piauí to Minas Gerais, Rio de Janeiro, and Mato Grosso do Sul), n. Bolivia (south to Cochabamba and n. Santa Cruz), and adjacent se. Peru (Tambopata Reserve in Madre de Dios). Also Panama. Mostly below 1000 m, less often up to 1500 m, rarely to 2100 m.

Myiozetetes similis

SOCIAL FLYCATCHER   PLATE: 44

Other: Vermilion-crowned Flycatcher

DESCRIPTION: 16.5–17 cm (6½–6¾"). Olive above with dark gray crown and sides of head, semiconcealed *red coronal patch,* and long broad white superciliary; *wing-coverts and inner flight feathers narrowly edged pale grayish to buffyish.* Throat white, remaining underparts bright yellow. W. and n. races (the small race *columbianus* of n. Colombia and most of Venezuela, and *grandis* of w. Ecuador and nw. Peru) average having the most pale edging on wing feathers. Immatures lack the coronal patch and may show some rufous edging on wings and tail.

SIMILAR SPECIES: Generally the most numerous and widespread of its genus. Often hard to separate from Rusty-margined Flycatcher; see discussion under that species. Cf. also Gray-capped Flycatcher, Lesser Kiskadee, and White-ringed Flycatcher.

HABITAT AND BEHAVIOR: Common to very common in shrubby clearings, gardens and residential areas, agricultural regions, and forest and woodland canopy and borders; a widespread bird, in places one of the more frequently seen. Often in small groups (the name "Social" is not inappropriate), with even larger numbers sometimes gathering at fruiting trees. Ranges from the ground (it regularly drops down onto lawns) to the canopy of tall trees. Noisy and excitable, often drawing attention by its varying, loud calls; most are harsh and unmusical, with a "kree-yoo," "ti-ti-ti-tíchew, chew," or "kree-kree-kree-kree" being most frequent. Social *never* gives the distinctive long-drawn plaintive call of Rusty-margined.

RANGE: W. Ecuador (Esmeraldas to El Oro and w. Loja) and extreme nw. Peru (Tumbes); n. and e. Colombia (Caribbean lowlands and south in Río Magdalena valley to Huila, but absent from Pacific slope; widely east of Andes), Venezuela, French Guiana (though seemingly absent from Surinam and Guyana), e. Ecuador, e. Peru, n. Bolivia (south to Cochabamba and n. Santa Cruz), much of Amaz. and e. Brazil (absent from most of the drainages of the Rios Tocantins and Xingu, and the upper Rio Paraguay basin; recorded south to n. Rio Grande do Sul), e. Paraguay (west at least to Caaguazú), and ne. Argentina (Misiones). Also Mexico to Panama. Mostly below 1000 m, in smaller numbers up to 1500 m.

Myiozetetes granadensis

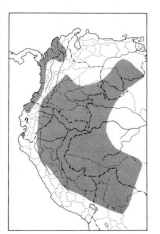

GRAY-CAPPED FLYCATCHER

DESCRIPTION: 16.5–17 cm (6½–6¾"). Olive above with *gray crown and nape,* semiconcealed orange-red coronal patch, dusky ear-coverts, and *only short and narrow white superciliary* (back only to just past eye); wings and tail dusky, wing feathers narrowly edged pale olive. Throat white, remaining underparts bright yellow. Females have crown patch reduced or lacking; immatures have olive-tinged crown, buffyish wing and tail-edging. *Obscurior* (east of Andes) slightly larger than *occidentalis* (w. Colombia and w. Ecuador). See V-28, C-39.

SIMILAR SPECIES: Social and Rusty-margined Flycatchers have much bolder, "black-and-white" head patterns. Dusky-chested Flycatcher is considerably smaller and browner, has *no* head pattern, shows chest streaking, etc. Cf. also Tropical Kingbird and Sulphury Flycatcher.

HABITAT AND BEHAVIOR: Fairly common in forest borders, shrubby clearings, and to a lesser extent around houses (but on the whole a less familiar bird than Social Flycatcher); most numerous near water and found almost exclusively in humid regions. Its calls are sharper and more emphatic than Social's (some are almost as strong as Great Kiskadee's) and include a "kip!" often repeated in series and a "kip-kee-kew."

RANGE: N. and w. Colombia (more humid Caribbean lowlands, and in Pacific lowlands), w. Ecuador (recorded south only to Pichincha; southward?), and extreme nw. Peru (an old record from Tumbes); s. Venezuela (Amazonas and w. Bolívar), e. Colombia (north to Meta and Vaupés), e. Ecuador, e. Peru, n. Bolivia (south to Cochabamba and n. Santa Cruz), and w. Amaz. Brazil (n. Roraima, w. Amazonas, and Rondônia). Also Honduras to Panama. To about 1100 m.

GROUP B   *Small; no* head pattern, chest *streaky.*

Myiozetetes luteiventris

DUSKY-CHESTED FLYCATCHER   PLATE: 44

DESCRIPTION: 14.5 cm (5¾"). *Uniform dark olive brown above,* somewhat grayer on head (*no* crown stripes) with semiconcealed yellow-orange coronal patch. Throat whitish, vaguely streaked dusky; remaining underparts bright yellow, *flammulated and clouded with olive on breast.*

SIMILAR SPECIES: Rather smaller than other *Myiozetetes* flycatchers, the scarce Dusky-chested has an unpatterned head and quite prominent blurry breast streaking, both marks setting it apart from others in the genus; Gray-capped is the most similar. Cf. also the markedly larger Sulphury Flycatcher.

HABITAT AND BEHAVIOR: Rare to locally uncommon in borders and canopy of terra firme and várzea forest, around treefalls, and at edges of lakes and rivers. Until recently considered a rarity, Dusky-chested Flycatcher has now been reported from a number of areas—it was probably overlooked and under-collected because of its obscure appearance and habit of remaining high in the canopy. Usually in pairs or small groups, most often independent of mixed flocks, though it regularly assembles at fruiting trees with other birds. Also sallies and hover-gleans to foliage after insects. Sometimes cocks its tail. Its excited-sounding calls, including a fast nasal "keeuw-keeuw, keep-kít" or simply a "keeuw," recall Gray-capped Flycatcher's.

RANGE: Locally in Surinam, French Guiana, and extreme ne. Brazil (Amapá); se. Venezuela (s. Bolívar) and extreme n. Brazil (n. Roraima); se. Colombia (north to Putumayo and Vaupés), e. Ecuador (Napo and Pastaza), e. Peru (recorded only from Loreto and Madre de Dios; probably more widespread), extreme nw. Bolivia (Pando at Camino Mucden and n. La Paz at Pampas de Heath), and Amaz. Brazil (south to Rondônia and n. Mato Grosso, and east to se. Pará and w. Maranhão at Açailandia). To 600 m.

NOTE: Meyer de Schauensee (1966, 1970), following the unpublished notes of J. T. Zimmer, transferred this species from the genus *Myiozetetes,* in which it had long been placed, to *Tyrannopsis.* However, recent evidence concerning its syrinx and nest shape (see Lanyon 1984), as well as its voice, demonstrate unequivocably that it is best left in *Myiozetetes.*

Conopias Flycatchers

A small group of flycatchers, basically similar to the more familiar *Myiozetetes,* but with proportionately longer bills. *Conopias* flycatchers are generally more forest-based than *Myiozetetes,* and their nests, so far as known, are made of grassy or fibrous material and stuffed into holes or tree cavities; sometimes old oropendola or cacique nests are apparently appropriated.

Conopias trivirgata

THREE-STRIPED FLYCATCHER

PLATE: 44

DESCRIPTION: 13.5–14.5 cm (5¼–5¾"). Disjunct range in Amazonia and se. South America. Bill fairly long and slender. Nominate race of the southeast is olive above with blackish crown and sides of head and long broad white superciliary (*no* coronal patch); wings and tail contrastingly dusky. Below bright yellow, *clouded olive on breast. Berlepschi* of Amazonia is smaller with a narrower bill, slightly paler olive back, and no olive on breast.

SIMILAR SPECIES: Amaz. race resembles Social Flycatcher but has all-yellow underparts with no white on throat, is smaller with proportionately longer and narrower bill, and lacks Social's usually quite prominent pale edging on wing feathers; their vocalizations differ markedly. Yellow-throated Flycatcher is larger, has blacker crown, and lacks contrast between rather dark back and wings.

HABITAT AND BEHAVIOR: Rare to locally uncommon in canopy and borders of humid forest; seemingly most numerous in middle Amazon region (from lower Rio Negro east to lower Rio Tapajós area; rare in w. Amazonia), and in e. Paraguay and the Iguazú area. Usually in pairs or small family groups which perch conspicuously and associate with mixed flocks of various arboreal birds. The most frequent call of the nominate race is a harsh, grating "jew" or "jeeuw," often repeated rapidly and excitedly; *berlepschi*'s vocalizations are similar.

RANGE: Very locally in Amazonia, where recorded from s. Venezuela (two 1992–1993 records from Río Pacuyacu in e. Sucumbios; P. Coopmans), e. Peru (recorded from Yarinacocha in Ucayali and the Tambopata Reserve in Madre de Dios), n. Bolivia (a single record from Chipiriri in Cochabamba), and cen. and e. Amaz. Brazil (near the Amazon from around Tefé east to the lower Rio Tapajós area, with a single recent sighting from n. Maranhão at Santa Inêz); more widely in se. South America, where known from se. Brazil (se. Bahia south to Paraná), e. Paraguay (west to Paraguarí), and ne. Argentina (Misiones and ne. Corrientes). Mostly below 300 m, but recorded at 960 m in Venezuela.

NOTE: The form found in Amazonia, *berlepschi* (Berlepsch's Flycatcher), possibly deserves full species status.

Conopias parva

YELLOW-THROATED FLYCATCHER

DESCRIPTION: 16.5 cm (6½"). Guianas west locally to ne. Ecuador and w. Amaz. Brazil; regarded as a species distinct from White-ringed Flycatcher. *Dark* olive above with black crown and sides of head, semiconcealed yellow coronal patch, and *long broad white superciliary which extends from forehead to encircle nape;* wings and tail dusky brown. Below (*including throat*) entirely bright yellow. See V-28, C-39.

SIMILAR SPECIES: *Myiozetetes* flycatchers have shorter bills, white throats, and different behavior and vocalizations. Three-striped Flycatcher is smaller, paler olive on back, not so black on crown, and lacks the coronal patch and "wrap-around" effect on nape.

HABITAT AND BEHAVIOR: Uncommon to locally fairly common in canopy and borders of humid forest (especially terra firme), sometimes out into tall trees in nearby clearings. Usually in pairs or small groups which remain high, characteristically perching atop leafy branches, scanning foliage and sallying out to snatch insects from leaf surfaces or branches (less often into air). Because they perch so high, Yellow-throated Flycatchers are often difficult to see except at forest edge. They regularly accompany mixed flocks but at least as often forage independently. The species is most often noted by tracking down its distinctive call, a loud, ringing, rhythmic "tre-tree-tree . . . ," sometimes repeated for long periods.

RANGE: Guianas, n. Brazil (locally from Amapá west to lower Rio Negro area in Manaus region, n. Roraima, and upper Rio Negro drainage), s. Venezuela (locally in Bolívar and Amazonas), and extreme e. Colombia (recorded only from e. Vaupés; probably more widespread), and ne. Ecuador (seen and tape-recorded in Aug. 1992 at Cuyabeno in e. Sucumbios; B. Whitney); south of the Amazon known only from 3 isolated localities (but likely under-recorded), 2 in ne. Peru in n. Loreto (Santa Cecilia [ANSP], and a sighting by E. O. Willis at Nuevo Andoas), and 1 in w. Amaz. Brazil (sightings south of Tefé near the Rio Urucu; C. Peres and A. Whittaker). Mostly below 1000 m.

NOTE: Because of marked plumage and vocal differences, here regarded as a species distinct from the widely disjunct, trans-Andean *C. albovittata*. If considered conspecific, the name *albovittata* has priority (*contra Birds of the World*, vol. 8, and the 1983 AOU Check-list). Some authors (e.g., Wetmore 1972 and the 1983 AOU Check-list) have used the genus name *Coryphotriccus* for *C. albovittata* and *C. parva*. *Coryphotriccus* was erected in recognition of their slightly larger bill compared to the other *Conopias* and their yellow crown patch (lacking in *C. trivirgata* and *C. cinchoneti*). However, Lanyon (1984) found the syringes of *parva* and *trivirgata* to be similar and suggested that *Coryphotriccus* be merged into *Conopias*.

Conopias albovittata

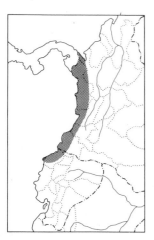

WHITE-RINGED FLYCATCHER

DESCRIPTION: 16.5 cm (6½"). *W. Colombia and nw. Ecuador.* Resembles the widely disjunct Yellow-throated Flycatcher (with which often considered conspecific) but has *white throat.* See C-39, P-23.

SIMILAR SPECIES: Yellow-throated Flycatcher has widely disjunct range *east* of Andes. White-ringed differs from *Myiozetetes* flycatchers in having a longer bill and different behavior and vocalizations. Note that while the white superciliaries of kiskadees and certain *Myiozetetes* may occasionally appear to "wrap around" the backs of their heads, they never do so as completely as in this species.

HABITAT AND BEHAVIOR: Uncommon in canopy and borders of humid forest, occasionally out into tall trees in adjacent clearings. Behavior much like Yellow-throated Flycatcher's, also habitually perching high and hard to see well. Likewise most easily found once its distinctive call is learned: a dry, fast, whirring or rattling trill "tre-r-r-r-r, tre-r-r-r-r . . . ," often repeated many times.

RANGE: W. Colombia (Pacific lowlands from Chocó to Nariño) and nw. Ecuador (Esmeraldas). Also Honduras to Panama. Mostly below 1000 m.

NOTE: See comments under Yellow-throated Flycatcher.

Conopias cinchoneti

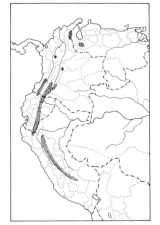

LEMON-BROWED FLYCATCHER

PLATE: 44

DESCRIPTION: 16 cm (6¼"). *Lower Andean slopes.* Above olive with *long, broad, pale yellow superciliary extending from forehead to nape* (almost joining at back of head); wings and tail dusky. Below entirely bright yellow, somewhat clouded olive on sides of chest.

SIMILAR SPECIES: No other *Myiozetetes* or *Conopias* flycatcher has a *yellow* superciliary (if present, theirs are white). Cf. Yellow-browed Tyrant (superficially alike but with very different behavior, habitat, distribution).

HABITAT AND BEHAVIOR: Rare to locally uncommon in clearings with scattered tall trees and at borders of montane forest. Usually occurs as well-separated pairs or family groups, often appearing to be absent from presumably suitable terrain. Conspicuous where found, Lemon-browed Flycatchers generally perch fully in the open on leaves or exposed limbs, usually well above the ground; they seem restless, rarely stay long in one place, and probably have very large home ranges. On occasion they accompany mixed flocks but more often remain independent. Their call is a distinctive high "whee-ee-ee-ee, wheedidididídí," with querulous complaining quality; a calling bird often pumps its head. In e. Ecuador RSR watched a group of 3 at an inactive colony of Russet-backed Oropendolas, 1 bird briefly hanging from the entrance of a nest, but whether they actually bred there is uncertain.

RANGE: Andes of w. Venezuela (north to Trujillo and w. Barinas), Colombia (quite locally; in W. Andes recorded only from Valle and Cauca, in Cen. Andes only at their n. end), nw. and e. Ecuador (on w. slope recorded only from Carchi, where seen and tape-recorded above Maldonado in 1989; M. B. Robbins), and e. Peru (south to Cuzco); Sierra de Perijá on Venezuela-Colombia border. Mostly 700–1700 m, locally down to 400 m on Pacific slope of Colombia, rarely up to 2100 m.

Myiodynastes Flycatchers

Rather large flycatchers with stout bills, the four species of *Myiodynastes* usually show a pronounced malar streak and have mainly rufous tails. They nest in crevices and holes in trees. The closest generic relative is apparently *Conopias*.

GROUP A

Indistinct chest streaking, *some buff on throat or chest.*

Myiodynastes bairdii

BAIRD'S FLYCATCHER

PLATE: 44

DESCRIPTION: 23 cm (9"). Arid lowlands of *sw. Ecuador and nw. Peru.* Rather heavy bill, base of lower mandible pinkish. *Broad black mask from forehead back through eyes onto ear-coverts,* surmounted by streaky

Myiodynastes chrysocephalus

pale sandy brown crown (palest above mask), with semiconcealed yellow coronal patch; back olive brown, becoming chestnut-rufous on rump; wings dusky, *feathers broadly edged rufous; tail mostly rufous-chestnut.* Throat whitish, becoming pale ochraceous on breast, indistinctly streaked gray especially on throat; belly pale creamy yellow.

SIMILAR SPECIES: Not likely to be confused in its limited range. Cf. Golden-crowned Flycatcher of montane areas (no overlap).

HABITAT AND BEHAVIOR: Fairly common in deciduous woodland, arid scrub with scattered taller trees, and gardens. Usually found in pairs, often perching rather high; generally quite conspicuous, sometimes even perching on phone wires. Its rather infrequently heard call is a throaty, steadily repeated (at 2- to 4-second intervals) "worr-sheeít . . . worr-sheeít . . . ," often given from a semiconcealed perch, mainly at dawn and dusk.

RANGE: Sw. Ecuador (north to cen. Manabí in the Bahía de Caráquez area, and inland into w. Loja) and nw. Peru (south to n. Lima at Paramonga). To 1000 m.

GOLDEN-CROWNED FLYCATCHER

DESCRIPTION: 20.5–21.5 cm (8–8½"). Mts. from Venezuela to Bolivia. N. races (south through Ecuador; *cinerascens* and *minor*) have crown brownish gray with semiconcealed yellow coronal patch, long broad white superciliary, and dusky sides of head; otherwise dull olive above; wings and tail dusky with fairly prominent rufous edging. *Lower cheeks and throat pale buff, separated by dusky malar stripe;* remaining underparts pale yellow, *breast clouded and flammulated with olive.* See V-28, C-39. S. nominate race (Peru and Bolivia) is larger and has reduced rufous wing- and tail-edging and less buff on throat.

SIMILAR SPECIES: Overall pattern and size recall Great Kiskadee or Boat-billed Flycatcher, neither of which shows a malar stripe or blurry breast streaking. Baird's Flycatcher has paler crown and blacker mask (hence more contrast), lacks distinct malar stripe, and is more ochraceous (not olive) on breast; the two do not occur together. Both Streaked and Sulphur-bellied Flycatchers are much more generally and heavily streaked.

HABITAT AND BEHAVIOR: Fairly common to common at borders and in openings of montane forest and in adjacent clearings with scattered tall trees. Usually found singly or in pairs, most often perched conspicuously on an exposed limb at low to moderate heights; sometimes joins mixed flocks but more often apart from them. Rather noisy, with several loud calls which can even be heard over the roar of a rushing mountain stream, the most frequent an often endlessly repeated "squeeé-yu" or "kiss-you."

RANGE: Coastal mts. of n. Venezuela (east to Sucre and Monagas), and Andes of w. Venezuela, Colombia, Ecuador (south on w. slope to w. Loja), e. Peru, w. Bolivia, and extreme nw. Argentina (1991 sighting from Santa Victoria in n. Salta; B. M. López Lanús); Sierra de Perijá on Venezuela-Colombia border, and Santa Marta Mts. of n. Colombia.

Also e. Panama. Mostly 1000–2500 m, lower (to 500 m) on Pacific slope of Colombia and Ecuador.

GROUP B

Heavily streaked throughout.

Myiodynastes maculatus

STREAKED FLYCATCHER

PLATE: 44

DESCRIPTION: 19.5–21 cm (7¾–8¼″). Base of lower mandible pinkish. *Mostly brown above streaked with dusky,* rump and *tail mostly rufous;* semiconcealed coronal patch yellow, *whitish superciliary,* broad blackish area across face and ear-coverts, bordered below by white lower cheeks and then a prominent dusky malar stripe; wings dusky with narrow rufous or buff edging. Whitish to dingy pale yellowish below, *broadly streaked dusky especially on breast, flanks, and crissum. Insolens* (migratory from n. Middle America to n. South America) has more olivaceous (not so rufescent) crown, more yellowish superciliary, and unstreaked crissum. *Solitarius* (breeding in s. South America, migrating northward) is darker above with broader, blacker streaks, is more boldly and extensively streaked below, has mostly whitish wing-edging, and has *mainly blackish tail* (only narrow rufous-chestnut edging).

SIMILAR SPECIES: Cf. very similar (but less numerous) Sulphur-bellied Flycatcher. Otherwise, this large and boldly streaked flycatcher is likely to be confused only with smaller (and notably smaller-billed) Variegated Flycatcher which is darker above (less "streaky") and has blackish crown.

HABITAT AND BEHAVIOR: Uncommon to locally common in secondary woodland, forest borders, clearings with scattered tall trees, and mangroves; in Amazonia mainly in várzea woodland and on river islands. Avoids, or is scarce in, very humid and extensively forested regions; seems particularly numerous in caatinga woodlands of ne. Brazil and in subtropical woodlands of e. Paraguay and ne. Argentina. In some areas regular around houses, even nesting under eaves. Usually noisy and quite conspicuous, though may perch stolidly and quietly for protracted periods. Has a variety of loud, harsh, nasal calls, the most frequent being a "chup" or "eéchup," but apparently all races also have an unexpectedly musical dawn song, a loud "wheeé-cheederee-wheeé" (sometimes lacking the last "wheeé") repeated quickly over and over, often starting well before first light. The song is sometimes also given at dusk.

RANGE: Widespread south to cen. Argentina (south to San Luis, La Pampa, and n. Buenos Aires); west of Andes south to nw. Peru (Piura), but absent or local in Pacific lowlands of sw. Colombia; Trinidad and Tobago, and Margarita Is. off n. Venezuela. Also Mexico to Panama. The s. race *solitarius* breeds north to Bolivia and cen. Brazil, migrating north during austral winter (mostly Apr.–Sept.) into range of other resident races, reaching e. Colombia, s. Venezuela, and Guianas (with single records from n. Chile in Atacama and sw. Peru in Arequipa). Mostly below 1500 m, but *solitarius* once recorded to 3000 m in Colombian Andes.

NOTE: *Solitarius* differs markedly in plumage from the other races of *M. maculatus,* and it has been suggested it might be a distinct species. However, J. T. Zimmer (*Am. Mus. Novitates* 963, 1937) found apparent intermediate specimens from s. Amaz. Brazil; in addition, *solitarius*'s voice does not appear to differ appreciably from that of other races.

Myiodynastes luteiventris

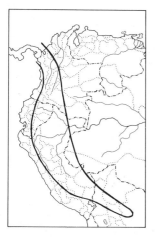

SULPHUR-BELLIED FLYCATCHER

DESCRIPTION: 20.5 cm (8″). Closely resembles more numerous and widespread Streaked Flycatcher. Differs in having its broad dusky malar stripe *narrowly joined across chin,* little or no rufous edging on primaries, *and lower underparts usually distinctly clear sulphur yellow* (paler and duller in some immatures) with unstreaked crissum (resembling *insolens* race of Streaked). See P-23.

HABITAT AND BEHAVIOR: Rare to locally fairly common n.-winter resident (mostly Oct.–Apr.) in canopy and borders of humid forest and secondary woodland and in clearings with scattered trees. Behavior similar to Streaked Flycatcher's; eats much fruit on its wintering grounds. In South America the Sulphur-bellied is generally quiet, inconspicuous, and perhaps often overlooked among the usually more numerous Streaked Flycatchers; before moving north, may give voice to its forceful but rather squeaky "squeez-ya" call.

RANGE: Nonbreeding visitor to w. Colombia (probably occurring mainly as a transient), e. Ecuador, e. Peru, n. Bolivia (south to Cochabamba and w. Santa Cruz), and extreme w. Brazil (Feb. 1992 sightings in Acre along the Rio Juruá; A. Whittaker). Breeds from sw. United States to Costa Rica, wintering in w. Amazonia. Mostly below 1000 m, though recorded as a transient to 2600 m in Colombia.

Legatus Flycatchers

The stubby-billed *Legatus* seems to form a bridge between *Empidonomus* (which, though markedly smaller, it resembles in plumage) and *Myiozetetes* (which has a similar syrinx; see Lanyon 1984). Its affinity with *Myiozetetes* is further indicated by its piratical nesting habits, for several *Myiozetetes* species are also occasionally known to do this.

Legatus leucophaius

PIRATIC FLYCATCHER   PLATE: 44

DESCRIPTION: 14.5 cm (5¾″). *Rather short bill. Uniform dark olive brown above,* duskier on head with semiconcealed yellow coronal patch, long whitish superciliary, whitish malar area, and dusky submalar streak; *wings plain* (feathers with faint pale edging), tail blackish (feathers sometimes with narrow rufous edging). Throat whitish, breast whitish with blurry dusky brown streaking, becoming pale yellow on lower belly and crissum.

SIMILAR SPECIES: Variegated Flycatcher has a similar pattern but is larger with a longer bill and has much more rufous on rump and tail and more white edging on wing feathers.

HABITAT AND BEHAVIOR: Uncommon to fairly common in borders of humid forest and secondary woodland and in clearings with scattered tall trees. Widespread and vocally conspicuous when breeding, Piratic Flycatchers are nevertheless sometimes hard to see as they tend to remain high in trees. Singing males perch on branches in the canopy, there tirelessly repeating a whining, querulous "weé-yee," sometimes followed by a rising "pírrirriree?"; this call is often given even through the heat of the day. Pairs usurp the pendant nests of various other species, especially those of oropendolas or caciques but also those of various flycatchers and others, harassing the rightful owners until the nest is abandoned. Adults have an almost entirely frugivorous diet.

RANGE: Widespread south to n. Argentina (in the northwest in Salta, Jujuy, and Tucumán; in the northeast from e. Formosa and e. Chaco east through Corrientes and Misiones) and s. Brazil (south to n. Rio Grande do Sul); west of Andes south to w. Ecuador (e. Guayas and nw. Azuay); apparently absent from much of interior ne. Brazil; Trinidad and Tobago. Also Mexico to Panama. Populations nesting in Middle America and s. South America are migratory, but details as to exactly where they go are not known (presumably both populations move to n. and Amaz. South America); present in Argentina and s. Brazil about Sept.–Mar. Mostly below 1000 m (recorded to 1700 m in w. Colombia).

Empidonomus and *Griseotyrannus* Flycatchers

Despite their plumage differences, this pair of slender flycatchers were long considered congeneric in *Empidonomus* (e.g., Meyer de Schauensee 1966, 1970). Lanyon (1984) erected a new genus, *Griseotyrannus,* for the Crowned Slaty Flycatcher, based mainly on several differences in syringeal morphology, and he thereby created the longest Latin binomial for any bird! Because of their strong vocal and behavioral similarities, we continue to associate the genera here.

Empidonomus varius

VARIEGATED FLYCATCHER

DESCRIPTION: 18–18.5 cm (7–7¼"). Resembles smaller Piratic Flycatcher; bill longer and proportionately narrower. Differs in having *back mottled and streaked* pale grayish brown and dusky; *wing-coverts and flight feathers prominently edged white;* and *rump and tail feathers broadly edged rufous;* see C-39. *Rufinus* (resident from Venezuela south to Amaz. and ne. Brazil) is slightly smaller and less boldly streaked below; see V-28.

SIMILAR SPECIES: Three widespread flycatchers of this flycatcher's "type" are boldly streaked below: Streaked, Variegated, and Piratic. Variegated is intermediate in size and differs from Piratic as enumerated above. Streaked differs in its larger size, paler upperparts (especially on crown), longer bill, and sharper, more contrasty streaking below.

HABITAT AND BEHAVIOR: Fairly common in forest borders, secondary and gallery woodland, and clearings and savannas with scattered trees; more a bird of wooded country than Crowned Slaty Flycatcher, which replaces it in more open savannas and lightly wooded terrain. Usually perches lower than Piratic Flycatcher and is generally in the open and easy to see; sallies both into air and to foliage and eats some small fruit. Quiet even when breeding; apparently its only vocalization is a very high, thin, weak "pseee" given at irregular intervals, sometimes in series; this call, almost inaudible at any distance, is apt to be thought an insect's. Wintering birds also occasionally vocalize.

RANGE: Widespread in e. and cen. South America south to n. Argentina (precise s. limits uncertain: recent records south only to Tucumán, Santa Fe, and Entre Ríos, but there are old records from as far south as La Rioja, San Luis, and La Pampa, these perhaps pertaining to migratory overshoots) and Uruguay (where evidently scarce); during austral winter (ca. Mar.–Sept.) nominate *varius* vacates the region from e. Bolivia and s. Brazil southward, at that time occurring north to Trinidad, w. Venezuela, e. Colombia, e. Ecuador, e. Peru, and w. Amaz. Brazil. There are also several remarkable records of overshooting migrants in the e. United States and se. Canada. Mostly below 1200 m.

Griseotyrannus
aurantioatrocristatus

CROWNED SLATY FLYCATCHER   PLATE: 44

DESCRIPTION: 17.5–18 cm (6¾–7"). *A slender gray flycatcher with contrasting black crown.* Brownish gray above with *black crown,* semiconcealed yellow coronal patch, gray superciliary, and dusky ear-coverts. *Uniform smoky gray below,* slightly paler and tinged yellowish on belly and crissum (especially in slightly smaller *pallidiventris* of interior ne. Brazil). Juvenile has more prominent and white superciliary, pale edging on wing feathers, and some rufous edging on rectrices.

SIMILAR SPECIES: In good light the contrasting black crown of this uniform-looking flycatcher should be apparent; Crowned Slaty also usually looks distinctively *flat-crowned.* It might also bring to mind various black-tyrants (especially in poor light) or even Grayish Mourner (though latter's habitat and behavior are very different).

HABITAT AND BEHAVIOR: Common in lighter woodland and scrub, savannas with scattered trees, and (in austral winter) clearings and borders of humid forest; one of the more numerous breeding birds in the chaco of n. Argentina and w. Paraguay. Found singly or in pairs, usually perching in exposed situations, often atop a bush or tree, sallying into the air much like a kingbird. Like Variegated Flycatcher, Crowned Slaty is rather quiet, but when breeding it gives a very weak "pseeek" call rather like Variegated's, sometimes delivered in a series.

RANGE: Breeds in n. and e. Bolivia (north to Beni), interior Brazil (e. Pará, Maranhão, and Piauí south through Goiás and much of Mato Grosso and Mato Grosso do Sul to w. Rio Grande do Sul), Paraguay (especially in chaco west of Río Paraguay), Uruguay, and n. and cen. Argentina (south to Mendoza, n. Río Negro, and w. Buenos Aires);

during austral winter s. breeders migrate north mainly into w. Amazonia, where recorded north to e. Ecuador, se. Colombia, and w. Amaz. Brazil (north as far as Manaus and Belém regions), with 2 records (of overshoots?) from Venezuela (in s. Amazonas and Aragua). To about 2000 m (in arid intermontane valleys of Bolivia).

NOTE: Formerly placed in the genus *Empidonomus.*

Tyrannopsis Flycatchers

With the transfer of the Dusky-chested Flycatcher back to the genus *Myiozetetes,* the Sulphury Flycatcher now comprises a monotypic genus. It is found locally in Amazonia. Although it superficially resembles the Tropical Kingbird, Lanyon (1984) suggests that, based on syringeal anatomy, its closest generic relative is the externally very different *Megarynchus;* like that genus, the nest of *Tyrannopsis* is cup-shaped.

Tyrannopsis sulphurea

SULPHURY FLYCATCHER   PLATE: 44

DESCRIPTION: 19 cm (7½"). Looks like *chunky, short-tailed Tropical Kingbird.* Bill rather short. Head mostly gray, somewhat darker and duskier on face, with semiconcealed yellow coronal patch and indistinct whitish superciliary; back dull brownish olive, *becoming even browner on wings and on rather short square tail.* Center of throat and upper chest white, *grayer on sides of throat* and with *olive mottling on sides of chest;* remaining underparts bright yellow.
SIMILAR SPECIES: Tropical Kingbird is larger and has a longer, distinctly notched tail; Sulphury is markedly duller overall, much browner above and with white throat set off from yellow belly by mottled "pectoral" area. Dusky-chested Flycatcher is much smaller with a stubbier bill and more uniformly dark and brown upperparts, and it shows more conspicuous olive flammulation across breast. Cf. also the smaller Gray-capped Flycatcher.
HABITAT AND BEHAVIOR: Uncommon and local at borders of humid forest and in savannas, agricultural regions, and even outskirts of towns, almost always associated with groves of moriche or buriti palms (*Mauritia flexuosa*), in which it nests. Usually rather inconspicuous, perching stolidly at varying heights (most often high) for much of the day, but noisier and easier to see early and late. Sallies into the air after insects and eats some fruit. Calls are quite loud and sharp and have a distinctive squeaky or sputtering quality; most frequent are a rapidly delivered "jee-peet! jee-peeteet, jeepeet!" or a "squeezrr-squeezrr-squeezrr-prrr."
RANGE: Locally in Guianas, e. and s. Venezuela (e. Sucre, Delta Amacuro, Bolívar, and Amazonas), e. Colombia (north to Meta), e. Ecuador (local), e. Peru (Loreto and Ucayali, with a few reports from the Tambopata Reserve in Madre de Dios), extreme nw. Bolivia (seen near Porvenir in Pando), and Amaz. Brazil (south to Rondônia, Goiás, and s. Mato Grosso); Trinidad. No evidence of migration. To about 400 m.

Tyrannus Kingbirds and Flycatchers

Conspicuous and often common flycatchers of open and semiopen country. Typical kingbirds have fairly stout bills, dusky ear-coverts, slightly forked tails, and are mostly yellow or whitish below. The Fork-tailed Flycatcher and Eastern Kingbird have a more "capped" appearance and smaller bills. The Fork-tailed Flycatcher (together with *T. forficatus*, Scissor-tailed Flycatcher, of the United States and Middle America) was formerly separated in the genus *Muscivora* on the basis of its long and deeply forked tail (e.g., Meyer de Schauensee 1966, 1970). However, various lines of evidence indicate the genera should be merged (e.g., Traylor 1977), the long tail of *Muscivora* merely being an adaptation to open habitats.

GROUP A

"Typical" neotropical kingbirds; note *largish bills, dark ear-coverts.*

Tyrannus melancholicus

TROPICAL KINGBIRD   PLATE: 44

DESCRIPTION: 21–22 cm (8¼–8¾"). *Head gray* with dusky ear-coverts and semiconcealed orange coronal patch; *above otherwise grayish olive,* wings and slightly forked tail brownish dusky, wing feathers edged paler. Throat whitish to pale grayish, becoming *olive to grayish olive on chest* and bright yellow on lower underparts.

SIMILAR SPECIES: One of the most abundant birds of semiopen and open terrain; learn it well so as to compare it with other less numerous kingbirds and other flycatchers. Cf. especially Sulphury Flycatcher and White-throated and Snowy-throated Kingbirds.

HABITAT AND BEHAVIOR: Very common and widespread in a variety of terrain ranging from forest borders and clearings (which it seems to find very rapidly) in mostly forested regions to agricultural regions; less numerous in w. Peru and sw. Ecuador. The Tropical Kingbird thrives even in noisy towns and cities, perching on wires and buildings, seemingly oblivious to all the commotion below—all it requires is a tree for nesting. One of the most frequently seen birds in many regions and one of the few that habitually perches out in the open, often on phone wires, in the heat of the tropical noonday sun. Pursues a variety of flying insects, often making spectacular long sallies after them; also eats some fruit. The frequently heard dawn song, given by resident birds throughout the year, is a short series of "pip" notes followed by a rising twitter, "piririree?"; often one of the earliest bird sounds to be heard, it is frequently given well before first light.

RANGE: Widespread in lowlands south to cen. Argentina (in small numbers to Neuquén and n. Río Negro), west of Andes south to w.-cen. Peru (Lima); Trinidad and Tobago, and on Netherlands Antilles. Also sw. United States to Panama. S. breeders (north to e. Bolivia and to São Paulo in Brazil) migrate northward during austral winter, moving into Amazonia (where flocks are regularly seen May–Sept.) and perhaps farther; breeders in n. Middle America are perhaps also somewhat migratory. In largest numbers below 1000 m, in lesser numbers in appropriate, often arid, habitat up to 2000–2500 m.

NOTE: Heine's Kingbird (*T. apolites*), known only from a single trade skin from "Rio de Janeiro," is believed to be a hybrid between the Tropical Kingbird and Variegated Flycatcher (*Birds of the World*, vol. 8).

Tyrannus albogularis

WHITE-THROATED KINGBIRD

DESCRIPTION: 21 cm (8¼″). Resembles the vastly more numerous Tropical Kingbird. Differs in having *notably paler gray head* which contrasts more with its dark mask; back paler and brighter olive; *throat pure white*, contrasting with mostly bright yellow underparts, with *only faint tinge of olive across chest*. See V-28, C-39.

SIMILAR SPECIES: In strong light Tropical Kingbird may also appear quite pale-headed and white-throated, and may show little olive on chest; the best mark then is White-throated's *pale crown* with *sharply demarcated black ear-coverts* and contrasting bright olive back.

HABITAT AND BEHAVIOR: Uncommon to locally fairly common in shrubby areas and the edge of gallery woodland, almost invariably near water and favoring stands of moriche or buriti palms (*Mauritia flexuosa*), less often in other palms such as *Scheelea* spp. When not nesting occurs more widely, though usually near water; it sometimes then is found in towns or cities. Behavior much like Tropical Kingbird's; migrating birds may occur in mixed flocks with that species. Vocalizations are also similar but higher and thinner (J. V. Remsen, *in* Hilty and Brown 1986). A pair breeds every year around the reflecting pool at the Ministry of the Exterior in Brasília.

RANGE: Breeds in n. Bolivia (Beni and n. Santa Cruz), interior and lower Amaz. Brazil (s. Mato Grosso and w. Mato Grosso do Sul east to Goiás and s. Piauí, north locally into the lower Amazon area and Amapá, and south to Minas Gerais and São Paulo), Guianas, and extreme se. Venezuela (se. Bolívar; Sucre as well?); during austral winter (at least May–Aug.) migrates into w. Amaz. Brazil and west to extreme se. Colombia (sightings from Leticia area), ne. Peru (Loreto and Ucayali), and e. Ecuador (several recent July sightings from Napo). To about 1000 m.

Tyrannus niveigularis

SNOWY-THROATED KINGBIRD   PLATE: 44

DESCRIPTION: 19 cm (7½″). *Sw. Colombia to nw. Peru.* Crown gray with blackish mask through eyes and semiconcealed yellow coronal patch; *back pale olive gray;* wings dusky, coverts and inner flight feathers edged whitish; tail blackish with almost no notch. *Throat white, becoming pale gray on breast* and clear pale yellow on belly.

SIMILAR SPECIES: Liable to be confused only with Tropical Kingbird, which differs in its larger size, markedly less pale underparts (grayer on throat, not so olive on breast, and brighter yellow on belly), more olive

(not so gray) back, and notched tail. Does not occur with White-throated Kingbird (latter only east of Andes).

HABITAT AND BEHAVIOR: Uncommon to locally (perhaps seasonally) common in semiopen agricultural areas with scattered groves or patches of scrubby woodland and in desert scrub; when not breeding also occurs at edge of humid forest. General behavior similar to Tropical Kingbird's; Snowy-throated's calls are shorter and drier, consisting of a sharp "kip!" sometimes lengthened into a snappy "kip, kr-r-e-e-e."

RANGE: Extreme sw. Colombia (sw. Nariño at Ricuarte), w. Ecuador, and nw. Peru (south to Ancash). May be somewhat migratory, moving into more humid regions in dry season; most or all records from north of Manabí, Ecuador, may pertain to migrants. Mostly below 500 m, locally up to 1200 m.

Tyrannus dominicensis

GRAY KINGBIRD

DESCRIPTION: 21.5 cm (8½"). Local in n. South America. *Bill quite heavy. Mostly gray above* with *dusky mask* through eyes and semiconcealed orange coronal patch; wings dusky, coverts and inner flight feathers edged whitish; tail dusky, slightly forked. *Below white,* tinged gray especially across breast. See V-28, C-39.

SIMILAR SPECIES: In poor light this bird's silhouette resembles Tropical Kingbird's, though Gray's bill is larger; when colors can be discerned they are of course easily distinguished. Eastern Kingbird is smaller and blacker above without the "masked" effect, and its tail is usually white-tipped (except in heavily worn individuals). Snowy-throated Kingbird (no overlap) is smaller with pale yellow (not white) belly.

HABITAT AND BEHAVIOR: Fairly common n.-winter resident (mostly Sept.–Apr.) in open and semiopen areas with scattered bushes and trees, savannas, and parks and residential areas; often most numerous near coast. In recent years a few have begun to breed in Venezuela, both along the coast and inland in the llanos; possibly they were formerly only overlooked, but breeding numbers do seem to be increasing. Gray Kingbirds are conspicuous birds, perching in the open on phone wires, fences, or atop bushes and trees, sallying after insects, also eating some fruit. Their most common call is a distinctive loud and frenetic "pe-cheer-ry."

RANGE: Nonbreeding visitor to w. and n. Colombia (south to Valle, Huila, and Meta; a few reports from Pacific coast at Buenaventura in Valle), much of Venezuela (south to n. Amazonas and n. Bolívar), Guianas, and extreme n. Brazil (seen at Maracá Ecological Station in Roraima); breeds locally in cen. Venezuela (south to Apure and n. Bolívar), and on Trinidad and Tobago, the Netherlands Antilles, and possibly in n. Colombia (Hilty and Brown 1986). Breeds mainly in West Indies and se. United States, wintering primarily in n. South America and Panama. Mostly below 500 m, but occasionally to 2500–3000 m in Colombian Andes.

GROUP B

Smaller bill and "*black-capped.*"

Tyrannus tyrannus

EASTERN KINGBIRD

DESCRIPTION: 20.5 cm (8″). *Mostly slaty above,* blackest on head, with semiconcealed coronal patch fiery orange; wings duskier, feathers narrowly edged whitish; *square tail broadly tipped white.* Below white, clouded gray across breast. See P-23. Immatures and worn-plumaged adults look much duller and more faded, and may have little or no white on tip of tail.

SIMILAR SPECIES: Fork-tailed Flycatchers in heavily worn plumage with tail streamers short or lacking may look somewhat similar but normally show some fork in tail; they also have a more obvious black-capped look, purer white underparts, and never show any white tipping on tail. Cf. also Gray Kingbird.

HABITAT AND BEHAVIOR: Locally common n.-winter resident (Sept.–May) in canopy and borders of humid forest and secondary woodland and in clearings, pastures, and parks with scattered trees; on migration can occur almost anywhere. Those familiar with Eastern Kingbird on its breeding grounds will hardly recognize it in South America. Here it becomes almost eerily silent and is largely frugivorous, though sallying for insects on occasion, and it is often found in large compact flocks which sometimes descend en masse to strip a tree of fruit. In Amazonia diurnal migrating flocks can be seen passing over the forest canopy, pausing along the shores of lakes and rivers; Fork-tailed Flycatchers sometimes accompany them.

RANGE: Nonbreeding visitor mainly to w. Amazonia, where it passes n. winter months (Dec.–Feb.) mostly in e. Peru and n. and e. Bolivia, migrating through Ecuador and Colombia. There are also a few records scattered across a wide area in s. Venezuela and Amaz. Brazil, casually east to Guyana and Surinam, and small numbers have been seen in the coastal lowlands of w. Peru (south to Mollendo in Arequipa) and south to n. Argentina (Salta, Tucumán, Formosa, and Misiones; recorded once as "abundant" in the last), more casually south to n. Chile (Arica) and e. Brazil (a single record from w. Bahia), accidentally even on Falkland Is. Breeds in North America, migrating through Middle America. Mostly below 800 m, higher on migration (then recorded to 2600 m in Colombia).

Tyrannus savana

FORK-TAILED FLYCATCHER   PLATE: 44

DESCRIPTION: Male 38–40 cm (15–16″), female 28–30 cm (11–12″), including *very long, deeply forked tail* (shorter in females, immatures, and molting birds). *Head and nape black* with semiconcealed coronal patch yellow; *back contrastingly pale gray,* wings dusky, tail black with outer web of outer pair of rectrices basally white. *Below pure white.* Immatures lack the extremely long tail feathers and have more brownish caps. Breeding races of Colombia and Venezuela (*sanctaemartae*

and *monachus*) have slightly paler gray backs and different emargination on outer primaries, deeply notched in *monachus,* nearly normal in *sanctaemartae.*

SIMILAR SPECIES: This spectacular and graceful flycatcher normally will not be confused, but a bird lacking tail streamers might be mistaken for an Eastern Kingbird or Sirystes.

HABITAT AND BEHAVIOR: Locally common in savannas and pastures with scattered bushes and trees when breeding. Highly migratory when not, and then can occur almost anywhere, especially as a transient (then sometimes even resting in forest canopy), though normally in open or semiopen situations. Conspicuous throughout the year. Fork-taileds typically perch low, often on fences or atop a shrub or small tree, thence making often spectacular long sallies after passing insects, whipping the tail around for additional maneuverability. Less often they drop to the ground. Often gregarious when not breeding, and when migrating in large loose flocks may stream over at considerable heights, gathering in enormous numbers (thousands or even more) at favored roosting sites (one is at the Caroni Swamp on Trinidad). They then consume substantial amounts of fruit. Unlike the true kingbirds, even when breeding Fork-tailed Flycatchers are rather quiet (though they are equally aggressive around the nest, often harrying away much larger birds), merely giving a weak "tic" note (sometimes in series), especially in flight.

RANGE: Widespread, as a breeding resident or migrant or both, in nonforested lowlands east of Andes south to cen. Argentina (Río Negro, with a few recent records south to ne. Chubut); west of Andes only in nw. Venezuela, and in n. and w. Colombia in Caribbean lowlands and the Río Cauca and Río Magdalena valleys; a few records of vagrants from w. Ecuador (Esmeraldas, Pichincha, and Azuay), coastal Peru (Lima and Arequipa), n. Chile (Arica), and the Peruvian altiplano near Lake Titicaca; casual on Falkland Is. Precisely delineating the limits of its breeding range is difficult because of migration, but known to nest in Colombia (east of Andes south to Meta and Vichada), much of Venezuela (south to n. Amazonas and n. Bolívar), s. Surinam (Sipaliwini), lower Amaz. Brazil (west at least occasionally to the Manaus area, and probably also in Roraima), and widely from n. and e. Bolivia (northwest to Beni) and cen. and se. Brazil (north to s. Mato Grosso, Goiás, and s. Piauí) southward into Argentina. S. breeders (nominate *savana*) migrate north during austral winter (Mar.–Sept.), spreading out over Guianas, Venezuela, Amazonia, and Trinidad and Tobago, but precise details (especially in Amazonia) still not well known. Also Mexico to Panama, where migratory in part, some birds reaching n. South America during northern winter (Oct.–Mar.); overshooting austral migrants occasionally reach West Indies and e. North America. Mostly below 1000 m, but occasionally to 2500–3500 m in Andes as a transient or wanderer.

NOTE: Formerly placed in the genus *Muscivora,* now subsumed into *Tyrannus* (e.g., *Birds of the World,* vol. 8). This forced a change in its species name as well: the species had been known as *Muscivora tyrannus,* but the specific epithet *tyrannus* was preoccupied by *Tyrannus tyrannus* (Eastern Kingbird). The next oldest species name for the Fork-tailed Flycatcher was *savana*.

Xenopsaris

A monotypic genus, becard-like but still of uncertain affinities. R. O. Prum and W. E. Lanyon (*Condor* 91[2]: 444–461, 1989) suggested that it, together with *Pachyramphus* and several other genera, be considered part of what they term the "*Schiffornis* assemblage." The merger of *Xenopsaris* into *Pachyramphus* has been advocated by some authors, but we agree with Traylor (1977) that the genus is best maintained. *Xenopsaris* is monomorphic (most *Pachyramphus* are sexually dimorphic), has a different tarsal scutellation, and lacks the short pointed 9th primary of all *Pachyramphus*. Further, its cup-shaped nest (see, *inter alia*, A. Cruz and R. W. Andrews, *Wilson Bull.* 101[1]: 71, 1989) differs strikingly from the suspended purse- or bag-shaped nests of all becards.

Xenopsaris albinucha

XENOPSARIS   PLATE: 45

Other: White-naped Xenopsaris, Reed Becard

DESCRIPTION: 13 cm (5"). *Crown black* with prominent white loral spot and pale gray nape; otherwise brownish gray above, *brownest on wings*, wing feathers with whitish edging; tail dusky, outer web of outer pair of feathers white. *Below pure white.* Sexes evidently alike. The "white nape" for which this species was formerly named (presumably from a very stretched study skin) is not evident in the field. Juvenile has browner crown, stronger brown tinge to upperparts (often with effect of scalloping), and creamy tinge to lower underparts.

SIMILAR SPECIES: Closely resembles male Cinereous Becard, which has more grayish underparts and purer gray (not so brownish) upperparts; the becard has vaguely pale-*tipped* rectrices (in the Xenopsaris it is the outer *web* of the outermost rectrix that is pale). The becard is also a less slender and shorter-tailed bird, with a thicker bill.

HABITAT AND BEHAVIOR: Rather rare and local in brushy riparian growth, lighter woodland, and borders, usually near water or in damp areas. Found singly or in pairs, usually not far above the ground; less arboreal than the becards. Male's song is a thin, high-pitched, and dainty whistle, "tsip, tsiweeé, tseee, ti-ti-ti-ti?" with variations, in quality unlike any of the becards'. It is apparently not often uttered; we have only once heard it, in Argentina. Perhaps most numerous in the pantanal of w. Mato Grosso do Sul, through even there not regularly encountered.

RANGE: Locally in w. and cen. Venezuela (recorded from w. Falcón, ne. Lara, Apure, and n. Bolívar; seems likely in adjacent ne. Colombia) and extreme n. Brazil (Roraima at the Maracá Ecological Station); locally in n. and e. Bolivia (a few sites in Beni and Santa Cruz), interior ne. and cen. Brazil (Ceará and w. Alagoas south through Piauí and w. Bahia to Mato Grosso do Sul), w. Paraguay, and n. Argentina (south to Tucumán, Córdoba, and Entre Ríos; at least formerly to n. Buenos Aires). To about 500 m.

NOTE: The English name of this species has presented problems. Prum and Lanyon (*Condor* 91[2]: 441–461, 1989) suggested that it might be called the Reed Becard. However, because it is *not* typically a species occurring in reedbeds, we do not find their suggestion compelling. Because there is only one member of the genus, a modifier ("White-naped") in its English name is not required, and in any case the species' nape is not actually white! We prefer, therefore, simply to call it the Xenopsaris.

Pachyramphus Becards

A fairly large genus of attractively patterned arboreal birds found widely throughout the neotropics. All males have the 9th (next-to-outermost) primary greatly shortened and narrowed; why is unknown. All becards have broad, somewhat hooked bills, usually pale bluish horn in color. All but two species are sexually dimorphic, males typically predominantly gray with much white in the wing, females more olive and brown with buff in the wing, or mainly cinnamon-rufous. Although not exactly crested, all species (especially those in the *Platypsaris* subgenus) frequently raise their crown feathers, resulting in a bull-headed or bushy-crested look; they also often pump or nod their heads like a *Myiarchus* flycatcher. Nests are large, untidy, globular structures, often conspicuous, suspended from a fork or the end of a branch.

The genus is of uncertain affinities: though it was long placed in the former Cotingidae, recent anatomical evidence prompted its transfer to the Tyrannidae (*Birds of the World*, vol. 8). R. O. Prum and W. E. Lanyon (*Condor* 91[2]: 444–461, 1989) suggested that the genus actually may be more closely allied to what these authors have termed the "*Schiffornis* assemblage."

Formerly, three species (Crested, Pink-throated, and One-colored) were placed in the genus *Platypsaris* (e.g., Meyer de Schauensee 1966, 1970), but we have followed Snow's (1973) merger of that genus into *Pachyramphus*. However, the species that comprised it do seem to form a cohesive group which is quite distinct from the other becards: they are larger and proportionately heavier-billed, they are much less vocal than typical *Pachyramphus* becards, and their nests are most often attached to the tip of a branch (not placed in a fork).

GROUP A   *Distinctive* becards (not necessarily closely related).

Pachyramphus viridis   **GREEN-BACKED BECARD**   PLATE: 45

DESCRIPTION: 14.5 cm (5¾″). Local in e. and s.-cen. South America; does not include Yellow-cheeked Becard of lower Andean slopes. Male has *crown glossy black* with white lores, narrow yellow eye-ring, and *sides of head and nuchal collar pale gray; remaining upperparts bright olive,* duskier on wings. Throat whitish, with *broad pectoral band bright yellow*

to *greenish yellow;* remaining underparts whitish indistinctly tinged buff. Female similar in general pattern but crown olive and *lesser wing-coverts mostly rufous-chestnut. Griseigularis* (se. Venezuela and lower Amaz. Brazil) differs from nominate race (remainder of range) in male's less distinct pectoral band and lack of the gray nuchal collar; female *griseigularis* also lacks the nuchal collar and shows almost no pectoral band; see V-27.

SIMILAR SPECIES: In its range confusion unlikely, for no other becard there has mainly olive upperparts. Cf. Yellow-cheeked Becard (no overlap).

HABITAT AND BEHAVIOR: Uncommon to locally fairly common in lighter woodland, gallery forest, borders, and clearings with scattered trees; widespread, though never really numerous nor very conspicuous. Usually in pairs, gleaning in foliage at varying heights. Male's song is a series of similar musical whistled notes, often with a crescendo, "tridídideédeédeédee!"

RANGE: Se. Venezuela (e. Bolívar); lower Amaz. Brazil (Marajó Is. upriver near the Amazon to around the mouth of the Rio Tapajós); e. and s. Brazil (north to s. Mato Grosso, Goiás, Ceará, and Rio Grande do Norte), e. and s. Bolivia (north to ne. Santa Cruz), Paraguay, n. and e. Uruguay, and n. Argentina (south to Tucumán, Santa Fe, and Entre Ríos). Likely occurs in Guyana as well. To about 1000 m.

NOTE: See comments under Yellow-cheeked Becard.

Pachyramphus xanthogenys

YELLOW-CHEEKED BECARD
Other: Green-backed Becard (in part)

PLATE: 45

DESCRIPTION: 14.5 cm (5¾"). *Foothills of Andes in e. Ecuador and e. Peru,* formerly considered conspecific with Green-backed Becard. Male has crown glossy black with white lores and at least a partial yellow eye-ring; *otherwise mainly bright olive above,* duskier on tail, and quite black on wings (coverts and inner flight feathers edged olive). *Cheeks and throat bright yellow,* becoming yellowish olive on breast; lower underparts whitish. Female has similar general pattern but crown grayish olive, lesser wing-coverts mostly rufous-chestnut, and throat grayish; it retains male's *yellow cheeks and mainly black wings.*

SIMILAR SPECIES: Barred Becard is markedly smaller, and both sexes show dark barring on underparts; male Barred differs further in having mostly black back and much white in wing. Cf. also geographically distant Green-backed Becard.

HABITAT AND BEHAVIOR: Uncommon to locally fairly common at borders of montane forest and in clearings with scattered tall trees in foothill zone along e. base of Andes. Usually in pairs, foraging in dense foliage well above the ground, generally not associating with mixed flocks; rather inconspicuous and probably often overlooked. Male's distinctive song is often given only at long intervals, usually from a high, hidden perch; it is a series of soft musical whistled notes, "du-du-didididididi." Numerous along the road to Loreto north of Archidona, Ecuador.

RANGE: E. slope of Andes in e. Ecuador (w. Sucumbios south to Zamora-Chinchipe), and in cen. Peru (Huánuco, Pasco, and Junín). Seems likely in extreme s. Colombia. Mostly 800–1400 m, rarely up to 1700 m.

NOTE: We regard *P. xanthogenys* (with *peruanus*) as a species distinct from *P. viridis* of the lowlands far east of the Andes. Not only are their ranges widely disjunct, but their habitats and plumage are quite different.

Pachyramphus versicolor

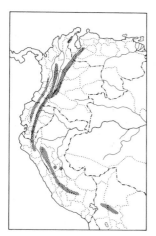

BARRED BECARD

PLATE: 45

DESCRIPTION: 13 cm (5"). *The most numerous and widespread becard in Andean forests;* chunky in shape and *relatively small.* Male *glossy black above* with gray rump; wing-coverts and inner flight feathers boldly spotted and edged white. *Lores, eye-ring, sides of head and neck, and throat greenish yellow,* fading to whitish on remaining underparts, *sides of neck and underparts with light dusky barring.* Female has *crown slaty;* otherwise olive above and on lores and sides of head and neck, with yellow eye-ring; wings blackish with *wing-coverts mostly rufous-chestnut* and rufous to buff edging on inner flight feathers; tail dusky. Below pale yellow *with faint dusky barring.* See V-27, C-35.

SIMILAR SPECIES: Often this species' barring on underparts is hard to see in the field, but even so males are easily known by their contrast between black crown and yellowish sides of neck, females by their contrasting gray crown and prominent rufous on wing. Cf. Yellow-cheeked Becard (found at lower elevations, only on e. slope).

HABITAT AND BEHAVIOR: Fairly common in canopy and borders of montane forest and second-growth woodland. Found singly or in pairs, often foraging more actively than other becards; frequently accompanies mixed flocks of tanagers and other insectivorous birds. Males have a musical and pretty song, typically a fast rising "treedidi-dee?," delivered softly at often long intervals through the day.

RANGE: Andes of w. Venezuela (north to Mérida), Colombia (not recorded in W. Andes north of Valle), Ecuador (on w. slope south to Chimborazo), e. Peru, and w. Bolivia (La Paz and Cochabamba); Sierra de Perijá on Colombia-Venezuela border. Also Costa Rica and w. Panama. Mostly 1600–2600 m.

Pachyramphus surinamus

GLOSSY-BACKED BECARD

PLATE: 45

DESCRIPTION: 13.5 cm (5¼"). A distinctive but rare becard of *ne. South America.* Male *glossy black above* with steel blue sheen on crown and some white at base of scapulars; *pure white below.* Female has *crown dark chestnut* indistinctly speckled black; sides of head dusky *contrasting with pale gray upper back* and *white lower back and rump.* Wings and tail black, wing feathers *broadly margined rufous,* outer tail feathers tipped buff. Below all white.

SIMILAR SPECIES: Striking black and white male is unlikely to be confused, though its pattern resembles certain antbirds' (none of which is

nearly so arboreal, however). Female's pattern somewhat recalls the larger Sirystes, which lacks rufous in wing, etc.

HABITAT AND BEHAVIOR: Rare and apparently local in canopy and borders of humid forest and in adjacent clearings with scattered large trees; in Surinam sometimes found in savanna woodland as well. This very distinctive becard remains poorly known in life; 3 seen near Bro-kopando in Surinam (GT) were feeding on fruit. May be more numerous north of Manaus, Brazil, where pairs are seen fairly regularly with mixed canopy flocks composed of various tanagers and other mainly insectivorous birds. Its song is a series of up to 8–10 very high-pitched "pwee" notes, accelerating and at first rising, then dropping off in pitch and volume (M. Cohn-Haft).

RANGE: Locally in Surinam, French Guiana, and lower Amaz. Brazil (recorded mainly north of the Amazon west to the lower Rio Negro in the Manaus area; south of the Amazon recorded from sightings south of Tefé on the Rio Urucu). Below about 300 m.

GROUP B

"Typical" becards: most males gray, black, and white; females usually very different.

Pachyramphus polychopterus

WHITE-WINGED BECARD   PLATE: 45

DESCRIPTION: 14.5–15 cm (5¾–6"). Males geographically variable, especially on underparts. In w. Amazonia (*nigriventris* and *tenebrosus*) *all black to blackish gray* (*tenebrosus* of e. Ecuador and adjacent areas the blackest), glossier above and especially on crown; wings with 2 bold white bars, the upper one broader; tail feathers broadly tipped white. Elsewhere underparts and rump are *grayer,* palest in *dorsalis* (sw. Colombia and nw. Ecuador) and nominate race (ne. Brazil); in addition to wing-bars, the latter races have white scapulars and edging to inner flight feathers. Female olive brown above, more *grayish brown on crown* and with *white supraloral and broken eye-ring;* wings dusky with *cinnamon-buff scapulars and broad edging to coverts and inner flight feathers;* tail dusky, feathers (especially outer ones) *broadly tipped cinnamon-buff.* Below pale yellowish, often clouded with olive especially on breast. Females in w. Amazonia have crown tinged rufescent. See V-27, C-35.

SIMILAR SPECIES: Male is only male becard in its Group *without white or gray on lores.* Black races are quite distinctive (though cf. male White-shouldered Tanager), but races with gray underparts are easily confused with male Black-and-white and Black-capped Becards (which see). Rather drab female can be confusing, but note its conspicuous wing and tail markings and relatively simple head pattern. Female Black-capped Becard is very similar but is slightly smaller and has an obviously rufous-chestnut crown (but beware tinge of rufous on crowns of w. Amaz. White-wingeds).

HABITAT AND BEHAVIOR: Uncommon to fairly common in lighter and secondary woodland, borders of humid forest, gallery forest, várzea forest and other semiopen riparian areas (in Amazonia), clearings and plantations, and mangroves. Widespread but never very conspicuous, pairs can be found foraging lethargically at all levels but not often far in the open; they sometimes accompany mixed flocks. Occasionally one will seem almost "fearless," methodically gleaning only a few feet away. The often-heard and pretty song, given by both sexes but much more often by male, is a leisurely short series of mellow musical notes, "teeu, tu-tu-tu-tu," with variations; it is delivered more slowly than songs of either Black-capped or Black-and-white Becards.

RANGE: Widespread in lowlands south to n. Argentina (south to Catamarca, Córdoba, and n. Buenos Aires) and Uruguay; west of Andes in n. and w. Colombia (but not in Pacific lowlands) and nw. Ecuador (Esmeraldas and Pichincha); Trinidad and Tobago. Also Guatemala to Panama. Apparently only a summer resident in s. part of range (e.g., Córdoba, Argentina, and Rio Grande do Sul, Brazil). Mostly below 1500 m, occasionally up to 2000 m or even higher.

NOTE: The well-established English names of the three similar becards—White-winged (*P. polychopterus*), Black-capped (*P. marginatus*), and Black-and-white (*P. albogriseus*)—are virtually meaningless. White-winged is no more "white-winged" than either of the others; Black-capped is likewise no more "black-capped"; and Black-and-white, with pattern and coloration almost identical to the others, is most assuredly not "black and white."

Pachyramphus marginatus

BLACK-CAPPED BECARD

PLATE: 45

DESCRIPTION: 14 cm (5½"). Mainly Amazonia. Male has crown glossy black with blue sheen, *back mixed black and gray* (relative amounts seem to vary individually), and pure gray rump; wings black with white scapulars, 2 wing-bars, and edging on flight feathers; tail black, outer feathers broadly tipped white. Supraloral spot and entire underparts uniform pale gray. Female like female White-winged Becard but with *rufous-chestnut crown.*

SIMILAR SPECIES: Over much of the area of overlap with White-winged Becard (basically Amazonia), male White-winged is mostly black and thus easily told from male Black-capped. Elsewhere note Black-capped's smaller size, pale gray lores, and forest canopy habitat (White-winged favoring borders and semiopen). Female White-winged's crown is at most tinged rufescent (not the obvious rufous-chestnut of Black-capped). Cf. also Black-and-white Becard.

HABITAT AND BEHAVIOR: Uncommon to fairly common in canopy and borders of humid forest (especially terra firme); probably often overlooked as it tends to remain well above ground and in heavy foliage. Usually in pairs, often with mixed flocks of various insectivorous birds. Male's song is a pretty, clear, whistled "teeu, wheedoweét; teeu, wheedoweét."

RANGE: Guianas, s. Venezuela (Bolívar and Amazonas), se. Colombia (north to Meta and Guainía), e. Ecuador, e. Peru, n. Bolivia (south to La Paz and Cochabamba), and Amaz. Brazil (south to s. Mato Grosso, Pará, and n. Maranhão); e. Brazil (Pernambuco south to se. São

Paulo); an isolated population in n. Venezuela (Carabobo). Mostly below 500 m, but recorded to 1000 m in Venezuela.

Pachyramphus albogriseus

BLACK-AND-WHITE BECARD

DESCRIPTION: 14.5 cm (5¾"). Local from Venezuela to Peru. Resembles Black-capped Becard (limited overlap). Male differs in having white (not pale gray) supraloral spot, *plain gray back* (never any intermixed black), and *lack of white on scapulars*. Female, unlike female Black-capped and White-winged, has more complex head pattern: *bright chestnut crown broadly margined with black,* and white supraloral extending back as a *broken but conspicuous eye-ring.* It also has no buff or rusty tinge on scapulars. See V-27, C-35.
SIMILAR SPECIES: Male White-winged Becard lacks the supraloral and always has black on back; female White-winged has much plainer head pattern.
HABITAT AND BEHAVIOR: Uncommon to locally fairly common in canopy and borders of montane forest; in w. Ecuador and nw. Peru also occurs in deciduous forest and woodland, sometimes even where quite scrubby. Behavior similar to other "black-and-white" becards'; usually more conspicuous in drier, semiopen habitats of Pacific lowlands than in humid forest. Its distinctive song is a pretty, mellow "chu-u-ree?" often repeated several times in succession.
RANGE: Mts. of n. Venezuela (Sucre west locally to Lara), and Andes of w. Venezuela (Mérida and Táchira), ne. and extreme se. Colombia (recorded only in E. Andes from Norte de Santander to Boyacá, and in Nariño, but likely more widespread), Ecuador (where also in Pacific lowlands from w. Esmeraldas southward), and e. Peru (south to Ayacucho; also in Pacific lowlands south to Lambayeque); Sierra de Perijá on Venezuela-Colombia border and Santa Marta Mts. of n. Colombia. Also Costa Rica and w. Panama. Mostly 1000–2200 m, locally down to near sea level in Ecuador and Peru.

Pachyramphus spodiurus

SLATY BECARD   PLATE: 45

DESCRIPTION: 14 cm (5½"). *Mainly w. Ecuador.* Crown black with whitish supraloral spot and frontlet; otherwise slaty gray above, back variably mixed with black; wings and tail blackish with *whitish edging on wing feathers* (but *no wing-bars*). Below uniform gray. Female bright cinnamon-rufous above, somewhat darker on crown, with whitish supraloral spot; *black greater primary-coverts* and outer primaries. *Mostly whitish below,* tinged buff on sides of throat and across chest.
SIMILAR SPECIES: This scarce species is often confused, particularly females; ideally identifications should be based upon seeing a pair. Both sexes resemble One-colored Becard, which is larger and heavier-billed and lacks Slaty's pale lores; male One-colored has *virtually plain wings.* Female Slaty closely resembles Cinnamon Becard and has similar size and shape; Cinnamon differs only in its reddish brown (not black) primary coverts and in its buffier (not so white) throat and belly.

HABITAT AND BEHAVIOR: Rare to locally uncommon in deciduous woodland and scrub, plantations and clearings, and humid forest borders; perhaps somewhat overlooked because of confusion with the more numerous One-colored and Cinnamon Becards. Slaty's behavior is similar to other "typical" becards', but it more often seems to forage close to the ground. Its song is a short, fast series of musical notes with a descending and slowing effect, "ti-ti-ti-ti-tee-tee-teh-teh-tu." Perhaps threatened by the destruction of much woodland across its small range, though there are several recent reports from relatively degraded areas.
RANGE: W. Ecuador (north locally to w. Esmeraldas and s. Pichincha) and extreme nw. Peru (Tumbes and n. Piura). To about 600 m.

Pachyramphus rufus

CINEREOUS BECARD

DESCRIPTION: 13.5 cm (5¼"). Male *mostly pearly gray above* with contrasting glossy black crown and white supraloral and frontlet; wings blackish, *feathers narrowly edged with white;* tail mostly slaty. Below grayish white, whitest on throat and midbelly. Female virtually identical to female Slaty Becard. See V-27, C-35.
SIMILAR SPECIES: The closely related Slaty Becard does not occur east of Andes. Male Cinereous most resembles Xenopsaris, which is more slender with a longer tail, has pure white (not so gray) underparts, and is more brown-tinged above (especially on wings). Male Black-and-white Becard is much darker generally with much more white in wings and tail. Female Cinereous closely resembles Cinnamon Becard, differing only in its black primary-coverts (reddish brown in Cinnamon) and its whiter throat and belly (not as buffy as in Cinnamon).
HABITAT AND BEHAVIOR: Uncommon and rather local in lighter woodland, forest borders, riparian areas, plantations and clearings with scattered trees, and mangroves; seems most numerous in Guianas. Usually found singly or in pairs, generally not with mixed flocks. Song is a fast series of ascending musical notes, commencing more slowly, almost trilled or dropping off at end, "teeu, teeu-twee-twee-twitwiti-tititi, trew."
RANGE: W. and n. Colombia (Caribbean lowlands, and south in Río Cauca valley to Valle and in Río Magdalena valley to Huila), much of Venezuela (except extreme south), Guianas, Amaz. Brazil (south to n. Mato Grosso, Pará, and probably Maranhão), extreme se. Colombia (Leticia area), and ne. Peru (Loreto); se. Ecuador (2 uncertain 19th-century records from Zamora-Chinchipe). Also e. Panama. Mostly below 1000 m (recorded to 1500 m in Colombia).

Pachyramphus castaneus

CHESTNUT-CROWNED BECARD   PLATE: 45

DESCRIPTION: 14–14.5 cm (5½–5¾"). Sexes alike. Mostly cinnamon-rufous above, darker and more chestnut on crown, with dusky lores and buffy whitish supraloral turning into a *gray stripe extending back from eye and encircling nape;* primary coverts brownish and primaries dusky. Below pale cinnamon-buff, whitest on throat and midbelly.

SIMILAR SPECIES: No other rufous becard has the gray band encircling nape; cf. especially Cinnamon Becard (mainly found *west* of Andes, no known overlap with Chestnut-crowned). In se. Brazil, cf. also the superficially quite similar Brown Tanager (*Orchesticus abeillei*).

HABITAT AND BEHAVIOR: Uncommon to locally fairly common at borders of humid forest and secondary woodland and in clearings with large trees left standing. Usually remains well above the ground but often conspicuous, perching in the open. Often in pairs, usually not with mixed flocks. The song is a soft and melodic "teeeuw, teeu-teeu" (sometimes only 1 or up to 4 "teeu"s), delivered in a characteristically slow, relaxed fashion.

RANGE: N. Venezuela (Sucre and Monagas west to Yaracuy and Falcón); locally in s. Venezuela (Bolívar and n. Amazonas); se. Colombia (north to Meta and Vaupés), e. Ecuador, e. Peru, n. Bolivia (south to La Paz and Cochabamba), and Amaz. Brazil (east to e. Pará and n. Maranhão, and south to Rondônia and n. Mato Grosso at Alta Floresta); s. Brazil (Bahia and s. Goiás south to n. Rio Grande do Sul), e. Paraguay (west to near Río Paraguay), and ne. Argentina (Misiones and ne. Corrientes). To about 1700 m (in Venezuela), but usually below 1200 m.

Pachyramphus cinnamomeus

CINNAMON BECARD

DESCRIPTION: 14 cm (5½"). *Nw. South America.* Closely resembles Chestnut-crowned Becard (no known overlap) but somewhat paler cinnamon-rufous above, not nearly as dark on crown (which is concolor with rest of upperparts), and *lacking* the gray band on head. Sexes alike. See V-27, C-35.

SIMILAR SPECIES: This relatively numerous species resembles females of several other scarcer becards found in its range. Female Cinereous and Slaty Becards are notably whiter below and have black (not more or less concolor rufous) primary-coverts. Female One-colored Becard is larger and has no whitish supraloral.

HABITAT AND BEHAVIOR: Fairly common to common at borders of humid forest and secondary woodland, in plantations, and in clearings with tall trees; avoids arid areas (unlike One-colored Becard). Usually in pairs, less often alone, generally remaining well above the ground and independent of mixed flocks. The song resembles Chestnut-crowned Becard's in quality but is usually delivered more rapidly with typically a longer series of terminal "teeu" notes.

RANGE: Nw. Venezuela (mainly in Maracaibo basin, also east of Andes in s. Táchira), n. and w. Colombia (widely in Caribbean and Pacific lowlands, and up Río Magdalena valley to Tolima; also along e. base of Andes south to w. Meta), and w. Ecuador (south to El Oro). Also Mexico to Panama. To about 1500 m.

GROUP C

Platypsaris subgenus: *larger,* more *bull-headed* and *stout-billed.* Males *gray to slaty;* females vary from *all rufous* to having *crown and back gray.*

Pachyramphus validus

CRESTED BECARD

PLATE: 45

DESCRIPTION: 18–18.5 cm (7–7¼"). S.-cen. South America. Very stout bill. Male *black above,* glossiest on crown; some white on scapulars, and semiconcealed white area on back. Supraloral spot and *underparts uniform pale smoky grayish.* Female has *dark gray crown contrasting with rufous of remaining upperparts;* primaries dusky. Supraloral spot and underparts uniform dull cinnamon-buff. Foregoing applies to nominate race of most of range; *audax* (e. slope of Andes and in adjacent lowlands) male has purer gray underparts, female a sooty black crown.

SIMILAR SPECIES: The largest becard, and in fact no more "crested" than other members of its *Platypsaris* subgenus (any of which can look bushy-crested). The rather plain male Crested is essentially 2-toned: black above, paler below. Female Pink-throated Becard has gray back, so its crown does not contrast. Cf. also Sirystes.

HABITAT AND BEHAVIOR: Uncommon in woodland and forest borders and in plantations and clearings with trees; rather local and on the whole not often encountered. Seen singly or in pairs, usually foraging well above ground, sometimes with mixed flocks. Not very vocal, only occasionally giving a few squeaky or twittery notes.

RANGE: E. and s. Brazil (e. Pará, Maranhão, and Ceará south to Rio Grande do Sul, and inland through Mato Grosso and Mato Grosso do Sul to Rondônia at Cachoeira Nazaré), Paraguay (mainly east of the Río Paraguay), n. Argentina (south in the northwest to La Rioja and w. Córdoba, in the northeast to n. Santa Fe and Corrientes), n. and e. Bolivia (north in lowlands to ne. Santa Cruz, and northwest on Andean slopes to La Paz), and se. Peru (north to Ayacucho). Apparently only a summer resident in s. part of range (e.g., in Córdoba, Argentina, and Rio Grande do Sul, Brazil). To about 2000 m (in Bolivia, where occasionally ranging even higher, to 3000 m).

NOTE: Formerly placed in the genus *Platypsaris* and called *Platypsaris rufus.* The merger of the genera *Pachyramphus* and *Platypsaris* forced a change in this species' specific name because the name of *Pachyramphus rufus* (Cinereous Becard) had priority. The next available species name for the Crested Becard was *validus.*

Pachyramphus minor

PINK-THROATED BECARD

PLATE: 45

DESCRIPTION: 17 cm (6¾"). Amazonia. Male *black above* with some white (often hidden) on bend of wing. *Mostly dark gray below* with *patch of rosy pink on lower throat and upper chest* (often surprisingly hard to see in the field). Female has *slaty gray crown and back contrasting with rufous wings and tail* and often some rufous on rump; supraloral spot and underparts uniform buff; see V-27, C-33.

SIMILAR SPECIES: Pink-throated marginally overlaps with somewhat larger Crested Becard along latter's n. range limit; male Crested lacks the pink and is not as dark a gray below, whereas female has rufous (not gray) back, *so it is the back and crown that contrast* (not the back and wings). Cf. also male of smaller White-winged Becard (which in

Amazonia is mostly blackish, showing little white on wings but with white in tail always obvious).

HABITAT AND BEHAVIOR: Uncommon to fairly common in canopy and borders of humid forest and secondary woodland, both in terra firme and várzea (usually more numerous in the former). Generally remains well above ground, and doubtless often overlooked as it seems surprisingly quiet. The most frequent vocalization is a clear, melodic "tuuuweeeit," obviously rising, sometimes followed by some twittering notes. A single bird or a pair will sometimes be found accompanying a mixed canopy flock.

RANGE: Guianas, s. Venezuela (Bolívar and Amazonas), se. Colombia (north to Meta and Vaupés), e. Ecuador, e. Peru, n. Bolivia (south to La Paz, Cochabamba, and n. Santa Cruz), and Amaz. Brazil (south to s. Mato Grosso, n. Goiás, and n. Maranhão). Mostly below 500 m.

NOTE: Formerly placed in the genus *Platypsaris*.

Pachyramphus homochrous

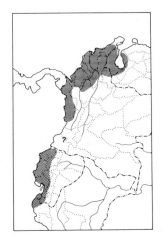

ONE-COLORED BECARD

DESCRIPTION: 16.5 cm (6½"). *W. Venezuela to nw. Peru.* Male *slaty gray above,* blackest on crown, wings, and tail, wing feathers very narrowly margined paler. *Below uniform gray;* a few males show a pink wash on lower throat. Female *uniform rufous above,* often with *some dusky around eye;* primaries dusky. Cinnamon-buff below, whitest on throat and midbelly. See C-35.

SIMILAR SPECIES: Neither sex is really "one-colored," both being appreciably paler below than above. Male distinctive in its range except for male of smaller Slaty Becard, which shows much more prominent white edging to wing feathers (One-colored's wing much plainer). Female easily confused with other "rufous" becards but is larger and more bushy-crested than any other in range; *it lacks any pale supraloral area* and usually shows dusky around eye.

HABITAT AND BEHAVIOR: Fairly common in humid and deciduous forest and forest borders, clearings with scattered trees, and (in sw. Ecuador) even in rather degraded dry scrubby woodland. Usually found in pairs, foraging at all levels but most often rather high. Frequently raises crown feathers into a rounded bushy crest, peering about alertly. Its song is a loud, sharp, sputtering "stet-ee-ee-teet-tsit-tsit-ts-tsít," variable but lacking the melodic quality of the true *Pachyramphus* becards.

RANGE: Nw. Venezuela (Maracaibo basin), n. and w. Colombia (Caribbean lowlands and south in Río Magdalena valley to e. Antioquia; south on Pacific slope only to s. Chocó); w. Ecuador (north to Esmeraldas) and extreme nw. Peru (Tumbes and n. Piura). Also e. Panama. Mostly below 900 m, but recorded to 1300 m in s. Ecuador.

NOTE: Formerly placed in the genus *Platypsaris. P. homochrous* may prove to be conspecific with *P. aglaiae* (Rose-throated Becard) of extreme sw. United States to w. Panama, and possibly with *P. minor* as well, but on the basis of presently available evidence we continue to favor treating them as allospecies in a superspecies complex.

Tityra Tityras

A trio of widespread, easily recognized, chunky and short-tailed birds found in lowland forests and woodlands, the tityras are mainly white or pale gray with black on head, wings, and tail. Like the becards, males have a shortened 9th primary; partly because of this, these genera have recently been placed in the Tityrinae subfamily of the Tyrannidae (*Birds of the World,* vol. 8). Formerly (e.g., Meyer de Schauensee 1966, 1970) both tityras and becards were classified as cotingas. Tityra nests are very different from becards', the tityras placing theirs inside a hole in a dead snag.

Tityra inquisitor

BLACK-CROWNED TITYRA

PLATE: 45

DESCRIPTION: 18–19 cm (7–7½"); southern birds larger. Bill black above, bluish to leaden gray below; *the only tityra always lacking red on bill and around eye.* Males from most of range (nominate group, with *erythrogenys* and *pelzelni*) have *crown and sides of head black;* otherwise pearly gray above, white tinged gray below; wings (except for tertials) and tail black. Females resemble males but have black only on crown, with pale buff frontlet and *rufous-chestnut sides of head;* back duller and darker gray, variably streaked with brown. Males of *albitorques* (seemingly disjunct range in w. Colombia and w. Ecuador, and e. Peru into w. Amaz. Brazil) have cheeks white and tail mostly white (with black reduced to a broad subterminal band); see C-35. *Buckleyi* (e. Ecuador and in Caquetá, Colombia) has white cheeks (like *albitorques*) but tail all black (like nominate group).

SIMILAR SPECIES: In most of range, both sexes of Black-crowned Tityra are readily known by their all-black bills; the species really should be called the "Black-billed Tityra." The red shown by the other 2 tityras is usually conspicuous, but note that in s. part of Black-tailed's range that species has a mostly black bill and reduced red around eye. No other tityra shows female Black-crowned's contrasting chestnut cheeks.

HABITAT AND BEHAVIOR: Uncommon to locally fairly common (seemingly more numerous southward) in canopy and borders of both humid and deciduous forest and woodland and in clearings with large trees. Regularly found in pairs, usually remaining well above the ground; most in evidence around clearings and at edge where more exposed perches are visible from ground. Sometimes several will gather at a fruiting tree, occasionally even with other tityras. Frequently seen in strong direct flight low over the canopy or across a clearing. Its calls are raspy, drier than the other tityras' (and less "grunty"), e.g. "zick-zick-zick."

RANGE: Widespread in lowlands south to n. and e. Bolivia (La Paz, Cochabamba, and Santa Cruz), e. Paraguay (west to near Río Paraguay), ne. Argentina (e. Formosa, e. Chaco, and Corrientes), and s. Brazil (n. Rio Grande do Sul); west of Andes south to sw. Ecuador (Guayas); seemingly absent from a wide area across n. Amazonia (extending from se. Colombia east across the Rio Negro drainage to most of Amapá). Also Mexico to Panama. Mostly below 1000 m.

NOTE: *Tityra leucura* (White-tailed Tityra) was described from a single immature bird taken in the 19th century on the upper Rio Madeira in w. Brazil. It has never been found since, and its status as a species seems dubious at best, especially given the geographic variation in tail color and pattern of *T. inquisitor.*

Tityra cayana

BLACK-TAILED TITYRA   PLATE: 45

DESCRIPTION: 21.5 cm (8½"). *Orbital area and most of bill red,* bill tipped black; *braziliensis* from e. Brazil and extreme e. Bolivia southward has orbital area reddish purple and bill mostly black with only its base reddish purple. Male has *crown and sides of head black;* otherwise pearly gray above and white tinged gray below; wings (except for tertials) and *tail black.* Female has similar pattern but is darker and more brownish gray above with variable amount of *black streaking* (often *prominent,* especially on nape and back); also shows some *narrow but conspicuous black streaking on breast.* Males of *braziliensis* are whiter generally, whereas females of that race are very different: they lack the black cap entirely, are more grayish brown above with head and back coarsely streaked black, and are *much more profusely streaked black below* (underparts are also more buff-tinged).

SIMILAR SPECIES: *Female is the only tityra with prominent streaking* (female Black-crowned may show a little on back). Male *braziliensis* Black-tailed has same pattern as males of sympatric race of Black-crowned Tityra, and this, combined with the reduced red on their bills and ocular areas, can cause confusion: however, male Black-crowned is smaller and grayer (particularly above) and never has *any* red or purplish on bill or face. Cf. also Masked Tityra.

HABITAT AND BEHAVIOR: Fairly common to common in canopy and borders of humid forest and secondary woodland, gallery forest, and clearings with trees and plantations. Generally widespread and conspicuous, often perching on high exposed branches or flying long distances in the open. Unlike Black-crowned Tityra, Black-tailed seems rather confined to humid regions. Its call, a nasal croak or grunt, most often doubled, "urt-urt," is frequently given in flight.

RANGE: Widespread in lowlands east of Andes south to n. and e. Bolivia (La Paz, Cochabamba, and Santa Cruz), Paraguay (mostly east of the Río Paraguay), ne. Argentina (south to e. Formosa, e. Chaco, and Misiones; probably also in Corrientes), and s. Brazil (south to n. Rio Grande do Sul); west of Andes only in nw. Venezuela (Maracaibo basin and Falcón); Trinidad. To about 1000 m.

NOTE: *Braziliensis* is so distinct from nominate *cayana* that it almost appears to deserve full species status (Brazilian Tityra), but intergrades are apparently known (*Birds of the World*, vol. 8).

Tityra semifasciata

MASKED TITYRA

DESCRIPTION: 20.5–21.5 cm (8–8½"). *Orbital area and most of bill red,* bill tipped black. Male's *forecrown and area around orbital region, including chin, black;* otherwise pale pearly gray above, white tinged pearly gray below; wings (except for tertials) black, *tail grayish white* with

broad black subterminal band. Female like male but lacks the black "mask" and has *darker gray back, fully brownish crown,* and is dingier and grayer below. Male *nigriceps* (w. Ecuador) is whiter generally, some with black spotting on hindcrown; female *columbiana* (n. Colombia and n. Venezuela) browner above. See V-27, C-35.

SIMILAR SPECIES: Male resembles male Black-tailed Tityra but has less black on head (none on hindcrown) and does not have all-black tail. Females likewise resemble female Black-tailed but are always *unstreaked* and also lack all-black tail. Cf. also Black-crowned Tityra.

HABITAT AND BEHAVIOR: Fairly common to common (generally most numerous west of Andes) in canopy and borders of humid forest and secondary woodland and in plantations and clearings with scattered trees. Behavior (including voice) similar to Black-tailed Tityra's; Black-tailed generally replaces this species in much of the Orinoco and Amazon basins, with Masked being found mainly at their periphery; locally, however, the 2 species do range together.

RANGE: N. and w. Venezuela (Distrito Federal west to Maracaibo basin), n. and w. Colombia (Caribbean and Pacific lowlands and up Río Magdalena valley to Huila; east of Andes only in w. Meta), Ecuador (west of Andes south locally to w. Guayas, Los Ríos, and nw. Azuay; east of them mainly along base of Andes), e. Peru, n. and e. Bolivia (south to La Paz, Cochabamba, and Santa Cruz), and Amaz. Brazil (almost entirely south of the Amazon, ranging south and east to s. Mato Grosso, Goiás, and Maranhão; north of it only along the Amazon and in Amapá), and French Guiana. Also Mexico to Panama. Mostly below 1300 m, occasionally up to 1800 m.

MANAKINS

THE manakins are a tyrannoid group found exclusively in the neo-tropics, where they range widely inside tropical and subtropical forests and woodlands. None is migratory. They are small chunky birds with short bills, short tails, and big eyes; the males of many species are very colorful or boldly patterned, but females of these are dull (usually olive), and some other species recently shown not to be "true" manakins (see below) are monomor-phic. Males of the true manakins engage in some sort of stereotyped display (in some very complex), either alone or in leks, to attract females. Females alone care for the young in most species; nests are simple cups attached to a fork in a branch.

Recent evidence has shown that the manakins almost unquestionably do not form a mono-phyletic unit (Prum 1989). Prum (op. cit.) concluded that the following genera are not "true" manakins: *Sapayoa, Schiffornis, Piprites, Tyranneutes, Neopelma,* and *Neopipo. Neopipo* (the Cinna-mon Tyrant-Manakin) seems certainly to be a tyrannid and is apparently the sister-group of the similar *Terenotriccus* (Ruddy-tailed Flycatcher). *Schiffornis,* together with certain other cotingid genera, apparently belongs in a group somewhat separate from any of the defined subfamilies. *Piprites* may be closest to the *Pachyramphus* becards, whereas the affinities of *Tyranneutes* and *Neopelma* remain uncertain. The relationships of the enigmatic *Sapayoa* remain completely un-resolved. While recognizing that it may not be technically entirely accurate, in view of the continuing controversy and the absence of well-defined alternative treatments, we retain all these problematic genera within the Piprinae.

Sapayoa

Long classified as a manakin, but new evidence indicates that the monotypic genus *Sapayoa* is of uncertain affinities; it assuredly is not a true manakin and probably should be placed outside the tyrannid group (S. M. Lanyon, *Syst. Zool.* 34: 404–418, 1985; and Sibley and Monroe 1990). *Sapayoa* superficially resembles certain of the duller true manakins—and we therefore place it for convenience's sake with them—but it is wider-billed and proportionately longer-tailed than any true manakin. Its nest remains unknown.

Sapayoa aenigma ### BROAD-BILLED SAPAYOA PLATE: 46
Other: Broad-billed Manakin

DESCRIPTION: 15 cm (6"). *W. Colombia and nw. Ecuador.* Rather broad, flat bill; *tail long* for a "manakin." *Uniform olive,* duskier on wings and tail, somewhat yellower on throat and midbelly. Males have usually concealed yellow coronal patch (absent in some birds, presumed either juveniles or mis-sexed specimens).
SIMILAR SPECIES: An inconspicuous and often confusing dull-colored bird of humid forest understory. About the same color as numerous

female manakins but larger and markedly longer-tailed and with different behavior (often with mixed understory flocks). Green Manakin of sympatric *litae* form is smaller with a more pronounced eye-ring and is more contrastingly yellow on belly. Thrush-like Mourner in area of overlap is larger, darker and browner generally, and duller (not yellow) on belly; unlike the sapayoa, it rarely accompanies mixed flocks. Cf. also Olivaceous and Pacific Flatbills; their bills are even wider than the sapayoa's and they both show prominent wing-edging and bars (sapayoa's wing is *essentially plain*).

HABITAT AND BEHAVIOR: Rare to uncommon in undergrowth of humid forest, favoring ravines and areas near streams. Usually seen singly or in pairs, often accompanying mixed flocks of *Myrmotherula* antwrens, Sulphur-rumped Flycatchers, etc. Generally rather quiet and unobtrusive, sapayoas perch vertically for often considerable periods before abruptly sallying to foliage in a manner reminiscent of a *Rhynchocyclus* flatbill. Foraging birds sometimes utter a soft, somewhat nasal, vaguely Long-billed Gnatwren-like trill; a slightly louder "chip, ch-ch-ch" call is also given (J. Guarnaccia).

RANGE: W. Colombia (Pacific slope from Chocó to Nariño, and east along humid n. base of Andes to middle Río Magdalena valley in Santander) and extreme nw. Ecuador (n. Esmeraldas). Also Panama. To 1100 m.

NOTE: As this species is not a true manakin (see above), we believe that it should no longer be called one. Given its still uncertain relationships, we suggest that employing its generic name is the best course.

Schiffornis Mourners

Rather plain birds inhabiting the forest understory, members of this genus were long considered aberrant manakins. However, they are now believed to be more closely related to the *Laniocera* and *Laniisoma* mourners, together with *Pachyramphus*, *Xenopsaris*, and *Iodopleura*, in what has been termed by R. O. Prum and W. E. Lanyon (*Condor* 91[2]: 444–461, 1989) the "*Schiffornis* assemblage," positioned separately between the true manakins, cotingas, and tyrant flycatchers. Prum and Lanyon proposed that the group name for *Schiffornis* be switched to "Mourner" to reflect this relationship, and we follow this suggestion as regards the group name, but we keep the genus with the rest of the manakins. All three *Schiffornis* species (there may be more) are retiring, inconspicuous, and infrequently seen birds, their most notable feature being a loud whistled song. The nest, very different from those of the true manakins, is a bulky cup placed on top of a broken-off stump or in vegetation close to the trunk of a tree.

Schiffornis turdinus

THRUSH-LIKE MOURNER   PLATE: 46
Other: Thrush-like Manakin, Thrush-like Schiffornis

DESCRIPTION: 15.5–16.5 cm (6–6½"). Variable geographically but usually *rather uniform and dingy*, always with *prominent large dark eyes* set

off by an indistinct paler eye-ring. Typical birds (including *amazonus*) are dull brownish olive above with wing feathers edged rufescent; uniform olive gray below. Most divergent are *panamensis* and *stenorhynchus* (n. Colombia and w. Venezuela): these are *markedly more rufescent above and on throat and chest, contrasting* with olive grayish lower breast and belly; see P-27. *Rosenbergi* and *acrolophites* of w. Colombia and w. Ecuador, and *aeneus* of e. slope of Andes in Ecuador and n. Peru, are *mostly dark brownish olive below,* with little or no gray tone. Nominate race of e. Brazil resembles the *amazonus* group but is distinctly larger.

SIMILAR SPECIES: This dull-plumaged, forest-understory inhabitant is seldom seen and often not recognized; with experience its round-headed, wide-eyed look is a consistent clue. The more rufescent races can be confused with Brownish Twistwing (*Cnipodectes*), whereas the dark and olivaceous races of w. Colombia and w. Ecuador recall the more purely olive Broad-billed Sapayoa. In s. Brazil cf. Greenish Mourner (which is always quite olive with contrasting rufescent wings). Despite its English name, Thrush-like Mourner is not particularly "thrush-like."

HABITAT AND BEHAVIOR: Uncommon to locally fairly common but retiring and hard to see (much more often recorded by voice) in lower growth of humid forest and mature secondary woodland, almost always remaining inside. Usually forages alone, hopping about in undergrowth, seizing insect prey in short sallies to foliage, and often clinging to upright stems; only rarely does it accompany mixed flocks. Mainly found through its distinctive voice, though individual songs are usually given at long intervals and hence are difficult to track down (it is often responsive to tape playback, however). These songs are strikingly variable geographically, though all have a characteristic clear, musical, whistled quality. Examples include "teeuu, wheet-wheet, wheet?" (*panamensis,* in Panama); "teeeeu, wheeeu-wheé-tu" (*wallacii,* in Surinam); a very slow "teeeeuuu . . . wheee-tú" (*rosenbergi,* in w. Ecuador); a more complex, faster, and more rhythmic "teeu, wheeu, wheé-tu-tu" (*aeneus,* in e. Ecuador); and a rather slow "teeuu, yooweé, tu, tu-wee?" (nominate, in ne. Brazil). The taxonomic significance, if any, of this complex variation remains to be elucidated.

RANGE: Widespread in more humid lowlands south to n. Bolivia (La Paz, Cochabamba, and Santa Cruz) and Amaz. and cen. Brazil (south to s. Mato Grosso and n. Goiás, and east to n. Maranhão); west of Andes south to sw. Ecuador (El Oro and w. Loja); e. Brazil (Pernambuco south to Espírito Santo and e. Minas Gerais); evidently absent from the llanos region of Venezuela and ne. Colombia. Also Mexico to Panama. To about 1500 m, occasionally slightly higher; in e. Brazil only in lowlands below about 500 m.

NOTE: More than one species is probably involved, but more field work needs to be done before this can be firmly established. In particular, the relationship of bright *panamensis*-type birds with dark *rosenbergi*-type birds in n. Colombia needs to be ascertained, as does that of dark *aeneus* (e. Andean slopes) with the *amazonus* group (Amaz. lowlands).

Schiffornis virescens

GREENISH MOURNER

Other: Greenish Manakin, Greenish Schiffornis

DESCRIPTION: 15.5 cm (6"). *S. Brazil and adjacent Paraguay and Argentina.* Resembles more olivaceous forms of Thrush-like Mourner but greener and not as dark; *wings and tail contrastingly rufescent.* Its indistinct pale eye-ring is generally even more apparent than Thrush-like's. The 2 species are not known to occur together, for in the area of apparent overlap in e. Brazil the Greenish occurs at higher elevations.

SIMILAR SPECIES: Female Blue Manakin is almost as large as this species and often occurs with it. It and the Greenish Mourner are quite similar, as the former's slightly elongated central tail feathers are often not apparent, but note mourner's duller green plumage, rufescent wings and tail, and dark (not reddish) legs.

HABITAT AND BEHAVIOR: Fairly common in lower growth of humid forest, mature secondary woodland, and gallery forest. General behavior very similar to Thrush-like Mourner's, and also much more often heard than seen. Its voice is similar, the most common song being a simple "teeeo, toweé?" or "teeeo, to, toweé?" (the latter has been transcribed as "pure mar-jor-eé"); we have noted no regional variation.

RANGE: S. Brazil (s. Bahia, s. Goiás, and e. Mato Grosso do Sul south to n. Rio Grande do Sul), e. Paraguay (west to Canendiyu and Paraguarí), and ne. Argentina (Misiones and ne. Corrientes). To about 1200 m.

NOTE: Sympatry between this species and *S. turdinus* has not been shown, and as with a number of other species pairs in the area (e.g., *Chiroxiphia pareola* and *C. caudata,* and *Mionectes oleagineus* and *M. rufiventris*), it probably does not occur. In Espírito Santo, for example, *S. virescens* seems confined to foothills above 500 m, with nominate *S. turdinus* in the lowlands below. This altitudinal replacement is much like what occurs with pairs of forms still considered subspecies of *S. turdinus* in nw. South America. We recognize that somewhat inconsistent criteria are being applied—but we reiterate that the field work needed to establish actual species limits in *S. turdinus* in South America has yet to be done.

Schiffornis major

VARZEA MOURNER

PLATE: 46

Other: Greater Manakin, Greater Schiffornis

DESCRIPTION: 15 cm (6"). *Near water in Amazonia. More or less uniform bright cinnamon-rufous,* paler below (especially on belly) and on rump; wings mainly dusky. Head with *variable amount of gray on face,* usually more or less confined to ocular area, in some birds extending to crown, a few with head entirely rufous; this variation cannot be correlated with age, sex, season, or locality.

SIMILAR SPECIES: Shape, behavior, and vocalizations are much like those of Thrush-like Mourner, but Varzea is always very much more brightly colored. Cinnamon Attila is similar in coloration, and these species frequently occur together, but the larger size, posture, and behavior of the attila are quite different, as are its calls.

HABITAT AND BEHAVIOR: Uncommon to locally fairly common in lower growth of várzea forest and borders. Behavior much like Thrush-

like Mourner's (found in terra firme undergrowth), and like that species much more often heard than seen. The Varzea's song, always relatively slow and complex, is very similar to certain versions of Thrush-like's, typically a leisurely "tee, towee-tee, towee?" or "teeoo, teewee? . . . teeoo . . . teeoo, teeweet." No geographic variation has been noted.

RANGE: Sw. Venezuela (s. Amazonas), extreme se. Colombia (recorded only from Leticia area in s. Amazonas, but likely more widespread), ne. Ecuador (numerous recent records from Napo), e. Peru, n. Bolivia (Pando and Beni), and w. and cen. Amaz. Brazil (south to Rondônia and n. Mato Grosso, and east along both banks of the Amazon to near the mouth of the Rio Tapajós). To 300 m.

NOTE: This species received its specific name *major* because at the time it was described, the larger species *turdinus* was placed in a different genus, *Heteropelma* (R. O. Prum and W. E. Lanyon, *Condor* 91[2]: 444–461, 1989). When the two are considered congeneric, as they surely are, the name "Greater" (obviously derived from *major*) becomes completely misleading. Prum and Lanyon (op. cit.) therefore suggested changing the modifying name of *S. major* to either "Varzea" or "Cinnamon." As *S. major* is so typical of várzea forests (being rarely or never found outside them), we select Varzea Mourner.

Tyranneutes Tyrant-Manakins

A pair of very plain, small "manakins" found in humid forest in Amaz. lowlands. The sexes are essentially alike in plumage. Small groups of males call persistently from certain perches at middle levels; they are usually within earshot of one another, but apparently otherwise do not interact. Generic relationships remain uncertain, but *Tyranneutes* does not seem to be a true manakin; it seems most closely related to *Neopelma* (R. O. Prum, pers. comm.).

Tyranneutes stolzmanni

DWARF TYRANT-MANAKIN   PLATE: 46

DESCRIPTION: 9 cm (3½"). *Very small and drab,* usually found and identified by its *distinctive voice.* Iris color variable but *always pale,* creamy whitish to hazel or pale grayish. Uniform olive above with *no coronal patch.* Throat and breast pale grayish olive, becoming pale yellow on belly.

SIMILAR SPECIES: Resembles various female *Pipra* manakins though differing from most of those by its pale iris. Some young male *Pipra* (e.g., Golden-headed, Red-headed, Round-tailed) acquire a pale iris while still in immature (olive) plumage; these may then closely resemble Dwarf Tyrant-Manakin but are larger. Most vaguely similar small tyrannids (including, for instance, Double-banded Pygmy-Tyrant and various *Hemitriccus* tody-tyrants) show wing-bars and have longer tails.HABITAT AND BEHAVIOR: Fairly common in lower and middle growth inside humid forest, rarely at edge or in adjacent clearings (then mostly to feed in fruiting trees); occurs in terra firme, várzea, and sandy belt forests. The inconspicuous Dwarf Tyrant-Manakin will hardly ever be found until the male's distinctive call is learned; then you realize that in appropriate habitat it is often numerous. That call is an oft-repeated, well-enunciated "jew-pit" or "ur-jit," delivered from perches 5–10 m above ground; birds sometimes vocalize at intervals through the heat of the day but often do not start before midmorning. Calling males often perch on unobstructed branches, but as they rarely move (when they do, movements are abrupt), they are often difficult to spot.

RANGE: S. Venezuela (Bolívar and Amazonas), e. Colombia (north to Meta and Vaupés), e. Ecuador, e. Peru, n. Bolivia (south to La Paz), and Amaz. Brazil (south to s. Mato Grosso and se. Pará, and east to n. Maranhão; north of the Amazon east only to the Rio Negro and Rio Branco). Mostly below 400 m, but recorded up to 800 m in s. Peru.

Tyranneutes virescens

TINY TYRANT-MANAKIN

DESCRIPTION: 8 cm (3"). *Ne. South America.* Resembles Dwarf Tyrant-Manakin; though not known to be sympatric, their ranges approach each other quite closely in Bolívar, Venezuela (where the Tiny is confined to the northeast, Dwarf west of the Río Caroní and Río Paragua), and n. Brazil (Tiny east of the Rio Negro and Rio Branco, Dwarf west of them). Tiny is *considerably smaller* and even shorter-tailed and has a *dark iris*. Male Tiny has a yellow coronal patch (lacking in Dwarf), but this is hard to see in the field and is vestigial or absent in females. See V-24.

SIMILAR SPECIES: Various female *Pipra* manakins are similar in shape and overall coloration but can generally be known by their larger size. Most vaguely similar small tyrannids show wing-bars and have longer tails, and many have pale irides.

HABITAT AND BEHAVIOR: Uncommon to locally fairly common in lower and middle growth inside humid forest. General behavior much like Dwarf Tyrant-Manakin's, but Tiny's voice is distinctly different, a burry, rather fast "Nicky the Greek" (R. Bierregaard) or "whippy-jebree" (D. Finch), given without inflection and repeated interminably at 3- to 6-second intervals. Generally this is given as the bird perches more or less motionless on a branch. D. Snow (*Ibis* 103a[1]: 112–113, 1961) describes a slow, "floating" display flight between branches, with yellow crest fully erect, and an odd sideways-peering display while perched. Regularly found at lower levels of Brownsberg Nature Park and numerous at Raleigh Falls Nature Park, both in Surinam.

RANGE: Guianas, se. Venezuela (e. Bolívar), and ne. Amaz. Brazil (south to the Amazon, and west to the lower Rio Negro region around Manaus). To 500 m.

Neopelma Tyrant-Manakins

Four species of dull-colored, flycatcher-like "manakins" which resemble certain *Myiopagis* elaenias (especially *M. viridicata*, Greenish Elaenia). All are much alike in appearance, but they have mainly allopatric ranges. There is no sexual dimorphism. These inconspicuous birds of lower and middle levels in woodland and forest are most notable for the male's vocalizations, given during display. Both insects and fruit are consumed, though the genus may be mainly insectivorous. Apparently no nest has been described. Their closest relative is probably *Tyranneutes,* and they are apparently not true manakins but rather are more closely related to the tyrant flycatchers (R. O. Prum and W. E. Lanyon, *Condor* 91[2]: 444–461, 1989).

Neopelma pallescens

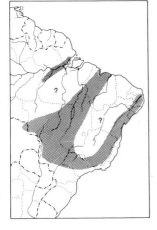

PALE-BELLIED TYRANT-MANAKIN   PLATE: 46

DESCRIPTION: 14 cm (5½"). *Mainly e. Brazil.* Iris pale grayish mauve. Plain olive above, with large coronal patch bright yellow bordered laterally with dusky. Throat whitish indistinctly streaked with gray, breast clouded with pale olivaceous gray, *belly creamy whitish.*
SIMILAR SPECIES: Stands out from its congeners (with which it overlaps only marginally) by virtue of its larger size and whiter (*not pale yellow*) belly. More apt to be confused with Greenish Elaenia (the 2 species are broadly sympatric); the elaenia in area of overlap (its nominate race) is much yellower on belly, shows considerable white on foreface (supraloral and ocular area), and has more prominent wing-edging.
HABITAT AND BEHAVIOR: Uncommon and apparently rather local in lower growth of deciduous and gallery woodland, often where there is heavy viny growth. This inconspicuous, dull-plumaged tyrant-manakin is most apt to be found when a male is displaying. So far as known, such males are solitary; they perch on low branches and intermittently utter a rather soft low nasal "wraah, wra-wra," and also periodically jump a few centimeters above their perch, often landing with reversed orientation. Can be found in appropriate habitat around Santarém.
RANGE: Locally in lower Amaz. Brazil (Amapá west along both sides of the Amazon to the lower Rio Tapajós region), and in cen. and e. Brazil (Maranhão south and west through Goiás to s. Mato Grosso and Mato Grosso do Sul, thence eastward through w. São Paulo, e. Minas Gerais, e. Bahia, Alagoas, and Pernambuco) and ne. Bolivia (ne. Santa Cruz on the Serranía de Huanchaca). To 700 m.

Neopelma sulphureiventer

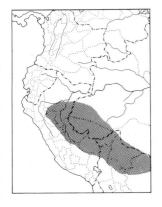

SULPHUR-BELLIED TYRANT-MANAKIN   PLATE: 46

DESCRIPTION: 13–13.5 cm (5–5¼"). Local in *sw. Amazonia. Iris pale,* grayish to cream to orange-brown. Plain olive above with pale yellow coronal patch. Throat whitish washed with gray, breast clouded grayish olive, *belly clear pale yellow.*
SIMILAR SPECIES: Pale-bellied Tyrant-Manakin (no known overlap) is somewhat larger, has darker eye, and is not yellow on belly. Greenish Elaenia is easily confused, but the elaenia shows yellowish wing-edging (the tyrant-manakin's wing is much plainer) and has more facial pattern (whitish supraloral and around eye); the extent of yellow in the crown of both species is similar, rarely showing as more than a stripe in either.
HABITAT AND BEHAVIOR: Uncommon and apparently local in lower

growth of humid forest, mainly in várzea, transitional, and riparian forest, often where there are bamboo thickets. A poorly known bird: what little has been discovered about this obscure bird, based mainly on a limited amount of data obtained in n. Bolivia (where it may be more numerous than elsewhere), was summarized by Remsen et al. (1988, pp. 370–372). Here it was found to be shy, and the call was "a series of 3–4 doubled, hoarse, almost frog-like, low-pitched, raspy scolding notes."

RANGE: E. Peru (locally from San Martín south to Ucayali, perhaps also southward), n. Bolivia (south to La Paz, Cochabamba, and n. Santa Cruz), and adjacent w. Brazil (Acre and w. Mato Grosso, probably also in Rondônia and w. Amazonas). To 450 m.

Neopelma aurifrons

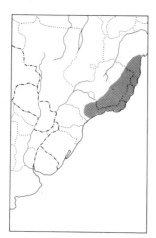

WIED'S TYRANT-MANAKIN

DESCRIPTION: 13 cm (5″). *Se. Brazil. Very* similar to Sulphur-bellied Tyrant-Manakin (would be indistinguishable in the field were they to occur together) but bill somewhat slighter and coronal patch, at least in males, somewhat more orange-yellow; iris pale grayish mauve.

SIMILAR SPECIES: Pale-bellied Tyrant-Manakin is a little larger and not yellow on belly. Cf. also Greenish Elaenia, from which Wied's differs in the same ways as Sulphur-bellied Tyrant-Manakin (which see).

HABITAT AND BEHAVIOR: Uncommon in understory of humid forest (often where there is a heavy growth of bamboo), secondary woodland, and shrubby borders. Like the other *Neopelma* tyrant-manakins, Wied's is generally inconspicuous and seldom seen unless males are displaying. These perch on branches 4–7 m above ground; several may occur in loose association (at least within earshot) but do not seem to interact. Males have intermittent calling sessions, giving a fast, spritely "chip, chip, dree-zee-zee, zéw" or "chip, chip, dree-dreuw" with numerous variations but always with some introductory "chip"s (sometimes a series of these alone). Calling birds do not move much and are often hard to spot. Small numbers can be found at upper levels of Itatiaia Nat. Park.

RANGE: Se. Brazil (s. Bahia south to e. São Paulo). To about 1400 m.

Neopelma chrysocephalum

SAFFRON-CRESTED TYRANT-MANAKIN

DESCRIPTION: 13 cm (5″). *Ne. South America*. Iris whitish to pale yellow; bill pale brownish flesh. Resembles Sulphur-bellied Tyrant-Manakin (no overlap) but *coronal patch larger* (wider and extending back to nape) *and decidedly rich golden yellow,* and grayer on sides of head (latter emphasizing the coronal patch). See V-24.

SIMILAR SPECIES: Does not overlap with any of its congeners. Cf. Tiny Tyrant-Manakin, which also has a yellow coronal patch but is much smaller and shorter-tailed and inhabits taller and more luxuriant forest. Greenish Elaenia has more prominent yellow wing-edging (Saffron-crested's wings are very plain), more white in facial area, etc.

HABITAT AND BEHAVIOR: Uncommon to locally fairly common in

lower growth of woodland and forest in savanna regions, and in areas with sandy soil; in some regions, e.g., north of Manaus, Brazil, seems confined to the rather scrubby vegetation (*campinas*) growing on such soil, and is absent from the surrounding, much more extensive areas of humid forest. General behavior much like other *Neopelma* tyrant-manakins'. Male's display is also similar, with scattered birds calling within earshot of each other from branches some 4–8 m above the ground in woodland with rather open understory, but vocalizations differ, Saffron-crested with a truly bizarre song. Most often heard is an interminably repeated nasal and squeaky "skeenh!" The song itself is an unmistakable and weird (often compared to a Jew's harp), *very* nasal and twangy "wrraaaaang, wrang-wrang-wrang." Both vocalizations are loud and carry far but can be quite ventriloquial and hard to track down. Sometimes the twangy song is given as the bird jumps off its perch and flares its crest. Numerous in savanna woodland in the Carolina region of Surinam and at the INPA campina north of Manaus.

RANGE: Guianas, s. Venezuela (Bolívar and s. Amazonas), extreme e. Colombia (e. Vaupés), and n. Brazil (mainly in the Rio Negro drainage south to the Manaus area, also in extreme n. Amapá). To 700 m (in Venezuela).

Neopipo Tyrant-Manakins

A single species of aberrant "manakin" found widely in Amaz. forests but everywhere seemingly rare and local. Its resemblance to the Ruddy-tailed Flycatcher (*Terenotriccus*) is remarkable. Although it has long been considered a manakin, R. O. Prum (pers. comm.) believes, based on anatomical evidence, that *Neopipo* is actually a tyrant flycatcher, in all likelihood the sister species of *Terenotriccus*.

Neopipo cinnamomea

CINNAMON TYRANT-MANAKIN   PLATE: 46
Other: Cinnamon Manakin

DESCRIPTION: 9.5 cm (3¾″). *A rare and very small "manakin" very like the much more common Ruddy-tailed Flycatcher. Legs blue-gray. Head and upper back gray*, crown slatier, with usually concealed yellow coronal patch (somewhat smaller and more orange-rufous in female), becoming brown on back and *cinnamon-rufous on rump and tail;* wings dusky with rufous edging and blurry wing-bars. Throat buffy whitish, *remaining underparts uniform cinnamon.*

SIMILAR SPECIES: This species so resembles Ruddy-tailed Flycatcher that it could easily be passed over in the field. Given a good view, look for its longer blue-gray legs (shorter and obviously pinkish in the flycatcher), narrower bill, lack of rictal bristles (quite prominent in the flycatcher), and the coronal patch. Cinnamon Tyrant-Manakin is also reported to have a more manakin-like shape and attitude, with large eyes, more rounded head, and slightly hunched posture (Hilty and Brown 1986).

HABITAT AND BEHAVIOR: Rare and local in lower growth inside terra firme forest, possibly mainly in areas with sandy soil. Despite its wide range, little seems to be on record about this enigmatic bird. One seen near Manaus, Brazil, made abrupt, typically manakin-like movements as it foraged with a small mixed flock (which included a Ruddy-tailed Flycatcher) in forest understory; it gave a short, low, whistled "weeo" call (A. Whittaker).

RANGE: Locally in Guianas, extreme s. Venezuela (s. Amazonas), extreme e. Colombia (Río Guainía in se. Guainía), e. Ecuador (few records), e. Peru (Loreto to Puno and Madre de Dios), and Amaz. Brazil (where seemingly very local but probably just scarce and underrecorded; south to n. Mato Grosso); seems likely in extreme n. Bolivia. To 1000 m (in Ecuador).

NOTE: Given *Neopipo*'s resemblance to *Terenotriccus*, and the fact that it apparently is not a true manakin, we prefer to cease calling it simply a manakin. Because it almost certainly is a tyrannid (see above), we propose calling it a tyrant-manakin. In fact it "looks" as much like a tyrant flycatcher as do *Tyranneutes* and *Neopelma*, both of which have long been called tyrant-manakins.

Piprites

A distinct genus of debated affinities, *Piprites* contains two species in South America, with a third (much like Wing-barred) in s. Middle America. Both are boldly patterned and easily recognized; they inhabit the canopy and borders of humid forest. The genus has long been placed with the manakins, though Snow (1975) pointed out several significant differences, and Sick (1985) went so far as to place it in the Cotingidae. Living birds most resemble, and behave like, becards. R. O. Prum (pers. comm.) believes *Piprites* almost certainly does not belong with the manakins, though its actual affinities remain uncertain. We thus use the genus as its group name.

Piprites chloris

WING-BARRED PIPRITES   PLATE: 46
Other: Wing-barred Manakin

DESCRIPTION: 12.5 cm (5"). Rather variable geographically, but typical birds (including *tschudii*) of nw. Venezuela, w. Colombia, and w. Amazonia east to w. Brazil are bright olive above with *yellow loral area and eye-ring* (imparting a bold spectacled look heightened by the large dark eye) and *gray nape and side of neck*; wings with 2 broad pale yellowish wing-bars and tertial tipping; short tail blackish tipped whitish. *Below mostly pale yellow*, clouded olive across breast. Nominate race (se. Brazil, e. Paraguay, and ne. Argentina) similar but with little gray on nape. *Chlorion* and *bolivianus* (Guianas and ne. Venezuela south through much of e. and cen. Amaz. Brazil to n. Bolivia) different below, with only throat and crissum yellow, *breast grayish and belly whitish*; see V-24, C-32.

SIMILAR SPECIES: Confusion with any of the true manakins is unlikely. Its pattern and coloration actually more resemble a flycatcher's or (especially) a becard's, though the piprites differs in its large round head and plump proportions with short tail.

HABITAT AND BEHAVIOR: Uncommon to fairly common (heard much more often than seen) in canopy and borders of humid forest and taller secondary woodland. Usually seen singly or in pairs, regularly accompanying mixed foraging flocks; gleans for insects like a becard. Best known from its distinctive and far-carrying voice, loud and rhythmic with an *unmistakable hesitating cadence,* "whip, pip-pip, pididip, whip, whip?," somewhat variable but always with the hesitation. Apparently all subspecies sound more or less alike.

RANGE: Locally in Guianas, lowlands and foothills of Venezuela (n. coastal mts. from Paria Peninsula westward, lower slopes of Andes and Sierra de Perijá, and more widely south of the Orinoco), n. and e. Colombia (more humid Caribbean lowlands, and east of Andes except in llanos region), e. Ecuador (an old record from Pichincha in w. Ecuador seems highly questionable), e. Peru, n. Bolivia (south to La Paz, Cochabamba, and Santa Cruz), and Amaz. Brazil (south to s. Mato Grosso, and east to n. Maranhão); se. Brazil (Espírito Santo south to n. Rio Grande do Sul), e. Paraguay (west to Paraguarí), and ne. Argentina (Misiones). Mostly below 1000 m, less often up to 1500 m.

Piprites pileatus

BLACK-CAPPED PIPRITES   PLATE: 46

Other: Black-capped Manakin

DESCRIPTION: 12 cm (4¾"). *Montane forests of se. Brazil and ne. Argentina. Bill and legs orange-yellow.* Male has *black crown and nape* contrasting with *rich chestnut back, rump, and wing-coverts;* wings otherwise dusky with yellowish green edging and prominent whitish speculum on primaries; *tail mostly rufous* with black central rectrices. *Sides of head and neck* (including frontal area and eye-ring), *throat, and breast cinnamon-buff,* becoming pale yellow on midbelly. Female similar but with olive back (though retaining chestnut on rump) and indistinct pale grayish wing-bars.

SIMILAR SPECIES: Strikingly patterned, this attractive species can hardly be confused.

HABITAT AND BEHAVIOR: Rare to locally uncommon in canopy and borders of montane forest, in more s. part of range often where *Araucaria* is present. Not well known, but behavior seems much like Wing-barred Piprites's, with single birds or pairs foraging in middle strata and subcanopy, sometimes with mixed flocks. Males give a distinctive, but oddly disjointed and patternless, fast rollicking "chik, chik, cheeút, chee-unh," variable in phraseology but always with the same chortling quality; females seem to give only a repeated "cheenh" with similar quality. This scarce and striking bird can be found at higher levels in Itatiaia Nat. Park, notably along the first part of the Agulhas Negras road.

RANGE: Se. Brazil (Rio de Janeiro south to n. Rio Grande do Sul;

reported occurrence in Espírito Santo remains unverified) and ne. Argentina (Misiones). To about 1800 m.

Heterocercus Manakins

Three species of large manakins, each occurring in a different part of the Amazon or Orinoco basin where they are characteristic of scrubby or várzea forests, primarily in blackwater or "sandy soil" regions. They are similar, differing only in crest color (males) and certain other plumage details. Note in particular their beautiful silky white and elongated gorgets (grayish in females) and rather strongly graduated tails, both unique among the manakins (and actually in the entire tyrant flycatcher assemblage as well; Prum 1992). Based on their syringes, Prum (op. cit.) considers *Heterocercus* to be most closely related to the genus *Pipra*. The nest of *Heterocercus* is a small cup suspended in a fork, very similar to that of other typical manakins (R. O. Prum, pers. comm.). *H. luteocephalus* (Golden-crested Manakin), known only from the lost or destroyed type specimen from an unknown locality, is now considered of doubtful validity; it may have been of hybrid origin.

Only the coronal patch (or crest) is colored in males of this genus, *not* the entire crown. Under normal field conditions the color is actually barely visible. We thus suggest a slight modification of each species' English name so as to indicate that the color does not encompass the entire crown (as, for example, in White-crowned and Blue-crowned Manakins).

Heterocercus linteatus

FLAME-CRESTED MANAKIN   PLATE: 46
Other: Flame-crowned Manakin

DESCRIPTION: 14 cm (5½"). *Mainly Amaz. Brazil.* Male has *head black with flame red coronal stripe* (usually hidden); otherwise dark olive above, wings and tail duskier. *Throat silky white, feathers lengthened at sides to form a ruffed bib;* narrow band of sooty-olive across chest; breast rich dark chestnut, becoming cinnamon-rufous on belly. Female entirely dark olive above, duskier on cheeks, with no crown stripe. *Throat gray* (less elongated at sides), remaining underparts dull cinnamon-buff, dingier on breast and tinged grayish olive on sides.

SIMILAR SPECIES: Not known to occur with any of its congeners; both sexes of Flame-crested Manakin are darker olive above than the others. Flashy males are easily recognized, whereas females can be known by their contrasting gray throat. Cf. smaller White-crested Spadebill.

HABITAT AND BEHAVIOR: Uncommon and rather local in lower and middle levels of deciduous and seasonally flooded várzea and riparian woodland and forest. Not well known in life, despite its having a rather broad range and being numerous at some sites (e.g., in se. Mato Grosso, Brazil; see Fry 1970). Displaying males flare their white gorget outward and may chase each other while calling loudly (Sick 1967).

RANGE: Amaz. Brazil (south of the Amazon from the Rio Xingu drainage and extreme se. Mato Grosso westward), extreme ne. Bolivia (ne. Santa Cruz west of the Serranía de Huanchaca), and ne. Peru (old records from along the Amazon in Loreto). To about 500 m.

Heterocercus flavivertex

YELLOW-CRESTED MANAKIN

PLATE: 46

Other: Yellow-crowned Manakin

DESCRIPTION: 14 cm (5½″). *Rio Negro and upper Orinoco drainages.* Male olive above with *golden yellow coronal stripe* (usually hidden) and slate gray lores and cheeks; wings and tail duskier. Like Flame-crested Manakin below. Female like female Flame-crested but brighter olive above and with more contrasting dark gray cheeks.

SIMILAR SPECIES: As it is not known to occur with any congener, both sexes are readily recognized, female by its contrasting gray throat. White-crested Spadebill has somewhat similar pattern.

HABITAT AND BEHAVIOR: Uncommon to fairly common in lower and middle levels of várzea, riparian, and gallery forest and woodland; also in scrubby woodland growing on sandy soil. Most often encountered singly as it moves about inside woodland, sometimes accompanying small mixed flocks. Males defend solitary display territories and have regularly used display perches some 2–5 m above ground. Here they sit quietly and motionless, often for protracted periods, at long intervals (often 5 minutes or more) emitting an explosive and very high-pitched "weeeeeeeeeit? pit-whít-cheeeu" or "weeeeeeee? whitcheeeu," not moving or even flaring their crest or gorget while calling. Males in full display bow forward with spread gorget, cock and spread their tail, and shiver rapidly back and forth for about a second (R. O. Prum). Both sexes also give a variety of other single or multisyllabic whistled calls of similar quality. Quite easily seen at Junglaven Lodge in Amazonas, Venezuela.

RANGE: Sw. Venezuela (Amazonas), e. Colombia (e. Vichada and ne. Meta south to Vaupés), and n. Amaz. Brazil north of the Amazon River (mainly in the Rio Negro drainage, also east to w. Pará on the lower Rio Trombetas; rather doubtfully recorded from Amapá). To 300 m.

Heterocercus aurantiivertex

ORANGE-CRESTED MANAKIN

Other: Orange-crowned Manakin

DESCRIPTION: 14 cm (5½″). Limited area in *e. Ecuador and ne. Peru.* Male much like male Yellow-crested Manakin but *coronal stripe orange* (not yellow) and duller generally, with mostly grayish head and throat grayish white (rarely or never elongated at sides), and *underparts uniform dull cinnamon-buff,* lacking darker chestnut on breast. Female similar to female Flame-crested Manakin but cheeks almost concolor with crown (not as dusky) and paler below.

SIMILAR SPECIES: Not known to occur with any of its congeners, so despite being relatively dull in color and pattern, should be readily

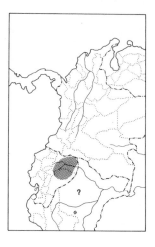

recognized. As with its congeners, posture and shape at times are vaguely thrush-like.

HABITAT AND BEHAVIOR: Rare and apparently local in lower and middle levels of várzea forest and woodland, mainly in blackwater drainages. Seemingly scarce everywhere; unlike Yellow-crested Manakin, museum specimens are few. The only vocalization that has been heard is a high, sibilant "wsiii." Small numbers can be seen at La Selva in Ecuador, where a displaying male or two perch regularly along the entrance boardwalk; occasionally one also can be found at a fruiting tree near the Río Napo.

RANGE: Locally in e. Ecuador (Napo and Pastaza) and ne. Peru (a single, somewhat uncertain, record from Chamicuros in sw. Loreto). To 300 m.

Chloropipo Manakins

Inconspicuous and fairly long-tailed manakins found in undergrowth of humid forest, all of them montane in distribution or found in foot-hills/lower slopes. None seems very vocal, and their displays, if they have any, remain undescribed. The genus is closely related to *Xenopipo*, and indeed Prum (1992) regards *Chloropipo uniformis* (Olive Manakin) and *Xenopipo atronitens* (Black Manakin) as sister taxa and suggests merging the genera, the name *Xenopipo* having priority. For now we continue to maintain the genera as distinct, in part because of *Xenopipo*'s extensive vocal repertoire (the *Chloropipo* manakins are, on the contrary, notably quiet birds).

GROUP A

Sexes *similar;* dull green to olive.

Chloropipo holochlora

GREEN MANAKIN
PLATE: 46

DESCRIPTION: 12 cm (4¾"). Iris dark; legs grayish. Nominate group (e. slope of Andes) *uniform moss green above* with indistinct pale eye-ring; throat, breast, and flanks olive, with *midbelly pale yellow. Litae* (w. Colombia and nw. Ecuador) is notably duller: more olive (not as pure green) above and somewhat darker olive on throat and breast (thus the pale yellow on midbelly contrasts more); see C-33.

SIMILAR SPECIES: Confusing. Much like a female *Pipra* manakin (in Amazonia, especially Blue-crowned) but longer-tailed and larger than most. Female of often sympatric Blue-backed Manakin is about the same size and shape but differs in its orangey (not grayish) legs. Female Yungas Manakin also can occur sympatrically with Green, but as with Blue-backed it differs in its purplish (not grayish) leg color. Broad-billed Sapayoa is even larger and longer-tailed, bigger-billed, and more uniform below (belly not contrastingly paler).

HABITAT AND BEHAVIOR: Uncommon in lower growth of humid forest, less often at borders. Infrequently encountered and not well known, though in some places quite often captured in mist-nets. Green

Manakin is usually solitary; sometimes accompanies mixed understory flocks and has occasionally been seen at fruiting trees. No display has been recorded. It is extremely quiet; RSR has never heard any vocalization, but R. O. Prum (pers. comm.) has on very rare occasions heard it utter a single harsh, growling "arrrn" when one bird displaces another at a fruiting tree.

RANGE: W. Colombia (Chocó to w. Nariño) and nw. Ecuador (south mainly to Pichincha; a single record from Quevedo in Los Ríos); e. slope of Andes and adjacent Amaz. lowlands in e. Colombia (north to w. Meta), e. Ecuador, and e. Peru (south to Puno). Also e. Panama. To 1300 m. Occurs in Amaz. lowlands primarily in Ecuador (and n. Peru?); in s. Peru ranges mainly in foothills (500–1100 m).

NOTE: R. O. Prum (pers. comm.) suggests that trans-Andean populations should perhaps be regarded as a full species, *C. litae* (Lita Manakin).

Chloropipo uniformis

OLIVE MANAKIN

DESCRIPTION: 13.5 cm (5¼"). A *dingy and dark* manakin found on the *tepuis of s. Venezuela and adjacent areas*. Rather long wings and long, narrow tail. Iris dark, legs dusky. *Uniformly rather dark olive,* slightly paler on belly, with an indistinct whitish eye-ring; underwing-coverts whitish (hard to see in the field). See V-24.

SIMILAR SPECIES: Female Scarlet-horned Manakin is somewhat smaller and shorter-winged, its tail is shorter and broader (though actually rather long-tailed for a *Pipra*), and its bill and legs are *flesh-colored* (not dusky). Female Black Manakin is virtually identical to Olive but has a larger bill; they would not be expected to occur together, Black being found at lower elevations in more open, scrubbier habitats. Cf. also the larger Thrush-like Mourner (not so olive generally, and with some rufous brown on wings).

HABITAT AND BEHAVIOR: Uncommon in stunted woodland and lower growth of humid forest. Not well known. Behavior seems to differ little from Green Manakin's, like that species quiet and difficult to observe. Small numbers have been seen coming to fruiting melastomataceous trees along the Escalera road in Bolívar together with Orange-bellied and Scarlet-horned Manakins, mainly at forest borders.

RANGE: Tepuis of s. Venezuela (s. Bolívar and n. and cen. Amazonas), extreme n. Brazil (Cerro Uei-tepui in Roraima), and adjacent Guyana. 800–2100 m.

GROUP B

Sexes *differ;* both species with white underwing.

Chloropipo flavicapilla

YELLOW-HEADED MANAKIN   PLATE: 46

DESCRIPTION: 12 cm (4¾"). *Local on Andean slopes in Colombia and e. Ecuador. Iris orange to red.* Male has *crown and hindneck bright golden yellow;* otherwise bright olive above. Cheeks and throat yellowish olive, paler on breast, becoming bright yellow on belly; underwing-coverts

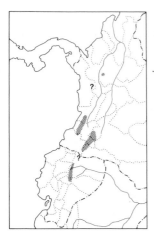

white (may show on bend of wing). Female similar but crown and nape not nearly as bright yellow (*though still distinctly yellower than back*) and breast duller; some females, probably young birds, have crown duller and virtually concolor with back. See C-32.

SIMILAR SPECIES: The lovely males are so yellow as to be easily recognized, whereas the distinctly yellowish crown of females should make them identifiable. Young birds may lack yellow on crown and the bright iris color; they thus resemble Green Manakin, though Yellow-headed is a paler and more yellowish olive above. Yellow-headed is basically a subtropical bird, occurring *above* range of Green. Female Jet Manakin is darker generally; these 2 species might overlap very locally in Ecuador.

HABITAT AND BEHAVIOR: Rare to uncommon and local in lower growth of montane forest and mature secondary woodland. Perhaps more inconspicuous than truly rare, but there are relatively few recent reports of this fine manakin. It may be threatened by deforestation, for much of its range lies in prime agricultural land, a great deal of which has been cleared. Like other *Chloropipo* manakins, its behavior is little known and it too appears to be very unvocal. Small numbers persist in patches of forest in the upper Río Pichindé valley above Cali.

RANGE: Andes of Colombia (locally on both slopes of W. Andes in Valle and Cauca, w. slope of Cen. Andes at their n. end in Antioquia, around head of Río Magdalena valley in Huila, and a sighting from e. slope of Andes in w. Putumayo) and on e. slope of Andes in n. Ecuador (a 19th-century specimen from Hacienda Mapoto in Tungurahua, and a few sightings from w. Napo in the Huacamayo ridge and Volcán Sumaco region). 1200–2400 m.

Chloropipo unicolor

JET MANAKIN

PLATE: 46

DESCRIPTION: 12 cm (4¾"). *E. slope of Andes in Ecuador and Peru.* Male *glossy blue-black above, duller black below* (with no gloss); underwing-coverts white. Female *uniform dark olive,* somewhat grayish on throat and belly; underwing-coverts white; shows a vague, pale eye-ring.

SIMILAR SPECIES: Male virtually unique in its limited range. The similar Black Manakin does not occur anywhere near it. Male of little-known nominate Andean Tyrant (males of which are black) resembles male Jet Manakin, but the tyrant is considerably larger, duller (not so glossy) black, and occurs at higher elevations than the manakin. Green Manakin replaces Jet at lower elevations on e. slope of Andes (with limited overlap?); it is not as *sooty* olive as female Jet, and has a contrasting pale yellow belly and dark (not white) underwing-coverts.

HABITAT AND BEHAVIOR: Uncommon in lower growth of montane forest. Like other *Chloropipo* manakins, Jet is rarely observed, though in some areas it is not infrequently captured in mist-nets. Its voice and display remain unknown.

RANGE: E. slope of Andes in Ecuador (north to Napo on lower slopes of Volcán Sumaco) and Peru (south to Puno). 930–1900 m, in Ecuador most numerous at 1500–1700 m.

Xenopipo Manakins

A fairly long-tailed manakin found locally in lighter woodlands of ne. South America. Seems closely related to *Chloropipo uniformis* (Olive Manakin); Prum (1992) goes so far as to suggest the merger of the genus *Chloropipo* into *Xenopipo*.

Xenopipo atronitens

BLACK MANAKIN   PLATE: 46

DESCRIPTION: 12 cm (4¾"). Local in woodland from ne. South America to s. Amazonia. Male has *pale bluish gray bill* with black tip; plumage *uniform glossy blue-black*, somewhat more brownish on wings and tail. Female *dark* olive green above and on throat and chest, becoming dull yellowish olive on lower underparts.
SIMILAR SPECIES: Male closely resembles male Amazonian Black-Tyrant, though that species has a larger bill; in the hand (*fide* R. O. Prum) the manakin can be seen to have fused outer toes (unfused in the black-tyrant). The black-tyrant favors riparian (not savanna) woodland and differs in behavior. Cf. also male Red-shouldered Tanager. Female Black Manakin looks very uniform and dark, especially compared to other female manakins that might occur with it; none of the very similar *Chloropipo* manakins occurs sympatrically with the Black.
HABITAT AND BEHAVIOR: Fairly common in often dense lower growth of scrubby forest and woodland, and in gallery forest; often occurs in areas with sandy soil. Black Manakin is seen singly, in pairs, or (less often) in small groups, regularly accompanying mixed flocks of understory birds. Its numerous calls are all loud and sharp and include a "skee! kip-kip-kip-krrr" with many variations and a dry, rattled "trrrrrrrrrup"; R. O. Prum (pers. comm.) considers its vocal repertoire to be more extensive than that of most other manakins. Male's display is evidently limited to calling and chasing other males (Sick 1967). Readily seen in dense scrub at Junglaven Lodge in Amazonas, Venezuela.
RANGE: Guianas, s. Venezuela (s. Bolívar and Amazonas), extreme e. Colombia (e. Guainía south to e. Vaupés; the Mozambique record, which was based on ANSP specimens, is in error), and Amaz. Brazil (north of the Amazon locally from the Rio Negro drainage eastward, south of it from the lower Rio Madeira to sw. Mato Grosso and the Rio Araguaia); isolated records from se. Peru (Pampas de Heath in Madre de Dios) and ne. Bolivia (ne. Santa Cruz on the Serranía de Huanchaca). To 1200 m.

Chiroxiphia Manakins

Fairly large and strongly sexually dimorphic manakins, the beautiful males with blue at least on the mantle. Immature males acquire the crown patch first, then the black and blue intrude into the green. The five species are basically allopatric in range (one occurs only in Middle America) and are found in deciduous or humid forest, mainly in the lowlands. Males have evolved a unique cooperative display (rather than competing directly for copulations) in which one bird, evidently the dominant male, acts as "ringleader" or "master of ceremonies." For a detailed account of the marvelous displays of two species, see Snow (1976).

GROUP A   "Typical" *Chiroxiphia* (underparts black).

Chiroxiphia pareola

BLUE-BACKED MANAKIN   PLATE: 46

DESCRIPTION: 12–12.5 cm (4¾–5″). *Legs orange* (somewhat paler in female). Male black with *patch of deep red on crown* and *pale azure blue mantle. Atlantica* (only on Tobago) somewhat larger with slightly longer red coronal patch. *Regina* (mostly south of the Amazon from e. Peru east to the w. bank of the lower Rio Tapajós; north of it recorded only from Codajáz and São Gabriel, both sites situated west of the Rio Negro) similar but with *coronal patch golden yellow.* Female olive above with an indistinct pale eye-ring, and duskier on wings; somewhat paler olive below, especially on belly, which is often yellowish.
SIMILAR SPECIES: Male distinctive, but cf. Yungas (recently split) and Lance-tailed Manakins; none of these occur together. Female Black Manakin has grayish (not orange to flesh) legs; note also its different shape (the Black is longer-tailed) and habitat. Female White-bearded Manakin is considerably smaller and shorter-tailed with deeper orange legs.
HABITAT AND BEHAVIOR: Uncommon to locally common in lower growth of humid forest and mature secondary woodland, sometimes coming out to edge and to clearings to feed at fruiting trees; in e. Ecuador restricted to terra firme forest. Despite their bright colors, males are usually hard to spot as they tend to remain within heavy cover; females are seen even less often. The full display of this beautiful bird is unforgettable. The arena is usually a pair of gently sloping branches about 1 m above the ground. Here males, usually 2, perch and at intervals throughout the day give a characteristic rich, throaty "ch-ch-ch-ch-chur-chereé," sometimes alternated with a more ringing "cooeee." When a female arrives, the males go into full display, jumping over each other and sidling on their perches ever more rapidly ("cartwheeling"), giving a more twangy "wr-r-r-ang-ang, wr-r-r-ang-ang . . ." ever faster and faster, suddenly halting when 1 bird calls a very loud "swee-ee-eék!" Thereupon only that male continues to display, crouching and vocalizing softly and periodically making short, slow, circular flights with rapidly fluttering wings; this may culminate in a copulation. The voice of *regina* is similar to that of the red-crowned races.
RANGE: Guianas, e. Venezuela (Bolívar), Amaz. Brazil (south to n. Goiás and sw. Mato Grosso, and east to n. Maranhão; absent from some of the Rio Negro drainage), extreme nw. and ne. Bolivia (Pando at Camino Mucden and ne. Santa Cruz on the Serranía de Huanchaca), se. and ne. Peru (Madre de Dios at Cerros de Pantiacolla [FMNH], and in Loreto), e. Ecuador, and se. Colombia (north to w. Meta); e.

Brazil (Paraíba south to Espírito Santo, perhaps to Rio de Janeiro); Tobago. To 750 m in Ecuador.

NOTE: Does not include *C. boliviana* (Yungas Manakin).

Chiroxiphia boliviana

YUNGAS MANAKIN

Other: Blue-backed Manakin (in part)

DESCRIPTION: 13 cm (5″). *Subtropical zone on e. slope of Andes in s. Peru and Bolivia.* Resembles Blue-backed Manakin (until recently considered conspecific) but tail notably longer and coronal patch of male slightly darker red. Leg color may also differ; all the long series of both sexes in ANSP are labeled as having legs "purplish brown" or "purplish flesh" (thus darker and less orange than in Blue-backed).

SIMILAR SPECIES: Nothing really similar in its montane range. Blue-backed Manakin occurs only at substantially lower elevations, and in the area where their ranges approach each other in s. Peru and Bolivia, Blue-backed males (*regina*) have a yellow coronal patch. Females would be difficult to distinguish in the field, except perhaps on leg color. Green Manakin (limited overlap in s. Peru) is quite similar, though differing in its grayish legs. Female Golden-winged Manakin is much smaller.

HABITAT AND BEHAVIOR: Locally fairly common in lower growth of montane forest. Not well known in life; general behavior probably differs little from Blue-backed Manakin's, though Parker and Remsen (1987, p.103) state that "song and display differ markedly." One call, given by males perched on their display branches, is a higher-pitched and less throaty, not so loud "chereeo" with variations (M. Foster recording); birds seen at that time were displaying alone (unlike other members of the genus), but this may not always be the case.

RANGE: E. slope of Andes in s. Peru (Cuzco, s. Madre de Dios on Cerros de Pantiacolla, and Puno) and w. Bolivia (south to Chuquisaca). 650–2150 m.

NOTE: Until recently *boliviana* was considered a race of *C. pareola* (e.g., Meyer de Schauensee 1966, 1970), but we regard it as a full species, following Parker and Remsen (1987); we also employ their suggested English name. The elevation preferences of the two species are very distinct, with *C. pareola* in the lowlands and *C. boliviana* in the foothills and subtropical zone; at Cerros de Pantiacolla, for instance, *C. pareola regina* was recorded (FMNH) at 450 m, with *C. boliviana* only at higher elevations (1100–1400 m).

Chiroxiphia lanceolata

LANCE-TAILED MANAKIN

DESCRIPTION: Male 13.5 cm (5¼″); female 13 cm (5″). *N. Colombia and n. Venezuela.* Resembles Blue-backed Manakin, but *both sexes have projecting pointed central tail feathers,* male's somewhat longer but even female's quite conspicuous. Male is somewhat sootier black below than male Blue-backed and has a slightly brighter blue mantle. See V-24, C-32.

SIMILAR SPECIES: Female White-bearded and Golden-collared Manakins are smaller and somewhat darker olive below (and thus more uni-

form overall); they have brighter orange legs and lack the projecting tail spikes.

HABITAT AND BEHAVIOR: Fairly common to locally common in lower growth of deciduous and semihumid forest, secondary woodland, and adjacent plantations. Behavior basically similar to Blue-backed Manakin's; Lance-tailed can also be a frustratingly difficult bird to see. Lance-tailed's display is essentially similar, though instead of "cartwheeling," both displaying males jump up and down alternately on their perches. Its vocalizations are, however, entirely different. Lance-tailed utters several calls with a much more mellow and semiwhistled quality, "doh" or "dee-o," often repeated, sometimes accelerated into a rolling "dowee-oh"; also gives a more nasal snarl. Numerous in Colombia's Tayrona Nat. Park and Venezuela's Guatopo Nat. Park.

RANGE: N. Colombia (Caribbean lowlands from Córdoba eastward) and n. Venezuela (Maracaibo basin east to Paria Peninsula, and on Margarita Is.). Also Costa Rica and Panama. Locally to 1700 m in Venezuela.

GROUP B

Larger and much bluer; se. South America.

Chiroxiphia caudata

BLUE MANAKIN   PLATE: 46
Other: Swallow-tailed Manakin

DESCRIPTION: Male 15 cm (6"); female 14.5 cm (5¾"). *Se. Brazil area.* Male's legs reddish flesh, female's duller and yellower; bill flesh-colored *Central tail feathers elongated,* male's somewhat longer. Male *rich pale cerulean blue* with contrasting black throat, face, nape, wings, and outer tail feathers; *entire crown scarlet* (including forehead); crissum dusky. Female *uniform olive,* slightly paler below; a few females have forecrown orange more or less intermixed with olive.

SIMILAR SPECIES: Larger than other *Chiroxiphia* manakins. The stunning male, *by far the bluest manakin,* is unmistakable. Female can be confused with Greenish Mourner, which is only slightly larger; note the mourner's "normal" tail, rufescent color on wings, pale ocular area, and dark (not yellowish) legs. In area of overlap with Blue-backed Manakin (Bahia and Espírito Santo, Brazil), Blue-backed occurs only in lowlands, whereas Blue is montane.

HABITAT AND BEHAVIOR: Fairly common to common in lower and middle growth of humid forest, secondary woodland, and borders. Behavior generally similar to Blue-backed Manakin's but seems easier to see, more confiding and perhaps more of an edge bird. Its wonderful display is also similar, though typically it is 3 (not 2) Blue Manakin males that perform the "cartwheel" in front of the female, each hovering briefly in front of her, then returning to the farther end of the line. Although the display may start slowly, it gradually accelerates, culminating in a veritable frenzy of motion which is brought to a sudden halt when one of the males, the "ringleader," gives a very sharp "eek-eek-eek-eek-eek!" Usually all males then fly off to nearby perches; they may resume dancing after an interval. Occasionally the ringleader remains and singly starts a slow "floating" flight display around the female; this sometimes leads to copulation. During the entire cartwheeling display, males utter a loud throaty "qua-a-a-a-a" call; at other times (even when not dancing) they, and also females, give a far-carrying "chorreeo" or "chorreeo, cho-cho-cho"; the latter is one of the more frequently heard bird sounds in its range. Blue Manakins are readily seen in lower levels of Brazil's Itatiaia and Serra dos Órgãos Nat. Parks. RANGE: Se. Brazil (s. Bahia, Minas Gerais, and s. Goiás south to Rio Grande do Sul), e. Paraguay (west to Canendiyu and Paraguarí), and ne. Argentina (Misiones and Corrientes). Mostly below 1500 m, in small numbers to 1900 m; north of Rio de Janeiro only above about 500 m.

NOTE: This species has recently been called the Swallow-tailed Manakin (e.g., Meyer de Schauensee 1966, 1970). However, we agree with Snow (1976, pp. 176–177) that this name is "wholly inappropriate," as no swallow's tail is shaped like this species'. We concur with his suggestion that *C. caudata* is much better named the Blue Manakin, it being the only predominantly blue manakin.

Antilophia Manakins

A large and long-tailed manakin found mainly in interior Brazil. Despite differences in display, the genus is close to *Chiroxiphia* (there are occasional hybrids between *Antilophia* and *C. caudata*, the Blue Manakin). Syringeal evidence also supports the close relationship of the genera (R. O. Prum, pers. comm.).

Antilophia galeata

HELMETED MANAKIN

PLATE: 46

DESCRIPTION: 14.5 cm (5¾"). *Interior cen. and s. Brazil.* Rather long, narrow tail. Male mostly deep black with *crimson red upstanding frontal crest, crown, nape, and midback.* Female uniform olive, somewhat paler and grayer below, with shorter but still easily visible *upstanding frontal crest.*

SIMILAR SPECIES: Spectacular male is unmistakable; female, though dull-plumaged, can readily be known by her frontal crest.

HABITAT AND BEHAVIOR: Fairly common to common in lower and middle strata of gallery forest and woodland, also locally in deciduous or swampy woodland. Although heard far more often than seen, Helmeted Manakin is usually not too difficult to observe once you manage to get inside its often nearly impenetrable habitat. Male's song is a distinctive series of fast, rich musical notes with a rollicking cadence, "whih-dip, whih-deh-deh-déhdidip," with many variations, either given as birds perch motionless on a branch or as they chase each other. Another frequent call, given by both sexes, is a throaty "wreee? pur." Unlike *Chiroxiphia,* the Helmeted Manakin seems to have no organized coordinated display. A good spot to observe this splendid manakin is in the woods around the public swimming pool in Brasília Nat. Park.

RANGE: Interior Brazil (cen. Maranhão and w. Bahia south to São Paulo, w. Paraná, and Mato Grosso do Sul), ne. Bolivia (ne. Santa

Cruz on the Serranía de Huanchaca) and ne. Paraguay (Concepción and probably Amambay). Mostly 500–1000 m.

Manacus Manakins

Small and boldly patterned manakins, males with characteristic length-ened throat feathers puffed out during display, the much duller females without long throat feathers. Two species occur in South America (a pair of others range in Middle America), where they are found in hu-mid tropical lowlands. Their ranges are allopatric or parapatric, with limited hybridization occurring where their ranges meet. Although these manakins usually are inconspicuous, at their leks males engage in elaborate displays, accompanied by remarkably loud sounds. Based on syringeal evidence, *Manacus* seems most closely related to *Chiroxiphia* and *Antilophia* (Prum 1992).

Manacus manacus

WHITE-BEARDED MANAKIN   PLATE: 47

DESCRIPTION: 10–11 cm (4–4¼"). *Bright orange legs* (both sexes). Male essentially black and white: *black above* with gray rump; *throat* (of-ten puffed out into a "beard") *and nuchal collar white*, becoming grayish white to grayish on lower underparts. Geographic variation involving the width of the collar and the extent of gray below is extensive, though overall pattern remains the same. Usually birds with narrower collars also have grayer underparts, e.g., *gutturosus* of e. Brazil, with gray extending up over entire breast, not more or less restricted to sides. The other extreme, e.g., *trinitatis* of Trinidad, has a broad white collar extending over the back and mostly white underparts. *Flaveolus* of Colombia's upper Río Magdalena valley has throat and collar tinged creamy yellow. Females of all races similar: plain olive above, paler and more grayish olive below, grayest on throat and yellowest on belly.
SIMILAR SPECIES: Male essentially unmistakable, but cf. closely re-lated Golden-collared Manakin. Female best known by its orange legs and small size. All female *Pipra* manakins have dark legs; female *Chi-roxiphia* are larger and have duller and yellower legs and a paler (not so dusky) bill.
HABITAT AND BEHAVIOR: Locally common in lower growth of sec-ondary woodland and forest borders and in shrubby campina and res-tinga woodland. Both sexes forage solitarily and usually quietly except for an occasional forceful "cheepu." Like other manakins, they sally upwards for fruit and occasionally insects. *Manacus* manakins, the noisiest in the family, are best known for their leks, and the sounds emanating from a displaying group can be heard from considerable distances. Each male has its own "court," a small area where the ground is cleared of leaves and debris and where it performs a variety of individual displays, usually with many other males in close proximity. The displays typically involve very fast back-and-forth flights between a pair of saplings (the male appears to bounce from one to the other),

then sidling up and down a sapling, often with wings fanned. All the while a variety of sounds are produced; most common are several distinctive whistled "peeoo" or "peeer" calls and other growling notes, but the most striking is a very loud firecracker-like snap, presumably produced mechanically by the wings. Wings of flying males also whirr. Leks, attended year-round, have decreased activity when birds are in molt. They represent one of the most exciting neotropical bird spectacles, especially where the birds are relatively habituated to the presence of observers (as at the Asa Wright Nature Center in Trinidad).

RANGE: Sw. Colombia (sw. Cauca and w. Nariño) and w. Ecuador (south to w. Loja); n. and e. Colombia (Caribbean lowlands west to Córdoba, Río Magdalena valley south to Huila, and widely east of Andes), e. Ecuador, ne. Peru (Loreto and San Martín), Amaz. Brazil (south to Rondônia and n. Mato Grosso, and east to n. Maranhão), sw. and s. Venezuela (Maracaibo basin, and Barinas east through Amazonas and Bolívar), and Guianas; e. Brazil (Alagoas south to Paraná), e. Paraguay (Canendiyu and Alto Paraná), and ne. Argentina (Misiones); Trinidad. Mainly below 1000 m, but regularly to 1300 m in sw. Ecuador.

NOTE: See comments under Golden-collared Manakin.

Manacus vitellinus

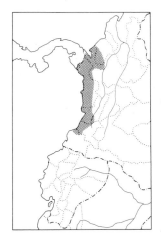

GOLDEN-COLLARED MANAKIN

DESCRIPTION: 10–11 cm (4–4¼"). *W. Colombia*. Male's pattern like White-bearded Manakin but with *bright golden yellow* replacing the white, and olive replacing the gray. Female very similar to female White-bearded, but Golden-collared brighter and more yellowish olive below with no grayish throat. See C-32.

SIMILAR SPECIES: Cf. White-bearded Manakin. Female also resembles female Lance-tailed Manakin, but latter is larger and has projecting central tail feathers.

HABITAT AND BEHAVIOR: Locally common in lower growth of secondary woodland and forest borders. Behavior and voice, including most aspects of its lek display, similar to White-bearded Manakin's.

RANGE: W. Colombia (Chocó and Córdoba south to sw. Cauca). Also Panama. Mostly below 1000 m.

NOTE: Closely related to *M. manacus* and sometimes regarded as conspecific (e.g., in *Birds of the World*, vol. 8), though more often they are treated as allospecies (e.g., in the 1983 AOU Check-list). As Haffer (1975, p. 75) states, they "are near the species level of differentiation." Very limited hybridization has been recorded along the contact zones between *M. manacus* and *M. vitellinus*, in both nw. and sw. Colombia. Some leks in these areas have males of either species at opposite ends with apparent "hybrids" in the middle; this would appear to indicate that the two types usually do recognize each other as "different."

Ilicura Manakins

An endemic manakin of se. Brazil, notable for its unusual plumage pattern and lengthened central feathers. Based on syringeal and behaviorial evidence, it is most closely related to *Masius* and *Corapipo* (R. O. Prum and A. E. Johnson, *Wilson Bull.* 99[4]: 521–539, 1987).

Ilicura militaris

PIN-TAILED MANAKIN   PLATE: 47

DESCRIPTION: Male 12.5 cm (5″); female 11 cm (4″). *Se. Brazil. Iris orange.* Elongated *central tail feathers* and striking pattern of male unmistakable; female duller and with central tail feathers shorter (tail looks *wedge-shaped*). Male has *deep crimson patch on forecrown*, otherwise black above with *scarlet lower back and rump* and contrasting olive inner flight feathers. *Sides of head pale gray*, becoming *grayish white on underparts*, whitest on belly. Female bright olive above; *sides of head and throat contrastingly gray*, remaining underparts pale grayish olive.
SIMILAR SPECIES: Female White-bearded and much larger Blue Manakins lack female Pin-tail's gray face.
HABITAT AND BEHAVIOR: Uncommon to locally fairly common in lower and middle growth of humid forest and mature secondary woodland. Usually seen singly, most often as it feeds on fruit in trees and shrubs, regularly at forest borders; also regularly accompanies mixed flocks. Males' display is described by B. K. and D. W. Snow (*Wilson Bull.* 97[3]: 273–282, 1985). Two or 3 males maintain small display territories within hearing distance of one another but perform independently. Each territory has numerous slender branches, some of them cleared of obstructing vegetation such as moss. The male's oft-repeated song is a simple series of 5–8 descending notes; singing birds posture with raised rump feathers. Two ritualized "snap-jumps" over a female crouching on the mating perch precede copulation. Away from the display area both sexes often give a call similar to male's song but with fewer (usually 3 or 4) notes; this often helps to locate foraging birds. Pin-tailed Manakins can be seen in Tijuca Nat. Park above Rio de Janeiro and at lower elevations in Itatiaia Nat. Park.
RANGE: Se. Brazil (Espírito Santo and s. Minas Gerais south to Paraná and e. Santa Catarina). Mostly 600–1200 m northward, but from Rio de Janeiro southward down to sea level.

Corapipo Manakins

A pair of small manakins found in n. South America, mainly in foothill forests. Males have distinctive snowy white bibs; immature males first acquire the white throat and a black mask on sides of face, then gradually become blacker overall. Their unique lek display incorporates spectacular flights above the canopy.

Corapipo gutturalis

WHITE-THROATED MANAKIN   PLATE: 47

DESCRIPTION: 9 cm (3½″). *Ne. South America.* Male's lower mandible flesh-colored. Male *glossy blue-black above;* inner webs of inner primaries white showing as a patch in flight, but concealed when perched.

Snowy white bib on throat ends in a point on upper chest; remaining underparts deep black. Female bright olive above; *mostly grayish white below,* tinged olive on sides and crissum.

SIMILAR SPECIES: Male unmistakable in its range; similar White-ruffed Manakin replaces it in nw. South America. Female whiter below than other sympatric female manakins, showing no yellow and very little olive on underparts.

HABITAT AND BEHAVIOR: Fairly common in lower and middle growth of humid forest, less often out to forest borders; occurs mainly in hilly areas. Tends to forage higher than many other manakins, with single birds or, less often, small groups accompanying mixed flocks of tanagers and other birds. Displays, described by R. O. Prum (*Ibis* 128[1]: 91–102, 1986), are focused on a mossy log on the forest floor, where up to 6 males may gather. The most common call, given by both sexes, is a high, thin "seeu"; this often helps to locate foraging birds. It is lengthened in the male's advertising call, usually delivered from perches near the display log. Displaying males adopt various postures, the most striking with the bill up exposing the white bib, or wings drooped exposing the white patch. Full display, a slow flight toward the log which sometimes almost seems to stall out, is accompanied by a mechanical "pop" sound and a repeated "tsee" call becoming louder as the bird nears the log. Upon landing the bird "bounces up" and lands again a short distance away facing the opposite direction. A variation of this approach consists of an amazing above-the-canopy flight display (first described by T. Davis, *Wilson Bull.* 94[4]: 594–595, 1982) in which a male rises steeply up to 25 m above the trees giving the "seeu" call, then plummets back into the forest, landing back on the display log. These marvelous displays can be witnessed at Brownsberg Nature Park in Surinam.

RANGE: Guianas, s. Venezuela (Bolívar and e. Amazonas), and ne. Brazil (Amapá, along Venezuelan border in Roraima, and at several sites north of Manaus). To 1300 m.

WHITE-RUFFED MANAKIN

Corapipo leucorrhoa

DESCRIPTION: 9.5 cm (3¾"). *N. Colombia and w. Venezuela.* Male resembles male White-throated Manakin (no overlap) but slightly larger with all-dark bill and with *white throat patch lengthened at sides to form a ruff* (not ending in a point). See C-32. Female mostly olive, somewhat paler below, with *sides of head and throat grayish* and belly pale yellowish. See P-27.

SIMILAR SPECIES: Male distinctive in range. Female much like various female *Pipra* manakins, though none of these show grayish on face and throat; cf. especially female White-crowned Manakin (with gray crown, red iris, etc.).

HABITAT AND BEHAVIOR: Uncommon and somewhat local in lower and middle growth of humid forest and forest borders, the latter especially when feeding at fruiting trees. Not well known in its South American range, where found mainly in foothills and where much of its original forest habitat has been destroyed. Males in Middle America have displays much like White-throated Manakin's (even including an above-canopy flight), though on the whole they seem much quieter.

RANGE: N. Colombia (Chocó; lower Río Cauca valley east across humid Caribbean lowlands and south in Río Magdalena valley to n. Tolima and w. Cundinamarca); w. Venezuela (lower Andean slopes of Mérida, Barinas, and Táchira); Sierra de Perijá on Venezuela-Colombia border. Also Honduras to Panama. To about 1200 m.

NOTE: Males of nominate *leucorrhoa* (all of its S. Am. range aside from Chocó, where *altera* occurs) differ from the Mid. Am. races (*altera* and *heteroleuca*) in having their 10th (outer) primary much shorter and narrower than the others: these differences may affect mechanical sounds made with the wings during display. Wetmore (1972) suggests that *C. altera* (with *heteroleuca*) should be considered a full species on the basis of this character; it would be called the White-bibbed Manakin, with *C. leucorrhoa* retaining the name White-ruffed Manakin. However, until the behavior, which remains unstudied, of nominate *leucorrhoa* is known actually to be different, we prefer to follow the traditional treatment of regarding them as conspecific. It is worth noting that displays of *C. gutturalis*, which is morphologically more divergent, seem to closely resemble those of *C. leucorrhoa altera*.

Masius Manakins

A monotypic genus, unusual among the manakins in being restricted to montane Andean forests. Although the male's plumage is very different, the genus is apparently most closely related to *Corapipo* and probably *Ilicura* (R. O. Prum and A. E. Johnson, *Wilson Bull.* 99[4]: 521–539, 1987).

Masius chrysopterus

GOLDEN-WINGED MANAKIN   PLATE: 47

DESCRIPTION: 11 cm (4¼"). *Andean slopes from Venezuela to n. Peru.* Longer-tailed than many other small manakins. Legs brownish flesh to purplish; bill paler flesh. Male of nominate group on e. slope of Andes black with *bright golden yellow forecrown, the feathers curling forward over bill*, extending back on midcrown and *becoming flame orange on nape;* black feathers on sides of crown somewhat elongated forming inconspicuous "horns"; tail feathers and *inner web of flight feathers mostly bright pale yellow* (often hidden on perched birds but conspicuous in flight); *midthroat and wider area on upper chest also pale yellow.* On w. slope of Andes (*coronulatus* and *bellus*), *nape feathers are blunt, shiny, and scale-like* and *brown to reddish brown.* Immature males first acquire the golden on throat and forecrown, then gradually become blacker. Female olive with *midthroat and patch on middle of upper chest pale yellow;* somewhat paler below, belly yellowish; see C-32.

SIMILAR SPECIES: Males of both types are essentially unmistakable. Females and young males usually show enough yellow on chin and frontal crest to be recognizable; their purplish legs are also often helpful.

HABITAT AND BEHAVIOR: Uncommon to fairly common in lower growth of montane forest and older secondary woodland. Inconspicuous and probably often overlooked, the Golden-winged Manakin's true numbers are better revealed by mist-netting. Occasionally one will forage for small fruits while accompanying a mixed flock composed primarily of various tanagers. Generally quiet, but a dry "tseet" note is sometimes given. R. O. Prum and A. E. Johnson (*Wilson Bull.* 99[4]: 521–539, 1987) described the male's displays. As in *Corapipo,* activities focus on a fallen mossy log or buttressed root. Their most frequent advertising call is a low nasal "harrnt" or "nurrt," sometimes varied to a "tseet-nurrt," given from a perch 2–5 m above ground. Displays, performed on the selected log or root, follow a stereotyped approach which includes a "rebound." On the log, males crouch head-downward with crest fully raised and "horns" flared, and then may bow from side to side.

RANGE: Andes of w. Venezuela (north to s. Lara), Colombia, Ecuador (south on w. slope to w. Loja), and n. Peru (Cajamarca and n. San Martín). Mostly 1200–2300 m, but regularly lower (to about 600 m) on Pacific slope in Colombia and Ecuador.

Machaeropterus Manakins

A trio of small manakins, their males with very striking patterns and colors, found in lowland and foothill forests. The bizarre Club-winged Manakin was formerly separated in the genus *Allocotopterus.*

Machaeropterus regulus

STRIPED MANAKIN

PLATE: 47

DESCRIPTION: 9–9.5 cm (3½–3¾"). Legs purplish flesh; iris dark red. Male with *shiny red crown and nape;* otherwise olive above. Throat whitish to dingy buff; *remaining underparts streaked reddish chestnut and white,* with stain of brighter red across chest. *Aureopectus* (s. Bolívar and w. Amazonas, Venezuela, and adjacent Brazil) has chest stain yellow. Nominate race (e. Brazil) is slightly larger, has no red chest stain, and has broader but sparser streaking below (so effect is of paler underparts). Female plain olive above; dingy whitish below with *more or less distinct brownish chest band* and *indistinct reddish streaking on lower underparts* (most pronounced on sides).

SIMILAR SPECIES: Male Fiery-capped Manakin has mainly golden crown. Female Fiery-capped lacks the reddish streaking below and brown on chest but does show some blurry *olive* breast streaking. No other female manakin shows any streaking below.

HABITAT AND BEHAVIOR: Uncommon to locally fairly common in lower and middle growth of humid forest and mature secondary woodland, less often out to forest borders, then mainly when feeding at fruiting trees. Generally inconspicuous, hard to spot even when calling. Descriptions of displays vary (geographically?) but usually involve 2 or more males perching some distance apart (but probably within earshot of each other) and vocalizing. In e. Ecuador males on territory in such dispersed leks give a soft whistled "whoo-cheet," repeated at

10- to 15-second intervals; no actual displays have ever been witnessed (R. O. Prum; RSR). In Brazil mechanical calls have been described as insect-like buzzes, often accompanied by short vertical jumps or by rotating around and actually under the perch (Sick 1967).

RANGE: W. and s. Venezuela (lower slopes of Sierra de Perijá, Maracaibo basin, lower Andean slopes north to Barinas; locally in Amazonas and s. Bolívar), n. and e. Colombia (humid Caribbean lowlands south locally on slopes of Río Cauca valley to Valle, also locally on w. slope of W. Andes in Chocó; locally in forested areas through much of e. lowlands), e. Ecuador, ne. Peru (south to n. Ucayali in the Pucallpa region), and south of the Amazon in w. Brazil (east to near the Rio Urucu south of Tefé); e. Brazil (e. Bahia south to Rio de Janeiro). To about 1300 m.

Machaeropterus pyrocephalus **FIERY-CAPPED MANAKIN**   PLATE: 47

DESCRIPTION: 9 cm (3½"). Legs purplish flesh; iris dark red. Male has *crown and nape golden yellow with red median stripe; back and rump rosy rufous,* cheeks and most of wings olive, inner flight feathers somewhat twisted and showing some whitish; *underparts pinkish white streaked with rosy plum color;* tail dusky olive. *Pallidiceps* (s. Venezuela, also probably extreme n. Brazil) like nominate but with less red in crown. Female uniform olive above; below paler and more yellowish olive with *effect of blurry olive streaking on breast and belly,* throat more grayish and belly pale yellowish.

SIMILAR SPECIES: Male's pattern recalls differently colored Striped Manakin (with solid red crown, etc.); they are sympatric only very locally (e.g., in ne. Peru). No female *Pipra* manakin shows blurry streaking below, though otherwise they are fairly similar; note also Fiery-capped's purplish leg color (dark in all *Pipra*).

HABITAT AND BEHAVIOR: Uncommon in lower and middle growth of humid forest, mature secondary woodland, and (especially when feeding) forest borders; in some areas (e.g., at the Tambopata Reserve in Madre de Dios, Peru) favors transitional forest. Inconspicuous and easily overlooked until male's song is recognized, and even then hard to track to its source. Its territorial call, given in a dispersed lek, is a rather high-pitched bell- or frog-like "pling" or "cling" (easily passed over as a frog or insect), usually given at long intervals. Males in full display (Sick 1967) perch in pairs, 1 of them hanging downward. The latter then twists very rapidly from side to side on its perch, becoming a blur and producing a loud "zssssss" sound, apparently from the enlarged secondaries.

RANGE: Locally in e. Peru (San Martín south to Puno and Madre de Dios), n. Bolivia (south to La Paz and ne. Santa Cruz), and very locally in Amaz. Brazil (Acre near Porongaba, Mato Grosso east to Goiás, and north along both banks of the lower Rio Tapajós to s. Amapá); s. Venezuela (recorded only from La Prisión on the lower Río Caura in nw. Bolívar) and extreme n. Brazil (Maracá Ecological Station in Roraima). To about 1200 m (in Peru).

Machaeropterus deliciosus

CLUB-WINGED MANAKIN

DESCRIPTION: 9.5 cm (3¾"). *Sw. Colombia and w. Ecuador.* Legs purplish flesh. Male *mostly rufous-chestnut*, darkest on breast and belly (almost blackish on lower belly and crissum), palest on head and throat; *crown scarlet;* wings and tail black, *inner flight feathers with considerable white and peculiarly thickened, stiffened, and twisted and bent toward their tips;* bend of wing yellow. Female olive above with *some cinnamon-rufous on face* and with *inner secondaries white on their inner webs;* throat dull whitish, breast and flanks olive, midbelly pale yellow; bend of wing yellow and underwing-coverts white; see C-32.

SIMILAR SPECIES: Male unmistakable, easily recognized even in flight as the wings flash so much white. No other sympatric female manakin shows Club-winged's rufous on face or white on inner flight feathers. Both sexes are stockier than other manakins of similar size and look "full-chested" (R. O. Prum).

HABITAT AND BEHAVIOR: Very local, but in some areas fairly common in lower and middle growth of montane forest (especially where mossy) and mature secondary woodland, mostly in foothills. Generally inconspicuous except at forest edge where it may emerge to feed at fruiting trees. Male's display is simple but bizarre, generally involving only a single bird though several are often within earshot of one another. They perch on open slender branches some 3–7 m above ground and give a "tip-beeuwww," sometimes with more than 1 initial "tip"; the "beeuwww" has a very odd ringing metallic quality. With each "tip" the wings quickly flutter downward, while with the "beeuwww" the wings are held upward for a longer time, almost meeting over the back. Both sounds are thought to be mechanically produced by the wings, presumably by the highly modified secondaries. Males also occasionally give a vocally produced clear and strident "keee" call. Club-winged Manakins are particularly numerous along the road above Junín in w. Nariño, Colombia; small numbers are also found along the entrance road into Mindo, Ecuador.

RANGE: W. slope of Andes in sw. Colombia (Valle southward) and w. Ecuador (recorded mainly south to Pichincha, and in El Oro west of Piñas; locally [only formerly?] in lowlands in southern Pichincha at Río Palenque and in Los Ríos near Quevedo). Mostly 400–1500 m.

NOTE: Formerly placed in the monotypic genus *Allocotopterus*. We agree with Snow (1975) that that genus is best merged in *Machaeropterus*. The modification in the secondaries of *deliciosus* is admittedly extreme, but *M. pyrocephalus* shows it to a lesser degree.

Pipra Manakins

Males of this well-known genus, widespread in humid forest in the lowlands and foothills, are strikingly patterned and usually brightly colored. Females are much plainer and usually some shade of olive or green. Immature males acquire color on the head or crown first, later on the body. Some females, presumably older individuals, may show traces of male plumage (see G. R. Graves, *Bull. B. O. C.* 101[1]: 270–271, 1981). Males of all species perform some sort of stereotyped display, some at communal leks, others more or less solitarily though always within hearing distance of others; the latter have been termed "exploded leks." Calls, some apparently mechanical, are important in display, as are various postures in which bits of color or pattern are shown off.

Syringeal morphology indicates that the genus *Pipra* is apparently polyphyletic (Prum 1992). Prum (op. cit.) would separate all the species in our Group A, the *P. serena* group, in the genus *Lepidothrix*, most closely related to the genera *Manacus, Antilophia,* and *Chiroxiphia*. He would also separate *P. pipra* (White-crowned Manakin) in the monotypic genus *Dixiphia*, most closely related to *Heterocercus*. For the present, however, we continue to employ the traditional arrangement, with all species still placed in *Pipra*. We follow J. Haffer (*J. f. Ornith.* 11: 285–331, 1970) and *Birds of the World*, vol. 8, in merging the monotypic genus *Teleonema* (Wire-tailed Manakin) into *Pipra*.

GROUP A

"*Crowned*" Group; *small*. Males typically have *blue or white crown patches,* and often *rumps* as well; females united by *viridian green upperparts*.

Pipra coronata

BLUE-CROWNED MANAKIN   PLATE: 47

DESCRIPTION: 8.5–9 cm (3¼–3½"). Males have 2 radically different "types" which intergrade in w. Amazonia. Males of the black-bodied type (nominate group, occurring in n. and w. Amazonia and west of Andes) are *sooty black* with *crown bright azure blue;* some Amaz. birds show greenish tinge on belly, whereas trans-Andean birds (*minuscula*) are deeper, more lustrous, black. The more southerly green-bodied type of n. Bolivia, e. Peru except in Loreto, and adjacent sw. Brazil (*exquisita* is typical) is *viridian green above* with *crown paler bright cerulean blue;* throat and chest viridian green becoming *bright pale yellow on middle of breast and belly*. What are apparently intermediate populations occur south of the Amazon in Brazil between the lower Rios Juruá and Madeira, and in n. Peru in the lower Río Ucayali/middle Río Marañón region. All females are essentially alike: *uniform viridian green to bluish green above;* throat pale greenish yellow, breast greenish, *belly pale clear yellow*. See C-32.

SIMILAR SPECIES: Males of both types are the only *Pipra* manakin, except Cerulean-capped, with solid blue crowns. Cerulean-capped, an inhabitant of cen. and s. Peruvian foothills (*above* range of Blue-crowned), is black-bodied; race of Blue-crowned in adjacent lowlands is green-bodied. Female Blue-crowneds are not easy to distinguish from other members of this Group, but the various species are almost always allopatric. Orange-bellied Manakin, an exception, mostly occurs at slightly higher elevations. Foothill-inhabiting Blue-rumped and Cerulean-capped Manakins could overlap with Blue-crowned along e. base of Andes; in se. Peru they are known (D. Stotz, pers. comm.) to come very close. Female *Pipra* manakins of other Groups are considerably duller and more olive above and show less yellow on belly.

HABITAT AND BEHAVIOR: Uncommon to locally common in lower growth of humid forest and mature secondary woodland, in Amazonia primarily in terra firme. Generally inconspicuous birds of the forest interior, Blue-crowned Manakins are most often recorded at fruiting trees, or from males' oft-repeated calls. Males sing from perches 2–5 m above the ground, the most common vocalization a soft "chí-wrrr," the first note almost like a hiccup. Males also give a high, thin, rising "wheeeeee" before display (R. O. Prum). In Middle America both sexes also have a more musical trill, "treereereeree," but this has not been heard in South America (R. O. Prum; RSR). Singing males alternate perching on several favored branches, and though usually solitary, may interact briefly with a second male.

RANGE: N. and w. Colombia (Pacific lowlands, and humid Caribbean lowlands east to middle Río Magdalena valley in e. Antioquia) and nw. Ecuador (south mainly to Pichincha, with 1 ANSP specimen from Quevedo in n. Los Ríos); e. Colombia (north to Meta and Guainía), s. Venezuela (Amazonas and Bolívar), e. Ecuador, e. Peru, n. Bolivia (south to Cochabamba), and w. Amaz. Brazil (north of the Amazon east to the lower Rio Negro, south of it east to the Rio Madeira). Also Costa Rica and Panama. Mostly below 1000 m, locally a bit higher in Colombia and Venezuela.

NOTE: R. O. Prum (pers. comm.) has suggested that trans-Andean populations may represent a separate species, *P. velutina* (Velvety Manakin).

Pipra isidorei

BLUE-RUMPED MANAKIN PLATE: 47

DESCRIPTION: 7.5 cm (3"). *E. slope of Andes from s. Colombia to n. Peru.* Male of nominate race (Colombia and Ecuador) black with *shiny white crown and nape* and *pale azure blue rump and uppertail-coverts. Leucopygia* of n. Peru (south of the Río Marañón) similar but with *milky white rump and uppertail-coverts* (bluest at upper and lower edges). Female viridian green above, *more yellowish green on crown,* and *paler and brighter on rump and uppertail-coverts* which contrast with dusky tail. Below somewhat paler and duller green, becoming pale yellow on midbelly.

SIMILAR SPECIES: Males of both races are virtually unmistakable unless the rump is hidden, in which case confusion is possible with larger and chunkier White-crowned Manakin. Female closely resembles female Blue-crowned Manakin, but Blue-rumped's crown is distinctly paler and more yellowish green (not concolor) and rump contrasts more with tail. Cf. also Cerulean-capped Manakin (which occurs farther south in Peru, not overlapping with *leucopygia*).

HABITAT AND BEHAVIOR: Uncommon to locally fairly common in lower growth of humid forest, mainly in foothills. Like other manakins in its Group, the lovely Blue-rumped is an inconspicuous bird of the forest interior, infrequently seen except when it comes to edge to feed at fruiting trees. Little is known about displays. A solitary male seen (RSR) above Archidona in Ecuador repeatedly gave a soft "wree?" call while perched on 3 slender horizontal branches 4–8 m above ground; for short periods this bird also crouched forward while conspicuously flaring its white crown feathers laterally and fluffing its blue rump feathers.

RANGE: E. slope of Andes in Colombia (recorded only from w. Meta, but surely also occurs southward), e. Ecuador, and n. Peru (San Martín and n. Huánuco). 700–1700 m.

NOTE: The taxon *leucopygia* may deserve full species status. No intergradation between it and nominate *isidorei* has been shown, and if *leucopygia*'s rump color is also employed in display, this would appear likely to serve as an effective isolating mechanism. If split, *P. leucopygia* could be known as the Milky-rumped Manakin.

Pipra coeruleocapilla

CERULEAN-CAPPED MANAKIN

DESCRIPTION: 8.5 cm (3¼"). *E. slope of Andes in cen. and s. Peru.* Resembles Blue-rumped Manakin, replacing that species southward; slightly larger and longer-tailed. Male has *crown and nape bright cerulean blue* (about same color as *exquisita* race of Blue-crowned Manakin) and *rump and uppertail-coverts deeper and more intense cerulean blue.* Female uniform bright grass green above; throat pale greenish yellow, breast greenish, belly pale yellowish.

SIMILAR SPECIES: Female probably indistinguishable from female Blue-crowned Manakin though slightly duller below; best to go by range and elevation. Female Blue-rumped Manakin (no overlap) is also very similar, though Cerulean-capped lacks its yellowish tinge on crown.

HABITAT AND BEHAVIOR: Uncommon to locally fairly common in lower growth of humid forest in foothills. Little known, but behavior probably much like Blue-rumped Manakin's. Small numbers can be seen along lower part of the Shintuya-Paucartambo road in Cuzco, Peru.

RANGE: E. slope of Andes in cen. and s. Peru (s. Huánuco south to Puno). 500–2100 m.

NOTE: The correct (*Birds of the World,* vol. 8; Sibley and Monroe 1990) spelling of the species name is *coeruleocapilla,* not *caeruleocapilla, contra* Meyer de Schauensee (1966, 1970).

Pipra serena

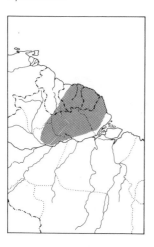

WHITE-FRONTED MANAKIN   PLATE: 47

DESCRIPTION: 9 cm (3½"). *Guianas south to n. Amaz. Brazil;* does not include Orange-bellied Manakin of the tepuis. Male black with *shiny white forehead* and bright azure blue lower rump and uppertail-coverts; spot on chest orange-yellow and *belly bright yellow.* Female bright grass green above, tinged blue on crown; throat and breast olive green contrasting with pale yellow belly.

SIMILAR SPECIES: Male virtually unmistakable, aside from similar Orange-bellied Manakin of the tepuis (which see). Female is greener (less olive) above than most other sympatric *Pipra* manakins (e.g., Golden-headed).

HABITAT AND BEHAVIOR: Locally common in lower growth of humid forest, coming to edge mainly to feed at fruiting trees, sometimes with other manakins. General behavior similar to other manakins in this Group. Male's primary call is an often-given, burry "prreee," sometimes doubled to "prreee-prrur" or given in series (when sometimes punctuated by a low bell-like "boop" note), delivered from a perch 2–6 m above ground. R. O. Prum (*Auk* 102[2]: 384–387, 1985) described its simple displays. These resemble Blue-crowned Manakin's, with protracted bouts of vocalizing and some stereotyped whirring flights between a series of perches. Males usually call and display solitarily, though some coordinated displays occur. A descending, rolling "puuu" or "puurrr" is occasionally given.

RANGE: Guianas (in Guyana known only from the southeast in the Acary Mts.) and n. Amaz. Brazil (Amapá west to the lower Rio Negro in the Manaus region). To 500 m.

NOTE: See comments under Orange-bellied Manakin.

Pipra suavissima

ORANGE-BELLIED MANAKIN
Other: Tepui Manakin

DESCRIPTION: 9 cm (3½"). *Tepuis of s. Venezuela and Guyana;* until recently considered conspecific with White-fronted Manakin. Male resembles male White-fronted Manakin but *lacks* the orange-yellow chest spot and has *belly yellow-orange.* See V-24 (but note that iris color incorrect on this plate: it is *dark,* as in White-fronted Manakin). Female very similar to female White-fronted Manakin; see V-24.

SIMILAR SPECIES: No overlap with White-fronted Manakin. Female Orange-bellied also resembles female Blue-crowned Manakin, which overlaps broadly with Orange-bellied but occurs at *lower* elevations. Female Blue-crowned differs in lacking the bluish tinge on crown and in being greener (less olive) on chest, but both distinctions require a close look in good light.

HABITAT AND BEHAVIOR: Locally common in lower and middle growth of montane forest and forest borders. Behavior similar to that of other manakins in this Group. Primary vocalization of males is a short, nasal, upward-inflected "yeep"; in response to tape playback they give 6–8 bright, rapid, rolling "peep" notes (P. Schwartz and T. A. Parker III recordings, *fide* R. O. Prum). Readily seen, perhaps especially when numerous trees are fruiting along the roadside in Feb.–Mar., along upper part of the Escalera road in e. Bolívar, Venezuela.

RANGE: S. Venezuela (Bolívar and Amazonas), n. Guyana, and extreme n. Brazil. 500–1400 m.

NOTE: We follow Prum (1990, 1992) in considering *P. suavissima* as a species separate from *P. serena. P. suavissima*'s syringeal anatomy is distinct, and male plumage and vocalizations are quite different. Further, *P. suavissima* differs in its entirely montane range. R. O. Prum (pers. comm.) suggested the English name of Orange-bellied Manakin. We regard the other proposed (Sibley and Monroe 1993) English name for *P. suavissima,* Tepui Manakin, as less than satisfactory, for two other manakin species, *Chloropipo uniformis* and *Pipra cornuta,* are also endemic to the tepui region.

Pipra nattereri

SNOW-CAPPED MANAKIN   PLATE: 47

DESCRIPTION: 8.5 cm (3¼"). *Cen. Amaz. Brazil.* Bill pale bluish; *iris yellowish white or pale yellow.* Male has *crown, nape, rump, and uppertail-coverts shiny white* in sharp contrast to bright grass green upperparts.

Throat and chest olive green *contrasting with bright clear yellow lower underparts,* including flanks. Female lacks the shiny white but otherwise resembles male; *female's crown is tinged blue* (nominate race; n. part of range south at least to Calama and Prainha) or pure green (*gracilis;* s. part of range).

SIMILAR SPECIES: Male unmistakable. Female known by the combination of its range, *pale* iris, and *bright* green and yellow plumage. Other similar sympatric manakins have dark eyes and are generally duller olive. Slightly larger and definitely larger-billed Opal-crowned Manakin, as well as very localized Golden-crowned Manakin, occur immediately east of this species' range.

HABITAT AND BEHAVIOR: Uncommon to locally common in undergrowth of humid forest, mainly or entirely in terra firme. Behavior generally similar to Blue-crowned Manakin's, likewise mainly in lower growth. Snow-capped's soft, short "chí-wrrr" is virtually identical to Blue-crowned's most common vocalization; a female-plumaged bird has been heard giving a more piercing and insistent "pweee?"

RANGE: Cen. Amaz. Brazil (mainly between the lower and middle Rios Madeira and Tapajós, toward s. end of range extending east into the upper Rio Xingu drainage and south to the Serra dos Parecís in s. Mato Grosso) and extreme ne. Bolivia (ne. Santa Cruz west of the Serranía de Huanchaca). Both this species and Opal-crowned Manakin are recorded from the upper Rio Xingu area (Sick 1985), but whether they occur in sympatry is unknown. To about 500 m.

Pipra vilasboasi

GOLDEN-CROWNED MANAKIN

DESCRIPTION: 8.5 cm (3¼"). Known only from *Rio Cururú in cen. Amaz. Brazil.* Male resembles male Snow-capped Manakin but *crown and nape glittering greenish gold.* Female apparently very similar to female Snow-capped and probably not distinguishable in the field except by range.

SIMILAR SPECIES: Not known to occur with either Snow-capped or Opal-crowned Manakins. Female Opal-crowned is slightly larger and appreciably heavier-billed.

HABITAT AND BEHAVIOR: Found in lower growth of humid forest, probably exclusively in terra firme. The only person who seems to have seen this beautiful manakin in life is H. Sick, who described the species in 1957. Its behavior and the male's call evidently resemble that of other manakins in the *P. serena* Group. Still known from only the type locality, the species may be threatened by deforestation, for that region is now being extensively developed for cattle ranching (D. Snow, in *Conservation of Tropical Forest Birds,* A. W. Diamond and T. E. Lovejoy, eds., ICBP, 1985, p. 65).

RANGE: Cen. Amaz. Brazil, where known only from Rio Cururú, a tributary of the upper Rio Tapajós, in sw. Pará. About 200 m.

NOTE: *P. obscura* (Sick's Manakin), described simultaneously with *P. vilasboasi* as another new species, is now believed to be the female or immature male of *P. vilasboasi* (*Birds of the World,* vol. 8, p. 275; Sick 1985).

Pipra iris

OPAL-CROWNED MANAKIN PLATE: 47

DESCRIPTION: 9 cm (3½"). *E. Amaz. Brazil. Bill notably heavy and pale bluish; iris pale buffyish or creamy* (both sexes). Male of nominate race (Belém region) is bright grass green above with *crown and nape bright silvery opalescent* (feathers shiny and somewhat flattened). Throat and breast green contrasting with bright yellow belly. Female like male but crown green without any opalescence. Male *eucephala* (e. bank of lower Rio Tapajós) lack nominate's narrow green frontlet (thus their opalescence extends to bill); female *eucephala* have *more bluish crown*.

SIMILAR SPECIES: The stunning male is unmistakable; even from below, when crown color may not be visible, its large bill is. Female is the only small, pale-eyed, bright green manakin in most of its range. In the upper Rio Xingu area, Opal-crowned possibly overlaps with the smaller and stubbier-billed Snow-capped Manakin; females of both have bluish-tinged crowns. Cf. also the rare Golden-crowned Manakin.

HABITAT AND BEHAVIOR: Uncommon to locally fairly common in lower growth of humid forest and mature secondary woodland, mainly or entirely in terra firme. General behavior similar to that of other members of this Group. The call of displaying males is also very similar, a rather rapidly repeated "chi-wir," usually given as the bird perches 3–6 m above ground and within hearing of at least 1 other bird. Small numbers of this exquisite manakin can be found in secondary forest along the road to Mosqueiro east of Belém, but here and elsewhere in its relatively limited range the species is threatened by ongoing deforestation.

RANGE: E. Amaz. Brazil (e. Pará in the Belém area east to nw. Maranhão and south to the upper Rio Xingu area, and on e. side of the lower Rio Tapajós; evidently not known from intervening regions). Below about 200 m.

GROUP B

Male *all black* with *extensive white crown;* female with *gray crown* (especially westward). *Iris red.*

Pipra pipra

WHITE-CROWNED MANAKIN PLATE: 47

DESCRIPTION: 9–10 cm (3½–4"). *Iris red* (deeper in males, often brighter and more conspicuous in females). Male *all deep black* with *white crown and nape* (some racial variation in extent of white on nape, the most in *occulta* of ne. Peru). Female olive green above with *crown and sides of head gray*. Mostly grayish below, tinged olive especially on breast and flanks. More e. races (e.g., wide-ranging nominate) show much less gray on head and neck (see V-24), whereas *coracina* (foothills from w. Venezuela to n. Peru) is much more yellowish olive below. Immature males in lower Amaz. Brazil (south of the Amazon from the lower Rio Tapajós eastward; *separabilis*) and e. Brazil (*cephaleucos*) have crown grayish white, underparts pure dark gray, and upperparts dark olive; this plumage seems not to occur in other races.

SIMILAR SPECIES: Male virtually unmistakable. Other female *Pipra*

manakins lack the gray on head and red iris. This species regularly occurs with members of our other manakin Groups.

HABITAT AND BEHAVIOR: Fairly common to common but somewhat local in undergrowth of humid forest; tends to be less numerous in w. South America, more numerous in the east. General behavior similar to other *Pipra* manakins', and like them inconspicuous except when males are displaying and vocalizing—calls and displays are relatively simple. Advertising males vocalize from branches 3–6 m above ground, usually in small loose groups. The most frequent call of males of nominate race (ne. South America) is a thin, slightly buzzy and spadebill-like "dzeee-ee-ee" or "dzeee-ee-ew"; displaying males engage in short stereotyped flights between branches, often with the crown patch spread outward and flattened. Displaying males in foothills of e. Ecuador (*coracina*) give a very different, loud "drrrrrr-eúw!"

RANGE: W. Colombia (Pacific slope in Valle and w. Cauca; humid Caribbean lowlands and on slopes above Río Magdalena valley south to Huila) and adjacent nw. Venezuela (slopes of Sierra de Perijá); Guianas, e. and s. Venezuela (mainly Bolívar and Amazonas, north to se. Sucre in the east, also in s. Táchira in the west), e. Colombia (mainly along e. base of Andes, also in far east in Vaupés and e. Guainía), e. Ecuador (mainly along e. base of Andes, locally in hilly lowlands of southeast), e. Peru (south to Cuzco), and Amaz. Brazil (south only to s. Pará, and east to n. Maranhão); e. Brazil (s. Bahia south to Rio de Janeiro). Also Costa Rica and Panama. To 1600 m.

NOTE: We suspect, based in part on the radical difference in males' vocalizations (see above), that ultimately *P. pipra* will be shown to be comprised of at least two separate species. The mainly foothill-inhabiting western and Central American birds would be called *P. coracina*, Sclater's Manakin.

GROUP C

Males with *golden to scarlet heads,* and usually a white iris; females *dull olive above.*

Pipra erythrocephala

GOLDEN-HEADED MANAKIN   PLATE: 47

DESCRIPTION: 9 cm (3½"). N. South America (*mainly north of the Amazon,* but locally south of the Río Marañón in Peru). Iris white (grayish or dark in females and immatures); *bill mainly flesh-colored or yellowish* (maxilla often duskier); legs dull pinkish. Male glossy black with *shining golden yellow head;* thighs red and white (hard to see except in display). Female dull olive above, paler and more grayish olive below, more yellowish on belly; see V-24, C-32.

SIMILAR SPECIES: Male unmistakable; other similar manakins have red heads. Drab female can be known in its range by its pale bill; female Blue-crowned and White-fronted Manakins are both brighter green dorsally. Cf. also the trans-Andean Red-capped Manakin (no known overlap in South America).

HABITAT AND BEHAVIOR: Fairly common to common in lower and middle growth of forest and secondary woodland; found in both humid and relatively deciduous forests. Females and males that are not displaying are relatively inconspicuous, most often noted at fruiting trees. Displaying males are noisy and draw attention to themselves but can be hard to spot as they may often perch motionless and then fly abruptly and rapidly. Males display in loose groups of up to 10 or more birds and have favored perches on branches 5–10 m up. They give a variety of sharp chips and buzzes as well as some complex trills; most frequent is a clear "pu." There are several stereotyped postures and movements, including rapid darting flights back and forth between perches, "sidling" to one side or backwards along a branch, jumps, and "about-faces"; displaying and calling reach a frenzy with the appearance of a female. In full display males often stand high on their perches, exposing the colorful thighs. Seems especially numerous on Trinidad.

RANGE: Guianas, most of Venezuela (evidently absent from the llanos region), n. and e. Colombia (humid Caribbean lowlands south in Río Magdalena valley to Santander, widely east of Andes), e. Ecuador, ne. Peru (south to n. San Martín and s. Loreto, occurring mainly north of the Amazon and the Río Marañón, south of the latter only west of the lower Río Ucayali and in n. San Martín at Moyobamba), and n. Amaz. Brazil (north of the Amazon); Trinidad. Also e. Panama. To about 1100 m, rarely higher.

Pipra rubrocapilla

RED-HEADED MANAKIN

DESCRIPTION: 10 cm (4″). Mainly Amazonia *south of the Amazon* (also in e. Brazil). *Iris hazel brown* (darker in females); legs dull pinkish. Male resembles male Round-tailed Manakin but smaller with red on head not extending over nape; thighs red and white (not yellow) and tail square (not rounded). Female very similar to female Round-tailed, distinguishable only by her smaller size and square tail shape (neither at all easy to discern in field).

SIMILAR SPECIES: Red-headed Manakin replaces Golden-headed south of the Amazon, with very limited possible overlap in Peru. Males are easy to tell apart, but females would be tricky; note Golden-headed's smaller size, shorter tail, and usually pale bill.

HABITAT AND BEHAVIOR: Fairly common to common in lower and middle growth of humid forest and mature secondary woodland. Behavior similar to other manakins' in this Group, especially Golden-headed's. Calls and displays are similar to that species'; the most common call is a loud, sharply emphasized "dzeek! dzeeuw" and a "drree-dit, dree-dee-dew."

RANGE: E. Peru (locally, recorded only from s. Loreto in drainages of the lower Ríos Ucayali and Huallaga, and in Madre de Dios at Cuzco Amazonico and the Tambopata Reserve), n. Bolivia (Pando, n. Beni, and ne. Santa Cruz), and s. Amaz. Brazil (south to Mato Grosso and n. Goiás and east to n. Maranhão); e. Brazil (Pernambuco south to Rio de Janeiro). To about 500 m.

NOTE: Sometimes considered conspecific with *P. erythrocephala* (Golden-headed Manakin), found north of the Amazon. However, the two differ in various characters (size, color of head, length of tail, color of underwing), and these likely serve as isolating mechanisms during display. In the 19th century *P. rubrocapilla* and *P. erythrocephala* were reported to have been collected at the same locality (Sarayacu, on the lower Río Ucayali in Peru), but as far as we are aware, actual sympatry has not been subsequently documented.

Pipra chloromeros

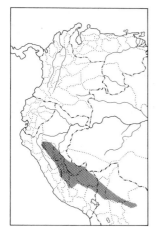

ROUND-TAILED MANAKIN   PLATE: 47

DESCRIPTION: 11 cm (4¼″). *E. Peru and n. Bolivia.* Iris whitish to grayish (dark in immatures and some females); legs dusky flesh. Male glossy black except for *brilliant scarlet head and nape,* nape feathers often somewhat protruding; thighs mostly yellow; underwing-coverts black. Female uniform olive above; somewhat paler and more grayish olive below, becoming yellowish on belly.

SIMILAR SPECIES: Red-headed Manakin is quite similar, and they occur together locally (e.g., at the Tambopata Reserve in se. Peru). Red-headed is smaller and has a square tail (Round-tailed's is indeed rounded, though this is hard to discern in the field). Red-headed male's thighs are red and white, and Round-tailed has greater extension of red on head.

HABITAT AND BEHAVIOR: Uncommon to locally fairly common in lower and middle growth of humid forest, both in lowlands and well into foothills. General behavior similar to that of other members in this Group; its displays have not been extensively studied but include raising up to show off the colored thighs (RSR). Calls are also similar and include a "peeeuw, pew-pew-pew" and a very sharp "ti-zeeeeék!" Numerous around Hacienda Amazonia in Cuzco, Peru.

RANGE: E. Peru (north to s. Amazonas and San Martín) and n. Bolivia (La Paz, Cochabamba, and w. Santa Cruz). To 1400 m in s. Peru.

Pipra mentalis

RED-CAPPED MANAKIN

DESCRIPTION: 10 cm (4″). *W. Colombia and w. Ecuador.* Similar to Round-tailed Manakin. Iris white (dark in females and immatures); legs brownish, bill dark. Male glossy black except for *brilliant scarlet head;* thighs and underwing-coverts yellow (hard to see except in display); some yellow around gape. See C-32. Female dull olive above, paler and more grayish olive below, more yellowish on belly; see P-27.

SIMILAR SPECIES: Male unmistakable in its range *west* of Andes, though resembling several other *Pipra* found east of them. The dull female can also be recognized by range. Female Blue-crowned Manakin is brighter (less olive) green above. Golden-headed Manakin is slightly smaller and has a pale bill (Red-capped's is always dark); they are not known to occur together in Colombia but might do so as they are known to be locally syntopic in Panama.

HABITAT AND BEHAVIOR: Fairly common to locally common in lower and middle growth of humid forest and mature secondary woodland. Inconspicuous except when displaying, tending to remain in the shady forest interior though sometimes emerging to borders while feeding in fruiting trees. Displaying males gather in loose groups at traditional leks where they are often very noisy. Their loudest call is a drawn-out "tsick, tseeeeeeeee-tsík!" given as a bird flies between display branches, the sharp "tsík!" as it lands on the second branch. Various other calls, some of them evidently mechanical and made with the wings, are also given.

RANGE: Pacific w. Colombia (cen. Chocó southward) and nw. Ecuador (now mainly in Esmeraldas; formerly south to Pichincha and Los Ríos, with 1 report from as far south as nw. Azuay). Also Mexico to Panama. Mostly below 500 m (higher in Middle America).

Pipra cornuta

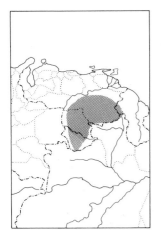

SCARLET-HORNED MANAKIN   PLATE: 47

DESCRIPTION: 12.5 cm (5"). *Tepuis of s. Venezuela and adjacent areas.* Iris white (dark in female and immatures); bill mostly pale flesh (browner in females). Male glossy black with *brilliant scarlet head, feathers on hindcrown elongated and projecting back and slightly upward,* with somewhat bifurcated effect; thighs scarlet. Female dull olive above with (*fide* J. P. O'Neill) a *slight tufted effect on nape;* somewhat paler and more grayish olive below, dull pale yellowish on belly.

SIMILAR SPECIES: Male unmistakable and *considerably larger and longer-tailed* than other manakins with similar color patterns. Female most likely confused with Olive Manakin, also endemic to tepui forests; Scarlet-horned may be large for a *Pipra,* but Olive is slightly bigger, longer-winged, and longer-tailed. Olive has dark soft-part colors (these paler, usually brownish flesh, in Scarlet-horned) and lacks Scarlet-horned's slight tuft on nape.

HABITAT AND BEHAVIOR: Uncommon to locally fairly common in lower and middle growth of humid forest and taller secondary woodland (generally not in stunted woodland). Behavior similar to that of other members of the Group, though males seem generally to display in smaller leks (D. Snow, *Bull. B. O. C.* 97[1]: 23–27, 1977; RSR). Display calls include a hoarse "sweeénk-aank" and a loud mechanical wing sound, "brrrt" (R. O. Prum). This spectacular manakin can be found in taller forest along the upper part of the Escalera road in e. Bolívar, perhaps most easily when melastomataceous trees are in fruit along the road (at least Feb.–Mar.).

RANGE: Tepuis of s. Venezuela (Bolívar and Amazonas south to Cerro de la Neblina) and adjacent Guyana (Alaroo River; elsewhere?) and extreme n. Brazil (upper Rio Branco area in Roraima). Mostly 900–1600 m. Early published records from near the Amazon are now considered erroneous. In fact there are no entirely verified locality records from Brazil, though the species seems almost certain to occur on the Brazilian slopes of certain tepuis such as Cerro de la Neblina.

GROUP D   Males differ from Group C in their "hooded" effect, with *yellow and/or red extending from face to belly;* females *brighter yellow below.* The *P. aureola* superspecies.

Pipra filicauda

WIRE-TAILED MANAKIN   PLATE: 47

DESCRIPTION: 11.5 cm (4½"), exclusive of tail filaments, which add about 4 cm (1½") to male, 2.5 cm (1") to female. *Iris white*. Male has *crown, nape, and upper back bright red*, contrasting with black remaining upperparts; some white on inner webs of inner flight feathers, showing mainly in flight; *shafts of tail feathers project as long wire-like filaments, curving downward and inward. Forehead, sides of head, and entire underparts bright golden yellow*. Female uniform olive above; somewhat paler olive below, becoming pale yellow on belly; *tail filaments elongated*.

SIMILAR SPECIES: Gaudy male unmistakable. Female readily known by combination of fairly large size, obvious white eye, and tail filaments (which though fine are usually quite easy to see).

HABITAT AND BEHAVIOR: Locally common in lower growth of humid forest, in Amazonia primarily in várzea and along streams in terra firme; elsewhere occurs in deciduous forest and sometimes quite scrubby gallery woodland, almost always near water. Despite its bright colors, Wire-tailed Manakin is inconspicuous and not seen regularly even in areas where mist-netting reveals it to be one of the more numerous understory birds. Calling males at their leks attract attention, however; the most common advertising vocalization is a short, attenuated, somewhat nasal "eeee-ew." Displays were described by P. Schwartz and D. Snow (*The Living Bird* 17: 51–78, 1978). They found that males perform either alone or with a partner, in which case coordinated displays are frequent. There are many short flights, some of them slow with butterfly-like flapping, and a "swoop-in" to a frequently used display perch on which males land with a loud "klok." Perched birds often ruffle their back feathers and raise their tails, often twisting from side to side. Then the tail feathers may actually brush the face or throat of the passive bird, be it a female or the male's display partner—it looks like tickling! This is believed to be the only instance among birds in which modified tail feathers are used primarily in a tactile, as opposed to a visual, manner.

RANGE: Venezuela (mainly in the west and north from the Maracaibo basin east to Miranda, also in s. Amazonas), e. Colombia, e. Ecuador, ne. Peru (south to the lower Río Huallaga area in San Martín, and along the lower Río Ucayali in s. Loreto), and w. Amaz. Brazil (north of the Amazon east to the Rios Branco and Negro, south of it east to the Rio Purus). Mostly below 500 m, but recorded higher (to 1000 m) in Venezuela.

NOTE: Formerly separated in the monotypic genus *Teleonema*, but shown by J. Haffer (*J. f. Ornith.* III: 285–331, 1970) to be closely related to *P. aureola* and *P. fasciicauda*, both of which have unmodified tails but similar color patterns. Syringeal evidence is supportive of this generic merger (Prum 1992).

Pipra fasciicauda

BAND-TAILED MANAKIN   PLATE: 47

DESCRIPTION: 11 cm (4¼"). Cen. Amazonia (*south of the Amazon*). *Iris white*. Male has crown, nape, and upper back bright red with some yellow showing through (especially on forecrown and back), contrasting with black remaining upperparts; wing feathers with white patch

on inner web (*forming stripe down the length of wing, conspicuous in flight*); *basal half of tail yellowish white* (its extent varying racially). Below mainly bright golden yellow, breast variably stained scarlet (most in *saturata* of ne. Peru, least in nominate race of se. Peru and w.-cen. Bolivia; *scarlatina* of n. Bolivia east through s. Amaz. Brazil and south to e. Paraguay and ne. Argentina roughly intermediate). Female rather bright olive above, somewhat paler olive below, *becoming pale yellow on belly*.

SIMILAR SPECIES: Dazzling males are unmistakable except for Crimson-hooded Manakin (see discussion under that species); they overlap only marginally, in e. Amazonia. Female can be known by its relatively large size for a manakin, staring white eye, and bright olive overall coloration with obvious yellow on belly; it is not distinguishable in the field from female Crimson-hooded. Cf. also female Blue-backed Manakin (with orangey legs, etc.).

HABITAT AND BEHAVIOR: Fairly common to common in lower growth of seasonally flooded várzea and transitional forest and in gallery forest and woodland. Displays and vocalizations are, as described by M. B. Robbins (*Wilson Bull.* 95[3]: 321–342, 1983), quite similar to Wire-tailed Manakin's. More Band-tailed males gather at lek sites, and vegetation at Band-tailed's leks is much denser. Band-tailed's tail feathers not being lengthened, these are not used in a tactile manner, but their pattern is conspicuous, especially during the "tail-up freeze" display; the wing-stripe is very prominent in various display flights. A Band-tailed lek lies just behind the buildings at the Tambopata Reserve in se. Peru; here these beautiful manakins are quite well habituated to the presence of observers.

RANGE: E. Peru (north to San Martín and s. Loreto), n. Bolivia (south to La Paz, Cochabamba, and Santa Cruz), Amaz. and interior s. Brazil (south of the Amazon from w. Maranhão west through upper drainages of the Rios Purus and Juruá, and south to s. Minas Gerais, n. São Paulo, and n. Paraná; apparently isolated populations in Ceará and Alagoas), e. Paraguay (west to Concepción and Paraguarí), and ne. Argentina (Misiones). To about 600 m.

Pipra aureola

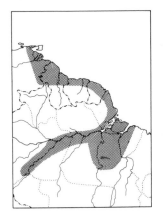

CRIMSON-HOODED MANAKIN

DESCRIPTION: 11 cm (4¼"). *Ne. South America*. Resembles Band-tailed Manakin, females indistinguishable in their limited area of overlap. Male *deeper red* (nearer "shining crimson") from crown to upper back and on breast; *belly mainly black* (not yellow); tail without white at base. Nominate race (e. Venezuela to lower Amaz. Brazil west to the lower Rio Xingu) is stained red on lower face and throat (see V-24); other races have throat yellow (more like Band-tailed). Note that the V-24 female should have a white eye.

SIMILAR SPECIES: Except for Band-tailed Manakin, male virtually unmistakable. Aside from Band-tailed, female Crimson-hooded is most likely confused with female Blue-backed Manakin, which has dark eye and is not as yellow on belly.

HABITAT AND BEHAVIOR: Uncommon in lower growth of swampy

and várzea forest and in tangled woodland along watercourses; perhaps most numerous on coastal plain of French Guiana, where considered "locally abundant" by Tostain et al. (1992, p. 138). General behavior seems similar to Band-tailed Manakin's, though Crimson-hooded has not been yet studied in any detail.

RANGE: E. Venezuela (Sucre south to e. Bolívar), Guianas (mainly in coastal regions), and lower Amaz. Brazil (north of the Amazon west to the Manaus area, south of it west to the Rio Madeira). Below 300 m.

COTINGAS

LIKE the manakins, the cotingas are an exclusively neotropical tyrannoid group found in tropical and subtropical forests, where almost all species are arboreal. Unlike the manakins, however, the cotingas are very diverse in size, ranging from very small (the Kinglet Calyptura) to among the largest of all passerine birds (the umbrellabirds and certain fruitcrows). Many male cotingas are exceptionally beautifully and brightly colored, whereas others can only be described as bizarre! Mating systems are diverse, with everything from simple monogamous pairing to extraordinarily complex lek systems being represented. Nests are, so far as known, simple cups, often surprisingly small or with quite flimsy construction, and sometimes placed directly atop a branch; in many cotingas only the female cares for the young.

Recent evidence (summarized in Sibley and Ahlquist 1990) has indicated that the following, all formerly considered as separate families, are better included in the Cotinginae: the single species of sharpbill (Oxyruncidae), the three species of plantcutter (Phytotomidae), and the two species of cock-of-the-rock (Rupicolidae). The genera *Laniisoma, Laniocera,* and *Iodopleura,* which share certain characters with other members of the "*Schiffornis* group" (Lanyon and Prum 1989; Prum 1990), may not be "true" cotingas but are here retained in their traditional position.

Oxyruncus Sharpbills

The Sharpbill has been the subject of considerable taxonomic interest. It had long been considered a monotypic family (Oxyruncidae), but recent DNA evidence suggests that it is best considered a cotinga (C. G. Sibley, S. M. Lanyon, and J. E. Ahlquist, *Condor* 86[1]: 48–52, 1984), though this conclusion was later questioned (S. M. Lanyon, *Syst. Zool.* 34[4]: 404–418, 1985). We follow Sibley and Monroe (1990) in considering it a cotinga. The Sharpbill has a very sharply pointed bill and boldly scaled and spotted plumage; its recumbent crest and the male's saw-edged outermost primary are reminiscent of certain tyrannids. With a highly disjunct (relictual?) distribution, the Sharpbill ranges in humid forest, mainly in hilly areas, from Costa Rica to s. Brazil. F. G. Stiles and B. Whitney (*Auk* 100[1]: 117–125, 1983) describe its behavior in Costa Rica.

Oxyruncus cristatus

SHARPBILL

PLATE: 48

DESCRIPTION: 16.5–17 cm (6½–6¾"). *Sharply pointed bill,* paler at base; iris reddish to orange (redder in males). Mostly olive above with 2 indistinct yellowish wing-bars; head and neck mainly whitish *with narrow blackish scaling* and with black-bordered orange to red crest (redder in males; crest usually flattened, with bright color concealed). Throat whitish narrowly scaled blackish; remaining underparts pale

greenish yellow, *profusely spotted black*. Nominate race (se. South America) is the yellowest below; all other S. Am. races have whiter underparts with yellowish tinge confined to flanks and crissum.

SIMILAR SPECIES: The very pointed bill plus the conspicuous ventral spotting render the Sharpbill virtually unmistakable. Cf. Speckled and Spotted Tanagers, Elegant Mourner (which has black crown and is *scaled* below), female Red-banded Fruiteater (which is obviously *streaked* below), and Scaled Fruiteater.

HABITAT AND BEHAVIOR: Uncommon to locally fairly common in canopy and borders of humid forest. Usually encountered singly, often while foraging with mixed flocks comprised mostly of various tanagers. Often perches quietly for protracted periods, then hops or jumps along major limbs or in outer canopy. Feeds on both insects and fruit, gleaning energetically, often hanging upside down, also probing into moss and dead leaves. The Sharpbill is rather stolid and inconspicuous; often its presence is first made known through the male's distinctive and far-carrying song, usually delivered from favored perches in the canopy. This drawn-out, high, thin, somewhat shrill and buzzy trill gradually slides down in pitch and fades in intensity, "zheeeeeeeeeeu-uuu'u'u'u-'u'u"; in se. Brazil it is somewhat more musical and sounds uncannily like the approach of a falling bomb (without the boom at the end!).

RANGE: Highly disjunct. Tepuis of s. Venezuela (Bolívar and e. Amazonas), Guyana, Surinam (on a few interior mountains, notably Brownsberg), French Guiana (locally on mountains in interior) and e. Amaz. Brazil (Amapá and locally in e. Pará); s. and e. Brazil (Alagoas; s. Goiás, Minas Gerais, and Espírito Santo south to Santa Catarina, and sightings from the Serra das Araras in s. Mato Grosso), e. Paraguay (west to Concepción, Caaguazú, and Guairá), and ne. Argentina (seen in 1986 near Iguazú Falls in n. Misiones; P. Kaestner); locally on e. slope of Andes in e. Peru (single localities in Amazonas, San Martín, Junín, and Madre de Dios [Cerros de Pantiacolla]) and w. Bolivia (southwest of Apolo in La Paz). Also Costa Rica and Panama (in the latter found east to Cerro Tacarcuna and Cerro Quía in Darién, both sites on the Colombian border), and seems likely within Colombian territory. To 1600 m (most numerous in foothills, 500–1000 m).

Phytotoma Plantcutters

Found in semiopen country of s. South America, the three species of plantcutters have a distinctive rounded bill with fine serrations along its cutting edge. Each has a short but expressive crest; males are mostly gray or black and rufous, with females much more streaked. Until recently the plantcutters were usually considered a separate family, the Phytotomidae. S. M. Lanyon and W. E. Lanyon (*Auk* 106[3]: 422–432, 1989) concluded that, on biochemical and morphological evidence, the family Phytotomidae was still worthy of recognition, and further suggested that three cotingid genera (*Ampelion, Doliornis,* and *Zaratornis*) should be incorporated into it. However, Prum (1990) concluded that *Phytotoma* should be placed with the cotingas, and this is the treatment followed here.

GROUP A

Undertail dark gray *tipped white.*

Phytotoma rutila

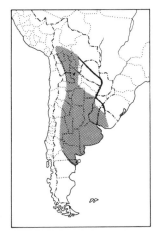

WHITE-TIPPED PLANTCUTTER   PLATE: 48

DESCRIPTION: 19–19.5 cm (7½–7¾"). Iris dull yellow to hazel. Male mostly gray above with sparse black streaking on back; wings and tail dusky, wings with *2 broad white wing-bars* (in fresh plumage may show 3), *tail feathers tipped white. Forecrown and entire underparts cinnamon-rufous,* with some gray on sides and flanks. Female pale brown above, *boldly streaked with blackish;* wings and tail dusky, wings with 2 (or 3) narrow whitish bars. Below pale drab buffyish to deep ochraceous buff, *conspicuously streaked blackish* (streaks sometimes finer). What are presumably young males resemble adults but are paler below and on forecrown and are more streaked generally.

SIMILAR SPECIES: No other plantcutter occurs in its range. Rather colorful male is not likely to be confused, but streaky female looks superficially finch-like (e.g., *Phrygilus* spp.). Sexes are usually found together in small groups, reducing the potential for confusion.

HABITAT AND BEHAVIOR: Locally fairly common to common in scrubby areas and in semiopen groves of acacia and other thorny trees, often around houses and in overgrazed areas. Seems to favor drier regions or areas with poor, often sandy, soil. Usually in small groups, perching conspicuously but quietly in or near tops of bushes and low trees, calmly allowing a close approach. Its weird call, uttered by both sexes, frequently draws attention; difficult to describe, though easy to recognize once learned, it is a dry, gravelly, mechanical-sounding "wree-ee-ee-eh" or "wraaaaaah."

RANGE: W. Bolivia (north to La Paz), n. and cen. Argentina (south to Mendoza, La Pampa, Río Negro, and in small numbers to ne. Chubut), and Uruguay; during austral winter (May–Sept.) there is some northward displacement, with birds reaching the lowlands of se. Bolivia (in Bolivia they are apparently resident only in the highlands and intermontane valleys), w. Paraguay (east to near the Río Paraguay), and extreme s. Brazil (1 record from w. Rio Grande do Sul). The n. limit of breeding in Argentina is uncertain, and the species may not be a breeding resident in Uruguay. To about 3500 m in Bolivia.

Phytotoma raimondii

PERUVIAN PLANTCUTTER

DESCRIPTION: 18.5 cm (7¼"). *W. Peru.* Iris yellow. Male like male White-tipped Plantcutter but with only a little rufous on forecrown (just above bill), and *throat and breast gray* (only the belly cinnamon-rufous). Females probably not separable in the field (but *no range overlap*).

HABITAT AND BEHAVIOR: Rare to uncommon and very local in

patches of low woodland sustained by subsurface water in otherwise mostly barren, sandy coastal desert. Behavior (including voice) much like White-tipped Plantcutter's, but Peruvian is now a *much* rarer bird. One of the few localities where this species has been found recently is south of Chiclayo in Lambayeque, several kilometers west of Mocupe along the road toward the coastal town of Lagunas. Here, at least in 1970s, it was numerous. Peruvian Plantcutter deserves formal threatened status; its range and habitat were never very extensive, and the latter has been seriously affected by firewood cutting and clearing for agriculture.

RANGE: Locally in nw. Peru (Tumbes south to n. Lima); has never been found within the present borders of Ecuador. To 550 m.

GROUP B

Undertail *rufous tipped blackish.*

Phytotoma rara

RUFOUS-TAILED PLANTCUTTER

PLATE: 48

DESCRIPTION: 19 cm (7½"). *Chile and s. Argentina.* Tail somewhat shorter and bill slightly larger and blacker than in other plantcutters. Iris red. Male has *crown chestnut* and back grayish olive brown heavily streaked black; sides of head blackish with mottled whitish patches on lower cheeks and at base of malar. Wings black with *large white patch on lesser coverts* and a second, narrower wing-bar; tail mostly black with *rufous inner web* on all but the broad tip (the rufous visible mainly from below). *Below deep cinnamon-rufous,* paling somewhat on belly. Female resembles female White-tipped Plantcutter but upperparts browner (not so gray) and tail pattern very different (*showing no white*); the rufous on female's tail is restricted to a wide band (visible mainly from below) across the middle of tail.

SIMILAR SPECIES: Does not occur in range of any other plantcutter. The streaky female vaguely recalls certain heavily streaked finches (e.g., Mourning or Plumbeous Sierra-Finch), but there are obvious differences in bill shape and behavior.

HABITAT AND BEHAVIOR: Uncommon to locally fairly common in shrubby areas, borders of low woodland, and agricultural areas with orchards and hedgerows; in at least some areas its presence is tied to that of *Berberis* (barberry) bushes. Usually occurs as scattered pairs, and often not very conspicuous, though sometimes perching on phone wires. In some regions considered an agricultural pest because of damage it may cause to fruit crops. Its call, a distinctive nasal and guttural "r-r-r-ra-ra-raáh," starts slowly and is more broken than other plantcutters' calls; as a result, its local name is *rara,* the source of its Latin name as well (it is not a "rare" bird!).

RANGE: Cen. and s. Chile (Atacama south to Magallanes) and s. Argentina (Neuquén and w. Río Negro south to w. Santa Cruz); may be extending its range southward, moving into young second-growth in areas recently cleared of forest; accidental on Falkland Is. Mostly below 1500 m, occasionally up to 2300 m.

Iodopleura Purpletufts

A distinctive genus of small cotingas found in the canopy of lowland forests. Male purpletufts have silky purple or violet flank tufts (white or absent in females), usually inconspicuous but flared out prominently during display. Their silhouette is characteristic, with a very stubby bill, short tail, and strikingly long wings. The nest (recalling a hummingbird's) is a tiny cup externally coated with cobwebs and placed on the top of a branch. The genus *Iodopleura* has traditionally been placed with the cotingas, but recent evidence indicates that it may belong in what has been termed the "*Schiffornis* assemblage," in a position separate from the true cotingas, the true manakins, and the true tyrant flycatchers (R. O. Prum and W. E. Lanyon, *Condor* 91[2]: 444–461, 1989).

GROUP A

Larger; *sooty and white pattern*.

Iodopleura isabellae

WHITE-BROWED PURPLETUFT   PLATE: 48

DESCRIPTION: 11.5 cm (4½"). A *small* cotinga with *short tail* and *long swallow-like wings*. Mainly brownish black above with *bold white facial markings* (loral spot, postocular stripe, and short malar streak); rump band white. *Throat and median underparts white,* sides and flanks broadly mottled and barred with dusky brown; flank tufts purple. Female like male except for white flank tufts.

SIMILAR SPECIES: Small size and distinctive pattern and behavior should preclude confusion, but cf. Dusky Purpletuft of ne. South America (no recorded overlap).

HABITAT AND BEHAVIOR: Uncommon in canopy and borders of humid forest, both in várzea and terra firme, sometimes out into tall isolated trees in adjacent clearings; probably often overlooked, as it usually perches well above ground. Most often in pairs, sometimes small groups, perching quietly, regularly on high exposed branches from which it occasionally sallies out after passing insects. Also eats much fruit. The call is a soft, thin "whee" or "eee," sometimes doubled or trebled (with quality of Long-tailed Tyrant).

RANGE: Sw. Venezuela (s. Amazonas), se. Colombia (north to Meta and Guainía), e. Ecuador, e. Peru, extreme n. Bolivia (Pando), and Amaz. Brazil (north of the Amazon east to the Rio Negro, south of it east to e. Pará and south to Rondônia and n. Mato Grosso). Published records from Alagoas in ne. Brazil are in error for the Buff-throated Purpletuft (Teixera et al. 1993). Mostly below 500 m, rarely up to 850 m.

NOTE: See comments under Dusky Purpletuft.

Iodopleura fusca

DUSKY PURPLETUFT

DESCRIPTION: 11 cm (4¼"). *Ne. South America.* Resembles White-browed Purpletuft but slightly smaller and *much darker and more uniform;* lacks White-browed's facial markings and has mostly dark under-

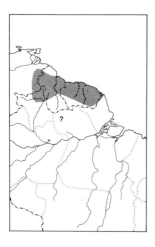

parts (*including throat*) with white restricted to median belly, crissum, and rump band.

SIMILAR SPECIES: Dusky Purpletuft's overall appearance and similar treetop-perching habits might lead to confusion with Swallow-winged Puffbird (*Chelidoptera tenebrosa*) though the latter is much larger and has rufous on belly and much more white on rump.

HABITAT AND BEHAVIOR: Rare in canopy and borders of humid forest. Behavior (including voice) reportedly similar to White-browed Purpletuft's, but this species seems to be scarcer and remains less well known. Perhaps less rare in French Guiana than elsewhere; at least there are numerous sightings from there (Tostain et al. 1992).

RANGE: Locally in se. Venezuela (e. Bolívar), Guianas, and n. Brazil in Roraima (sightings from Maracá Ecological Station and [D. Stotz] Colonia do Apiau) and north of Manaus. Probably occurs elsewhere in n. Amaz. Brazil. To 500 m in Venezuela.

NOTE: Possibly conspecific with *I. isabellae,* but until intergradation between the two has been shown, it seems best to maintain them as full species. If considered conspecific, the name *fusca* would have priority, and White-rumped Purpletuft would be the best name for the expanded species.

GROUP B

Smaller and grayer; rare in e. Brazil.

Iodopleura pipra

BUFF-THROATED PURPLETUFT   PLATE: 48

DESCRIPTION: 9.5 cm (3¾"). *E. Brazil.* Markedly smaller than other purpletufts but with the same short-tailed, long-winged shape. *Ashy gray above,* crown feathers blacker and somewhat elongated (regularly raised as a crest, *fide* D. Stotz), and wings and tail duskier. *Median throat, chest, and crissum pale cinnamon-buff;* lower underparts white *coarsely barred with gray,* and with lilac flank tufts. Female like male but lacks flank tufts (some may show a trace of white or lilac). *Leucopygia* (ne. Brazil) similar to nominate race (se. Brazil) but with white rump band; a few birds from nominate's range also have white on rump (Collar et al. 1992).

SIMILAR SPECIES: No likely confusion in its small range.

HABITAT AND BEHAVIOR: Rare and local in canopy and borders of humid forest, secondary woodland, and cacao plantations. Not well known (especially *leucopygia*), but general behavior apparently much as in its larger relatives, though thought to be somewhat more active (D. Stotz). Like them, Buff-throated Purpletuft tends to perch on high exposed branches and occurs most often in pairs; it reportedly sallies to the air less often (E. O. Willis and Y. Oniki). Eats many mistletoe berries. Reported to have a high, fine "si-si" call (Sick 1985). Small numbers can be found in coastal ne. São Paulo north of Ubatuba and near the base of the mts. along the Ubatuba-Taubate highway. Overall numbers, which never seem to have been large, must have declined substantially because of deforestation; the species deserves formal threatened or endangered status (probably especially *leucopygia*).

RANGE: Locally in e. Brazil (Paraíba, e. Pernambuco, and Alagoas; Espírito Santo south to se. São Paulo). The single record from Minas

Gerais (Lagoa Santa) is regarded as doubtful (Collar et al. 1992). To 1000 m.

NOTE: E. O. Willis and Y. Oniki (*Rev. Brasil. Biol.* 48[2]: 161–167, 1988) present information on nesting and behavior of the nominate form. Two 19th-century specimens, supposedly procured in Guyana, provided the basis for the description of the form *leucopygia*. There have been no subsequent Guyana records, and it was supposed (Snow 1982) that the specimens were mislabeled and had in fact been obtained somewhere in e. Brazil. Recent (late 1980s) records from ne. Brazil (*fide* D. Teixera) confirm that this indeed was the case. *Leucopygia* might be viewed as deserving recognition as a full species (White-rumped Purpletuft), though the occasional presence of some white on the rumps of examples of nominate *pipra* from se. Brazil would seem to argue against this.

Calyptura Calypturas

The smallest cotinga and one of South America's smallest passerines, the unique Kinglet Calyptura bears an uncanny resemblance to the holarctic kinglets (*Regulus*), though they are totally unrelated. Sadly, the calyptura has not been recorded for over a century and may now be extinct.

Calyptura cristata

KINGLET CALYPTURA   PLATE: 48

DESCRIPTION: 8 cm (3¼"). *Very rare (if not extinct?) endemic in se. Brazil.* Mostly bright olive above with *orange-red to yellow-orange coronal stripe bordered laterally by a broad black stripe;* forehead and rump band yellow. Wings and *very short tail* dusky, wings with 2 prominent white wing-bars and tertial tipping. *Below mostly bright yellow,* clouded with olive on breast.

SIMILAR SPECIES: In the welcome event that the distinctive calyptura is ever relocated, it should be easily identified. Specimens are vaguely manakin-like in shape, but whether in life the calyptura actually resembles a manakin is unknown.

HABITAT AND BEHAVIOR: Virtually unknown, with no 20th-century records; it may be extinct. From the sketchy comments of Descourlitz (1852, *in* Snow 1982), the calyptura was found not only in forest but also in second-growth and foraged actively, mostly at middle levels. The description of its call, "brief, sharp, and disagreeable," does not give one much to go on! Possibly best searched for in or near the Serra dos Órgãos, near where several of the old specimens were supposedly obtained (but note that Black-hooded Antwren, also supposedly taken in the same region, was recently rediscovered in *coastal* woodland); D. Stotz (pers. comm.) suspects it might also persist near Ubatuba in ne. São Paulo. Confirming the continued existence of the Kinglet Calyptura (there have been a few rumors, *fide* D. Stotz) would cause much excitement in the ornithological world, and is the greatest prize yet awaiting the growing cadre of field ornithologists in se. Brazil.

RANGE: Se. Brazil (Rio de Janeiro, where in the 19th century recorded from Rosário, Cantagalo, and Nova Friburgo; also reported from Espírito Santo, but this remains unconfirmed). To about 900 m.

Laniisoma Mourners

A monotypic genus of uncertain affinities, though long considered a cotingid. R. O. Prum and W. E. Lanyon (*Condor* 91[2]: 444–461, 1989) recently concluded that *Laniisoma* is best considered part of the "*Schiffornis* assemblage" (which besides that genus also includes *Laniocera, Pachyramphus, Xenopsaris,* and probably *Iodopleura*). For the present, we leave *Laniisoma* where it has traditionally been placed, with the cotingas. A basically olive and yellow bird with bold scaling below, it ranges at low densities and very locally in humid foothill forests. *Laniisoma*'s remarkable nestling plumage with its long filamentuous "spines" is surely one of the most bizarre of all bird plumages; it was admirably illustrated by M. Woodcock (*in* Snow 1982).

Laniisoma elegans

ELEGANT MOURNER   PLATE: 48
Other: Shrike-like Cotinga

DESCRIPTION: 17.5 cm (6¾″). Local and scarce in foothill forests. Lower mandible pale greenish, maxilla blackish. Nominate race (se. Brazil) has *crown black;* otherwise olive green above with narrow, pale grayish green eye-ring. *Bright yellow below* with variable amount of *coarse black scaling across chest, down flanks, and on crissum.* Female similar but with crown dusky and virtually *all* of underparts scaled with black. Immature similar to female but with *large rufous spots on tips of wing-coverts.* Birds found along and near e. slope of Andes (*buckleyi* group) similar, but males show *little* scaling below (only sparse markings on flanks); see C-34. Females of *buckleyi* group have crown usually *concolor* (olive) with rest of upperparts (though some dusky may show); their underparts are like nominate's.
SIMILAR SPECIES: Sharpbill, more spotted below and scaly on face, has a very different bill. Female Barred Becard is markedly smaller, more finely barred below, and shows a rufous area on wing. Cf. also Scaled Fruiteater and various *Pipreola* fruiteaters.
HABITAT AND BEHAVIOR: Rare in humid forest and tall secondary woodland; generally lethargic and inconspicuous, apt to be overlooked unless calling. Ranges at all levels inside forest, less often at edge; it is usually seen singly. The call in Peru is a peculiar, rather insect-like, very thin and high "psiiiiiiiiieeeee," repeated persistently (but often only at long intervals) in morning and early afternoon hours by males perched in the subcanopy (Parker and Parker 1982).
RANGE: Locally on lower e. slope of Andes in extreme w. Venezuela (sw. Barinas and se. Táchira), e. Colombia (n. Boyacá and apparently also w. Meta), e. Ecuador, e. Peru (Amazonas to Pasco, probably also farther south), and w. Bolivia (La Paz); se. Brazil (Espírito Santo, se. Minas Gerais, Rio de Janeiro, São Paulo, and e. Paraná; several early specimens are labeled as from "Bahia"). Mostly 400–1350 m, once in Peru to 1800 m.
NOTE: The generally employed English name for this species, Shrike-like Cotinga, is very misleading. As Snow (1982, p. 35) states, "the Shrike-like Cotinga owes its

English name to a translation of its not very appropriate generic name. . . . There is nothing to suggest that it is in fact shrike-like in any way." R. O. Prum and W. E. Lanyon (*Condor* 91[2]: 459, 1989) suggest that as the genus is closely related to the *Laniocera* mourners, it too is best called a mourner. "Elegant," from its Latin modifying name, *elegans,* then becomes, as they suggest, a logical English modifier. It has been suggested (Collar et al. 1992) that the two highly disjunct populations represent separate species: birds of se. Brazil would remain the Elegant Mourner (*L. elegans*), and those of the Andes would be the Buckley's Mourner (*L. buckleyi*).

Phibalura Cotingas

A very distinctive cotinga with strikingly long, deeply forked tail and boldly barred plumage, found mainly in se. South America. Its surprisingly inconspicuous cup-shaped nest is made mostly of lichens and is usually placed on top of a branch in the semiopen.

Phibalura flavirostris

SWALLOW-TAILED COTINGA
PLATE: 48

DESCRIPTION: 21.5−22 cm (8½−8¾"). *Mainly se. Brazil area.* Virtually unmistakable, with *long, slim, deeply forked tail.* Bill straw yellow; legs yellowish. Crown black *bordered laterally by a grayish stripe* and with a semiconcealed maroon-red coronal patch; partial white collar behind ear-coverts, and pinkish eye-ring. Back and rump yellowish olive *coarsely barred with black;* wings and tail mainly bluish black. *Throat and malar area bright yellow; breast white, coarsely barred black;* belly pale yellow, sparsely spotted black. Female similar but with grayer crown, more olive on wings and tail, and more uniform underparts (throat duller yellow and speckled black, belly more densely spotted and barred).

HABITAT AND BEHAVIOR: Rare to locally uncommon in forest borders, partially or lightly wooded areas, and clearings and gardens with scattered trees, where it often nests. Regularly perches on exposed limbs and usually in the semiopen, not normally inside forest. Apparently feeds mainly on mistletoe berries. In nonbreeding season found in loose groups of up to 15−20 birds, but when nesting separates out more as individual pairs (though active nests have been found quite close to each other). Even when breeding, the species seems very quiet. In flight, when the forked tail is held closed in a virtual point, it can look uncannily like a *Pyrrhura* parakeet. Small numbers can be found in Itatiaia Nat. Park in Brazil and at Caraça in Minas Gerais. The species may well have undergone a general decline recently and perhaps deserves formal threatened status.

RANGE: Se. Brazil (Espírito Santo and cen. Minas Gerais south to Rio Grande do Sul; also recorded from s. Goiás, perhaps as an austral migrant), e. Paraguay (west to Guairá; few recent records), and ne. Argentina (Misiones; few recent records); w. Bolivia (foothills of La Paz, where recorded from only 2 specimens, with an additional third lacking locality data). Apparently an austral migrant at least to some extent, e.g., occurring in Rio Grande do Sul only during austral summer (Belton 1985); may be an altitudinal migrant as well, nesting in mountains, descending during austral winter. To 1400 m.

Carpornis Berryeaters

A pair of cotingas endemic to the forests of e. Brazil, the two species of berryeaters basically replace each other altitudinally (often with a gap between them), Black-headed occurring lower, Hooded higher. Both have black heads and otherwise mainly olive or yellow plumage.

Carpornis cucullatus

HOODED BERRYEATER   PLATE: 48

DESCRIPTION: 22.5–23 cm (8¾–9"). *Se. Brazil.* Iris brown. *Head, neck, and breast black,* contrasting with *bright yellow nuchal collar and lower underparts. Mantle rich chestnut brown,* becoming olive on rump; wings and tail blackish with olive edging, wings with 2 pale yellow wing-bars. Female like male but with dusky-olive head, neck, and breast; mantle olive *suffused with chestnut;* and sides and flanks faintly scaled with olive.

SIMILAR SPECIES: Cf. Black-headed Berryeater.

HABITAT AND BEHAVIOR: Uncommon in subcanopy and (especially) middle levels of montane forest. Heard much more often than seen, Hooded Berryeater ranges solitarily inside forest, usually perching quite vertically, looking rather slender and trogon-like. Evidently it eats mostly the soft fruits of epiphytic plants (Snow 1982), but birds have also been seen capturing large insects. Its loud, far-carrying calls are one of the characteristic sounds of the wet forests of Brazil's Serra do Mar, though individual calling birds are well separated from each other and the species is never numerous. The call, an abrupt whistled "weeok, wee-ków!," is given at fairly long intervals; the species has the local onomatopoeic name of *corocochó.* Regularly found at the Nova Lombardia Reserve in Espírito Santo and in the Serra do Mar of São Paulo (e.g., at Fazenda Intervales and above Ubatuba).

RANGE: Se. Brazil (Espírito Santo south to Rio Grande do Sul). Mostly 500–1500 m.

Carpornis melanocephalus

BLACK-HEADED BERRYEATER   PLATE: 48

DESCRIPTION: 20.5–21 cm (8–8¼"). *E. Brazil. Iris red. Head, neck, and throat black,* contrasting with *plain olive green upperparts.* Breast dull pale olive, becoming yellower on remaining underparts, *faintly barred with dusky-olive.* Female similar but with some olive on crown and sides of head.

SIMILAR SPECIES: Female of dark-eyed Hooded Berryeater is much brighter yellow below with less barring and has wing-bars and more extensive hood.

HABITAT AND BEHAVIOR: Rare to uncommon and local in subcanopy and middle levels of humid forest; occurs at elevations almost entirely

below those of Hooded Berryeater. General behavior similar to Hooded's but seems less vocal and thus is encountered less often. Black-headed's call is a loud, whistled "tuhweéo"; birds can sometimes be decoyed in to a whistled imitation. Small numbers are found at the Sooretama Reserve in n. Espírito Santo and on Ilha Cardoso in se. São Paulo, but overall numbers have declined greatly because of extensive deforestation in e. Brazil's coastal lowlands; the species deserves formal threatened status. Hooded Berryeater appears to have declined less, for its primary habitat is montane forest, which remains comparatively intact.

RANGE: E. Brazil (Alagoas, and from e. Bahia south to ne. Paraná). Mostly below 300 m, locally up to about 500 m.

Ampelion Cotingas

A pair of rather sluggish cotingas found in the Andes, Red-crested in the temperate zone, Chestnut-crested more locally in the subtropical. Sexes are alike. Both species sport striking nuchal crests, Chestnut-crested's broader, and have rather short and heavy, mainly whitish to bluish gray, bills. S. M. Lanyon and W. E. Lanyon (*Auk* 106[3]: 422–432, 1989) suggested that the genus (as well as *Doliornis* and *Zaratornis*) was most closely related to the plantcutters (*Phytotoma*) and that these genera be removed from the cotingas and placed with the plantcutters in the family Phytotomidae. However, we follow Prum (1990) and Sibley and Monroe (1990) in continuing to treat *Ampelion* as a cotinga genus.

Ampelion rubrocristatus

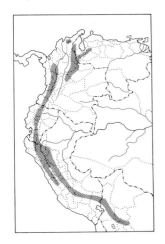

RED-CRESTED COTINGA   PLATE: 49

DESCRIPTION: 21–21.5 cm (8¼–8½"). *Bill chalky white with black tip; iris bright red. Mostly plumbeous gray,* blacker on head, wings, and tail; *semiconcealed nuchal crest of long maroon feathers* usually laid flat over nape (and thus inconspicuous) but sometimes protruding straight out to rear and occasionally flared transversely in spectacular fashion. Some whitish streaking on rump and lower belly, and crissum whitish boldly streaked with black; a *broad white band across tail* is visible mainly in flight and from below. Streaky immature is browner above with whitish back and (especially) rump streaking, no nuchal crest, and mainly yellowish white underparts coarsely streaked with brownish gray.

SIMILAR SPECIES: Adult virtually unmistakable. Immatures, however, can be confusing, though they always show the tail-band (never seen in White-cheeked and Chestnut-crested Cotingas).

HABITAT AND BEHAVIOR: Uncommon to fairly common at borders of montane forest and secondary woodland, also in patches of low woodland and hedgerows with scattered trees in agricultural terrain; occurs regularly up to treeline, e.g., in patches of *Polylepis*-dominated woodland. Generally widespread and conspicuous, though never really numerous, Red-crested Cotinga often perches upright at or near the top of a bush or tree and frequently allows a close approach; it may remain motionless for protracted periods. Most often seen in pairs. Eats mostly fruit, including much mistletoe, but also makes short sallies after flying insects. Although usually quiet, may give a distinctive short, guttural, frog-like "rrreh" (T. A. Parker III) or "trrrrrrrr" (Hilty and Brown 1986), sometimes in flight.

RANGE: Andes of w. Venezuela (north to Trujillo), Colombia, Ecuador, Peru (south on w. slope to Lima), and w. Bolivia (south to w. Santa Cruz); Sierra de Perijá on Venezuela-Colombia border and Santa Marta Mts. in n. Colombia. Mostly 2500–3700 m.

Ampelion rufaxilla

CHESTNUT-CRESTED COTINGA   PLATE: 49

DESCRIPTION: 21 cm (8¼"). A *strikingly patterned* cotinga of subtropical Andean forests. Bill bluish gray with black tip; iris bright red. Forehead grayish, most of crown black with *ample nuchal crest of long bright chestnut feathers* (usually at least somewhat exposed, often quite conspicuous and sometimes flared, fan-like); *remainder of sides of head and neck, and throat, cinnamon-rufous.* Otherwise olivaceous gray above, indistinctly streaked dusky on mantle and rump; wings and tail blackish with rufous-chestnut patch on shoulders. Chest gray; *breast and belly pale yellow boldly streaked blackish.*

HABITAT AND BEHAVIOR: Uncommon and rather local in canopy and borders of montane forest. Behaves much like Red-crested Cotinga but tends to perch higher above the ground and is more of a true tall forest bird (though usually at its edge). Its usual call, often given with crest fully exposed, is a dry, raspy, nasal "reh, r-r-r-r-réh," very reminiscent of a plantcutter's.

RANGE: Locally in Andes of w. Colombia (Cen. Andes, and W. Andes in Valle and Cauca) and on e. slope of Andes in e. Ecuador (sightings from w. Sucumbios along the La Bonita road [J. C. Mathews], and Zamora-Chinchipe in Podocarpus Nat. Park; 1 1992 specimen [ANSP] from west of Zumba in s. Zamora-Chinchipe), e. Peru, and w. Bolivia (La Paz and Cochabamba). 1750–2700 m.

Zaratornis and *Doliornis* Cotingas

A pair of scarce and very local cotingas, both found only at high elevations (mainly in woodland near treeline), primarily in the Andes of Peru; an undescribed *Doliornis* species has recently been found in Ecuador (see below). They are here retained in separate genera, following the evidence presented by S. M. Lanyon and W. E. Lanyon (*Auk* 106[3]: 422–432, 1989); other recent authors (notably Snow 1973 and Snow 1982) had advocated their merger into *Ampelion,* which these birds generally resemble in plumage and behavior.

Zaratornis stresemanni

WHITE-CHEEKED COTINGA   PLATE: 49

DESCRIPTION: 21 cm (8¼"). Local in *Andes of w. Peru.* Bill bluish gray; iris bright red. *Crown black* contrasting with *white face;* above otherwise buff broadly streaked with dusky brown, wing and tail feathers

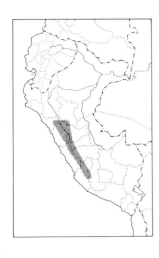

narrowly edged paler. *Throat and chest uniform brownish gray; remaining underparts ochraceous buff broadly streaked dusky,* brightest on unstreaked crissum.

SIMILAR SPECIES: Immature Red-crested Cotinga, which is somewhat similarly streaked, lacks the white cheeks and always shows a white tailband; it and White-cheeked occur together at some localities.

HABITAT AND BEHAVIOR: Rare to uncommon and very local in groves of *Polylepis* woodland, occasionally also in relict patches of more mixed temperate-zone forest. Behavior similar to *Ampelion* cotingas': sluggish, often perching for prolonged periods on partially exposed branches at or near the top of low trees. White-cheeked Cotinga apparently feeds primarily on 2 species of orange-flowered mistletoes and appears to be the primary dispersal agent for their seeds (T. A. Parker III, *Bull. B. O. C.* 101[1]: 256–265, 1981). The song is a nasal, rather frog-like "reh-reh-eh-reh-rrrrrrrrrrr-ré-ré," given most often early in the morning as the sun first illuminates a woodland (T. A. Parker III). Found in woodland patches along the Santa Eulalia road well above Lima. Ever-increasing destruction of *Polylepis* groves for firewood poses a threat to this species in some areas; a population exists in Huascarán Nat. Park in Ancash, but the park itself is in need of better protection.

RANGE: W. Peru (La Libertad at Tayabamba south locally to Ayacucho at Pampa Galeras). 2700–4240 m.

Doliornis sclateri

BAY-VENTED COTINGA

DESCRIPTION: 21.5 cm (8½"). Local on *e. slope of Andes in Peru.* Bill black with base of lower mandible bluish gray; iris gray. *Crown and nape black* with semiconcealed maroon-chestnut nuchal crest; upper back grayish, becoming grayish brown on remaining upperparts, brownest on wings and tail. *Throat and sides of head and neck gray;* remaining underparts brown, with *rich rufous-chestnut crissum.* Female similar but lacks black crown.

SIMILAR SPECIES: Distinctive in its limited range; cf. Red-crested Cotinga.

HABITAT AND BEHAVIOR: Rare to locally uncommon near treeline in canopy and borders of montane forest and in patches of low woodland. Not well known. Usually in pairs, perching stolidly and inconspicuously near tops of trees. Has been seen to eat the small fruits of a melastomataceous shrub (T. A. Parker III, *in* Snow 1982). The only call that has been noted is a raspy "shhh" note, varying in length and intensity (R. Rivera, *in* Snow 1982).

RANGE: Locally on e. slope of Andes in e. Peru (Puerto del Monte in San Martín; east of Tayabamba in e. La Libertad; Carpish Mts. in Huánuco; Pozuzo-Chaglla trail in Pasco; Maraynioc in Junín). Mostly 2500–3450 m, once to 3600 m.

NOTE: Specimens (ANSP) representing an undescribed species of *Doliornis* cotinga were obtained in 1992 in e. Ecuador (se. Carchi and extreme s. Zamora-Chinchipe). The new species has also been observed in Podocarpus Nat. Park.

Ampelioides Fruiteaters

A monotypic genus of arboreal cotinga found locally in humid Andean forests. It is notable for its complex plumage pattern and unusual in that females have the more strikingly patterned underparts. *Ampelioides* superficially resembles the genus *Pipreola* but is shorter-tailed and even plumper, with a heavier and noncolorful bill; vocally it is quite different.

Ampelioides tschudii

SCALED FRUITEATER

PLATE: 49

DESCRIPTION: 19 cm (7½"). Iris yellow; upper mandible black, lower mandible pale olive to grayish. Crown and sides of head black, *lores and long moustachial stripe yellowish white, joining pale yellow nuchal collar;* above black *conspicuously scalloped with bright olive* and with some black and yellow barring on uppertail-coverts; wings mostly black, greater-coverts bright olive forming wide band; tail mostly black, feathers tipped creamy whitish. *Throat whitish;* remaining underparts pale yellow, *feathers broadly edged olive giving scalloped effect.* Female basically similar in pattern but with olive crown, and *underparts with feathers edged black giving even more boldly scalloped effect;* see C-34.
SIMILAR SPECIES: Plump shape, short tail, and overall scalloped pattern make recognition of this fancy cotinga easy.
HABITAT AND BEHAVIOR: Rare to locally uncommon in subcanopy and middle levels of montane forest and forest borders. Rather inconspicuous and sluggish, the Scaled Fruiteater is usually found singly or in pairs and is most apt to be encountered when accompanying mixed flocks of tanagers, various tyrannids, etc. It regularly hops along horizontal limbs searching for insects and also eats much fruit. The song is a loud, far-carrying, and rather raptor-like whistle, "whee-e-é-é-é-eeur" or "ee-ee-ee-ee-oo-ow," fading and dropping toward the end (sounding vaguely like a falling bomb), sometimes repeated at regular 5- to 10-second intervals; it is notably lower-pitched than the calls of *Pipreola* fruiteaters, lacking their sibilant quality.
RANGE: Locally in Andes of Colombia (mostly in W. Andes, north to Antioquia; also in Norte de Santander, and at head of Río Magdalena valley), Ecuador (south on w. slope to w. Loja), e. Peru (south to s. Madre de Dios on Cerros de Pantiacolla [FMNH] and in Cuzco around Hacienda Amazonia), and w. Bolivia (La Paz); Sierra de Perijá on Venezuela-Colombia border and Sierra de Macarena in e. Colombia. Mostly 900–2000 m.

Pipreola Fruiteaters

An attractive group of colorful Andean forest birds, with one outlying and divergent species on the tepuis. *Pipreola* fruiteaters are plump and chunky with rather short tails. Their soft-part colors are usually distinctive, the bills showing some red. All but the tepui endemic are predominantly some shade of green, males often with black on head and/or some red or orange on chest, females more subdued and usually barred or streaked below. Fruiteaters are notably lethargic and are often difficult to find; their high-pitched vocalizations frequently reveal their presence but are notably hard to track down.

GROUP A

Large and boldly barred below; male has *black hood.* Iris color varies.

Pipreola arcuata

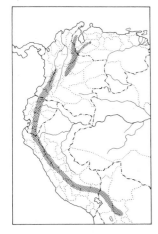

BARRED FRUITEATER
PLATE: 49

DESCRIPTION: 23 cm (9"). A *large* fruiteater of *temperate-zone* Andean forests. Iris color of both sexes variable geographically (and also individually?), usually bright red to orange-red in Colombia and Ecuador, red or yellow in Venezuela, chestnut in n. Peru, and pale yellow to creamy white in *viridicauda* of s. Peru and Bolivia. Bill and legs coral red. Male with *head, throat, and chest glossy black;* above otherwise bright olive, with some black and yellow barring on uppertail-coverts; wings with *large pale yellowish spots on greater-coverts and tertials,* tail with broad black subterminal band and narrow white tipping. *Breast and belly evenly barred black and pale yellow.* See V-26, C-34. Female lacks black on head and chest and has *entire underparts* (including throat) *evenly barred black and pale yellow.*

SIMILAR SPECIES: This, the largest fruiteater, is *mostly found at higher elevations* than the others (Green-and-black and Band-tailed come closest). No other fruiteater shows the black barring below.

HABITAT AND BEHAVIOR: Uncommon in montane forest and forest borders. Usually found singly or in pairs, notably sluggish and unsuspicious. The Barred Fruiteater is most often discovered independent of mixed flocks, but it sometimes joins feeding aggregations at fruiting trees. Its call is so extremely high-pitched that one is apt to ignore it as not coming from a bird; strangely, however, it seems rather far-carrying, and like other fruiteaters' calls it is ventriloquial and very hard to track down. It is a high, thin, "almost hissing" (Hilty and Brown 1986, p. 443) "see-e-e-e-e-e-e-ah"; it is quite long (about 2½ seconds) from Ecuador north, reportedly shorter in Peru.

RANGE: Andes of w. Venezuela (north to sw. Lara), Colombia (in W. Andes recorded only from Cauca), Ecuador (south on w. slope to Pichincha), e. Peru, and w. Bolivia (La Paz and Cochabamba); Sierra de Perijá on Venezuela-Colombia border. Mostly 2000–3300 m.

GROUP B

Both sexes moss green with "hooded" effect, *dark iris,* and *coral red legs.*

Pipreola riefferii

GREEN-AND-BLACK FRUITEATER
PLATE: 49

DESCRIPTION: 17.5–18.5 cm (6¾–7¼"). *Generally the most numerous fruiteater from Ecuador northward.* Bill and legs coral red, iris dark. Male with *entire head, throat, and chest black* suffused with green (especially on throat and chest), *margined on neck and around bib with narrow border of bright yellow;* otherwise bright moss green above, *ter-*

tials narrowly tipped whitish. Lower underparts bright pale yellow; *chachapoyas* and *confusa* of e. Ecuador and n. Peru are more or less mottled and streaked with green across entire belly, but midbelly clear yellow in nominate group found to north and in w. Ecuador (see V-26, C-34). *Tallmanorum* (thus far known only from Huánuco, Peru) is rather different, being *markedly smaller* with a red iris; it lacks the green suffusion on bib and has a clear yellow midbelly. Female like male but with *head and bib green* like back, without the bib's yellow margin, and with entire lower underparts streaked and mottled with green.

SIMILAR SPECIES: In Peru cf. Band-tailed Fruiteater. Otherwise most resembles Black-chested Fruiteater, but both sexes of latter have whitish (not dark) irides and grayish (not red) legs and lack tertial tipping; male Black-chested further differs in lacking yellow margin to bib. Barred Fruiteater is substantially larger, and both sexes show prominent barring below.

HABITAT AND BEHAVIOR: Fairly common to common in lower and middle levels of montane forest, forest borders, and secondary woodland; sometimes also ventures out, seemingly more often than other fruiteaters, into shrubby regenerating clearings. Usually found singly or in pairs, though occasionally more will gather at a fruiting tree; sometimes follows mixed flocks. Rather stolid and unsuspicious, the Green-and-black Fruiteater often perches motionless for protracted periods. Like other *Pipreola*, as far as known it eats only fruit, sometimes taken in a clumsy hover but more often while perched. Its frequently heard song, easily passed over as an insect's, is a very thin, high-pitched, and sibilant "tsi-tsi-tsi-tsi-tsi . . ." series (continuing for up to 4−5 seconds); the last note in the series is sometimes lengthened (e.g., "tsi-tsi-tsi-tsiiiiiiiiyiii").

RANGE: Mts. of n. Venezuela (Aragua to Miranda) and Andes of w. Venezuela (north to s. Lara), Colombia, Ecuador (south on w. slope to El Oro), and e. Peru (south to Huánuco); Sierra de Perijá on Venezuela-Colombia border. Mostly 1500−2700 m, lower on Pacific slope.

NOTE: The recently described form *tallmanorum* (J. P. O'Neill and T. A. Parker III, *Bull. B. O. C.* 101[2]: 294−299, 1981) is quite different from *chachapoyas*, the next race of *P. riefferii* found to the north. When more is known of *tallmanorum*, it may prove more appropriate to treat it as a distinct species (Huanuco Fruiteater).

Pipreola intermedia

BAND-TAILED FRUITEATER

DESCRIPTION: 19 cm (7½"). *Peru and Bolivia.* Resembles Green-and-black Fruiteater but *notably larger* than its actually or potentially sympatric races (*tallmanorum* and *chachapoyas*). Male differs in lacking the green suffusion on bib and in having the yellow margin around bib brighter and deeper, and *quite prominent black chevrons on sides and flanks* (in addition to the green mottling). Unlike Green-and-black, both sexes have a *wide black subterminal tail-band* (somewhat less obvious in female) *and whitish tail-tipping.*

HABITAT AND BEHAVIOR: Fairly common in lower and middle levels of montane forest and forest borders. Behavior similar to Green-and-black Fruiteater's (even their vocalizations are much alike). In their area of overlap (La Libertad and Huánuco, Peru), Band-tailed tends to occur at higher elevations, though they can occur together; at 1 site, both species have even been observed feeding in the same fruiting tree. Regularly noted on the Paty Trail in the Carpish Mts. in Huánuco, Peru.

RANGE: E. slope of Andes in Peru (north to e. La Libertad) and w. Bolivia (La Paz and Cochabamba). Mostly 2300–3000 m.

GROUP C

Both sexes emerald green with *yellow iris*, coral red bill, and *olive-gray legs*. Males superficially appear diverse; females (except Black-chested) yellow-streaked to throat. The *P. aureopectus* superspecies.

Pipreola lubomirskii

BLACK-CHESTED FRUITEATER   PLATE: 49

DESCRIPTION: 17 cm (6¾"). *Local, mainly on e. slope of Andes from s. Colombia to n. Peru.* Male with *head, throat, and center of chest glossy black,* contrasting with bright green upperparts and sides of chest. Breast and belly bright yellow with mottled green streaking on flanks. Female uniform bright green above *and on throat and chest;* lower underparts prominently streaked with green and bright yellow; see C-34.

SIMILAR SPECIES: Not found with any member of its Group, none of which has the male's *solid black bib* nor female's *solid green bib.* Both sexes of much more common Green-and-black Fruiteater differ in soft-part colors (dark eye and red legs in Green-and-black) and have pale tertial tipping; male Green-and-black also has a prominent yellow margin to bib.

HABITAT AND BEHAVIOR: Rare to locally uncommon in lower and middle levels of montane forest, occasionally out to forest borders. Phlegmatic, retiring behavior similar to other fruiteaters'. The song is a very high, thin, piercing "pseee, pseeét."

RANGE: E. slope of Andes (mainly) in s. Colombia (slopes around head of Río Magdalena valley in Huila, and in se. Nariño), e. Ecuador, and n. Peru (west of the Río Marañón in Cajamarca). 1500–2300 m.

NOTE: See comments under Golden-breasted Fruiteater.

Pipreola pulchra

MASKED FRUITEATER   PLATE: 49

DESCRIPTION: 18 cm (7"). *E. slope of Andes in Peru.* Male mostly bright green above (*including crown*), *darker from sides of head to upper throat. Lower throat and center of chest orange,* connected to broad yellow band arching up onto sides of neck, and margined narrowly with black; lower underparts bright yellow with mottled green streaking on sides and flanks. Female uniform bright green above; *entire underparts green narrowly streaked with yellow.*

SIMILAR SPECIES: Not sympatric with any other member of its

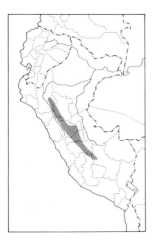

Group; Masked's range comes closest to Black-chested, but that species is recorded in n. Peru only west of the upper Río Marañón, with Masked only east of it from Amazonas southward. Male Scarlet-breasted Fruiteater has much brighter scarlet patch on chest, shows tertial tipping, and lacks the black mask and partial yellow "collar." Female Scarlet-breasted likewise shows tertial tipping and has a yellower throat contrasting with more solidly green breast.

HABITAT AND BEHAVIOR: Rare to uncommon in lower and middle levels of montane forest, sometimes also at forest borders and in mature secondary woodland. Behavior (including voice) much like other subtropical-zone fruiteaters'. Can be seen in small numbers in the Divisoria area of the Cordillera Azul, east of Tingo Maria in Huánuco, Peru.

RANGE: E. slope of Andes in Peru (Amazonas south to n. Cuzco on the Cordillera Vilcabamba). 1500–2200 m.

NOTE: See comments under Golden-breasted Fruiteater.

Pipreola jucunda

ORANGE-BREASTED FRUITEATER

DESCRIPTION: 18 cm (7″). *W. slope of Andes in s. Colombia and Ecuador.* Resembles Masked Fruiteater (no overlap) but male with *entire head and throat glossy black* (no green on crown) and breast more fiery orange. See C-34. Females indistinguishable in the field.

SIMILAR SPECIES: Male Golden-breasted Fruiteater lacks black on head. Females are very similar, but Golden-breasted has pale tertial tipping (lacking in Orange-breasted) and shows more yellow streaking on throat.

HABITAT AND BEHAVIOR: Uncommon to locally fairly common in lower and middle growth of montane forest and forest borders, especially in mossy cloud forest. Behavior much like other fruiteaters'. Its song is an extremely high-pitched, thin, hissing "see-e-e-e-e-e-e-e-e-e-e" (Hilty and Brown 1986) or "pseee-eeet." Most easily found above Junín in w. Nariño, Colombia; rather scarce, at least in readily accessible areas, in Ecuador.

RANGE: W. slope of W. Andes in s. Colombia (north to s. Chocó) and w. Ecuador (south to e. Guayas; in recent years recorded south only to Pichincha). 600–1700 m.

NOTE: See comments under Golden-breasted Fruiteater.

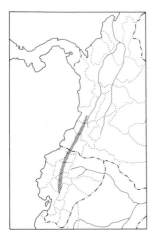

Pipreola aureopectus

GOLDEN-BREASTED FRUITEATER

DESCRIPTION: 16.5–17 cm (6½–6¾″). *Venezuela and Colombia.* Male above bright green, sometimes tinged bluish especially on nape and mantle; tertials tipped whitish. Chin also green, *throat and center of chest bright golden yellow;* lower underparts paler lemon yellow, with mottled green streaking on sides and flanks. Foregoing is *festiva* of n. Venezuela (see V-26); nominate race (Andes of w. Venezuela and Colombia) has more green streaking across midbelly; *decora* (Colombia's Santa Marta Mts.) like *festiva* but with narrow yellow line arching

up beneath ear-coverts (see C-34). Females of all races are bright green above with *pale tertial tipping; below entirely streaked green and yellow* (yellowest on throat and midbelly).

SIMILAR SPECIES: Male Handsome Fruiteater has black head and fiery area on chest, whereas female is barred (not streaked) below with a golden patch on upper chest. Male Orange-breasted Fruiteater also has a black head (and throat) and is truly orange (not golden) on chest; female Orange-breasted is very like female Golden-breasted Fruiteater but *lacks* tertial tipping.

HABITAT AND BEHAVIOR: Fairly common but somewhat local in lower and especially middle growth of montane forest across n. portion of its range, but seemingly rare and decidedly local in Andes. In the latter it overlaps with Orange-breasted Fruiteater, but that species is considerably more numerous. Behavior similar to other fruiteaters'; voice much like Orange-breasted's. Quite readily seen around Colonia Tovar in n. Venezuela and in Santa Marta Mts. (where the only fruiteater present).

RANGE: Mts. of n. Venezuela (Carabobo to Aragua), and Andes of w. Venezuela (Lara to Táchira) and very locally in Colombia (recorded from E. Andes in Norte de Santander, n. end of Cen. Andes in Antioquia, and W. Andes from Antioquia to w. Nariño); Sierra de Perijá on Venezuela-Colombia border and Santa Marta Mts. in n. Colombia. Mostly 1000–2300 m.

NOTE: It has been suggested (e.g., *Birds of the World*, vol. 8) that the four species we here consider the *P. aureopectus* superspecies should be treated as a single, polytypic species. However, as Snow himself (1982, p. 69) later pointed out, there is now evidence of "extensive sympatry" in *P. aureopectus* and *P. jucunda* in the W. Andes of Colombia. Whether these species actually occur syntopically has not yet, to our knowledge, actually been demonstrated (*P. aureopectus* tends to occur at slightly higher elevations in the area of overlap), but they certainly range very close to each other, with no evidence of intergradation.

GROUP D

Males diverse, though all share a *fiery red chest patch;* females all have green *barring* on lower underparts.

Pipreola frontalis

SCARLET-BREASTED FRUITEATER   PLATE: 49

DESCRIPTION: 15.5–16.5 cm (6–6½″). *Andes of e. Ecuador to w. Bolivia.* Iris yellow; male's bill and legs coral red to orange, female's much duskier. Male of nominate race (Bolivia and s. Peru north to Junín) mostly bright green above, frontlet more blackish; tertials tipped pale yellowish. Upper throat yellow, becoming *fiery red on lower throat and center of chest; remaining underparts mainly yellow* with some green mottling on flanks. Female has upperparts like male's but with frontlet yellow. *Throat yellow, breast virtually solid green* (faint yellow shaft streaks are barely apparent); belly yellow barred with green. *Squamipectus* (Ecuador south to n. Peru in San Martín) is rather different, being markedly *smaller* though with longer bill. Male differs in having *crown shiny dark bluish green* and less red on throat; female has much

less yellow on forecrown, less contrasting yellow throat (with considerable green scaling), and more yellow scaling on green breast.
SIMILAR SPECIES: Fiery-throated Fruiteater is quite similar, particularly resembling the small n. race of Scarlet-breasted, but is *even smaller*. Males are best told by their green (not mainly yellow) lower underparts; females are hard to separate aside from the size difference, though Fiery-throated shows no yellow at all on forecrown (remember that female *squamipectus* has very little) and is paler yellow on belly. Fiery-throated mostly occurs at lower elevations than Scarlet-breasted. Cf. also (in Peru) Masked Fruiteater.

HABITAT AND BEHAVIOR: Uncommon to locally fairly common in middle levels and subcanopy of montane forest. Behavior much like other fruiteaters' but rather more arboreal than most and more apt to accompany mixed flocks. What is evidently the song of male *squamipectus* is a very high, thin, and *short* "psiii."

RANGE: E. slope of Andes in Ecuador (north to w. Napo), Peru (San Martín, and from Huánuco south), and w. Bolivia (La Paz, Cochabamba, and w. Santa Cruz). Mostly 1100–2000 m, in small numbers lower (recorded by Snow [1982] down to 670 m in Peru).

NOTE: Two species may be involved, for no intergradation between *squamipectus* and the rather different nominate form has been demonstrated in n. Peru, though the explanation for this might only be that the intervening region between their ranges remains ornithologically little known. Should *P. squamipectus* be regarded as a full species, it would be best called the Bluish-fronted Fruiteater.

Pipreola chlorolepidota

FIERY-THROATED FRUITEATER   PLATE: 49

DESCRIPTION: 13 cm (5"). *A very small fruiteater of Andean foothills.* Iris grayish white to bluish gray; bill salmon tipped dusky (more blackish in female); legs orange. Male bright green above, tertials tipped whitish. *Throat and chest scarlet* (almost with effect of a "breast plate"), *contrasting with green of remaining underparts,* belly somewhat more yellowish. Female with upperparts like male's; *below rather uniformly and coarsely scaled green and yellowish,* greenest on breast.
SIMILAR SPECIES: Cf. larger Scarlet-breasted Fruiteater (which usually occurs at higher elevations). Fiery-throated is so small that females can easily be mistaken for manakins (their shapes are not dissimilar), perhaps especially a female Blue-backed (whose legs are also orange). However, no manakin is scaled or barred below, and none shows pale tertial tipping.
HABITAT AND BEHAVIOR: Rare to locally uncommon in lower and middle growth of humid forest in foothills near e. base of Andes. Has been observed accompanying mixed flocks of various tanagers, furnariids, etc., and at fruiting trees, but on the whole not a well-known species. We do not know its voice.
RANGE: Foothills along e. slope of Andes in s. Colombia (sightings from w. Caquetá), Ecuador, and n. and cen. Peru (south to Pasco). Mostly 600–1200 m, in small numbers lower (to 250 m in Ecuador).

Pipreola formosa

HANDSOME FRUITEATER

DESCRIPTION: 16.5 cm (6½"). *N. Venezuela.* Iris dark; bill salmon red; legs grayish olive. Male has *head and throat glossy black,* contrasting with bright green of remaining upperparts; tertial spots whitish. *Patch on chest fiery orange;* remaining underparts bright yellow, washed with green on flanks. Female lacks black on head and throat; above otherwise like male. Throat green, *small patch on chest golden yellow; remaining underparts more or less evenly barred green and yellow.* See V-26.

SIMILAR SPECIES: Male unmistakable in range; no other fruiteater in n. Venezuela has orange on chest. Female is the only small fruiteater in its range that looks *barred* below (Golden-breasted is *streaked*), and no other shows the fairly conspicuous chest patch.

HABITAT AND BEHAVIOR: Fairly common in lower and middle growth of montane forest and forest borders. Usually seen singly or in pairs, perching quietly in lower growth or coming out to a fruiting tree at forest edge; seldom with mixed flocks. Readily found near Rancho Grande in Henri Pittier Nat. Park.

RANGE: Mts. of n. Venezuela (Paria Peninsula west to Yaracuy). 800–2200 m.

GROUP E

Both sexes unique; confined to *tepuis.*

Pipreola whitelyi

RED-BANDED FRUITEATER   PLATE: 49

DESCRIPTION: 16.5–17 cm (6½–6¾"). *An unmistakable fruiteater of the tepuis.* Iris orange (male) to ochre (female); bill and legs salmon red, female's duller. Male mostly dull grayish green above with *tawny-gold forehead and long superciliary arching around ear-coverts; wings and tail mostly tawny brown. Below mostly gray* with *broad orange-red pectoral band,* crissum ochraceous. Female very different, moss green above with *paler greenish yellow echoing male's head pattern;* wing and tail feathers edged paler olive. Below yellowish white *boldly streaked with black.*

SIMILAR SPECIES: Female might be confused with Sharpbill or various spotted tanagers, but apart from bill differences it is obviously streaked (not spotted or scaled) below.

HABITAT AND BEHAVIOR: Rare to uncommon in middle levels of montane forest and forest borders. This fruiteater's inconspicuous general behavior is much like its congeners; it usually remains inside forest but sometimes comes out to the edge at fruiting trees. Its song is a drawn out, very high and thin "pss-ee-ee-ee-ee-ee-ee," given at long intervals from high in trees (T. Davis). Small numbers of this species, arguably the most distinctive of the tepui endemics, can be found along the Escalera road in e. Bolívar, but even there it can be difficult to locate.

RANGE: Tepuis of s. Venezuela (e. Bolívar) and adjacent Guyana (Mt. Twek-quay). 1300–2230 m.

Porphyrolaema Cotingas

A monotypic genus reminiscent in shape and behavior of the genus *Cotinga* but with a heavier, stubby bill. Males have a different color pattern, and the fringing on the upperparts of both sexes is unique.

Porphyrolaema
porphyrolaema

PURPLE-THROATED COTINGA   PLATE: 50

DESCRIPTION: 18–18.5 cm (7–7¼″). W. Amazonia. Male *black above,* feathers of scapulars, back, and rump *fringed white;* a single broad white wing-stripe and edging on tertials. *Throat deep purple; remaining underparts white,* center of chest stained purple, with some black barring on lower flanks. Female mostly dark brown above, *feathers fringed buffy whitish, crown irregularly barred buff and blackish. Throat bright cinnamon-buff, remaining underparts narrowly and evenly barred black and buff,* crissum pale cinnamon-buff.
SIMILAR SPECIES: Male essentially unmistakable; female recalls females of various *Cotinga* cotingas, none of which is truly barred below (they are scaled or spotted) or shows a deep buff throat.
HABITAT AND BEHAVIOR: Rare to uncommon in canopy and borders of humid forest, both in terra firme and várzea. Behavior much like *Cotinga* cotingas', often perching on high exposed branches where it takes the early morning sun, but at other times generally inconspicuous and seen most often at fruiting trees. Unlike *Cotinga* cotingas, however, the Purple-throated seems to often occur as pairs, implying a difference in its breeding strategy (its nest is as yet unknown). The infrequently heard call, a high, plaintive "preeeeeeer" repeated over and over but easily overlooked, is reminiscent of a common vocalization of Dusky-capped Flycatcher (Hilty and Brown 1986).
RANGE: Se. Colombia (recorded only from w. Caquetá and the Leticia area, but likely more widespread), e. Ecuador, e. Peru (south to Madre de Dios), and w. Amaz. Brazil (east to the lower Rio Negro area near Manaus and n. Mato Grosso at Alta Floresta); should occur in extreme nw. Bolivia. Mostly below 400 m, but recorded to 900 m in n. Peru.

Cotinga Cotingas

A distinctive and well-known genus of arboreal birds found in humid lowland forests (the "blue-cotingas"), males famed for their vibrant blues, the shades of which vary from species to species. Females are brown and more obscure, usually quite scaly, but easily recognized to genus by their distinctive silhouette: a small, rounded, dove-like head, plump shape, and upright posture. There are five South American members of the genus (two additional species in Middle America); all except the distinctive Spangled Cotinga have allopatric ranges. None seems to produce any vocal sounds. Their food is mostly (entirely?) large fruits. Nests are placed on high horizontal branches, either in a fork or next to an epiphytic plant, and females care for the young alone.

GROUP A

Males *deeper*, more *cobalt* blue; *more extensive purple below*. Females *conspicuously scaled and spotted*.

Cotinga maculata

BANDED COTINGA

PLATE: 50

DESCRIPTION: 20 cm (7¾"). *Se. Brazil*. Male *mostly bright deep cobalt blue above*, black bases of feathers showing through irregularly; most of wing (except lesser-coverts) and tail black. *Underparts mostly bright deep purple*, with *band of cobalt blue across upper breast;* lower belly also cobalt blue. Female dusky brown above, feathers tipped and scaled whitish, often with an indistinct whitish eye-ring. Below pale grayish buff, feathers with darker centers, giving *a bold spotted and scaled effect*.
SIMILAR SPECIES: The only *Cotinga* in its limited range. Female of sympatric White-winged Cotinga is much grayer and more uniform looking and shows bold white on wing.
HABITAT AND BEHAVIOR: Rare to locally uncommon in canopy and borders of humid forest, to a limited extent also out into adjacent secondary woodland. Sometimes perches on high exposed branches in early morning, but more often seen in fast direct swooping flight or when visiting fruiting trees; there several may gather, occasionally with White-winged Cotingas. Banded Cotinga is now severely threatened by deforestation and seems even scarcer than White-winged; small numbers remain in the Sooretama Reserve and the adjacent Rio Doce Reserve in n. Espírito Santo, this area likely forming the species' primary remaining stronghold.
RANGE: Se. Brazil (s. Bahia south locally to Minas Gerais and Rio de Janeiro). Below 200 m.

Cotinga cotinga

PURPLE-BREASTED COTINGA

DESCRIPTION: 18 cm (7"). *Ne. South America*. Much like Banded Cotinga (no overlap) but *markedly smaller*. Male differs in having *entire throat and breast purple* (no intervening blue band). Female very similar aside from the size difference. See V-26, C-34.
SIMILAR SPECIES: Male's hue is a considerably deeper, more cobalt, blue than either Plum-throated's or (especially) Spangled Cotinga's, and its purple extends much lower down on underparts. Female is more difficult to identify, but Plum-throated and Spangled are noticeably larger and much less conspicuously scaled or spotted below.
HABITAT AND BEHAVIOR: Rare to locally uncommon in canopy and borders of humid forest, including (primarily?) forest and woodland in areas with sandy soil ("sandy-belt forest" or "savanna forest"). Behavior similar to other *Cotinga* cotingas'; like them most often seen in early morning when perched on a high exposed branch, where it may remain for protracted periods, or when feeding at a fruiting tree. Males' wings emit a characteristic sharp and often surprisingly loud whirr in flight.
RANGE: Guianas, s. Venezuela (e. Bolívar and s. Amazonas), extreme e. Colombia (e. Guainía to Vaupés), and n. and e. Amaz. Brazil

(mainly north of the Amazon from the Rio Negro drainage eastward, south of it from the lower Rio Tapajós east to n. Goiás and w. Maranhão). To 800 m (in Venezuela).

Cotinga nattererii

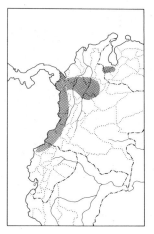

BLUE COTINGA

DESCRIPTION: 18.5 cm (7¼″). *Nw. Venezuela to nw. Ecuador.* Male generally resembles male of geographically distant Banded Cotinga but somewhat smaller, the blue somewhat paler and more turquoise, and the purple on underparts reduced to a large throat patch and another patch down middle of lower breast and belly. Females of the 2 species are very similar, though Blue is more cinnamon-buff on belly. See P-26.

SIMILAR SPECIES: The only *Cotinga* cotinga found west of Andes in South America, thus readily recognizable.

HABITAT AND BEHAVIOR: Uncommon in canopy and borders of humid forest and secondary woodland. Behavior much like other *Cotinga* cotingas'. Blue Cotinga appears more likely than its congeners to occur up into the foothills.

RANGE: Extreme w. Venezuela (Maracaibo basin in Táchira and Mérida), n. and w. Colombia (humid Caribbean lowlands east to middle Río Magdalena valley in Santander and w. Boyacá, and south on Pacific slope to Nariño), and nw. Ecuador (Esmeraldas). Also Panama. To 1000 m.

GROUP B

Males *paler,* more *turquoise* blue; *only throat purple.* Females more uniform, *scaling and spotting reduced.*

Cotinga maynana

PLUM-THROATED COTINGA   PLATE: 50

DESCRIPTION: 19.5 cm (7¾″). W. Amazonia. Iris yellow (evidently duller in immatures and some females), but this usually not very evident in the field. Male *almost entirely bright shining turquoise blue* (scattered pink feather bases showing through); flight feathers black, and some black on tail; *small throat patch shining plum purple.* Female grayish brown above, feathers narrowly and inconspicuously scaled with buff. Below slightly paler grayish brown, *becoming more ochraceous on belly,* feathers of breast and, to a lesser extent, throat and belly darkcentered, imparting a somewhat scaly look.

SIMILAR SPECIES: Male Spangled Cotinga has paler blue plumage with considerable scattered black showing through and has more extensively black wings and a markedly larger area of purple on throat. Female Spangled is similar to Plum-throated (both being more uniform and less scaly below than other female *Cotinga*) and at times they are hard to distinguish. Female Spangled is slightly darker and more grayish (less brown) overall, is decidedly less ochraceous on belly (only a buff tinge), and has underwing-coverts dull buff (in Plum-throated brighter cinnamon-buff; in good light this is sometimes quite evident in flight).

HABITAT AND BEHAVIOR: Uncommon to fairly common in canopy and borders of humid forest, in both terra firme and várzea but in most areas especially the latter, and in tall trees of adjacent cleared areas. Behavior much like other *Cotinga* cotingas'; sometimes feeds with Spangled Cotinga in the same tree. Especially numerous and quite readily seen in the lowlands of e. Ecuador.

RANGE: Se. Colombia (north to Caquetá and Vaupés), e. Ecuador, e. Peru, n. Bolivia (Beni and n. La Paz), and w. Amaz. Brazil (north of the Amazon east to w. bank of the lower Rio Negro, south of it east to Rondônia and w. bank of the lower Rio Madeira). Mostly below 700 m, exceptionally to 1200 m in Ecuador.

Cotinga cayana

SPANGLED COTINGA

PLATE: 50

DESCRIPTION: 20 cm (8″). Widespread from Amazonia to Guianas. Male *mostly pale shining turquoise blue* with black bases of many feathers showing through especially on head, back, and scapulars; *wings and tail mostly black,* feathers edged with the same pale blue; *large patch on throat and upper chest bright magenta purple.* Female *rather dark grayish brown above and on throat and breast,* feathers narrowly scaled whitish. Lower underparts somewhat paler grayish brown, feathers edged buffy whitish.

SIMILAR SPECIES: Male Plum-throated Cotinga is not as pale a blue, looks quite uniform (with virtually no black showing through), has much smaller throat patch, and shows much less black on wing. Female resembles female Plum-throated Cotinga (they often are hard to distinguish in the field, regularly occur together, and even feed simultaneously in the same tree), but Plum-throated is not so dark and ashy-looking generally and shows more buff on belly and brighter buff underwing-coverts.

HABITAT AND BEHAVIOR: Uncommon to fairly common in canopy and borders of humid forest and woodland, tending to be more numerous eastward and usually outnumbered in w. Amazonia by Plum-throated. General behavior much like other *Cotinga* cotingas'.

RANGE: Guianas, s. Venezuela (Bolívar and Amazonas north to Delta Amacura, and in sw. Táchira), e. Colombia, e. Ecuador, e. Peru, n. Bolivia (south to La Paz and Cochabamba), and Amaz. Brazil (south to Rondônia, n. Mato Grosso, and n. Goiás; east to w. Maranhão). To 600 m.

Xipholena Cotingas

A trio of magnificent cotingas (the "purple-cotingas") found in the canopy of humid lowland forests, mainly in e. South America. Males are among the most striking neotropical birds, with stiff glossy body feathers and contrasting white wings; two species have highly modified greater wing-coverts which, quetzal-like, are lengthened and partially cover the flight feathers. Females are drab and gray with distinctive white edging on wings. Their behavior (including nesting) and ecology are much like the *Cotinga* cotingas'.

Xipholena punicea

POMPADOUR COTINGA

DESCRIPTION: 19.5 cm (7¾"). Mainly Guianas and cen. Amazonia. Iris pale yellow. Male *mostly shining crimson-purple* with *mainly white wings;* some of the purple scapular feathers are stiff, pointed, and elongated ("spear-like"), extending down over the white flight feathers. Female *mostly uniform ashy gray,* whiter on lower belly and crissum; *wingcoverts and inner flight feathers conspicuously edged with white.*

SIMILAR SPECIES: Stunning adult males are unmistakable at any distance in reasonably good light—even in poor light the contrasting white wings are normally evident. No other *Xipholena* cotinga normally occurs with this species. Birds in female plumage (some of them immature males) are unfortunately seen more often than full adult males; they can be known by their overall gray appearance with rather conspicuous pale eye and white edging on wing. Females of other *Xipholena* cotingas are more mottled or scaled below (not so smoothly gray).

HABITAT AND BEHAVIOR: Uncommon to locally fairly common in canopy and borders of humid forest and woodland (the latter especially in areas with sandy soils). Pompadour Cotingas are most numerous north of the Amazon from Guianas to e. Colombia; they are much less common in w. Amazonia, where the scatter of records either represent localized populations (in areas with sandy soil?) or merely wandering birds. They are often very conspicuous, especially the males whose white wings flash against the dark green of the forest canopy at astonishingly long distances. Both sexes often perch on high exposed branches, particularly in early morning. They seem somewhat more gregarious than *Cotinga* cotingas, not only gathering in small groups when feeding at fruiting trees but also when males are displaying. Then several (usually 2 or 3) males engage in a "ritual chase" in which a male slowly flies at another perched bird which flutters off a short distance and lands again. This process is repeated over and over in a relatively restricted area (see Snow 1982 for fuller discussion); sometimes a female or two are perched nearby, but they never seem to participate actively. Pompadour Cotingas are mainly silent, but a hollow mechanical rattle is sometimes heard (D. Stotz).

RANGE: Guianas, s. Venezuela (Bolívar and Amazonas), extreme e. Colombia (e. Guainía to e. Vaupés, also once in n. Arauca), Amaz. Brazil (north of the Amazon from the Rio Negro drainage east to Amapá, south of it from the Rio Juruá and south of Tefé east to the lower Rio Madeira and south to Rondônia and s. Mato Grosso), and ne. Bolivia (ne. Santa Cruz on the Serranía de Huanchaca); 1 record from se. Ecuador (an immature male taken at "Río Corrientes" in 1964 [ANSP]). To 1300 m (in Venezuela).

Xipholena lamellipennis

WHITE-TAILED COTINGA

DESCRIPTION: 20.5 cm (8″). *Lower Amaz. Brazil south of the Amazon.* Iris pale yellow. Male *mostly shining purplish black,* feathers very stiff and pointed (with an odd, matted effect); wings and *tail entirely white* (the tail somewhat longer than in other *Xipholena* cotingas); elongated dark scapular feathers as in Pompadour Cotinga. Female like female Pompadour Cotinga but *more mottled with grayish and whitish on breast.*

SIMILAR SPECIES: Usually this striking cotinga is not sympatric with other *Xipholena* cotingas, though it and Pompadour have been recorded from several localities in w. Pará, Brazil. Male Pompadour's body plumage is much more purple (less black), and its tail is dark (not white); female Pompadour is "smoother" gray below with no mottled effect. Female *Cotinga* cotingas lack white edging on wing feathers and have a dark iris.

HABITAT AND BEHAVIOR: Rare to locally uncommon in canopy and borders of humid forest. Little is known about this relatively poorly studied species' behavior, but it seems much like Pompadour Cotinga's. Snow (1982) describes a solitary male's display flight in which it repeatedly fluttered up into the air from canopy perches. Substantial numbers occur in the still quite extensive upland forests south of Santarém, but it has doubtless declined considerably in the more deforested Belém region to the east.

RANGE: Lower Amaz. Brazil south of the Amazon from the Rio Tapajós drainage (including its w. bank) east to n. Maranhão. Below 400 m.

Xipholena atropurpurea

WHITE-WINGED COTINGA

DESCRIPTION: 19 cm (7½″). *E. Brazil.* Iris pale yellow; bill dark purplish. Male *mostly blackish purple,* more brownish purple on tail, and purer purple on crissum; *wings mainly white.* Female like female Pompadour Cotinga but breast more mottled with whitish. Looks quite short-tailed.

SIMILAR SPECIES: Occurs far from the range of either of the other *Xipholena* cotingas. Male's body plumage is intermediate between the purple of Pompadour and the blackish of White-winged; its elongated scapulars are comparatively rudimentary so its pure white wing stands out even more than theirs. Female Banded Cotinga looks much scalier below, lacks the white edging on wing feathers, and has a dark eye.

HABITAT AND BEHAVIOR: Rare to locally uncommon in canopy and borders of humid forest and mature secondary woodland. Behavior appears similar to other *Xipholena* cotingas', though no flight display has yet been described. In flight males (only?) often have a characteristic, rather loud wing-whirring which White-tailed and Pompadour Cotingas seemingly lack. White-winged is now threatened by deforestation in much of its range but probably not quite to the extent of the often-sympatric Banded Cotinga: the former's range is larger (small numbers persist even in Alagoas, well to the north of Banded's range), and it seems more numerous in at least 1 major stronghold for both, the Sooretama/Rio Doce Reserves in n. Espírito Santo.

RANGE: E. Brazil (Paraíba, e. Pernambuco, and Alagoas; se. Bahia, Espírito Santo, and n. Rio de Janeiro). To 700 m.

Carpodectes Cotingas

These stunningly white, somewhat dove-like cotingas (the "white-cotingas") appear to be the trans-Andean allies of the *Xipholena* cotingas; there are two additional, slightly smaller species in s. Central America. Females are grayer. *Carpodectes* and *Xipholena* seem similar behaviorally, and their females are much alike in plumage. Male *Carpodectes,* however, have very soft feathers, completely different from the hard glossy texture of *Xipholena*'s feathers.

Carpodectes hopkei

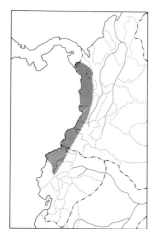

BLACK-TIPPED COTINGA

Other: White Cotinga

PLATE: 50

DESCRIPTION: 23.5–24 cm (9¼–9½"). *W. Colombia and nw. Ecuador.* Iris orange. Male *pure snowy white;* outer primaries and central tail feathers minutely tipped black (the black inconspicuous in the field, when one is simply dazzled by the bird's whiteness). Female slightly smaller, *mainly gray above,* blackish on wings and tail, *wing-coverts and inner flight feathers conspicuously edged with white.* Throat and breast somewhat paler gray, becoming grayish white on belly.

SIMILAR SPECIES: Unmistakable male is so white that it can often be spotted from tremendous distances. Female looks rather like female of geographically distant Pompadour Cotinga; were they to occur together they would be hard to distinguish, though Black-tipped is markedly larger.

HABITAT AND BEHAVIOR: Uncommon in canopy and borders of humid forest, sometimes, especially to feed, out into adjacent second-growth or clearings with scattered tall trees. Often very conspicuous (especially males), perching high on exposed limbs or flapping slowly between tree tops on broad, rounded wings. Regularly found in small groups of up to 6 or more birds, both when congregating at fruiting trees and when moving through canopy. They are not known to vocalize. Small numbers can be found in the partially deforested terrain around Buenaventura, Colombia.

RANGE: W. Colombia (Pacific lowlands from Chocó southward) and nw. Ecuador (mainly in Esmeraldas, in smaller numbers, and, mainly formerly, south into w. Pichincha). Also in e. Panama. To about 700 m; once recorded in Colombia at 1450 m.

NOTE: In some recent literature known as the White Cotinga, an almost equally good name though males are only slightly whiter than other members of the genus. The male's black wing-tips, though inconspicuous, are unique. We follow Ridgely (1976) and the 1983 AOU Check-list in employing "Black-tipped."

Conioptilon Cotingas

A recently discovered species and monotypic genus (G. H. Lowery and J. P. O'Neill, *Auk* 83[1]: 1–9, 1966), thus far found only in the lowland forests of se. Peru. Its closest relative has been supposed to be *Carpodectes* (see also Snow 1982), which we agree is generally similar. *Conioptilon*'s plumage and behavior, however, differ markedly from that of *Carpodectes;* further, unlike that genus, *Conioptilon* is monomorphic and quite vocal. One of *Conioptilon*'s unusual features is its abundant powderdown patches which *Carpodectes,* as well as most passerine birds, lack. Nothing seems to be known about nesting.

Conioptilon mcilhennyi

BLACK-FACED COTINGA   PLATE: 50

DESCRIPTION: 23 cm (9″). *Local in se. Peru.* Virtually unmistakable. *Crown, face, and throat black* (latter with short spiny feathers), facial area with whitish border; otherwise *dark gray above,* more blackish on wings and tail (latter more silvery gray from above); remaining *underparts much paler gray* with somewhat ruffled or flammulated effect on breast, becoming white on lower belly and crissum. Sexes alike.

HABITAT AND BEHAVIOR: Fairly common but local in subcanopy of humid forest, almost invariably in swampy or seasonally flooded forest along lake or river margins (not in terra firme). Usually in independent pairs, though regularly congregating with other frugivorous birds at fruiting trees; only rarely with mixed flocks. Flight is swooping, the birds often hover-gleaning as they snatch at fruit; behavior in many ways much like Purple-throated Fruitcrow's. The call is a distinctive, ascending, whinny, rather loud and far-carrying, "o-o-o-e-e-eeé?," reminiscent of one of the vocalizations of Smooth-billed Ani (*Crotophaga ani*). The Black-faced Cotinga is numerous along the upper Río Manu in Manu Nat. Park and is present in small numbers near the Manu Lodge; it has also been found at Cuzco Amazonico near Puerto Maldonado (but, inexplicably, never at the nearby Tambopata Reserve).

RANGE: Se. Peru (s. Ucayali at Balta; s. Madre de Dios in Manu Nat. Park and near Puerto Maldonado, rarely near Shintuya). Seems likely to occur in adjacent w. Brazil and nw. Bolivia. 300 m, rarely to 450 m.

Laniocera Mourners

A pair of mourners found inside lowland forest on either side of the Andes. Both superficially resemble two *Rhytipterna* mourner species (Grayish and Rufous), but the genera are now believed not to be closely related. Lanyon (1985) concluded that, based on anatomical considerations, *Rhytipterna* should be placed in the Tyrannidae near *Myiarchus,* whereas *Laniocera* appears to be a true cotingid. Even more recent evidence (Prum and Lanyon 1989) indicates that *Laniocera* may belong in what has been termed the "*Schiffornis* assemblage," in a position between the cotingas and the tyrant flycatchers. We retain the genus's placement in its usual position with the cotingas. As yet no nest has been found; its construction would be of interest.

Laniocera hypopyrrha

CINEREOUS MOURNER

PLATE: 51

DESCRIPTION: 20 cm (8″). *East* of Andes. Narrow golden eye-ring. *Mostly ashy gray,* somewhat paler below; wings duskier with *2 rows of large cinnamon-rufous spots,* tail feathers and tertials also tipped with cinnamon-rufous; crissum tinged rufous, with faint dusky barring. *Pectoral tuft either pale yellow or orange-rufous,* but often hidden beneath wings; this seems to be individually variable and is not correlated with age or sex. Immatures show some rufous on breast (more on younger birds) intermixed with a variable number of black spots; based on the large number of specimens that show it, this plumage is retained for a considerable time.

SIMILAR SPECIES: Grayish Mourner, often found in the same areas, lacks the conspicuous rufous wing-spotting; it also has a somewhat flatter-crowned (less rounded) head shape, with a "fiercer" expression (not "soft" and dove-like as in Cinereous). Cf. also Screaming Piha.

HABITAT AND BEHAVIOR: Rare to uncommon in lower and middle growth inside humid forest and woodland; seems more numerous eastward. Usually inconspicuous and not often seen, though one is occasionally spotted accompanying understory flocks of antshrikes and antwrens. Males deliver a tirelessly repeated song from regularly used perches: a high, ringing "teeyr, teeoweét, teeoweét, teeoweét . . ." (up to 10 "teeoweét"s in succession, then a pause before starting up again). This carries far and is quite ventriloquial, and is often given in the heat of the day.

RANGE: Guianas, s. Venezuela (Delta Amacuro west through Bolívar and Amazonas), e. Colombia (north to s. Casanare and e. Guainía), e. Ecuador, e. Peru, n. Bolivia (south to La Paz, Cochabamba, and Santa Cruz), and Amaz. Brazil (south to s. Mato Grosso, and east to n. Maranhão); e. Brazil (se. Bahia and Espírito Santo). Mostly below 500 m, occasionally up to at least 900 m on e. slope of Andes.

Laniocera rufescens

SPECKLED MOURNER

DESCRIPTION: 20 cm (8″). *W. Colombia and nw. Ecuador. Mostly rufous brown,* breast feathers often scaled with dusky (more pronounced in immatures, and sometimes intermixed with a few black spots); *wing-coverts dusky,* feathers with *large rufous tips.* Male has pale yellow pectoral tuft (often hidden behind wing), usually lacking in female and immature (in which rarely orange-ochraceous?). See C-35.

SIMILAR SPECIES: Rufous Mourner is about the same size and is often found with Speckled, but it is more uniform rufous overall, never showing any of Speckled's prominent dusky and rufous pattern on wing-coverts. Their facial aspects are slightly different, Speckled having a rounder head with a "softer" expression. Cf. also the larger Rufous Piha.

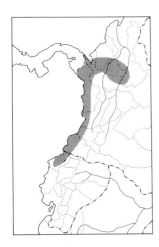

HABITAT AND BEHAVIOR: Rare to locally uncommon in lower and middle growth inside humid forest and mature secondary woodland. Behaves much like Cinereous Mourner, which replaces Speckled east of Andes. Speckled Mourner's voice is also similar, with the same odd ringing quality, a repeated "tlee-yeeí, tlee-yeeí, tlee-yeeí . . ." (or "tee-wheeít"), up to 12–15 couplets, then a pause before starting up again. RANGE: N. and w. Colombia (humid Caribbean lowlands east to middle Río Magdalena valley in Santander, and Pacific lowlands) and nw. Ecuador (Esmeraldas). Also Mexico to Panama. To 1000 m.

Lipaugus Pihas

Eight plainly attired cotingas found in humid forest, both in the lowlands and in montane areas. Here they perch lethargically for often long periods; their posture is quite upright, unlike the *Turdus* thrushes which they otherwise superficially resemble. Gray, rufous, and olive predominate, with only one, the bizarre Rose-collared Piha, having any bright color; Rose-collared is also the only sexually dimorphic species. There exists an unusual parallel: one rufous piha is found west of the Andes together with rather similar *Laniocera* and *Rhytipterna* mourners which are also rufous; east of the Andes an equally similar trio of gray species occur, also one from each genus. Most pihas are very vocal and are best known from their calls, but a few seem notably quiet. The affinities of *Lipaugus* have been long debated, but recent anatomical evidence indicates that, unlike the *Rhytipterna* mourners, they are true cotingas (see Lanyon 1985). We concur with Snow (1982) that the construction of their flimsy, dove-like nests (quite similar to those of some other obvious cotingas) also indicates that they are indeed cotingas. Prum (1990) suggests that the genus *Lipaugus* is polyphyletic and that *L. subalaris* and *L. cryptolopha* (Gray-tailed and Olivaceous Pihas) should be separated in their own genus, for which the name *Lathria* would be available. We follow Remsen et al. (1982) in considering *Chirocylla*, a monotypic genus in which the Scimitar-winged Piha was formerly placed (Meyer de Schauensee 1966, 1970; *Birds of the World*, vol. 8), and which was distinguished by the male's strangely modified and curved primaries, as best merged into *Lipaugus*.

GROUP A

"*Olive green*" pihas; local in Andes.

Lipaugus subalaris

GRAY-TAILED PIHA

PLATE: 51

DESCRIPTION: 23.5 cm (9¼"). *Local in foothills on e. slope of Andes from s. Colombia to Peru.* Mostly olive green above with *conspicuous but narrow pale yellow eye-ring;* rump more grayish, *tail pure pale gray;* bend of wing and underwing-coverts pale yellow. Throat and breast olive green, slightly paler on chin, with whitish shaft streaks; *lower underparts pale gray.* Males have semiconcealed black coronal patch.
SIMILAR SPECIES: Olivaceous Piha is similar but much yellower on belly and has olive (not gray) tail.

HABITAT AND BEHAVIOR: Rare to locally uncommon in understory and middle levels of humid forest in foothills along e. base of Andes. Favors lower elevations than Olivaceous Piha; the two have never been found at precisely the same site. Unknown in life until the mid 1980s when J. Fitzpatrick (pers. comm.) and his FMNH coworkers found it locally quite numerous on Cerros de Pantiacolla in s. Peru. There it foraged alone and was very inconspicuous, only rarely associating with mixed flocks, perching motionless for long periods, sallying to foliage for insects and regularly hover-gleaning. Occasionally one was also seen at a fruiting tree. Male's call (subsequently also heard in Ecuador; RSR and others) is a clear and ringing 2-noted whistle, "churrrrrrr-ee!" delivered at long intervals (often several minutes); a shorter and softer version ("chreeee?") is given less often. Small numbers occur along the Loreto road north of Archidona in Ecuador.

RANGE: Very locally on e. slope of Andes in s. Colombia (seen near Florencia in w. Caquetá; Mocoa in w. Putumayo), Ecuador, and Peru (northeast of Jirillo in San Martín, Enenas in Pasco, and Cerros de Pantiacolla in s. Madre de Dios). 600–1400 m.

Lipaugus cryptolophus

OLIVACEOUS PIHA

DESCRIPTION: 23.5 cm (9¼"). *Local on lower Andean slopes from s. Colombia to Peru.* Resembles Gray-tailed Piha, differing in its *pure olive green rump and tail* (with no gray), *yellower belly* (with no gray), and in having few or no pale shaft streaks on breast. See C-33.

SIMILAR SPECIES: Coloration of Olivaceous Piha is reminiscent of various tanagers (e.g., Olive and Lemon-spectacled), but the piha is larger and its sluggish behavior markedly different.

HABITAT AND BEHAVIOR: Uncommon in understory and middle levels of montane forest, less often out to borders. Very lethargic and inconspicuous, the Olivaceous Piha tends to forage alone and only infrequently is found with mixed flocks. It may perch stolidly for long periods, then fly out to foliage or a branch for an insect; sometimes several will congregate at a fruiting tree. No vocalization seems to be known.

RANGE: Andes of s. Colombia (w. slope of W. Andes from Valle southward, and around head of Río Magdalena valley in Huila), Ecuador (south on w. slope to Pichincha; locally along entire e. slope), and on e. slope of Andes in Peru (south to Huánuco). Mostly 1200–2200 m, locally (mostly on w. slope) down to 900 m.

GROUP B

Non-Andean pihas; color variable.

Lipaugus vociferans

SCREAMING PIHA   PLATE: 51

DESCRIPTION: 24.5–25.5 cm (9½–10"). *A large, very uniform, thrush-like bird found widely in tropical forests east of Andes.* Basically *plain gray,* somewhat duskier on wings and tail, paler gray on belly. Immatures are tinged brown or rufous on wings (especially) and underparts.

SIMILAR SPECIES: Closely resembles Grayish Mourner (a flycatcher),

and sometimes difficult to distinguish in the field, especially when not vocalizing. The piha is markedly larger, tends to have a grayer iris (never the mourner's reddish brown), always has a stouter bill, and has a slightly paler throat. Thrushes found in the Amaz. lowlands are essentially brown; none is so uniformly gray.

HABITAT AND BEHAVIOR: Common in understory and middle levels inside humid forest and woodland, both in terra firme and várzea, but only rarely coming out to edge. For a bird with such a powerful and unmistakable voice, the Screaming Piha is surprisingly hard to see. Away from males' leks, it tends to be solitary and rather sluggish, perching erectly, occasionally flying out after an insect or to pluck a fruit in a trogon-like hover. Fruit likely comprises the major portion of its diet. Occasionally one accompanies a mixed flock. The male's voice is perhaps the best-known sound of Amazonia (it is a familiar background sound even on movie soundtracks), and it carries so far that in many regions one is almost always within earshot. The most common call is a very loud, ringing "weee, weee, weee-ah," usually preceded by several guttural "grah" notes which are not audible for nearly as far. Leks usually are composed of 4–10 males which perch some 5–10 m up on open branches; despite this, birds are often quite difficult to spot as they tend to remain nearly motionless for long periods.

RANGE: Guianas, s. Venezuela (s. Sucre south through Bolívar and Amazonas), e. Colombia (north to Meta and Guainía), e. Ecuador, e. Peru, n. Bolivia (south to La Paz, Cochabamba, and n. Santa Cruz), and Amaz. Brazil (south to s. Mato Grosso and n. Goiás, and east to n. Maranhão); e. Brazil (Pernambuco south to Espírito Santo). Most numerous below 500 m, in smaller numbers in Andean foothills up to 1000 m; recorded to 1400 m in Venezuela.

Lipaugus lanioides

CINNAMON-VENTED PIHA

DESCRIPTION: 28 cm (11″). *Se. Brazil.* Resembles Screaming Piha. Larger and *more brownish gray overall* (brownest on wings, tail, and crissum), with somewhat scalier effect on crown.

HABITAT AND BEHAVIOR: Uncommon to locally fairly common in understory and middle levels inside humid forest. In Espírito Santo, Cinnamon-vented Piha occurs mainly or entirely in foothill areas (it is, for example, numerous at the Nova Lombardia Reserve above Santa Teresa), whereas Screaming Piha is only found in the lowlands; they have not been found together. Cinnamon-vented remains a poorly known bird, but it apparently does not form large leks like Screaming Piha; otherwise general behavior and comportment of the 2 species seem much alike. Cinnamon-vented's voice is similar in its loud arresting quality, a typical sequence being "skeeo-skeeo, skeeo-skeeo, skeeo-sheét."

RANGE: Se. Brazil (Espírito Santo and cen. Minas Gerais south to ne. Santa Catarina; sightings from se. Bahia require confirmation, and are perhaps the result of confusion with Screaming Piha). To 1400 m in Minas Gerais.

Lipaugus unirufus

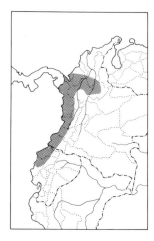

RUFOUS PIHA

PLATE: 51

DESCRIPTION: 23.5 cm (9¼"). *W. Colombia and nw. Ecuador.* Bill blackish with some buffy brown on lower mandible. *Uniform cinnamon-rufous,* slightly paler below, palest on throat.

SIMILAR SPECIES: This species closely resembles Rufous Mourner (a flycatcher) and is sometimes found with it. The mourner is somewhat smaller and more slender, and has a more "flat-crowned" head and an all-blackish, less heavy bill (the piha's may show pale at base). These distinctions are all subtle, and the 2 species are best distinguished by their characteristic vocalizations. Note, too, that the piha is most numerous in the lowlands, whereas the mourner ranges regularly up into the foothills.

HABITAT AND BEHAVIOR: Uncommon to locally fairly common at lower and middle levels inside humid forest. Usually rather inconspicuous, the Rufous Piha often perches lethargically and quietly for long periods, then briefly becomes more active while foraging. It feeds mostly on fruit. Unlike Screaming Piha, it seems not to form true leks, though several calling males, scattered more or less at random through the forest, may perch within earshot of each other. Calls of the Rufous are similar in quality to the Screaming's though rather more variable, typically an explosive, loud, whistled "peeeéa," "wheeeéo," or "chow-eeéo," sometimes in excited-sounding series. Birds may call sporadically throughout the day, often in response to some sharp noise or disturbance.

RANGE: N. and w. Colombia (humid Caribbean lowlands east to Río Magdalena valley in Santander, and Pacific lowlands; an isolated population in the Serranía de Macuira, on the Guajira Peninsula) and nw. Ecuador (south at least formerly to n. Manabí and w. Pichincha; recently only in Esmeraldas). Also Mexico to Panama. Mostly below 700 m, in smaller numbers to 1000 m.

Lipaugus streptophorus

ROSE-COLLARED PIHA

PLATE: 51

DESCRIPTION: 22.5 cm (8¾"). *Tepuis of s. Venezuela area.* Male gray, slightly paler below and especially on belly, with *very conspicuous magenta-pink collar and crissum.* Female lacks the pink collar and has *crissum rufous.*

SIMILAR SPECIES: Spectacular male is unmistakable. Female might be confused with Screaming Piha (overlap possible, though Rose-collared generally occurs at higher elevations); Screaming shows gray crissum concolor with rest of underparts.

HABITAT AND BEHAVIOR: Uncommon in canopy and middle levels of humid forest, sometimes at edge. Rose-collared is unusual among the pihas in that it regularly perches in the semiopen at forest borders. It is the only sexually dimorphic piha, and what are apparently pairs have been observed (Snow 1982). One call, given at long intervals by the male, is a loud and very sharp "skreéyr!" (T. Meyer), with quality of a Golden-crowned Flycatcher. Small numbers are found at the top of the Escalera road in e. Bolívar.

RANGE: Tepuis of s. Venezuela (e. Bolívar) and adjacent w. Guyana and extreme n. Brazil (Roraima). 1000–1800 m.

GROUP C

Largest and *longest-tailed* pihas; mainly or all *gray*. Andes.

Lipaugus uropygialis

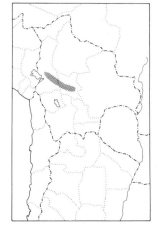

SCIMITAR-WINGED PIHA   PLATE: 51

DESCRIPTION: 30 cm (11¾"). *A large piha of Bolivian Andes. Mostly gray*, darker above and duskier on wings, tail very long; *rump, lower flanks, and crissum rufous-chestnut*. Male's primaries are narrow and so strongly recurved as to be visible in the field given a reasonably good view; female's primaries are much less modified.

SIMILAR SPECIES: Unlikely to be confused in its limited range. Scimitar-winged probably replaces Dusky Piha (or is its ecological equivalent), despite the very large gap between their ranges.

HABITAT AND BEHAVIOR: Uncommon in middle levels of montane forest and forest borders. A poorly known bird; as of early 1980s only 10 specimens were known (see Remsen et al. 1982). Birds seen have usually been perching quietly inside or, less often, at edge of forest; they have usually been alone, sometimes loosely associating with a mixed flock. What is believed to be Scimitar-winged Piha's call (though seen nearby, these birds have never been observed actually vocalizing) is reminiscent in quality to that of other pihas, an excited-sounding "wheeo, wheeo, whee-wheé, whee-wheé, whee-wheé!," sometimes with extra "whee"s or "whee-whee"s (RSR and R. A. Rowlett). Small numbers were noted in early 1980s in the Chapare area along the Cochabamba-Villa Tunari road, and in the yungas below Sacramento Alto in La Paz.

RANGE: E. slope of Andes in w. Bolivia (La Paz and Cochabamba). 1800–2575 m.

NOTE: Formerly placed in the monotypic genus *Chirocylla*.

Lipaugus fuscocinereus

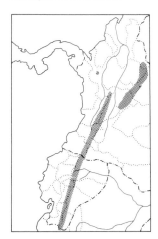

DUSKY PIHA

DESCRIPTION: 32.5 cm (12¾"). *A large, plain gray piha found locally in Andes from Colombia to n. Peru.* Resembles Scimitar-winged Piha (and equally *long-tailed*) but lacks modified primaries and has *no chestnut on rump or crissum*. Above uniform gray, duskier on wings and tail; throat somewhat paler gray, becoming uniform olivaceous gray on remaining underparts. See C-33.

SIMILAR SPECIES: Occurs at much higher elevations than other pihas in n. South America. Dusky Piha can be confused with much more common Great Thrush (they are about the same size and have similar proportions and overall coloration), but note the thrush's orange bill, eye-ring, and legs and its different behavior.

HABITAT AND BEHAVIOR: Rare to uncommon and local in canopy, middle levels, and borders of montane forest. Although specimens are relatively numerous, Dusky Piha is now seemingly local and is only infrequently encountered; deforestation has doubtless reduced its numbers in many areas. Where it persists, the Dusky Piha often is found in small groups which are active and fairly conspicuous (notably so for a piha), flying about in canopy and borders, sometimes accompanying other fairly large birds (e.g., Mountain Caciques, Turquoise Jays, and Hooded Mountain-Tanagers). In n. Colombia, S. Hilty observed an apparent lek, with the birds flying back and forth in treetops, loudly calling "whee-a-wheee" or "whee-a-wheeee-a-wheeeea" with whistled quality reminiscent of Screaming Piha (Hilty and Brown 1986). Small numbers can be found in the Cuyuja area east of Quito, Ecuador.

RANGE: Locally in Andes of Colombia (E. Andes from Norte de Santander south to Cundinamarca; Cen. Andes; W. Andes only at their n. end on the Cordillera de Paramillo), and on e. slope of Andes in Ecuador and extreme n. Peru (Cerro Chinguela in Piura). Mostly 2000–3000 m.

Tijuca Cotingas

A pair of fairly large, piha-like cotingas found only high in the mountains of se. Brazil. The genus seems most closely related to *Lipaugus* (Snow 1982). Despite their extremely restricted ranges, neither *Tijuca* appears truly endangered, mainly because little of their montane forest habitat has been modified by human activities.

Tijuca atra

BLACK-AND-GOLD COTINGA   PLATE: 51

DESCRIPTION: 26.5–27.5 cm (10½–11"). *Se. Brazil. Male's bill orange,* female's duller orange-brown. Male *deep black* with *a large patch of bright golden yellow on primaries* (conspicuous even when bird is perched). Female slightly smaller, *uniform dull olive,* somewhat brighter and yellower on belly and flight feathers.

SIMILAR SPECIES: Male virtually unmistakable, though in rapid flight it could be confused with smaller Golden-winged Cacique; cf. also male Yellow-legged Thrush. In its range female is only uniform olive bird its size; cf. markedly smaller Olive-green Tanager. Cf. also the range-restricted Gray-winged Cotinga.

HABITAT AND BEHAVIOR: Locally fairly common in canopy and middle levels of montane forest. One of the great specialties of the high se. Brazilian mts. where, at least from Sept. to Jan. (all year?), calls of singing males may echo from all around; they can, however, be frustratingly hard to see. That most strange and memorable song, a drawn out, eerie, high-pitched, and ringing "eeeeeeeeeee-yeeeé," lasts about 3 seconds; after a pause of several seconds, it is repeated, over and over. It carries surprisingly far, and often birds can be heard faintly, almost subliminally, calling from high on a ridge when you are in a valley far below. The call is ventriloquial and usually given from a hidden perch in dense foliage; the birds seem shy, easily taking alarm and flying off. Calling intensity is greatest, and birds most apt to be partially in the open, in the early morning and late afternoon and on days when the mts. are enshrouded in clouds. Females and silent males are only rarely encountered. Numerous at higher levels of Itatiaia Nat. Park, where it can be observed along the lower part of the Agulhas Negras road.

RANGE: Se. Brazil (Rio de Janeiro, extreme e. São Paulo, and adjacent s. Minas Gerais). Mostly 1200–1700 m.

Tijuca condita

GRAY-WINGED COTINGA

DESCRIPTION: 24 cm (9½″). Very local in *the high mts. of se. Brazil*. Resembles female Black-and-gold Cotinga. Gray-winged is smaller with a more slender bill, yellow wash on rump, yellower underparts, *markedly grayer wings,* and *gray (not olive) tail*. Evidently not sexually dimorphic. Note its *very* restricted range (even smaller than Black-and-gold's).

HABITAT AND BEHAVIOR: Rare to uncommon and very local in elfin cloud forest in Rio de Janeiro on 2 mountain ranges, Serra dos Órgãos and Serra do Tingua, on both of which it occurs only *above* the preferred elevational range of Black-and-gold Cotinga. The areas this cotinga inhabits are reached only after long hikes. In 1980 D. Scott and M. de L. Brooke discovered what little is known about the Gray-winged Cotinga (summarized in Snow 1982; see also D. A. Scott and M. de L. Brooke, *Bird Conserv. Int.* 3[1]: 1–12, 1993). It appears to be exceptionally wary and elusive, flying off at the slightest disturbance. Males vocalize from within dense foliage of the low elfin-forest canopy. The song bears a slight resemblance to Black-and-gold's but is shorter, more explosive, and more clearly bisyllabic, e.g., "sooee-wheeé"; it is given sporadically throughout the day but most often in early morning and late afternoon.

RANGE: Se. Brazil in Rio de Janeiro. 1370–1980 m.

NOTE: A recently described species: D. Snow, *Bull. B. O. C.* 100(4): 213–215, 1980. This description was based on a long-unrecognized female specimen, taken in 1942, housed in the MZUSP; it remains the only specimen in existence.

Procnias Bellbirds

A distinct genus of large cotingas, one species found in s. Central America, the others with mainly allopatric distributions in the canopy of lowland and foothill forests of n. and e. South America. Rather strangely, none occurs in the Andes. There is marked sexual dimorphism, males with some bizarre ornamentation on or about the head or throat. Females are much more plainly attired, and immature males require several years to attain full adult plumage. Bellbirds are entirely frugivorous, and they have extremely wide gapes, apparently an adaptation for eating large fruits. Advertising males regularly use perches high in the forest canopy from which they make their presence known over wide distances through their extraordinarily loud vocalizations, "bell-like" in only one species (White). Females are, by contrast, silent, and they alone care for the young.

Procnias nudicollis

BARE-THROATED BELLBIRD

PLATE: 51

DESCRIPTION: Male 28 cm (11"); female 26.5 cm (10½"). *Se. South America*. Male *pure white* with *ocular area and extensive throat patch bare bright greenish blue* with inconspicuous narrow black bristles. Female olive above with *blackish crown and sides of head. Throat blackish* narrowly streaked with white; remaining underparts pale yellowish coarsely streaked with olive. The extent and deepness of the blackish on throat seem to vary (individually?); in some birds white streaking is prominent, obscuring the black. Crown always seems to be solidly blackish. Males require 2 years to acquire adult plumage; mainly olive, female-plumaged birds (but already with blue throats) sometimes sing and display.

SIMILAR SPECIES: Male unmistakable. Female so closely resembles female Bearded Bellbird (they overlap in ne. Brazil) that they probably cannot be distinguished in the field. Female Bearded's crown is dusky-olive, dark but never as truly blackish as in Bare-throated.

HABITAT AND BEHAVIOR: Locally fairly common in canopy and borders of humid forest. Sluggish and, aside from displaying males, most apt to be seen when feeding at a fruiting tree. "Singing" males are surprisingly difficult to spot, mainly because they tend to perch in dense foliage of high tree crowns where even their stunning white plumage is hard to locate. They sing and display from open, exposed perches only rarely. Males have permanent calling territories and 2 basic vocalizations; they appear to vocalize, at least intermittently, throughout the year (even through the austral winter in e. Paraguay). Both vocalizations are ventriloquial and *very* loud. The main "bock" or "bonk" call is delivered with the gape wide open, whereas a series of up to 6–8 repeated "clink-clink-clink . . ." or "tonk-tonk-tonk . . ." metallic notes are given with the bill closed (though the bare throat pulses visibly with each call). Often several males (only one of them fully adult?) call in fairly close proximity to each other. Although the species is still fairly numerous in certain protected areas, Bare-throated Bellbird numbers have unquestionably declined, a decline attributable to deforestation and (perhaps especially) to heavy trapping pressure. Males are, especially in Brazil (where they are known as *arapongas*), surprisingly popular as cage-birds; in some areas one hears far more bellbirds calling from cages in towns than from what is left of the surrounding forests.

RANGE: E. Brazil (Alagoas south locally to Rio Grande do Sul, and inland to s. Mato Grosso), e. Paraguay (west to Concepción), and ne. Argentina (Misiones). Apparently only a summer visitor to Rio Grande do Sul, Brazil (Belton 1985). To about 1000 m; may engage in altitudinal movements, but details uncertain.

Procnias averano

BEARDED BELLBIRD

PLATE: 51

DESCRIPTION: Male 28 cm (11"); female 26.5 cm (10½"). *Local in Trinidad, Venezuela, and ne. Brazil*. Male *mostly grayish white* with coffee brown head, *black wings,* and *remarkable bare black throat covered with*

clusters of long, narrow, stringy wattles. Female very similar to female Bare-throated Bellbird but with *crown dusky-olive* (not blackish). Male of nominate race (ne. Brazil) differs from *carnobarba* of remainder of range in having almost pure white body plumage.

SIMILAR SPECIES: Male unmistakable. Bearded overlaps with Bare-throated Bellbird (females very similar; see above) only in Alagoas, ne. Brazil, where Bare-throated ranges mainly in hill country, Bearded in remnant lowland forests. Female Bearded also resembles female White Bellbird (they occur together in se. Venezuela), but White is more olive generally, lacks Bearded's dusky effect on crown and ear-coverts, and has olive (not slaty) throat streaking.

HABITAT AND BEHAVIOR: Uncommon to locally fairly common in canopy and borders of humid forest and mature secondary woodland. General behavior much like Bare-throated Bellbird's, and presence also mainly made known by male's resounding vocalizations. Its main calls are quite similar to Bare-throated's (the unbelievably loud "bock" with open gape and the repeated "tonk-tonk-tonk . . ."), but Bearded also gives a bisyllabic call (apparently not part of the repertoire of Trinidad birds); in n. Venezuela this is a more musical "kay-kong" or "kring-krong," in s. Venezuela (see Snow 1982) an unmusical, slightly hissing "bisset, bisset. . . ." Calls of nominate race of ne. Brazil unknown. Can, with patience, be seen in the valleys of Trinidad's Northern Range, and also much in evidence (at least when males are calling) along the upper part of the Escalera road in Venezuela.

RANGE: N. Venezuela (Paria Peninsula west locally in coastal mts. to Falcón and Zulia) and extreme ne. Colombia (slopes of Sierra de Perijá); se. Venezuela (s. Bolívar and extreme se. Amazonas) and adjacent w. Guyana and extreme n. Brazil (Roraima); ne. Brazil (Maranhão and Piauí east locally to Pernambuco and Alagoas); Trinidad. To about 1900 m; apparently engages in seasonal (elevational?) movements, but details uncertain.

Procnias alba

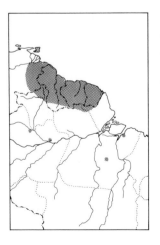

WHITE BELLBIRD

DESCRIPTION: Male 28.5 cm (11¼"), female 27.5 cm (10¾"). *Ne. South America.* Male *all pure white; a single large, fleshy, black, sparsely white-feathered wattle* springs from base of maxilla and hangs down side of bill (usually to the right). See Meyer de Schauensee and Phelps (1978, p. 236). Female *uniform olive above*, duskier on ear-coverts. Below pale yellowish *coarsely streaked with olive*, streaking finer on throat. *Wallacei* (local in e. Amaz. Brazil) has somewhat larger bill but otherwise is similar.

SIMILAR SPECIES: Male unmistakable. Rather similar female Bearded Bellbird has crown dusky-olive (not concolor with upperparts) and throat streaked blackish (not olive).

HABITAT AND BEHAVIOR: Uncommon to locally fairly common in canopy and borders of humid forest. General behavior much like the other 2 bellbirds', but calling males tend to be more conspicuous because they perch more often in the open. This is *the* bellbird, the species for which the group was named and the only one with "bell-like" vocalizations, all much more musical than in other bellbirds. Most frequent is a very loud, truly bell-like "kóng-kay!," the first note usually uttered as the bird leans right with the wattle hanging down normally, the second just after the bird swings rapidly to the left, briefly flipping the wattle, which soon returns to its usual position. A drawn out "doi-i-i-i-ing," usually followed by a fainter short note, is also given. In Surinam, where this spectacular bird is well known and usually readily seen on Brownsberg Plateau, it is known as the *gón-gee*. White Bellbirds are usually numerous along the lower and middle Escalera road in se. Venezuela but are replaced at higher elevations by the Bearded Bellbird; at some points one can hear both species simultaneously.

RANGE: Guianas and se. Venezuela (e. Bolívar); a recently discovered population in e. Amaz. Brazil (on the Serra dos Carajás in se. Pará) is perhaps the source of an old record from near Belém in e. Pará; 2 records from the lower Rio Negro probably refer to wanderers; has also wandered to Trinidad. To about 1250 m, occasionally higher (in Venezuela).

Gymnoderus Fruitcrows

The bizarre Bare-necked Fruitcrow has no evident close relative, and its bare wrinkled skin on the sides of the neck is unique. Both it and the quite different Black-faced Cotinga have patches of powderdown in their plumage; this causes a distinctive pale bloom on the plumage. The fruitcrow is generally numerous and conspicuous along Amazonian and Guianan rivers and lakeshores. Its nest is a small, inconspicuous cup made of lichens and placed on top of a large limb, usually in a tree standing in or at the edge of water. Despite the specific name *foetidus*, the Bare-necked Fruitcrow does not have any offensive smell, even during specimen preparation (F. Sornoza).

Gymnoderus foetidus

BARE-NECKED FRUITCROW

PLATE: 52

DESCRIPTION: Male 38 cm (15″), female 33 cm (13″). Bill bluish gray, black at tip. Male *mainly black* with *silvery gray wings* (very conspicuous, especially in flight); feathers of crown, face, and upper throat short and plush-like; *sides of neck and ocular area unfeathered, cobalt blue to bluish white, the skin elaborately crinkled and folded.* Female smaller and slatier gray generally, with wings the same color as back, and sides of neck with less crinkled bare bluish skin; see C-XIII. Immatures are scaled with white below; young males' wings are less silvery.
SIMILAR SPECIES: Virtually unmistakable. Female vaguely recalls female Amazonian Umbrellabird, but fruitcrow's profile is of a small head and thin neck, very different from umbrellabird's.
HABITAT AND BEHAVIOR: Fairly common along borders of rivers and lakes, on river islands, and in canopy and edge of várzea forest. The Bare-necked Fruitcrow is a conspicuous bird, seen most often flying

high overhead with characteristic deep, rowing wing-strokes, the male's silvery wings flashing in the sun and visible from great distances. Perched birds often hop from branch to branch, toucan- or cracid-like. Although solitary birds are frequently seen in flight, this species seems more likely to be in small groups when perched. It seems to make no vocal sounds.

RANGE: Se. Colombia (north to Meta and Amazonas), e. Ecuador, e. Peru, n. Bolivia (south to La Paz, Cochabamba, and n. Santa Cruz), most of Amaz. Brazil (south to s. Mato Grosso and Goiás, and east to Maranhão; but seemingly absent from much or all of the Rio Negro drainage), Guianas, s. Venezuela (locally in w. Bolívar and Amazonas) and adjacent Colombia (e. Vichada). To 500 m.

Querula Fruitcrows

A distinctive, monotypic genus whose closest relative is uncertain. It is widespread, and usually numerous, in lowland forests. The nest is a sparse, flimsy-looking cup, often surprisingly conspicuous, usually placed in the crotch of a somewhat isolated tree.

Querula purpurata

PURPLE-THROATED FRUITCROW   PLATE: 52

DESCRIPTION: Male 28 cm (11"), female 25.5 cm (10"). Bill mostly leaden blue. *All black,* adult males with *large throat patch* (extending to sides of neck) *shiny reddish purple.*

SIMILAR SPECIES: In poor light male's purple throat can be hard to make out; then it and all females and immatures can be confused with various mainly black caciques. The fruitcrow's chunky and short-legged shape is, however, very different, as is its much less pointed bill. In flight, note also the fruitcrow's broad and rather rounded wings and short tail.

HABITAT AND BEHAVIOR: Fairly common to common in middle levels and canopy of humid forest and mature secondary woodland, sometimes out into borders and adjacent clearings with large trees. Almost always occurs in groups of 3–6 birds in which purple-throated adult males are normally a minority. These groups are usually quite conspicuous, even bold, as they troop about with various large birds such as toucans or caciques and oropendolas. They have a characteristic swooping flight with long glides. These noisy birds give a variety of often quite loud calls, including a distinctive drawn out "ooo-waá" or "kwick-oo, ooo-waá," or (most often in flight) a "wak-wak-wheéawoo." Some are reminiscent of the "warm-up" call of Screaming Piha. A flock can sometimes be lured in by imitating these calls; they may then perch overhead, sometimes quite close, and lean forward as they call and peer down at the "intruder," the males flaring and ruffling their vivid purple gorgets.

RANGE: N. and w. Colombia (humid Caribbean lowlands east to middle Río Magdalena valley in Santander and e. Caldas, and Pacific lowlands) and w. Ecuador (recorded south to e. Guayas, but no recent reports south of Pichincha); se. Colombia (north to Meta and Vaupés), e. Ecuador, e. Peru, n. Bolivia (Beni and Pando), most of Amaz. Brazil (south to n. Mato Grosso and Goiás, east to Maranhão; but seemingly absent from much of the Rio Negro drainage), Guianas, and se. Venezuela (Bolívar). Also Costa Rica and Panama. Mostly below 700 m (recorded up to 1200 m in Colombia).

Haematoderus Fruitcrows

The relationships of the spectacular Crimson Fruitcrow, a rare resident of humid forest in ne. South America, remain obscure. We suspect that, despite its large size, it may be most closely related to the *Xipholena* cotingas.

Haematoderus militaris

CRIMSON FRUITCROW

PLATE: 52

DESCRIPTION: 33–35 cm (13–14"). *Local in ne. South America.* Heavy reddish bill. Adult male *mostly shining crimson*, the feathers very long, glossy, and stiffened; wings and tail dusky brown, but latter partly concealed by elongated uppertail-coverts. At times shows a bushy crest. Female and immature male *rosy crimson on head, neck, and entire underparts* (the feathers not as stiff or lanceolate as male's), with entire mantle, wings, and tail dusky brown.

SIMILAR SPECIES: Female could possibly be confused with much smaller and more slender-billed *Phoenicircus* red-cotingas.

HABITAT AND BEHAVIOR: Rare in canopy and borders of humid forest. The magnificent Crimson Fruitcrow is still not a very well known bird, though in recent years a few have been regularly seen in the Manaus, Brazil, area, especially from the INPA/WWF canopy observation tower north of the city. R. O. Bierregaard, Jr., D. F. Stotz, L. H. Harper, and G. V. N. Powell (*Bull. B. O. C.* 107[3]: 134–137, 1987) reported on their observations from Manaus; these are summarized here. From the tower, single birds (usually males) have favored perches in canopy emergent trees, most often in the shade just below the actual canopy, where they may remain for protracted periods. Their normal undulating flight is reminiscent of a large woodpecker's or umbrellabird's, but flight displays, involving a spiral ascent followed by a long descending glide, have also been observed. Although they are generally quiet, a short, low-pitched, owl-like hooting (sometimes doubled) has been heard. A sharp, loud "bok" call is also given (A. Whittaker). Despite being called a "fruitcrow," to date the species has only been seen to feed on large insects such as cicadas. Additional data on flight displays, feeding, and the first observation of nesting behavior are given by A. Whittaker (*Bull. B. O. C.* 113 [2]: 93–96, 1993).

RANGE: Guianas and ne. Brazil (north of the Amazon west to around Manaus; south of the Amazon from the lower Rio Tocantins east to the Belém area, from which there are no recent reports); also a remarkable record of a single bird obtained in 1988 at Cachoeira Nazaré in Rondônia, w. Brazil (Stotz et al. ms.) and an almost equally surprising sighting in 1984 at Cerro de la Neblina in extreme s. Venezuela (Willard et al. 1991). Below 200 m.

Pyroderus Fruitcrows

A very large and spectacular cotinga with simple but striking plumage pattern and coloration; this genus seems most closely related to the *Cephalopterus* umbrellabirds. It is found locally in foothill and subtropical forests.

Pyroderus scutatus

RED-RUFFED FRUITCROW

PLATE: 52

DESCRIPTION: 36–43 cm (14–17″), females averaging smaller. *Large.* Male's bill usually bluish gray (blackish in some birds); female's dusky. Nominate race (se. South America) and *granadensis* (n. and w. Venezuela south into Colombia's upper Río Magdalena valley) *mainly black with large flame-red bib of shiny feathers on lower throat and upper breast* (with a somewhat crinkled effect); often a few chestnut spots on underparts. *Occidentalis* (w. Colombia and nw. Ecuador) smaller with *mainly rufous-chestnut lower underparts* (see C-XIII); *masoni* (e. Peru) and *orenocensis* (e. Venezuela and Guyana) similar but somewhat duller below.

SIMILAR SPECIES: In poor light could be confused with an umbrellabird.

HABITAT AND BEHAVIOR: Rare to locally uncommon in forest and forest borders, mainly in humid or montane forest but locally (e.g., in e. Venezuela) in somewhat drier regions. Mostly solitary and usually inconspicuous, ranging through forest at all levels but only infrequently in the open. Has a heavy, somewhat ponderous flight; unlike the umbrellabirds, it rarely flies above the canopy. Sometimes quite unsuspicious, occasionally even approaching an observer with seeming curiosity. Usually silent away from its leks. Lekking display is spectacular but unfortunately has only rarely been witnessed; P. Schwartz's observations in Venezuela were summarized in Snow (1982). Seven to 8 males were in attendance, with closely grouped display perches up to 6 m above the ground. The displaying males give a very deep, booming call in chorus, "oomm-oomm-oomm"; rarely a single "oomm" may be given away from the lek. Calling males lean forward and extend the ruff, which hangs out away from the body; they may then straighten up and flare the bib laterally. Deforestation has reduced some populations, but no subspecies yet seems truly threatened; it is perhaps most readily seen on either side of Iguazú Falls.

RANGE: Se. Venezuela (e. Bolívar) and adjacent Guyana; locally in coastal mts. of n. Venezuela (east to Distrito Federal) and Andes of w. Venezuela, w. Colombia, and nw. Ecuador (where very rare, with only a few records, once south to Santo Domingo de los Colorados in

w. Pichincha); Sierra de Perijá on Venezuela-Colombia border; e. slope of Andes in Peru (Amazonas south to Junín); se. Brazil (s. Goiás and s. Bahia south locally to n. Rio Grande do Sul), e. Paraguay (west to Concepción, San Pedro, and Paraguarí), and ne. Argentina (Misiones). Nominate race and *orenocensis* up to 850 m; other races mostly 1200–2200 m.

Cephalopterus Umbrellabirds

The most bizarrely ornamented of the cotingas. The three umbrellabirds (one species is found only in Costa Rica and Panama) are unmistakable large black birds with strangely modified crests and (in the South American species) extraordinary long, pendent wattles.

Cephalopterus ornatus

AMAZONIAN UMBRELLABIRD   PLATE: 52

DESCRIPTION: Male 48–49 cm (19″), female 41 cm (16″). *Iris whitish;* bill mostly pale bluish gray, blackish on ridge. *Entirely glossy black* with *unmistakable "umbrella-shaped" crest* (upstanding and often recurved over bill, sometimes so far as almost to obscure it, but more often held straight up, almost spike-like; white shafts of frontal feathers show quite prominently), and *wide pendent wattle hangs from lower throat* (some 8–10 cm [3–4″] long, but usually held in tightly against body so *not* very conspicuous). Female similar but smaller and less glossy with *crest smaller but still very evident,* no white feather shafts, and wattle short.

SIMILAR SPECIES: Confusion unlikely; Long-wattled Umbrellabird occurs only *west* of Andes. In the lowlands cf. Bare-necked Fruitcrow; along e. base of Andes cf. Red-ruffed Fruitcrow.

HABITAT AND BEHAVIOR: Rare to locally fairly common in 2 distinctly different habitats: along rivers in Amazonia and the upper Orinoco drainage (favoring islands with extensive stands of *Cecropia* trees and adjacent várzea forest), and in humid forest and forest borders along e. base of Andes. Amazonian populations are better known. Here umbrellabirds are seen singly or in small groups, either perched high in trees (seldom long in the open) or during their slow, undulating, woodpecker-like flight. Moving about in trees, they make big, somewhat awkward, toucan-like hops, then may perch stolidly but alertly for considerable periods. They often seem exceptionally wary and flush at the slightest disturbance, perhaps because of persecution; foothill birds seem somewhat tamer. In at least parts of Amazonia they favor certain stands of trees; at some of these, groups of 2–5 males gather to display. They perch on branches some 10–25 m above the ground, often, especially in the early morning, quite in the open. Periodically they give a deep, moaning "boom" (sometimes likened to the bellowing of a bull), usually when leaning forward with expanded crest and wattle enlarged and hanging downward. Some (ritualized?) chasing and displacing occur. The Amazonian Umbrellabird is now reduced in numbers and quite local across much of its range; this decline is presumably mainly attributable to persecution, for to date there has been little modification at least of its riverine habitat (though there has been more in Andes).

RANGE: Locally in s. Guyana (Kanuku Mts.), s. Venezuela (Amazonas and Bolívar), e. Colombia (north to Boyacá), e. Ecuador, e. Peru, n. Bolivia (south to La Paz, Cochabamba, and n. Santa Cruz), and Amaz. Brazil (north of the Amazon east only to the Rio Negro drainage, south of it east to the Rio Xingu drainage, and south to s. Mato Grosso). To about 1500 m on e. slope of Andes.

Cephalopterus penduliger

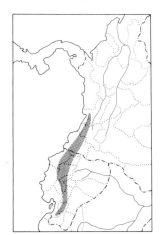

LONG-WATTLED UMBRELLABIRD

DESCRIPTION: Male 41 cm (16″), female 36 cm (14″). *Sw. Colombia and w. Ecuador.* Resembles Amazonian Umbrellabird (latter found only *east* of Andes). Smaller with a proportionately shorter tail, and iris dark brown (not whitish). Male has shafts of crest feathers black (not white), and *wattle is much longer* (usually 20–30 cm [8–12″] long, but substantially extensible). See C-XIII.

SIMILAR SPECIES: Cf. Red-ruffed Fruitcrow.

HABITAT AND BEHAVIOR: Rare and local in canopy and borders of humid forest, occasionally out into trees of adjacent clearings; sometimes found in stunted, mossy "cloud" forest. Long-wattled is not well known, but its behavior apparently differs little from Amazonian Umbrellabird's, especially the latter's foothill population. Usually solitary or in pairs, typically rather wary and hard to see, though occasionally perching boldly right in front of an observer, peering about intently and even seeming curious. Nothing seems to be on record about voice or display, which must be spectacular. Overall numbers of the Long-wattled Umbrellabird continue to decline, attributable both to direct persecution (it is shot for food by country residents) and to deforestation. It almost certainly deserves formal threatened status. Most areas where it persists in reasonable numbers are remote; some occur around El Placer in Esmeraldas, Ecuador (along the railroad between Ibarra and San Lorenzo).

RANGE: Locally on w. slope of W. Andes in sw. Colombia (north to Valle) and w. Ecuador (south to El Oro). Mostly 500–1400 m, occasionally wandering lower, even out into adjacent lowlands (but because of deforestation, this rarely occurs now).

Perissocephalus Capuchinbirds

Surely one of the weirder-looking birds in the world, the Capuchinbird seems rather closely related to the *Cephalopterus* umbrellabirds and the *Pyroderus* fruitcrow. It is notable for its remarkable lek display; its twig nests are small and sparse, and all of those found have been situated very close to the lek. For more details on behavior, see B. K. Snow (*Ibis* 114[2]: 139–162, 1972) and Snow (1982).

Perissocephalus tricolor

CAPUCHINBIRD

Other: Calfbird

DESCRIPTION: Male 35.5 cm (14″), female 34.5 cm (13½″). *A strange-looking* (Snow [1982, p. 153] aptly calls it "grotesque"), *large cotinga of ne. South America.* Bill blackish above, pale bluish gray below, with *bare crown and face pale bluish gray. Mainly cinnamon brown,* brighter and more rufous on lower underparts; wings dusky with white under-wing-coverts; tail black.

SIMILAR SPECIES: Unmistakable. Because most of the head is feather-less, it looks disproportionately small, giving the bird a unique and ungainly silhouette.

HABITAT AND BEHAVIOR: Uncommon to locally fairly common in hu-mid forest. Away from its leks, the Capuchinbird is an inconspicuous and rather solitary bird, ranging through the forest at varying heights but most often in subcanopy and middle levels. It eats much fruit but also consumes large insects. Its lek behavior is extraordinary. Three to 4 males gather to display in understory trees (the same ones for many years), usually perching 8–12 m above the ground where they emit one of the most amazing sounds made by a bird, termed the "moo" call by B. Snow, though that really doesn't do it justice. It is a loud and far-carrying (audible for over a kilometer) "grrrrrrrrr, aaaaaa-ooo," to our ear more reminiscent of a distant motorboat than (despite its old name, "Calfbird") of a calf. The "grrrrrrrrr" is given as the male leans forward and inhales, the "aaaaaa" as it stands high on its perch and fluffs out its plumage so that the bare head is ringed by feathers; it then relaxes with the final "ooo," ending by leaning backward and lowering its tail. Capuchinbirds and their marvelous leks can be readily observed at Su-rinam's Brownsberg Nature Park.

RANGE: Guianas, s. Venezuela (Bolívar and Amazonas), and ne. Brazil (north of the Amazon from Amapá west to the Manaus area and the upper Rio Negro drainage); may occur in far e. Colombia. Mostly below 600 m (recorded up to 1400 m in Venezuela).

Phoenicircus Red-Cotingas

A pair of beautiful cotingas found from Amazonia to the Guianas, ranging in humid forest and usually rare. They are unusual in that males are distinctly smaller than females. Generic relationships are un-certain, and we thus leave the genus in its traditional place among the cotingas. The genus shows a foot structure typical of the manakins (Snow 1982) and the wings are rather small and short relative to the birds' size, and lek display is quite manakin-like though with some cotinga-like aspects. P. W. Trail and P. Donahue (*Wilson Bull.* 103[4]: 539–551, 1991) present much information on the behavior and ecology of both species.

Phoenicircus carnifex

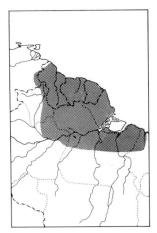

GUIANAN RED-COTINGA

PLATE: 52

DESCRIPTION: Male 22 cm (8½″), female 23 cm (9″). *Ne. South America. Iris red.* Male's *crown and prominent flat crest bright scarlet;* back blackish brown, becoming rufous brown on wing-coverts and inner flight feathers, dusky on outer flight feathers; rump and tail bright red, tail tipped brownish. *Throat and breast brownish maroon,* becoming rosy red on lower underparts. Female's *crown and tail dull reddish;* otherwise brownish olive above and on throat and chest, latter merging into *rosy red of lower underparts.*

SIMILAR SPECIES: Cf. somewhat larger Black-necked Red-Cotinga (with at most limited overlap).

HABITAT AND BEHAVIOR: Uncommon to apparently locally common in lower and middle levels of humid forest. Behavior, including lekking, is much like that described for Black-necked Red-Cotinga, but the primary vocalization given at the lek is a rather different "pee-chew-eet" (P. Trail). The call given by both sexes away from the lek, a sharp, abrupt "cheék!" or "wheék!," sometimes draws attention to them; the call is somewhat reminiscent of a Golden-olive Woodpecker's (T. Davis). Perhaps most numerous in French Guiana.

RANGE: Guianas, extreme s. Venezuela (e. Bolívar), lower Amaz. Brazil (north of the Amazon west to around Manaus, south of it from west of the lower Rio Tapajós east to nw. Maranhão). To about 600 m.

Phoenicircus nigricollis

BLACK-NECKED RED-COTINGA

DESCRIPTION: Male 23 cm (9″), female 24 cm (9½″). *W. and cen. Amazonia.* Resembles Guianan Red-Cotinga but larger, and both sexes have dark iris and are *more boldly patterned;* the patterns of both species are similar. Male *deep black on back and wings* (instead of brownish); bright scarlet on crown, rump, and tail with tip of tail black; throat black, *contrasting with bright scarlet remaining underparts.* Female brighter reddish on crown and tail than female Guianan, brighter and more bronzy olive above, and *brighter red below.* See C-33.

SIMILAR SPECIES: Males are among the most dazzling of all Amaz. birds. Females have enough of male's pattern and coloration to be readily recognized.

HABITAT AND BEHAVIOR: Rare to locally uncommon in lower growth and middle levels of humid forest, mainly in terra firme. In most areas Black-necked Red-Cotinga is an elusive and shy inhabitant of remote forests, usually encountered only occasionally as the odd solitary foraging bird. In the early 1980s a lek of this stunning cotinga was discovered not far from Explornapo Lodge on the lower Río Napo near Iquitos, Peru; here it is quite readily seen. The following is summarized from notes provided by B. Whitney, supplemented by Trail and Donahue (*Wilson Bull.* 103[4]: 539–551, 1991). The lek is situated in terra firme forest. Between 8 and 20 males (some subadult) congregate loosely on horizontal limbs some 6–15 m above the ground, usually remaining almost motionless. At intervals one utters an explosive penetrating "skeéyh!," sometimes given in series and always with the red rump feathers fluffed out; many males may follow suit, producing a calling bout that may continue for several minutes before all again fall silent. Males also have a swift twisting display flight in which the wings are vibrated to produce a strange, high-pitched whirring. Calling is most intense during early morning. Foraging birds of both sexes regularly utter a call similar to that given at the lek.

RANGE: Extreme s. Venezuela (sw. Amazonas), se. Colombia (north to Caquetá and Vaupés), e. Ecuador, ne. Peru (Loreto and San Martín), and w. and cen. Amaz. Brazil (north of the Amazon east to w. bank of the lower Rio Negro, south of it to the lower Rio Tapajós and on the middle Rio Xingu). May overlap with Guianan Red-Cotinga along the lower Rio Tapajós and Rio Xingu. To 400 m.

Rupicola Cocks-of-the-rock

A pair of splendid large cotingas, one found on Andean slopes, the other in the Guianan shield region of ne. South America. Their bright plumage, unique fan-shaped crests, and unusual courtship behavior place them among the most famous of neotropical birds. Long separated in their own family (Rupicolidae), but most authorities now place the cocks-of-the-rock with the cotingas (e.g., *Birds of the World*, vol. 8). Their nesting behavior is, however, notably different: females plaster their cup-shaped mud nests to the side of a damp rock face, usually near the males' leks.

Rupicola peruviana

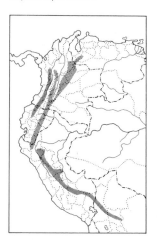

ANDEAN COCK-OF-THE-ROCK   PLATE: 52

DESCRIPTION: 30.5 cm (12″). *A spectacular, large, chunky bird of ravines and adjacent Andean forests. Bushy, somewhat laterally compressed frontal crest,* female's smaller, mostly conceals bill, which is yellowish in male, dark with yellow tip in female; legs orange-yellow in male, dusky in female. Iris of male varies from yellow in north to bluish white in south (female's is always bluish white); that of *sanguinolenta* (w. Colombia and nw. Ecuador) is mostly red with yellow inner and outer rims. Male *mostly bright orange to reddish orange;* wings and tail black, with *innermost flight feathers pearly gray and very wide* (shingle-like). *Sanguinolenta*'s body plumage is *intense blood-red* (see C-33). Female *mostly orangey brown,* wings and tail duller and browner (inner flight feathers widened like male's). Female *sanguinolenta* (and to a lesser extent *saturata* of s. Peru and Bolivia) notably redder, *almost brick red or carmine.*

SIMILAR SPECIES: Unmistakable; only possible confusion lies with Guianan Cock-of-the-rock (but the two are never found together). Even females can be easily known by their distinctive shape (especially the unusual crest) and orangey or reddish tone.

HABITAT AND BEHAVIOR: Uncommon to locally fairly common in ravines and along forested streams in montane areas, ranging into nearby forest to forage. Usually remains inside forest at lower and middle levels, but ascends higher in fruiting trees and sometimes enters or crosses clearings. Rather shy and inconspicuous, all too often seen only briefly, flying away after being flushed, or hurtling down a valley in swift direct flight. Cocks-of-the-rock are seen to best advantage at their display leks, which unfortunately is not easy as the birds are wary and easily disturbed. Unlike Guianan Cock-of-the-rock, displaying Andeans are entirely arboreal. In Colombia, the Benalcazars (*in* Snow 1982) studied a lek attended by 6 males, divided into 3 "pairs" which performed "confrontation displays." They faced each other, bowing and jumping and flapping their wings, occasionally snapping their bills, all the while giving a variety of squawking or grunting calls—a cacaphony of bright color, rapid motion, and weird sounds, raised to a veritable frenzy by the approach of a female. Leks elsewhere, e.g., in Colombia's Cueva de los Guácharos Nat. Park, may have considerably more displaying males. Foraging birds of both sexes give a loud, querulous "uankk?" in flight or when disturbed. With patience and reasonable luck, cocks-of-the-rock can be seen along the road to Mindo and the Chiriboga road in nw. Ecuador and along the railroad tracks below Machu Picchu in Peru; they are especially numerous and comparatively tame along the lower part of the Shintuya-Paucartambo road in s. Cuzco, Peru.

RANGE: Andes of w. Venezuela (north to w. Barinas near the San Isidro tunnel [*fide* B. Swift and others]), Colombia, Ecuador (south on w. slope to Cotopaxi east of Quevedo), e. Peru, and w. Bolivia (La Paz and Cochabamba). 500–2400 m.

Rupicola rupicola

GUIANAN COCK-OF-THE-ROCK

DESCRIPTION: 27 cm (10½"). *Ne. South America.* Generally resembles Andean Cock-of-the-rock (no overlap) but smaller, mostly because of its *markedly shorter tail. Laterally compressed frontal crest in both sexes* (female's smaller), mostly concealing bill. Iris orange to orange-yellow. Male *mostly intense orange* with narrow maroon subterminal band on crest feathers; lengthened filamentous uppertail-coverts partially conceal the mostly blackish tail; wings mostly blackish with large white speculum (showing mostly in flight); *inner flight feathers dusky with white border* and very wide (shingle-like), their *outer webs ending in long orange filaments.* See C-33. Female *uniform dark dusky brown.*

SIMILAR SPECIES: Nothing similar in range, but female might at a glance or in poor light be taken for an umbrellabird. Female Guianan is duller and darker than female Andean Cock-of-the-rock; the 2 species do not overlap.

HABITAT AND BEHAVIOR: Uncommon to locally fairly common in lower and middle growth of humid forest, primarily near rocky outcrops where males gather to display and females nest. Foraging birds move solitarily through forest, where even the gaudy males are surprisingly inconspicuous. Often such birds are located subsequent to revealing their presence through their often-given and distinctive "waa-oww" call. Guianan Cocks-of-the-rock come into their own at their communal leks; here reportedly up to 40 or even 50 males (more usually 5–10) gather, producing a fantastic spectacle. Males have individual "courts" which consist of several low display perches over a more or less circular area of bare ground up to 2 m in diameter. They spend much time displaying at each other, engaging in various stereotyped movements, bill snapping, and ritualized chases, all the while uttering various loud calls (e.g., an explosive, penetrating "ka-krrow!"). Not until a female appears do the males drop to the ground, landing with a great squawk and thrashing of wings. Each male then crouches and "freezes," remaining more or less motionless, apparently trying to remain perpendicular to the female, which usually remains perched in the trees above. A fine lek can be visited at the Voltzberg in Surinam's Raleigh Falls Nature Park; the species can also be seen along the lower Escalera road in Bolívar, Venezuela.

RANGE: Guianas, s. Venezuela (Bolívar and Amazonas), locally in e. Colombia (e. Vichada to Vaupés), and n. Brazil (upper Rio Negro region south locally to about 100 km north of Manaus in the Balbina area, and east locally through Amapá). Mostly below 1200 m (recorded up to 2000 m in Venezuela).

NOTE: For a discussion of lek display, with dazzling photographs, see P. W. Trail (*Am. Birds* 39[3]: 235–240, 1985).

BIBLIOGRAPHY

American Ornithologists' Union. 1983. *Check-list of North American Birds,* 6th ed.

Arballo, E. 1990. Nuevos registros para avifauna uruguaya. *Hornero* 13(2): 179–187.

Bates, J. M., M. C. Garvin, D. C. Schmitt, and C. G. Schmitt. 1989. Notes on bird distribution in northeastern Dpto. Santa Cruz, Bolivia, with 15 species new to Bolivia. *Bull. B. O. C.* 109(4): 236–244.

Bates, J. M., T. A. Parker III, A. P. Capparella, and T. J. Davis. 1992. Observations on the *campo, cerrado* and forest avifaunas of eastern Dpto. Santa Cruz, Bolivia, including 21 species new to the country. *Bull. B. O. C.* 112(2): 86–98.

Belton, W. 1984. Birds of Rio Grande do Sul, Brazil. Part 1. Rheidae through Furnariidae. *Bull. Am. Mus. Nat. Hist.* 178(4): 369–636.

———. 1985. Birds of Rio Grande do Sul, Brazil. Part 2. Formicariidae through Corvidae. *Bull. Am. Mus. Nat. Hist.* 180(1): 1–241.

Bettinelli, M. D., and J. C. Chebez. 1986. Notas sobre aves de la Meseta de Somuncurá, Río Negro, Argentina. *Hornero* 12(4): 230–234.

Bond, J. 1951. Notes on Peruvian Fringillidae. *Proc. Acad. Nat. Sci. Phil.* 103: 65–84.

———. 1953. Notes on Peruvian Icteridae, Vireonidae, and Parulidae. *Not. Nat. (Phil.)* 255: 1–15.

———. 1955. Notes on Peruvian Coerebidae and Thraupidae. *Proc. Acad. Nat. Sci. Phil.* 107: 35–55.

———. 1956. Additional notes on Peruvian birds 2. *Proc. Acad. Nat. Sci. Phil.* 108: 227–247.

Bond, J., and R. Meyer de Schauensee. 1942. The birds of Bolivia. Part 1. *Proc. Acad. Nat. Sci. Phil.* 94: 307–391.

Brooks, A., R. Barnes, L. Bartrina, S. H. M. Butchart, R. P. Clay, N. I. Etcheverry, J. C. Lowen, and J. Vincent. 1992. Project Canopy '92, Preliminary Report. Unpublished.

Canevari, M., P. Canevari, G. R. Carrizo, G. Harris, J. R. Mata, and R. J. Straneck. 1991. *Nueva Guía de las Aves Argentinas.* Buenos Aires: Fundación Acindar.

Cardiff, S. W. 1983. Three new bird species for Peru, with other distributional records from northern Departamento de Loreto. *Gerfaut* 73: 185–192.

Cardoso da Silva, J. M., and Y. Oniki. 1988. Lista preliminar da avifauna da Estação Ecológica Serra das Araras, Mato Grosso, Brasil. *Bol. Mus. Par. Emílio Goeldi,* Zool., nov. sér., no. 4(2): 123–143.

Chapman, F. M. 1917. The distribution of bird life in Colombia. *Bull. Am. Mus. Nat. Hist.* 36: 1–729.

———. 1926. The distribution of bird life in Ecuador. *Bull. Am. Mus. Nat. Hist.* 55: 1–784.

Clark, R. 1986. *Aves de Tierra del Fuego y Cabo de Hornos, Guía de Campo.* Buenos Aires: Literature of Latin America.

Collar, N. J., and P. Andrew. 1988. *Birds to Watch: The ICBP World Checklist of Threatened Birds.* Cambridge, England: International Council for Bird Preservation.

Collar, N. J., L. P. Gonzaga, N. Krabbe, A. Madroño Neito, L. G. Naranjo, T. A. Parker III, and D. C. Wege. 1992. *Threatened Birds of the Americas: The ICBP/IUCN Red Data Book.* Cambridge, England: International Council for Bird Preservation.

Cracraft, J. 1985. Historical biogeography and patterns of differentiation within the South American avifauna: Areas of endemisim. *In* P. A. Buckley et al., eds., *Neotropical Ornithology.* AOU monograph no. 36, pp. 49–84.

Cuello, J. 1975. Las aves del Uruguay (Suplemento 1). *Comun. Zool. Mus. Hist. Nat. Montevideo* 10(139): 1–27.

Cuello, J., and E. Gerzenstein. 1962. Las aves del Uruguay (lista sistemática, distribución y notas). *Comun. Zool. Mus. Hist. Nat. Montevideo* 6(93): 1–191.

Darrieu, C. A. 1986. Estudios sobre la avifauna de Corrientes 3. Nuevos registros de aves Passeriformes (Dendrocolaptidae, Furnariidae, Formicaridae, Cotingidae, y Pipridae) y consideraciones sobre su distribución geográfica). *Hist. Nat.* 6(11): 93–99.

———. 1987. Estudios sobre la avifauna de Corrientes 4. Nuevos registros de Aves (Passeriformes, Tyrannidae) y consideraciones sobre su distribución geográfica. *Neotropica* 33(89): 29–35.

Darrieu, C. A., and A. R. Camperi. 1990. Estudio de una colección de aves de Corrientes 1 (Dendrocolaptidae, Furnariidae). *Hornero* 13(2): 138–146.

———. 1992. Estudio de una colección de aves de Corrientes 3 (Tyrannidae). *Hornero* 13(3): 219–224.

Davis, S. E. 1993. Seasonal status, relative abundance, and behavior of the birds of Concepción, Departamento Santa Cruz, Bolivia. *Fieldiana, Zool.*, new series no. 71: 1–33.

Davis, T. J. 1986. Distribution and natural history of some birds from the departments of San Martín and Amazonas, northern Peru. *Condor* 88(1): 50–56.

Davis, T. J., C. Fox, L. Salinas, G. Ballon, and C. Arana. Annotated checklist of the birds of Cuzco Amazonica, Peru. 1991. *Occ. Papers Mus. Nat. Hist. Univ. Kansas* 144: 1–19.

de la Peña, M. 1988–1989. *Guía de Aves Argentinas,* vols. 5–6. Buenos Aires: Edit. L.O.L.A.

Donahue, P. K., and J. E. Pierson. 1982. *Birds of Suriname: An Annotated Checklist.* South Harpswell, Maine.

Dubs, B. 1992. *Birds of Southwestern Brazil: Catalogue and Guide to the*

Birds of the Pantanal of Mato Grosso and its Border Areas. Kusnacht, Switzerland: Betrona-Verlag.

Dunning, J. S. 1982. *South American Land Birds: A Photographic Guide to Identification*. Newtown Square, Pa.: Harrowood Books.

———. 1987. *South American Birds: A Photographic Guide to Identification*. Newtown Square, Pa.: Harrowood Books.

Feduccia, A. 1973. *Evolutionary trends in the Neotropical ovenbirds and woodhewers*. Ornithol. Monogr. no. 13: 1–69.

ffrench, R. 1991. *A Guide to the Birds of Trinidad and Tobago*, 2d ed. Ithaca, N.Y.: Cornell University Press.

Fitzpatrick, J. W. 1976. Systematics and biogeography of the Tyrannid genus *Todirostrum* and related genera (Aves). *Bull. Mus. Comp. Zool.* 147(10): 435–463.

Fjeldså, J. 1987. *Birds of Relict Forests in the High Andes of Peru and Bolivia*. Copenhagen: Zoological Museum, University of Copenhagen.

———. 1992. Biogeographic patterns and evolution of the avifauna of relict high-altitude woodlands of the Andes. *Steenstrupia* 18(2): 9–62.

Fjeldså, J., and N. Krabbe. 1986. Some range extensions and other unusual records of Andean birds. *Bull. B. O. C.* 106(3): 115–124.

———. 1989. An unpublished major collection of birds from the Bolivian highlands. *Zool. Scripta* 18(2): 321–329.

———. 1990. *Birds of the High Andes*. Copenhagen: Zoological Museum, University of Copenhagen.

Friedmann, H. 1948. Birds collected by the National Geographic Society's expeditions to northern Brazil and southern Venezuela. *Proc. U. S. Natl. Mus.* 97: 373–570.

Frisch, J. D. 1981. *Aves Brasileiras*, vol. 1. Verona, Italy: Mondadori.

Fry, C. H. 1970. Ecological distribution of birds in northeastern Mato Grosso State, Brazil. *Ann. Acad. Bras.* 42: 275–318.

Goodwin, D. 1976. *Crows of the World*. Ithaca, N.Y.: Cornell University Press.

Gore, M. E. J., and A. R. M. Gepp. 1978. *Las Aves del Uruguay*. Montevideo: Mosca Hnos., S.A.

Graham, G. L., G. R. Graves, T. S. Schulenberg, and J. P. O'Neill. 1980. Seventeen bird species new to Peru from the Pampas de Heath. *Auk* 97(2): 366–370.

Graves, G. R., and R. L. Zusi. 1990. Avian body weights from the lower Rio Xingu, Brazil. *Bull. B. O. C.* 110(1): 20–25.

Gyldenstolpe, N. 1945a. The bird fauna of the Rio Juruá in western Brazil. *Kungl. Svenska Vet.-Akad. Handl.*, ser. 3, 22(3): 1–388.

———. 1945b. A contribution to the ornithology of northern Bolivia. *Kungl. Svenska Vet.-Akad. Handl.*, ser. 3, 23(1): 1–300.

———. 1951. The ornithology of the Rio Purús region in western Brazil. *Ark. Zool.*, ser. 2, 2: 1–320.

Haffer, J. 1974. *Avian Speciation in Tropical South America*. Publ. Nuttall Ornithol. Club no. 14: 1–390.

―――. 1975. *Avifauna of Northwestern Colombia, South America.* Bonn. Zool. Monogr. no. 7: 1–181.

Haverschmidt, F. 1968. *The Birds of Surinam.* Edinburgh and London: Oliver & Boyd.

Hayes, F. E., P. A. Scharf, and R. S. Ridgely. Ms. (in prep.) Austral bird migrants in South America: a Paraguayan perspective.

Hellmayr, C. E. (in part with C. B. Cory or B. Conover). 1924–1938. Catalogue of birds of the Americas. *Field Mus. Nat. Hist., Zool. Ser.,* vol. 13, parts 3–11.

―――. 1929. A contribution to the ornithology of northeastern Brazil. *Field Mus. Nat. Hist., Zool. Ser.* 12: 235–501.

Hilty, S. L., and W. L. Brown. 1983. Range extensions of Colombian birds as indicated by the M. A. Carriker, Jr., collection at the National Museum of Natural History, Smithsonian Institution. *Bull. B. O. C.* 103(1): 5–17.

―――. 1986. *A Guide to the Birds of Colombia.* Princeton, N.J.: Princeton University Press.

Holt, E. G. 1928. An ornithological survey of the Serra do Itatiaya, Brazil. *Bull. Am. Mus. Nat. Hist.* 57: 251–326.

Hudson, W. H. 1920. *Birds of La Plata,* vol. 1. New York: E. P. Dutton & Co.

Humphrey, P. S., and D. Bridge. 1970. Apuntes sobre distribución de aves en la Tierra del Fuego y la Patagonia Argentina. *Rev. Museo Arg. Cienc. Nat. "Bernardino Rivadavia"* 10(17): 251–263.

Humphrey, P. S., D. Bridge, P. W. Reynolds, and R. T. Peterson. 1970. *Birds of Isla Grande (Tierra del Fuego), Preliminary Smithsonian Manual.* Lawrence, Kans.: Univ. Kans. Mus. Nat. Hist.

Isler, M. L., and P. R. Isler. 1987. *The Tanagers: Natural History, Distribution, and Identification.* Washington, D.C.: Smithsonian Institution Press.

Johnson, A. W. 1967. *The Birds of Chile and Adjacent Regions of Argentina, Bolivia, and Peru,* vol. 2. Buenos Aires: Platt Establ. Gráficos.

―――. 1972. *Supplement to the Birds of Chile and Adjacent Regions of Argentina, Bolivia, and Peru.* Buenos Aires: Platt Establ. Gráficos.

Koepcke, M. 1961. Birds of the western slope of the Andes of Peru. *Am. Mus. Novitates* 2028: 1–31.

―――. 1970. *The Birds of the Department of Lima, Peru,* 2d ed. Wynnewood, Pa.: Livingston Publishing Co.

Krabbe, N. 1992. Notes on distribution and natural history of some poorly known Ecuadorean birds. *Bull. B. O. C.* 112(3): 169–174.

Kratter, A. W., M. D. Carreño, R. T. Chesser, J. P. O'Neill, and T. S. Sillett. 1992. Further notes on bird distribution in northeastern Dpto. Santa Cruz, Bolivia, with two species new to Bolivia. *Bull. B. O. C.* 112(3): 143–150.

Kratter, A. W., T. S. Sillett, R. T. Chesser, J. P. O'Neill, T. A. Parker III, and A. Castillo. 1993. Avifauna of a chaco locality in Bolivia. *Wilson Bull.* 105(1): 114–141.

Lanyon, W. E. 1978. Revision of the *Myiarchus* flycatchers of South America. *Bull. Am. Mus. Nat. Hist.* 161(4): 427–628.

———. 1984. A phylogeny of the kingbirds and their allies. *Am. Mus. Novitates* 2797: 1–28.

———. 1985. A phylogeny of the Myiarchine flycatchers. *In* P. A. Buckley et al., eds., *Neotropical Ornithology*. AOU monograph no. 36, pp. 360–380.

———. 1986. A phylogeny of the thirty-three genera in the *Empidonax* assemblage of Tyrant Flycatchers. *Am. Mus. Novitates* 2846: 1–64.

———. 1988a. A phylogeny of the thirty-two genera in the *Elaenia* assemblage of Tyrant Flycatchers. *Am. Mus. Novitates* 2914: 1–26.

———. 1988b. The phylogenetic affinities of the Flycatcher genera *Myiobius* Darwin and *Terenotriccus* Ridgway. *Am. Mus. Novitates* 2915: 1–11.

———. 1988c. A phylogeny of the flatbill and tody-tyrant assemblage of Tyrant Flycatchers. *Am. Mus. Novitates* 2923: 1–41.

Laubmann, A. 1933. Bietrage zur avifauna Paraguay. *Anz. Ornithol. Ges. Bayern* 2: 287–302.

———. 1939. Wissenschaftliche Ergebnisse der Deutchen Gran Chaco-Expedition. Die Vogel von Paraguay, vol. 1. Stuttgart: Strecker und Schroder.

———. 1940. Wissenschaftliche Ergebnisse der Deutchen Gran Chaco-Expedition. Die Vogel von Paraguay, vol. 2. Stuttgart: Strecker und Schroder.

Marchant, S. 1958. The birds of the Santa Elena Peninsula, S.W. Ecuador. *Ibis* 100: 349–387.

Marín, A. M., L. F. Kiff, and L. Peña G. 1989. Notes on Chilean birds, with descriptions of two new subspecies. *Bull. B. O. C.* 109(2): 66–82.

Mayr, E., and W. H. Phelps, Jr. 1967. The origin of the bird fauna of the south Venezuelan highlands. *Bull. Am. Mus. Nat. Hist.* 136(5): 269–328.

Meyer de Schauensee, R. 1948–1952. The birds of the Republic of Colombia, parts 1–5. *Caldasia* 22–26: 251–1212.

———. 1959. Additions to the birds of the Republic of Colombia. *Proc. Acad. Nat. Sci. Phil.* 111: 53–75.

———. 1964. *The Birds of Colombia*. Narberth, Pa.: Livingston Publishing Co.

———. 1966. *The Species of Birds of South America with Their Distribution*. Narberth, Pa.: Livingston Publishing Co.

———. 1970. *A Guide to the Birds of South America*. Wynnewood, Pa.: Livingston Publishing Co. (Reprinted by International Council for Bird Preservation, 1982.)

Meyer de Schauensee, R., and W. H. Phelps, Jr. 1978. *A Guide to the Birds of Venezuela*. Princeton, N.J.: Princeton University Press.

Mitchell, M. H. 1957. *Observations on Birds of Southeastern Brazil*. Toronto: University of Toronto Press.

Moscovits, D., J. W. Fitzpatrick, and D. E. Willard. 1985. Lista preliminar das aves da Estação Ecológica de Macará, Território de Roraima, Brasil, e áreas adjacentes. *Pap. Avuls. Zool.* (São Paulo) 36(6): 51–68.

Narosky, S. 1978. *Aves Argentinas, Guía para el Reconocimiento de la Avifauna Bonaerense*. Buenos Aires: Asociación Ornitológica del Plata.

———. 1983. Registros nuevos o infrecuentes de aves Argentinas. *Hornero* 12(2): 122–126.

Narosky, S., A. G. DiGiacomo, and B. L. Lanús. 1990. Notas sobre aves del sur de Buenos Aires. *Hornero* 13(2): 173–178.

Naumberg, E. M. B. 1930. The birds of Matto Grosso, Brazil. *Bull. Am. Mus. Nat. Hist.* 60: 1–432.

———. 1935. Gazetteer and maps showing collecting stations visited by Emil Kaempfer in eastern Brazil and Paraguay. *Bull. Am. Mus. Nat. Hist.* 68: 449–469.

Nores, M. 1992. Bird speciation in subtropical South America in relation to forest expansion and retraction. *Auk* 109(2): 257–346.

Nores, M., and D. Yzurieta. 1980. *Aves de Ambientes Acuáticos de Córdoba y Centro de Argentina*. Córdoba, Argentina: Secretaría de Estado de Agricultura y Ganadería.

———. 1981. Nuevas localidades para aves Argentinas, parte 1. *Hist. Nat.* 2(5): 33–42.

———. 1982. Nuevas localidades para aves Argentinas, parte 2. *Hist. Nat.* 2(13): 101–104.

Nores, M., D. Yzurieta, and R. Miatello. 1983. Lista y distribución de las aves de Córdoba, Argentina. *Bol. Acad. Nac. Cienc.* (Córdoba) 56(1–2): 1–114.

Novaes, F. C. 1957. Contribução a ornitologia do noroeste do Acre. *Bol. Mus. Par. Emílio Goeldi*, Zool., nov. sér., no. 9: 1–30.

———. 1960. Sobre uma coleção de aves do sudeste do estado do Pará. *Arq. Zool. São Paulo* 11: 133–146.

———. 1974, 1978. Ornitologia da Territorio do Amapá, 1 and 2. *Publ. Avuls. Mus. Goeldi* 25: 1–121; 29: 1–75.

———. 1976. As aves do rio Aripuañá, estados de Mato Grosso e Amazonas. *Acta Amazônica* 6(4). Suplemento: 61–85.

———. 1978. Sobre algumas aves pouco conhecidas da Amazonia Brasileira 2. *Bol. Mus. Par. Emílio Goeldi*, Zool., nov. sér., no. 90: 1–15.

Olivares, A. 1969. *Aves de Cundinamarca*. Bogotá: Universidad Nacional de Colombia.

Olrog, C. C. 1979a. Notas ornitológicas, 11. Sobre la colección del Instituto Miguel Lillo. *Acta Zool. Lill.* 33(2): 5–7.

———. 1979b. Nueva lista de la avifauna Argentina. *Opera Lilloana* 27: 1–297.

———. 1984. *Las Aves Argentinas, "Una Nueva Guía de Campo."* Buenos Aires: Administración de Parques Nacionales.

O'Neill, J. P. 1974. "The birds of Balta, a Peruvian dry tropical forest locality, with an analysis of their origins and ecological relationships." Ph.D. dissertation, Louisiana State University. 284 pp.

O'Neill, J. P., and D. L. Pearson. 1974. Estudio preliminar de las aves de Yarinacocha, Dept. de Loreto, Peru. *Publ. Mus. Hist. Nat. "Javier Prado,"* Ser. A Zool. 25: 1–13.

Oren, D. C. 1990. New and reconfirmed bird records from the State of Maranhão, Brazil. *Goeldiana,* Zoología Núm. 4: 1–13.

Ortiz-Von Halle, B. 1990. Adiciones a la avifauna de Colombia de especies arribadas a la Isla Gorgona. *Caldasia* 77: 209–214.

Parker, T. A., III. 1982. Observations of some unusual rainforest and marsh birds in southeastern Peru. *Wilson Bull.* 94(4): 477–493.

Parker, T. A., III, J. M. Bates, and G. Cox. 1992. Rediscovery of the Bolivian Recurvebill with notes on other little-known species of the Bolivian Andes. *Wilson Bull.* 104(1): 173–178.

Parker, T. A., III, A. Castillo U., M. Gell-Mann, and O. Rocha O. 1991. Records of new and unusual birds from northern Bolivia. *Bull. B. O. C.* 111(3): 120–138.

Parker, T. A., III, and J. P. O'Neill. 1980. Notes on little known birds of the upper Urubamba valley, southern Peru. *Auk* 97(1): 167–176.

Parker, T. A., III, and S. A. Parker. 1982. Behavioral and distributional notes on some unusual birds of a lower montane cloud forest in Peru. *Bull. B. O. C.* 102(2): 63–70.

Parker, T. A., III, S. A. Parker, and M. A. Plenge. 1982. *An Annotated Checklist of Peruvian Birds.* Vermillion, South Dakota: Buteo Books.

Parker, T. A., III, and J. V. Remsen, Jr. 1987. Fifty-two Amazonian bird species new to Bolivia. *Bull. B. O. C.* 107(3): 94–107.

Parker, T. A., III, T. S. Schulenberg, G. R. Graves, and M. J. Braun. 1985. The avifauna of the Huancabamba region, northern Peru. *In* P. A. Buckley et al., eds., *Neotropical Ornithology.* AOU monograph no. 36, pp. 169–197.

Partridge, W. H. 1953. Observaciones sobre aves de las provincias de Córdoba y San Luis. *Hornero* 10: 23–73.

Paynter, R. A., Jr. 1972. Biology and evolution of the *Atlapetes schistaceus* species-group (Aves: Emberizinae). *Bull. Mus. Comp. Zool.* 143(4): 297–320.

———. 1978. Biology and evolution of the avian genus *Atlapetes* (Emberizinae). *Bull. Mus. Comp. Zool.* 148(7): 323–369.

———. 1982. *Ornithological Gazetteer of Venezuela.* Cambridge, Mass.: Museum of Comparative Zoology.

———. 1985. *Ornithological Gazetteer of Argentina.* Cambridge, Mass.: Museum of Comparative Zoology.

———. 1988. *Ornithological Gazetteer of Chile.* Cambridge, Mass.: Museum of Comparative Zoology.

———. 1989. *Ornithological Gazetteer of Paraguay.* Cambridge, Mass.: Museum of Comparative Zoology.

———. 1992. *Ornithological Gazetteer of Bolivia,* 2d ed. Cambridge, Mass.: Museum of Comparative Zoology.

Paynter, R. A., Jr., and M. A. Traylor, Jr. 1977. *Ornithological Gazetteer of Ecuador.* Cambridge, Mass.: Museum of Comparative Zoology.

———. 1981. *Ornithological Gazetteer of Colombia.* Cambridge, Mass.: Museum of Comparative Zoology.

———. 1991. *Ornithological Gazetteer of Brazil.* Cambridge, Mass.: Museum of Comparative Zoology.

Pearman, M. 1993. Some range extensions and five species new to Colombia, with notes on some scarce or little known species. *Bull.
B. O. C.* 113(2): 66–75.

Pearson, D. L., D. Tallman, and E. Tallman. 1977. *The Birds of Limoncocha, Napo Prov., Ecuador.* Quito: Instituto Linguístico de Verano.

Peña, L. E. 1961. Explorations in the Antofogasta ranges of Chile and
Bolivia. *Postilla* 49: 3–42.

Peres, C. A., and A. Whittaker. 1991. Annotated checklist of the bird
species of the upper Rio Urucu, Amazonas, Brazil. *Bull. B. O. C.*
111(3): 156–171.

Peters, J. L. 1951–1970. *Check-list of the Birds of the World,* vols. 7–15
(many vols., or parts thereof, have different authors). Cambridge,
Mass.: Museum of Comparative Zoology.

Phelps, W. H., and W. H. Phelps, Jr. 1963. Lista de las aves de Venezuela y su distribución, 2d ed., vol. 1, part 2, Passeriformes. *Bol. Soc.
Venez. Cienc. Nat.* 24(104, 105): 1–479.

Pinto, O. M. de O. 1932. Resultados ornitológicos de uma excursão
pelo oeste de São Paulo e sul de Matto-Grosso. *Rev. Mus. Paulista*
17(2): 641–708.

———. 1937. Catálogo das aves do Brasil, parte 1. *Rev. Mus. Paulista*
22: 1–566.

———. 1944. *Catálogo das Aves do Brasil,* parte 2. São Paulo: Secre-
tario Agricultura.

———. 1952. Sumula histórica e sistemática da ornitologia de Minas
Gerais. *Arq. Zool. São Paulo* 8: 1–52.

———. 1954. Resultados ornitológicas de duas viagens científicas ao
Estado de Alagoas. *Pap. Avuls. Zool.* (São Paulo) 12: 1–98.

———. 1978. *Novo Catálogo das Aves do Brasil,* parte 1. São Paulo.

Pinto, O. M. de O., and E. A. de Camargo. 1954. Resultados ornitológicos de uma expidição ao Territorio do Acre pelo Departamento
de Zoologia. *Pap. Avuls. Zool.* (São Paulo) 11: 371–418.

———. 1957. Sobre uma coleção de aves de região de Cachimbo (Sul
do Estado do Pará). *Pap. Avuls. Zool.* (São Paulo) 13: 51–69.

———. 1961. Resultados ornitologicos de cuatro recentes expedições
do Departamento do Zoologia ao nordeste do Brasil, com a descri-
ção de seis novas subespecies. *Arq. Zool. São Paulo* 11(9): 193–284.

Prum, R. O. 1990. Phylogenetic analysis of the evolution of display
behavior in the Neotropical Manakins (Aves: Pipridae). *Ethology*
84: 202–231.

———. 1990. A test of the monophyly of the Manakins (Pipridae)
and of the Cotingas (Cotingidae) based on morphology. *Occ. Papers Mus. Zool. Univ. Mich.* 723: 1–44.

———. 1992. Syringeal morphology, phylogeny, and evolution of the
Neotropical Manakins (Aves: Pipridae). *Am. Mus. Novitates* 3043:
1–65.

Prum, R. O., and W. E. Lanyon. 1989. Monophyly and phylogeny of
the *Schiffornis* group (Tyrannoidea). *Condor* 91(2): 444–461.

Rand, D. M., and R. A. Paynter, Jr. 1981. *Ornithological Gazetteer of
Uruguay.* Cambridge, Mass.: Museum of Comparative Zoology.

Remsen, J. V., Jr. 1984. Natural history notes on some poorly known Bolivian birds, part 2. *Gerfaut* 74: 163–179.

———. 1986. Aves de una localidad en la sabána humeda del norte de Bolivia. *Ecol. en Bolivia* 8: 21–35.

Remsen, J. V., Jr., and T. A. Parker III. 1983. Contribution of river-created habitats to bird species richness in Amazonia. *Biotropica* 15(3): 223–231.

———. 1984. Arboreal dead-leaf-searching birds of the neotropics. *Condor* 86(1): 36–41.

Remsen, J. V., Jr., T. A. Parker III, and R. S. Ridgely. 1982. Natural history notes on some poorly known Bolivian birds. *Gerfaut* 72: 77–87.

Remsen, J. V., Jr., and R. S. Ridgely. 1980. Additions to the avifauna of Bolivia. *Condor* 82(1): 69–75.

Remsen, J. V., Jr., C. G. Schmitt, and D. C. Schmitt. 1988. Natural history notes on some poorly known Bolivian birds, part 3. *Gerfaut* 78: 363–381.

Remsen, J. V., Jr., and M. A. Traylor, Jr. 1989. *An Annotated List of the Birds of Bolivia*. Vermillion, South Dakota: Buteo Books.

Remsen, J. V., Jr., M. A. Traylor, Jr., and K. C. Parkes. 1986. Range extensions for some Bolivian birds, 2 (Columbidae to Rhinocryptidae). *Bull. B. O. C.* 106(1): 22–32.

———. 1987. Range extensions for some Bolivian birds, 3 (Tyrannidae to Passeridae). *Bull. B. O. C.* 107(1): 6–16.

Ridgely, R. S. 1976. *A Guide to the Birds of Panama*. Princeton, N.J.: Princeton University Press.

———. 1980. Notes on some rare or previously unrecorded birds in Ecuador. *Am. Birds* 34(3): 242–248.

Ridgely, R. S., and J. C. Gaulin. 1980. The birds of Finca Merenberg, Huila Department, Colombia. *Condor* 82(4): 379–391.

Ridgely, R. S., and J. A. Gwynne. 1989. *A Guide to the Birds of Panama, with Costa Rica, Nicaragua, and Honduras*, 2d ed. Princeton, N.J.: Princeton University Press.

Robbins, M. B., and R. S. Ridgely. 1990. The avifauna of an upper tropical cloud forest in southwestern Ecuador. *Proc. Acad. Nat. Sci. Phil.* 142: 59–71.

Robbins, M. B., A. P. Capparella, R. S. Ridgely, and S. W. Cardiff. 1991. Avifauna of the Río Manití and Quebrada Vainilla, Peru. *Proc. Acad. Nat. Sci. Phil.* 143: 145–159.

Rocha O., O. 1990. Lista preliminar de aves de la Reserva de la Biosfera "Estación Biológica Beni." *Ecol. en Bolivia* 15: 57–68.

Rodríguez, J. V. 1982. *Aves del Parque Nacional Los Katíos*. Bogotá: INDERENA.

Rosenberg, G. H. 1990. Habitat specialization and foraging behavior by birds of Amazonian river islands in northeastern Peru. *Condor* 92(2): 427–443.

Ruschi, A. 1979. *Aves do Brasil*. São Paulo: Editora Rios.

Schulenberg, T. S. 1986. Adiciones a la avifauna de Pampa Galeras. *Bol. de Lima* 48: 89–90.

———. 1987. New records of birds from western Peru. *Bull. B. O. C.* 107(4): 184–189.

Schulenberg, T. S., S. E. Allen, D. F. Stotz, and D. A. Wiedenfeld. Distributional records from the Cordillera Yanachaga, central Peru. *Gerfaut* 74: 57–70.

Scott, D. A., and M. de L. Brooke. 1985. The endangered avifauna of southeastern Brazil: A report on the BOU/WWF expeditions of 1980/1981 and 1981/1982. *In* A. W. Diamond and T. E. Lovejoy, eds., *Conservation of Tropical Forest Birds.* International Council for Bird Preservation Technical Publication 4: 115–139.

Short, L. S. 1968. Sympatry of Red-breasted Meadowlarks in Argentina, and the taxonomy of meadowlarks (Aves: *Leistes, Pezites,* and *Sturnella*). *Am. Mus. Novitates* 2349: 1–30.

———. 1971. Aves nuevas o poco comunes de Corrientes, Republica Argentina. *Rev. Museo Arg. Cienc. Nat. "Bernardino Rivadavia"* 9: 283–309.

———. 1975. A zoogeographic analysis of the South American Chaco avifauna. *Bull. Am. Mus. Nat. Hist.* 154(3): 165–352.

———. 1976. Notes on a collection of birds from the Paraguayan Chaco. *Am. Mus. Novitates* 2597: 1–16.

Sibley, C. G., and J. E. Ahlquist. 1985. Phylogeny and classification of New World Suboscine Passerine Birds (Passeriformes: Oligomyodi: Tyrannides). *In* P. A. Buckley et al., eds., *Neotropical Ornithology.* AOU monograph no. 36, pp. 396–428.

———. 1990. *Phylogeny and Classification of Birds, A Study in Molecular Evolution.* New Haven: Yale University Press.

Sibley, C. G., and B. L. Monroe, Jr. 1990. *Distribution and Taxonomy of Birds of the World.* New Haven: Yale University Press.

———. 1993. *A Supplement to Distribution and Taxonomy of Birds of the World.* New Haven: Yale University Press.

Sick, H. 1955. O aspecto fitofisionómico da paisagem do medio Rio das Mortes, Mato Grosso e a avifauna do região. *Arq. Mus. Nac. Rio de Jan.* 42: 541–576.

———. 1967. Courtship behavior in the Manakins (Pipridae): A review. *The Living Bird,* 6th an.: 5–22.

———. 1979. Notes on some Brazilian birds. *Bull. B. O. C.* 99(4): 115–120.

———. 1985. *Ornitologia Brasileira, Uma Introdução,* vols. 1 and 2. Brasilia: Editora Universidade de Brasília.

———. 1993. *Birds in Brazil, A Natural History.* Princeton, N.J.: Princeton University Press.

Sick, H., A. de Rosario, and T. Rauh de Azevado. 1981. Aves do Estado de Santa Catarina. *Sellowía, ser. zool.,* no. 1.

Smith, W. J., and F. Vuilleumier. 1971. Evolutionary relationships of some South American ground tyrants. *Bull. Mus. Comp. Zool.* 141(5): 259–286.

Snethlage, E. 1914. Catálogo das aves amazônicas. *Bol. Mus. Par. Emílio Goeldi,* Zool., nov. sér., no. 8: 1–534.

Snow, D. 1978. The classification of the manakins. *Bull. B. O. C.* 95(1): 20–27.

———. 1982. *The Cotingas: Bellbirds, umbrellabirds, and other species.* Ithaca, N.Y.: Cornell University Press.

Snyder, D. E. 1966. *The Birds of Guyana.* Salem, Mass.: Peabody Museum.

Steinbacher, J. 1962. Beitrage zur Kenntnisder vogel von Paraguay. *Abh. Senckenb. Naturf. Ges.* 502: 1–106.

———. 1968. Weitere Beitrage uber vogel von Paraguay. *Senckenb. Biol.* 49: 317–365.

Stephens, L., and M. A. Traylor, Jr. 1983. *Ornithological Gazetteer of Peru.* Cambridge, Mass.: Museum of Comparative Zoology.

———. 1985. *Ornithological Gazetteer of the Guianas.* Cambridge, Mass.: Museum of Comparative Zoology.

Stiles, F. G., and A. F. Skutch. 1989. *A Guide to the Birds of Costa Rica.* Ithaca, N.Y.: Cornell University Press.

Stiles, F. G., and S. M. Smith. 1980. Notes on bird distribution in Costa Rica. *Brenesia* 17: 137–156.

Storer, R. W. 1989. Notes on Paraguayan birds. *Occ. Papers Mus. Zool. Univ. Mich.* 719: 1–21.

Stotz, D. F., and R. O. Bierregaard, Jr. 1989. The birds of the Fazendas Porto Alegre, Esteio and Dimona north of Manaus, Amazonas, Brazil. *Rev. Brasil. Biol.* 49(3): 861–872.

Stotz, D. F., R. O. Bierregaard, M. Cohn-Haft, P. Petermann, J. Smith, A. Whittaker, and S. V. Wilson. 1992. The status of North American migrants in central Amazonian Brazil. *Condor* 94(3): 608–621.

Taczanowski, M. L. 1884–1886. *Ornithologie du Peru.* 3 vols. Berlin: R. Friedlander & Sons.

Teixera, D. M., J. B. Nacinovic, and G. Liogi. 1988. Notes on some birds of northeastern Brazil (3). *Bull. B. O. C.* 108(2): 75–79.

———. 1989. Notes on some birds of northeastern Brazil (4). *Bull. B. O. C.* 109(3): 152–157.

Teixera, D. M., J. B. Nacinovic, and F. B. Pontual. 1987. Notes on some birds of northeastern Brazil (2). *Bull. B. O. C.* 107(4): 151–155.

Teixera, D. M., J. B. Nacinovic, and M. S. Tavares. 1986. Notes on some birds of northeastern Brazil. *Bull. B. O. C.* 106(2): 70–74.

Teixera, D. M., R. Otoch, G. Luigi, M. A. Raposo, and A. C. C. de Almeida. 1993. Notes on some birds of northeastern Brazil (5). *Bull. B. O. C.* 113(1): 48–52.

Terborgh, J. W., J. W. Fitzpatrick, and L. Emmons. 1984. Annotated checklist of bird and mammal species of Cocha Cashu Biological Station, Manu National Park, Peru. *Fieldiana, Zool.,* new series 21: 1–29.

Todd, W. E. C., and M. A. Carriker, Jr. 1922. The birds of the Santa Marta region of Colombia: A study in altitudinal distribution. *Ann. Carnegie Mus.* 14: 1–611.

Tostain, O., J.-L. Dujardin, C. Erard, and J.-M. Thiollay. 1992. *Oiseaux de Guyane.* Brunoy, France: Société d'Études Ornithologiques.

Traylor, M. A., Jr. 1958. Birds of northeastern Peru. *Fieldiana, Zool.* 35: 87–141.

———. 1977. A classification of the Tyrant Flycatchers (Tyrannidae). *Bull. Mus. Comp. Zool.* 148(4): 129–184.

———. 1982. Notes on Tyrant Flycatchers (Aves: Tyrannidae). *Fieldiana, Zool.*, new series 13: 1–22.

Traylor, M. A., Jr., and J. W. Fitzpatrick. 1982. A survey of the Tyrant Flycatchers. *The Living Bird*, 19th an.: 7–50.

Vaurie, C. 1971. *Classification of the ovenbirds* (Furnariidae). London: Witherby.

Vaurie, C. 1980. Taxonomy and geographical distribution of the Furnariidae (Aves, Passeriformes). *Bull. Am. Mus. Nat. Hist.* 166(1): 1–357.

Venegas C., C., and J. Jory H. 1979. *Guía de Campo para las Aves de Magallanes*. Punta Arenas: Instituto de La Patagonia.

Voous, K. H. 1983. *Birds of the Netherlands Antilles*. Curaçao: De Walburg Press.

Vuilleumier, F. 1967. "Speciation in high Andean birds." Ph.D. dissertation, Harvard University. 444 pp.

———. 1969. Systematics and evolution in *Diglossa* (Aves, Coerebidae). *Am. Mus. Novitates* 2381: 1–41.

———. 1985. Forest birds of Patagonia: ecological geography, speciation, endemism, and faunal history. *In* P. A. Buckley et al., eds., *Neotropical Ornithology*. AOU monograph no. 36, pp. 255–304.

———. 1991. A quantitative survey of speciation in Patagonian birds. *Ornitol. Neotrop.* 2(1): 5–28.

Weske, J. 1972. "The distribution of the avifauna in the Apurímac valley of Peru with respect to environmental gradients, habitat, and related species." Ph.D. dissertation, University of Oklahoma. 137 pp.

Wetmore, A. 1926. Observations on the birds of Argentina, Paraguay, Uruguay, and Chile. *Bull. U.S. Natl. Mus.* 133: 1–448.

———. 1972. *The Birds of the Republic of Panama, part 3, Passeriformes: Dendrocolaptidae (Woodcreepers) to Oxyruncidae (Sharpbills)*. Washington, D.C.: Smithsonian Institution Press.

Wetmore, A., R. F. Pasquier, and S. L. Olson. 1984. *The Birds of the Republic of Panama, part 4, Passeriformes: Hirundinidae (Swallows) to Fringillidae (Finches)*. Washington, D.C.: Smithsonian Institution Press.

Wiedenfeld, D. A., T. S. Schulenberg, and M. B. Robbins. 1985. Birds of a tropical deciduous forest in extreme northwestern Peru. *In* P. A. Buckley et al., eds., *Neotropical Ornithology*. AOU Monograph no. 36, pp. 305–315.

Willis, E. O. 1976. Effects of a cold wave on an Amazonian avifauna in the upper Paraguay drainage, western Mato Grosso, and suggestions on Oscine-Suboscine relationships. *Acta Amazônica* 6(3): 379–394.

———. 1977. Lista preliminar das aves da parte noroeste e areas vizinhas da Reserva Ducke, Amazonas, Brasil. *Rev. Brasil. Biol.* 37(3): 585–601.

———. 1988. Behavioral notes, breeding records, and range extensions for Colombian birds. *Rev. Acad. Col. Ciencias* 16: 137–150.

Willis, E. O., and Y. Oniki. 1981. Levantamento preliminar de aves em treze áreas do Estado de São Paulo. *Rev. Brasil. Biol.* 41(1): 121–135.

———. 1985. Bird specimens new for the State of São Paulo. *Rev. Brasil. Biol.* 45(1/2): 105–108.

———. 1988. Aves observadas em Balbina, Amazonas, e os prováveis efeitos da barragem. *Ciencia y Cultura* 40(3): 280–284.

———. 1990. Levantamento preliminar das aves de inverno em dez áreas do sudoeste de Mato Grosso, Brasil. *Ararajuba* 1: 19–38.

———. 1991. *Nomes Gerais para as Aves Brasileiras.* Rio Claro, Brazil: Sadia S.A.

Woods, R. W. 1988. *Guide to the Birds of the Falkland Islands.* Shropshire, England: Anthony Nelson Ltd.

Zimmer, J. T. 1931–1955. Studies of Peruvian birds, 1–66. *Am. Mus. Novitates.*

INDEX TO ENGLISH NAMES

INDEX TO SCIENTIFIC NAMES